The Birdwatcher's Companion

Christopher Leahy

THE BIRDWATCHER'S
An Encyclopedic Handbook

COMPANION
of North American Birdlife

Illustrated by Gordon Morrison
PREFACE BY ROGER F. PASQUIER,
INTERNATIONAL COUNCIL FOR BIRD PRESERVATION

BONANZA BOOKS
New York

For Dorothy E. Snyder

This 1984 edition is published by Bonanza Books,
distributed by Crown Publishers Inc., by arrangement
with Farrar, Straus, and Giroux.

Manufactured in the United States of America

Library of Congress Cataloging in Publication Data

Leahy, Christopher W.
  The birdwatcher's companion.

  Bibliography: p.
  Includes index.
  1. Bird watching—North America.   2. Birds—North
America.   I. Title.
QL681.L34   1984   598′.07′2347   84-21587
ISBN 0-517-459957

h g f e d c b a

Contents

Illustrations

COLOR PLATES

(following page 278)

1. Ecological niches
2. Display
3. Cryptic coloration

(following page 598)

4. Plumage variations
5. Aberrant plumages
6. Endangered birds of North America

FIGURES

Preface

Roger Tory Peterson has said that although birds do not change, bird-watchers do. Perhaps not since the origin of the modern field guide a half century ago have birders changed as much as in the last few years. Today the well-stocked bird lover's library has not only one or more local field guides but guides of equal quality for the remotest corners of the earth, directories of bird clubs and useful contacts, manuals on attracting and feeding birds around the house, self-proclaimed bibles listing sources for all the paraphernalia required for an avian outing, checklists of the birds of the world, family and species monographs, how-to compendia, catalogues from bird-tour companies—and, one hopes, an introduction to ornithology. Birders whose shelves have reached carrying capacity must now be looking for a synthesis that gives, in a readily accessible format, all the information they really want. For me, Christopher Leahy's *The Birdwatcher's Companion* is the answer.

Here one will find accounts of the families of North American birds, the people for whom they were named, the ecological principles they illustrate, and the amusing or obscure terms they generate (see, for example, Grandry's corpuscles, Gynandromorphism, or Kelso's Rule). Taking the long view, as we are invited to by Leahy's subtitle, *An Encyclopedic Handbook of North American Birdlife,* this is what we expect to find in such a book: there were, after all, bird encyclopedias before there were birdwatchers. Aristotle's *History of Animals* was one, and the first printed book about birds was issued in 1467, contemporary with Gutenberg; it was a pedagogic work based on the *Etymologies* of Saint Isidore of Seville, originally written in the seventh century.

What distinguishes Leahy from Aristotle, Isidore, and all the encyclopedists of the intervening centuries is that he deals with birding as well as with birds. The *Companion* is useful to readers of every level. It advises the beginner on the choice of optical equipment and the techniques of watching birds in different locales and in different seasons. Accounts of forty-four North American avian hot spots will whet the novice's appetite for trips farther afield. Before setting forth, he would be wise to read Etiquette and Birdsmanship (not at all the same thing). Increasing proficiency should inspire the birder to undertake a Big Day. Curiosity about changing populations may lead to Censuses, Christmas Counts, and Banding. Finally, the reader may find a place in the Hard Core and can contrast the nature of Birdwatching in North America and Great Britain.

Along the way, I hope the reader will delve into the longer entries on more ornithological topics such as Abundance, Egg, Flight, Migration, Navigation, and Young. These are scientifically accurate, up-to-date, and eminently literate. Even the problems of Taxonomy, as described here, are comprehensible and worthy of the layman's interest. The *Companion* provides an excellent grounding in all facets of ornithology.

The accounts of persons, famous or obscure, should remind the reader that ornithology remains one of the few sciences to which the amateur may still make a valuable contribution. Many entries in the *Companion* indicate the limits of current knowledge and the kinds of information that can be gathered by nonprofessional observers. What can be more satisfying than to develop one's skills and add to one's own knowledge—and possibly the world's—while pursuing objects of such beauty and charm as the birds?

How far to carry a hobby remains the choice of each bird lover, but every user of the *Companion* should read the entries on Conservation and Man-made Threats to Birdlife. As the people who know and care most about birds and their habitats, it is our responsibility to do all we can to assure their preservation. Leahy is eloquent and realistic on the prospects for North America's rarest species, as well as on the still-widespread birds that, like ourselves, are now at risk due to mankind's mismanagement of our shared environment.

The Birdwatcher's Companion has a valuable place in the crowded field of recent books for the North American birder. Whether one wants a complete analysis of how birds raise their young, or only to know who Xantus was, in the *Companion* the answer is easy to find and is given with precision, authority, and wit.

ROGER F. PASQUIER

Introduction

Authors of books that claim to be "encyclopedic" are assailed as they write by two unreasonable exhortations. On the one hand, conscience insists that *everything* be included; on the other, the ego whispers that the author's own interests should be fully elaborated and short shrift given to topics he considers obscure or boring. Both of these errant urges have been resisted more or less successfully in the present instance, but the reader may still be curious about the premises on which the information in this book has been selected and presented.

The inspiration for the *Companion* is rooted in two desires that—as a veteran reader and writer about birds—I have long expected someone else to fulfill. One is the practical wish to own a single reference book that I could hold in one hand but that would tell me, for example: whether birds have a well-developed sense of taste; what "agonistic" means; what color a dipper's eggs are; what "pomarine" means; how to pronounce "parula"; who Bendire was; how many species of woodpeckers there are in the world; what kind of bird a "hagdon" is; what special birds I might hope to see in the Pribilof Islands; how to measure a bird; when to visit the Florida Keys in order to be sure of finding a Black-whiskered Vireo; whether or not I should subscribe to *The Condor*; how to cook a scoter . . . and other such information, from the critical to the trivial. The other worthy ideal involves my desire for readable, non-technical (yet pithy and accurate) accounts of the basic elements of birdlife—accounts that can be read for pleasure as well as information after a thought-provoking day in the field or simply for the fun of discovering some of the more bizarre peripheries of the bird world. These still seem to me to be worthwhile goals, and while I never expected to attempt their realization myself, I have tried my best to do so in the *Companion*.

No work of this kind can claim to be "original" in the sense that a novel may be or a scientific paper documenting new discoveries. It is essentially a collection of other people's work, and the author's creativity is seen mainly in the selection of information, the organization of the material, and the words he chooses to summarize his sources. My main debt then is to the hundreds of ornithologists and other biologists and naturalists from whose work I derived the *Companion*. Many of these men and women are cited directly in the main text, particularly where verbatim quotations or summaries of original assertions demand this courtesy, and the names of the rest appear in the Bibliography. I am especially indebted to the authors of some of the major modern secondary sources on birdlife whose admirable works I virtually inhaled during the course of this project. They gave me an invaluable perspective, guided me to many crucial primary sources, and kept me humble.

The individual to whom I am most and immeasurably beholden is Mr. James Baird, director of the Conservation Department of the Massachusetts Audubon Society and a fount of ornithological wisdom, who read through the *entire* typescript making countless critical contributions relating both to profound issues and to minute details. Anyone tempted to underestimate Mr. Baird's resolve and good humor should try reading even the shortest alphabetical reference book through from A to Z.

Mr. Arthur Wang unfailingly displayed all of the cardinal virtues of good editors, including especially a high degree of literacy and taste, infinite patience, and the ability to apply pressure politely.

Gordon Morrison worked many hours of overtime without compensation on the *Companion*'s illustrations. He cheerfully made dozens of revisions in his work right up through its final stages and seemed to thrive on frank appraisals, evincing character traits not exhibited by all artists of his competence and reputation.

Mr. Roger F. Pasquier also read the typescript through—at astonishing speed—and furnished numerous valuable suggestions.

Jim Lane cast his expert eye over the BIRD FINDING entries, thereby improving them significantly.

Mr. Jack Lynch took on the onerous task of copy-editing the *Companion* with its multiple subheadings, eccentric features, and ornithological obscurities. He did so with uncommon thoroughness, allowing me to correct a number of substantive points as well as compensating for my abundant lapses in matters of punctuation and the like.

Others who have freely contributed their time and expertise to the crucial details or broad philosophical aspects of this book are: Peter Alden, Arthur Argue, Gabriel Behringer, Thomas Davis, Richard Forster, Dr. Norman Hill, Kathryn Leahy, Trevor Lloyd-Evans, Dr. John Peterson, Dr. Raymond Paynter, Dr. William Satterfield, Dr. Paul Spitzer, and Peter Vickery.

Since I was not always wise enough to heed the advice of the generous people named above, all errors noted in the *Companion* can be attributed to my own ignorance and/or carelessness.

Finally, I thank the Massachusetts Audubon Society, for allowing me the time and support without which I never could have written such a long book.

CHRISTOPHER LEAHY

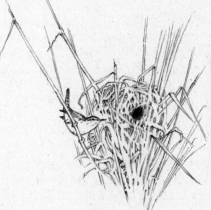

The Birdwatcher's Companion

How to Use This Book

Most readers will not feel the need for elaborate instructions on how to use a book with an alphabetical format—ALBATROSS will surely be found under A somewhere between ACCIPITER and ALCID; M is clearly the likely place to look for MIGRATION; and so forth all the way to ZYGODACTYL. However, anyone who has ever used an encyclopedia knows that a subject is not always treated under its own name and that a considerable exercise of wits and an extended expedition within the uncharted archipelago of the cross-references are sometimes necessary to find the required information in what the author or editor considers the proper location. This common frustration results from the necessity, in compendiums such as this one, of striking a balance between excessive consolidation and excessive repetition. On the one hand, it is galling for readers to have to scan a long entry called CARE OF PLUMAGE when all they are interested in is ANTING. On the other hand, it is not practical for the author to repeat the same information about down under FEATHER, PLUMAGE, MOLT, and YOUNG, DEVELOPMENT OF as well as under DOWN itself. There is no perfect solution to this problem—the author's subjective judgment regarding the organization of material can never coincide precisely with the reader's—but confusion and fruitless labor can perhaps be minimized. An effort has been made in this book to include brief definitive entries for the great majority of specific subjects as well as to provide the appropriate cross-reference(s) when necessary, so that readers will find at least some information (perhaps all they require) where they first think to look. Further effort has been expended to purge the *Companion* of excessively broad or extraneous headings, again in order to minimize entries that offer nothing but a command to look elsewhere (AIR, BIRDS IN: see FLIGHT!).

The following summary of the book's organization, contents, and features will help users of the *Companion* understand: what is included and what is omitted; where to look first for specialized information; and how the author has approached the presentation of various subjects.

SCOPE. The geographical scope of the *Companion* is the continental United States and Canada. Defined in this way, North America is nearly equivalent to the Nearctic region. However, several isolated transitional areas at the margins of the Nearctic provide so many exceptions to generalizations about the rest of the continent that they are treated separately under BAJA CALIFORNIA, BERMUDA, and GREENLAND, thus highlighting the distinctive qualities of their respective avifaunas and relieving the text of myriad phrases beginning: "except for Greenland (or Baja or Bermuda), which . . ." Appendixes I and II list species of Canada and the continental United States only.

Wherever possible, North American birds are used in examples of avian phenomena. However, many broad subjects and those dealing with various extremes of birdlife cannot be adequately treated without alluding to other avifaunas. No one hoping to learn about INCUBATION, for example, should be cheated of an awareness of megapodes simply because no member of this fascinating family occurs in North America. Likewise the Ostrich is essential to any comprehensive discussion of size variation among birds.

LONG ENTRIES. Broad subjects are treated in essay form with the aim of summarizing present knowledge or current practice in a particular field. Though subheadings are freely used to allow the information seeker to find facts readily, the longest entries are also meant to be read through at leisure as one might read a chapter of a book or a magazine article. Major entries on general subjects are listed immediately below, except for those dealing with parts, systems, and functions of a bird's body, which are given separately in the next section.

ABUNDANCE	ENDOPARASITE	NAVIGATION
AGE	EVOLUTION OF BIRD-	NEST
AGGRESSION	LIFE	NOMENCLATURE
AVICULTURE	EXTINCT BIRDS	OPTICAL EQUIPMENT
BANDING	FALCONRY	ORNITHOLOGY
BATHING	FEATHER	PARENTAL CARE
BIRD CLUB	FLIGHT	PESTS, BIRDS AS
BIRD FEEDING	FLOCK	PHOTOGRAPHY
BIRD FINDING	FOOD/FEEDING	PLUMAGE
BIRDHOUSE	HUMAN CULTURE,	POPULATION
BIRDWATCHING	BIRDS IN	PREDATION
CARE OF DISTRESSED	HYBRIDIZATION	PREENING
BIRDS	ILLUSTRATION	RECORDING OF BIRD
CENSUS	IMAGINATION, BIRDS IN	SOUNDS
COLOR AND PATTERN	INCUBATION	SIZE
CONSERVATION	INTELLIGENCE	SLEEP
DISEASE	INTRODUCED BIRDS	SONG
DISPLAY	LAWS PROTECTING	SPECIATION
DISTRIBUTION	BIRDLIFE	SPEED
DOMESTICATED BIRDS	LISTING	SWIMMING/DIVING
DOMINANCE	MAN-MADE THREATS	TAXONOMY
ECTOPARASITE	TO BIRDLIFE	TERRITORY
EGG	MIGRATION	YOUNG, DEVELOP-
ENDANGERED BIRDS	MOLT	MENT OF

One of the inherent inadequacies of reference books containing many entries is that they inevitably include a wealth of information from which the reader never benefits because he doesn't know it exists and therefore has neither the occasion nor the ability to look it up. Entries from the *Companion* that may fit this description include:

ANTING

ATLAS, BREEDING-
  BIRD

BIRD CALLS (made by
  humans)

BIRDSMANSHIP

CANNIBALISM

CANOPY FEEDING

CAPTURE (of wild
  birds)

CHRISTMAS COUNT

CHUMMING

CLIMBING

COLLECTING (bird
  specimens)

COMFORT MOVE-
  MENTS

DISPERSAL

DRINKING

DRUNKENNESS

DUCK STAMPS

DUETTING

DUSTING

EDIBILITY

ESCAPES

ETIQUETTE FOR BIRD-
  WATCHERS

EXOTIC SPECIES

FLIGHTLESSNESS

FOLLOWING SHIPS

GUANO

HIBERNATION

HOMOSEXUALITY

HOPPING

IRRUPTION

LATIN NAMES

MARKING

MEASUREMENTS

MOBBING

MOON WATCHING

MORTALITY

MUSEUMS

NAMES, COLLOQUIAL

NAMES, VERNACULAR

NEST FAUNA

NOMADISM

NOUNS OF ASSEM-
  BLAGE

OBSERVATORY

ODOR

PAIR FORMATION

PIRACY

PLAY

POLITICS, BIRDS IN

POLLINATION

RADAR

SCRATCHING

SMOKE/FIRE

SUNNING

TAMENESS

VERIFICATION OF
  RECORDS

WALKING/RUNNING

WEATHER

PHYSIOLOGY AND ANATOMY. For the most part, the principal components of a bird's body are treated within long entries describing the body systems, functions, or regions. Organs and other structures or physiological phenomena that are unique to or highly specialized in birds are defined briefly under their own headings and then (in most cases) cross-referenced to the appropriate longer entry. Main headings are allotted to basic organs common to most or all vertebrates for the convenience of the reader, but these are followed only by a cross-reference to the applicable system (EYE: see VISION; or BRAIN: see NERVOUS SYSTEM). No attempt has been made to be anatomically exhaustive: the avian gall bladder (some birds have one, others do not) is not mentioned in the main text. A few body parts, e.g., TONGUE, are treated with thoroughness apart from their systems. These, along with all longer entries covering systems, functions, and body regions, are listed below.

BILL
BROOD PATCH
BULLA
BURSA OF FABRICIUS
CIRCULATORY SYSTEM
COLOR AND PATTERN
DIGESTIVE SYSTEM
ECHOLOCATION
EMBRYO
ENDOCRINE SYSTEM
ENERGY
EXCRETORY SYSTEM
FAT
FEATHER
FECAL SAC
FLIGHT
FRIGHT MOLT

GRANDRY'S CORPUS-
    CLES
GYNANDROMORPHISM
HEARING
HERBST'S CORPUSCLES
KERATIN
LEG/FOOT
MOLT
MUSCLES
NERVOUS SYSTEM
NOSTRILS
OIL GLAND
OPERCULUM
OSSIFICATION
PELLET
PIGEON'S MILK
PLUMAGE
REPRODUCTIVE SYSTEM

RESPIRATORY SYSTEM
SALT GLAND
SEX, CHANGE OF
SKELETON
SKIN
SMELL
STOMACH OIL
SYRINX
TAIL
TASTE
TEETH
TEMPERATURE, BODY
TONGUE
TORPIDITY
TOUCH
VISION
WING

TERMS. In addition to exclusively ornithological terms (e.g., NIDIFU-
GOUS) and birdwatching jargon (e.g., JIZZ), the *Companion* contains a
number of widely used biological terms relating to habitat, anatomy, behavior, etc. In general, these are words that occur frequently in ornitholo-
gical/birdwatching contexts but may not be well understood by the general reader. All such terms used within the text of the *Companion* are
defined under their own headings.

FAMILY ACCOUNTS. The *Companion* does not attempt to treat comprehensively taxonomic groupings below the family level—that is, the
reader can expect to find an entry on thrushes in general under THRUSH,
but will find no entry such as THRUSH, GRAY-CHEEKED that gives a full account of an individual species. The exceptions to this general rule are those
families that contain only a single North American species. In such cases,
e.g., DIPPER, the family account refers particularly to the native form and
thus becomes hardly distinguishable from a species account. When one of
these sole North American family representatives does not bear its collective family name, the comprehensive entry will be found under the generic
or species name rather than that of the family. For example, the lone
North American babbler is described in detail under WRENTIT, not
BABBLER, and our only cracid is covered under CHACHALACA, not CURAS-
SOW.

The family accounts are written in a standardized format giving in
sequence the following information: taxonomic definition; number of species contained in the family both worldwide and in North America (approximate in many cases due to differences in taxonomic opinion); charac-

teristic morphological and behavior traits; nest; eggs; voice; distribution; and derivation of the English family name.

A few groups within large, varied families are so distinct from other members of their family (if only superficially) that they have been accorded full family treatments as described above. The family-type entries are listed below; those marked with asterisks are sole North American representatives or distinctive subgroups of larger families (noted in parentheses).

ALBATROSS

ANHINGA

ANI* (cuckoo)

AUK

AVOCET

BARN OWL

BECARD* (cotinga or tyrant flycatcher)

BLACKBIRD

BOOBY

BUSHTIT* (tit or long-tailed tit)

CARACARA* (falcon)

CHACHALACA* (curassow)

CORMORANT

COWBIRD* (blackbird)

CRANE

CROW

CUCKOO

DIPPER

DUCK

FALCON

FLAMINGO

FRIGATEBIRD

GNATCATCHER* (Old World warbler)

GOOSE* (duck/goose/swan)

GREBE

GROUSE

GULL* (gull/tern)

HAWK

HUMMINGBIRD

IBIS

JACANA

JAEGER

JAY* (crow)

KINGFISHER

KINGLET* (Old World warbler)

LARK

LIMPKIN

LOON

MEADOWLARK* (blackbird)

MIMIC THRUSH

NIGHTJAR

NUTHATCH

OLD WORLD WARBLER

ORIOLE* (blackbird)

OSPREY* (hawk)

OWL

OYSTERCATCHER

PARROT

PELICAN

PHAINOPEPLA* (silky flycatcher)

PHALAROPE* (sandpiper)

PHEASANT

PIGEON

PIPIT

PLOVER

QUAIL* (pheasant)

RAIL

ROADRUNNER* (cuckoo)

SANDPIPER

SHEARWATER

SHRIKE

SKIMMER

SOLITAIRE* (thrush or silky flycatcher)

SPOONBILL* (ibis)

STARLING

STILT* (avocet)

STORK

STORM-PETREL

SWALLOW

SWAN* (duck/goose/swan)

SWIFT

TANAGER

TERN* (gull/tern)

TIT

TREECREEPER

TROGON

TROPICBIRD

TURKEY

TYRANT FLYCATCHER

VERDIN* (penduline tit)

VIREO

VULTURE

WAGTAIL* (pipit)

WAXWING

WEAVER

WOODPECKER

WOOD WARBLER

WREN

WRENTIT* (babbler)

STANDARD ENGLISH BIRD NAMES. The *Companion* contains an entry for all North American English generic bird names. Some of these (e.g., AUK and WOODPECKER) are also family names and are followed by comprehensive family accounts. Others (e.g., RAZORBILL and FLICKER) pertain to only a single species or a small group and are accorded only brief taxonomic and etymological definitions and perhaps a sentence or two on unique characteristics when these exist.

The phrase "standard English name" is used consistently in the text to refer to the "official" vernacular (common) English names recognized by the American Ornithologists' Union or (in a few cases) other nomenclatural authorities.

NAME DEFINITIONS AND ETYMOLOGY. The meaning and origin of standard English generic bird names are noted under the appropriate headings—unless they are obvious: the derivation of WOODPECKER does not require lengthy explication. When these are family names (e.g., FALCON), the etymology is given at the end of the entry.

Unusual adjectives used in standard English names, e.g., POMARINE or HEPATIC, are also defined under their own headings, but obvious modifiers, e.g., "Common" or "White-throated," are omitted.

Etymology of Latin (scientific) bird names is not attempted in the *Companion*, but some excellent sources for this information are noted in the Bibliography under BIOGRAPHY (Gruson, 1972, and Choate, 1973) and under LATIN NAMES (Borror, 1960, and Jaeger, 1960).

BIOGRAPHIES. The lives of all the men and women whose names appear in current Latin or English species names of birds that occur regularly in North America have been sketched briefly. Also included are accounts of a number of men who, though uncommemorated in ornithological nomenclature at the species level, were responsible for describing and/or naming a significant number of North American species. And a few entries are devoted to men with neither of the above qualifications but of such towering reputation in American ornithology/birdwatching that they demand inclusion. Towers, of course, are perceived to be of different heights depending upon the perspective of the viewer and many prominent names will inevitably be missed as a result of the author's slant.

All men and women profiled are deceased and only a few can be said to belong to the modern era.

For further discussion of biographical subject matter and a list of useful references, see BIOGRAPHY.

COLLOQUIAL BIRD NAMES. Over a hundred of the best-known and most colorful "local" or "folk" names for birds are listed alphabetically and briefly defined under NAMES, COLLOQUIAL. Even widely used colloquialisms such as "shag" and "chewink" are to be found in this collective entry and not as separate headings in the text.

NOUNS OF ASSEMBLAGE, or collective nouns relating to birdlife, e.g., "gaggle of geese," are listed alphabetically under NOUNS OF ASSEMBLAGE rather than scattered as main headings throughout the text.

FALCONRY TERMS, such as "eyass" and "ostringer," are defined at the end of FALCONRY and not under headings of their own in the main text. A few exceptions are made for terms that have gained a broader usage, e.g., HACKING.

BIRD-FINDING LOCALITIES. The *Companion* contains brief descriptive entries on forty-four of the best-known birdwatching hot spots of North America, as follows:

ADAK (see ALEUTIAN ISLANDS)
ALEUTIAN ISLANDS
ANHINGA TRAIL (see EVERGLADES)
ATTU (see ALEUTIAN ISLANDS)
BATHURST INLET
BAXTER STATE PARK
BEAR RIVER MARSH NATIONAL WILDLIFE REFUGE
BIG BEND
BONAVENTURE ISLAND
BRIGANTINE NATIONAL WILDLIFE REFUGE
BROWNSVILLE (see RIO GRANDE VALLEY)
BULL'S ISLAND
CAPE MAY
CHIRICAHUA MOUNTAINS (see SOUTHEASTERN ARIZONA)
CHISOS MOUNTAINS (see BIG BEND)
CHURCHILL
CORKSCREW SWAMP
DELTA MARSHES
DRY TORTUGAS
EDWARDS PLATEAU

EVERGLADES NATIONAL PARK
FALCON DAM (see RIO GRANDE VALLEY)
FLORIDA KEYS
GALVESTON ISLAND
GAMBELL
HAWK MOUNTAIN
HIGH ISLAND
HORICON MARSH
JAMAICA BAY
LOXAHATCHEE NATIONAL WILDLIFE REFUGE
MACHIAS SEAL ISLAND
MADERA CANYON (see SOUTHEASTERN ARIZONA)
MALEUR NATIONAL WILDLIFE REFUGE
MILE-HI (see SOUTHEASTERN ARIZONA)
MONOMOY NATIONAL WILDLIFE REFUGE
MONTEREY
MOUNT LEMMON (see SOUTHEASTERN ARIZONA)
MOUNT PINOS
NEWBURYPORT/PLUM ISLAND

NEWPORT BAY
PLUM ISLAND (see NEWBURYPORT)
POINT PELEE
PRIBILOF ISLANDS
RAMSEY CANYON (see SOUTHEASTERN ARIZONA)
REELFOOT LAKE
RIO GRANDE VALLEY
ROCKPORT
ROCKY MOUNTAIN NATIONAL PARK
SALTON SEA
SANIBEL ISLAND
SANTA ANA NATIONAL WILDLIFE REFUGE (see RIO GRANDE VALLEY)
SAPSUCKER WOODS
SONOITA CREEK (see SOUTHEASTERN ARIZONA)
SOUTHEASTERN ARIZONA
TAMIAMI TRAIL
WOOD BUFFALO NATIONAL PARK
YELLOWSTONE NATIONAL PARK
YOSEMITE NATIONAL PARK

PERIODICAL LITERATURE. The majority of North American ornithological and birdwatching periodicals, as well as a few foreign journals published in English and a selection of more general science or natural history publications that often contain articles about birdlife, are listed in the Bibliography under PERIODICALS along with the addresses of their subscription offices.

The best-known ornithological and birdwatching periodicals are also described briefly in entries of their own. See PERIODICALS in the main text for a listing of these.

DEFINITIONS OF LATIN TAXA. Rather than crowd the main text with repetitive entries defining each of the North American orders, suborders, families, etc., a taxonomic list of the North American avifauna is included as Appendix I. The list makes the relationship of a given taxon to all others apparent at a glance: *Dendroica*, for example, is immediately seen to be a genus in the family Parulidae, order Passeriformes, containing numerous species and subspecies. In addition the list has been annotated to show pertinent facts about the various taxa, e.g., extinct species and number of species in a given family worldwide and in North America.

For easy reference, alphabetical listings of all North American orders, suborders, and families with the pages on which they appear are given under ORDER, SUBORDER, and FAMILY. For further details of this system, see the introduction to Appendix I.

CLASSIFICATION AND NOMENCLATURE. In the absence of a recently revised standard checklist of North American birds, the taxonomy and nomenclature of the *Companion* have been derived from a number of authoritative sources, especially the A.O.U. *Check-list of North American Birds*, 5th edition (1957 and Supplements); *Checklist of Birds of the World* by Peters et al. (1931 et seq., and particularly those volumes and revisions that have appeared after 1957); and recent opinions published in the ornithological literature. Where two or more bird names are in wide usage and where significant taxonomic controversies exist, the attempt has been made to explain or at least note the major options both in the main text and in Appendix I.

As the *Companion* went into the final stages of publication, the A.O.U. published a species list, the phylogeny and nomenclature of which will be followed in the forthcoming 6th edition of the A.O.U. *Check-list*. It has not been possible to revise the entire text in accordance with the nomenclature and taxonomic preferences stated in the new standard. However, most of the changes made were anticipated and are noted at least as options within relevant entries, and Appendix I has been amended to reflect the species concepts of the new A.O.U. list, but see the introduction to Appendix I for further details.

PRONUNCIATION. Guides to pronunciation are provided only when the word in question is likely to be unfamiliar to the general reader, when the pronunciation is not obvious, or when two or more pronunciations are popular. In the latter case, all widely used pronunciations are given and no attempt made to dictate "correct" usage.

Pronunciations are indicated not by phonetic symbols but by substituting words or syllables with familiar, relatively unambiguous pronunciations for potentially problematic ones. Syllables to be emphasized are set in capital letters, and if two emphases occur in a word, they are shown as having equal weight, though they will usually be unequal in reality.

This system is not intended to convey phonetic niceties, but merely to allow the reader to say a word with which he is unfamiliar.

For other sources on pronunciation of both English and Latin names, see the Bibliography under LATIN NAMES.

BIBLIOGRAPHY. The Bibliography includes not only works cited in the text but also a selection of books and papers deemed to be of particular interest or pertinence to the various entry subjects. The arrangement of the Bibliography parallels the format of the main text, with all references appearing under headings that correspond to major entry headings in the body of the *Companion*. (Not all entries, of course, have corresponding bibliographies.) Under the subject headings in the Bibliography, individual works are arranged alphabetically by author. The reader wanting to look up the citation "(Emlen, 1967)" from the entry headed NAVIGATION will turn to the NAVIGATION heading in the Bibliography and will then locate the author's name alphabetically. The reader who wishes a comprehensive work on navigation by birds or who wants to review principal references on the subject can turn directly to the Bibliography without referring to the NAVIGATION entry in the main text.

In order to avoid excessive duplication of references that are relevant under two or more headings (applies particularly to major secondary sources), some textual citations are cross-referenced to bibliographical headings different from the entry headings under which they appear. The citation "(Fisher and Peterson, 1964–BIRD)" appearing in the entry on ABUNDANCE means that this particular reference is given not under ABUNDANCE in the Bibliography (as would usually be the case), but under BIRD, where various general titles are listed.

APPENDIXES. Appendix I consists of a coded phylogenetic list of all bird species that occur regularly in North America. Appendix II lists all bird species that have occurred as vagrants or "accidentals" in North America and whose occurrence has been convincingly documented. Appendix III is a calendar of some of North America's principal birdwatching places, events, and birds. The use and special features of the appendixes are detailed in introductions to each.

ILLUSTRATIONS. Ninety-one species representing forty-five North American bird families are depicted in the *Companion*'s illustrations.

Both figures and color plates illustrate avian phenomena treated in the text and in most cases are associated with specific entries, e.g., MOBBING (Fig. 14) or DISPLAY (Plate 2). However, captions are also provided to describe the details of each illustration.

The twenty-five black-and-white figures were executed on Strathmore bristol board (3-ply, medium surface), using 2H, HB, and 2B pencils for the line and tone work throughout. The six color plates and the book jacket illustration were begun in much the same manner and transparent washes of acrylic and watercolor added. The combination of the two mediums allows the artist to closely control color intensity by building up multiple washes and thus avoid sacrificing the detail and sensitivity of the line art.

Abbreviations

Like other major fields, ornithology/birdwatching is immersed in an alphabet soup made from the initial letters of organizations which it has engendered. The following is a brief guide to abbreviations for the most prominent bird-related institutions. Many of the institutions have entries of their own in this volume.

A.B.A.	American Birding Association
A.O.U.	American Ornithologists' Union; the analogous British organization is abbreviated B.O.U.
B.B.C.	Brookline Bird Club; and of course other bird clubs with an initial B
C.O.C.	Cooper Ornithological Club
D.V.O.C.	Delaware Valley Ornithological Club
E.B.B.A.	Eastern Bird Banding Association
F.O.N.	Federation of Ontario Naturalists
I.C.B.P.	International Council for Bird Preservation
I.O.C.	International Ornithological Congress
M.B.O.	Manomet Bird Observatory
M.C.Z.	Museum of Comparative Zoology
N.B.B.A.	Northeastern Bird-Banding Association
P.R.B.O.	Point Reyes Bird Observatory
W.B.B.A.	Western Bird Banding Association
W.O.S.	Wilson Ornithological Society

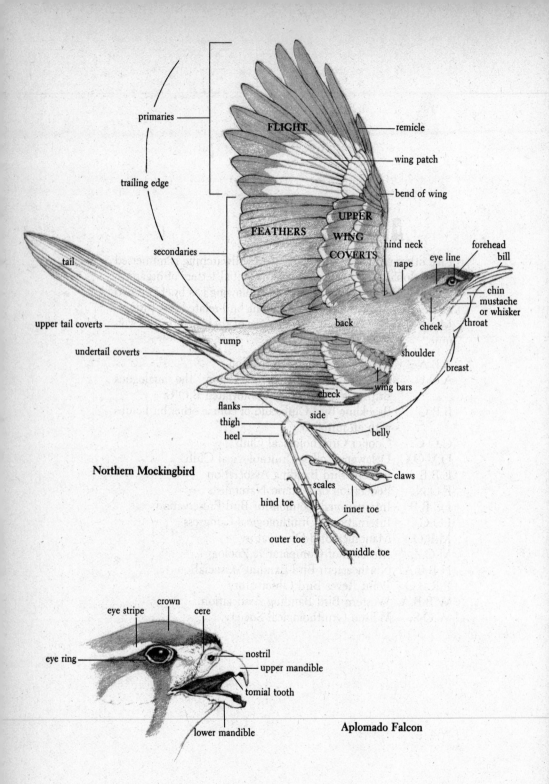

primaries

trailing edge

secondaries

FLIGHT

remicle

wing patch

bend of wing

FEATHERS

UPPER
WING
COVERTS

hind neck

eye line

forehead

bill

nape

tail

chin

mustache
or whisker

throat

cheek

upper tail coverts

undertail coverts

rump

back

shoulder

breast

check

wing bars

side

flanks

thigh

heel

belly

Northern Mockingbird

scales

claws

hind toe

inner toe

outer toe

middle toe

eye stripe

crown

cere

eye ring

nostril

upper mandible

tomial tooth

lower mandible

Aplomado Falcon

A

ABERRANT (ab-AIR-ent). Abnormal; deviant. Sometimes used to describe untypical plumages or structural malformations in birds. See PLUMAGE; ALBINISM; MELANISM; LEUCISM; SCHIZOCHROISM; XANTHOCHROISM; ERYTHRISM; and Plate 5.

ABERT (AY-bert), James William, 1820–97 (Abert's Towhee: *Pipilo aberti*). One of a number of officers in the Army Corps of Engineers who collected birds for Spencer BAIRD while on duty in the West. Baird repaid this service by naming one of Abert's New Mexico specimens for its collector.

ABNORMALITY. It is not unusual for banders and feeder owners to encounter birds with physical handicaps or deformations. Some of these—e.g., lost or broken wings and legs or damaged eyes, resulting from accidents, encounters with predators, frostbite, etc.—reflect the inherent hardship of avian life. And the resiliency of apparently fragile and vulnerable organisms is also exemplified in the fact that many birds survive such handicaps with surprising adaptability. Other abnormalities due to disease or genetic defects are noted less frequently, possibly because they often prove fatal shortly after birth. However, even some avian "monsters" with extra legs or wings or bizarrely deformed mandibles are sometimes able to function satisfactorily.

For reviews of various abnormalities recorded in birds, see Hicks (1934), Michener (1936), Nickell (1965), and Pomeroy (1962; illustrations of bill deformations).

For plumage abnormalities, see ALBINISM; MELANISM; ERYTHRISM; LEUCISM; XANTHOCHROISM; PLUMAGE; and Plate 5. See also DISEASE.

ABRASION. In an ornithological context, the wearing away by normal friction of the edges of a feather. In many species, marked plumage changes result from abrasion. The speckled basic (winter) plumage of adult Common Starlings, for example, is produced by the pale tips of body feathers acquired in the pre-basic (post-nuptial) molt. Most of these tips wear off by spring, leaving a nearly spotless alternate (breeding) plumage.

Individual feathers may become worn "to the bone"—i.e., down to a nearly vaneless shaft—thus altering the protective and insulation capacity of the plumage (see TEMPERATURE, BODY).

Some light-colored species—e.g., many small sandpipers—seem par-

FIG. 1. *Topography of a bird.* Mostly field terms; for technical terms, see Fig. 25.

ticularly pale and/or "scaly" when freshly molted, because of body feathers with dark centers and broad pale edges; such birds appear darker and more uniformly colored as the feather margins become abraded.

Body feathers with dark centers and pale edges are very common among many families of birds, whereas pale feathers with dark borders are comparatively infrequent. The chemical composition of melanin, the dark pigment in feathers, inhibits wear and therefore offers a clue to the evolution of this "rule."

ABUNDANCE (of individual birds/species). It should surprise no one that the question of how many individual birds are alive on this planet at any given moment has yet to be answered with any degree of certainty. True, there are a few species, e.g., Whooping Crane, whose distributions have been fully discovered and whose total populations are so small that we know precisely how many individuals presently exist (see ENDANGERED BIRDS). But estimates even for so scarce and well-studied a species as the large California Condor (20–30 birds) have an error factor equal to half or a third of the total population. The populations of certain seabirds, e.g., Laysan Albatross, Greater Shearwater, Northern Fulmar, Northern Gannet, Common Puffin, Roseate Tern, that nest locally in compact colonies—most of which are known—can be estimated with a high degree of accuracy simply by counting nest sites. But when we consider even so limited a goal as calculating the number of Black-capped Chickadees in Massachusetts during a given month—not to mention the number of songbirds in Canada or the planet's total avian population—we begin to appreciate the difficulty of the task. To begin with, simply counting accurately the number of small woodland birds in a ten-acre plot involves much patience and labor (see CENSUS) and leaves the counter with little confidence that absolute accuracy has been achieved. Once there are reasonably reliable counts for a range of species and habitats, one can begin to make some tentative extrapolation—but consider some of the variables involved:

• The populations of all birds fluctuate greatly in the course of the year, hitting a low before birds of the year have hatched—when only individuals that have survived the ravages of age, winter, and predation exist—and peaking at the end of the breeding season, when in most cases juvenile birds outnumber adults by at least several fold.

• Even small-scale censuses show that some habitats support many more birds than others—from as few as 13 birds (adults of all species) per 10 acres of woods or farmland to over 1,000 individuals in the same amount of exceptionally rich habitat (Lack, 1966–POPULATION).

• Bird populations in a given locality change drastically during the year not only due to seasonal fluctuations effected by reproduction but also due to bird movements. Areas of arctic tundra which teem with breeding shorebirds and other birds are nearly (or totally) barren of birdlife for six or more months of the year. And the already rich resident avifauna of Central

America is increased no-one-knows-how-many times by the flood of North American migrants that arrive on their wintering grounds there each fall.

• Population densities of different species vary greatly, making it impossible to extrapolate total bird populations from what is known about one or a few species.

• Bird populations increase and decrease in cycles and according to ecological variations (see POPULATION). Northern finches and raptors experience alternating "booms" and "busts"—a continually shifting pattern brought about by fluctuations in the amount of food available to the potential consumers.

Some "guesstimates": Despite the inherent difficulty in counting birds, the question of "how many" exerts a powerful fascination, partly no doubt because there are obviously so many and partly because it would be very useful in judging the health of a given species (as well as of the whole environment) to know whether bird populations are declining drastically (as many earnestly contend), holding their own, or even (certainly true in some cases) increasing. Readers wanting more detail or insights than can be included here should refer to the references cited in the Bibliography, from which the following figures are taken.

• The world's total avian population has been reckoned (by broad extrapolation) at around 100 billion birds (Fisher, 1951–BIRDWATCHING)— give or take some hundreds of millions!

• The total population of wild land birds in the contiguous United States at the beginning of the breeding season has been estimated (Fisher and Peterson, 1964–BIRD) at 5–6 billion birds, jumping to perhaps 20 billion with the addition of birds of the year.

• In a notably careful survey running the length of Finland and considering all habitats, Merikallio (1958) came up with a total of 64 million adult breeding birds, with the two commonest species (Chaffinch and Willow Warbler) making up 10 percent of the whole.

• There are about 44 species of birds (scarce, local and/or conspicuous, colonial seabirds; see above) whose total populations are accurately known (Fisher and Peterson, 1964–BIRD).

• The Red-billed Dioch or Quelea, a tiny African waxbill finch (family Estrildidae), is arguably the most abundant bird species in the world. It occurs in locust-like plagues in the dry savannas south of the Sahara, where it wreaks havoc on grain crops. Single invasions of a particular region have been estimated to be 100 million birds strong and the total population is currently estimated at about 10 billion.

• The Wilson's Storm-Petrel is another candidate for the most numerous bird in the world, not according to any census but in view of its enormous colonies, large (antarctic-subantarctic) breeding distribution, and wide oceanic range, over much of which it is (seasonally) abundant (Fisher, 1951–BIRDWATCHING).

• The Common Starling and the House Sparrow have been nominated as the world's most abundant land birds (Fisher, 1951–BIRDWATCH-ING), but other authorities point out that while their distribution is exceedingly wide, their occurrence is relatively localized.

• The domestic chicken population is estimated at about 4 billion—roughly equal to that of our own species.

• The most abundant species of North American bird in recorded history was the Passenger Pigeon; about 3 billion are thought to have been alive at the time of Columbus.

• Based on its extremely broad distribution, local population densities, and vast wintering roosts, the Red-winged Blackbird has been judged the most numerous of living native North American land birds (Pettingill, 1970–ORNITHOLOGY).

• The Red-eyed Vireo might be the most abundant of eastern North American deciduous-woodland birds (Peterson, 1948–BIRDWATCHING). Of course, any land-bird species with high population density and broad distribution (e.g., Yellow and Yellow-rumped Warblers, House Wren, Black-capped Chickadee, American Robin, Brown-headed Cowbird, or Chipping Sparrow) can enter this contest without fear of being too badly defeated.

For rarest North American birds, see ENDANGERED BIRDS. For numbers of species, see SPECIES and Appendix I.

ACADIAN (uh-KAY-dee-un) (Flycatcher). Acadia was a French colony consisting of present-day Nova Scotia, Prince Edward Island, and parts of neighboring New Brunswick and Maine; in 1755 its inhabitants were forced by the British to flee and many settled in coastal Louisiana (see H. W. Longfellow's *Evangeline*). It would be gratifying to report that the Acadian Flycatcher breeds in eastern Canada and winters along the Gulf coast. In fact, however, it has never been recorded in Nova Scotia and winters from Costa Rica to northern South America. Its type was collected "near Philadelphia," and it is commonest as a breeding bird in southeastern North America.

ACCIDENTAL. A term used to describe bird species which occur in a given place only very infrequently and irregularly. Such occurrences may result from unusually severe weather patterns: storm-driven birds from the tropics, the Arctic, Europe, and Asia have been recorded as "accidentals" on all North American shores and far inland. Or they may represent aberrations in individual birds which, for example, have not followed their normal migration routes.

The use of the term in reference to a particular species varies geographically. The occurrence of Fork-tailed Flycatcher, which is not normally found north of southern Mexico, would be regarded as accidental anywhere in North America. A Black-throated Sparrow would be accidental in Virginia, but not in southern Arizona.

For a list of species which have occurred "accidentally" in North America, see Appendix II.

ACCIPITER (ak-SIP-ih-ter). A genus of hawks characterized by short, rounded wings, long tails, and long legs. There are about 50 species of accipiters worldwide, of which three—Northern Goshawk, Cooper's Hawk, and Sharp-shinned Hawk—occur in North America. The accipiters are forest raptors that feed mainly on birds and are superbly adapted for the speed and agility required to follow fast-moving prey amidst a maze of tree trunks. Because of generally similar plumage patterns and coloration—particularly among immatures and females—and a characteristic sexual dimorphism in size which puts females of smaller species in the same size range as males of larger species (see DIMORPHISM), the three species are occasionally difficult to identify in the field. It is common to hear honest birdwatchers report that they have seen "an accipiter" or "a medium-sized accipiter."

The word derives from a Latin verb meaning "to seize" and was used by Pliny to refer to the hunting habits of a species of hawk.

For family characteristics, see HAWK.

ADAK. See ALEUTIAN ISLANDS.

ADAMS, Edward, 1824–55 (Yellow-billed Loon: *Gavia adamsii*). A British naval doctor and naturalist who accompanied several exploratory expeditions to the American Arctic. Not least of these was the voyage of the *Enterprise* (1850–55) during which the Northwest Passage was discovered. In addition to dispensing medical services, Adams collected numerous natural history specimens, including several species that proved new to science. One of these, the Yellow-billed Loon, was named for him.

ADAPTATION. Adjustment, by an organism, sometimes in a striking and/or highly specialized way, to a particular way of life. A widely applicable term that may relate to structure, function, and/or behavior. Cryptic coloration, night vision, and canopy feeding, for example, are all adaptive characteristics of certain groups of birds.

ADDLE (or addled). An addle egg is one that has become rotten or the living contents of which have died or been destroyed. "Addled" has become the popular adjective form.

ADULT. Generally used loosely in avian contexts to refer to birds which have acquired their definitive plumage (see MOLT, *Sequence and Terminology*). This may or may not be indicative of sexual maturity; some species become sexually mature before fully acquiring their definitive plumage.

AFTERFEATHER. A secondary, usually much smaller feather which branches from the shaft of the body feathers of most birds below the beginning of the vane (see Fig. 9). In a few cases, almost as prominent as the main feather or entirely absent; presumably provides additional insulation.

AFTERSHAFT. The shaft of the AFTERFEATHER and sometimes used (imprecisely) as a synonym for it; also called the hyporachis.

AGE. *Longevity* in birds can be determined with precision in two ways: (1) by recording the life spans of birds which are born and die in captivity, and (2) by banding birds of known age (e.g., nestlings) and recovering the bands upon their deaths. These two methods yield two different kinds of information on the ages of birds. The first tells us something of a bird's *potential* life span; i.e., the greatest age a given species may achieve under ideal circumstances. The champions in this category are often cited. The longest reliably recorded avian life was that of a male Andean Condor (*Vultur gryphus*) named Kuzya, which took up residence in the Moscow Zoo as an adult in captivity in 1892 and died 72 years later. An Eagle Owl (*Bubo bubo*) lived in captivity for 68 years, and a Siberian Crane for 62. Other families with representatives surviving 50 years or longer in captivity are the hawks and eagles, the pelicans, the owls, the corvids (raven), and the parrots. The last are renowned for long life and there are many apocryphal accounts of psittacine Methuselahs. *The Guinness Book of World Records* (1980) notes (with reservations) the assertion of Mrs. Bella Ludford of Liverpool, England, that her pet parrot (*Amazona*) Jimmy was born in captivity in 1870 and survived for 104 years.

Certain conditions of captivity which are not encountered in the wild—e.g., lack of exercise, an artificial diet, air pollution in city zoos—may, of course, prevent a long life from being even longer, but in general, hazards to life in the wild are far greater and the chances of recording extreme "natural" ages therefore much smaller.

Banding records give good indications of *average* life spans of birds as well as providing a few record ages under "natural" conditions. The greatest known longevity in the wild is found in the albatrosses, some species of which regularly exceed 40 years of age (Fisher, 1975), and it has been suggested (Tickell, 1968) that some individual Wandering Albatrosses may reach a "natural" age of 80. A Herring Gull (*Larus argentatus*) and a European Oystercatcher (*Haematopus ostralegus*) are apparently tied for second place at present at 36 years. Arctic and Sooty Terns are also known to have passed 30 in the wild, and individual loons, herons, hawks, swans, geese, and ducks have survived to over 20 in nature. The longest wild passerine life span on record is that of a Common Starling banded as an adult 20 years before its death (Rydzewski, 1962); and swallows, finches, and tits have reached 15, 10, and 8 respectively. A captive Northern Cardinal is reported to have lasted to 28½ (Terres, 1980–BIRD).

It should be emphasized that (1) the "natural" ages of many birds which are long-lived in captivity (e.g., owls, parrots) are so far unknown and new data will doubtless continue to break existing records, and (2) many of the records cited above are extremes of old age, at least for wild birds. From 2 to 5 years is probably close to the average life span of most adult songbirds.

Life expectancy increases greatly after the highly perilous period between egg and fully functional adult when predation, disease, accidents, and vulnerability to exposure take a high toll. It then tends to level off, since wild birds normally meet their end in sudden death, and old age is reached so infrequently as to be a negligible factor in avian actuarial tables.

The implication of the record ages and of banding data is that large birds live longer on the whole than small birds.

AGE DETERMINATION. For methods of aging bird species in which plumage characters are not reliable for this purpose, see BURSA OF FABRICIUS; OSSIFICATION.

AGGRESSION. Aggressive gestures are common among birds, but actual physical assaults by one bird on another are infrequent, and except when they kill their own kind for food (see PREDATION), birds very rarely inflict maiming or mortal injury on each other. The avian "aggressor" is almost invariably on the defensive, the two commonest scenarios in which the urge to fight is aroused being: (1) defense of territory, usually against a rival of the same species or a species with similar nesting requirements (e.g., cavity nesters), and (2) defense of the nest from predators.

Territorial aggression is most evident among birds during the breeding season (see TERRITORY), and a functional link has been established between levels of testosterone (the male sex hormone) and an aggressive urge toward other males of the same species. Territorial song may be considered aggressive behavior to the extent that it acts as a warning to other members of the singer's species to "stay out or else!" When this warning is ignored, the trespasser is often chased "off the property" but only seldom touched physically, much less injured. In fact, it is not unreasonable to suppose that there may be selective pressure against harming members of one's own species. In colonial situations, where constant territorial conflict is routine because of the "close quarters," extended "fights" are more common. Gulls, for example, may grab each other's bills or wings and play "tug-of-war" for many minutes or even hours. But again, such animosities only rarely result in serious injury or death. It is, of course, the innate territorial aggressive urge of roosters that is exploited by "sportsmen" who enjoy watching cockfights. It should be remarked that long, sharp steel spurs must be fixed to the birds' legs in order to provide the desired bloodshed and "fight to the finish."

Courtship rituals also involve acting out of aggressive urges. This tendency is perhaps most conspicuous among "lek" species such as the Ruff and many grouse. The involved rituals enacted by companies of males of such species on their "dancing grounds" usually include aggressive gestures and even innocuous contact (see DISPLAY; LEK; DOMINANCE). Even the more common male/female courtship ritual often begins aggressively with the male treating a prospective mate as a rival; the female must gradually encourage a more benign reaction by behaving in a way that "defuses" the male's attack response (see COURTSHIP).

Though less flamboyant than sex-related aggression, physical threats are also common among birds defending feeding territories. No one can watch a flock of feeding sandpipers, blackbirds, or finches for long without witnessing an "angry" bill thrust by a bird whose neighbor has infringed on the former's innately perceived feeding space (see FLOCK). The gesture is usually all that is required to assert these "rights."

Nest defense is the circumstance in which birds regularly punish each other (and other animals) physically. As in territorial defense, threatening behavior usually precedes actual contact, but the aggression level is much more likely to escalate in the case of nest defenders. The degree of punishment likely to be inflicted in defense of eggs or young varies widely according to species and circumstance. Many hawks, eagles, and falcons will unhesitatingly kill an avian intruder large enough to be deemed a threat and do as much damage as possible to a human one. Gulls, terns, and jaegers typically "dive-bomb" and "splash" humans invading a colony, and may make actual contact with bill or wing if these warnings are ignored. While most smaller birds will flee before human intrusion, many species—notably the larger tyrant flycatchers—will follow and physically abuse raptors or nest-robbing birds, even ones many times their own size.

The avian animosity engineered by Alfred Hitchcock for his film The Birds with the aid of a lot of trained crows and drugged gulls is, of course, pure fantasy as well as a clever exploitation of our atavistic fear of all non-human or non-domesticated animals. Though it is hard to fathom why crows and gulls would want to attack their chief benefactors, it must be admitted that many bird species do have reason enough to hate us (see MAN-MADE THREATS TO BIRDLIFE). But birds lack the intellectual equipment to launch a concerted attack on humankind even if they possessed sufficient emotional equipment to perceive injustice or feel resentment.

AGONISTIC. Relating to aggressive behavior between members of the same species. The threat displays of male birds defending their territories or the antagonistic gestures of lek displays are examples of agonistic behavior. See AGGRESSION; LEK; DISPLAY; and Plate 2.

AIGRETTE (AY-gret or ay-GRET) (also spelled aigret and egret). The long, delicate, and particularly beautiful plumes acquired by various species of herons during the breeding season. Around the turn of the century, these feathers were in such demand as ornamentation for hats, fans, and other items of feminine apparel that Great, Snowy, and Reddish Egrets were brought to the brink of extinction by commercial plume hunters (see CONSERVATION).

AIR SACS. Thin-walled extensions from the bronchi of the lungs, which fill most of the space of the body cavity not occupied by the viscera (see RESPIRATORY SYSTEM). The term is also used to refer to the inflatable pouches on the necks of some birds which function in courtship display and temperature control (see DISPLAY; TEMPERATURE, BODY).

ALAR (AY-lar). From *ala*, the Latin noun for "wing." Used as a technical adjective meaning "of the wing." A wing stripe is an alar characteristic of many sandpipers.

ALBATROSS (pl.: albatross or albatrosses). Standard English name for all members of the family Diomedeidae (order Procellariiformes). There are 13 species of albatrosses worldwide, 2 of which (Black-footed and Laysan) occur regularly off our Pacific coast, while 4 others have occurred as accidental stragglers in either the Atlantic or the Pacific (see Appendix II). The Short-tailed Albatross was once a regular visitor to the western Pacific from northeast Asian breeding colonies but has since been exploited to the brink of extinction (see ENDANGERED BIRDS); there are a few recent records from California, Washington, and Oregon. No species of albatrosses breed in North America.

Albatrosses are among the largest and most graceful of seabirds with heavy bodies and extraordinarily long, narrow wings, adapted to soaring on strong oceanic winds (see FLIGHT, *Dynamic Soaring*). They measure from about 2½ to 4½ feet in length, and the wingspan of two species is probably the greatest of any living bird, averaging over 10 and possibly reaching 13 feet in extreme individuals (see SIZE). Their general coloration runs to combinations of black, white, and various shades of brown with touches of yellow and pink on bill and legs. As with the other tubenoses, the hind toe (hallux) of the albatrosses is tiny or absent, and the front three toes are webbed. Their nasal "tubes" are located on either side of the bill ridge (culmen), rather than on top as in the SHEARWATERS and STORM-PETRELS, and they walk erect on land, another point of distinction from those two families, whose members must shuffle along on their tarsi. Despite their ethereal bearing, albatrosses are the most ravenous of marine carnivores and scavengers, known for their gluttonous consumption of squid, fish, crustaceans, ships' wastes, and whale carcasses. Some species follow ships for days or even weeks and they figure in many marine legends (see, for example, Coleridge's "The Rime of the Ancient Mariner").

Albatrosses nest in colonies on remote oceanic islands or desolate coasts; their courtship rituals are elaborate and often comical (see DIS-PLAY). The nest may be simply an unlined scrape in the earth, sometimes with dirt or vegetation pulled up by the sitting birds, or a high (to one foot) mud cup (Black-browed). They lay a single egg that is white in most species, brown-spotted in a few.

The voices of albatrosses are heard mainly on the breeding grounds or when flocks are feeding at sea. Squeaks, brayings, moans, and clucks are standard sounds in the repertoires of most species. They also make hollow "woody" noises by snapping or "fencing" with their long bills.

The two species that visit North American waters regularly breed on islands in the tropical Pacific Ocean and range widely over those warm seas and to the food-rich waters of the North Pacific. Most albatrosses, however, are birds of the cold antarctic and subantarctic oceans and breed during the southern summer (our winter) and disperse around the high latitudes of the South.

"Albatross" evolved from an Arabic word for "bucket." The Spanish version was *alcatraz* and referred to the bucket-like gular pouch of the pelicans. The term was then applied indiscriminately to other large seabirds and finally settled in its present form on the distinctive diomedeids.

ALBINISM (AL-buh-nizm). An abnormal lack of pigment resulting in white or whitish external features. Total albinos have pink irises (and other parts), because blood vessels at the surface become visible in the absence of other pigmentation. The feathers of totally albino birds are uniformly and completely white. More common, however, is *partial* albinism, in which only some features are white. Birds in this condition may appear splotchy or have a symmetrical pattern. See Purple Martins in Plate 5.

Nero (1954) documents "albinistic" male Red-winged Blackbirds in which the absence of melanin leaves a pinkish or reddish (salmon) coloration instead of white; presumably this pigment is present in normal birds as well but is masked by the usual black plumage.

Though often due to the emergence of a recessive genetic character and therefore present at birth and transmitted to offspring, albinism can also appear in individuals born with normal coloration. In this case the cause is a malfunction in body chemistry, which may in some cases be related to dietary deficiencies or physical trauma. Albinism is recorded in certain groups of birds more often than in others—notably ducks, geese, and swans, quail and pheasants, crows, thrushes, swallows, New World blackbirds, and fringillid finches—whereas it is unrecorded in many other families.

See also LEUCISM; SCHIZOCHROISM; and Plate 5.

ALBUMEN. The egg white. A gelatinous or semi-liquid substance surrounding and protecting the yolk. See EGG; EMBRYO.

ALCID (AL-sid). A member of the bird family Alcidae. The name by which the murres, murrelets, guillemots, puffins, auks, auklets, and dovekies are referred to collectively, e.g., "a small alcid" or "an alcid flight." See AUK.

ALEUTIAN (uh-LOO-shun) **ISLANDS.** A chain of volcanic islands (the submerged extremity of the Aleutian Range that separates the Bering Sea from the Pacific Ocean) running in a graceful curve southwest from the Alaska Peninsula, ending well west of the Chukotski Peninsula of Siberia, and reaching within a few hundred miles of the Russian Komandorskie Islands. The outermost Aleutians are effectively within the Palearctic region and host many bird species typical of that fauna both as residents and (mainly) as vagrants from South Asian–Siberian migration routes. A number of endemic alcids of the region are also of great interest to birdwatchers.

    The outer Aleutians are essentially treeless, typically fogbound, and offer accommodations that are simple at best, primitive at worst. Nevertheless, they have become a kind of Holy Land to those bird listers whose goal is to see 700 or more species in "North America." Adak and Attu (the westernmost island) hold U.S. military installations (ergo, airstrips) and are the most-visited of far-Aleutian birding meccas. See Appendix II for Alaskan-Palearctic vagrants and Appendix III for best seasons. See also GAMBELL; PRIBILOF ISLANDS. See *Birding*, 8:305–12 and 12:30–35, for descriptions and lists of Adak and Attu, respectively.

ALEXANDRE, M. M. (Black-chinned Hummingbird: *Archilochus alexandri*). A little-known French physician who sent biological specimens home from Mexico during the mid-nineteenth century.

ALIMENTARY SYSTEM. See DIGESTIVE SYSTEM.

ALLANTOIS (al-LAN-toh-iss). A membranous sac which develops from the hind gut of embryonic birds and other animals. It receives the urinary waste products and supplies oxygen to the embryo through connecting blood vessels. At its greatest development during incubation, the allantois lines almost the entire inside of the egg, surrounding the embryo and yolk sac, but it dries up before hatching time and is left behind together with its connective tissue. See EMBRYO and Fig. 8.

ALLEN, Arthur A., 1885–1964. One of four distinguished American ornithologists with the same surname (see following entries). Arthur A. Allen is perhaps best remembered as a founder of the Cornell LABORATORY OF ORNITHOLOGY, as a pioneer of bird photography, and as the author of many popular (as well as scientific) books and articles about birdlife.

ALLEN, Charles A., 1841–1930 (Allen's Hummingbird: *Selasphorus sasin*). An amateur ornithologist from Milton, Massachusetts, who moved to California for his health. There he collected specimens for professional eastern naturalists. One of these, a hummingbird which he recognized as distinct from the similar Rufous, was eventually named for him by H. W. Henshaw.

ALLEN, Joel A., 1838–1921. One of the supporting pillars of American ornithology, whose death heralded the passing of the generation of great nineteenth-century bird men that included BAIRD, BREWSTER, and COUES. J. A. Allen is generally acknowledged as the "father of the American Ornithologists' Union" and served as its president for its first seven years. His professional life was devoted mainly to the curatorships of mammals and birds, first at the Museum of Comparative Zoology at Harvard and then at the American Museum of Natural History, where he ultimately assumed the role of "Dean of the Scientific Staff." Allen served as editor for 8 volumes of the *Bulletin of the Nuttall Ornithological Club* (the club was the predecessor of the A.O.U.), 28 volumes of *The Auk*, 3 editions of the A.O.U. *Check-list of North American Birds*, and 22 volumes of the *Bulletin of the American Museum of Natural History*. His own bibliography comprises some 1,450 technical papers, mainly dealing with birds and mammals but also including important work on reptiles and evolution. He was a major influence in the stabilization of American scientific nomenclature and formulated ALLEN'S RULE.

Allen began as a boy naturalist from a strict Puritan New England family and became a protégé of Louis Agassiz. He was a shy man with no talent for public speaking and little inclination to popular writing. Consequently, he was little recognized outside the scientific community and today tends to be confused with the small host of other ornithological Allens (see preceding and following entries). But his influence in nearly all realms of our ornithology was immense and, as noted by one of his eulogists (Witmer Stone), his peers regarded his death as "a calamity."

ALLEN, Robert Porter, 1905–63. Ornithologist, National Audubon Society conservationist, early student of raptor migration, and author of several definitive studies of North American wading birds (e.g., see the Bibliography–FLAMINGO) and widely read natural history "classics" (e.g., *On the Trail of Vanishing Birds*).

ALLEN'S RULE. The generalization (formulated by J. A. Allen) that representatives of bird and mammal species living permanently in warmer climates tend to have larger external appendages (e.g., bills) than their counterparts living in cooler climates. The ecological significance of this formula is that heat loss from external appendages has been minimized through adaptive size reduction of these parts in populations constantly subjected to lower temperatures. The greater bill size (both length of culmen and depth) of southern races of Red Crossbills compared with that of their northern counterparts exemplifies Allen's rule. There are many exceptions. For example, the bills of Clapper Rails of the Atlantic coast become shorter on average as one moves south (Ripley, 1977–RAIL).

For a related concept, see BERGMANN'S RULE. See also SPECIATION.

ALLOPATRIC (al-loh-PAT-rick). Separated geographically; usually refers to closely related species or subspecies whose breeding ranges, although adjacent, do not overlap. In this situation the possibility of interbreeding cannot be tested because the two forms do not normally meet. See SYMPATRIC; SPECIATION.

ALLOPREENING. The preening of one bird by another; also referred to as "mutual preening." It has been recorded in at least nineteen orders of birds, including, among other families, the albatrosses, shearwaters, stormpetrels, boobies, cormorants, herons, storks, ibises, ducks, geese, and swans, New World vultures, hawks and eagles, pheasants and quail, rails, gulls, auks, pigeons, cuckoos, parrots, owls, swifts, wrens, New World blackbirds and orioles, weaver finches, starlings, and crows and jays.

The activity is usually performed by two birds of the same species (often mated pairs), but it may involve a group of birds or two birds of different species. In the latter case, it is thought by some authorities to involve redirection of aggressive urges. See PREENING and Harrison (1965).

ALPINE. In natural history, usually refers to the habitat above the tree line of the highest mountains. The characteristic vegetation of such areas is relatively sparse, low, often creeping, and has much in common both in form and in species composition with that in arctic regions. The term "arctic-alpine" is often used to imply this relationship between high altitude and high latitude. The rosy finches of the Rocky Mountains and Alaska are typical alpine birds. They breed on the stony barrens near the snowfields and descend to lower elevations during the winter. See ARCTIC; TUNDRA; LIFE ZONES. See also BIOME; DISTRIBUTION; and Fig. 5.

ALTERNATE PLUMAGE. Generally synonymous with "nuptial," "breeding," or "summer" plumage. See MOLT, *Sequence and Terminology.*

ALTITUDE. Our perception of the relative height of bird flight is strongly subject to distortions of circumstance. We are impressed (as we should be) when we watch an eagle disappear from view somewhere between 8,000 and 9,000 feet above us (Terres, 1980–BIRD) and when we hear of nocturnal land-bird and shorebird migrants routinely traveling at 5,000 to 10,000 feet (see MIGRATION). Yet many small birds that live above the tree line on our highest mountains double or triple these altitudes as they flit from one lichen-encrusted stone to another. Of course, in terms of energy expenditure, there is a great difference between the minor exertions of alpine songbirds and the heroic effort required to flap over the Himalayas. And it is no coincidence that the holders of the altitude records listed below are all strong-flying or soaring birds, most of which either inhabit mountainous regions or must traverse them in migration.

SOME RECORD ALTITUDES ATTAINED BY BIRDS

• 37,000 feet: The highest documented bird flight—Rüppell's Griffon Vulture (*Gyps rueppelli*) in collision with an airplane over the Ivory Coast (West Africa), November 29, 1973 (Laybourne, 1974).

• Approximately 28,000 feet: A flock of Bar-headed Geese (*Anser indicus*) heard calling above the Himalayan peak Makalu (elev. 27,842 feet) (Swan, 1970).

• 26,000 feet: Alpine Choughs (*Pyrrhocorax graculus*)—highest known altitude for a songbird, recorded by the British expedition to Mount Everest in 1924 (McWhirter, 1980). The birds followed the climbers' camp as it ascended, probably scavenging leftovers, as is typical of this species, which habitually forages above the snow line. A good candidate for highest nesting record as well, but data are lacking.

• 21,000 feet: Highest recorded altitude for small land-bird migrants; detected by radar over Norfolk, England (Lack, 1960–MIGRATION).

• 21,000 feet: North American altitude record; a Mallard (*Anas platyrhynchos*) collided with a commercial airliner, July 9, 1963, over Nevada (Terres, 1980–BIRD).

Records of all types of birds both on high mountains and in flight between 10,000 and 20,000 feet, while not "usual" perhaps, are relatively numerous in the literature.

HOW DO THEY DO IT? No human being can engage in strenuous exertions above 20,000 feet without supplementary oxygen. How do birds, especially those that normally live near sea level, fly in the rarefied atmosphere prevailing at the altitudes listed above? According to Tucker (1968), birds may hyperventilate and drastically reduce body temperature when circumstances demand it, thereby increasing oxygenation of the blood and availability of oxygen to the lungs.

ALTRICIAL (al-TRISH-ul). Refers to young birds which are helpless—usually naked, with eyes closed and totally dependent on their parents—for a period after hatching. Contrast with PRECOCIAL. See YOUNG, DEVELOPMENT OF.

ALULA (al-YOU-la). A small group of feathers attached to the first "finger" of the wing. The number of feathers varies from two to seven (three or four in most passerines). It is used as a braking and steering mechanism both in flight and underwater. Also called the "bastard wing." See WING; FLIGHT; SWIMMING/DIVING; and Fig. 25.

AMERICAN BIRDING ASSOCIATION (A.B.A.). A birdwatching organization based in North America with a current membership of about 5,000 enthusiasts. It is dedicated to the promotion of birding as a sport or pastime and to developing its members' field expertise. Its bimonthly magazine, *Birding,* offers articles on field identification, tricks of the trade, birding adventures, bird finding, summaries of technical literature of interest to birders, biographies of prominent birders, book reviews, and the philosophy and rules of bird listing. Since the A.B.A.'s major emphasis is on birding for fun, much of its attraction derives from the lure of the list, and each year it publishes the tallies of birders who have seen the most species in individual states and provinces and the world. For a sample of a *Birding* article and more on "the numbers game," see LISTING. See also SOCIETIES, ORNITHOLOGICAL; BIRD CLUB.

AMERICAN BIRDS. A bimonthly publication of the National Audubon Society (950 Third Avenue, New York, NY 10022). Two issues are devoted mainly to regional bird censuses, but the other four are devoted to a unique bird-reporting analysis by regions of the entire North American continent, supplemented by authoritative articles on field identification, distribution, taxonomy, and technical matters of interest to serious "field ornithologists." One issue is devoted to recording the previous year's CHRISTMAS COUNT.

AMERICAN ORNITHOLOGISTS' UNION (A.O.U.). The preeminent scientific ornithological organization of North America. It was founded in 1884 (incorporated in 1888) largely under the auspices of the ornithological elite which comprised the Nuttall Ornithological Club of Cambridge, Massachusetts. The A.O.U. published (and continues to revise) the authoritative *Check-list of North American Birds,* as well as lengthy ornithological monographs and *The Auk,* a quarterly journal of ornithology.

This organization has always represented the cutting edge of scientific bird study not only on this continent but worldwide. Accordingly, it is now possible to trace the course of modern ornithology over the last century by examining a sequence of issues of *The Auk* from the early numbers to the latest. In the beginning they contained many articles with titles such as "The Birds of Southeastern Dakota" (Agersborg, *Auk* [1885], 2:276–89), reflecting the descriptive, phenological, and conservation-oriented emphasis in the ornithology of the day. While important articles of this kind still appear in *The Auk,* they are now likely to be outnumbered by papers such as "Hormonal Induction of Feather Pigmentation in Ptarmigan" (Höhn and Braun, *Auk* [1980], 97:601–7) and other documents of the most meticulous research. Reflective of the academic thrust of the A.O.U. is the fact that its membership is largely drawn from colleges and universities rather than from the ranks of birdwatchers.

Serious birdwatchers of the older generation can still be heard to complain of what they consider a shift of emphasis in this venerable journal away from their subjects of interest, though of course the annals of field ornithology—from the trivial to the scientific—continue to be recorded in many other periodicals.

For more on the history of the A.O.U., see its 1933 publication, *Fifty Years Progress of American Ornithology.*

AMNION. In birds, a fluid-filled sac within the eggshell which encloses the embryo. See EGG.

ANATID (an-AT-id). A term of convenience for any member of the Anatidae, the family of birds containing the swans, geese, and ducks. In the plural, refers to these species collectively—e.g., "Sixteen species of anatids were recorded, including Whistling Swan and White-fronted Goose." See DUCK; GOOSE; SWAN; and Appendix I.

ANATOMY. For descriptions of the various bodily parts, see individual systems: RESPIRATORY SYSTEM; SKELETON; MUSCLES; etc.

ANHINGA (an-HING-guh). Standard English name for a single American species, *Anhinga anhinga,* and a collective term for all members of the family Anhingidae (order Pelecaniformes), known in most of the English-speaking world as the darters. There are 1–4 species of anhingas worldwide (depending on taxonomic opinion), all in the genus *Anhinga,* only one of which occurs in the New World.

Anhingas, which average about 32 inches in length, resemble cormorants that have fallen into the "skinny mirror" at the carnival, with almost absurdly elongated wings, tail, neck, and bill. Like the other members of the order Pelecaniformes, they have webs between all four toes and reduced nostril openings in the bill—both adaptations to underwater habits. An unusually elaborate system of neck muscles and a sharply pointed bill enable anhingas to spear fish underwater with extraordinary agility.

Anhingas are birds of wooded rivers, bayous, and swamps. Characteristic activities are swimming with all but head and neck submerged, perching singly or in groups with wings outspread to dry (feathers lack waterproofing oil), and soaring very high in the air.

Anhingas eat frogs and aquatic crustaceans and insects in addition to fish.

The nest of the native anhinga is a surprisingly small stick platform in an arboreal colony. Alternatively, these birds will adopt an abandoned heron nest. The 3–5 (rarely 2) eggs are blue with a white, chalky coating covering the surface.

Anhingas are normally silent but can make guttural croaks if the occasion arises.

The distribution of the anhingas is essentially pantropical and they tend to be migratory in temperate zone extremities of their range.

The name for the single New World species, Anhinga, derives from Tupi, a common language of native tribes of the Amazon Basin.

ANHINGA TRAIL (Florida). See EVERGLADES.

ANI (AH-nee). Standard English name for 3 of the 4 members of the subfamily Crotophaginae (family Cuculidae [cuckoos]; order Cuculiformes), 2 of which breed in North America.

Anis are medium-sized (11 to 14 inches), uniformly shiny and black, loose-plumaged birds with uniquely arched upper mandibles. The only obvious clues to their membership in the cuckoo family are their long, highly mobile tail and their hunchbacked manner of perching. They are birds of hot, open, scrubby country and feed mainly on insects. They sometimes follow grazing livestock and catch the insects that are flushed by the foraging animals, and are even known to pick ticks from the backs of cattle. Unlike the "true" cuckoos, they are often gregarious.

Both of the North American species build a communal nest, a rather large, messy cup of sticks, lined with fresh leaves and placed in a low tree or shrub, usually in a tangle of branches and foliage. Several females contribute eggs to this one nest and alternate incubation duties. A single female may lay 4–7 (Smooth-billed) or 3–5 (Groove-billed) eggs and one nest may contain up to 29 or 15 eggs, respectively. The eggs are light greenish to bluish and covered (except rarely) with a thin, white, chalky coating, which becomes scratched and stained to some degree during incubation.

Ani calls are: a "surprised" or "inquisitive" whining whistle—*wooo leeek!* (Smooth-billed); and a sharp, abrupt, metallic *whleenk*, often uttered in a staccato, flicker-like series (Groove-billed). Also other assorted calls.

All three anis are birds of the New World tropical lowlands; the North American range of our two look-alike species is normally restricted to southern Florida (Smooth-billed) and southern Texas (Groove-billed), though both have been recorded in adjacent Gulf states.

The name "ani" was coined by the indigenous tribes of Brazil.

See references in the Bibliography under CUCKOO.

ANISODACTYL (AN-ih-so-DAK-til). Describes the commonest form (invariable in passerines) of a bird's foot, with three toes directed forward and one behind. See LEG/FOOT; SKELETON, *Bones of the Leg.*

ANNA de Belle Masséna, 1806–c. 1896 (Anna's Hummingbird: *Calypte anna*). The wife of the Duc de Rivoli of France was a noted beauty of her day, and therefore aptly immortalized by one of her countrymen, the great naturalist Lesson, in the name of this spectacular species. See also RIVOLI.

ANTICRYPTIC. Blending with the natural background or disguised as harmless so as to be ignored by potential prey (compare PROCRYPTIC). In the second sense, little known in birds; however, it has been suggested that the Zone-tailed Hawk mimics the Turkey Vulture in form, coloration, and manner of flight in order to capture prey which recognize the vulture as unthreatening. If so, this could be considered an anticryptic phenomenon. See MIMICRY for discussion.

ANTING. The application by birds of the body fluids of ants (or other substances) to their plumage; in "passive anting" a bird squats on an ant nest and allows the insects to crawl over its plumage (see Fig. 16), sometimes while anting "actively" or going through the motions.

Typically, an anting bird crushes an ant in its bill and rubs it vigorously on parts of its plumage, particularly the underside of the wing tips, the undertail coverts, and the base of the tail feathers. The ant fluid may be spread on the head and other parts from the wing tips, but certain parts of the body—e.g., the belly—are anted directly only infrequently.

More than 200 species of birds (worldwide) have been observed anting. It is practiced chiefly by passerines but a few non-passerines are known to engage in anting—or at least anting-like behavior.

The purpose of anting is not yet fully understood. It is known that ants which emit chemicals (especially formic acid) as a defense technique are favored over ants whose main defense is stinging. It has also been demonstrated that formic acid kills feather mites. It is therefore the consensus theory that anting is an avian form of delousing. The activity is often followed by preening and bathing.

In the absence of ants, birds will use mothballs, citrus fruits, vinegar, still-glowing embers, and other substances, most of which produce a burning sensation, as does formic acid. This kind of stimulation apparently "releases" the anting impulse, and since individual birds must discover the effect for themselves, some members of a species ant regularly while others seldom or never learn the behavior.

An alarming side effect of certain birds' fondness for a burning sensation is a propensity for picking up flaming tinder and transporting it elsewhere—in some cases to nests constructed in buildings (Mayfield, 1966; Goodman, 1960).

ANTIPHONAL (an-TIFF-uh-null) **SONG.** Song composed of closely spaced phrases sung alternately by the male and female of a pair of birds. In "classic" antiphonal song, each bird sings a characteristic *different* phrase and the phrases are so closely spaced that the effect is of a single song. In North America, male and female Plain Chachalacas, Bobwhite, California and Gambel's Quail are recorded as responding to one another with similar calls at brief intervals; this appears to be the nearest any North American bird approaches true antiphonal song. See Thorpe, 1972–SONG. See also DUETTING; SONG, *Multiple Vocalizations.*

APATORNIS (AY-pah-tor-niss or AP-ah-tor-niss). An extinct genus of birds (order Ichthyornithiformes; family Apatornithidae), two species of which have been described from fossils found in Upper Cretaceous deposits in Kansas and Wyoming. Similar to *Ichthyornis,* but apparently not as strong a flier. See EVOLUTION OF BIRDLIFE.

APICAL (APE-ih-cul or AP-ih-cul). Near the tip. The bill of a Sandwich Tern has a yellow apex or apical area. Opposite of BASAL.

APLOMADO (ah-plo-MAH-doh) (Falcon). Spanish for "lead-colored." That a Spanish name be given to an essentially Neotropical falcon is entirely appropriate, though the overall color of this striking species is more blue-gray than lead-colored.

APOSEMATIC (AP-uh-seh-MAT-ic). Protective, especially in the context of color or pattern. There are various forms of aposematic plumage types in birds. The species in Plate 3 are protected by mimicry of their habitat; other species may escape predators by flashing a momentarily disconcerting patch of bright color (e.g., the white rump of a Common Flicker). The kind of aposematic coloration that warns of a bad-tasting meal, very common in insects, is unrecorded in birds, though it apparently applies to some egg patterns and colors.

APTERIA (app-TEER-ee-uh) (sing.: apterium). Areas of a bird's skin from which no contour feathers grow; they are sometimes down-covered. The apteria vary in size and shape among different types of birds. For a more detailed description, see FEATHER TRACTS.

ARANSAS (uh-RAN-zuss) National Wildlife Refuge (Texas). A 54,289-acre federal reserve located on the Blackjack Peninsula of the Texas coast near Tivoli. Its principal claim to fame is as the wintering ground of the rare Whooping Crane (see ENDANGERED BIRDS), but it also is host to a good selection of regional breeding birds and (especially) migrant and wintering water birds.

ARCHAEOPTERYX (arky-OP-tuh-ricks) (*A. lithographica*). The oldest-known animal considered by most authorities to be a bird. Fossil remains dating from the early Jurassic Period (138 million years ago) were found in Bavarian Germany in the mid-1800's. The first of these were originally identified as reptiles and indeed the skeleton is still considered more reptile-like than bird-like; yet the fossils clearly show that quintessentially avian characteristic—feathers. For more on the significance and anatomy of *Archaeopteryx*, and for a recent challenge to its title as the world's oldest bird, see EVOLUTION OF BIRDLIFE. For its taxonomic position, see TAXONOMY.

ARCTIC. Geographically, the Arctic extends from the North Pole south to 66° 33′ N. latitude, north of which the sun does not rise above the horizon on midwinter day (December 22) and remains above the horizon on midsummer day (June 22). Biologically, however, the Arctic is better delineated by a climatological boundary, the 10° C. (50° F.) isotherm, i.e., that part of the Northern Hemisphere in which the mean temperature for the hottest month of the year (July) does not exceed 10° C. Because of variations in temperature over the earth's surface, this line is very irregular, extending south more than 10° of latitude below the Arctic Circle in the Bering Sea and to above 70° N. in northern Scandinavia. It roughly coincides with the line above which standing trees will not grow, i.e., the line above which tundra prevails.

Though only a very few bird species (Common Raven, ptarmigan) are equal to the arctic winter, the avian *breeding* fauna of the Arctic is surprisingly rich. Loons, grebes, waterfowl, hawks and eagles, falcons, plovers, sandpipers, jaegers, gulls, auks, owls, warblers, and finches are all well represented north of the Arctic Circle during the brief (about six-week) nesting season, taking advantage of prodigious summer insect populations and the marine life that thrives in cold arctic oceans. The brevity of the breeding season is mitigated to some degree by the fact that birds can forage in daylight for nearly 24 hours during much of June and July.

For discussion of particular arctic habitats and the bird species that occupy them, see MUSKEG; TAIGA; TUNDRA; and accounts of the families noted above. See also SUBARCTIC; BIOME; DISTRIBUTION; and Fig. 5.

ARCTIC-ALPINE ZONE. One of Merriam's life zones; transcontinental in northernmost Canada and Alaska and extending southward on the summits of the highest mountains; above the Hudsonian Zone. See LIFE ZONES and Fig. 6.

ASPECT RATIO. The proportion of wing length to breadth; more specifically, the figure obtained by dividing a wing's length by its average width. Birds with high aspect ratios—i.e., those with long, narrow wings (e.g., many seabirds)—are aerodynamically more efficient and can glide long distances without flapping, especially with the aid of wind. See FLIGHT and Fig. 22.

ASPERGILLOSIS (ASS-pur-jill-OH-siss). A respiratory disease contpacted by birds and other animals by eating or inhaling the spores of a fungus (*Aspergillus fumigatus*) which grows on decaying plant material. In rare instances it is "caughp" by breeders of domestic birds. See DISEASE.

ATLAS, BREEDING-BIRD. A system for mapping the occurrence of breeding-bird *species* in a given area, as distinct from a breeding-bird census, which attempts to determine or estimate numbers of *individual* birds in a given area. The atlas concept was pioneered in Europe and is now being used in a few places in North America, e.g., Massachusetts, New York, Maryland, Maine, Vermont, Connecticut, New Jersey, Florida (planned), California, Michigan, Ontario, and the Maritime Provinces (planned).

The Massachusetts system, based on the British, works as follows: The state is divided (as are all states) into a U.S. Geodetic Survey topographic grid, scored along lines of latitude and longitude. Each topographic quadrangle is further divided for atlas coverage into six equal parts which are assigned to individuals or groups for coverage. Species are recorded according to specified criteria of *possible breeding* (e.g., a bird present in suitable habitat during the breeding season), *probable breeding* (e.g., a single male apparently on territory in suitable habitat), and *confirmed breeding* (e.g., the finding of an active nest or unambiguous evidence such as a bird carrying nesting material, or a fecal sac). Most atlas organizers allow five seasons in which to gather the requisite data. This is then fed into a computer, which ultimately prints out a map that shows at a glance the possible, probable, or (ideally) confirmed nesting distribution of each species throughout the state.

The beauty of the system is that it requires only a single confirmation for each species in each block without regard for the species' abundance. Thus, experienced birdwatchers at a favorable season (mid-June through early July is the period of maximum "confirming" activity in Massachusetts) can verify nesting of a number of species in a single morning's work; and the resulting data do not require any strained extrapolations. The central problem is getting adequate coverage (a likelihood of confirming the majority of breeding species present) for all blocks, and therefore places with a small area, large population, and high density of birders (e.g., Britain and Massachusetts) lend themselves far better to "atlasing" than places where the coverage area exceeds the coverage capacity, such as many western states. In such cases it may be more practical to use a larger grid system, e.g., one record required per topographical quadrangle, excepting perhaps areas of localized habitats.

ATTU (at-TOO). See ALEUTIAN ISLANDS.

AUDUBON (in English, AW-duh-bonn), John James, c. 1785–1851 (Audubon's Shearwater: *Puffinus lherminieri*). The name the world associates inextricably with birds belonged to an artistic genius who, like many of his kind, was as eccentric as he was brilliant. He was born at Les Cayes, Santo Domingo (now Haiti), the acknowledged bastard of a well-to-do French merchant-slaver, Jean Audubon. The artist once described the mother he never knew as being "a lady of Spanish extraction . . . as beautiful as she was wealthy," but this appears to be another example of the autobiographical imagination which encouraged him to let it be rumored that he might just be the lost Dauphin of France. Who exactly his mother was remains a matter of speculation. She may have been Jeanne Rabin, a French chambermaid or "a free . . . creole woman." In any case there is a strong likelihood that she was at least part black, the best evidence of which is the length to which family and early biographers went to cover it up. In addition to the name by which history knows him, Audubon was also called Jean Rabin and various combinations of Jean Jacques La Forêt (La Forest) Audubon.

Like many another genius (one thinks of his near-contemporary U. S. Grant), Audubon was a failure at workaday occupations such as family and business; even his early labors as an itinerant portraitist amounted to little except, probably, to hone his drafting skills. To the world's immeasurable benefit, his *raison d'être*, the double elephant folio edition of *The Birds of America* announced in 1827, consumed Audubon body and soul until its completion in 1838. These plates, engraved largely by Robert Havell, Jr., of London from Audubon's original watercolors and hand-colored under the artist's direction, comprise 497 bird forms (many of Audubon's "species" have been "lumped") painted life size. They also contain a wealth of carefully rendered plants (especially those by the teen-age Joseph Mason), mammals, reptiles, insects, and other life forms plus a fine series of period land- and townscapes. A small selection of the original watercolors, including a series showing one of the copper engravings and a hand-painted print therefrom, is on permanent exhibition at the New-York Historical Society (New York City), which owns the collected originals and occasionally mounts a comprehensive show.

As was common practice at the time, *The Birds of America* was sold by subscription and published serially. Thus, while between 175 and 200 complete, bound sets of the 27″ x 40″ double elephant folio edition are thought to have once existed, an unknown number of incomplete sets were also published. Many of the complete sets have since been broken up and the individual leaves sold for increasingly impressive sums. The original subscribers paid $1,000 for the four huge volumes containing 435 plates—a grand enough sum in the 1830's. However, today a single plate can command as much as $4,500 (game birds bringing the highest prices) and a complete elephant folio recently sold at auction for $440,000.

After completing *The Birds of America,* which brought its creator fame and a measure of financial security, Audubon embarked in 1859 on a smaller, octavo edition in collaboration with the Philadelphia lithographer J. T. Bowen. The rapid completion of this project could not be matched in the production of another famous edition, the chromolithographs in the original double elephant size begun by Julius Bien just before the Civil War. Unscrupulous business partners and the war halted publication when only 15 numbers containing 105 plates (150 species) had been issued. A plethora of popular editions (in all sizes, price ranges, and degrees of quality) have appeared since. See the Bibliography for some notable ones. (For a definitive history of Audubon's struggles with his monument and a meticulous accounting of editions and prints known to be extant, see Fries, 1973.)

Also begun right after the publication of the elephant folio was Audubon's collaboration with his friend the Reverend John BACHMAN on *The Viviparous Quadrupeds of North America:* but the master's eyesight and energy were beginning to fail, and many of the paintings for this work were done by his son John Woodhouse Audubon. He grew senile in the last two years of his life and died at Minniesland, his home overlooking the Hudson in upper Manhattan.

Though Audubon represented himself abroad as a colorful frontier character, "an American woodsman," acting and dressing the part with long flowing tresses and rustic, fur-trimmed attire, he was not the naïve, rude "natural genius" he sometimes pretended to be. He had studied drawing briefly under the great Jacques Louis David in Paris before coming to his father's farm in Pennsylvania at the age of seventeen, and his shrewdness in promoting himself and his paintings in the highest circles of European society is verified by the publicity he quickly generated and his success at peddling such an expensive work. His wit and intelligence came through in many of his dramatic (some think overdramatic) compositions and in his writings. Both his *Ornithological Biographies,* written (with William MACGILLIVRAY supplying the scientific detail) to accompany *The Birds of America,* and his journals, edited by his granddaughter, Maria A. Audubon, contain many passages which are movingly evocative of the early-nineteenth-century American wilderness and its inhabitants. Audubon was among the first to lament the sad destruction of the former.

AUDUBON SOCIETIES. The Audubon movement began as a militant lobby for bird preservation, responding to the largely unheeded slaughter of the continent's avifauna that continued well into this century. For a brief sketch of the society's origins, see CONSERVATION; for longer histories, see the Bibliography–CONSERVATION.

The name Audubon alone assures the automatic association between birds and Audubon Societies in the minds of the general public, but the leaders of the Audubon movement in the modern era have long realized that the most serious threats to birdlife are ones that unselectively threaten all life on earth—e.g., air and water pollution, habitat destruction, indiscriminate use of chemical pesticides, and careless disposal of both organic and inorganic wastes. The widespread awareness of these threats to the environment has coincided with a burgeoning of popular interest in and proprietary attitude toward living organisms other than human beings. This is clearly reflected in the enormous increase in "nature" publications and TV programs and in the increased popularity of outdoor activities. The Audubon Societies promote a wide spectrum of aesthetic and recreational experiences in order to stimulate people's innate (but often dormant) appreciation of the natural world, to educate them in the details and functions of the ecosystem, and to elicit support for maintaining a livable planet and holding the line against reckless exploitation of unrenewable natural resources.

Though they share similar goals, there are really several Audubon movements. The National Audubon Society, with a nationwide membership, is the largest and publishes two periodicals with national circulation: *Audubon*, a monthly magazine famed for its fine photography, and *American Birds*, a journal of field ornithology, published six times a year. The national organization is based in New York City and has affiliates throughout the U.S.

The Canadian Nature Federation (formerly Canadian Audubon Society) is similarly organized north of the border, with affiliates in each province. Of these the Federation of Ontario Naturalists (F.O.N.) and the Manitoba Naturalist Society are the largest, each publishing its own glossy magazine. The provincial organizations in turn have local branches.

The Audubon Societies of Massachusetts, Maine, New Hampshire, Connecticut, Rhode Island, New Jersey, Arkansas, Indiana, Michigan, Central Atlantic States, and Florida are independent organizations that set their own environment agendas. Though these tend to concentrate on local issues, the larger state Audubon Societies are among the country's major conservation forces. The Massachusetts Audubon Society (father of the present national organization), for example, has 27,000 members, departments of education, research, environmental affairs, natural history, and publications, maintains 12,000 acres of wildlife sanctuaries statewide, and has a voice in national and even international issues.

AUK. Standard English collective name for the family Alcidae (order Charadriiformes), though no living species is currently known by the name "auk" in North America. There are 21 or 22 (depending on taxonomy) species of auks worldwide, 19 of which breed in North America, with another (Craveri's Murrelet, considered conspecific with Xantus' Murrelet by some) occurring as a visitor to southern California in the fall. Not included in these totals is the Great Auk, which was eradicated for food and feathers by 1844 (see EXTINCT BIRDS).

The auks are small to medium-sized (6½ to 14 inches; the Great Auk measured about 30 inches) birds with narrow wings, short to medium-length bills, and front three toes fully webbed. Excepting the puffins, they hobble awkwardly on their tarsi when on shore (which they visit only to breed) rather than walk upright. Their plumage is generally patterned in black (or sooty brown) and white, though two western species have a rusty-brown alternate (breeding) plumage. Their legs, mouth linings, and bills are often brightly colored, and a number of species have elaborate bill modifications and facial plumes (see Plate 2).

Auks occur exclusively in the marine environment except (in a few cases) while nesting. Most nest in dense colonies, building no nest but laying their eggs on rocky ledges, in crevices, or under rocks. A few species (e.g., puffins) excavate burrows in the earth and provide a sparse lining of vegetation, feathers, and/or other debris. The great majority of auks nest within feet of the sea, but the Kittlitz's Murrelet nests on talus slopes near the tops of mountains above the tree line. Most remarkable of all is the preferred site of the Marbled Murrelet, which nests in coniferous trees, laying its egg on a pad of moss up to 148 feet from the ground (see NEST for details of discovery). The size, shape, color, and markings of auk eggs are all remarkably variable—even among individuals in the case of the last two characteristics. The eggs of the two murre species are long and strongly pyriform, an adaptation usually supposed to have evolved in conjunction with their predilection for nesting on narrow cliffside ledges: when the eggs are kicked by parent birds, they tend to roll in a circle rather than over the edge. Murre eggs are also noted for their impressive variation in color and markings (see Fig. 7). Auk eggs in general may be white, yellowish, buff, green, or olive; unmarked, finely speckled, heavily splotched, and/or scrawled in gray, buff, reddish, purplish, brown, or blackish; and the markings may be well defined or fuzzy, evenly distributed, concentrated at the large end, or cover the surface so thoroughly that the egg appears almost wholly dark. Most auks lay a single egg as a rule; the Ancient Murrelet and the guillemots (*Cepphus*) are exceptional in regularly laying two and the latter unique in sometimes producing three.

Auks are seldom heard at sea, but on the breeding grounds they utter low moans, guttural growls, quacks, and croaks; a few species give piping cries and shrills.

The auks are the quintessential birds of the northern seas, just as penguins are of the Antarctic. Most species breed in the Arctic and disperse to sea—but not far south—after nesting; a few species breed as far south as Baja California and a couple regularly cross the Tropic of Cancer in winter. The group reaches its greatest diversity by far on the west coast of North America and a number of species are endemic to this region. Several species have a circumpolar arctic breeding distribution.

"Auk" derives from Old Norse names for some of these birds and may have been inspired by the croaks they utter in their breeding colonies. Ornithologically, the term is synonymous with ALCID.

See also AUKLET; DOVEKIE; GUILLEMOT; MURRE; MURRELET; PUFFIN.

AUK, THE. Quarterly journal of the American Ornithologists' Union. For a general description of materials published, see AMERICAN ORNITHOLOGISTS' UNION. For the subscription address as of 1982, see the Bibliography under PERIODICALS.

AUKLET. Standard English name for 6 species of auks, 3 of them in the genus *Aethia* (family Alcidae; order Charadriiformes), all of which breed along the North Pacific coasts of North America. Except for the three congeneric species, the name has no taxonomic integrity and is not even a reliable diminutive, since one species (Rhinoceros) averages larger than several of the medium-sized auks (the other auklets are under 10 inches). All of the auklets, except Cassin's, have unusual bill modifications and/or head plumes in alternate (breeding) plumage. All nest in rocky crevices (most species) or burrows excavated in earth (Cassin's and Rhinoceros).

For family characteristics, see AUK.

AUKLET, THE. A parody of *The Auk*, sometimes published on the occasion of the annual convention of the American Ornithologists' Union. The quality of its humor varies enormously from subtle send-ups of ornithological research to sophomoric puns and "jokes."

AURICULARS (awe-RIK-yeh-lerz). The ear coverts. The area of feathers covering the ear openings near the center of the "cheeks." Often visible in the field as a distinctly outlined patch below and behind the eye. Male Golden-winged Warblers have black auriculars. See Fig. 25.

AUSTRAL (AWE-strull). Southern; see LIFE ZONES and Fig. 6.

AUTOLYCISM (awe-TALL-ih-sizm). Coined by Meinertzhagen to describe uses birds make of other animals, including other birds and human beings. In the strictest sense excludes close beneficial or detrimental relationships such as SYMBIOSIS or PARASITISM. Examples of autolycism are:

gulls following a tractor to feed on exposed insect larvae; swifts nesting in chimneys; a bird using fur or another species' feathers for nest construction.

AVES. See AVIS.

AVIAN (AY-vee-un). Referring to birds, e.g., "Feathers are a uniquely avian characteristic."

AVIARY (AY-vee-air-ee). A place where birds are kept in captivity. The term often implies a relatively large, though enclosed area in which a variety of species are able to fly freely. A "bird house" at a zoo could also be called an aviary, but a small cage housing a canary generally would not. See AVICULTURE.

AVIATION (birds as hazards to). See PESTS, *Hazards to Aircraft.*

AVICULTURE. Here defined broadly as the practice of keeping birds for any purpose. The branch of aviculture which involves rearing birds for food is, however, treated under DOMESTICATED BIRDS. And FALCONRY and COCKFIGHTING are also described separately. Although the widespread practice of keeping caged birds as pets is noted here, the term "aviculturist" is usually restricted to one engaged in breeding birds in captivity, often with a serious purpose in mind.

CAGE BIRDS. A great many people who have little or no interest in observing birdlife in nature keep birds in captivity for a variety of reasons. Doubtless the most common of these is the simple amusement and company that a pet bird can provide. Originally, of course, native birds—especially those with fine songs—were trapped for this purpose. And while this is now forbidden by law in much of Europe and all of North America, it remains a common custom throughout much of the world. The species most commonly kept as pets are now bred in captivity especially for the pet market and can be bought cheaply in an astonishing array of color variations which may include no trace of the original plumage characteristics of their species. The best-known pet cage birds are: the Canary, derived originally from the wild Serin (*Serinus canaria*) of the Canary Islands, the Azores, and Madeira and justly famed for its voice, which, along with its plumage characteristics, has been "improved" in captivity; the Budgerigar (*Melopsittacus undulatus*), or "parakeet" as it is often called in America, native of arid regions of Australia and capable of making some word-like sounds with training; the Cockatiel (*Nymphicus hollandicus*), another native of the Australian interior; the Hill or Talking Mynah (*Gracula religiosa*), a resident of humid forest in southern Asia, and a truly remarkable vocal mimic, which not only enunciates words but copies the tone of the imitated sound; and several species of handsomely colored waxbill finches (family Estrildidae), e.g., the Gouldian Finch (*Chloebia gouldiae*) and the Zebra Finch (*Taeniopygia guttata*).

A somewhat different circumstance prevails in the case of some of the larger parrots which are becoming increasingly popular in North America for their exotic quality and brilliant plumage as well as the ability (of a few species) to "talk." These birds are mainly *not* bred in captivity for the commercial market, but captured from the wild from Australia (cockatoos), Africa (Gray Parrot), and Latin America (*Amazona* parrots and macaws). It is difficult to imagine these bizarre creatures as wild birds unless one has seen them flying free in their native habitat—to most people they seem to be native to zoos, pet shops, and the exotic-bird plate in the encyclopedia. In fact, however, the numbers of several macaw species are dwindling drastically due in large measure to habitat destruction but also to the capture of fledglings, which bring fancy prices as ornaments for the gardens of tropical hotels and as exotic pets in the Temperate Zone. The Yellow-headed Parrot (*Amazona ochrocephala*) of Mexico and Central America seems also to be under pressure due to its well-known "talking" ability.

"EXOTIC COLLECTABLES." Some aviculturists collect birds more or less in the way that a philatelist collects stamps, i.e., with a taste for the beauty and/or rarity of particular species. Tropical countries are major sources of imports both because of the wide array of colorful bird species found in the tropics and because of the lax enforcement or total lack of bird trapping and exporting regulations. While most exotic-bird collectors are completely scrupulous with regard to dealing in rare species and do not try to evade import-export laws, it is nonetheless a fact that a lucrative trade in birds such as rare Australian parrots and waxbills continues to thrive.

WATERFOWL AND PHEASANTS. These birds are relatively easy to keep in captivity, especially for collectors of means with some acres of parkland which can be developed as suitable habitat. Assembling private synoptic collections of anatids or phasianids on a worldwide or more local scope is a widespread (if not common) practice in the Western world. The most famous of such collections is the Severn Wildfowl Trust in Slimbridge, Gloucestershire, England, founded by Sir Peter Scott in 1946. Though it is open to the public, Slimbridge (and most other large waterfowl collections) is more than an assemblage of pretty ducks. It serves as a base for research into breeding biology and other aspects of behavior, population dynamics, hybridization, disease, and the like and also acts as a gene reserve and breeding center for rare and endangered species. In North America a great many much smaller collections are kept by hobbyists simply for fun.

It would be pointless to deny that pheasants (or ducks) are kept and bred at least in part for the splendor of the males' plumage. However, many pheasant species occupy extremely narrow Asian ranges and are threatened by overpopulation and habitat destruction, and they too benefit from captive breeding programs.

ENDANGERED SPECIES. Many rare birds are unfortunately far less easy to rear in captivity than waterfowl and pheasants. Indeed, the "sluggish" breeding biology of species such as the California Condor may play a major role in their continuing decline. Nevertheless, encouraging results have been achieved recently in carefully controlled scientific captive breeding programs designed to increase populations of Peregrine Falcons (Cornell Laboratory of Ornithology, Ithaca, N.Y.) and Whooping Cranes (Patuxent Wildlife Research Center, Md.). The fact that such quintessentially wild species can be reared and (apparently) returned successfully to the wilderness permits us to hope that we may be able to offset to some degree the by-products of the man-made environment which were responsible for the decline of these and other species.

Many of our largest and most sophisticated zoos also consider it a principal goal to obtain and breed species of birds and other animals from all over the world whose wild populations are threatened. While it is hoped that captive-bred species can eventually be returned to their native ranges and habitats, it may be crucial to much of the life on earth that genetic diversity is maintained, i.e., that unique organisms not be allowed to disappear (see EXTINCT BIRDS).

AVICULTURE: PROS AND CONS. Modern avicultural practices can be viewed as a net boon to society. They have made it possible to maintain populations of rare bird species, taught us a great deal about the habits and biology of species nearly impossible to study in the wild, greatly expanded the availability of certain food sources (poultry and eggs), provided educational experiences (public zoos), aided medical research (laboratory birds), and allowed people to enjoy pet birds without detriment to wild native species.

It is unfortunate therefore that "bird fanciers" retain one smudge on an otherwise gleaming escutcheon—the exploitation (legal in many instances) of wild bird populations, particularly in "underdeveloped" parts of the world. Most people would regard the sale and keeping of captive-bred "budgies" and canaries as harmless at worst and at best as serving a genuine human need. But the importation of wild exotics, which currently runs to millions of birds annually in the U.S. alone and which yields huge profits—proportional in many cases to the rarity of a species—is a practice which any conscientious aviculturist would be hard-pressed to defend—especially since as many as 80 percent of the birds captured for this purpose may die before reaching their prospective "owners" (Nilsson, 1980).

AVIFAUNA. The birdlife of any given place or era, e.g., North American avifauna, Pleistocene avifauna, urban avifauna, Nearctic avifauna, backyard avifauna.

AVIS (pl.: Aves) (AY-viss [veez] or AH-viss [veez/vaze]). The Latin word for "bird"; and in the plural, the name of the class of animals that consists exclusively of birds. For a definitive description of the class, see BIRD.

AVOCET (AV-uh-set). Standard English name for 4 members of the family Recurvirostridae (order Charadriiformes), which is sometimes referred to as the avocet family and also includes the STILTS. The American Avocet is the sole species of avocet in North America.

Avocets are tall (average about 15 inches), gracefully proportioned shorebirds with stilt-like legs, upturned bills, and elegantly patterned plumage. Like the stilts, avocets are colonial nesters and often feed together in flocks, "swishing" their bills in bottom muck to disturb small vertebrates (fish, frogs) and large invertebrates (shrimp, insects). They are good swimmers (front three toes almost fully webbed) and even dive occasionally.

A sparsely lined depression in sand or mud in shortgrass marsh or in the open is the typical avocet nest. The 2–5 (usually 4) eggs are brownish yellow, normally rather densely covered with distinct, dark brown spots.

The call of the American Avocet is a loud, high *klee-eep* or *plee-eek*.

Avocets occur in all the major zoogeographic regions of the world, in general breeding neither in the warmest nor in the coldest climates. In North America, they are most abundant and widespread in the West, where they nest along lakeshores and marsh edges and migrate to the coast for the winter.

The origins of the lovely name are lost.

AXILLARS (or axillaries). A small group of stiffened feathers in the "armpit." The black axillars of the Black-bellied Plover, which stand out strikingly against the pale gray of the basic (winter) plumage, are a classic field mark, used by birdwatchers worldwide.

B

BABBLER. Standard English name for about 150 species of birds in the essentially Old World family Timaliidae (order Passeriformes), which also includes the akalats, illadopses, jeries, chatterers, babaxes, laughing thrushes, mesias, barwings, minlas, fulvettas, sibias, yuhinas, oxylabes, log runners, whipbirds, quail thrushes, eupetes, and several other forms. All of these are known collectively as "babblers." Peters et al. (1931 et seq.–CHECKLIST) consider the babblers to be a subfamily (Timaliinae) under a very broad definition of the family Muscicapidae. There is only one North American babbler: the Wrentit (*Chamaea fasciata*), long an ornithological puzzle and, until recently, placed in a family of its own, the Chamaeidae (see WRENTIT).

"Babbler" refers to the raucous, varied, and long-winded vocal habits of many members of the family.

BACHMAN (BOCK-mun), Rev. John, 1790–1874 (*Haematopus bachmani*: Black Oystercatcher; Bachman's Warbler: *Vermivora bachmanii*; Bachman's Sparrow: *Aimophila aestivalis*). A Lutheran minister born in Rheinbeck, New York, but residing in gentlemanly comfort for most of his life in Charleston, South Carolina. Over his long career as a prominent naturalist he knew both Wilson and Agassiz, but he is best remembered for his complex and intimate association with AUDUBON. They first met in 1831 when the pastor put Audubon up for a few weeks during one of the latter's collecting expeditions. Bachman's sister-in-law, Maria Martin, did some botanical and entomological details such as the flame azalea and the Florida atala and buckeye butterflies which rather overwhelm Audubon's drab Swainson's Warbler in Havell's Plate CXCVIII. Audubon's two sons married Bachman's two (alas, short-lived) daughters. And Audubon and Bachman collaborated on a number of natural history projects, of which the greatest was their *Viviparous Quadrupeds of North America*. Audubon named the oystercatcher and the warbler, currently the rarest in North America, for his friend. It was Bachman who discovered the warbler and his sparrow near Charleston. Maria Martin painted the *Franklinia* tree in which the pair of warblers in Havell's Plate CLXXXV are placed. The tree, named for Benjamin Franklin by the Bartram brothers, is almost as rare as the warbler; it is now widely cultivated, but was found in the wild only recently in one locality after having been "lost" since 1790.

BAIRD, Spencer Fullerton, 1823–87 (Baird's Sandpiper: *Calidris bairdii*; Baird's Sparrow: *Ammodramus bairdii*). A central figure in American ornithology in the latter half of the nineteenth century (see also BREWER; CASSIN; COUES; RIDGWAY; George Newbold LAWRENCE) and, perhaps more than any other single person, responsible for bringing knowledge of the North American avifauna from the pioneering stages of Wilson and Audubon to the comprehensiveness and meticulous classification of the modern era. In the Historical Preface to his *Key . . .* (1890), Elliott Coues outlines the "Bairdian Epoch" in American ornithology, and at Baird's death, J. A. ALLEN called him the "Nestor of American Ornithology."

Baird began as a boy naturalist in Pennsylvania, took his first degree in natural history, made friends before he was twenty with the aging Audubon, and rapidly developed talents as a linguist, administrator, politician, and writer. He published extensively not only on birds but on mammals, reptiles, and fishes. He became the secretary of the Smithsonian

Institution in Washington, D.C., and persuaded Congress to build the National Museum of Natural History to house the collections he accumulated so assiduously. He created and headed the U.S. Commission of Fish and Fisheries and founded the marine science laboratory at Woods Hole, Massachusetts. Through his connections in the government and his relationship by marriage (son-in-law) to the Inspector General of the Army, he was responsible for the remarkable involvement of government surgeons (see BIOGRAPHY) in the collecting of zoological specimens in the West. These collections along with his own field work provided the basis for a government report (part of the survey for the railroad route to the Pacific) on birds of the U.S. Later reissued as *The Birds of North America* (1859), this work included 738 forms, constituting the first truly comprehensive, scientifically organized checklist of the avifauna. Baird's other major ornithological works are noted in the Bibliography. In addition to his achievements, he was remembered as a friend and supporter of other naturalists.

BAJA CALIFORNIA. A long, narrow peninsula extending more than 700 miles south from the southern border of California and contiguous in its northeastern extremity with Arizona and the Mexican state of Sonora. Baja itself is divided into two Mexican states, Baja California Norte (north) and Baja California Sur (south), with their common border along the 28th parallel. Both are bounded to the west by the Pacific Ocean and to the east by the Gulf of California (the Sea of Cortez). Baja's total area is 55,619 square miles.

Much of this peninsula's character is captured in the words "dry" and "rugged." Its picturesque coastlines give way to scrub desert and a broken cordillera of arid mountains which reaches above 10,000 feet on its highest peak. The most humid northerly sections and mountaintops receive all of 10 inches of rain a year and, except for isolated patches of highland pine forest, the vegetation consists largely of cactus, ocotillo, creosote scrub, and other desert plants. Though parts of Baja burst into Elysian bloom briefly, following the short annual rains, its normal aspect is one of barrenness and ferocious heat. Its length can now be traveled by car, but the less adventurous might prefer to visit via one of several ferries from the Mexican mainland or from the deck of a cruise ship.

In the present context, Baja California is of interest chiefly because it is considered part of North America by the compilers of the A.O.U. *Check-list of North American Birds.* Within recorded ornithological history the peninsula contained five species of birds which occurred nowhere else in the world: Guadalupe Storm-Petrel (*Oceanodroma macrodactyla*), Guadalupe Caracara (*Polyborus [Caracara] lutosus*), Black-fronted (Xantus') Hummingbird (*Hylocharis xantusii*), Gray Thrasher (*Toxostoma cinereum*), and San Lucas Robin (*Turdus confinis*). The storm-petrel and the caracara, known only from Guadalupe Island and vicinity, have been extinct since early in the century and the robin is now widely considered a pale race of the American Robin (*Turdus migratorius*). The hummingbird and thrasher are still alive and remain "good species" and many endemic subspecies still occur, especially on some of the offshore islands. Black and Least Storm-Petrels are *breeding* endemics of islands in the Sea of Cortez and off the Pacific coast of Baja, and the only "North American" records for a few species of birds (e.g., Townsend's Shearwater: *Puffinus auricularis*) were made on the peninsula or its offshore waters.

The North America of the present book does *not* include Baja California and species known from nowhere else on the "continent" are not included in Appendixes I and II.

See Grinnell, "Distributional Summation of the Ornithology of Lower California," *Univ. Calif. Publ. Zool.* (1928), 32:1–300.

BALDPATE. An alternative name, still in wide usage, to the standard English name American Wigeon. The pate (crown) of this duck is not bald in the sense of showing bare skin, but merely covered in white feathers.

BANDING. The placement of a numbered metal band on the leg or (less frequently) wing of a bird in an effort to individualize the bird and thereby discover certain facts of its life history. In Britain the practice is called "ringing."

ORIGINS. It is fruitless to guess when the first curious naturalist may have tried to keep tabs on a bird by tying a bit of colored yarn to its leg. We know for certain, however, that John James Audubon tied silver strands on the legs of young Eastern Phoebes near Philadelphia in 1803, and observed their return the following spring—so it is entirely fitting that the title of First North American Bird Bander go to him.

More organized efforts began in Western Europe in the 1890's, with the first serious banding operation generally credited to Christian Mortensen of Viborg, Denmark, in 1899 and the first banding station established in 1903 at Rossitten on the Baltic coast of Germany. Some small individual operations began in America not long afterward, but banding did not become centralized in the U.S. and Canada until the early 1920's. Like nearly everything else, bird banding has expanded enormously since the world wars (see *Results,* below), though, except for Japan, its appeal is still largely restricted to developed Anglo-Saxon countries.

PURPOSES. In essence, the value of bird banding lies in allowing us to keep track of an individual bird (or many individual birds) in more than one time and place during the course of its life. If we band a nestling Herring Gull in 1981 and it is found dead in the summer of 2001, we have proven that Herring Gulls live to be *at least* 20 years old. If we band a

Manx Shearwater in Boston and retrap it on its arrival back at its breeding hole in England, we get a fair idea of the speed at which the species travels, its navigational skills, and its homing instincts. If a Blackpoll Warbler is banded in Canada, retrapped along the New England coast, and found dead in South America, we begin to discover the migration route of at least some members of this species. In all these cases, the more individuals of a species which are both banded and recovered, the clearer their behavior patterns become. If we band nestlings from a colony of cormorants, for a period of years we can not only reckon average life span, homing abilities, migration routes, and wintering grounds, but also assemble data on dispersal, mortality rates, and other characteristics of that particular population. In addition to being of intrinsic scientific interest, such information is crucial to the formulation of policies governing hunting, pest control, and endangered species.

PROCEDURES. The collection and analysis of large amounts of reliable information requires centralized organization and regulated standards as well as the skill, care, and enthusiasm of individuals.

Permission to band birds must be obtained first from the federal government (Bird Banding Laboratory, U.S. Fish and Wildlife Service, Laurel, MD 20708, or Canadian Wildlife Service, 400 Laurier Avenue West, Ottawa 4, Ontario, Canada) and then from the appropriate state or provincial fish and game or conservation agency. Applicants must be eighteen or older, have some experience in bird study, and supply the names of three professional ornithologists or licensed banders as personal references—this to assure that new licensees possess the minimal prerequisites of skill in bird identification and the ability to keep accurate records. Licensed banders remain subject to the federal and state regulations governing keeping, breeding, collecting, or transporting wild birds, their nests or eggs (see LAWS).

Paraphernalia and Techniques. Once banding permits are obtained from the appropriate government agencies, the Bird Banding Laboratory supplies the bander with bands, reporting forms, and the official procedural guide, the *Bird Banding Manual*, all without charge. Banders are responsible for supplying their own bird-capturing equipment and other accessories; in most countries, they must also purchase the bands from the controlling agency.

The typical bird band is a short cylinder of light metal (usually aluminum alloy) ranging from less than 2 mm. to 30 mm. in diameter, to accommodate the varying leg sizes of different species. Of critical concern is that the band not encumber or in any way harm the bird. It is split lengthwise so that it can be opened and then reclosed by pliers around a bird's leg (usually the tarsus). Each band is inscribed with a number and an indication of where reports should be sent (see end of entry). Plastic color bands are used when field recognition is important, and various types of plastic or metal wing clips, neck rings, and bill markers—all harmless to the birds—are used in special situations (see also MARKING).

Numerous trapping devices have been developed over the years to catch birds (see CAPTURE), and very infrequently birds may be "tranquilized" by "treated" bait for banding purposes. By far the most widely used method of catching birds up to the size of a Sharp-shinned Hawk is the setting of mist nets. These nets consist of a relatively open mesh made of fine but strong black silk or nylon. Different strengths and mesh sizes are used depending on the size of the birds to be captured. A typical mist-net setup is 30 to 40 feet long and consists of five "trammels" strung horizontally about a foot apart one above the other between the poles. The netting is made to hang loosely so that a long pocket is formed along the lower margin of each trammel. The effect is not unlike a series of flimsy, sagging badminton nets, except that against vegetation the mesh is all but invisible. A bird crossing a trail along which a net has been strung blunders into the net, falls into the pouch area, and becomes enveloped in the fine mesh. The bander carefully untangles the captive, records its vital statistics (see below), affixes the right-sized band to its leg, and releases it. Normally this is a quick and completely painless (though no doubt slightly traumatic) experience for the birds involved. Banders are obligated to check their nets frequently to prevent birds from becoming too badly entangled and to make sure they are not running more nets than they can humanely handle when many birds are likely to be caught, e.g., during migration.

Perhaps the commonest and certainly the most convenient method of banding large birds is to concentrate on nestlings. The dangers risked in trying to band juvenile goshawks in their treetop nests or young gannets on a precipitous cliff face are not inconsiderable, but they are trivial compared to grappling with adults of such powerful, "well-armed" species.

Collecting and Processing Data. The minimum information a bander must record includes the identity of the species, sex and age (when known), the place of its banding, and the band number. Other information, such as a bird's degree of fat accumulation or its subspecies, results in more precise deductions if the bird is recaptured or found dead elsewhere. Some of these things may be obvious from superficial examination; others require knowing what to look for where, e.g., the bursa of Fabricius and ossification of the skull (age) and a cloacal protuberance (sex).

The unusual closeness to the bird, the difference in perspective, and the impossibility of judging physical attitude and gesture (see JIZZ) can make identification of birds "in the hand" surprisingly difficult, even for those who consider themselves proficient at field identification. And of course some species, such as *Empidonax* flycatchers and certain immature warblers, are hard to label under *any* circumstances. A compensating factor is the ability of the bander to examine his captive bird minutely from every angle, take measurements, and observe clues, such as wing formula, which are invisible in the field. The *Bird Banding Manual* and banding journals (see below) record a broad spectrum of minute but definitive characters, and perceptive banders continue to discover new ones.

Obviously, the more information that is recorded about an individual bird, the greater the possibility of learning something useful. However, banders must resist any temptation to record data that they are "almost" sure of, since a mistake could lead to completely false conclusions about a bird's behavior.

All of the information collected by the bander is recorded on standardized forms supplied by the Bird Banding Laboratory, where all data are sent for analysis by computer. This information center makes it possible for researchers to use not only the data that they collect but also that of hundreds of other banders across the continent.

RESULTS. Although much can be learned by the analysis of initial bandings, the greatest rewards come when a bird falls into human hands at least twice—once when it is trapped and banded and again when it is captured, killed, or found dead. A disparity in the dates and/or places of the successive contacts with the bird is also necessary—we learn very little when, as often happens, a bander re-nets a bird he has just banded.

It is easy enough to band a lot of birds, but there are a number of factors which work against a second recorded recovery. The sheer abundance of birdlife is one limitation. Since only a tiny percentage of birds can be banded, the chances of banded birds being reported a second time are slight. Furthermore, many thousands of birds must be banded each year simply to balance the number of birds which end up at the bottom of the sea or buried in the leaf litter of an Amazon rain forest. The uneven distribution of bird banders and people who are likely to return a band also limits the percentage of interesting returns and distorts the data that *are* collected. Many of the people most likely to hold a banded bird in their hands in Latin America would be unlikely to guess its significance correctly, even if they could read the inscription on the band. The true explanation, after all, is as strange as almost any invented one, and countless bands probably end up as ceremonial jewelry or mementos of supposed religious significance. If our perception of world bird distribution were limited to banding records, we would be given to assume that most birds occur in heavily populated regions of the Western world, particularly those where bird banders are numerous.

It should also be obvious that it is *accumulated* recoveries of a given species in a given place, at a given time, etc., which yield credible theories, not isolated returns. If a Canada Warbler banded in Ontario is recovered a year later in Mexico, we have no way of knowing whether it is a migrant, winter resident, or vagrant there, whether it is common or not, its time of arrival or departure, its rate of travel, or the mortality rate of the species. If, however, *numerous* banded Canada Warblers are netted and re-netted during a certain period of the winter over successive years in a particular locality in Peru, we can make reasonable assumptions about all of these things and even shed some light on the single Mexican record. Unfortunately, banding stations are scarce in Mexico and Peru, as they are throughout the wintering grounds of most Northern Hemisphere migrants, and data from these tropical regions are proportionately scarce.

In spite of these formidable limitations, bird banding has been one of our principal sources of facts about birdlife. And as the number of competent banders increases our insight expands. Approximately 1,138,397 birds were banded in 1981 in North America by about 2,500 master banders. Out of the total 30–40 million birds banded in North America to date, roughly 10 percent have been recovered. As noted, the recovery rate varies greatly according to circumstances—from as high as 20 percent for popular sport species to fractions of 1 percent for recoveries from tropical wintering grounds.

There are some short-term, "flashy" data yielded by bird banding, e.g., prodigious speeds or journeys of which some birds are capable. But a great deal of the valuable information about birdlife derived from banding is attributable to patient, long-term efforts and the great advantage of a collective information system—aided immensely these days by what used to be called an "electronic brain." Governments and philanthropic institutions are unlikely to deem the plumage sequence of the Cape May Warbler or the life span of the Red-legged Kittiwake worthy of a grant or a scientist's time. But over the years—with a class of graduate students working here, a retired backyard bander there—such worthwhile minutiae accumulate in the banding literature, where they wait to take their place in a work of grander ornithological or ecological significance.

Banding Stations and Publications. These provide the easiest access to more information about bird banding. If you are lucky enough to live near a bird observatory, you have the opportunity to witness a large-scale banding of migratory birds. During peak periods these operations often need to recruit capable volunteers. Many colleges and conservation organizations run periodic banding demonstrations, and most individual banders are glad to share their enthusiasm with anyone who shows an interest, especially budding banders.

The following publications are also sources of detailed information and can tell you of banders or stations in your area (addresses given in the Bibliography under PERIODICALS):

The Journal of Field Ornithology (formerly *Bird-Banding*): the leading national quarterly published by the Northeastern Bird-Banding Association

North American Bird Bander: quarterly (merger of major continental banding publications, including *Western Bird Bander, E.B.B.A. News, Inland Bird Banding News,* and *Ontario Bird Banding)*

If You Find a Banded Bird, the number of the band should be reported to the proper authorities (see below). If the bird is dead you can remove and mail the band itself; release live birds after carefully noting the band numbers. You need not worry about identifying the bird since the band number is unique to the bird wearing it and its species will have been recorded by the bander. In return for your effort, the banding office will send you the bird's "vital statistics."

Pigeons are banded by pigeon racers for identification rather than scientific purposes. You can discover the owner of a racing pigeon that strays into your life by looking up the letter code on the band in an official *Band List,* published annually by the International Federation of American Homing Pigeon Fanciers, Inc., and the American Racing Pigeon Union, 107 Jefferson St., Belmont Hills, PA 19004. Be warned, however, that pigeons that have wandered from their appointed course are usually of little interest to their owners.

Owners of private waterfowl collections also usually band their birds, which not infrequently escape when their clipped flight feathers are replaced in the next molt. Finding the source of these strays may involve more research and long-distance charges than it is worth.

All birds banded for scientific purposes in the U.S. and Canada have "Avise Bird Band Wash, D.C." inscribed on their bands; on smaller species it may appear on the inner surface. Postmen know that envelopes so addressed are to be delivered to the Department of the Interior, which, in turn, sends them on to the bird banding laboratory in Maryland.

BANNER MARKS. Bright, pale (often white) areas or "flashes" in a bird's plumage, normally concealed when a bird is in repose but revealed when it takes flight or otherwise displays the area. Examples are the white rump patches in many woodpeckers and other birds, the white spot in the tips of the tail feathers of many warblers, and the bold striping which becomes apparent in the spread wings of a Willet. Some of these markings may play a part in a species' courtship display, but they are also thought to surprise and momentarily distract potential predators and/or to direct their attention to parts of the body which, if seized, will not cause mortal injury. See COLOR AND PATTERN.

BANTAM. Any number of dwarf breeds of the domestic chicken originating near the town of Bantam, Java. These popular chickens are now raised throughout the world.

BAPTORNIS. A fossil genus containing a single species (*B. advenus*), described from remains found in the famous Upper Cretaceous Niobrara chalk beds of Kansas in the 1870's. *Baptornis* was apparently a flightless, fish-eating, grebe-like bird measuring about 1½ feet in length. See EVOLUTION OF BIRDLIFE.

BARB. One of the main branches which project laterally from the rachis of a feather. In contour feathers, the barbs interlock by means of the barbules and barbicels to form a smooth, continuous vane. Less frequently called the ramus. For more detail, see FEATHER and Fig. 9.

BARBICEL. A projection extending laterally from the barbule of a contour feather. Sometimes the term is used to include the hooked projections (hamuli) borne on the forward-pointing barbules and sometimes it is confined to the shorter, straight projections borne by both forward- and rearward-pointing barbules. For more detail, see FEATHER and Fig. 9.

BARBULE. One of the branches which project laterally from the shafts of the barbs, the main branches of the rachis of a feather. In contour feathers, the barbules that project forward toward the feather tip clasp by means of hooks (hamuli) onto the ridged edges of the rearward-pointing barbules, thus forming a smooth, continuous vane. Less frequently called the radius. For more detail, see FEATHER and Fig. 9.

BARN OWL. Standard English name for 3 members of the family Tytonidae (order Strigiformes) as well as a collective name for the family as a whole. One species is resident in North America.

Many of the characters by which taxonomists separate barn owls from "true" owls are either internal (e.g., structure of the pectoral girdle; see SKELETON) or inconspicuous (the pectinate—i.e., comb-like—middle claw, like that of the nightjars). However, even a casual observer of a barn owl would remark the heart-shaped facial disk (which gives the bird a slightly creepy expression), the long legs and toes, and the rather uniform, lightly speckled (rather than heavily streaked or barred) plumage—all characters lacking (or nearly so) in true owls.

Differences notwithstanding, barn owls have much in common with true owls: nocturnal habits; a taste for live vertebrate prey, especially small rodents; eyes placed in the front of the head; unusually soft plumage; silent flight; the practice of swallowing prey whole and regurgitating indigestible parts in compact pellets; and a reversible outer toe.

Barn owls nest in cavities in either banks or trees or on the ground as well as in barns and other man-made structures. They add nothing but owl pellets to these "nests." The 3–11 (usually 4–7) white, unmarked eggs are not as round as the eggs of the true owls.

The barn owls' dry scream has been likened to the sound of ripping canvas.

The family as a whole and *the* Barn Owl (*Tyto alba*) are both cosmopolitan in distribution, though they are absent from the colder regions and higher mountains. Thus in North America the species barely reaches southern Canada and does not occur in much of the Rockies. See the Bibliography under OWL.

BARROW, Sir John, 1764–1848 (Barrow's Goldeneye: *Bucephala islandica*). A highly competent British administrator, and sometime mathematician, teacher, explorer, engineer, geographer, and diplomat, who rose from relatively humble origins to become Second Secretary of the British Admiralty. Much of his long career was spent in South Africa. He visited the Arctic in his youth, but his lasting contribution to that region was his encouragement of the Admiralty's efforts to find the Northwest Passage.

BARTRAM, William, 1739–1823 (*Bartramia longicauda*: Upland Sandpiper). Son of John Bartram (1699–1777), who was botanist to King George III and whose scientific prestige and botanical garden attracted ambitious and eminent naturalists from far and wide, making Philadelphia a kind of Athens of early American biology. William, like many other young men with his interests, was a failure at practical forms of livelihood. In addition to being a devoted naturalist, however, he was a skillful artist and writer and by this combination of gifts attained a fame equal to or greater than his father's. Though he illustrated Bartram's early *Elements of Botany* (1803), he had wider interests than his father, and during his travels noted details on many "new" life forms. He recorded 215 species of birds in eastern North America, the most comprehensive listing to that time, and set down details of life history in many cases. One of his most interesting avian anecdotes is a detailed description of a King Vulture he encountered in Florida, a record which remains the best argument for including this Neotropical species in our avifauna. The younger Bartram recorded his adventures in *Travels through North and South Carolina, Georgia, East and West Florida*, a highly readable account of his four-year ramble in the wilderness which was acclaimed by European (as well as American) readers, including Wordsworth and Coleridge. William Bartram is often credited with giving Alexander Wilson the encouragement he needed to tackle his ground-breaking *American Ornithology*.

BASAL (BAY-sul). In a biological context, the region nearest the main body. For example, the base or basal area of the bill of a bird is the part of the bill nearest the skull. A field mark of the Glaucous Gull is the pale bill base or basal area. Opposite of APICAL.

BASIC PLUMAGE. Generally synonymous with "non-breeding" or "winter" plumage. See MOLT, *Sequence and Terminology.*

BASTARD WING. The ALULA.

BATHING. Almost all birds wet their feathers in some manner on a regular basis as part of their ritual of plumage maintenance. Some desert birds seldom or never take water baths, and gallinaceous birds substitute dust baths at least in most instances. Most authorities seem to agree that birds bathe not as a direct cleaning process as humans do, but more as preparation for preening and oiling the feathers. As is true of most other forms of bird behavior, bathing is not done haphazardly but rather in a sequence of characteristic gestures which vary consistently among different types of birds. Observations of both captive and wild young birds suggest that the urge to bathe is innate, though some of the particular gestures of the wetting and drying process may be learned or at least triggered by watching older individuals.

Most songbirds bathe while standing in shallow water (e.g., in a birdbath), and water birds dunk and flutter in their preferred element. But birds are also known to bathe by fluttering in wet vegetation (leaf bathing and dew bathing) and by simply exposing their plumage to the rain. (Larks may use *only* this method; Simmons, in Thomson, 1964–ORNITHOLOGY). Highly aerial birds bathe on the wing. Swallows and many species of flycatchers wet themselves by flying over water and splashing themselves by touching the water surface; and hummingbirds will hover under natural drips or even lawn sprinklers.

As noted, the specific gestures which accompany bathing vary. Songbirds tend to dip the head while standing in the water to flip water onto the back and then splash on the water by shaking the bill in it and by fluttering the wings rapidly, thus wetting the flight feathers; the tail is also immersed and fluttered (see Fig. 16). Swimming birds usually dip their head and neck while sitting on the water, allowing the water to roll down onto their backs; this is alternated with beating the wings on the surface. Some species practice various combinations of these basic gestures. In all cases the body feathers are "fluffed," i.e., raised.

The object is not to soak the feathers—though Berger (Van Tyne and Berger, 1976–ORNITHOLOGY) mentions young Blue-winged Warblers which did just this and were unskilled at drying themselves; a bathing bird is already more than usually vulnerable to predators and one unable to fly because of sodden plumage would be easy prey indeed. Water birds depend on the air trapped in their feathers to stay afloat and would sink if soaked "to the skin."

Both during and after the wetting procedure, birds flap, shake their body, and vibrate their wings and tail to throw off excess water. Following the bath, they typically do a thorough preening job, which eliminates the rest of the water, arranges the ruffled feathers, and spreads the preen oil over the plumage. It is thought that wetting and preening permits the efficient removal of old oil and facilitates the smooth and even distribution of fresh oil by the bill from the preen gland. Vultures, hawks, cormorants, and anhingas characteristically hold out their wings "spread-eagle" to the sun for drying.

See also PREENING; OIL GLAND; SUNNING; DUSTING.

BATHURST INLET (Northwest Territories, Canada). Spectacular high arctic wilderness scenery, wildflowers, mammals (musk-ox, caribou, wolf), and birdlife, with comfortable accommodations at a converted Hudson's Bay Company post (Bathurst Inlet Lodge). About 340 miles north of Yellowknife; 100 miles south of Victoria Island, Coronation Gulf; access strictly by private air service (through the lodge). Mainly upland (dry) tundra with magnificent cliffscapes, lakes, and "fjords." Bird specialties include breeding Yellow-billed, Arctic, and Red-throated Loons, Whistling Swan, Golden Eagle, Peregrine Falcon, Gyrfalcon, Rock and Willow Ptarmigan, Golden Plover, Baird's and White-rumped Sandpipers, Northern Phalarope, Glaucous and Thayer's Gulls, Hoary Redpoll, Harris' Sparrow, Lapland Longspur, and Snow Bunting. See also ARCTIC; TUNDRA; and the Bibliography under ARCTIC.

BAXTER STATE PARK (Maine). About 20 miles northwest of Millinocket; 216 square miles consisting mainly of coniferous forest and including Mount Katahdin. Good for many northward-breeding specialties such as Spruce Grouse, Yellow-bellied Flycatcher, Gray Jay, Boreal Chickadee, Swainson's and Gray-cheeked Thrushes, Mourning, Tennessee, Bay-breasted, and Blackpoll Warblers, Rusty Blackbird, Pine Siskin, and Red and White-winged Crossbills.

BAY DUCK. Collective term for the ducks in the genus *Aythya* (family Anatidae; order Anseriformes), of which 5 species (the scaups, Canvasback, Redhead, and Ring-necked Duck) breed in North America and 2 others (Common Pochard and Tufted Duck) occur as migrants in the Aleutians. These species are sometimes placed with the typical or surface-feeding ducks in the subfamily Anatinae, sometimes with other diving ducks in the Aythyinae, and sometimes in the tribe Aythyini with the other POCHARDS.

The term is an apt one, for while the bay ducks breed in a variety of habitats—from tundra to prairie marsh to wooded pond—they all favor sheltered coastal waters as their wintering grounds.

Except for the Greater Scaup, all resident North American bay ducks are restricted to the New World; only the Lesser Scaup reaches (and crosses) the Equator. Both scaup species breed north of the Arctic Circle, though not exclusively.

BEAK. Essentially synonymous with BILL. In more restrictive usage, refers particularly to larger bills, especially the hooked beaks (or bills) of birds of prey. In general "bill" is the preferred term in ornithological/birdwatching contexts.

BEARDLESS. The smallest North American flycatcher (3½ inches) is "beardless" in that it lacks the bristles that line the upper margin of the gape in most members of its family (Tyrannidae). These so-called "rictal" bristles are widely supposed to aid flycatchers in capturing their prey and, if so, it may be significant that the Northern Beardless Tyrannulet (Beardless Flycatcher) feeds at least partially on fruit and picks insects from leaves and branches in the manner of a warbler, rather than snatching flies from the air.

BEAR RIVER MARSH National Wildlife Refuge (Utah). One of the most spectacular water-bird concentration sites in the world, consisting of over a hundred square miles of diked wetlands in the delta of the Bear River at Great Salt Lake. Excellent birding prevails throughout the year. (Birders and other tourists are most numerous in the summer.) The greatest spectacle occurs in the fall (peak in September) when millions of migrant waterfowl stop over on their way south from northern breeding grounds. The fall migration also brings a greater diversity of other migrants, such as shorebirds. Breeding specialties include Eared and Western Grebes, White Pelican, White-faced Ibis, Cinnamon Teal, Long-billed Curlew, American Avocet, Wilson's Phalarope, Franklin's Gull, and Yellow-headed Blackbird. Winter highlights include Bald and Golden Eagles.

BECARD (see below for pronunciation). Standard English name for about 16 species of passerine birds which occur exclusively in the tropics. Traditionally these frugivorous/insectivorous birds have been placed in the Neotropical family Cotingidae, a family that has often served as a repository for species of uncertain affinities.

The members of this taxonomic potpourri vary extravagantly in size (3½ inches to 1½ feet), form, coloration, and behavior. Some authorities now believe that the becards, all contained within two genera (*Pachyramphus* and *Platypsaris*), belong in fact with the tyrant flycatchers (family Tyrannidae).

Only one becard, the 6-inch Rose-throated (*Pachyramphus* [*Platypsaris*] *aglaiae*), reaches North America as a summer resident of southeastern Arizona, southwestern New Mexico, and (rarely) the lower Rio Grande Valley of Texas. It eats both fruit and insects, as befits its ambiguous status; builds a large, untidy, globular nest woven of coarse plant fibers and wool, lined with fine plant down and bark strips, and suspended from the end of a branch; and lays 4–6 white, lavender, or buff eggs marked with rather fine brownish, reddish, or gray speckles, blotches, and scrawls.

The becard "song" is a distinctive (in North America), rather quiet, descending two-syllable whistle, sometimes accompanied by some unmusical "conversational" sounds.

The French *bécarde* means "shrike," and while becards are totally unshrike-like in behavior and unrelated taxonomically, many species are gray and white and (like other tyrant flycatchers) have heavy, hooked bills. Of the two pronunciations heard commonly in North America, BECK-erd is the closest to the sound of the French name noted above; buh-KARD is heard with at least equal frequency, however.

BEGGING (by young birds). See YOUNG, DEVELOPMENT OF.

BEHAVIOR. See listings under "Long Entries" in the "How to Use This Book" section, p. 4.

BELL, John Graham, 1812–89 (Bell's Vireo: *Vireo bellii*; *Amphispiza belli*: Sage Sparrow). A well-known collector and taxidermist from New York State who accompanied his friend John James Audubon on the latter's expedition up the Missouri River in 1843. He was also known and liked by eminent ornithologists of the next generation, e.g., BAIRD, RIDGWAY, CASSIN, and LE CONTE. Audubon named the vireo for him, Ridgway the sparrow, and an ornithologist named Giraud added a Mexican warbler species now known as the Golden-browed Warbler (*Basileuteris belli*).

BENDIRE (BEN-dye-er), Charles Emil (born Karl Emil Bender), 1836–97 (Bendire's Thrasher: *Toxostoma bendirei*). After abandoning ecclesiastical studies in Germany, Bendire emigrated with his brother to the U.S. while still in his teens. He joined the army, serving competently and bravely in the Civil and Indian wars, eventually attaining the rank of major. He was part of the group of army ornithologists who corresponded with and were encouraged by Spencer BAIRD. Bendire's specialty was eggs, of which he amassed a large collection (8,000 specimens), and he was eventually considered a ranking oologist of his day. On giving his collection to the National Museum, he was made Honorary Curator of the Department of Oology by Baird. Late in his life he began chronicling the *Life Histories of North American Birds* (U.S. Natl. Mus. Bull., vol. 1, no. 1, Washington, D.C., 1892). Even Mr. BENT, on whose shoulders the completion of this herculean labor ultimately fell, did not live to see its completion. Bendire's friend Elliott Coues named the southwestern thrasher for him.

BENT, Arthur Cleveland, 1866–1954. The chief biographer of North American birds in his well-known volumes of *Life Histories* (see throughout the Bibliography), published by the Smithsonian as National Museum Bulletins between 1919 and 1968. From a "frail youth" of modest circumstances Bent transformed himself through hard work into a highly successful businessman of apparently limitless energy. His interest in birds began during his childhood in Massachusetts, and in 1910 he decided to complete the monumental task Charles BENDIRE had made a slim start on in 1892. Between 1901 and 1930, Bent traveled extensively throughout North America acquiring a comprehensive perception of the avifauna. In 1948 he partially retired in order to give more time to the project. He lived to see the nineteenth volume (Wood Warblers) published in 1953, having completed the manuscript of the twentieth (Blackbirds, Orioles, and Tanagers). The last volume of the series (Finches) was completed by a number of ornithologists under the editorship of O. L. Austin, Jr.

BERGMANN'S RULE. The observation (formulated by a nineteenth-century German zoologist) that overall body size tends to be greater in representatives of bird and mammal species living permanently in cooler climates than in those living in warmer climates. Put simply, American Kestrels in Maine (*Falco sparverius sparverius*) are larger on the average than those in Florida (*F. s. paulus*). The ecological principle followed is that large bodies retain heat more efficiently than small ones, and that there is therefore an adaptive size increase in populations constantly subjected to lower temperatures.

BERMUDA. A group of small islands in the northwestern Atlantic Ocean at the edge of that great pelagic desert, the Sargasso Sea, and about 570 miles east of Cape Hatteras, North Carolina. The fishhook-shaped chain measures about 22 miles long and contains a total of about 21 square miles. Perched atop an ancient submarine volcano, Bermuda is a typical atoll composed of a white limestone derived from the bodies of reef-building organisms; the climate is mild year-round (annual mean temperature about 70° F.) due to the proximity of the Gulf Stream, and the general ambience is that of the Caribbean. The islands have been under British influence continuously since the late seventeenth century, and though Bermuda continues to be widely pictured as a kind of oceanic Elysium, the pressures of immigration from other Commonwealth countries, an ever-increasing birth rate, and the tourist industry, on which the island's economy depends, make present-day Bermuda hardly more idyllic than any of the larger landmasses.

The predominant vegetation was a forest of the endemic Bermuda cedar (*Juniperus bermudiensis*) until this species was almost completely destroyed by a scale insect accidentally introduced from California. A resistant strain of the cedar has emerged and reforestation by cedars is underway; meanwhile the ubiquitous, fast-growing Australian casuarina has been extensively planted to provide windbreaks and greenery. David Wingate, the island's Conservation Officer, is attempting to preserve and restore patches of native forest in several parts of Bermuda.

In the present context, Bermuda is of interest chiefly because it is considered part of North America by the compilers of the A.O.U. *Check-list of North American Birds.* Like many another small, isolated group of oceanic islands, Bermuda has never had a rich native landbird fauna but was once teeming with colonial seabirds. With the arrival of human colonists and their mammalian attendants (rats, cats, dogs, and pigs) the latter have been reduced to remnant populations of: the endangered Bermuda Petrel (*Pterodroma cahow*; see CAHOW), an endemic form, sometimes considered a race of the Black-capped Petrel (*P. hasitata*); and the White-tailed Tropicbird (*Phaethon lepturus*). Neither of these species breeds anywhere on the North American mainland.

One endemic land-bird form, a subspecies of the White-eyed Vireo, survives on Bermuda. Bird species not previously known to science and thought to have been endemic to Bermuda have been described from semi-fossilized bones, but it is not known whether these early residents disappeared as the result of natural catastrophes or fell victim to the early depredations of man and his associates. The five commonest resident land birds of present-day Bermuda are: Mourning Dove (a recent natural colonist), Great Kiskadee (flycatcher; introduced), Eurasian Goldfinch (introduced), Eurasian House Sparrow (introduced), and Common Starling (introduced). Eastern Bluebird (presumed early colonizer), Gray Catbird (early colonizer), and Northern Cardinal (presumed to have been an early introduction) are all present in lesser numbers. In spring and especially fall migration, the island's copses and shorebird habitat are sometimes crowded with birds, and the chain is inevitably a refuge for windblown vagrants from Europe (e.g., House Martin), the Caribbean (e.g., Noddy Tern), and even Asia (e.g., Siberian Flycatcher: *Muscicapa sibirica*) and the Pacific (only "North American" record for White or Fairy Tern: *Gygis alba*).

The North America of the present book does *not* include Bermuda, and species occurring there but known from nowhere else on the continent are *not* included in Appendixes I or II.

BEWICK (BYOO-ik), Thomas, 1753–1828 (Bewick's Wren: *Thryomanes bewickii*). English naturalist and master wood engraver commemorated by his friend and fellow artist-naturalist John James Audubon. Though Bewick's artistic competence was broad, he is best known for two books of engravings on natural history subjects: *The General History of Quadrupeds* and *History of British Birds.*

BIG BEND National Park (Texas). 708,281 acres of desert, canyon country, and mountain woodland located in the great curve in the Rio Grande which forms the southwestern border of Texas. Access via Alpine (west) or Marathon (east). The avian superstar here is the Colima Warbler, whose North American breeding range is restricted to the Chisos Mountains in the park. The deciduous (oak-maple) woodland at Boot Springs (6,500 feet) is *the* locality for this specialty. The habitat and avifauna are similar to that of SOUTHEASTERN ARIZONA, noted for a large variety of "Mexican" bird species.

BIG DAY. A birdwatching game invented (or at least made famous) by Ludlow GRISCOM in which a single party of birders tries to record as many species as possible during a twenty-four-hour period. There is no limit to the size of the area covered or the methods of transportation used—a Texas big day using airplanes and a neighborhood big day on foot are equally valid—but a standardized itinerary is usually evolved so that totals for succeeding years can be fairly compared. One-man big days are theoretically permissible but credibility is enhanced if two or more participate; on the other hand, more than five probably cramps efficiency. Party members are not allowed to work different areas simultaneously and usually remain within earshot of each other at any given locality so that they can make a quick departure when the habitat has yielded the requisite species. A species need only be seen *or* heard by *one* member of the party to be counted, so that the fun is enhanced by the expertise and known honesty of each participant. The traditional big day begins and ends at midnight, but revisionists have also tried starting and ending at noon (Singapore Big Day).

In addition to field competence and indefatigability, a successful big day depends on favorable weather, visiting the widest possible variety of habitats, timing stops to coincide with factors such as tides and species habits, a good score on a few local "stakeouts," and good migration—preferably a "wave." The best timing for a big day—that period during which the largest number of species are likely to be in a given area—varies of course from region to region, though classically it is a spring event.

The first big days took place in May in Dutchess County, New York. See Jaques, *Birds Across the Sky* (1942), Chapter 1, for an "outsider's" description of one of the early Griscom efforts.

Notable big day totals include:

231 species, California, April 29, 1978
229 species (total "adjusted" to 202 to comply with "95% rule"—
    see citation below), Texas, April 28, 1973
193 species, Manitoba (inland), May 24, 1980

For details on these and other high counts in many localities, see *Birding* (1981), 13:1. See also ROUNDUP; CHRISTMAS COUNT.

BILL. A bird's bill (or "beak") is analogous to our jaws, though it is used differently in many respects and bears little obvious resemblance in form. It consists of two bony frontward extensions of the skull—one above and one below the mouth—covered with a horny or leathery sheath made of keratin, which, like our fingernails, is a product of the upper layer of the skin (epidermis). In most animals the upper jaw is called the maxilla and the lower the mandible, but in birds the two parts of the bill are known as the upper and lower mandibles. The upper mandible is of a single piece in most birds, though in a few (e.g., tubenoses, frigatebirds, jaegers) it is divided into sections. The lower mandible is made up of two identical pieces (rami) which extend outward from the skull, meet usually at the midpoint of the bill's length or beyond, and are fused at the tip. This meeting place is called the "gonys" (see Fig. 25) and is conspicuous as a distinct angle in the profile of the lower mandible of the larger gulls. Both mandibles have two sharp edges, called the "tomia," often equipped with some form of serration for holding food securely. In most birds the upper mandible is slightly longer, deeper, and wider than the lower mandible, so that there is a slight overlap from above. Nostril holes are evident in all but a few species and in all North American birds occur nearer the base of the bill than the tip. (For nostril structure, shape, and variation, see NOSTRILS.)

Bill wear is compensated for by formation of new keratin much in the way our outer skin layer flakes away and is imperceptibly replaced; and broken bills can also "grow out" at least in some cases.

The young of species with unusually long or peculiarly shaped bills (e.g., curlews and spoonbills) begin life with these features much reduced and inconspicuous; the adaptations take shape as the birds mature. Bill length is subject to age and sexual dimorphism; sandpiper bills, for example, are, as a rule, longer in older females, shorter in younger males of the same species.

Malformations of the bill, including crossed mandibles (in species other than crossbills) and abnormal extensions of one mandible or the other, are seen occasionally in wild birds. This is usually the result of an

FIG. 2. *Specialized bills and feeding techniques.* The crossbills have evolved a unique and complex technique for prizing open the scales of unripe cones. It involves insertion of the long, sharp upper mandible between cone scales; a twisting head motion in which the opposed crossed mandible tips pry the scales apart; and *lateral* play of the mandibles which also acts to separate the scales. Once the pine seed is revealed, a cartilaginous cutting "tool" on the tip of the thick crossbill tongue detaches it at its base. The laterally flattened oystercatcher bill is in effect an oyster knife which can be inserted between the shells of a closed bivalve to sever the adductor muscle(s) holding the shells together. The Black Skimmer "slices" calm shallows with its knife-thin lower mandible until it encounters an edible object such as the luckless killifish illustrated; it then snaps the shorter upper mandible closed on its prey with a characteristic downward/backward jerk of the head before raising it out of the water to be swallowed. For more detail on these techniques and other specialized feeding methods, see FOOD/FEEDING.

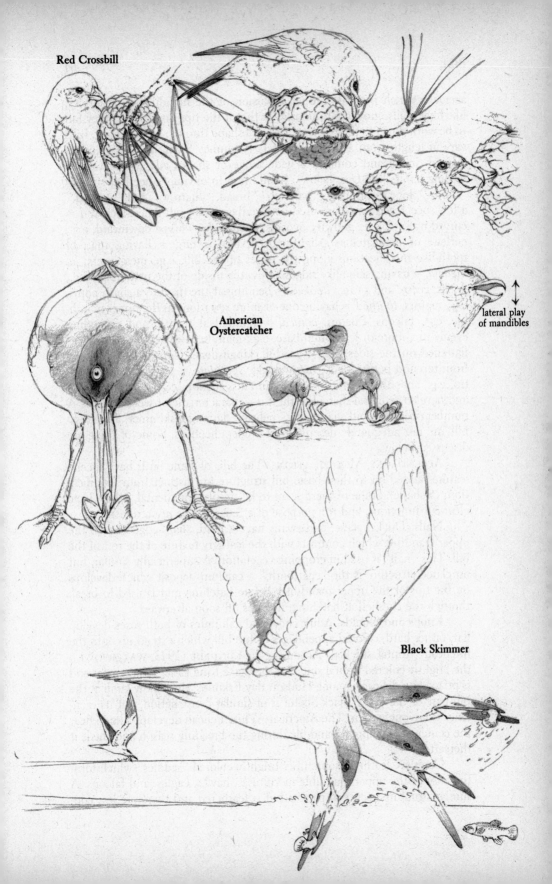

Red Crossbill

American
Oystercatcher

lateral play
of mandibles

Black Skimmer

accident which prevents proper occlusion of the mandibles. Mandibles, like fingernails, grow continuously, so that if the tips don't meet, they fail to be worn down to their normal size and shape through constant use. Bills vary in length from a few millimeters (Chimney Swift) to over 9 inches (Wood Stork) and come in a wide range of shapes adapted to various feeding habits (see *Use*, below). In addition to obvious adjectives such as "short," "long," "straight," "curved," "broad," "narrow," and "pointed," a few specialized terms are used to describe certain bill types: *recurved* = curved upward, e.g., godwits, avocets; *decurved* = curved downward, e.g., curlews or gnatcatchers (slightly decurved); *serrate* = having rows of tooth-like modifications along the edges of the bill, e.g., mergansers; *lamellate* = having seine-like ridges across the inside of the mandibles, e.g., ducks, geese, and swans; *hooked* = bending at the tip into a sharp point, e.g., raptors; *toothed* = having one or more serrations in the upper mandible, e.g., falcons, trogons; *conical* = pointed at the tip and expanding evenly to a more or less round base, e.g., many seed-eaters; *compressed* = flattened on the sides, e.g., Razorbill, kingfishers; *depressed* = flattened from top and bottom, e.g., many ducks; *spatulate* = wide and flat at the tip, e.g., spoonbills; *terete* = round in cross section, e.g., hummingbirds; and *beveled* = chisel-shaped at the tip—characteristic of woodpeckers. A number of bizarre bill shapes, e.g., pelican, flamingo, skimmer, and crossbill, are not adequately described by single adjectives. Some of these are discussed below.

APPENDAGES, MODIFICATIONS. The bills of some birds have special features added on to their basic bill structure (as distinct from modifications of shape). Some of these seem to be simply ornamental, others have clear-cut functions, and the purpose of a few remains mysterious.

Nails. Ducks, geese, and swans have a hard, sharp-edged tip to the upper mandible which contrasts with the leathery texture of the rest of the bill. This "nail" is used in cropping vegetation. A superficially similar, but unrelated structure is the "egg tooth," a calcium deposit which develops on the tips of the upper mandibles before hatching and is used to break through the eggshell at hatching; it drops off soon afterward.

Knobs and Shields. Adult coots and gallinules of both sexes develop flat, rather hard, colored appendages of the bill which extend up onto the forehead (frontal shields). According to Kortright (1943–WATERFOWL), the brightly colored frontal shield of the drake King Eider is largely fat and is prized as a delicacy among Hudson Bay Eskimos; the yellow knob at the bill base of the drake Black Scoter is of similar construction, but its esculence is unvouched for. The American White Pelican develops a knob near the center of the upper mandible during the breeding season and sheds it thereafter.

Ceres are leathery, sometimes brightly colored "saddles" which form the base of the upper mandible in vultures, hawks, eagles, and falcons. A similar structure occurs in parrots but is feathered and therefore less conspicuous. In both cases the nostrils open through the cere, but the function of the latter is unknown. Pigeons also have a naked cere at the base of the bill which in some species (e.g., Rock Dove) develops into a soft prominence, called an "operculum" by some authorities.

Seasonal Sheaths are developed as part of the breeding "plumage" of many alcids, notably the puffins. It is typically larger and more brightly colored than the "winter" bill and is shed and reacquired annually.

Throat Pouches made of leathery skin and hanging from the forked portion of the lower mandible are conspicuous among cormorants but reach their highest development in the pelicans. When the pelican enters the water headfirst, the flexible lower mandible and attached sac is forced open like a wide-necked pouch into which the fish are scooped; when the pelican surfaces the pouch is contracted and the water seined out through the sides of the mandibles.

USE. Because a bird's bill is inevitably associated with its mouth and because birds spend a great deal of time eating, it is natural to associate bill functions with food. Perhaps, therefore, it should be emphasized that many of the things birds do with their bills—including catching and preparing food, but also carrying, digging, and nest building—are things we would do with our fingers and hands. The most generalized bill function is a pliers-like grasping, performed to some extent by all birds. No modern birds have true teeth or chewing capacity and must therefore either swallow their food whole or pull or break it into manageable pieces. However, gripping of slippery prey such as fish is aided in many cases by tooth-like serrations of the mandible edges. These are highly developed and conspicuous in the mergansers but also appear on the bills of herons and a few other birds.

Another widespread bill action, for which a *pointed* bill is handy but not essential, is pecking, used to hack up nuts and other hard-shelled foods, to chop large pieces of food into manageable bits, to dig in the earth or tree trunks, and to repel enemies; ground-feeding birds (e.g., grouse, quail, sparrows) use a sharp pecking motion as they pick up grain and seeds. Many birds, members of the crow family for example, survive very well with simple bills adapted for grasping and pecking but without highly specialized catching or feeding modifications.

Others use one or a combination of other basic bill actions which follow.

Tearing large prey into pieces small enough to be swallowed is typical of birds with strong hooked bills, such as day-flying raptors (including shrikes), owls, and to some extent tubenoses, jaegers, and gulls.

Probing is most highly developed among shorebirds (including woodcocks and snipes), many of which have sensitive, relatively soft bill tips for "feeling" and grasping subterranean life forms. The great variety of bill shapes and lengths in this group shows adaptation to feeding "niches" at different depths. Ibises probe in a similar manner. Another kind of probing is practiced by hummingbirds, which can penetrate deep calyxes of flowers with their long bills in order to sip nectar with their even longer tongues; hummingbird bills are also ideal for picking insects off plants and out of the air, forceps-like.

Stabbing at prey is favored by many water birds with long sharp bills, e.g., anhingas, herons, rails, cranes. In many cases what seems to be a spearing motion is in fact a fast grab, but fish eaten by Western Grebes are apparently all pierced by that species' very sharp bill before being swallowed (Palmer, 1962–GREBE).

Husking seeds has been perfected by finches, some of which have a specially reinforced skull structure to withstand the strain of crushing very hard fruit pits.

The interior of a seed-eater's bill is adapted to facilitate the husking/crushing process. The edges of the lower mandible fit into grooves along the inside of the upper mandible when the bill is closed. A seed to be husked is maneuvered into one of these grooves (i.e., right or left side) by the tongue. The sharp edge of the lower mandible is then brought up to bear on the seed's husk. After the outer husk is pierced, the tongue revolves the seed and the husk is "shorn" from the kernel by the same sharp mandibular edge. This procedure is performed very rapidly, and larger-billed finches can hold more than one seed in their mouths at once and husk each sequentially. The size and hardness of seeds which a species can deal with depends on the size of its bill and the development of its jaw muscles, cranial structure, etc. Since large-billed species can eat small, soft seeds as well as large, hard ones, they have a wider choice of food in general than do smaller finches.

The massive bill of the Eurasian Hawfinch can exert a pressure of up to 100 pounds per square inch, and the similar "nutcracker" borne by our Evening Grosbeak may be comparable.

Straining animal and vegetable matter out of water or mud is achieved with the aid of a series of ridges (lamellae) running across the interior of the bill. This adaptation is found in ducks, geese, and swans and flamingos.

Some bills are peculiarly adapted to highly specific feeding methods; for details of these, see FOOD/FEEDING. See also Fig. 2.

Display. Most bills are "horn-colored," which ranges from pinkish brown to blackish gray. However, bright bill color, including the various appendages noted above, occurs in many families and in some cases becomes heightened during the breeding season. Bill noises are also included in some courtship rituals. Black-browed Albatrosses, for example, accompany one of their nuptial "dances" with loud bill snapping.

BILLING. A courtship ritual involving "affectionate" bill gestures between a pair of birds. Such caresses accompanied by vocalizations are practiced with relish in public by Common Pigeons and give rise to the human lovemaking metaphor, "billing and cooing." The more aggressive bill-whacking gestures performed by some albatross species, among others, are not normally referred to as billing.

BILL NOISES. See SONG, *Non-vocal Sounds.*

BINOCULARS. See OPTICAL EQUIPMENT.

BINOMIAL (or binominal). Literally, a name consisting of two words. In the Linnaean system of biological nomenclature, all species are referred to by a Latin binomial, the first word being the name of the genus and the second the name of the specific members of that genus. Thus the Common Goldeneye is scientifically labeled *Bucephala clangula.* See NOMEN-CLATURE; TAXONOMY; TRINOMIAL.

BIOCHORE (BY-oh-core). A major ecological formation on land characterized by a general vegetation type, e.g., forest, open wetland, open dry land, etc. A biochore is a subdivision of a BIOCYCLE, and in turn may be divided into BIOTOPES. No species of bird inhabits the whole of any biochore, though we may speak of certain families of birds as being largely "forest birds" (e.g., the trogons) or largely "open-country birds" (e.g., larks). See also BIOME.

BIOCYCLES. The three major subdivisions of the BIOSPHERE: sea (marine); fresh water (aquatic); and land (terrestrial). The biocycles may be subdivided into BIOCHORES and BIOTOPES.

BIOGEOGRAPHY. The distribution of living plant and animal life; or the study thereof. Compare ZOOGEOGRAPHY. See DISTRIBUTION.

BIOGRAPHY. Numerous fascinating human stories are related to the progress of American ornithology—far more than can be included in the present book. However, there are two good reasons to learn about the most prominent ones: (1) Curiosity. It is natural when contemplating, for example, Lucy's Warbler to wonder who Lucy was. Sometimes the fruits of such inquiry are meager—as when the person commemorated is little known or unexceptional—but in other cases the life of a bird's namesake proves to be the most spectacular attribute of the species. (2) The names, both Latin and English, of North American birds embody to a great extent the history of the discovery, classification, description, and illustration of the native avifauna.

In a time when interest in birds has reached an all-time high and nearly every family owns an illustrated field guide, it is easy to imagine Adam and Eve recognizing Prothonotary Warblers and Calliope Hummingbirds as they strolled around their garden. It is good to remember therefore that the differentiation of these species and the rest of our bird-life has been accomplished almost entirely within the last 250 years, before which there was just an unknown diversity of "red birds," "yellow birds," or "wiskedjaks," which were distinguished only to the extent that they were useful or detrimental to human survival. Furthermore, as with other aspects of American history, the pioneering period of ornithological investigation is a particularly fascinating one. Though not very distant in years, the eighteenth and much of the nineteenth century are definitely removed from us by change. Many of the exploits of the early naturalists bring those times to life with greater verisimilitude than the deeds of the legendary public figures which crowd the textbooks.

Information about the people of American ornithology is given here in three ways: (1) People for whom species are currently named or who named a significant number of species or who fit neither of these categories but whose reputation merits inclusion (in the admittedly subjective judgment of the author) are listed as entries in the main text. All such entries describe persons now dead. (2) Modern ornithologists are increasingly tied to the lab and the library and their contributions therefore tend to be better reflected in their writing than in recountings of their adventures in the field. Therefore, prominent *modern* ornithologists, living and dead, are recorded here (with few exceptions) only in the Bibliography. (3) The bibliography for the present entry provides a list of references which chronicle the doings of the whole range of American bird men, in many cases far more thoroughly than it has been possible to do here.

In reviewing the range of people for whom North American birds have been named a few facts stand out.

• Except for Anna Blackburne, the only women commemorated are those we might call "loved ones"—the daughters, wives, or beautiful aristocratic patronesses of the men who did the naming. These are commemorated exclusively by their *first* names. Even this was not always considered flattering. At least once Audubon was rebuffed when he offered to name a pretty bird after a pretty lady of his acquaintance; having one's name associated with a bird was "not quite nice" in some circles. There is not a single woman among the *authors* of North American bird species.

• In contrast to the general scarcity of women is the plethora of doctors. Of the 90-odd people whose names are used for North American bird species, over 20 percent were closely connected to medicine—of which the great majority at least completed medical school, and one, William HAMMOND (flycatcher), was a U.S. Surgeon General. Not a few of the doctors were also in the army; for an explanation and account of this circumstance, see BAIRD in the main text and Hume (1942). For what it is worth, doctors are today very well represented in birdwatching circles; without supporting statistics (but with extensive field experience) the author ventures that doctors far outnumber birders of other professions, e.g., lawyers.

• Finally it is impossible not to be impressed with the haphazardness with which fame-by-bird descends and is withdrawn. An obscure English lady botanist (Ms. Blackburne) is remembered in the name of one of the most exquisite North American wood warblers because she was known by a German systematist (Gmelin); while poor John Selby, the English ornithological illustrator, is cast into nomenclatural limbo because what Audubon thought was Selby's Flycatcher was really an immature Hooded Warbler.

This kind of injustice is mitigated somewhat by the fact that it falls with almost equal cruelty on the great as on the slight. Mark CATESBY has no memorial bird and even the giant Audubon has lost much ground at the species level. Audubon's Caracara, Audubon's Woodpecker, and Audubon's Warbler are now mere subspecies or less. His shearwater—which does not even breed on the continent—is all that's left him and some would call it "Dusky."

BIOLOGY. All animal and plant life, e.g., the biology of the earth or of North America; also the science of same.

BIOMASS. The total *weight* of organisms in a specified area. Biomass may be measured by land unit, e.g., weight per acre or cubic foot; by habitat; and by groups or organisms, e.g., insect mass per acre of rain forest. The measure is useful in comparing fundamental differences in biological structures and functions. We know, for example, that the number of species of birds tends to increase as one moves into the tropics, but in many instances biomass—the total weight of birds—remains the same as in equivalent habitats in the Temperate Zone. In these instances we can deduce that there must be fewer individuals of more species in parts of the tropics.

BIOME (BY-ome). One of the main types of biological community characterized by soil conditions and climate which produce a distinctive form of vegetation which, in turn, is inhabited by characteristic animal forms. The major North American biomes are: tundra, coniferous forest, deciduous forest, grassland, southwestern (U.S.) pine-oak woodland (see Plate 1), pinyon-juniper woodland (and hills and mountain slopes of western U.S.), chaparral (western U.S.), and desert. Each of the biomes may be subdivided on the basis of geography, e.g., arctic tundra vs. alpine tundra, or differences in plant associates, e.g., sagebrush desert vs. creosote scrub desert.

Many species of birds are characteristic of or confined to one of the various biomes, while others span two or more: Wrentits and chaparral are almost inseparable in North America, while the Common Crow occurs to some extent in most biomes. Compare LIFE ZONES; see also DISTRIBUTION and Fig. 6.

BIOMETRICS (or biometry). Biostatistics; the application of statistical techniques to the study of life forms.

BIONOMICS. A largely obsolete synonym for "ecology."

BIOSPHERE. That part of the earth from the upper layers of the crust to the lower layers of the atmosphere which supports any form of plant or animal life. Subdivided into BIOCYCLES; BIOCHORES; etc.

BIOTA. The combined flora and fauna of any given area. The "biota of your backyard" including its birdlife is as acceptable a usage of the term as the "biota of the Canadian Arctic." Compare BIOME and BIOTOPE.

BIOTOPE. A geographical area containing a characteristic ecological community of plants and animals which may be usefully compared with other, similar communities. A rain forest biotope in coastal British Columbia will bear certain similarities with (as well as many differences from) a rain forest biotope in the Amazon Basin; e.g., conclusions about composition and behavior of the respective avifaunas may be drawn. A subdivision of a BIOCHORE. See also BIOME.

BIRD. Collective name for all members of the vertebrate animal class Aves. Though there are many traits that we strongly associate with birds—e.g., wings, bills, nest building, egg laying, song—only one character is unique to them: feathers. This does not mean that birds—both as a class and within the great variation of avian forms—have not evolved many unique adaptations to particular life styles. For example, the modification of the avian forelimb for flight is very different from the homologous bat wing (see WING). Furthermore, birds can be characterized by a *combination* of features that typifies no other class, viz.: warm-bloodedness (birds and mammals only); four-chambered heart; feet and lower leg usually scaled and featherless; teeth lacking (except ARCHAEOPTERYX and perhaps other fossil forms); mandibles covered with a horny sheath (bill); large breastbone usually with prominent keel (see FLIGHT); air sac system filling spaces of body cavity (see RESPIRATORY SYSTEM); pneumatized bones; absence of bladder; internal fertilization; hard-shelled (calcareous) eggs with large yolk, incubated externally.

Birds evolved from reptiles, apparently emerging in the Upper Jurassic Period (see EVOLUTION OF BIRDLIFE). Between 8,600 and 8,700 species (depending on taxonomic interpretation) are living at present, breeding on all of the continents, occupying a full range of ecological niches, and variously adapted for existence on land, water (including the open ocean), ice, and air, with a majority of species adapted for perching and feeding in trees and/or shrubs. Birds presently achieve greatest diversity in South

America, where nearly 3,000 species have been recorded. About 702 bird species occur regularly in North America (as defined on p. 3); about 140 others have been recorded as vagrants (see Appendix II).

The deepest roots of the word "bird" have disappeared, but the Old English form was *bridd*, which was a very broad term encompassing young animals of many (or any) kinds.

For entries treating broad aspects of birdlife, see "How to Use This Book," pp. 4–6.

BIRDATHON. A fund-raising event in which a subscriber agrees to pay a designated amount of money for each species of bird a given person can see during a fixed time period, usually a day. Someone who agrees to contribute 25 cents per bird species, for example, would have to pay out 25 dollars if the birder under contract found 100 species. A bird observatory or some other worthy cause gets the money.

BIRD BANDING. See BANDING.

BIRD-BANDING. Now called *The Journal of Field Ornithology*, a quarterly journal of the Northeastern Bird-Banding Association. For the address of its subscription office as of 1982, see the Bibliography under PERIODICALS. See also BANDING.

BIRD CALLS (made by humans). Sound, sometimes made with the aid of a mechanical device, to attract wild birds. Hunters have long used instruments made of wood or metal which, when blown into, reproduce the call of their intended victims. Crows, for example, may be attracted by imitating their distress call. The effect of wooden decoys is enhanced by signaling flocks of waterfowl with enticing quacking sounds; and shorebird shooters have used a variety of tin whistles which, with some practice, could be made to imitate the calls of yellowlegs, godwits, various plovers, and the like.

Birdwatchers also make noises to attract birds. A metal plug inserted into a small wooden cylinder (patented as the "Audubon Bird Call") makes a squeaking noise when twisted, which may provoke curiosity in some birds. Squeaking sounds can also be made orally or by kissing the back of the hand in hopes of the same effect. By far the most widely used and effective of oral bird calls is "pishing" or "spishing," a hissing or "shushing" sound uttered in a pulsating rhythm. That a wide variety of birds respond to this technique in many instances cannot be disputed. *Why* they respond is less clear. Simple curiosity may be a factor among notably curious species such as titmice and jays. It has also been suggested that pishing sounds resemble alarm calls of many species and therefore elicit a mobbing response from birds within hearing range. Birds thus attracted often add their own alarm calls, intensifying the general excitement and enhancing the cumulative effect. Sustained and somewhat aggressive pishing seems to work best, and it is not unusual during migration to be able to attract dozens of individuals of many species. Certain families and species are particularly responsive. Chickadees, nuthatches, and kinglets are usually among the first to arrive. Woodpeckers, flycatchers, jays, wrens, mimids (especially Gray Catbird), thrushes, vireos, warblers, and sparrows are also susceptible. Effectiveness varies dramatically and there is still a great deal of myth and mystery connected with the phenomenon. For example, in the Neotropics, North American migrants respond much more readily than resident species—an experience which can be demonstrated but is difficult to explain. Pishing is not practiced by European birdwatchers and is viewed with a mixture of suspicion and derision by many of them. The fact that it is seldom tried there with any enthusiasm reinforces the belief that it doesn't work. Casual experiments show, however, that shy woodland birds *will* respond well to the "irate jay" form of pish in at least some parts of Europe.

Like peering with an (apparently) vacant expression into the air or wading about in fetid marshland, pishing may direct a certain amount of not altogether approving human attention to the birdwatcher. But the effect of the technique depends on a certain emotional commitment and unembarrassed vigor, and fainthearted birders will do as well to remain silent.

See also RECORDING OF BIRD SOUNDS.

BIRD CLUB. In the broadest sense, any organization which promotes the study and/or enjoyment of birdlife among a group of people. The range is from the venerable Nuttall Ornithological Club of Cambridge, Massachusetts, which gave birth to the American Ornithologists' Union in 1888 and continues to present programs and publish work of scientific interest and value; to the National Audubon Society, a conservation organization with a membership (open to the public) of about 450,000 and two impressive publications (see PERIODICALS); to the smallest neighborhood birding group which meets, as the spirit moves its members, for birding and chitchat.

Many clubs publish local checklists, organize field trips, and give programs. They are a great resource for beginning birdwatchers, newcomers to an area who want to learn some of the region's "hot spots," and anyone seeking a little sociable fun in the field.

According to Rickert (1978), there are more than 820 bird clubs in North America. The same source lists these (plus the clubs of Hawaii, Mexico, Central America, Bermuda, the Bahamas, and the Caribbean) along with their addresses, publications, meeting and field trip schedules, and state or provincial maps showing club locations.

BIRDER (birding). A relatively new term that has become popular as an alternative to "birdwatcher" with its unflattering (to some) overtones of passivity, eccentricity, frivolity, and even effeminacy. A birder is one who "birds" or "goes birding" in a serious and energetic manner, whether to hone his or her field-identification skills or amass an impressive list.

The strong identification of "birding" with "listing" has recently forced the hippest of field ornithologists to resort to the anti-snobbery of calling themselves "birdwatchers."

For another interpretation and some discussion of the term's history, see J. A. Tucker, *Birding* (1981), 13:38 (editorial; also responses in subsequent issues).

See also BIRDWATCHING; LISTING.

BIRD FEEDING. Humans have been feeding birds, at least inadvertently, for at least as long as they have had agriculture. Flemish genre paintings of the fifteenth century, for example, show magpies and sparrows nibbling at kernels spilled from grain barrows and crusts in dooryards. But it is only since about the 1930's that bird feeding has become a highly organized pastime complete with specialized (and expensive) merchandise and written guides dealing with the growing technology in the field. Polls have revealed that between 20 and 50 percent of the households in American cities and towns are engaged in bird feeding. In some cases, this amounts to nothing more than throwing the stale bread out the kitchen window, but in many others, it is a full-fledged hobby. It has been documented (DeGraaf and Thomas, 1974) that 20–25 percent of American households feed wild birds in some fashion, accounting for the sale of millions of tons of birdseed at a retail cost of about $170 million. And this fails to account for further millions spent on the almost infinite variety of complex and beautiful dispensers now available.

The appeal of bird feeding is easy to understand. Birds are attractive, amusing, companionable, and provide a contact with the natural world which is generally lacking in the lives of many urban and suburban dwellers. Dealing with the intricacies of feeder placement, catering to special tastes, dispensing different consistencies of feed, and discouraging pests can keep a dedicated gadgeteer in nearly perpetual motion for life. And for many, there is a sense of helping fellow creatures to survive life's cruelties. A number of full-length books have been devoted totally to the skills and pleasures of this new pastime. What follows is but a skeletal outline.

EFFECTS ON BIRDLIFE. Given the explosive increase in bird feeding, it is reasonable to speculate that there have been correspondingly enormous effects on bird populations. That there have been effects, no one would deny. What kinds of effects and their magnitude are matters still principally addressed by guesswork, educated and otherwise. It is not unusual to hear enthusiastic, though unsubstantiated claims that: (1) feeding has increased bird populations; (2) feeding is responsible for the northward extension of the range of the Northern Cardinal and the Tufted Titmouse; (3) birds are forsaking their normal habitat and becoming hooked on store-bought millet in suburbia; etc. Many such claims are as hard to refute as they are to prove. However, to counter the more extravagant theories and to ease any incipient guilt regarding your feeding operation, the following should be borne in mind: (1) Feeders may increase the survival rate of weaker individuals, thereby adding somewhat to the total population of a given species. But there are other pressures, potentially fatal, on birds besides finding an adequate food supply and there is no evidence as yet that feeder bird species are increasing. (2) Changes in habitat and climate may have been as important (or more so) to the recent northward movement of the Northern Cardinal and the Tufted Titmouse. Northern Mockingbirds, after all, which generally stay clear of feeders, have undergone an analogous increase during roughly the same period. (3) Except for inherently weak individuals, birds do not *depend* on your feeder or *forget* how to find food for themselves; they simply take advantage of the easiest supply of food available. If you stop feeding, the healthy members of your clientele will resort to wild food sources (or to your neighbor's feeder) without hesitation. Only those which need a "crutch" to survive are likely to fall prey to real life.

If your pleasure depends on the Florence Nightingale rationale for feeding, you can take solace from the probability that migrants such as warblers, tanagers, orioles, and thrushes which have remained in winter climes "by mistake" doubtless owe their survival, in many cases, to the emergency rations to be found at feeders. When spring arrives they will probably return to breeding grounds near their birthplace but may also come back to your orange slices on schedule each winter—undeniably beneficiaries of bird feeding.

To put the humanitarian issue in proper context, it should be noted finally that the phenomenon of well-off Americans supplying birds unnecessarily with tons of grain that might go to truly starving people is morally ambiguous at best.

WHICH BIRDS TO EXPECT. This depends on a variety of factors, such as where you live and what kind of food you put out. One of the intriguing things about feeding birds is the knowledge that virtually anything is possible. It would only be risking contradiction by a resident of Key West to announce that you can rule out frigatebirds. However, it is possible to narrow the field in a general way. Water birds, of course, are only likely if you have a substantial body of water nearby, but it should perhaps be mentioned that if you can continue to maintain some open water on your property when the other ponds and lakes in your region are frozen over, you may attract a variety of wild ducks which will soon be as glad to eat bread from your hand as "puddle" Mallards.

True "feeder birds" are land birds. Among these, the species which are *least* likely to put in an appearance at your feeder are the migratory insect-eaters such as cuckoos, swifts, nightjars, flycatchers, swallows, wrens, pipits, gnatcatchers, vireos, and warblers. Many of these will visit feeders if faced with starvation, and a few (e.g., Yellow-rumped Warbler) are even regular customers, but others would literally die amidst plenty because they don't recognize a sunflower seed or suet as food. Owls and most large diurnal raptors are also unlikely (for exceptions, see *Predators*, below). This leaves grouse, quail and pheasants, doves, hummingbirds, woodpeckers, larks, corvids, titmice, nuthatches, mimic thrushes, true thrushes, starlings, blackbirds and orioles, tanagers, and finches. Not all of the species in these families come regularly to feeders, and some families are far better represented than others or are more frequent in particular regions of the country, but the remaining possibilities are still very wide. Some species seem particularly susceptible to the temptation of artificially proffered goodies. One species or another of dove, woodpecker, chickadee, nuthatch, jay, and several finches are almost certain to appear very promptly if you live where they are fairly common.

REGIONAL DIFFERENCES. The area of the country in which you live will largely determine the dramatis personae of your avian groaning boards. In the northern U.S. and southern Canada, influxes of winter finches such as the Pine Siskin, redpolls, Evening Grosbeak, and crossbills, which have exhausted supplies in their native coniferous forests, eat feeder owners to the doorstep of the poorhouse one year and are ill-represented or totally absent the next. The Southwest is unparalleled for hummingbirds. Denverites get rosy finches when the snow drives them (the rosy finches) from their high-altitude breeding areas; and southern Floridians can expect anything from a bulbul to a macaw.

WHEN TO FEED. In general, avian intelligence leaves much to be desired, but birds are quick to take advantage of a free meal. Once a bird discovers that a copious and inexhaustible banquet is to be had at your feeder, it will return regularly, and this behavior will, in time, attract other birds. Since your food source is likely to be more reliable than any "natural" one, you can count on good attendance even in the warmer months when "wild" food is abundant.

On the other hand, there is no doubt that a cover of snow or other environmental effect which makes food scarce or hard to get at will increase feeder custom. Some people feel that they "ought" to feed birds in the winter lest they starve, but this is a moral obligation with which no one need be burdened.

KINDS OF FOOD. There are probably few edible substances which feeder birds have not been offered by experiment-minded "station managers" (e.g., spaghetti!). The staples, however, are as follows:

Seed and Grain. Sunflower seeds, with and without hulls, millets (seeds of several species of grasses), and thistle seeds are among the most attractive food to doves, finches, tits, jays, and other regular feeder birds. Some seeds are in special demand by certain species (Evening Grosbeaks, for example, are mad for sunflower seeds). Some, e.g., thistle, are more expensive than others. Cracked corn and other coarse grains (usually in the form of chicken scratch feed) are especially popular with grouse, pheasants, quail, jays, and blackbirds. Mixtures which include most or all of the above are sold in grocery stores as well as feed stores. However, it has recently been demonstrated (Geis, 1980) that these mixtures contain ingredients such as sorghum, wheat, oats, and rice to which the majority of feeder birds are indifferent. The same study revealed that white proso millet and black oil-type sunflower seeds are outstanding favorites and that peanut hearts are gobbled by starlings but little else. This U.S. Fish and Wildlife report also contains a list of food preferences species by species and many other details of interest for the "serious" bird feeder.

Fruit. Oranges, bananas, pears, apples, grapes, and raisins are frequently offered on bird tables and any other soft fruit is probably equally effective. Not surprisingly, they are particularly attractive to species which normally feed on fruit, such as thrushes, the Yellow-breasted Chat, tanagers, orioles, and certain finches. Migrant fruit-eaters which remain up North when most of their kind have left for tropical wintering grounds are more likely to be drawn to feeders offering their preferred food. Such birds are often celebrities of the winter birding scene and may (if the word gets out) attract a flock of avid human fans.

Suet and Cooking Fats. Both of these are appealing to most species but particularly to tits, woodpeckers, starlings, and lingering insect-eaters.

Sugar Water and Honey. Primarily used to attract hummingbirds, but also appealing to orioles, warblers, and a surprising assortment of other species (even woodpeckers!). It is important that these substances be used with some care to ensure the health of the birds they attract. (See *Hazards*, below, for proper "formula" and other considerations pertaining to this specialized type of feeding.)

Bread. A staple of human charity toward birds and a symbol of the days before bird feeding became an industry. It still works, fresh or stale, and apparently the least nutritious type of white bread is the most popular. However, other bakery products, from Danish pastry to dog biscuits, will not be scorned. Caution: this class of food is especially popular with avian lowlife such as pigeons and House Sparrows, not to mention mammalian undesirables such as rats.

Peanut Butter. Immediately popular with titmice, nuthatches, woodpeckers, starlings, and many other species; for rumored ill effects, see *Hazards*, below.

Water. For drinking and bathing, water may bring a greater variety of birds to your yard than your feeder. It is best placed in the shade and near cover, into which bathers can duck when you let your cat out. A drip fountain seems to increase popularity, and if you can continue to offer open water when the temperature drops below freezing your yard will virtually throb with avian gratitude. Birdbath heating elements are available commercially. Glycerin, sometimes touted as a means of keeping birdbaths "open" in winter, has one major drawback—it doesn't work. Cleaning birdbaths thoroughly and often is crucial, as they are an ideal medium for bacterial growth to which the birds might be susceptible. Then too, in warm weather, a stagnant "bath" may well add to your yard's mosquito population.

FEEDERS. You can now spend almost any amount of money you desire on elaborate feeding apparatus. Feeders come equipped with the latest technology in squirrel baffles, intricate compartmentalization which excludes certain species to the benefit of others, and convenient gizmos for cleaning and filling. Architecturally, some are so grand that one's house may suffer by comparison. The thrifty and lovers of simplicity will recognize, of course, that feeding birds does not require a feeder. Simply throwing your offerings on the ground is likely to be highly effective; however, it does deprive you of a measure of control which feeders provide. For example, food spread on the ground is vulnerable to wastage from the effects of weather and the depredations of undesirable guests such as squirrels. Furthermore, not all birds prefer to feed on the ground, and certain substances such as suet and peanut butter are most conveniently offered in some kind of container. By raising a feeder on a pole, nailing it to a tree trunk, or suspending it on a wire, you can minimize waste, exclude uninvited visitors, and make your offering more attractive to certain species. Feeders may also enhance your enjoyment. Window feeders, for example, allow almost intimate contact between observer and bird, and some feeders are designed to force titmice and other agile species to perform acrobatic stunts for their supper. All of this may be achieved with minimum expense by the application of a little ingenuity and effort. The chief considerations in making a homemade feeder are (1) keeping food dry in wet weather: drainage holes and/or roof; (2) stability: platforms poorly suspended will dump their contents onto the ground when the first starling lands on the edge; and (3) convenient refilling: climbing trees or poles in a blizzard with a bucket of seed can be tiresome. Everything else is a matter of taste. Suet can be suspended in mesh fruit bags, placed in simple "cages" of folded hardware cloth nailed to a tree, or spread onto pine cones or into bark crevices; effective seed dispensers can be made from milk cartons, cans, plastic bottles, or any other container; and a feeding tray or table need be nothing more than a piece of wood with drainage holes and raised edges to minimize scattering of feed.

Hummingbird feeders are also available in elaborate and expensive designs, but again, homemade versions (e.g., a test tube wired at an angle to a branch) are just as effective. To help hummers find your feeder, adorn it with something red and, if possible, position it near flowers that you have seen hummingbirds visiting. Once they have found the feeder and realize that it is a consistent food source, hummers will visit it regularly and remember it from year to year. The most important precaution in hummingbird feeding is keeping the syrup clean. It ferments rapidly and soon becomes poison rather than nourishment. Water for the solution should be boiled and residues in feeders removed frequently. When starting out, you may have to dump several untouched solutions before the local hummers discover your feeder. For a discussion of the correct syrup formula and more detail on potential health problems, see *Hummingbird Formulas*, below.

Once you have made (or bought) your feeder you should give some thought to where you're going to put it: (1) Having several feeders in different situations will appeal to a greater variety of birds, make it more convenient to watch the activity from your house, and make possible a kind of segregation if necessary (see *Pests*, below). (2) Place feeders where you can see them easily from inside. (3) Sunny spots, sheltered from the wind, are preferred. (4) Some birds prefer to feed closer to the cover of vegetation, which, however, makes handy hiding places for cats; other birds want to have an open view—if possible, provide both.

PESTS. Gluttony and covetousness are the characteristic sins of most feeder pests. Some gobble more expensive provisions than, so to speak, they are worth; others aggressively hog feeder space, keeping the more genteel clientele away; quite a few do both. The best solutions lie in separation of offerings, placement of feeders, and the odd mechanical device.

Rats. Sometimes attracted to food spread on the ground. If you have reason to believe that your rat population is a small one, you can try to trap them (not always as easy as it sounds). However, you may discover some alarming facts about rat populations. Selective poisoning is also possible but, of course, should be undertaken with the utmost caution. Needless to say, the best solution is simply to stop feeding on the ground.

Squirrels. Though regarded by most as "nicer" than rats, squirrels are far worse pests at feeders. The eastern gray squirrel is probably enemy No. 1. They have a voracious appetite for almost anything, and they are so agile that only a feeder hovering unattached in midair with no climbable surface within 20 feet can be considered truly squirrel-proof. A more practical solution called a "squirrel baffle" comes in various forms. Slippery metal collars with no graspable edges can be placed around poles which support standing feeders; slippery, tippy baffles, placed along the suspen-

sion wires of hanging feeders, are also popular; and there are some ingenious inventions on the market which, for example, close off the food supply when a heavy squirrel steps on the platform but remain open under the
modest weight of small birds. When all your baffles are in place, sit back
and prepare to enjoy watching the squirrels get around them all.

Trash Birds. This term is defined in the eye of the beholder. To some
bird lovers there is no such thing; many feeder owners, however, include at
least pigeons, starlings, and House Sparrows; and not a few include doves,
jays and crows, and all blackbirds. Their faults are the same as squirrels',
but the corrective measures differ. (1) All the birds named above prefer
coarser foods; therefore, separate the gross stuff—cracked corn, bread,
etc.—from the *haute cuisine* and the pests will tend to feed with their own
kind, leaving the classier types largely unmolested. (2) Most of the pests
are relatively large species and not sufficiently agile to negotiate cylindrical
hanging feeders with short perches. (3) Some pest species seem to feel
more secure feeding away from human habitation. Place a diversionary
feeder with favorite foods in a location remote from your main operation.

Predators. Some categorize Sharp-shinned and Cooper's Hawks, kestrels, and shrikes as pests and worse—avian malefactors which ruthlessly
destroy innocent chickadees. This view is humane in origin but grievously
flawed as an interpretation of the relationships among living organisms. It
is simply a hard fact of life that most animals function partly as food for
other animals. Prolific species such as chickadees can and do withstand
high mortality rates and thereby sustain a variety of other life forms. If
chickadees were not checked, they would become intolerably abundant.
One of the natural checks on chickadee fecundity is the Sharp-shinned
Hawk, and the grace and skill with which it performs its ecologically essential service is one of nature's most elegant achievements. The feeder
with a small predator in attendance is a feeder of distinction. The compulsive vigilante who refuses to be enlightened should then be warned: the
predacious species are all protected by laws which impose heavy fines for
killing birds of prey (see LAWS).

HAZARDS. Some feeding practices have proven detrimental rather
than beneficial to the birds they attract. They are avoided by observing
simple precautions.

Disease. It has been suggested that aspergillosis, a bacterial infection
which originates in decaying plant matter and is common among birds,
may on occasion be picked up from fruits left to rot at feeding stations.
Salmonellosis and other bacterial diseases may infect stagnant water in
birdbaths. The solution, of course, is frequent cleaning of receptacles and
changing of food and water.

Choking and Bloating. It is alleged that undiluted and especially
frost-congealed peanut butter and certain large seeds sometimes choke
birds at feeders. The alarm has also been sounded regarding the unwhole-

some effect on the avian tummy of "inflatable" foods such as oatmeal. It is probably safe to say that birds exercise much more control over how they eat than do most humans—and therefore show a correspondingly low incidence of food-related deaths. Furthermore, many choking records originate in imaginative autopsies rather than eyewitness accounts of strangling chickadees. Peanut butter and oatmeal can probably be offered without undue concern, but peanut butter is easily "thinned" if you wish to be extra cautious.

Cold Metal Surfaces. Birds' eyes and tongues may freeze to feeder parts made of iron (e.g., suet dispensers); greasing such surfaces will prevent this kind of accident.

Hummingbird Formulas. Particularly in the Southwest, where hummers are abundant and their species varied, providing them with artificial nectar has long been one of the most popular feeding practices. With experience it became clear that the most *attractive* potion consisted of two parts water, one part sugar, and enough red food coloring to make the transparent feeder glow like a flower. Leery of feeding refined sugar to their hummers, some people suggested honey as a more "natural" alternative. Over the years the salubriousness of all three of these items has been questioned: the 2-to-1 solution as too rich for livers; the red dye as a carcinogen; and the honey as the cause of a fatal disease which attacks the tongue. Only the charge against honey has been thoroughly documented, and though the disease *may* be preventable by ensuring a very fresh honey supply, it may be best not to take chances—most of the claims made for its superiority over sugar water are spurious anyway. Red dye will attract birds more quickly but can probably also be eliminated with little long-range effect on the success of your operation. A strong sugar solution also helps in the initial attraction problem but is not essential in the long run. Since the effects of both the dye and the sugar-heavy solution are cumulative rather than immediate, their temporary use to get things started is probably permissible.

Summer Suet. In warm weather suet tends to liquefy and can dangerously mat birds' plumage. Woodpeckers seem particularly vulnerable. Best reserved as a winter offering.

Cutting Off the Supply. As noted, most birds would return to finding "wild" food without difficulty in most cases if you suddenly stopped feeding. However, if you have built up a large dependent flock over months of feeding, you could at least be accused of a certain callousness if you abandon your operation abruptly during the harshest season. Having a feeder is not unlike taking on a number of pets—your responsibility will inevitably impinge somewhat on your freedom.

ORGANIC BIRD FEEDING. You can combine bird feeding and horticulture by planting your property with trees, shrubs, and herbs which bear edible nectar, fruits, or seeds as well as provide cover and nesting materials.

Most of the plant species listed here are widespread and many are cultivated as garden ornamentals in the Temperate Zone. A host of others
occur in subtropical and arid regions of North America and the lists below
are by no means complete. They can easily be expanded by watching what
birds eat in the field and bringing seeds or cuttings into your yard.

The following trees, shrubs, and vines are highly attractive to fruit-
eating birds:

Apples, pears, chokeberries, crab apples (*Malus* [*Pyrus*])
Barberries (*Berberis*)
Bayberry (*Myrica pennsylvanica*)
Blueberries (*Vaccinium*)
Buckthorns (*Rhamnus*)
Cherries (*Prunus*)
Curlewberry (*Empetrum nigrum*)
Currants (*Ribes*)
Dewberries, blackberries, raspberries, etc. (*Rubus*)
Dogwoods (*Cornus*)
Elderberry (*Sambucus canadensis*)
Firethorn (*Cotoneaster pyracantha*)
Grapes (*Vitis*)
Greenbrier (*Smilax*)
Hawthorns (*Crataegus*)
Hollies (*Ilex*)
Honeysuckles (*Lonicera*)
Huckleberries (*Gaylussaccia*)
Mountain ash (*Pyrus americana*)
Poison ivy (*Rhus radicans*)
Privet (*Ligustrium*)
Red cedar (*Juniperus virginiana*)
Roses (*Rosa* spp., especially *R. multiflora*)
Russian olive (*Eleagnus angustifolia*)
Shads (Juneberries or serviceberries) (*Amelanchier*)
Viburnums (*Viburnum*)
Woodbine (Virginia creeper) (*Parthenocissus quinquefolia*)
Yew (*Taxus canadensis*)

Trees and shrubs visited frequently by seed-eating birds include:

Alders (*Alnus*)
Birches (*Betula*)
Firs (*Abies*)
Hemlock (*Tsuga canadensis*)
Pines (*Pinus*)

Spirea (*Spirea*)
Spruces (*Picea*)

   The following common plants (both wild and cultivated) bear flowers
attractive to hummingbirds. Experiments have shown that red flowers are
most attractive to hummers, followed by yellow; blue flowers are less appealing, though some species, e.g., delphiniums, are quite popular.

Azalea (*Rhododendron*)
Bee balm (*Monarda*)
Bellflower (*Campanula*)
Bouncing bet (*Saponaria*)
Butterfly bush (*Buddleia*)
Canna
Cardinal flower (*Lobelia cardinalis*)
Century plants (*Agave*)
Columbine (*Aquilegia*)
Coralbells (*Heuchera sanguinea*)
Cornflower (*Centaurea*)
Day lily (*Hemerocallis*)
Delphinium
Erythrina (flowering tree spp.)
Figwort (*Scrophularia*)
Flowering tobacco (*Nicotiana*)
Four-o'clock (*Mirabilis*)
Foxglove (*Digitalis*)
Fuchsia
Gladiolus
Hamelia
Hollyhock (*Althaea*)
Iris
Jasmines (*Jasminicum*)
Jewelweed (*Impatiens*)
Larkspur (*Delphinium*)
Lilac (*Syringa*)
Lily (*Lilium*)
Louseworts (*Pedicularus*)
Matrimony vine (*Lycium*)
Milkweeds (*Asclepias*)
Mint (*Mentha*)
Monkey flower (*Mimulus*)
Morning glory (*Ipomoea*)
Nasturtium (*Tropaeolum*)
Oriental poppy (*Papaver orientale*)

Painted cup (*Castilleja*)
Pelargonium
Penstemon
Petunia
Phlox
Poinciana
Ragged robin (*Lychnis*)
Rattlesnake root (*Prenanthes*)
Red-hot poker or torch lily (*Kniphofia*)
Scabious (*Scabiosa*)
Scarlet runner bean (*Phaseolus coccineus*)
Scarlet sage (*Salvia splendens*) and other *Salvias*
Snapdragon (*Antirrhinum*)
Solomon's seal (*Polygonatum*)
Spiderflower (*Cleome*)
Sweet william (*Dianthus barbatus*)
Tritoma
Trumpet creeper (*Campsis radicans*)
Virginia bluebell (*Mertensia*)

A well-planned weed patch made up of local species can be more attractive to both birds and humans than a sterile lawn and borders of cultivated flowers. Composites such as thistles, goldenrods, St.-John's-worts (*Hypericum*), and asters have showy flowers and an abundance of seed in the fall and winter. Slightly less attractive species—e.g., pokeweed (*Phytolacca americana*), various knotweeds (*Polygonum*), amaranth (*Amaranthus*), and large grasses such as foxtails (*Setaria*), panic grass (*Panicum*), and barnyard grass (*Echinochloa crusgalli*)—can be made to look quite presentable if planted carefully.

BIRD FINDING. With the recent "explosion" of the North American birdwatcher population (see BIRDWATCHING) and the great mobility its members enjoy, it is now commonplace to encounter birders in the farthest corners of the continent—or the world—in search of new ornithological adventures. This has sparked a new service literature—bird-finding guides, a list of which is given in the Bibliography.

Of course, bird finding is not the exclusive province of ornithological jet-setters. In fact, anyone who has not honed his finding skills in seeking the avian specialties of his yard, home town, county, state, and region is unlikely to be very successful at ferreting out the feathered denizens of rain forests and other exotic habitats beyond. The key to seeing the greatest possible number of species is the same whether you are listing the birds of your neighborhood or the world—namely, to examine all ecological niches in as many habitats and as many geographical regions as possible (see DIS-

TRIBUTION). And, of course, it helps to learn as much as you can about the habits of the birds you seek. Many species are highly specific in their feeding, breeding, and migratory behavior and quite a few are inordinately secretive—presenting what some birders consider an "unfair" advantage. It is finding these "tough birds" which brings the greatest rewards to the serious "lister," "twitcher," or "tick hunter." Anyone can buy a ticket to Africa or South America and come home with an enormous list of relatively common birds. But the birder who knows what to look for, along with how, when, and where to look for it, in his own region is the type who plays the sport best and gets the most satisfying thrills.

Most beginning birders reading this book probably entertain the goal—however vaguely—of seeing as much of the splendidly diverse North American avifauna as possible. Having practiced the above dictum about learning one's backyard birds first, he will eventually want to explore the following major geographical/biotic regions of the continent: (1) the northeast coast (Maritime Provinces, New England) for exclusively Atlantic tubenoses, gulls, and alcids; (2) the northern coniferous forest (northern New England, southern Canada) for specialties of this biome such as Spruce Grouse, three-toed woodpeckers, Bohemian Waxwing, Gray Jay, and a variety of breeding thrushes, wood warblers, and northern finches; (3) the southeastern woodlands (pine *and* hardwood) for the likes of Red-cockaded Woodpecker, Carolina Chickadee, Brown-headed Nuthatch, Carolina Wren, Swainson's and other wood warblers, and Bachman's Sparrow; (4) southern Florida for great water-bird concentrations and Caribbean specialties (both breeding and vagrant) in the Keys; super-listers will also want to check out the numerous officially "listable" exotics in the Miami area; (5) southern Texas for Mexican land-bird specialties and a great wealth of birdlife generally; (6) southwestern deserts for such dry-country birds as Gila Woodpecker, Le Conte's Thrasher, Cactus Wren, Verdin, Phainopepla, and Black-throated Sparrow; (7) southeastern Arizona for species of largely Mexican distribution, especially highland ones, e.g., hummingbirds, Elegant Trogon, Red-faced Warbler; (8) the western mountains (Rockies, Sierra Nevada, Cascades, etc.) for montane endemics, e.g., White-headed Woodpecker, Williamson's Sapsucker, Mountain Chickadee, Hammond's Flycatcher, Clark's Nutcracker, Cassin's Finch, and rosy finches; (9) the central prairies for grouse species, Dickcissel, Le Conte's and Baird's Sparrows, Lark Bunting, Clay-colored Sparrow, McCown's and Chestnut-collared Longspurs; (10) the Pacific coast for numerous water-bird species, especially pelagics, shorebirds, gulls, and alcids; (11) Alaska for its endemic specialties (alcids, McKay's Bunting, etc.) as well as myriad coastal, coniferous forest, and arctic species; and (12) the Arctic for breeding shorebirds, jaegers, ptarmigan, raptors, and a few passerine specialties such as Hoary Redpoll. The mobile bird-seeker will also want to visit areas where great concentrations of birdlife occur, such as coastlines, swamps and marshes, and places where migrating birds pass or stop. And if truly serious, he or she will have to make pilgrimages (some definitely out of the way) to look for very local species such as California Condor, Yellow-billed Magpie, and Colima, Golden-cheeked, and Kirtland's Warblers. Of course, these regions and localities overlap at their margins and each contains many species other than their avian "highlights." Furthermore, with the aid of the migration phenomena, birders can see a large percentage of American bird species in their own backyard, as it were, especially if they live near the coast. But for a comprehensive view of North American birdlife, a bird finder must, like many of his quarry, become a bird of passage.

The guides listed in the Bibliography give highly specific details not only on what birds are where ("The wide shoulders along Farm Road 2004 are particularly good for Sprague's Pipits"—Jim Lane on the Texas coast) but on how and when to look for them, whom to ask for advice in a given area, and (occasionally) where to stay.

The present book does not even attempt to compete with these comprehensive and meticulous bird-finding guides. However, the neophyte birder unfamiliar with the names of North American birding "meccas" ("Patagonia" in birder-ese usually refers to southeastern Arizona, not Argentina) will find a selection of more than 50 such famous localities included as entries here with brief descriptions of the habitat(s) they comprise and their bird specialties. For a list of these "hot spots," see p. 9. For timing your birding expeditions, see the Birdwatcher's Calendar, Appendix III. See also references in the Bibliography under SANCTUARY.

BIRDHOUSE (or nest box). Attracting cavity-nesting birds by setting out homemade nesting sites is an ancient tradition. Native Americans hung hollowed-out gourds to attract Purple Martins. In Europe the practice of putting out specially made clay or wooden flasks for birds to nest in can be traced at least as far back as the Middle Ages.

The custom did not originate from altogether altruistic impulses. The medieval Europeans *ate* the first broods of the birds which used their birdhouses (usually House Sparrows and Common Starlings), and the Amerinds were motivated (according to Audubon) by the territorial aggressiveness of the martins which kept the vultures away from their deer kills. Even today, many people erect martin houses (see below) not solely for the company of the birds but for their (alas, highly exaggerated) taste for mosquitoes (see below). But if the practice was initially self-serving, there can be no doubt that putting up nest boxes near one's home for the simple pleasure of it has also appealed to us for a long time. It is especially appealing today as the trend to push the natural world away and hem ourselves in with layers and piles of man-made trash continues unabated. And for those whose pleasure depends on the notion that they are providing quarters for birds which would otherwise be homeless, there is some experimental evidence that this is indeed the case. The majority of cavity nesters depend upon the abandoned holes of woodpeckers (which generally excavate a new site each year), and these sites are of course much scarcer than those used by species which construct their own nests in trees or on the ground. In a number of forest localities it has been shown that the number of birds seeking cavity sites far exceeds their availability and that almost as many birdhouses as are erected are occupied. This is not true everywhere, but it is a reliable indication that you can expect to have a fair degree of success in redressing the avian housing shortage.

WHAT KIND OF BIRDS. More than fifty species of North American birds have been reported nesting in "artificial situations," and over thirty-five species are known to do so with some degree of regularity. In any given place, the variety will, of course, be considerably less. The construction chart below includes the species you are most likely to attract.

SOME BASIC GUIDELINES. There is nothing complicated or tricky about making and locating a successful birdhouse, and specific construction details are given below, accompanied by Fig. 3. However, naturalists have learned a few things since they began putting out nest boxes in a methodical way (in nineteenth-century England), which both encourage occupancy and enhance your tenants' welfare.

• The young of most cavity nesters are born naked (see YOUNG, DEVELOPMENT OF) and are therefore particularly sensitive to extremes of heat and cold. Accordingly, it is important that the materials, plans, and location of your nest box do not increase the birds' vulnerability to the elements. These considerations are incorporated in the more specific guidelines given below.

• Even if there is a housing shortage (as described above) in your area, most birds have strong territorial instincts which will normally deter them from nesting too close to other birds, especially ones of their own species. Recent studies have revealed that even Purple Martins, which we encourage to live together in homemade apartment houses (see below), would not nest in such density given their preference. Other studies indicate that 4–5 cavity nesters per acre seem to be average for many localities and this may be a reasonable guideline to follow on your property. Except for the martins, make "single dwelling units" and space them widely.

• In addition to the location suggestions for particular species given under *Construction*, below, pay attention to just where you put your bird box. Try to allow for a fairly clear flight path to the entrance. Place it so that the entrance hole is not exposed to the prevailing direction of wind-driven rainstorms (easterly in most parts of the continent) or any other prevailing winds of your region. In most cases, this will mean that the preferred direction will be south, southwest, or west. Make sure the box rests vertically or slanted *slightly* toward the ground; if tilted toward the sky, it is more vulnerable to precipitation.

• Cavity nests can provide easy prey for cats; if you have one or live in the suburbs, make sure your birdhouse is cat-proof. A metal pole or "cat guard" of some kind (see, for example, under *Construction*) will discourage Felix as well as raccoons, snakes, and other potential molesters.

• To reduce nest parasites, some of which winter over in old nests, remove the contents of your nest boxes at the end of the breeding season. If you do this conspicuously, it may also win you housekeeping points with your neighbors—Audubon said that he could judge the quality of country inns by the state of the martin houses traditionally erected on the hostelry signboards. The construction plans below provide for easy cleaning.

• Though it is possible to encourage certain species and discourage others by methods of construction and location, it is not really possible to keep out some "undesirable" birds. This is especially true of the usual species so termed—the House Sparrow and Common Starling. Both of these introduced pests are extraordinarily uncritical in judging the suitability of a nest site; often occupy a box very early in the season before native migratory birds have arrived; usually prevail in contests with more desirable species over a suitable site; and of course are very common in many areas. The only solution to this problem is to actively discourage the unwanted tenants. You can block the entrance holes until the species you want to encourage have returned in the spring. And if starlings or House Sparrows begin to build, simply remove nest material as the birds collect it. If eggs or young are present, only your personal sentiments may prevent you from destroying them. Neither the law nor responsible conservation organizations advocate the protection of these aliens.

CONSTRUCTION OF A SIMPLE NEST BOX. The design and building instructions which follow are adapted from the Massachusetts Audubon Society's Public Service Information Sheet, "Nest Boxes for Birds." They result in a well-tested, easy-to-make birdhouse which can be modified or "fancied up" according to the taste of the builder. The instructions are numbered to correspond with the plans in Fig. 3.

1. This *bluebird box* is made from a single board, 1″ x 6″ x 48″; pine or spruce is recommended. Measure and cut the pieces as shown one at a time to allow for the width of the saw cut. *Then:* Drill four ¼″ ventilation holes in each side, 1″ below the roof line; cut off the corners of the floor board as drainage holes; drill an entrance hole of the desired diameter in the front board, making sure the distance from the *center* of the hole to the bottom of the front board is that given in the chart (below) under "Distance—Hole to Floor" for the species you are aiming to attract.

2. Nail one of the three 5½″ strips as shown on each of the side boards, 1″ (or the *thickness* of the front board) in from the edge.

3. Nail the back to the floor, then attach the sides to the back and floor. Note that the sides are supposed to extend beyond the front edge of the floor board, as this is where the front board will lie. Attach the roof so

that it will be flush in back but overhang in front, providing shade and shelter from rain.

4. Nail the last strip across the top of the box just below the roof overhang and cut it flush with the sides.

5. Cut a ⅜" notch at the center of the bottom edge of the front board. Then slip the front board into position under the roof strip and resting on the two side strips. Make a pencil mark on the front edge of the floor board where the *top* of the notch meets it. Then remove the front and drive a front-support nail in (to the depth shown) at the pencil mark.

6. Attach the extension board to the back *with screws* so that it projects 3" above the roof.

7. Note that the finished box does *not* include a perching peg below the entrance hole as called for in some plans. Such pegs are not only unnecessary but actually encourage predation by giving the nest robber a place to sit while it goes about its unseemly business. If the wood used is smooth-planed and you wish to offer the occupants a better gripping surface, simply score the surface under the entrance hole (inside as well as outside) with a knife or file. If you wish to stain the house, use a non-insecticide stain and coat only the outside. Houses placed in the open should be light-colored or painted with reflective paint to obviate the danger of overheating.

8. Shows how a simple cat/raccoon baffle can be attached to a pole mount.

Wood Duck boxes are built on the same principle (see Fig. 3, lower left), but with a few specific modifications to accommodate the requirements of the species.

• A tunnel entrance should be provided for protection from predators, especially raccoons.

• Top rather than front is removable (as shown).

• Ventilation holes in *bottom*.

• Use unplaned boards; roughen the inside of the front board from floor to hole or put screen or hardware cloth in this area so that ducklings can climb out of the box after hatching.

• Line the bottom of the box with about 4" of wood shavings and sawdust—*not* leaves, grass, or other "nesting material."

• Boxes to be sited over water should be affixed to wooden poles (preferably cedar) no less than 4" in diameter or on metal pipes (require U-bolt clamps).

• The best location for Wood Duck boxes is over open water at least 20' from shore and out of reach of any overhanging limbs. Such locations are naturally safeguarded against predators and provide efficient, safe access to open water for ducklings. Quiet, open water with good marshy or

FIG. 3. *Birdhouses.* See building instructions above.

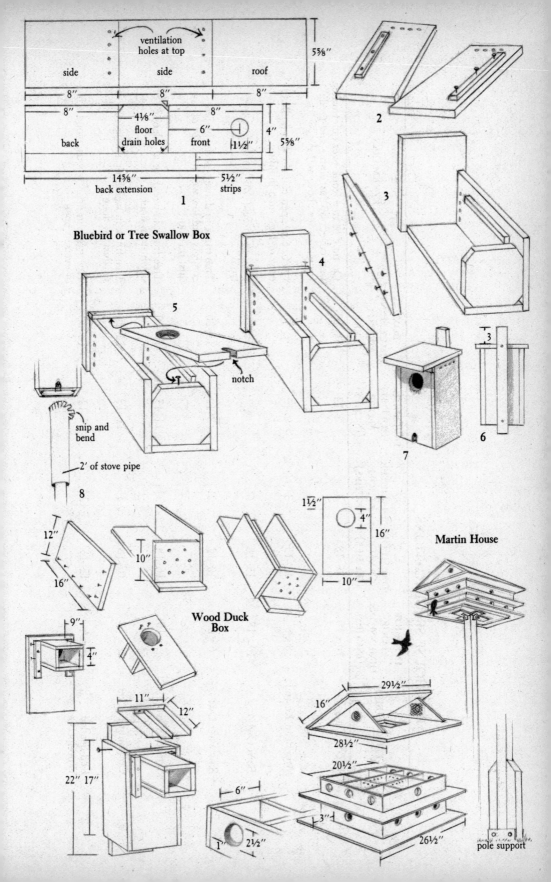

ventilation holes at top

side

side

roof

5⅝"

8"   8"   8"

8"   8"

4⅛"

floor
drain holes

6"   front

1½"

4"

5⅝"

back

14⅝"

back extension

5½"

strips

1

Bluebird or Tree Swallow Box

2

3

4

5

notch

snip and bend

2' of stove pipe

8

6

7

3

1½"   4"

16"

10"

12"

10"

16"

Wood Duck Box

Martin House

9"   4"

11"   12"

22" 17"

6"

1"   2½"

29½"

16"

28½"

20½"

3"

26½"

pole support

BIRDHOUSE SPECIFICATIONS

TYPE OF BIRD	INTERIOR FLOOR DIMENSIONS (INCHES)	DEPTH OF CAVITY (INCHES)	DIAMETER OF HOLE (INCHES)	DISTANCE— HOLE TO FLOOR (INCHES)	BOX PLACEMENT HEIGHT (FEET)	SITE/REMARKS
Wood Duck	10 x 10	15–18	4	8–12	4–20	On pole or tree trunk over quiet water, near cover; sawdust lining and predator guard; see above and Fig. 3
American Kestrel	8 x 8	12–15	3	9–12	10–30	On tree in open country or woodland edge or high on a building
Barn Owl	10 x 18	15–18	6	4	12–18	Near open fields on building or tree trunk
Saw-whet Owl	6 x 6	10–12	2½	8–10	12–20	Tree trunk in dense woods; prefers conifers and low wet areas; 2" of sawdust on floor
Screech Owl	8 x 10	16–18	3¼	11–13	12–20	Tree trunk in woods or at edge; 2" of sawdust on floor
Common Flicker	7 x 7	16–18	3¼	11–13	12–20	Tree trunk in woods or at edge; 2" of sawdust on floor
Red-headed Woodpecker	6 x 6	12–15	2	9–12	12–20	Tree trunk in open woods, wood edge, or even in open

Hairy Woodpecker	6 x 6	12–15	1½	9–12	12–20	Tree trunk in woods
Great Crested Flycatcher	6 x 6	8–10	2	6–8	8–20	Tree trunk in woods
Bluebirds, Tree and Violet-green Swallows, Prothonotary Warbler	5 x 5	6–8	1½	5–6	4–12	In open or near wood edge; warbler in swampy woods, usually low; see Fig. 3
Purple Martin	6 x 6	6	2½	1	15–20	On pole in open field; near water; see above and Fig. 3
Chickadees and other tits, nuthatches, and Downy Woodpecker	4 x 4	8–10	1¼	6–8	8–15	Tree trunk in or at edge of woods; line with sphagnum, sawdust, and/or wood chips for best results with tits
House and Bewick's Wrens	4 x 4	6–8	1	4–6	5–10	Wood edge or open woods
Carolina Wren	4 x 4	6–8	1¼	4–6	5–10	Wood edge or open woods

wooded cover nearby is ideal Wood Duck habitat. Boxes are best placed in such sites in winter when the ice is solid. Be sure that the pole is set deep enough in the bottom of the pond or marsh to withstand flood or ice movements, and that the box is at least above spring flood line. Do not place the pole in the path of a strong current.

• Boxes fixed to trees are more vulnerable to predators but are workable provided: the trees are near water and no less than 10"–12" in diameter; the boxes are placed 8'–10' from the ground (where prospecting ducks look for them); tunnel entrances are provided; and the top cover is secured. (The above guidelines are adapted from the recommendations of the Massachusetts Division of Fisheries and Wildlife.)

Martin houses are also essentially a variation on the principles governing the construction of the "basic house" above. See Fig. 3, lower right, for details. Note especially the ventilation holes in the central cubicle and roof. All tiers, including the roof, should be fastened with hooks and eyes for easy removal and cleaning.

Because martin houses are most attractive (to the birds) when raised 15'–20' off the ground, the "support system" for the structure is very important for both the birds' safety and the landlords' convenience. The foundation on which the bottom floor of the house rests should be 20½" square and 2½" thick. Centered on its underside, attach a cross made of a double thickness of ¾" boards 3" x 6". Attach four heavy angle irons (one to each spoke of the cross) spaced to meet the 4" x 4" center pole. The pole itself can be hollow—i.e., made from ¾"-thick hard-pine boards. The base is the other essential point of security. This consists of two 8'-long 4-by-4's buried in the ground to a depth of 4' and held apart by another 4-by-4 buried between them. The house pole is fitted between the two support poles and metal plates are bolted across the opening between the support poles and across the base of the house pole. In addition, a pipe or large bolt runs through the tops of the support poles and the house pole, holding the latter at another point. This bolt serves as a hinge or lever in lowering the martin house for cleaning at the end of the season.

Purple Martins, like other swallows, are "aerial insectivores," meaning they feed exclusively on the wing on flying insects. The ideal site for a martin house, therefore, is in the middle of a large open field—not in or near woods or other shelter. Nearby bodies of water and additional open perching places also increase real estate value from the martin point of view.

A Word about Martins and Mosquitoes. A lot of publicity issues from certain quarters claiming that Purple Martins are man's best hope in winning the war against mosquitoes. Since martins do indeed eat a great quantity of flying insects, the assumption is not illogical, and since its adherents are advocating biological rather than chemical control of pest insects, the motives are essentially noble ones. Unfortunately, martins and mosquitoes are simply not abroad at the same time of day. Martins are mainly diurnal, mosquitoes mainly crepuscular and nocturnal. (For more on this sad truth, see Kale, 1968.) One should be particularly wary of extravagant claims made by those offering martin houses for sale. None of this should diminish anyone's enthusiasm for Purple Martins one iota. They are beautiful, interesting, and charming birds—well worth attracting.

BIRD SHELVES. Phoebes, American Robins, and Barn Swallows build partly with mud and prefer flat, level surfaces on which to nest. In nature, a rocky shelf or broad horizontal branch may fill this requirement but man-made structures are often ideal. These species occupy sheltered eaves or similar shelves on houses or barns. A simple 6″ x 8″ platform, sheltered from the weather and otherwise oriented favorably as described in the instructions for the basic nest box, may attract these birds and possibly Song Sparrows, which normally build a conventional grass cup.

For attracting birds with plantings and offering food, see BIRD FEEDING.

BIRDING. The bimonthly publication of the American Birding Association, containing features and articles on field identification, bird finding, summaries of ornithological literature with relevance to birding, birding ethics (e.g., whether "heard only" birds should be counted on one's life list), personality profiles, photo quizzes, book reviews, and annual summaries of the longest state, provincial, North American, and international species lists compiled during the preceding twelve months. As its title implies, *Birding* is directed mainly at the sporting element of the birdwatcher population. For a sample article, see LISTING. For the address of its subscription office as of 1982, see the Bibliography under PERIODICALS. For "birding," the activity, see BIRDWATCHING.

BIRD LICE. Chewing lice in the insect order Mallophaga, which live their entire life cycles on the bodies of birds, eating bits of skin, feathers, and some body fluids. For more detail, see ECTOPARASITE.

BIRDLIME. See LIME.

BIRD OF PREY. Generally understood to refer to hawks, eagles, falcons, and their relatives (except perhaps for the vultures) and owls. Often defined as birds which hunt, kill, and eat other animals or other vertebrates or other "warm-blooded" animals, but there are too many exceptions to this formula to sustain the validity of it. Many herons, corvids, and specialized species of other families (e.g., roadrunners) fit this definition but are not thought of as birds of prey. Both Ospreys and mergansers hunt, kill, and eat fish, yet the former is certainly a bird of prey, while the latter is certainly not. A better definition is birds equipped with talons and/or hooked bills adapted for holding and tearing meat; this would admit the shrikes and vultures, which might be disputed, but would exclude other carnivores. Essentially synonymous with "raptor." See PREDATION.

BIRD SKIN. The usual form in which specimens of birds are preserved in museum collections for a variety of purposes vital to the study of birdlife. Novice birdwatchers and those with a particularly deep empathy for living things of all kinds are often dismayed the first time they see a large scientific collection—drawer upon drawer filling cabinet after cabinet sometimes occupying room after room, all filled with stuffed bird carcasses, most of which were intentionally collected. Most soon realize, however, that the number of birds sacrificed to science is barely discernible next to the carnage of migrant birds produced by a single skyscraper or TV tower during a single night or even the combined annual death toll from the continent's picture windows, and that what is learned from the preservation of intelligently collected specimens is significant compensation. For a detailed discussion of the function of skin collections, see Parkes (1963–MUSEUM).

The usual method of preparing a bird skin is (very briefly) as follows: The bird is laid on its back and the feathers parted manually down the center of the breast and belly. An incision is made through the skin running from the top of the breastbone to just above the vent. The skin is then worked back with fingers and scalpel from the muscular body to which it adheres. This internal carcass is detached at the knee and shoulder joints and at the base of the tail, and the skin is inverted over the neck and head to the base of the bill. The carcass is then detached from the base of the skull, so that only the skull and lower wing and leg bones remain attached to the feathered skin. These and the inside of the skin itself are now cleaned of any remaining muscle, fat, and other perishable tissue, and the whole interior is treated with a drying agent. The skin is then turned "right side to," with the cleaned skull remaining in the head. Finally a "body" composed of cotton or other stuffing substance is made in proportion to the original one, fitted into the cavity, and the incision is sewn up. The specimen is laid on its back, its bill pointing forward (in short-necked birds), its wings folded, its legs crossed, its plumage arranged, and—a crucial step without which all effort would be wasted—a label is attached giving as much information as is known about the specimen—e.g., place and date of collection, age, state of sexual organs, colors of soft parts, stomach contents, weight before skinning, measurements of various parts, species and subspecies, and the name of the collector. Few specimens, in fact, are labeled this thoroughly, but any ornithologist will affirm that a specimen's value is proportionate to the thoroughness with which it is labeled.

All of this may sound simple enough—especially if you are not squeamish about "innards"—but the preparation of a good bird skin is in reality a minor art, as you will quickly discover if you ever have the opportunity to try it. In the old days when collecting and preparing 50 birds in a weekend was routine for the serious amateur collector, a skilled hand was said to be able to turn out a "passable" skin in ten or fifteen minutes (for hard cases). These gentlemen typically omitted to sew up the incision in small birds, however, and how passable they were in fact is a matter of highly subjective judgment.

For a lengthy—and often entertaining—account of how bird skins were made in the old days, see Coues (1890). For detailed modern technique, see Anderson (1965). See also MUSEUM; COLLECTING.

BIRDSMANSHIP. A matter of style. Conducting oneself to the best advantage in birding and ornithological situations. Encompasses all aspects of the birdsman's world, e.g., dress, comportment in the field, public speaking, dinner conversation. For the seminal work on the subject, including many instructive anecdotes, see Bruce Campbell's definitive essay reprinted in Peterson (1957–BIRDWATCHING).

A single example must serve here. The late Robert Smart, a birdsman of repute, was scoping the sea one breezy November morning when another birder, scanning nearby, called out—with that crisp air of infallibility that only second-rate field men seem able to master: "Red Phalaropes, moving right, two o'clock, about halfway to the horizon."

"Excellent," said Bob, shifting his scope to the flock in question and managing to convey both enthusiasm and regret over not having found the birds himself: "Where exactly from the Sanderlings?"

BIRD'S NEST SOUP. An expensive Asian delicacy made from the nests of several species of Old World swifts in the genus *Collocalia;* the nests are made of viscous, solidifying saliva, secreted by the swifts for this purpose. The saliva itself is relatively tasteless and is improved in most soup recipes by the addition of vegetables and condiments. Swift spittle is considered an aphrodisiac by the Chinese. See EDIBILITY for other avian dishes.

BIRDWATCHING. Usually refers to the regular, somewhat methodical seeking out and observation of birds, whether for pure aesthetic pleasure or recreation or out of a more serious, quasi-scientific motive. That is, usually does *not* apply either to people who may feed birds but are not particularly interested in which species they attract or to professional ornithologists, most of whom spend at least as much (usually much more) time in the laboratory and library as they do observing birds in the field. The relatively new, but rapidly evolving ethological branch of ornithology intrinsically involves long hours of watching birds, yet the practitioners of this discipline are known as "bird behaviorists," implying the specialized education that "birdwatchers" usually lack.

The semantics, history, and social implications of "birdwatcher"/"birder"/"ornithologist" are rather complex and potentially amusing. It should be noted, first, that a "serious" birdwatcher of today could easily instruct an "ornithologist" of 150 years ago—due, of course, to the accumulation of knowledge which the early ornithologists helped to discover. Nevertheless, modern "birders" should neither feel nor be disparaged by modern ornithologists.

In North America an interest in birds has always been associated with very different values than it has in Europe and especially England, where birds and man meet on a more nearly equal footing than in any other Western country. Until after World War II, birdwatching in America was regarded as a pursuit of: (1) the rich (perhaps because many early conservationists, e.g., Teddy Roosevelt, were American aristocrats); (2) the eccentric (because of field clothes? because only a crazy would spend time peering up into trees at tiny, flitting forms?); and in males (3) the somewhat effeminate (not enough physical contact for a proper sport!). In spite of the dramatic increase in environmental education and the popularity of "nature appreciation" here recently, there is still some stigma felt by any boy over ten who would just as soon watch birds as play baseball. In much of Europe, these negative values attached to an interest in natural history are not apparent—the idea of a father and son going birdwatching in the morning and to a rugby match in the afternoon surprises no one (mothers and daughters are a different case—see below). Pretentious analyses of this difference, involving Americans' relatively recent subjugation of their "wilderness," will not be indulged in here.

Another interesting difference between American and European birdwatchers involves how each perceives his/her avocation. In a recent (1980) book aimed at British birdwatchers, Alan Richards observes: "In the early 1950's ornithologists tended to believe that all birdwatching should yield some scientific return; in more recent years this attitude has disappeared and birdwatching is usually done for sheer pleasure and interest." With some notable exceptions the situation in America has been just the reverse. In the 1950's (and later) ornithologists here expected nothing whatever of birdwatchers, and birdwatchers expected nothing of scientific value of themselves—only fun; only recently have young American birdwatchers in any numbers begun "watching" (rather than simply listing) birds and carrying notebooks into the field to record their observations.

Another British comment (Homes, 1964) points up a second English/American contrast: "Many [British] birdwatchers never progress ... beyond proficiency in the field identification of birds ... and in learning to do so by ear as well as by sight." Many American birdwatchers have gotten a lifetime of enjoyment out of their hobby without mastering more than the most obvious field marks and most distinctive bird songs; people who do more have been referred to here as "professional birdwatchers." Given this difference, it is fascinating that most American birdwatchers

insist on being called "birders" (see also LISTING), as implying a more serious, aggressive approach to the activity, whereas in British usage "bird-
watcher/birdwatching" still prevails (Richards records a growing popularity for "birder/birding," however).

To summarize the reality behind some of the above distinctions:
American birdwatching (birding) is largely a form of competitive sport involving how many species of birds one can see in a day, year, life, state, or
the world; a great deal of driving and talking are usually involved in a day's
birding and relatively little attention is paid to individual birds. European
birders (birdwatchers) concentrate more on honing field identification
skills under difficult conditions; they tend to walk (and slog) more, write a
great deal in notebooks (field marks, behavior, phenological data), are not
very tolerant of idle conversation while "watching," and are usually suspicious of listers; they consider good notes on a particular species better evidence of a good day in the field than a long species list. Obviously there are
distinct advantages to both of these approaches to birdwatching.

SOME DEMOGRAPHICS

• Birdwatching is a strongly male-dominated activity wherever it is
practiced. The most adept and ardent birders often begin as obsessive pre-
adolescent boys. The sexual balance is changing slightly for the better
since the 1960's.

• In America, a special gathering of birdwatchers—for example, at a
migration watch point—is likely to consist mainly of middle-aged or older
people; groups of older children or teenage birdwatchers are practically
unheard of. In Europe, birdwatching hot spots tend to be overwhelmingly
dominated by young people, mostly teenagers and people in their twenties;
busloads of schoolchildren with binoculars on excursions organized specifically for birdwatching are commonplace. At least in Britain and the Scandinavian countries, there is a recognized pattern of a widespread interest in
natural history developing among kids which fades in many as they get
older. In America, the tendency seems to be the reverse, though this pattern too has changed somewhat recently.

• The old stereotype of the well-to-do birdwatcher is not entirely
without foundation today. To compete successfully in listing circles, a certain minimum of leisure and mobility are necessary. The "professions" are
well represented among birders, particularly doctors, who have always figured prominently in American ornithology (see BIOGRAPHY).

• WASP's probably still make up the majority of the Western birdwatching community; a black birdwatcher is still a rara avis.

• Birdwatching is largely restricted to "developed" countries of the
North Temperate Zone, especially North America, northern Europe (including Russia), and Japan.

For more detail on variations and accouterments of birdwatching as
well as some of the scientifically useful projects in which birders make an

essential contribution, see ATLAS; CENSUS; CHRISTMAS COUNT; BIG DAY; BIRD FINDING; FIELD GUIDE; IDENTIFICATION; FIELD PROBLEM; OPTICAL EQUIPMENT; PHOTOGRAPHY; RECORDING; BIRD FEEDING; BIRD CLUB; PERIODICALS.

The Bibliography contains "how to" books as well as some of the best "birding adventure" books. Other relevant titles will be found in the Bibliography under other headings, e.g., BIRD FINDING.

BITTERN. Standard English name for all members of the subfamily Botaurinae (family Ardeidae [herons]; order Ciconiiformes). There are 13 species of true bitterns worldwide, though the name is sometimes applied to a number of other herons not in the subfamily Botaurinae. Two species of bitterns, the American and the Least, breed in North America.

The bitterns are secretive, semi-crepuscular marsh birds, more often heard than seen. The American Bittern is widespread in wetlands from subarctic Canada to Central America. The Least Bittern barely reaches Canada and is essentially absent from the Great Plains but reaches South America as a breeding bird.

The Least Bittern has a dark (melanistic or erythristic) color phase once thought to be a separate species, called Cory's Least Bittern.

"Bittern" derives from a Greek term relating to the remarkable sound that the Eurasian Bittern makes. It resembles the lowing of an ox, a fact that inspired the Latin bittern genus *Botaurus*—from *Bos taurus*, the European wild white ox or aurochs. The characteristic sound of the American (*Botaurus*) Bittern is less bovine but even more remarkable and has given rise to nicknames such as "dunk-a-doo," "stake driver," and "thunder-pump."

For family characteristics, see HERON.

BLACKBIRD. Standard English name for about 23 of the approximately 90 members of the family Icteridae (order Passeriformes). The name is often used to refer to all of the largely black members of the family, i.e., the cowbirds and grackles, as well as the species actually called blackbirds. It has also been applied to the family as a whole, encompassing the orioles, oropendolas, caciques, meadowlarks, and Bobolink. The icterids are so diverse in form, coloration, and behavior that it is almost impossible to discuss them in terms of their common traits. Therefore the "black blackbirds," including the grackles, are considered together in this entry and the others under COWBIRD; ORIOLE; MEADOWLARK; BOBOLINK.

Ten species of "black blackbirds" breed in North America, including 5 which are called blackbirds, 3 species of grackles, and 2 of cowbirds. One additional species (the Tawny-shouldered Blackbird) has been recorded as an accidental straggler (see Appendix II).

The blackbirds range in size from 6½ inches (Brown-headed Cowbird) to 18 inches (Great-tailed Grackle). In most species the bill tapers to a sharp point. The males of all species are largely black, most are "shiny," several have strong green and purple iridescence, and three have areas of brilliant red or yellow feathering. Except in the Common Grackle, females are mainly dull grayish or brownish and are streaked in some species. The blackbirds are essentially ground feeders, walking deliberately over fields, lawns, and the margins of marshes or lakes, picking up virtually any form of animal or plant life that they are capable of swallowing, including worms, insects, mussels, snails, crayfish, frogs, lizards, bird's eggs and nestlings. Several species (especially the grackles) wade in shallow water and catch small fish. All blackbirds also have great appetites for seeds, especially grain, and Red-winged Blackbirds and Brown-headed Cowbirds eat more vegetable than animal food. The blackbirds are very (many people would say excessively) gregarious, gathering in wintering flocks of mixed species that sometimes number in the millions of birds. These blackbird armies can be serious pests at stockyards, in grainfields, and occasionally in their vast noisy night roosts (see PESTS).

Most of the blackbirds nest in loose to rather crowded (Tricolored Blackbird) colonies. The tree-nesting species (grackles, Rusty Blackbird) make rather bulky cups of twigs and coarser grasses. The marsh nesters usually weave cup-shaped baskets around upright cattail or rush stems, in some cases using soggy dead materials which tighten into a neat structure as they dry. Many blackbird nests are cemented with mud or dung and all have an inner lining of finer plant fibers, fresh grasses, and/or hair. The cowbirds never make nests, the females of both species laying their eggs in the nests of a wide variety of land-bird and (less usually) water-bird species (see COWBIRD). Blackbirds lay 3–7 (usually 4–5) eggs, except for the cowbirds, which may lay 10–12 eggs (or perhaps as many as 30) in a given season (see COWBIRD for more detail). Blackbird eggs are rather glossy and extremely variable, even within one species (e.g., Red-winged Blackbird). The ground color varies from white to pale blue, green, pinkish, purplish, or brown. They may be immaculate (Bronzed Cowbird) or sparsely or densely speckled, spotted, or scrawled with what look like letters of the old Arabic alphabet.

Blackbird songs are generally rather harsh with loud squeaks, whistles, and clarion calls, yet some (e.g., Red-winged Blackbird) are pleasantly exuberant and the cowbirds' odd liquid sounds border on the subtle.

Blackbirds are restricted to the New World and range from the Arctic to the Straits of Magellan, achieving their greatest diversity in South America. Several of the North American species breed from coast to coast. Most are migratory from the northern parts of their range but winter largely in the warm southern U.S., where a majority of native species are resident year-round.

"Blackbird" is, of course, perfectly apt for a few members of the Icteridae, but hardly appropriate with regard to species like the meadowlarks and orioles. A further complication is the name of the abundant and wide-spread Eurasian thrush that replaces the American Robin in much of the Palearctic. This species is called simply Blackbird in Britain, where (according to Mother Goose) four and twenty of them were once baked in a pie and set before the king.

BLACKBURNE, Anna (Blackburnian Warbler: *Dendroica fusca*). An eighteenth-century botanist and keeper of a natural history museum in her native Lancashire, England. Her brother, Ashton, collected birds for her while visiting New York, New Jersey, and Connecticut. The exquisite wood warbler was named for her twice, first in Latin by Johann GMELIN (*Motacilla blackburniae*, a name soon discarded) and then in English by the zoologist Thomas Pennant.

BLACKPOLL (Warbler). Standard English name for a single species of wood warbler, *Dendroica striata* (family Parulidae), which breeds exclusively in coniferous forests continentwide in boreal North America and winters in South America (see Fig. 13). The "poll" is the top and back of the head including the nape; this region is black in male Blackpoll Warblers in alternate (breeding) plumage. See WOOD WARBLER.

BLIND. A small building, tent, wall, or other structure with narrow "windows" behind which hunters, birdwatchers, or photographers can conceal themselves and thereby get close to birds or other animals without alarming them. In Britain usually called a "hide." See PHOTOGRAPHY.

BLUEBIRD. Standard English name for the 3 small, cavity-nesting thrushes in the genus *Sialia* (family Turdidae; order Passeriformes); also used for the 2 species of leafbirds in the genus *Irena* (family Irenidae; order Passeriformes)—the fairy bluebirds of Asia.

The American bluebirds are among our most popular songbirds, owing to their colorful plumage, pleasant song, and fondness for man-made habitats, especially agricultural lands and structures. There is even a North American Bluebird Society (Box 6295, Silver Spring, MD 20906), which promotes the erection of nest boxes and relates the adventures of dedicated bluebirders in its quarterly journal, *Sialia.*

Bluebirds are readily attracted to birdhouses, though care must be taken to keep potential bluebird sites from being occupied by starlings or House Sparrows (see BIRDHOUSE). The decline of the Eastern Bluebird in the Northeast is partly attributable to these introduced competitors.

In the northern parts of its breeding range, the Eastern Bluebird is among the earliest birds to return in the spring and has therefore become a traditional herald of that season.

The range of the Mountain Bluebird reaches beyond the Arctic Circle and that of the Eastern Bluebird to Nicaragua. Among them the three bluebirds are distributed continentwide.

For family characteristics, see THRUSH.

BLUETHROAT. Standard English name for a single species of small thrush, *Luscinia* (*Erithacus*) *svecicus* (family Turdidae or Muscicapidae), that breeds across the northern Palearctic region and just reaches the Nearctic in western Alaska. The Alaskan population winters in southern Asia. The name is apt for adult males in alternate (breeding) plumage. For family characteristics, see THRUSH.

BOBOLINK. Standard English name for a single species in the New World blackbird family (Icteridae), *Dolichonyx oryzivorus*. It undertakes the longest migration of any North American land-bird species, its greatest mileage being from southern Canada to the Argentine pampas. The name is a shortened form of a folk name, "Bob Lincoln," and echoes the species' bubbling song. Thoreau recorded a Cape Cod boy's reaction to a singing Bobolink: "What makes he sing so sweet, Mama? Do he eat flowers?" See BLACKBIRD.

BOBWHITE. Standard English name in North America for a single species of quail, *Colinus virginianus*. Three Latin American species of the same genus have "bobwhite" in their names, e.g., Spot-bellied Bobwhite. The name is a close approximation of the surprisingly loud whistled call. See QUAIL.

BOHEMIAN (Waxwing). Bohemia is a region (once a kingdom) in western Czechoslovakia, where *Bombycilla garrulus* occurs only as a winter visitor. It is the alleged home of the gypsies and the name may refer to this species' habit of wandering unpredictably and at irregular intervals south of its normal wintering range. See IRRUPTION; WAXWING.

BONAPARTE, Charles Lucien, 1803–57 (Bonaparte's Gull: *Larus philadelphia*). A nephew of Napoleon I, he tackled the description of the North American avifauna in his *American Ornithology* during an eight-year stay in America. He was well educated in science and is generally acknowledged to have been one of the foremost ornithologists of his time. His American reputation is eclipsed somewhat due to his appearance on the scene between the two giants of early American ornithology, Wilson and Audubon. He continued to study and write about birds and other zoological subjects on returning to Europe, but much of his later life was consumed by politics, especially the independence of Italy. The Bonaparte's Gull was described and named by George ORD, one of WILSON's chief patrons.

BONAVENTURE ISLAND (Quebec). The most famous seabird colony of eastern North America, located 2.2 miles (3.5 kilometers) off the east coast of the Gaspé Peninsula. Bonaventure is a 160-square-mile (416-square-kilometer) island with a spectacular cliff face to the north and east. It holds the largest colony of Northern Gannets in the world (25,000 pairs) as well as Leach's Storm-Petrel, Common Murre, Common Puffins (a few), Razorbills, and Black-legged Kittiwakes. It is a major tourist attraction in this remote corner of Quebec and a favorite feature of natural history "screen tours." The island is now a reserve of the Ministère du Loisir, de la Chasse et de la Pêche of Quebec and of the Canadian Wildlife Service, and the breeding birds are protected from disturbance by visitors. An interpretive center in the adjacent mainland village of Percé highlights Bonaventure's fascinating flora (450 species) as well as the avifauna. Day tours of Bonaventure begin by boat from Percé. Visitors can take naturalist-led tours or hike on their own around and across the roughly circular island. Overnight stays on Bonaventure are not permitted.

BONES. See SKELETON.

BOOBY. Standard English name for 6 members of the family Sulidae (order Pelecaniformes), all in the genus *Sula*. The other 3 species of the family are called gannets and have often been distinguished in the genus *Morus*. Four species of boobies visit the southernmost coasts of North America with varying degrees of regularity. The Northern Gannet breeds on islands along the northeast coast and winters offshore in the Atlantic and Gulf of Mexico.

The boobies and gannets are large (30 to 40 inches) pelagic seabirds, most of them boldly patterned in white, black, and shades of brown and often with brightly colored feet and facial skin. Like the other members of their order, they have webs between all four toes; they lack external nostril openings in the bill.

Sulids are strong fliers that soar over the ocean and dive intermittently on fish and squid from heights of up to 100 feet (Northern Gannet).

All boobies and gannets are colonial. All, except for the Red-footed Booby, some populations of Masked Boobies, and the gannets, nest on bare ground, sand, or rock with only a ring of guano deposited by the sitting birds for a "structure" and no lining. The exceptional boobies make stick nests in the tops of bushes or trees (to 35 feet). Gannets make a mound of seaweed and other flotsam on bare rock. All boobies and gannets lay 1 or 2 (rarely 3) pale blue to green eggs, covered at laying with a white, chalky coating. The latter is soft at first but dries quickly and becomes stained and scratched off in places.

These birds are not often heard except on the breeding grounds. There is a marked sexual dimorphism in the structure of the trachea and syrinx in the Masked and Blue-footed Boobies, so that the males give a whistling call and the females a "resonant trumpeting" (Palmer, 1962). The other species make only harsh quacks, squeaks, screeches, and hisses.

The boobies are pantropical in distribution, whereas the gannets are restricted to colder waters of the Northern and Southern Hemispheres (see GANNET).

Boobies are named for their stupidity in dealing with mankind. Having little experience with human behavior on their remote breeding islands, they reacted with curiosity rather than alarm at the approach of hungry mariners. For their innocence they were clubbed on the head for immediate consumption or thrown alive into the "booby hatch," a small hold under the poop deck where a supply of fresh meat was customarily stored.

BOOMING (booming ground). The wild, somewhat mournful sound produced by male Greater Prairie Chickens on their spring courtship "dancing" (or booming) grounds (see LEK). The sound is connected with the inflation of the bright orange neck pouches and is often likened to the sound of blowing across the top of a small empty bottle. While not inaccurate, this description leaves out the eerie plaintiveness of the sound, especially when uttered in random chorus and echoed by a dozen or more birds. Forbush (1925–29–STATE BOOKS) says of the now extinct eastern race (Heath Hen) that it "ends in the air like a Scotch ballad." One of the fine wild sounds of the North American prairies, now, alas, all too seldom heard.

BOREAL (BOR-ee-yul) (Owl, Chickadee). In the most general sense, simply "northern," deriving from Boreas, the Greek god of the north wind. In technical usage, it refers to the Arctic-Alpine, Hudsonian, and Canadian life zones combined or sometimes the last two only. The ranges of the Boreal Owl and the Boreal Chickadee in North America are essentially coextensive with the Boreal Zone. Other bird species typical of the boreal forest are Merlin, Spruce Grouse, three-toed woodpeckers, Gray Jay, Gray-cheeked Thrush, Bohemian Waxwing, Northern Shrike, Blackpoll Warbler, Pine Grosbeak, and Fox Sparrow. See also LIFE ZONES; TAIGA; MUSKEG; SUBARCTIC.

BOTTERI (BOT-er-ee), Matteo, 1808–77 (Botteri's Sparrow: *Aimophila botterii*). A well-known Yugoslavian (Dalmatian) professional collector who worked principally in southeastern Europe and Mexico. He eventually founded a natural history museum and became a professor of natural history at Orizaba in the Mexican state of Veracruz. The sparrow, the range of which is largely in Mexico, was named for him by one of the systematists to whom he sent specimens.

BOTULISM (BOT-chew-lizm). A virulent and deadly bacterial infection which occasionally kills large numbers of waterfowl. See DISEASE.

BRACE. A hunting term meaning two dead game birds of the same species. For example, six grouse, regardless of sex, are referred to as "three brace" of grouse. See NOUNS OF ASSEMBLAGE.

BRAIN. See NERVOUS SYSTEM.

BRANDT, Johann Friedrich von, 1802–79 (Brandt's Cormorant: *Phalacrocorax penicillatus*). A prolific zoologist, paleontologist, and geographer who made his reputation in St. Petersburg (Russia), though a native of Germany. He described and gave the Latin name to the cormorant which now memorializes him.

BRANT. Standard English name in North America for a species of small goose, *Branta bernicla*, which breeds in the High Arctic and winters along the Atlantic and Pacific coasts. The dark race of western North America (*B. b. nigricans*) was once considered a distinct species called Black Brant. Brant are esteemed as table birds and are also remarkable for their fondness for eelgrass, a taste that almost doomed eastern populations of the species during the eelgrass blight of the 1930's. The standard English name for this goose in Europe is Brent Goose. The origin of both names is unclear; it may be related to "burnt" and "brand" in reference to its coloration (a scorched Snow Goose). For family characteristics, see GOOSE.

BREEDING CYCLE. See COURTSHIP; DISPLAY; PAIR FORMATION; REPRODUCTIVE SYSTEM; SONG; TERRITORY; NEST; LAYING; EGG; EMBRYO; INCUBATION; HATCHING; PARENTAL CARE.

BREEDING IN CAPTIVITY. See AVICULTURE.

BREEDING PLUMAGE. The alternate or nuptial plumage, which results from either feather wear or a pre-nuptial molt (see MOLT). In many species it is much gaudier, especially in males, than the basic or winter plumage.

BREEDING SEASON. The time period (weeks or months) during which birds mate, lay eggs, and rear young in any given locality. Though a few tropical species seem to breed according to no discernible schedule, the great majority of birds have fixed breeding seasons (or at least patterns), which are ultimately related to some environmental factor(s) affecting reproductive success. The fact that the majority of temperate zone birds breed during the warmer months reflects the advantages which longer days, abundant food, dense cover, and simple warmth offer in rearing young. Of course, the relationship between the season and the calendar is different in the North Temperate Zone from that in the South, and while Greater Shearwaters and Wilson's Storm-Petrels are experiencing the very height of their breeding seasons in South Atlantic and subantarctic islands, northern breeding grounds are deep in the silence of winter. Exceptions to the warm weather breeding season rule are some seed-eating birds, e.g., crossbills, Mourning Dove, and Common Pigeon, which feed their young mainly on seeds (see also PIGEON'S MILK). Because they can obtain food for nestlings year-round, these species are freed from bondage to the seasons and have been recorded breeding in every month of the year.

In the tropics, where the temperatures remain mild and the days of about equal length year-round, it is wet and dry seasons which govern the abundance of food and cover, and tropical birds too tend to have fixed breeding seasons based on these variables. In tropical rain forests, where rainfall is uniform at all seasons, different species will breed at different times throughout the year but most individual species still follow a characteristic breeding calendar. This is a little mysterious, and obviously depends on factors perceived by birds but not as yet by humans.

It is important to make the distinction between the breeding season in a particular place—e.g., roughly April through August in Massachusetts—and the usually much shorter breeding season for any given species: Louisiana Waterthrushes in Massachusetts breed between mid-April and about mid-June. Of course, multiple-brooded populations (see BROOD; NEST) have longer breeding seasons than those which rear only a single brood.

The time of the full breeding season is shared by some species occupying the same niche, one species breeding early, another late, perhaps a third still later (see DISTRIBUTION, *Temporal Effects*), and the breeding season may vary (usually by only a few days) from year to year depending on whether the season is "early" or "late."

BREWER, Thomas Mayo, 1814–80 (Brewer's Blackbird: *Euphagus cyanocephalus*; Brewer's Sparrow: *Spizella breweri*). Though he was interested in birds from boyhood until his death, Brewer's capabilities could never be contained in a single field. He was an M.D. (Harvard), a newspaperman (Boston *Atlas*), an influential figure in the Whig Party, a partner in a successful publishing house, and an electee of the Boston School Committee. In addition to all this, he kept active in ornithological circles. He was a friend of Nuttall's and won Audubon's praise for data and specimens tendered. His chief interest was eggs, but his great work on the subject was never completely published due to the cost of printing the plates. He wrote most of the text of his joint ventures with Baird and Ridgway

(see the Bibliography under BAIRD). Gruson (1972–BIOGRAPHY) notes
that he was something of a "curmudgeon," and among the younger generation of field ornithologists, could tolerate only William BREWSTER.

BREWSTER, William, 1851–1919 (Brewster's Warbler, originally described as a full species; now recognized as the "dominant" hybrid form of
Blue-winged and Golden-winged Warbler parentage; see HYBRIDIZATION).
Perhaps the most prominent of New England naturalists around the turn
of the century. His chief interest was birds, of which he amassed a significant collection and about which he wrote a number of faunal works. He
was one of the founders (and president for forty years) of the Nuttall Ornithological Club at Harvard. This organization was the progenitor of the
American Ornithologists' Union, of which he was also a founder and president. Brewster's father was a successful banker, a circumstance that allowed the son—after giving "business" a year's trial—to live his life as a
gentleman farmer and devote his energies to birds. Brewster was admired
but also liked by his associates—reputedly the only member of the younger
generation who could get along with the cranky Thomas BREWER.
Though Brewster did some collecting in the South and in the American
tropics, his reputation is strongly tied to New England, on account of both
his faunal studies and his literary evocations of New England country life
(see the Bibliography).

BRIDLED (Tern, Titmouse). In most cases refers to dark linear head
markings which suggest a horse's bridle. In both the Bridled Tern and the
Bridled Titmouse, the line runs from the gape through the eye. Also used
to describe the white eye ring and line that characterize the "ringed" (or
"bridled") phase of the Common Murre in breeding plumage.

BRIGANTINE National Wildlife Refuge (New Jersey). 13,204 acres,
largely of coastal marshes, located immediately northwest of Atlantic City;
some woodland. Principally known for concentrations of water birds at all
seasons and especially for rare migrants such as the Ruff, Curlew Sandpiper, Spotted Redshank, Bar-tailed Godwit, and Gyrfalcon (winter). The
avian wealth and drivable dikes, encompassing bird-filled wetlands, make
Brigantine a mecca for birdwatchers nationwide and a frequently visited
locality for the large northeastern birding community.

BRISTLE (Bristle-thighed Curlew). In birds, a more or less stiff, hair-like
feather, lacking a vane and sometimes completely barbless (see Stettenheim, 1973–FEATHER, and Fig. 9). A number of the flank feathers of the
Bristle-thighed Curlew bear only a few barbs at the base and extend downward an inch or more beyond the contour of the belly plumage. Though
certainly no field mark, these bristles are visible in the wild at very close
range or with the aid of a telescope.

BROKEN-WING ACT. Describes the characteristic gestures of certain forms of distraction display, especially among the shorebirds, e.g., Killdeer. For evolution and other details, see DISPLAY.

BROOD. A brood consists of all the young hatched from a single clutch of eggs, e.g., Pintails normally rear broods of from 7 to 9 ducklings. "Brooding" is the practice by parent birds of "sitting on" (altricial) nestlings in order to maintain sufficient body temperature in the latter as well as to shade them and prevent overheating in direct sunlight, shield them from precipitation, and conceal them from predators. The term is sometimes used loosely to mean INCUBATION, i.e., "brooding of eggs," but is probably more useful if restricted to the narrower definition.

Parent birds which are "in the mood" to sit on nestlings—an innate response which normally follows the laying and subsequent hatching of the eggs—are said to be "broody."

Birds which rear only one "family" in a season are said to be "single-brooded"; those rearing two, "double-brooded"; etc. The brood pattern varies from species to species and among populations of the same species according to climate (length of season). Single and double broods are the rule among the majority of North American birds and more than three broods in a season (treble-brooded) is rare. For more detail on brooding rhythms, see NEST, *Pattern and Timing*. See also PARENTAL CARE.

BROOD PARASITISM. Describes the laying of eggs by one bird species in the nest of another, "host" species which rears the "changeling(s)," often at the expense of some or all of its own young. This behavior has also been called "nest parasitism," but this term is easily mistaken to mean nest piracy—the appropriation of one species' nest by another—or the infestation of a nest by arthropod parasites (see NEST FAUNA); "social parasitism" is yet another synonym. See PARASITISM for general definitions.

In North America some ducks and the two common *Coccyzus* cuckoos are known to be "nonobligate" brood parasites, but only the Redhead and Ruddy Duck avail themselves of this alternative with any frequency.

Worldwide, "obligate" brood parasites—those that never build a nest of their own—are recorded from 5 families: the ducks (1 species); the cuckoos (many, but not all species); the honeyguides (perhaps all 11 species of this Old World family); the New World blackbirds (5 out of 6 cowbird species); and the weavers (a few species, notably the whydahs of Africa).

Though brood parasitism has evolved independently in several families, its practice varies significantly among them, both in specific habits and in effect. The Black-headed Duck of South America, the only precocial obligate brood parasite species, does not displace eggs or young from the host's nest, takes no food from the host parents, and becomes fully independent within 2 days of hatching; it has therefore been called "the most perfect of avian parasites" (Weller, 1968). But Smith (1968) describes actual benefits derived by hosts of the Giant Cowbird in Panama. All of the other brood parasites inflict some degree of harm on their hosts by removal of host eggs or young (by parent or young parasites) or by consuming food intended for a nest's rightful inhabitant. The response of the host also varies from apparently complete obliviousness of the deception and sacrifice of its own young to the needs of the (often much larger) parasite; to rearing the parasite *along with* some of its own young; to evicting the parasitic egg; to covering over a parasitized nest with successive "floors" (an often-recorded response by Yellow Warblers to Brown-headed Cowbird parasitism); to abandonment of a parasitized nest.

No summary of brood parasitism can be considered complete without mentioning the well-studied case of the Common Cuckoo of Eurasia (*Cuculus canorus*). The habits of this common and widespread Old World parasite have been familiar in a general way for centuries, providing a common metaphor for sexual insults and many a verse, both good and bad. Only in this century, however, have the subtleties of the cuckoo's "art" been fully appreciated. One of the most intriguing facts of this (and some other cuckoo) species is the degree to which it has perfected "egg mimicry." Though it generally parasitizes hosts much smaller than itself, it has evolved the ability to lay small eggs which (in varying degrees) are also shaped, colored, and patterned to match those of the species victimized. This adaptation has apparently led to the evolution of "clans" of cuckoos which specialize in particular host species, e.g., "wren cuckoos" that consistently lay remarkably wren-like eggs. In some brood parasites the gape color/pattern of nestlings also mimics that of the host nestling, further enhancing anonymity and discouraging rejection by host parents. The clan system is imperfect in that the inevitable interbreeding of members of different clans results (for example) in "wren cuckoo" eggs being laid in pipit nests, increasing the risk of recognition, but as noted below, total success for all cuckoos is not in the best interests of its species. Another cuckoo characteristic that may aid its success is the strong resemblance in form, coloration, and manner of flight of several species (including the Eurasian ones) to small hawks (accipiters). It is suspected that songbirds frequently "mob" male cuckoos, not because of their parasitic habits, but out of an instinctive response to a supposed predator, and that this "false alarm" may distract the host species from the laying of the cuckoo's eggs.

For an account of the habits of North America's most successful brood parasite, see COWBIRD.

Although brood parasites tend to lay many more eggs in a season than "normal" birds under "normal" circumstances and in many cases are highly "successful" in the sense that they occur in substantial numbers with a broad distribution, it should be obvious that if cuckoos or cowbirds, for example, were too successful, they would soon put their hosts and therefore themselves out of business. Local examples of such imbalances do, in fact, occur, a notable North American one being the threat posed by Brown-headed Cowbirds to the continued existence of Kirtland's Warbler (see ENDANGERED BIRDS)—a situation which may be attributable ultimately to human influences on the ecosystem. On the whole, however, a brood parasite's boom at the expense of host species is thwarted by: (1) the imperfection of deceptive adaptations, facilitating (2) the ability of many individuals of many host species to recognize and reject parasite eggs; (3) asynchrony between parasite laying season and host nesting season allowing some potential host species to successfully rear at least one brood without danger of parasitism; and (4) the ability of many hosts to rear one or more of its own young along with that of a brood parasite. See also PARASITISM; DUMP NEST; COWBIRD; CUCKOO.

BROOD PATCH. Also called "incubation" patch. An area of skin on the belly of a bird modified during the breeding season to facilitate incubation of the eggs. It is located for the most part in the area(s) of the abdomen which lack(s) feather tracts (apteria), but down and/or some contour feathers are usually lost or plucked. The resulting area of bare skin becomes somewhat thickened due to an increase in blood vessels as the patch develops. There may be from one (all passerines) to three discrete patches, the number and location varying among different groups of birds. Development begins a few days to a week before laying begins, and lost feathers return with the following pre-basic (post-nuptial) molt. As would seem logical, it is usually only the parent with incubating responsibilities which develops brood patches, but there are exceptions.

All North American species, except pelicans, tropicbirds, frigatebirds, gannets and boobies, cormorants and anhingas (i.e., the Pelecaniformes), and Crested Auklet, develop brood patches.

See also INCUBATION and R. E. Bailey, *Condor* (1952), 54:121–36.

BROWNSVILLE (Texas). See RIO GRANDE VALLEY.

BUDGERIGAR (or Budgerygah, in Australia) (Budgie). Standard English name for a small (7 to 8 inches) parrot, *Melopsittacus undulatus*, abundant throughout most of the drier regions of Australia and a very popular "talking" cage bird in Europe and North America. Its natural coloration is largely vivid grass green with a yellow, partially barred head, a blue tail, and a brown scaly back, but in captive breeds the green may be replaced with blue or the birds may be entirely white, blue, or yellow. See AVICULTURE; SONG, *Vocal Mimicry*.

BUFFLEHEAD. Standard English name for a single species of sea duck, *Bucephala albeola*, which breeds exclusively and winters largely in North

America (continentwide). The name comes from "buffalo head," though not, apparently, from our round-headed American bison but rather from the European wild ox or buffalo. The Latin genus name of this species and the goldeneyes (*Bucephala*) has the same origin. See DUCK.

BULBUL. Standard English name for most of the approximately 120 members of the family Pycnonotidae (order Passeriformes), one of which, the Red-whiskered Bulbul, was accidentally introduced near Miami, Florida, in 1960 and continues to maintain a small population there.

The bulbuls are cut from a "normal" passerine pattern with few remarkable characteristics, but with a wide assortment of color patterns—some quite striking. Many species are gregarious; most are birds of the forest and forest edge. They have broad tastes in small invertebrates and fruits. Their songs are often rather noisy, with some tuneful themes but little musical distinction. As a family, bulbuls are essentially restricted to the Near East, Africa (including Madagascar), and the Orient.

The Red-whiskered Bulbul is a medium-sized (8 inches), surpassingly abundant species of India and adjacent countries. It builds a cup nest of small sticks, dead leaves, and debris bound with spider silk and lined with finer fibers. The site is a shrub or low tree. The 2 or (usually) 3 eggs are white or pink to light purple, profusely but often finely marked with various shades of brownish-purple speckles and blotches.

According to Newton (1893–96–ORNITHOLOGY), the name "bulbul" probably originated in Persia, where it referred to a songbird with a reputation similar to the nightingale's; this species may or may not have been what we now call a bulbul. Later the name may have echoed the call of a particular pycnonotid species and then been adopted for all of its relatives.

BULLA. Generally, a blister-like structure in bone or other tissue. Many male ducks have such an enlargement in the syrinx at the base of the windpipe (trachea). It may function in the production of characteristic whistling calls, which bulla-less female ducks never utter.

BULLER, Sir Walter Lawry, 1838–1906 (New Zealand Shearwater: *Puffinus bulleri*). A native of New Zealand who practiced law and bird study both in his homeland and in England. Published *A History of the Birds of New Zealand* in England in 1871–74 and *A Manual of the Birds of New Zealand* in 1882.

BULL'S (a.k.a. Bull) **ISLAND** (South Carolina). 5,000 acres of fine southeastern (pine and swamp) woodland, ponds, and coastal water-bird habitat. Located at the southern end of Cape Romain National Wildlife Refuge with headquarters at McClellanville (about twenty miles south of Georgetown). Once a "good" locality for the exceptionally rare Bachman's Warbler, which, alas, is now nearly impossible to locate anywhere (see ENDANGERED BIRDS). Spectacular concentrations of both breeding and wintering water birds (herons, waterfowl, shorebirds, etc.) and southeastern woodland specialties, e.g., Red-cockaded Woodpecker, Brown-headed Nuthatch, and Bachman's Sparrow. Access by boat only, from Moore's Landing.

BUNTING. Standard English name for a large, very heterogeneous assortment of finches. In British terminology, the name "sparrow" is reserved for the WEAVERS (e.g., House Sparrow), whereas the emberizine finches (including the New World sparrows and longspurs) are called "buntings." In North America only three emberizines, the Lark, Snow, and McKay's Buntings, are so named, and the word is mainly used for the smaller, brightly colored cardinaline finches, e.g., Indigo and Painted Buntings.

　　As this attempt at definition makes clear, the classification and nomenclature of the finches is a tangled thicket. For further elucidation and general characteristics of all types of buntings, see FINCH.

　　The nativity of "bunting" is lost in the shifting sands of vernacular nomenclature. It may have first been applied to the Old World Corn Bunting, referring to that species' speckly plumage (*bunt* is German for "mottled" or "speckled"); Choate (1973–BIOGRAPHY) relates the more charming theory that it was a kind of "pet name" (for Corn Bunting), as in "Bye-Bye Baby Bunting," and therefore in the same tradition as "Robin Redbreast."

　　For family characteristics, see FINCH.

BURSA OF FABRICIUS. A sac or pocket which opens via a duct from the upper (dorsal) wall of the last section of the cloaca (proctodeum). All young birds have such a bursa, but it gradually shrivels, and its opening to the cloaca disappears as a bird reaches sexual maturity. Its function in a bird's system is not completely understood. The fact that, like the thymus, it is best developed in youth suggests that it may have an influence on growth or it may produce white blood cells and/or antibodies to control disease. Its usefulness to the ornithologists is more clear-cut: it is a means of determining age, especially in large birds—e.g., waterfowl. The investigator spreads open the bird's vent and examines the dorsal wall of the cloaca. If the opening to the bursa is present, the bird is immature. It is even possible by measuring the degree to which the sac is involuted to fix age within a year. As may be imagined, the delicacy of the procedure makes it impractical with small birds.

BUSHTIT. Standard English name for a single species, *Psaltriparus minimus*, which traditionally has been classified in a subfamily (Psaltiparinae) among the tits (family Paridae; order Passeriformes). Some authorities believe it belongs in the family Aegithalidae, known collectively as the long-tailed tits, and also sometimes considered a subfamily (Aegithalinae) of the "true" tits. The black-eared "morph," or color phase, of the species, which predominates locally, was once considered a distinct species, Black-eared Bushtit (*P. melanotis*).

In general form and coloration, Bushtits are rather tit-like with small pointed bills, short but strong legs, and generally grayish coloration. However, at less than 4 inches they have proportionally longer tails. Bushtits are birds of scrub oaks, chaparral, and riparian brush.

They are highly gregarious, often traveling in feeding flocks of 50 or more individuals, sometimes in company with kinglets and other small songbirds. Such flocks move rapidly through brush or copses, nervously but deftly probing bark crevices and gleaning leaves in search of insect food. They also eat some berries.

The presence of Bushtits is often first detected by the faint lisping twitter produced by the flock as a whole; it is the only sound the species makes.

The Bushtit nest is typically located in a bush or tree from 4 to 50 feet from the ground. It consists of a distinctive, rather untidy, pendulous sack which may be a foot long, though it is often only half as long. The entrance is near the top. It is made with grasses, mosses, lichens, leaves, and a great variety of other materials, bound with spider silk and heavily lined with feathers, fur, and plant down. Bushtits may lay as many as 15 immaculate white eggs per clutch (usually 5–7).

The Bushtit occurs exclusively from southwestern British Columbia south into Baja California and Guatemala and east in North America to western Colorado and Texas. It is non-migratory. The other seven species of long-tailed tits occur in Eurasia.

See Bent (1946–TIT).

BUTEO (BOO-tee-oh [Latin genus] or BYOO-tee-oh [vernacular English collective term]). A genus of broad-winged, short-tailed hawks. In a broader sense, any hawk with these characteristics, whether or not it belongs to that genus. Thus the Common Black Hawk (*Buteogallus anthracinus*) may be included among North American "buteos." This broader usage is analogous to the British term "buzzard." (See discussion under HAWK.)

C

CAECUM (SEE-kum) (pl.: caeca). A narrow sack or, as frequently described, "a blind tube" which opens onto the digestive tract where the small intestine meets the large. Sometimes in pairs; notably present in species which feed largely on plant tissue (e.g., grouse). See DIGESTIVE SYSTEM.

CAGE BIRD. Avian house pet. Usually small species either bred domestically or imported from other countries. For favored species and other details, see AVICULTURE.

CAHOW (kuh-HOW). Widely used name for a species of gadfly petrel (*Pterodroma cahow*), also known as the Bermuda Petrel. This bird, sometimes considered a subspecies of the Black-capped Petrel (*Pterodroma hasitata*), has always been restricted to the islands of Bermuda and due to pressure from man, rats, and tropicbirds seemed until recently to be facing certain extinction. However, due to careful research into its habits and current threats to its existence and careful management of the vestigial population, it has tentatively begun to gain some ground (for more detail, see ENDANGERED BIRDS). The name echoes one of the species' calls.

CALAMUS (KAL-uh-mus) (pl.: calami). The lower, hollow portion of the shaft of a feather before the beginning of the vane. See FEATHER and Fig. 9.

CALL (or call note). A vocal sound, often brief, uttered by a bird on a regular basis and distinct from its "song." A given species usually has a repertoire of different call notes which convey alarm signals and other messages within a migratory or feeding flock or between parents and young birds. Many species have highly distinctive call notes by which they can be readily identified. See SONG, *Calls*; also BIRD CALLS; GOOD CALL/BAD CALL.

CAMBRIDGE BAY (Northwest Territories). Perhaps best accessible high arctic birding spot in the world, located on southeastern Victoria Island on Coronation Gulf. Regular jet flights from Edmonton, Alberta, via Yellowknife, N.W.T.; simple but expensive food and accommodations and a limited network of roads. The habitat is barren stony tundra with clumps of dense matted vegetation (e.g., purple saxifrage and silvery oxytrope) and pocked with pothole ponds and sedgy sloughs. Specialties that can be expected in or not far out of town are: White-fronted Goose, King Eider, Rock Ptarmigan, Black-bellied Plover, Buff-breasted Sandpiper, Ruddy Turnstone, Red Knot, Sanderling, Baird's and White-rumped Sandpipers, Red Phalarope, Sabine's and Thayer's Gulls, Long-tailed and Pomarine Jaegers, and Snowy Owl as well as low arctic species (see BATHURST INLET). Prime time: mid-June to mid-August. The enemy is the weather: fog frequently envelops Cambridge Bay suddenly for unpredictable, often prolonged periods; be prepared to wait to get in and be stranded once you get there. See ARCTIC; TUNDRA; and the Bibliography under ARCTIC.

CAMOUFLAGE. See COLOR AND PATTERN, *Concealment*.

CANADIAN ZONE. One of Merriam's life zones; corresponds closely to the coniferous forest biome. See LIFE ZONES and Fig. 6.

CANARY. In its wild form, *Serinus canaria* is closely related to the widespread European Serin (*Serinus serinus*) but is restricted to Madeira, the Azores, and, of course, the Canaries. It was first introduced as a cage bird in Europe in the sixteenth century and has become popular worldwide for its loud, musical, and varied song. In its natural state its plumage is streaky with grayish back, wings, crown, and tail but it has been artificially bred to produce a pure-yellow strain as well as an astonishing number of variations involving color, song, and even feather structure. In the wild the famous song is often given accompanying a courtship flight. See AVICULTURE.

CANNIBALISM. The eating of an individual of a given species by another individual of the same species. With reference to birds, most often applied to the eating of "extra" young birds in the nest by the parent birds or other nestlings. This is recorded in a number of families (e.g., boobies, pelicans, storks, eagles, owls), especially when hatching is staggered and the earliest hatchling dominates in size and parental attention. In seasons of short food supply, the youngest/weakest birds of a brood are often allowed to languish in favor of the survival of the older/stronger birds and cannibalism may serve as an even more "efficient" means to the same end.

In another context, certain rapacious species (e.g., gulls) may kill and eat young, sick, or injured members of their own species.

CANNON NET. A device for trapping flocks of medium-sized to large ground-feeding birds such as waterfowl or shorebirds; the net is attached to rockets which propel the net over the flock, enclosing it before the birds have time to take flight. The simultaneous firing of the rockets is achieved by electric remote control. The technique requires a situation where birds are feeding or roosting at close quarters or a place to which they can be lured by bait.

CANOPY FEEDING. A practice peculiar to several species of herons in which the wings are spread forward to shade the area of water in which a feeding bird is standing, presumably affording some advantage in catching prey. It has been suggested that the canopy acts as a trap of sorts, with fish attracted to a suddenly available patch of shade. It also seems plausible that the gesture may act as a simple sun shade for herons feeding in the open, where glare off the water obstructs a clear view of activity below the surface. It is not yet clear to what extent either or both of these possibilities explain this distinctive behavior.

Canopy feeding is most highly evolved in the Black Heron (*Melanophoyx ardesiaca*) of Africa, but it is also characteristic of the Reddish Egret

Fig. 4. *Canopy feeding* is characteristic feeding behavior for the Reddish Egret. Whether the shadow cast is simply a sunshade or acts as a lure to these silversides and other fish—or both—is still unclear.

(see Fig. 4) and a less elaborate form of wing shading is occasionally practiced by the Louisiana Heron and the Snowy Egret. See Hancock and Elliott (1978–HERON).

CANVASBACK. Standard English name for a single species of bay duck, *Aythya valisineria*, which breeds exclusively in North America. It was praised by Audubon and by many other epicures before and since for its excellent flavor. The light color and mottling of the back plumage give it a resemblance to canvas. See DUCK and A. H. Hochbaum's classic 1944 monograph, *The Canvasback on a Prairie Marsh* (recently reissued by the University of Nebraska Press).

CAP. An area of contrasting color on the crown, e.g., the black "cap" of the male Wilson's Warbler; or including the entire top of the head from the bill through the nape, e.g., the Black-capped Chickadee or Black-capped Vireo. See Fig. 14.

CAPE MAY (New Jersey). One of the oldest and best-known migratory bird localities in North America, this peninsula projects into Delaware Bay south of Atlantic City. It comprises: barrier beach, dunes, salt marsh, freshwater ponds, pastureland, scrubby copses, and coastal pine-oak woodland. This diversity of habitats, its coastal location, and the cul-de-sac the point makes for southward-bound migrants make Cape May a magnet for a superb variety of bird species, especially raptors, shorebirds (including a notable woodcock flight in early November), and frequently spectacular numbers of passerines of many species. The peak of popularity among birdwatchers is in the fall (late August–early November), but the area is also interesting for wintering water birds and is far from boring during spring migration. For a detailed and readable account of this locality's birdlife, see Stone (1937).

CAPON (KAY-pon). A rooster which has been castrated and then fattened for the dinner table.

CAPTIVITY (birds in). See AVICULTURE.

CAPTURE (of wild birds). Men have always caught and killed birds for food. In many large seabird colonies or on remote islands where large predators were unknown to the native birds, this required no more effort or ingenuity than it takes to club a tame bird over the head and haul it back to the campfire or ship's galley. Boobies are so named for what sailors perceived as their foolish innocence, and the "booby hatch" was originally the opening to a hold under the poop deck of a ship where *live* boobies were stored to provision extended stays at sea. In most cases, however, birds were too wary (or became so) to be simply picked up or subdued on the spot, and over time a number of techniques and devices—from the rudimentary to the sophisticated—have been invented to trick birds into captivity.

Fire and other forms of bright light have long been known to both attract birds and render them helpless in certain circumstances. Natives of Central America catch hundreds of songbird and shorebird migrants by lighting bonfires on high mountain peaks at the proper season; and both primitive hunters and bird banders are aware that roosting birds can often be captured easily in large numbers at night with the aid of a torch or flashlight. Even nocturnal birds such as nightjars may be dazzled by light and allow themselves to be approached and even picked up, and banders use this effect to net resting shorebirds at night.

Several cultures have concocted substances from plants which are so sticky that birds perching on "limed" branches are held fast. And putting soporific chemicals in drinking water has also proven effective for capturing certain types of birds.

A major breakthrough in bird-catching technique was the invention of snares and nets, once made out of animal hair, more recently out of fine synthetic fibers. Inconspicuous slip loops placed where birds walk, for example, catch birds well, though setting such snares and recovering them consumes much time and effort. Variations are, of course, practically innumerable. Greenland Innuit catch Dovekies out of the air above their nesting colonies using long-handled dip nets, and similar methods have been widely adapted to catch both flying and sitting birds. More ingenuity but less physical exertion are required in using devices such as "clap" or "bow" nets, which consist of a furled net fixed to the ground at one edge and attached to a pole hinged to a peg or bow along the opposite edge. A pull cord is then tied to the bow or pole and held by the would-be trapper concealed nearby. When the bird is lured to the baited catching area, the furled net is pulled over it. A rocket-powered modification of this principle is used to capture whole flocks of large birds (see CANNON NET for details). Probably the most widely used bird-trapping device today is the exceedingly fine nylon mist net, which, when properly set, is virtually invisible and effectively entangles most small to medium-sized birds that fly into it (see BANDING for details of operation).

In addition to nets are what might be termed "structural" traps, all of which require some initiative on the part of the victim, usually elicited by means of bait or a lure. Perhaps the simplest of such traps is a box propped up over a baited area with a stick. A string is attached to the stick and held by the trapper, who watches from his hiding place until a bird comes to feed on the bait and then pulls out the peg, letting the box fall over the quarry. Some very elaborate structural bird traps have been invented, most of them relying on a funnel or lobster-trap principle, whereby the birds are lured or encouraged to wander into a wide "mouth" and soon find themselves unable to return or unable to perceive the narrow escape route (see HELIGOLAND TRAP and DECOY for more detail on such traps).

It should be emphasized that, except for a few introduced and pest species, it is illegal to trap birds in North America without a federal permit, and these are granted only for such legitimate purposes as BANDING, FALCONRY, and emergency control of bird PESTS. See LAWS for particulars.

See Pettingill (1970–ORNITHOLOGY) for further description and a good bibliography of trapping methods.

CARACARA (CAH-ruh-CAH-ruh). Standard English name for all 9 members of the subfamily Polyborinae (family Falconidae; order Falconiformes).

Taxonomists assure us that the caracaras are so closely related anatomically to the falcons that they should be placed in the same family. Superficially, however, they seem to be made up of equal parts of hawk and vulture. The single North American species, Crested Caracara, *Polyborus plancus* (*Caracara cheriway*), is typical, with long legs, a heavy bill for tearing flesh, and a broad area of bare skin over the face and base of the bill; this, like the vultures' naked heads, probably evolved in conjunction with the eating of greasy, decomposing carrion. Caracaras are nearly omnivorous, taking all kinds of waste matter, and small animals (alive as well as dead) including insects; they have even been known to eat some vegetable matter and wade in shallow water to catch fish.

The nests of caracaras are bulky, messy accumulations of sticks and other plant matter placed in trees, in cacti, on ledges, or on open ground and lined (if at all) with dung, bits of carrion, and other organic debris. The 2–3 (rarely 4) eggs are white to buff or lavender, usually densely speckled, the whole overlaid with heavy dark splotching covering almost the entire surface.

The vocal repertoire of the caracara subfamily as a whole contains a broad selection of croaks, squeaks, and screams as well as some rather haunting "well-articulated" phrases. The subfamily name, a Tupian word, is derived from the common call of the Crested Caracara, which is usually described as a rattle.

The caracaras are restricted to the New World and are most diverse in South America, whence one species reaches Antarctica. The Guadalupe Caracara, once endemic to Guadalupe Island off Baja California, became extinct about 1900. Our one handsome species is a permanent resident in southern Florida, Texas, Arizona, and New Mexico.

CARDINAL. Standard English name for 8 species of finches in several genera, all in the family Fringillidae or Emberizidae (see FINCH and Appendix I). One of these, the Northern Cardinal, is common virtually throughout eastern North America as well as in the extreme Southwest. It is one of the most familiar and best-loved of American songbirds, not least, perhaps, because it seems to prefer man-made habitat such as hedgerows and suburban plantings and visits bird feeders readily. Within the last twenty-five years it has undergone a marked northward extension of its range (see DISTRIBUTION).

Since the male Northern Cardinal is almost totally vivid red with a prominent crest, it is justly compared to the Roman Catholic Church official of the same name. However, in the illogical way of the coining of vernacular names, 7 species of large South American finches—only one of which is totally red in any plumage and several of which are uncrested—

have been called "cardinals" because of their taxonomic relationship. One of these is known as the Yellow Cardinal! For family characteristics, see FINCH.

CARDIOVASCULAR SYSTEM. See CIRCULATORY SYSTEM.

CARE OF DISTRESSED BIRDS (young, sick, injured, oiled). It is a credit to our species that the word "human" carries a strong connotation of sympathy for our fellow creatures. This is nowhere more clearly manifested than in the common inclination to try to "nurse" birds or other wild animals on which some misfortune has fallen. The present entry offers some practical suggestions which may help you succeed in the praiseworthy effort to save a bird's life, but it must begin with a series of *warnings*.

DO YOU KNOW WHAT YOU'RE GETTING INTO?

Nature Is a Harsh Mother and puts enormous pressure on most organisms, including birds, to be nearly perfect in function. Injuries to which humans can readily adjust—a limp, blindness in one eye—are likely to put a bird at a fatal disadvantage in surviving the threats of predation which it meets daily. A bird which has truly been "cured" or successfully reared must be able to participate fully in the role characteristic of its species in the wild, to find enough to eat, to reproduce, and to avoid predators. This goal may be simply impossible for human nurses to achieve in cases in which birds have suffered some form of physical damage.

The Odds of saving (in the above sense) a bird with a serious problem may be reckoned at about 10 to 1 *against* success, and in many cases, e.g., unfledged nestlings, the success rate is substantially lower. This grim statistic is stated not to discourage would-be Florence Nightingales, but to prepare them for the difficulty of the task and the frustration of possible failure. Children, who are often injured animals' best friends, are especially likely to embark on a salvation project with overly high hopes and to be badly disappointed by the death of their charge.

Long Hours and Considerable Patience are necessary in treating many bird patients. Very young birds, for example, must be fed almost constantly (see below) and in most cases—not understanding the benevolent intentions of their keepers—birds will make feeding and dressing of wounds as difficult as possible, at least at first. Administering effective animal care, even to a single individual, is not unlike taking on a part-time (or even full-time) job. Putting a sick or injured bird in a box with a dish of water and a piece of lettuce or a dog biscuit, though well-intentioned, is just not good enough. Inadequate care may simply prolong suffering or be worse for the bird than leaving it in the wild.

Humans Are Inadequate Parents for young birds despite the best of intentions. We tend to think of the natural "cruelties" from which we can protect helpless baby birds, but forget that we are incapable of giving them an introduction to the ways of their species in the wild. This puts human-reared birds at some disadvantage (at least initially), even if we wean them as soon as possible.

State and Federal Laws now prohibit keeping wild birds (except pigeons, starlings, and House Sparrows) even for the bird's own good unless a special permit has been issued. The nearest office of your state fish and wildlife department can tell you what permits, if any, are required for the temporary keeping of sick and injured birds.

If you have read the above caveats, and still think you can cope with what your child or cat just brought in, here is some advice on how to do so effectively.

"BABY" BIRDS. The first and most frequent mistake made by saviors of bird "orphans" is coming to the rescue prematurely. Young songbirds leave the nest before they can fly or fend for themselves and are fed and defended by their parents until they can fly and find food for themselves—usually in about three weeks. If you find such a bird, it is best to leave it where it is and assume the parents are off fetching it food or waiting for you to go away. If someone brings you such a bird, tell him or her to take it back to where it was found. *Touching young birds does not discourage parent birds from caring for them.*

Not infrequently nests containing young birds are blown or otherwise dislodged from their places in trees. Here again the best solution is to leave the birds in the wild. Find the original nest site and replace the nest—tie it in place with string, if necessary. If the nest has been destroyed, any reasonable substitute that will hold the young securely will do. Both active fledglings and fallen nestlings are vulnerable to cats and dogs; anything you can do to minimize this hazard will greatly improve a young suburban bird's chances for survival.

If you are certain that a young bird has been abandoned or don't know where it came from and think you have the time and patience to give it proper care (see PARENTAL CARE to get an idea of what you are in for), read on.

Living Quarters. Nestlings unable to grasp a perch will need a "nest" such as a shallow box or basket lined with paper tissues; the lining should be changed often. As soon as a bird can sit on a perch, it will benefit from as much space and freedom as you can allow it, though it should, of course, be protected from pets and other household hazards. A mobile fledgling should be taken outside in good weather and allowed to explore its real world. A fenced yard or portion thereof is ideal. For the first week after your bird has left the "nest" it should be brought in at night and in very bad weather (e.g., hard rain).

Temperature. Birds cannot maintain their own body temperature until their feathers are well grown. In the wild, birds which are born naked are kept warm (brooded) by their parents. Placing your homemade "nest" on a heating pad or electric frying pan (set low enough so that you can comfortably touch the surface) is a necessary substitute. Light bulbs at the proper distance can also be arranged to serve as a heat source but extreme care should be taken to avoid creating a fire hazard. Be sure that birds exposed to direct sunlight have a place to find shade. Birds which hatch with a full covering of natal down (e.g., ducks, gallinaceous birds) are more independent thermally but do need a "warm place" (light bulb) where they can rest periodically.

Food and Feeding. Young birds' principal nutritional need is protein, and this is usually delivered by parent birds in the form of insects or other invertebrates, even among species which eat mainly seeds or fruits as adults. Canned dog food or raw beef kidney are convenient substitutes for the adoptive human parent to offer. The kidney should be cut into strips of pure meat (i.e., without fat or connective tissue); a robin-sized bird can swallow pieces measuring ¼ x ¼ x ½ inch. Vary this meat diet with bits of hard-boiled egg, pieces of carrot and fruit (e.g., apple, blueberry), and, if you can manage it, earthworms, caterpillars (non-hairy types), or other "wild" foods. Doves and seed-eating species should be given a few grains of earth, charcoal, and/or crushed hard seeds to aid digestion. Twice a week add a small amount of multivitamin in powder or liquid form to the food. Different authorities have worked out a variety of specific diets for various species of birds. Terres (1980) includes diet suggestions with his treatments of individual bird families, and variations on the above basic diet are also given in other references in the Bibliography.

Songbirds will usually "cheep" and open their mouths to be fed when you come near or jostle the nest and you will have to place the food well down in the throats of young nestlings as the parent birds do. This is best accomplished using a pair of *blunt-tipped* forceps or a small paintbrush for holding and placing small bits of food. The nestlings will usually make a swallowing gesture when food is placed in their throats until they are "full," but they are capable of eating almost constantly at this stage and you should not worry about overfeeding. Older birds may not open their mouths as readily but can usually be induced to do so by pressing *gently* the corners of the mouth between thumb and index finger; then place the food well down in the throat to induce swallowing.

Naked nestling songbirds are sometimes fed as often as every 5 minutes during daylight hours in the wild. Many authorities recommend a feeding every 15 to 20 minutes, and one feeding every half hour is probably the minimum. To compensate for the unlikelihood that you will be getting up with the birds (i.e., 4:30–5 a.m.), keep feeding your charges in the evening right up to the time you go to bed. The number of feedings can be reduced as the bird matures, since it will be able to eat more at each feeding. By the time it has a covering of feathers, for example, one feeding an hour will probably be sufficient. By this time the bird should ideally be loose in your yard, so that it will begin to learn to feed itself, and you should encourage this tendency to seek independence.

Young raptors (hawks, owls, etc.) need a meat diet (raw beef, chicken, fish) and "roughage" consisting of bones, fur, etc., for proper digestion. If you can't supply the latter in the form of mice or chicken heads, buy some *veterinary* (not ordinary) bone meal at a pet store and include it along with the meat.

Chicks of so-called precocial species, including ducks and geese, grouse and pheasants, have longer incubation periods and are much more independent at hatching. They too need protein, but are capable of picking up their own food from the start, though they may need some encouragement at first. Duck or chick mash, chopped hard-boiled egg, and "wild" invertebrates are staples of a good diet for such birds.

Water. Young birds get sufficient liquid with their food and it can be dangerous to pour liquids down their throats. If you have some reason to suspect dehydration, moisten their food a little before giving it to them. A pan of water should be provided for bathing, however, once your bird is "out of the nest." This should not be offered in a confined space where it will be spilled immediately and the bird become waterlogged. Swimming birds should have the opportunity to exercise this characteristic, ideally from the beginning. Ducks, for example, learn to forage from the water within hours after birth in the wild.

Handling young birds too much—children quite naturally want to fondle their charges—should be avoided.

Duration of Dependence varies according to the species of bird and the stage of growth at which it came into your care. Most songbirds spend an average of ten days to two weeks in the nest and another three weeks during which they are fed at least in part by their parents. Some larger birds such as members of the hawk family, however, remain dependent for much longer. See the table under YOUNG, DEVELOPMENT OF, to judge the likely term of adoption for the species you have.

SICK, INJURED, AND OILED BIRDS. Adult birds which come into human hands because they are hurt or diseased require somewhat different treatment than do young birds. In considering how to proceed, you should try at the outset to assess the seriousness of the bird's problem. Individuals that have been struck by a car or have hit a window may be only temporarily stunned, and protecting them from predators for a few hours or days may indeed increase their life spans significantly. Some internal maladies may likewise respond well to a safe and controlled environment and a good diet. Problems such as broken wings, internal injuries, or advanced diseases may already be beyond the stage at which the best of care can be expected to return the bird to the wild. In such cases you should think seriously about leaving the bird in the wild and letting nature take its course or seeking professional help (see below). If you think you can handle the situation, the following may prove useful.

Space. Adult birds need room to exercise, including flying (if they are able), in order to remain healthy. A room, *large* cage, or fenced yard is therefore an important requirement. Keeping an adult bird in a little closed box is detrimental to its recovery.

Food and Feeding. Many birds have rather specific feeding habits and require fish or freshly killed mammals, whereas most songbirds have a very varied diet consisting of fruit, seeds, insects, and a host of other items. Terres (1980) gives very thorough accounts of food preferences species by species and an effort to approximate these is advisable. However, providing a balanced diet consisting of adequate protein and vegetable nutrients should be your goal and this can be achieved without collecting wild edibles each day. Meal worms (obtainable at pet stores) are excellent for birds which eat insects, and, of course, store-bought meat, fruits, and seeds are just as good as wild ones for the species which eat them. See under *"Baby" Birds* (above) for convenient dietary supplement.

Some adult birds will not feed themselves at first and must be force-fed as described above. As they improve and get used to their artificial surroundings they should be able to feed themselves and should not be encouraged to wait to be fed. Adult birds need be fed only three or four times a day.

Water should be provided in a shallow but large container for bathing and drinking.

Curtailing Infection. Birds with superficial wounds should heal satisfactorily, the chief risk being infection. The wound and any surrounding feathers matted with blood can be gently cleaned and a small amount of first-aid (antibiotic) cream or ointment applied. However, keep in mind that the bird will undoubtedly try to preen the injured area, so that any substance applied to it should be non-toxic.

Broken Bones. This problem will usually be beyond the capabilities of most people to rectify. Unless a break is mended very skillfully, the ability of the bird to escape predators or catch food (raptors) will be seriously (probably fatally) impaired. Whipping up a makeshift splint from the Boy Scout handbook will probably not suffice. Mutchler (1972) gives some splinting techniques that have proved effective with large species, but it is cruel to "play doctor" with an injured animal, and the most humane treatment of birds with serious breaks is to deliver them into the hands of experienced animal-care practitioners or to destroy the crippled individual (see below).

Oiled Birds. Water birds are very vulnerable to even small amounts of petroleum in their plumage. It mats the feathers, destroying the natural insulation that allows them to maintain body temperature while swimming and diving in the frigid ocean (see MAN-MADE THREATS TO BIRD-LIFE). If the oiling is extensive, even professional treatment will probably not suffice to save a bird's life. But experience with recent oil spills has improved our ability to help oiled birds. If you find a bird with more than a spot of oil on its plumage, your best course of action is to take it to an animal-care center (preferably one experienced with this problem) or to "euthanize" the victim humanely (see below). If the amount of oil is small, clean the feathers as thoroughly as possible with detergent (Dawn has proven an effective oil remover); rinse out the cleaning agent thoroughly; then keep the bird warm and well-fed (see above) until it has a chance to coat the affected area with the natural body oils necessary for effective insulation. Then, if the bird seems healthy, return it to its normal habitat. This should all take place as soon as possible, i.e., three to four days.

EUTHANASIA. Despite the best of intentions and meticulous care, many birds will not respond to treatment and will become clearly moribund. Rather than prolong probable suffering you may wish to put the bird to sleep. A painless method for small birds is to soak several balls of cotton in motor ether (available at auto-supply stores; chloroform is not obtainable without prescription) and place them with the bird in a container with an airtight lid for at least fifteen minutes. The bird will "go to sleep" painlessly. (Do not allow the cotton or ether to come in contact with the bird, as this might be painful.)

HYGIENE. The notion that birds carry disease is widely exaggerated (see DISEASE); however, many wild birds (especially sick ones) are host to a variety of small invertebrates on their bodies (see ECTOPARASITE), which, while mostly not transmittable to human beings, can make contact with an avian patient less pleasant. Pet stores sell "flea powders" specially made for dusting cage birds and these work just as well for wild birds when the instructions are carefully followed. If you don't notice a lot of parasites, the procedure is not necessary.

Follow the usual sanitary precautions of covering any cuts you may have on your hands and washing your hands thoroughly after handling a bird, whether or not it seems sick.

PROFESSIONAL HELP. Some conservation and humane organizations operate animal-care facilities, and you may have one nearby, particularly if you live near a large city. These vary greatly in scale of operations and treatment specialties and in most cases simply do not have the staff, facilities, or funds to accommodate all of the requests they receive. The professionals employed at such facilities see a great deal of animal suffering and are expert in treating many problems but are usually not very sentimental about sick or injured animals. They will usually reserve the right to put to sleep any animal you give to them, if they deem it in the animal's best interest. They will almost always refuse to pick up an animal at your home; you will have to provide delivery, if they accept the animal at all. Though a few veterinarians will look at a sick or injured bird, most have neither the training nor the inclination to treat wild animals.

If you are dealing with the life and death of a bird for the first time and seek professional help, their attitude may seem unsympathetic or callous. Try to remember the limitations of most animal-care centers noted above and the fact that during the spring your call about an "abandoned" bird may be one of hundreds received that day.

CARINA (kuh-RYE-nuh) (carinate [KAIR-uh-nate]). A keel-like ridge, a basic form found on parts of many species of plants and animals. In birds it usually refers to the keel of the breastbone (sternum) found to some degree in all non-ratite birds (see RATITE); carinate—literally, having a carina—is sometimes used as a synonym for non-ratite.

CARNIVOROUS. Flesh-eating; usually reserved for those animals (and a few plants) that catch and eat live prey, usually to the exclusion of other food. Thus vultures, which prefer carrion, may be excluded from classification as true avian carnivores. Members of the hawk, owl, and shrike families usually spring to mind at the mention of carnivorous birds, but herons, some ducks, and a variety of other water birds are equally carnivorous, as in the broadest sense are many insectivores. Compare HERBIVOROUS.

CAROLINIAN ZONE. The Upper Austral Zone east of the 100th meridian; between the Transition and Lower Austral zones. See LIFE ZONES and Fig. 6.

CASPIAN (Tern). The Caspian Tern was originally described from a specimen collected at the Caspian Sea. The species is not, of course, restricted to the Caspian Sea; in fact, it is one of the few nearly cosmopolitan species of birds.

CASSIN, John, 1813–69 (Cassin's Auklet: *Ptychoramphus aleuticus*; Cassin's Kingbird: *Tyrannus vociferans*; Cassin's Finch: *Carpodacus cassinii*; Cassin's Sparrow: *Aimophila cassinii*). One of the prominent Philadelphia bird men who helped shape American ornithology after the pioneering efforts of Wilson and Audubon. Cassin was a businessman by profession but pursued his interest in birds with the avidity and competence of a full-time ornithologist. Coues comments on his "bookishness," by which he apparently meant his meticulous scholarship manifested in his curatorship of the bird-skin collection of the Philadelphia Academy of Natural Sciences—the largest then in existence—and in his numerous publications. He was ornithologist on Admiral Perry's "opening" voyage to Japan in 1853–54. Cassin named a number of bird species after colleagues and was certainly well commemorated in turn.

See the Bibliography under BAIRD.

CASTINGS. In some organisms, used as a synonym for droppings, i.e., feces; in birds generally refers to regurgitated wastes and synonymous with PELLET.

CASUAL. Of infrequent and irregular occurrence; a necessarily subjective term used in field guides and in studies of bird distribution to describe the status of a species which occurs too frequently to be termed "accidental" but appears at unpredictable intervals.

CATBIRD. Standard English name for 2 species of mimic thrushes (family Mimidae), each in its own genus. The Gray Catbird, *Dumetella carolinensis*, breeds exclusively in North America; one of its many calls suggests a cat's meow. The Black Catbird, *Melanoptila glabrirostris*, is a permanent resident of the Yucatán Peninsula and adjacent islands, ranging south to northern Guatemala. The name catbird is also applied to a species of Australian bowerbird, and to an African babbler/flycatcher. For family characteristics, see MIMIC THRUSH.

CATESBY (KATES-bee), Mark, c. 1680–c. 1750. Author and illustrator of *Natural History of Carolina, Florida and the Bahama Islands*, a large-format work in two volumes and an appendix consisting of 220 plates comprising 109 bird species as well as many species of plants, mammals, reptiles, fish, and insects: the first comprehensive, illustrated (engraved by Catesby himself and hand-colored), accurate (given the pre-Linnaean state of early-eighteenth-century biology) work on the natural history of North America. All of the three early editions (1743/48, 1754, 1771) are now exceedingly rare. Almost nothing is known of Catesby's life. He was English, apparently relatively well-to-do (his sister was the wife of the secretary of the governor of the Virginia colony); he was well connected in London scientific circles; his chief field of expertise was botany; he was self-taught as an artist; and he visited the New World twice between 1712 and 1726 for a total of eleven years.

CENSUS. Birds are counted for three basic reasons: (1) scientific inquiry, (2) wildlife management, and (3) fun. In studying the animal communities of a particular habitat, for example, a census of the total population of breeding and/or wintering birds of all species might be desirable. Or in studying a particular species it is often useful to know how many pairs occupy a given unit (acre, square mile, etc.) of their preferred habitat. Simply by recording numbers of birds at a particular place and time and comparing totals over a period of time, patterns of abundance for species, seasons, weather conditions, changes in habitat, or other contributing factors can be discovered. Finally, spending a day in the field trying to see as many species and individuals as possible can be great sport and is recognized as such by a growing number of North Americans (see BIG DAY; CHRISTMAS COUNT; ROUNDUP).

Several census methods have become standard for counting birds. The most straightforward, of course, is a simple counting of all individual birds in a population. Though virtually impossible in censusing most birds—especially small species in large areas of dense habitat—this method is sometimes workable in counting species (e.g., seabirds) which nest colonially in the open. In such situations, aerial photographs can be taken and occupied nests counted at leisure, or census teams can walk through the colony counting according to a prescribed method which minimizes omission and duplications.

Arboreal "rookeries" of large species such as herons can be accurately censused by determining the number of occupied nests.

The procedure for counting small birds in dense habitats is usually some form of sampling method, whereby the number of birds in a limited area is determined and figures for a broader area or an entire population extrapolated from it.

Plot samples usually involve a square section of uniform habitat marked off by grid lines along which counters walk, attempting to count all birds (or all of a particular species) on their assigned route. To ensure reasonable accuracy, the procedure is repeated a number of times and, especially in the case of a breeding census, counts are taken when birds are most conspicuous (usually early morning).

Strip samples follow a similar basic procedure but are taken along a longitudinal section of uniform habitat (or through a cross section of different habitats), often, for example, along a road. The census taker counts birds seen or heard within a given distance (usually 100 feet) of his route.

Rarely, an attempt is made to trap and mark or band all individuals in a designated area to reduce the error factor inherent in sight-and-sound censuses. In this case the labor involved must be weighed against the degree of improvement in accuracy.

Though the best data consist of absolute numbers, much can be learned by careful comparisons of *relative abundance*. Sea watches, during which migrating water birds passing a given point over a given time are counted and meteorological conditions noted, yield valuable information about population fluctuations as well as bird movements. Even birding a particular area regularly, keeping careful notes and comparing results of successive visits, can have value if methods (time spent, distances traveled, habitats visited, etc.) are consistent and recorded carefully enough to permit valid comparisons (see CHRISTMAS COUNT). A widely practiced version of this kind of "structured birding" is to drive along a set route, stopping every mile (or other fixed distance) and recording every bird seen and/or heard at each stop. No valid conclusions can be drawn from this about total birds in a population, but relative abundance from year to year can be gauged.

See also ATLAS and other entries noted above.

CENTURY RUN. Synonym for BIG DAY.

CERE (seer). The raised, fleshy base of the upper mandible in the members of the Falconiformes (vultures, hawks, eagles, falcons, etc.), through which the nostrils open. A similar, but feathered, structure is typical of the parrots and owls. Among members of the hawk and falcon families, the cere is often bright yellow or orange, though in juvenile birds it may be duller. Its function, if any, is unclear. See also OPERCULUM.

CERULEAN (suh-ROO-lee-un) (Warbler). A shade of relatively pale blue, as the clear blue of a cloudless sky or the softer, grayer tone on the head and neck of *Dendroica cerulea.*

CHACHALACA (CHA-chuh-lack-uh). Standard English name for all 9 members of the genus *Ortalis,* one of which, the Plain Chachalaca (*O. vetula*), is the sole North American representative of the guan family (Cracidae; order Galliformes). Like all of the guans, chachalacas are fairly large (to 2 feet), long-tailed, partially arboreal gallinaceous birds which feed mostly on fruits, buds, and other plant matter. *Unlike* most of their relations, the chachalacas are birds of shrubby brushlands rather than forest.

They typically construct a surprisingly small, flimsy, stick platform nest, sparsely lined with fresh leaves and placed near the end of a branch but within the densest foliage of a small tree. They normally lay 3 immaculate white eggs.

The Plain Chachalaca is restricted in North America to the acacia scrublands of the southern Rio Grande Valley of Texas.

The name is from a Nahuatl (indigenous Mexican) word via Spanish and echoes the insistent raucous "songs" of these birds (see SONG, *Multiple Vocalizations*).

See Delacour and Amadon (1973–GALLINACEOUS BIRDS).

CHALAZA (kuh-LAY-zuh). Two fibrous cords of albumen which connect a developing embryo, yolk, etc., to the egg membrane (see Fig. 8). Its basic function is to stabilize the embryo as it passes through the oviduct. Since the developing embryo must remain at the top of the egg mass as it tumbles down, the chalaza becomes twisted as the egg turns. For more detail, see EGG.

CHAPARRAL (chap-uh-RAL or SHAP-uh-ral). In the broadest sense, relatively dry, dense, evergreen shrublands such as occur in the western and southwestern U.S. and northwestern Mexico. The chamisal scrubland on the dry western slope of southern California and northern Baja California has been designated as the coastal chaparral biome.

The term derives from *chaparro,* a Spanish word for the dwarf scrubby oaks which are characteristic of the habitat. It is generally agreed that rainfall in typical chaparral is between 10 and 30 inches a year—too little for forest and too much for desert—but neither the plant nor the animal communities are closely defined. Most authorities agree that scrub oaks, mountain mahogany (*Cerocarpus*), manzanita (*Arctostaphylos pungens*), and chamisal (*Adenostoma fasciculatum*) are typical chaparral plants, but sagebrush, mesquite, madrone, and even the pinyon-juniper association of arid mountain slopes may be included. Species which might reasonably be called "chaparral birds" are: Greater Roadrunner, Northern Beardless Tyrannulet, Dusky Flycatcher, Bushtit, California and Curve-billed Thrashers, Pyrrhuloxia, and Sage Sparrow.

CHAPMAN, Frank M., 1864–1945. Curator of Birds at the American Museum of Natural History for fifty-four years. Chapman's outstanding career was described by Robert Cushman Murphy as follows: "He was a creative museum-builder, a life-long conservationist, a taxonomist and bio-geographer, a student of bird behavior and always an educator" (*Auk*, 67:312). Chapman's best-known published works are the several editions of his *Handbook* (see the Bibliography), and his distributional studies of the birds of Colombia (1917) and Ecuador (1926) continue to support his reputation as a scientist. His total output comprised 17 books and 225 articles.

He was born into a well-to-do New Jersey family and spent six years of "servitude" as a banker before becoming J. A. ALLEN'S assistant at the American Museum. Though he was reserved with some people and in later life, Chapman's personality was essentially robust (Murphy compares his temperament to the "Latin" one); he was an athlete when young, a keen businessman—despite his preference for birds—and a man of strongly held opinions.

CHARACTER DISPLACEMENT. When two similar, closely related species breed in the same area, certain of their differentiating morphological characteristics may become more prominent than in areas where either one breeds alone. For example, Smith (1966–SPECIATION) found that *Larus* gulls breeding on Baffin Island use iris color to distinguish their own species from the other very similar species with which they nest in close association. The iris color of the Kumlien's race of the Iceland Gull (*L. glaucoides kumlieni*) proved to be highly variable: darkest in birds nesting among light-eyed Herring and Glaucous Gulls and lightest when nesting among dark-eyed Thayer's Gulls.

CHAT. Standard English generic name for a variety of passerine bird species in several families, viz., the Australian chats (Epthianuridae or Sylviidae), the monotypic Caribbean endemic Palmchat (Dulidae), a number of small Palearctic and African thrushes (Turdidae or Muscicapidae), and a few species tentatively placed among the wood warblers (Parulidae). The name is often used in a combined form, e.g., Stonechat, robin-chat, and frequently reflects uncertainty about the phylogeny of the bearer. The Rufous Bush-Chat (or Warbler) of southern Europe and Africa, the Palm-chat of the Caribbean, and the New World chats in the genera *Icteria* and *Granatellus* are all anomalous forms. The Yellow-breasted Chat (*Icteria virens*), a seemingly unique species, is the only North American "chat" and is traditionally placed among the wood warblers.

"Chat" is a broad reference to vocal disposition and quality, appropriate enough in the case of the Yellow-breasted Chat but not descriptive of all chat songs.

CHECK. A pale (usually white) area usually at the base of the primary feathers of certain birds which appears as a squarish mark on the folded wing of a bird at rest (see Fig. 1). A "classic" field mark for female and immature Black-throated Blue Warblers, but present in a number of other North American species, e.g., the shrikes.

"CHECK!" An exclamation of delight at being able to add a bird to one's life list; in Britain "tick!" is preferred. See TICK; LISTING.

CHECKLIST. In a biological context a very broad term which includes everything from a simple listing of vernacular names of species in a particular region to lengthy, technical, profusely detailed taxonomic works. Many local bird clubs print small cards entitled, for example, "Birds of the Genesee Valley," with spaces for "checking" species seen on a particular day, month, year, etc.; state or regional faunal lists are often in the form of "annotated checklists" which document in detail the status and abundance of species and subspecies which have occurred therein. The A.O.U. *Check-list of North American Birds* (5th ed.) is a nearly 700-page work (plus Supplements) listing in phylogenetic order all of the species and subspecies of birds for which there are substantiated records for the U.S., Canada, Greenland, Baja California, and Bermuda, including the range of each form and appropriate taxonomic notes; it is the standard reference for taxonomy and nomenclature of North American birds. *A Checklist of the Birds of the World*, by J. L. Peters et al. (1930–   ), will, when completed, consist of fifteen volumes and list the species and subspecies of all the birds of the world and their ranges. See the Bibliography for other examples.

CHICK. A downy, relatively independent (precocial) young bird, during the period between hatching and flying. The young of ducks, gulls, shorebirds, gallinaceous birds, and others are usually called "chicks," as distinguished from the largely naked, helpless (altricial) young typical of songbirds, which are called NESTLINGS.

CHICKADEE. Standard English name for the 7 North American members of the genus *Parus* (family Paridae; order Passeriformes) that have black caps and black throats. In British usage, these and all other members of their family are known as "tits"; the Gray-headed Chickadee of Alaskan and Canadian tundra edge is mainly a Palearctic species and its English name in Europe is Siberian Tit.

The chickadees range almost throughout the continent (absent from treeless habitats), with the ranges of two species overlapping in several regions. They are among the most common, familiar, and adored of native songbirds due to their expressive-seeming "faces," their active, acrobatic feeding behavior, their willing association with humans, and their "cheerful" calls. They are invariably among the first birds to appear at a new feeding station and with a little patience can be coaxed to take seeds from the hand.

Most species have a call that (with a little imagination) can be heard as *chick-a-dee*; most also have a clear whistled "song."

For general characteristics of the family, see TIT.

CHICKEN. General name for the domestic barnyard fowl, especially the young and hens. Most of our chicken breeds are presumed descendants of the Red Jungle Fowl of Asia, *Gallus gallus* (Phasianidae), which has been kept by man for thousands of years. See DOMESTICATED BIRDS.

CHICKEN HAWK. Pejorative colloquial name used, in its broadest sense, to refer to any of the medium-sized to large hawks, all of which are presumed by the ignorant to ravage poultry yards habitually. The Cooper's Hawk is the only species to which the name can be applied with any justification, since it feeds principally on medium-sized birds and knows an easy kill when it sees one. The other accipiters and several species of buteos are known to take chickens very infrequently.

CHIRICAHUA MOUNTAINS (Arizona). See SOUTHEASTERN ARIZONA.

CHISOS (CHEE-sose) **MOUNTAINS** (Texas). Sole breeding area in North America for the Colima Warbler; see BIG BEND.

CHLAMYDIOSIS (kluh-MID-ee-OH-sis). (Once considered a viral disease—ornithosis/psittacosis.) A bacterial disease that occasionally produces severe epidemics in a wide range of bird species and may cause a form of viral pneumonia in people who handle a lot of birds, e.g., poultrymen and aviculturists. For further detail, see DISEASE, *Ornithosis and Psittacosis*.

CHRISTMAS COUNT. A popular (amateur) census of birdlife taken each year by a growing number of enthusiastic birdwatchers between December 20 and January 2. The tradition began in 1899 as a modest affair involving a handful of participants, but today tens of thousands of birders take more than 1,250 individual counts, recording hundreds of *millions* of individual birds of more than 600 species. The event is sponsored by the National Audubon Society and the U.S. Fish and Wildlife Service, and the results are published in a special issue of the N.A.S. bimonthly *American Birds.*

Though the great majority of participants still take part in Christmas Counts for the fun of it, the sheer scope which the phenomenon has attained has made the data collected of some scientific significance. In order to make the count as useful in this regard as possible, it is carried out under specific guidelines. Each local census is restricted to a circle with a diameter of fifteen miles which may not overlap another count circle. Numbers of individual birds as well as species are recorded and the habitats, weather, number of counters, and miles traveled by car and foot are noted. Fed into a computer, these data can give a rough approximation of densities of wintering bird populations on any selected scale and clearly point out cyclical movements of birds such as invasions of winter finches and their extent.

The variation in "styles" of Christmas Counts throughout the vast and varied continent (not to mention counts now being conducted in Hawaii and the Neotropics) can be imagined. In frozen interior Alaska or Newfoundland a couple of hardy souls may be responsible for an entire circle, braving the harsh climate for the sake of reporting a few individual birds of even fewer species. Other counts, especially those in the warmer (hence "birdier") parts of California, Texas, and Florida, have become star events, attracting hundreds of participants and top birding talent. The competition among these super-counts to record the highest number of bird species doubtless improves the thoroughness with which habitats are investigated in the regions involved. The count traditionally ends with a convivial gathering at the end of the long birding day, during which an official tally for one or more circles is compiled orally from the lists of individual teams, bird tales are swapped, field competence impugned, old counts relived, and much warming refreshment consumed.

See Robbins (1966) for a detailed history of the Christmas Count.

CHROMATOGRAPHY (KR-muh-TOG-ruh-fee). A method of chemical analysis in which different components of a solution are made to separate out and show as bands of different colors on a medium such as filter paper. The term has been extended to include separations which do not involve color differences. The technique is used with rewarding results in investigating taxonomic affinities among birds. See TAXONOMY, *Taxonomic Characters;* ELECTROPHORESIS.

CHUCK-WILL'S-WIDOW. Standard English name for a single species of nightjar, *Caprimulgus carolinensis,* which breeds exclusively in North America. The name is a literal approximation of its call. See NIGHTJAR.

CHUKAR (CHUCK-er). Standard English name for a single species of Mediterranean partridge, *Alectoris chukar,* which has been introduced with some success into its preferred dry, rocky, barren habitat in the western U.S. In the A.O.U. *Check-list* (1957) (and consequently in many field guides) it is confused with the Rock Partridge, *Alectoris graeca,* a very similar species which ranges from the extreme eastern Mediterranean into Asia. The name "chukar" derives from the species' chicken-like clucks (or "chucks").

For family characteristics, see PHEASANT or QUAIL. See also PARTRIDGE.

CHUMMING. In birdwatching parlance, the ladling of a loathsome concoction of putrid fish entrails upon offshore waters in the hope of attracting interesting pelagic birds. Though "chum" in an advanced stage of decomposition is preferred, the oily livers of freshly caught fish will serve. Heating the brew is said, by a few who have tried it, to increase its volatility, thus improving its effectiveness, since tubenoses are attracted by the odor (see SMELL).

Chumming is a worthwhile technique, but even the most seaworthy birders often find themselves nearer the rails than the petrels when it is used in rough weather.

CHURCHILL (Manitoba). Wet tundra, rocky shore, and boreal forest habitats at the mouth of the Churchill River, on the western shore of Hudson Bay. The best accessible (by plane and train from Winnipeg) low arctic breeding locality in North America. Though situated below the Arctic Circle, Churchill's vegetation and birdlife and other fauna are authentically arctic. It is especially famed for its diversity of breeding shorebirds, but its broad, flat marshy expanses also hold loons, waterfowl, Yellow Rail, terns, Smith's Longspur, etc.; its willow and alder copses provide nesting localities for Harris' Sparrow, Common and Hoary Redpolls; its islands of spruce forest contain Spruce Grouse, Gray Jay, Boreal Chickadee, Blackpoll Warbler, Pine Grosbeak, Fox Sparrow, and other typical passerines; and the area also hosts almost the entire spectrum of high arctic species which pass through in migration. In 1980 the rarely seen, exquisite Ross' Gull was found breeding there. Mammalian attractions include beluga (white) whales in the Churchill River and polar bears (September–November). For further detail, see J. Jehl and B. Smith, *Birds of the Churchill Region* (Winnipeg, 1970). See also ARCTIC; TUNDRA; MUSKEG; and the Bibliography under ARCTIC.

CHYME (kyme). Food which has been reduced to a semi-liquid state by the digestive processes in the stomach of a bird. This unpleasant substance is sometimes vomited forth—notably by the tubenoses and vultures—as a defense technique.

CIRCADIAN (sur-KAY-dee-un) **RHYTHM.** Changes which occur within an organism that are synchronized with the progression of a natural day (approximately twenty-four hours), regardless of proximate external stimuli such as changes in light or temperature. The concept is related to the question of an intrinsic "time sense" in birds and other life forms, and there is some experimental evidence to indicate that organisms do indeed function partially according to an "internal clock," though little is known about how the mechanism works. See Gwinner (1975) and Harker (1958).

CIRCULATORY SYSTEM. As in humans, the means of supplying nutriment and oxygen carried in the blood to all the tissues of the body and removing wastes. Blood is pumped from the heart through the arteries into the network of minute "hair-like" capillaries through which the tissue takes sustenance and returns impurities. The "dirty" blood passes from the capillaries to the veins, is purified by various organs, reoxygenated by the lungs, and returns to the heart.

There are a number of anatomical details in the more intricate reaches of this system which are peculiar to birds. On the whole, however, the avian circulatory system functions essentially like our own and only a few differences stand out in a non-technical context.

THE HEART. A bird's heart is located in the center of the chest (thoracic) cavity. As in man, it is the muscular organ which pumps blood continuously throughout the circulatory system. Though they evolved separately, the hearts of both birds and men have four chambers, two each for "incoming" and "outgoing" blood. The route the blood takes through a bird's body is also similar to that in man: out left ventricle of heart → arteries → capillaries in all parts of the body → veins → in right atrium of heart → out right ventricle → lungs → in left atrium, etc.

HEART SIZE. The weight of the heart in proportion to body weight tends to be greater in birds than in mammals and has been found to vary significantly among birds: (1) Fast fliers and those capable of long-sustained flight tend to have larger hearts than do weak fliers—here, size of heart is apparently more significant than development of wing muscles. (2) Residents of high altitude tend to have larger hearts than those of low. (3) Residents of cold climates tend to have larger hearts than those of warm, even if of the same species. (4) Males tend to have larger hearts than females. (5) Species with louder songs tend to have larger hearts. (6) Heart size tends to increase slightly in winter.

RATE OF HEARTBEAT. In birds, heartbeat is rapid compared to that of mammals of comparable size, and varies over a much greater range both among individuals (as much as hundreds of beats per minute) and among species. Though rates lower than the human average of 72 beats per minute are known in larger birds (Ostrich as low as 38 beats per minute), the average for passerines tends to be between 300 and 500 beats per minute and hummingbirds routinely exceed 1,000. As with heart size, rate of heartbeat varies according to circumstances: (1) Not surprisingly, it increases under stress and exertion. (2) It is greater in smaller birds than in larger. (3) It increases in cold weather. (4) It tends to be higher in an incubating bird than in one simply perched.

BLOOD. Compared to animals below them on the phylogenetic tree, birds' blood is rich in red blood cells (erythrocytes) at between 1.5 and 5.5 million per cubic millimeter (Stresemann, 1927–34), which is in the lower range of that for mammals. Richness varies among species and among individuals depending on circumstances, such as size, sex, and temperature.

THE LYMPHATIC SYSTEM. A bird's lymphatic system is as inscrutable to the layman as the human one. Among myriad other functions, it produces a type of white blood cells (lymphocytes), transports fats and proteins, and combats harmful bacteria. Only a few species of birds have the lymph glands that are prominent in humans and other mammals.

Certain details of the circulatory system have been used in making taxonomic judgments.

CIRCUMBOREAL. Refers to the distribution of organisms which occur worldwide from the southern limit of the Boreal Zone (45°–50° N.) north. One of the few such instances among birds is the Red Crossbill, which breeds not only throughout the circumboreal region but also into the New World tropics as well. Compare CIRCUMPOLAR; HOLARCTIC.

CIRCUMPOLAR. In a distributional context, ranging continuously around the earth near the North or South Pole. Many antarctic seabirds are circumpolar in distribution. The breeding range of the Snow Bunting may be described as "circumpolar arctic." Compare CIRCUMBOREAL; HOLARCTIC.

CLARK, William, 1770–1838 (Clark's Nutcracker: *Nucifraga columbiana*). Frontiersman, surveyor, naturalist, Indian fighter, gentleman farmer, and friend (from the army) of Meriwether LEWIS, with whom he made the first overland crossing of the U.S. to the Pacific coast. Following this successful adventure, Clark was appointed Superintendent of Indian Affairs, and became governor of the Missouri Territory and a hero of the War of 1812.

CLASS. The major taxonomic category between the phylum and the ORDER—i.e., a subdivision of a phylum and a grouping of orders. All birds, living, extinct, and fossil, belong to the class AVES. For a definition of this class, see BIRD. For a phylogenetic breakdown of a single bird species, see TAXONOMY. For a phylogenetic listing of all North American species in the class Aves, see Appendix I.

CLASSIFICATION. See TAXONOMY; NOMENCLATURE; and Appendix I.

CLAW. A modified scale present at the ends of the toes of all species of birds and adapted for a variety of functions according to the habits of the species. See LEG/FOOT; SPUR.

CLEMENCIA. Clémence Lesson (Blue-throated Hummingbird: *Lampornis clemenciae*). Wife of the preeminent French naturalist René P. Lesson (1794–1849), the author of many species and subspecies of New World birds, one of which—a very elegant one—bears the name of his wife.

CLIMBING. Though many species of birds which live and/or feed in trees "climb" in the sense of hopping upward with the aid of a wingbeat or two, only a few families have evolved special adaptations for climbing. Woodpeckers have relatively large feet and heavy claws, with two toes placed forward and (except for the two species of three-toed woodpeckers, which have only a single hind toe) two behind. The stiffened, wedge-shaped woodpecker tail is also well suited to vertical climbing and is used for support and to stabilize the body in its jerky progress up a tree trunk.

Woodpeckers ascend and descend in a series of hops with the body held vertically, though the hop itself may take them to one side as well as upward/downward. They will, on occasion, perch on a thin horizontal branch or even a wire, but never fail to look awkward doing so.

Flickers, which spend most of their time on the ground feeding on ants, nevertheless retain their climbing "gear" and in effect "climb" (i.e., hop) over the earth in the same manner used to ascend trees.

The Brown Creeper, like the woodpeckers, hops vertically up tree trunks and has a specially modified supporting tail. But its feet are more like those of typical perching birds, with three forward toes and one behind—all, however, equipped with long curved claws adapted for clinging. In contrast to the more or less random ascent route of most woodpeckers, treecreepers characteristically take a spiral course beginning at the base of a trunk; when they have reached a certain height they fly directly down to the base of another trunk and repeat the pattern.

Nuthatches have long toes and claws but do not have a propping type of tail—indeed, they hardly have a tail at all. Their climbing technique is different from that of the treecreepers or woodpeckers and allows more versatile movement. One foot is always placed higher than the other, so that no matter which way a nuthatch moves, one foot is always clinging from above and the other supporting from below. This allows it to move with the head up, down, or sideways.

The Black-and-White Warbler, though lacking any foot or tail modifications, climbs and gleans tree trunks and branches in a manner essentially similar to that of the nuthatches; investigation has revealed that its leg musculature is indeed modified in accordance with this habit. See also LEG/FOOT; TAIL; WOODPECKER; TREECREEPER; NUTHATCH.

CLINE. Also termed "character gradient." In species with ranges spanning broad geographical areas or climatic zones, it is often possible to trace a *gradual* change in mensural and/or morphological characteristics—e.g., from smaller to larger, or darker to lighter. Populations of birds at either end of this cline may be strikingly different though linked by populations that grade imperceptibly one into the other. The extremes may be taxonomically differentiated as subspecies, but the precise racial boundaries may be difficult or impossible to define.

CLIPPING (of wing). Severing of the primary feathers of *one* wing to keep captive birds flightless so that they need not be enclosed in cages. The procedure is painless and not permanently damaging since the feathers grow back with the next molt. Compare PINIONING.

CLOACA (klo-AY-kuh). In birds, reptiles, amphibians, and many fish, the terminal enlargement of the digestive tract through which solid wastes, urine, and the products of the reproductive system all pass prior to excretion, egg laying, or copulation. In mammals, of course, the digestive passage is completely separate from the urinary and genital passages. "Cloaca" is sometimes used as a synonym for the cloacal opening or "vent."

CLUBS, BIRD. See BIRD CLUB; SOCIETIES, ORNITHOLOGICAL.

CLUTCH. All of the eggs laid and brooded by a given bird (or birds, in the case of communal nests) during a single incubation period. Also known as a "set." For number of clutches per season and eggs per clutch, see EGG; NEST.

COB. A male swan of any species.

COCK. In the broadest sense, the male of any bird, and in Britain widely used in this way, e.g., "a cock siskin." In North America, usually reserved for the male chicken, i.e., a rooster; opposite of "hen."

COCKADED (Red-cockaded Woodpecker). A cockade is an emblem or badge, often of a bright color, worn in the hat as a symbol of office or other affiliation. In the case of the endangered woodpecker (Plate 6), it refers to the tiny (frequently invisible) wisp of red feathers on the side of the male's head.

COCKFIGHTING. A "sport" in which two roosters, bred and trained with the aim of developing their natural sexual aggressiveness, are fitted with razor-sharp steel spurs and made to fight each other in a ring or pit. Illegal now in all parts of the U.S. and Canada, but still widely practiced in clandestine meetings.

COCK NEST. Synonymous with DUMMY NEST.

COHORT. A little-used tertiary taxonomic division between SUBCLASS and SUPERORDER. Also used to designate age groups in populations: the 1980 "crop" of Song Sparrows is the 1980 "cohort." See TAXONOMY.

COLIMA (cuh-LEE-muh) (Warbler). A small state on the Pacific slope of Mexico that lies within the breeding range of *Vermivora crissalis* and is the TYPE LOCALITY for this species.

COLLECTING (bird specimens). The killing, by shotgun or other means, of birds, which are then prepared as "study skins" and preserved as a record of occurrence in a given place and time. In the previous century, before the advent of modern field guides and optical equipment, professional and amateur bird students alike pursued their interest by collecting and preserving as many specimens as they could. For an excellent account of the nineteenth-century approach to the subject, see Part I, "Field Ornithology," of Coues's *Key to North American Birds* (1890).

Until very recently, a specimen was considered the only acceptable scientific documentation of species' occurrence, and it is still necessary and desirable in the case of species and subspecies which cannot be identified with certainty from obvious characters. However, federal and state laws and regulations require thorough review of any proposal for the scientific collecting of birds before permits are issued. Despite the fact that birds numbering in the millions are killed each year by hunters, the scientific collecting of birds has come under close scrutiny in recent years. In fact, birds collected under scientific collecting permits in any given year represent a small fraction of the number killed at picture windows each year, or the equivalent of one night's "kill" at the Empire State Building or one of several TV towers.

For the greatest North American museum collections of bird skins, see MUSEUM. See also BIRD SKIN.

COLLECTIONS (of live birds). See AVICULTURE.

COLLOQUIAL BIRD NAMES. See NAMES, COLLOQUIAL.

COLONY (colonial birds). The broadest collective term (see NOUNS OF ASSEMBLAGE) for birds which breed in close association with other members of their own (and sometimes other) species. Most conspicuously colonial birds are water birds: many tubenoses (albatrosses, shearwaters, petrels, storm-petrels), Pelecaniformes (pelicans, cormorants, boobies, etc.), herons, ibises, storks, some waterfowl, stilts and avocets, gulls and terns, skimmers, and alcids. But some swifts, swallows, and blackbirds are strongly colonial and not a few other passerines (e.g., Pinyon Jay, Kirtland's Warbler) breed in close association with a few other birds of their species and are sometimes said to be "semi-colonial" or "loosely colonial."

Colonial birds are afforded a measure of nest security because they can mount a collective alarm and defense against predators and as a consequence many such species lay fewer eggs than do solitary nesters without diminishing breeding success.

Not to be confused with communal nesters (see NEST; ANI).

COLOR AND PATTERN. Including the nature of avian color—both of feathers and of "soft parts"—and the adaptive significance of color and pattern among some North American species.

WHAT IS COLOR? The colors of birds (and everything else) are different wavelengths of light selectively reflected from different substances. White light consists of all wavelengths together and therefore a substance which reflects them all appears white. A substance which reflects none of them lacks all color and appears pure black. When some but not all of the wavelengths are reflected, we see one of the colors in our visible spectrum—red, yellow, green, blue, and all possible combinations thereof. The color we see in a given object or substance may be simply the result of the light-absorbing and light-reflecting properties of its chemical makeup. This is called chemical, pigmentary, or biochromatic color (pigments or biochromes) (Fox, 1953). Our perception of color is also affected by the structural composition of the material from which light is reflected, which may, for example, scatter the light in such a way as to make certain wavelengths visible to us while others are diverted out of the line of our perception. This effect is called structural or schemochromatic color (schemochromes).

Both pigmentary and structural colors occur in many different forms and may exist alone or in combination to produce a particular chromatic effect. The breadth of possibilities thus implied is amply demonstrated in the seemingly infinite variety of bird coloration.

Pigments account for most of the colors we see in the plumage, bills, legs, skin, and irises of birds. Most belong to one of three groups of organic compounds: the melanins, the carotenoids, and the porphyrins, all of which occur very commonly throughout the animal kingdom. Some specific pigmentary compounds (e.g., eumelanin and carotene) have been identified and may be responsible for only very particular areas of coloration.

Melanins are the commonest pigments in birds. They are almost insoluble, and occur as minute granules on both feathers and "soft parts." They are responsible for most of the "earth tones" exhibited by birds—especially blacks, grays, and shades of brown, but also including some "off pinks" and yellows. Melanins are also the chief pigments in human hair and skin.

Carotenoids are the most widespread of organic pigments, occurring throughout the plant as well as the animal kingdom. Unlike the other pigments noted here, the carotenoids must be ingested by birds in plant food, for they are not synthesized by the body. The carotenoids give most of the yellows, oranges, and reds seen in birds, including the yellow of egg yolk (carotene).

Porphyrins are also very common throughout the animal kingdom, including birds. They are responsible for some greens, reds, and a range of browns (especially pinkish buffs).

Dietary deficiencies and metabolic imbalances may upset the pigment-producing process in a bird's system. For instances of both excesses and insufficiencies, see ALBINISM; MELANISM; LEUCISM; SCHIZOCHROISM; ERYTHRISM; XANTHOCHROISM; and Plate 5.

Structural Color produces *all* whites and blues in birds' plumage and the various forms of iridescence—the now-you-see-it-now-you-don't head colors of most male hummingbirds as well as the multicolored oil-on-water iridescence of the Common Starling, the grackles, and others.

White results from an absence of pigment in the feathers, allowing the reflection of all wavelengths of sunlight from a colorless surface. The quality of the whites, whether dull or glossy, depends on the structural details of individual feathers and the texture of the plumage as a whole (see below).

The romantically inclined will be pleased to learn that the blue of bird feathers owes its existence to the same phenomenon that makes the sky blue; the technically inclined may prefer a brief description of the "Tyndall phenomenon" by which it is achieved: White light falling through a perfectly clear atmosphere would produce no color. But the upper atmosphere is filled with minute particles which pick up and scatter (i.e., reflect) the shortest (blue) light waves; when larger particles are encountered nearer the earth, the longer yellow and red waves are scattered, giving us brilliant sunsets. In bird feathers the light-scattering elements are not particles but tiny air pockets (vacuoles) in a layer of cells in the feather barbs (see FEATHER). This layer lies beneath the outer transparent covering and above a core of cells darkened by melanin granules. The blue light is scattered by the vacuoles and the rest of the spectrum is absorbed by the melanin beneath. Most non-iridescent greens in feathers appear in the same way except that the outer covering of the barb contains yellow pigment instead of being transparent, so that the blue light is reflected through a yellow medium, giving green. When a Blue Jay's feather is dipped in alcohol and the air in the vacuoles is displaced by the liquid, the feather appears a dull blackish.

Iridescent Colors result from the structure of the barbules and are produced according to the principle of "interference" of light waves, the mutual change that occurs when two light waves intersect. The barbules are twisted and flattened in such a way as to reflect light only at certain angles and sometimes, as in the case of hummingbirds, with spectacular intensity. The colors originate in the microstructure of the surface of the barbules. In hummingbirds, at least, this consists of extraordinarily thin successive films of minute elliptical "platelets" arranged mosaic-like in a dark matrix. Interference of light waves occurs by reflection and refraction in these films in a manner similar to that produced by a film of oil on water or soapy water over air (e.g., soap bubbles). In the multicolored iridescent neck feathers of pigeons the interference occurs between the light reflected from transparent surface carotene and a layer of granular melanin immediately below. Other kinds of birds showing different iridescent effects produce them by variations of the basic principle. The details of this complex phenomenon are too numerous to give here, but are explicated and illustrated with admirable lucidity and at the length they deserve in Greenewalt (1960–HUMMINGBIRD).

In many if not all cases, the iridescent feathers lack the interlocking structure of the barbules of "normal" feathers; they are, therefore, relatively weak and tend to occur as body feathers rather than flight feathers.

Texture. The appearance of plumage coloration is strongly influenced by the size of feathers and the angle at which feathers and their constituent barbs lie. Short feathers projecting vertically, as from the heads of many ducks, give a soft velvety effect. When feathers, barbs, and/or barbules are arranged with flat surface facing outward, the effect is increased shininess—not to be confused with iridescence. The brightly colored (red or yellow) crown feathers of woodpeckers show this quality on close inspection.

While a number of bird species are unicolored and clear primary hues are not infrequent in avian coloration, the plumages of most species are to some degree combinations of the effects described above. Variations of hue and intensity of color, for example, are often the result of mixtures of pigments present in individual feathers. Dark melanin granules, for example, among a carotenoid pigment result in a range of dull olive greens and browns or dull reds. Structural blue combined with biochromal red yields purple. Melanin forms a part of the structure of at least some forms of iridescence, serving as a refraction and/or absorption medium as well as providing background color as in the "iridescent black" granules.

And striking plumage patterns are often the results of mixed effects—iridescence next to "matt" color; primary hues next to muted tones; dark patterns against light—as exemplified by males of many species of ducks.

Special Effects also modify coloration in a few cases. Particles of powder down, for example, covering the surface of the plumage softens tones slightly and makes them less glossy. The roseate bloom which appears on the breasts of some species of gulls and terns early in the breeding season may be a pigment produced seasonally from the oil gland and applied with the bill like "rouge." The "soft parts" and irises of many heron species vivify dramatically during the very acme of breeding season excitement. This effect is at least in part due to a hormonally triggered increase in blood vessels at the surface of affected areas. And the color has been seen to change in response to an immediate stimulus, so that when the legs of a Green Heron or the loral skin of a Snowy Egret intensifies it seems, in essence, to be "blushing." However, it has been shown that an increase in pigments is also involved, which may help to explain how a Louisiana Heron's bill base changes in the breeding season from dull yellow to bright blue.

CoLOR SPECIFICATION. Redheads, Ruby-throated Hummingbirds, Vermilion Flycatchers, American Robins, Orchard Orioles, Scarlet Tanagers, Northern Cardinals, and Rose-breasted Grosbeaks all display "red" in some plumage. An observer can attempt to describe the shade of red with adjectives such as dark, light, brownish, scarlet, etc., but he will be understood only if these names apply to an accepted standard, however arbitrary. It doesn't really matter if a given shade is "truly" rufous as long as it is always labeled as such. A widely used standard is the Villalobos system, which "rests on a sound theoretical basis" and is represented in abbreviated form in the introduction to Palmer's *Handbook of North American Birds,* Vol. 1 (1962).

PURPOSES OF COLOR AND PATTERN. One should always exercise caution when attempting to explain striking natural phenomena. Clearly adaptive plumage characteristics, such as the cryptic forest-floor coloration of most nightjars, encourage us to look for similar "reasons" for *all* eye-catching colors or designs, when, in fact, many may have evolved simply in the absence of any selective pressure *against* them.

However, the stunning variety in plumage color and pattern inevitably excites our curiosity, especially when certain "motifs" seem to be repeated consistently in correlation with factors of habitat or behavior. A few of the better-known "functions" of color and pattern are therefore described briefly below.

Physiological Benefit. It has been suggested that species with dark plumage may benefit from superior heat absorption and that the pale coloration of many desert birds may aid temperature control, in addition to providing a measure of concealment against pale arid landscapes (see below and DESERT). Due to the chemical composition of melanin, black feathers are stronger than pale feathers and a glance through a modern field guide reveals that wing tips or all flight feathers are frequently darker (often black) than other body feathers.

Recognition. Distinctive plumage colors and patterns allow males and (more often) females to recognize potential mates of their own species; some displays involving these feathers may release appropriate breeding behavior, e.g., the urge to copulate. These same characteristic species colors/patterns serve as warning to territorial trespassers. Other recognitive functions are as follows:

• Brightly colored/patterned bills and gapes release begging and feeding responses in young and parent birds, respectively, and feeding nestlings in cavities or other dark locations is doubtless facilitated by the white or bright yellow gape margins seen in many species.

• The white or pale gray coloration of gulls, terns, and gannets congregated at a food source may act as a signal—visible for miles against the dark sea—to other seabirds in the area, making food seeking more efficient; likewise "kettles" of dark vultures against a pale sky may alert other scavengers to a kill (or a dump).

• Species such as shorebirds which maintain tight flocking formations may be aided in their synchronous movements by contrasting "flags" in wings and tail which release "following" instincts.

• Conspicuous coloration as a warning to potential predators of unpalatability or toxicity is relatively common among insects, but only scantily documented for a few bird species.

For mimetic coloration, rare among birds, see MIMICRY.

Distraction. Many birds have bright (often white) flashes or "banner marks" which are concealed when the birds are at rest but instantly revealed when the bird spreads its feathers in flight. The white rumps of woodpeckers, the white outer tail feathers of pipits, juncos, and other passerines, and the spots on the tail corners of *Dendroica* warblers are familiar examples. These may serve to momentarily startle a predator, allowing crucial seconds for escape, and/or induce an attacker to strike at expendable parts of the body.

Concealment (see Plate 3). Many birds are so colored/patterned as to blend with their characteristic habitat. Some animals (e.g., toads, anglefish) use such "camouflage" to capture prey which wander unsuspectingly within reach (anticryptic). But cryptic coloration in birds largely serves the opposite function, that of concealing them from potential predators (procryptic).

Perhaps the most interesting thing about the phenomenon is the many ways in which near-invisibility is achieved. To begin with, one should recognize that brilliant color and bold patterns may be as cryptic against the proper background as somber colors and uniform patterns. Gerald Thayer (1909) taxes our credulity when he suggests that the salmon pink of American Flamingos is adapted to conceal flocks of this species against brilliant Caribbean sunsets, but an adult male Scarlet Tanager in nuptial plumage moving amidst the vivid contrast and moving shadows of its treetop habitat is not nearly as conspicuous as the inexperienced observer might expect. Conversely, even the most highly evolved cryptic coloration stands out like the proverbial sore thumb against the "wrong" background.

The *extent* of concealing color/pattern among birds ranges from the not-as-obvious-as-you-might-think (Scarlet Tanager) to the impossible-to-find-even-when-you-know-where-to-look (nightjars). A great many species, e.g., ducks (females), sandpipers, vireos, sparrows, etc., match in a very general way the colors and textures of the habitats in which they are normally found. In a few species (the American Bittern is the favorite example, followed closely by the nightjars and the American Woodcock) the background mimicry reaches a high degree of fidelity providing (1) that the species in question is in the appropriate habitat at the appropriate season—bitterns are much more conspicuous against green cattails than against brown; and (2) that appropriate behavior reinforces coloration: a bird trying to be invisible *must* remain motionless; many species crouch low to the ground to minimize giveaway shadows; and a few have a concealment "display" such as the vertical freeze posture of the American Bittern.

A number of species whose habitat tends to be snow-covered for at least part of the year have evolved white plumage, and in some cases the concealing elements must change according to the season and/or the habits of the species. Snowy Owls do not alter their plumage seasonally, but Snow Buntings, which winter somewhat farther south and on a more regular basis, become mottled with brown following the breeding season. The ptarmigan, by contrast, which do not migrate, change with the seasons in an unusual sequence of molts (see MOLT): their plumage is at its whitest in winter, brownest at midsummer, and patchy (like the snow cover) betweentimes.

Concealing coloration may also change with age. Most precocial chicks are clothed in a highly cryptic natal down whether their parents make use of the same phenomenon (gallinaceous birds, sandpipers, etc.) or not (gulls, terns).

Countershading or obliterative shading takes advantage of the fact that under normal circumstances a bird's upper surface will be under direct light while the undersurface remains in shadow. The shading of many plumages reverses this, being darkest above and palest below, thus neutralizing the contrast and "flattening" the bird's form to blend more easily with background patterns. An adult Herring Gull in full sun demonstrates this effect, though in many passerines the gradation from darkest to palest is more gradual.

Disruptive patterning juxtaposes contrasting patches of color of irregular shape, making the outline of a bird ambiguous and encouraging the eye to relate parts of the bird's coloration to elements of the background rather than bringing them together in the shape of a bird. The *Charadrius* plovers against their stony-ground habitat are probably the best North· American examples of disruptive patterning.

A few species seem to combine most of the cryptic elements in a single "act." The waterthrushes, for example, have a general resemblance to their background color, are countershaded, have disruptive eye and breast stripes, *and* heighten the last effect by adding a bobbing motion which seems to mimic the motion and play of light of their preferred moving-water habitat.

For birds which seem to mimic other birds rather than habitat, see MIMICRY.

Sighting Lines. The prevalence in birds' facial patterns of lines which pass through the eye or from eye to gape is undeniable. It has been suggested (Ficken et al., 1971) that such marks help a bird coordinate its bill movement with the movements of its prey.

COLOR/PATTERN TERMINOLOGY. For definitions of technical terms often used in discussion of adaptive coloration, see PROCRYPTIC; ANTI-CRYPTIC; PHANERIC; EPIGAMIC; EPISEMATIC; APOSEMATIC.

For aberrant color/pattern, see ALBINISM; MELANISM; LEUCISM; SCHIZOCHROISM; ERYTHRISM; XANTHOCHROISM; and Plate 5.

See also DISPLAY; PLUMAGE; and Plate 4.

COMB. A fleshy, featherless, usually brightly colored, serrated crest adorning the heads of some gallinaceous birds from the base of the bill to the rear of the crown. Combs undoubtedly function in sexual display and are usually more prominent in the male than the female. In North America, only cock domestic fowl are adorned with combs.

COMFORT MOVEMENTS. Collective term for a variety of actions and gestures made by birds, usually in association with PREENING or resting. The commonest comfort movements are: shaking of the body or parts thereof, notably the head and tail; ruffling and resettling of the body feathers; "shuffling" of the wings, a distinctive motion in which the folded wings are "sawed" alternately back and forth over the back; yawning; and stretching. The last type of movement has several standard variations, especially: (1) stretching both wings upward simultaneously; (2) stretching both wings downward simultaneously; (3) stretching one wing and the leg of the same side outward and downward, usually with the same side of the tail fanned; and (4) stretching both legs while lowering head and neck and arching the back. Closely related species of birds tend to practice similar stretching gestures.

For a detailed account of comfort movements in the duck family, see McKinney, *Behavior* (1965), 25:120–220.

COMIC (COMMIC) TERN. Combination of "Common" and "Arctic" (Tern), used by birdwatchers to refer to birds which belong to one of these two similar species but which cannot be identified with certainty as one or the other.

COMMENSALISM. Close association between two or more organisms of different species which is detrimental to neither. In some cases (and definitions) one of the "commensals" derives an advantage without harming (or aiding) the other(s). Insects which live in a bird's nest without any direct contact with its owner share a commensalistic (or commensal) relationship with the bird. Cattle Egrets, which feed on insects flushed from pasture vegetation by cattle, are also commensals, as are their benefactors. Compare SYMBIOSIS; PARASITISM.

COMMISSURE. In birds, the line along which the upper and lower mandibles close.

COMMUNICATION. See SONG.

CONDOR. Standard English name for the two largest species of New World vultures (family Cathartidae): the Andean Condor (*Vultur gryphus*) and the California Condor (*Gymnogyps californianus*). The name derives from the Peruvian (Quechua) word *cuntur,* which apparently refers to all vultures and which was corrupted by the Spanish to *condor.* For characteristics of the family, see VULTURE. For details of the nearly extinct California Condor, see ENDANGERED BIRDS.

CONDOR, THE. Quarterly journal of the Cooper Ornithological Society. For a general description of materials published, see COOPER ORNITHOLOGICAL SOCIETY. For the address of its subscription office as of 1982, see the Bibliography under PERIODICALS.

CONGENERIC. Belonging to the same genus. The three phoebes are all placed in the genus *Sayornis* and are thus congeneric.

CONSERVATION. The protection of natural resources, including birds and other living organisms, whether for humanitarian reasons or to prevent the extinction of valuable and/or aesthetically desirable life forms.

HISTORY OF BIRD CONSERVATION IN NORTH AMERICA. Though the humane instinct has existed at least from the beginning of recorded history, wildlife conservation as an influential social consensus is a relatively modern phenomenon. Its roots are planted in three characteristics of "advanced" civilizations: (1) The transformation of wilderness from a threat and an obstruction to a beneficial, spiritual resource; in North America this happened concurrently with the "conquest" of the frontier and the pattern of its progress is still discernible: in the northeastern states, where the North American wilderness was first encountered and beaten into submission, the conservation movement today reaches maximum effectiveness, while in Alaska, where the wilderness still holds a tenuous dominion, conservationists are widely reviled. (2) The flourishing of a moral (though not always religious) conviction that killing things, especially "higher" animals, is wrong. (3) The realization that wanton destruction of wildlife almost inevitably redounds to the detriment of human beings.

The earliest American bird conservation initiatives resulted from isolated cases in which it was realized that "if we kill any more, there won't be any left to kill." Thus as early as 1616 the government of Bermuda passed a law prohibiting the further destruction of the Bermuda Petrel or Cahow, whose abundance had recently been sacrificed to feed starving colonists during a severe winter.

Late in the seventeenth century a few citizens of the North American colonies began to notice a decline in some game birds and urged self-control, and in 1708 New York passed seasonal hunting restrictions on the Wild Turkey, Heath Hen, Ruffed Grouse, and quail, but only for those few counties where these species were already scarce.

In 1818 a Massachusetts law extended protection in a vague way to birds which ate "noxious" insects as well as those which were "useful" as food. In the 1850's and 1860's about a dozen states (northeastern and midwestern) passed laws protecting specific songbird species which passed muster as "friends of the farmer" or were at worst "small and harmless."

More significant than these early laws, which tended to be vague and enforced only near large cities if at all, was the appearance, beginning before the middle of the nineteenth century, of illustrated bird books. Many of these, such as DeKay's *Birds of New York* (1844), covered regional avifaunas, and though they were not meant to be hauled along on outdoor excursions (see FIELD GUIDE), they contained descriptions of what we now call field marks and species "histories," aimed at both satisfying and encouraging a growing curiosity and enthusiasm in the public. By the 1870's and 1880's periodicals such as *The Atlantic, Harper's,* and *Scribner's* magazines regularly contained "nature" pieces, often about birds. *St. Nicholas* magazine encouraged young people (especially boys) to regard birds as their friends rather than as amusing targets, even going so far as to organize a kind of club for young "Bird Defenders." The pious moralizing and shameless sentimentality and anthropomorphism ("old grandmother To-whee Bunting"—Samuels, 1868) would not go down well with current subscribers to *Ranger Rick,* but the popularity of this style of birdy lore in the last century is beyond dispute.

Encouraging as this wave of "nature appreciation" may sound out of context, it in no way mitigated the slaughter of wagonloads of Passenger Pigeons, Eskimo Curlews, and other game species by market gunners and sportsmen, or the appetite for fresh game on the table (see EDIBILITY), or the enthusiasm of male adolescents for collecting songbirds, their nests and eggs. Even serious students of birdlife and most of the early conservationists did most of their birdwatching through the sights of a shotgun. Then around 1875 there arose a phenomenon which seemed to spell doom for many of the world's most decorative bird species—though it would ultimately prove their salvation—the desire of all ladies of fashion to wear birds on their hats!

The advertisements for feather fashions are more amusing than shocking to the modern sensibility: there stands a pretty young lady—elegant, well corseted, with an air of self-conscious superiority—apparently unaware that there is a dead grebe squatting among the silk flowers of her bonnet. But what now seems a peculiar and callous fad reigned unhindered for twenty-five years and survived under fire for at least ten more. It made the fortunes of many milliners, earned good livings for plume hunters, and decimated populations of the most popular species, especially the plumed egrets. If it is difficult to put in perspective the 5–20 million birds per year which ended as frills, consider Frank CHAPMAN recording forty *species* of "hat birds" on an afternoon's stroll in New York City in 1886. To the hunters, clean, cured bird skins brought from a few cents apiece for small or less desirable species to five dollars for a Roseate Spoonbill, and the treasured "aigrettes" were sold separately. In addition to egrets, gulls and terns were much in demand for their graceful wings. Smaller, colorful species were also popular (a dress made from the iridescent throat feathers of 3,000 hummingbirds was admired in a society column), and even woodpeckers and owls found their niche in *haute couture.*

By the 1880's it was clear to those few who cared that the combination of millinery fashion, the appetite for bird flesh, and shooting for sport would inevitably lead to the extinction of some species (as indeed it did—see EXTINCT BIRDS) unless something was done. In 1883 the American Ornithologists' Union was founded and almost immediately organized a Committee for the Protection of North American Birds, which served to enlist the efforts of prominent ornithologists—many of them wellborn and influential—in the incipient conservation movement. In 1886 the first Audubon Society was founded in New York and almost immediately attracted nearly 40,000 supporters, among them such cultural "lights" as Oliver Wendell Holmes and a new breed of sportsman-naturalist whose prototype was President Theodore Roosevelt. Another enlightened patrician of this ilk, George Bird Grinnell, who owned and ran Forest and Stream Publishing Company, produced the first *Audubon* magazine in 1887.

In spite of all this pro-avian activity—which was accompanied by a continued proliferation of popular bird books and articles and even some natural history in public school curricula—the country at large was still opposed or at best indifferent to the idea of bird protection. This was made manifest by the failure of the Audubon Society and its magazine in 1889 and the declaration by conservationist William Dutcher that 1895 represented the "low tide of bird protection." In 1896, however, the Audubon movement rallied with the formation of the Massachusetts Audubon Society under the direction of William Brewster. Other states followed this example and at the turn of the century formed a national federation which included twenty local Audubon societies (see AUDUBON SOCIETIES). In 1899 Frank Chapman started *Bird-Lore* magazine, a comparatively nononsense publication dedicated exclusively to the "study and protection of birds," and a voice for the bird conservation movement which the milliners and shooters were unable to shout down.

The early years of the new century saw the enactment of the first bird protection laws with teeth, mostly patterned after a "Model Law" proposed by the A.O.U. in 1886. This document clarified the distinction between game birds (ducks and geese, rails and coots, Wild Turkey, grouse, pheasants and quail, and shorebirds in those days) and non-game; recommended prohibitions against the destruction of nests and eggs of non-game species (except the House Sparrow); and allowed the necessity of licensing scientific collectors.

As happens even today, emotions and rhetoric over conservation reached apoplectic intensity. In a display of congressional wisdom still entirely familiar, U.S. Senator Reed of Missouri announced on the floor in August 1913 that he "really, honestly want[ed] to know why there should be any sympathy or sentiment about a long-legged, long-beaked, long-necked bird that lives in swamps and eats tadpoles and fish and crawfish and things of that kind; why should we worry ourselves into a frenzy because some lady adorns her hat with one of its feathers, which appears to be the only use it has."

The most pious of the conservationists replied to the likes of Senator Reed by calling them "human fiends," "bloated epicures" "sensualists," and worse.

It is impossible to designate a single event which turned the tide in favor of the conservationists—the shooting to death of Audubon warden Guy Bradley by a plume hunter in Florida in 1905 doubtless converted many skeptics—but by the start of World War I, the milliners were having to make do with game birds and illicit imports, and market gunning was largely history. The early conservationists had good reason to congratulate themselves, and we owe them much, though we can smile in hindsight at their innocence of what was to come.

MODERN CONSERVATION. Originally bird protection amounted to simply prohibiting humans from killing non-game birds for whatever purpose. Though large numbers of North American migrants are still killed for food in Latin America each year despite the enactment of migratory bird treaties, direct destruction of birds by humans in the U.S. and Canada is a relatively minor concern of today's conservationists. The hunting of game birds (now including only ducks, geese, and swans, quail and pheasants [most of the last are stocked artificially], some grouse, rails, woodcock, and snipe, some doves and crows) is now regulated by state and federal law as to season and bag limits and taxed; and many hunters consider themselves conservationists out of enlightened self-interest. Wearing birds and market gunning are gone, probably forever, and while some boys of all ages continue to shoot at birds for fun and the occasional songbird stew doubtless gets served in rural areas, these misdemeanors are not considered threatening to the population of any bird species.

Most present-day conservationists, however, would probably trade the new problems for the old without a moment's thought. Overpopulation, draining and filling of wetlands, reckless lumbering practices, pesticides, and oil spills are just a few of the by-products of the post-industrial age which threaten not only birds but all life forms, including ourselves (see MAN-MADE THREATS TO BIRDLIFE). Since today's life-threatening phenomena tend to affect entire habitats or ecosystems (including the world ecosystem), conservation efforts have had to become more holistic in approach. Because of the overwhelming dominance of human life on the planet, we have also had to try to deliberately manage the survival of particular species, rather than simply removing a threat and letting nature control the recovery.

Most conservationists' energies today are devoted to three basic approaches:

1. *Ecosystem preservation.* It is far more practical to protect whole systems of interdependent organisms, including birds, than to try to focus on a single species or class. This theory has been enforced by our growing awareness that major biomes such as rain forests not only are walk-in zoos and botanical gardens full of exotic organisms, but also may help maintain the global climate and contain an enormous diversity of genetic material which may prove crucial to such human necessities as agriculture and medicine. Saving habitat is simple in theory: buy land and maintain its integrity—by force if necessary. But the pressures of human hunger and development are in continual conflict against its effective execution.

2. *Monitoring, correcting, and safeguarding against environmental deterioration.* Many of the miracles that we have worked in the last 200

years have been shown to have disastrous consequences and, perhaps worse, many consequences undoubtedly exist that we are yet unable to measure. No one can predict, for example, what the long-term effects of the large quantities of oil we have spilled in the oceans will be. Common sense tells us that there will probably be some, but shortsightedness and perhaps fear encourage us to think that it has just gone away—"out to sea." Much more support is needed—for basic research, to correct our mistakes and to inform the public.

Despite the inescapable logic of giving meticulous protection to the only habitable environment we know of, the current trend in the U.S. as this book goes to press is to lift the few safeguards we have managed to install in favor of transient short-term gains, to cut off funds for environmental investigation and repair work, and to condemn environmentalists as spoilsports and impeders of human progress.

3. *Captive breeding.* The populations of some birds have fallen so low due to habitat destruction and other factors, some of them as yet unknown (see ENDANGERED BIRDS), that the last hope for their survival is artificial breeding programs directed and run by both public and private wildlife research institutions. Briefly stated, the goal of such projects is to increase the numbers of rare species under controlled conditions free of many of the hazards—natural and man-made—of the real world and then eventually to acclimate birds born in captivity to suitable parts of their former range. The Peregrine Project at Cornell University and the captive breeding of Whooping Cranes at the Patuxent (Maryland) Wildlife Research Center (U.S. Fish and Wildlife Service) have met with some encouraging successes (see ENDANGERED BIRDS), though, as may be imagined, human rearing of "wild" birds is a tricky business—requiring expert knowledge, rare insight, and a dedication that is born of a deep concern for the right of an animal or plant to exist.

WHAT CAN I DO? Traditionally conservation has been a people's movement. Its life force has always come from individuals who care about the quality of the environment they live in or about the welfare of their fellow animals. By contrast, the "enemy" is usually a large collective entity made up of people who don't live near what they intend to destroy and can't see the forest *or* the trees for the profits. The experience of the last twenty years has shown that many people *do* feel strongly about maintaining the beauty and diversity of the continent even at some expense to their so-called standard of living. But they are often ill-informed on the issues about which they have a voice and therefore are often not present when the votes are counted. *THEREFORE:* Keep up on local news about environmental issues. Join your local conservation commission and other conservation organizations. Subscribe to a national conservation periodical to keep posted on national issues which will affect your area. Write to your representatives at all levels of government—expressions of thoughtful concern are not discarded as crank mail; often such letters are exactly what a congressman or senator needs to support an issue he favors. Do some research on your own if there is a matter which concerns you. Rachel Carson almost single-handedly alerted the world to the dangers of the promiscuous use of lethal pesticides, though she was untrained in either chemistry or entomology. Her lack of credentials was, of course, quickly pointed out by the self-interested and some of her figures were criticized by scientists. But her main premise was sound and was ultimately vindicated here by the federal ban on the use of DDT (see MAN-MADE THREATS TO BIRDLIFE).

Many organizations once noted for saving birds have (without relinquishing any concern for birdlife) come to the conclusion that the best way to save birds today is to save the whole planet. These and other nonprofit organizations which have been broadly environmentalist from their inception badly need your support. A few of the best-known are listed below.

> International Council for Bird Preservation
>   Smithsonian Institution, Washington, DC 20560
> National Audubon Society
>   950 Third Avenue, New York, NY 10022
> World Wildlife Fund
>   1319 18th St. N.W., Washington, DC 20036
> The Nature Conservancy
>   1800 North Kent St.
>   Arlington, VA 22209
>   (national office; many local offices nationwide)

See also AUDUBON SOCIETIES.

CONSPECIFIC. Belonging to the same species; frequently used in arguing the validity of species/subspecies: "Are Rose-breasted and Black-headed Grosbeaks conspecific?"

CONTOUR FEATHER(S). The outer layer of feathers including flight and tail feathers which give a bird its characteristic form. See PLUMAGE.

CONURE. A generic English name sometimes used for most of the species of New World parakeets. The term is popular with aviculturists, much less so with ornithologists/birdwatchers; however, see in Forshaw (1973–PARROT).

CONVERGENCE (convergent evolution). The development of similar form and/or structural details and/or behavioral traits in unrelated groups of organisms due to adaptation to similar living conditions. In a broad context, the development of the forearm into a wing in both bats and birds is an example. In birds a number of uncanny look-alikes from different families have evolved in this manner. Two frequently cited examples are: (1) the North American meadowlarks (American blackbird family: Icteridae) and African longclaws (lark family: Alaudidae), all open-country species; and (2) the Dovekie (auk family: Alcidae) of the arctic and subarctic oceans and several species of diving petrels (diving petrel family: Pelecanoididae) of Southern Hemisphere oceans.

COOPER, William, 1798?–1864 (Cooper's Hawk: *Accipiter cooperii*). Independently wealthy, taken with natural history from boyhood, schooled in zoology in Europe, Cooper was a founder of the New York Lyceum of Natural History and a man of substantial reputation in the scientific community of his day. He was a student of paleontology, malacology, botany, and herpetology as well as ornithology. His dwindling prominence results from his scanty bibliography. He edited the last two volumes of Lucien Bonaparte's *American Ornithology*; Bonaparte described as a new species a hawk that Cooper had collected and named it for him. He is also commemorated by *Tringa cooperi*, a sandpiper collected and described by Spencer Baird; it has proved to be unique (a hybrid?), no one having seen its like since. William Cooper's son, James, also became a well-known naturalist, one of the surgeon-collectors whom Baird sent West with the army and railroad surveys. James was interested in everything, but his name is now most often heard in the context of the Cooper Ornithological Society of California (see following entry).

COOPER ORNITHOLOGICAL SOCIETY. A nonprofit organization based in California that promotes the scientific study of birds and has a special interest in the birds of Mexico, Central and South America, and the Pacific. It was founded in 1893 and its name commemorates Dr. James G. Cooper, an early California ornithologist, and son of William COOPER, for whom Cooper's Hawk was named. The society publishes a quarterly journal, *The Condor*, which contains scientific papers, bird notes of more general interest, book reviews, etc. Membership is by invitation but the public may subscribe to *The Condor*; for address, see the Bibliography under PERIODICALS.

COOT. Standard English name for 9 members of the rail family (Rallidae; order Gruiformes), all in the genus *Fulica.* Some authorities distinguish the coots in a subfamily of their own, the Fulicinae. One species, the American Coot, breeds in North America and two others have occurred as accidental stragglers (see Appendix II).

All species of coots have a uniformly slaty-black plumage with yellow, red, or white bills and some form of frontal shield (an elaborate horny caruncle in one South American species). Their most distinctive external feature is their peculiarly lobed toes which are adapted for swimming. Coots are equally at home swimming and diving like a duck and walking along lake margins like a rail. They appear to be weak fliers, but some populations undertake long migrations. Like the rails, coots feed on a wide variety of plant and animal foods.

The coots achieve their greatest diversity in South America, where seven species are resident. However, at least one species of coot is abundant on every major landmass in the world excluding the Arctic and Antarctic. The American Coot is found south of the boreal forest throughout North America, though in much of the East it occurs as a migrant only. Its general abundance may be attributable in part to its unpalatability—it is said to be muddy-tasting.

The origins of "coot" are uncertain, though it is known to be involved (as descendant or ancestor) with "scoter"—scoters are widely known as "coots" today by east coast hunters. The naïve, comical "expression" of coots and their distinctive, awkward head-bobbing gesture when swimming have made "coot" a metaphorical term for a "fool" and to "coot along" implies slow, halting progress.

For family characteristics, see RAIL.

COPULATION. In birds, accomplished by contact of the inverted cloacas of male and female of a species, aided in a few groups (e.g., ducks) by a penis-like structure. See REPRODUCTIVE SYSTEM.

CORKSCREW SWAMP (Florida). A 10,895-acre National Audubon Society Sanctuary near Immokalee, northeast of Naples. Famous among birders for its boardwalk, which traverses Florida's largest stand of bald cypress and allows excellent studies of swampland birdlife (e.g., Limpkin, Wood Stork, Pileated Woodpecker, Barred Owl, and many other species). Also of great interest to the birder-*botanist*.

CORMORANT. Standard English name in North America for all members of the family Phalacrocoracidae (order Pelecaniformes). There are 29 species of cormorants worldwide, most (or all) in the genus *Phalacrocorax*, of which 6 breed in North America.

Cormorants are moderately large (2 to 3 feet), usually black, swimming and diving birds, with fairly long, cylindrical, hooked bills. Like the other members of their order, they have webbing between all four toes and no nostril openings in the bill. All species have throat pouches and brightly colored patches of facial skin at the base of the bill in breeding plumage.

Cormorants are gregarious by nature and are customarily seen standing in erect battalions on rocks or pilings—often with their wings spread out to dry—or swimming, partially submerged, with only the head, neck, and part of the back showing above the surface. They feed mainly on fish but also take amphibians, marine/aquatic invertebrates, and even some plants. In migration cormorants fly in long V formations and are often mistaken for geese.

All cormorants are colonial breeders that prefer offshore islands or remote peninsulas, where they nest on the ground or in arboreal "shaggeries" (cormorantries), often in company with herons and other wading birds. Ground nesters assemble piles of seaweed; tree nests are made largely of sticks. The 2–4 (rarely 6) eggs are pale blue or green and unmarked, with a white, chalky coating that typically becomes scratched and stained during incubation.

Cormorants are generally silent but are capable of some guttural croaks uttered in the various "emotional" incidents of the breeding season.

Some species of cormorants are strictly marine (e.g., Brandt's), others largely prefer fresh or brackish water (e.g., Neotropic), while a few (e.g., Double-crested) are apparently equally at home in fresh or salt water.

The family is distributed worldwide in coastal areas except for the islands of the central Pacific Ocean. In North America cormorants are familiar along all coasts except icebound arctic ones, as well as on many large lakes and rivers of the interior. Northern populations of some species are migratory, but few North American birds winter beyond coastal waters. Cormorant populations have increased dramatically along the northeast coast and in the Great Lakes within the last decade. The reason for the increase (upward fluctuation in food-fish supply? lack of persecution?) is as yet undetermined, but fishery authorities are beginning to worry about adverse effects of overabundant cormorants on overscarce anadromous fish species such as salmon, and about predation at hatcheries and seines.

"Cormorant" is derived from one or more Romance-language variations of the Latin *corvus marinus*, i.e., "sea crow." "Shag" is the standard British name for all but one species of cormorant, and this name is widespread here as a colloquial name among east coast fishermen.

CORMORANTRY. A breeding colony of cormorants, also called a shaggery. Other specific names for bird colonies are given under NOUNS OF ASSEMBLAGE.

CORNELL. See LABORATORY OF ORNITHOLOGY.

CORNEOUS. Horny; having a hard texture such as that of a bird's bill.

CORNIPLUME. A horn-like tuft of feathers, such as the "ears" of several owl species, the "crests" of the Double-crested Cormorant, and the "horns" of the Horned Lark.

CORVID(S). Any member of the bird family Corvidae. In the plural, a name by which the crows, ravens, jays, magpies, and nutcrackers can be referred to collectively. Fifteen species of corvids breed in North America. See CROW (includes ravens); JAY; MAGPIE; NUTCRACKER.

CORY, Charles B., 1857–1921 (Cory's Shearwater: *Calonectris diomedea*). Wellborn, well educated, and independently wealthy (until ruined at the age of forty-six), Cory spent his life collecting bird specimens, especially in North America and the Caribbean, and writing faunal works on the areas he knew best. His vast accumulation of bird skins became the nucleus of the collection at the Field Museum of Natural History (Chicago Natural History Museum). On Cory's personal attributes, Gruson (1972–BIOGRAPHY) is eloquent: "Cory was the blithe spirit of American ornithology ... A wit, raconteur, tireless ballroom dancer, sportsman, yachtsman, marksman, hypnotist, belletrist, writer of songs and light operas."

COSMOPOLITAN. Loosely defined: occurring worldwide, i.e., at least in the Northern, Southern, Eastern, and Western Hemispheres. In a more restrictive sense: occurring in all of the major zoogeographic regions (see DISTRIBUTION; ZOOGEOGRAPHY).

It can be stated as a truism that the broader the taxonomic grouping, the more likely it is to be cosmopolitan, i.e., *most orders* of birds are cosmopolitan, and *many families* of birds are so, whereas relatively few genera can claim the distinction and even fewer species. The Great Egret, Osprey, Peregrine Falcon, Common Gallinule,* Snowy Plover,* Black-winged Stilt,* Gull-billed, Caspian, Sandwich, Roseate, and Least Terns, Barn Owl, and Barn Swallow have cosmopolitan breeding ranges; the Black-bellied Plover, Ruddy Turnstone, Red Knot, Sanderling, Northern Phalarope, Common Tern, and all three jaeger species breed in the Temperate Zone worldwide (all but the Common Tern in the Arctic) and migrate to equally cosmopolitan wintering grounds; the House Sparrow has become cosmopolitan by a combination of introduction and an ability to spread to nearly any place of human habitation.

* Subject to a broad taxonomic interpretation.

COSTA, Louis Marie Pantaléon, Marquis de Beau-Regard, 1806–64 (Costa's Hummingbird: *Calypte costae*). A Sardinian (French Savoyard) military officer, diplomat, and historian. He owned a collection of hummingbird specimens.

COTINGA (kuh-TING-guh). Collective name for any member of the family Cotingidae (order Passeriformes), which includes the berry-eaters, fruit-eaters, purpletufts, pihas, becards, tityras, fruit crows, umbrella birds, and bellbirds as well as species in many genera (including *Cotinga*) known simply as "cotingas," e.g., Swallow-tailed Cotinga. One species of becard breeds north to the extreme southwestern U.S. but is now considered by some authorities to belong taxonomically among the tyrant flycatchers (see BECARD). All of the other cotingas are of Neotropical distribution.

The Cotingidae constitute a kind of taxonomic potpourri, containing an amazing assortment of avian forms and behavior patterns, belonging in many cases to species of uncertain phylogeny. The family contains about 73 species including the becards.

"Cotinga" is a native Amazonian (Tupi) name, apparently referring to the immaculate white plumage of the White Bellbird (*Procnias alba*).

COUES (cows), Elliott, 1842–99 (Coues' Flycatcher: *Contopus pertinax*). One of the foremost—easily the most interesting—of the American ornithologists of the late nineteenth century. Coues was born in New Hampshire, graduated from the college and medical school of what is now Georgetown University in Washington, D.C., and almost immediately began a writing career which eventually included almost 1,000 works, several of them major volumes. He was the most eminent of the army surgeons who collected specimens for Spencer BAIRD while on duty in the western states and became secretary and naturalist of the (U.S.-Canadian) Border Commission, out of which experience came two of his own ornithological works, *Birds of the Northwest* and *Birds of the Colorado Valley*. He also published extensively on western mammals. As secretary and naturalist for the Geological and Geographical Survey of the Territories, Coues added papers on the history of the exploration of the American West to his extensive bibliography. He was a founder of the American Ornithologists' Union and his 1882 *Check-list of North American Birds* was the basis for the A.O.U. publication of the same name, the first edition of which appeared shortly thereafter. What set Coues apart from the other brilliant naturalists of his time was his personality, which has been described as "electrifying." He was physically handsome, and had a highly developed sense of humor, boundless energy, and a greater than average taste for the eccentric. The most notable example of this characteristic was his passionate conversion late in his life to the cult of the infamous theosophical charlatan Madame Blavatsky. He took to spiritualism with the same zest he brought to his other interests but was eventually banished from the movement for publishing the details of a Blavatskian hoax. Coues has remained unchallenged as the best writer among American ornithologists and much of what was in his personality is evident in the eloquent, witty, and opinionated introductory chapters to his *Key to North American Birds*. Besides being a landmark in American ornithology, this volume contains a fine evocation of what being a nineteenth-century naturalist was like, from how to clean your collecting gun ("elbow grease"), to the wisdom (none) of taking "stimulation" when afield, to the perils of skinning a putrid bird (festering sores), to the excesses of the overzealous "splitters" who dominated taxonomic theory in Coues' time.

COUNTERSINGING. The vocal response of a male bird on territory to another singing male on adjacent territory. Also sometimes used in the sense of ANTIPHONAL SONG.

COUNTING. The ability to estimate accurately the number of birds in a passing flock is a useful skill for participants in sea watches and other kinds of censuses. By practicing with beans and other inanimate objects of varying number and size, one can develop a high degree of precision in this perceptual technique. See Arbib in *American Birds*, 26:706. See also CENSUS. For counting ability *of birds*, see INTELLIGENCE.

COURTSHIP. An early stage in the breeding cycle, beginning with male and female birds of a given species coming together and leading to copulation. A few migratory species arrive in established pairs on the breeding ground (see PAIR FORMATION), but for most species courtship begins with the attraction of the female by the male's territorial song or display. Once he has attracted a potential mate to his territory, the male follows her around, displaying to her, and attempts to copulate. He is usually rejected at first, but if the female remains on his territory, pair formation is established, and the female will permit copulation within a few days. In the brief period of chaste betrothal, the male may let up on his song or even stop singing altogether. But once allowed his connubial privileges, he resumes his territorial behavior with renewed enthusiasm, which does not normally abate until the eggs hatch.

Display rituals are a crucial element of courtship. They take many forms, each with a special significance—e.g., attraction, enforcement of the pair bond, preparation for copulation—and they may continue even after the young have hatched. For more detail, see DISPLAY. See also COURTSHIP FEEDING; LEK; PAIR FORMATION; SONG; TERRITORY.

COURTSHIP FEEDING. A ritual of the breeding cycle during which a male bird offers food to its mate. It has been recorded in some herons, gulls, doves, cuckoos, and a few passerines. It has been observed preceding, during, and after copulation, but, contrary to the implication of its name, may take place even after the young have hatched. The female usually calls and begs in response to the offering of food by the male.

COVERTS (KUV-erts). Contour feathers which overlap the primary and secondary feathers of the wings and also the main tail feathers (rectrices) from above and below. The coverts are divided into several named sections, e.g., the greater secondary coverts (see WING; TAIL; and Fig. 25).

The feathers covering the ear holes are called the ear coverts.

COVEY (KUV-ee). A widely used collective noun referring to a mother and young or a flock of small game birds, especially quail.

COWBIRD. Standard English name for 6 species of New World black-birds (family Icteridae; order Passeriformes), all but 1 (or 2, depending on taxonomy) in the genus *Molothrus*. Two of these species breed in North America; the rest are Neotropical in distribution.

All but one of the cowbirds are brood parasites, and the exception, the Bay-winged Cowbird of South America, often appropriates the nest of other songbirds. This antisocial behavior is biologically redressed by the Screaming Cowbird, which lays its eggs exclusively in the nests of its only non-parasitic congener.

The life history of the Brown-headed Cowbird has been well studied (see especially Hann, 1941; Payne, 1965; and Friedmann, 1929, 1969, 1971); it apparently represents the most successful form of avian brood parasitism to have evolved in the New World.

Like other brood parasites, Brown-headed Cowbirds do not engage in any form of nest-building behavior or develop brood patches. But females do occupy a defined territory in which to parasitize; all individuals occupy restricted breeding and wintering ranges for life; and males erect their shiny plumage in nuptial display. However, both sexes are promiscuous. Fertilized females locate hosts by watching for nest-building activity, typically that of small to medium-sized songbirds. The species is known to have parasitized the nests of at least 214 bird species, including (possibly by accident) shorebirds and ducks, but its most frequent hosts are small tyrant flycatchers, *Hylocichla* thrushes, vireos, wood warblers, tanagers, and finches. Only rarely does it parasitize cavity nesters. The Bronzed Cowbird is known to parasitize only 62 species of birds, mainly finches and members of its own family, but some of the Neotropical hosts of this species—which reaches its northernmost distribution in the southwestern U.S.—may remain undiscovered.

Typically, the female cowbird waits until the host's nest is complete and a clutch begun before slipping onto the nest before dawn—while both parent birds are away—and depositing a single egg (white speckled with brown) within a few seconds. Much variation is recorded in this sequence of events—some cowbird eggs being laid before the host nest is complete or after the host young are hatched—but the preceding is apparently the most successful. Later in the day (or on the preceding or following day) the parasite removes one of the host's eggs, piercing it with its bill and eventually eating the contents; there are a few records of cowbirds removing nestlings of the host species as well. The best available evidence indicates that the female cowbird parasitizes additional nests until a "clutch" of up to 6 eggs is completed and that she usually produces 2–3 "clutches" a season, or a total of 10–15 eggs; however, Nice (1949) records a total of 25 eggs in 7 clutches for a single cowbird. It is unusual for the female cowbird to lay 2 (or even 3) eggs in a single nest, but a nest may be visited by several parasites and contain as many as 8 cowbird eggs (Byers, 1950).

Unlike the avian brood parasites in other families (see BROOD PARASITISM), cowbirds do not exhibit any form of egg or nestling mimicry, nor are they shown any hostility by prospective hosts unless they are perceived to be menacing the nest after incubation or brooding is well established.

The responses of cowbird hosts vary among different species and individuals. About half of individuals parasitized accept the changeling as one of their own and rear it faithfully even when it results in the starvation of other nestlings. The most frequent negative response to being parasitized is to desert the nest, but certain species—Pettingill (1970–ORNITHOLOGY) cites the American Robin and Gray Catbird—can recognize cowbird eggs and remove them. A relatively rare solution—habitual with the Yellow Warbler—is to build a new nest over the parasitized one, covering the host's eggs as well as the cowbird's.

The cowbird incubation period is unusually short and the nestling fast-growing and usually larger than its foster siblings, so that even if the cowbird egg is laid after the host's young are hatched, the parasite has a chance of survival. Cowbird nestlings do not instinctively push host eggs out of the nest (as does that most famous of brood parasites, the Eurasian Cuckoo) or kill the nestlings directly (as do the honeyguides), but it often starves members of the normal brood by consuming more than its share of the food brought by the parent and will sometimes deliberately evict a rightful tenant. In most cases, however, the host is able to fledge some of its own young as well as the cowbird. Both rejection by hosts and the success of host young in a parasitized nest are, of course, in the best interest of the parasite, since its abundance depends on that of host species. In general the cowbird populations and their effect on host species populations reach a natural equilibrium, but abnormally high cowbird populations can be detrimental locally, notably in the case of Kirtland's Warbler (see ENDANGERED BIRDS). It is probably fair to say that human agricultural and livestock-rearing practices are principally responsible for its present high density.

The distribution of the Brown-headed Cowbird once coincided largely with that of the plains Bison and the species was once known as "buffalo bird." Both of our cowbirds continue to seek bovine company, following cows as well as other livestock to catch the insects they flush while grazing and (at least in the case of the Bronzed Cowbird) picking ticks from the backs of their mammalian associates. However, cowbirds are largely granivorous and the pastoralization of the vast eastern forests (whether for livestock or crops) has enabled the Brown-headed Cowbird to expand its range to continentwide and into open habitats with and without cows. Their fecundity and fondness for grain have made them pests of feedlots and grainfields. This species now breeds throughout North America south of the Arctic and is a permanent resident in the southern part of its range. The Bronzed Cowbird is essentially a Middle American species.

For other icterids, see BLACKBIRD; ORIOLE; GRACKLE; MEADOWLARK; BOBOLINK; see also PARASITISM; BROOD PARASITISM; and related references.

CRAKE. Name in wide usage worldwide for most species of small, short-billed rails. Although the Eurasian Corn Crake, a casual straggler to North America, is the only species on the current A.O.U. *Check-list* to bear this name, many species in the genera *Porzana, Laterallus,* and *Coturnicops,* to which our Sora, Black Rail, and Yellow Rail belong, respectively, are called "crakes."

CRANE. Standard English name for all 14 members of the family Gruidae (order Gruiformes), 2 of which breed in North America; a third species has occurred accidentally (see Appendix II).

The cranes range in size between 30 and 60 inches and are superficially much like the herons and storks, with very long legs and neck; fairly long (but not *very* long) bill; broad powerful wings; and a short tail. Many crane species have patches of bare red skin on the forehead and elongated and/or curled secondary feathers that are used in display. Like the storks and unlike the herons (usually), they fly with necks extended. The cranes feed in uplands, including cultivated fields, more habitually than the other long-legged wading birds and are virtually omnivorous, with a strong taste for tuberous roots as well as small vertebrates and large invertebrates. They are renowned for their courtship dances and are regarded as sacred in the Orient, where they have proven inspirational for many generations of traditional painters and poets (see HUMAN CULTURE).

Cranes' nests consist of piles of plant material—a considerable heap when built in shallow wetlands or merely a hollow with a sparse lining in drier sites. The usually 2 (atypically 1 or 3) eggs are yellowish buff to olive with reddish-brown splotches and speckles and similar but paler (lavender or grayish) subsurface markings.

Wild, bugling cries and less spectacular honking or grunting calls are both typical.

Cranes range to the High Arctic in the Holarctic region and to the tropics in Africa, Asia, and Australia. They are absent from Central and South America, the Malaysian and Polynesian archipelagos, and New Zealand.

The two North American species, Sandhill and Whooping Cranes, are virtually North American endemics, both breeding to near or beyond the Arctic Circle and wintering near the southern border of the U.S. The latter is, of course, our most famous ENDANGERED BIRD.

"Crane" is recognizable as a name for these birds a long way back, as in the Old English *cran.* Beyond this the word mavens find Indo-European roots such as *gar* (to cry out), referring presumably to the distinctive utterings produced in gruiform courtship rituals.

CRAVERI, Federico, 1815–90 (Craveri's Murrelet: *Endomychura craveri*). A native of Turin, Italy, Professor Craveri spent twenty years in Mexico, where he taught chemistry in Mexico City. He also toured the country extensively, collecting rock and animal specimens, which he shipped back to the Academy of Science in his home town. While investigating Raza Island in the Gulf of California (apparently to assess the guano potential), he collected a small alcid. It was eventually named for him by his countryman Count Tommaso A. Salvadori, director of the Zoological Museum in Turin.

CRÈCHE (kraysh or kresh). In general usage the term means a nursery or foundling home. Ornithologically it refers to the "pooling" of precocial chicks of the same age from a number of nests in a colony. Among North American species, Common Eiders and Royal and Sandwich Terns are known to form crèches. See YOUNG, DEVELOPMENT OF.

CREEPER. Standard English generic name, alone or in combination, for many species in several families of birds worldwide. In North America it applies unambiguously to our only member of the treecreeper family (Certhiidae), the Brown Creeper (*Certhia americana*). For a discussion of this problem of vernacular nomenclature and a family account, see TREE-CREEPER.

CREPUSCULAR (cre-PUS-kya-ler). In the context of animal behavior, the term means active in low levels of light, especially at dusk. No North American bird species is *exclusively* crepuscular, but some species of owls, swifts, and nightjars are particularly active or conspicuous in the twilight hours before sunset and dawn. The Black Skimmer, which can feed best in calm water (see SKIMMER and Fig. 2), usually takes advantage of the low wind levels characteristic of dawn and dusk and is therefore largely crepuscular in its feeding habits.

CREST. An adornment of feathers, usually peaked, on the top of the head; not readily distinguishable from a "tuft," e.g., Tufted Titmouse, nor very reliable as to general contour, e.g., Double-crested Cormorant. Only seven North American species can claim to be "nomenclaturally crested": Double-crested Cormorant, Crested Auklet, Great Crested Flycatcher, Brown (Wied's) Crested Flycatcher, Crested Caracara, Crested Mynah (introduced), and Blue Jay (*Cyanocitta cristata*); Black-crested Titmouse is now widely considered a subspecies of Tufted Titmouse. Many other species, e.g., Scaled Quail, Royal Tern, Belted Kingfisher, are crested without acknowledgment. For a detailed analysis of the geographical distribution of crests and other appendages, see Pidler in the 1973 edition of *The Auklet*, p. 9.

CRISSUM (Crissal Thrasher). The undertail coverts; the area of feathers between the vent and the rectrices (see Fig. 25). On the Crissal Thrasher this area is dark chestnut, contrasting sharply with its generally gray-brown coloration; no other thrasher has a distinctive crissum.

CROP. A sac-like appendage opening into the gullet (esophagus) where food is stored temporarily before digestion or regurgitation. Absent in most birds but well developed in North American species of doves and gallinaceous birds. More loosely, any enlargement of the gullet used for food storage. Also called the ingluvies. See DIGESTIVE SYSTEM.

CROSSBILL. Standard English name for 3 species of cardueline finches (family Fringillidae; order Passeriformes), 2 of which breed and winter in North America.

The most striking distinction between the crossbills and the other "winter finches" that breed in northern coniferous forests is, of course, the former's peculiarly elongated and crossed mandibles. Though crossbills frequently eat seeds of fruit (after slicing the pulp in two with a scissor-like action), pick up seeds or insects in an unexceptional manner, and even take suet from feeders, the unique function of their unusual bills is to pry open the scales of *closed* cones. Different species (and subspecies) of crossbills have bills of varying size and strength, which correspond to the heaviness of the preferred cones to be "cracked." The relatively delicate-billed White-winged Crossbill prefers larch cones; the massive-billed Parrot Crossbill of Europe specializes in the toughest of green Scotch pine cones. For a detailed description of the cone-opening procedure, see FOOD/FEEDING and Fig. 2.

The crossing of the mandibles takes place gradually after hatching, the upper mandible beginning to lengthen by the fourteenth day, but no crossing is evident for about four weeks. At this time the lower mandible starts to bend to one side and soon sticks up beyond the upper. Only the horny sheath of the bill, not the bones beneath, is bent and curved. The feet of crossbills are also specially adapted—notably large with heavy claws—to hold cones while prying them open.

The lives of the crossbills are dictated to a large extent by the northern cone crops. Different populations time breeding so that hatching coincides with an abundance of ripe cones. Since cones provide easy meals at all seasons, both Red and White-winged Crossbills can breed throughout the year. The young are altricial but unusually downy at hatching and can withstand being uncovered for brief periods in ambient temperatures at least as low as $-35°$ C. (-30 F.).

Like other "winter finches," crossbills are given to periodic "irruptions" during which they appear (and even remain to breed) south of their "normal" winter range—sometimes in large numbers. This phenomenon is also tied to the success of the northern cone crops in relation to the size of crossbill populations (see IRRUPTION). Seasonal incursions of crossbills and the birds' fascinating feeding adaptation have long been observed. The English diarist R. Carew wrote in 1607: "... there came a flocke of birds into Cornwall, about Harvest season, in bignesse not much exceeding a sparrow, which made a foule spoyle of the apples. Their bills were thwarted crosswise at the end, and with these they would cut an apple in two at one snap, eating onely the kernels."

Both of our native crossbills have circumboreal distributions. The White-winged breeds well beyond the Arctic Circle, but does not generally range south of northern forests except in irruption years (though there is a recent summer record for the mountains of New Mexico and a disjunct, non-migratory population in Hispaniola). The Red does not nest so far north, but ranges south in the mountains until the pines run out in the Nicaraguan highlands.

For general family characteristics, see FINCH. See also Griscom's monograph on the Red Crossbill, *Proc. Boston Soc. Nat. Hist.*, 41:77–210.

CROW. Standard English name for about 30 members of the family Corvidae (order Passeriformes). Also used in a broader collective sense to refer to the approximately 36 species of the genus *Corvus*, including the jackdaws, rooks, and ravens as well as the crows, and to refer to the family as a whole, including the jays, magpies, tree pies, choughs, and nutcrackers as well as the above-named forms. Including the two ravens, 5 species of crows breed in North America, and a sixth, Mexican Crow, is a regular visitor in numbers from south of the border.

The *Corvus* crows are among the largest songbirds, ranging in length from the comparatively diminutive Jackdaw (13 inches) to the Common Raven, which, excepting species with inordinately long tail feathers (e.g., the lyrebirds), can fairly claim to be the largest passerine bird in the world. All crows are husky birds, with stout (sometimes massive) bills; powerful, broad wings; sturdy legs and feet well adapted to walking; and short to moderately long tails. The plumage of most species of crows is entirely glossy black, but several have broad areas of gray feathering, one has extensive white on the nape and breast, and brown and iridescent blue overtones are not uncommon.

Crows are virtually omnivorous except for green plants. Insects, crustaceans, shellfish, small vertebrates of all kinds (including nestling birds), eggs, carrion (including dead fish), garbage, fruit and grain are all staple items of the crow diet. They tend to gather in large foraging flocks sometimes containing hundreds of individuals. Several crows soar freely and engage in playful aerobatics.

Many crow species nest in colonies. They make large, bulky stick cups in trees and shrubs, on rock ledges (Common Raven) and abandoned buildings. Most species plaster the cup with mud and/or dung and then provide an inner lining of bark strips and other fine plant material, wool, hair, etc. The 3–8 eggs (average 4–5 in most species) are pale or moderately dark green or blue (rarely white), sparsely to very densely speckled and splotched with olive and dark brown.

Crow calls are notably harsh and guttural for songbirds, but individual species tend to have a fairly wide repertoire of calls. Crows in captivity have proven themselves to be excellent vocal mimics of the human voice and other sounds (see SONG) but rarely exhibit this talent in the wild. The combination of their abundance and fondness for grain earns crows little love among farmers (see PESTS), and they are also traditional targets for sport shooting in many parts of the world.

To the extent that the term can be applied to any bird, the crows have a reputation for being "smart" (see INTELLIGENCE). There are many elaborate hunting tales recounting the cleverness of crows in avoiding decoys and recognizing the hunter's intent. And these casual observations are supported by experimenters who have found that crows are able to learn "tricks" based on reinforcement more quickly and easily than birds from other families. Some taxonomists believe the crows to be the most highly evolved of all bird families. Their cleverness and "personality," in combination with their blackness, have made crows almost as ubiquitous as owls in folklore and superstition (see IMAGINATION).

Crows show broad habitat tolerances and are widely distributed, though they are absent in South America, New Zealand, and many oceanic islands. The American (Common) Crow and Common Raven range continentwide in North America; our other species are much more local. The northern populations of American Crow are migratory; otherwise crows are relatively sedentary.

"Crow" comes straight from the call, though as Choate (1973–BIOGRAPHY) points out, "crowing" suggests more the sound of a rooster than a crow these days.

See also JAY; MAGPIE; NUTCRACKER.

CROWN. The top of the head, technically including the area above the eye between the forehead (front) and the nape. See Fig. 1.

CRUS (rhymes with "bus") (pl.: crura [KROOR-uh]). The part of the leg between the knee and the ankle. On a bird, the section above the "tarsus," called the "drumstick" on table birds. See LEG/FOOT.

CRYPTIC. In reference to birds usually refers to plumage pattern and coloration which conceal a species from predators. See COLOR AND PATTERN and Plate 3; see also PROCRYPTIC; ANTICRYPTIC; PHANERIC.

CRYPTIC SPECIES. Synonymous with SIBLING SPECIES.

CUCKOO. Standard English name for about 75 members of the family Cuculidae (order Cuculiformes); also includes the ANIS and ROADRUNNERS. Three species of cuckoos breed in North America and 2 others have occurred as accidental stragglers (see Appendix II).

Cuckoos are slender birds with long tails and relatively long, slender bills. They exhibit great variations in form and color worldwide but all of the North American species measure about a foot in length, are brown above, paler below, and have colored fleshy eye rings and some form of spotting on the tips of the outer tail feathers. The feet of cuckoos have two toes (I and IV) pointing to rearward while the other two point forward (zygodactyl).

Our cuckoos are rather skulking in habits and therefore are not often seen by the casual observer. Their favorite food is hairy moth larvae such as those of the pestilent gypsy moths, tent caterpillars, and webworms, but they also eat other insects, spiders, small vertebrates, and fruit. The cuckoos are among the most solitary of birds, never flocking with members of their own or other species.

The American cuckoos do lay their eggs in the nests of other birds, but only occasionally rather than habitually as do some of their Old World relatives (see BROOD PARASITISM). Their own nests are loose stick platforms or shallow cups lined with finer plant material and placed in low trees and shrubs. The 1–5 (usually 2–3) eggs are unmarked, light blue to green with a dull finish.

Our cuckoos make a series of low, unmusical, rather "woody" clucks (Yellow-billed and Mangrove) or a softer, shorter (3–4 notes) hooting or cooing (Black-billed). It is only the Common Cuckoo of Eurasia that "says" *CUCK-oo* and inhabits clocks.

Cuckoos are distributed almost worldwide (absent from arctic tundra) but reach their greatest diversity in the tropics. The single North American genus (*Coccyzus*) is restricted to the New World. Two of our species are long-distance migrants that winter in the tropics, and the third is a local permanent resident in southern Florida, where its preferred habitat is mangroves.

For origin of name, see under voice, above.

CULMEN. The ridge of the upper mandible from base to tip. See Fig. 25.

CURLEW (KERR-loo or KERR-lyoo). Standard English name for all but one of 8 species of large, long-billed sandpipers in the genus *Numenius* (family Scolopacidae; order Charadriiformes). The exceptional curlew is the WHIMBREL (*N. phaeopus*).

Including the Whimbrel, 4 species of curlews breed in North

America, though one, the Eskimo Curlew, may now be extinct due to overshooting in the last century (see ENDANGERED BIRDS). Three other species have occurred here as accidental stragglers (see Appendix II). All curlews have brownish plumage, varying in tone and marked with streaks and spots, and all have long (female Long-billed to 8¾ inches) decurved bills that they use for probing in mud or soil. Some curlews prefer upland habitats, including cultivated fields, while others prefer coastal dunes, marshes, and flats. They eat small organisms (insects, crabs, etc.) which they pick up from the surface of the ground, as well as subterranean fare which requires probing; in the Arctic they also feed on fruits, e.g., curlew-berry (*Empetrum nigrum*).

Curlews breed throughout the Holarctic region (mainly in the Arctic) and migrate over or winter in most of the rest of the world.

"Curlew" echoes the splendid plaintive fluting of these birds—a sound that has inspired more than one poet.

For family characteristics, see SANDPIPER.

CURSORIAL. Adapted for walking or running; particularly of species in which this is the preferred form of locomotion. Ostriches are quintessentially cursorial, having no other choice; in North America, the Roadrunner and Wild Turkey fit the definition.

CYGNET (SIG-net). The young of any species of swan, applied to birds in immature plumage as well as downy chicks; a diminutive form of *cygnus*, the Latin word for "swan."

D

DABBLING DUCK. Collective name for the "surface-feeding" ducks in the subfamily Anatinae or the tribe Anatini, including the teal, pintails, shovelers, wigeons, and Mallard. All are primarily freshwater ducks that feed from the surface of the water by "dabbling" with their flattened, lamellate bills after bits of vegetation and aquatic invertebrates. See also DUCK.

DAMAGE (caused by birds). See PESTS.

DARTER. Standard English name—except in North America—for members of the family Anhingidae, which are here called anhingas. The single American species, *Anhinga anhinga*, the Anhinga, has (by the perversely stubborn) been called the American Darter. The name refers to the fast fish-spearing motion of neck and bill. See ANHINGA.

DDT (dichlorodiphenyltrichloroethane). A "miracle" insecticide formerly widely used in North America and eventually proven to have disastrous effects on the reproductive capability of large raptors (especially fish-eaters) and other organisms including humans. It was banned in the U.S. in 1972 but is still being sold and used elsewhere, especially in "underdeveloped" nations. For more detail on its effects, see MAN-MADE THREATS TO BIRD-LIFE, *Pesticides.*

DECOY. Originally (sixteenth-century Holland) a trapping method by which wild ducks were encouraged to "mob" a trained dog which would lead them into a trap. Later the same term was applied to tame ducks which lured their kind to within gunshot range. Today in North America, usually applied to wooden, composition, or plastic replicas of waterfowl (also crows, pigeons, and shorebirds) which are placed close to where shooters wait in concealment. An imitative call may be used to enhance the effect (see BIRD CALLS). Old painted wooden decoys have become valuable items of folk art, collected at considerable expense.

DEFECATION. See DIGESTIVE SYSTEM; EXCRETORY SYSTEM; GUANO; BIRDLIME; EXCREMENT.

DEFINITIVE (plumage). A plumage which has ceased to change with age, though it continues to change seasonally according to a consistent sequence. See MOLT, *Sequence and Terminology.*

DEGLAND, Dr. Côme Damien, 1787–1856 (*Melanitta deglandi:* White-winged Scoter). French author of *Ornithologie Européene* (1849), which was "panned" by Bonaparte and other ornithologists of the day. He also ran a natural history museum in Lille. The White-winged Scoter is now lumped by most authorities with the so-called Velvet Scoter (*M. fusca*) of Eurasia and Dr. Degland's name now signifies only a subspecies, *M. f. deglandi.*

DELAWARE VALLEY ORNITHOLOGICAL CLUB (D.V.O.C.). One of the most venerable of North American bird clubs (founded in 1890), the D.V.O.C. meets at the Philadelphia Academy of Natural Sciences. It publishes a newsletter and an annual scientific journal, *Cassinia,* and offers both local and international field trips.

DELTA MARSHES (Manitoba). An impressive expanse of prairie marshland filled with associated birdlife at the mouth of the Assiniboine River, where it empties into Lake Winnipeg, northeast of the city of Winnipeg. The Delta Research Station is located here and has produced an extensive literature on prairie waterfowl. See, for example, *Life in a Prairie*

Marsh and other titles by A. H. Hochbaum. Among local breeding birds of the marshes and nearby lakeshore and prairies of interest to birders are: Western, Red-necked, and Horned Grebes, Canvasback, Redhead, Lesser Scaup, Avocet, Willet, Upland Sandpiper, Marbled Godwit, Wilson's Phalarope, Franklin's Gull, Burrowing Owl, Sprague's Pipit, Western Meadowlark, Yellow-headed Blackbird, Le Conte's and Clay-colored Sparrows, and Chestnut-collared Longspur.

DERTRUM. The tip of the upper mandible.

DESERT. Broadly defined, deserts are places of excessive heat (during daylight hours) and extreme dryness in which plant and animal species are relatively few and often markedly adapted to the harsh conditions of their habitat. Based on relatively predictable biological (especially vegetational) differences that coincide with differences in moisture levels, deserts have been more specifically defined as regions that receive 10 inches (250 mm.) or less of rain per year (arid), and some authorities extend the category to include areas that receive as much as 20 inches (500 mm.) of rain annually (semi-arid). Frequency of rainfall, evaporation rate, cloud cover, dew level, and other climatic factors apart from the amount of annual rain also mitigate extreme aridity in some localities.

Deserts cover approximately one fifth of the earth's land surface and are concentrated mainly in the subtropical zone. In some places they are extending themselves due to overgrazing, the destruction of moisture-retaining vegetation (forests, etc.), and possibly a fluctuation in the atmosphere of the planet.

Though the popular image of a desert includes a strong element of pale sand dunes, deserts in reality take a great variety of forms—flat or rugged topography; rocky or sandy texture; and black, red, or varicolored in hue. This diversity is reflected in the fact that the vocabularies of Bedouins and other desert dwellers contain many words referring to different desert types, just as Innuit peoples have terms for all the different kinds of snow and ice conditions.

The North American desert is largely confined to the southwestern quarter of the continent. It is sometimes known as a whole as the Sonoran Desert or divided into major subregions, viz.: Chihuahuan, Sonoran, Arizona, Mojave, and Great Basin deserts, all of which also have distinctive subdivisions.

As noted, desert animals (as well as plants) tend to be specialized to suit their extreme environment. Among the most notable characteristics of desert birds worldwide are marked adaptive coloration that blends cryptically with the local soil tones (arguably a protective adaptation in response to the desert's general scarcity of cover in which to escape predators) and some form of modification that enhances conservation of body moisture.

Because North American desert birds seem to have few obvious adaptive features of the latter kind and also on the basis of certain botanical elements, our deserts are thought by some authorities to be relatively "young" as compared with Old World deserts.

Udvardy (1958–DISTRIBUTION) identifies 29 North American species as desert birds, of which 22 represent monotypic genera, and this taxonomic distinction is another characteristic of desert birds worldwide. Of course, many broadly adapted bird species (e.g., Turkey Vulture) occur in arid habitats in addition to those that are restricted to them. Among our best-known dry-country birds are: White-tailed Hawk, Inca Dove, Greater Roadrunner, Elf Owl, Costa's Hummingbird, Gila Woodpecker, Vermilion Flycatcher, Verdin, Cactus Wren, Le Conte's Thrasher, Phainopepla, Gray Vireo, Lucy's Warbler, Pyrrhuloxia, Varied Bunting, Black-throated and Rufous-winged Sparrows, and White-necked Raven. This last species exemplifies another—apparently anomalous—characteristic of many desert animals: blackness. Examined superficially, heat-absorptive black would seem to be the worst possible coloration for animals exposed to hours of scorching sunshine (see GLOGER'S RULE). But studies have confirmed that the solar energy accumulated most efficiently by black plumage may balance the high energy expenditure required to maintain adequate body temperature during the characteristically frigid desert night and fuel foraging activity in the still-cold desert morning. Black species can easily seek shade and remain inactive in the intense heat of midday when their color might otherwise work to their disadvantage. That desert "black birds" usually are not species that are vulnerable to large predators is consistent with the fact that they tend to be highly conspicuous against desert landscapes. For a comprehensive discussion, see Serventy (in Farner et al., 1971–75, Vol.1–ORNITHOLOGY).

See TEMPERATURE, BODY; COLOR AND PATTERN. See also BIOME; DISTRIBUTION; and Fig. 5.

DETERMINATION. In comparative biology, a judgment about the identity of a given form. In the case of poorly defined subspecies of birds, for example, a taxonomist may compare a specimen with hundreds of others in a museum collection, as well as consider factors such as locality and date of collection, in order to properly "determine" its identity—to make an accurate "determination."

DIAL-A-BIRD. See RARE BIRD ALERT; VOICE OF AUDUBON.

DIATRYMA (dye-uh-TRY-muh). A fossil genus of huge flightless long-legged birds with massive skulls and bills. Four species have been described from skeletal remains from the Paleocene and Eocene epochs. A species which lived in what is now Wyoming (*D. steini*) stood over seven feet tall.

DÍAZ (DEE-az), Augustín, 1829–93 (*Anas diazi*: Mexican Duck). A Mexican soldier, engineer, geographer, and teacher who served prominently on the commission to establish the U.S.-Mexican boundary and who made an early geographical map of Mexico for his government. The Mexican Duck, sometimes considered a race of a variable species including the Mallard, Black Duck, and Mottled Duck, was named for Díaz by Robert RIDGWAY.

DICKCISSEL (DIK-siss-ul or dik-SISS-ul). Standard English name for a single species of finch, *Spiza americana* (family Fringillidae, Emberizidae, or perhaps Icteridae; see Raikow, *Bull. Carnegie Mus. Nat. Hist.* no. 7, 1978). It is an open-country species which breeds exclusively in North America and winters in South and Central America, where it is sometimes encountered in flocks of thousands. Its breeding distribution in North America fluctuates significantly (see NOMADISM).

The name is a fairly close approximation of its song. See FINCH.

DIGESTIVE SYSTEM. The digestive apparatus, by which food is broken down into fuel for all bodily functions, is basically a flexible tube running from the mouth to the vent; it is enclosed and protected along most of its length by the sternum and rib cage (see SKELETON). The tube is enlarged and modified in several places to facilitate stages of the breakdown process. These modifications vary according to the eating habits of different species.

The breakdown of food is accomplished by both chemical and mechanical processes, and the raw material and wastes are pushed through the system by rhythmic, wave-like contractions of the muscles in the walls of the tube. All of the above is true of both birds and men. The differences between the avian and human digestive systems lie chiefly in the equipment which each has evolved to accomplish similar goals.

The first major step in human digestion takes place in the mouth, where solid food is tasted, chewed into small pieces, moistened with saliva, and passed through the gullet (esophagus) to the stomach. Lacking teeth and with comparatively little sense of taste, birds tend to swallow their food whole or, in the case of seed-eating birds, after crushing with a heavy bill. Salivary glands are present in most birds but are reduced in number or totally lacking in many water birds, whose food is premoistened.

The Esophagus of a bird, rather than being simply a connecting passage to the stomach, as in humans, may also be used for temporary storage of food. In most species the gullet simply expands as it becomes full, but in some cases there is a permanent enlargement in this part of the digestive tract. In gallinaceous birds, doves, and parrots, this has developed into a distinctive, pouch-like appendage, the crop, or ingluvies. This allows birds to "gorge" when and where food is plentiful, or gobble a meal or two quickly in vulnerable situations, and digest later at leisure. It is also a handy means of carrying fresh food back to the nest to be regurgitated for young birds.

The Stomach, a single pouch in man, is divided into two sections in birds. In the first, the proventriculus, the same digestive juices which act in the human stomach (principally the enzyme pepsin in combination with hydrochloric acid) are secreted and the whole passes on to the second, large stomach—the ventriculus or gizzard. In birds which prefer soft foods, this organ is not very different from the proventriculus in function. But in birds which feed on solid substances such as seeds, the tough, hard muscular walls of the gizzard, aided by swallowed sand and gravel, serve a function similar to that of human teeth (see GRIT). Fur, bones, fish scales, and other substances which the gizzard cannot properly pulverize are separated out at this point in the digestive process to be regurgitated in a compact mass (see PELLET) and the now more or less liquefied remainder, called chyme, enters the small intestine.

The Intestines, small and large, of both birds and humans are responsible for the final stage of transforming food into usable fuel and releasing it to the rest of the body. In birds, this happens mainly in the small intestine, where bile from the liver and enzymes from the pancreas are added to the chyme, which is thereby transformed into proteins, fats, and carbohydrates. These are absorbed through the intestinal walls into the bloodstream, leaving little but water, to be absorbed from the relatively short large intestine, and waste products, to be expelled through the vent (see EXCRETORY SYSTEM).

In some species of birds which feed principally on vegetation (e.g., ptarmigan), the small intestine is larger than usual in order to accommodate the great quantity of material which must be digested to supply sufficient energy. These and other vegetarians usually have well-developed caeca (sing.: caecum), narrow sacs which open where the small intestine meets the large. These hold concentrations of bacteria and secrete additional enzymes needed to break down plant tissue.

See also FOOD/FEEDING.

DIMORPHISM (dye-MORF-ism). Literally, the occurrence of two distinct forms or "morphs." Many species of birds are "sexually dimorphic," i.e., the males and females differ strikingly in plumage and/or mensural characteristics (e.g., the pair of Vermilion Flycatchers in Plate 4). Seasonal dimorphism is also common, as exemplified by the summer and winter plumages of the Black Guillemot, also shown in Plate 4. Compare POLYMORPHISM; see PLUMAGE; COLOR AND PATTERN. See also the Bibliography.

DIPPER. Standard English name for all 4 or 5 (depending on taxonomy) members of the family Cinclidae (order Passeriformes), one of which breeds in North America.

Dippers superficially resemble large (average 6 inches), stocky wrens, with their compact form, short wings, and frequently "cocked-up" tail. Closer inspection, however, reveals a slightly hooked bill which is laterally flattened; an unusually thick feather coat and underlying down; somewhat pointed wings; and rather large, strong feet with short, stout claws. All dippers are brown or gray, some with patches of white. Most of these features are adaptations to the dippers' unique life style. They are quintessentially birds of fast-water streams and rivers and make their living swimming and walking underwater on the stream bed, picking aquatic insect larvae, snails, small fish, and the like from among the submerged rocky crannies. They can dive to a depth of at least 20 feet. Periodically they rise to the surface, float buoyantly to a nearby rock, and preen their feathers, all the while bobbing in a characteristic abrupt "curtsy" quite different from the "teetering" of the Spotted Sandpiper and waterthrushes. Dipper songs are also wren-like, i.e., "bubbly" and loud (audible above the splash of rushing water); they also make a variety of loud calls.

Dippers build domed nests of moss and other plant material, lined with dead leaves, with the entrance hole "aimed" toward the water. These may be tucked in streamside crevices, under a waterfall, or placed on a large rock in the midst of the torrent. The 3–6 (usually 4–5) eggs are glossy white and unmarked.

Dippers occur throughout much of the Holarctic, though in most cases they are restricted to mountainous regions with permanent streams; they also range throughout the Neotropical highlands. The American Dipper occurs in our western mountains from arctic Alaska through Central America.

DISEASE. Birds are beset by a wide variety of health problems, brought on by equally diverse causes. Malnutrition, vitamin deficiency, accidental injury, poison, extreme weather conditions, internal and external parasites—alone or in combination—can bring on death or weaken the constitution, making a bird's system more vulnerable to disease. Many of these causal factors are discussed under separate headings (see, for example, WEATHER; ENDOPARASITE; ECTOPARASITE; MAN-MADE THREATS TO BIRDLIFE). The present entry is confined to a summary of common illnesses of birds which result from infections of microorganisms such as bacteria and viruses.

Though the immediate reaction to disease in any context tends to be a negative one, we should remember that it plays an important role in the complex business of population balance. Like predation, disease tends to cull weak individuals, such as those with genetic malformations, from the breeding population, ensuring that such disadvantages aren't passed along to future generations. It also helps ensure that no one organism becomes "too successful"; a plague of chickadees, after all, would be no more desirable than the bacterial kind.

Much of what we know about sickness in wild birds is a result of the study of diseases of poultry, pets, or other domestic or captive birds. However, in many cases the conditions under which such birds live (e.g., indoors, in great density, and/or with artificial food sources) produce health problems that are rare among free-living birds, and these are omitted here.

. Bacteria are an extremely important, vastly diverse group of microorganisms, similar in some ways to the fungi, but sometimes placed in a kingdom of their own between the plants and the animals. They are crucial to such beneficial processes as soil formation, sewage decomposition, and plant growth, as well as being the source of many important diseases in both plants and animals. The following diseases frequently afflict wild birds:

BACTERIAL DISEASES

Tuberculosis. The microorganism *Mycobacterium avium* is frequently taken into birds' systems with their food and the bacilli are spread very effectively by excretion in the feces. Gallinaceous birds and raptors seem to be particularly susceptible, but the disease is far more prevalent among domestic birds than wild ones. The organism spreads through the lymph and blood systems, forming tissue-destroying tubercles in intestines, liver, spleen, and other organs, often causing fever, emaciation, weakness, and death.

Erysipelas. The bacterium *Erysipelothrix rhusopathiae* commonly affects young domestic pigs and other vertebrates as well as birds. It causes disease of the skin and subcutaneous tissue which results in fever and red blotches on the body. The organism lives in the soil and probably infects through open wounds.

Salmonellosis. Several of the many species of *Salmonella* bacterium are eaten in birds' food and spread through the diarrheal symptoms which develop. Liver, spleen, and lung disease and death may result or the disease may persist at a low level over a long period. Since it is ingested from droppings of other birds, heavily patronized feeding operations—especially ground-feeding areas—may become abnormally infected if not cleaned regularly. This is the same organism which causes many cases of "food poisoning" and diarrhea in humans.

Botulism (Western Duck Sickness). The *Clostridium botulinum* bacterium causes another kind of "food poisoning" but is much more virulent and has a much more disastrous effect on bird populations than *Salmonella.* It thrives best in warm, stagnant, alkaline waters where large amounts of decaying vegetable or (especially) animal matter are present. Wildfowl are therefore particularly susceptible, especially during the summer, but it has been diagnosed in many other kinds of birds. As in humans, it causes violent and usually fatal symptoms and has occurred in a number of famous outbreaks in western North America in which millions of ducks and other water birds perished.

Ornithosis and Psittacosis. Until recently these ailments were thought to be caused by two large viruses in the genus *Miyagawanella*. They are now known to be forms of a bacterial disease, chlamydiosis (from the genus of the infecting organism, *Chlamydia*). Though responsible for fatal epidemics among a wide variety of bird species, external and even internal symptoms are often lacking or inconspicuous. Eventually, victims may show runny eyes and nose, lethargy, and bloody diarrhea. The disease is characteristically transmitted by inhalation of infected particles in breath, by ingestion of infected excretion, and by ectoparasites; it is known to be often contracted in the nest. Pigeons, chickens, and a variety of cage birds are frequently cited hosts of the ornithosis form of the infection, and the psittacosis form is, as its name implies, restricted to members of the parrot family. See below for symptoms in humans.

Chlamydiosis. See above.

VIRAL DISEASES. Viruses are submicroscopic agents of disease in plants and animals which can survive only within the particular tissue they infect. Defining viruses—even to the extent of deciding whether they are living or non-living—in order to control them is a chief aim of medical science and the investigation is still in its infancy. The following viral diseases are common among birds:

Fowl Pox (Avian or Bird Pox). Infects only birds and these non-fatally, producing warts on head and feet.

Encephalitis. A general term for inflammation of the brain which can be caused by a variety of factors. Several viral forms are known in birds. Perhaps the most significant of these is equine encephalomyelitis, which is transmitted by mosquitoes and other blood-feeding organisms. For implications for humans, see below.

Dermatitis. Blistering on the feet of a number of species of colonial seabirds is caused by several viruses which are transmitted from foot to ground to foot.

Newcastle Disease. A highly contagious major killer of domestic fowl, much less apparent in wild birds (occasional cases in waterfowl); however, the causal virus (NDV) has been found to occur, apparently benignly, in a wide variety of wild species.

Duck Plague. Known mainly from northern Europe until 1969, when diagnosed in domestic ducks in northeastern U.S. A major outbreak occurred in North Dakota in the winter of 1972–73, killing over 40,000 ducks and geese within a few weeks. Restricted to members of the Anatidae; survivors apparently retain an immunity (Leibovitz, 1971).

OTHER DISEASES. Common bird diseases which are neither bacterial nor viral in origin are:

Aspergillosus. Transmitted by a fungus (*Aspergilla fumigatus*) which occurs as a mold on decaying plant material. Birds eat or inhale the spores, which destroy tissue in the respiratory system and many other parts of the body. The disease is known from many species of birds and occasionally occurs in large epidemics with heavy mortalities, particularly among waterfowl and gallinaceous species. It has been suggested that fruit or other vegetable matter left to rot in bird feeders could be a source of aspergillosis—one of many good reasons to keep feeders clean. For implications for humans, see below.

Colds (Coryza). Birds, like humans, are subject to the common cold, an inscrutable disease which can be caused by a variety of infections, including viruses. Its symptoms in birds (inflammation of the respiratory membranes with discharge of mucus, fever, and chills), the conditions under which it is contracted (cold/wet weather, close contact with other individuals, inhalation of infected mucus particles), and its course (usually short-lived, rarely becoming a more serious respiratory infection) will all be familiar to the reader.

BIRD DISEASES AFFECTING PEOPLE. Man is susceptible to all of the "bird diseases" described above, but the risk of catching something from birds is very small in any case and practically nonexistent unless you are in close and prolonged contact with birds or places where they nest. Considering the number of potential disease vectors which are destroyed by insect-eating birds and the amounts of carrion and organic waste matter which is neutralized by various avian scavengers, there can be little doubt that on balance birds are a net benefit to human health. However, there are instances in which birds can transmit disease to humans and these are worth noting.

Ornithosis/Psittacosis (Chlamydiosis). Not uncommon among people who handle a lot of birds, e.g., poultry farmers, aviculturists, and bird banders. It produces a type of viral pneumonia in man which, though potentially fatal, is effectively treated with antibacterial drugs such as tetracycline.

Histoplasmosis. Contracted by inhaling spores from a fungus (*Histoplasma capsulatum*) which grows on bird droppings. Therefore, bird colonies, poultry yards, and (especially) enclosed spaces where droppings collect are likely infection sites. Symptoms include enlargement of the liver and spleen, fever, and anemia; however, 95 percent of people who are exposed develop an immunity without suffering any symptoms.

Encephalitis. Birds are known carriers of equine encephalomyelitis (to which most individuals become immune), and migrating species might theoretically transport the South American strains of the disease to North America. Transmitting encephalomyelitis from a bird to a human also requires a horse (where the virus originates) and at least two blood-feeding vectors such as a mosquito or tick—one to infect the bird (from the horse or other carrier) and another to infect the human from the bird. The importance of the bird's role in this complex transaction is being studied; however, inoculating the horses, rather than attacking either birds or mosquitoes, will probably continue to be the best means of preventing human cases of equine encephalomyelitis.

DISJUNCT. In reference to distribution or range, discontinuous; existing in widely separated populations. The Sandhill Crane, for example, has a disjunct distribution in North America with unconnected breeding populations in arctic Canada and Alaska, north-central and western U.S., and Florida; the cosmopolitan range of the Gull-billed Tern is made up of a series of disjunct populations. See DISTRIBUTION.

DISPERSAL. In an ornithological context, used in a potentially confusing variety of ways, all having to do with the movement of birds. Perhaps the most orthodox usage is that describing the characteristic wanderings of young birds in all directions from their nest sites and the tendency of young birds to "disperse" more widely than their elders after the breeding season, thus ensuring the distributional "dispersal" of the species (see MIGRATION; DISTRIBUTION). Some other uses of the term which appear in the literature are: (1) The irregular "dispersals" or IRRUPTIONS of northern species of raptors and "winter finches" in large numbers to areas south of their normal wintering range. (2) The gradual "dispersal" or invasion of certain "southern" species—e.g., Northern Cardinal, Tufted Titmouse, Northern Mockingbird, various species of herons—into regions north of their previous breeding ranges. (3) The "dispersal" of vagrant birds by severe weather conditions, e.g., hurricanes, out of their normal range; by this means tropical seabirds and migrant land birds are regularly carried far out of their normal range to boreal shores temporarily and in a few cases such "dispersals" have resulted in range expansions, as in several species blown to Greenland from Europe by easterly gales. (4) The "dispersal" of a population of birds over a given area or habitat: "Most of the rookery dispersed over the salt marsh and mud flats within a three-mile radius to feed after 6 a.m." Not to be confused with DISPERSION.

DISPERSION. A spatial concept describing the density and configuration of birdlife in a given area or habitat. The "dispersion" of feeding shorebirds—i.e., how closely they associate with one another in a marsh or on a mud flat—may depend upon the density of the food source and also be governed by certain behavioral or "psychological" factors (see FLOCK and V. C. Wynne-Edwards, *Animal Dispersion in Relation to Social Behaviour* [London, 1962]). Not to be confused with DISPERSAL.

DISPLACEMENT ACTIVITY. Birds respond in an innately prescribed way to certain signals ("releasers"; see INTELLIGENCE). When two conflicting signals are received—e.g., the presence of a perched owl in daytime which provokes both fear (flee) and aggression (attack)—birds may respond to the ambiguity by doing something totally irrelevant, such as feeding or preening. These "inappropriate" gestures are called "displacement activities." See Fig. 14.

DISPLAY. See Plate 2. In the broadest sense, any innate, stylized visual signal made by a bird the function of which is to trigger or "release" appropriate behavior in the intended object of the signal. Under this definition, the gaping or pecking motions of juvenile birds can be called "begging display." The most conspicuous examples of bird display are complex, prolonged rituals in a sexual or defensive context. These frequently involve the actual "display" of some prominent plumage or other characteristic, but the gestures involved often give no hint of the intended outcome—at least to the human witness.

All birds engage in some form of display, though there is much variation both in size of repertoire and in intricacy of ritual. Certain kinds of "choreography" may be characteristic of particular families of birds, e.g., the bowing and leaping courtship dances performed by members of the crane family. But each species has its stereotyped variation which in turn may be modified slightly by individual birds.

ORIGINS. Some courtship displays are so theatrical and exuberant that it is tempting to interpret them as spontaneous expressions of sexual energy or even imaginative ballets inspired by avian affection. In reality, many displays seem to have evolved out of half-realized movements made by birds in ambivalent situations. In forming pair bonds, for example, birds are normally torn between attraction to a potential mate and aggression toward a potential rival, especially in cases in which the plumages of male and female are alike. Within the aggressive impulse is yet another ambivalence, namely, whether to stay and fight or to flee. Viewed as a series of discrete gestures, courtship dances can often be seen to consist of recognizable expressions of all these motivations, as well as apparently irrelevant gestures such as presenting nesting material or preening—displacement activities which over time have become integrated into the courtship ceremony. Likewise, so-called distraction displays are amalgams of protective and escape movements though they have come to function as distractions to nest predators.

INTERSEXUAL DISPLAY. The reproductive cycle, which necessitates frequent and varied interactions between two or more birds, is the richest source of specialized displays.

Function. Courtship displays performed by males alone serve not only to identify the displaying species and attract the attention of unmated females but also as "no trespassing" signs to other males. As the mating ritual proceeds, the genetically prescribed movements, usually accompanied by appropriate sounds, dissipate aggressive urges, thus permitting the successful completion of the many details of reproduction—copulation, nest building, feeding of young, etc.—which mated birds do *together*. In many cases, each of these is accompanied by its own specialized ritual—pre-copulatory display, post-copulatory display, food-bringing display, incubation-relief display—which, in effect, are simple operating instructions, allowing birds to fulfill their biological roles with a comparatively rudimentary mental capacity. "Displays of affection" such as mutual preening and "billing" may lack the emotional depth imputed to them by some humans, but they do serve to maintain pair bonds during the breeding season and in some species for life.

Sexual Roles. Many water-bird species in which the sexes look alike—e.g., loons, grebes, tubenoses, pelecaniforms, gulls and terns—perform courtship displays in which the sexes are equally active. Such pairs may perform in tandem, like the Western Grebes "racing" in Plate 2; or face each other in a mirror-image tableau, as in the gannets' "greeting" ceremony; or take different parts in a more or less fixed ritual and periodically change roles, as in the "dance" of the Black-footed Albatross.

The displays of most ducks, shorebirds, hummingbirds, and passerines, by contrast, are dominated by the male. While he engages in some form of plumage display accompanied by song and/or movements (sometimes including aerial maneuvers), the female remains composed: sometimes appearing completely indifferent or even impatient, sometimes expressing her reaction with displacement activities such as feeding or preening, and sometimes responding with ritualized gestures of submission alternating with solicitation.

Among North American grouse species (excluding the ptarmigan) and a few species of shorebirds, females are excluded altogether from courtship display—except, of course, for the finale of copulation. Cock Ruffed, Spruce, and Blue Grouse perform in pristine isolation from carefully chosen perches or openings in the forest; the sounds accompanying these rituals carry well through the dense vegetation to be heard by other displaying males. Males of Sage and Sharp-tailed Grouse, the prairie chickens, and a few species of shorebirds (most famously the Ruff) gather in the spring to "dance" *together* in communal "arenas" or "leks." As with the other grouse, the females play no part in the display itself (though they do visit the display area to be fertilized by the one or two cocks that emerge as dominant) and the nest sites are chosen outside the "stage" area.

Forms of Courtship Display. The often bizarre and elaborate antics of birds engaged in sexual display are among the most fascinating and entertaining aspects of birdlife. The diversity of courtship rituals in any avifauna is always as great as the number of species it contains—more so, in fact, since many species have several acts in their repertoire. Virtually every avian attribute and external anatomical feature—plumage, bill, legs, eyes, flight, voice—is active in one ritual or another, and not a few adaptations apparently function solely in display. Many "breeding" or "nuptial" (alternate) plumages are in prime condition only long enough to secure a territory and attract a female. In addition to more colorful or contrasting contour feathers, the display "costume" may include decorative features which irresistibly suggest makeup, jewelry, and fancy clothes to human observers. Egrets, for example, acquire exquisite back plumes; many alcids, like the Tufted Puffin in Plate 2, develop facial tufts and colorful bill sheaths. The roseate bloom on the breasts of some species of gulls and terns may be applied as "rouge" provided by the oil gland only during the breeding season; and the color of so-called soft parts—bills, legs, fleshy eye rings, and facial skin—intensifies greatly in a wide range of species, though sometimes very briefly during courtship. Other features—the colored air sacs of frigatebirds and some grouse, the brilliant crown tufts of the Ruby-crowned Kinglet, the epaulets of Red-winged and Tricolored Blackbirds—are present year-round but are revealed to full effect only in the ardor of sexual display (or the ire inspired by territorial transgression). Finally, much of any species' repertoire of songs, calls, mechanical sounds, and physical agility is reserved for performance during courtship.

Not all birds engage in extravagant displays. The most brilliantly colored passerine species (e.g., wood warblers, tanagers, orioles) find it sufficient simply to erect their most exciting feathers and dance a modest (though characteristic) jig accompanied by appropriate sound effects. And of course many species, e.g., wrens, many flycatchers and sparrows, haven't a bright feather on their bodies, yet manage to court successfully on the basis of subtle plumage patterns in combination with song and gesture.

At the other extreme are courtship rites which are impossible to ignore. These frequently involve stylized movements which birds use in no other context (see above for origins) and in some cases are so unusual that the human observer is overcome with awe or with laughter. The most distinctive rituals are categorized below; almost all are accompanied by some vocal and/or mechanical sound.

FLIGHT DISPLAYS

Soaring: Anhingas and the Roseate Spoonbill soar en masse over their colonies; many hawks and eagles do so over territory during the mate-attracting phase of the breeding cycle.

"Volplaning"—i.e., gliding down from a height with wings held motionless, outstretched: Loons, especially the Red-throated, volplane over territory with wings held stiffly upward, calling as they descend; pairs of Chimney Swifts perform a similar, if more buoyant version of this activity. Red-billed Tropicbird pairs volplane one above the other with the upper bird's wings held down, lower bird's up, so that they almost touch; some sandpipers volplane down from song flights and anhingas do so from com-

munal soaring flights. Perhaps the most readily seen volplaning display is that of the Mourning Dove, which performs over a long breeding season and occurs continentwide.

"Butterflying": Most North American plovers incorporate a very distinctive, slow, shallow wingbeat in their flight displays, as do male Vermilion Flycatchers and American Goldfinches.

Hovering: Replaces a tall singing perch for many open-country species, e.g., Bobolink, larks, pipits, longspurs, tundra-breeding shorebirds. Singer may hover hundreds of feet in the air.

Plummeting: The American Woodcock and Common Snipe descend from the top of their aerial displays in erratic swoops, making characteristic sounds as they do so (see SONG); Upland Sandpipers sometimes fold their wings and drop from nuptial flights; and Common Nighthawks plummet and "pull out," making a characteristic noise with their wings.

"Sky dances": Male hummingbirds describe characteristic patterns in the air before mates (see Plate 2), calling and in a few cases making feather noises as well; Leach's Storm-Petrels perform eerie circling (chasing?) flights accompanied by haunting calls over their nesting burrows at night.

Aerobatics: Perhaps the most thrilling of aerial displays are the stunt maneuvers performed by most species of hawks and eagles. A familiar variation is a series of continuous undulations (shallower in accipiters; deeper in buteos and eagles). Some species will also fold their wings and plummet from as high as 1,000 feet, pulling out sharply and rising to repeat the dive. The most remarkable display stunt of any North American bird may be the "tumbling" of Bald Eagle pairs: the male flies above the female, she turns on her back and presents her talons, which the male grasps in his; then they fall down through space in a tumbling roll.

Chasing: Many species from loons to passerines chase each other (or male chases female) as part of the courtship ritual; "three-bird chases" are characteristic of many waterfowl.

DANCING. Pairs (and sometimes small groups) of albatrosses (including the Black-footed), cranes, some pelecaniforms, and many gulls and shorebirds engage in more or less conspicuous formalized earthbound displays. These involve a great diversity of actions, including bill fencing, gaping (to show color of mouth lining), wing posturing, "curtsying," pointing, stretching, and presentations of food or nest materials. Owing to their size and the exaggeration of many of their movements, the albatrosses and cranes are especially famous as "dancers."

As noted elsewhere, male Sage and Sharp-tailed Grouse and the two species of prairie chickens gather in leks (called "strutting grounds," "gobbling grounds," or "booming grounds"—according to the characteristic sounds and gestures made) and perform a rather staid sequence of stamping motions, the culmination of which is the inflation of brightly colored air sacs at the neck or breast.

The Ruff, a largely Eurasian sandpiper, is also noted for an elaborate lek display, and males of some other North American shorebirds (e.g., Willet) gather in (less formal?) display grounds. See LEK.

The Great Blue Heron (including the Great White) and the Reddish and other egrets sometimes "dance" among members of their species early in their breeding cycle (Palmer, 1962–HERON).

WATER DISPLAYS

Racing: Loons and grebes, with legs placed near the end of their bodies, are capable of standing nearly erect and paddling furiously across their breeding lake or pond in this vertical posture. Pairs do this in tandem as one act of their courtship display (see Plate 2). Fulvous and Black-bellied Whistling (Tree) Ducks also do a tandem "race" as a post-copulatory ritual.

Other: The courtship displays of loons, grebes, and waterfowl are essentially aquatic dances. In the first two families, the sexes share equally in the ritual, while among the waterfowl the male dominates, and often many males display to a single female. The goldeneyes execute a very distinctive combination of head and neck motions involving "inflating" the head feathers until the head is nearly spherical, stretching the neck forward, and then wrenching the head violently over the back ("head throwing"); in one version, this is accompanied by splashing, which exposes the bright orange legs and feet. Other bay and sea ducks do less exaggerated forms of this display. The drake Ruddy Duck inflates a tracheal air sac and then slaps its enlarged chest with the bill near the waterline, making a distinctive sound (by hitting the air sac?) and simultaneously producing a cluster of bubbles. In another irresistible courtship maneuver of this species, the male races toward the female while clapping its long stiff tail on the water behind, leaving (briefly) a series of rings ("the ring rush").

DEFENSIVE DISPLAY. Called upon to defend themselves, their mates, young, eggs, or territory, birds, like other animals, may respond straightforwardly by attacking, harassing, sounding a vocal alarm, or fleeing. They may also, however, react with more complex and subtle behavior the result of which is to deceive the source of the threat. Like those connected with the breeding cycle, such defensive displays evolved out of ambivalent intentions in stressful situations, especially the quandary of whether to flee or remain and fight. That ambivalence is a major influence in display is nowhere clearer than in the frequent appearance of "defensive" gestures in courtship rituals. Defensive displays may be grouped for convenience under three headings.

Threat Display. Most if not all birds have characteristic threat postures which they assume when confronting a member of their own species invading their territories and also perhaps in other threatening situations. Many passerines, for example, crouch and "flatten" themselves, compress their body feathers, and adopt "nervous" gestures like flipping the wings or tail or raising and lowering the crown feathers. The tendency to erect body feathers, with the effect of making the potential victim seem larger or otherwise more impressive, is also common. Blue-footed Boobies, for example, create an imposing presence by raising the head and neck feathers, making them "bristle like porcupine quills" (Palmer, 1962–BOOBY). Nestling hawks and owls and cornered adults (like the Red-tailed Hawk in Plate 2) will often spread their wings and display their talons as well as raise feathers, all gestures aimed (often successfully) at intimidating would-be attackers. Several American blackbird species—e.g., Bronzed Cowbird, the grackles, and the Red-winged Blackbird (see Plate 2)—"puff up" in displays which function effectively to deter predators as well as warn territorial rivals and attract mates.

Perhaps the most impressive achievement in the evolution of threat displays—at least in human terms—is the "snake display" performed by some species of titmice. When the hole nest is invaded, the sitting bird gapes wide, hissing and swaying in a serpent-like manner, and finally "strikes" upward, simultaneously hitting the nest wall with its wings.

Distraction Display. This type of display by nesting adults diverts the attention of predators from eggs or young. It is most highly evolved (or at least most conspicuous) among open-country ground nesters, but it has been observed in some form in most bird families, including cavity nesters. The basic effect, performed with greater or lesser skill by different species, is of an injured or ill bird flopping helplessly over the ground and crying out in anguish. The Killdeer's "broken-wing act"—the epitome of pathos and verisimilitude—is the best-known North American example of this form of display. Plate 2 shows an American Avocet's version.

A variation is the "rodent run" practiced by small rails, shorebirds, and not a few songbirds. It consists of darting off the nest and *running* vole-like through the ground vegetation. The Green-tailed Towhee is said to have refined the technique by raising its long tail over its back in emulation of a ground squirrel (Van Tyne and Berger, 1976–ORNITHOLOGY).

Freezing should perhaps be mentioned here, though in one sense it might be termed "anti-display." It involves simply remaining motionless in the face of perceived danger. It is innate in many juvenile birds, often released by a special parental call, and is reinforced in many cases by cryptic coloration. For more detail on this and other defensive adaptations related to plumage markings, see COLOR AND PATTERN, *Concealment*, and Plate 3.

See also COURTSHIP; PAIR FORMATION; SONG; TERRITORY.

DISTAL. Farthest away from the main body. The white patch in the wing of a Yellow Rail is in the distal secondaries. Opposite of PROXIMAL.

DISTRACTION. In an avian context, a form of display in which a parent bird simulates injury or sickness, drawing the attention of a potential predator to itself and away from its eggs or young. Practiced to some degree among most birds, but most conspicuous among open-country species, e.g., shorebirds. See DISPLAY and Avocet in Plate 2.

DISTRIBUTION. Where birds live and why—a very broad subject, ultimately touching on nearly every other entry in this book.

Anyone who remembers writing something like the following in his or her sixth-grade geography book—

> Chris Leahy
> 15 Rockaway Street
> Marblehead
> Essex County
> Massachusetts
> U.S.A.
> North America
> Western Hemisphere
> Earth
> Solar System
> Milky Way Galaxy
> Universe
> Infinity

—will probably appreciate the many levels of inquiry presented to the would-be student of bird distribution. Consider, for example, that:

• Some species of birds are found only in small areas of very specialized habitats, while others are tolerant of many kinds of environment.

• Some species occur only on a single mountain peak, while others are distributed nearly worldwide.

• Some stay put year-round, while others travel great distances between breeding and wintering grounds.

• Some never leave regions of constant high temperature and humidity, while others never breed beyond the isotherm which marks a mean annual temperature of 50° F. or less (see ARCTIC).

• Some will not cross a narrow river or strait even when good habitat is clearly visible on the far side, while others spend their entire lives beyond the sight of land except for a few months every other year when they return to isolated oceanic islands to nest.

• Whole families of birds are restricted to certain regions of the globe and ocean and no other, while other families are represented in all major regions.

These are only some of the readily observed facts of bird distribution. The questions of "how" and "why" that they pose are generated exponentially.

HISTORY OF BIRD DISTRIBUTION. Bird distribution began, of course, with the evolution of the first bird. The fossil evidence that we have uncovered so far suggests that this probably happened in what we now call the Old World (Eurasia and Africa) sometime during the 30 million years of the Jurassic Period, which ended about 135 million years ago (see EVOLUTION OF BIRDLIFE). If we could watch a time-lapse film showing how the first bird or birds evolved into the present worldwide avifauna of 8,600-odd species and the climatic and geological events which accompanied that evolution, we could see quite clearly why bird species now live where they do. But we were only a gleam in the Creator's eye (as it were) during the greater portion of avian evolution and were not even making notes (much less movies) until about 5,000 years ago. If, then, we wish to trace the course of bird distribution from its beginnings, we must try to unravel the crisscrossed trails of evolution *backward* from present distribution and a few fossil remains. This is a highly speculative undertaking. The meager fossil record does not even begin to describe the intricate vicissitudes of evolutionary history. It is clear from modern examples such as the Cattle Egret—which in the space of about a hundred years has expanded its range from Africa throughout the New World tropics and now thrives as far north as coastal Maine—that hundreds of thousands of overlapping population shifts have occurred within the earth's avifauna over the millennia. Hundreds of species, some no doubt common and widespread, have long since disappeared, leaving no trace of their existence and condemning us to puzzle over the relationship between their ancestors and descendants. Furthermore, our understanding of the phylogeny of living species is far from perfect, especially regarding the great order of perching birds (Passeriformes). In tracing the Wrentit's ancestry, it makes a great difference, after all, whether it is taken to be a titmouse (as first supposed), a unique form in a family of its own (as it is defined in the 1957 A.O.U. *Check-list*), or, as many authorities now agree, the sole New World member of the babbler family (Timaliidae).

MAJOR INFLUENCES ON BIRD DISTRIBUTION. It may be that we will never be able to completely untangle the long interwoven skeins of evolution, much less map the successive distributions of bird species past and present. However, there are a number of basic influences on distribution which are plainly evident today or can be reasonably inferred and which help us guess at the distribution patterns of the past.

In considering the nature of distribution it is important to realize (1) that it is a part of the evolutionary process and is thus always changing—rapidly in some cases (e.g., the Cattle Egret), imperceptibly in others; (2) that the distribution of any given bird species is influenced by varying *combinations* of some or all of the factors noted below; and (3) that not all species respond in the same way to apparently identical distributive "opportunities"—i.e., "psychological" factors seem to predispose some species to expand their ranges and others to remain confined to a limited area despite a lack of physical inhibitions.

Physiographical Barriers. Many truly pelagic birds are ill disposed to come within sight of land much less to attempt to cross a landmass in getting from one ocean to another; similarly, many land-bird species are inhibited from crossing bodies of water. (During the Pleistocene, expanses of inland seas, created during several interglacial periods, doubtless made such a barrier between birds of eastern and western North America.) These tolerances vary widely from species to species, some fearing to cross the narrowest barrier between similar habitats while others seem oblivious to such inhibitions as long as other influences (see below) are not involved. Presumably, however, if North America and Europe "drifted" together again, their avifaunas would soon intermingle.

High mountain ranges in themselves probably do not constitute barriers to bird movements, but crossing them usually means leaving a preferred environment and passing through several alien ones before again reaching suitable habitat (see *Adherence to Niche/Habitat*, below). Birds (e.g., the Brown-capped Rosy Finch) can also be isolated on the tops of mountains—unwilling to travel to adjacent "islands" of alpine habitat.

Physical Capability. Flightless birds are obviously at a distinct disadvantage in undertaking large-scale shifts in distribution. Though there are no flightless species in North America (see FLIGHTLESSNESS), the gallinaceous species are not equipped to make long-sustained flights; they are nearly all non-migratory and are unlikely to turn up as pioneers in areas very distant from their present ranges. At the opposite extreme are species such as the Black-headed and Little Gulls, Eurasian species which have been recorded in North America only within the last fifty years and now breed locally in the northern U.S. and Canada. These species are strong fliers, well able to survive the rigors of an ocean crossing, regardless of where their travels take them. There are several theories as to precisely how they arrived in North America.

Adherence to Niche/Habitat. In the course of evolution, many species have become strongly adapted to fill a certain role (niche) in a highly specialized habitat, e.g., desert, coniferous forest, fast-moving rivers, to which they become essentially restricted. This kind of distributional enforcement is inextricably connected to variations in soil, temperature, and rainfall, which to a large extent dictate the vegetation (or lack of it). The vegetation in turn influences the food, nest-site, and nest-building preferences of the birds in the habitat and in some species these preferences become exclusive. Thus Cactus Wrens are never found in deciduous forest or Scarlet Tanagers in the desert though no barriers or physical incapacities exist to prevent either species from going where it will.

Food. A factor of perhaps preeminent importance in niche/habitat adherence is food. Some species (e.g., many corvids) are practically omnivorous and their distribution is therefore unrestrained by their feeding habits, but many species have more restrictive tastes and tend to be found only in association with their principal food source. Birds such as flycatchers and warblers, which depend largely on insects, must shift their distribution southward in cold weather or perish from starvation. Crossbills sustain themselves mainly on conifer seeds and are seldom found away from cone-bearing trees. In years when northern cone crops fail or are insufficient to sustain crossbill populations, the birds move south seeking a new supply; occasionally some birds will remain south of their normal breeding range to nest. A few species are extremely fussy eaters, and their fate is therefore rather precariously tied to the welfare of another organism. The population of Brant which winters along the Atlantic coast of North America suffered a precipitous decline when its favorite food, eelgrass (*Zostera marina*—a saltwater submergent in the pondweed family, Majadaceae), was nearly wiped out by disease in 1931 and 1932; fortunately some of these geese switched to seaweed, and learned to graze fields, and made a recovery—as did the eelgrass. Everglade Kites and Limpkins specialize on the large "apple" snails in the genus *Pomacea.* The fondness of Bald Eagles and Ospreys for fish was a significant factor in their recent decline due to the effects of waterborne DDT (see MAN-MADE THREATS TO BIRDLIFE). Some narrow eating habits, of course, are less precarious: the American Woodcock's strong preference for earthworms (75 percent of its diet) is probably indulged at low risk.

Dispersal. When breeding success surpasses the death rate in a given bird population, the competition for food and nest sites would in some cases increase to intolerable levels if some young birds did not move into new breeding areas. The population explosion of large gulls in the Northeast, for example (see *Environmental Changes*, below), has resulted in occupation of virtually all suitable nesting sites in many parts of their ancestral range and a pronounced expansion southward.

There is a measure of "accident" in some distributional shifts. Wilson's Phalarope was, until recently, largely restricted to the central prairies of North America as a breeding bird, with only sporadic nesting records east of the Great Plains. Its migration route was also mainly west of the Mississippi. It was traditionally known as an accidental or very rare spring and fall migrant along the Atlantic coast (Griscom and Snyder, 1955–GRISCOM). Since the 1960's records of the species during migration have increased dramatically, and it now nests very locally in New Brunswick (probable), in New York, and in a salt marsh on the north shore of Massachusetts. How to explain this apparently sudden range expansion? Increased breeding success in the West? An unusual number of individuals blown off course in a given year or sequence of years? The gradual reoccupation of a range that dwindled in prehistoric times? An increase in suitable open-country wetland habitats as eastern forests have been cut? All of the above?

Competition among Bird Species. How a bird species is distributed *within* its preferred habitat (or the scope of its niche) is strongly influenced by the number of its avian competitors. A widely ranging species may share its habitat with only a few others in some areas and thus be able to exploit a greater variety of food sources, nest sites, singing perches, etc., than it could where rival species made stronger claims on some of these.

On a broader scale, pioneer males of a given species—of which there is often an excess—may be pressured by competition (see POPULATION) to spread to a new habitat or an unexploited niche in the species' traditional area, thus taking a first step toward becoming a distinct species with a "new" distribution and/or habitat preference.

Environmental Changes. When habitat is destroyed, the birds which depend upon it experience an alteration in their distribution. There is evidence that Whooping Cranes were once widespread in the prairie and taiga wetlands of North America, for example, but were reduced to their present extremely limited distribution by drainage of marshes for agriculture and other encroachments of civilization (see ENDANGERED BIRDS).

Very often, of course, the narrowing of one species' range coincides with the broadening of another's. When a forest is cleared, open-country birds gain the ground that the forest birds lose. Some species, e.g., the misnamed Prairie Warbler, specialize in second-growth formations which spring up after burns or logging. The distribution of such species therefore fluctuates to a much greater extent than those which live in more stable habitats.

Altering habitat is only one of the ways in which human society affects the distribution of birdlife. Open dumping of refuse and the enormous increase in offshore fishing operations are credited with the spectacular range extensions of Herring and Great Black-backed Gulls, formerly northern species which now breed as far south as the Carolinas. Their abundance along the New England coast resulted in the altered distribution of less aggressive species such as the Laughing Gull and some terns.

The unified suburban "green belt" which now accompanies the eastern megalopolis from southern cities to New England is suspected of at least encouraging the recent northward spread of the Northern Mocking-

FIG. 5. *Major North American biomes.* Because of the scale of the map and the complexity of the pattern, some detail has been sacrificed: alpine tundra exists above tree line atop the highest peaks of the western mountains (usually over 10,000 feet) as well as on the highest peaks of the Northeast; the southwestern pine-oak woodland (depicted in Plate 1) occurs at moderate elevations (5,000–8,000 feet) in the hills and mountains of Oregon, Colorado, Utah, California, and in southern Arizona and New Mexico it contains a variety of "Mexican" bird specialties. Many of the plant and animal associations of southern Florida and the southernmost end of the Rio Grande Valley of Texas do not fit neatly into any of the major North American biomes. See BIOME; ECOTONE.

After F. A. Pitelka, in *The American Midland-Naturalist* (1941).

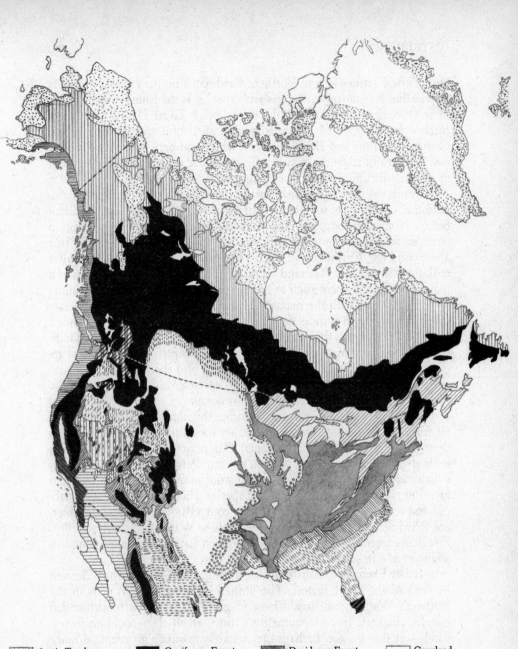

 Arctic Tundra

Tundra–Coniferous Forest Ecotone

Creosote Scrub Desert

Sagebrush

Coniferous Forest

Coniferous-Deciduous Forest Ecotone

Coniferous Forest–Grassland Ecotone

Coniferous Forest–Sage Grass Ecotone

Coastal Chaparral

Pinyon-Juniper Interior Chaparral

Deciduous Forest

Oak-Pine Ecotone (subclimax)

Southeastern Pinewoods (subclimax)

Deciduous Forest–Grassland Ecotone

Moist Coniferous Forest

Grassland

Grass-Sage Ecotone (subclimax)

Desert (Mesquite) Scrub (subclimax)

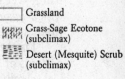 Mixed Subtropical

bird, Tufted Titmouse, and Northern Cardinal; a similar effect is probably responsible for drawing such "eastern" species as the Blue Jay and "Baltimore" Oriole westward across the once treeless Great Plains. And man's careless introduction of highly adaptable alien bird species such as the Common Starling and House Sparrow, which compete with native species (see INTRODUCED BIRDS), may drastically reduce populations to the extent of altering distribution—at least temporarily.

Temporal Effects on Distribution. The passage of time affects distribution of birdlife in at least three distinct ways. (1) As noted earlier, distribution is an ever-changing phenomenon. In many species, distribution changes significantly within a generation for a variety of reasons (see above) and the distribution of the world avifauna has been shown to alter radically within a few thousand years, especially with the intervention of a major geoclimatic event such as an ice age. (2) Bird distribution changes with the seasons, with the majority of species from the North Temperate Zone moving south during the winter months, many to the Neotropics. Obviously this means that there are more or fewer of both species and individuals in a given area at different seasons. Except for northernmost regions, all parts of North America support: (a) bird species which are present year-round (permanent residents); (b) species which only breed in the region and migrate afterward (summer residents); (c) species which arrive from the north and are present only during the non-breeding season (winter residents); and (d) those which neither breed nor winter but only pass through during migration (transients). There are also a few anomalies, such as pelagic species (e.g., Wilson's Storm-Petrel, Greater Shearwater) which arrive in the North Atlantic during our summer after their Southern Hemisphere breeding season. (3) Bird species which occupy the same habitat and overlapping niches may reduce competition by nesting on different schedules. Berger (1954) cites the Yellow Warbler (earliest), Willow Flycatcher (second), and American Goldfinch (latest) as exemplifying this phenomenon in southern Michigan.

Other Factors. The distribution of some species seems to be defined by none of the above factors. The limited breeding grounds of both the Kirtland's Warbler and Ross' Goose (Fig. 13) are *apparently* surrounded by ideal habitat, free of competitors, into which they could easily expand—yet they do not. Perhaps they innately maintain an ancestral range which was once restricted by factors no longer present. Perhaps they continue to be restricted by factors we have yet to perceive.

DEFINING BIRD DISTRIBUTION. In an effort to analyze the complex patterns of bird distribution, scientists have proposed a number of theoretical schemes. These approach the problem in two basic ways: (1) by dividing the earth into distinctive areas—based on climate, vegetation, faunal homogeneity, or other factors—with which birds (and other life forms) are then categorically associated, e.g., tropical birds, coniferous-forest birds, Nearctic birds (see below); and (2) by defining the distribution of individual species, again according to a number of factors—e.g., geographical and ecological. The main schemes are as follows.

Zoogeographic Regions. This concept divides the earth into six major regions, in each of which the animal life can be seen to have (in very general terms) an evolutionary identity distinct from all the others. The regions are the Palearctic, Ethiopian, Oriental, Australasian, Neotropical, and Nearctic. (The boundaries of the last closely coincide with those of North America.) An additional region, the Holarctic, was suggested by Heilprin in 1887; it combines the Nearctic and Palearctic, which share a large proportion of species. (See ZOOGEOGRAPHY for origins of the concept and Fig. 24 for location of the regions.) A number of faunas, such as those of isolated island groups (Galápagos, Hawaii, Madagascar, etc.), and oceanic organisms do not fit within the major regions, and the ranges of numerous species overlap two or more regions (indeed, some occur in all of them; see COSMOPOLITAN). Nevertheless, the theory embodies a significant measure of "distributional truth" and is much more realistic in making broad faunal comparisons than trying to compare "artificial" geographical entities such as countries or even continents. One way of demonstrating how the zoogeographic scheme works is to note that all but a few *orders* of birds occur in all the major regions (i.e., are cosmopolitan); that only about a quarter of bird *families* are cosmopolitan, while about a quarter are restricted to a single region; but that only a few *genera* and a *very* few *species* are distributed throughout, while a high proportion of both of those categories are regional endemics.

Zoogeography also provides a broad framework on which to consider the origins of animal groupings and their subsequent changes in distribution with evolution. And it is a handy way of referring to the elements of our own avifauna—the Plain Chachalaca is an essentially Neotropical species, wagtails are today largely Palearctic breeders, while vireos are doubtless of Nearctic origins. (See *Origins of North American Birdlife*, below).

Latitudinal Zonation is another form of zoogeographical division, articulated by Darlington (1957), which recognizes affinities and differences among animal groups in distinctive zones of latitude, which, of course, are closely related to climatic changes: the tropics, the North and South Temperate Zones, the Subarctic/Arctic, and the mainly oceanic Antarctic. Looked at from this perspective, we can see that some families of birds, e.g., trogons, are distributed mainly throughout the tropical regions of the earth (pantropical) and that sandpipers are conspicuously concentrated as breeding birds in the Arctic/Subarctic. It also becomes clear that whereas there is a relatively sharp distinction between tropical and north temperate avifaunas, south temperate birdlife seems to be a kind of avian outwash plain from the tropics with few distinct bird groups above species level. Another "latitudinal insight" is that the tropics contain a spectacularly greater diversity of bird species than any other zone and that numbers of *individuals* also have a tendency (far less pronounced) to diminish as one approaches the poles.

Oceanic Zones. The distribution of pelagic birds does not fit into either the regional or the latitudinal concepts which apply to the land-masses, but is divisible into distinctive zones of its own, largely on the basis of water temperature. Marine organisms on which true seabirds depend are most abundant in cold water, with the result that arctic and (especially) antarctic seas support a wide variety and impressive concentrations of such species. Movements of cold water such as the Labrador and Humboldt currents penetrate the lower latitudes here and there, bringing their rich plankton contents and avian dependents along, but in general the warm tropical seas are relatively barren of birdlife. The northern oceanic zone has nurtured the evolution of numerous alcid species (unique to the Northern Hemisphere) while the antarctic seas are characterized by a wealth of penguins and tubenoses (Procellariiformes)—both zones support species of cormorants, gannets, gulls, and skuas; and a few species (e.g., Wilson's Storm-Petrel, Greater, Sooty, and other shearwaters) migrate between the polar seas (see MIGRATION). Though comparatively depauperate as noted, the avifauna of tropical oceans does have a distinctive ornithological character, defined by the unique occurrence of the well-named tropicbirds, the frigatebirds, a proliferation of booby species, and a few tubenoses (e.g., Black-capped Petrel, Audubon's Shearwater).

Altitudinal Zones. Baron Alexander von Humboldt (1845–62) was the first to draw attention to certain similarities between moving northward (or southward) from the tropics to the poles and moving up the slopes of high mountains. In both cases the temperature drops as the elevation/latitude rises and the forms of the vegetation and the animal life change accordingly. Another way of looking at this phenomenon is to note that (very generally speaking) as one approaches the tropics from the poles the distinctive vegetational zones in effect "climb" the mountains—at 70° N. tundra occurs at sea level, but at 30° N. it is not encountered below 10,000 feet. In general, it would be misleading to cite similarities between the avifaunas of arctic and alpine tundra, but it can be noted that, for example, "northern" birds (e.g., Black-throated Green Warbler) breed *only* in the mountains in the southern extremities of their ranges.

Life Zones, postulated by C. H. Merriam (1894–LIFE ZONES), were an attempt to prove a direct correlation between changes in temperature and plant and animal distribution. The limits and names of the North American life zones are given under LIFE ZONES and shown in Fig. 6. This early attempt to formulate scientific principles of distribution was widely accepted in the early part of this century, but, though still useful in broadly defining distribution of species, the temperature correlation has proven to be a too simplistic solution to this complex phenomenon. Birds and other organisms are influenced by many factors besides temperature (see above).

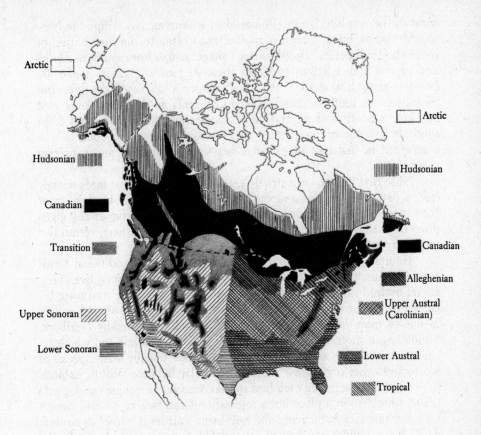

Arctic

Arctic

Hudsonian

Hudsonian

Canadian

Canadian

Transition

Alleghenian

Upper Austral
(Carolinian)

Upper Sonoran

Lower Sonoran

Lower Austral

Tropical

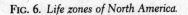

FIG. 6. *Life zones of North America.*

Biomes and Ecotones. Biomes may be defined as distinctive, stable communities of plants and animals, usually named for their characteristic (climax) plant formations, e.g., tundra biome, chaparral biome. Since these plant communities and their associated animal life are products of diverse factors (e.g., soil, humidity, as well as temperature), the biome concept represents a more realistic approach to distribution than the earlier life zone theory (see above). The major North American biomes are listed under BIOME (see also Fig. 5). Of course, many species inhabit more than one biome.

The transition between one biome and another usually occurs over a zone in which aspects of both are represented as well as elements unique to the transition zone. These zones are called *ecotones* and tend to contain richer faunas and floras than the "pure" communities they separate. The birdwatching cliché that "birds like edges" reflects this characteristic.

Range is the geographic distribution of a particular organism or grouping of organisms beyond which they are entirely absent. We can speak of the ovenbird family (Furnariidae) as ranging only within the New World tropics, but the term is applied most often to the distribution of species and subspecies. The Western Tanager ranges from southern Alaska and central Saskatchewan to Costa Rica: its total or "gross" range. Its breeding range is western North America from southern Alaska to central Saskatchewan, south to northern Baja California and western Texas, east to western South Dakota and Nebraska. Its winter range extends from southern Baja and central Mexico to Costa Rica; it normally occurs only as a transient in that part of its range between its breeding and wintering grounds.

Note that "range" is a strictly geographical term. Most birds occupy only a particular habitat and ecological niche within the boundaries of their ranges. The ranges of hundreds of bird species overlap at any given point on the earth (except at sea and at the polar extremities), yet no two ranges are exactly alike.

Habitat, Niche, Community, and Ecosystem are additional terms commonly used to describe where birds (and other organisms) live. They are all useful in describing specific phenomena, but can be confusing because of their interrelationships. Within a bird's range (see above), it lives in one or more *habitats*, which may be defined very broadly (seashore, woodland) or more narrowly (sandy beach, oak woodland) and which include the non-living as well as living components. Usually many species of birds (and other organisms) share a particular habitat. Within habitats each organism (including each bird species) occupies a unique (*ecological*) *niche*, which is not a place but a role: what it eats, where it nests, how it uses and modifies both living and non-living entities it comes in contact with. A *community* is a unit of interrelated organisms which can be defined according to its components (plant community, animal community, lichen community, bird community) and on any scale (the Sonoran Desert community, tide pool community). The collective interrelations of plant and animal communities together with the non-organic elements of habitat (rock, water, temperature) make an *ecosystem*, and again it is equally appropriate to speak of the global ecosystem or the salt marsh ecosystem. For other related (and potentially confusing) terms, see BIO- (e.g., BIO- SPHERE); ZOOME.

The details of bird distribution within an ecosystem, community, or habitat—i.e., how a bird recognizes its proper nesting habitat, how it defines its niche in competition with other members of its community; relative numbers of species/individuals a given habitat can support—these and many other fascinating aspects of distribution are beyond the scope of the present book, but see the Bibliography, especially Odum (1971), Milstead (1972), MacArthur (1964, 1971), Marshall (1957), Balda (1969), Ricklefs (1966), Wiens (1969).

ISLANDS AND BIRD DISTRIBUTION. When a portion of a major landmass becomes separated from the mainland, there is a tendency for the diversity of plant and animal species to diminish. Bird species on a small island, for example, which are unwilling or unable to cross to and from the mainland may not have a sufficient "gene pool" among the island population to permit survival. Species which *do* survive tend to expand into the empty niches left by the less adaptable forms.

Remote islands (Galápagos, Hawaiian) tend to be colonized by wide-ranging pelagic birds and by windblown strays from distant mainlands. Without competition for niches, the immigrant land birds (as well as the plant, insect, and other organisms which also arrive by wind and water) tend to evolve into distinct forms (eventually species) and to fill the wealth of niches. If the island has a wide range of habitats, the diversity of bird species may evolve to a comparable width. Such island life forms are, of course, unique—endemic to their particular island or island group—and eventually become incapable of interbreeding with (and distinct in appearance from) the mainland ancestor from which they originally evolved. Ocean islands, such as the Antilles, which are close but not too close to the mainland usually have a combination of endemics and resident populations of strong-flying continental species. But on the Hawaiian Islands—more than 2,000 miles from any mainland coast—98 percent of the resident birds (excluding introductions) occur nowhere else in the world.

ORIGINS OF NORTH AMERICAN BIRDLIFE. Despite the difficulties involved in tracing avian lineages, some highly educated guessers have speculated very convincingly about the origins of some bird families. Mayr (1946) thought it impossible on the evidence available to postulate the origins of twenty-nine families worldwide, including most water birds and some families of cosmopolitan distribution such as hawks, nightjars, and swallows. Of the bird families which currently occur in North America, he believes that the American vultures, grouse,* turkeys, limpkins, wrens,* mimic thrushes, waxwings,* silky flycatchers (e.g., Phainopepla), vireos, and wood warblers evolved in North America. Families with asterisks are the only ones which have reached the Old World—one species each in the case of the wrens and waxwings. The shallow sea bed of the Bering Strait that periodically bridges the watery gap between what are now Alaska and Siberia during times of low sea level is believed to have been a major route for interchange of New and Old World avifaunas. Excepting the grouse, all of the families listed above now occur in the Neotropical region as well.

Families Mayr believes to have originated in South America are the hummingbirds, guans (e.g., chachalacas), tyrant flycatchers, tanagers, and American blackbirds/orioles. None of these families occurs in the Old World; all reach greatest diversity in the Neotropics.

The pheasants and quail, cranes,* pigeons and doves, cuckoos, barn owls, typical owls, kingfishers, larks,* crows and jays, tits,† nuthatches,† treecreepers,† babblers,* thrushes, Old World warblers (e.g., the kinglets), pipits and wagtails,* and shrikes* originated in the Old World according to Mayr. Those marked with asterisks do not reach the Neotropics or only barely so; daggers mark families which reach only the highlands of Mexico and Central America. The only bird species in the New World considered to be a member of the large and diverse babbler family is the Wrentit, which occupies a narrow range in the chaparral of coastal Oregon and California and Baja California.

See also SPECIATION.

DIURNAL (dye-UR-nl). In the context of animal behavior, the term means "active by day," which describes the great majority of bird species. Contrast NOCTURNAL; see also CREPUSCULAR.

DIVING. See SWIMMING/DIVING.

DODO (doe-doe). One of at least 3 species of turkey-sized, flightless pigeon-like birds endemic to islands of the Mascarene group in the Indian Ocean. The extirpation of these last members of the family Raphidae in the late seventeenth and early eighteenth centuries shortly followed the arrival of Europeans. The Dodo was a heavy, ungainly species with blue-gray plumage, short legs, a heavy hooked bill, and small, useless wings and was confined to the island of Mauritius. Little was recorded of its habits except its fearlessness of men, which gained it quick extinction and immortalization as a symbol of stupidity.

DOMESTICATED BIRDS. Restricted here to birds which have been bred in captivity for many generations for the sake of some product useful to human beings. For other instances of tamed and wild birds kept and bred in captivity, see AVICULTURE; FALCONRY; COCKFIGHTING. The following domestic birds are familiar throughout North America. Only the species from which they originally derived, their range in the wild, and the principal use of the domestic breeds are given. In addition to their importance as food, most of these species are extensively bred in ornamental forms purely for show, many are also a source of feathers for decoration and stuffings, and a few are used in sport and ritual. For information on the nearly innumerable breeds which have been developed and other details, see the Bibliography.

Barnyard Geese and Ducks come in a great variety of shapes and colors but derive on the whole from a relatively few species. Chief among these are:

GREYLAG GOOSE (*Anser anser*) breeds from Europe through central Asia and winters in North Africa, through northern India and southern China; still common as a wild bird throughout much of its range despite its popularity as a game bird. Delacour (1964–WATERFOWL) thinks that the Greylag is probably the oldest domesticated bird, as it appears in Egyptian frescoes dated from about 4,000 years ago, but this opinion has been offered for most of the birds under discussion here. The many domestic versions may resemble the wild bird—i.e., largely brownish gray with white lower belly and undertail—or be totally white or some combination of the two. The legs and in some races the bills of wild greylags are pink; in domestic breeds both are usually bright orange; domestics also tend to be larger than the wild birds, sometimes (e.g., Toulouse Goose) spectacularly so; Greylags are used mainly for meat and down.

SWAN GOOSE (*Anser cygnoides*) breeds from central Siberia to Kamchatka in the north, to central Asia and Mongolia in the south; winters eastward to northern China and Japan; not very well known to Western ornithologists and now apparently becoming scarce due to overhunting. Another species long in "domestic service," beginning at least 3,000 years ago in China. The usual domestic incarnations are either all white or brown and white like the "original" and have a very prominent knob at the forehead; they are often called Chinese Geese, are kept for their meat, and are also useful—due to their large size and loud voice—as "watch geese."

Greylag and Swan Geese are often interbred.

MALLARD (*Anas platyrhynchos*) breeds throughout most of western North America (increasingly eastward), Europe, and Asia to above the Arctic Circle; winters south to central Mexico, North Africa, and southern China. Mallards, too, were domesticated by the ancient Egyptians and the classical cultures, whence to Europe and America. Domestic Mallards may be much larger than wild ones, retain their normal colors or show varying degrees of albinism (e.g., Pekin Ducks) or melanism; a frequent melanistic variation is nearly all black or iridescent green with a white breast. Many different breeds are cultivated for meat, eggs, and ornamental characteristics.

MUSCOVY DUCK (*Cairina moschata*) is resident from southern Mexico to northern Argentina. The conquistadores first brought Muscovies to Europe from South America, where they had been domesticated by the natives of Colombia and Peru—probably for centuries. The nearly all-black and metallic-green (with white wing patch) plumage of the wild Muscovy is seldom seen in domestic birds, which may be all white, patchy black and white, tan, or blue-gray. It is a large species in its natural state and like other domestics is often selectively bred to near-monstrous proportions. Domestic drakes tend to develop great, hideous red facial caruncles. They will interbreed with other domestic species and when paired with female Mallards, for example, produce hybrids with good-quality meat. This is their principal use.

The name Muscovy is either a corruption of a South American Indian name or the result of a confusion about the species' origins by the namer (Linnaeus).

Domestic Turkeys all derive from a single species, the Wild Turkey of North America, *Meleagris gallopavo*. This species once ranged throughout the open deciduous forests of North America south to southern Florida and central Mexico, but is now reduced to scattered populations within its former range due largely to the destruction of its habitat. It is still locally common, however, has been successfully reintroduced into many areas, and remains a popular game bird.

Our Thanksgiving turkeys arrived on our tables by a circuitous route. Turkeys were domesticated by the native peoples (e.g., Aztecs) of Mexico for an unknown period before the arrival of the Spanish conquistadores. The Spanish introduced the Mexican breeds into Europe in the sixteenth century and these were eventually carried back to North America by early colonists, where—possibly together with northeastern wild birds—the domestic American stocks developed. There are six major domestic breeds, including the Bronze (similar in plumage to wild birds), the White Holland, the Narragansett, the Bourbon Red, the Black, and the Slate (gray). The present great popularity of turkey meat began only in about 1935, previous to which turkeys were bred here mainly for show. Today they represent a major segment of the poultry industry. For origin of the name, see TURKEY.

Chickens are descended from one of four forest-dwelling gallinaceous species in the genus *Gallus* (family Phasianidae), all from India and southern Asia. They seem to have been domesticated in India before 3000 B.C. and eventually moved westward via China and the Middle Eastern civilizations. Chickens reached North America during the earliest phases of colonization, but there is evidence that they were present in South America (via Asia) in pre-Columbian times. The raising of domestic poultry for both meat and eggs is, of course, a major industry today in North America. More than 100 breeds of chickens are recognized; perhaps only 30 of these are raised for food, the rest being of ornamental interest. Well-known American breeds include Plymouth Rock (white or barred with black), Rhode Island Red (state bird of Rhode Island), and Wyandotte (usually white). The Leghorns, another familiar breed, originated in Europe.

In addition to their importance as food, chickens have long been and continue to be (e.g., in Latin America) frequent victims of animal sacrifice and blood sport (see COCKFIGHTING).

Guinea Fowl belong to the strictly African family Numididae, which contains seven species in five genera. Domestic guineas apparently all descend from the widespread species *Numida meleagris*. Guinea fowl were introduced several times into Europe and then to America, but have not "developed" and consequently look very much like their wild ancestors. They are used largely for food.

Pigeons, now ubiquitous in a stunning assortment of color varieties throughout North American population centers, all come from the Eurasian Rock Dove, or Common Pigeon (*Columba livia*), which still breeds in its original cliffside habitat throughout much of the Old World. Beginning as early as 3000 B.C. and perhaps long before, pigeons figured in Persian and Egyptian civilizations as sacred symbols as well as food sources. Uninspiring as it may be to contemplate from our present vantage point, the dove of Genesis was more likely a Common Pigeon than any more exotic columbid. Though young pigeons do occasionally grace gourmet menus as "squab," the species is more likely to be bred in ornamental show varieties, used in sport (pigeon racing), or kept as pets. Lamentably, they are also a significant nuisance, particularly in urban areas, where in addition to their general messiness they have been cited as carriers of histoplasmosis and chlamydiosis, both diseases that can affect humans.

DOMINANCE. Birds, mammals, and other animals which engage in social interaction set up natural hierarchies, based on an individual's ability to dominate others. The rank of a given individual within a particular group is typically established by means of a physical contest, though sometimes simple presence—as in the case of a very large individual among small ones—is enough to establish dominance. In some species, notably the turkeys, grouse, and other gallinaceous birds, courtship displays are social events at which the "peck order" of a particular population of birds is reaffirmed or rearranged. Prolonged physical contests, such as those between rutting sheep or deer, are rare among birds, though elaborate ritualized fighting occurs in some species (e.g., Ruffs) and a sharp peck or blow with a spurred wing or leg to show a subordinate bird its place is not uncommon. There tends to be a general correspondence between position in the peck order and sexual success, the alpha or top-ranked male attracting more females and therefore having a greater likelihood of perpetuating his genes. However, all males in a display situation are likely to be "primed" for copulation, and with numbers of available females present, the establishment of dominance rarely if ever translates into "winner take all."

Dominance is not restricted to male sexual hierarchies. The original "peck order" is that among barnyard hens. And interspecific dominance contests are common where food is abundant. Anyone who has watched the interactions that take place at a bird feeding station knows that battles for preferred positions or even the entire feeder take place almost constantly and are not always won by the larger species. Though sheer size does often confer dominance, age, sex, hormonal levels, and place also affect who prevails over whom.

Even in stable flocks of a single species, disputes over dominance occur regularly, especially as younger generations overtake older. But a certain fixity also obtains in such hierarchies once dominance has been clearly established. This inhibits constant challenges within the ranks and even allows the alpha individual to sustain a defeat or two without losing position.

For another form of individual dominance, see TERRITORY. For genetic dominance, see SPECIATION; HYBRIDIZATION.

DORSAL. Upper (surface); the dorsal aspects of a bird are principally those of the back or mantle but also include the top of the bill, head, tail, etc.; the lower or under portions are VENTRAL.

DOTTEREL (DOT-er-ul). Standard English name in North America and Europe for a single species of tundra-breeding, essentially Palearctic plover, *Eudromias morinellus.* Eight other species (all but two in the genus *Charadrius*), mainly of Australian and South American distribution, have "dotterel" in their English names. *The* Dotterel breeds locally in extreme northwestern Alaska; these birds presumably winter in Asia.

The name "little dolt" refers to the species' alleged stupidity. Dotterels were once widely trapped in nets for food in Europe. The trappers believed that the birds imitated any action they made and, thus distracted, were easily caught. The belief was based on the "fact" that when men stretched out their arms, the dotterels followed suit. In reality the trappers were mimicking the broken-wing distraction display typical of many plovers. Doubtless, the birds *were* easy enough to net, since they rely on cryptic coloration and "sitting tight" for protection and are reluctant to leave the vicinity of the nest, once flushed. Still, it seems there were "dotterels" among the hunters as well as the plovers. See PLOVER.

DOVE. Standard English name for about 140 members of the family Columbidae (order Columbiformes), which also includes the pigeons. There is no real (i.e., morphological/taxonomic) distinction between a dove and a pigeon; for such distinctions as exist and the general characteristics of the family, see PIGEON.

Five native North American columbids are officially named "doves" and two (or three) others so called have been "successfully" introduced.

"Dove" may come from the German *dubo,* "dark-colored" (Gruson, 1972–BIOGRAPHY), or the Anglo-Saxon *dufan,* "to dive" (Choate, 1973–BIOGRAPHY).

DOVEKIE. Standard English name in North America for a single small auk, *Alle* (*Plautus*) *alle,* which breeds on arctic coasts and islands from northwestern Greenland east to Novaya Zemlya and south to Iceland; it is the smallest alcid of this region. Dovekies breed largely in teeming high arctic colonies and are a principal food source for other inhabitants of the barren lands, including some Innuit populations. In spite of their small size they are fully equal to the harsh conditions on their North Atlantic pelagic wintering grounds but are vulnerable during migration to onshore storms and are sometimes driven onto coastal beaches and even far inland (see Snyder, 1960–MORTALITY). Helpless to take off except from water, many become victims of gulls and other predators. Others are adopted by humans, glad to take a little "penguin" under their protection; Dovekies are soon killed by this form of kindness and are much more likely to survive if released immediately in the ocean or another large body of water from which they can take off.

The standard English name in Europe is Little Auk. "Dovekie" is a Scandinavian whaler's name meaning "little dove," but it was originally applied to the Black Guillemot (*Cepphus grylle*); the smaller alcids were called *rotche* in that area. The switch was apparently made by New World seamen, many of whom today call Black Guillemots "sea pigeons." For family characteristics, see AUK.

DOWITCHER. Standard English name for all 3 species of long-billed sandpipers in the genus *Limnodromus* (family Scolopacidae; order Charadriiformes), 2 of which breed in North America. Some taxonomists place the dowitchers in the subfamily Scolopacinae with the woodcocks and snipes.

The North American dowitchers (Long-billed and Short-billed) are comparatively short-legged shorebirds with "rusty" underparts in alternate (breeding) plumage, which is replaced by drab gray and dirty white in basic (winter) plumage. The two species are notoriously difficult to distinguish in the latter plumage; however, see Prater et al. (1976–FIELD GUIDE).

"Dows" probe in mud and soft sand with a characteristic "sewing machine" motion duplicated only by the Stilt Sandpiper. The Long-billed nests in western Alaska and Siberia, and normally appears in eastern North America only during the fall passage; it shows a stronger preference for inland freshwater habitats than its sibling species. The Short-billed breeds in marshy tundra in the Low Arctic of central and eastern Canada as well as southern Alaska. Both dowitchers winter along the southern coasts of the U.S. and in the American tropics.

Two theories are commonly advanced on the origins of the name "dowitcher." It may be an anglicization of the Iroquois name for the birds or a corruption of *deutscher*, referring to the popularity of roast dowitchers among New York Dutchmen of an earlier age. The species must have enjoyed a much broader ethnic appeal than this analysis implies, for by 1909 dowitchers had been decimated by market gunners. With full protection they have recovered their former abundance.

For family characteristics, see SANDPIPER.

DOWN. Small, soft, tuft-like feathers with a short, often negligible rachis and free-branching barbs which form no vane (see FEATHER). Individual down feathers are technically known as plumules, plumulae, or plumaceous feathers. In all its forms, down serves mainly in the conservation of body heat. It is not confined to feather tracts.

The definition of the different types of down is a confusing business, made more so by a baroque terminology. Only a few undisputed generalizations will be hazarded here.

(1) There is a difference between natal down feathers (neossoptiles) and adult (teleoptile or definitive) down feathers. (2) Natal down does not occur in all species. (3) When it does occur, it may be scattered over the skin of a nestling or, as in precocial chicks (e.g., of ducks and shorebirds), form a dense continuous coat. (4) The barbs of the natal down feathers of many species emerge in a ring from the top of their calamus and have no rachis whatever; other neossoptiles (e.g., of ducks) have a well-developed rachis. (5) Many but not all natal down feathers are simply specialized tips connected to the incoming juvenal "pinfeathers" and are dropped as the vanes of these unfold from their sheaths. (6) The natal down coat of precocial chicks is often cryptically colored and patterned to resemble habitat near the nest, which conceals them from predators. (7) Most owls and many falconiforms have two successive coats of down as nestlings, followed by the "adult feathers" of the juvenal plumage. (8) Adult down feathers have a rachis which is shorter than the longest of its barbs and may be negligible. (9) Adult down is usually completely concealed. (10) Adult down is best developed in water birds and is used as nest lining by the overwhelming majority of North American swans, geese, and ducks (see NEST).

Humans appreciate the highly effective insulating capacity of down and use it (as well as adult feathers and man-made down-like substances) in clothing, blankets, sleeping bags, and the like. In Nordic countries, down is "harvested" from the nests of the Common Eider. Female ducks have a quantity of easily detachable down beneath their breast feathers with which they line their nests. When "down pickers" remove the first lining, it is promptly replaced by the sitting bird and this too may be harvested and replaced without noticeably affecting breeding success or unduly depleting the female's store of down.

See also FEATHER; PLUMAGE; MOLT.

DRAKE. A male of any species of duck; "duck" then becomes specific for females. This terminology is still current in some hunting circles and in Britain, e.g., "two drake Gadwalls and a Pintail duck."

DRIFT. The phenomenon in which migrating birds, whether disoriented or "on course," are forced in a given direction by the prevailing wind. Seabird "wrecks," in which migrating alcids, phalaropes, petrels, and other species are blown far inland by onshore gales, could be considered one extreme form of drift; but the "piling up" of numbers of land-bird migrants along the coast of North America in fall when the prevailing winds are westerly is a better example of the term's usual import. See Baird and Nisbet, *Auk* (1960), 77:119-49.

DRINKING. Water is essential to the survival of birds and all other organisms. A great many birds obtain sufficient water in the solid foods they eat and are seldom or never seen to drink. And the capacity of some species—even ones which live in a dry habitat and eat dry food, e.g., seeds—to go without drinking for long periods is well documented. This is in part explained by the fact that birds do not excrete quantities of liquid urine as mammals do, but reabsorb most fluids internally. Nevertheless, anyone who owns a birdbath knows that birds do drink from time to time, some species more often than others.

There are two basic avian drinking methods. By far the commoner is to take a mouthful of water and then tilt the head back, allowing the water to pass into the esophagus. When the head is tilted the glottis "automatically" closes, preventing the water from flowing into the windpipe (trachea); the same involuntary reflex ensures the safe swallowing of food. A few birds, notably the pigeons, can suck in water as mammals do without raising their heads. Other species, e.g., hummingbirds, are known to drink from wet vegetation, and aerial species such as swifts and swallows can snatch a mouthful of water from a pond or lake while on the wing.

See Bartholomew, *Proc. XVth Int. Ornith. Congr.,* 1972, pp. 237–54.

DROPPINGS. Matter excreted through the vent consisting of both urine and feces. See DIGESTIVE SYSTEM; EXCREMENT; EXCRETORY SYSTEM; GUANO.

DRUMMING. Usually refers to a sequence of booms and "thunder rolls" which the Ruffed Grouse produces by beating its wings rapidly from a stationary perch. Precisely how the sound is produced was long in dispute, but it has now been demonstrated that the sound comes solely from the interaction of the cupped wings and the air. Drumming is most strongly associated with the courtship and territoriality of the cock grouse in spring and usually resumes for a brief period in fall; but the sound has been heard throughout the year, day and night, and, according to some sources, is at least occasionally performed by the hen. This is one of the great "voices" of the northern forests of North America, often described as more felt than heard and so pervasive that it is often difficult to judge the location of the drummer. The term is occasionally used for other non-vocal bird sounds, such as the rapping of woodpeckers; and grouse "drumming" is also known as "booming."

DRUNKENNESS. Birds occasionally become intoxicated from eating fermented fruit or nectar, and instances of fatalities occurring due to the resulting loss of control have been recorded. Robins, waxwings, and other frugivores that habitually depend on "old" fruits of mountain ash, crab apple, or other species in winter are sometimes killed outright by the alcoholic toxins contained in the fruit or fly into windows or other objects after becoming tipsy. Similarly, *Agave* blossoms, which are very popular with a wide range of nectivorous birds in warm climates, ferment rapidly when filled with rain and then "boiled" by the hot sun. In at least one case, a highway near such an organic cocktail lounge was littered with squashed corpses of avian tipplers that apparently were rendered less sensitive to the danger of passing traffic and/or lost some motor coordination. See Phillips, *Audubon* (1959), 61:6.

DRY TORTUGAS (Florida). The outermost of the Florida Keys, 68 miles west of Key West, and the best place in North America to see Sooty and Noddy Terns, which nest on Bush Key. Access is by boat (8–9 hours one way) or plane (1½ hours round trip) to Fort Jefferson on Garden Key, where the birds are easily watched and birders can camp if they wish (no tourist facilities available). The waters around the Tortugas are good hunting grounds for other tropical seabirds, such as frigatebirds, Brown, Masked, and Red-footed Boobies, White-tailed Tropicbird, and Black (Lesser) Noddy; West Indian land-bird vagrants are also recorded occasionally. During migration, windblown migrants seek safe haven on these barren, coral semi-deserts and occasionally spectacular concentrations of these disoriented, exhausted, and starving birds occur.

DUCK. Standard English name for about 50 members of the family Anatidae (order Anseriformes), but also a collective term for about 80 additional members of the family which do not include "duck" in their names.

There are about 30 species of ducks that breed in North America, and another 6 that occur as migrants to western Alaska, as vagrants, or as escapes (see Appendix II). Taxonomists have grouped and reorganized the ducks into a bewildering number of subfamily or tribal assortments. No attempt will be made to explicate the variations in this entry, but for one version, see Appendix I; for another, see the A.O.U. *Check-list* (5th ed., 1957); and for yet another, see Delacour (1954–64–WATERFOWL). For some enlightenment on individual groups, see DABBLING DUCK; BAY DUCK; SEA DUCK; WHISTLING DUCK; STIFFTAIL DUCK; MALLARD; GADWALL; PINTAIL; SHOVELER; TEAL; WIGEON; POCHARD; BUFFLEHEAD; GOLDENEYE; OLDSQUAW; EIDER; SCOTER; MERGANSER.

The ducks are a highly varied group of medium-sized (10 to 18 inches) water birds, mostly with a broad, flat bill (mergansers exceptional) ending in a small hook or "nail" and lined with sieve-like lamellae (see BILL); the front three toes are webbed. Coloration ranges from rather drab (e.g., Black Duck) to spectacular (e.g., male Wood Duck). Many ducks have a brightly colored patch in the secondaries, called the speculum. Most can be described as either diving or surface-feeding species, both types eating a wide variety of plant and animal foods.

Dabbling ducks, bay ducks (genus *Aythya*), eiders, scoters, the Old-squaw, and the Harlequin Duck typically nest in a hollow on the ground near water, concealed in shore vegetation or (especially in tundra species) in the open. The Wood Duck, Bufflehead, goldeneyes, mergansers, and Black-bellied Whistling (Tree) Duck usually nest in tree cavities. The Ful-vous Whistling Duck deposits plant material on a flattened clump of swampland vegetation. And the stifftails (genus *Oxyura*) make floating nests anchored to emergent vegetation, heap up plant matter on the shore, or use the top of a muskrat lodge or an old nest of other duck species. All but the whistling ducks and the stifftails line their nests with down from the female's breast and (in some species) some scraps of handy plant mate-rial. Many ducks (e.g., the Ruddy Duck and Hooded Merganser) occa-sionally lay eggs in the nests of other ducks (see DUMP NEST). Ducks typi-cally lay large clutches of eggs; 3–21 is the range for North American species, but 6–12 is average for most. These vary considerably in size and shape, are often somewhat glossy with a waxy (waterproof?) coating. They may be white, yellowish, buff, olive, bluish, or greenish and are always un-marked (see Fig. 7).

Ducks produce many variations of the stereotypical "quack," of course, but also make a wide range of cooing, whistling, grunting, and croaking sounds. Oldsquaw flocks are characteristically noisy, whence the species' name; less chauvinistic auditors have likened this wild sound to a distant kennel of hounds. The whistling ducks and wigeons give pleasant, somewhat plaintive, piping notes in flight or when alarmed.

Ducks occur worldwide in both salt and fresh water and the majority of species are migratory.

"Duck" comes from an Old English word meaning "diver."

DUCKLING. The young of any species of duck until fully fledged. Analo-gous to "gosling" and "cygnet" (swan).

DUCK STAMPS. A stamp issued annually (on or about July 1) by the U.S. federal government to raise revenues for the conservation of water-fowl through the purchase of wetland. By law all wildfowl hunters over sixteen years of age must buy a stamp and help support refuges and other efforts to maintain populations of ducks, geese, and swans. The Migratory Bird Hunting Stamp Act, passed by Congress in 1934, was a response to the precipitous decline in waterfowl numbers during the "dust bowl" pe-riod of the early 1930's. Currently the stamp issue brings in about $12 million annually. The design for each year's stamp is chosen from entries in a contest sponsored by the federal government and open to anyone. The stamps are invariably fine depictions of waterfowl themes and are popular with non-hunting collectors who make up an additional source of support for wildfowl conservation.

For more on hunting regulations, see LAWS.

DUCKS UNLIMITED. A private, nonprofit sportsman's organization founded for the purpose of acquiring and protecting habitat for nesting and migrating waterfowl. Its existence testifies to the fact that responsible hunting practices can be compatible with the goals of the conservation movement.

DUETTING. A pair of birds singing together: either the same song in unison or in closely synchronized, alternating phrases (ANTIPHONAL SONG). Duetting/antiphonal singing seems to be principally a tropical phenomenon, practiced, for example, among a number of Neotropical wrens and African warblers (*Cisticola* species). The phenomenon is not common in North America, but has been recorded in several species of quail (Stokes and Williams, 1968–SONG) and in Brown-headed Cowbirds (Brackbill, 1961–SONG). See Thorpe (1972–SONG). See also SONG, *Multiple Vocalizations*.

DUMMY NEST. A phenomenon, especially characteristic of wren species, in which the male, arriving on territory ahead of the female, constructs a series of shells (i.e., external nest structures). When the female arrives, she is taken on a songful tour of inspection, following which she selects a nest and lines it or makes more substantial improvements in preparation for egg laying. After the breeding season the dummy nests may be used by young and adult birds as "dormitories." In North America, House, Winter, and Long-billed Marsh Wrens habitually make dummy nests, and the practice has also been recorded in the Prothonotary Warbler (Terres, 1980–BIRD). "Cock nest" is a synonym.

DUMP NEST. A phenomenon, characteristic of some ducks and gallinaceous species, in which several females lay eggs in a single nest that is ultimately abandoned. In at least some cases, dump layers are birds with no nest of their own, and also tend to be species which sometimes practice parasitism (nonobligate parasites). In a nest where only a few extra eggs are dumped, the owner may incubate the clutch, even if it includes eggs of a different species. However, when the egg pile reaches intimidating proportions—one Redhead nest was found with 87 eggs (Weller, 1959)—the hen abandons it.

Dump nesting should not be confused with the communal practices of anis and a few other birds that deliberately lay in a single nest and share incubation duties. See NEST.

DUNLIN. Standard English name for a species of small sandpiper, *Calidris (Erolia) alpina*, with a circumboreal distribution. The name means "little dun (i.e., grayish-brown) thing" and applies to the basic (winter) plumage only. The alternate (breeding) plumage is so much more colorful that it was once considered characteristic of a separate species. The name

Red-backed Sandpiper, once popular in North America, refers to this brighter incarnation.

DUSTING (dust bathing). Some species of birds actively and regularly fill their plumage with fine dry soil or sand and then remove it by shaking and preening in a ritual known as "dusting" or dust bathing. The practice seems to be most prevalent among birds of open country, such as larks, gallinaceous birds, and some (emberizine) sparrows, but has also been recorded in some hawks, owls, nightjars, wrens, Wrentit, and House Sparrow. Some "dusters," e.g., gallinaceous birds, apparently never bathe in water, and larks bathe only by exposing themselves to the rain. But other birds both bathe and dust. According to Simmons (1964), dusting and ANTING are mutually exclusive as far as is known, except for one species of Australian mudnest-builder (family Grallinidae).

While some dusting gestures—fluffing of feathers, shaking of bill in dust, flicking of wings—are similar to water-bathing gestures, the process is not truly analogous either in performance or in function. The ritual varies from species to species. Songbirds typically make a hollow in the dust by scratching with their feet and rotating their bodies, and the dust is applied by a combination of direct wallowing and the water-bathing gestures just described. Gallinaceous birds and others use bill and feet both to gather dirt around them and to "drive" it into or throw it onto their plumage. After a thorough dusting, birds shake and flap vigorously to rid themselves of the dirt. House Sparrows typically dust in small groups, while for the majority of species it is a solitary activity.

The purpose of all this is far from clear. Present evidence (e.g., Healy and Thomas, 1973) suggests that dusting helps keep plumage fluffy (hence air-retentive for good insulation) by removing excess moisture and preen oil. It is also a means of flushing out ECTOPARASITES such as bird lice.

For related behavior, see BATHING; PREENING; SUNNING; ANTING; OIL GLAND.

E

EAGLE. Standard English name for about 60 members (including hawk eagles) of the family Accipitridae (order Falconiformes), which also includes the hawks. Three species of eagles breed in North America; and another has occurred as a straggler from Asia (see Appendix II).

Ornithologically the term "eagle" refers to the largest of the diurnal birds of prey. These do not form a unified taxonomic group, however, and in some cases it would not be inaccurate to describe them as large or very large hawks (see HAWK for the confusing etymology of this term).

Like other members of their family, eagles have powerful wings and legs; a broad wing area; a heavy, hooked bill for tearing flesh; and long, sharp claws for dispatching and/or carrying prey.

The Golden Eagle is distributed throughout the Holarctic region and has been a symbol of majesty and might from the beginning of recorded history. It preys mainly on small animals (e.g., rabbits), but it is widely (and mistakenly) thought to be a major threat to livestock among ill-informed ranchers. It has suffered grave losses in North America recently from "sport" shooting from airplanes. The Bald Eagle, our national emblem, has suffered from a different form of human stupidity, the indiscriminate use of pesticides, which it ingests with its preferred food, fish (see MAN-MADE THREATS TO BIRDLIFE); it is now on the endangered species list in most states. Both eagles are now protected by federal statutes (see LAWS), which carry stiff fines and jail sentences for violators.

Like hawks, eagles construct large stick nests to which they add materials each season. Old eagle nests consequently may attain almost ridiculous mass and weigh two or more tons (see NEST). For other details of nesting and voice, see HAWK.

Aquila, the Latin word for "eagle," connotes dark color and the north wind (Choate, 1973–BIOGRAPHY); this became *aigle* in French, from which it is but a short step to "eagle."

See references in the Bibliography under HAWK.

EAR. See HEARING.

EATING. See FOOD/FEEDING.

ECDYSIS (EK-duh-sis). The shedding of old feathers in the molting process (compare ENDYSIS and see MOLT).

ECHOLOCATION. Bats, marine mammals, and some amphibians and insects can navigate in total darkness, even in the presence of numerous obstacles, by making noises and judging the time taken for the sound waves to bounce off surrounding objects and return to their highly sensitive ears. The only bird species in which the use of echolocation has been confirmed are the Oilbird (*Steatornis caripensis*) of South America and Asian swiftlets in the genus *Collocalia*, all of which breed and roost in dark caves. It is suspected, but not proven, that the regular *peent*'s uttered by Common Nighthawks while hunting on the wing may be a means of echolocating insect prey.

ECLIPSE (plumage). In the broadest sense, refers to a drab basic plumage acquired by male birds in a pre-basic (post-nuptial) molt that makes a hiatus between the splendor of the preceding and following alternate (breeding) plumages. The term is usually directed more specifically to the unusually brief basic plumage that occurs in most male duck species. Typically this is acquired in the midst of the breeding season but has been shed in favor of the alternate plumage by fall or early winter. See MOLT.

ECOLOGY. The study of the interrelationships of plants, animals, and all the factors which make up the environment in which we live. Ecological studies of birds, for example, include such factors as: habitat preference, food sources, relative abundance, migration habits, details of the breeding cycle—how all these factors are shaped by the environment and how they, in turn, affect it.

ECOSYSTEM. All of the factors, including organisms, geology, climate, etc., which make up a particular environment or the earth's environment as a whole. Birds are, of course, a conspicuous and significant component of the global ecosystem and also of the smaller interlocking ecosystems which make up the whole.

ECOTONE (EE-koh-tone). A zone of transition between two major environments and their respective organic communities. Between forest and prairie, for example, there is likely to be an area which is neither one nor the other. An ecotone may have a fairly uniform character of its own with few apparent similarities with either extreme; or take the form of interlocking fingers of the two merging environments. In some instances ecotones are particularly rich in organisms since they contain elements of the communities they bridge as well as ones unique to themselves.

The birdwatcher's truism that birds like "edges" is related to the ecotone concept.

ECTOPARASITE. An organism which lives on the surface of the body of another organism to the detriment of the host. (For parasites which live internally, see ENDOPARASITE.)

Birds are host to an astonishingly populous and varied fauna of invertebrate ectoparasites. Thousands of species and subspecies of flies, fleas, lice, ticks, and mites have been identified as living to some degree and in various ways on the bodies of birds. A single small songbird may have an unwelcome guest list numbering dozens of individuals of several species, and in the breeding season, its nest is likely to contain several times more. This will confirm for some the prejudice that birds are "dirty" and dangerous, yet most birds are able to control these pests to a tolerable level (at least from the bird's viewpoint) and no bird parasite is known to transmit disease to man.

A few of the more frequent parasite life styles are worth noting in a general way.

Some bird parasites, notably the bird lice (order Mallophaga) and feather mites (Acarina), live out their entire life cycles on the bodies of their hosts. Others feed on the host only at intervals or during one stage of their development and live in the nest, in the ground, on another host, on flowers, or elsewhere during other stages. Consequently, *how* birds become infested also varies.

Parasites which live exclusively on bird hosts are passed directly from bird to bird by direct contact. This occurs, of course, between parent birds and their young and also between raptors and their avian prey (hawks and eagles, vultures, and owls usually accommodate an unusually rich variety of pests). Bird lice occasionally hitch rides from host to host on the bodies of larger and more mobile louse flies (Hippoboscidae). Parasites which live part of their lives "ex-avis" contact birds in diverse manners. The eggs of some flies are laid in birds' nests and progress through larval and pupal stages during a single breeding season, parasitizing nestlings as larvae and quitting the nest as adults; other flies overwinter in the nest as larvae. Many parasites live in the nest but visit their hosts only at night. And most ticks fall off their host after a single blood meal and must find a new host for the next feeding.

A wide range of tolerances is exhibited by invertebrates which parasitize birds. Some adult chiggers are equally content to feed on the blood of birds, mammals, or reptiles. Bird lice and feather mites are not only restricted to birds but usually to certain types of birds (see below). Some are habitat-specific and may be attracted, for example, only to marsh-haunting birds or birds of arid scrub; the nest fly (Neothopilidae) prefers nests made partly of mud such as those of many thrushes.

Families and species of bird lice tend to parasitize particular orders and families of birds exclusively and to parallel the phylogenetic relationships of their hosts. Thus, loon lice may be different from grebe lice, but are likely to be more closely related to each other than to gull lice. The parallel has proved so consistent that comparison of lice has been used to argue taxonomic relationships. The fact that the lice which colonize flamingos are similar to those found on waterfowl is a clue to the much disputed affinities of these groups of birds.

Food preferences of ectoparasites also vary. Fleas, flies, ticks, chiggers, and some lice suck blood, but feather mites and certain lice attack feathers (both the webs and the core of the shaft), and skin debris, body grease, and other bodily fluids are specialties of a number of species.

It may seem that a bird's chances of surviving the onslaughts of this army of tiny attackers are slim, and there is no question that ectoparasites can cause debilitation and death. Some are vectors of diseases fatal to birds; the toxic saliva of some ticks can cause death; an unusually heavy burden of any type of blood-sucking parasite can readily kill nestlings and severely weaken adult birds, making them more vulnerable to larger predators and disease; and the feather-eaters and itch mites, which cause birds to scratch until raw, sometimes cause extensive feather loss resulting in impaired flying ability and exposure.

Still, birds are not totally defenseless. Preening appears to be crucial, and birds unable to preen through some disability are more vulnerable to parasites. Practices such as dusting, smoke bathing, sunning, and anting may be, at least in part, methods of pest control. And, finally, among the array of tiny creatures which inhabit birds and their nests are a number which feed not on birds but on bird parasites! One is reminded of that venerable lyric summary of invertebrate biology:

> Big fleas have little fleas
> Upon their backs to bite 'em.
> Little fleas have smaller fleas,
> And so, *ad infinitum*.

The principal ectoparasites are listed below with brief descriptions of their appearance, habits, and importance. Flies, fleas, and bird lice are insects; ticks and mites belong to the same class as spiders (Arachnida).

Flies (order Diptera)

Blowflies (family Calliphoridae). Adults similar in appearance to greenbottle or bluebottle flies; larvae of species in two genera (*Apaulina* and *Protocalliphora*) live in nest and suck blood of young at night; prefer hole nesters; may occur by the hundreds and cause death.

Botflies (family Oestridae). Adults large, hairy, somewhat bee-like; eggs are laid on nestlings; larva hatches and burrows into skin, where it feeds until ready to pupate; not a major pest in birds in the Temperate Zone.

Mosquitoes (family Culicidae) and other flies which suck blood as adults occasionally attack birds and may have some importance in transmitting disease among them.

Louse Flies (family Hippoboscidae). Most important fly parasites on birds, but a few species attack mammals; adults smaller than housefly; may be winged or wingless; flat and "leathery"-looking; wingless forms crawl through feathers and resemble crab lice; adults remain for life on host; larva hatches and matures within body of the female fly and pupates as soon as "born"; pupa may overwinter in nest or in ground; tend to be habitat-specific, but all species can be found on bird predators; about 100 bird-feeding species worldwide; known from 18 orders of birds.

Fleas (order Siphonaptera). Resemble mammal fleas; about 20 species and subspecies attack North American birds; mainly habitat-specific, a few host-specific; larvae feed on debris in nest; adults suck blood of hosts; raptors which eat mammals may have mammal fleas.

Bird Lice or Chewing Lice (order Mallophaga). Perhaps most important of bird ectoparasites; small, usually flattened, wingless; more than 800 North American species in several families known from more than

500 bird species; mostly on birds—only a few prefer mammal hosts. Most birds are host to a number of species in different body "niches"—head and neck lice, fat, rounded, sluggish with clasping mouth parts; wing and back lice, slender, agile to elude preening bird—do not suck blood but bite off bits of skin or eat feathers and pith of rachis; spend entire life cycle on bird, attaching eggs to feathers and dispersing by contact between birds; a few live in throat pouches of cormorants and pelicans; heavy infestation may coincide with debilitation of host; die with the host; highly host-specific and phylogeny parallels that of hosts, thus useful as taxonomic characters. It has been observed that prodigious "blooms" of lice sometimes occur on moribund birds, apparently as an effect rather than a cause of the individual's condition.

Ticks and Mites (order Acarina). Many important bird parasites in about a dozen families of this large order; behavior patterns very variable with regard to host specificity, feeding and breeding habits; may occur in nests in spectacular numbers; a few groups should be emphasized.

Hard and Soft Ticks (families Ixodidae and Argasidae). Typical ticks which lay eggs away from host and feed on blood during two nymphal stages and the adult stage; hard ticks gorge once during each stage, then drop off and find new host for next meal; soft ticks usually live in nest and take successive meals at night; species of both types may favor particular places of attachment, e.g., around eyes; both can transmit disease or inject a toxic saliva which can cause fatal paralysis.

Chiggers (family Trombiculidae). Very small; adults usually adventitious and tolerant of wide variety of prey, including birds, reptiles, man, and other mammals; larval stage usually more host-specific; generally have blood-sucking habits similar to those of ticks; tend to cluster on areas of head; a few species invade respiratory system by way of nostrils; other species predatory on feather mites.

Itch Mites (family Sarcoptidae). Mostly mammalian pests but a few species attack birds; some invade internal systems, others burrow beneath skin and cause severe irritation and mange, which is often aggravated by scratching of host, causing feather loss and/or infection.

Feather Mites (Analgesidae and several other families). Important parasites, which, of course, are restricted to birds; like bird lice, spend entire life cycle on host; lay eggs on feathers or within quills; often host-specific and habitat-specific on individual bird, different species preferring different types of feathers and even different parts of particular feathers; heavy infestation may severely damage plumage.

See also NEST FAUNA.

EDIBILITY (of birds, eggs, nests). In the present era of Migratory Bird Acts, strict hunting seasons, and heightened "eco-consciousness," the notion of eating birds suggests to most North Americans the grocery store

much more strongly than the wilderness. Yet as late as 1882, one O. A.
Taft, proprietor of a hotel and restaurant at Point Shirley, Boston Harbor
(famous for its "game" menu), could bet an assembled company of friends
that they could not name an edible North American bird that he could not
produce instantly. He reportedly had no takers. Lest the reader have too
narrow a conception of what Mr. Taft considered edible, a menu of his establishment which has been preserved (Garland, 1978) includes the following species (translated where possible by the present author): Owls
"from the North," Chicken Grouse (Prairie Chickens) "from Ill.," Upland
Plover, Dough Birds (Eskimo Curlew), Brant Birds (Marbled Godwit?),
Willet "from Jersey," Godwit, Jack Curlew (Whimbrel), Jack (Common)
Snipe, Sand Snipe (Dowitcher?), Rock Snipe (Purple Sandpiper?), Golden
Plover, Beetle-head (Black-bellied) Plover, Redbreast Plover (Knot),
"Seckel-bill" (Long-billed) Curlew, Chicken Plover (Ruddy Turnstone),
Summer (Lesser) Yellowlegs, Winter (Greater) Yellowlegs, Reed Birds
(Bobolinks) "from Del.," Ringneck (Killdeer?), Snipe, Rail (Clapper?)
"from Del.," Brown Backs (Pectoral Sandpiper), Grassbirds (Baird's Sandpipers), and Peeps (small sandpipers). The pièce de résistance of this particular bill of fare is Hummingbirds Served in Walnut Shells! A good
crowd easily—and apparently frequently—disposed of a thousand such
"game birds" of an evening at Taft's. And though by the 1890's a few
voices were being raised against the slaughter required to stock such
sumptuous larders (see CONSERVATION), one could still buy songbirds and
shorebirds in market game stalls here in the first decade of the present
century. Even today, the occasional (illegal) deep-dish robin pie or other
such fare finds its way to the table, especially in rural areas.

Feather hunting and "pure sport" have, of course, taken their toll of
birds (see EXTINCT BIRDS), but the most important single encouragement
to man's inclination to kill birds is that they are extraordinarily good to eat.
Some are better than others, of course; many—consider vultures, for example—do not recommend themselves because of their habits; yet it is not
unreasonable to suppose that every species of North American bird has
been eaten at least once by someone.

Taste. It is gospel among some hunters that how a bird tastes depends upon where it lives and what it eats. By this rule nearly all seabirds
are despised by some as "fishy" and coots rejected as "muddy." Though
there is some truth to this generalization—as most people who have sampled cormorant flesh will affirm—it is belied by certain ingenious methods
of cleaning and preparing "strong" birds which make them very tasty or at
worst innocuous. The author has heard recipes for virtually every species of
seabird in the North Atlantic from experienced gourmands of Newfoundland. Many of these involved immediate evisceration and "blooding" and
often the use of marinades ("pickles") in which strips of breast meat are
cured for weeks or longer before cooking.

Another recipe, this one for the notoriously unpalatable scoters (or "coots" as they are called along the coast of New England), was offered by R. W. Hatch in the December 1924 issue of *Field and Stream*.

> The easiest way is to place the coot in a pot to boil with a good flat iron or anvil. Let it boil long and merrily, and when you can stick a fork in the flat iron or the anvil, as the case may be, then the coot will be ready to eat. If that takes too much patience, take the goodly coot and nail it firmly to a hardwood board. Put the board in the sun for about a week. At the end of that time, carefully remove the coot from the board, throw away the coot, and cook the board.

Other New England coot fanciers allow that it is preferable to roast the coot with a brick in the cavity and when the latter becomes soft, it (the brick) is ready to eat.

In addition to insisting that birds are what they eat, common knowledge also holds that the bigger and/or older a bird, the tougher and "gamier" the meat. Here again there is both support and refutation from those who have dined on ancient swans and the like.

A more scientific note is sounded by Cott (1946 and 1951), who shows that there is some correspondence between cryptic coloration and palatability in birds (and eggs) and that some very conspicuous birds are notably distasteful (see also Meinertzhagen, 1951–COLOR AND PATTERN).

Game Birds. Many species in the duck, turkey, grouse, pheasant, rail, and dove families are still shot legally in parts of North America (see LAWS for specifics). Though many sportsmen shoot for fun alone, all of these species are valued by at least a few for their flesh, and some are very tasty indeed. Most wildfowl eaters agree that Canvasback, teal, and Brant deserve special praise among waterfowl, provided, of course, they have fed in the right places and are prepared properly. The epicurean merits of sea ducks have been discussed above.

Shorebirds. The steep decline of shorebird populations by the turn of the last century is directly attributable to market gunning. With protection, many species have recovered well, others not at all. The Eskimo Curlew or Doughbird, once of "sky-darkening" abundance, may now be extinct, a consequence of its superb flavor (second, according to many, only to the Passenger Pigeon). By all accounts most of the sandpipers and plovers make excellent eating.

Songbirds. Larks, thrushes, "ortolans" (buntings), and many other passerines have been traditional food in civilized Europe for centuries and are still trapped and eaten in large numbers in France, Italy, Greece, and elsewhere. They are usually skinned, roasted on small spits, and eaten bones and all. There is no point in denying that they are delicious. Many southern European householders set window traps for House Sparrows, which some claim are only marginally inferior to ortolans. House Sparrows are not protected by law in North America.

In Latin America, people of all social strata who have never heard of migratory bird treaties shoot migrant warblers and other birds and prepare them by methods similar to those just described. There is no satisfactory way to estimate how many birds perish in this manner.

Museum curators, having skinned a bird for their collection, have been known on occasion to cook and sample the remains; in a statistically insignificant survey made by the author, they too have a generally high opinion of the flavor of small North American songbirds. Evidently Cott's "bright color/bad taste" hypothesis does not hold for breeding-plumaged wood warblers.

Eggs. "Egging" at seabird colonies was once widespread; it was at least partially responsible for the demise of the Great Auk and allegedly brought about the virtual absence of Herring Gulls along the New England coast early in this century. Eskimos and other North American natives are still allowed by law to harvest the eggs from seabird colonies (as well as the birds themselves).

Seabird eggs, like their parents, are widely thought to be "fishy." This may be the case under certain circumstances, but in the experience of many, a fresh Herring Gull egg is superior in taste to a supermarket hen's egg.

Plover, gull, and quail eggs are familiar European delicacies—the latter, at least, being provided by domestically bred birds.

Cott (1954) says that eggs of larger colonial nesters taste better in general than those of smaller solitary nesters and that (as with birds) cryptically colored eggs tend to taste better than conspicuous ones. The latter (he says) are likely to be bitter.

Nests. Only the nests of a few species of Asian swiftlets in the genus *Collocalia* are eaten by man (see BIRD'S NEST SOUP). They are made almost entirely of the bird's sticky saliva. Since the amount of spittle used by some of our native swifts in cementing their nest materials together is comparatively small and the toil of removing it from the other nest materials comparatively great, savory bird's nests have remained an imported delicacy in North America.

EDWARDS PLATEAU (Texas). An approximately 20,000-square-mile elevated block of limestone in south-central Texas (the "hill country") pitted with sinkholes, traversed by cool, clear streams, and covered with pleasant juniper/scrub oak woodland. The breeding range of the Golden-cheeked Warbler is exclusively restricted to this habitat. Other specialties of the region, only slightly less restricted in North American range, are the Cave Swallow (breeds in caves and sinkholes) and Black-capped Vireo (oak-juniper scrub). The area also contains many species of both eastern and western affinity. Austin is situated at the eastern end of the plateau and San Antonio just off the southeastern edge.

EGG. In one sense, simply the female reproductive cell or ovum. A bird's egg, however, consists of the ovum, including its attached food supply (yolk), surrounded by a mass of gelatinous and nearly liquid "egg white" (albumen), the whole enclosed in a hard calcium shell.

FORMATION AND STRUCTURE (see Fig. 18). A bird's egg originates as a germ cell within a small sac (follicle), many of which, together with "supportive" tissue, make up the female reproductive organ or ovary (see REPRODUCTIVE SYSTEM for a different perspective on this process). In addition to germ cells, the lining of the follicles contains other types of cells, some of which develop into the egg yolk. As the yolk grows preceding ovulation, the follicles expand into a spherical shape, and the ovary as a whole takes on the appearance of a tiny whitish or yellowish cluster of grapes.

The Yolk when fully formed ranges in color from pale yellow to deep orange-red. It consists essentially of protein and fat granules arranged in concentric layers of white yolk (narrower layers; less fatty) and yellow yolk. The germ cell (the nucleus of the unfertilized ovum; also called the germinal spot or vesicle) remains on the surface of the yolk but is connected to its core (latebra) by a narrow column of white yolk of which the core itself also consists. Once fertilized, the germ cell will divide—the first step in EMBRYONIC DEVELOPMENT—and as the embryo continues to grow it will take most of its nourishment from the attached yolk.

Ovulation. When the ovum reaches full size it bursts the skin of the follicle and passes through the wide mouth (infundibulum) of the oviduct and into the uppermost reaches of this tube for fertilization by the male reproductive cell (spermatozoon). Whether fertilized or not, the ovum then passes into the magnum, an enlarged chamber of the oviduct with muscular walls containing mucous glands from which is secreted the albumen.

Albumen consists of protein and carbohydrate (i.e., a glycoprotein) dissolved in water and is secreted in four layers around the yolk. The layers are alternately thin (i.e., almost watery) and thick (more gelatinous) and together serve to cushion the developing embryo and its food supply, to retain essential water, and to provide an additional source of nutriment. The first (innermost) layer of albumen encloses the yolk closely and develops at opposite ends into fibrous cords of albumen, called the chalazae. These structures, unique to birds, hold the yolk in a stable position with the germ cell (later the embryo) on top as the developing egg tumbles through the spirally ridged walls of the oviduct. The outer ends of the chalazae are connected to an outer fibrous layer of albumen (which is ultimately linked at both ends to the shell membranes), so that in order to

FIG. 7. *Eggs.*

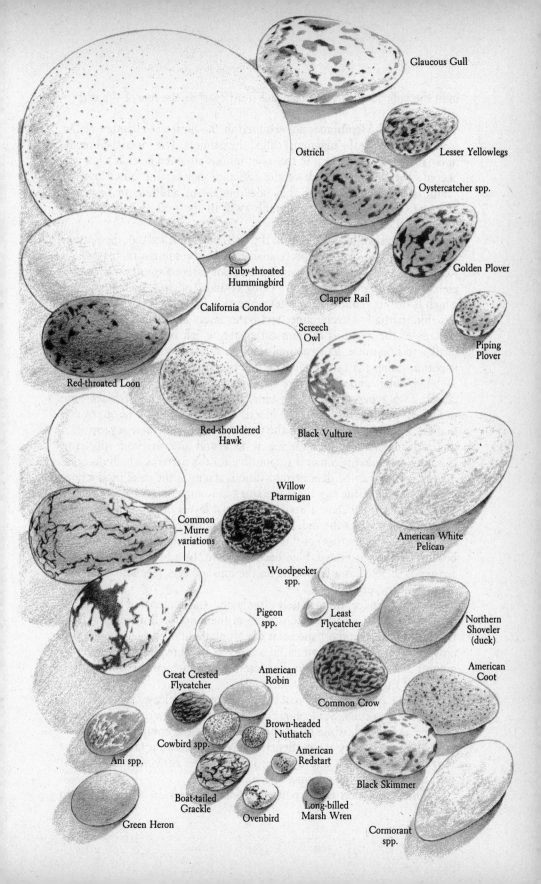

Glaucous Gull

Ostrich

Lesser Yellowlegs

Oystercatcher spp.

Ruby-throated
Hummingbird

California Condor

Golden Plover

Clapper Rail

Screech
Owl

Piping
Plover

Red-throated Loon

Red-shouldered
Hawk

Black Vulture

Willow
Ptarmigan

Common
—Murre
variations

American White
Pelican

Woodpecker
spp.

Pigeon
spp.

Least
Flycatcher

Northern
Shoveler
(duck)

American
Robin

American
Coot

Great Crested
Flycatcher

Common Crow

Brown-headed
Nuthatch

Cowbird spp.

American
Redstart

Ani spp.

Black Skimmer

Boat-tailed
Grackle

Green Heron

Ovenbird

Long-billed
Marsh Wren

Cormorant
spp.

hold the yolk stationary the chalazae must *twist* as the rest of the egg revolves.

The Shell Membranes are acquired in the narrower chamber of the oviduct (following the magnum) called the isthmus. The inner shell membrane fuses with extensions of the outer fibrous albumen layer at what will become the "pointed" ends of the egg and encloses the outer layer of "thin" albumen. The outer shell membrane—in addition to being attached to the inner shell membrane—will in the next step become attached to the eggshell itself.

The Eggshell is secreted from the walls of the shell gland, the portion of the oviduct (in some respects analogous to the human uterus) which follows the isthmus. The suspended calcium carbonate salts that are secreted quickly harden into interlocking crystals (calcite), the cohesion of which is further reinforced by interconnecting protein fibers. The eggshell has thin, partially organic inner and outer layers but all but a small percentage of the whole is calcium carbonate, which is also the essence of chalk and limestone. Its structural strength notwithstanding, the eggshell is porous rather than solid, allowing the contents to "breathe."

Egg colors and patterns are also secreted from the walls of the shell gland. Two types of pigment—blue/green and red/brown/black—are produced, possibly from bile and blood, respectively. The blue/green coloration is deposited throughout the shell and when it is present provides a uniform coloration, though varying in shade and intensity from species to species. The darker pigment is responsible for the patterns which decorate many eggs and can be deposited at various stages in the shell production. On the surface of the egg these markings can range in color from pink to black and also may show through superficial layers of eggshell in muted tones. In some cases the red/brown/black pigment appears uniformly in the surface layers (cuticle) of the egg, altering the underlying color—white becomes yellow or brown; blue becomes olive. In a few species a chalky coating is secreted as a final icing on the finished egg. (See also *Color* and *Texture*, below, and Fig. 7).

The Air Space. Immediately after laying, the contents of the eggshell cool and contract, causing a separation of the inner shell membrane from the outer in what in most species is the blunter end of the egg. It is in this air space that the full-grown embryo takes its first breath of air before beginning the hatching struggle. For internal development beyond the formation of the air space, see EMBRYO.

LAYING. The completion of the nest seems to "release" the egg-laying urge in many species. Some, however, delay laying for a day or more after the nest is finished, while others begin laying before completion.

Many species lay at a particular time of day. Dawn is favored by most songbirds, but pigeons and doves reputedly prefer early afternoon and at least a few species the evening.

The commonest laying pattern is one egg every 24 hours, but 2- to

3-day intervals are not uncommon among falconiforms and intervals of up to 7 days are recorded for the Masked Booby. The female may sit on the nest for about an hour while depositing a given egg but otherwise tends to ignore the nest until the clutch is complete. The male usually continues to be songful during the laying period and copulation often occurs throughout it.

Some species will lay replacement eggs if their first clutch is removed or destroyed and will, in fact, continue to lay almost indefinitely if eggs continue to disappear. Mallards have been induced to lay up to 100 eggs in succession. Such birds are known as *indeterminate layers.* Some gulls, plovers, pigeons, and others, on the other hand, will lay only a fixed number and are therefore called *determinate layers.*

CLUTCH SIZE. The number of eggs laid varies mainly according to genetic determination, simple physical factors, and selective elements that optimize success. To begin with, particular species and families are "programmed" genetically to lay a certain number of eggs per clutch. A single egg per clutch is typical of the tubenoses, tropicbirds, gannets and boobies, frigatebirds, most alcids, some doves, and the odd species in other families. Most passerines average clutches of 3–6 eggs, but totals of 8 or more are not uncommon among tits, nuthatches, wrens, and kinglets. The champion layers are the ducks and gallinaceous birds, among which clutches of 12–15 are not unusual; a Bobwhite clutch of 28 has been recorded. Other groups of birds fall between the extremes—for details, see egg identification references in the Bibliography.

The inherent breeding biology of a species also affects clutch size: colonial nesters whose chicks have high survival rates often lay only 1–2 eggs, while less "secure" species must lay more eggs to compensate for the high attrition rates among eggs, juveniles, and/or adults.

The fact that small birds or those with small brood patches cannot incubate more than a few eggs successfully is an example of a simple physiological clutch-size determinant.

Modifying these deep-seated factors are environmental elements such as geography, climate, and food supply. It has been shown, for example, that: (1) northward-breeding passerines average larger clutches than their southern counterparts—compensating for the fact that their shorter season restricts them to fewer broods; (2) first nests of the season contain larger clutches on the average, maximizing the success of the brood during the optimal period when food supplies are most reliable; (3) island populations of some species lay consistently smaller clutches than their counterparts on the coast of the mainland at the same latitude (Crowell and Rothstein, 1981)—perhaps a means of restricting populations where habitat is limited.

For number of clutches/broods per season, see NEST.

SUPERFICIAL CHARACTERISTICS OF EGGS

Size. In general, the larger the bird, the larger its egg, but there are some anomalies (e.g., the Ruddy Duck is much smaller than the Canvasback but lays a larger egg).

The fossil eggs of the gigantic extinct Elephant Bird, *Aepyornis*, are as large as 14.5" x 9.5" (36.8 cm. x 24.1 cm.) and are thought to have weighed up to 27 pounds (12.27 kilos).

The largest egg of a *living* bird worldwide is that of the Ostrich (the largest bird), both in diameter—average 7" x 5.5" (17.8 cm. x 14 cm.)— and in weight—3 pounds (1,400 grams). The largest native North American bird's egg is that of the Trumpeter Swan—4.3" x 2.8" (10.9 cm. x 7.1 cm.), closely rivaled by the California Condor's—4.3" x 2.6" (10.9 cm. x 6.6 cm.). The egg of the successfully introduced Mute Swan is slightly larger than either—4.5" x 2.9" (11.43 cm. x 7.37 cm.).

Hummingbirds unquestionably lay the smallest eggs of any living birds, though which species holds the absolute world record is unresolved. The egg of the Bee Hummingbird (*Mellisuga helenae*—a Cuban endemic and the world's smallest bird) is often cited: 0.45" x 0.32" (1.14 cm. x 0.81 cm.) or thereabouts, but lengths as short as 0.25" (0.64 cm.) are reported for the family. In North America the competition for smallest egg may be too close to call, given normal variation. The egg of the Calliope Hummingbird (smallest North American bird) is recorded at 0.48" x 0.33" (1.22 cm. x 0.84 cm.); that of Costa's Hummingbird at 0.49" x 0.32" (1.25 cm. x 0.81 cm.); both of which may, however, be edged out by the slender egg of the White-eared Hummingbird, measured at 0.49" x 0.31" (1.25 cm. by 0.79 cm.). The smallest hummingbird eggs weigh in at about 0.5 gram (0.0176 ounce).

Because precocial young develop more fully in the egg, their eggs tend to be larger in relation to the size of adult birds than those of altricial species. The eggs of a Baldpate, for example, are significantly larger than those of the similar-sized Common Crow.

Egg size may also vary within a given species according to clutch size (more eggs = smaller ones); season (some songbirds lay slightly larger eggs in succeeding clutches during a given breeding season, while some seabirds' eggs are smaller on the average as the season advances); and age of the female (the eggs of some birds tend to be slightly larger as the female ages).

SHAPE. Most, but by no means all, eggs are "egg-shaped," i.e., with one end slightly more pointed than the other. But the range of variation even within this one, readily visualized shape is broad, and several terminologies have been used to describe different shapes with varying degrees of exactness. The account below is based on the now widely used system of Preston (1969) and attempts to sort out some of the ambiguity. Preston's terminology recognizes four basic shapes, each with a longer and shorter variation.

1. *Elliptical,* long elliptical, spherical (substituted for short elliptical). An ellipse is a geometric form widest at the middle of its long axis and

with equally rounded ends. When this shape is "shortened" to the point of eliminating its longer dimension, it ceases to be an ellipse and becomes a circle or, in the case of a three-dimensional shape, a sphere; hence the substitution of "spherical" for "short elliptical." "Round" is another substitute for "spherical." Among North American birds only some owls lay eggs which approach spherical shape; most are better described as elliptical. Hummingbirds provide the best North American examples of long-elliptical eggs.

2. *Sub-elliptical*, long sub-elliptical, short sub-elliptical. Longer and more tapered toward both ends with greatest width not at the midpoint of the long axis. Cranes' and rails' eggs are typically sub-elliptical. Grebes' eggs exhibit an extreme of long sub-elliptical, sometimes called "biconical" or "fusiform," with both ends somewhat pointed and widest about the midpoint.

3. *Oval*, long oval, short oval. In the strictest sense "oval" means explicitly "egg-shaped," i.e., broader, more rounded at one end, tapering gradually to a more pointed end. One source of confusion here is that elliptical shapes are often referred to as "oval" in popular usage. As noted, the majority of bird's eggs fit one of the three oval types. "Ovate" may give a mildly technical ring to "oval" but adds nothing to the meaning.

4. *Pyriform*, long pyriform, short pyriform. Pyriform literally means "pear-shaped" and is essentially an extreme form of oval with one *very* broad end, one *very* pointed end, and a tendency for the strongly tapered sides to be relatively straight (or even slightly concave). This form has also been labeled "conical." Murres and many shorebirds lay distinctly pyriform eggs. It is often suggested that in the latter group this shape is an adaptation to efficient incubation, since the four pyriform eggs that sandpipers usually lay form a neat, tight circle when clustered with their pointed ends together; it has also been noted that pyriform objects roll in a circle, a useful adaptation for birds such as murres which lay their eggs on a bare, narrow cliff shelf.

On the whole, basic egg shapes tend to conform within bird families; however, there is also significant variation among members of the same species and even age and seasonal variation in shape among individuals.

Shape no less than structure (see *Formation*, above) contributes to the inherent strength of an egg. It has been estimated that a chicken's egg can withstand pressure of 10 tons per square inch *evenly applied*. This is demonstrated in the parlor trick in which the "volunteer" is challenged to crush a raw hen's egg between his hands along the long axis. The results are usually impressive but can also be messy if the pressure is not applied at the egg's "pointed" ends. Another proof of egg strength is the presence of uncracked starlings' eggs on suburban lawns in the spring. In most cases these are "laid" prematurely by inexperienced females as they fly over.

COLOR AND PATTERN. The normal ground colors of North American bird's eggs are white (i.e., without visible pigment), blue to green, or brown. Depending on where in the shell the pigment occurs and the developing of different pigments (see *Formation,* above), a wide range of hues and shades is possible. In the palest forms, for example, brown can produce a dirty yellow or pink as well as dark umbers. Though many eggs are "plain," the majority have some kind of marking, again in a form of brown pigment. The markings are classified by oologists into categories such as scribbled, scrawled, speckled, spotted, and blotched and may occur in characteristic patterns. The eggs of many species, for example, are "wreathed," i.e., have a concentrated circle of markings at the blunter end which passes through the "shell gland" first and picks up the bulk of the pigment.

There is close color/pattern conformity in some bird families; for example, all North American owls have white or off-white, unmarked eggs. But there is also much variation, not only among species in a family but among individuals of a species. In fact, no two bird's eggs are exactly alike.

Because the eggs of birds' nearest phylogenetic ancestors, the reptiles, are white, it is generally assumed that bird's eggs were originally white and evolved color and pattern in accordance with various survival pressures. Birds such as terns and plovers which nest in the open usually lay eggs cryptically colored and patterned to blend with the ground, making them less obvious to predators. The fact that many cavity nesters have unmarked or sparsely marked eggs suggests a possible relationship between color and exposure to the sun—but this theory is hard to justify in view of the numerous exceptions. The great individual variation in the patterns of murres' eggs may have recognition value for individuals looking for their own eggs in a crowded colony. And some brightly colored eggs may advertise an unpleasant taste.

TEXTURE. Loon, swan and goose, many hawk, alcid, chachalaca, stork, jaeger, and some gull eggs have a *granular* texture (mostly rather fine). Duck eggs have a *waxy* or *greasy* coating which may be a kind of waterproofing. The California Condor's egg is finely *pitted*. Gannets, cormorants, Anhinga, pelicans, flamingos, and anis lay eggs with a superficial white *chalky* coating which tends to scratch or flake off at least partially during incubation. Except for the pelicans, the underlying shell color of these eggs is green/blue. Woodpeckers have notably smooth and *shiny* eggs.

Other North American species have smoothly textured eggs that vary from non-glossy (i.e., "eggshell" or matt) through various degrees of glossiness.

IDENTIFICATION AND COLLECTING. A number of field guides currently on the market, comprehensively illustrated in color (see the Bibliography), make it easy for anyone with a moderately well-developed critical faculty to identify bird's eggs at least to family if not to species.

On the other hand, the opportunity to practice one's oological expertise is now strictly limited by law and (one hopes) by personal ethics. Among wild bird species, only the eggs of the Common Starling, Common Pigeon, and House Sparrow are unprotected by federal law (see LAWS), and the risk of disturbing birds or attracting the attention of nest-molesting species will keep scrupulous naturalists from satisfying their curiosity about "live" eggs too zealously.

HUMANE CONCERNS. A popular "science" lesson among parents and teachers is to artificially incubate commercially purchased eggs, so that the hatching can be watched by wide-eyed youngsters, who thereby derive firsthand experience with the wonders of life. Regrettably, once the hatchling has performed, it rapidly becomes less wonderful, and frequently suffers a lingering death from starvation or rough handling, or it may just be callously flushed down the toilet. There are *two* lessons in life in the above scenario—they cancel each other out.

EGG BLOWING. The practice of emptying a bird's egg of its contents while keeping the eggshell essentially intact for the purpose of preserving it in a collection. This is best achieved, of course, when the embryo is in an early stage of development and the contents of the egg largely liquid or gel. The simplest method is simply to carefully poke a smallish hole with any fine-pointed implement into both ends of the egg. Usually the hole in the blunter end is made somewhat larger and the mouth is applied to the sharper end. Serious oologists, however, are equipped with impressive kits of drills, tiny saws, and blowing tubes of different sizes to perform the task with maximum efficiency and end up with the best possible specimen. See EGG COLLECTING.

EGG-BOUND. Refers to a condition in which a bird is unable to lay an egg that is in its oviduct, due, for example, to an obstruction or malformation of the egg.

EGG COLLECTING. Before it was prohibited by law (see LAWS), collecting birds' eggs was a popular hobby among men and boys in northern Europe and America. Good collections not only included a large species representation (with as many rarities as possible) but also displayed the greatest possible range of variation in the eggs of a given species and often different-sized clutches of the same species. Clandestine egg collectors are still a bane to conservation authorities in parts of Europe (especially Britain), but on the whole the passion for the activity seems largely to have died out in North America. A recent exception was the theft of a nest and eggs of Ross' Gull from its newly established breeding station at CHURCHILL, Manitoba. The culprit apparently cut the entire nest and the grassy tussock on which it was placed from the tundra with a sharp tool between 7 p.m. and 3 a.m., managing to elude a guard posted to protect the site. It is estimated that the eggs might bring as much as $10,000 to $20,000 in the oological underground.

Since the rarest birds inevitably lay the rarest eggs, we can be grateful that the thrill of risking jail and a stiff fine for stealing a bird's egg that can be admired by only a handful of other egg-loving criminals appeals only to a kinky few.

See L. F. Kiff, "Bird Egg Collections in North America," *Auk* (1979), 96:746–55.

EGGSHELL. See EGG.

EGG TOOTH. A small, hard (calcareous) protuberance on the tip of the bill which develops in the embryos of all birds to help break through the eggshell. It is also present in reptiles and a few frogs. In birds, it is usually situated on the upper mandible, but may be on the lower (e.g., in oyster-catchers, avocets, and plovers) or on both (a few species of auks and wood-peckers). The egg tooth usually falls off or is reabsorbed within the first week after hatching (sometimes during the first day) but may remain longer. All North American birds develop this structure; it is lacking only in the Ostrich and the megapodes of Australasia. See Clark, *Wilson Bull.* (1961), 73:268–78.

EGRET (ee-GRETT, EE-grett, even EGG-rett). Standard English name for 8 species of herons (family Ardeidae; order Ciconiiformes), all but one (according to some authorities) in the genus *Egretta*. Four species of egrets breed in North America and 2 others have occurred as accidental stragglers (see Appendix II).

The plumage of all egrets is largely or totally white (the Reddish Egret has both white and dark color phases) and all but the Cattle Egret develop long, exceedingly delicate plumaceous feathers as part of their breeding display. These graceful plumes or "aigrettes" were in great demand around the turn of the century as decorations for women's fashions. This taste created a thriving trade for plume hunters and nearly extirpated the egrets (see CONSERVATION for details of the feather trade).

Aside from their whiteness and inordinately decorative plumage, the egrets resemble the other HERONS.

"Egret" derives from a diminutive form of Old High German and Old French words for "heron."

EIDER (EYE-der). Standard English name for 4 species of sea ducks (family Anatidae; order Anseriformes), all of which breed in North America. They are sometimes included with the bay ducks and other sea ducks in the subfamily Aythyinae, or in the subfamily Merginae or tribe Mergini, both of which exclude the bay ducks (genus *Aythya*).

All of the eiders have unusual head shapes and color patterns and the drakes are among the handsomest of sea ducks. All four species breed primarily in the Arctic (all but Common Eider exclusively so) and migrate relatively short distances south of pack ice in the winter. The eiders dive in shallow water, feeding on mollusks and other bottom life.

The down which the female Common Eider plucks from her breast to line her nest is harvested in Iceland and other Scandinavian countries for mattresses, pillow stuffing, and clothing linings. Harvesters usually take two linings and leave the third in place; the only ill effect on the birds seems to be inconvenience.

For family characteristics, see DUCK.

EISENMANN, Eugene, 1906–81. Born in Panama City into a family prominent in business and politics, Eugene Eisenmann left his native country at the age of ten for New York City, which became his home for the rest of his life. He graduated from Harvard College and Law School and then joined a Wall Street law firm, from which he retired in 1956. His interest in birds began during his boyhood in Panama, and that country's ornithology occupied his attention all his life. A member of all the major North American ornithological societies, he became president and editor of the Linnaean Society, editor of *The Auk*, and a key member of the Committee on Classification and Nomenclature of the American Ornithologists' Union. Mr. Eisenmann's best-known published work is "The Species of Middle American Birds," *Transactions of the Linnaean Society of New York* (1955), 7:1–128, a slender checklist that revolutionized the taxonomy of that region's avifauna and reified Eisenmann's principles in the coining of standard vernacular names: essentially that birds be named for distinctive features and ones that occur in all races of the species in question.

"Gene" Eisenmann was one of those men whose vast influence cannot be measured by the length of his bibliography. He was a mentor to the young and many of today's prominent ornithologists are his protégés. He was a walking encyclopedia of Neotropical ornithology. He was a dedicated solver of taxonomic quandaries and very generous with his time to anyone similarly engaged. Perhaps his truest measure is taken in the hundreds of acknowledgments in the ornithological literature in which his name appears and the fondness with which he is remembered by his legion of friends.

ELECTROPHORESIS (ee-LEK-tro-for-EE-sis). The movement of minute particles suspended in a liquid under the influence of an electric field. Charles G. Sibley (1960, 1970–TAXONOMY) and others have subjected the different proteins suspended in egg white to electrophoresis in order to discover phylogenetic relationships of bird species. The size, shape, and electric charge of the proteins and the combinations in which they are present are unique in different forms of birds, and because these characters are genetically determined, they provide more reliable clues to taxonomic affinities than superficial structural characters, which often vary and converge (see CONVERGENCE) by adaptation.

The actual techniques of electrophoresis are complex and require sophisticated equipment, but essentially a sample of egg white is put on a medium such as filter paper or acetate and a controlled electric current is directed onto it, for a set time period. The proteins separate into a unique linear pattern which can be dyed, analyzed, and compared with the electrophoretic patterns produced by the egg whites of different species under identical conditions.

EMARGINATE. In ornithological parlance, usually refers to the abrupt tapering of the outer web of a primary feather between its midpoint and tip (see Fig. 9). This character is occasionally used in identifying hard to distinguish species, such as the *Empidonax* flycatchers, in the hand. See WING FORMULA.

EMBERIZID (em-bur-EE-zid or em-bur-EYE-zid). Any member of the family Emberizidae (order Passeriformes), and in the plural, the family as a whole. The emberizid *finches* include the longspurs, New World sparrows, juncos, towhees, buntings, and some grosbeaks. Some taxonomists place the emberizid finches in a subfamily (Emberizinae) under the Fringillidae; however, the current trend is to enlarge the Emberizidae as a family to include the tanagers and perhaps the wood warblers, honeycreepers, and New World blackbirds and orioles.

For a systematic breakdown of the confusing taxonomy and nomenclature of finches, see FINCH and Appendix I.

EMBRYO (embryonic development). The embryonic development of a bird begins immediately after fertilization with the division of the nucleus (germinal vesicle) of the female reproductive cell (ovum). This nucleus is visible as a germinal spot (blastodisk) about ⅛ inch in diameter on the top surface of the yolk of a newly laid egg (see EGG, *Formation and Structure*, and Fig. 8). Within the first 24 hours of incubation, this unimpressive spot shows vestiges of circulatory, nervous, and digestive systems and during the second day a head of sorts with eyes becomes visible. For the first few days, a bird embryo remains a large-headed, long-tailed, tadpole-like creature hardly distinguishable, except by an embryologist, from a human fetus at a similar stage of development. But well before half the incubation period has elapsed, unmistakably avian features, such as a bill and feather tracts, can be discerned. And for the last few days before hatching, the embryo essentially resembles a full-grown chick crammed into much too small a space.

One of the first features to develop is a system of veins, through which the embryo draws nourishment from the fats and proteins which, together with water (about 50 percent), make up the yolk. The percentage of the total egg volume taken up by this food supply at the start of incubation depends upon the state of development at which hatching will take place. Most North American passerines have a relatively short incubation period of about 12–15 days, but at hatching the young are blind, naked, and helpless. In these species, the yolk takes up only about 20 percent of the egg. So-called precocial species, such as ducks, shorebirds, and gallinaceous birds, take longer to hatch (from 3 to 7 or more weeks; see INCUBATION), and require a larger yolk (about 35 percent of total volume), but emerge from the shell with a full coat of protective down and are almost immediately able to fend for themselves.

The yolk is gradually consumed by the developing embryo until, shortly before hatching, the yolk sac and what little of its contents is left

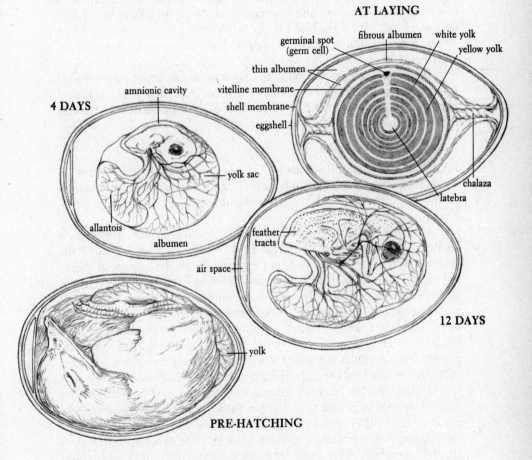

FIG. 8. *Embryonic development.* Four stages from the laying of a fertilized egg to just before hatching.

pass into the body of the young bird through the umbilical opening. This yolk remnant can nourish the nestling for several days after hatching, allowing time for the parents or chick to establish the new feeding routine.

The egg white (albumen), which is 90 percent water, cushions the yolk and embryo, retains vital moisture, and provides an additional source of protein. It too is consumed during the incubation period.

The embryo takes its necessary oxygen through the porous walls of the eggshell until, just before hatching, the bill is poked through into the air space at the wider end of the egg (see Fig. 8) and the young bird takes its first real breath. Excretory products (largely urine) flow into a special sac, the allantois, a kind of external bladder which develops out of the hind gut of the embryo. Furthermore the tissue of the allantois is thickly threaded with blood vessels which carry oxygen to the embryo. Eventually, of course, these excretory and respiratory functions are taken over by kidneys and lungs within the bird's body. Adult birds have no urinary bladder and by hatching time most of the allantois has dried up and remains in the shell.

Barring disease or accident, the success of the embryonic progress from germinal spot to bird—an enormously complex process barely hinted at here—requires only that the temperature of the embryo be kept close to that of the parents (see INCUBATION).

EMPIDONAX (em-PID-uh-nacks) ("empi"). A New World genus of about 16 species of small (4 to 6 inches), famously nondescript tyrant flycatchers (family Tyrannidae; order Passeriformes), 10 of which breed in North America.

The "empis," as they are fondly called by birdwatchers who enjoy a challenge, present one of the great field identification problems in the North American avifauna. They are exceedingly similar in general shape, coloration, and JIZZ. All are drab with prominent wing bars and eye rings. All are readily identifiable during the breeding season by song and habitat preference and some (notably the Buff-breasted, Western, and Yellow-bellied Flycatchers) can be "called" with a high degree of certainty on color (and distribution) alone. Several of the others are distinctive enough to the practiced eye as adults but remain inscrutable in immature plumage. Short of murder or the bird's suicide, there are two traditional ways to deal with the identification of "empis." One is to catch the bird in question (for which one needs a permit from the federal authorities; see BANDING) and compare the lengths of the primary feathers (see WING FORMULA), which vary distinctively among the different species. The other approach is to study all members of the genus intensively, noting the minutest variations in plumage color (brownish olive or olive brown?), form of eye ring, mandible color, tone and extent of wing bars, and tail gestures—for all ages and in all light conditions. The field ornithologist with this level of detailed expertise can, under good conditions, often make a highly educated guess about the identity of any given *Empidonax*.

For identification, see Phillips, Howe, and Lanyon, *Bird-Banding* (1966), 41:190–99.

ENDANGERED BIRDS. See Plate 6. The U.S. Fish and Wildlife Service (Department of the Interior) publishes periodically a register of species and subspecies of plants and animals of the world which have been identified as endangered. The Endangered Species Act of 1973 defines its subject as "any species which is in danger of extinction throughout all or a significant proportion of its range." The Service also lists "threatened" species and subspecies, defined as "any species which is likely to become an endangered species within the foreseeable future"; as well as "rare" species and subspecies, defined as "although not presently threatened with extinction . . . in such small numbers throughout its range that it may be endangered if its environment worsens. Close watch of its status is necessary."* An "Endangered Species Technical Bulletin" is published monthly to report the latest news on particular species.

The register for Tuesday, May 20, 1980 (Vol. 45, No. 99), lists as endangered 27 species *and subspecies* of birds which occur in North America (very rarely or irregularly in 3 cases). No North American species are listed as threatened. The following seven endangered birds are full species which breed exclusively in North America. If they become extinct in North America they will have ceased to exist on the planet.

California Condor (*Gymnogyps californianus*). *Former Range*: Permanent resident from Washington State south to northern Baja California and east at least as far as Texas. Though it has never been abundant or wide-ranging in historical times, it undoubtedly ranged much more widely prior to 1,000 years ago, and it may have existed in Arizona and Utah as late as the 1880's. *Present Range*: Now restricted to coastal mountain ranges of southern California from Los Angeles County north to Monterey County, east rarely to the foothills of the Sierra Nevada. *Habits*: Nests in caves or (rarely?) in large tree cavities or stumps; lays its single egg on sand or litter on the ground; at best rears only a single young every other year; apparently does not re-nest if egg is lost (breakage is frequent); only sporadically returns to same nest site in successive breeding years; spends much time roosting in dead trees or rocks near nest sites; soars over a wide range on sunny days in search of carrion—its only known source of food. *Main Reasons for Decline*: Many theories have been advanced for the condor's decline, principal ones being: a shortage of food (carcasses)

---

* The International Council for Bird Preservation produces its own thoroughly annotated list of endangered species of the world, known as the Red Data Book (most recent edition, 1981). It uses the categories "Endangered," "Vulnerable," and "Rare," which correspond closely in definition to the Department of the Interior's "Endangered," "Threatened," and "Rare."

in the managed rangeland that now makes up much of its habitat; poisoning by DDT, Agent 1080 (used by ranchers for ground-squirrel control), and/or lead; shooting; collisions with high power lines; unknown habitat inadequacies; or all of the preceding. As Snyder (1980) points out, there is a dearth of evidence to support any of these hypotheses, owing largely to the difficulties inherent in obtaining the relevant data. It is not even known whether the condors are suffering from reproductive failure (not enough young produced to replace old birds) or increase in mortality. It has recently been established that Common Ravens at least occasionally raid condor nest sites and eat eggs. *Current Status:* The total condor population is currently (1982) estimated at between 25 and 30 individuals ranging over about 50,000 square miles (apparently adequate), and it seems to be in precipitous decline. Snyder (1980) cautions that no more than six years may remain to reverse this trend if the decrease continues at the rate calculated since 1945. Effective efforts have been made to provide the birds with additional carcasses, but recently the condors have paid these little attention. Given their high profile, it is unlikely that anyone could shoot a condor *by mistake.* What to do in the condors' eleventh hour is still hotly debated, but recently those experts favoring a crash captive-breeding program have prevailed. Efforts to capture a pair of adult birds during the spring of 1982 were unsuccessful, however.

Whooping Crane (*Grus americana*). *Former Range:* Bred from Hudson Bay to northern Mackenzie, N.W.T., in the north, south through the Great Plains to Iowa and Nebraska and in Gulf coastal marshes (at least in Louisiana) in recent times; may once have ranged continentwide; wintered in the Gulf states from Florida to Texas and south into central Mexico. *Present Range:* A single population now breeds in Wood Buffalo National Park, a 17,300-square-mile wilderness reserve south of Great Slave Lake in Mackenzie and northern Alberta; winters on the Blackjack Peninsula, part of the Aransas National Wildlife Refuge near Rockport, Texas. *Habits:* Makes large (4 to 5 feet in diameter) mound nests in open water in wilderness marshlands in subarctic plains or (formerly) coastland; lays 1–3 (usually 2) eggs; feeds on plant tubers and a variety of large invertebrate and small vertebrate organisms. *Main Reasons for Decline:* Like the condor, probably never abundant in historical times, with low reproductive rate. A large, conspicuous, and "meaty" bird, it was undoubtedly shot for food during the frontier period in the Midwest and continued to be a good target for "slob hunters" until well into this century. However, human settlement—dissipation of wilderness and draining of marshes for farmlands—was probably the major factor in the species' decline. *Current Status:* Following a low point in the winter of 1951–52, during which only 21 birds survived, the cranes have gained steadily and as of the winter of 1981–82 were numbered at 73 wild individuals. This is due in no small measure to nationwide publicity and the grace and beauty of the species, which have created enormous public sympathy, such that even the U.S.

Air Force dares not contemplate an action that would ruffle the feathers of a whooper. Much credit is due local conservationists (especially N. J. "Ding" Darling) and the federal government for taking steps to protect the cranes' vulnerable winter range.

Whooping Cranes normally rear successfully only one of the two (rarely three) eggs laid in a season. With this fact in mind, U.S. and Canadian wildlife authorities in 1967 began removing single eggs from crane clutches at Wood Buffalo and hatching them at Patuxent Wildlife Research Center in Maryland. This effort resulted in a flock of 22 *captive* cranes capable of producing their own eggs. In 1975 biologists began placing these "extra" whooper eggs in the nests of incubating Sandhill Cranes on the Grays Lake National Wildlife Refuge in Idaho with the hope of establishing a second wild population of Whooping Cranes. As of the 1980 breeding season, 7 young whoopers had been reared by the Sandhills and followed their adoptive parents to their wintering grounds in New Mexico. Four of these are now (1981) mature males theoretically capable of holding territory. The climax of this experiment will, of course, be for the orphan whoopers to breed and successfully rear their own offspring.

Eskimo Curlew (*Numenius borealis*). *Former Range:* Bred in Mackenzie, N.W.T., west (probably) to western Alaska; migrated eastward in the fall to staging points near Ungava Bay, and perhaps James Bay, and the Maritime Provinces and then crossed the western Atlantic over the Lesser Antilles to winter quarters in southern Brazil, Paraguay, and Argentina. In the spring the preferred route passed up through the Mississippi drainage. *Present Range:* Unknown, but certainly very small and within the vast boundaries of its historical range. *Habits:* Nests in a virtually unlined depression in barren tundra; winters on shortgrass pampa. In migration frequently associated with the Golden Plover and Whimbrel in close-cut or well-grazed pastures, plowed fields, coastal marshes, and dunes. *Main Reasons for Decline:* Though mention has been made of a conversion from grazed pastures to agriculture along its midwestern migration route, it can be stated unequivocally that, like the Passenger Pigeon, the Eskimo Curlew was simply, thoughtlessly, shot out of existence. Before its decline it was renowned for its great abundance, delicious flavor (see EDIBILITY), and fearlessness of man. Heavy hunting is recorded from the Ungava region; on South American wintering grounds; along the Atlantic coast of the U.S., when weather forced it to interrupt its transoceanic southern migrations; and in spring in the midwestern U.S., whence wagonloads were carted off to market. An abrupt decline was noted in the 1870's; large flocks had ceased to occur by the late 1880's; and by the turn of the century the possibility of extinction had been raised. Unlike most species of shorebirds which were wantonly killed for food and sport in the last century, the Eskimo Curlew never recovered. *Current Status:* Unknown; certainly extremely rare if still surviving. Recent reliable records since 1960 are as follows: April 3, 1960: Galveston Island, Texas (good sight record of single bird); March–April 1962: Galveston Island, Texas (3 or 4 seen and conclusively photographed); April 11, 1963: Rockport, Texas (sight record of 2 birds by experienced observers); September 4, 1963: Barbados, West Indies (bird shot; preserved at Philadelphia Academy of Natural Sciences); August 15, 1976: North Point (James Bay), Ontario (inconclusive but "reasonably convincing" sight record of 2 birds by experienced observers —Hagar and Anderson, 1977). Other sight records in the 1960's and 1970's from Texas and New England at the proper season are intriguing but lack the authority of the sightings noted above.

Bald Eagle (*Haliaeetus leucocephalus*). *Former Range:* Virtually throughout North America from tree line in the north to northern Mexico and Baja California in the south. *Present Range.* Withdrawn from much of its former range though healthy local populations still remain (see *Current Status*, below). *Habits:* Seldom seen away from large bodies of water— salt or fresh; still or running—where it can find its preferred food, fish. Characteristically nests high in living trees; usually lays 2 eggs. *Main Reasons for Decline:* DDT, highly concentrated in fish tissues, severely damaged breeding success of this eagle—our national emblem—in all but the remotest parts of the country (see MAN-MADE THREATS TO BIRDLIFE); encroachment on habitat due to population growth and some trophy shooting have also contributed in some degree to decline. *Current Status:* There has been a notable recovery of the species since the ban of DDT in the U.S., but it is still listed as endangered except in Alaska, Washington, Oregon, Minnesota, Wisconsin, and Michigan, in all of which it is listed as threatened.

Bachman's Warbler (*Vermivora bachmanii*). *Former Range:* Southern Indiana and southern Missouri east to Virginia, south to northern Arkansas and Alabama; nesting proved in five states; wintered in Cuba, and perhaps the Isla de Pinos, Bahamas. *Habits:* A bird of mature swamp woodlands, breeding in marginal thickets (mainly cane). Feeds mainly low. A typical wood warbler in most respects. *Main Reasons for Decline:* Probably never abundant, though locally common (150–200 in migration, Key West, July–August 1887–89), but shot by late-nineteenth-century collectors in large numbers (e.g., 46 in one area in 1890) in migration. Its present scarcity does not seem to be attributable to destruction of its breeding habitat, which, though lumbered in some areas, still exists in sufficient quantity to support a healthy Bachman's Warbler population. Destruction of its wintering habitat, about which little is known, on Cuba and the Isle of Pines is a more likely cause of the species' decline. This may also be the exceptional case in which overcollecting contributed to extinction. *Current Status:* No more than 6 per year have been recorded anywhere since the 1950's, with records decreasing to the present. Most recent sightings are from I'on Swamp near Charleston, South Carolina (a male and female in the spring of 1977), and a spring record of a female from Cuba (April 6, 1980; see Ripley and Moreno, 1980).

There have been intimations (Shuler, 1977) that the National Forest Service, which "manages" the I'on Swamp, has traditionally acted in the interest of the lumber industry rather than that of Bachman's Warbler in discharging its responsibility.

Kirtland's Warbler (*Dendroica kirtlandii*). *Former Range:* Not known to have ranged far beyond its current distribution but may have occurred more widely in the extensive appropriate habitat in Canada. *Present Range:* Breeds in north-central Michigan (east of Grayling; see Fig. 17) and possibly very locally elsewhere; winters in the Bahamas; rarely seen on migration. *Habits:* Nests in loose colonies, building a lined cup on ground under cover of low (young) jack pines between 6 and 12 feet tall—essentially to the exclusion of all other habitats; thus its distribution normally tends to shift to areas where there have been burns in the recent past; its habitat is now managed for its protection by the U.S. Forest Service in the 4,000-acre Huron National Forest; habits typical of wood warblers in most other respects. *Main Reasons for Decline:* The small total population of this species has remained relatively stable during the period of recorded ornithological history. Its present threatened status has been caused mostly by Brown-headed Cowbirds. This species lays its eggs in the nests of small birds, which raise the cowbird "orphans" to the detriment of their own progeny (see BROOD PARASITISM; COWBIRD). Cowbirds were responsible for a 60 percent decline (to 201 singing males) of the species over a ten-year period ending in 1971. Blue Jays have also been found to take a heavy toll of Kirtland's young (Harwood, 1981). There is also some reason to fear that habitat destruction amounting to total clearing of vegetation for resort communities and sugarcane fields in much of the Bahamas may have drastically reduced food sources for wintering (as well as native) birds, including Kirtland's warbler. *Current Status:* Following a program to control parasitism by Brown-headed Cowbirds, the Kirtland's population has recovered somewhat from its low point in the early 1970's. In the spring of 1980, 242 singing males were recorded. This tiny population remains extremely vulnerable, however, its future depending on continuing management of its breeding grounds and maintenance of wintering habitat.

Red-cockaded Woodpecker (*Picoides* [*Dendrocopus*] *borealis*). *Former Range:* Northern Oklahoma, Tennessee, and southern Maryland south to eastern Texas, the Gulf coast, and Florida Keys; has been recorded as far north as Pennsylvania and New Jersey. *Present Range:* Though the limits of its range remain unchanged, the species has become increasingly isolated in islands of habitat throughout much of it. *Habits:* Life cycle inextricably bound to pine forest; prefers open stands of long-leaf, loblolly, shortleaf, and slash pines; feeds largely on wood-boring (pine-associated) insects, and nests, when possible, 20 to 100 feet up in pines infected with "red heart," a fungus disease which attacks the core of older pines. *Main Reasons for Decline:* The management of southern pine woods for timber and pulp—removal of diseased trees, prevention of new infestations, i.e., the current profit-oriented trend toward "healthy" forest plantations—deprives this woodpecker of suitable nesting and feeding habitat. Chemical control of fire ants may diminish food resources and affect the species' reproductive success. *Current Status:* 3,000–10,000 birds in 2,500 colonies estimated in 1971. A 13 percent decline in sample colonies between 1971 and 1975. Private and government efforts are being made to manage woodland in favor of the species.

The following four endangered subspecies represent the entire North American populations of more widespread species.

Florida Everglade Kite (*Rostrhamus sociabilis plumbeus*). *Former Range:* Southern Florida. *Habits:* A bird of marshes and lake-margin rush beds that feeds, almost exclusively, on large freshwater "apple" snails (*Pomacea paludosa*). *Main Reason for Decline:* Drastic decline in snail populations, due to expedient draining of wetlands in Florida, reduced these birds in the 1950's to a few pairs (approximately 10 individuals in 1965) on the shores of Lake Okeechobee. *Current Status in North America:* This is a hardy and resilient species and with protection and management it has established stable breeding populations in Everglades National Park, Loxahatchee National Wildlife Refuge, and National Audubon Society property at Lake Okeechobee. The total Florida population was estimated at over 100 birds in 1970 and has remained stable or increased since. *Status of the Species Worldwide:* The Everglade Kite remains abundant in its preferred habitat in much of Latin America from Mexico to Argentina and Cuba; because of its highly specialized food preferences, however, it will always be vulnerable to drainage of wetlands.

American and Tundra Peregrine Falcons (*Falco peregrinus anatum* and *F. p. tundrius*). These two races are the only Peregrine Falcons which breed in North America except for *F. p. peali*, which breeds in the Aleutian Islands of Alaska and the Queen Charlotte Islands off western Canada. *Former Range: Tundrius* is an arctic race (not recognized by all authorities) which breeds from Alaska to Greenland north of the tree line; *anatum* once occupied the remainder of North America south into Mexico (in the cordilleras) in suitable habitat; *tundrius* winters in Latin America—at least as far south as the Beagle Channel; *anatum* winters in the southern half of the U.S. and perhaps into the northern Neotropics. *Present Range:* Pure *F. p. anatum* is extinct as a breeding species in eastern North America (however, see below). Populations in the West are currently (King, 1981) estimated as follows: boreal U.S. and Canada: about 50 pairs; western Texas to central Mexico: 100+ pairs; Gulf of California: 35–50 pairs. Because of its more remote habitat, *tundrius* did not decline as drastically but is much reduced and also considered endangered. *Habits:* Feeds mainly on medium-sized birds; nests on rock ledges in wilderness but has also bred on city skyscrapers, where its main prey was pigeons. *Main Reason for Decline:* Reproductive rate drastically reduced due to high levels of DDT deposited in the tissues of its prey, resulting in the production of thin, breakable eggshells. *Current Status:* Though DDT is now banned or controlled in the U.S. and Canada, it continues to threaten Peregrines on tropical wintering grounds, where it is still widely used. The Peregrine Project based at the Laboratory of Ornithology at Cornell University, in cooperation with the National Audubon Society and the U.S. Fish and Wildlife Service, has generated widespread public concern about the species. The Laboratory has been engaged in an extraordinarily successful program of inducing captive Peregrines to lay eggs, which are then artificially incubated; the young are reared until they are about 30 days old, and then placed in artificial nest sites where unseen humans feed them until they fledge. Since 1975, 220 young Peregrines have been released into the wild in this manner, and in the spring of 1980 two pairs of captive-bred Peregrines successfully reared young in New Jersey—the first east of the Mississippi since the 1950's—and a pair was in residence on Mt. Desert Island, Maine. There were further successes in the 1981 season, including a new nesting site in the White Mountains of New Hampshire. These captive-reared birds are of "mixed genetic stock" and not "pure" *anatum. Status of Species Worldwide:* The Peregrine Falcon is cosmopolitan in distribution, with about 18 races recognized, several of which (in addition to *tundrius* and *anatum*) have also suffered population declines. The nominate race, *F. p. peregrinus,* of Europe, was also endangered by DDT, but has recovered encouragingly in the British Isles.

American Ivory-billed Woodpecker (*Campephilus principalis principalis*). *Former Range:* East Texas to southeastern North Carolina south and up Mississippi drainage to southern Illinois and Ohio. *Present Range:* Possibly single individuals or pairs remain in wilderness areas in South Carolina, Florida, Louisiana, and/or Texas, but no confirmed breeding site is known (or at least recorded). *Habits:* Occupied large territories (*maximum* density: 1 pair per 16 square miles) in mature river-bottom forests, feeding principally on the larvae of wood-boring beetles; nest hole high in trees; its ideal habitat was diseased forest, heavily infested with its preferred food. *Main Reason for Decline:* Destruction and "cleaning" of extensive southern hardwood forests. *Current Status:* Perhaps extinct; last pair photographed May 22, 1971; unconfirmed sightings of individuals since. *Status of the Species Worldwide:* The only other race of the Ivory-billed Woodpecker is the Cuban Ivorybill (*C. p. bairdii*), which is also critically endangered. It is presently restricted to mixed montane pine-hardwood forest in eastern Cuba (Oriente Province), where 12–13 pairs survived up to 1956. As of 1974 it was estimated that no more than 6 pairs survived.

The following five endangered species or subspecies have never bred in North America (at least in historical times) but have been recorded here.

Short-tailed Albatross (*Diomedea albatrus*). Once occurred commonly off the Pacific coast of North America and bred by the millions mainly in the Isu Islands of Japan. Now reduced to a single colony of about 57 pairs and perhaps another 100 non-breeders on Torishima (in the Isus). There have been a handful of records off our west coast (Alaska, British Columbia, Oregon, California) in the 1960's and 1970's; most recent confirmed record in North America was a bird photographed off Westport, Washington, May 3, 1970.

Cahow or Bermuda Petrel (*Pterodroma cahow*). Sometimes considered a race of the Black-capped Petrel (*Pterodroma hasitata*), the Cahow has always been restricted to the islands of Bermuda. With settlement, it was reduced to nesting on a few small offshore islands near Castle Harbor. It was a major food source for starving colonists during periods of famine in the seventeenth century, and rats, pigs, and other companion animals of man contributed to its decline. It also suffers from competition with White-tailed Tropicbirds, which share breeding habitat with the petrel. Arriving about two weeks later than the Cahows and finding petrel chicks in a suitable nesting burrow, the tropicbirds kill the chicks and take over the site. The effects of DDT on breeding success were thought to doom the tiny remnant population as late as the 1960's. However, due to the efforts of a single man, David B. Wingate, a Bermuda conservation officer, who studied the problem, promoted public awareness of the bird's plight, and instituted a plan for conservation, the Cahow is now increasing slowly but steadily with chick production averaging 12 per year.

The Black-capped Petrel as a whole is listed as "Vulnerable" by the I.C.B.P. (King, 1981).

Thick-billed Parrot (*Rhynchopsitta pachyrhyncha*). Breeds locally in coniferous forests of north-central Mexico and possibly nested as far north as southern Arizona and New Mexico in pre-colonial times. Irregular invasions have occurred into the latter area since, with over 1,000 birds recorded in the Chiricahua Mountains of southeastern Arizona in 1917–18. The last reliable U.S. record is from 1935, though there are rumors of sightings as late as 1945. The dwindling of Mexican populations is probably largely due to cutting of their high-elevation pine forest habitat for lumber. The much-repeated notion that they require abandoned holes of the nearly extinct Mexican endemic Imperial (Ivory-billed) Woodpecker (*Campephilus imperialis*) is probably overstated.

Greenland White-tailed (Sea) Eagle (*Haliaeetus albicilla groenlandicus*). Breeds only in southwestern Greenland north as far as Disko Bay. As of 1974 the Greenland population was estimated at 200 adults and a smaller number of juveniles. This essentially Palearctic species has withdrawn from much of its world range with encroachment of human settlement and attendant firearms; the Greenland race appears to be dwindling for similar reasons. The great "erne" is an accidental visitor to the northern coastal extremities of North America. See Appendix II.

The following eleven endangered, threatened, or rare subspecies make up only a part of the North American population of their species, the rest of which is not presently considered endangered.

Aleutian Canada Goose (*Branta canadensis leucopareia*). Breeds in the Aleutian Islands, Alaska; winters on the Pacific coast of North America. Apparently recovering well with release of captive-bred birds and listed as only "Rare" by I.C.B.P. (1981).

Attwater's Greater Prairie Chicken (*Tympanuchus cupido attwateri*). Resident locally, coastal prairies of Texas. Population currently stabilized at low levels and therefore listed as only "Rare" by I.C.B.P. (1981).

Masked Bobwhite (*Colinus virginianus ridgwayi*). Formerly resident in southern Arizona, as well as Sonora, Mexico; extinct in U.S. since early twentieth century, and near extinction throughout its range. Some efforts made to reintroduce birds from Mexico into southern Arizona since 1937, but all have failed due to lack of sufficient protected habitat.

Mississippi Sandhill Crane (*Grus canadensis pulla*). Resident Mississippi; fewer than 50 birds remaining in a localized population near the Gulf coast.

California Clapper Rail (*Rallus longirostris obsoletus*). Coastal salt marshes of northern California; 5,000 birds or fewer remaining. Listed as "Vulnerable" by I.C.B.P. (1981).

Light-footed Clapper Rail (*R. l. levipes*). Coastal salt marshes of southern California and northern Baja California. Perhaps 250 birds remain.

Yuma Clapper Rail (*R. l. yumanensis*). Salton Sea, California, and locally on Colorado, Gila, and Salt rivers, Arizona; south along Pacific coast of Mexico to Nayarit. Apparently on the increase or stable and no longer listed by I.C.B.P. (1981).

San Clemente Loggerhead Shrike (*Lanius ludovicianus mearnsi*). Restricted to one small island off the coast of southern California that has suffered severe habitat alteration due to the introduction of goats. Only 16 individuals recorded in 1974 and reproductive success apparently poor.

Cape Sable Seaside Sparrow (*Ammospiza maritima mirabilis*). Brackish coastal marshes of southwestern Florida. Almost wiped out by the hurricane of 1935, but currently population may contain almost 3,000 birds. Thus listed as "Rare" by I.C.B.P. (1981).

Dusky Seaside Sparrow (*A. m. nigrescens*). Salt marshes of central eastern coast of Florida (near Merritt Island). Effectively extinct. As far as known, remaining birds are all males and all in captivity.

San Clemente Sage Sparrow (*Amphispiza belli clementeae*). Restricted to San Clemente Island off coast of southern California. Current population consists of perhaps 20–30 adults and continues to decline due to habitat destruction by goats.

The following species or subspecies are considered "Rare" (as defined above) in North America by the U.S. Department of the Interior, though none is listed in the most recent (1981) edition of the I.C.B.P. Red Data Book.

Florida Great White Heron (*Ardea herodias occidentalis*)
Short-tailed Hawk (*Buteo brachyurus*)
Prairie Falcon (*Falco mexicanus*)
Northern Greater Prairie Chicken (*Tympanuchus cupido pinnatus*)
Lesser Prairie Chicken (*T. pallidicinctus*)
Greater Sandhill Crane (*Grus canadensis tabida*)
Florida Sandhill Crane (*G. c. pratensis*)
California Black Rail (*Laterallus jamaicensis coturniculus*)
Golden-cheeked Warbler (*Dendroica chrysoparia*)
Ipswich Savannah Sparrow (*Passerculus sandwichensis princeps*)

See also EXTINCT BIRDS; CONSERVATION; MAN-MADE THREATS TO BIRDLIFE.

ENDEMIC (en-DEM-ik) (endemism). In a biological context, "endemic" means restricted in distribution to a given area. The term can be applied to any taxon and to an area of any size. The bird family Parulidae (wood warblers) is endemic to the New World but not to North America. The Bay-breasted Warbler is a *breeding* endemic of North America or the Nearctic region but winters in the Neotropics. Whether it is considered a full species or a racial variation, the Brown-capped Rosy Finch is endemic to a few peaks of the central Rocky Mountains above timberline. Most of our native grouse, woodpeckers, corvids, and tits are North American endemics.

The medical meaning of "endemic," most often used in describing the occurrence of disease, is quite different: that bilharzia is "endemic" in Venezuela does not mean that the parasitic condition is restricted to that country, but that it is constantly present there.

ENDOCRINE SYSTEM. Endocrine glands produce chemicals called hormones and secrete them directly into the bloodstream; *exocrine* glands produce substances other than hormones and secrete them (usually by means of a duct) externally or to other parts of the body: the liver, which secretes bile to the intestines for digestion, and the oil gland, which secretes oil from a bird's rump, are both exocrine glands.

The endocrine system is linked by *function* rather than tissue. It works in close conjunction with the nervous system to stimulate and balance a great diversity of bodily functions. Many of these are subtle and therefore little understood or undiscovered. The following brief description of these glands gives the name, location, characteristic hormones, and some of the main functions of a bird's endocrine glands. Those familiar with the human endocrine system will recognize many similarities.

The Pituitary Gland is suspended on a stalk from the hypothalamus at the base of the brain; secretes several hormones which act specifically on other endocrine glands as well as oxytocin, pitressin, prolactin (see PIGEON'S MILK), and vasopressin. The pituitary is a kind of master gland which stimulates activities in many of the other glands and is regulated by them in return. It plays a significant role in the breeding cycle: stimulating sexual function, e.g., the development of a brood patch, and promoting behavioral characteristics such as courtship rituals. It is also known to be responsible for more mundane necessities such as water retention and the muscular contractions required for egg laying. Many pituitary functions known in mammals have yet to be confirmed in birds.

The Thyroid Gland rests at the base of the neck; secretes thyroxin when stimulated by the pituitary gland. The thyroid has many general metabolic functions, e.g., blood production, pulse rate, physical growth. It also controls feather development and coloration and molt sequences and may influence the urge to migrate.

The Parathyroid Glands are very small and are located near the thyroid, though precise location and number vary (usually 2 or 3); they produce parathormone, which monitors calcium and phosphate levels in the blood and is therefore crucial to bone and eggshell development.

The Ultimobranchial Glands, also tiny, lie near the parathyroids and secrete a hormone called calcitonin, the function of which is poorly understood.

The Adrenal Glands come in pairs (sometimes joined) near the top of the kidneys. In birds, as in humans, adrenaline is the emergency hormone; it can rapidly raise the amount of sugar in the blood, supplying extra fuel for the muscles, and increase heart rate and blood pressure.

The Pancreas is a large gland which rests in a loop of the small intestine. It serves both an exocrine function—the secretion of digestive enzymes—and an endocrine function—the secretion of insulin. Insulin is instrumental in releasing energy from blood sugars.

The Gonads (testes and ovaries) are the sex glands and also have both exocrine and endocrine roles. As exocrine glands they produce the male and female reproductive cells (see REPRODUCTIVE SYSTEM). As endocrines they produce male and female sex hormones (testosterone and several estrogens, respectively). These work in close association with the pituitary gland and like it have a wide influence throughout the body, affecting growth, behavior, blood chemistry, and changes in internal and external structures, particularly those associated with breeding conditions.

ENDOPARASITE. An organism which lives inside the body of another organism to the detriment of the host. (For parasites which live on the surface of the body, see ECTOPARASITE.)

For obvious reasons, endoparasites in birds are far less conspicuous than ectoparasites; nevertheless, they occur in great variety, sometimes in great numbers, and are occasionally responsible for significant mortalities.

Internal parasites usually enter the body of the host via one of three routes widely used by different types of organisms: (1) Filarial worms (a type of roundworm—phylum Nematoda) and a variety of single-celled organisms are transmitted from the bloodstream of an infected bird by mosquitoes or other biting insects. (2) Other types of roundworms and tapeworms (subclass Cestoda) have a more or less dormant infective stage, e.g., an egg which is eaten inadvertently by a feeding bird and develops in its preferred site in the host's body. Gallinaceous birds and other ground foragers ingest parasites in this way. (3) Many endoparasites, including some roundworms, some tapeworms, and all flukes (class Trematoda) infect an intermediate host, which is then eaten by a bird. A typical fluke life cycle runs as follows: All flukes have snails as their first intermediate host; with some, the snails are ingested by birds, which then become infected; schistosome flukes transform into an infective stage in the snail, become free-swimming in the water, and enter a bird's body directly through the skin; most flukes, however, require a second intermediate host, such as a fish or aquatic insect, which must be eaten by a bird (or other predator) in order to develop into its final stage; fluke eggs deposited in the digestive tract of the bird are excreted into the water, hatch, and find their appropriate host snail to complete the cycle.

Virtually all organs and spaces in the body are vulnerable to attack by endoparasites, though the digestive tract is especially popular.

Wild birds apparently have a high tolerance for internal parasites and are known, in some cases, to support thousands of them with no noticeable ill effects. Paradoxically, there are also instances in which death seems to have been caused by a relatively minor infestation. Poultry yards seem to be more vulnerable to certain common endoparasites than wild bird populations.

For a more detailed, but still highly readable review of the commoner avian endoparasites, see Soulsby's review in Thomson (1964–ORNITHOLOGY).

ENDYSIS (EN-duh-sis). The acquisition of new feathers, replacing those which are being dropped in the molting process. Compare ECDYSIS, and see MOLT.

ENERGY (expenditure). Attempts have been made to calculate energy expended by birds in flight. There are many variables, such as flying conditions, wing shape, and manner of flight, which make such calculations tricky at best. Some of the data can be interpreted to show that birds cannot possibly produce sufficient energy to fly any distance. Other figures, seemingly closer to reality, indicate energy expenditure in birds to be many times (perhaps thirty times) greater in some cases than that of mammals of comparable weight.

It is obvious, of course, that small, non-soaring migrants which travel thousands of miles must expend great amounts of energy, even under the most favorable conditions, and it has been proven that they store fat prior to their journeys from which to draw the necessary energy (see especially Nisbet et al., 1963–FAT).

The data on bird energy expenditure which exist are expressed in formulas involving ergs per unit of time per unit of muscle or total body weight and often by other technical means, beyond the scope of this book. However, see the Bibliography.

See also FAT; METABOLISM; TEMPERATURE, BODY.

EPIGAMIC (EP-ih-GAM-ik). Characters or behavior patterns which promote reproduction are said to be epigamic. The inflated neck pouches of various grouse species (see Plate 2) are epigamic characters; ritualized precopulatory calls and gestures between mated birds are epigamic behavior patterns.

EPISEMATIC. Behavior and, more usually, color or pattern which aid recognition are said to be episematic. The red spot on the bill of many large gulls is an episematic feature. It is recognized by juvenile gulls, which peck at it, signaling the adult to regurgitate food.

ERYTHRISM (eh-RITH-rizm). In birds, refers to the conspicuous presence of reddish (rufous) pigment in the plumage. The phenomenon is most often seen in normal color variations such as the erythristic (red) phase of the Screech Owl and Cory's Least Bittern and the red forms of the Ruffed Grouse (see Plate 5). However, abnormal erythrism (akin to MELANISM or ALBINISM) has also been recorded, for example in prairie chickens and in Rufous-sided Towhees (see the Bibliography).

ESCAPES. Usually refers to species not native to North America which appear in the wild having escaped or been released from captivity. Wing-clipped birds in waterfowl collections which regain their ability to fly, for example, may depart and take up with nearby free-living populations of similar species. Florida supports a broad exotic avifauna originating mainly from the "jungle garden" type of zoos which are popular tourist attractions there. Cage birds are frequently released because the owner becomes bored with them or for more genuine, if misplaced, humanitarian reasons.

Escaped birds cause two kinds of problems: (1) If they are able to breed successfully and proliferate, they may compete for habitat with native species and/or become pests (see INTRODUCED BIRDS). (2) Records of migratory species which might plausibly reach North America as "natural" vagrants are made ambiguous by birds which have escaped from some form of captivity. This difficulty arises most often in the case of Palearctic waterfowl, many species of which are kept in collections in eastern North America. In a few cases the origins of escaped individuals can be established by inquiring of known collectors about recent losses. However, a negative response doesn't lessen the measure of doubt.

If suspected vagrants are evaluated according to the following criteria, it is usually possible to see where the burden of proof should be: (1) Is the species frequently kept in captivity in North America? (2) Is it a migratory species or a permanent resident within its normal range? (3) Is it particularly susceptible to a weather pattern (e.g., hurricanes) which might explain its occurrence outside its normal limits, and has any such weather pattern occurred recently? (4) Is the species abundant within its normal range or comparatively scarce? (5) Does the individual bird show any signs of having been in captivity, i.e., unusual tameness or (in the hand) callused feet, broken feathers, or other symptoms common among captive birds?

For the sake of a "clean" record, species which are kept in captivity with some regularity in North America, but which also could plausibly occur as vagrants, should be placed on a hypothetical list (even if collected or photographed) and the circumstances of occurrence detailed.

For another perspective on this problem, see Ryan (1972). See also EXOTIC SPECIES; VERIFICATION OF RECORDS.

ESTUARY. The region within the tidal zone at the mouth of a river where salt and fresh water dilute each other. Estuarine areas give rise to unique forms of vegetation, e.g., salt marsh and mangrove swamp, and are favorite spawning areas for marine fishes and invertebrates. They are therefore enormously rich feeding areas for water birds, especially herons, certain ducks, shorebirds, gulls, and terns.

ETHOLOGY (ee-THOLL-uh-jee). The study of the *behavior* of a bird or other organism within the context of its natural environment. In his definitive essay on ethology (1969), Niko Tinbergen cites Darwin as a prototype ethologist and quotes Julian Huxley's nomination of Konrad Lorenz as "the father of modern ethology." Some of the most significant ethological studies of Darwin, Lorenz, and Tinbergen were based on bird species: Galápagos finches, Greylag Geese, and gulls, respectively.

ETIQUETTE FOR BIRDWATCHERS. It is always surprising to find birdwatchers and other naturalists abusing the very resources from which they derive pleasure—but it happens. The departure of the Common Black Hawks that once nested regularly along Sonoita Creek in Patagonia, Arizona, is directly and unequivocally attributable to harassment by birders, and other local rarities have suffered similar fates as a result of the disturbance of sitting birds either directly or by the use of tapes (see RECORDING OF BIRD SOUNDS). It probably must be taken for granted that there will be a few yahoos in any interest group, and the slob birders are doubtless best checked by the responsible majority of the birding community. A knottier problem has arisen with the vastly increased popularity of bird listing. These days, property owners must think twice before alerting the public about a rarity on their land, lest they find their privacy invaded and their acreage trashed by battalions of birders laying siege for as long as the avian celebrity remains on the premises. In many such cases, damage and inconvenience are less the result of individual callousness than simply by-products of large numbers of people in a limited space. Birders have always had to endure being thought a little odd. Far worse would be to gain a reputation as destructive. It would limit our freedom of access and the anti-environmentalist sentiments currently popular among the ignorant would gain credibility.

A "Country Code" of conduct for outdoor recreation is a time-honored tradition in Britain. One always has the feeling that those who most need such standards either never become aware of them or choose to ignore them, but for the record, here is a suggested "Birders' Code."

A BIRDWATCHERS' CODE OF CONDUCT

1. Ask permission before entering private property and abide by what you are told. If part of a large group looking for a rarity on someone's land, be an active part of the group's conscience about impact on the land and the owner's privacy.

2. Leave gates, chains, etc., as you found them.

3. Keep to paths, especially on active croplands.

4. Don't disturb livestock.

5. Leave no litter.

6. Respect other life forms:
   - Don't flush birds unnecessarily.
   - Don't approach active nests too closely.
   - Don't use tapes to excess when disturbance of breeding birds is in question
   - Don't pursue your bird at the expense of other organisms, e.g., plants underfoot.

7. Respect other birdwatchers and naturalists:
   - Keep talk to a minimum or at least at low volume—a particularly tough one for American birders. If you are obliged to lead a group, keep your lectures brief and dulcet.
   - Don't flush birds for a photo or a better look when others are present.
   - Don't assume that all birders benefit from the sounds issuing from your tape recorder; many prefer to pursue their quarry without resorting to mechanical trickery; botanists and hikers trying to capture a semblance of wilderness are likely to be even less sympathetic to taped bird calls.

- Don't slam car doors.
- Leave your dog at home.

See also Glinski (1976), Tucker (1981), Wauer (1974), and Balch (1981).

EURASIA. Europe and Asia combined. Though we sometimes speak of the "continents" of Europe and Asia, the boundaries between the two are more ethnic and political than physiographical. Therefore many species of animals are common to both and may be said, for example, to have a Eurasian breeding distribution.

The term also provides one solution to the problem of synonymy in vernacular names. Thus the American Woodcock, *Scolopax* (*Philohela*) *minor*, is distinguished in the vernacular from its near relative the Eurasian Woodcock, *S. rusticola.*

EURYOECIOUS (yury-EE-shuss). Able to exist in a wide diversity of habitats. The Common Crow is a euryoecious species. Compare STENOECIOUS.

EURYPHAGOUS (you-RIF-a-gus). Tolerant of many different kinds of food. Gulls, Starlings, and crows are among the most euryphagous of birds. Compare STENOPHAGOUS; MONOPHAGOUS; OMNIVOROUS.

EUSYANTHROPIC (yoo-sigh-an-THRO-pik). Living with man. Barn Swallows, Chimney Swifts, phoebes, and other species which often, even preferably, nest in or on houses are eusyanthropic. Compare EXANTHROPIC; SYNANTHROPIC.

EVERGLADES National Park (Florida). A 1,400,533-acre flat "river of grass" dotted with ponds and wooded "hammocks" of West Indian vegetation, the whole making up the southwestern tip of the Florida peninsula. Among a number of trails created by the Park Service to accommodate the thousands of tourists that visit annually is the boardwalk called Anhinga Trail not far from the park's entrance. It is particularly noted for the tameness of its wildlife, including Anhingas, Purple Gallinules, and herons as well as alligators. Other avian specialties of the Everglades include: Roseate Spoonbill, Limpkin, Mottled Duck, Swallow-tailed Kite, Short-tailed Hawk (in North America, breeds exclusively in Florida), Bald Eagle, White-crowned Pigeon, Smooth-billed Ani (occasionally), Gray Kingbird (breeding season), and the Cape Sable race of the Seaside Sparrow. See Smith and Matusek's 1975 *Guide to the Everglades* (Tampa); also Lane's Florida guide (1980–BIRD FINDING). See also FLORIDA KEYS for additional specialties of southern Florida.

EVOLUTION. In biology, the process by which organisms change over time by altering the patterns of their cumulative ancestral traits through random mutation, often in response to environmental pressures. That all species including ourselves are descended from other life forms and have a common ancestor in the first simple organism to appear on earth is inherent in the concept of evolution. The evolutionary scenario suggested by Charles Darwin in his *On the Origin of Species* (London, 1859; many current reprints) depicts gradual, continual change taking place in minute increments over millions of years, but many modern evolutionary biologists now believe that organisms are more likely to change in relatively rapid bursts of adaptation followed by long periods during which they do not change at all.

Evolutionary theory has been from its inception and continues to be at odds with the theological notion of special creation, wherein all species are believed to be unrelated and immutable works of a deity.

See EVOLUTION OF BIRDLIFE; SPECIATION; NATURAL SELECTION.

EVOLUTION OF BIRDLIFE. Due to three relatively recent discoveries—the realization that ancient animal forms are preserved in stone; the ability to determine the stone's age; and evolutionary theory—the perspective with which we are able to consider our present avifauna is enormously broader than it was only 150 years ago. It is now clear, for example, that birds are direct descendants of reptiles, that they were living throughout the earth tens of millions of years before man emerged from apedom, and that compared to the avian heyday several hundred thousand years ago, the modern era supports a scant diversity and population of birds which continues to decline.

Doubtless many more insights lie buried than we have yet unearthed—for example, we still have no fossil showing a stage between a scale and a feather. But what we have managed to examine and classify has proven fascinating.

THE FOSSIL RECORD

Perspective. Since our only reliable source of data on prehistoric birdlife is fossilized remains, we should remember that this form of evidence does not present anything like a thorough and balanced overview of the past. For one thing, there isn't very much of it. Then as now, the fragile bird skeletons which evolved as concomitants to flight were undoubtedly pulverized in predators' digestive tracts or scattered and broken by scavengers and weather far more often than they fell intact into preservative sediment or tar. Furthermore, fossils tend to present a habitat bias. Lake-bed sediments, after all, can be expected to contain a certain number of fossilized lake birds but not to yield many clues as to what kinds of birds inhabited the lakeside forests. Finally, it should be noted that paleo-ornithologists are themselves *rarae aves*, with the result that old bird bones have been looked for and studied less than either modern birds or ancient reptiles.

Sites. North America boasts some of the world's most productive known fossil repositories. During the Cretaceous Period, 50 percent of the continent was submerged below sea level, so that much of the surface rock of what is now the western U.S. is limestone formed by the accumulation of the calcareous skeletons of hard-shelled protozoans called foraminifera. The Niobrara chalk beds, a part of this internal ocean floor in western Kansas, yielded admirably whole skeletons of the famous Cretaceous toothed birds (see below) late in the nineteenth century.

Another exemplary fossil boneyard is the great asphalt deposit or tar pits at the 23-acre Rancho La Brea (= tar in Spanish) near Los Angeles, which was first excavated in 1906–13. Along with mastodons, saber-toothed tigers, and other Pleistocene mammals, 83 species of birds, including the great vulture TERATORNIS, have been recovered from this mire. California is also rich in sedimentary fossil beds, and other sites important to ornithology have been excavated in Oregon (especially Fossil Lake), Wyoming, New Mexico, Texas, Florida, and New Jersey.

Highlights. The chart beginning on p. 250 encapsulates avian ancestry insofar as it has been deduced from the recovery of fossil remains and may help the reader get his bearings in the sometimes confusing geological chronology, with its incomprehensibly long and subdivided eras, periods, and epochs. The following overview attempts to sketch what might be called the "shape" of the fossil record to date and includes brief descriptions of those extinct bird species whose skeletons have excited the most wonder. (For an excellent series of photos and artistic reconstructions of many of the birds mentioned here, see Van Tyne and Berger, 1976–ORNITHOLOGY.)

The oldest and in many ways the most important bird fossil that has yet been found is that of *Archaeopteryx lithographica,* four specimens of which, including complete skeletons, have been liberated from Upper Jurassic sediments in Germany, the first of them in 1857. In addition to being the first-known feathered animal, the significance of *Archaeopteryx* lies in the fact that its skeleton is more that of a reptile than a bird. It has, in fact, been described by more than one authority as a kind of small (pigeon-sized) dinosaur, but it now resides securely and uniquely in a subclass of its own, Archaeornithes—Ancient Birds— while *all* other birds, including more recent fossils, are placed in the subclass Neornithes—Modern (True) Birds. *Archaeopteryx* does not represent the transitional species between reptiles and birds—that link is still missing—but it does clinch the reptilian origins of birdlife. As the chart on p. 247 shows, *Archaeopteryx* is more than a little reptilian, based on skeletal details, yet other features seem to reflect, as it were, a clear "intention" of becoming a typical bird. Foremost of these is that most quintessentially avian characteristic—feathers. *Archaeopteryx*'s claim to "world's oldest bird" was challenged in 1981 by James Jensen, a paleontologist of Brigham Young University. Dr. Jensen reiterates doubts about *Archaeopteryx* being a "true" bird, but

FEATURE	MODERN BIRDS	MODERN REPTILES	ARCHAEOPTERYX
Feathers	Yes	No	Yes
Bill	Yes	No	No
Large eye sockets and sclerotic rings	Yes	Few	Yes
Toothed jaw	No	Yes	Yes
Hollow (pneumaticized) bones	Yes	No	No
Extensive fusion of backbone	Yes	No	No
Pygostyle	Yes; few exceptions	No	No
Long, bony tail	No	Yes	Yes
Wishbone (furcula)	Yes	No	Yes
Fusion of pelvic girdle	At least partial	No	No
Extensive fusion of hand/wrist bones (carpometacarpus)	Yes	No	No
Uncinate processes connecting ribs	Except screamers	Rare	No

more significantly he has unearthed fossil bones in a Colorado quarry which he claims are contemporaneous with *Archaeopteryx* and also more bird-like. He has dubbed his new old bird *Paleopteryx thomsoni*.

Fossils from the next (Cretaceous) period—including species resem-
'ing loons, grebes, ibises, geese, flamingos, cormorants, rails, sandpipers,
·lls—indicate that water birds, at least, had been evolving apace and
.ent directions in the 3 to 15 million years between *Archaeopteryx*
..d the next known fossil bird, *Gallornis straelini*, a large goose/flamingo.

It may be recalled at this point that many of the extinct "birds" which have been described and assigned a place in official phylogeny are in actuality a few pieces of petrified femur or the like, which compare well with grebe femora or ibis femora. When entire skeletons are unearthed, giving us clear impressions of what some prehistoric bird actually looked like, the specimens in question are likely to become the centerpieces for the period from which they came. In the Cretaceous such stardom is still reserved for two toothed water birds from the Kansas chalk beds, the small (8 inches tall) gull-like *Ichthyornis* and the much larger (almost 5 feet long) loon-like *Hesperornis*. The latter was flightless but presumably was descended from flying ancestors of which *Archaeopteryx* was a progenitor—another measure of the extent of avian evolution by the time of the Cretaceous. For other Cretaceous birds, see APATORNIS; BAPTORNIS.

The 70 million or so years of the Tertiary Period saw great diversification of the earth's habitats, due in part to widespread mountain building and climatic changes which stimulated plant evolution. According to Brodkorb (1971): "By the end of the Miocene, all of the nonpasserine families were probably established, as well as most, if not all of the passerines." This means that all of the major kinds of birds with which we presently share the earth may have been fully evolved as long as 11 million years ago. It is also probable that the Pliocene was the "golden age of birds," with more species alive than at any other time, before or since.

Indisputably the most impressive avian forms that we know of from the Tertiary are the species of *Diatryma*, powerfully built, long-legged terrestrial predators, some of which stood as high as 7 feet. The remains of these and similar giants have been found in Paleocene and Eocene deposits in New Mexico, Wyoming, and New Jersey and have been classified somewhat tentatively as crane relatives. Another gigantic avian relic from this period is a seabird from California with a wingspan as great as 16 feet (modern-day Wandering and Royal Albatrosses have a maximum documented wingspan of between 11 and 12 feet, the greatest of any *living* bird species). Of more interest to ornithologists are the tooth-like structures which arise out of the jawbones, giving the species its Latin name, *Osteodontornis*.

A smaller but hardly less interesting species of which we have a clear image is *Neocathartes*, a long-legged vulture and another gift of Eocene rock from Wyoming. Though it was capable of flight, its proportions indicate that it probably foraged largely on foot with intermittent short glides.

In the Quaternary Period (from the Pleistocene to the present), the gradual cooling of the earth's climate begun in the Tertiary culminated in a series of cataclysmic glacial advances across the Northern Hemisphere. It is reasonable to suspect that it was these inexorable ice sheets which hastened the doom of the many "older" bird species that vanished during the Pleistocene, and they certainly were a major influence in shaping the earth's present avifauna. The *total* Pleistocene avifauna is estimated (Brodkorb, 1971) at 10,600 species, as compared to about 8,650 living today. No new species of birds are thought to have evolved since the end of the Pleistocene, a mere 25,000 years ago; and since 78 have become extinct within the last 300 years, the decline of bird diversity begun with the glaciers continues—largely under human auspices.

Brodkorb once estimated (1960) that the total number of bird species that have *ever* lived (based on the more than 900 known extinct fossil species and including the present avifauna) is 1,630,000, and this impressive statistic is widely quoted. However, he later (1971) "greatly revised" his estimate downward and now believes 154,000 to be a more realistic total.

REPTILES AND BIRDS. Even if the "lizard bird" *Archaeopteryx* had remained locked in Jurassic slate, the evolutionary descent of birds from reptiles would not be in serious question. Spotty though it is, the fossil record is clear enough on the fact that reptiles throve in great diversity tens of millions of years before rudimentary avian models such as *Archaeopteryx* emerged (see chart, p. 251). And modern birds and reptiles share enough fundamental characters to clinch their common descent: The presence of a *single occipital condyle* (an oval bone process which connects the base of the skull to the first cervical vertebra [atlas])—mammals, including humans, have two occipital condyles; the presence of a *single* small bone, the *columella,* in the middle ear (tympanum)—humans have three; an *ambiens muscle* which is attached to the pelvis, its tendon facilitating grasping or perching with the toes; *uncinate processes* uniting the rib cage (see SKELETON and Fig. 19)—found only in birds and extinct or primitive reptiles; an *egg tooth*; and eggs containing particularly *large yolks* are all characters shared uniquely by reptiles and birds. Of course, modern birds have evolved away from many reptilian features such as toothed jaws and long bony tails; they have established characters unique to their class, especially feathers; and they possess some features, such as warm-bloodedness and a four-chambered heart, which are associated with "higher" animals, i.e., mammals, and which are lacking in reptiles. But this in no way contradicts the evidence of birds' reptilian ancestry.

Exactly *which* ancient reptiles birds evolved from is a knottier problem—at present we simply lack the fossil links necessary to complete a chain of descent from a particular reptile species to *Archaeopteryx.* However, two major theories dominate the argument at present. The majority opinion holds that birds, as well as dinosaurs, descend from a group of small, broadly adapted, carnivorous, toothed reptiles which were apparently common during the Triassic Period. These creatures are collectively called pseudosuchians—order Thecodontia ("socket-toothed"); suborder Pseudosuchia ("false crocodiles")—and a number of skeletal characteristics of such fossil pseudosuchian species in the genera *Euparkeria* and *Ornithosuchus* agree well with those of *Archaeopteryx.* Ostrum (1974) dissented from this, however, citing greater skeletal resemblance between *Archaeopteryx* and small dinosaurs (coelurosaurs—order Saurischia, suborder Theropoda) which lived contemporaneously with *Archaeopteryx* in the Jurassic Period.

EVOLUTION OF FEATHERS AND FLIGHT. The close relationships between reptilian scales and feathers and between modern bird feathers and flight are undisputed. The scales of some of the fossil pseudosuchians seem to bear the pattern of a feather impressed on their surface (Swinton, 1960–61), and the processes of scale and feather formation are very similar in modern reptiles and birds. Likewise, the adaptive elegance with which feathers suit flight in present-day birds seems obvious, though it is equally clear that feathers also serve other functions. Reconstructing the step-by-step transition from scale to feather and earthbound to airborne is an even more speculative undertaking than exploring the roots of the avian family tree. Three theories relating to feather and/or flight evolution—equally plausible, though so far equally unprovable—are summarized here: (1) That early reptiles such as the pseudosuchians which walked or ran on their hind legs began to climb trees, which, with the necessity of moving deftly to pursue prey among the branches, initiated a selective process that favored the development of perching/grasping feet—i.e., with a back-ward-pointing toe (hallux)—and wings with which the creature could efficiently glide or flap/hop from branch to branch; the elongation and lightening of forearm scales would have been additional selective advantages in this scenario. The long wing-claws of *Archaeopteryx*, which would be useful to a climbing bird with only limited flying abilities, can be construed as supporting this theory. (See Marsh, 1880, and Osborn, 1900.) (2) That small active terrestrial reptiles flapped their arms as they ran, again resulting in elongation of scales, the hind edges of which in effect "frayed" into feathers. (See Nopsca, 1923.) (3) That body feathers developed initially among *reptiles* as a means of thermoregulation (see TEMPERATURE, BODY) and that the "flight" feathers evolved as an efficient means of trapping (by enclosure) fast-moving prey such as large insects and small vertebrates, which were then picked up in the toothed mouth; only subsequently did wings become adapted to flight. (See Ostrum, 1974.) *Archaeopteryx* has been used as evidence supporting all three theories. Whether it hopped through the trees using its wings as a sort of parachute, or flapped its way from tree to tree, or stayed on the ground and used its wings only to ensnare prey is, of course, most germane to any flight evolution theory. Unfortunately it is not clear from the fossil skeletons known so far whether it had a prominent keel on its breastbone (a characteristic of strong fliers) or none; but other skeletal elements of *Archaeopteryx* seem to indicate that at best it was capable of short flapping flights.

The following chart attempts to place the evolution of birdlife in the context of the history of all life on earth and some of the major geological/climatic/biological events which have occurred during the emergence of an avifauna—all, it need hardly be repeated, to the extent of our present knowledge!

EVOLUTION OF BIRDLIFE

AZOIC TIME
Before 3–5 billion years ago; no evidence of life.

CRYPTOZOIC TIME

3–5 billion years ago to 600 million years ago; scanty evidence of life: calcareous algae, worm tubes, possibly sponges.

PHANEROZOIC TIME

600 million years ago to present: 10 percent of earth's history to date.

PALEOZOIC ERA: 600 million to 225 million years ago. Evolution of life from earliest marine plants and invertebrates to presence of all current invertebrate classes plus fishes, amphibians, and reptiles. Reptiles emerged in the Pennsylvanian (late Carboniferous) Period (about 300 million years ago) and by the end of the Permian Period (280–225 million years ago) had greatly diversified.

MESOZOIC ERA: 225 million to 70 million years ago.

TRIASSIC PERIOD: 225 million to 195 million years ago

MAJOR TRENDS/EVENTS	EVOLUTION OF BIRDLIFE
North American climate mild; deserts extensive. Forests of conifers and cycads; tree ferns and horsetails abundant. Amphibians decline; dinosaurs (including thecodonts) dominant by end of period.	No birds.

JURASSIC PERIOD: 195 million to 135 million years ago

Sierra Nevada and Cascades arise. Climate mild; deserts widespread. Cycads dominant plants; conifers still abundant. Age of Reptiles: present on land, in sea, and in air; great dinosaurs.	*Archaeopteryx:* first known bird.

CRETACEOUS PERIOD: 135 million to 70 million years ago

50 percent of North America under water: extensive limestone deposits/fossil beds laid down in West. Rockies arise. Climate turns cold late in period. Flowering plants appear; deciduous forests become dominant; sequoias widespread. *Tyrannosaurus* and other dinosaurs thrive at first, becoming extinct by end of period. Marsupials and primitive placental mammals evolve.	*Apatornis, Baptornis, Hesperornis,* and *Ichthyornis.* Also birds resembling modern loons, cormorants, ibises, rails, and sandpipers.

Cenozoic Era: 70 million years ago to present.

TERTIARY PERIOD

Paleocene/Eocene Epoch: 70 million to 38 million years ago

MAJOR TRENDS/EVENTS	EVOLUTION OF BIRDLIFE
Early mountain building followed by erosion; much of Atlantic and Gulf lowlands submerged. Seed-bearing plants continue dominant. Early 1-foot-high horse (*Eohippus*), camels, elephants, dogs, cats evolve.	Few bird fossils from Paleocene: first hawks, also loons, tropicbirds, vultures, gulls, and terns. Eocene sees major evolution of birdlife, with nearly all known orders established by its close: albatrosses, pelicans, ibises, flamingos, grouse, pheasants, cranes, auks, cuckoos, owls, kingfishers, and a few passerines (e.g., starlings); also *Diatryma, Neocathartes.*

Oligocene Epoch: 38 million to 26 million years ago

Coastal lowlands emerge; active vulcanism along Pacific coast. Climate continues mild. Modern-type forests. Mammals dominant, especially cat and dog families; also three-toed horse, mastodon, anthropoid ape.	First known grebes, shearwaters, boobies, storks, turkeys, limpkins, plovers, parrots, pigeons, nightjars, swifts, Old World warblers, and ploceid sparrows. A few genera of present-day birds appear. Many species of cranes and rails.

Miocene Epoch: 26 million to 12 million years ago

Sierras and Rockies rise again. North America at first very warm, cooling toward end. Forests reduced, plains and deserts arise. More modern tree species evolve. Golden Age of Mammals: great diversity of camels, great ape in Europe.	Most modern bird families probably exist; more modern genera evolve.

Pliocene Epoch: 12 million to 2–3 million years ago

Last lifting of Appalachians, Rockies, Sierras, Cascades. Climate continues to cool. Mastodons migrate from Old World to New; forerunner of modern horse; gorilla; beginning of Old Stone Age.	Birds reach maximum diversity; emergence of many modern genera and species. Moas, ostriches, rheas, tinamous, larks, swallows, nuthatches, emberizids, and (perhaps) woodpeckers appear.

QUARTERNARY PERIOD

Pleistocene Epoch: 2–3 million to 10 thousand years ago

Ice Age: glaciers cover northern half of North America 4–5 times, greatly altering earth's surface; Great Lakes, many other modern geological features formed. Climate cold except for tropics. Four species of elephants, camels, saber-toothed tiger in North America early in epoch; many large mammals and other forms die out with advance of ice. Rise of *Homo*.	All modern birds in existence by end of epoch. Glaciation causes: demise of some large, ancient forms; division of populations in North America, promoting speciation; retreat of species from North, perhaps leading to evolution of migration.

Holocene (Recent) Epoch: 10,000 years ago to present

MAJOR TRENDS/EVENTS	EVOLUTION OF BIRDLIFE
Last of ice retreats; northern areas reforested; deserts expand. Climate warmer and drier. Development of agriculture and domestication of animals. Humanity spreads to all parts of earth. Gross decline in populations of large mammals; widespread human-related habitat destruction and pollution of the biosphere. Capacity to destroy all life developed, tested.	Between 8,600 and 9,000 species of birds. New subspecies evolve. Last 300 years see extinction of 78 species, mostly through human agency. Current extinction rate greater than at any other time.

EXANTHROPIC (EX-an-THRO-pik). Preferring to live apart from humanity. Forest-dwelling raptors, such as the Northern Goshawk, tend to be exanthropic. Some populations of robins may be exanthropic while others appear to prefer the company of man. Compare EUSYANTHROPIC; SYNANTHROPIC.

EXCREMENT. In birds, urine and feces are voided together through a single anal opening, or vent. Bird droppings therefore usually consist of solid, dark wastes (feces) in a white, chalky, semi-solid material (urine). The excreta of the nestlings of many passerine birds are enclosed in a gelatinous membrane or fecal sac for easy disposal by the parents.

The excrement of certain seabirds is commercially exploited (see GUANO); where bird droppings collect in enclosed spaces, they may present a health hazard (see DISEASE).

The presence of certain groups of birds, e.g., grouse and geese, may be reliably confirmed by the unique forms of their droppings.

EXCRETORY SYSTEM. Excretion of solid waste in the form of feces is the final stage of the digestive process, for which see DIGESTIVE SYSTEM. The processing of birds' liquid wastes in the form of urine, on the other hand, has evolved as with us in conjunction with the reproductive system, and the two functions are often discussed together as the *urogenital system.* Unlike mammals, however, birds have only a single opening, the cloacal vent, through which pass both solid and liquid wastes, as well as the products of the reproductive system.

A bird's urinary system consists of a pair of kidneys each connected by a narrow tube or ureter to the cloaca. The kidneys lie protected within the pelvic region close to the backbone; birds have no bladder.

Urinary systems in general remove excess water, salts, and nitrogen wastes from the body. But birds reabsorb almost all of the water in the kidneys and ureters, leaving a white, nearly solid substance very different in appearance from human urine. This is voided, together with the feces, through the vent.

For another method of salt excretion, see SALT GLAND.

EXOTIC SPECIES (exotics). Terms used to describe birds or other organisms that are not native to a given ecosystem. They usually imply human agency, either through accident or design. For example, a Fork-tailed Flycatcher blown to Maine by a hurricane may be "exotic," but in birding/ornithological jargon, it would be described as a "vagrant" or an "accidental straggler" rather than as an exotic. For such species with a claim to inclusion on the North American checklist, see Appendix II. The Mute Swan, initially an exotic, is native to a climate similar to that of northeastern North America, has established a firm foothold as a breeding bird in the latter region, and therefore has evolved over time to the status of an INTRODUCED BIRD. The quintessential exotic bird, then, is a species that initially arrived on our shores as a captive, survives at liberty, usually breeding at least locally, is not well adapted on the whole to the ecosystem in which it finds itself and therefore has limited viability in its adoptive avifauna. There are, of course, ambiguous cases. The Red-whiskered Bulbul, escaping from captivity in southern Florida in 1960, would seem to be a classic exotic, doomed to a brief celebrity among Dade County listers. However, the species turns out to be an enormously resourceful (hence abundant) resident of its native India and southeastern Asia, thriving in parts of its range in a climate very similar to that of the Miami area. Small numbers of this bubul seem to be eking out a successful living there, and while the species does not seem to be expanding its range, it may end up being a kind of subtropical Mute Swan. A few species, e.g., the Spot-billed Duck, have occurred here both as exotics and as vagrants.

Some of the better-known and most successful North American exotics, many living in the warm climate and cage-bird paradise of southern Florida and most having nested at least once, are listed below along with their place of origin. The majority are illustrated on p. 303 of Peterson's new *Field Guide to the Birds East of the Rockies.*

For other perspectives on non-native species, see AVICULTURE; ESCAPES; INTRODUCED BIRDS; VAGRANT; VERIFICATION OF RECORDS; and Appendix II.

Scarlet Ibis, *Eudocimus ruber* (South America)
Black-necked Swan, *Cygnus melanocoryphus* (South America)
Black Swan, *Cygnus atratus* (Australia)
Swan (Chinese) Goose, *Anser cygnoides* (northern Asia)
Bar-headed Goose, *Anser indicus* (central Asia–India)
Egyptian Goose, *Alopochen aegyptiacus* (Africa)
Spot-billed Duck, *Anas poecilorhyncha* (Asia)
Mandarin Duck, *Aix galericulata* (northern Asia)
Golden Pheasant, *Chrysolophus pictus* (central China)
Southern Lapwing, *Vanellus chilensis* (South America)
Gray-necked Wood Rail, *Aramides cajanea* (Latin America)

Budgerigar, *Melopsittacus undulatus* (Australia)
Canary-winged Parakeet, *Brotogeris versicolurus* (Central and South America)
Orange-chinned Parakeet, *Brotogeris jugularis* (Latin America)
Monk Parakeet, *Myiopsitta monachus* (South America)
Yellow-headed Parrot, *Amazona ochrocephala* (Latin America)
Red-crowned Parrot, *Amazona viridigenalis* (Mexico)
Hispaniolan Parakeet, *Aratinga chloroptera* (Hispaniola)
Green Parakeet, *Aratinga holochlora* (Middle America)
Orange-fronted Parakeet, *Aratinga canicularis* (Middle America)
Black-hooded (Nanday) Parakeet, *Nandayus nenday* (South America)
Blossom-headed Parakeet, *Psittacula roseata* (southern Asia)
Rose-ringed Parakeet, *Psittacula krameri* (India and Africa)
Masked Lovebird, *Agapornis personata* (Africa)
Cockatiel, *Nymphicus hollandicus* (Australia)
Hill (Talking) Mynah, *Gracula religiosa* (Asia)
Java Sparrow, *Padda oryzivora* (Malaysia)
Common Waxbill, *Estrilda astrild* (Africa)
Spotted Munia, *Lonchura punctulata* (southern Asia)
Chestnut Munia, *Lonchura malacca* (southern Asia)
Red-whiskered Bulbul, *Pycnonotus jocosus* (India–southern Asia)
Spot-breasted Oriole, *Icterus pectoralis* (Middle America)
Troupial, *Icterus icterus* (South America)
Red-crested (Brazilian) Cardinal, *Paroaria coronata* (South America)

EXTINCT BIRDS. It is probably a healthy exercise, when considering the extinction of species in this age, to remember that many thousands of life forms have ceased to exist from wholly natural causes—dinosaurs spring inevitably to mind. And further that some organisms—especially primitive forms which, as it were, are "past their prime"—will pass into oblivion both without human assistance and in spite of it. At the same time it should be noted that we may be about to witness extinction of species on an unprecedented scale due to the rapid and widespread destruction of the planet's tropical rain forest (which contains about 50 percent of the species of living organisms) and other manifestations of the recent quantum leap in human technology. We should also not kid ourselves about the implications of such losses. Extinctions to date can be dismissed by the callous as marginal aesthetic deprivations, but if the extinction rate accelerates to the degree now predicted by many biologists, there can be no doubt that the potential for human food, medical, and other vital (economically calculable) resources will be measurably diminished and the prospects for our own survival possibly made problematical (see Ehrlich and Ehrlich, 1981).

That said, there will be no further attempts here to argue for or against "moral" issues of extinction: whether man can or cannot be considered a "natural" cause of a species' demise, etc. Rather, the facts will be presented, to be philosophically pondered by the reader.

Seventy-eight full species and over fifty subspecies of birds have ceased to exist on the planet since the beginning of the eighteenth century, the greatest proportion of them (about 35 percent) taking their final bow between 1850 and 1900. A significant proportion of the whole have been island forms, which evolved in the absence of human and other predators and therefore succumbed all too quickly when man arrived with his usual contingent of rats and domestic animals—not to mention guns. For example, the island of Hawaii has to date lost ten full species of endemic birds since 1859, as opposed to four to date in all of North America.

However significant, the phenomenon of high extinction rates on islands has little to do with extinction in North America. The four full species which have become extinct in North America in the historical period were recorded confidently for the last time between 1844 and 1918. In addition, one subspecies (Heath Hen) expired in 1932. A brief account of each follows:

Labrador Duck (*Camptorhynchus labradorius*). *Former Range and Status*: Apparently ranged from the southern coast of Labrador, where it bred, as far south as Chesapeake Bay in winter. It was known to science for less than 100 years, so that its distribution is known only where it was hunted, and nothing at all was discovered of its breeding biology. Early accounts indicate that it was never abundant but common enough so that "a fair number" made it to the New York market in the years from 1840 to 1860; it has also been stated that it was not uncommon along the coasts of New England and Long Island in winter. *Main Causes of Extinction*: Unknown. There is no doubt that it was shot for sport and meat, and there is also a suspicion that colonies may have been raided in the St. Lawrence for meat and eggs. However, the bird's rapid demise will probably never be accounted for completely. *Date(s) of Extinction*: The last verifiable specimen was taken in 1875, with a lost specimen reported as shot in 1878.

Great Auk (*Pinguinus impennis*). *Former Range and Status*: Bred in Norway, Iceland, southern Greenland, and down the east coast of North America at least as far as the St. Lawrence; wintered regularly to Cape Cod and was recorded as a straggler as far south as Florida. The species was abundant within its normal range until the late eighteenth century. The largest North American colony, on the Funk Islands off the east coast of Newfoundland, was decimated between 1830 and 1841. *Main Causes of Extinction*: There is no ambiguity about the disappearance of the Great Auk. It was extirpated by white men for food and commercial gain. The species had long been traditional food on fishing and other vessels in Britain and Scandinavia. The adults and young were killed and salted down or kept alive on board as a source of fresh meat, and the eggs were also collected. Another widespread use of the birds was as bait. This kind of depredation alone was responsible for the extinction of the auk in the British Isles long before the discovery of the American colonies. But the inevitability of its doom was probably not settled until the late 1700's, when commercial hunters began to systematically devastate the colonies, not only for marketable game but for oil and feathers for mattress stuffing. These operations were carried out indiscriminately throughout the breeding season, and continued unabated well after the threat of extinction was obvious. The Great Auk was flightless, awkward on land, and unafraid of men and could be herded and clubbed with a minimum of inconvenience. *Date(s) of Extinction:* The last record of the species is from Iceland in 1844; the last North American record is from the Funks in 1841.

Passenger Pigeon (*Ectopistes migratorius*). *Former Range and Status:* Bred throughout the northern forests from Manitoba to Nova Scotia, south to Kansas and West Virginia; wintered from Arkansas and North Carolina south to central Texas and northern Florida. Its abundance is legendary, numerous reliable sources reporting migrating flocks in excess of one or even two billion birds and nesting colonies miles in extent with a hundred or more nests to a single tree. *Main Causes of Extinction:* Like the Great Auk, the Passenger Pigeon was killed unmercifully for food, for the market, and for the hell of it. In addition, its forest habitat was being converted to farmland. The species was so numerous that its extirpation, and particularly the suddenness with which it occurred, was probably impossible for men to imagine at the time. Even modern authorities suggest that disease or a migratory "wreck" may have played a part in the disappearance of the last millions, which took place in a mere twenty years. Most agree that the bird's breeding success depended on its gregarious habits and that the reproductive rate dropped with the size of the colonies. This would explain in part the suddenness of the final exit. *Date(s) of Extinction:* The last well-verified shooting of a wild Passenger Pigeon took place in Wisconsin in 1899. "Martha Washington," hatched at the Cincinnati Zoo, was the last survivor. She succumbed on September 1, 1914, at the age of twenty-nine.

Carolina Parakeet (*Conuropsis carolinensis*). *Former Range and Status:* Once occurred throughout most of the eastern U.S. from the Great Plains to the eastern seaboard and from the tip of the Great Lakes and western New York south to the Gulf coast and southern Florida. Before it declined, it occurred regularly in flocks of 200–300. *Main Causes of Extinction:* Probably a combination of habitat destruction and decimation by shotgun, but there is little documentation from the period. The favored nesting sites were tree hollows in forested swamps and river bottoms, much of which was cleared by the ax in the eighteenth and nineteenth centuries. The bird was also, and with some justification, regarded as a pest on grain and fruit crops and was, as Audubon put it, the victim of "severe retaliation on the part of the planters." However, the species was never shot on a large scale for food, sport, or ornamentation and dwindling habitat may have been the dominant cause of extinction. *Date(s) of Extinction:* The last specimen reportedly shot in the wild is from Kansas (!) in August 1904; the last known survivor died in the Cincinnati Zoo on February 21, 1918. There were numerous sight records and rumors until at least 1936; a few from the 1920's sound convincing but Nicholson (1948) has noted that, even then, exotic parrots were escaping from their cages in Florida.

Heath Hen (*Tympanuchus cupido cupido*), the eastern race of the Greater Prairie Chicken. *Former Range and Status:* From southern New England (southern New Hampshire) south along the coast probably as far as Virginia. Originally common albeit rather local due to the scarcity of its preferred prairie-type habitat except along the coast. *Main Causes of Extinction:* It has been suggested that this subspecies may initially have increased with the clearing of forest which came with European colonization. But this gain (if it occurred) was soon counterbalanced by shooting, the depredations of domestic animals, and settlement. A bill passed by the Massachusetts legislature in 1831 to protect the bird (during the breeding season only!) was inspired by its obvious decline. *Date(s) of Extinction:* The Heath Hen may have been extinct on the mainland by 1850 (though there was a report from New Jersey in 1869). It was officially reported extinct in 1876 except for an estimated 120–200 birds left on the "great plain" of Martha's Vineyard, Massachusetts. This population fluctuated violently during the early twentieth century, perhaps reaching a high of 2,000 birds in 1916 but repeatedly reduced by fires. There was a final rally in 1921, with over 400 birds estimated, but two wet and cold breeding seasons reduced them to a mere 54 by 1924. In spite of renewed protection efforts, the population continued to decline. A single bird appeared on the "booming field" until March 11, 1932, and none was seen thereafter.

In addition to the above species and subspecies, four others, officially listed as "endangered," have at best a tenuous hold on existence. The Eskimo Curlew, American Ivory-billed Woodpecker, and Bachman's Warbler may already have passed into oblivion, and the Dusky Seaside Sparrow population now contains only males. See ENDANGERED BIRDS; also CONSERVATION; MAN-MADE THREATS TO BIRDLIFE.

EXTIRPATE (EKS-tur-pate or eks-TUR-pate). To exterminate or eradicate. Often used in ornithological contexts to describe the man-made extinction of a bird species, e.g.: "The Passenger Pigeon was extirpated by wanton overshooting."

EYE. See VISION.

EYE LINE. Either a linear, usually pale mark running above the eye or a usually dark mark running through the eye. See EYE STRIPE.

EYE RING. An area of contrasting feathers (e.g., Ruby-crowned Kinglet) or unfeathered skin (e.g., Black-billed Cuckoo) encircling the eye of a bird; cited as a field mark for many species of birds. See Fig. 1.

EYESHINE. A reflection of colored light from an animal's eye. Most nightjars show a brilliant eyeshine when fixed by headlight or flashlight beams and some species can often be located in this manner by walking or driving along little-used country roads after dark. For physiology of eyeshine in general, see VISION, *Eyeshine*.

EYE STRIPE. Used for both a superciliary stripe or line (i.e., a linear, usually pale mark running *above* the eye, e.g., Red-eyed Vireo) and a usually dark mark running *through* the eye (e.g., Blue-winged Warbler). There is some tendency in popular guides to call the supercilium an eye stripe and a mark *through* the eye an eye line, but the terminology is not at all consistent and many birdwatchers reverse the meaning of the terms.

EYRIE (or aerie, many alternate spellings) (EYE-ree). The nest of a large bird of prey, generally with an implication of remoteness and inaccessibility, such as the cliffside sites preferred by Gyrfalcons, Peregrines, and Golden Eagles. It would not be incorrect, however, to refer to an Osprey's nest atop a utility pole as its eyrie.

F

FALCON (FALL-cun or FAW-cun; birders sometimes say FAL-cun). Standard English name for about 30 members of the family Falconidae (order Falconiformes) and in a general sense referring to all members of this family (about 58 species worldwide) with the exception of the 8 living species of CARACARAS. Five species of falcons (all in the genus *Falco*) currently breed in North America; one (Aplomado Falcon) that once bred is now probably only a rare visitor to the Southwest; and another (Eurasian Kestrel) has been recorded as an accidental visitor.

Falcons range in size from the tiny (6 inches) falconets of the Old World to the 20-inch Gyrfalcon. They are usually boldly patterned and in some cases (e.g., American Kestrel) highly colored. Like their close relatives, the hawks and eagles (family Accipitridae), falcons have powerful wings and legs, a short, heavy, hooked bill for tearing flesh, long, sharp claws for holding prey, and a fleshy cere and eye ring—both usually bright yellow or orange in adult birds. In general form, all falcons are characterized by long, powerful wings and long tails. All are predators on other animals, though specific food preferences and manner of hunting vary among species. Some (especially the Peregrine) are famed for the incredible velocity of their "stoop"; however, see SPEED.

A falcon's nest consists of a scrape on open ground, a hollow on a rocky ledge, the ledge of a city office building, the abandoned stick nest of a corvid, hawk, or eagle, or in a few cases (e.g., American Kestrel) a tree (or other) cavity. No nest material is added. The 2–8 (usually 3–5) eggs have a white to pale buff or yellowish ground color, which, however, is normally obscured by fine speckling of reddish/brownish that in turn may be heavily overlaid with dark brown splotching sometimes covering almost the entire surface.

Falcon calls are staccato piping notes, high-pitched in smaller species, more "throaty" in larger; also various harsh cackles.

Falcons have captured the human imagination at least since the time of the ancient Egyptians, and the swift and graceful hunting techniques of the larger species inspired the development of the ancient, aristocratic sport of FALCONRY.

Because of their susceptibility to DDT (see MAN-MADE THREATS TO BIRDLIFE) Peregrines recently approached the brink of extinction throughout much of the world. But thanks to the efforts of dedicated falconers and scientists (and of course the banning of DDT), the species is beginning to make a comeback (see ENDANGERED BIRDS).

The falcons are truly cosmopolitan as a family, ranging from the Arctic to the Antarctic and finding a niche in every major biome. Most of our North American species (American Kestrel, Merlin, and Peregrine) range throughout the continent as residents, migrants, or winterers, with the Gyrfalcon largely restricted to arctic barrens and the Prairie Falcon to open country in the West.

"Falcon" comes from the same root as the Latin word *falx*, "sickle," the connotation being the curved talons and/or bill of these raptors.

FALCON DAM (Texas). See RIO GRANDE VALLEY.

FALCONRY. The ancient sport of flying falcons, hawks, and eagles at live prey. Often called the "sport of kings" because of its immense popularity with the medieval aristocracy. Though game killed by falcons has often found its way to someone's table, the practice of falconry has always been mainly a source of pleasure rather than food.

HISTORY. Falconry is recorded in ancient texts, paintings, and sculpture from at least 2000 B.C. in China and from the seventh century B.C. in the Middle East, where legend attributes its origins to a prehistoric Persian king. The sport was also practiced within the first millennium B.C. in Japan and perhaps in North Africa. Though falconry has never been proven to have existed in any New World culture until the modern era, there is some evidence that the inhabitants of what is now Latin America may have trained birds to hunt. Aristotle and Pliny confirm the practice of falconry in classical times, and it is believed to have reached England by way of France around A.D. 860. It flourished as a sport among the higher social orders in Europe and was employed on a more practical level by those of a lower station, who were allowed to use Northern Goshawks and smaller accipiters to provide game for the table. With the decline of feudalism and (especially) the advent of readily available firearms in the seventeenth century, the popularity of falconry waned greatly, but the tradition has been maintained locally in Western societies by a few dedicated sportsmen of all classes. And in the oil-rich sheikdoms of the Middle East it thrives today as it always has.

SPECIES USED AND PREY. The large falcons have historically been thought of as the greatest sporting birds, with the Peregrine preferred above all others for its flying style, gentle behavior, and capacity to be trained. The Gyrfalcon, traditionally reserved for kings or sheiks, has always been appreciated for its size and majesty, but south of its native arctic tundra habitat, its heartiness declines, and its far-ranging hunting style becomes impractical, especially for the modern falconer. Among the less tractable (though very agile and exciting) accipiters, the Northern Goshawk is favored for its ability to catch small game (e.g., rabbits, grouse) for the table. Smaller species such as Merlins, hobbies, and the sparrow hawks (*Accipiter*) put on a good show but are not capable generally of capturing prey that humans care to eat. On the whole, the species most popular in a given region are those best adapted to the prevailing habitat. For example, Saker Falcons, native to the arid wastes of the Palearctic region, are favored for chasing bustards in the deserts of North Africa.

The prey at which falcons are flown also varies with the fauna and traditions of the region. "Coursing" the diminutive dorcas gazelle with large falcons and salukis (the highly bred, greyhound-like Arab dog) was the favorite sport in the Middle East until the gazelles became scarce, due at least in part to over-hunting. In Europe and America medium-sized to large birds such as ducks, pheasants, partridges, herons, and crows and smaller mammalian game such as rabbits were and are the chief targets of falconers hunting for both meat and sport. Smaller hawks were flown on songbirds and shorebirds, though "larking"—as setting hobbies or Merlins on high-flying Skylarks was called—was not considered "serious" falconry. Eagles have always been prized for their inherent grandeur and trained to take jackrabbits and even larger game. On the Asian steppes, Golden Eagles are still used to capture foxes and wolves, the pelts of which are a source of livelihood for subsistence falconer-hunters. Eagles and their smaller cousins, the buteos or broad-winged hawks, are generally deemed to be less exciting to watch than the falcons and accipiters, though they are equally efficient hunters using their own methods. However, because of the characteristic docility and relative abundance of some species, the buteos have come to be among the birds most frequently used by American falconers (see below).

CAPTURE, TRAINING, AND FLYING. Normally hawks are either caught as immatures during their first fall migration or taken from the nest before they are able to fly. Once captured, wild birds are traditionally (but no longer invariably) fitted with a leather hood that covers their eyes; kept in a special building called a "mews"; and gradually accustomed to the falconer's glove, the sights and sounds of humanity, the touch of the "master," and the habit of being fed on the glove at the sound of a whistled signal. The bird is then trained to fly to the falconer's gloved fist to be fed, to fly at a lure that is swung on a cord, and finally flown free after live quarry in the field.

Whereas the first part of a wild bird's training involves acclimating it to captivity, the chief aim in raising birds taken from the nest is to attempt to teach them as many of the lessons they would learn naturally in the wild while at the same time preserving their "tameness." These "eyasses" are cared for in the first month with minimal human contact. Once able to fly well, they are given their freedom for a period, during which they are said to be "at hack." As soon as they are able to catch prey on their own, they are recaptured (if possible) for further training. This consists mainly of releasing live birds (usually pigeons) for the falcon to stoop on, in the process learning to "wait on" (i.e., fly above) the falconer in anticipation of stooping.

Because wild-caught birds tend to have the greatest determination to hunt, some falconers are of the opinion that birds trained from infancy are never as satisfactory as those reared initially among their own kind. Bedouin falconers captured passage hawks, trained them quickly and hunted with them, and then released them to complete their migration to their wintering grounds. This practice reflected an unwillingness to keep birds regarded as invested with supernatural powers in prolonged captivity, but it also freed the nomadic captors from the chores of feeding and caring for the birds year-round. American falconers often use Merlins in this way.

In the old days, once a bird was trained, it was usually carried into the field hooded and released when prey was spotted or flushed. Today birds are usually released in appropriate habitat to "wait on"—in the case of falcons at a height of 200–300 feet, or with accipiters to take up perches and scan for prey as they would on their own. European falconers of yore normally went afield on horseback, allowing them to reach a bird with prey quickly. This permitted the falconer to retrieve the falcon before it ate too much of its victim and thereby dulled its appetite for another stoop; in some cases the falconer was able to release larger game unharmed to be chased another day. Falcons thus deprived are always rewarded with a morsel of food. The Arabs still ride to the hunt but nowadays in jeeps modified to carry and protect their falcons. Western falconers generally go on foot, though they may use dogs to point up and flush game for their birds.

MODERN FALCONRY IN NORTH AMERICA. Though a few falconers may have practiced their sport here since colonial times, the birth of modern North American falconry can be dated for convenience in the 1920's, when the first continentwide organization was founded. Today there are perhaps as many as 2,500 licensed falconers in the U.S. and Canada, though perhaps as little as half this number are active. They are distributed fairly evenly over all regions, except for the minority of states and provinces where this method of taking game is not permitted. The North American Falconers' Association publishes a yearly journal and a quarterly publication called *Hawk Chalk* (chalk = droppings), which between them keep members informed on the latest regulations, husbandry techniques, and scientific work relating to raptors, as well as providing a forum for an exchange of views and a vehicle for anecdotes from the field.

Modern falconry is defined as "the pursuit of wild game with a raptor" and, though one courts inaccuracy to generalize about a group made up of self-avowed individualists, it is probably safe to say that most falconers come from the ranks of the traditional hunting community. The typical falconer (if such exists) is fiercely dedicated to his sport and his birds, committed to sound conservation practices, and is something of an elitist. He tends to consider himself a more highly skilled, dedicated, and "natural" sportsman than the rifle (or even bow) hunter and a far more knowledgeable, realistic, and unsentimental naturalist than the average birdwatcher. One need not subscribe to every detail of this flattering self-image to believe that falconers today are as deeply in thrall to the powerful beauty and romance of their sport as they always have been.

No one becomes a falconer casually. Those who begin with a mild interest are soon discouraged by the great difficulties and expenditure of time involved in acquiring, training, and keeping a bird and the burden of legal stipulations that must be satisfied. All falconers are bound by federal regulations, which in many cases are made more restrictive—never less—by state laws. Though state regulations vary, qualification as a licensed falconer is basically achieved through comprehensive written examinations and a sponsor/apprentice system. There are three levels of falconers; apprentice, intermediate, and master, each with its own specified duration, requirements, and prescribed species. At each level, written tests must be passed, and some states require field trials as well. Would-be falconers must also acquire (or make themselves) a minimum of essential equipment (e.g., jesses, hoods, perches, hawk house, etc.) and satisfy a strict standard of housing and maintenance for their bird(s). A master falconer is permitted to keep up to three birds at a time, but keeping so many fit is so time-consuming that many falconers limit themselves to a single bird. In addition to earning state and federal licenses, the falconer must also satisfy any applicable hunting regulations. If he intends to fly his bird at waterfowl, for example, a falconer must buy whatever licenses and duck stamps are required by his country and state and is restricted to the prescribed season. In many cases gun and falconry seasons are identical, a situation falconers generally deplore, since they sometimes lose birds to gunners unable to resist potting an unwary raptor that has been trained to hunt with man.

Falconers are allowed to trap any species of hawk or falcon that is neither on the endangered species list (see ENDANGERED BIRDS) nor under special protection locally, and even protected species may be taken under special circumstances, as when a permit is issued to capture a particular Golden Eagle that habitually kills livestock. They may also capture Great Horned Owls. There are provisions for taking young birds from the nest (leaving the majority of the brood), trapping birds of the year (passage hawks) during the fall migration, or receiving captive-bred birds from licensed breeders. Under no circumstances, however, may raptors (or any other native or endangered birds) be sold.

According to both the law and the falconer's code, hawks are always "slipped" at specific prey, but once a bird has left the fist, there is always the chance that it will be diverted from its intended victim and take a non-game species or one that is out of season. To cover this contingency, most states have adopted "let it lay" regulations, which provide that the hawk be allowed to feed on such kills and that whatever remains then be left for other animals and to decompose—just as would happen in a natural raptor/prey encounter.

By far the most popular species among modern North American falconers is the docile, yet spirited, Red-tailed Hawk, whose abundance also favors its widespread use. Next in popularity is an essentially Neotropical, dry-country species, the Harris' or Bay-winged Hawk, which reputedly combines the Red-tailed's even temperament with the agility of a large accipiter. Another reason for this bird's popularity is the ease with which it is bred in captivity and thus its ready availability. Accipiters are very exciting to fly but commensurably difficult to train (see White, 1951, for a vivid confirmation). Apprentice falconers often cut their teeth on the small, colorful American Kestrel.

Falconry probably will always remain drenched in ancient tradition—it is part of the mystique of the art. But today's falconers also reap both the rewards and the detriments of the modern world. Techniques of rearing and caring for birds in captivity have improved immeasurably since the Middle Ages (especially in the last ten years), and some ancient rituals practiced out of superstitious faith, rather than for their effectiveness, have been winnowed out. Falconers can now recover many of their lost birds by attaching tiny radio transmitters to legs or plumage and thereby tracking birds that stray. On the other hand, early falconers did not have to contend with slob hunters, low-flying aircraft, power lines, pesticides, and all the other hazards that a free-flying hawk must now suffer.

The falconer himself is also under some pressure, mainly from the sentimentalist element of the wildlife protection movement which sees his sport as a kind of organized cruelty, comparable to cockfighting. The falconer's defense is that, unlike gun or bow hunting, falconry is a non-consumptive sport, the falconer simply modifying a natural process, so that he can observe its beauty and share in the experience. Of course, some people are simply uncomfortable with the fact that some animals kill others as a way of life; they shudder to think that anyone could possibly enjoy the natural beauty of this predatory behavior. But the falconer—unlike the cockfighter—does not gamble on his birds and is not interested in the bloody and competitive aspects of his birds' behavior. His pleasure comes as much from the ability of prey species frequently to avoid the falcon's talons as from the performance of his own bird; he exults in the evolutionary beauty of the predator/prey equilibrium. Furthermore, all of us can be grateful for the crucial contribution of American falconers to the Peregrine recovery program, currently realizing some encouraging successes. The captive breeding and reintroduction of this magnificent species might still be in its infancy were it not for the hawkers' expertise. Of course, like all groups, falconers are not without their "bad eggs." There is no denying that Peregrine and other nests have been robbed by unscrupulous hawkers. And the avidity of Arab falconers has without question contributed to the perilous present status of some desert wildlife, notably the dorcas gazelle and species of bustards. But compared to the toll taken by gun hunters, the falconer's harvest is minute, and would occur in any case (in fact, would be greater) if his birds were living in the wild.

The literature of falconry is extensive and contains medieval classics as well as modern texts, "how to" books as well as more evocative experiential prose. Beebe (1976) is a highly regarded current work on North American falconry, and other books and articles, both summary and comprehensive, are given in the Bibliography.

Anyone wishing to watch falconry in action must exert some initiative. Falconers are generally not interested in public audiences at their occasional meets and couldn't care less about encouraging the popularity of their obsession. Most would tell you that falconers are born, not made.

FALCONERS' JARGON. Like many venerable practices, falconry has evolved its own special language, unintelligible to the uninitiated. Some of the commonest falconry terms are defined below. Terms relating to specialized gear are omitted.

Austringer: One who flies accipiters, especially Northern Goshawks, as differentiated from hawkers who use only falcons (members of the subfamily Falconinae).
Bate, bating: An attempt by a hawk to fly from a perch to which it is tethered. As a display of fright or temper this behavior is characteristic of birds in the early stages of training, but seasoned hawks also bate in a fit of pique or out of simple boredom.
Brancher: A juvenile hawk sufficiently mature to perch (e.g., on a branch) near its nest, but not yet fully independent.

Cadge: Formerly a frame or box with padded perches for transporting birds of prey. This contraption was carried by a "cadgeman" in the old days, and the birds thus given a free ride. This may be the source of the current "cadge," meaning to get for nothing, e.g., to cadge or "bum" a cigarette. Today usually means simply a portable perch used to carry birds into the field.

Eyass (EYE-us) (also eyas and eyess): A juvenile hawk that is captured from the nest, as opposed to a bird captured after fledging and on the wing. Birds captured in the former manner continue to be called eyasses even after reaching adulthood.

Hacking: See entry in main text.

Haggard: A hawk captured from the wild after it has completed at least one molt (first pre-alternate or pre-nuptial); i.e., an adult; more loosely, any wild adult hawk.

Imping: See entry in main text.

Intermewed: Refers to a hawk that has undergone a molt in captivity.

Jack: A male Merlin

Jerkin: A male Gyrfalcon.

Mantle: To mantle is to stretch the wing and leg simultaneously to one side; reputedly a sign of contentment.

Mews: Traditionally the place where hawks were kept while they molted. Now simply the "hawk house," where the birds live permanently.

Mutes: Hawk droppings.

Passage hawk: A bird of the year captured during its first fall migration or "passage."

Stoop: See entry in main text.

Tiercel (or tercel): Originally the mate of a "falcon" when the latter term was reserved for the female. Now a male hawk of any species that is used in falconry. The term derives from male hawks being characteristically smaller than their mates, usually by about a third.

Yarak: A hawk's state of readiness to hunt, detectable in certain bodily gestures, particularly among accipiters, buteos, and eagles.

For more on the birds used in falconry, see FALCON; HAWK; PEREGRINE, etc.

FALL WARBLERS. Species of wood warblers in juvenal plumage or after the pre-basic (post-nuptial) molt, many of which are notoriously difficult for the tyro birdwatcher to distinguish. A male Hooded Warbler is, therefore, never a "fall warbler," even though it may be seen during the autumn migration.

FAMILY. The major taxonomic category between ORDER and GENUS; orders may be divided into suborders and families; families into subfamilies, tribes (occasionally), and genera (see TAXONOMY and Appendix I). A family may also be defined as a grouping of phylogenetically related genera. All Latin family names end in -*idae*. There are about 170 families of birds worldwide, the precise number being a matter of taxonomic opinion. Authorities tend to agree on the composition of the more primitive families—there is no dispute over what species belong in the loon family or the flamingo family—but the familial breakdown of the huge order Passeriformes (perching birds) is open to considerable speculation.

The 75 families of birds which breed or occur regularly in North America are listed below in alphabetical order. For a "definition" of these —which orders they belong to; which and how many genera and species they contain; and their phylogenetic position—note the page number given after each family, which refers to Appendix I. With a few exceptions, the family concepts below reflect the A.O.U. *Check-list of North American Birds*, 5th ed. (1957). Those families marked with an asterisk are reduced to subfamily or tribe level in the 6th ed. of the A.O.U *Check-list* (1983).

Accipitridae, p. 799
Aegithalidae, p. 816
Alaudidae, p. 813
Alcedinidae, p. 811
Alcidae, p. 807
Anatidae, p. 800
Anhingidae, p. 798
Apodidae, p. 810
Aramidae, p. 803
Ardeidae, p. 798
Bombycillidae, p. 814
Caprimulgidae, p. 810
Cathartidae, p. 799
Certhiidae, p. 817
Charadriidae, p. 804
Ciconiidae, p. 798
Cinclidae, p. 814
Columbidae, p. 808
Corvidae, p. 823
Cracidae, p. 802
Cuculidae, p. 809
Diomedeidae, p. 796
Emberizidae, p. 817
Falconidae, p. 800
Fregatidae, p. 797
Fringillidae, p. 822

Gaviidae, p. 797
Gruidae, p. 803
Haematopodidae, p. 804
Hirundinidae, p. 814
Hydrobatidae, p. 797
*Icteridae, p. 821
Jacanidae, p. 804
Laniidae, p. 814
Laridae, p. 806
*Meleagrididae, p. 803
Mimidae, p. 815
Motacillidae, p. 814
Paridae, p. 816
*Parulidae, p. 819
Pelecanidae, p. 798
Phaethontidae, p. 797
Phalacrocoracidae, p. 797
Phasianidae, p. 802
Phoenicopteridae, p. 799
Picidae, p. 811
Ploceidae (Passeridae), p. 822
Podicipedidae, p. 797
*Polioptilidae, p. 816
Procellariidae, p. 796

Psittacidae, p. 808
Ptilogonatidae, p. 814
Pycnonotidae, p. 814
Rallidae, p. 803
Recurvirostridae, p. 806
Remizidae, p. 816
*Rynchopidae, p. 807
Scolopacidae, p. 804
Sittidae, p. 817
*Stercorariidae, p. 806
Strigidae, p. 809
Sturnidae, p. 822
Sulidae, p. 798
*Sylviidae, p. 816
*Tetraonidae, p. 802
*Thraupidae, p. 819
Threskiornithidae, p. 798
*Timaliidae, p. 816
Trochilidae, p. 810
Troglodytidae, p. 814
Trogonidae, p. 811
*Turdidae, p. 815
Tyrannidae, p. 812
Tytonidae, p. 809
Vireonidae, p. 821

Except for the Ploceidae (weaverbirds), the Pycnonotidae (bulbuls), and the Sturnidae (starlings and mynahs), which together contribute 5 introduced species to the North American avifauna, all of the above families are native.

Representatives of 6 additional families have occurred in North America as accidental stragglers. These families are: the Burhinidae (thick-knees); the Upupidae (hoopoes); the Jyngidae (wrynecks), now usually considered a subfamily of the Picidae (woodpeckers); the Prunellidae (accentors); the Muscicapidae (in the narrow sense of Old World flycatchers); and the Coerebidae (honeycreepers), sometimes placed with the wood warblers (Parulidae) or allied with the tanagers (Thraupidae or Emberizidae). These vagrant species are listed in Appendix II.

Members of 45 North American bird families appear in the illustrations in this book. For illustrations and descriptions of the bird families of the world, see references in the Bibliography under BIRD, especially Austin and Singer (1971).

FAT. Migratory birds typically acquire a heavy layer of subcutaneous fat in a bout of voracious feeding before their journeys. These reserves are essential fuel during long uninterrupted flights, which last more than twenty-four hours and span vast stretches of open ocean in many instances. The amount of fat laid down varies from species to species, with short-distance migrants usually putting on considerably less than half their "normal" weight as fat (e.g., White-throated Sparrow: 23–28 grams "normal" weight vs. 24–33 grams pre-migratory [fat] weight), while a long-distance migrant such as the Blackpoll Warbler more than doubles its "normal" weight (from 11–12 grams to 27 grams). See Nisbet et al. (1963) and MIGRATION.

FAUNA. The animal life of any given place or era. Fauna + flora = BIOTA. Avifauna is the birdlife of any given place or era.

FEAR OF MAN. See TAMENESS.

FEATHER. See Fig 9. A very elaborate modification of the outer layer (epidermis) of a bird's skin, made almost entirely of a light, strong, horny substance called keratin. Feathers are unique to birds, are variously modified in form to serve different functions (e.g., flight, temperature control, display), and in the aggregate make up a bird's PLUMAGE, which covers nearly the entire surface of its body.

EVOLUTION OF THE FEATHER. Authorities differ as to how feathers evolved from reptilian features. Some believe that the first feathers were elongated scales adapted for flight; others think that down evolved first from filaments found among the scales of some reptiles and paralleled development of "warm-bloodedness." In either case, it is clear that the first phase of feather formation in the skin is identical to that of scale formation

FIG. 9. *Feather form and structure.* The Cooper's Hawk primary at center is magnified to three different levels to demonstrate how the vane of contour feathers achieves its neat, smooth cohesion. The other drawings show different types of feathers (as labeled), and at the top, the rictal bristles which fringe the gapes of most nightjars are shown "in action."

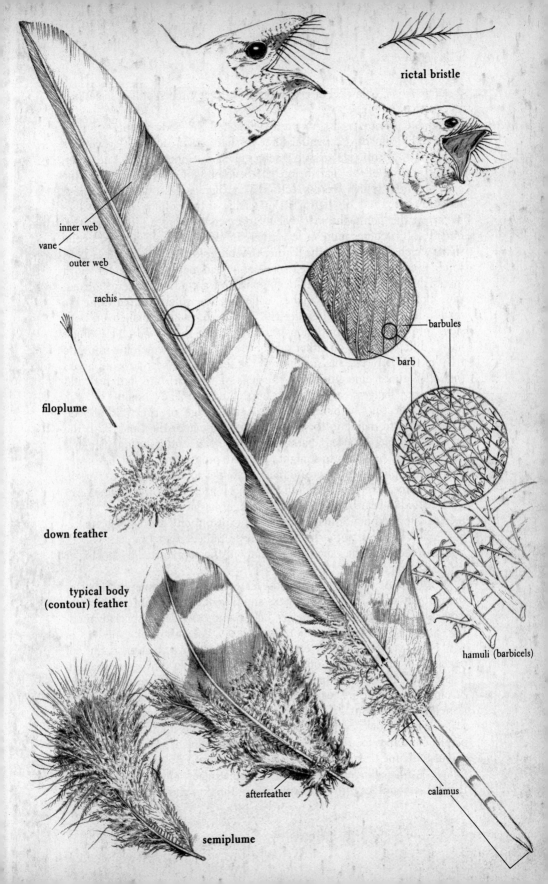

rictal bristle

inner web

vane

outer web

rachis

barbules

barb

filoplume

down feather

typical body
(contour) feather

hamuli (barbicels)

afterfeather

calamus

semiplume

(see *Formation,* below). For evolution of feathers from reptilian scales, see EVOLUTION OF BIRDLIFE.

BASIC STRUCTURE. A typical wing, tail, or body feather consists, when fully formed, of a central spine or shaft, from each side of which a thin, relatively soft *vane* or web emerges along its upper length. The lower, hollow portion of the shaft before the beginning of the vane is called the *calamus* and is round in cross section. The calamus has a hole (*umbilicus*) at its lower tip and another on its underside at the point where the vanes begin. At this point, the shaft begins to taper, contains a pithy core (*medulla*), and becomes more or less square in cross section. This part of the shaft, which continues to the feather tip and holds the full length of both vanes, is called the *rachis.* The two vanes, which may be of different width in certain feathers (e.g., primaries), consist of a continuous series of narrow, closely interlocked branches, called *barbs,* which diverge from the rachis angled toward the feather tip. The barbs in turn branch on both sides into a close-set continuous series of much shorter *barbules,* which have a different shape on either side of the barb. Those emerging from the front of the barb (i.e., the side nearest the feather tip) bear a row of hooks (*hamuli*); those emerging from the rear of the barb are flattened and curled or flanged along the upper edge. The hooks of the forward-projecting barbules grip the ridged edge of backward-projecting barbules to maintain the smooth, even surface of the vane. Both the forward-pointing (hooked) barbules and the rearward-pointing (flanged) barbules also bear short, straight, pointed projections called *barbicels,* which probably serve to increase the Velcro-like adhesiveness of the mesh. (Some sources refer to the hamuli as barbicels as well and the barbules can then be said to bear both hooked and straight barbicels.) This intricate but precise intermeshing of hooks and edges explains why it is so easy to "repair" the vane of a feather which has been pulled apart (see PREENING), but the delicacy of the vane "fabric" can only be appreciated by looking at it under a microscope.

At the base of the rachis of most feathers are a few rows of soft barbs, the barbules of which have no hooks and do not therefore interlock into a vane. Down feathers (see *Formation,* below, and DOWN) and specially modified feathers such as SEMIPLUMES and FILOPLUMES also lack vanes.

FORMATION. The first external sign of feather formation is the appearance of small bumps on the skin of an embryo during incubation. These result from the formation in the lower skin layer (dermis) of pimple- or nipple-like structures called *feather papillae,* which push up the outer skin layer (epidermis). This is identical to the beginnings of reptilian scales, which, however, take a different course at this point. In birds, each papilla continues to grow outward, taking the shape of a pointed cylinder, and at the same time it recedes into the skin, forming a cavity, the *feather follicle.* As the cylinder grows it hardens (keratinizes) into a feather sheath. It eventually pushes through the surface of the skin and the central dermal pulp is reabsorbed, leaving in essence a hollow tube. Along the inner wall of this hollow sheath a lining of straight longitudinal ridges develops within which the barbs of the first (natal) down feathers (if any) are formed. Eventually the top of the sheath splits open, releasing the barbs, each of which emerges separately from around the top edge of the calamus of this first feather like a fringe around a cuff. Meanwhile from the same follicle, a second dermal papilla is developing into another sheath just below the first down feather. The barb ridges of this second feather, however, rather than growing straight and vertical as before, grow in descending half-spirals along either wall of the sheath and finally meet and fuse with a central ridge which has formed along the (interior) upper surface. The ridge will be the rachis of a feather of the first full (juvenal) plumage. As before, the top of the feather sheath splits and the new barbs emerge, bearing the down feather at their tip. The barbs of the new feather having been fully formed within the sheath, the vane simply unfurls once it has emerged and the down feather quickly drops off. Succeeding feathers begin, as before, but are not connected to the preceding feather as was the initial down feather. In molt, the worn feathers are dropped before the new sheath emerges from the surface of the skin.

The somewhat complex subject of adult down feathers as opposed to the natal (neossoptile) down is discussed under DOWN. See also PLUMAGE and specific feather types, e.g., PRIMARY, FILOPLUME, etc., and MOLT.

For good illustrations of the formation process, see 'Espinasse (1964).

FEATHER MITES. Important arachnid parasites belonging to several families of the order Acarina. Feather mites spend their entire life cycle on the bodies of birds, eating feather parts and sometimes causing severe damage to plumage. For further details, see ECTOPARASITE.

FEATHER TRACTS (and apteria). Except for the ratites, penguins, and toucans, which have feathers evenly distributed over the surface of the skin, birds' feathers grow in discrete tracts or *pterylae* separated by feather-less areas called *apteria* (see PLUMAGE). Because the feathers normally overlap the apteria, the arrangement is not visible unless a bird is examined in the hand. The number of tracts/apteria and their respective sizes and shapes have proven to conform more or less among closely related species and are thus of significance as taxonomic characters.

The major feather tracts and apteria are as follows:

Capital tract. Top of the head from bill base to beginning of neck and over the face to the "jawline."

Spinal or dorsal tract. From the top of the neck (where capital tract leaves off) down across the back to the beginning of the upper tail coverts (caudal tract).

Ventral tract. From the chin (base of lower mandible) down the underside of the neck to the breast, where it forks (around the mid-ventral apterium) and continues to just above the vent.

Cervical apteria. The sides of the neck, separating the capital and spinal tracts from the ventral.

Lateral apterium. Covering much of a bird's sides from the outer margins of the spinal (dorsal) tract around to the outer margins of the ventral tract.

Mid-ventral apterium. The space enclosed by the fork in the ventral tract from the breast or even neck to somewhere on the lower belly. The form of the spinal and ventral tracts relative to the lateral and mid-ventral apteria varies widely among different groups of birds.

Humeral tract. A narrow strip running across the wing bases above (dorsally); the tract from which the scapulars arise (see Fig. 25).

Alar tract. The margins of both surfaces of the wings from which the flight feathers and coverts arise. Alar apteria sometimes occur in the center (or elsewhere) of both of the wings, separating the alar and humeral tracts.

Femoral tract. A narrow strip running along the thigh separated from the lower portion of the spinal tract by the lateral apteria.

Crural tract. Covering most of the feathered portion of the legs (variable); separated from the femoral tract by a narrow apterium.

Caudal tract. From the end of the spinal tract/uropygium/upper tail coverts around the tail to the base of the undertail coverts; it includes the circle of feathers (anal ring) surrounding the vent and gives rise to the rectrices as well as the tail coverts.

An accurately labeled diagram of the feather tracts and apteria is much clearer than a verbal description. Such a diagram is located on p. 7 of Palmer's *Handbook of North American Birds,* Vol. 1 (1962).

FECAL (FEE-kl) **SAC.** A gelatinous pouch into which the feces of nestling (mainly passerine) birds are excreted. The adaptation would seem to be an aid to nest sanitation. Adult birds remove the sacs from the cloacae of their young and usually eat them or carry them away from the nest, at least during the early stages of the brooding period. See PARENTAL CARE.

FEEDER. A contraption for dispensing seeds, fruit, syrup, or other substances to attract wild birds. It may be a simple shelf or platform on which to place food, but these days it is much more likely to be an elaborate structure providing shelter, a variety of perches, food-dispensing mechanisms, and baffles to discourage non-avian visitors or birds of insufficient beauty or charm. See BIRD FEEDING.

FEEDING (of birds by humans). See BIRD FEEDING.

FEEDING HABITS. See FOOD/FEEDING.

FEEDING OF YOUNG. See PARENTAL CARE, *Feeding.*

FERAL. In general, wild or untamed; but usually refers to domesticated animals which have "gone wild." Feral birds such as barnyard Mallards and pigeons seem to retain more of the characteristics of domestication, e.g., trust of man, than do feral cats and dogs.

FERRUGINOUS (feh-ROO-jin-uss) (Owl). Literally, iron-colored; rusty, e.g., the Ferruginous (Pygmy) Owl or (in breeding plumage) the Curlew Sandpiper, *Calidris (Erolia) ferruginea*. Ideally, the shade should be darker and duller than "rufous."

FERTILIZATION. In birds, as in humans, the conjunction of male and female reproductive cells (sperm and ova); in birds this takes place in the upper end of the female's oviduct, following copulation. See REPRODUCTIVE SYSTEM.

FIELD GUIDE. A book designed to be carried outdoors and used to identify species of birds or other particulars of natural history. A field guide is typically portable, if not "pocket-sized"; illustrated with diagnostic drawings or photos of the forms under consideration; and filled with concise descriptions of physical details, habits, distribution, and other facts pertinent to identification.

Birds inspired the composition of the first field guides, though early works were not so named. The prototype of the genre may be Thomas Nuttall's *A Manual of the Ornithology of the United States and Canada*, first published in two smallish volumes in 1832–34. More recognizable progenitors of modern identification aids were Chester Reed's *Bird Guides*, first published in 1906. These handy (3½ by 6 inches) volumes, illustrated by the author, showed and described one species per page. The paintings are more than passable, even by current standards, and the pithy texts cram description, habits, song, nest, and range into about six square inches. Frank Chapman's *Handbook of Birds of Eastern North America*, published in 1930 and (ultimately) illustrated by Louis Agassiz Fuertes, incorporated much more specific detail in the species accounts, consistent with the increasing sophistication of field ornithology.

It need hardly be explained that these worthy volumes were eclipsed in 1934 by the appearance of *the* field guide (the first so named)—Roger Tory Peterson's *A Field Guide to the Birds* (Eastern North America). This seminal work combined clear, diagrammatic illustrations with a unique system which uses arrows on the plates to point to diagnostic field marks and a concise text that emphasizes differences among similar species. In spite of predictions that sales of the guide would not repay the costs of printing it, it eventually sold over 2 million copies. At this writing the Peterson Field Guide Series contains 26 titles with two new ones due within a year. These cover almost all aspects of natural history and include five bird guides (Eastern North America, Western North America, Texas, Europe, and Mexico). In 1980 a new edition of the Eastern guide was published with a completely revised text and all new plates by Mr. Peterson.

In 1966 *Birds of North America*, by Chandler Robbins, Bertel Bruun, and Herbert Zim and illustrated by Arthur Singer, posed the first serious challenge to the preeminence of the Peterson guide. It offered a new format and fewer diagrammatic illustrations, covered all North American species in one small volume, and has become as indispensable to the dedicated American birdwatcher as *the* field guide. Another North American bird guide series that has attained richly deserved popularity is Richard H. Pough's *Audubon Bird Guides* (three volumes: Land Birds, Water Birds, and Western Birds). The two-volume *Audubon Society Field Guide to North American Birds* (Eastern Region, by John Bull and John Farrand, Jr.; Western Region, by Miklos D. F. Udvardy), a recent addition to the market with color photos in place of painted illustrations, has been an instant success with the public, though much less useful for field identification than the guides noted above.

Other bird guides currently in print which are pertinent to the North American avifauna are listed in the Bibliography.

FIELD IDENTIFICATION. The art of recognizing species of live birds in the wild—as opposed to identifying birds "in the hand," e.g., those trapped in a mist nest or museum specimens. Field identification is the essence of one kind of interest in birds. See IDENTIFICATION; BIRDWATCHING.

FIELD MARK. A characteristic, such as color, shape, or specific marking (eye rings, wing bars, breast stripes, etc.), by which a species can be distinguished in the field from similar species. In many cases, a number of field marks taken together are necessary for a conclusive identification. The black "armpits" of the Prairie Falcon are a field mark which serves to distinguish that species from the other large falcons. Compare JIZZ.

FIELD PROBLEM. Refers to an inherent difficulty in identifying certain species of birds. To novice birdwatchers, most of the sparrows and the "confusing fall warblers" often present frustrating field problems. However, some field problems—e.g., separating "medium-sized" accipiters, or the two scaup species at a distance, or immature jaegers—can tax or defeat the expertise (and patience) of even the most brilliant field ornithologist. See FIELD IDENTIFICATION; BIRDWATCHING; JIZZ.

FIGHTING. See AGGRESSION; TERRITORY; POPULATION.

FILOPLUME (FYE-low-ploom). A soft (not stiff), hair-like feather, i.e., one which lacks a vane or whose vane is insignificant. Two types of filoplumes are recognized. The first typically emerges in small groups from around the base of the body feathers and is normally completely concealed by them; this type usually has a tuft of vane at the tip and is present in nearly all birds. The second type has no vane at all and extends beyond the body feathers, most often in the head and neck region; these are present in many species but are difficult to see except on close inspection. Other hair-like feathers are sometimes called filoplumes but usually have more or less extensive vaning, e.g., bristles or certain long, narrow display plumes. See FEATHER and Fig. 9.

FINCH. The standard English "catchall" name covering almost all bird species with conical, seed-eating bills as well as a number without. It is used in referring collectively to members of several different families (e.g., Fringillidae, Emberizidae, Estrildidae, Ploceidae) and occurs in many individual species names (e.g., rosy finches, goldfinches). Traditionally, all North American "finches" (except the two introduced WEAVER FINCHES—the Eurasian House and Tree Sparrows) have been lumped in the family Fringillidae, which in its most expanded definition contains about 436 species worldwide, about 70 of which are native residents of North America. Under this definition, the Fringillidae family is the largest in the world (with the possible exception of the Muscicapidae, which in the broadest interpretation would include between 1,350 and 1,400 species) and without exception is the largest in North America. This taxonomic "reading" of the fringillids comprises such a great diversity of form and behavior (cardinals, buntings, Dickcissel, Pine Grosbeak, crossbills, seedeaters, towhees, sparrows, juncos, longspurs, etc.) that it is impossible to generalize about the common traits of its members. Therefore a more recent interpretation of these birds, which breaks them into smaller groups, is followed here.

EMBERIZID FINCHES. Include the cardinal-grosbeaks (subfamily Cardinalinae), the sparrow-buntings (subfamily Emberizinae), and in some taxonomies the tanagers (subfamily Thraupinae); these last are treated separately under TANAGER.

Cardinal-Grosbeaks (subfamily Cardinalinae). Include Northern Cardinal, Pyrrhuloxia, the *Passerina* buntings (including Blue Grosbeak), the *Pheucticus* grosbeaks (Rose-breasted and Black-headed), and Dickcissel in North America—a total of 10 of the world's approximately 37 cardinaline finches. The Dickcissel is now believed by some authorities to belong in the New World blackbird and oriole family (Icteridae).

These birds all have fairly heavy to very heavy bills, and in most species the males are very colorful at least in alternate (nuptial) plumage. The male Painted Bunting, for example, is arguably the most gaudy North American bird.

Most species of cardinal-grosbeaks forage with equal facility on the ground or in shrubbery and trees (depending, of course, on preferred habitat), where they feed on a wide variety of insects (e.g., moth larvae, grasshoppers, beetles), fruits, and seeds. Most come readily to feeders. Their songs are loud whistles or more gentle, protracted warbles (Dickcissel buzzy and sparrow-like).

The nests of these finches are comparatively small, loose or compact cups made of thin twigs, coarse grasses, dead leaves, and often bits of paper, cotton, snakeskin, or other miscellaneous debris and lined with finer grasses, plant fibers, and hair. The 2–5 (average varies) eggs vary widely among species: ground color white to pale blue or green; immaculate to heavily blotched, speckled, and streaked with brown or reddish.

The cardinal-grosbeaks are confined to the New World and achieve their greatest diversity in the Neotropics. As a whole, this group is widely distributed south of the coniferous forest zone in North America, though only one species (Blue Grosbeak) has a continuous continentwide distribution here. Two pairs of closely related species—Rose-breasted/Black-headed Grosbeak; Indigo/Lazuli Bunting—replace each other east/west. All but Northern Cardinal, Pyrrhuloxia, and the southern Florida population of Painted Bunting migrate from their North American breeding ranges to winter in Latin America.

For name derivations, see CARDINAL; PYRRHULOXIA; BUNTING; DICK-CISSEL.

Sparrow-Buntings (subfamily Emberizinae). Include the longspurs, snow buntings, Lark Bunting, New World sparrows, juncos, seedeaters, and towhees in North America, a total of 48 of the world's approximately 315 emberizine finches. Six others (four buntings and two grassquit species) have been recorded as accidental stragglers (see Appendix II).

The sparrow-buntings, like their cardinaline relatives, have conical bills adapted for crushing seeds, but these never reach the massive proportions seen in some of the cardinal-grosbeaks and fringillid finches (see below), and in some cases (e.g., Seaside Sparrow) they are relatively long and slender. The birds vary widely in size (4 to 10 inches) and form (compare, for example, SEEDEATER; SPARROW; TOWHEE) and while many are boldly patterned and even highly colored (e.g., Rufous-sided Towhee, several Old World buntings), they never exhibit the brilliant reds and blues which appear in the plumage of the cardinal-grosbeaks or fringillid finches.

The emberizine finches are quintessentially ground birds, hopping and scratching energetically in leaf litter, grass, or on bare soil for food. Most species prefer open-country habitats, but several (especially the towhees and Olive Sparrow) are typically found in dense underbrush or on the forest floor. The mainstay in the diets of most of these finches is seeds, but all species at least supplement their vegetarian regimen with a significant proportion of insects and other invertebrate food. Fruit is also a regular food item of many species, and the large towhees even take small salamanders, lizards, and snakes. The Seaside and Sharp-tailed Sparrows feed *primarily* on invertebrates, including many aquatic forms such as amphipods and crabs, and this departure from "normal" sparrow behavior probably explains their notably long, narrow bills.

Many open-country sparrow-buntings nest exclusively on the ground, and even those which favor shrubland or woodland rarely nest higher than

5 feet (exceptional Song and White-crowned Sparrow nests placed 25 and 35 feet in trees, respectively, have been recorded). The emberizine nest is usually the typical songbird cup, made loosely or compactly of small sticks, coarse grasses, bark strips, dead leaves, and the like and lined with hair, fur, fine plant fibers and down, and occasionally some feathers. A number of ground nesters (Savannah Sparrow, Lark Sparrow, juncos, Chestnut-collared Longspur) make a shallow hollow in the earth and line it or fill it with a frail, rudimentary cup. Sharp-tailed Sparrows weave a semi-dome structure around the stems of emergent sedges or rushes. Some emberizines have fairly musical songs with a strong cadence and bell-like quality; others utter barely perceptible insectile buzzes and clicks.

The sparrow-buntings lay between 2 and 8 eggs per clutch, the average for most species being 3–5 or fewer. The eggs vary by species from pale white to light blue/green and from immaculate to densely speckled or prominently blotched or scrawled with reddish/brownish or purplish/blackish.

The sparrow-buntings achieve their greatest diversity in the Holarctic region, but also occur in South America, Africa, and southern Asia. They are absent (except for introduced members of European species) from Australasia. In North America, this subfamily breeds from the High Arctic to the subtropical extremities of southern Texas and Florida. Many species range continentwide. The great majority are migratory but winter largely (or wholly) in North America and in the main move no further south than the central plateau of Mexico.

For name derivations, see SPARROW; BUNTING.

FRINGILLID FINCHES. As defined in Peters et al. (1931–   ) this family contains two subfamilies worldwide, the Fringillinae and the Carduelinae. The former contains only 3 species, 1 of which (Brambling) occurs here as a migrant in the Aleutians (Alaska). The cardueline finches here include the siskins, goldfinches, redpolls, rosefinches, rosy finches, crossbills, and Pine and Evening Grosbeaks, a total of 14–16 North American species (depending on taxonomy of the rosy finches) out of the approximately 129 members of the Carduelinae worldwide. Four other species of cardueline finches have been recorded as accidental stragglers (see Appendix II). The cardueline finches are now widely believed to constitute a family of their own, the Cardueliidae.

Except for the crossbills, the cardueline finches have conical bills that vary in form from the relatively narrow, thin bills of the siskins to the massive crushing mechanism borne by the hawfinches and Evening Grosbeak (see BILL). The birds themselves range in size from the 3¾-inch Lesser Goldfinch to the 10-inch Pine Grosbeak. Many male carduelines are brightly colored as adults.

In contrast to the emberizines, most of these finches are essentially arboreal (rosy finches exceptional), though they all feed readily on the ground when that is where the food is, e.g., at a feeding station. The main content (up to 97 percent in some species) of the cardueline diet is seeds, though all are known to take some insects during the warm seasons, and berries are also eaten by some species. In contrast to the sparrow-buntings, which normally find seeds on the ground, the carduelines usually extract seeds from their source in cones, catkins, or flower heads. The bills of the various species are generally adapted for dealing with preferred seed types: the crossbills have evolved a highly specialized apparatus for prizing apart cone scales and extracting the seeds—described in detail under FOOD and illustrated in Fig. 2. A number of the carduelines (e.g., rosy finches, Pine Grosbeak) have throat pouches in which to temporarily store food for feeding of young or eventual digestion.

Most carduelines have rich, melodious, if somewhat chaotic-sounding songs, though some (e.g., redpolls) make more "tinkling" and sparrow-like noises and the rosy finches produce no sound that deserves to be labeled anything but a "call."

The cardueline nest is typically placed off the ground (except rosy finches)—from the barely elevated weed clumps tenanted by some pairs of Lesser Goldfinches to the 70–80-foot-high treetop sites occasionally favored by the grosbeaks and rosefinches (*Carpodacus* spp.). A relatively bulky cup nest is the rule, made loosely with sticks (Evening Grosbeak) or more compactly of grasses, stems, bark strips, dead leaves, etc., lined with finer plant fibers, hair, fur, feathers, moss. The rosy finches build mainly of mosses and coarse grasses and place the nest in a rock crevice. Many northern carduelines use a lot of lichens, and the American Goldfinch is strongly partial to thistle and other plant down. The House Finch often (but not always) nests in a cavity which, as its name implies, is frequently an opening in a man-made structure. The 2–6 (average 4–5) eggs are white or pale blue, immaculate or sparsely spotted and/or scrawled in brownish/purplish, the markings typically concentrated at the large end.

The carduelines are well represented in North and South America and Eurasia and several European species have been successfully introduced in Australasia. They are particularly prevalent in the Temperate Zones—both of latitude and of altitude. In North America, these finches breed throughout the continent except for the Southeast. The Hoary Redpoll is one of the few passerines to breed in high arctic barrens and one of the few birds of any kind to routinely endure arctic winters. The rosy finches show a similar hardiness in their preferred alpine habitat. Most species are at least partially migratory, though most North American populations winter within the continent. The so-called WINTER FINCHES are subject to periodic IRRUPTIONS south of their "normal" range.

See also SISKIN; ROSY FINCH; GOLDFINCH; ROSEFINCH; CROSSBILL; GROSBEAK.

COLOR PLATES 1–3

Plate 1. A stylized depiction of the *ecological niches* occupied by some of the bird species of the pine-oak woodland biome of the southwestern U.S. The Elegant (Coppery-tailed) Trogon [1] forages for fruit and large insects mostly at moderate heights and under the forest canopy. The Cooper's Hawk [2] is an agile forest predator adept at chasing and seizing birds even within a dense stand of trees. Montezuma (Harlequin) Quail [3] forage in coveys over the ground in the open pine-oak woods, feeding on pine nuts, acorns, grass seeds, and some insects as well as digging for the edible tubers of the nut sedge (*Cyperus esculentus*). Like most small owls, the Whiskered Owl [4] usually nests in tree cavities (e.g., woodpecker holes) and catches large insects and small rodents by night, both in the canopy and on the ground. Rivoli's (Magnificent) Hummingbird [5] visits flowers near the ground for nectar but also "flycatches" in midair and picks insects from the outer foliage of tall trees. Acorn Woodpeckers [6] climb along the trunks and branches of oaks in this Arizona canyon and specialize in eating acorns, which they store in holes drilled for that purpose in trunks, telephone poles, and even buildings; they also take grasshoppers and other insects and sip nectar from sycamores and other trees; an Acorn Woodpecker was doubtless responsible for the hole in which the Whiskered Owl now nests. Sulphur-bellied Flycatchers [7] tend to perch under the canopy at the top of a tall tree but periodically dart out to take an insect from the air or (more characteristically) to glean the surface of leaves while hovering. The other flycatcher of this habitat is the elegant Black Phoebe [8], which is typically found near water; it makes short sallies from a low perch, usually to nab insects flying *below* it and occasionally even to catch small fish from the surface of the water. Violet-green Swallows [9] are also insectivores but concentrate their energies on the unseen myriads of tiny invertebrate prey which "dance" in the air high overhead. Noisy flocks of Mexican (Gray-breasted) Jays [10] are ceaselessly on the move through these woodlands, searching high and low for whatever is edible: insects, nestling birds, eggs, carrion, picnic remains, and—as befits an oak-associated species—acorns. The Canyon Wren [11] is at the edge of its rocky cliffside niche here; its *raison d'être* is to glean crevices on rock faces (sometimes buildings) for spiders and other invertebrates; its ringing, down-scale song is one of the quintessential sounds of southwestern canyonlands. Lesser Goldfinches [12] are essentially open-country birds which are especially fond of thistle and other weed seeds; thus they feed at the edge of the woods here and would typically nest fairly low in a tree near the stream. The Painted Redstart [13] is one of the most spectacular of the exotic "Mexican" species which reach the northern extremity of their range in these southwestern mountains; it is normally easy to spot this bird hopping nervously over the branches and foliage of the oaks with its wings and tail fanned, ever ready to launch a twisting, swooping, aerial attack on some flying insect. Despite their bright plumage and relative abundance, Hepatic Tanagers [14] are not so readily seen, since they usually move rather deliberately amid thick foliage, picking up insects and fruit as the occasion arises. The ground is home to the Yellow-eyed (Mexican) Junco [15], an attractive, often very tame sparrow which walks and pecks at fallen seeds (or bread crumbs) in the open or scratches in leaf litter like a towhee; juncos also *nest* on the ground.

Each of these species (along with the other members of the southwestern pine-oak avifauna) occupies its own unique ecological space. Food items, feeding and breeding localities, and behavioral traits may be shared by many different birds, but no two combine them in exactly the same way. Among them, the birds which are characteristic of this habitat exploit a high percentage of the natural resources available to them without competing unduly with each other. See DISTRIBUTION.

Plate 2. *Display.* Birds have evolved a great variety of plumage and behavioral adaptations in conjunction with their breeding habits—particularly courtship rituals. Many auks such as the Tufted Puffin [1] acquire bizarre head plumes and bill modifications at the start of the breeding season. These are worn by both sexes and presumably help the birds recognize their own species. Despite the finery, the puffins' courtship rituals are not elaborate. In Red-winged Blackbirds [2], only the male wears any bright feathers. His brilliant red-and-yellow "epaulets" are worn year-round but are only "used" during the breeding season. In full display, male redwings spread their wings and tails and erect virtually every feather on their bodies, simultaneously uttering their ringing *kong-ka-ree* song. The epaulets then bulge into almost spherical "wing lights" and can even be lifted frontward like flaps. In addition to species recognition, this conspicuous performance attracts the attention of prospective mates and acts as a warning to other male redwings that they should not trespass on the displayer's territory. Male Lesser Prairie Chickens [3] do not defend territories but gather together early on spring mornings and perform stylized "dances" in open country—while the females remain on the sidelines, apparently indifferent to the proceedings. The nuptial gathering places are known as LEKS. Though regular inflation of the cocks' rosy neck sacs adds a touch of color to the ritual, it is the "dance" and the "music" that deserve most attention. With wings fanned downward and tails cocked high, the males stamp the ground furiously, raise their head fans smartly, blow up their sacs, and give out with a chorus of gobbling sounds. Western Grebes [4] also "dance"—but in pairs (usually) rather than in "stag" assemblies—and on the water rather than on land. The "race" shown here is only the showiest and most energetic of half a dozen displays performed by this species during the breeding season. At home neither on the ground nor on the water, hummingbirds "dance" in the air, different species performing characteristic display flights. The Ruby-throated Hummingbird [5] plunges back and forth in a great "horseshoe," chirping ecstatically, its brilliant gorget flashing periodically when the light hits it at the proper angle.

Courtship is not the only context in which birds "display." The American Avocet [6] is attempting to lure an intruder away from her eggs or young by flapping and calling as if injured. When a potential predator has been distracted and led away from the nest area, the "cripple" resumes good health to avoid falling victim herself. The young Red-tailed Hawk [7] is trying to protect *itself.* Cornered on the ground—unable to take off or perhaps injured—it sits back on its tail, raises its formidable talons and broad wings, and erects its body feathers in a threat display meant to be as intimidating as possible. See DISPLAY.

Plate 3. *Cryptic coloration* is common among birds but varies greatly in its subtlety and degree of mimesis. Among the most cryptically colored of all birds are the nightjars, which both roost and nest on the ground during the day and defend themselves from potential predators by remaining motionless and blending with their surroundings. The complex coloration and patterning of the plumage of the Chuck-will's-widow [1] is an almost uncanny reflection of the irregular shapes and play of light on the forest floor; even the nightjar shape and typical posture—suggesting a piece of a rotting limb—aids the deception. Equally effective as a concealment device is the high degree of background matching attained in both the eggs and the nest of many birds that nest in exposed situations, e.g., the beach-dwelling Least Tern [2]. Another almost perfectly cryptic plumage is that of the Snowy Owl [3]—as anyone who has tried to find one in a snowbound landscape can attest; unlike the "chuck's," this deception involves little or no patterning but rather a simple likeness in coloration between the bird and the landscape in which it most often occurs. Presumably, the advantage of the owl's concealment is in improved ability to catch prey rather than in avoidance of predators. The plumage of the King Rail [4] is less precise in its mimicry of habitat but blends well in a generalized way with the wetland habitats in which it normally occurs; the prominent barring on the bird's flanks may be compared to a zebra's stripes—conspicuous out of context, but becoming cryptic against the light and shadows of its usual milieu, in this case the vertical-linear vegetation of marshland. The Louisiana Waterthrush [5] combines a number of general concealment "techniques." Its brown upperparts blend well with the shady forest floor and stream bank habitat in which it is typically found. It is "countershaded," its shadowed white underparts blending with its darker but better-lit upperparts. This gives it a flat "unsculptured" form which melds more easily into the backdrop of habitat. Its patterning is "disruptive," tricking our eye into associating parts of the body with parts of background rather than bringing them together in the form of a bird; the linear pattern on the waterthrush's breast resembles the rippling shadows of the stream it characteristically haunts, and the birds improve on this cryptic device by keeping their bodies in constant bobbing motion. For a more detailed account of cryptic coloration and associated behavior in birds, see COLOR AND PATTERN.

FISCHER von Waldheim, Johann Gotthelf, 1771–1853 (*Somateria fischeri*: Spectacled Eider). A German polymath—geologist, physician, paleontologist, zoologist, and authority on the history of printing. Though of humble origins, he became a protégé of Humboldt and Cuvier and eventually became prominent in the natural science establishment of Moscow. The spectacular duck which commemorates him was named by Johann BRANDT, another Russified German scientist.

FISHING. The majority of birds which wade, swim, and/or dive and not a few land birds (including, occasionally, some owls, flycatchers, corvids, warblers, and blackbirds) eat at least some fish. For specific fishing techniques, see SWIMMING/DIVING; BILL; CANOPY FEEDING (and Fig. 4).

FIXED ACTION PATTERN (F.A.P.). The behaviorist's term for the instinctive, highly stereotyped patterns of stimulus and response which govern the rituals of daily life of birds and other animals. A bird which, so to speak, is "in the mood" to eat, court, copulate, fight, etc., must receive the correct sound, gesture, or color signal which acts as a "releaser" of the intended behavior. See INTELLIGENCE.

FLAMINGO. Standard English name for all 5 (or 6 depending on taxonomy) members of the family Phoenicopteridae. The flamingos were once classified (with apparent logic) as a suborder in the order containing the storks and herons (Ciconiiformes). However, it is now widely accepted that they are more closely related to the waterfowl (order Anseriformes) but require an order of their own (Phoenicopteriformes).

All flamingos are pink with black wing tips; have almost absurdly long legs with neck to match and (unlike herons and storks) full webs between the three front toes. They stand almost 5 feet tall with neck extended normally. Perhaps their most extraordinary characteristic is their odd, thick bill, which is bent sharply downward at the middle. The interior of this device is lined with rows of lamellae which act as a sieve as the birds strain bottom mud in shallow water with their heads upside down. Their principal diet is diatoms, fly larvae and pupae, algae and bacteria, as well as some small fish, shrimps, etc. Their pink color is derived from a pigment in their normal food sources and fades when these are unavailable, e.g., in captivity. So bizarre are flamingos in reality that their appearance as organic croquet mallets in *Alice in Wonderland* by Lewis Carroll hardly stretches one's credulity further.

Colonial nesters, flamingos build a unique nest in—or at least surrounded by—shallow salt water. It consists of a mud cone with the top hollowed out to accommodate the single (rarely 2) egg, which is pale greenish with a white chalky coating.

According to Palmer (1962), flamingo flocks engage in a convivial "fowl-like gabble," and individual birds give a honk reminiscent of a Greylag Goose. The flocking flight call is likened to "a chorus of frogs" and a courtship call is rendered as *eep-eep cak-cak, eep-eep cak-cak.*

Flamingos are generally associated with warm climates, though they range well into the Temperate Zone in Patagonia and to lakes in the high puna zone of the Andes. One species, the American (Greater) Flamingo (*Phoenicopterus ruber*), may possibly have bred in "the old days" on the Florida Keys but there are only yarns to verify this speculation. They undoubtedly once occurred on the Gulf coast as stragglers from Caribbean colonies, and they may still do so, but it is now hard to distinguish these from birds which have escaped from Hialeah Park and elsewhere in Florida.

"Flamingo" originates from the Latin word for "flame," referring of course to the birds' color; Spanish flamenco dancers are so named because their strutting movements resemble those of courting and "marching" flamingos.

FLAMMULATED (FLAM-you-lay-ted) (Owl). Literally "inflamed" or perhaps "tinged with flame" (color). A rather overstated description of the hints of rufous in the facial disk and elsewhere in the gray plumage of the Flammulated Owl. It is possible that this small screech owl was named for its rarer red phase.

FLEDGE (fledged, fledgling). To grow feathers and, therefore, a verb unique to birds; does not include the downy covering with which some species are born. A young bird confined to the nest is a "nestling"; once out of the nest it is a "fledgling" until it is independent of its parents. When it has acquired its first true feather coat (juvenal plumage) or makes its first flight, it is said to be "fledged." See MOLT; YOUNG, DEVELOPMENT OF; FEATHER.

FLICKER. Standard English name for the 6 species of woodpeckers in the genus *Colaptes* (family Picidae; order Piciformes), one of which, the Common Flicker, breeds throughout North America.

The flickers nest in tree cavities as do other woodpeckers, but they forage mainly on the ground, pursuing their preferred food, ants. In 1973 the Committee on Classification and Nomenclature of the American Ornithologists' Union "lumped" three forms of North American flickers (Red-shafted, Yellow-shafted, and Gilded) into a single species, Common Flicker (see SPECIATION; HYBRIDIZATION; and Short, 1965–HYBRIDIZATION.)

The flicker is among the most familiar of birds and has acquired a very long list of colloquial names. Ironically, the one that became official is of uncertain origin. Gruson (1972–BIOGRAPHY) associates the name with "striking," i.e., "pecking"; Choate (1973–BIOGRAPHY) suggests a connection with an old Anglo-Saxon usage meaning a "fluttering of birds."

For family characteristics, see WOODPECKER.

FLIGHT. Although all bats and a great many insects are skillful fliers—and a few birds are hopelessly earthbound—the words "bird" and "flight" are almost inextricably associated in the human mind. And for good reason. There can be no question that in the evolution of birdlife the power of flight has reached its greatest natural refinement and versatility.

EVOLUTION OF FLIGHT. The earliest adaptations among vertebrate animals to traveling through the air were kite-like modifications consisting of webs of skin stretched across the angles of front and/or hind limbs. This model is still with us in the form of flying squirrels, flying fish, and a few species of reptiles and amphibians. It allows these animals to "glide" or "sail" over much greater distances than can be traversed by simply jumping, but the duration of their flight is largely dependent on the height from which they launch themselves and the initial power they expend in takeoff.

Sustained flight, powered by a greatly modified forearm or wing, first evolved among reptiles such as the various pterodactyls familiar from the painted skies in museum reconstructions of the Jurassic and Cretaceous periods. Structurally, the reptilian wing was very different from the modern bird wing (for comparative anatomy of insect, reptile, bird, and bat wings, see WING). It still made use of the "stretched-skin kite" design but it did provide what only the lowly insects had by then achieved: the ability, once launched upon the air, to stay there.

The first *feathered* wing we know about belonged to *Archaeopteryx*, a very reptile-like bird of the Upper Jurassic which may have been a far weaker flier than some of its fully reptilian contemporaries (see EVOLUTION OF BIRDLIFE). Its wing was an early experiment in what has proven to be the earth's most efficient flying mechanism.

DEFYING GRAVITY. The wings of flying birds, though widely variable, are all adapted in structure and shape to take advantage of a physical phenomenon called "lift." When air passes over a convex surface such as an inverted saucer or a bird's wing in a normal, outstretched position, it travels faster across the top than across the hollow undersurface. This creates pressure from below and a vacuum above, which will raise the object in question if it is not too heavy. An inverted saucer exposed to a strong wind will be "lifted"—briefly. But a bird's wing, with its rigid, blunt but rounded leading edge, its smoothly curving convex surface (camber), and its tapered, flexible trailing edge, is adapted to "catch" lift and then control it in precise opposition to the downward pull of gravity. Adaptations to lightness in a bird's body, such as a fused and simplified skeleton and the hollowness of some of its larger bones (see SKELETON, *Pneumatization*), complement the force of lift in making a bird airborne.

Lift will not occur, of course, unless there is a continuous stream of air passing across the surfaces of a bird's extended wing. Gulls on a beach can sometimes be seen to simply raise their wings and be borne aloft by a strong wind. But in most cases birds must propel themselves into the air until the air pressure they encounter is great enough to raise their weight. This explains why we see birds "taxi" over the surface of the water or the ground and also why it is expeditious to "fall" off a high cliff or leap from the top of a tree. The alternative to these launching techniques is a powerful, rapid flapping of the wings, requiring a great expenditure of energy (see *Taking Off*, below).

Conquering gravity is only the first step in the complex art of flying. Once aloft, a bird must be able to move through the air, to maintain stability while moving, and to execute certain basic maneuvers efficiently and safely in a manner appropriate to the proportions of its body.

MOVING THROUGH THE AIR. Just as lift balances weight in getting a bird off the ground, another opposing force is needed if a bird is to overcome inertia and the resistance the air puts up against any body moving through it (drag). Evolution has provided all modern flying birds with an aerodynamically efficient form and a smoothness of surface which minimizes drag to a great degree. And we shall eventually see that some birds are capable of using natural air movements such as thermals and updrafts

FIG. 10. *Mechanics of flight.* The diagram at upper right shows how the breast muscles act in conjunction with the skeleton to raise and lower a bird's wings. Some of the details have been simplified or stylized for the sake of clarity. Our model is flying directly at us and is raising one wing while it lowers the other—something birds *never* do in actual flight. To the left of the dotted divider, the *supracoracoideus* muscle (or *pectoralis minor*) has just contracted, pulling on the tendon which passes through a hole formed at the juncture of the scapula, coracoid, and clavicle (not shown) bones and is ultimately attached to the base of the humerus. The wing, in effect, is hoisted by rope (tendon) and pulley (bone) powered by the supracoracoideus. To the right of the dotted divider, it is the *pectoralis* (*major*) which is contracting, hauling the humerus down in the powerful downstroke. The two breast muscles work in synchronized opposition, the pectoralis relaxing as the supracoracoideus contracts and vice versa. The "cutaway" loon shows the form of the pectoralis (major) muscle as it lies attached to and covering the breastbone (sternum). Note that the supracoracoideus muscle is completely obscured below the pectoralis from this view, as is the "rope and pulley" mechanism shown upper right. Of course, birds move their wings in many subtle ways in addition to up-and-down strokes of flight, but (except for two prominent tendons) the complex musculature of the wing has been omitted here.

A Bufflehead is shown in "stop-action" poses depicting the configuration of a single wingbeat. The top line shows the downstroke and the bottom the upstroke. Note that the wing tip moves down and forward and then up and back, inscribing a narrow, diagonal figure 8. Another detail of the flying process is demonstrated by the meadowlark at bottom. In order to gain maximum lift from air pressure, the primary feathers are held tightly closed in the downstroke, then opened, like venetian blinds, allowing less air resistance as they return to their position. Especially in larger birds, the wing tips are also curved upward in the midst of both strokes (as shown in the 4th and 5th "frames" in the top row of Buffleheads), creating a propeller-like action which pulls the bird along.

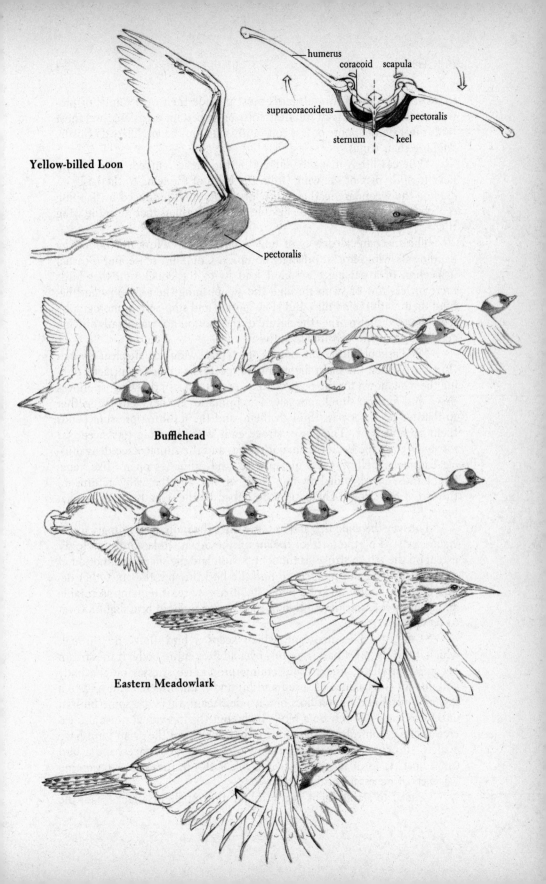

humerus

coracoid   scapula

supracoracoideus

pectoralis

sternum   keel

Yellow-billed Loon

pectoralis

Bufflehead

Eastern Meadowlark

to assist their efforts. But all birds must provide their own source of propulsion (or thrust) at least intermittently or on certain occasions, and most
birds must do this more or less constantly when in the air. They do this by
flapping their wings.

Whereas lift is managed largely by the broad, curved, relatively inflexible *inner* part of the wing (from the bend of the wing to the base, including the secondary feathers), the forward motion produced by flapping
is accomplished mainly by the flexible primary feathers that form the wing
tip.

The mechanical details of how a bird achieves forward motion by
flapping its wings are surprisingly complex. Common sense and a casual
inspection of a passing cormorant lead us to the conclusion that birds
more or less row or swim through the air, pushing the air below and behind them with their wings. But slow-motion and stop-action photography
have revealed that neither the nature of the motion nor the details of wing
action support this sensible hypothesis.

The basic physical components of a typical wingbeat are clear enough
(Fig. 10). When the main flight muscle (pectoralis major) contracts, pulling the wing down for the power stroke (see MUSCLES), the wing tip moves
down *and forward* simultaneously. The primaries are held closed together
so that air does not pass through them, and the resulting pressure bends
them up and back. The power stroke ends with the wing tips swept far
forward. Then the pectoralis major relaxes and the supracoracoideus muscle contracts, pulling the wing upward, the primaries open "like venetian blinds," and, aided by the force of the air, the wing returns to
the top of the stroke. The pattern described by the wing tip is a diagonal
figure 8.

The way the wing tips and in some cases the individual primary feathers are twisted by the force of the air on the down stroke (and to a lesser
extent on the return stroke) is thought to simulate the shape and motion of
a propeller blade and in effect *to pull* the bird through the air. Other details of the wingbeat and of a bird's stabilizing systems remain inscrutable
and a comprehensive description of the aerodynamics of bird flight has yet
to be written.

STABILITY. The airstream, which keeps a bird aloft and through
which it travels, must pass smoothly over a bird's entire body. If the stream
becomes turbulent, uneven and counterproductive stresses on the body
will disrupt the balance of speed and lift and if uncorrected will lead to a
loss of control and a rapid loss of altitude. Again, there are some built-in
anti-turbulence feathers on a bird's body, but the individual must also exercise certain controls. As mentioned, the contours of the avian form have
evolved to permit a smooth, even flow of air over all surfaces, and a bird
can adjust its form by muscular control of the feather coat—becoming
"sleeker" if necessary or desirable.

Crucial to stable flight is controlling the "angle of attack," i.e., the angle at which the wing meets the oncoming air. As the angle of attack increases, so does lift, but so also does turbulence. If the angle is increased too much, turbulence overcomes lift and the bird "stalls." To prevent stalling at a high angle of attack, a bird may raise its alula, the small group of feathers at the bend of the wing; this forms a "slot" which, in effect, corrects the flow of air, stabilizing the stream as it passes through the opening and over the wing surface. In some birds, notably broad-winged soaring birds, additional "slots" are apparent between the emarginate tips of the outer primaries.

Another constant source of turbulence is the eddies of air which are created along the trailing edges and tips of the wings in flapping flight. These "wing-tip vortexes" drag against forward motion and also swirl up onto the upper wing surfaces, disrupting the smooth flow of air over them. In wings which are long in proportion to their width, such as those of an albatross, such turbulence is minimized by the shorter surface over which the air must travel. In broad-winged birds, the problem is again corrected by the wing "slots," which "cut" the air into fast, uniform streams.

FORM AND FUNCTION. Though basic principles of flight must be obeyed by all birds, and mastery of basic maneuvers such as landing and taking off (see below) are necessary for all, it is clear, if we compare warblers, woodpeckers, eagles, and albatrosses, that the *manner* in which basic principles are followed and maneuvers executed varies widely according to a bird's particular "equipment." Length, breadth, and shape of body, wings, and tail, body weight, development of muscles, form of bill and feet—all in proportion to one another—determine the characteristic way different birds move in the air and their relative competence in various situations. Several of these physical relationships are essential in discussing the many flight styles which have evolved.

Aspect Ratio is the wingspan divided by average breadth. Albatrosses and other birds with long, narrow wings have *high* aspect ratios which permit maximum lift with minimum drag and turbulence. This arrangement allows long-distance gliding with little necessity for flapping, which these birds cannot do with any force. This technique is greatly assisted by winds over the sea (see *Dynamic Soaring,* below). Most birds with low aspect ratios (e.g., songbirds) are incapable of gliding for any distance without rapidly losing altitude and must flap almost constantly. Soaring birds such as eagles have *low* aspect ratios but can catch maximum lift with their broad, strongly cambered wings with additional help from rising air currents (see *Soaring,* below). They are thus able to hold flapping energy in reserve.

Wing Loading is the proportion of wing area to body weight. Birds with low wing loading (lower weight/greater wing area)—vultures are good examples—tend to be more buoyant and capable of slow reconnaissance flight with little flapping, again aided by thermals. Loons, with heavy bodies and smaller wing areas, have heavy wing loads and also a relatively low aspect ratio because of their short (though narrow) wings and so have to propel themselves by constant, rapid wingbeats. If it seems that loons (like grebes and auks) received short shrift in flying apparatus, it will be remembered that their short, narrow, powerful wings and heavy bodies are ideal for deep diving, an activity which would prove futile to an albatross and fatal to a vulture.

Muscles. Not nearly as apparent as aspect ratio or wing loading is muscle development. The size and shape of a hummingbird's wings do not suggest great aerial competence. But when driven by enormously developed pectoral muscles (the greatest, proportionally, of any bird), they become uniquely powerful propellers.

BASIC MANEUVERS. All birds must be able to perform the following operations if they are to be successful fliers. Once again, method and competence are married to physical equipment. In addition, many commonplace actions, whether routine (e.g., landing) or subtle (e.g., pursuing prey through dense woods), are not entirely instinctive but rather are skills which must be learned and perfected for the sake of survival.

Taking Off. Birds with high aspect ratios, e.g., shearwaters, are masters of flight once airborne, but their long, narrow wings are not designed for flapping; they depend on "taxiing" over the sea surface on powerful legs until they can catch enough lift. Heavy birds with comparatively small wings, such as alcids, also have trouble taking off from a level surface and tend to perch or nest where they can simply drop off into the air.

Most birds, however, begin their takeoff at a more nearly vertical angle to the ground, thrusting downward with their legs for a boost and beating their wings powerfully in a horizontal plane back and forth to initiate the necessary airstream. This is a very different motion from the figure 8 of normal flapping flight and is controlled by different muscles (mainly the supracoracoideus).

Altitude. To rise, a bird can shift its wings (and thus its center of gravity) forward, raising its head and lowering its tail. Ordinarily, though, it will raise its angle of attack as described above. Soaring birds are often assisted in gaining altitude by a variety of atmospheric aids (see *Soaring*, below). Losing altitude requires less effort, of course, but must be controlled by the mechanisms of speed and direction described below. (For height records, see ALTITUDE.)

Speed. A bird can accelerate by simply flapping faster and/or by streamlining its body to minimize drag. Depending on its needs, it can fold back the wing tips only, leaving the base of the wing extended for lift to maintain altitude. Or, like a Peregrine stooping, it can fold its entire wing close to its body and drop, gaining great speed through inertia and minimal drag. In slowing down, a bird applies an appropriate amount of drag by raising its angle of attack, putting wings, tail, and body before the wind (see *Landing*, below).

Turning. Altering body symmetry, e.g., folding one wing or twisting the tail to one side, will effect a turn, because the air then strikes part of the body with greater force than other parts. Birds soaring in the slipstreams of ships are easily seen making continual adjustments to fluctuating updrafts in this manner. More abrupt, directed changes of course require a shift in body weight and the twisting of the tail in a rudder-like action in addition to the appropriate wing movements to control stability and speed as well as direction.

Landing. Birds begin to lose speed in preparation for landing by increasing drag. They may, for example, tilt the trailing edge of the wing into the wind—the original "flaps"—or spread the tail to the same effect. If aiming for an elevated perch rather than a level surface, most birds will approach from below, raise their angle of attack, and then swoop up to the stalling point with wings fully extended and tail held vertically and spread. Simultaneously, the alula is extended to break the stall, the legs are thrust forward to meet the branch or perching surface, and the wings flap rapidly forward, halting all forward momentum. Anyone who has watched a young bird overshoot a perch and crash into the adjacent shrubbery will appreciate the muscle coordination and skill required for a successful landing. Coming to rest on water or land usually is accomplished by a similar method, minus, of course, the up-swoop. Water birds can afford less precise landings because their final contact is cushioned—grebes and alcids, for example, often bounce several times on choppy seas or aquaplane for several feet on calm water. Other aquatic birds, e.g., cormorants and ducks, extend their webbed feet forward and "waterski" in as they make their stopping flaps.

Birds which are well adapted for soaring, when landing into the wind—e.g., a hawk on a treetop or a gull on a parking lot—may be able to maintain lift without forward motion and then simply drop gracefully into place. Less buoyant birds can do the same thing by hovering briefly before dropping onto their perch.

SPECIAL FLYING TECHNIQUES

Soaring might be defined as maintaining altitude without self-propulsion (flapping). By the laws of flight, then, it requires some other source of lift. One source is air currents diverted upward after meeting a surface. Winds hitting a cliff face, for example, are deflected upward and birds can sail along the edge of a precipice effortlessly suspended by these updrafts. Winds blowing out over a cliff face, i.e., offshore, can create upward-curling eddies below the edge which can also be used for support. A coastal or offshore gull or gannet colony is a good place to watch this method of soaring. Another is a ridge of mountains during a hawk migration. Similar updrafts over sea waves are also exploited. Pelicans are expert at sailing in formation along the crest of the wave line at tropical beaches, and shearwaters ply the air in the troughs of swells so skillfully that their wings do actually "shear" the surface occasionally with no loss of stability. Another variation is practiced by the gulls which ride the slipstream along the gunwales of large boats, flapping only to drop on a proffered potato chip.

Thermal Soaring (Fig. 20) depends upon columns of rising warm air (thermals) which are generated at irregular intervals from the earth's surface. As the column rises it expands toward the top and is finally set free by surrounding cold air. (Picture a bubble of air rising from the bottom of a glass container of boiling water.) Within the bubble there is a revolving circle of warm air with a continual updraft of cold air through the center. Finding one of these thermals, some birds can "ride" the rising ring of moving air to the desired height and then drift off in the desired direction, finding another thermal when they get too low. Vultures, eagles, and buteos depend on thermals in searching wide areas for prey without expending too much energy. These and other raptors as well as pelicans, cranes, and storks also need them to efficiently cover the long distances they travel during migration.

Since thermals are not generated over water, migrating soaring birds must skirt large lakes or other bodies which lie along their route, and shorelines are therefore often good places to watch thermal soaring in action. When a large group of birds enters a thermal it swirls upward with it, showing the actual form and movement of the air mass. They may rise out of sight into the clouds, but at a given moment a single bird leaves the spiral and heads off in the appropriate direction, followed by the rest of the birds in a line, like a string unwinding from a top. Such whirlpools of birds are called "kettles" in North America.

Dynamic Soaring (Fig. 22) exploits the fact that winds blowing over the surface of the sea are slowed by the waves at the surface and gradually increase in velocity with altitude. Relatively heavy birds such as albatrosses, fulmars, and shearwaters with high aspect ratios (best for control and stability) can gain speed high in the fastest air and then plunge downwind; when they reach the slower air near the sea surface they then use their momentum to head up again, simultaneously turning into the wind, which blows them back aloft. The entire sophisticated maneuver is performed without a single flap. A variation of this technique is used in flying across the wind. One of the great spectacles of birdwatching along the coast is a flight of pelagic birds executing these dynamic arcs across the horizon in a gale.

Hovering is essentially flying in place. A number of bird species have developed the technique as a way of watching for and lining up on their prey from above. In a strong wind, gulls, jaegers, and certain hawks, such as Rough-legged Hawks, White-tailed Kites, and American Kestrels, can simply glide into the wind, flapping only often enough to keep their air speed equal to the wind speed. Most hovering, however, is powered by a rapid horizontal beating of the wings with the body held more or less vertically; this is simply an extended version of the taking-off motion (see above) and requires a tremendous investment of muscular energy. Warblers and other insectivorous birds may hover momentarily while chasing an insect or during indecisive moments before perching. A few species—kingfishers, terns, American Kestrel—have evolved the extra muscular stamina to sustain the action longer. Hummingbirds, of course, are the master hoverers. As noted above, they have the largest flight muscles in relation to body size of any bird and their flight feathers take up almost their entire wing—all flap and little lift. Their precision maneuverability is achieved with the aid of their broad tails. Even with this special design, hummingbirds must feed constantly and often become torpid during the night to conserve energy for such high-power hovering.

V Formation is standard travel procedure for cormorants, cranes, ducks, geese, and swans and is practiced less habitually by gulls. The same destabilizing eddies which rise up over the trailing edge of a bird's wing as it flaps (see *Stability*, above) can give a bird flying in its wake added lift, saving energy on long journeys. The lead bird, of course, misses the advantage, which perhaps explains why we often see the leadership shift in migrating flocks. The fact that we see no small birds in V formations suggests that they do not generate enough helpful ascending air to encourage the evolution of the pattern.

See also EVOLUTION; FEATHER; WING.

FLIGHTLESSNESS. It is tempting to liken a bird that can't fly to a fish that can't swim, but this is not really a very good analogy. With very few exceptions, such as the swifts, birds tend to be at least as well adapted to life on the ground or in the water as they are to an aerial existence. Some birds, e.g., gulls, seem equally adept at all three. It is not very surprising therefore to find that there have always been and continue to be birds which have evolved terrestrial life styles at the expense of their power of flight.

Though doubtless a precursor of a stronger-flying form, the first known bird, *Archaeopteryx*, was a poor flier whose wings mastered the air only to the extent that they enabled their owner to glide from tree to tree, much as a flying squirrel does today. A later diving bird, *Hesperornis* of the Cretaceous Period, probably evolved from flying ancestors, yet it may have had no externally visible wings at all and passed its life on and under the water while strong-flying reptiles flapped and soared overhead. Terrestrial flightless birds often show a conspicuous protective adaptation which compensates for their inability to escape into the air. In many cases this adaptation takes the form of great size. The giant *Diatrymas* of the Paleocene and Eocene epochs stood to 7 feet and had powerful legs and massive heads and bills to offset the uselessness of their puny wings. The much more recent Elephant Bird of Madagascar is thought to have weighed half a ton, and the largest of the giant moas of Australasia to have stood as tall as 13 feet—proportions that would inhibit most predators. Most of the living ratite birds, the Ostrich, Emu, cassowaries, and rheas, are also very large, though the kiwis of New Zealand rely on secretive nocturnal behavior rather than size for protection.

On isolated islands or lakes, species of flightless grebes, cormorants, ducks, and rails evolved in the absence of predators and consequently lacked any effective defense when man and his attendant rats, pigs, cats, and dogs disembarked in their domains. Many unique species, e.g., the Dodo and Great Auk, have ceased to exist through a combination of human callousness and their inability to fly from it; and almost without exception those that survive are severely threatened.

Unique among modern flightless birds are the penguins, which, unlike the Ostrich and other ratites, did not lose the power of flight but rather adapted it to swimming. The term "ratite" implies the lack of a keel on the breastbone, to which the flight (pectoral) muscles of flying birds attach (see Figs. 10 and 19). Penguins have both keel and flight muscles, but their wings have become flippers, and they fly through the water rather than in the air.

If we survey the present world avifauna, it becomes clear that the ability to fly is not represented in a simple "have" or "have not" fashion but is highly variable among different species. Some birds, e.g., albatrosses, vultures, alcids, are powerful fliers under the proper conditions but are unable to get off the ground in others. Many species fly well enough but do so relatively infrequently, spending most of their energy in the water (grebes) or on the ground (many gallinaceous birds). Even within a single family, great variation in flying ability may be apparent. Many cuckoo species are graceful fliers and long-distance migrants, yet the anis seem barely able to cross a road despite a furious flapping of their short wings followed by a long *Archaeopteryx*-like glide; and the roadrunners, though apparently more capable than the anis, almost never take to the air, but prefer to run—even for their lives.

The only passerine bird species suspected of being flightless was the Stephen Island Wren, a member of a small family of birds (Xenicidae or Acanthisittidae) endemic to New Zealand. It reputedly ran around on the ground like a mouse, but its habits were little known and it became extinct soon after it was discovered in 1894; its wing structure suggests that it may have been capable of weak flight.

Since the demise of the Great Auk (see EXTINCT BIRDS) no flightless bird species have occurred in North America.

FLIGHT PATTERN. The manner in which birds fly, often highly distinctive among different families of birds and even diagnostic at the species level. For example, almost all woodpeckers travel in a series of regular swooping undulations, alternating bursts of flapping with a glide of about equal length. The Spotted Sandpiper can be distinguished in flight from any other North American species from as far away as it can be seen by its highly distinctive flight pattern, consisting of a furious "whir" of shallow beats with wings held stiffly, interspersed with periods of glide. Only small shearwaters fly in a similar manner in North America.

Flight pattern is an element of JIZZ, crucial to skillful field identification.

FLIGHT YEAR. A year in which unusually large concentrations of a given species occur. The phenomenon is associated mostly with northern species—e.g., Great Gray, Hawk, and Boreal Owls, alcids, winter finches, Bohemian Waxwings—due to inadequate food supplies, overpopulation, or the like. See IRRUPTION.

FLOCK (flocking). "Flock" is a broad collective term which applies to groups of any kind of bird, as well as to certain other animals, e.g., sheep; for more specific and less conventional collectives referring to birds, see NOUNS OF ASSEMBLAGE.

Flocking as a pattern of behavior may be practiced by normally solitary species under certain circumstances—e.g., Downy Woodpeckers often travel with mixed feeding flocks of titmice, nuthatches, kinglets, etc. Or it may be characteristic of at least one major phase in the life of a species—e.g., Snow Buntings migrate and feed in flocks before and after the breeding season, though they are not gregarious while nesting. A number of water birds—e.g., Double-crested Cormorants—spend their entire life cycle in close association with others of their own kind, though not necessarily with the same individuals. Other species—e.g., Merlin, Yellow-billed Cuckoo—are just as determinedly solitary and are seldom found in even small groups.

Leaving aside colonial nesting (for which, see COLONY), flocking is associated with three basic activities: feeding, travel, and defense.

Feeding Flocks of foraging birds such as blackbirds move in a systematic "leapfrogging" progress across fields; birds at the rear of the flock pass over the heads of their fellows when they have gleaned a certain area of ground and land at the front rank. These flocks are normally silent or nearly so. Other species (e.g., many finches, waxwings) will arrive at a feeding site—a fruiting tree or seed-bearing conifer—en masse but feed individually (though closely) without following any apparent group dynamic. Such flocks tend to be noisier. Mixed flocks of forest birds, which often include titmice, creepers, nuthatches, kinglets, vireos, warblers, and representatives of other families, move noisily through the trees, feeding according to preference, seemingly oblivious to each other, and sometimes at some distance from their companions. Seabirds of several species frequently congregate to exploit abundant food sources such as fish schools or wastes dumped by boats. Groups of Double-crested Cormorants and American White Pelicans appear to have taken this one step further when they engage in cooperative "fish drives" (see FOOD/FEEDING, *Feeding Flocks*).

Traveling Flocks include flights of birds (e.g., crows, herons) to feeding grounds and back to communal roosts, but reach greatest development during migration. A noteworthy feature of migratory flocks is the degree to which their membership may be "exclusive." In the great majority of cases, birds migrate only with their own species, though mixed flocks of closely related species (e.g., cormorants, scoters, swallows, waxwings)— usually with one species clearly predominating—are not unusual. Arctic shorebirds flock in different age groups, the adults leaving the breeding grounds a month or more before the birds of the year. Especially in spring, many passerine species (e.g., Red-winged Blackbirds) travel only with their own sex, a fact which may be related to the males' need to establish a territory on the breeding grounds before the females arrive. Canada Geese and other anatids migrate in congregations which are subdivided into family groups; the composition of the larger flocks may change but the family units (parents and offspring of the year) leave, winter, and return together.

Despite the tendency of most species to some form of segregation, migratory flocks containing mixed ages, sexes, and relationships also occur and, as noted, certain species are fundamentally solitary, even in migration.

Defensive Flocks are formed quickly in response to a common threat and usually consist of birds that are gregarious in another context. Mixed colonies of seabirds, for example, will rise together to harass an eagle, and foraging flocks of forest birds (described above) join forces to "mob" owls and jays for the same reason (see Fig. 14). Starlings and small sandpipers often arise in unison and form dense flocks, thus thwarting the intentions of predators such as Merlins and Sharp-shinned Hawks, which are confused by a mass of shifting forms and must "cut out" an individual bird in order to follow and kill it successfully.

Flock Dynamics. No one who has seen moving aggregations of birds can fail to be impressed with the high degree of cohesion and simultaneity of motion. Though some behaviorists (e.g., Tinbergen, 1951–INTELLIGENCE) have theorized that flocking is merely a by-product of instinctive activities such as feeding and migration, it is now widely believed that there is also a separate "flocking instinct." This is not to deny that certain details of flocking behavior (e.g., appropriate calls) need to be learned by individual birds.

A few specific flocking phenomena deserve emphasis.

"Following" describes an action initiated by one or a few birds in a flock and immediately imitated by the rest. This is best seen in flocks as they cease one activity, e.g., feeding or resting, and begin another, e.g., drinking or preening.

Communication is a major element of cohesion in most flocks, though there are exceptions (see *Feeding Flocks*, above). Individuals in migratory and some feeding flocks often keep up a steady utterance of short notes; and alarm notes, warning of danger, are heeded in unison even when issued by a different species.

Spacing of precise dimensions is strictly observed in most flocks, each bird having in effect a tiny territory or "individual distance," which it will not permit to be transgressed. This is easily observed in sparrows feeding on the ground, swallows on a wire, or shorebirds working a beach or mud flat. At the other extreme, birds on the edge of a flock may allow themselves to lag or to wander some distance, but only to certain (apparently instinctual) limits. Except for aggressive encounters or where heat conservation is at stake (e.g., swallows or titmice huddling in a roosting cavity for warmth), birds rarely make physical contact with other members of a flock.

"*Schooling*" *movements*, such as the sharp, split-second turns executed in apparent perfect harmony by flocks of sandpipers, may be under the control of the central nervous system instead of (or as well as) being simply an unusually precise "following" action.

Benefits of Flocking. The prevalence of flocking among birds is an indication that the practice has advantages which favor survival. A few obvious ones are as follows.

• Large numbers of birds congregated at an abundant food source (e.g., at sea) serve as a conspicuous signal to other birds searching for food within visual range.

• Flocks have increased sensitivity (multiple eyes, ears) to potential dangers, such as predators.

• Aggressive flocks discourage predation by mobbing raptors, nest robbers, or other "enemies."

• Close cohesion and rapid "schooling" movements frustrate falcons, accipiters, and other predators which take prey on the wing.

• Migrants which travel in V formation save energy by taking advantage of air currents created by the preceding birds (see FLIGHT).

• Navigational accuracy is improved in flocks where a "consensus" orientation is maintained, and presumably young birds benefit from traveling in flocks of experienced individuals (see NAVIGATION).

FLORIDA KEYS. A string of coral islands stretching southwestward from the southeastern tip of Florida and connected by the remarkable 165-mile Overseas Highway (the tail end of U.S. 1). The keys are noted for a number of essentially Caribbean water-bird and land-bird species, most of which occur regularly in North America only in southern Florida: Magnificent Frigatebird, Great White Heron (now considered a color phase of Great Blue Heron), Reddish Egret, White-crowned Pigeon, Mangrove Cuckoo, Antillean (Common) Nighthawk (now regular Key West), Gray Kingbird, and Black-whiskered Vireo. Many more widespread species (especially water birds) are also present. And West Indian vagrants can be expected at any season (see Appendix II).

FLYCATCHER. See TYRANT FLYCATCHER for New World flycatchers (Tyrannidae); OLD WORLD FLYCATCHER for Muscicapidae.

FLYWAY. A relatively narrow route along a prominent topographical feature, such as a large river valley or seacoast, which migratory birds follow to their destinations. It was once thought that most migration was concentrated in major flyways, e.g., the Mississippi Flyway, the Atlantic Flyway, but recent studies using RADAR and other techniques (see MOON WATCHING) have revealed that, on the whole, migration takes place over much broader areas of airspace. This is not to say that migrating birds do not make use of prominent landmarks for navigation, but rather that the once popular mental picture of masses of birds funneling down from northern breeding grounds into narrow travel corridors separated by vast areas of empty sky is a distorted view of the phenomenon. The concept continues to bear the federal government's stamp of approval due to the convenience it lends to regional waterfowl management programs. See MIGRATION.

FOLKLORE (birds in). See IMAGINATION.

FOLLOWING SHIPS. Many species of seabirds associate with boats of all sizes. Gulls have learned from long association the advantage to be gained by visiting even a small rowboat where fish are being caught and cleaned. And the incredible largesse offered by modern fishing operations has proven so attractive to seabirds that it is given much of the credit/blame for the enormous increase and range expansion of several North Atlantic gull species. The albatrosses, shearwaters, and gulls which follow larger, relatively high-speed vessels, such as large fishing boats or liners, not only profit from the refuse which is disposed of overboard but can also take advantage of the updrafts of air which are pushed up along the sides and stern of a moving ship to get a little "free" lift (see FLIGHT) and save energy. Fulmars seem to ride the side currents for the sheer joy of it (see PLAY) and will race along the rails, sometimes within reach of the passengers, and then cut sharply across the bow as if seeing how close they can come before allowing themselves to be blown astern for another run. Albatrosses, which are particularly adept at exploiting air currents in various ways (see FLIGHT, *Dynamic Soaring*, and Fig. 22), have been known to follow liners for weeks at a time over hundreds of miles of ocean. Gulls, too, are devoted followers, sometimes making transatlantic crossings in the company of ships, which may explain why European Lesser Black-backed Gulls are found with unusual frequency at outlying landfalls such as Bermuda, Nantucket Island (Massachusetts), and centers of shipping activity such as New York Harbor.

It is interesting, though problematical, that the urge to follow ships occurs in varying intensity even among closely related species. Wilson's Storm-Petrels, for example, are inveterate ship followers, while Leach's Storm-Petrels will never fly in the wake for any distance, though it comes readily enough to feed on refuse. Some species, e.g., jaegers, will follow for short distances, but typically seem to lose interest quickly and move off.

A tangential phenomenon is the transportation of small land-bird migrants which frequently wander (or are blown) out of their prescribed migratory routes and take refuge on ships at sea. A majority of these birds perish due to starvation or an excess of salt ingested with food they find on deck, but it has been proven that a few "hitchhike" all the way to the British Isles, explaining in part why so many North American land-bird vagrants occur in the Scilly Isles, the first land encountered on the southwest approach to England.

FOOD (birds, eggs, nests as). See EDIBILITY.

FOOD/FEEDING. Birds, like all other animals, must eat to live, and if we analyze what most birds do during an average day, we would be justified in concluding that they live to eat. Food is the reason that the falcon stoops, the dipper dips, the woodpecker pecks, and the turnstone turns stones. Only the rituals of the breeding cycle even begin to claim a bird's time and attention to the extent that the activities associated with feeding do. Having largely replaced hunting and gathering with fast food, most post-industrial humans forget that such an all-consuming obsession with food is the norm in the animal kingdom—even for the majority of their own species. To most of us, a meal is an event, like writing a letter. To a bird, however, the urge to feed is instinctual and nearly continuous; it is more a function—like breathing or reproduction—than a series of events.

BORN TO EAT. All birds come into the world with certain anatomical "tools" that are characteristic of their species and serve their particular feeding priorities—e.g., specialized bills (see Techniques of Finding and Obtaining Food, below). But they are also born with a knowledge of specific ways of feeding and these are triggered—also innately—by stimuli in their normal surroundings (see INTELLIGENCE; FIXED ACTION PATTERN). For example, when chicks of gallinaceous birds, ducks, or sandpipers hatch, they almost immediately begin pecking or dabbing at small objects. Experiments indicate that at least in some cases this action is "released" merely by the size of the object and its degree of contrast with its background. By trial and error and perhaps some parental example, the instinctive pecking eventually provides a meal, which, of course, reinforces the urge to peck. All of the complex feeding habits exhibited by birds are chiefly governed by similar patterns of stimulus and response, rather than the human eat-if-you-are-hungry mode. This is vividly demonstrated by the phenomenon of raptors catching, killing, and then discarding prey they neither need nor want to eat. The urge to forage simply exceeds appetite. This practice dismays those who like to think that nature does not abide waste or tolerate "wanton" killing, but it is a natural enough "side effect" of the rather mechanical operation of much animal behavior.

Though the greater proportion of hunting and feeding behavior is instinctual, birds which exercise complex skills in getting their food (e.g., predators) must practice their techniques. Teaching by parent birds is apparently limited to "encouragement" in this context (see INTELLIGENCE), but young birds do learn the locations of reliable food sources in their natal area from their parents.

WHAT BIRDS EAT. The record of what birds eat is far from complete—think of the effort involved in identifying the minutest plant and animal forms that birds doubtless ingest. But present evidence points to the conclusion that birds eat *everything*. Since sand, pebbles, shell, salt, and/or water are included in most species' "diets," their menu is not even restricted to organic substances. Only some of man's improbable concoctions such as plastic seem to be totally lacking in appeal.

One way to demonstrate the catholicity of animal tastes in food is to try to think of feeding opportunities they don't exploit. After all, we find birds taking food from deep in mud (godwits); from the upper layers of soil (American Robin); from ground surfaces (raptors, sandpipers, gallinaceous birds, doves, many finches); from rock surfaces (Purple Sandpiper, dippers); from leaf litter (Wood Thrush, towhees); from grasses (many sparrows); from tree trunks (woodpeckers, Brown Creeper, Black-and-White Warbler); from foliage at all levels (wide range of passerines); from lake and ocean bottoms (swans, Brant, some ducks); from stream beds (dippers); from deep waters (loons, auks, some ducks; see SWIMMING/DIVING); from the water's surface (many ducks, tubenoses, phalaropes); from crevices, including those in man-made structures (wrens, tits); and from the air (falcons, swifts, nightjars, swallows, and flycatchers). Of course many species exploit two or more of these major food sources.

A similar comprehensiveness is revealed if we enumerate broad classes of matter which birdlife takes for food: seeds (gallinaceous birds, doves, many finches); leaves of flowering plants (doves, grouse); lichens (ptarmigan); seaweed (sea ducks, Glaucous Gull); moss (Purple Sandpiper); freshwater algae (ducks); flowers (parrots); nectar (hummingbirds, orioles); fruits (grouse, thrushes, waxwings, Phainopepla, tanagers, orioles, many finches); bark (sapsuckers); sap (sapsuckers and a variety of passerines); plankton (storm-petrels and other seabirds); jellyfish (gulls, other seabirds); annelids, e.g., earthworms and sea worms (woodcock, many other long-billed shorebirds, American Robin); an enormous range of crustaceans, e.g., amphipods, barnacles, shrimp, isopods (many water birds) and crabs (gulls); spiders (wrens, many other "insectivores"); ticks (anis); insects (the majority of birds eat some, many feed on them almost exclusively); mollusks (loons, grebes, ducks, geese, gulls, shorebirds); starfish and sea urchins (gulls); fish (most water birds, kingfishers, occasionally flycatchers, grackles, dippers, etc.); amphibians (herons, some hawks, some ducks, kingfishers, crows); reptiles (hawks, some owls, herons, cormorants, ducks, turkeys, cranes, rails, roadrunners, crows, and even small passerines—albatrosses are known to eat an occasional sea snake); birds (hawks, falcons, owls, shrikes, and occasionally herons, gulls, corvids, and other large omnivores); eggs (turnstones, gulls, skuas, corvids, wrens); mammals (hawks, falcons, jaegers, owls, shrikes, occasionally herons, gulls, corvids, and other large omnivores—the largest live prey taken by any North American bird are young deer and antelope, which are occasionally attacked by Golden Eagles); carrion (vultures, some hawks, gulls, corvids); animal blood, fat, and oils (many tubenoses in addition to raptors and carrion eaters); garbage (vultures, some eagles, gulls, and some corvids), and even excrement (vultures, petrels, gulls, and alcids).

This is by no means an exhaustive account of what birds eat, but it hints at the range. Of life forms with which most people are familiar, only the fungi are apparently little eaten by birds. Another generality that emerges from this overview is that, though many species of birds are essentially vegetarians, most are sustained primarily by animal food and virtually all at least occasionally balance their diets with some high-protein invertebrates.

Variation in Diet. Birds eat different things according to the habit of their species, their age, where they live, and the availability of acceptable food.

Some bird species are notably fussy eaters. Limpkins and Everglade Kites, for example, prefer large freshwater snails to other foods and tend to live only where these flourish. Of course, such narrow tastes can be dangerous if the favorite food disappears for some reason. When the eelgrass beds of the east coast suffered a plague in the 1930's, the Brant populations which were sustained almost exclusively by this one plant species also declined drastically. The survival risk implicit in such narrow diets probably explains why most species have evolved more flexible tastes; the Brant did, and just in the nick of time.

At the other extreme, some species and/or families (e.g., gulls, many corvids) are nearly omnivorous and will eat plant material, live vertebrates and invertebrates of all kinds, as well as carrion and waste products. Though it might balk at a dead skunk, the Ruffed Grouse is known to have eaten parts of at least 414 species of plants and 580 species of animals (Van Tyne and Berger, 1976–ORNITHOLOGY).

Most birds have characteristic but not severely restrictive food preferences. Ospreys prefer fish, hummingbirds nectar, and a great many species are partial to insects or seeds. But Ospreys will eat any of a wide variety of fish species, depending on what is available, and faced with a general dearth of fish will readily take small mammals and birds. A Magnolia Warbler would quickly starve if it demanded the same *species* of insects on its Mexican wintering grounds that it habitually consumes in Canada, where it breeds. Therefore, its tastes must encompass hundreds of species of many families of insects, not to mention spiders and other invertebrates and even occasional sips of nectar. On the other hand, Magnolia Warblers are still slaves to their food preferences to a large extent. Since both invertebrates and nectar are in short supply during the Canadian winter, birds which feed on them must move south to warmer climes (see MIGRATION; DISTRIBUTION).

Other birds have solved this problem by staying put and adapting their feeding habits to prevailing conditions. Some woodpeckers, for example, shift from a largely insect to a largely fruit and seed diet as the season changes. Almost universally, nestlings are fed "meat," even in species whose mature tastes run to plant food. Pigeons and doves, which nourish their nestlings on a high-protein crop secretion (see PIGEON'S MILK), and crossbills, which often rear young during the winter months and feed them exclusively conifer seeds, are among the few exceptions. Some authorities believe this supports the theory that the earliest birds fed on animal substances exclusively (as do most modern reptiles) and only gradually evolved vegetarian forms.

Roles of the Senses in Finding Food. Indisputably, the sense most crucial to finding food for the majority of birds is sight, but there are important exceptions. After debates going back 200 years, it has finally been proven that the Turkey Vulture can locate at least some types of carrion by its odor (see SMELL); but this talent is much less developed in its near relative, the Black Vulture. Owls, hunting at night, depend to a large extent on their sense of hearing to zero in on their prey, and Barn Owls are known (Payne, 1962–HEARING) to be able to capture a mouse in total darkness, guided only by the sounds made by the animal, a feat made possible by the owls' acute hearing and remarkable asymmetrical ear apparatus (see HEARING).

The range of certain birds' hearing and certain gestures they make while foraging have led some authorities to infer that woodpeckers, woodcock, and American Robin (for example) locate their quarry underground or in a tree trunk by hearing its movements.

TECHNIQUES OF FINDING AND OBTAINING FOOD. So great is the extent to which birds' lives are occupied in finding food that the evolution of avian anatomy can be read as the development of a variety of food trapping, harvesting, and processing machines. Any mutation which inhibited food getting would obviously reduce its bearer's odds for survival and therefore its own likelihood of being perpetuated. It can also be fairly stated that most well-established avian features can be shown to assist the nearly perpetual search for a meal, however indirectly. It might be argued that birds do not catch food or eat with their feathers, but of course without them, many raptors and insect-eaters could not catch their respective prey.

The feet of a Northern Goshawk (see Fig. 12) are well adapted to grasping branches and are even useful in walking in the few circumstances in which a goshawk needs to do so. But their most important function is to catch and kill food.

Given its proximity to the mouth, it is perhaps not surprising that a bird's bill reflects its owner's specific feeding habits more vividly than any other obvious physical character: an ibis's bill is a probe, a duck's bill a strainer, a phalarope's bill forceps, a hawk's bill shears, an anhinga's bill a lance, a nightjar's gape a funnel, a nutcracker's bill a hammer, and so forth—the specialized tools of master food getters. The uses of many bills are easily guessed at—long, slender bills are clearly designed for probing, whether in mud (snipe) or flowers (hummingbird); while a grosbeak's bill is obviously useless as a probe but it is an ideal crushing mechanism. Some bills have evolved as all-purpose tools. A gull's beak is a kind of avian Swiss Army knife, capable of shearing an eel in two, tearing flesh, hammering into a crab's carapace, grasping a purloined cormorant egg, and picking dainty morsels from a raft of floating garbage. For a more comprehensive discussion of some of these self-evident functions, see BILL.

Some of the methods and "tools" by which birds search out and obtain their food are more complex and/or less obvious to the casual observer and merit a brief description.

Flight Mannerisms. An unusually slow flight has evolved in the harriers and the Turkey Vulture as a means of effectively scanning large areas for their preferred prey. Some seabirds, most buteos and vultures soar on rising air currents for a similar purpose. And the American Kestrel, some hawks and kingfishers hover in midair, keeping their heads stationary to watch for movements of small, quick prey below. See FLIGHT, *Soaring* and *Hovering*, and Fig. 20.

Nightjars have small bills but enormous gapes (2 inches fully opened in Chuck-will's-widow; see Fig. 9) and fly through the air with their mouths open, swallowing numbers of insects (from tiny flies to large beetles) and even an occasional small bird. It has been widely suggested—but not conclusively shown—that the long, stiff, modified feathers (rictal bristles; see FEATHER) that border the upper half of the gape in most nightjar species serve to enlarge their effective "funnel" and also detect the presence of insects flying nearby in the dark. The latter hypothesis gains some support in the fact that the nighthawks (genus *Chordeiles*), which on the average fly during daylight hours more frequently than other nightjars, lack rictal bristles.

Canopy Feeding is practiced by some heron species and consists of raising the wings to create a shadow over shallow water. This may serve the dual purpose of attracting fish and cutting surface glare for the heron. See CANOPY FEEDING and Fig. 4.

Foot Movements are used in several bird families to flush prey within reach. Herons and some shorebirds stir the bottom in shallow pools and pick up any disturbed invertebrates. The characteristic "spinning" of phalaropes is an elaboration of this technique. Some gulls are reputed (Meyerriecks, 1966) to "paddle" the earth with their feet to bring earthworms to the surface. And "foot flushing" is also recorded in some ground-feeding songbirds.

The Long Tongues of most woodpecker and hummingbird species can be extended into a tree cavity or flower calyx as much as several inches with the aid of an extendible bone and muscle structure known as the HYOID APPARATUS. This mechanism is attached at the base of the tongue, coils around the back and top of the skull, and is anchored at the nostrils. The actual tongues of these birds bear a variety of specializations—barbs, brushes, grooves, saliva—that help to capture and/or swallow particular food types (see TONGUE for details).

Wing Flashing, i.e., lifting the wings suddenly, is apparently used by species of herons and mockingbirds to startle aquatic life and insects into motion, so that they can be seen and eaten. Mockingbirds also use this gesture (see Fig. 1) in confrontations with snakes and other threatening situations.

The Bills of Avocets are strongly recurved toward the tip and vertically flattened. When a bird lowers its bill into the water, the upturned third of the bill becomes parallel to the surface and is swept rapidly back and forth amidst the surface algae or in bottom sediment, flushing invertebrates to be caught and eaten. This action is analogous to the foot motions of other shorebirds (see above).

The Bills of Spoonbills are strongly flattened vertically and widened into a spatula shape at the tip. The interior of the "spoon" is lined with sensitized tissue. Spoonbills feed by wading in shallow water and sweeping their partially opened bills from side to side in bottom sediment and vegetation. When live organisms (small fish, mollusks, crustaceans, etc.) are felt by the bill, the mandibles close on the prey.

Skimmers are unique in having a lower mandible which is significantly longer than the upper—an adaptation to an equally unique method of feeding. The birds fly low over calm water (often at dawn and dusk and in flocks) and "shear" the surface with the tip of the lower mandible, which is laterally flattened to nearly razor sharpness. When a fish or other edible object is encountered by this blade, the upper mandible closes down on it instantaneously. (The action is vividly shown in Fig. 2.) Skimmers will often retrace a stretch of water they have just "plowed," apparently to take advantage of fish which rise to investigate the initial disturbance.

See also INTELLIGENCE, *Tool Use.*

Feeding Flocks. Flocks of cormorants, sometimes containing hundreds of birds, will form a line at the edge of a school of fish swimming near the surface and systematically advance on their prey. The flock members do some "leapfrogging" such as that practiced by foraging blackbird flocks (see FLOCK), but they also dive continuously so that a large proportion of the flock is always beneath the surface.

American White Pelicans, which do not dive for fish from the air as do Brown Pelicans, form semicircles of half a dozen birds, surround a school of fish, and by splashing and beating their wings "drive" them into shallow water where they are readily caught. Flocks of American Avocets and Black-necked Stilts also engage in fish drives.

Seabirds of several families (e.g., gulls, terns, jaegers, shearwaters, storm-petrels, gannets) are sensitive to the sight of congregations of birds over the ocean which indicate the presence of food, in the form of either a school of small fish driven to the surface by marine predators or a fishing boat cleaning its catch. It has been theorized that the light color of many seabirds against the dark sea contributes to the success of this form of cooperation. A similar practice is followed by vultures and other scavengers that are alerted to the presence of carrion by a conspicuous column of their kind marking a distant carcass.

Mixed flocks of small forest birds may stir up more live food as they move through vegetation than would a single bird, and thus benefit all participating individuals. This advantage may also explain the flock feeding of American Avocets, which flush food by agitating bottom sediment with their bills (see above).

Secondary Feeding, i.e., taking advantage of a food source generated by another animal.

• Anis, Bronzed Cowbirds, and Fish Crows reportedly pick ticks and other ectoparasites off cows and other ungulates.

• Frigatebirds, jaegers and skuas, and some gulls and eagles habitually steal food caught or found by other birds, though all such "kleptoparasites" can and frequently do obtain food on their own. (For further detail, see PIRACY.)

• Many species of birds, including herons, ducks, phalaropes, and kingfishers, have been observed following other bird species which stir up edible plants and animals while foraging for themselves. Swans, for example, which can reach bottom vegetation in deep water with long necks, are sometimes attended by dabbling ducks which pick up floating plant parts dislodged by the swans.

• Numerous small birds (e.g., hummingbirds, vireos, warblers, kinglets) sip sap from the holes made by sapsuckers.

• Cattle Egrets, anis, and gulls follow feeding livestock to catch the insects flushed by the larger animals. Cattle Egrets have, of course, made a "profession" of this practice. In Europe small songbirds have been observed to use small mammals in a similar way (e.g., Eurasian Robins and moles), and elsewhere various insectivorous birds have been seen to "use" trains and automobile traffic with similar motives.

• Humans have inadvertently created many new food sources for birds, the most copious of which, e.g., open garbage dumps and the refuse of a burgeoning fishing industry, have been credited with or blamed for increasing populations of birds such as fulmars and (especially) gulls. A number of our labor-saving machines dispense bird food as by-products. Gulls, American Robins, and other birds frequently follow plows to pick up grubs and the like from the turned soil. Many seabirds follow ships—even in the absence of fish spoils or garbage—to pick up marine tidbits churned to the surface by the screws. Pelagic birds follow pods of whales and dolphins and schools of tuna and other large fish to take advantage of small prey driven to the surface as well as "leftovers." Some insectivorous birds have learned to wait along busy roadsides and pick up insects disabled by passing cars; this in turn sometimes results in dead birds, which may attract crows, whose corpses invite vultures, and so on.

How Much Birds Eat. The quantity of food ingested by birds is directly related to how much energy they can store and the level of energy required by a species' particular life style. As anyone would guess, large birds eat more in absolute quantity than small birds. However, in general, the smaller the bird, the more it eats *in proportion to its body weight*. This is because small birds tend to have a higher metabolism, i.e., "burn fuel" faster than large birds. Therefore, while an eagle may eat 2 pounds of meat a day and a pelican 4 pounds of fish (Terres, 1980–BIRD), these amounts constitute only about a quarter and a half of body weight, respectively. By contrast, a hummingbird that consumes twice its weight or more per day in nectar and insects may have taken in under a half ounce of food. Within this generality based on size, there are many exceptions because of differing life styles. Small, but comparatively sedentary birds such as doves, for example, may consume less in relation to body weight than eagles do. Another generality about avian food consumption is that birds eat more in cold weather and less in hot. This, too, is related to expenditure of energy, which is greater when low temperatures require more effort to maintain sufficient body heat.

A more vivid way of conveying how much birds eat is to report what is likely to be found in a bird's stomach at any given moment during a normal day. It is not unusual for a dabbling duck's stomach to contain between 50,000 and 100,000 seeds or plant parts, and 185 blue mussels have been taken from the digestive tract of a single Common Eider.

The stomachs of insectivorous birds may contain hundreds of caterpillars or 5,000 or more small insects such as ants or mosquitoes. These totals are all the more impressive when we consider that birds can pass food through their digestive tracts in 30 to 90 minutes, so that the above totals represent only a fraction of a day's consumption.

WHEN AND HOW OFTEN BIRDS FEED. The feeding schedules of species and individual birds differ markedly according to a number of variables. Obviously, hummingbirds and small songbirds, which must consume a large proportion of (or more than) their body weight per day, must feed almost constantly during daylight hours. Observers of such species maintain that this is indeed the case, and it has been proven that at least some hummingbirds go into a kind of coma after dark to lower their metabolism during the nightly fast (see TORPIDITY). As with the amount of food needed, there is a general reverse correlation between the size of a bird and the number of meals. It should be remembered, however, that birds such as eagles or vultures must spend much more time hunting and/or killing their food than, for example, insect- or seed-eaters, and therefore food-associated activities may take up a large proportion of their day despite the fact that relatively little time is spent actually eating.

Obviously, food availability affects how often birds eat (though it does not usually reduce time spent searching for food). Many birds can gorge themselves when food is available and hold it for a short period undigested in their crops (see DIGESTIVE SYSTEM) for use when snow covers food supplies or in the case of vultures when no carrion can be located. A few birds (penguins, chicks of many tubenoses) can accumulate vast fat stores and live for weeks or even months without a meal.

Under normal circumstances, the majority of bird species have some kind of regular feeding routine. Most feed only during daylight, but of course owls and nightjars have evolved nocturnal feeding schedules, and a few species prefer the twilight periods near sunrise and sunset (see CREPUSCULAR). Some routines are based on environmental factors: shorebirds tend to feed on exposed flats at low tide and roost in marshes or fields at high water; vultures must wait for thermals to be generated to begin their hunting day (see FLIGHT); plankton tends to rise toward the surface of the sea during the night and is followed by the many larger marine organisms that feed on it, so that many pelagic birds feed most actively in the dark or in the early morning hours; earthworms also rise to the surface at night, encouraging American Robins and woodcock to seek them mainly near dawn and dusk; at midday, robins usually seek other fare.

Every birdwatcher and feeder owner is aware that early morning and late afternoon are periods of increased feeding activity for most diurnal birds and has probably also noticed other apparent peaks of activity during the middle of the day. Small birds which must forage constantly nonetheless tend to adhere to a fairly fixed routine, especially when the food source is dependable—feeder birds show great regularity in their visits even though they may hunt food elsewhere throughout the day. Another phenomenon noticed by feeder owners is the apparent sensitivity of birds to approaching bad weather, which results in unscheduled—often frenzied—visits to the seed and suet bins.

PREPARATION OF FOOD. With no teeth and little sense of smell or taste, most birds swallow their food whole, leaving hard substances to be pulverized by the powerful muscles and grit reserves in the gizzard (see DIGESTIVE SYSTEM). Indigestible substances such as shell, bone, feathers, and hair are then regurgitated in a consolidated mass (see PELLET).

There are, however, some conspicuous exceptions to this general rule. Hawks, eagles, and falcons usually pluck feathers or areas of fur and pull small pieces of meat from their prey. They also tend to eat somewhat selectively—often discarding or ignoring the entrails, for example. Owls by contrast tend to bolt prey whole or in the case of large animals tear off and swallow large pieces.

The versatile gulls will gulp their food when possible and in many cases manage to swallow fish which clearly stretch their flexible esophagi to the limit. But they will also hack and tear pieces out of very large items, e.g., a seal carcass, as will skuas and some of the larger tubenoses.

Some gulls learn the effectiveness of dropping hard-shelled items (mollusks, crabs, sea urchins) from the air in order to crack their shells, but competence in the technique varies: certain individuals show poor judgment as to the surface on which they drop their prey, while others habitually fly to suitably hard "cracking grounds." Crows are also known to use this system.

Birds which take large insects (including caterpillars) sometimes remove struggling legs which would impede consumption and are frequently seen to whack their prey against a branch or rock to kill it, remove hairs, or otherwise improve its consistency.

Some seed-eating birds habitually crack the hard outer husks of seeds by either hacking them on a branch or stone (tits, "nuthacks," jays) or crushing them under the pressure of their heavy, specially modified bills (e.g., grosbeaks; see BILL for a description of the process).

A few unusually sophisticated preparation methods deserve emphasis:

The ability of some birds to avoid toxic chemicals deposited in the exoskeletons of certain insects from their food plants has been proven in at least one instance. "Bullock's" Orioles have been recorded as squeezing out the "uncontaminated" insides of monarch butterflies, thus avoiding the cardiac glycocides concentrated in their wings and "skin." The origin of the poison is the milkweed plants (*Asclepius* spp.) on which the butterflies' larval stage feeds. In many if not most cases the effect of the toxin is to discourage birds from eating monarchs after an encounter or two with the bad-tasting cathartic. A similar fastidiousness is demonstrated by birds which wipe irritating spines off caterpillars and the toxic slime from slugs (Hartley, in Thomson, 1964–ORNITHOLOGY).

The bills of oystercatchers are laterally flattened toward the tip. This thin, sharp tool is inserted chisel-like between the shells of live bivalves and then shears the powerful adductor muscle(s), which otherwise would hold the shells closed "as tight as a clam" (see Fig. 2). Anyone who has tried to open an oyster or hard-shelled clam without proper tools will appreciate the finesse in this evolutionary achievement. Occasionally a bivalve gets the better of the bird by closing tightly on its bill before the muscle is severed and while the mollusk is still anchored in the sand; when the tide comes in, the oystercatcher drowns.

The bills and feet of Everglade (Snail) Kites are specially adapted for extracting from their shells the large snails on which they feed exclusively. Their long toes and claws are ideal for holding the round, slippery shells and the long, slender, strongly decurved upper mandible serves to penetrate the columellar muscle by which gastropods hold on to their shells. Lang (1924) reports that Snail Kites in Guyana wait until a captured snail raises its hard operculum of its own accord before stabbing their bills into the soft muscle and then wait again for the pierced muscle to relax so that the shell can be shaken free. But Snyder and Snyder (1969) observed a more active procedure in Florida whereby the bill is inserted under the closed operculum and severs the columellar muscle.

Crossbills have evolved the most interesting bill modification of any North American bird species; its precise workings have been debated in print at least since the eighteenth century. A description of the crossbills' unique means of extracting cone seeds should perhaps begin by noting that they do not always need to employ all of the several aspects of their technique. They are, for example, perfectly willing simply to pick seeds out of a fully opened pine cone, munch spruce buds, or even gobble suet from a feeder, as do seed-eaters with less elaborate equipment. The full play of a crossbill's talents is exercised only in extracting seeds from *green, tightly closed, unripe cones*. In attacking such a cone, the crossbill plucks it and takes it to a horizontal perch, where it holds it down firmly with one of its unusually large, powerful feet so that the long axis of the cone lies slightly at an angle to the long axis of the bird. The tip of the longer upper mandible (which curves downward) is then wedged between two of the cone scales so that the curve of the lower mandible rests on the surface of the cone and the tip of the upper mandible is fixed on the *inside* surface of a scale. The bird then twists its head in such a way that the force exerted against the stable lower mandible forces the scale apart on the tip of the upper mandible. Simultaneously, the two mandibles are forced apart by special jaw muscles—not in the usual vertical plane of birds opening their bills, but in a horizontal (lateral) motion that contributes essential force to the separating process. Once the scales have been forced apart, the unusually large, protrusible tongue reaches into the cavity and detaches the firmly anchored, unripe seed with the aid of a special cartilaginous cutting tool which forms the tongue tip. Needless to say, this procedure is very difficult to observe in wild (or even captive) crossbills, nor is it easily illustrated. Fig. 2 shows the dynamics of the head/bill maneuver in relation to the already opened pine scales. Watching crossbills feed at close range, one is most aware of the head-twisting motion, which is very vigorous and rapid and accompanied by loud cracking noises as the pine scales give. It is also possible to see the fat, parrot-type tongue come into play, but the lateral motion of the mandibles and the cutting action of the tongue tip are normally invisible. The crossbill's unique mandibles are also used as shears to slice through soft fruits such as apples to get at the pips.

STORING FOOD. Woodpeckers, tits, nuthatches, and members of the crow family habitually store food. The degree to which it is retrieved by the storers for later use apparently varies and has only been thoroughly studied in a few species. Eurasian Nutcrackers are known to recover a majority of the nuts they bury in caches in the ground both for sustenance during the winter and to feed young in the spring. There is evidence that this is also true of the North American Clark's Nutcracker, which is known to store food in communal caches and displays an excellent memory in returning to these sites even when they become obscured by heavy snow cover. Acorn and Lewis' Woodpeckers store huge quantities of acorns and other nuts in the trunks of trees, telephone poles, and the like—the former drilling shallow holes into which the acorns are riveted. These species are known to retrieve stored items and to defend their caches against theft by other birds, indicating that such reserves are at least a hedge against starvation.

Several species of carnivorous birds occasionally store carcasses to which they return. The shrikes do this most conspicuously, hanging small mammals and birds on thorns or in crotches and feeding on them over a period of days. There are instances of them revisiting these "larders" after a period of months, but whether this qualifies as true storage in the sense of laying by crucial food reserves is doubtful.

That many stored materials go unrecovered is demonstrated, for example, by the sprouting of oak trees where jays were known to have buried acorns (see SEED DISPERSAL). Tits, nuthatches, and treecreepers have also been seen eating the stores secreted in bark crevices by other tits and nuthatches. To explain why birds would store food to which they did not "intend" to return, some authorities hold that it satisfies the urge to forage and feed after a bird's appetite has been sated.

See also DRINKING; GRIT.

FOOD CHAIN/FOOD WEB. A way of describing interrelationships among life forms and, especially, the transfer of energy from one organism to another. The "classic" food chain begins with green plants, which manufacture energy from sunlight by means of photosynthesis. The next link in the chain is a leaf beetle (for example), which eats and derives energy from the plant; a Sulphur-bellied Flycatcher eats the beetle; a Cooper's Hawk catches and devours the flycatcher. The hawk, which concentrates the combined energy of the organisms below it on the chain and is not likely to be consumed by a larger organism, is said to be "at the top of the food chain." The cumulative effect of a food chain can be harmful as well as beneficial if there is something amiss in the lower links. Pesticides entering aquatic food chains after being washed out of croplands reach ever higher levels as increasing amounts pass from microorganisms to aquatic invertebrate larvae to small fish to big fish and finally to Ospreys or Bald Eagles or Brown Pelicans, which may be poisoned outright or rendered incapable of reproduction (see MAN-MADE THREATS TO BIRDLIFE).

"Food web" is a metaphor for the "interconnectedness" of the innumerable food chains which make up a particular system, whether a microhabitat or the world ecosystem. If we return to our original example, it is obvious that there are hundreds of thousands of plant species and even more plant-eating insects, that both plants and insects are eaten not only by many species of birds but by an awesome variety of other organisms as well, and that even the corpse of the hawk at the top of many food chains is a juncture in the web, providing sustenance for blowfly maggots, carrion beetles, and perhaps vultures as well as returning nutriment to the soil which will eventually be absorbed by green plants, and so ad infinitum.

FOOD PASS. A habit of some species of raptors, especially the harriers, in which an item of food is transferred from the talons of one bird to those of another. The receiving bird sometimes turns upside down in the air, as in the tumbling nuptial display of some eagles (see DISPLAY), and indeed food passing is part of the courtship ritual of the harriers; however, it has also been observed between adult and young birds.

FOOT. See LEG/FOOT.

FOREST. A plant formation which consists of an extended area of tall, relatively closely spaced trees. A fully mature (climax) forest, including all of the shrubby and herbaceous plants typically associated with it, may constitute a BIOME, e.g., the coniferous forest biome (see DISTRIBUTION and Fig. 5). The presence of forest implies a certain degree of warmth, humidity, and soil fertility, as demonstrated by the absence of large or dense trees in tundra, desert, and savanna. In some contexts, "forest" is used to mean *only* climax tree formations and subclimax tree formations are contrasted as "woodland," but this distinction is not made consistently.

Forest birds are, of course, those which inhabit (especially breed in) forest. Thus it is possible to speak of both Pine and Kentucky Warblers as "forest species," though the former typically occupies the upper stories of coniferous forest and the latter prefers the deciduous forest floor.

FORM. In a strict nomenclatural sense, a variation below subspecific rank, a "variety," e.g., the "blue form" of the Lesser Snow Goose. But also widely used to refer to species/subspecies/varieties of uncertain nature: "Authorities disagree on the taxonomic status of these forms." Also a collective for all entities below genus rank, e.g.: "That genus contains a great diversity of forms."

FORMULA MUSCLES. Muscles of the pelvis and legs used in classification. See MUSCLES.

FORSTER, Johann Reinhold, 1729–98 (Forster's Tern: *Sterna forsteri*). A talented German who gave up the church for natural history (see also BENDIRE). He worked as a teacher, natural historian, and translator in England and ended as a professor of mineralogy at the University of Halle in Germany. The central event in his life was a disastrous sailing as a naturalist on Cook's second voyage around the world (for details, see Gruson, 1972–BIOGRAPHY). Forster was the first to attempt to catalogue the American avifauna (as well as the rest of its animal life) in *A Catalogue of the Animals of North America* (1771); he listed 302 species of birds. The tern was named for him by Thomas NUTTALL.

FOSSORIAL (fah-SORE-ee-ul). Adapted for digging or burrowing in the earth. The Burrowing Owl, which digs its own nest chambers as well as taking over those made by prairie dogs and other mammals, and the Belted Kingfisher and Bank Swallow, which excavate cavities in the sides of earth banks, are all birds of fossorial habits.

FOWL. Once a general term for any kind of bird (e.g., Chaucer's "Parlement of Foules"). Now usually refers to birds which are used for food (e.g., wildfowl or waterfowl) and especially domesticated species, i.e., barnyard fowl (chickens), guinea fowl.
   "Fowl" is cognate with the Latin *volucris*, "one capable of flight."

FOWL DISEASES. See DISEASE.

FRANCOLIN (FRANK-uh-lin). Standard English name for most of the approximately 38 species of partridges in the genus *Francolinus* (family Phasianidae; order Galliformes). The Black Francolin (*F. francolinus*), resident from Turkey to Bangladesh, has been introduced as a game bird, with established local populations in Louisiana and Florida. For family characteristics, see PHEASANT.

FRANKLIN, Sir John, 1786–1847 (Franklin's Gull: *Larus pipixcan*). British naval commander best known for his terribly arduous and vain attempts to reach the North Pole and navigate a Northwest Passage. He came within a few miles of achieving the latter with the *Erebus* and *Terror* before becoming hopelessly trapped in the ice and perishing along with the entire expedition. Franklin's travels resulted in a vastly improved knowledge of the geography of the American Arctic. He and his companion Sir John Richardson traced the coast of the Arctic Ocean from Coppermine to 149° 37′ W. on the Alaskan coast in 1829, and the more than forty expeditions sent to search for his ill-fated final expedition accumulated much new data over the ten years before the mystery was solved. It is one of the ironies of commemorative zoological nomenclature that the great arctic explorer's name should be given to a gull which breeds in the American prairies and winters largely in tropical seas.

FRIGATEBIRD. Standard English name for all members of the family Fregatidae (order Pelecaniformes). There are 5 species of frigatebirds worldwide, one of which, the Magnificent Frigatebird, visits southernmost coasts of Atlantic and Pacific North America and breeds at one locality between Key West, Florida, and the Dry Tortugas. The Lesser Frigatebird of the tropical Pacific has been recorded here once—from Maine!

In appearance, frigatebirds are unique. They are among the largest seabirds (length about 3 feet), with long, pointed wings (wingspan 7½ feet), long, forked tail, and a long, prominently hooked bill. They carry the lightest wing loads (weight in proportion to wing area) of all birds, allowing them to soar slowly over vast areas of ocean and expend minimal energy in search of food. Their feet are small, weak, and (as in the other Pelecaniformes) webbed between all four toes—but only at the base. Frigatebirds never alight at sea, and their feet are used only to grasp perches on roosts or breeding grounds. There are no external nostril openings in the bill. Male frigatebirds have an extendible red throat pouch which they inflate in courtship like a great balloon.

Frigatebirds breed in colonies, placing stick platforms in trees and shrubs (when available), on the ground, and in rocky niches on barren islands. The single egg (rarely 2) is white and unmarked.

They are usually silent at sea, but the adults utter a strange, far-carrying guttural/whistling sound on the breeding grounds, and the cackling and whining of nestling birds can create a respectable din. Males also make a drumming sound that may be a product of their inflated throat sacs.

Frigatebirds range over tropical seas worldwide. They are essentially non-migratory, but undertake lengthy peregrinations especially when immature. The name is, of course, a metaphorical evocation of their graceful sailing before the wind.

FRIGHT MOLT. The shedding of feathers as a result of extreme stress—usually fright but perhaps also occasionally out of frustration. Apparently the muscles which control the feathers are relaxed and the feather

tip itself may be forcibly released from its follicle. The tail feathers (rectrices) are those most regularly lost in this manner, but breast and back
feathers may also be shed. In the case of a predator grasping a bird by its
tail, there would of course be survival value in being able to leave the tail
behind as efficiently as possible. But birds are also known to undergo a
fright molt from non-extremities while being gently handled. Some types
of birds, e.g., some pigeons and gallinaceous species, seem to "jump out of
their feathers" more routinely than others.

For a detailed review and discussion of this phenomenon, see Juhn,
Wilson Bull. (1957), 69:108.

FRINGILLID (frin-JILL-id). Any member of the finch family, Fringillidae
(order Passeriformes), and in the plural the family as a whole. Some taxonomists regard the longspurs, New World sparrows, juncos, towhees,
buntings, and some grosbeaks as a separate family, the Emberizidae, which
leaves only the cardueline finches—goldfinches, siskins, redpolls, rosy
finches, rosefinches (*Carpodacus*), crossbills, and two grosbeaks—plus one
member of the subfamily Fringillinae, the Brambling, as North American
fringillid finches.

For a systematic breakdown of finch taxonomy, see FINCH and Appendix I.

FRONT. The forehead; the area on a bird's head between the base of the
upper mandible and the crown. Beginning birdwatchers often assume the
term refers to the breast and are therefore puzzled by names such as
White-fronted Goose. See Fig. 25.

FRONTAL SHIELD. A relatively hard (horny or leathery), often brightly
colored extension of the bill onto the forehead (front) present in a few
species of birds, e.g., King Eider drakes, Common Gallinule, and American Coot. See BILL.

FRUGIVOROUS (froo-JIH-vor-us). Fruit-eating. Tanagers, for example,
are largely frugivorous.

FUERTES (FWAIR-teez), Louis Agassiz, 1874–1927. The greatest American bird portraitist with the *possible* exception of Audubon. A native of
New York State, Fuertes was instinctively drawn to both birds and art as a
child. His talent was skillfully nurtured by Elliott COUES, the artist Abbott
Thayer, and Frank CHAPMAN. He had a long association with Cornell
University, as had his father, and eventually became a lecturer there on
birds. Fuertes was a highly skilled technician, but his greatest gift was generally acknowledged to be his ability to capture a bird's "jizz," i.e., to paint

the living essence of a given species, rather than simply its color, pattern, and general shape. He was also admired by all who knew him for his personal warmth, his intelligence, his enthusiasm for nature and his work, and his generosity with his talents. Fuertes was killed in an automobile collision at a railroad crossing when only fifty-three, thus depriving the world of untold works by a great artist in his prime. For some of the many works illustrated by Fuertes, see the Bibliography under ILLUSTRATION and STATE/PROVINCIAL BOOKS.

FULMAR. Standard English name for 2 species of petrels in the genus *Fulmarus,* one of which, the Northern Fulmar (*F. glacialis*), occurs throughout the coldest waters of the Holarctic region. The two Giant Petrels in the genus *Macronectes* are sometimes called Giant Fulmars. Darwin once opined that the Northern Fulmar was the most abundant bird in the world. Anyone who has been at sea in the midst of a fulmar migration or on a fishing boat in the heart of its pelagic range can understand how he might have formed that opinion—though, almost certainly, it was never the case.

The Atlantic population of the species has undergone a dramatic increase within the present century, particularly on the eastern side, where it has markedly extended its range southward. Some authorities have speculated that this phenomenon is related to increases in fishing activity, but if so it is hard to explain the relatively slight increase and range extension in the western Atlantic.

The purveyors of ornithological etymology agree that "foul" is involved in the significance of the name, referring to the obnoxious (but effective) procellariiform practice of vomiting foul-smelling STOMACH OIL onto molesters.

For family characteristics, see SHEARWATER; see also Fisher (1952–SHEARWATER).

FULVOUS (FULL-vuss) (Tree Duck). Yellowish brown; tawny.

FURCULA (FER-kew-luh) (pl.: furculae). The fused clavicles (collarbones) typical of birds; also known as the wishbone or merrythought. See SKELETON, *Pectoral Girdle,* and Fig. 19.

G

GADFLY PETREL. Collective name for 26 species of petrels which make up the genus *Pterodroma* (family Procellariidae), most of which breed on islands in south temperate seas and range within the Southern

Hemisphere. No gadfly petrel breeds in North America; the endangered Bermuda Petrel or Cahow (*P. cahow*) nests exclusively in Bermuda, and 6 other species in the genus have been recorded as visitors or vagrants.

A gadfly is, first: a fly (family Tabanidae, Oestridae, or Muscidae) which bites or buzzes in the ears of cattle, making them "gad," i.e., dash about wildly; second: a person who annoys other people (as a gadfly annoys cattle). The petrel doubtless takes its name from the notion of rushing about aimlessly (gadabout petrel might be better), from either its far-flung oceanic wanderings or the fast, erratic, swooping, careening flight characteristic of *Pterodroma*.

For family characteristics, see PETREL.

GADWALL. Standard English name for a single widespread species of dabbling duck, *Anas strepera*. No one has yet been able to suggest a credible origin for this name. See DUCK.

GALLINACEOUS. Chicken-like. The members of the order Galliformes—which includes the chachalacas, grouse, quail, pheasants, and turkeys—are commonly referred to collectively as gallinaceous birds.

GALLINULE (GAL-uh-nool or GAL-uh-nyool). Standard English name in North America for 2 members of the rail family (Rallidae; order Gruiformes), both of them in the genus *Gallinula*. In the Old World the name is reserved for certain of the large, heavy-billed rails in the genus *Porphyrio*.

To North Americans, the gallinules (and coots) seem rather distinct from our species of rails, with a different type of coloration in adult birds and a more duck-like "jizz," due in large measure to the fact that they are more often seen swimming in the open than are the rails. Placed in context with the rails of the world, however, they do not represent an extreme variation. Like the other rails, gallinules eat a combination of plant and small invertebrate animal foods. The Common Gallinule is distributed through much of the Old World as well as the New, though its North American distribution is peculiar: widespread east of the Mississippi; much more restricted and local in the West. The Purple Gallinule is essentially a bird of the New World tropics and is restricted in North America to the southeastern region.

"Gallinule" is an anglicization of a Latin word meaning "little hen," referring to the gallinules' walk-and-peck method of feeding when on land. The Common Gallinule is officially known as the Moorhen in the Old World.

For family characteristics, see RAIL.

GALVESTON ISLAND (Texas). The northernmost of a string of barren islands which line the southern coast of Texas (southeast of Houston).

Most of the east end of the island is occupied by the city of Galveston (Kempner Park in the center is a notable haven for land-bird migrants during the storied spring migrations of the Texas coast; see HIGH ISLAND and ROCKPORT), but the west end is largely composed of beach, pastures, sloughs, marshes, and flats which abound in all kinds of water birds. In addition to the impressive fact that more than 300 bird species have been observed on the island over the years, Galveston's greatest claim to ornithological fame is that it hosted some of the latest reliable occurrences of the Eskimo Curlew (1959–63); see, however, ENDANGERED BIRDS.

GAMBEL, William, 1819–49 (Gambel's Quail: *Lophortyx gambelii; Parus gambeli:* Mountain Chickadee). A doctor–bird collector of the mid-nineteenth century and sometime colleague of BAIRD, CASSIN, and NUT-TALL. Remembered particularly for his collections in California and northern Mexico. For a summary of some of Gambel's frontier adventures, including Indian raids and a sojourn as surgeon on an ox train led by Daniel Boone, see Gruson (1972–BIOGRAPHY). Gambel described his own quail, but it was his mentor Nuttall who named it for him. RIDGWAY added the chickadee.

GAMBELL. A settlement on the northwestern extremity of 90-mile-long St. Lawrence Island in the Bering Sea. The island is characterized by its barrenness, bad weather, inhospitable natives, lack of decent accommodations, and annual (spring; see Appendix III) visits by a large number of North American bird listers. The explanation for the last, apparently anomalous, characteristic is that, while St. Lawrence is a U.S. possession and thus officially part of North America, it lies closer to the Siberian Chukotski Peninsula than to the Alaskan mainland and is a frequent host to Palearctic bird species that rarely or never occur farther east. If your yen for a "good tick" is matched by your tolerance for physical discomfort, you can visit Gambell in the company of experts on Palearctic and Asian avifaunas under the auspices of several bird-tour agencies. See Appendix II for Alaskan-Palearctic vagrants. See also ALEUTIAN ISLANDS; PRIBILOF ISLANDS.

GAME BIRD. In the broadest sense, any bird which is hunted for sport or food. There are a number of more specific definitions:
   Ornithological. An English name for the Galliformes, i.e., a synonym for "gallinaceous bird."
   Sporting. There is a hunter's tradition which excludes ducks and geese from the strictest usage of "game bird"; they are instead "waterfowl." This leaves the gallinaceous birds, the shorebirds (now protected), woodcock and snipe, the rails, and the pigeons and doves as "true" game birds.

Legal. Those species of birds for which there is a hunting season or which are not protected: ducks and geese, gallinaceous birds (many of them introduced for this purpose), woodcock and snipe, rails, pigeons and doves, and crows. Many other birds, including small land birds, were of course hunted for food and sport before protection, and this tradition doubtless continues in remoter parts of North America where the "pioneer spirit" still prevails. See LAWS.

GANDER. A male goose of any species.

GANNET. Standard English name for 3 species of seabirds in the family Sulidae (boobies), one of which, the Northern Gannet, breeds and winters in coastal and offshore waters in eastern North America. The three gannets are very similar in appearance (they constitute a superspecies) and occupy separate ranges, one in the North Atlantic and two in south temperate seas (South African region and Tasmania/New Zealand). Their preference for cold waters sets them apart from the other boobies, all of which normally occur only in tropical seas.

Their large size and striking plumage, together with their habit of nesting colonially on picturesque wilderness isles and of plunging into the sea for fish from heights of up to 100 feet, make the Northern Gannet one of our most popular seabirds.

Gannets were once thought to be related to geese, whence the present name, which arises from the same root as "gander."

For family characteristics, see BOOBY.

GAPE (gaping, gaper). Sometimes used synonymously with COMMISSURE or to refer to the softer rictal region at the corners of the mouth. Usually the gape is associated with the *open* mouth, especially of nestling birds begging for food. This gaping gesture, together with the calls of the young birds, stimulates a feeding response in the parent birds. Juvenile birds, even when fully fledged and out of the nest, can often be recognized by the enlarged, fleshy, often brightly colored corners of the mouth; such birds are sometimes called "gapers."

GASTRULATION. A complex process which occurs early in embryonic development (following the blastula) and consists of movement of cells to their appropriate positions in the embryo.

GAUSE'S RULE. The principle that no two (or more) organisms with exactly the same ecological requirements can coexist in the same environment permanently, since the inevitable competition will always favor one species over the other. Therefore one normally finds birds and other ani-

mals occupying different ecological "niches" in any given habitat. See DIS-
TRIBUTION and G. F. Gause, *The Struggle for Existence* (Baltimore,
1934).

GENERA (JEN-er-uh). Plural of GENUS.

GENETICS (jeh-NET-iks). A major facet of biology, dealing with the nature of heredity; the means by which the traits of any organism persevere
or vary through succeeding generations. This is not the place to attempt a
summary of such a vast subject matter, single facets of which have generated many books fatter than this one. However, for aspects of bird study
to which genetics is relevant, see HYBRIDIZATION; INTELLIGENCE; AVICUL-
TURE; PARENTAL CARE; SONG; SPECIATION; DISTRIBUTION; TAXONOMY.

The distinction between "genetic" traits or characters (e.g., the ability to find a remote wintering area without previous experience) and those
acquired during an individual's life span by observation and practice (e.g.,
the ability of some gulls to break shellfish by dropping them on pavement)
is a frequent topic in ornithological as in other biological literature.

GENITALIA. Birds lack external sexual organs, though in a few cases, notably ducks, geese, and swans, males have a penis-like organ which is ex-
truded during copulation; females of these species have a rudimentary clitoris. All sexual as well as excretory functions take place through a single
anal opening, the vent or cloacal aperture. See REPRODUCTIVE SYSTEM.

GENOTYPE (JEE-no-type). The sum of an organism's genetic characteristics as opposed to its external appearance (phenotype). For further discussion, see PHENOTYPE.

GENUS (JEE-nuss) (pl.: genera [JEN-er-uh]). The major taxonomic category
between the FAMILY and the SPECIES. Families may be divided into subfamilies and genera; genera into subgenera and species. A genus can also
be defined as a grouping of phylogenetically related species. The 300+
genera of birds that occur regularly in North America appear in phylogenetic order in Appendix I. See TAXONOMY.

GEOGRAPHICAL VARIATION. Differences which have evolved in
animal forms living in different places. The Savannah Sparrow exhibits
marked geographical variation over its broad North American range in
color, size, and other characters. See SPECIATION; DISTRIBUTION; and
Plate 4.

GILA (HEE-luh) (Woodpecker). Of desert regions, such as that of the
Gila River of Arizona, near where the type specimen of this species of

woodpecker was collected; the word has no other meaning in Spanish and is perhaps derived from a native American word.

GIZZARD. The second of two enlargements in a bird's digestive tract which together function like the human stomach; it could also be described as the lower of a bird's two stomachs. Also called the ventriculus. See DIGESTIVE SYSTEM and Fig. 19.

GLAUCOUS (GLAW-kuss) (Gull, -winged Gull). Bluish, referring to the pale blue-gray mantle color of adult Glaucous, Glaucous-winged, and other "white-winged" gulls.

GLOGER'S RULE. The generalization that representatives of bird or mammal species that breed in warmer, more humid climates tend to be darker in color than those breeding in cooler, drier climates. For example, the pale plumage of the desert-dwelling races of the Horned Lark (e.g., *Eremophila alpestris leucansiptila*) contrasts strikingly with that of races such as *E. a. merrilli* and *E. a. strigata* from the humid Northwest. The implications of Gloger's rule are not well understood and a glaring anomaly to its premise exists in the form of the many desert-inhabiting species that are partially or totally black (see DESERT). Mayr (1963–SPECIATION) says that the "physiological basis [of Gloger's Rule] is not clear."

The rule was first articulated by C. W. L. Gloger in *The Variation of Birds under the Influence of Climate* (1833). Compare ALLEN'S, BERGMANN'S, and KELSO'S RULES; see also Plate 4.

GNATCATCHER. Standard English name for the 11–12 members (depending on taxonomy) of the family Polioptilidae (order Passeriformes). Some taxonomies include this group among the Old World warblers (family Sylviidae); others as part of the broadest definition of the family Muscicapidae. Two species of gnatcatchers breed regularly in North America and a third, Black-capped Gnatcatcher, has bred in southeastern Arizona and was collected with young by a graduate student at the University of Arizona.

The gnatcatchers are all small (average 4 inches), with a comparatively long, slender bill and a long, mobile tail, frequently held in a "cocked-up" position. All are colored in combinations of black, slate, and/or blue-gray and white.

They feed in the hyperactive manner common to tits and warblers, gleaning the interstices of tree trunks and the undersides of leaves as well as catching flies on the wing. Their diet consists almost entirely of insects, but like most insectivores, they occasionally partake of a berry or seed.

Several gnatcatcher species have soft warbling songs, but in general they are not very songful, and their nasal buzzy calls are heard far more frequently.

The tiny (2 to 2½ inches) gnatcatcher nest is sited on a limb or in the fork of a tree or shrub 2 to 80 feet from the ground. It is a neat, rather deep cup made of plant fibers, bark strips, grasses, etc., bound with spider silk and "shingled" on the outside with lichen flakes (Blue-gray Gnatcatcher); it is lined with plant down, fur, and/or feathers. The 3–5 (usually 4) eggs are pale blue and variably marked (lightly/heavily; densely/sparsely) with reddish or purplish.

The gnatcatchers are restricted to the New World, most species occurring in the tropics. Of the North American species, the Blue-gray Gnatcatcher breeds across the southern third of the continent (farther north in the East) and winters southward as far as Central America; the Black-tailed is resident in the arid lowlands of the Southwest. While gnatcatchers doubtless catch their share of gnats, the name is no more definitive than warbler or sandpiper.

GOATSUCKER. Widely used English name, especially in North America, for the nightjar family, Caprimulgidae (literally "goat milkers"); perhaps excluding the nighthawks. The superstition that members of this family (e.g., Whip-poor-wills) suck at the teats of goats during the night goes back at least to Aristotle. See NIGHTJAR.

GOBBLING GROUND. Dry, grassy fields where males of the Lesser Prairie Chicken come early on spring mornings to perform their distinctive courtship displays; the "dances" involve a characteristic cackle or "gobbling" sound, which, according to Pough (1957–FIELD GUIDE), lacks the "resonance and volume" of the Greater Prairie Chicken's "booming."

GODWIT. Standard English name for all 4 species of large, long-billed sandpipers in the genus *Limosa* (family Scolopacidae; order Charadriiformes). Three of these breed in North America and the remaining species has occurred with relative frequency as an accidental straggler (see Appendix II).

Godwits are statuesque shorebirds cryptically patterned with splotches and streaks and colored in rich earth tones. The godwits tend to probe much more deeply with their long bills than do the curlews, frequently working them down to the base into mud or soil in search of worms, shellfish, crustaceans, and the like.

Hudsonian and Bar-tailed Godwits breed in arctic tundra and their migrations are among the longest of any birds (see Fig. 13). The Marbled Godwit nests wholly on the central prairies of southern Canada and the northern U.S. and migrates to the coasts for the winter, even reaching New

England in small numbers and occurring as far south as northern South America.

The call of both Hudsonian and Marbled Godwits can be "translated" as *god-WIT*.

For family characteristics, see SANDPIPER.

GOLDENEYE. Standard English name for 2 of the 3 members of the sea duck genus *Bucephala* (family Anatidae; order Anseriformes). Both of these—the Common Goldeneye (*B. clangula*) and Barrow's Goldeneye (*B. islandica*)—nest in tree cavities in coniferous zone forest, the Common preferring boreal lowlands and Barrow's adapted to western alpine forests (also rocky barrens of Greenland and Iceland). The distribution of the Common Goldeneye is Holarctic, that of Barrow's essentially Nearctic, though it is a permanent resident in Iceland. North American populations of both winter along Atlantic and Pacific coasts.

Barrow's Goldeneye favors streams on its breeding grounds, where it dives for the larvae of aquatic insects. The Common Goldeneye prefers crustaceans, insects, and other invertebrate life of still northern waters. Both species feed heavily on mollusks on their marine wintering grounds.

The eyes of all adult goldeneyes are bright yellow and are discernible from a surprising distance.

GOLDFINCH. Standard English name for 5 species of cardueline finches (family Fringillidae; order Passeriformes), 2 in the Old World genus *Carduelis*, 3 in the New World genus *Spinus*. (Some taxonomies include all in *Carduelis*.) Three species of *Spinus* goldfinches breed in North America and the Eurasian (*Carduelis*) Goldfinch has been introduced here unsuccessfully a number of times and in a number of localities.

The goldfinches eat mainly small seeds, but also a few insects and berries. They make notably thick-walled nests with much soft fibrous material such as plant down and feathers. Lawrence's Goldfinch of the Southwest tends to breed in loose colonies. The American Goldfinch is one of the most familiar and appreciated of American songbirds. In some regions, this species delays its nesting until late summer to coincide with the availability of thistle seeds for feeding its young and thistle down for nest lining. At 3½ inches, the Lesser Goldfinch is one of the smallest North American songbirds.

The male American Goldfinch is the only form in this group which truly merits its name.

GONADS. The sexual glands, testes (male) and ovaries (female), which produce reproductive cells, spermatozoa (male) and ova (female), as well as sexual hormones which stimulate other phenomena of the reproductive cycle. In female birds, only the left ovary and its companion oviduct usually develop. See REPRODUCTIVE SYSTEM.

GONYS (GO-niss). The ridge formed where the two rami of the lower mandible come together, making a conspicuous angle in the outline of the lower margin of the bill in some birds, e.g., the larger gulls, Razorbill. See Fig. 25.

GOOD CALL / BAD CALL. Birdwatching terminology referring to quick, accurate identification or lack thereof. Ludlow GRISCOM may have pioneered the concept. He was always "calling" an anonymous speck on a distant phone wire or a grayish water bird in a distant bay from a speeding car. He is said to have once accurately "audioed" (called by call) a Bridled Tern flying overhead along the coast of Massachusetts. An appropriate response from an admiring companion would have been: "Good call, Ludlow!"

Bad calls are rarely announced but give off an odor of embarrassment for several minutes after they are revealed. You are standing at the bow during a pelagic trip in the North Atlantic in late September. You pick up a buoyant white form on the horizon and as it comes into focus you detect a bold pattern of contrasting triangles emblazoned across its wings and mantle. "Sabine's!" you cry triumphantly to the assembled bird clubs of six states. "Sabine's Gull!" The bird turns and heads straight for the boat and just as you are beginning to feel some unease about your snap call, your archrival—an insufferable fool whose reputation in the field rests solely on his arrogant posturing and uncanny luck—says calmly but loudly, "Immature kittiwake." Silence.

See also IDENTIFICATION.

GOOSANDER (GOO-san-der or goo-SAN-der). Standard English name, except in North America, for *Mergus merganser*, which we call Common Merganser. The name Goosander is apparently of Scandinavian origin and means "goose-duck"; it is a large duck (22 to 27 inches), measuring about an inch longer on the average than a Brant.

GOOSE. Standard English name for 27 members of the family Anatidae (order Anseriformes), including the so-called South American "sheldgeese" in the genus *Chloephaga* and such odd forms as the Magpie "Goose" of Australia and the Egyptian "Goose" of Africa and Asia Minor, all usually placed in the subfamily Tadorninae (or tribe Tadornini) with the shelducks. All 7 native (or regularly occurring) North American goose species (including Brant) are "true geese" in the subfamily Anserinae (or tribe Anserini).

Geese are medium-sized to large, essentially vegetarian water birds, many of which spend as much time (or more) "grazing" in wild and cultivated fields as they do in the water. Like the other members of their family, geese have lamellate bills, flattened in some cases like ducks' bills (Canada Goose, Brant) or somewhat arched and narrow (e.g., Snow

Goose). All geese are relatively stout-bodied and long-necked. Honking V formations of Canada Geese are familiar sights throughout North America, heralding the change of seasons. These and the Brant are popular game birds.

Most goose species are solitary nesters, but some (e.g., Ross') are loosely colonial. The nest is a scrape in the open, lined with down and small contour feathers from the female's breast and bits of handy vegetation; sometimes a low rim is scraped up from the sides by the sitting bird. Canada Geese are also known to use the tops of beaver and muskrat lodges, stumps, and even abandoned raptor nests 10 to 20 feet off the ground. The 2–11 (usually 3–6) eggs are white to yellowish and unmarked.

High, usually quavered, bugling or honking notes are typical goose sounds, characteristically uttered in chorus from flocks on the wing. Geese also make defensive hisses and low "conversational" mutterings.

The geese are distributed worldwide, but largely restricted to the Temperate Zones, north and south. All North American geese breed in the Arctic, all but Canada Goose exclusively so. And all except the large, semi-domesticated population of Canada Geese are migratory.

"Goose" comes to us almost unchanged from Old Norse and Old English words referring specifically to these birds.

GORGET (GOR-jet). An area of brightly colored feathers covering the throat; often used to refer to the brilliantly iridescent throats of hummingbirds; originally the part of a suit of armor which protected the throat.

GOSHAWK (GOSS-hawk). Standard English name for about 18 of the larger members of the genus *Accipiter*, one of which, the Northern Goshawk (*A. gentilis*), has a Holarctic distribution and ranges throughout much of the northern and mountainous regions of North America. The "gos" is famed for its magisterial bearing, its deft capture and dispatch of birds and mammals, and its ferocious defense of its nesting territory. Its skill and panache as a hunter make this species a favorite of falconers.

"Goshawk" means "goose hawk," implying (erroneously) the species' preferred prey.

For family characteristics, see HAWK.

GOSLING. A young goose of any species; applied to birds in immature plumage as well as downy chicks.

GRACE Coues (Grace's Warbler: *Dendroica graciae*). Miss Coues was the sister of Elliott COUES, the brilliant ornithologist of the later nineteenth century. Spencer BAIRD named this western warbler species for her.

GRACKLE. Standard English name for 11 species of New World blackbirds (family Icteridae; order Passeriformes) as well as for a species of starling endemic to Ceylon. Three species of icterid grackles breed in North America.

The grackles are black birds with a multicolored iridescence and fairly long to very long tails.

Together the North American species occur throughout the continent south of the boreal forest except for the Far West. They winter in staggering multitudes in the Southeast, where they are justly regarded in some cases as significant PESTS.

"Grackle" comes from the Latin *graculus,* which has referred to several black birds as diverse as the Jackdaw (the call of which it was meant to echo) and the cormorant.

GRAMINIVOROUS (GRAM-ih-NIV-er-us). Refers to eaters of grass, e.g., sheep and the grazing species of geese.

GRANDRY'S CORPUSCLES. Ovoid masses of nerve endings of about 1.5 hundredths of a millimeter in length in the lower layer of skin (dermis). Known so far only in birds, they apparently function as receivers of tactile sensation. Generally similar to Herbst's corpuscles but presumed to have an exclusive function which has yet to be precisely defined. See TOUCH; HERBST'S CORPUSCLES.

GRANIVOROUS (gran-IH-ver-us). Feeding on grains and/or other seeds. Some ducks, geese, gallinaceous birds, doves, blackbirds, and finches are largely granivorous, at least for part of the year or in situations where this form of food is readily available.

GRASSLAND. Any upland habitat in which the principal vegetation is grasses. A number of bird species are partial to grassland as a breeding habitat, e.g., Upland Sandpiper, Sprague's Pipit, meadowlarks, Bobolink, Dickcissel, Grasshopper Sparrow, Lark Bunting, McCown's and Chestnut-collared Longspurs. Grassy wetlands, e.g., salt marshes, stands of *Phragmites* reed, are not usually called grassland. See also PRAIRIE; SAVANNA.

GREBE (greeb). Standard English name for all members of the family Podicipedidae, the sole family in the order Podicipediformes. There are 20 species of grebes worldwide, 6 of which breed in North America.

The grebe family is a varied one, containing small (9 inches), drab, and short-billed species as well as large (29 inches) species with long, sharp bills and ones with a colorful breeding plumage. Shared characteristics include: peculiarly lobed toes (see Fig. 12) with flattened claws adapted for strong swimming at the surface and underwater (see SWIMMING/DIVING), a dense glossy plumage, short wings, and a negligible tail.

Because of their peculiarly adapted legs/feet, grebes are most at home in the water, and extremely awkward on land, which they visit, if at all, only to nest. They fly little except during migration; several Latin American species are flightless. They have the unusual ability to reduce their buoyancy and sink below the surface by "squeezing" the air from their plumage. Once underwater, they can swim surprising distances, often seeming to disappear altogether, a practice that has generated superstitious names such as "water witch" and "hell-diver." Grebes are said to submerge for "divers" reasons and return to the surface for "sun-dry" reasons; for more detail, see SWIMMING/DIVING.

Grebe's nests are heaps of wet dead vegetation piled up at the margin of a lake or pond or floating and anchored to emergent vegetation. The 2–10 (most species average 3–5) eggs are notably long and "biconical" (see Fig. 7); they are white and unmarked when laid, but become stained from the soggy plant material of the nest. Grebes are among the few birds which cover their eggs when they leave the nest, and it has been suggested that the rotting plant material used may generate enough heat to aid incubation.

Grebes are seldom heard except on their breeding grounds, where most species give extended, sometimes tremulous braying or crooning "songs" as well as shorter whistles, squeaks, and wheezes.

The origins of "grebe" may be another of the many bird names to have arisen out of a generalized term for a seabird, or it may be a corruption of the Breton word *krib*, meaning "crest" and probably referring to the Great Crested Grebe of the Old World.

GREENLAND. The world's largest island, measuring 1,650 miles in its longest dimension, 800 miles in its widest, and containing a total of 840,-000 square miles. Of the latter, 727,360 square miles are buried under a vast glacier (the largest in the Northern Hemisphere) and most of the remainder which is not *permanently* icebound lies above the Arctic Circle. Since the early eighteenth century Greenland was under the political control of Denmark, but in 1979 home rule was granted to the native Innuit.

In the present context, Greenland is of interest chiefly because it is considered part of North America by the compilers of the A.O.U. *Checklist of North American Birds*. This decision is readily defensible on a number of grounds. Greenland is separated from Ellesmere Island in the Canadian Arctic Archipelago by a strait as narrow as 25 miles, which is normally frozen. It is connected to North America by a ridge on the ocean floor, the top of which is nowhere more than 600 feet beneath the surface, making Greenland contiguous with our continental shelf. The geology of the whole island is virtually identical to that of the nearby Laurentian Shield of Canada. The vast majority of its plant species are of North American affinities. The majority of its approximately 60 breeding bird species are represented in the Nearctic region, and about half of these leave Greenland in late summer and fall to winter in North America.

Greenland has no endemic bird species, but it is the westernmost breeding locality for a number of Palearctic birds, such as Barnacle and Pink-footed Geese, White-tailed Sea Eagle, Meadow Pipit, and Fieldfare (since 1937 only). And a number of other Eurasian species—e.g., Gray Heron, Eurasian Spoonbill—appear in the A.O.U. *Check-list* solely because of their accidental occurrence in Greenland.

The North America of the present book does *not* include Greenland, and species known from nowhere else on the continent are not included in Appendixes I and II.

For a general notion of the depauperate Greenland avifauna, see TUNDRA.

GREGARIOUS. Characteristically found in flocks; Evening Grosbeaks, Common Starlings, and many shorebirds, for example, are normally gregarious; Peregrine Falcons and Belted Kingfishers are not. See FLOCK.

GRIFFIN (Griffon, Gryphon). An ancient imaginary beast, perhaps originating with the Hittites. A lion with an eagle's beak, wings, and talons (on the forelegs) and, occasionally, a serpent's tail; in some accounts, eight times as large as a lion. Among various ancient cultures (Greek, Syrian, Roman) it was thought to range throughout Asiatic Scythia; to be a guardian of gold mines and other treasures; to pull the chariot of the sun; and to be the enemy of horses.

One of the Gryphon's most recent appearances is in Lewis Carroll's *Alice in Wonderland*, where it plays straight man to the Mock Turtle.

Also standard English name for Old World vultures in the genus *Gyps*, especially *Gyps fulvus, the* Griffon Vulture.

GRINNELL (grih-NELL), Joseph, 1877–1939. Grinnell's scientific achievements are inextricably associated with the fauna of California, but his influence in elevating ornithology to a "full-fledged" science was nationwide. He was the director of the Museum of Vertebrate Zoology at the University of California at Berkeley, long-time editor of *The Condor*, and president of the American Ornithologists' Union, 1929–32. His bibliography comprises 554 titles, mostly on avian subject matter but not a few on mammals. Despite this prolific output and his heavy administrative load, he was also an ardent and able field man. A number of subspecies of North American birds and mammals are named for Grinnell, e.g., Grinnell's Waterthrush (*Seiurus noveboracensis notabilis*) and a Baja California race of Loggerhead Shrike (*Lanius ludovicianus grinnelli*).

Not to be confused with George Bird Grinnell (no relation), 1849–1938, the patrician outdoorsman, Indian authority, and early conservationist, who greatly influenced the establishment of the National Parks system and early bird protection laws.

GRISCOM, Ludlow, 1890–1959. The patron saint of modern American birdwatching. As an ornithologist at the American Museum of Natural History in New York and at Harvard, Griscom's main professional contribution was the elucidation of the Mexican and Central American avifaunas. But the achievement of his life was to show that "birding" did not need to be practiced with a gun—except in cases where field identification is impossible and a specimen is required for the record—and that the great majority of birds can be identified with absolute accuracy by a practiced and intelligent observer. Griscom's brilliance in the field, his eloquent enthusiasm for the "sport" of field ornithology, and his large circle of protégés largely spawned the legions of present-day birdwatchers and their need for good optical equipment and comprehensive field guides. Griscom's love of field work is reflected in his best-known works, which were mainly distributional in nature (see the Bibliography).

GRIT. Small pieces of rock, shell, or other hard substance ingested by birds to assist the digestion process in the gizzard (ventriculus) (see DIGESTIVE SYSTEM). Seeds, buds, and other coarse vegetable matter are pulverized by contractions of the powerful muscles of the stomach walls aided by digestive "juices." The grit acts in combination with rhythmic contractions of the tough, coarse muscles which line the stomach walls to pulverize the seeds, buds, and other coarse vegetable matter. Relatively little of it is ever excreted with waste products and therefore it accumulates in the stomach throughout the bird's life.

Gallinaceous birds, doves, and seed-eating finches are perhaps most readily associated with this digestion technique, but grit of varying coarseness has been found in a wide variety of both land and water birds. The practice of picking up grit contributes to the susceptibility of birds in ingesting lead shot pellets, with serious consequences to many game birds, especially ducks (see FOOD/FEEDING; MAN-MADE THREATS TO BIRDLIFE, *Lead Poisoning*).

GROSBEAK. Standard English name for about 24 species of large-billed cardinaline (Emberizidae) and cardueline (Fringillidae) finches. Three "cardinal-grosbeaks" (Rose-breasted, Black-headed, and Blue) and 2 "finch-grosbeaks" (Evening and Pine) breed in North America.

The name is largely one of convenience, referring to the large seed-crushing bill, and has little taxonomic significance.

For general family characteristics, see FINCH.

GROUND DOVE. Standard English name for 14 species of small (6 to 9 inches), short-tailed members of the family Columbidae (order Columbiformes), all in the genera *Columbina* (*Columbigallina*) or *Claravis* (some authorities include several other species from two other genera). All are confined to the New World. One species, the Common Ground Dove, breeds in southeastern and southwestern North America, and another, the Ruddy Ground Dove, has occurred as an accidental straggler (see Appendix II).

Like many other doves and pigeons, ground doves habitually feed on the ground; unlike most others, they also often *nest* on the ground.

For general characteristics of the family, see PIGEON; for provenance of "dove," see DOVE.

GROUSE. Standard English name for about 10 members of the family Tetraonidae (order Galliformes) and used in a more general sense to refer to the whole family, which includes the ptarmigan and prairie chickens. There is no taxonomic affinity (except the familial one) among the various "grouse," which occupy 7 different genera. All 5 North American species of grouse are endemic.

Members of the grouse family are mostly medium-sized (average 15 inches), chicken-like birds with a short bill and short legs and wings. They often have elaborate or strikingly patterned tails (see Plate 5) as well as facial wattles and inflatable colored sacs on the neck—all of which are used in nuptial display (see Plate 2). Many species of grouse have evolved foot adaptations for coping with walking and scratching in snow. The tarsi and feet are heavily feathered in some cases (ptarmigan), making them resemble rabbits' feet; other species develop little comb-like projections (pectinations) from the sides of the toes which act as "snowshoes" (see LEG/FOOT and Fig. 12).

Grouse inhabit both forest and open country. They feed mainly on seeds, buds, shoots, and other vegetable matter and in most cases have unusual courtship rituals involving "dances" and strange sounds.

The typical grouse nest is a shallow scrape on the ground lined sparsely (if at all) with handy plant fragments. Large clutches of eggs are characteristic of grouse, and nests with as many as 17 eggs have been found, though 6–12 is the norm. The eggs may be whitish, yellowish buff-brown, or pinkish, with markings highly variable among different species: immaculate, very finely speckled, spotted, or heavily splotched with pale brown to black.

Everyday grouse vocalizations are mostly variations on chicken-like cluckings and gobblings with some squeaks and rattles given in alarm. Displaying males produce unique "instrumental" (i.e., non-vocal) sounds using their wings and inflatable neck pouches (see SONG; DISPLAY; BOOMING; DRUMMING; GOBBLING GROUND; STRUTTING GROUNDS; and Plate 2 for further detail).

The grouse family is restricted to the Holarctic region. Our grouse occupy the northern forests (coniferous and mixed), the prairies, and western sagebrush plains.

The origins of "grouse" have so far remained obscure.

See references in the Bibliography under GALLINACEOUS BIRDS.

GUANO. Originally, the excrement of the Guanay Cormorant (*Phalacrocorax bougainvillii*) and other island-nesting seabirds of the west coast of South America. Guano, which accumulates to great heights at the largest colonies, is commercially "mined" for fertilizer and gunpowder and was once Peru's chief export and source of income. By the end of the nineteenth century, however, reckless exploitation had depleted supplies of guano built up over the centuries (see pp. 286–95 of Murphy, 1936–SEABIRD). Presently an attempt is being made to extract guano in equilibrium with its accumulation.

The excrement of other species of colonial birds has been exploited elsewhere in the world, but the food preferences of the seabirds and the aridity of the west coast of South America are ideal for the production of nitrogen-rich guano.

The term is also used loosely now for any kind of excrement, e.g., "bat guano."

GUILLEMOT (Eng.: GILL-uh-mott; French: GEE-mo). Standard English name for the 3 species of auks in the genus *Cepphus* (family Alcidae; order Charadriiformes), 2 of which breed and winter in North America.

All of the guillemots are largely black in alternate (breeding) plumage, becoming substantially white after the breeding season. They breed on rocky islets and remote rocky coasts and winter more inshore than other alcids—most of which are essentially birds of the open ocean. The Pigeon Guillemot inhabits the North Pacific, and is replaced in the North Atlantic and most of the north coast of the U.S.S.R. by the Black Guillemot.

The name literally means "little William," a diminutive of the French name Guillaume; its origin is apparently in pure whimsy. In British usage, the murres (genus *Uria*) are also called guillemots.

For family characteristics, see AUK.

GUINEA FOWL (or guinea hen). Species of gallinaceous birds in the family Numididae, which are largely African in natural distribution. Domesticated in North America for meat and eggs. See DOMESTICATED BIRDS.

GULAR (GYOU-ler). Referring to the throat. The red inflatable pouch on the throat of a male frigatebird, for example, may be called a gular sac.

GULL. Standard English name for the great majority of the approximately 45 members of the subfamily Larinae (family Laridae [gulls and terns]; order Charadriiformes). The great majority of gull species belong to the genus *Larus*. Two species are known as KITTIWAKES.

Twenty species of gulls breed in North America (including Black-headed Gull; see Vickery, 1977), 4 are regular visitors, and 2 others have occurred as vagrants.

Gulls range in size from 8 to 30 inches, though most are medium-sized to large. Their plumage is invariably in tones of black, white, and gray (brown in immatures). Their bills and legs are often bright red or yellow and some species acquire a rosy "bloom" during the breeding season (see COLOR AND PATTERN). A large proportion of gull species also acquire dark (gray, brown, black) head feathers in the alternate (nuptial) plumage. Gulls' bills are relatively short but vary from rather thin and delicate to fairly massive. The first three toes are fully webbed and the hind toe (hallux) is small or vestigial.

Gulls are among the most successful birds in the modern world. They are strong fliers and swimmers, and some species make shallow dives from the air. Their diet tends to be nearly all-encompassing. They seek food not only over the world's oceans, lakes, and rivers, but also inland, where some species follow the farmer's plow and consume the grubs of crop-eating beetles. A statue to the California Gull in Salt Lake City, Utah, commemorates that species' "heroic" efforts in stemming the plagues of large grasshoppers which threatened Mormon crops in 1848 and 1855.

Gulls nest colonially, different species preferring a wide variety of breeding habitats: marshes, beaches, tundra, and cliffs are typical locations and islands are often favored. The nest itself may be a fairly well-shaped cup of grasses, seaweed, and/or other available material; a simple pile of the same material on which the eggs are laid; or a plover-type scrape with a sparse lining of debris. Franklin's Gull builds a floating raft of marsh vegetation anchored to emergent plants, and Bonaparte's Gull makes a loose cup of sticks lined with grass, moss, and lichens, placed in a spruce tree in the boreal forest. The color and markings of the 2–5 eggs (usually 3 in most species) are variable among both species and individuals. Many are some shade of olive or buff with fairly profuse dark brown splotches and many paler subsurface markings, but they can also be nearly white, unmarked, sparsely marked, or finely speckled.

Gulls make a great variety of loud, penetrating sounds, from extended buglings and mewings to short nasal ejaculations.

The gulls provide a striking example of man's potential effect on animal populations. At the turn of the last century, Herring Gulls bred mainly in the Arctic and visited the New England coast only in winter. Though summering birds may have attempted to breed further south before the mid-nineteenth-century, shooting and egg hunting inhibited such range expansion. In the 1920's, Herring Gulls established a few small breeding colonies as far south as Massachusetts, and owing at least in part to commercial fishing practices and the open dumping of human refuse, these pioneers have replicated themselves exponentially into the burgeoning gull population which currently clogs our harbors, beaches, lakes, and sanitary landfills and occupies breeding habitat at the expense of other bird species, especially terns. Herring Gulls and Great Black-backed Gulls (another "arctic" species) now breed well down the Atlantic coast at least to the Carolinas. Other species of gulls have shown similar spectacular recent increases.

Gulls breed worldwide from the Arctic to the Antarctic, and inhabit most watery ecological niches from the high seas (some species strictly pelagic) to Andean lakes above 10,000 feet. They tend to be especially numerous along shorelines and near human habitation, where they are useful (if now often overabundant) scavengers.

"Gull" derives from Celtic names for these birds. These may originally have described the wailing noises made by gulls or their gluttonous appetites.

GYNANDROMORPHISM (juh-NAN-droh-MORF-izm). A genetic abnormality in which characteristics of both sexes are combined in a single individual. Avian gynandromorphs are very rare, but birds showing normal male plumage on one side of the body and normal female plumage on the other (bilateral gynandromorphism) have been recorded.

GYRFALCON (JURR-fall-kun). Standard English name for a single species of falcon (*Falco rusticolus*) which breeds, usually on a cliffside, throughout much of the Arctic; a few individuals occasionally wander south as far as northern Europe, Russia, and the U.S. Occurs in a range of color variations from nearly black to ivory white. It is a more robust and powerful bird than the Peregrine and is widely and justly regarded as the most splendid of the falcons.

In medieval falconry, it was reserved for kings (Kubla Khan is said to have owned 200), and Arab princes will still pay exorbitant sums for them, their royal worthiness being enhanced today by increasing scarcity and strict protection throughout most of the breeding range. In spite of their distinguished reputation, modern falconers find them harder to train and less spectacular in action than the Peregrine.

Gruson (1972–BIOGRAPHY) traces the name to Old High German *girvalke*, which means (O regal moniker!) "greedy falcon."

For family characteristics, see FALCON.

H

HABITAT. A flexible term for a restricted part of the environment in which a given plant or animal prefers to live—often (but not always) associated with a broad plant community; e.g., coniferous forest is the preferred habitat of the Gray Jay. Surf-washed rocks are the characteristic habitat of the Purple Sandpiper for most of the year, though its *breeding* habitat, barren tundra, is quite different. Habitat preferences of other species are broader. Semipalmated Sandpipers are found feeding in nearly all watery situations: mud flats, marsh and pond edges, riverbanks, sandy beaches, even coastal rocks. Mud flats are ideal habitat for many marine organisms and therefore excellent feeding habitat for a great variety of shorebirds. For related ecological concepts, see NICHE; BIOME; DISTRIBUTION.

HACKING. In falconry, the practice of setting young, captive, fledged falcons free for a period of weeks to allow them to develop full powers of flight and a wild spirit. During the hacking period (when birds are said to be "at hack") they are sometimes equipped with bells on their legs to hinder any efforts to capture their own food and to force them to come back to the food set out by the falconer at a fixed perch.

The term is also used today in the broader sense of reintroducing birds into the wild after a period of captivity. Injured birds, for example, rapidly grow accustomed to kindly human benefactors and "free" meals and must therefore be "hacked back" into the wild if they are to survive.

HACKLES. Long, narrow feathers of the neck; especially those of domestic roosters, which are key components in certain fishermen's flies. The golden nape of adult Golden Eagles, which contrasts with the dark body feathers, is made up of hackle-like feathers.

HALCYON (HAL-see-on). A literary word for kingfisher and, by a combination of fanciful metaphor and bad ornithology, an adjective meaning calm, peaceful, e.g., "halcyon days."

A minor Greek goddess, Halcyone, threw herself into the sea out of grief for her drowned husband, Ceyx (both *Halcyon* and *Ceyx* have been adopted as names of kingfisher genera). Taking pity, the gods turned them both into kingfishers. From this legend arose the belief that kingfishers nest on the surface of the sea for a period of two weeks near the winter solstice and have the power to calm the waves to facilitate the incubation process.

HALLUX (HAL-iks) (pl.: halluces). The first digit or "big toe" of a bird's foot. In most species, the hallux is the hind toe, opposed to three others pointing forward. Several other arrangements also exist, however, and not a few birds (e.g., many shorebirds) typically lack a hallux altogether or bear only a vestigial one. See LEG/FOOT and Fig. 25 or SKELETON and Fig. 19.

HAMMOCK. A land form/plant community typical of the southeastern U.S., especially Florida. Sprunt (1954–STATE BOOKS) defines a hammock as "a wooded island in a sea of grass," and quotes another definition: "a dense growth of trees other than pines in comparatively dry soil . . . in a region where open pine forests predominate" (Dr. Roland Harper). The botanical composition of hammocks varies and the term is modified accordingly, e.g., "palm hammock." Hammocks are likely to contain woodland bird species, e.g., Red-bellied Woodpecker, Barred Owl, which are not typical of the surrounding open country.

HAMMOND, William A., 1828–1900 (Hammond's Flycatcher: *Empidonax hammondii*). In the legion of army doctor-birders (see BIOGRAPHY), Hammond was unquestionably the most eminent in his profession. He was a distinguished neurologist, professor of medicine, and an active and innovative (though underappreciated; see Gruson, 1972–BIOGRAPHY) U.S. Surgeon General. As with many other amateur ornithologists of his day, Hammond's interest was fostered through his army service and Spencer BAIRD. It was the exotic John XANTUS, befriended by Hammond, who described and named the western highland "empi" for him.

HAMULUS (HAM-yuh-luss). A hook, e.g., those on the barbicel of a feather. See FEATHER.

HARD CORE (pronunciation in New England: "hahd coah"). Indefatigable in the pursuit of a "good bird"; also, such birders as an elite, "*the* hard core." The quintessence of this state of being is embodied by those hardy souls who spend thousands of dollars in transportation costs and guide fees, camp in an execrable environment with inadequate sanitation and hostile natives in arctic Alaska, driven by the hope of adding an immature Scarlet Rosefinch (or other species abundant throughout the Palearctic region) to their North American lists. Dr. Norman Hill, author of *The Birds of Cape Cod*, deems these folk and their kind "the flinty haht (heart) of the hahd coah."

HARLAN, Richard, 1796–1843 (Harlan's Hawk: *Buteo jamaicensis harlani*; once considered a full species, now considered a highly variable western form of the Red-tailed Hawk). A Philadelphia naturalist, doctor, and friend of AUDUBON, who named this hawk. He was a distinguished physician, but an unexceptional naturalist. According to Gruson (1972–BIOGRA-PHY), he had the courage to take Audubon's part in the Wilson-Audubon feud, an incident of rhetorical arson ignited by WILSON and fanned after his death by Audubon and Wilson's mentor George ORD.

HARLEQUIN (Duck, Quail). Standard English name for two North American bird species, a duck (*Histrionicus histrionicus*) and a quail (*Cyrtonyx montezumae*), also known as Montezuma Quail. The Harlequin, a traditional clown character of the Italian commedia dell'arte, always appears in varicolored tights. His name is therefore an apt metaphor for the plumage of the male *Histrionicus*, arguably the most strikingly patterned duck in existence, and that of the male *Cyrtonyx*; males of both species are also decidedly "clown-faced."

HARRIER. Standard English name for the 13 species of hawks in the genus *Circus* (family Accipitridae; order Falconiformes), 1 of which, the Northern Harrier, *C. cyaneus* (formerly called the Marsh Hawk here and still known as the Hen Harrier in the Old World), breeds in North America.

The harriers are among the most graceful of raptors, all with exceptionally long wings, tails, and legs and a characteristic slow "tippy" manner of flight. They course over marsh, prairie, and tundra, periodically dropping suddenly to catch a small mammal, reptile, amphibian, or bird on the ground or in shallow water. The harriers also nest on the ground and sometimes form communal roosts in marshlands or other open-country cover after the breeding season.

The genus *Circus* is distributed worldwide except for the usual oceanic islands and frigid antipodes, and the Northern Harrier breeds throughout most of the Holarctic region.

"Harrier" means simply "hunter," though it derives from "harry," originally a military term meaning to plunder or harass.

For family characteristics, see HAWK.

HARRIS, Edward, 1799–1863 (Harris' Hawk: *Parabuteo unicinctus*; Harris' Sparrow: *Zonotrichia querula*). An amateur naturalist and gentleman horse breeder of New Jersey who accompanied his friend John James Audubon on his expeditions to the Florida Keys and up the Missouri River. On more than one occasion he provided Audubon with crucial financial support, for which we all have reason to be grateful to him. Audubon called him "one of the finest men of God's creation" and wished that "he was my brother." He also named the hawk after him (originally *Buteo harrisi*); Nuttall named the sparrow.

HATCH. To break through and emerge from an eggshell, as: "All the chicks (were) hatched (out) yesterday." Also, speaking of the egg, to break open as a result of the efforts of the embryo, as: "All the eggs hatched yesterday."

Hatching may be described as the final act of a bird embryo or the first act of a young bird, and preparation for this major transition begins early in the incubation period. As embryonic moisture evaporates through the porous eggshell, an air space is created between the inner and outer shell membranes at the blunt end of the egg. The embryo itself develops two temporary structures, the egg tooth and the hatching muscle, that aid the final escape from the egg. And the eggshell becomes weaker through the transfer of minerals to the embryonic skeleton.

Two or three days before hatching, the chick-to-be thrusts its bill into the air space and begins taking air into the lungs—though it continues to depend for part of its oxygen exchange on the allantois (see EMBRYO). In this first act of the hatching process, the embryo realigns its body from the crosswise to lie along the long axis of the egg, the most favorable position for forcing an exit from the blunt end. Aided principally by the leg and neck muscles and by the special hatching muscle attached to the back of the skull, the embryo's body soon begins to make convulsive thrusting motions that end in forcing the bird's bill against the inside of the shell. With the help of the horny egg tooth (located at the tip of the upper mandible in most species), the egg is eventually cracked or "pipped." The internal hammering continues until enough of the shell is cracked to cause the end of the egg to fall away and to allow the chick to emerge exhausted on the floor of the nest. Having fulfilled their function, the hatching muscle and the egg tooth will soon disappear, the latter dropping off or in some species being reabsorbed into the bill proper (see EGG TOOTH for more detail on this structure).

From pipping to full emergence the hatching process may take from as little as a half hour (small passerines) to as much as 6 days (albatross), but among small to medium-sized birds it consumes a few hours to most of a day on average. In most cases, eggs in a clutch do not hatch simultaneously but in sequence, reflecting the intervals in laying and the subsequent start of incubation.

Parent birds of some species may pick bits of shell away or poke into the initial cracks as the embryo struggles from within, and Ostriches are said to crack their eggs with their breastbones and pull the chicks out with their bills (Armstrong, in Thomson, 1964–ORNITHOLOGY), but in most cases, chicks must make their way into the world unassisted.

After the embryo has broken into the air space, it often begins "peeping," a sound that may trigger the shift in parental behavior from the "incubation mode" to the "brooding/feeding mode." Some parents will even bring food to these noisy eggs before they have been pipped.

For egg formation and pre-hatching development, see EGG; EMBRYO; INCUBATION; for post-hatching behavior and development, see YOUNG, DEVELOPMENT OF; PARENTAL CARE.

HATCHLING. A bird which has just emerged from its egg. See CHICK; NESTLING.

HAWK. Standard English name in North America for about 50 members of the family Accipitridae (order Falconiformes) and used in combination in the names of a number of other birds of prey, e.g., Northern Goshawk. "Hawk" is also popularly used to refer to any member of the Accipitridae except the vultures, condors, and eagles and even to the members of the Falconidae, i.e., in a loose context it is possible to say that Swallow-tailed Kites and Peregrine Falcons are both types of "hawks." In a slightly more restricted usage, the family Accipitridae is referred to as the hawk family, including the accipiters, buteos, eagles, kites, and harriers, but not the falcons and caracaras, cathartid vultures, or Osprey. There are currently 15 species of resident North American birds of prey called "hawks" (including Northern Goshawk), all either "buteos" or "accipiters"; other native members of the hawk family (Accipitridae) include 5 kites, 1 harrier (formerly Marsh Hawk), and 3 eagles.

Hawks vary greatly in size (8 to 12 inches in length; to nearly 4 feet if the eagles are included), but all have powerful wings and legs and a short, stout, hooked bill for tearing flesh and long, sharp claws for grasping and in some cases killing prey. All species have a fleshy eye ring and a "saddle" of skin at the base of the bill (cere) through which the nostrils open (see Fig. 1); both of these are often bright yellow or orange in adult birds. Many hawks are boldly patterned and handsomely colored and in action often display admirable agility and grace.

Hawks and eagles are all predatory on other animals, though the choice of prey (ailing antelopes to insects) and methods of hunting vary widely among different species. They never take plant food.

The typical hawk's nest is a large, bulky, sometimes carefully constructed cup of sticks, lined with moss, roots, grasses, and finer plant material. The site varies with the habitat of species and populations: on the ground, in marshland, on rocky cliffs, or in trees. Nests are often re-used and "improved" with additional materials year after year and sometimes become massive structures over time (see EAGLE; NEST). The 1–8 eggs (average 2–4 in most species) are notably round (short sub-elliptical; see Fig. 7). Color and marking very variable among both species and individuals: whitish to pale buff to pale bluish; unmarked to fine pale speckling to very heavy dark brown splotching covering almost the entire surface.

Vocalizations of hawks and eagles include harsh screams, plaintive fluted whistles, whinnies, and chatters.

Hawks are distributed worldwide and throughout all North American biomes. Except for the Northern Goshawk and the Rough-legged Hawk, all our species are endemic to the New World; most are migratory.

English names of day-flying birds of prey have undergone a lamentable corruption since a precise usage evolved among falconers in medieval Britain. North Americans must bear the blame for this degeneration. Originally "hawk" was reserved for the bird hunters in the genus *Accipiter*; "falcon" referred strictly to the members of the Falconidae—swift raptors with pointed wings; "harrier" described only the long-winged, long-tailed open-country raptors of the genus *Circus*; and broad-winged soaring raptors, mostly in the genus *Buteo*, were called "buzzards." In America "hawk" was substituted for all these more precise names and of course "buzzard" was reassigned to the New World vultures (Cathartidae). At present the official nomenclatures have begun to restore some of the useful distinctions. North American birdwatchers are now enjoined to speak of American Kestrels, Merlins, Peregrines, and Northern Harriers instead of Sparrow Hawks, Pigeon Hawks, Duck Hawks, and Marsh Hawks. But it is doubtful whether buteos will ever be called "buzzards" here. See also KITE.

"Hawk" can be traced to Old German and Old English verbs related to "have" and meaning to grasp or seize.

HAWKING. Another name for falconry. Also, flying over an area, eying the ground or water carefully in search of prey. Some hawks (e.g., Northern Harrier) do this habitually, but so do many other birds. Gull-billed Terns, for example, characteristically "hawk" over marshes and mud flats.

HAWK MOUNTAIN Sanctuary (Pennsylvania). A narrow spur of the Kittatinny Ridge in the eastern Appalachians, along which tens of thousands of day-flying raptors (mostly Broad-winged Hawks) pass between late August and mid-November (see Appendix III for peak dates). This famous flyway was once the site of an annual "varmint shoot" by ignorant farmers and "sportsmen" of the region, but it is now a protected area visited by thousands of hawk watchers annually. It is located about 17 miles north of Reading, Pennsylvania, and is reached via the town of Hamburg. For more details on Hawk Mountain birds and the saga of raptor preservation, see Broun (1949) and Harwood (1973).

HAZARD TO AVIATION. See PESTS.

HEARING. Bird ears are like human ones in their location in the sides of the head and in having three interconnected chambers, the outer, middle, and inner ears (for details of avian ear anatomy, see references in the Bibliography under HEARING and appropriate chapters in major secondary sources under ORNITHOLOGY). In general, birds lack the fleshy external sound-catching appendage so prominent in mammals, and their ear holes are totally concealed under normal circumstances under the feathers called ear coverts (auriculars) (see Fig. 25). However, some owls have a flap of skin called an operculum or concha along the front margin of the ear hole that can close over the opening or be erected to catch sounds *from behind*. Owl ears are also unique (as far as known) in being asymmetrical both in position (one higher than the other) and in internal structure; these may be adaptations for finding prey in the dark (see below).

To minimize obstruction of sounds, birds' auricular feathers lack barbules and can be erected from the sides of the head—though this is rarely witnessed.

Birds are among the most vocal of animals, and it is therefore not surprising that they possess acute hearing. Courtship and territorial songs, vocal signals between parents and young, alarm notes, threat sounds, calls among flocking birds, and sounds made by predators are important elements in the lives of birds and would be useless, of course, unless they could be heard.

To understand the useful comparison between human hearing and that of birds, the reader will recall that sound is recorded as the rate at which sound vibrations pass through the air, called cycles per second (c.p.s.). The more vibrations or cycles per second, the higher the frequency or pitch. The normal human ear hears sounds between about 20 and 17,-000 c.p.s. (20,000 maximum). The known hearing range for all birds is between 34 and 29,000 c.p.s. *However*, the range of any individual bird species is significantly less than ours: we hear about nine octaves; birds average about five.

As logic suggests, bird species tend to hear about the same range of sounds they can produce. Many small songbird species can sing and hear sounds of higher frequency than we are capable of hearing. However, these same birds miss several lower octaves which we hear easily. For example, these avian tenors and sopranos often cannot hear the relatively low-frequency human voice, so that loquacious birdwatchers usually disturb their fellow birders more than their quarry.

At least some birds can also hear "faster" than we can. Slowing down a recorded bird song often reveals notes we couldn't hear at normal speed, though birds which mimic other birds (see SONG) have been shown to include these fast notes in their imitations.

Birds use their hearing not only in communicating but also in locating food. Payne (1962) revealed how Barn Owls can zero in on mice in the dark by precisely locating the position of their squeaks; and there is some evidence that robins, plovers, and other birds which hunt over the ground for invertebrates can *hear* their prey as it moves under the surface, and that woodpeckers can hear grubs and other wood-inhabiting insects moving in bark and trunks.

It has recently been shown (Kreithen and Quine, 1979) that domestic pigeons can detect "infrasounds"—e.g., vibrations made by meteorological or tectonic disturbances—perhaps from thousands of miles away. This would explain instances of birds "predicting" earthquakes and may also aid homing ability (see NAVIGATION).

ECHOLOCATION, highly developed in bats, has been verified in a few species of cave-dwelling birds in South America (Oilbird) and Asia (swiftlets).

HEART. See CIRCULATORY SYSTEM.

HEAT (regulation of). See TEMPERATURE, BODY.

HEATH HEN. Standard English name for the extinct eastern subspecies of the Greater Prairie Chicken, *Tympanuchus cupido cupido*. Today the species is associated with undisturbed grasslands of central North America, but in colonial times the Heath Hen thrived in ericaceous (blueberry, huckleberry, etc.) barrens, characteristic of burned-over areas in the East. The destruction of the eastern population may be blamed unequivocally on the stupidity of overshooting; this was essentially accomplished by the early 1800's, when hunting the species for the market ceased to be profitable in the East. After this period, only a few remnant populations remained. The last of these was on the glacial outwash plains near the south shore of the island of Martha's Vineyard, Massachusetts, near present-day Katama. The last bird here succumbed sometime after March 11, 1932.

For other details, see EXTINCT BIRDS; also PRAIRIE CHICKEN.

HEEL PADS. See LEG/FOOT.

HEERMANN (HAIR-mahn in German; HERE-mun in North American), Adolphus L., c. 1827–65 (Heermann's Gull: *Larus heermanni*). Heermann was a boy naturalist and grew to attain all the characteristics of the successful nineteenth-century bird man; he was a doctor, a member of the Philadelphia Academy of Arts and Sciences, and an officer in the U.S. Army. These circumstances inevitably brought him into contact with Spencer BAIRD, with whom he worked on the zoological portions of the Pacific Railway Survey. He collected birds and eggs in Florida, Mexico, and California and according to Gruson (1972–BIOGRAPHY) died by the cruel (but intriguing) combination of advanced syphilis and an accidental self-inflicted gunshot wound. He collected the beautiful Pacific coast gull which commemorates him and which was named by his contemporary John CASSIN. For a fuller biography, see Stone, *Cassinia* (1907), 9:1–6.

HELIGOLAND (HELL-ih-goh-LAND) **TRAP.** A famous, rather elaborate trap for land-bird migrants which takes its name from the tiny German island in the North Sea where the contraption was pioneered as a banding tool in the early part of this century. It is essentially an enormous funnel made of chicken wire or other mesh fencing material. The mouth is 20 or more feet high and once birds have entered they are driven up into a box fitted with devices to facilitate getting hold of the trapped birds so that they can be banded. Heligoland traps are usually placed near low, dense vegetation so that birds can be flushed from one side into the trap on the other. Bait in the mouth of the funnel is also used.

Mist nets have replaced trapping methods such as this one at most bird-banding stations. See MIST NET; CANNON NET; BANDING; CAPTURE.

HEN. The female of any species of bird, especially of the gallinaceous birds (grouse, quail, pheasants, etc.) and more especially of the domestic chicken. The corresponding term for the male is "cock." It is not uncommon in Britain to hear expressions such as "a hen Reed Bunting" or "a cock Siskin." But this usage is rare at best in North America.

HENSLOW, John S., 1796–1861 (Henslow's Sparrow: *Passerherbulus henslowii*). English botanist, geologist, clergyman, and teacher. He was a principal in the establishment of Kew Gardens. Perhaps most notably, he was one of Charles Darwin's teachers and recommended him as a young naturalist for a post on the *Beagle*. He was also a friend of Audubon, who named the sparrow for him.

HEPATIC (Tanager). Pertaining to the liver. The liver is normally dark, dull red or purplish brown; the male Hepatic Tanager in breeding plumage is brick orange—with some dusky shading on back, wings, and cheek. It would be surprising to find a truly liver-colored Hepatic Tanager and alarming to find a Hepatic Tanager-colored liver. Perhaps the coiner of this name was thinking of the yellow female or immature male and the jaundice produced by a malfunction of the liver.

HERBIVOROUS (her-BIH-ver-us). Describes a preference for plant food. Plant-eating animals are known as "herbivores." Ptarmigan and other grouse are examples of herbivorous birds.

HERBST'S CORPUSCLES. Ovoid masses of nerve endings about 1.5 hundredths of a millimeter in length in the lower layer of skin (dermis), so far known only in birds. They apparently serve as receivers of tactile sensation. See TOUCH; GRANDRY'S CORPUSCLES.

HERON. Standard English name for about 40 members (including night herons and tiger herons) of the family Ardeidae (order Ciconiiformes), which also includes the egrets and bitterns. Twelve members of this family breed in North America, and two species of egrets have occurred here accidentally (see Appendix II).

The herons are relatively small (11 inches) to large (4½ feet) wading birds characterized in general by long legs and neck, long, pointed bill, broad wings, a short tail, and in many species long beautiful plumes on head, back, and/or chest which develop during the breeding season (see Fig. 4). They consistently feed in shallow water or marshland, perhaps preferring fish, but by no means eschewing frogs, snakes, small birds and mammals, and any invertebrate large enough to be worth the trouble.

Herons are popular as characters in fables and fairy tales due to their distinctive, somewhat humanoid form and their manner, which in turn is now dignified, now stealthy, now relaxed. And their delicate plumage and graceful movement both in the air and on the ground doubtless explain their prominence in the ancient tradition of Oriental brush painting (see HUMAN CULTURE). The species with the most beautiful plumes (egrets) were hunted to the brink of extinction around the turn of the century for the sake of ladies' fashions (see CONSERVATION). Most species have rebounded strongly with protection.

Most heron species nest in colonies, usually placing their stick platforms in trees or bushes but also on rocky ledges or clumps of wetland vegetation. The structure is a notably flimsy affair when first built but becomes larger and more substantial in succeeding years. If any lining is added it usually consists of a few leaves and other plant debris. Herons lay 2–7 (usually 3–4) pale to fairly deep greenish blue (American Bittern to olive brown), unmarked eggs.

Most herons are usually silent, except in the social atmosphere of the breeding colony. Their repertoire consists mainly of throaty croaks, squawks, and the occasional hiss. The Green Heron and the night herons call more often, the first giving a distinctive, sharp *kuke* when disturbed and the latter uttering its familiar *quok* en route to and from feeding grounds. For the most unusual of heron sounds, see BITTERN.

The heron family is distributed worldwide except for the barrens above tree line and they reach their greatest North American diversity in the Southeast, but occur continentwide wherever there is water. A number of "southern" species (Snowy and Great Egrets, Little Blue and Louisiana Herons) have extended their range markedly northward in the last quarter century. The recent phenomenal range expansion of the Cattle Egret is in a class by itself (see DISTRIBUTION).

"Heron" may be traced back through various ancient words, all referring specifically to the birds themselves.

HESPERORNIS (HESS-purr-OR-niss). Literally, "western bird." A genus of extinct birds (order Hesperornithiformes; family Hesperornithidae), four species of which have been described from fossils uncovered in Upper Cretaceous chalk beds in Kansas and Montana. All were large (4 to 5 feet), flightless, swimming and diving birds, superficially resembling modern loons. O. C. Marsh, the famous turn-of-the-century paleontologist who described the first *Hesperornis*, erected a new subclass (Odontoholcae) defined by the presence of this bird's most distinctive feature: teeth set in grooves in the jaws; but it is now usually placed in the subclass Neornithes with all "true birds," both fossil and recent. Compare ARCHAEOPTERYX; ICHTHYORNIS; see also EVOLUTION OF BIRDLIFE; TAXONOMY.

HETEROCHROISM. Technical term for abnormal color differences. See ALBINISM; MELANISM; LEUCISM; ERYTHRISM; XANTHOCHROISM.

HIBERNATION. In the sense of a prolonged, regular, seasonal period of dormancy in which life functions are dramatically reduced, hibernation is documented for only one bird species, the Poor-will (*Phalaenoptilus nuttallii*); but similar metabolic phenomena are recorded for a few others. See TORPIDITY.

HIGH ISLAND (Texas). A knoll of high ground with live oaks along the predominantly marshy Texas coast northeast of Galveston. Such copses, known locally as "hummocks," form the only satisfactory sanctuary for migrant woodland birds arriving from the long spring journey across the Gulf of Mexico. In good weather the migrants disperse inland, but when bad weather forces them to put down on the nearest land, High Island (as well as other localities along the Gulf coast) occasionally becomes deluged with millions of exhausted birds. See Appendix III for prime dates.

HINCKLEY, Ohio. Site of an annual celebration on March 15, the approximate date of the spring return of hundreds of Turkey Vultures (or "buzzards" as they are known locally) to an area of breeding cliffs about 20 miles south of Cleveland.

HOARY (Redpoll). Whitish, especially with age. If anything, redpolls become darker with age, since between molts the pale edges of the feathers wear away, making the brown centers more prominent. However, the Hoary Redpoll is generally paler (hoarier) than the Common Redpoll, especially with regard to the rump, which is always unstreaked in the Hoary and usually appears streaked in the Common.

HOLARCTIC REGION. The Nearctic and Palearctic zoogeographic regions combined. A bird species such as the Northern Shrike, the range of which is continuous (except for current ocean barriers) around the world north of the tropics, is said to have a Holarctic distribution. See ZOOGEOGRAPHY; DISTRIBUTION.

HOLOTYPE. When the author of a new species (or other taxon) designates a particular specimen as the basis for his description at the time of publication, that specimen is called the holotype. Compare LECTOTYPE; see also NOMENCLATURE, *Types*.

HOME RANGE. The total area which a bird inhabits while resident in a given place. The home range may be essentially the same as the breeding territory (in species with large territories in which they feed, gather nesting material, etc., as well as nest); or contain the breeding territory but extend far beyond it (many colonial nesters); or be totally separate from the breeding area, e.g., on wintering grounds.

   Though species of raptors may avoid hunting within another individual's home range, the latter differs from a territory mainly in not being defended (see TERRITORY).

   On the average, the home range is larger than the territory and may be very large indeed (28 square miles recorded for one Golden Eagle), but size varies among both species and individuals.

HOMOIOTHERMAL (HO-moy-o-THERM-ul) (or homoiothermic or homoiothermous). Warm-blooded; i.e., capable of maintaining a constant body temperature independent of the environment. Only mammals and birds are "homoiotherms," and the young of bird species which are born naked are in fact "cold-blooded" and therefore dependent on their parents for maintenance of body temperature until at least partially fledged. Compare POIKILOTHERMAL. See TEMPERATURE, BODY.

HOMOSEXUALITY. In bird populations in which one sex greatly outnumbers the other, homosexual pairing sometimes occurs. The phenomenon is particularly prevalent among captive birds. During the mating season in a colony of birds such as gulls, in which males and females are superficially similar, a certain amount of sexual confusion—females mounting males, males mounting other males—is not very unusual. Hunt et al. (1980) have recorded a high incidence of female-female pairing among Western Gulls on Santa Barbara Island, California (again, probably due to a skewed sex ratio). When one member of such pairs was fertilized by a promiscuous male, the two females successfully reared broods by sharing responsibilities.

HOOD. Either a feathered crest, e.g., Hooded Merganser, or an area of distinctly colored feathers covering part of the head and neck, e.g., Hooded Warbler, Hooded Oriole. A Laughing Gull may be said to have a black "hood" in breeding plumage.

   In falconer's parlance, a leather headpiece of varying design which covers the eyes of hawks to keep them docile.

HOOTING. A general term for the "song" of all owls; some, e.g., Great Horned Owls, "hoot"; others screech, wail, howl, and even ululate.

HOPPING. The manner in which most perching birds (order Passeriformes) move when on the ground. By contrast, most non-passerines walk (see WALKING/RUNNING). Notable exceptions (i.e., passerines which usually walk rather than hop) in North America include: Horned Lark, ravens, crows, and magpies (jays regularly both hop and walk), pipits and wagtails, starlings, meadowlarks, grackles, cowbirds, and blackbirds, and the Savannah Sparrow. Of course, a great many arboreal or aerial species, e.g., warblers or swallows, do not normally spend any time on the ground and so rarely hop or walk. Other species, e.g., American Robin, though normally hoppers, will occasionally run. It is generally supposed that ground-haunting birds evolved the habit of hopping in order to move efficiently among small obstructions, such as rocks, encountered frequently in their preferred habitat.

HORICON MARSH (Wisconsin). 35,000 acres of freshwater marsh in southeastern Wisconsin (near Waupun), protected as a water-bird refuge by both state and federal governments. The greatest avian event at Horicon is the concentrations of waterfowl, especially when Canada and Snow Geese occur in March and April (peak: first two weeks in April); the fall flight, late September to early November (peak: mid-October), is less spectacular. The refuge also contains a heronry and an interesting assortment of midwestern marsh birds, e.g., Sedge (Short-billed Marsh) Wren and Yellow-headed Blackbird.

HORNED LARK. Standard English name for the 2 members of the lark genus *Eremophila* (family Alaudidae; order Passeriformes). One of these, *the* Horned Lark (*E. alpestris*), is widespread in the Holarctic region, occurring in virtually every open-country habitat: some 20 subspecies have been distinguished in North America alone.

The name derives from the species' characteristic corniplumes—small, pointed tufts of feathers projecting from the top of the head above and behind the eyes in adult birds.

For family characteristics, see LARK.

HORNEMANN, Jens Wilken, 1770–1841 (*Acanthis hornemanni*: Hoary Redpoll). Eminent Danish botanist: co-author (with eight others) of the fourteen-volume *Flora Danica*. The redpoll was named by the Dutch ornithologist C. P. Hoelboll, a contemporary of Hornemann's and for a time governor of Greenland. Mr. Hoelboll's name is attached to a subspecies of the *Common* Redpoll (*Acanthis flammea hoelbolli*) and was once used as the accepted common name for the Red-necked Grebe. Unfortunately, the governor's name has long been misspelled by taxonomists as Holboell, but the error has now been officially corrected.

HOST. In a biological context, an organism which is parasitized by another. Many songbird species are "hosts" to the brood parasitism of the Brown-headed Cowbird. See PARASITISM; COWBIRD.

HOVERING. Remaining stationary in midair, usually by rapid beating of the wings. A flight technique used for hunting terrestrial animals by a number of raptors, including the shrikes, and characteristic of the flight of hummingbirds. See FLIGHT, *Special Techniques.*

HUDSONIAN ZONE. One of Merriam's life zones; corresponds closely to the tundra/coniferous forest ecotone. See LIFE ZONES and Fig. 6.

HUMAN CULTURE, BIRDS IN. It is far beyond the scope of the present book to treat this vast and fascinating subject with anything like thoroughness. All the subtopics below merit full-length books of their own, and in most cases such books already exist. The aim here is to sketch a broad outline and to prick the reader's curiosity; the Bibliography lists some sources in which he may find satisfaction.

The ubiquity, variety, and abundance of birds have always made them familiar to human beings. They are more universal even than trees (for many Eskimos have lived and died without ever seeing a full-sized tree) or mountains (for inhabitants of coral atolls never see mountains) or even the sea (which many inland cultures know only from legend). Since birds are also good to eat, are decorative, and can be trained to participate in several sports, it is hardly surprising that birdlife figures prominently in the whole spectrum of human activities. But that bird themes should be so pervasive in our cultural life—in our painting, music, literature, religion, and folklore—requires further explanations, of which I think there are essentially four: (1) Birds lend themselves very readily to anthropomorphic characterization—the wise owl, the vain peacock, the noble eagle—much more so even than most of our nearer relatives the mammals. Perhaps the fact that birds walk erect on two legs as we do is partly responsible for our tendency to "humanize" them. (2) Only birds among the other animals are as vocal as ourselves and often *seem*, at least, to sing for pleasure as we do, as well as for communicating (see SONG). (3) Birds lead a conspicuous family life with many habits—elaborate and silly courtship rites, nest building, food bringing, family "outings"—that remind us of ourselves. Many mammals have these habits, but one sees them less often. (4) Birds can fly—the one non-human attribute that we unreservedly and universally envy.

These speculations about the prominence of avian themes in human culture apply to all the categories below and so will not be emphasized again in each case.

PAINTING. There are two discernible kinds of "bird painting": (1)

bird portraiture in which birds are treated for their own sake as the main objective of a painting and (2) works of art by acknowledged masters in which birds figure—sometimes very prominently—in the composition. The best examples of the former may exhibit exquisite draftsmanship together with fine perceptions of light, texture, composition, and other values. But their intent is altogether different from that of the latter and so this form of bird painting is treated separately under ILLUSTRATION.

There is little exaggeration if any in the statement that you can find birds wherever you look in the history of art. They occur most often as genre elements included, so to speak, to show the world as it is (or was). Some of the most realistic depictions of birds (i.e., those in which the species or at least the family is recognizable) appear in hunting scenes, the first of which are Paleolithic cave paintings—about 17,000 years old—among the oldest works of art we know of. Herons and kingfishers are clearly portrayed in the limestone relief of a hippopotamus hunt in the tomb of Ti (c. 2400 B.C.) of the Old Kingdom of Egypt; and one of the treasures of Tutankhamen's tomb (c. 1360 B.C.) is a painted chest showing the young king hunting bustards (among many other animals) and attended by two Griffon Vultures. Hunting scenes with birds also show up in classical Etruscan, Greek, and Roman wall paintings, in medieval tapestries and illuminated texts (falconry was a very popular genre subject in the Middle Ages), and continue to appear in serious works of art until nearly the present day (e.g., Winslow Homer's *Right and Left,* showing a pair of Common Goldeneyes in the foreground being dispatched from a distant boat on a wintry sea). The hunt continues to be a central theme in the "primitive" art of African, Australian, South American, and Innuit cultures. In the fifteenth century common dooryard birds such as crows, magpies, and sparrows became prominent in carefully drawn scenes of daily life such as the Limbourgs' *Les Très Riches Heures du Duc de Berry* and later in the town-and-country scapes of Brueghel. Though recognizable species occasionally appear in later landscapes (e.g., Rubens' *Landscape with the Château of Steen*), birds are more likely to be used as vague evocations of nature, e.g., the anonymous avian shapes in flight added with a few strokes of the brush by Claude, Constable, or the Impressionists. The American Luminist Movement (1850–75) made liberal use in its seascapes of the kind of little wide-V "sea gull" that all schoolchildren learn to make and stick picturesquely in their skies. A grisly variation on the obligatory seascape gulls depicts black-and-white birds (Cape Petrels?) hovering over the carnage in Turner's *The Slave Ship.*

The purely decorative qualities of birds also appealed to some of the earliest-known artists, e.g., Greek seventh-century-B.C. perfume vases in the shape of an owl or motifs on painted black-figure Attic kylikes (sixth century B.C.). The highly formalized garden scenes in late-fourteenth- and early-fifteenth-century tapestries and frescoes made good use of the forms and bright colors of such birds as peacocks and Golden Orioles (*Oriolus*). And these "ideal" birds were also popular in sensual arcadian scenes in the Renaissance (e.g., Titian's *Bacchanal*, 1518) and in the romantic eighteenth-century nymph-scapes of Watteau and Fragonard. On Baroque ceiling frescoes, cupids and angels usually outnumber birds, but not infrequently a flight of swallows or some other suitably idyllic avian phenomenon is included, as in Guercino's ceiling fresco *Aurora* (1620's) in the Villa Ludovisi in Rome. Somewhat ironically, some of the most detailed depictions of birds in art are found in Dutch still lifes of the seventeenth century. Like the sumptuous flower and food arrangements of the same Baroque tradition, birds of many species, carefully chosen for the variety of their colors and patterns, are shown to exquisite advantage—except that they are all dead.

A few painters have recognized the potential of birds in enhancing fantastic themes. The unrivaled master of feathered fantasy is Hieronymus Bosch, who, to judge by the precision with which he painted actual species and the variety of them he uses, seems to have been more than a little interested in birdlife. Birds appear in many of his paintings as elements of genre (see above), but in his famous *Garden of Delights* triptych he uses a staggering variety of birds—real and imaginary—in three of art's most fantastic landscapes. In the Eden and Hell side panels, he gives us fairly standard idyllic (egrets, birds of paradise) and horrific (owls and other night birds) avian images, respectively. But in the center panel, showing the Adamite conception of how life should be lived, birds are far more than peripheral decorations. Giant finches, woodpeckers, hoopoes, jays, and owls wade about in crowded pools with the same spirit of frolicsome liberation that their human brethren display; a smiling duck drops fruits into a man's mouth, spoonbills squawk in delight at riding on a goat's back, a robin (*Erithacus*) is entirely content to carry a man with a huge seed pod on his head. Except that it seems a trifle overcrowded, here is a world of perfect contentment for man and bird (and a great many other things).

Before leaving fantasy, we should probably give a respectful nod to the twentieth-century fantast Henri Rousseau, whose haunting jungle scenes (e.g., *The Dream*) often include a bird or two of imaginary species which help to evoke an aura of primitive innocence.

Finally, it should be mentioned that birds in paintings are often symbols for concrete entities, e.g., saints or Satan, or for emotions or phenomena, e.g., the volatility of the spirit or spring. Bosch's owls, for example, stand specifically for evil/the underworld, omnipresent but often unnoticed in the human sphere, and his eggs, which bear surprising contents in many of his works, are alchemistic devices. Birds in early ecclesiastic paintings are also included in many cases to represent a specific aspect of Christianity, e.g., the bleeding pelican which appears in painted crucifixions (see IMAGINATION, *Religion*). The less literal form of symbolism is exemplified in Brancusi's gleaming abstract bronze, *Bird in Space* (1919), which embodies the sleek grace that man admires in the flight of birds.

Arguably the most exquisite of painted birds are those done in the tradition of the Northern Sung Dynasty painter-emperor Hui Tsung of eleventh-century China. The exquisite egrets among lotuses and fierce goshawks perched in flowering plum trees also stand for qualities which they suggest to human observers, though no one can deny their decorative appeal. The elegant lines and harmonious forms are meant to express Buddhist teachings such as transmigration of the soul and the insubstantiality of the ego, as well as simply delighting the eye.

MUSIC. The songs of some of the famous European songbirds, e.g., Common Cuckoo and Nightingale, have been incorporated now and then as themes in classical music. These species plus the European Quail (*Coturnix*) can be heard in the second movement of Beethoven's Pastoral Symphony (see Howes, 1964, for other birdsong motifs). Plaintive calls such as those of various plover species and the Eurasian Curlew have purportedly inspired music intended to evoke the mood of a lonely landscape or the like, much in the way the "emotional" qualities of birdsong are often used in poetry (see below). On the whole, however, bird "music" does not correspond very closely to the characteristic range of melodies and rhythms of Western music and therefore is seldom transposed successfully or at least recognizably. Other musical traditions, e.g., Oriental flute music, seem to lend themselves much more naturally to the use of birdsong.

The occurrence of birds in musical *lyrics* is, of course, an altogether different matter. As with recording avian appearances in poetry (see below), noting instances of birds in human song would require the lifetime services of a professional bibliographer. Suffice to say that bird lyrics may be found throughout all (or very nearly all) musical traditions, from the oldest folk songs to Gilbert and Sullivan's tit-willow (not to be confused with the Willow Tit, *Parus montanus*), to "Listen to the Mockingbird," to the Beatles' "Blackbird" (White Album).

LITERATURE. Here distinguished from both ornithological "literature," i.e., technical writing, and "nature writing" on the subject of birds; also from fairy tales and other fanciful writings about birds, which are discussed under IMAGINATION. The present subject matter is "real" birds in fiction and poetry.

Fiction. Excepting the odd parrot on a sea captain's shoulder or caged canary used as a prop, birds in fiction usually serve as background scenery and mood-setting devices. Novelists with an eye for nature or a fondness for outdoor action frequently conjure the seacoast with some gulls wheeling and crying; it is very difficult to describe spring without a certain amount of exuberant birdsong; and some ecstatic avian caroling from field or forest is as indispensable as the perfume of wildflowers to love alfresco. There is also, evidently, a strong compunction, when writing about tropical landscapes, to include some "strange" and/or colorful birds for the sake of verisimilitude.

Such use of birds, if well done, may enhance a reading experience for someone who knows something about birdlife or it may hand him a laugh if the author has skipped his ornithological homework. But overall the impact of birds in English and American fiction must be accounted negligible.

A few oddities where birds assume a more prominent role than usual may be mentioned.

Gulliver's Travels by Jonathan Swift. The hero is "boxed" by a Brobdingnagian "Linnet somewhat larger than an English Swan" and in the same country narrowly escapes a "kite," which sounds suspiciously like a kestrel.

The Narrative of Arthur Gordon Pym by Edgar Allan Poe. Some fairly detailed and (on the whole) accurate accounts of south polar oceanic birds which add a suitably bizarre touch to the later chapters. Poe also invents a few species of his own, e.g., a "Black Gannet."

Green Mansions by W. H. Hudson. Some touches involving tropical forest birds help the reader pass through the soggy romantic wilderness; Hudson's reminiscences of his naturalist boyhood on the Argentine pampa (especially *Far Away and Long Ago*) are far superior, from an ornithological *and* a literary perspective.

An American Tragedy by Theodore Dreiser. The Adirondack wilderness setting of the famous drowning scene (Book II, Chapter 47) is alive with birds that either call ominously or provide a counterpoint to the grim occasion with their fine songs or bright plumage. Though Dreiser uses his avian images to good effect, he is an indifferent ornithologist. But his inclusion of a Caribbean endemic (Yellow-shouldered Blackbird) in the avifauna of upstate New York is more than compensated by that sinister corvid, the "weir-weir," which hops about the branches of dead trees during the murder, going "Kit, kit, kit Ca-a-a-ah!"

Birds of America by Mary McCarthy. The central character is a young birdwatcher (= sensitive) and the novel is about a phase of his late adolescence. It gets some good mileage out of the "personalities" and habits of a number of bird species.

The literate ornithologist-birdwatcher can only lament that Vladimir Nabokov, the only great naturalist who was also a great novelist, was fascinated with lepidoptera, not with birds. See, however, under *Poetry.*

The above does not, of course, pretend to be a comprehensive survey of birds in fiction. Perhaps this may inspire someone to make one. The subject seems to be that rarest of phenomena, an unexplored facet of English literature.

Poetry. It is in poetry that birds and literature seem to form a natural alliance. The poet's need to conjure place and express emotion concisely but vividly finds a ready answer in birds' deep and varied symbolic (as well as real) presence in human experience. There is also a nice kinship between verse and birdsong which blends effectively with the poet's anthropomorphic metaphor in a poem such as Hardy's "The Darkling Thrush." Song may also be used to good effect in devising a poem's structure, as in the onomatopoeic lines in Whitman's "Out of the Cradle Endlessly Rocking," cited below. Finally, poets, as the ultimate wordsmiths, must appreciate the ample selection of useful and telling "sounds" present in the names of any avifauna. Words such as loon, albatross, fulmar, shag, vulture, harrier, falcon, plover, gull, thrush, and sparrow serve the poet at least as well as they serve the taxonomist or birdwatcher.

Birds have been part of the tradition of Western poetry from its beginning. They appear in the lyrics of Homer (before 800 B.C.) and Catullus (first century B.C.), are mentioned in *Beowulf*, the first English epic (early eighth century), and by the end of the thirteenth century had fully assumed their archetypal function as symbols of renewal and the joy of nature in the famous anonymous rondel which begins:

> Sumer is icumen in,
> Lhude sing cuccu!

From this point on, the English avifauna—particularly the Skylark (*Alauda arvensis*), the (Barn) Swallow (*Hirundo rustica*), the Eurasian Robin (*Erithacus rubecula*), the Nightingale (*Luscinia megarhynchos*), the Eurasian Blackbird (*Turdus merula*), and the Song Thrush (*Turdus philomelos*), as well as the Common Cuckoo (*Cuculus canorus*)—is generously represented in every period, form, poetic usage, and in every length and quality of verse in the English language. From Chaucer to contemporary poets in England and America, the challenge is to find one who has *not* included a bird at least once.

Until well into the eighteenth century, the ornithological versatility of Shakespeare remained unchallenged—in fact, it may remain so today. At least one scholar (Gelkie, 1916) has taken the trouble to confirm that more than sixty species are distributed throughout the plays and many of the sonnets. But more impressive than Shakespeare's "list" is the resourcefulness with which he makes use of his considerable knowledge of both the habits of common species and the folklore and superstition which surrounded them. He works dozens of changes on the familiar spring/love/birdsong theme, but also has birds appear as omens, jokes, character analogues, in genre scenes, and in examples of nature's simple wisdom.

Without doubt, the greatest literary bird refuge of all was the age of Romantic poetry, beginning with Blake's outrage at a caged Robin Redbreast (in "Auguries of Innocence") and ending (perhaps) with Thomas Hardy's pathetic darkling thrush. The Romantics are characterized by their love of nature's rich, wild imagery and a strong sense of "song," so it is hardly surprising to find birdlife generally abundant in their poetry or that the period produced the best-known (and perhaps best) "bird poems" of all time: Shelley's "To a Skylark" and Keats's "Ode to a Nightingale." Also hatched between the late eighteenth century and the death of Queen Victoria were Coleridge's deliverance-bearing albatross (in "The Rime of the Ancient Mariner"), Burns's "green-crested Lapwing" ("Afton Water"), a well-stocked and songful (but largely unlabeled) variety from Wordsworth, Tennyson's "Throstle," Browning's unlikely Gannet, Swinburne's "sister swallow" ("Itylus"), Gerard Manley Hopkins' kestrel ("Windhover"), to name a very few.

In modern poetry, man seems to take precedence over nature, but this is due more to a change of context than to any marked shift in theme. After all, Shelley's Skylark and Keats's Nightingale are never glimpsed. They are simply metaphors for an unblemished—totally anthropomorphic—ecstasy, which is contrasted with the melancholy that inevitably tempers man's joy. The tendency among many modern poets is to omit nature and look at man in contexts of his own making—contexts such as war and cities, which are generally inhospitable to birdlife.

Nature is hard for a poet to ignore, however, and so we have Yeats's exquisite "The Wild Swans at Coole"; the very rich and frequent avian imagery in Dylan Thomas (e.g., "Over Sir John's Hill"), T. S. Eliot's Sweeney placed ironically among Keats's Nightingales, and many other examples.

In examining American "bird poetry" it is hard to disagree with Welker (1955), who found little to praise. Most is sentimental doggerel— the kind of "ladies' verse" sometimes published in newspapers: "Our merry friend the chickadee / Chirps his song from the tall pine tree / Chick-a-dee-dee-dee, Chick-a-dee-dee-dee," etc.

It is only respectful to remember that Alexander Wilson was a poet before he was an ornithologist and left us several stanzas on the Osprey:

> True to the season, o'er our sea-beat shore,
> The sailing osprey high is seen to soar
>
> . . . . .
>
> She rears her young on yonder tree,
> She leaves her faithful mate to mind 'em;
> Like us, for fish, she sails to sea,
> And, plunging, shews us where to find 'em . . .

And Poe's "The Raven" must be noted in passing, though the bird of the title is a pet and a literary device, not the subject of the poem.

Admirers of Emerson and Longfellow are bound to bring up the former's "The Titmouse" and various avian musings of the latter, e.g., "Birds of Passage": "I hear the beat / Of their pinions fleet."

But there is really only one nineteenth-century bird poem worth the name, Walt Whitman's "Out of the Cradle Endlessly Rocking." Whitman was both a serious student of natural history and (much more importantly in this context) a serious poet. And the mockingbird in "Out of the Cradle ..." is not "nature observed" or a banal metaphor for some transcendental human quality. It is a voice of knowledge calling a boy out of his innocence:

> O solitary me, listening—nevermore shall I cease
> perpetuating you ...

And Whitman uses the rhythmic repetitions of the mocker's song in his lyric. *Leaves of Grass* contains many birds, used skillfully to evoke the wilderness, but there is only one "Out of the Cradle Endlessly Rocking."

Other first-rate American poets have used avian themes or images, but few are cited among their makers' best work. The poetry-reading naturalist may want to look up the following, if he does not know them; these are not, with a few exceptions, poems *about* birds, but serious poetry which uses bird imagery in a variety of ways.

Emily Dickinson: "At Half Past Three a Single Bird"; "The Robin Is the One"; "To Hear an Oriole Sing"; "I Dreaded That First Robin So"; "A Bird Came Down the Walk"; and many other poems with bird themes.

T. S. Eliot: "Cape Ann" (the last part of *Landscapes*).

Robert Frost: "The Oven Bird"; "Looking for a Sunset Bird in Winter"; "A Minor Bird"; "On a Bird Singing in Its Sleep."

Vladimir Nabokov: "Pale Fire" (first stanza) in *Pale Fire*; not, of course, a "bird poem."

Robert Penn Warren: *Audubon* and "Ornithology in a World of Flux" in *Some Quiet, Plain Poems*.

Wallace Stevens: "Thirteen Ways of Looking at a Blackbird" and "The Bird with the Coppery, Keen Claws."

See the Bibliography for works on the subject of birds in art, literature, and other manifestations of human culture. See also IMAGINATION.

For natural history writing with birds as a principal theme, see the Bibliography under BIRDWATCHING.

HUMMINGBIRD. Standard English collective name for the approximately 320 members of the family Trochilidae (order Apodiformes), of which 14 species breed in North America, another is a regular visitor, and 7 others (including the Cuban Emerald, Green Violetear, Plain-capped Starthroat, and Bahaman Woodstar) have been recorded here as vagrants (see Appendix II).

The world's largest hummingbird measures 8½ inches in length, but most members of this family are small or very small—including the world's smallest bird, the 2¼-inch Bee Hummingbird (*Melisuga helenae*). The size range of North American species is 2¾ inches (Calliope) to 5¼

·inches (Blue-throated). The Rufous Hummingbird breeds in southern Alaska and is therefore the member of its largely tropical family that ranges farthest north.

Most of the hummingbirds' most striking physical adaptations are related to their mode of feeding, which consists of hovering in midair while probing the calyxes of flowers for nectar or picking insects off vegetation or out of the air.

Hummingbirds' bills are exceedingly thin and pointed and come in a wide range of lengths and variations in shape, though the bills of North American hummers are of medium length and slightly to fairly strongly decurved. Their tongues are exceptionally long, extensible, and grooved, becoming tubular toward the tip with an apical brush. Thus the nectar is not sucked through the bill (as with a soda straw) but "pumped" along the tongue with the aid of capillary action.

Hummers have long, narrow wings and highly developed flight muscles which take up a quarter to a third of total body weight and power a wingbeat as fast as 80 beats per second in the case of smaller species. (Oddly enough, this is *slower* than the wingbeats of most birds when measured in relation to body weight!) Due to hummingbirds' small size and low body weight, "their twin propellers" give them extraordinary maneuverability: they can remain stationary as they probe blossoms for nectar; they can move backward if necessary; and they are capable of precision aerobatics in courtship displays and fly-catching forays. Some species attain speeds of at least 27 m.p.h. and perhaps up to 50 m.p.h. or more.

The broad, stiff tails of hummingbirds act as a rudder, crucial in fast changes of direction. Many tropical species have elaborately modified rectrices used in courtship and other displays, but the tails of North American hummers are slightly rounded to modestly forked. The legs and feet are so small as to be practically nonexistent—one of the few visible characters hummers share with their order-mates, the swifts.

Every schoolchild knows that hummingbirds "drink" nectar, but even many birdwatchers are unaware that a substantial part of all hummers' diet consists of insects and spiders that they catch in the bill without the aid of the tongue.

Hummingbirds have the highest metabolism of any warm-blooded vertebrate, with the possible exception of the shrews. So high is their rate of energy consumption that they must feed almost continuously during the day, store a supply of food in their tiny crops, and not infrequently (perhaps on days when food has been scarce) lapse into a state of torpidity for the night.

Tropical hummingbirds come in a spectacular variety of plumage variations. There are a few dull species, and females are usually drab in comparison with their resplendent mates, but the spectrum of brilliant, metallic-iridescent colors represented in the family as a whole is nearly complete, and the assortment of feathered tufts, puffs, frills, streamers, and spangles exhibited would be the envy of a Hollywood costumer. As befits the temperate climate in which they live, North American species depart only in a few cases from the basic hummer design, consisting of bright, metallic-green upperparts and an electric-iridescent gorget and/or crown. This male finery is displayed in courtship flights characteristic of each species (see Plate 2). Hummingbird voices are also used in courtship, but song is one of the few avian gifts denied the family. To the human ear, hummer voices are no more than combinations of high-pitched twitters or squeaks, occasionally assembled into a phrase that approaches one of the more insipid wood warbler songs.

Hummingbirds build cup nests of plant flakes (e.g., lichen) bound together with spider silk and lined with plant down. These are placed on a branch in the open. They lay 2 (rarely 1 or 3) white, unmarked, notably elongate eggs (see Fig. 7) which are tiny compared to those of most other birds (see EGG) but large in relation to the size of the layers.

In spite of their small size, hummingbirds are very aggressive, always ready to attack rival members of their own species, much larger birds of other species, the family dog, or even a full-grown human if any of these are perceived to be invading breeding territory or competing for food.

The distribution of the hummingbird family is strictly confined to the New World and extends from southwestern Alaska (Rufous) to the Straits of Magellan (one species). However, diversity diminishes in proportion to distance from the Equator. In North America only a single species (Ruby-throated) breeds east of the Mississippi, the other 14 residents being concentrated in the West and particularly in the mountains of the Southwest, where several Neotropical species reach the northern extremity of their range. No hummer breeds on the prairies of the Great Plains. Hummers occur in most major biomes, including the desert, and their seasonal distribution is governed in part by the presence of blooming flowers. Most of our species are migratory and the Ruby-throat undertakes the crossing of the Gulf of Mexico and continues to wintering grounds in Central America.

The name comes not from the voice but from the audible whir of the wings. North Americans may be surprised to learn that only a little over a quarter of hummingbird species are called "hummingbirds." Various ornithologists have revealed their sentimental side by giving the rest such whimsical monikers as: coquette, hermit, mango, wood nymph, mountain gem, plumeleteer, brilliant, sunbeam, sun angel, trainbearer, comet, sylph, fairy, and woodstar.

HUNTING (of birds). Before prohibited by law, the taking of a wide variety of bird species—including large numbers of songbirds—for food, feathers, and decoration was commonplace in North America. Bird shooting as a sport is now restricted to upland game species (turkeys, grouse, quail, pheasant), waterfowl, most rails, one race of Sandhill Crane, woodcock and snipe, and some dove species. Some of the most popular species in the first category are introduced from the Old World (e.g., Common Pheasant), and their populations are artificially maintained by stocking in regions where they have not become naturally self-sustaining.

Present-day hunters generally acknowledge that at least minimal conservation practices—e.g., ensuring that bag limits are consistent with the ability of a given species to maintain its population—are in the best interests of their sport. And any excesses committed by the unconvinced are redressed by both state and federal hunting laws. This is not to imply that few birds fall to the gun these days. For example, hundreds of thousands of hunters collectively bag tens of millions of Mourning Doves annually in the U.S.; hundreds of thousands of woodcock and tens of thousands of rails are also taken. See periodic Special Science Reports (Wildlife), available from the U.S. Fish and Wildlife Service, Washington, D.C.

See also LAWS; CONSERVATION; MAN-MADE THREATS TO BIRDLIFE; ENDANGERED BIRDS; EXTINCT BIRDS; EDIBILITY; INTRODUCED BIRDS.

HUTTON, William, mid-nineteenth century (Hutton's Vireo: *Vireo huttoni*). Except for the vireo, which he collected in California and which was named for him by CASSIN, Hutton has left few traces. He was one of the many enthusiastic and talented young naturalists who collected specimens for the National Museum in the last century, particularly in the West.

HYBRIDIZATION. See Fig 11. The interbreeding of two genetically different forms, usually species or distinctive subspecies. The resulting offspring (if any), which shares the characteristics of both parents, is called a "hybrid" or "cross" between the two forms involved. The interbreeding of a male Mallard and a female Black Duck would, if successful, produce young which would be designated as Mallard X Black Duck or *Anas platyrhynchos* X *Anas rubripes* hybrids.

FIG. 11. *Hybridization.* This illustration shows the results of crossbreeding between the Mallard and four other species of ducks, a group in which hybridization occurs with unusual frequency, especially in captivity. *All males* are shown in order to demonstrate the plumage mixes—in the wild the cooperation of a female would, of course, be necessary in each case. All of the birds depicted were drawn from documented records. Though in general hybridization is most likely between closely related species (e.g., Mallard X Pintail or X Gadwall—all in the genus *Anas*), "improbable" crosses such as the Mallard X Common Eider do occur in rare instances even in the wild. A fascinating phenomenon is the occasional appearance in a hybrid of characters—perhaps of an atavistic nature—which appear in *neither* parent. A "bimaculated" duck (top left) with pale areas and sometimes "bridling"on the head is a well-documented form of this intriguing aberration, and the Mallard X Eider (lower left) also shows some "original" plumage traits.

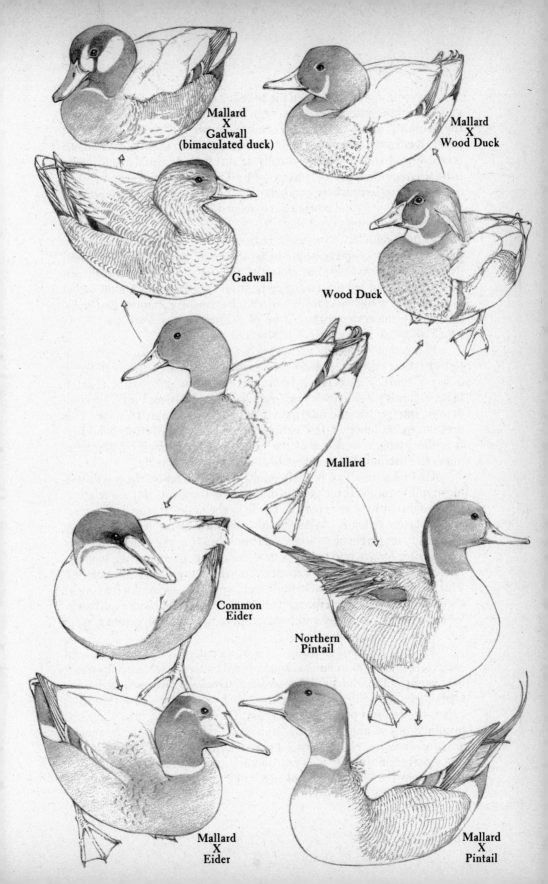

Mallard
X
Gadwall
(bimaculated duck)

Mallard
X
Wood Duck

Gadwall

Wood Duck

Mallard

Common
Eider

Northern
Pintail

Mallard
X
Eider

Mallard
X
Pintail

Hybridization occurs when the so-called isolating mechanisms, which normally inhibit interbreeding between unlike forms, break down or when topographical or ecological barriers are eliminated, allowing distinct but closely related populations to meet and interact. Both of these phenomena occur only infrequently or very locally, so that hybrids are relatively rare in natural circumstances (see SPECIATION). They are much more frequent among captive birds where choosing the "right" mate may be impossible or choice is limited and where closely related species normally of separate distribution are brought together.

Certain families or orders of birds are more prone to hybridization than others. Ducks and geese are by far the most "ambitious" hybridizers, with more than 400 different crosses to their credit—though a high percentage of anatid hybrid records come from waterfowl collections. Other families with a high incidence of hybridization—e.g., grouse and hummingbirds—share the characteristic of a brief and/or weak pair bond, which of course allows "freer" selection of a mate.

Forms that are closely related (phylogenetically) are more likely to interbreed than distant relatives. For example, hybrids between different orders of birds—e.g., between hawks and owls—are unknown, and interfamily hybrids are extremely rare (recorded in gallinaceous birds). By comparison, intergeneric and interspecific hybrids are relatively frequent. This does not mean, however, that closely related forms are *likely* to hybridize. It is the strength/weakness of the isolating factors which chiefly determines the likelihood of interbreeding, not genetic similarity.

There is a variety of possible results which can follow the interbreeding of unlike forms. If the genetic difference is too great (i.e., the relationship too distant) the eggs may be sterile or the embryos may be defective and die before hatching. When healthy offspring do result they are often sterile, i.e., incapable of reproducing themselves. On the other hand, it is also possible for a hybrid to be "better" than either parent, owing to inheritance of dominant strong characteristics which overshadow weaknesses. This phenomenon is called "hybrid vigor" or "heterosis" and is, of course, the goal in artificially interbreeding domestic fowl. The resulting hybrids, for example, may be larger and faster-growing than their progenitors, obvious merits for the poultry farmer.

A hybrid can look more like one of its parents, or share superficial characters equally, or in rare instances show features which are not present in *either* parent. Audubon's "Bimaculated" Duck—a presumed Mallard X Gadwall hybrid with a bright tawny cheek patch not characteristic of either species—was probably such a case. These traits have been explained hypothetically as atavistic—i.e., "throwback" characters from an ancient ancestor—and have been recorded more recently.

Apart from this rare phenomenon, the appearance of a hybrid which results from the interbreeding of two "pure" forms is usually predictable according to a fixed pattern of gene dominance within the chromosomes of each bird. When a pure Golden-winged Warbler interbreeds with a pure Blue-winged Warbler, for example, the first-generation hybrids (so-called Brewster's Warblers) are largely white below but lack a black cheek mark and throat. This is because the color-of-underparts gene is "dominant," i.e., *stronger*, in Golden-winged, and prevails over the "recessive," i.e., *weaker*, color-of-underparts gene of Blue-winged. The reverse is true in the case of the face and throat markings. The first-generation Brewster's hybrids may then interbreed with other hybrids or with pure Blue-wings or Golden-wings, resulting in offspring which can be typically Golden-winged, typically Blue-winged, or various hybrid mixtures. It is only when two hybrid birds interbreed that the two sets of recessive genes can combine in one individual to produce the so-called Lawrence's Warbler with black facial and throat markings and yellow underparts. It is therefore easy to understand why Brewster's type hybrids are much commoner in nature than Lawrence's type. (For a diagram of Golden-winged X Blue-winged Warbler hybrids, see Pough, 1949–FIELD GUIDE.)

Succeeding hybrid generations need not always be confined within the genes of *two* pure forms. Hybrid ducks involving at least five different species are known and crosses involving many more components are theoretically possible, though of course very unlikely except in captivity.

Male bird hybrids are recorded more often than female, and there is a theoretical basis for believing that they are in fact more frequent; however, it is also true that male plumages are more likely to be noticed and that females with impaired sexual function are sometimes "cock plumaged" (see SEX, CHANGE OF).

The hybrids most frequently encountered in the wild involve forms with a close common origin which have evolved separately on either side of some ecological or topographical barrier. When the barrier is bridged or removed, and the forms have an opportunity to mingle, they may ignore each other sexually, indicating complete differentiation into distinct species; or they may engage in an orgy of interbreeding which results in the two once distinct forms melding into one; or a relatively stable "zone of secondary hybridization" may develop in which hybrid birds, distinct from either "pure" form, are common. The last situation occurs in North America in the case of "Myrtle" and "Audubon's" Warblers; "Bullock's" and "Baltimore" Orioles; "Red-shafted," "Yellow-shafted," and "Gilded" Flickers; and "Slate-colored," "White-winged," "Oregon," and "Gray-headed" Juncos. By definition such hybrids are of local occurrence and are, like other hybrids, rarely encountered except in the restricted zones of overlap. Since a species is defined by its reproductive isolation from other species, this manifestation of hybridization is significant taxonomically (see SPECIES; SPECIATION).

For a listing of known hybrids, see Gray (1958).

HYOID APPARATUS. Specialized system of bones and muscles of the avian tongue. See TONGUE.

HYPERPHAGIA (HY-per-FAY-gee-uh). A technical term for overeating; in humans usually neurotic and unhealthful, but normal in some avian contexts. Perhaps the best example is the eating binge in which many migrants indulge, preceding their departure, in order to store energy in the form of fat to fuel their long flights. See Nisbet et al. (1963–FAT) and MIGRATION.

HYPERSTRIATUM (HY-per-stree-AY-tum). Part of the basal ganglia of the brain; unique to birds. Its exact function is not yet known. See NERVOUS SYSTEM, *Brain;* INTELLIGENCE.

HYPORACHIS (HY-po-RAY-kiss). Technical term for the shaft of the afterfeather, a smaller, subsidiary feather stemming from the calamus of a main body feather. See AFTERFEATHER; FEATHER; and Fig. 9.

I

IBIS. Standard English name for about 24 members of the family Threskiornithidae (order Ciconiiformes), which also includes the SPOONBILLS. Also formerly a misnomer for the single native North American STORK, once officially designated as Wood Ibis (now Wood Stork). Three species of ibis breed in North America, and another is an accidental visitor.

Ibises are large (20 to 40 inches) wading birds with long legs, a long, decurved bill, broad, strong wings, and a short tail. Except for the Scarlet Ibis of South America, they tend to be uniformly dark or white but often with some black in the primaries, iridescent highlights in the plumage, and/or brightly colored "soft parts." They feed on small fish, shrimp, insects, the occasional small frog or snake, and some plant material by probing in marshland muck with their specially adapted bill.

An ibis nest is a bulky stick platform in low trees, shrubs, or (less typically) on the ground in wetlands; marsh nests tend to be of cattails, sedges, etc. Ibises lay 2–4 eggs: moderately dark blue and unmarked in the Glossy Ibis; yellowish buff to olive with irregular light to dark brown blotches and speckles in the White Ibis.

Ibises have only a rudimentary vocal apparatus, but are capable of some harsh grunts (*urnk*), cooing sounds, and hisses.

Ibises are distributed worldwide, mostly in warmer climates. They have traditionally been thought of as "southern" birds in North America as well, but the Glossy Ibis has extended its range dramatically in recent years and now breeds north to the coast of Maine.

"Ibis" can apparently be traced to ancient Egypt, where the Sacred Ibis of the Nile (*Threskiornis aethiopicus*) was revered as the animal form of Thoth, the god of wisdom and magic.

ICHTHYORNIS (IK-thee-OR-niss). Literally "fish bird"; an extinct genus of birds (order Ichthyornithiformes; family Ichthyornithidae), 7 species of which have been described from fossils found in Upper Cretaceous deposits in Kansas, Montana, and Texas. The species of *Ichthyornis* are thought to have resembled small (8 inches in height) gulls or terns, hence their name, referring to presumed feeding habits. Their pronounced keel suggests they were strong fliers. A stray reptile bone in one fossil led archaeologists to believe for many years that *Ichthyornis* was toothed, but this is now in question. See EVOLUTION OF BIRDLIFE.

ICTERID (IK-tuh-rid). Any member of the New World family Icteridae (order Passeriformes), including the blackbirds, cowbirds, grackles, orioles, oropendolas, caciques, meadowlarks, Bobolink, Troupial, and perhaps Dickcissel, and a useful collective term for the family as a whole. See also TROUPIAL.

General descriptions of the icterids are given under BLACKBIRD; COWBIRD; GRACKLE; ORIOLE; MEADOWLARK; BOBOLINK.

IDENTIFICATION. Well into the twentieth century bird identification was something that a "field ornithologist" did in his study at the end of a day or when foul weather kept him indoors. Having spent the day exploring the woods and wetland borders, shotgun under arm, eager to live up to Dr. COUES's injunction to bag "all you can get," the first "birders" returned home, measured their specimens, noted the color of their "soft" parts, plugged their mouths with cotton, and then set about preparing them as "bird skins." This done, if the collector was puzzled by any of his new acquisitions, he took the specimen in question in one hand, Coues's *Key to North American Birds* (or other reliable reference) in the other, and proceeded to identify his bird. Did the long-tailed flycatcher in hand have "three or four primaries emarginate; crown spot yellow in black cap" or merely "one primary emarginate; crown spot flaming in ashy cap"? If the former, it must be a Fork-tailed Flycatcher; if the latter, a Scissor-tailed.

Birds are still identified "in the hand" by ornithologists and bird banders using keys that systematize mensural details or combinations of obscure plumage details. Indeed, this is the only foolproof procedure for reliably distinguishing certain species and subspecies, not to mention the ages and sexes of many birds. But during the 1920's Ludlow GRISCOM and a rapidly expanding group of his protégés began to prove that the great majority of bird species could be positively identified in life with the aid of a pair of field glasses and a comprehensive knowledge of field marks. This insight, aided by the appearance of illustrated FIELD GUIDES and ever-improving optical equipment, gave rise to a new era in field ornithology, now known (with fewer elitist overtones) as "birdwatching."

Birdwatching and its sportier variation, "birding," suggest many things to many people (see BIRDWATCHING), but identifying species is central to everyone's notion of the activity. Many now-obsessive birders can remember a particular bird—a Magnolia Warbler glimpsed at scout camp or a spoonbill noticed on a business trip to Florida—that unaccountably inflamed a dormant curiosity about nature and made them desperate to find a book that would tell them what they had seen. Once you have identified your first bird, it is difficult to stop wondering about this world of hitherto unnoticed beauty that has suddenly materialized or to resist the satisfaction derived from the possession of arcane knowledge and the ease with which herons and ducks, woodpeckers and orioles yield their identities to your increasingly sophisticated scrutiny in the early months. But the hook of addiction is not firmly set until the reddest of Northern Cardinals, the most radiant of Yellow Warblers have become just the slightest bit boring and you find yourself scanning the sparrow pages of your field guide, or concluding that all sandpipers suddenly look puzzlingly different rather than puzzlingly alike, or taking an interest in those tiny moving objects near the horizon that some show-off is presuming to name. For the animus that drives the serious modern birdwatcher is not a yearning for aesthetic thrills or scientific discovery; it is not even the "lure of the list" (though all these may be important ancillary rewards). Rather, it is the evolutionary accident that many birds look a great deal like many other birds.

This truth soon appears in rudimentary form to the novice birder in the realization that mockingbirds and shrikes, for example, are superficially similar. But the paragon among today's birders is he who holds in his mind every field mark, every call note, every nuance of gesture and posture (see JIZZ), every fact of distribution, seasonality, and extralimital occurrence of every species that could possibly paddle, flap, or hop into his line of vision. He knows where, when, and how to look for birds; he sees them and hears them with an acuity astounding to the uninitiated; he identifies them at a distance or in motion confidently, rapidly, and (it usually proves) accurately. There is often a degree of swagger in his manner, but he readily and humbly admits his infrequent errors.

A unique pleasure of being a birdwatcher in the first decades of the phenomenon's existence is to watch the horizons of field identification pushed back. The legendary Griscom died puzzling over field problems now routinely solved by dedicated adolescent birders. This casts no disgrace on Griscom's reputation; it is the logical result of an increased number of sharp eyes, ears, and brains scrutinizing birds in the field with the kind of systematic fervor that Griscom pioneered. One effect of the continual breaking of identification barriers is that rarities become less rare: Have the Eurasian stints suddenly become more frequent visitors to North America? Probably not, but there are certainly more people around who recognize one when they see it. Another mark of advancing sophistication is the growing obsolescence of the standard field guides among birders of the upper echelons of birdernity. Members of this airy realm now take their instruction from journals of field ornithology (see PERIODICALS) and contemplate "postgraduate" field guides that will unlock all the mysteries of unsongful *Empidonax* flycatchers and immature gulls and "peeps," and largely ignore "fall warblers," most of which have long since ceased to be confusing to them.

There is a grumpiness in some quarters about the alleged snobbery of so-called "professional birders." "We," say the self-styled amateurs, "bird for fun," the implication being that the better you play the game, the less enjoyable it becomes. This is nonsense, of course, and the goal of total identifiability—however unattainable—is a healthy one, both intellectually and spiritually. If the hyperbirder is exceptionally liable to any character flaws, they are hubris (e.g., listing no unidentified alcids or jaegers for a day's sea watch) and humorlessness (e.g., discussing the possibility of a hybrid Kumlien's X Thayer's Gull with a straight face for more than three minutes).

Those scanning this entry for the "how to" section will be disappointed, for, in the author's opinion, bird identification skills cannot be taught. There is undeniably a knack to the business, but there are no tricks that can be transferred verbally from one who knows them to one who does not in the way that, say, magicians can share expertise. Everyone must start from scratch, though in fact some begin before scratch by being born with keen eyesight and hearing, the most useful of birding faculties, which unfortunately are not available on demand. Making the best of his inherited traits, the would-be bird identifier should: (1) Buy the best pair of binoculars and the best telescope he can afford, learn how to use them as if they were essential prostheses, and keep them in the best condition. (2) Memorize—no, inhale—all available bird guides and all other literature relevant to identification (omitting books that purport to explain how to watch birds). (3) Spend every available minute of your life out looking for birds and examining them critically for their distinctive qualities. (4) Form an intimate friendship with someone as intelligent, as enthusiastic, and approximately as knowledgeable about bird identification as you are. If, after five years of following these guidelines faithfully, you are still saying things like "That Swamp Sparrow is much browner than the one in the book," you may have to resign yourself to remaining a novice birder for life. Happily, there is no shame in this; looking at birds seems to yield equal pleasure at all levels of expertise.

See Griscom, "The Historical Development of Sight Recognition,"

ILLUSTRATION   360

Birding, 8:77–80. See also BIRDWATCHING; LISTING; FIELD GUIDE; OPTI-
CAL EQUIPMENT.

ILLUSTRATION (of birdlife). Defined here as the depiction of birdlife
for its own sake—in an attempt to distinguish ornithological painting from
birds that appear for a variety of reasons in works in the mainstream of the
classical painting tradition (see HUMAN CULTURE) and also from symbolic
depictions, e.g., the thunderbird/eagles, painted for eons by native Americans (see IMAGINATION). The unfortunate but inevitable implication of
this definition is that paintings of birds (i.e., *about* birds) can never aspire
to be more than minor works of art. For a fascinating tour—but no convincing way out—of this labyrinthine problem, compare Sutton (1962),
Eckelberry (1963), and Mengel (1980).

Leaving "What is art?" "Why won't curators hang Fuertes next to
Matisse?" and other vexed questions to these three articulate bird painters—artists all—it may yet be possible in the limited space afforded here to
suggest an approach to evaluating the qualities to be found in "bird art," a
genre that has never been more popular. We might begin by examining
the abilities and probable intentions of the artist-craftsman. Some men
(women are as scarce in bird painting as in classical painting) learn to draw
birds out of devotion to their subject matter, knowing and caring little
about "art" and acquiring only as much knowledge of light, composition,
draftsmanship, and atmospherics as is necessary to produce a comment
such as: "Now *that's* a Blue Jay!" or "Why, you can see every feather!"
Many such "bird artists" produce admirable—often much prized—work,
which, however, does not aspire to be more than a "lifelike" and decorative depiction of an attractive animal. Other men are artists *first*—
schooled in the traditions and techniques of painting—but also have a
deep understanding of the natural world and are committed to using their
gifts and experience to express their acute perceptions.

The line just drawn is not a sharp one. Any trained artist who sets out
to make a living painting birds will invariably spend at least his early years
doing illustrations, which, because of their purpose (field identification,
scientific description), allow for little interpretation. Such work cannot be
expected to show an artist's depth or range no matter how fine his sensibi-
lities or sophisticated his technique. Contrariwise, the most talented of
bird portraitists sometimes produce works of some depth and subtlety out
of fortuitous combining of raw talent and their feeling for their subject. As
a general guideline, however, we can expect even the most straightforward
field sketches of the artist-who-paints-birds to contain a difficult-to-define
quality (artistic imagination? aesthetic insight?) that is usually lacking in
the grandest, most colorful designs of the bird painter.

Sadly, the public, and particularly the American public, is severely
handicapped in its ability to develop any subtle discernment regarding bird

painting. The best bird guides and the most magnificent of illustrated monographs can show only one aspect of an artist's ability and very little of his "vision." The sentimental animal prints now hawked in airports and in nature magazines at exorbitant prices do little to educate the public taste. And the most expressive works of our best natural history artists are mostly sealed from our view in the homes of the few who can afford to buy them as originals, because, justly or not, few art museums will hang a painting of a bird even alongside a minor artist in a mainstream tradition. So what we see in infinite succession are bird portraits, some very fine, many incompetent or excruciatingly dull, but all of them too limited in concept truly to measure up to the term "bird art." Some hint of what we are missing appears in the examples of Bruno Liljefors' work reproduced in the September 1978 issue of *Audubon* magazine, in some of Robert Verrity Clem's plates for *The Shorebirds of North America* (1967), and in Charles Tunnicliffe's *A Sketchbook of Birds* (1979). The student of bird painting is encouraged to seek out these exemplary and accessible sources, and no aficionado of *American* bird painting can attempt to say an authoritative word without a thorough knowledge of the work of: John James AUDUBON (still in some respects the greatest), Major Allan Brooks, Mark CATESBY (the first), Robert Verrity Clem, John Henry Dick, Don R. Eckelberry, Louis Agassiz FUERTES (the father of modern bird painting), A. E. Gilbert, Francis Lee Jaques (pronounced Jakes), J. Fenwick Lansdowne; Robert M. Mengel, Roger Tory Peterson, Terry M. Shortt, Arthur Singer, George Miksch Sutton, Guy Tudor, and Alexander WILSON. The list is far from complete and no slight is intended in the omission of many artists (especially young ones) whose reputation is not yet the equal of their talent. The work of some of the men noted above may be continually before you in the form of their popular field guide illustrations; however, see also the finely illustrated volumes noted in the Bibliography under STATE/PROVINCIAL BOOKS and BIRD. Some less well-known examples of bird illustration are noted in the Bibliography for this entry, which also contains sources on the history of bird art from cave painting to illuminated manuscripts, to early woodcuts, to Audubon, to the modern era—for which there is no room here.

IMAGINATION, BIRDS IN. An astonishing variety of fanciful bird imagery permeates human culture. It has occurred throughout our history and crops up in almost all societies, both primitive and modern. And it enlivens human endeavors from the most frivolous amusements to practical matters of daily life to the most solemn rituals. On the whole, this imagery owes very little to ornithological truth; rather its integrity tends to lie in ancient cultural traditions, and this in turn explains why it is impossible to make clear-cut distinctions between the bird images we find in religion, mythology, fairy tales, heraldry, superstition, and so forth. Often they all have their roots in man's primordial striving to explain his world and his touching need to invest his surroundings with a complex animism.

PRIMITIVE BELIEFS AND RITUALS. When we can't perceive the reason for something, we tend to attribute it to some force or power which is "supernatural" or at least more powerful than ourselves. Often, we also try to associate it with things we *do* know that seem to have some connection. Birds lend themselves very well to association with the supernatural. We have watched them soar out of sight into the "heavens" or "space" or "never-never land." They live in ways which until very recently were mysterious to us—disappearing (or perhaps transforming themselves) for parts of the year. And both their physical and behavioral characteristics—seemingly as varied as human personalities—beg to be invested with the animism—the "souls"—which we long to give them.

The Great Spirit is thought of among many native American tribes as a "sky father" or as being embodied in the sun, both of which lend themselves to strong association with birds, especially powerful, high-soaring species such as eagles. A more concrete figure among Amerinds is a hero of sorts commonly referred to as a "trickster." He is usually the creator of the universe and of people and acts as their protector, but he is also the source of great mischief, such as bringing on the flood and inventing death. For the Indians of the northwest coast, this being was embodied in Yetl, the raven (or, rarely, crow), which would seem logical in many cultures since the "tricky" or "clever" nature of corvids is well known wherever they occur. For many northeastern tribes, the Gray Jay or "wiskedjak" was the trickster's animal form.

The best-known of North American bird spirits is the thunderbird, which occurs in the beliefs of tribes virtually throughout the continent. He is seen as the embodiment of the life force, which engages in continuous battle with a man-eating serpent. The thunderbird is therefore the protector of humanity and also the guardian of fire, and, like those other thunderers, Zeus and Thor, he is also the spirit of war.

The Micmacs and other tribes of northeastern North America have a legend of a huge bird which once made great winds with its wings so that the people could not venture onto the sea to catch food. A young brave discovers the source of the trouble and contrives to break the bird's wing "by accident." This results in a total lack of wind, which brings on the stagnation of the ocean, a fate as bad as the original one. Finally, the people fix the broken wing and, when the great bird has healed, set it free but exhort it to flap more gently.

A common means of exhorting or appeasing powerful bird deities is to dance, adorned, in the case of the thunderbird, in eagle feathers and imitating many of that bird's mannerisms.

Courtship dances in many "primitive" cultures throughout the world also have strong avian themes. In New Guinea and elsewhere brilliant feathers may be worn—as they are by the birds themselves—to attract a mate and in some instances the elaborate courtship rituals of birds such as cranes are mimed by their human counterparts.

RELIGION. With the development of civilization, animal deities are gradually replaced by gods with human forms. The early Egyptians believed that the figures in their pantheon were originally animals but evolved human bodies over time. Therefore, these gods are usually represented with human bodies and the heads of particular sacred animals. Ra, one of Egypt's chief deities, the great god of the sun, often appears with a falcon's head, as does Horus, another sun god. The Sacred Ibis (*Threskiornis aethiopicus*) was the animal of Thoth, the time measurer and inventor of numbers—hence the god of wisdom and magic (also the moon god)—and Thoth appears in hieroglyphs and paintings with the head of an ibis.

The deities of classical Greece and Rome are even more fully evolved into (idealized) human form, and most of the bird-man creatures (e.g., the Harpies) as well as assorted monsters with some bird features (e.g., the Griffin) principally appear in more secular mythical contexts (see below). However, Pallas Athene, one of the most important of the Greek deities, was associated with the owl (*Athene* is used as the name of a genus of Old World owls) and is sometimes represented as winged, as is her daughter Nike, the goddess of victory, portrayed in the famous statue Nike of Samothrace (c. 200 B.C.). Like the thunderbird, Athene is associated with thunder and lightning and war, but was also the goddess of wisdom and the protector of cities.

The major Greek and Roman gods would on occasion transform themselves into animals, as Zeus did when he visited Leda, queen of Sparta, in the guise of a swan. As a result of these avian attentions, Leda bore two eggs, one of which hatched into Helen and the other into Castor and Pollux. The classical tradition is also full of people or lesser gods being transformed into birds or other animals (see *Myth*, below).

Among the "modern" religions widely practiced today, the main holy figures have human forms, but there is a sharp divergence in the perception of the relationship between humans and the other animals. In Islam (Mohammedanism), Judaism, and Christianity, man is seen as a superior being made in the image of the one true God. Birds and other animals are therefore traditionally held in rather low esteem—at best thought to have been created for man's benefit—among believers and do not appear with any prominence in the religious literature. Of the more than 400 bird species known in modern Israel, only 40 are mentioned in the Bible, of which about half are noted in Leviticus and Deuteronomy as "unclean." In this light it is perhaps not surprising that in Islamic, Judaic, and Christian countries, birds which are not proscribed as food have been recklessly destroyed, though conservation efforts have stemmed this cultural tradition in North America and Western Europe.

By contrast, the Oriental Hindu and Buddhist traditions espouse reverence for all life and consider human life simply a part (and a very transitory one) of a living whole. As a result of this less anthropocentric tradition, wild birds in India exist unmolested alongside burgeoning cities and villages, many of whose people are in need of edible protein but will not sacrifice the life of a fellow creature to get it. Certain birds, e.g., cranes, are objects of particular reverence throughout most of Asia. The Hindu-Buddhist tradition holds that we pass through a series of lives, in each of which we learn something of value to guide us ultimately to the blissful non-existence called nirvana in Sanskrit. For example, a soul might pass through one life as a falconer, the next as a falcon, and the next as a teal, each experience adding a measure of enlightenment.

There is one prominent vestige of the superhuman bird-man tradition in Judeo-Christian belief, namely, the angels. These are normally thought of as beautiful "winged creatures" rather than "part bird," which would be considered an unsatisfactory description of God's messengers. Nevertheless, their wings are always painted and described as bird-like—rather than butterfly-like, for example—and the feature seems to inspire artistic invention. The upper-echelon angels in Milton's *Paradise Lost* are given multiple sets of wings of many gorgeous colors, and angels' wings in ecclesiastical painting (see, for example, the angel in Fra Angelico's Annunciation fresco in the monastery of San Marco in Florence) are also often spectacular, doubtless reflecting (at least in part) the artists' perception of the beauty of birds' wings.

In addition to angels, the Bible contains a few bird images of note. In Genesis, Noah sends a raven, a kingfisher, and a dove to look for the land which would signal the subsiding of the waters and God's wrath. The last returned with an olive branch from the top of Mount Ararat. An English tradition says that the (Eurasian) kingfisher flew high into the sky, thus acquiring its blue back, and too near the sun, thus "scorching" its breast, and for its foolishness Noah made it stay out on the roof of the ark and catch its food from the water.

Other bird species, while not specifically mentioned in the Bible, have come to be symbolic of certain biblical themes and often appear as such in ecclesiastical painting: the (Eurasian) Goldfinch, because of its association with thistle (= thorns), came to stand for the Passion of Christ; doves represent purity as well as peace and are therefore often depicted in the company of the Virgin; the eagle is a symbol of the Resurrection as well as the personal sign of St. John the evangelist; the pelican is sometimes associated with Christ because of the erroneous notion that it can feed its young with blood from its own breast. A number of species, e.g., the Barn Swallow, have traditionally been credited with trying to ease

Christ's suffering by pulling thorns from the Crown or nails from the Cross, drawing blood from their own breasts in the process; and the peculiar mandibles of the crossbills have also been attributed to the pulling of crucifixion nails.

MYTH. Though religions invariably take their substance from a body of myths, myths are also generated in secular contexts, though the line between religious and secular myth is often hard to draw. The thunderbird is both an attempt to explain inscrutable natural phenomena (thunder is a huge eagle flapping its wings) and a deity which influences the fate of humanity. As has been shown, these mythical forces appear under different names again and again throughout time and all over the world in religious ritual, and the same is true of secular myths. An enormous bird of prey, usually with gorgeous plumage, has been associated for ages with the workings of the heavens, especially the movements of the sun. The first of these to achieve mythical prominence was the Garuda, the bearer of the Hindu sun god Vishnu; it became known by different names throughout Asia and was believed to feed on elephants, among other prey. The Simurgh, a similar creature of Persia, also shared behavioral traits (e.g., elephant eating) with the Rukh (Roc). And the fire-bird tradition has its most splendid culmination in the storied Phoenix and its Chinese incarnation, the Fung-whang, which is a popular motif in Chinese and Japanese art.

The best-known mythical birds are further described under PHOENIX, ROC, GRIFFIN, and HALCYON, and those which are important in religious myth are discussed above. A few other bird myths are briefly accounted for below:

Harpies. Literally "snatchers" (Greek); originally wind or death spirits (*Odyssey*) but evolving into loathsome, predatory birds, with the faces of ugly women, which figure malevolently in the saga of the Argonauts, etc. The world's largest raptor, the Harpy Eagle (*Harpia harpyja*), takes its names from this myth.

Sirens. Creatures from Greek mythology, not unlike the Harpies. Sometimes depicted as birds with narrow heads, or women with birds' legs and/or wings. Two or three of this species were supposed to live on an island between that of Circe and the rock of Scylla (*Odyssey*) in the Strait of Messina and to have lured sailors to their death by their sweet songs. Odysseus (warned by Circe) foiled them by having his men plug their ears with wax. Orpheus saved the Argonauts from them by singing more beautifully than they.

Stymphalian Birds. The sixth labor of Hercules was to rid marshlands at Arkadian Stymphalos of man-eating birds, part eagle, part stork, which had lethal arrow-like feathers. This he did by banging brass cymbals supplied by Athene (see above) which flushed the birds, enabling him to shoot them. (Compare control methods under PESTS.) The Stymphalian birds may have been a metaphor for pestilence thought to emanate from stagnant marshland.

The Tengus. Mischievous creatures, half man, half eagle, with long red bills and eyes like lightning, still familiar in Japanese legend. The tengus are the protectors of all remote and lonely places on earth and delight in promoting war. They dance to the music of the thunder and are extremely skillful with weapons, a talent they occasionally teach to a human captive. Originally considered the natural enemies of Buddhism, tengus were said to transform themselves into priests and to play other tricks in order to thwart Buddha's pacifist ideals.

Quetzalcoatl. The feathered serpent, a widespread figure in Middle American pre-Columbian mythology, originating with the Toltecs of Mexico. He discovered corn, art, science, and the calendar and was symbolized in Aztec and Mayan rituals by the wearing of the long plumes of the Resplendent Quetzal (*Pharomachrus mocinno*). To their everlasting grief, the Aztecs at first confused the Spanish conquistadors with the predicted return of the power of this benign figure.

The Caladrius. An avian phenomenon of the Middle Ages, the caladrius was said to be totally white and capable of predicting whether a sick person would live or die. Faced with the patient, the bird would turn its back on him/her if doomed, but if curable would take the disease on itself, fly up to the sun, and vomit the poison forth. White (1954) notes the similarity of this name with the current plover genus *Charadrius*, but also that the species, or even family, of this useful bird seems always to have been vague. This leads us to speculate that a caladrius may have been an albino of any (or many) species. The birds were apparently sought out in shops for diagnostic purposes. Unless the shopkeeper demanded money down, the customer would find out which bird was the caladrius, obtain his diagnosis, and walk out without having made a purchase.

FOLKLORE AND SUPERSTITION. As we have seen, many fanciful ideas about birds have arisen out of attempts to understand natural phenomena, whether as awesome as creation and the sun or as relatively mundane (though crucial) as crop fertility. Because birds have been known for ages as having seasonal comings and goings among peoples of the Temperate Zone, because many species adapted well and quickly to human agricultural practices, and because they seemed to embody "sky powers," birds have always been a source of various degrees of folk wisdom. Some was truly observed and retains validity to this day, while the rest has proven to be wholly imaginary. It is instructive that the lore of uneducated, simple rural "folk" has often been closer to fact than the elaborate divinations and "scientific" hypotheses of more sophisticated thinkers. A sampling of bird beliefs both wise and wonderfully inaccurate follows:

Predicting the future by observing birdlife is a fixture in many primitive traditions and was an accepted branch of science/magic (ornitho-

mancy) in classical times. An augur divided the sky into four quadrants
and would then predict, say, the outcome of a battle based on how many
birds of what species appeared in the different quadrants and what they
were doing. Reading other bird signs was simply a matter of common
sense, as when Shakespeare's Cassius notes that the eagles which had followed his legions and fed from his soldiers' hands had been replaced on
the eve of the confrontation at Philippi by ravens, crows, and kites which
"downward look on us, as we were sickly prey" (*Julius Caesar,* Act V,
Scene I). In Western cultures, older people may still remember telling fortunes by seeing a number of crows or other birds and repeating the rhyme:
"One for sorrow, two for mirth, three for a wedding, four for a birth." A
more specific superstition holds that upon hearing the first call of the dove
in spring, you will find a hair the color of your future mate's if you step
back three paces.

Similarly complex divination rituals involving particular species of
birds and their actions are still practiced locally in Southeast Asia. And
some of our common superstitions involving birds are predictive (see
below).

Certain types of birds have long been associated with forces of good
and evil, especially the latter. Owls are still widely believed to presage
death or disaster. And ravens, crows, jays, and magpies are also associated
frequently with misfortune or mischief. Owl and raven gods have the most
ancient lineage (see *Primitive Beliefs and Rituals,* above); both owls and corvids seem to embody more human-like spirits than most birds; and owls'
nocturnal habits and the blackness of ravens and crows doubtless contribute to their bad reputations.

Similarly, luck or the lack of it is perceived in the presence, actions, or
numbers of birds. A bird (like a black cat) crossing one's path to the left or
right is lucky or unlucky depending on the bent of one's superstition. It's
good luck to see a red bird (Northern Cardinal) fly up, bad luck if it flies
down. Wrens nesting near a house are good luck. It's bad luck to break a
bird's egg (or to bring eggs into the house after sunset), but good luck to
break off the larger piece of a wishbone. Owls hooting in the daytime (or
any time) are bad luck; to drive away a Screech Owl, take off your right
shoe and turn it upside down. A bird flying against a house is an ill omen.
Putting salt on a bird's tail is lucky (!) as well as a means of catching it.
The first bluebird of spring is lucky and three birds flying in a line is good
for business. If you wish for luck when you see three birds on a wire, it will
come true if the birds don't fly away; a similar advantage is attached to
throwing three kisses to the first robin of spring.

Particular birds have long been thought to influence or at least predict the weather and seasons. Farming activities have been scheduled to
coincide with the return of certain birds from their wintering grounds and
of course the notion has considerable validity because of the rather precise

timing of migratory movements (see MIGRATION); geese, cranes, and swallows were especially useful in this way.

A number of North American species have been known as "rain birds." The word "plover" and the plover genus *Pluvialis* both imply a connection (now inscrutable) with rain. The Red-throated and other loons are known as "rain geese" in cultures as disparate as those of the Indians of the northwestern U.S. and Scottish Highlanders: both contend these birds are especially noisy before a rain. Black-billed and Yellow-billed Cuckoos are said to do the same and are widely known therefore as "rain crows." Swallows feeding low are said to precede rain. There is nothing intrinsically suspicious in these observations as long as one sorts out proper cause and effect. No doubt swallows often do fly low preceding a storm, reflecting the movement of aerial insects out of the wet or turbulent upper air. Most rain birds seem to make their "predictions" as the impending weather change has become only too clear.

Fertility, both human and agricultural, has also been associated with birds. Cranes, for example, are thought by some to be good for crops, while dangling and waving a bird or image thereof over the belly of a barren woman is only one of a number of bizarre solutions which have evolved to rectify that situation.

That spirits of human dead inhabit the bodies of birds is another venerable folk belief, stemming no doubt from birds' ethereal qualities, their association with the heavens, and their great variety. Some cultures believe that all or most birds serve this purpose, while others think it to be true of only particular species. It is a common maritime tradition that storm-petrels represent the souls of drowned seamen.

The notion that nightjars suck the teats of goats or other milk-giving domestic animals was accepted as fact by Aristotle and has persisted in rural areas to the present. The teats are said to whiten and the animal to gradually waste away when visited by a Whip-poor-will or other bird in this family. This superstition is utterly without foundation, and except for the nocturnal habits and generally odd appearance of nightjars, it is hard to imagine what can have lent this belief credence for so long; perhaps it is thought too strange not to be true.

SYMBOL. In addition to evoking certain powers, events, or particular figures in religion, folklore, and art, birds have also been widely used as concrete symbols, as in the heraldry of a family or nation, and this custom often relies on the perceived characters of certain species. The eagle is the favorite symbol of nations wishing to project an image of both nobility and might.

Symbols are by nature superficial and rely on appearance and inference rather than fact. Benjamin Franklin's naïve suggestion that we adopt the Wild Turkey—a beautiful, gentle species which stands for plenty rather than war—as our national emblem would never have been approved by the Congress in any era. The Bald Eagle, by contrast, is an ideal national bird, as long as we are careful to overlook the fact that it is fond of carrion and that we very nearly accomplished its extermination by the indiscriminate use of DDT.

FANTASY. Encouraged by all the traditions sketched above and the seemingly endless and often bizarre variations in bird form, inventors of tales have created fanciful avifaunas of their own, related in some cases to recognizable legendary birds or wholly produced out of the mind of the human creator. These tale makers have been so prolific that it is impossible to give a concise account which conveys the richness of make-believe birdlife in the various languages. Talking birds, birds which come to the aid of princes, birds which cause trouble, birds which lay golden eggs, the Simurgh-like Nunda in Swahili tales, the witty storks of Aesop, the vain crow of La Fontaine, Andersen's storks, the Grimm brothers' *Fundvogel*, Disney's Donald Duck, Hitchcock's avian uprising, *Sesame Street*'s Big Bird, and Snoopy's feathered pal Woodstock—these and the rest of their kind probably make up a fanciful class of animal life with more forms and of greater taxonomic complexity than the world's actual current avifauna of 8,600 species.

See also HUMAN CULTURE.

IMMATURE. Not fully adult, either generally or in some specific aspect of development. Some species of birds, for example, may acquire adult plumage while they are still sexually immature. Used in field guides to describe the plumage or plumages between juvenile and adult plumage. Because plumage sequence varies widely among species, it is not a very precise term and is often misused by birdwatchers to refer to any individual bird not in "full breeding plumage." See PLUMAGE; MOLT.

IMPING. Chiefly a method of mending damaged flight feathers, especially in birds of prey. The technique was first developed among falconers and involved the use of metal pins (imping needles) on which a broken feather could be rejoined. Today, imping is used not only by falconers but by animal care specialists to rehabilitate a wide range of damaged birds.

In the modern method, the base of the feather shaft (calamus) remaining attached to the bird is cleanly cut and glue placed in the hollow center. A replacement feather (perhaps taken from a dead individual of the same species) is cut to the right length and its sharpened end inserted into the glue-filled hollow of the basal section.

Imping has also been used as a marking technique; dyed feathers have been imped into the tails of ducks, for example, so that they can be identified on sight. See MARKING.

IMPRINTING. A form of rapid learning which occurs soon after hatching, during which a bird normally attaches its own identity to that of the parent birds. In abnormal or experimental situations, chicks may attach

themselves to the wrong species, humans, or even inanimate objects. See
INTELLIGENCE, *Instinct* and *Learning.*

INCERTAE SEDIS. Literally, "doubtful place"; a Latin taxonomic term
applied to a form of uncertain phylogeny. The Yellow-breasted Chat (*Icteria virens*) is traditionally placed among the wood warblers (family Parulidae), but it is untypical of that family in many ways, and a taxonomic
checklist might list it at the end of the wood warblers under the heading
"Incertae Sedis." The term is also applied to higher taxa (genera, families,
etc.). See TAXONOMY.

INCUBATION. The embryos of birds are "warm-blooded" and therefore, once they leave their mother's body, they must still be kept at a constant, relatively high temperature (see below)—unlike the eggs of insects,
for example, or amphibians, which are laid in a suitable site and left to
mature on their own. The term for this egg-warming process is "incubation." Except for the "ingenious" megapodes (see below), and brood parasites such as cowbirds, which let other birds incubate their eggs for them,
all bird species keep their own eggs at the proper temperature by covering
them in such a way that their body heat is transferred more or less directly
to the developing embryo. On occasion (e.g., early in the egg-laying period) birds will "sit on" (cover) their eggs but not apply full body heat; this
is not true incubation.

 PHYSICAL PREPARATION. As with copulation, nest building, and food
gathering, the instinct to incubate is initiated by hormonal changes triggered by external stimuli (e.g., increased daylight) associated with the
onset of the breeding season—and by specific behavior "releasers" (see IN-
TELLIGENCE), such as the appearance and "feel" of the actual eggs. The
most significant physiological adaptation to incubation is the development
of a *brood patch* (incubation patch)—an area (or up to three adjacent
areas) at the center of a bird's abdomen in which the skin becomes slightly
thickened and the tissue markedly vascularized (density of blood vessels
increases) and generally more edematous (filled with fluid), allowing more
body warmth to pass directly to the embryos. The region where the brood
patch develops—the midventral apteria (see FEATHER TRACTS)—is normally relatively free of feathers year-round, but any down which normally
occurs there in some species and perhaps some marginal contour feathers
are shed with the development of the patch (see BROOD PATCH for further
specifics). A few birds, notably members of the order Pelecaniformes (pelicans, boobies and gannets, cormorants, etc.), ratites, and some alcids do
not develop brood patches, and it has been suggested (Tucker, 1943) that
gannets compensate for this lack by applying their large webbed feet to the
eggs.

 Both male and female birds may develop brood patches, though this
varies from species to species. While it would satisfy our sense of logic to

find that males or females which develop patches incubate and those which don't, don't, Skutch (1957) presents evidence that this is far from the case, at least among passerines: males without patches are known to incubate in some cases, whereas some *with* patches do not!

Although this incubation patch is widely called a brood patch and the patch does remain while nestlings are being brooded, it is clear that its greatest development coincides with the incubation period, after which the tissue involved returns to normal.

TIMING. The incubation period is usually timed from the laying of the last egg in a clutch to the hatching of that same egg (usually, but not always, the last to hatch) (Nice, 1954), though this method of measurement is considered less than ideal when precise heat transfer/development rate data are wanted (Kendeigh, 1963).

The incubation period varies widely—from 80 or more days (the largest albatrosses) to as little as 10.5 days recorded for some small passerines—the period for most of the latter is under 16 days. The Black-footed Albatross has the longest incubation period of any "North American" species (to 67 days); many native passerines incubate for as little as 11 days. The time required for incubation is subject to many variables, but a few broad generalities have been hazarded:

• Larger species, even within the same families, tend to have longer incubation periods.

• Cavity nesters tend to have longer incubation periods than species which nest in the open.

• Fully altricial species (see YOUNG, DEVELOPMENT OF) tend to have shorter incubation periods than other (semi-altricial, precocial) types, correlated with the fact that they are less developed at hatching.

The onset of true incubation is also variable. It may begin after the first egg is laid or not until several days after the last egg is laid; the norm lies in between. In most cases incubation begins with the completion of the clutch.

Some birds (e.g., pigeons) seem to have an innate sense of the "correct" length of the incubation period and will stop sitting if the eggs do not hatch on schedule. However, Skutch (1962) has shown that birds in a wide range of families will incubate for twice the normal period (on average) in an effort to hatch defective eggs.

The percentage of the total incubation period during which the eggs are covered is another variable, but comes to between 60 and 80 percent in most birds. The rhythm of coverage often changes according to atmospheric conditions, since eggs can be left more often or for longer periods when the ambient temperature is high; birds tend to sit tighter and more continuously at night and in bad weather. At least in some birds, the incubation period decreases as the season advances, possibly due to warmer air temperatures.

INCUBATION BEHAVIOR. As noted, the principal duty of an incubating parent is to keep the developing embryos at a constant temperature. The "proper" temperature for the majority (about 75 percent) has proven to be 35° C. (95° F.) (Irving and Krog, 1956), i.e., slightly lower than the body temperature of the parent bird (see TEMPERATURE, BODY).

We tend to think of incubation as a warming process, but especially with nests in the open in warm climates, shading the eggs is also crucial. It has been shown that in general embryos are much better able to withstand extremes of cold than of heat.

In addition to sitting, parent birds of most species turn their eggs regularly—in some cases several (up to eleven) times an hour. The internal structure of the egg is so "designed" that no matter how many times the egg is turned, the embryo remains uppermost (see EMBRYO and Fig. 8).

Sitting birds usually do a fair amount of fidgeting while in the nest—adjusting their posture, shaking their feathers, picking at their nest, and in dense colonies taking a poke at a neighboring bird. "Off-duty" birds behave much as they do at other seasons—feeding, sleeping, etc. Males sing enthusiastically during this period and many continue certain "programmed" rituals of courtship, such as bringing nesting material or food to the sitting mate. As would seem prudent, incubating birds are normally silent; however, grosbeaks, vireos, and other species not infrequently sing their version of "The Incubation Blues" while on the nest.

A very few species cover their eggs when leaving the nest: ducks and other anatids with down, grebes with the wet vegetation of their nests, and one species of *Charadrius* plover with sand. Obviously this provides a measure of concealment and helps keep the eggs at a constant temperature.

DIVISION OF LABOR AND WORK RHYTHM. Bird species have evolved virtually all possible variations in the manner in which they discharge their incubation duties. One analysis (Van Tyne and Berger, 1976–ORNITHOLOGY) based on the available data shows that on a worldwide basis male and female birds share incubation in 54 percent of species; the female alone incubates in 25 percent; the male alone in 6 percent; and it varies between male, female, and both in about 15 percent of species. However, Pettingill (1970–ORNITHOLOGY) states that among North American species "incubation by the female alone is far commoner than incubation shared by both sexes."

When incubation is shared, the parents may switch off relatively frequently (several times a day) or do long stints (to several days—e.g., many tubenoses). Often the schedule is on some form of day shift/night shift basis.

When only a single parent incubates, it may remain on the nest almost continuously—fasting or being fed by the partner; or take fairly long recesses to feed, etc., at fairly long intervals; or take a great number of shorter recesses. It stands to reason that eggs attended by both parents would get better coverage than those attended by a single parent, would therefore hatch faster, and perhaps aid species survivability—but once again nature sets reason on its ear. Skutch (1962) showed that some species in which both parents incubate spend *less* total time on the eggs than others in which only one parent does. He concluded that the number of incubators bears little if any intrinsic relationship to breeding success.

The above is by no means a complete analysis of incubation rhythms. Among Sanderlings, only one parent incubates a given clutch—but it may be either one (Parmelee, 1970). Some *Alectoris* partridges (including the Chukar) sometimes incubate two nests simultaneously, the male sitting on one, the female on the other. The eggs laid by a single Bushtit may be incubated by other adult Bushtits in addition to the parents. And anis and Acorn Woodpeckers have communal nests with a number of females laying and a number of adults (male and female) sharing incubation.

For a schematic outline of the various incubation patterns, see Skutch (1957) or Van Tyne and Berger (1976–ORNITHOLOGY, pp. 492–93: same but with additions).

THE MEGAPODE METHOD. The superficially chicken-like members of the Australasian/Polynesian family Megapodiidae (megapodes, Mallee Fowl, Brush Turkeys, etc.) bury their eggs in the warm ash of active volcanoes or sun-warmed sand or sizable mounds of decaying vegetation and avoid the ennui of sitting on eggs altogether. The adults gauge the incubation temperature—apparently with their ultra-sensitive tongues (!)—and make adjustments by airing the fermenting plant material when it is too hot and building up more insulation or allowing more sun exposure when the air becomes cooler.

For related aspects of the nesting period, see NEST; EMBRYO; YOUNG, DEVELOPMENT OF.

INCUBATION PATCH. Same as BROOD PATCH.

INCURSION. Sometimes used as a synonym for IRRUPTION, e.g., an "incursion" of Great Gray Owls.

INDIVIDUAL VARIATION. Differences which may occur between two members of the same population of a given species, as opposed to racial or geographical variation in which whole populations or many populations share common differences which distinguish them from other populations. Individual variation is crucial to the biological selection process. Variations which help an individual survive tend to perpetuate themselves, as they give advantage to one successful generation after another. Variations which are detrimental to an individual's survival tend to be "selected out" because of the disadvantaged individual's diminished capacity to reproduce itself. See SPECIATION.

INGLUVIES (in-GLOO-veez). The crop. See DIGESTIVE SYSTEM.

INJURY FEIGNING. See DISPLAY, *Distraction Display*.

INSECTIVOROUS (IN-sek-TIV-er-uss). Insect-eating; feeding mainly on insects. Not surprisingly, most flycatchers are largely insectivorous; hummingbirds and kestrels are partially insectivorous.

INSTINCT. A very broad, general term, used in non-technical contexts to describe behavior which is inherited, rather than learned by an individual bird or other organism. For relevance to birdlife, see INTELLIGENCE.

INSTRUMENTAL SOUNDS. Non-vocal sounds, such as bill noises. For a breakdown of those made by North American birds, see SONG.

INTELLIGENCE. Terms such as "booby," "dodo," and "birdbrain" carry the unmistakable implication that birds are not very smart. And by human standards this is indeed true. If we define intelligence as the ability to understand, to reason, to make deductions from apparent facts, to use symbols and deal in abstractions, it is very clear that birds have none at all. On the other hand, birds are highly perceptive of sights and sounds and can be trained to act "cleverly" by learning to perform fairly complex tasks in response to fairly subtle stimuli. A famous series of experiments (Kohler, 1950) has demonstrated, for example, that birds can be trained to recognize numbers in the form of differently shaped dots, flashes of light, a series of sounds, or even a combination of flashes and sounds—but also that they never learn that there is any natural relationship between numbers, e.g., that 4 is more than 3.

Because we tend to view a bird's world using our own brains, and because birds often seem "alert" or "curious"—qualities we associate with intelligence—we often mistake mechanical reactions based on instinct or "rote" learning experiences for deductive reasoning.

INSTINCT. Almost everything a bird does is "programmed," so to speak, into the genes it inherited from its parents. Its behavior throughout its life is essentially a combination of innate abilities (e.g., the ability to fly) and a series of unchanging, highly predictable responses to objects and events. For some reason the former is easier for us to accept than the latter. We take it for granted that when birds reach a certain age they know "automatically" how to fly. But when we see young birds with their mouths open and cheeping at the approach of a parent bird, which proceeds to stuff some food into one or more mouths, we explain the scene in human terms: "the children are hungry; they recognize their beloved parents; they cry and beg for food and the solicitous parents give them what they want."

The behaviorist's version of this domestic scenario may not be as appealing, but he has proven it to be accurate. In another famous series of experiments, the Dutch ethologist Niko Tinbergen showed (1953) that Herring Gull chicks respond not to their parents but only to their bills, or rather to a long, thin object with a contrasting red spot pointing downward. Chicks which had never seen adult Herring Gulls responded to such objects, proving that the reaction is completely innate. When the chick sees the bill-like object, it "begs" and pecks at the red spot. When the parent bird is pecked on the bill it regurgitates food. No red spot—no pecking; no pecking—no food. Herring Gull chicks do not respond to blue bills nor would an adult respond to "unconventional" pleas for food, no matter how pathetic.

Such instinctual give-and-take is known in the behavior trade as *fixed action patterns*, and stimuli which, like a gull's red bill spot, provoke a predictable response are called *releasers*. F.A.P.'s and releasers are the very stuff of avian life—the genetic "programs," as it were, behind display, song, feeding, copulation, etc.—and serve in all the thousands of situations in which complex, constantly tormented humans would bring to bear emotion and reason. Not that birds are utterly will-less automatons. A female which is not stimulated to copulate, for example, will not behave in such a way as to "release" her potential mate's mounting instinct. But her lack of interest would not be the result of her "deciding" she was not in the mood. Nor would the male become "discouraged"; as long as his state of sexual readiness continued, he would respond energetically as soon as the right signals were received.

LEARNING. Authorities agree that birds are capable of adding to their instinctual behavior by a few limited kinds of learning. But it is often difficult to tell where innate abilities leave off and learned skills begin. This is not very surprising, since learning and innate ability are normally very closely associated in any complex task, but many such activities involving growing birds are particularly misleading to the human perception. Anyone who has watched young birds "learning" to fly assumes he is witnessing a textbook example of "practice makes perfect." However, captive young pigeons have been denied this practice, as well as the opportunity to watch other birds, and when they were of the age when their siblings were flying skillfully, they were released and found to do just as well. In other words, the clumsiness of juvenile birds may have more to do with immaturity of muscle coordination than with lack of experience. In similar situations we are encouraged to conclude that parents are "teaching" their young because we see an adult bird perform an activity which the juvenile bird duplicates. With study, however, this proves to be simply an example of the "following response" (see FLOCK), akin to the human propensity to yawn when others do.

Ambiguous cases to the contrary notwithstanding, certain forms of learning in birds have been convincingly identified, though whether they are functionally distinct or all part of a single faculty is still debated.

It has been proven that young birds begin to recognize calls of adults while still in the egg. Immediately after hatching, young birds become very strongly attached to the first moving object of a certain size which they see and hear. Normally this is one of the parent birds, and the fixation initiates the chicks into a sense of identity with their own species and leads them into their characteristic life patterns as exemplified by their parents. But if, instead of first seeing their parents, young birds are immediately exposed to a different bird species, a human, or even an inanimate object such as a box or a football, their attachment to such unlikely "parents" is no less ardent. If such chicks continue to be encouraged in their devotion to a football and are deprived of any contradictory learning experiences, they may develop a permanent attachment and even, as they mature, direct sexual behavior to the stand-in. This striking early learning pattern, made famous by Konrad Lorenz—who has often been photographed trailing a brood of devoted goslings—is called *imprinting*.

As young birds gain experience with age, they begin to distinguish shapes and actions which are harmless—e.g., leaves and their movements—from those which are threatening. This basic form of learning is technically known as *habituation* and is demonstrated very clearly by trained falcons or House Sparrows becoming relaxed among noisy, fast-moving humans, which most "wild" birds continue to fear.

A more active form of learning involves imitation of the behavior of adult birds and practice. Experiments have shown, for example, that, though born with an innate knowledge of their song, at least some species never learn to sing it correctly unless they hear it "properly" sung and try to repeat it (see SONG).

Birds also learn by *trial and error*—the ability, for example, to recognize and avoid eating certain kinds of caterpillars which once (or repeatedly) made them violently ill. This is a form of *conditioning*, which "rewards" an animal for doing the "right" thing and "punishes" it for doing the "wrong" thing, thereby forming habitual patterns of behavior.

Insight learning and tool use. Insight learning is, so to speak, the ability to put 2 and 2 together without any previous experience with 4. It is approached by the birds whose "counting" achievements are noted above; it *may* be exemplified in a gull's "figuring out" that dropping a clam on the street from aloft will result in a meal. Other evidence of the dawning of this kind of mentality in birds has been demonstrated in the lab (e.g., Pastore, 1954). If birds are, in fact, capable of insight learning, it is as close as they come to true intelligence.

Some of the most intriguing examples of apparent insight learning in birds involve the use of "tools" to obtain food. The best-publicized example of this is the practice among *some* African populations of Egyptian

Vultures of breaking Ostrich eggs by dropping rocks on them—well documented and photographed for *National Geographic* in 1969 by the van Lawick-Goodalls. Perhaps equally famous is the Woodpecker Finch, one of the *Geospiza* finches of the Galápagos Islands that helped inspire Darwin's theory of evolution. This bird habitually uses cactus thorns to probe for grubs burrowed in holes beyond the reach of its short finch bill. Other instances of tool use include the use of bark scales by Brown-headed Nuthatches to pry off other bits of bark under which invertebrate prey are expected (Morse, 1968); the tearing off of bits of newspaper by laboratory Blue Jays to rake food pellets into their cages (Jones and Kamil, 1973); and similar behavior in several families of Australian birds (see Green, 1972). Because these skills tend to be discovered and "taught" only among certain populations and because of the significance of the dawning of tool use in human evolution, it is tempting to jump to the conclusion that an unusually bright vulture or finch or jay had a brainstorm one day, thereby improving the "cultural" standard of its local population. However, as Alcock (1970) and others point out, the apparent "cleverness" of these birds more plausibly originates in accidents which result in strong positive reinforcement: the vulture, unable to pick up the huge Ostrich egg in its bill, picks up a nearby rock instead in a redirection of its frustration; on rare occasions the rock is dropped on the Ostrich egg, yielding a meal and conditioning the vulture to drop rocks on eggs. Similarly, a frustrated *Geospiza* finch may once have picked up a bit of nesting material, displacing its unavailing efforts to pull a grub from its hole; the nest stick probes the hole by accident, yielding a grub, and a Woodpecker Finch is born.

THE BIRD BRAIN. Though large in relation to body size compared to that of all other animals except mammals, the bird brain is developed differently from the brains of more "thoughtful" life forms. The cortex—that great wrinkly mass of "gray matter" which dominates the appearance of the human brain and is known to be the source of our subtler tricks of ratiocination—is only a smooth, thin, covering layer in birds. For early investigators, that pretty much settled the matter of avian intelligence. It has since been discovered, however, that a bird's "mind," such as it is, seems to originate in the relatively well-developed *corpus striatum*, which lies beneath the thin cortex. More specifically, avian intelligence seems to be located in a part of the corpus striatum called the *hyperstriatum* and learning centered in the bulge on the hyperstriatum called the *wulst*. For further comparison of the avian and human brains, see NERVOUS SYSTEM.

INTERNATIONAL COUNCIL FOR BIRD PRESERVATION (I.C.B.P.). The oldest international conservation organization in the world (founded 1922). Made up of ornithologists and environmentalists, the I.C.B.P. provides expertise on ornithological matters to governments and conservationist organizations worldwide, funds research and efforts to pro-

tect endangered bird species, promotes legal action to prevent wanton destruction of habitat, and disseminates information to the public. It has national sections in 65 countries. Its main headquarters are in Cambridge, England: 219C Huntingdon Road, CB3 ODL.

INTERNATIONAL ORNITHOLOGICAL CONGRESS (I.O.C.). An official gathering of ornithologists from all over the world held in a different city and country on each occasion, currently at intervals of four years. The first congress was held in Vienna in 1884 and the last (18th) in Moscow. The institution is governed by a committee of 100 members and each meeting is chaired by a distinguished ornithologist. Like other conventions, the I.O.C. serves social as well as professional functions. Papers are given (and later published in some form of *Proceedings*), ideas exchanged, job opportunities advertised, and field trips taken. Occasionally positions are taken on international ornithological issues.

INTRODUCED BIRDS. Defined here as birds which have been released intentionally by man in North America for a specific purpose and which have become established at least locally or temporarily. For the much larger number of species which have escaped from captivity or domestication and in some cases established "wild" populations, see EXOTIC SPECIES; ESCAPES; DOMESTICATED BIRDS.

Bird introductions are generally made for one of three reasons: for sport (upland game shooting); to correct some perceived flaw in the ecosystem; and as an aesthetic improvement.

So far, those responsible for pursuing any of these purposes have kept their narrow gaze fixed steadfastly on the benefits they believed would accrue from introducing non-native species and have for the most part ignored the possible detrimental consequences both to native birdlife and to man (see PESTS). Though some of the effects of introducing alien species have become obvious, the subject has not been studied in much detail.

INTRODUCTION FOR SPORT. A number of alien upland-game-bird species have been released in North America in an attempt to enliven the hunting "potential" of a township, state, or the country as a whole. In addition to importing species from other parts of the world, state and federal game authorities have transplanted native species such as the Sharp-tailed Grouse to other parts of the country. Most introductions fail to establish themselves because their new habitat lacks some essential characteristic of their native one. The following, however, have adapted well, and for the most part are able to maintain their population levels without further introductions. The exception to these generalities is the Common Pheasant, hundreds of thousands of which are raised annually for release in heavily hunted areas where the "native" (i.e., formerly introduced) population cannot sustain itself against the hunting pressure.

Species	Natural Range	Est. in North America
Plain Chachalaca *Ortalis vetula*	Rio Grande Valley, Texas, south to northern Nicaragua	Sapelo and Blackbeard Is., Georgia
Chukar *Alectoris chukar*	Rocky, arid areas, southeastern Europe through Middle East	Southern British Columbia through Great Basin to southern California and New Mexico
Black Francolin *Francolinus francolinus*	Central Asia through eastern India	Locally in Louisiana and Florida
Common Pheasant *Phasianus colchicus*	Ukraine through central Asia to southern China	Common and widespread esp. in farmland throughout much of the North Temperate Zone of North America; local in southern regions
Gray Partridge *Perdix perdix*	Most of Europe to central Siberia	Common to abundant locally in farmland, Nova Scotia to British Columbia south to northern California and Michigan

INTRODUCTION FOR ECOLOGICAL BENEFIT. Without doubt, the two most "successful" introduced birds in North America are the House (English) Sparrow and the Common (European) Starling. While the people who released these two avian pests on the continent found them pleasing birds, most of them also made great claims for the beneficial habits of the birds. The House Sparrow, which was introduced more than 100 times, mostly in the northeastern U.S. and Canada in the 1850's and 1860's, was, among other benefits, to save eastern shade trees from the ravages of the larvae of two species of geometer moths—the spring cankerworm (*Paleacrita vernata*) and the elm spanworm (*Ennomos subsignarius*). The sparrows did eat a lot of these inchworms in New York and Philadelphia, but they also apparently displaced the native bird species which normally checked the numbers of another pest, the white-marked tussock moth (*Hemerocampa leucostigma*). These moths rapidly increased to equal or surpass the ill effects achieved by the geometers. All of these lepidopterous pests are still with us, but to them has been added a much more pernicious destroyer of grain and fruit crops. Perhaps the most serious effect of the introduction of the House Sparrow, however, was the decline of a number of hole-nesting native bird species. House Wrens, Purple Martins, and Cliff Swallows, among others, were extirpated by the aggressive sparrows in some regions; and, though reduced from the plague proportions their populations reached around the turn of the century, they are still major competitors of hole-nesting birds. Needless to say, their aesthetic appeal has dwindled—even many fervent bird lovers revile them as the cockroaches of the avifauna. Their decrease is attributed to the passing of the horse as transportation, since they found a principal source of food in the undigested grain in "road apples." This decline can hardly be considered a defeat. The species is unquestionably the most widespread introduced bird in the world (domesticated species excepted), ranging virtually throughout the New World south of the Arctic, except for the Amazon Basin, and well established in Australia, New Zealand, and Asia as well as its native Europe. The House Sparrow shows clearly the multiple folly of introducing alien species: (1) They rarely (if ever) work the miraculous cures promised. (2) They are apt to produce an upset in the ecological balance which will cause more trouble than the original problem. (3) They may turn out to be agricultural pests themselves. (4) They are likely to compete with native species. These caveats apply to all introduced animal life, not just birds.

The Common Starling of Eurasia was introduced from the 1870's to about 1900, but not as often as the House Sparrow, nor did it spread as rapidly and widely. Its song and plumage, both once regarded as very fine, had more to do with the starling's introduction than those of the House Sparrow, but its alleged "value" in devouring legions of crop pests (beetle larvae, etc.) was also advertised. Alas, in North America about 50 percent of its diet consists of vegetable matter and, with the increase in its numbers, it has become a serious vineyard and orchard pest. Because starlings assemble for the night (after the breeding season) in prodigious roosts in cities and suburbs, the species surpasses the House Sparrow in two forms of pollution: noise and "guano." It is also a hole nester and, along with the House Sparrow, is a major nest-site competitor of the Eastern Bluebird. In the East, starlings are no longer seen in the massive flocks of fifty years ago, and it would appear that their populations have declined markedly after the initial "explosion" characteristic of introduced species freed for a time of limiting factors (see POPULATION). The causes of this apparent stabilization are not clear, but a combination of newly adapted ecological constraints is probably responsible. These did not take effect in time to slow the spread of the species westward, and the starling has now established strongholds across the entire continent north to Alaska and south to Baja California.

The Eurasian Tree Sparrow and Crested Mynah, close relatives of the House Sparrow and Common Starling, respectively, may also have been introduced at least partly with "beneficial" rationales. The former arrived in St. Louis in 1870 and the latter near Vancouver around 1897. Both are potential pests, but neither has increased (except initially) or spread very far.

Species	Natural Range	Est. in North America
Eurasian House Sparrow *Passer domesticus*	Europe, Asia, and North Africa	Virtually throughout to about 50° N. (sporadically north-ward), esp. near human habitation
Eurasian Tree Sparrow *Passer montanus*	Europe and most of Asia	St. Louis, Missouri, and adjacent Illinois
Common Starling *Sturnus vulgaris*	Europe, Asia, and North Africa	Throughout North America south of 50° N.
Crested Mynah *Acridotheres crista-tellus*	Widespread southern Asia	Vancouver, British Columbia, and vicinity

INTRODUCTION FOR AESTHETIC REASONS. One of the minor aberrations of Western civilization is the passion for introducing all the birds of the Bible, Shakespeare, or one's native land (usually England) onto some hapless distant shore. This damn-fool notion has attained its apogee in New Zealand, where 13 species native to Great Britain are now the dominant songbirds throughout the man-made agricultural habitats of that country, to the great detriment of the vastly more interesting native species. North Americans have largely been spared the effects of this whimsical presumption. Though hundreds (probably thousands) of attempts have been made to add "nice" species to the native avifauna, only a small population of Skylarks (*Alauda arvensis*, native throughout the Palearctic region south of the Arctic Circle) has become established—at the southern end of Vancouver Island, British Columbia. The Eurasian Goldfinch (*Carduelis carduelis*) may also have been widely introduced and was established briefly on Long Island, but no longer survives there.

There remain a few species which were introduced for a combination of reasons and might as well be called escapes, exotics, and/or domestic birds as introduced birds. However, since they were more or less deliberately "feralized," they are included here.

Species	Natural Range	Est. in North America
Mute Swan *Cygnus olor*	Throughout most of Eurasia	Southern New England and south along the coast to Chesapeake Bay, locally in Great Lakes
Rock Dove *Columba livia*	Britain, southern Europe, and North Africa to China	Throughout, near human habitation
Spotted Dove *Streptopelia chinensis*	Southeast Asia	Los Angeles and Orange counties, California
Ringed Turtle (Barbary) Dove *Streptopelia "risoria"*	An aviary-bred pale form of the African Collared or Pink-headed Dove (*S. roseogrisea*)	City of Los Angeles, California, and several Florida cities

Finally, two potential advantages of introduction should be mentioned. The *reintroduction* of native species such as the Wild Turkey and Peregrine Falcon into areas where they had been extirpated by hunting, habitat destruction, or other man-made phenomena has proven successful in some cases and may offer new hope for restoring native endangered species.

It has also been suggested that species endangered in undeveloped countries, where there is currently no control over habitat destruction or hunting, might be introduced into appropriate habitats elsewhere in the world, including North America, as an alternative to extinction. The rare Great Indian Bustard, for example, might be protected on a reserve in the southwestern U.S.

INVASION. Often used as a synonym for IRRUPTION, but perhaps more properly restricted to more or less permanent range extensions such as the recent "invasion" of North America by the Cattle Egret.

IRIDESCENCE. See COLOR AND PATTERN.

IRIS (pl.: irises or irides [EYE-ruh-deez]). The pigmented part of the eye surrounding the dark pupil; used as a field mark for some species of birds. The *yellow* iris of Bendire's Thrasher, for example, is helpful in distinguishing it from the similar Curve-billed Thrasher, which has an *orange* iris. It is, of course, the iris that is referred to in names such as Red-*eyed* Vireo. As a rule, juvenile birds have dark irises, which become more colorful or paler in some species as they mature.

For the function of the iris and more detail on eye color, see VISION.

IRRUPTION. An irregular movement of large numbers of birds following the breeding season into areas beyond their normal range due to inadequate food supply. "Irruption" is the most orthodox term for this phenomenon, but such movements have also been called invasions, incursions, and influxes. Cornwallis (1964) pointed out that all of these terms describe the birds' *arrival*, though of course their departure from their usual range is just as marked; he suggested the term "irregular migration," but so far "irruption" remains the preferred usage. Years in which irruptions of a particular species occur are commonly known as "flight years." Irruptions, as described below, are a fairly well-defined phenomenon and should not be confused with other movements and fluctuations in the numbers of certain species as a result of: bad weather (Dovekie "wrecks," flocks of hurricane-driven Sooty Terns); intermittent range expansions (Carolina Wren); local breeding population increases not related to food scarcity (Black- and Yellow-billed Cuckoo populations tend to increase in areas where outbreaks of gypsy moths and/or tent caterpillars are occurring); or the characteristically erratic behavior of certain species (Dickcissel; see NOMADISM).

A list of the most frequently irruptive of North American species is given below. Most are birds of the tundra or boreal (coniferous) forest; however, some species which inhabit deciduous or mixed forest (e.g., Blue Jay) also fit the pattern, and irruptions from mountain coniferous habitats to lower elevations are undertaken by Clark's Nutcracker and the Pinyon Jay. The families best represented among irruptives are the hawks (Accipitridae), the owls (Strigidae), and especially the cardueline finches (Fringillidae); however, eight other families are represented in the list below.

The characteristic which these species share, aside from the irruptions themselves, is a fairly restricted food preference which is subject to sharp fluctuations—irregular or cyclical—in abundance. For example, the biology of many northern raptors is strongly influenced by the population cycles of the small rodents (e.g., lemmings and voles) with which they feed themselves and their young. Similarly, crossbills are dependent on cone crops in their native boreal forests. When rodents and conifer seeds are abundant, populations of raptors and crossbills increase, but when the food source declines precipitously, the birds cannot find enough to eat within their usual range and must seek new supplies beyond it. Since rodent populations rise and fall with some regularity, the irruptions of rodent-dependent species are somewhat predictable—Snowy Owls winter southward in large numbers about every four years. Cone crops, on the other hand, vary according to irregular tree growth cycles tied to such climatic factors as rainfall and temperature. The irruptions of crossbills and other "winter finches" are therefore highly unpredictable and may also be much more dramatic, if a long series of abundant crops is followed by a lean year. What makes individual birds "decide" to irrupt is more difficult to determine. Lack (1954–POPULATION) has suggested that the unusually high density of birds triggers an innate urge to move.

Birdwatchers who live south of the ranges of irruptive species logically tend to perceive these movements as proceeding from north to south. But this is not always the case. Many birds of the boreal forest (e.g., Red Crossbill) are somewhat nomadic within that continentwide belt of conifers, so that there is often much east-to-west exploration before the depleted reserves of a whole region compel an advance southward. Similarly, in the last century, poor cone crops in the mountain pine forests of Mexico forced irruptions of Thick-billed Parrots *northward* into southeastern Arizona, though owing to habitat destruction on the birds' breeding grounds, they have not appeared north of the border in any numbers since the winter of 1917–18.

The details of irruptive behavior vary from species to species. In some cases the participants have been shown to be nearly all immature birds, which conforms with a tendency in birds of the year to wander farther afield than adults after they leave the breeding grounds (see MIGRATION); however, in other instances adults predominate. There is no doubt that a large percentage of some irruptive hordes fail to find an adequate supply of food and die of starvation. Yet many also survive to return to their normal area of residence. Crossbills and some other finches not infrequently will stay on well south of their usual breeding grounds to breed for a year or more. Irruptions may also be implicated in more lasting population shifts. Evening Grosbeaks were virtually unknown in New England and the Maritime Provinces of Canada until the winter of 1889–90, during which the first of a series of irruptions from the west arrived in the region. Though its abundance still varies from winter to winter, the species is now regular at that season and nests regularly (if sporadically) throughout the Northeast.

The following list includes those North American species whose populations are subject to the most conspicuous irruptions. Populations of other species also fluctuate and move according to the availability of food, but on a small scale that does not justify the use of the term "irruption."

Northern Goshawk
Rough-legged Hawk
Willow Ptarmigan
Snowy Owl
Hawk Owl
Great Gray Owl
Long-eared Owl
Short-eared Owl
Boreal Owl
Thick-billed Parrot
(Northern) Three-toed Woodpecker
Black-backed (Three-toed) Woodpecker
Blue Jay
Steller's Jay
Pinyon Jay

Clark's Nutcracker
Black-capped Chickadee
Boreal Chickadee
Red-breasted Nuthatch
Bohemian Waxwing
Northern Shrike
Evening Grosbeak
Purple Finch
Cassin's Finch
Pine Grosbeak
Common Redpoll
Pine Siskin
Red Crossbill
White-winged Crossbill

ISOCHRONAL (eye-SOCK-ruh-nl) **LINE**. A line on a map connecting points at which a given event happened at a given time. If the average arrival dates of a migrant bird species are plotted on a map for different regions of North America and all the marks representing the same dates are connected, the rate of movement of the species and the "shape of its progress" across the continent are revealed.

ISOLATING MECHANISM. A characteristic which limits the possibility of hybridization among species. This may take the form of a functional incompatibility, as when two animals are physiologically unable to copulate, or, between more closely related forms, a distinctive signal. Familiar isolating mechanisms in birds are plumage colors and patterns, song, and courtship displays. The development of reliable isolating mechanisms is crucial to the process of SPECIATION, and closely related species which share a habitat or breeding range tend to have the most strongly marked differentiating features. See Smith (1966–SPECIATION).

ISOPHENE (EYE-suh-feen). In an ornithological context, an imaginary line which connects similar forms in a cline of a variable species. Visualize, for example, a hypothetical species which occurs throughout North America but becomes gradually darker the farther south it occurs. A line drawn between the points where the darkest individuals occur from west to east is an isophene. The same, of course, would apply to lines connecting the occurrences of the lightest or any equivalent individuals.

J

JACANA (see below for pronunciation). Standard English name for all 7 or 8 members of the family Jacanidae (order Charadriiformes), 1 of which, the Northern (or Middle American) Jacana, has bred sporadically in southern Texas.

Jacanas look like a cross between a shorebird and a rail. Most species are generally dark in coloration with contrasting frontal shields and/or wattles near the base of the bill. Several species, including the American one, have vividly contrasting "flashes" in the webs of the primaries. The most striking characteristic of the family is enormously elongated toes, adapted for walking easily over the leaves of emergent vegetation, which gives rise to the apt nickname "lily trotter" (see Fig. 12). Like rails, jacanas take a broad assortment of foods, including small fish, invertebrates, and some seeds.

The jacana nest is a rather flimsy layer of water weeds laid on top of floating aquatic plants, e.g., water lettuce (*Pistia*). The 3–4 yellowish-brown eggs are heavily inscribed with fine and/or heavy, irregular scrawls.

Jacanas break into a mirthful cackle when flushed or interacting with their fellows, and can also make a sharp whistle.

The distribution of the jacanas is essentially pantropical, and they are notably intolerant of low temperatures. Even winters near the southern Texas coast periodically prove too harsh for the small populations of Northern Jacanas that establish residence there in mild years.

"Jacana" is indisputably derived from a name given the bird by South American indigenes and entered our language via the Portuguese. There all agreement ends. The Tupi-Guarani word was apparently something like *jassana*, probably with little or no emphasis on any syllable. The "official" Portuguese rendition is close to ZHA-seh-nah. Southwestern birders, presuming it to be a Spanish word, often say hah-CAH-nuh, and eastern elitist bird-tour leaders insist upon jah-CAH-nuh (or jah-KAH-ner, as in CU-ber). The variations are limited only by imagination; jah-KAY-nuh is popular locally, and from some eccentric corner has come the refreshing JACK-a-naw. All of this makes a strong case for "lily trotter."

JAEGER (YAY-ger). Standard English name in North America for all 3 members of the genus *Stercorarius* (family Stercorariidae; order Charadriiformes), all of which breed in North America. The family also includes the skuas (genus *Catharacta*).

The jaegers are rather elegant, gull-like birds with aggressive, raptorial feeding habits. All have a horny cere-like "saddle" on the upper mandible (referred to in the name POMARINE Jaeger) and adults in breeding plumage all have elongated and modified central rectrices which are distinctive in each species. If these tail feathers are included, jaegers range in size between 16 and 24 inches. Their front three toes are fully webbed and the hind toe (hallux) is minute.

On their arctic breeding grounds, jaegers catch and eat lemmings and other rodents and small songbirds and shorebirds; they take eggs and nestlings of other species; and they also pick up insects and other invertebrates, feed on carrion, and eat arctic berries. At sea, where jaegers spend most of their lives, they habitually harass gulls, terns, and other seabirds, forcing them to drop or disgorge food, which the jaegers then retrieve for themselves. The smallest species (Long-tailed Jaeger) does this less than the others. All species also feed on fish, marine invertebrates, floating carrion, and ships' refuse.

The Latin name *Stercorarius* means "excrement eater," and there are many less delicate mariner's terms (e.g., jiddy hawk) which similarly characterize the jaegers. Birds being harassed by jaegers frequently defecate in the air, and unquestionably jaegers do occasionally follow and retrieve the falling excrement, but whether they do this "on purpose" or mistake the excrement for dropped food is open to argument.

The jaegers are among the aerial masters of the bird world; their agility in pursuing a tern or gull with piratic intent is rivaled only by some of the falcons.

A jaeger nest consists of a shallow hollow in the tundra with little or no lining. It contains 1–3 (usually 2) eggs, which may be tan, olive, or brown, rather sparsely and erratically splotched with dark brown. Jaegers are solitary nesters or sometimes loosely colonial.

Jaegers are seldom heard at sea; on the breeding grounds they make high-pitched gull-like or hawk-like whistles as well as dry clicks and sharp squeals.

The breeding distribution of all three jaegers is circumpolar arctic; after the brief arctic nesting season they disperse over the oceans of the world; they are seldom seen from land at this time except during onshore storms.

"Jaeger" means "hunter" in modern German and Dutch and can be traced back to Old Norse roots with the same meaning. In British usage all of the jaegers are called "skuas." See also SKUA; POMARINE.

JAMAICA BAY Wildlife Refuge (New York City). A water-birding hot spot accessible by subway from Manhattan (IND Rockaway to Broad Channel); by road only a few miles southeast of Kennedy Airport. 312 species of birds have been recorded from the refuge. It is particularly noted for breeding herons, egrets, and Glossy Ibis and for migrant waterfowl and shorebirds. Permits to visit Jamaica Bay must be obtained at the visitors' center at the entrance to Gateway National Park (of which the refuge is a part). Best visited April–October, especially after July when "fall" shore-bird migration begins.

JAY. Standard English name for about 40 members of the family Corvidae (order Passeriformes), 8 of which breed in North America.

Jays are medium-sized to moderately large (7 to 28 inches) songbirds with sturdy, nutcracking bills, strong legs and feet, and (Pinyon Jay excepted) long (or *very* long) tails. A number of species are crested and most have a conspicuous—often predominant—area of blue feathering.

Jays are widely, and justly, famed for handsome plumage, a fearless nature, incessant noisiness, and omnivorousness. They gobble seeds, fruits, insects, small reptiles, young birds, and eggs with equal relish, though overall they consume more plant than animal food. The Gray Jay of the boreal forest is notorious as a camp robber that will not only steal bacon from your plate but also make off with your favorite fishing lure and "cache" it in the crotch of a tree. Jays customarily travel in feeding flocks when not nesting. Though some species are broadly adaptable, most New World jays prefer pine and oak habitats.

The typical jay nest is a bulky cup of twigs, sometimes lined with mud (Steller's and Blue Jays), always with an inner lining of moss, plant down, grasses, roots, feathers, and/or hair. The site may be fairly low in a shrub or high in a tree. The 2–7 (usually 3–5) eggs vary in color and markings among different species and individuals: pale to dark buff, greenish, bluish, or olive; unmarked (Mexican Jay occasionally) or sparsely to densely speckled and/or splotched with buff to dark brown.

Jays are well known for their harsh, raucous, frequently uttered screams, but they also make mewing noises, clicking sounds, and resonant whistles and are accomplished mimics, especially of hawk calls.

Jays are distributed throughout the Holarctic and Neotropical regions—absent elsewhere except for one "primitive" Southeast Asian species. Most of the American jays belong to exclusively New World genera and are sometimes distinguished taxonomically from "typical" jays of the Old World. The Gray Jay, Blue Jay, and Pinyon Jay are endemic to North America.

"Jay" may derive from a Latin nickname, "Gaius," much in the way that the Gray Jay is called "Whiskey Jack" from the American Indian name "wiskedjak." The jay of Europe, where the name originated, has no call which sounds like *jay* and does not have a "gay" plumage—two other derivations that have been suggested.

JIZZ. A distinctive physical "attitude," totally apart from any specific field mark, which may help in certain critical field identifications. It is essentially an amalgam of shape, posture, and behavior. Knowledge of a species' "jizz" comes only after long experience with it and that of similar species in the field. In some cases, it is more reliable than rote observation of detail. The use of jizz is crucial, for example, to the skillful discrimination of diurnal raptors in flight. The origin of the term is uncertain; perhaps a corruption of "gestalt."

JOURNALS, ORNITHOLOGICAL. See PERIODICALS and the bibliography for that entry.

JUNCO. Standard English name (and Latin genus) for 3 species of emberizine finches (family Emberizidae or Fringillidae; order Passeriformes), 2 of which breed in North America. The taxonomy of the juncos has recently been rearranged (see Appendix I).

The juncos are easily recognized as a group by their uniform gray and/or brown upperparts, paler (usually clear white) belly, and pink (at least partly so) bill. Two species have pale irises. All but one (Central American) species have white outer tail feathers.

Juncos are widespread, often abundant birds which breed largely in boreal or montane coniferous forests and winter at lower altitudes and latitudes in woodland edges and brush. They are frequent visitors to winter feeders.

"Junco" comes from the same root as *Juncus*, the Latin generic name for members of the rush family (Juncaceae). *Junco* was apparently a Spanish bird name implying "bird of the rushes" (perhaps the Reed Bunting of Europe?), and then found its corrupt way to the present birds, which may feed in grasses, but rarely if ever in rushes or reeds.

For general family characteristics, see FINCH.

JUNGLE FOWL. Any of 4 species of forest-dwelling, chicken-like birds in the genus *Gallus* (family Phasianidae) native to India and parts of Southeast Asia. It is from one or several of these species that all our breeds of domestic chickens are descended. See DOMESTICATED BIRDS.

JUVENAL, JUVENILE (both: JOO-vuh-nl). Originally, perhaps, alternate spellings (American and British, respectively) of a general term relating to youth. They have evolved distinct ornithological usages, which, however, are frequently confused.

"Juvenal" plumage refers specifically to the first coat of teleoptile feathers acquired by a young bird. It supplants the natal down (if any) in the pre-juvenal (post-natal) molt and in turn is replaced in many species (almost immediately) by the first basic (first winter) plumage in a first prebasic (post-juvenal) molt. The juvenal plumage differs from all other adult plumages in texture and in the shape of the remiges and rectrices.

A "juvenile" bird is one that is older than a nestling or chick but has not yet achieved sexual maturity or its first basic (first winter) plumage, i.e., a "juvenile" bird wears "juvenal" plumage.

Birdwatchers often use "juvenile" (or "juve") to refer to a bird in a distinctive juvenal plumage and sometimes (mistakenly) to one in first basic or other immature plumages. See also MOLT; MATURITY.

K

KEEL. The narrow median process of the breastbone which provides additional surface area for the attachment of breast (pectoral) muscles; most prominent in strong-flying species; absent in ratite birds. See SKELETON; FLIGHT; and Figs. 10 and 19.

KELSO'S RULE. The generalization that the ear openings and the flaps of skin which cover them in owls are larger among members of northern populations, smaller in southern. See Kelso, *Wilson Bull.* (1940), 52:24–29.

KERATIN (KAIR-uh-tin). The tough protein of which the outer layer of human skin, hair, and nails and birds' bills (rhamphothecae), legs (podothecae), and feathers are largely composed. It is highly insoluble and contains much sulphur.

KESTREL. Standard English name for 13 members of the genus *Falco* (family Falconidae; order Falconiformes), 1 of which, the American Kestrel (*F. sparverius*), is a New World endemic and a common resident throughout North America. The Eurasian Kestrel (*F. tinnunculus*) has been recorded twice as an accidental straggler to the east coast and Alaska.

Our native kestrel is an exquisite little raptor which hovers gracefully over open spaces (even highway medians) as it searches for the small rodents and large insects that it prefers to eat. Unlike most members of its family, it nests habitually in cavities and can be induced to inhabit a nest box (see BIRDHOUSE).

"Kestrel" may come down through centuries of corruption from the Latin verb *crepitare,* "to rattle or crackle," which is suggestive of the distinctive kestrel call. The American Kestrel was once widely known as the Sparrow Hawk, which is not a particularly apt (though not wholly inaccurate) description of the species' food preference, and is also a confusing synonym for a Eurasian "hawk" (*Accipiter nisus*).

KETTLE. A flock of migrating hawks or other soaring birds spiraling upward on warm air currents. Because of the form of the rising "thermals," the birds riding them take on the form of an inverted cone and suggest the whirlpool effect created when one vigorously stirs a kettle of liquid (see FLIGHT, *Thermal Soaring*, and Fig. 20). In parts of Europe the formation is called a "screw."

KILLDEER. Standard English name for a single species of plover, *Charadrius vociferus*, which is very common at some season nearly throughout North America. It breeds and winters nearly throughout the New World to the Subarctic and Subantarctic, though it nests only locally in the Neotropics. The name is a close approximation of the species' call, not a description of unlikely predatory habits. See PLOVER.

KINGBIRD. Standard English name for 10 or 11 species of tyrant flycatchers in the genus *Tyrannus* (family Tyrannidae; order Passeriformes), 7 of which breed in North America. An additional species (Loggerhead Kingbird) has been recorded as an accidental straggler (see Appendix II); many authorities now consider the form of the Tropical Kingbird which reaches southern Texas a distinct species, Couch's Kingbird.

The kingbirds are relatively large (approximately 9 inches), open-country flycatchers with broad, heavy bills, a dark "mask" through the eye, and a bright red or orange crown patch (usually concealed). Of all the members of their family, the kingbirds best deserve the name "tyrant." They usually choose conspicuous perches from which to chase flying insects and this serves double duty as a sentinel post. When potential nest robbers, such as crows or hawks, approach, kingbirds typically sound a loud alarm and fly at the intruder remorselessly until it has been "escorted" to a safe distance.

"Kingbird," of course, carries the same implication of dominance as "tyrant flycatcher."

For family characteristics, see TYRANT FLYCATCHER.

KINGFISHER. Standard English name for most of the 86 members of the family Alcedinidae (order Coraciiformes) as well as a collective name for the family as a whole. Three species of kingfishers breed in North America.

Kingfishers range in size from 4 to 18 inches (North American species, 7 to 16½ inches). The most striking physical characteristic of kingfishers is a long, straight, pointed—sometimes massive—bill connected to a head of the same scale. The rest of the body often looks disproportionately small. The legs and feet are particularly small and oddly modified: toes III and IV are fused for most of their length and II and III are fused at the base (syndactyl); these three toes point forward (II is lacking in some species) and toe I (hallux) points rearward. Some species are dull-plumaged, but most are boldly patterned in bright, sometimes brilliantly metallic colors. The plumage of North American species is sexually dimorphic, with the female Belted wearing the gaudier version. Many species are crested. Their wings are short, rounded, and strong, though as a rule kingfishers fly only short distances between perches.

Despite their name, kingfishers are not true water birds, but land birds (related to bee-eaters, hoopoes, and motmots), many of which have evolved the habit of diving into shallow water after fish. Thc ·gh all three North American species are strongly piscivorous, the majority of species worldwide are not, many living, for example, in arid or forested habitats and feeding mainly on large insects, small reptiles, and the like. The typical manner of catching prey (of whatever kind) involves hovering above a prospective victim and then diving down to snatch it, though some species (e.g., Green Kingfisher) seldom hover but plunge directly from a perch overhanging the water. The Belted Kingfisher is known to take shellfish, small mammals, frogs, young birds, and even fruit in addition to fish. Food is swallowed whole and indigestible items regurgitated in pellet form.

Kingfishers are solitary and nest in holes in earthen banks which they excavate themselves and which are notable for the loathsome accumulation of excrement and putrifying food scraps they contain by the time the young are grown. These unsanitary habits do not seem to have any negative effect on reproductive success. The 3–8 (usually 4–6) eggs are white, glossy, and unmarked.

Kingfisher calls consist of harsh chatters or rattles.

The family is distributed worldwide, being most diverse in warmer climates. In North America, the Belted Kingfisher ranges throughout the continent and even breeds in the Arctic (Alaska/Yukon); the other two native kingfishers (Green and Ringed) are essentially Neotropical species which reach the northern limits of their range along our southern border.

The name, of course, connotes fishing expertise and, as noted above, does not suit most members of the family.

See also HALCYON.

KINGLET. Standard English name for the 2 North American members of the genus *Regulus* (family Sylviidae; order Passeriformes). Audubon's attempt to give us an additional kinglet and name it for Baron Cuvier (see Havell Plate LV) is discounted as an error of memory by most authorities.

Kinglets (including Old World *Regulus* spp.) are tiny (3¼ to 4½ inches), but rotund songbirds with short, slender bills and rather short tails. Their plumage is largely olive green with prominent wing bars, and the males of all species (and females of some) have bright, erectile crown patches of red and/or yellow feathers. Kinglets are hyperactive gleaners of vegetation and live largely on small insects, though they occasionally take fruit, seeds, and sap. They are among the regular constituents of mixed forest flocks of foraging chickadees, nuthatches, warblers, woodpeckers, etc.

Kinglet songs are surprisingly loud and mellifluous considering the size of the resonating chamber. Their calls are high and lisping or "dry" and wren-like.

The kinglet nest is usually suspended from a fork but may also rest on top of a branch. It is a small (3 to 4 inches in diameter), fairly deep cup, almost spherical in shape, made of mosses, *Usnea* lichen, pine needles, grasses, hair, fibers, etc., bound with spider silk and lined with fine plant fibers, hair, and feathers.

The 5–11 (usually 7–9) eggs are white or yellowish buffy with ill-defined, rather pale brownish or reddish speckles often forming a "wreath" at the larger end.

The kinglets range throughout much of the Palearctic region and North America and penetrate the Neotropics as far as the Guatemalan highlands. Both North American species breed in coniferous forest, mostly in Alaska, Canada, New England, and the Rockies, and migrate through or winter in the rest of the continent. The Ruby-crowned Kinglet breeds well above the Arctic Circle in the Northwest.

Like the Latin generic name *Regulus*, "kinglet" is literally "little king," and refers to the bright "crown."

For the other American sylviid, the Arctic Warbler, see OLD WORLD WARBLER.

KIRTLAND, Jared P., 1793–1877 (Kirtland's Warbler: *Dendroica kirtlandii*). A productive and prestigious physician, zoologist, and legislator, born in Connecticut, but active for much of his adult life in Ohio. He was a founder of the Cleveland Medical College and *the* founder of the Cleveland Academy of Natural Sciences. He found a surprising amount of time to collect and mount birds and correspond with Spencer BAIRD, who named the warbler for him. Gruson (1972–BIOGRAPHY) quotes Kirtland's biographer as opining that this pillar of society led "the happiest [life] of which I have any knowledge."

KISKADEE. Standard English name for 2 species of tyrant flycatchers in the genus *Pitangus*. Both are largely Neotropical in distribution, but one, the Great Kiskadee, *P. sulphuratus*, breeds commonly in the Rio Grande Valley of Texas and has been introduced *all too successfully* in Bermuda. The name is a good imitation of this species' loud, frequently uttered call. See TYRANT FLYCATCHER.

KITE. Standard English name for about 26 members of the family Accipitridae (order Falconiformes), 5 of which breed in North America. The kites are a rather loose grouping that includes a great diversity of forms (the 5 North American species are all in different genera) and does not have the taxonomic unity of, for example, the falcons. In form and habits, some species of kites are accipiter-like, some falcon-like, some almost buteo-like, and others, e.g., the splendid Swallow-tailed Kite, are unique.

Physical characteristics and general habits of the kites are like those of the other members of their family (see HAWK). The kites are distributed worldwide, except for the coldest regions, but in North America are found mainly in the southern half of the U.S. Several North American kites have suffered severe declines in the last century and the native race of the Everglade Kite is officially endangered (see ENDANGERED BIRDS).

"Kite" is one of many pleasing bird names whose etymology is too obscure to be very interesting. It is widely repeated that it may come from an old Indo-European word meaning "to shoot," referring (?) to the "swooping" action characteristic of some kites when hunting.

KITTIWAKE. Standard English name for 2 species of pelagic gulls traditionally distinguished from other gulls in the genus *Rissa* (or *Larus*). One of these (Black-legged) occurs throughout the world's northern oceans, while the other (Red-legged) breeds only on islands in the Bering Sea, including the Aleutians and Pribilofs. Both kittiwakes are particularly graceful in form and flight and both nest on narrow ledges of precipitous cliffs.

The name approximates both species' calls.

For general family characteristics, see GULL.

KITTLITZ, Friedrich H., 1799–1874 (Kittlitz's Murrelet: *Brachyramphus brevirostris*). A German soldier-naturalist who traveled widely, collected specimens, and wrote ornithological treatises on such widely separated places as Chile and the Philippines. According to Gruson (1972–BIOGRAPHY), ill health and the resulting delays in publication denied him the recognition which he may have deserved. He collected his alcid on a Russian expedition to Kamchatka; it was named for him by his fellow German-Russian zoologist Johann Friedrich von BRANDT.

KLEPTOPARASITISM. A technical term for stealing by one animal from another. For examples among birds, see PIRACY.

KNOT. Standard English name for 2 of 18 species of relatively small sandpipers in the genus *Calidris* (family Scolopacidae; order Charadriiformes), one of which, the Red Knot, breeds in North America. The Great Knot, a largely Asian species, has been recorded in Alaska as an accidental straggler (see Appendix II).

The Red Knot is the largest of the North American *Calidris* sandpipers, in basic (winter) plumage more resembling a Black-bellied Plover than any species of "peep." In alternate (breeding) plumage its breast is dowitcher "red." Knots prefer sandy beaches and rocky shorelines to marshy situations, though they appear occasionally on mud flats. This taste may reflect their breeding preferences, for they are among the few shorebird species (Sanderling and Ruddy Turnstone are the others) to tolerate the stony barrens of northernmost Greenland and similar ultra-high arctic habitat.

The Red Knot has a circumpolar breeding range and migrates and winters over the remainder of the planet, including the New Zealand and Fuegean antipodes. The population which nests in northern Greenland and adjacent Canadian islands winters in Europe, making a routine stop in Iceland to rest and feed.

The charming notion that "knot" comes from King Canute (or Cnut) of Denmark, whence knots were once thought to come, has, alas, been authoritatively dismissed. The Oxford English Dictionary suggests an association with "gnat." The call note of the Red Knot might be rendered as *knut*.

L

LABORATORY OF ORNITHOLOGY (at Cornell University, Ithaca, N.Y.). According to Dr. Arthur A. ALLEN, the laboratory's first director, this now famous institution was named by the eminent entomologist James G. Needham in order to justify the appointment of an ornithologist to a zoology department renowned mainly for its work on insects. It became a separate department of the university in 1955 and was the first institution in North America to offer a doctorate in ornithology. It has distinguished itself in the fields of research, field investigation, teaching, conservation, photography, illustration, and public relations—all in the interests of birdlife. It encompasses the Library of Natural Sounds (established by Dr. Peter Kellogg and Albert Brand), perhaps the most comprehensive collection of bird and other animal sounds in the world, and in 1962 it published the first volume of its annual periodical, *The Living Bird*, a major ornithological journal that concentrates on field studies. Over the years almost all of the prominent names of twentieth-century American ornithology have been associated in some way with the Laboratory of Ornithology.

See also SAPSUCKER WOODS.

LAMELLAE (luh-MELL-ee) (sing.: lamella). In reference to birds, transverse ridges along the inside edges of the bill which act as a sieve in aquatic feeding situations. Characteristic of swans, geese, and ducks (family Anatidae) and a few other water birds. Bills with lamellae are described as "lamellate" (LAM-uh-late).

LAND BIRD. A term of convenience without taxonomic or other scientific significance for birds that do not habitually frequent aquatic or marine habitats except by chance or to bathe and/or drink. The Osprey, kingfishers, dippers, and waterthrushes are generally considered "land birds" despite their close association with watery habitats. North American waterbird families are listed under WATER BIRD; all other families consist of land birds. See also WALKING/RUNNING; PASSERINE; SONGBIRD.

LARID (LAR-id). Any member of the bird family Laridae. In the plural, a name by which all gulls and terns can be referred to collectively; e.g., "We saw seven species of larids, including Heermann's Gull and Elegant Tern."

LARK. Standard English name for the 66–75 members of the family Alaudidae (order Passeriformes), only 1 of which, the Horned Lark, is native to North America. An Old World species, the Skylark, has been successfully introduced on Vancouver Island, British Columbia.

Most larks are relatively small (average 7 inches), open-country, ground-haunting birds with drab grayish or brownish upperparts that blend cryptically with their preferred habitat. Many species have streaked breasts, and not a few have bold areas of black on face, breast, wings, and/or tail. A very long, straight, sharp claw on the hind toe (hallux) is typical of many larks and other terrestrial songbirds. Leg length and bill shape are quite variable within the family. They often occur in flocks after the breeding season and forage over the ground for seeds, insects, and the occasional snail. They walk, rather than hop, as most passerines do. As if to compensate for their drab plumage, larks are accomplished songsters, in many cases performing lengthy arias while hovering or circling high in the air. The Skylark is such an excellent musician that it inspired one of the most famous poems in English literature (see HUMAN CULTURE); and it has been widely introduced in British colonies because of its cheerful evocation of the British countryside.

Larks make a grass cup in a depression on the ground, usually near a clump of vegetation or a rock and lined with finer grasses, hair, and plant down. The 2–7 (usually 3–4) eggs are pale gray, buff, or greenish, very densely speckled or splotched with buff, olive, or dark brown. "A lark's nest" is also one of the many polite elimination euphemisms, such as "rest stop" or "call of nature." The British are to blame for "I'm off to look for a lark's nest," the connection presumably being that the errand is one preferably accomplished alone.

The larks occur on all continents and achieve considerable diversity in the steppes, deserts, and farmlands of the Old World.

For distribution and other particulars of North American species, see HORNED LARK; SKYLARK.

LATIN (SCIENTIFIC) NAMES. The widespread publication of stan-dardized English bird names in field guides has for the most part relieved birdwatchers of the burden of learning the scientific names of the species they pursue. However, there are still many discrepancies and ambiguities in the use of common names (see NAMES, VERNACULAR), especially in the more remote parts of the world, where there is not enough of a birdwatch-ing community to develop a popular consensus in the matter. Further-more, there are occasions when the use of Latin nomenclature facilitates the discussion of a field problem, e.g., how to distinguish among the gray-headed *Oporornis* warblers or the characteristics of the longer-billed *hen-dersoni* race of the Short-billed Dowitcher.

The fear and loathing with which many people regard Latin/Greek names is understandable. Few people today have had even a smattering of the classical languages, so that Latin names are mostly meaningless to the majority. Then too, as with all other foreign languages, the rules of Latin pronunciation (though simple) are quite unlike those of English, creating an intimidating risk of making a fool of oneself in front of the more knowl-edgeable.

The only way to become acquainted with the meaning of scientific names is to learn a little Latin and Greek etymology. Fortunately this does not require enrolling in a language school. Many technical names are sim-ply descriptive, referring to color or size or number, and therefore certain roots appear over and over again: *atr-* is a Latin prefix meaning black; thus *Spizella atrogularis* (Black-chinned Sparrow). Decoding technical names can also be fun. Many of the early namers *did* have thorough classical educations and gave free rein to their imaginations in their nomenclatural inventions. "Prairie chicken" is a pleasant name, but it pales beside its Latin equivalent, *Tympanuchus*, which according to Coues (1903–COUES) refers to the kind of drum played during pagan bacchanals—a wonderful evocation of both the sound and the purpose of courtship dances of male prairie chickens (see DISPLAY). For anyone interested in acquiring the ru-diments of scientific Latin, Borror (1960) is highly recommended. For those who prefer to have their Latin and Greek interpreted for them, Gru-son (1972–BIOGRAPHY) and Choate (1973–BIOGRAPHY) are comprehen-sive for the North American avifauna and very readable.

Pronouncing scientific names is less straightforward than understand-ing them. There are, of course, rules, but when comprehensive they are rather extensive, some are downright perverse, and they vary from au-thority to authority and from country to country. The result is that while speaker A insists his Latin pronunciation impeccably follows *the* rules, speaker B pronounces things differently with equal self-confidence. The lack of a comfortable standard can be frustrating, but the more positive view is that if your pronunciation is logical, allows a listener to write down a fair approximation of what you have said, and agrees with local conven-tions, only a fussbudget would be so narrow-minded as to declare you "wrong." A set of rules is, of course, essential, if only to have a standard to depart from. Again, for a good, concise set, see Borror (1960).

One obstacle that English speakers uniquely face in pronouncing technical names is that their vowel sounds are different not only from Latin but from all the modern languages which derive from Latin (Spanish, French, Italian) as well as most others, e.g., German. For example, a long "a" in English is pronounced as in "jay," while in all the other languages mentioned it is pronounced as in "swallow." The greatest perversity of makers of Latin pronunciation rules for English speakers is to insist that we should say *Tringa* FLAY-vuh-peas (*flavipes*), when the rest of the world instinctively says FLAV-uh-pace.

LAWRENCE, George Newbold, 1806–95 (Lawrence's Goldfinch: *Carduelis* [*Spinus*] *lawrencei*). Coues put Lawrence as one of the "peers" of the mid-nineteenth-century ornithologists along with BAIRD, BREWER, and CASSIN. His present reputation results mainly from his early descriptions of species of the Neotropical avifauna. Lawrence began collecting birds early in his life, and had the good fortune to be the son of a successful businessman, so that he could pursue bird study unencumbered by the need to make a living. He eventually was able to donate more than 8,000 specimens to the American Museum of Natural History. He was one of Baird's collaborators on the ornithological volume of the *Pacific Railroad Reports* (see BAIRD). The uncle of the Lawrence of warbler fame; see following entry.

LAWRENCE, Newbold Trotter, 1855–1928 (Lawrence's Warbler— originally described as a full species, now known as the rare recessive hybrid of Golden-winged X Blue-winged Warbler parentage). An amateur New York ornithologist, honored by a college classmate, Harold H. Herrick (another amateur New York ornithologist), who shot and described the first-known of these striking aberrations. The nephew of George Newbold Lawrence; see preceding entry.

LAWS PROTECTING BIRDLIFE. All native species of North American birds are protected to some extent by federal and state laws. Even among introduced species which have established themselves successfully, only three—the Common Pigeon, Common Starling, and House Sparrow—are not protected. The great majority of species are *fully* protected, meaning that it is illegal for anyone to harm, harass, kill, capture, possess, buy, sell, barter, or transport birds—alive or dead—or parts of them (e.g., feathers), or their nests or eggs, without obtaining special permits or except in emergency situations. This is the essence of several *federal* bird protection acts (see below). Concerning these prohibitions and the specific exemptions and permit requirements discussed below, the states may make laws which provide *more* protection than federal regulations require but they may not elect to lengthen seasons, exempt species, or otherwise lessen protection.

PERMITS. Some species may be killed, captured, possessed, etc., after obtaining permits which must be issued by both federal and state authorities. Of these the best-known are the so-called game birds. Most species of anatids (ducks, geese, and swans), Wild Turkey, some species of grouse, most species of quail, the three widely introduced phasianids (Common Pheasant, Chukar, and Gray Partridge), the "little brown" race of the Sandhill Crane, most rails, Common Coot, American Woodcock, Common Snipe, and most species of doves and pigeons may be hunted during a restricted season in prescribed areas. The federal *closed* hunting season (i.e., the period during which hunting of birds is *not* permitted) runs from March 10 to September 1. Federal law also forbids certain hunting methods, e.g., the use of live decoys, poisons, explosives, bait, or chasing game birds in motor vehicles (snowmobiles, cars, airplanes, or boats). The number of birds which can be killed (bag limit) is also controlled, and such birds usually cannot be sold by the hunter. There are numerous other regulations governing the hunting of game birds in North America (see, for example, DUCK STAMPS). These vary considerably from place to place and the would-be hunter should check details with his own state or provincial authorities.

Other activities involving wild birds for which special permits can be obtained from the federal government, mostly subject to rather strict guidelines, are:

• Falconry: Federal and state permits may be issued to persons who have passed written examinations in falconry to capture and keep certain native non-endangered raptors (accipitrids, falconids, and the Great Horned Owl). Applicants must also be sponsored by licensed falconers and demonstrate that they have proper facilities for keeping and transporting the birds. The quarry which falconers may pursue is limited to game species and they may hunt only during prescribed seasons. (See FALCONRY for more detail.)

• Banding and marking birds for scientific purposes, e.g., migration studies (see BANDING; MARKING).

• Collecting live or dead specimens, their nests or eggs for scientific or educational purposes (see COLLECTING).

• Taxidermists need no permits to mount legally killed game birds or the three alien unprotected species (see above). However, they must be reasonably satisfied that any "trophy birds" were taken in strict accordance with state and federal hunting laws. They cannot under any circumstances mount a protected bird, either for themselves or for someone else, unless state and federal permits are obtained. Such permits are so hard to come by that no one should bother applying unless he/she can present some extraordinary extenuating arguments. Of course, all of the strictures that apply to professional taxidermists also obtain in the case of would-be amateur bird stuffers.

• Exporting or importing permits are required for all birds with the exception of some waterfowl (see *Exemptions,* below).

• Killing or capturing of "pest" birds (with the usual exceptions of the Common Pigeon, Common Starling, and House Sparrow and a few other species; see *Exemptions,* below) requires federal permits. Any control measures permitted by the federal authorities must also be approved by state authorities; the government must approve the method of control and disposition of any birds killed or captured. Such control situations are considered "emergencies" and normally involve serious threats to agriculture, livestock, fish cultures, or human health (see PESTS).

• Keeping dead, sick, or injured birds of any species except Common Pigeons, Common Starlings, and House Sparrows requires permission from federal and state authorities. Persons wishing to care for sick, or injured, or juvenile birds can usually obtain the necessary permit from the nearest U.S. Fish and Wildlife office without undue difficulty (see, however, under CARE if you are considering undertaking this responsibility).

• Special permits may be issued at the discretion of the Secretary of the Interior in emergency situations or in cases not covered above which serve the interest of the birds involved, e.g., research projects.

EXEMPTIONS. Some special exemptions from the federal permit requirements noted above are as follows:

• Indigenous inhabitants (Amerinds) of Canada and Alaska may take birds and their eggs "for their own nutritional and other essential needs" without permits. This activity is regulated in the U.S. by the Department of the Interior.

• Blackbirds, cowbirds, grackles, crows, and magpies may be controlled without federal permit when they seriously threaten trees, crops, livestock, or wildlife or when they are a nuisance (see PESTS). However, state permits may be required for such actions, and methods of control and disposition of the birds are under regulation.

• Scaring or herding pest species requires no permits, with the exception of eagles and other threatened or endangered species, which are protected from all molestation and harassment.

• Public wildlife-related organizations, e.g., zoos, museums, scientific or educational institutions, state or municipal game authorities, may buy or accept live or dead birds or parts thereof or their nests and eggs without a permit if they have been legally obtained.

• Transactions involving captive-reared Mallards (properly tagged) and some other species of waterfowl do not require a permit, though hunting them does.

• Most members of the family Anatidae (ducks, geese, and swans) may be imported with a permit from the U.S. Department of Agriculture—i.e., such transactions are exempt from federal bird protection laws (see below).

• Feathers of legally hunted game birds (see above) can be put to such commercial uses as fishing flies, pillows and mattresses, and feathers and skins of legally taken *game birds* (e.g., ones mounted by a taxidermist) can be owned or imported for *personal use* without a permit. *However*, it is illegal to buy, sell, or barter mounted specimens of such birds or to use their feathers for ornamentation.

• Grandfather clauses make it possible for persons who legally owned objects or substances before the passage of laws which forbid such ownership to continue to legally possess them. Therefore birds (alive or dead) or parts thereof or their nests and eggs which were legally acquired prior to the date of the acts protecting them (see below) may be kept and transported (they must be marked, if shipped) by the owner. *However*, documentation of when they were acquired is mandatory and such goods cannot be imported, exported, sold, or bartered without a federal permit. The offspring of live birds held under a grandfather clause are *not* exempt. Also raptors acquired by falconers (including endangered species) before the enactment of federal regulations restricting their acquisition may be kept by their owners subject to the stipulations noted above.

PENALTIES. Most violations of the regulations described above are treated as misdemeanors punishable by a fine not exceeding $500 and/or imprisonment not longer than 6 months. Felony convictions involving the illegal taking and selling or bartering (or intent to do so) of protected birds is punishable by a maximum fine of $2,000 and/or 2 years in prison. Persons convicted of pursuing, molesting, disturbing, shooting, shooting at, wounding, poisoning, capturing, or killing a Bald or Golden Eagle are subject to a $5,000 fine and/or 1 year in prison for a first offense and $10,-000 and/or 2 years in prison for subsequent offenses.

THE U.S. BIRD PROTECTION ACTS. Several federal laws have been enacted since the early decades of this century to protect North American bird species. Each successive law extends protection, so that today almost all birds are protected in some way and some much more strictly than others. The provisions of the various acts overlap, and the average citizen need not be concerned in most cases with disentangling fine distinctions from the government "legalese" in which they are of necessity written, as long as he/she understands the implications described above. The exception is in the case of "grandfather clauses" (see above), for which it is important to know *when* the various laws took effect. For the record then: North American birds are protected by the Migratory Bird Treaty Act of 1918, amended in 1936; the Bald Eagle Act of 1940, amended in 1962 to include the Golden Eagle; the Endangered Species Preservation Act of 1966; the Endangered Species Conservation Act of 1969; and the Endan-

gered Species Act of 1973, amended in 1977. Regulations governing falconry were instituted in 1976 under the Migratory Bird Treaty. A list of
the birds protected by federal law as of 1970 can be obtained by writing
the U.S. Government Printing Office for Wildlife Leaflet No. 494. See
also ENDANGERED BIRDS.

INTERNATIONAL CONVENTIONS. The full security of migratory birds
requires, of course, that they be legally protected in all countries in which
they breed, winter, or visit during migration. Accordingly, the U.S. is a
signatory of international treaties with Canada (1916), Mexico (1936,
amended in 1972), Japan (1976), and the U.S.S.R. (1976, including not
only migratory birds but their environment). In general, these treaties pro-
claim protection for species which migrate between the signatories, the
major exception being cases in which such species are "injurious to agriculture and constitute plagues."

It should be noted that we as yet have no treaties with any of the
countries of Central or South America, where a large percentage of North
American migrant birds winter. It is also important to realize that enforcement of the migratory bird protection treaty in Mexico—where all edible
species (including songbirds) have been traditionally hunted for centuries—is far down on the list of priorities of the responsible agencies.

In spite of the current high visibility of the environmental movement
in North America, the public's awareness of what people can or cannot do
to or with the birds with which they coexist is often imperfect. For example, an article in a Massachusetts town newspaper in 1981 gave a cheerful
account of a teenage lad whose greatest delight was potting Blue Jays with
his .22. Blue Jays, it was agreed by all concerned, are noisy pests. The
teenager was clearly unaware that he was breaking a federal law punishable
by heavy fines and a jail sentence (he was subsequently enlightened); but
perhaps more significantly, no one at the newspaper was aware that any
laws were being violated. Another widespread misconception is that any
bird which makes a nuisance of itself, and particularly birds of prey, may
be destroyed at will by an indignant citizen. Though there are provisions
for dealing with bird pest problems which reach emergency proportions
(see PESTS) and dispensatory permits may be issued by federal authorities
in exceptional cases (see above), the citizen emphatically does *not* have a
legal right to destroy birdlife at will.

The extent of the existing legislation is such that anyone in doubt
about whether he can do something to or with any bird, live or dead, or a
part thereof, or its eggs or nest, on his property or off—had best assume
that he *can't.*

LAYING. The deposition of an egg or eggs; oviposition. The actual void-
ing of an egg from the end of the oviduct ("vagina") is accomplished by

wave-like (peristaltic) contractions of the vaginal wall. In most birds, this "labor" takes from one to several minutes; at least some brood parasites (cuckoos), which must transact their business quickly to minimize detection, reputedly lay in a few seconds; at the other extreme, turkeys and geese are said to take 1–2 hours (Weidmann, 1964).

For variations in laying schedules and other related details, see EGG; EMBRYO; INCUBATION.

LAZULI (LAZZ-yoo-lye or LAZZ-yoo-lee) (Bunting). The word has the same Middle Eastern origins as "azure," connoting the blue of a clear sky, a fair description of the dominant color of an adult male Lazuli Bunting.

LBJ. "Little Brown Job." Small birds of obscure markings and drab coloration that are therefore difficult to identify. For the beginner birdwatcher, most of the sparrows are spoken of in frustration as LBJ's. The term may have been coined during the tenure of Lyndon Baines Johnson, the late thirty-sixth President of the United States.

LEACH, William E., 1790–1836 (Leach's Storm-Petrel: *Oceanodroma leucorhoa*). A world authority on the Crustacea and a broadly knowledgeable naturalist who revised the literature of his day on birds and insects as well as his specialty in his curatorial posts at the British Museum. Like many early naturalists, he began his career by taking an M.D., but he never practiced. The storm-petrel was named by L. J. VIEILLOT, the French systematist.

LEADING LINE. A topographic feature, e.g., a coastline or mountain ridge, which diverts diurnal migrants from their intended course. Birds migrating over land on arriving at the coast may be "led" to right or left even when this takes them away from the most direct line of travel. See MIGRATION; NAVIGATION.

LEAD POISONING. Fatal to large numbers of game birds annually in North America, especially certain species of dabbling ducks that swallow spent lead shot pellets as food or grit. Lead is fatally toxic in very small amounts and causes a lingering death from starvation. For more detail, see MAN-MADE THREATS TO BIRDLIFE, *Lead Poisoning*.

LEARNING. See INTELLIGENCE.

LE CONTE (luh-KONT), John, 1818–91 (Le Conte's Sparrow: *Passerherbulus caudacutus*). Son of a wealthy Georgia plantation owner who was a dedicated amateur scientist, John Le Conte took a degree in medicine and practiced briefly, but soon dedicated his life to the teaching of chemistry and physics, eventually becoming president of the University of California at Berkeley. He absorbed some of the family interest in natural history, but unlike his cousin, John L. Le Conte (see the following entry), did not distinguish himself professionally in that field. His sparrow was named for him by AUDUBON.

LE CONTE, John Lawrence, 1825–83 (Le Conte's Thrasher: *Toxostoma lecontei*). Like his cousin John (no initial) Le Conte, after whom Audubon named a sparrow (see the preceding entry), John L. was wealthy, trained as a doctor of medicine, was influenced by a scientifically inclined father, John E. Le Conte (a noted amateur zoologist and botanist), and forsook the medical profession to pursue other interests, in this case entomology. His scientific reputation rests mainly on his work with beetles and on the biogeographic theories that emerged from his studies of insects. He also published in the fields of geology, paleomammalogy, and ethnology and was the first biologist to map the faunal regions of the western U.S. He served as the Chief Clerk of the U.S. Mint at Philadelphia under President Hayes. The desert thrasher that commemorates this Le Conte was named for him by yet another naturalist in his family, his cousin George N. LAWRENCE of goldfinch fame.

LECTOTYPE. When the author of a species (or other taxon) fails to designate a type specimen in his published description, one must be chosen subsequently from the original type series according to the rules of scientific nomenclature. Such a specimen is known as a lectotype. Compare HOLOTYPE; see NOMENCLATURE, *Types*.

LEG/FOOT. The awkward title of this entry reflects two facts: (1) that where the "foot" stops and the "leg" begins varies greatly among different kinds of animals and (2) that for the most part the leg and the foot function as a unit, one being useless or nearly so without the other. Lest the reader be in doubt about the limb under discussion, it is that which begins at the top of the thigh and ends at the tip of the claws (or toenails).

STRUCTURE. A fair notion of variation in leg/foot structure can be gained by comparing the human and avian versions. Using the human

FIG. 12. *Specialized foot types* are adaptations suited to distinctive avian life styles. The ptarmigan grow "snowshoes" of stiff feathers on their feet during the fall, which allow them to cope more efficiently with their snowbound winter habitat. Cooper's Hawks and other accipiters have long toes and exceptionally long talons for seizing and killing prey—mostly other bird species. Grebes have legs set far back on their bodies for maximum (torpedo-like) propulsion during dives as well as uniquely lobed toes which spread into "paddles" on the rearward "power stroke" and turn into narrow blades, slicing effortlessly through the water, on the return stroke. The almost absurdly long, narrow, broadly splayed toes and long legs of the jacanas are perfectly suited to "lily trotting," i.e., padding securely over floating leaves of aquatic vegetation.

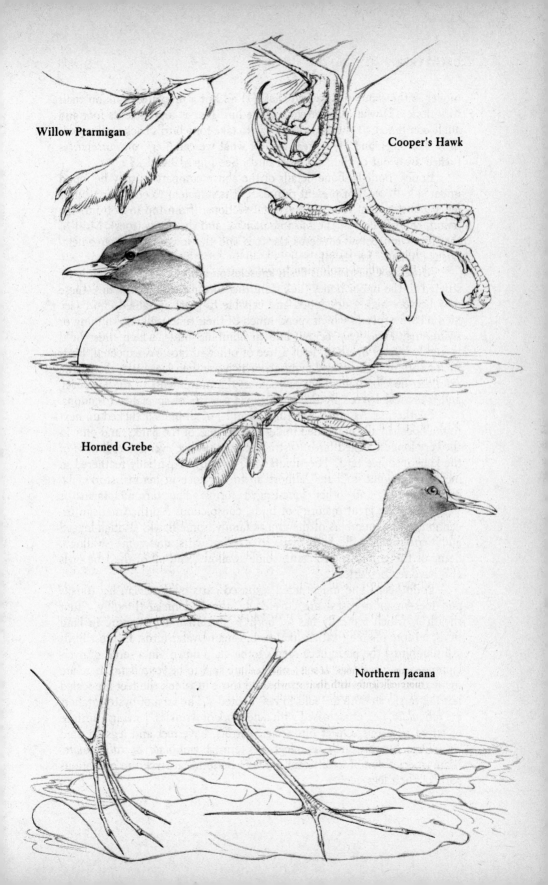

Willow Ptarmigan

Cooper's Hawk

Horned Grebe

Northern Jacana

model as the standard, we find that: (1) all but a few birds walk on their toes alone; (2) what birdwatchers call a bird's leg is more like its foot and ankle combined; (3) what we are likely to take for a bird's backward knee is in fact its heel; and (4) a great deal of what we call "leg" on ourselves is tucked away out of sight on most birds. See Figs. 19 and 25.

Bones. Bone-by-bone details of the above comparison may be found under SKELETON. For present purposes, it is sufficient to consider a bird's leg as consisting of four main skeletal sections: (from top to bottom) the *femur*, the *tibiotarsus*, the *tarsometatarsus*, and the *digits* (toes). Most of the discussion below concerns the toes and the lower leg, or tarsometatarsus ("tarsus" for short).

Muscles. Conspicuous fleshy muscles on a bird's leg are generally restricted to the upper bones (i.e., from the "drumstick" or *crus* up); these may be very highly developed and capable of great sustained effort (see MUSCLES) in species which spend much of their time walking/running or swimming/diving (see below) and in climbing birds, which must hold themselves erect on the side of a tree or other surface. As expected, birds such as hummingbirds and nightjars, which use their legs little, show little muscular development there. Of course, the movements of the lower leg and toes are powered by the muscles via a series of specialized tendons.

Feathering. As noted, the thigh (femur) of all birds is tucked up next to the body, totally concealed under the feathers of the flanks, and only in the very longest-legged birds (Ostrich, cranes) do we ever get a glimpse of the knee in a live bird. The tibiotarsus is wholly or partially feathered in most species, but is "bare" almost up to the knee in herons, storks, flamingos, stilts, and other long-legged forms. The tarsometatarsus is "naked" in the great majority of birds, conspicuous North American exceptions being members of the grouse family, some hawks (Rough-legged and Ferruginous), the barn owls, true owls, swifts, and some swallows. Some of the grouse (ptarmigan), some swallows, and all of the true owls also have feathered *toes*.

Podotheca. The unfeathered, exposed parts of the avian leg (tarsus and toes in most cases) are covered by the *podotheca* (literally, "foot sheath"), which typically has a "horny" (fingernail-like) texture in land birds, a more pliable (leather-like) feel in many water birds. In most birds (all songbirds) the podotheca seems to be "laid down" in a series of overlapping scales, and legs/feet so covered are said to be *scutellate*; there are many different scutellation patterns and those in which the feet are scaled but the tarsus smooth are said to be "booted." The tarsi of oystercatchers are *reticulate*, i.e., crisscrossed with a network of wrinkles, leaving a surface of raised polygons. Other birds, e.g., parrots, have feet and legs covered with little bumps; such legs/feet are termed *granulate* or *tuberculate*. Many species combine different types of podothecal structure on various parts of their legs/feet.

Claws. Except in the case of some albatrosses, birds' toes end in some form of claw or nail, a modified scale, the form of which is also highly variable consistent with its use (see below). Most perching birds have sharp, curved claws of moderate length. Bird claws, like human fingernails, grow continuously but are kept short by natural wear rather than by clipping or biting.

Spurs. A few birds, notably the turkeys and pheasants (as well as domestic chickens), have sharp, bony spurs which project from the rear of the tarsus and are covered (but not dulled) by the podotheca. These reach greatest development in males, are used in breeding combat with rivals, and are of course the weapons upon which COCKFIGHTING aficionados have "improved."

Heel Pads. Nestling kingfishers, woodpeckers, and members of a few other families hatch with horny, bumpy, or ridged structures covering the rear of the "heel" joint. Nestling birds rest on their "heels" and the pads are shed when the young leave the nest, but little written speculation exists about the origin or function of heel pads.

Number and Position of Toes. The vast majority of birds have four toes; none has more; and only one, the Ostrich, has as few as two. In a number of non-passerines, the first digit (hallux), which normally points rearward, has become much reduced in size and/or "elevated" on the tarsus above the level of the other toes through disuse. A few species (e.g., some albatrosses, plovers, most alcids, stilts, all oystercatchers, some flamingos, some kingfishers, kittiwakes, Sanderling, and three-toed woodpeckers) lack a hallux altogether and in others it is a barely discernible vestige.

Birds' toes are numbered and designated as in Figs. 1, 19, and 25. The arrangement of the toes tends to conform among broad categories of birdlife and is therefore of some significance as a taxonomic character. The principal toe arrangements are as follows:

Anisodactyl: Three toes (II–IV) pointing frontward and the hallux (I) pointing rearward. This is the most frequent pattern among birds in general and is universal among passerines.

Zygodactyl (or "yoke-footed"): Two toes (II and III) pointing forward and the other two (I and IV) pointing rearward; this is apparently an adaptation allowing for improved climbing and holding ability and is characteristic of woodpeckers (except three-toed), parrots (which climb around tree branches and often hold food with their feet), and cuckoos. Owls and the Osprey are also considered "zygodactyl" but are able to move their outer toe (IV) forward to the anisodactyl position.

Heterodactyl: Similar to zygodactyl but with toes III and IV pointing forward and I and II rearward, an arrangement unique to the trogons.

Syndactyl: Toes III and IV joined at the base, forming an unusually long "sole"; kingfishers.

Pamprodactyl: All four toes pointing forward; most swifts, which habitually cling to vertical surfaces and use their feet for little else.

Tridactyl: Sometimes used to describe birds which lack toe I (see above).

MODIFICATIONS AND USE. As with other parts of their anatomy, the many striking adaptations seen in the legs and feet of birds have evolved in conjunction with characteristic modes of behavior.

Perching Feet. Most living species of birds have feet with a well-developed rearward-pointing hind toe (I) and are otherwise well adapted for holding firmly to a branch or other perch. The group containing most of these is in fact named for this characteristic—"perching birds," order Passeriformes. This does not mean that non-passerines cannot perch effectively—most can; or that perching birds are all arboreal—many, e.g., longspurs, meadowlarks, are mainly terrestrial. Nevertheless, even the feet of the ground-loving pipits and larks are better suited to grasping a perch than are (for example) the feet of boobies, herons, sandpipers, and woodpeckers.

Long Legs. Characteristic of birds which wade in relatively deep water (herons, storks, cranes, some sandpipers, etc.) and also of "cursorial" species for which walking and running are specialties. The Ostrich and the coursers are perhaps the world's champion long-legged runners. In North America, the long legs of the Crested Caracara, Northern Harrier, Wild Turkey, Upland Sandpiper, and Greater Roadrunner are related to terrestrial rather than wading habits. See also WALKING/RUNNING.

Webbed Feet. Enable many water birds to swim and dive faster and more efficiently by providing more surface area to "push" back the water. The webbing is part of the podotheca (see above) but appears as a fairly thick, leathery membrane spanning the space between the toes. This character has evolved separately in many families of birds only distantly related. The loons, albatrosses, shearwaters and petrels, storm-petrels, flamingos, ducks, geese, and swans, jaegers, gulls, and skimmers have *palmate* feet, i.e., with webbing between the three forward-pointing toes. The tropicbirds, boobies and gannets, cormorants, anhingas, and pelicans and frigatebirds—which together make up the order Pelecaniformes—have webbing between all four toes (frigatebirds only at the base) and are known collectively as the *totipalmate* swimmers. The frigatebirds as well as some herons (see Fig. 25), storks, ibises, Limpkin, plovers, and sandpipers, which have only partial webbing between any number of toes, are called *semipalmate(d)*.

Lobed (Lobate) Feet. Another form of natural paddling adaptation and, like webbing, occurs in various "styles" and in diverse families. Perhaps the most "unconventional" of these is the grebe foot, with each toe a unified paddle ending appropriately with a flattened nail (see Fig. 12). Before bringing the foot forward from the paddle stroke, grebes' toes twist 90 degrees, allowing their thin lateral surface to knife through the water on the return stroke. Grebes' legs are also flattened (laterally) to minimize resistance when swimming and diving. These marvelous legs/feet are placed far back at the end of the body for maximum torpedo-like propulsion in the water. This makes them nearly useless on land, though several grebe species run erect on the water in one of their courtship rituals (see Plate 2) and at least one species (Eared) has been seen to perform this tiptoe race overland in an emergency.

Coots and phalaropes also have lobate toes, but the foot is not so fully transformed as in the grebes. The effect is rather as if full webs began to bridge the spaces between the toes but remained incomplete, and neither the claws nor the flexibility of the toes is strongly modified in these birds. See also SWIMMING/DIVING.

Long Toes/Claws. The toes of rails are somewhat elongated, giving added support in walking over the soft surface of their marshy habitat. The gallinules of the same family have even longer toes, which permit them to pad about on a shaky floor of floating aquatic leaves such as pickerelweed or water lilies. The undisputed champions of lily-trotting adaptation, however, are the jacanas. To their long toes are appended long, straight claws, the rear one longer than the toe to which it is attached (see Fig. 12). These remarkable feet, together with their owners' light build and long legs, enable jacanas to step about on a bed of floating water lettuce as if it were the firmest ground.

Larks, pipits and wagtails, longspurs, snow buntings, and some other ground-dwelling passerines, which spend little or no time perching in trees, have moderately to very long hind claws. These may improve stability in moving rapidly over the earth.

The long rear claws of nuthatches and creepers are strongly curved, pointed, and sharp, giving stability and extra maneuverability in their characteristic foraging over tree trunks.

"Snowshoes." Another adaptation to traveling easily over a soft substrate is the extra fringe of stiffened feathers which ptarmigan acquire on the margins of their already feathered toes. Other grouse, whose feet are not feathered, grow a comb-like edging from the podotheca of the front toes. Both types of avian "snowshoes" allow grouse to travel over the top of soft snow in which they might otherwise flounder.

Talons. The name commonly used to designate the unusually long, sharp, strongly curved claws on raptorial feet—i.e., feet used by avian hunters to catch and kill live prey. In most cases, eagles, hawks, and owls execute their victims instantaneously upon seizing them (usually on the ground) by simply closing their powerful feet. This applies crushing pressure while the knife-like talons simultaneously pierce the prey's body. (Victims not killed by the talons are quickly dispatched by a bite to the base of the skull.) A thoughtful assessment of the feet of the Cooper's

Hawk, shown in Fig. 12, inevitably yields the conclusion that these birds deal a very sudden death. Peregrines and other large falcons which kill birds on the wing knock their victims to eternity with a sharp blow from their large, heavy feet delivered at the climax of a stoop at 80 (or perhaps over 200) m.p.h. (see SPEED); they may also "rake" their prey with their long rear talon.

Digging/Scratching Feet. Gallinaceous birds, which live largely by scratching in the earth in search of seeds or insects, and the wide range of species—Burrowing Owl, Bank Swallow, kingfishers—which sometimes or invariably excavate their own nest burrows by digging, tend to have strong (though not necessarily large) feet and comparatively blunt heavy claws.

Less Conspicuous Leg/Foot Modifications. Many bird species have special foot adaptations which are visible only on the closest inspection—not to mention those which require a millimeter rule or dissection to detect. In the former category are the spiny soles of the Osprey, an invaluable aid in holding slippery fish. Herons and nightjars have a small "comb" on the lower surface of the claw of their middle (III) toe, apparently a PREEN-ING tool. Crossbills (see Fig. 2) have unusually muscular feet and stout claws for gripping pine cones firmly while they apply their specialized extracting tools (see FOOD).

Even in the hand, the feet of the Black-and-White Warbler seem to be those of a normal parulid with none of the obvious adaptations to a climbing life style shown by woodpeckers or nuthatches. On dissection, however, Black-and-Whites do show an unusually developed "clinging muscle."

How Come Their Feet Don't Freeze? Anyone who has seen ducks or gulls standing—apparently comfortably—on the ice has asked himself this question. In answering it, it should first be noted that sometimes birds' feet *do* freeze. Land birds (especially) occasionally lose a toe or an entire foot to exposure at below-zero temperatures. But water birds which winter in the Temperate Zone have the capacity to "automatically" reduce blood flow to their nether extremities as the temperature falls. There is also evidence (Irving and Krog, 1956–INCUBATION) that such birds can lower the temperature of the blood flowing to unfeathered parts, which further minimizes heat loss (see TEMPERATURE, BODY). Finally, there is little fleshy muscle and relatively few nerve endings in a bird's foot, so that pain or other sensations are registered little if at all from the legs/feet. On the coldest days birds on the ice often sit on their feet.

Birds' feet can apparently withstand an ordeal by fire as well as ice. Norris-Elye (1945–TEMPERATURE) relates an account of Gray Jays which could stand atop a red-hot stove for at least eight seconds without evincing any discomfort.

For perching mechanism, see MUSCLES. See also WALKING/RUNNING; HOPPING; FOOD/FEEDING; CLIMBING; SWIMMING/DIVING.

LEK. Originally coined to describe the courtship arena of the Eurasian Black Grouse, the term is now used to describe any place where a number of male birds gather to perform display rituals. In North America, lek-type "dancing grounds" are characteristic of the Sage and Sharp-tailed Grouse and the two species of prairie chickens. In the other grouse species (except the ptarmigans) the cocks display alone but may be heard by birds on adjacent display grounds, an arrangement that has been termed an "exploded lek." As is typical of lek performances, the males of these species affect highly stylized postures and gestures—spreading wing and tail feathers, inflating colorful air sacs on the neck—accompanied by a concert of arresting sounds. Lek behavior probably serves to establish hierarchy among males of a population and to facilitate pair formation. Females of lek species do not display but attend the rituals, waiting on the sidelines to serve the one or two males that emerge from the bizarre contest as dominant.

The Ruff (a largely Eurasian species of sandpiper now known to breed in Alaska) is another bird famous for lek displays performed by males wearing strikingly individualized plumage "ruffs," and cranes and some hummingbird, parrot, and passerine species also engage in their own versions of lek behavior.

The word "lek" derives from the Swedish *leka*, which in certain contexts refers to "sex play."

See also DISPLAY; DOMINANCE; and Plate 2.

LEUCISM (LOO-sizm). Abnormal paleness in the plumage of a bird resulting from the "dilution" of normal pigmentation (see COLOR AND PATTERN). It is also called "imperfect albinism" and, like true albinism, may in some cases be related to abnormal diet. Leucistic birds retain their characteristic pattern but appear slightly or extremely "washed out." See Plate 5; also ALBINISM; SCHIZOCHROISM; and references in the Bibliography under ALBINISM.

LEWIS, Meriwether, 1774–1809 (Lewis' Woodpecker: *Asyndesmus lewis*). Lewis' immortality resides, of course, not in his woodpecker, but in his leadership with William CLARK of the heroic three-year exploration of an overland route to the Pacific coast of the U.S. commissioned by Thomas Jefferson. He was a Virginia aristocrat by birth, a soldier by training, but a gifted observer by nature and he recorded (as the President had asked) an immense quantity of detail on the natural history, ethnology, geography, trade and settlement potential of the "new" lands he traversed. The expedition's discoveries were published by Jefferson in a presidential message (1806), and the journals of the explorers have been published in several forms and editions; see, for example, Allen's *History of the Expedition under the Command of Captains Lewis and Clark* (a condensation of

1814 reprinted by Elliott Coues in 1893). Following his famous adventure, Lewis was appointed governor of the vast Louisiana Territory, in which office he died—possibly by his own or another's hand.

L'HERMINIER (LAIR-min-yay), Félix-Louis, 1779–1833 (*Puffinus lherminieri:* Audubon's Shearwater). A French naturalist who did much of his work on the French colony of Guadelupe (Leeward Islands, West Indies). He developed seminal theories of taxonomy and nomenclature for which he was made Royal Naturalist by the government in Paris. Unaccountably (Gruson, 1972–BIOGRAPHY, suggests snobbery) his ideas were largely ignored in England and America, to the detriment of the advancement of science in these countries. L'Herminier was also a practicing physician. He shares a shearwater with Audubon courtesy of fellow Frenchman and systematist R. P. Lesson. The German ornithologist F. H. O. Finsch later described this species *again* and named it after Audubon. By the rules of synonymy (see NOMENCLATURE) the Latin name reverted to *P. lherminieri* when the duplication was discovered, but Audubon's name stuck in the English vernacular.

LICE. See ECTOPARASITE.

LICHTENSTEIN, Martin Heinrich Karl, 1780–1857 (Lichtenstein's Oriole: *Icterus gularis*). A German doctor of medicine who began his career as physician to the Dutch governor of the Cape of Good Hope and tutor to the latter's children. While in Africa, Lichtenstein found the time to travel about and make extensive zoological collections, which he shipped back to Europe. After returning to Germany, he published a number of catalogues describing not a few new species and also wrote a book about his peregrinations as a naturalist. These works soon gained him an international reputation as a zoologist and he was eventually appointed director of the Berlin Zoological Museum.

It has been erroneously stated that the oriole in question—now called Altamira Oriole throughout most of its largely Neotropical range—was named for Martin Lichtenstein's father, Dr. Anton August Heinrich Lichtenstein, a theologian and teacher who became headmaster of the classical college of Hamburg. The elder Lichtenstein was also a naturalist and gained a reputation in German zoological circles by publishing a descriptive catalogue of rare, mainly African animals.

LIFE BIRD ("lifer"). A species of bird seen by a birdwatcher for the first time in his or her life. Certain "moral criteria" may apply to adding a new species to one's "life list." For example, some feel that honor requires one to find and identify one's own "life birds," while others are content to check off species which have been found and identified for them.

In the heady atmosphere of big-time, competitive listing, where critical identifications must often be made, it is considered wise to have each "new bird" witnessed by a "competent observer."

Birding, the quarterly publication of the American Birding Association (see PERIODICALS), has published a number of lengthy discussions concerning what may be ethically counted and when.

See also LISTING.

LIFE CYCLE. See REPRODUCTIVE SYSTEM; EGG; EMBRYO; INCUBATION; YOUNG, DEVELOPMENT OF; PARENTAL CARE; COURTSHIP; PAIR FORMATION; TERRITORY; AGE; MORTALITY.

LIFE LIST. The record—whether by simple check marks or richly annotated—of all the species of birds which a birdwatcher has seen during his or her life. A life list of substance (e.g., 600–700+ in North America; 4,000+ in international competition) carries a measure of prestige in listing circles and is a means of access to birding fraternities. See LISTING; 600 CLUB.

LIFE ZONES. A system devised by C. H. Merriam in the 1890's which attempts to correlate plant and animal distribution in North America with latitudinal and altitudinal zones of temperature. Merriam believed that an organism's distribution could be predicted by calculating such factors as heat totals during the breeding season and mean temperature maximums. The results are shown mapped (in simplest form) in Fig. 6. It has since been demonstrated that the distributions of many organisms (especially lowland ones) are not consistent with the theory, but reference to life zones was de rigueur in the early part of the century, and a basic knowledge of them is still useful in reading biological literature. Compare BIOMES (mapped in Fig. 5).

Except for the Subtropical and Lower Austral zones (see below), each life zone encompasses 7.2° F. (4° C.) of mean temperature at midsummer, roughly equivalent to 400 miles of north-south distance in North America and 2,500 vertical feet. Thus, traveling north at sea level can be roughly equated biologically with traveling up a mountain; i.e., traveling from lowland forest in tropical Mexico north to the arctic tundra can be compared (again only roughly) with climbing from rain forest at sea level to the alpine zone on one of Mexico's high mountains.

From coldest to hottest (both in descending latitude and in descending altitude) the life zones are: Arctic-Alpine; Hudsonian; Canadian; Transition (called Alleghenian east of the 100th meridian); Upper Austral (often called Carolinian east of the 100th meridian and Upper Sonoran in the West); Lower Austral (and Lower Sonoran); and Subtropical (including only southern Florida in North America).

LIME. At least two meanings connected with birdlife. Accumulations of bird droppings at nest sites—especially colonial ones—are called birdlime on account of their whitish color and chalky consistency (see GUANO).

A more interesting "birdlime" is the sticky substance used for centuries and almost universally as a means of catching birds. This trick is described by Aristotle (fourth century B.C.) and may have been used by Chinese boys long before. The localities from which birdlime is known, together with its raw constituents, include: ancient Rome (Pliny says it was made from mistletoe berries); Northern Europe (rotten holly bark); Southern Europe (fig sap); Algeria (thistle sap); Africa (fig sap or *Euphorbia* "milk"); India (fig sap); Japan (holly and other bark); Polynesia (breadfruit sap); other Pacific islands (berries); South America (a variety of plants). The preparation process usually includes mortaring, boiling and/or chewing and/or mixing with olive or other oil. The African *Euphorbia* recipe is said to be strong enough to hold a hornbill. Typically birdlime is spread on branches where birds are known to perch, or an artificial sticky tree is constructed and placed in a likely spot, sometimes using food or a caged bird of the desired species as bait. Or a glob of lime is fixed to the end of a long, light pole and birds picked off their perches.

For other types of bird snares, see CAPTURE.

LIMPKIN. Standard English name for the only member of the family Aramidae (order Gruiformes), which is essentially restricted to the Neotropical region but reaches North America as a permanent resident throughout much of the Florida peninsula and adjacent Gulf coast.

The Limpkin might be described as a "crane-rail," being larger (25 inches) and longer-legged than any rail but shorter, more secretive, and more cryptically colored than any crane. Like the rails, it has a preference for nocturnal/crepuscular habits (especially in North America), but its call is a far-carrying cry like a crane's. It feeds almost exclusively on large "apple" snails, such as the ones favored by the Everglade Kite.

Limpkins nest in clumps of emergent marsh vegetation or in low trees or shrubs, making a loose, dish-shaped platform of Spanish moss (*Tillandsia*), vines, dead leaves, and the like. Their 4–8 eggs are buff to olive with reddish to dark brown blotches, smaller speckles, and paler subsurface markings.

The highly distinctive Limpkin call is a penetrating wail, reminiscent of howling alley cats or the mournful complaints of tortured souls. Limpkins also make some harsh guttural sounds, sometimes uttered in a marked rhythm. They call mainly between dusk and dawn.

The name is usually associated with the species' gait, but may also have originated in an indigenous South American language.

LINCOLN, Thomas, 1812–83 (Lincoln's Sparrow: *Melospiza lincolnii*). A gentle, retiring, well-to-do Maine farmer who as a young man accompanied Audubon on his Labrador expedition. Though he acquired no fame during his life, Lincoln seems to have been extraordinarily well-regarded by those who knew him. Describing the discovery of the "first" Lincoln's Sparrow, for example, Audubon wrote: "Chance placed my young companion, Thomas Lincoln, in a situation where he saw it alight within shot, and with his usual unerring aim, he cut short its career. On seizing it, I found it to be a species I had not seen; and supposing it to be new, I named it *Tom's Finch*, in honor of our friend Lincoln, who was a great favorite among us." Gruson (1972–BIOGRAPHY) notes that Lincoln also gave Audubon the dog that figured along with his master in the well-known portrait called "Old Woodsman."

LINNAEAN SOCIETY. One of the aristocrats of American bird clubs (founded in 1878), the Linnaean Society meets monthly at the American Museum of Natural History in New York City. It publishes a newsletter and offers field trips.

LINNAEUS (luh-NEE-us). Latinization of Linné, Karl von, which see.

LINNÉ, Karl von, 1707–78. Generally known by the Latinized form of his name: Linnaeus. The founder of the modern system of binomial nomenclature under which all plants and animals are now classified. The seminal work in the method is Linnaeus' *Systema Naturae*, first published in 1735, the 10th edition (1758) of which marks the starting point for the classification of all organisms under the Linnaean system. Binomial nomenclature has been improved upon as the complex interrelationships of living things have emerged under increasingly sophisticated scientific study, but the elegant simplicity of Linnaeus' original idea remains (see NOMENCLATURE). He seems to have been a born plant lover and classifier. He was known as "the little botanist" as early as age eight. Though he became famous throughout the Western world at an early age, his entire career was spent in Swedish academia (mainly the University of Uppsala). He was educated as a physician and practiced briefly (and successfully) in Stockholm but returned to university shortly after the publication of his great work. His other major works include *Genera Plantarum* (1737), *Species Plantarum* (1753), as well as a *Flora* (1745) and *Fauna* (1746) of Sweden and two volumes of "observations" made on his botanizing expeditions around his native country. Linnaeus had no special interest in birds, but as the world's "head classifier," he received specimens from everywhere and named an enormous number of forms throughout the plant and animal kingdoms. In spite of the countless additions and revisions since Linnaeus' death, a glance through a systematic checklist, such as the A.O.U. *Checklist of North American Birds*, reveals that he has a lasting memorial in biological nomenclature.

LISTING   416

LISTING. The competitive branch of birdwatching in which one competes against oneself and/or others for the greatest number of species seen in a given place and/or time. Some listers reinforce their interest by keeping detailed notes on phenological phenomena such as arrival and departure dates of migrant species near their homes or, among the more widely traveled, by recording faunal information for little-known localities. For most, however, sport and diversion are the chief attractions.

A national organization, the American Birding Association (A.B.A.), sets official standards for validity of records, organizes field trips to good birding localities on the continent, and provides a forum for discussion of listing issues in its bimonthly publication, *Birding*. In addition to printing an annual tally of the longest state, provincial, North American, and international species lists, *Birding* contains a variety of features and articles of value and interest to birders (see BIRDING, publication). An example is reprinted in part below by permission of the A.B.A. It articulates, far better than any description, the "lure of the list."

Bird-listing is a much-discussed topic in the birding world, especially among A.B.A. members. Some birders malign listing, some can take it or leave it, some are disgusted by it, and others are compulsive about it. Because I find myself in the latter category, I would like to take this opportunity to tell others how, in my opinion, listing enhances the sport of birding.

First, I will list the lists that I keep. For a lister, listing lists is really fun, and it is something I seldom get a chance to do. Here they are:

1. U.S. Life List (526)
2. Minnesota Life List (341)
3. Month Lists (2,468; average, 206/month)
4. County Lists (11,924 for 87 counties; average, 137)
5. Season Lists (Spring, 312; Summer, 274; Fall, 292; Winter, 160)
6. Breeding-Bird List (235)
7. Yard List (3 residences) (highest, 135)
8. Early Spring Dates
9. Average Spring Dates
10. Late Fall Dates
11. Average Fall Dates
12. Bell Ringers (birds seen in all months) (74)
13. January 1 List (98)
14. Day List (for each field trip) (highest, 177—May 22, 1976—Big Day)
15. Record Daily List by Month
16. Year List (since 1947) (highest, 296—1977)

Lists 2 through 16 refer to lists kept in the State of Minnesota, and Lists 1 through 13 are cumulative. All of these lists are self-explanatory, with the probable exception of 13. This is kind of a special list kept since 1949. It is a cumulative total of all species seen on January 1, the traditional day to take a field trip to start a new year list. The figures in parentheses are my personal species totals.

Possibly, the first question many people will ask is, "Why keep so many lists?" My first and best answer is that list-keeping is fun because it gives you a chance to compare one year with the next, one day with another day, one area with another, and on, and on, ad infinitum; secondly, lists give me (and others) a good picture of the present distribution of birds in the state. I believe that there need be no other justification for lists. Probably the list that has become the most fun for me is the County List. My goal, to see at least 100 species in each county, has been accomplished in 82 of the 87 counties of Minnesota, with my average for the 87 counties being 137 species. The real fun of county listing is that it gets me into many different areas of the state, areas that probably would not be covered during regular birding trips. Some years ago I became somewhat tired of always going to the same place at the same time of year. County listing provided the means to break the routine and get into new unbirded areas. To further enhance county listing, I started a town list. This is a list of all the named places in the state. To get to each of these places you have to cover the county "like a blanket." There are 1,828 named places in Minnesota—so far I have been in all but 166 of them!

I have seen a number of birders become bored with seeing "the same old bird time after time." Although the thought of being bored by birds never occurred to me, one way in which I have escaped the possibility of boredom is by listing. Listing provides new challenges and an interest in seeing that "same old bird" in new areas and at different times of year. . . .

—From Robert B. Janssen, "Listing: Minnesota Style,"
Birding (August 1979), 11 (4)

A few stars in the listing galaxy deserve special mention. The source for the records noted below is the 1981 (October) Supplement to *Birding*.

• Stuart Stokes of Australia has seen more species of birds than anyone ever: 6,150, or about 70 percent of the living bird species of the world. G. Stuart Keith of New York held this record for many years (he was the first person to have seen over half of the world avifauna), but now trails by nearly 700 species.

• Joseph Taylor of New York was the first person to see 700 species of birds in North America. This long-awaited *coup de liste* occurred on

Attu Island in the Aleutians (Alaska). The 700th species was the Grey-streaked (or -spotted) Flycatcher (*Muscicapa griseisticta*), a vagrant from the Palearctic.

• Paul W. Sykes, Jr., of Florida has seen more species of birds *in North America* than anyone ever: 733, or about 89 percent of all species for which there are valid records for the region as defined on p. 3. At least 14 other birders have now seen over 700 species in North America and over 60 have topped 650.

• Kenn Kaufman, then just out of high school, broke the "Big Year" record in 1973, seeing 671 species between January 1 and December 31 in North America. His accomplishment is the more notable considering that he spent less than $1,000 total and did most of his traveling (69,000 miles) by thumb.

• Jim Vardeman set out to see 700 species of birds in North America between January 1 and December 31, 1979. Mr. Vardeman spared no expense, hiring the best local authorities to find critical species anywhere, anytime, at a moment's notice, to add a species, and publishing his own newsletter chronicling his progress. He failed to meet his goal by a single species. His adventures are recorded in *Call Collect, Ask for Birdman*. Mr. Vardeman also currently holds the record for most birds seen during a ten-day period: 1,035; his itinerary included parts of Australia, Africa, Europe, and South America.

See also BIRDWATCHING.

LOCOMOTION. See FLIGHT; CLIMBING; HOPPING; WALKING/RUNNING; SWIMMING/DIVING.

LOGGERHEAD (Shrike, Kingbird). A loggerhead is a dunce (blockhead), but as a biological term the word seems to be used in the sense of big-headed. Both the shrike and the kingbird (see Appendix II) have relatively, but not spectacularly, large heads, and the possibility of a lost folk connotation remains.

LONGEVITY. See AGE.

LONGSPUR. Standard English name in North America for 4 species of emberizine finches, 3 (or in some taxonomies all) of them in the genus *Calcarius* (family Emberizidae or Fringillidae; order Passeriformes). All are birds of open country from high arctic barrens to grasslands of the Great Plains.

All but one of these sparrow-like birds breed and winter exclusively in North America. The exceptional Lapland Longspur, which ranges widely in the Holarctic, is known in British usage as the Lapland BUNTING.

The name describes the elongated claw of the hind (I) toe, a feature that the longspurs have in common with other terrestrial songbirds, e.g., the larks.

For family characteristics, see FINCH.

LONG-TAILED TITS. Standard English collective name for the 8 species of birds in the family Aegithalidae (order Passeriformes), often considered a subfamily (Psaltriparinae) of the "true" tits (family Paridae). For the single North American representative, see BUSHTIT.

LOOMERY. Collective term in British usage for a breeding colony of murres, deriving from an Old Norse word for these and other seabirds. For other colonial collectives, see NOUNS OF ASSEMBLAGE.

LOON. Standard English name in North America for all members of the family Gaviidae, the sole family in the order Gaviiformes. There are 4 species of loons worldwide, all of which occur in North America.

Loons are moderately large (about 2 to 3 feet), slender, and elongate birds with narrow but powerful wings, long, sharp bills, very short but stiff tail feathers, and the three front toes webbed. They are strong swimmers, divers, and fliers, but extremely awkward on land, which they visit only to nest. All loons of both sexes acquire a surpassingly handsome alternate (breeding) plumage which is replaced during the winter with a drab gray and white basic plumage. In form, loons are similar to and perhaps descended from some of the earliest-known birds, e.g., HESPERORNIS.

These unmistakable water birds are denizens of frigid lakes, rivers, inlets, and wet tundra on their arctic and boreal breeding grounds, but all winter at sea, mainly along temperate zone coasts. They feed mainly on fish, but also take crustaceans, mollusks, sea worms, aquatic insects, and even a little plant matter—proportions of each depending on the abundance of local food sources. With the exception of the penguins, the loons hold the world record for deep dives—to 200 feet or more (see SWIMMING/DIVING).

The loons' flamboyant courtship rituals include both aerial displays and "water ballets," usually performed by pairs in unison (see DISPLAY).

The nests of loons may be no more than bare scrapes at the water's edge but in marshy situations or in shallow water a mound of wet vegetation may be pulled together with the bill; these heaps may be built up to considerable size if the water level rises. The 1–3 (usually 2) eggs are notably dark brown or olive with rather sparse black spots and speckles and a coarse surface texture (see Fig. 7). Young loons are transported on the backs of their parents during the first two to three weeks after hatching.

Loons are rather noisy birds, famous for their extended wailing or yodeling cries, which have been likened variously to demented laughter, the cries of banshees, or the quintessential "call of the wild." These calls are most typical of the breeding grounds, where they are heard at all times of day and night. All species also make various clucking or quacking sounds both during flight displays and in migration.

The loons are a Holarctic family. All four species breed in the Arctic and/or Subarctic; one (Red-throated) is circumpolar in distribution and two (Common and Arctic) regularly reach the Tropic of Cancer in winter.

The name is generally supposed to derive from Scottish and Scandinavian words meaning "lame," referring to the awkward hobbling gait of loons on land. Madmen are named for loons, not vice versa. In Britain, the standard English name for the group is diver.

LORE(S). The area between the base of the upper mandible and the eye. The Solitary Vireo has white lores; the Black-throated Gray Warbler has a diagnostic yellow loral spot. See Fig. 25.

LOWER AUSTRAL ZONE. One of Merriam's life zones; called Lower Sonoran Zone west of the 100th meridian. See LIFE ZONES and Fig. 6.

LOXAHATCHEE National Wildlife Refuge (Florida). A vast (145,635 acres) marsh just west of Palm Beach and Delray Beach. Florida wetland birds (e.g., herons Limpkin, rails) are of course in conspicuous evidence, but the refuge is probably best known for Everglade (Snail) Kites and the extremely local and retiring Masked Duck. Smooth-billed Anis may also be seen.

LUCIFER (Hummingbird). The "light bringer," Satan's name as an archangel before his fall. With regard to the tiny, essentially Mexican hummingbird species, the name refers to the dazzling magenta gorget of the male.

LUCY Baird Hunter, 1848–1913 (Lucy's Warbler: *Vermivora luciae*). The daughter of Spencer Fullerton BAIRD, the eminent ornithologist who also named two other warblers for ladies of his acquaintance (see GRACE; VIRGINIA).

LUMPING (lumper). In an ornithological context, the practice of combining bird forms (especially subspecies) into larger taxonomic units (especially species). Taxonomists gain reputations as "splitters" or "lumpers" according to whether they perceive fine distinctions among closely related birds and classify them accordingly or, contrariwise, lump two or more apparently distinct forms into one.

Modern ornithology has been able to demonstrate that, in many cases, birds which seem superficially very different—e.g., "Baltimore" and "Bullock's" Orioles (see Plate 4)—are in fact well-marked racial variations of the same species—namely, Northern Oriole (*Icterus galbula*)—just as superficially very *similar* forms—e.g., Boat-tailed and Great-tailed Grackles—may be biologically distinct.

For obvious reasons, instances of the former are not popular with those birdwatchers whose main pleasure comes from accumulating a long list of species (see LISTING). Some listers become so enraged by what they perceive as taxonomic larceny that they refuse to consider the scientific rationale for the decision.

LUTINO (loo-TEE-noh). A bird exhibiting a color aberration in which yellow pigmentation is abnormally apparent due to a lack of some other pigment in the plumage. Used especially with reference to captive parrots in which the condition occurs routinely. See XANTHOCHROISM and Plate 5.

M

MacGILLIVRAY, William, 1796–1852 (MacGillivray's Warbler: *Oporornis tolmiei*). Like an uncanny percentage of early naturalists, the Scotsman MacGillivray began as a doctor of medicine (see BIOGRAPHY). He soon heeded his irresistible calling, however, and eventually became a distinguished curator and professor of natural history (universities of Edinburgh and Aberdeen and Royal College of Surgeons, Edinburgh). His interest was not confined to birds, and he wrote extensively on other matters related to his field. Audubon paid him (late and loathly) for writing a significant part of his *Ornithological Biographies*. Aububon's attempt to name a new warbler after MacGillivray was not entirely successful, for John TOWNSEND had already described the species and named it after *his* friend William TOLMIE. In the end both of these admirable Scotsmen were commemorated, one in Latin and one in English.

MACHIAS SEAL ISLAND (New Brunswick). A 15-acre treeless island off the northeast coast of Maine, best known among North American birdwatchers as a reasonably accessible place to see breeding Common Puffins. Leach's Storm-Petrels (in burrows by day, active and "songful" at night during the breeding season), Arctic Terns, and Razorbills also breed here. Access via fishing/lobster boat from Cutler, Maine. Landing only possible in calm weather; permission to stay on the island must be obtained from the Department of Marine, St. John, New Brunswick; fog is frequent. Prime puffin time is mid-May to mid-August.

MADERA CANYON (Arizona). See SOUTHEASTERN ARIZONA.

MAGPIE. Standard English name for approximately 11 members of the crow family (Corvidae; order Passeriformes), 2 of which breed in North America. The name has little taxonomic integrity—the magpies are contained in 5 different genera—but large size, a long tail, brightly colored and/or boldly patterned plumage, and jay-like garrulousness are traits that most magpies share.

Except for their proportions and bold plumage pattern, the Black-billed and Yellow-billed Magpies of North America are typical crows. They are birds of open country; are nearly omnivorous (especially with regard to animal foods); make bulky stick nests bound with mud; score high on avian-level I.Q. tests; have a large repertoire of mainly harsh calls and some skill at mimicry; pick up and hide found objects, including human possessions; and in general accommodate readily to the human presence. Our magpies also tend to nest in loose colonies and usually add a dome to their nests. They are known to pick ticks from the backs of wild and domestic animals and also feed at open wounds.

The distribution of the genus *Pica*, of which our two magpies are the only members, is peculiar. The Black-billed Magpie ranges throughout almost the entire Palearctic region, where it is common in the lowlands and well into the mountains. In North America the same species is largely restricted to the West. The Yellow-billed Magpie by contrast is extremely local, breeding exclusively in the fertile valleys (mainly the Sacramento and San Joaquin) west of the Sierra Nevada in California. Its appearance and behavior are very similar to its black-billed congener.

The "mag" of magpie is a shortened form of Margaret and the name as a whole is therefore part of the same tradition that spawned several British bird names: Jack the Daw, Robin Redbreast, Maggie the Pie. The exact significance of "pie" is less clear. It was used historically in France to refer to the Black-billed Magpie, but the widely repeated notion that it may imitate some magpie call must be doubted, since no such call is commonly uttered. The more recent etymology of "pie" refers to the bird. The baked dish, being an assortment of odds and ends, was named after the magpies' habit of making such collections; and "pied," used in many English bird names (Old World species: Pied Wagtail, Pied Flycatcher), refers to the splotchy black and white plumage worn by magpies.

For additional family characteristics and references, see CROW; JAY.

MALAR (MAY-ler) (region, stripe). The region of the lower cheek or side of the throat from the base of the bill to the corner of the jaw; bordered below by the gular region and above by the loral region and auriculars. A malar stripe—also known as a whisker or mustachial stripe—runs through this region. See, for example, the Black-whiskered Vireo and many species of sparrows. See also Fig. 25.

MALEUR National Wildlife Refuge (Oregon). 165,276 acres of flat, arid butteland and scrub (sage, greasewood) pocked with shallow saline lakes and rush beds. Excellent concentrations and variety of migrant water birds in spring (March and April) and fall (September and October) and a fine assortment of western breeding species. Noted especially for the Trumpeter Swan, Sandhill Crane, and Sage Grouse. The Western Grebe, White Pelican, White-faced Ibis, Cinnamon Teal, Golden Eagle, Prairie Falcon, Long-billed Curlew, American Avocet, Wilson's Phalarope, California Gull, Say's Phoebe, Rock and Canyon Wrens, Sage Thrasher, and Yellow-headed Blackbird are also routine. Breeding species best found May through July. Access via Burns, Oregon.

MALLARD. Standard English name for a single widespread species of dabbling duck, *Anas platyrhynchos.* The name originally referred only to the male of the species, translated from Old French and Old English as "wild drake." For family characteristics, see DUCK.

MANDIBLE. In the narrowest technical usage, the lower jaw, paired with the upper jaw or maxilla. More commonly, however, both parts of the bill are referred to as the mandibles, upper and lower, e.g.: the upper mandible of the Black Skimmer is strikingly shorter than the lower mandible. See BILL and Fig. 25.

MANGROVE. A distinctive type of tropical swamp forest consisting of an association of several species of trees with ovate, shiny, leathery, dark green leaves and smooth, light bark, supported by a remarkable structure of stilt roots which give a mangrove "swamp" its characteristic gothic, haunted quality. Trees from several families are typically grouped collectively as "mangroves," though one species, *Rhizophora mangle,* may be designated as "*the* mangrove." Mangroves thrive in brackish water and are therefore characteristic of tidal river mouths. In North America this tropical formation occurs only in southern Florida, where it is the preferred habitat of the Mangrove Cuckoo. Mangroves are also inhabited by a great variety of other water-associated birds, such as anhingas, herons, ibises, certain raptors, kingfishers, Prothonotary Warblers (winter), and waterthrushes (winter).

MANKIND AND BIRDLIFE. See AVICULTURE; BANDING; BIRDATHON; BIRDWATCHING; COCKFIGHTING; CONSERVATION; DOMESTICATED BIRDS; EDIBILITY; FALCONRY; HUMAN CULTURE; HUNTING; ILLUSTRATION; IMAGINATION; LAWS; LISTING; MAN-MADE THREATS TO BIRDLIFE; ORNITHOLOGY; PESTS.

MAN-MADE THREATS TO BIRDLIFE. It has been a long time since we could claim that humankind was locked in an equal life-or-death struggle with nature. In fact, long after nature surrendered to our tools, machines, master plans, and fecundity, we continued to "conquer" her—if not out of necessity precisely, then for profit and pleasure. The rightness of this urge to exploit the biosphere was bolstered by the notion, popular in Western religions, that the earth was created for our benefit.

By the late nineteenth century the expiration of several bird species (see EXTINCT BIRDS) and the impending man-induced doom of a number of others made it clear to a few people that men with rapacious appetites for killing represented a mortal threat to wildlife. In the first half of this century these "conservationists" managed to convince the public at large that this was true, that it was a bad thing, and that legislation should be passed to rigidly restrict the killing of animals. Today in North America the major threat to wildlife is no longer the clear, direct one of men killing animals, but the rather more insidious and ill-defined one of a sophisticated technology working beyond our control killing organisms gradually, indirectly, in ways we didn't predict and in many cases still don't understand. "Conservationists" have become "environmentalists," having realized that the new dangers threaten ourselves as well as other animals.

With this brief historical perspective, consider the following man-made threats to birdlife.

HUNTING. Shooting for the game markets as well as for sport and individual use in the late nineteenth and early twentieth century is generally credited with the extinction of the Passenger Pigeon and the Heath Hen and the mortal decline of the Eskimo Curlew. It also drastically reduced the numbers of many other native shorebirds and upland game birds before effective conservation laws were passed. The Great Auk was hunted to extinction for its eggs, meat, and feathers, and populations of Great, Snowy, and Reddish Egrets and Roseate Spoonbills were drastically reduced by plume hunters between about 1875 and 1900 (see EXTINCT BIRDS; ENDANGERED BIRDS; CONSERVATION). Game and conservation laws now restrict hunting to certain species of birds (chiefly the ducks, geese, grouse, pheasants, quail, rails, and doves); to certain clearly defined seasons; to a limited number of birds; and to licensed hunters using approved methods (see LAWS for further details). In North America responsible hunters now consider themselves conservationists and support research on and propagation of game species and protection of their habitat.

The most popular upland game bird on the continent is the introduced Ring-necked (Common) Pheasant, which is reared in large numbers in captivity and released for the benefit of sportsmen.

HABITAT DESTRUCTION. This may be the single greatest threat to wildlife on the planet. It occurs in direct proportion to population growth and development, though it takes many forms: draining of wetlands for highway construction, destroying prairie lands for agriculture, clearing second-growth woodland for house lots, cutting down primeval redwood forest for lumber. It was a major factor in the decline of the Whooping

Crane, Everglade Kite, and (probably) Bachman's Warbler and the probable extinction of the American Ivory-billed Woodpecker and Dusky Seaside Sparrow. It is particularly threatening to species with highly restrictive habitat preferences: prairie chickens need shortgrass prairie, Red-cockaded Woodpeckers need diseased pine trees, Golden-cheeked Warblers need virgin stands of cedar, Seaside Sparrows need salt marshes. Without these specific requirements, the birds which depend on them will likely perish.

There has been considerable public sympathy recently for the preservation of unique habitats in North America, as people have recognized their intrinsic beauty as well as their value in maintaining biological diversity. This is commendable, but it should not be allowed to mask the fact that habitat destruction elsewhere in the world (e.g., the chopping of tropical rain forest at the rate of about 30 acres per minute) is of more than just local concern. Wood Thrushes and Hooded Warblers, which breed in North America, winter almost exclusively in Middle American rain forests. Furthermore, it has been argued that the survival of tropical forests is crucial to such fundamental matters as the planet's oxygen supply, its climate, and its genetic diversity—about 50 percent of the world's species of plant and animal life occur exclusively in tropical rain forest, a habitat covering only about 6 percent of the earth's surface.

PESTICIDES AND OTHER CHEMICAL POISONS. The careless use of highly toxic chemicals to control arboreal and agricultural insect pests stands as one of the chief follies of the modern era. Those who continue to urge heavy reliance on non-specific, highly toxic, persistent pesticides argue that they are the most effective and efficient means of controlling pest insects such as mosquitoes, caterpillars, and leaf beetles. Opponents reply that such pesticides are: (1) insufficiently specific, killing "good" insects as well as "bad" along with other insect-controlling organisms such as birds, amphibians, etc., and potentially destabilizing entire ecosystems, making them highly vulnerable to unpredictable new problems; (2) difficult to control in application, especially when sprayed from airplanes and carried by winds away from target areas; (3) highly persistent and mobile both in soil, whence it is washed into bodies of water, and in animal tissue, where it accumulates and increases in concentration as it is passed up a food chain (see below) (pesticide residues have been detected in the tissue of humans living in the remotest reaches of the earth); (4) often applied carelessly and without sufficient warrant, as when thousands of acres are sprayed in a knee-jerk reaction to an outbreak of eastern equine encephalitis, in a futile attempt to kill the mosquitoes that may bear the disease, instead of requiring and enforcing the inoculation of horses, which would stop the disease in mid-cycle; (5) effective against noxious insects *only in the short term*, since insect populations readily produce resistant generations which in turn require the use of even deadlier pesticides or heavier applications of the original one.

DDT (dichlorodiphenyltrichloroethane), once considered a miracle chemical essential to man's struggle against competitive insects, has been shown to have been the principal cause of the precipitous decline of certain bird species in North America during the 1960's and early 1970's as well as being implicated in human health problems. DDT washed by rain from uplands into lakes and rivers became highly concentrated in the tissues of large fish. Bird species, especially the Brown Pelican, Bald Eagle, and Osprey, feeding heavily on these, accumulated still higher concentrations—enough in some cases to kill the birds outright. A more insidious effect of the pesticide was to create a hormone imbalance in the birds' systems which inhibited the ability to produce calcium for eggshells. Affected females laid soft-shelled eggs, which could not survive incubation, or even eggs with no shells at all. Peregrine Falcons feeding on fish-eating ducks and insectivorous birds also fell prey to the DDT miracle. The decline in populations of the four species mentioned above during years of maximum DDT use was dramatic, as has been the recovery of some populations since the ban on DDT in 1972.

Because of the persistence of DDT, we may continue to discover more subtle but no less pernicious side effects of its indiscriminate use for a long time to come. And DDT is only one of many toxic chemicals which were ladled freely into the environment, the effects of which, in many cases, we are just beginning to discover. Among those proven dangerous are aldrin, dieldrin, endrin, toxaphene, BHC (benzene hexachloride) HCB (hexachlorobenzene), heptachlor epoxide, PCB's (polychlorinated biphenyls), and that most obscene of chemical weapons applied in Vietnam by Dr. Strangelove—Agent Orange.

Another ugly twist to this sad story is that some American chemical corporations, forbidden to sell their poisons in North America, have not scrupled at passing them off on third world countries to the detriment of the latter's people and wildlife. One need not expect corporations profiting from the export of DDT to appreciate the fact that North American migrant birds are still being exposed to pesticide poisoning on their Latin American wintering grounds.

A more direct form of poisoning kills Golden Eagles and other raptors drawn to poisoned carcasses of "controlled" prairie dogs set out to attract coyotes.

LEAD POISONING. One of the oldest and most severe man-made threats to many game-bird species is lead pellets from shotgun cartridges, the inevitable remains of the thousands of rounds of ammunition spent during the hunting season. Fatal lead poisoning has been recorded in a wide range of gallinaceous birds and waterfowl, which ingest the shot along with other GRIT. But particularly susceptible are those species of dabbling ducks that feed largely on the hard, round seeds of aquatic plants to which shot pellets bear a strong resemblance. Terres (1980–BIRD) notes the case of 110,000 Mallards succumbing to lead poisoning *on a single oc-*

casion in Illinois, and Bellrose (1964) estimates that waterfowl deaths from this source may account for 2–3 percent of North American populations.

Lead toxins enter the bloodstream of their victims via the stomach and intestinal walls after being pulverized from the shot pellets in the gizzard (see DIGESTIVE SYSTEM). Effects include liver and kidney damage and paralysis of the muscles of the digestive tract. Within a few days affected birds develop diarrhea and begin to lose their appetite; they soon become pathetically weak and unable to function normally but may take three weeks or more to die of starvation. A single lead pellet is sufficient to cause death in some instances (Wetmore, 1919), but dead ducks found in heavily hunted areas normally contain 10–40 times this number. Each season thousands of tons of lead shot are added to what has been accumulating in wetlands in significant amounts for more than a century.

The solution to the problem is, of course, the replacement of lead shot with an acceptable, non-toxic substitute. A soft iron shot has been tested on birds in the laboratory with good results, but legislation banning the use of poisonous ammo has not been passed to date. The issue puts the commitment of the hunting community to sound conservation practices to a clear test—one they have yet to pass.

OIL SPILLS. It does not require much imagination to understand that petroleum, sea water, and swimming birds do not mix well. Loons, grebes, tubenoses, sea ducks, alcids, and other oceangoing species which are caught in the thick phlegm of an oil spill quickly become hopelessly mired, totally unable to function, and thus are doomed to a slow death by starvation, exposure, and poison. Even birds with apparently negligible oil stains may be dangerously liable to total loss of body heat because the oil creates a gap in the insulation system that maintains a bird's body temperature on the cold ocean. Ingestion of oil can also kill—postmortem examinations of some alcids found dead on beaches with no oil at all on their plumage have revealed lung and intestinal tissue clotted and destroyed by oil.

In recent years, conservationists have had all too many opportunities to experiment with techniques of cleaning oiled birds. After a major oil spill, hundreds of thousands of dead and dying seabirds wash up on our beaches—probably a small fraction of those that perish offshore. And in spite of improved cleaning methods, the survival rate among oiled birds is very low.

The millions of tons of oil which we have put into the oceans was not all spilled by accident. Much of it results from the deliberate flushing of tanks and oily bilges at sea. In the winter of 1956, a year in which no major oil spills were reported, 7,500 fatally oiled seabirds washed up on the beaches of Nantucket Island (Massachusetts) alone. This form of pollution has been "limited" by international convention, but no one suggests that the practice has been effectively curtailed. Think of this the next time you get "tar" on your feet at the beach.

In the current panic to exploit native oil resources here, some are willing to risk the living resources of offshore fishing banks for a problematical and very limited return of petroleum. On Georges Bank off the coast of New England, the fishery and the large concentrations of whales and seabirds which are attracted by it are being wagered against the possibility of finding enough oil to meet the energy needs of the U.S. for 3–4 weeks.

It is still common for people to sigh in relief when a euphoric newscaster reports that the latest oil spill is being blown or carried "out to sea" away from bathing beaches. We still know very little about the long-range effects of oil on the marine environment, but we do know that when the oil sinks to the bottom of the ocean, it has a devastating and long-term effect on benthic (bottom-dwelling) organisms.

For how to treat oiled birds, see CARE.

COMPANION ANIMALS. The dogs, cats, rats, pigs, goats, and other animals which have followed the spread of Western civilization around the world have at times posed serious threats to wildlife. Their arrival has been particularly devastating among endemic island species such as the Laysan Island Rail, which, due to the absence of predators on its native island, had lost the ability to fly. However, any burrow-nesting or ground-nesting bird is potentially threatened by these animals. Pigs, for example, were a factor in the decline of the Bermuda Petrel or Cahow (*Pterodroma cahow*) and rats often menace petrel, tern, and alcid colonies. Suburban neighborhoods, which may support several dogs and/or cats per household, are treacherous breeding areas for songbirds.

MAN-MADE STRUCTURES. Skyscrapers and television towers represent hazards to low-flying nocturnal migrants. Especially on foggy nights, the bright lights of city buildings may attract thousands of birds which become disoriented, unable to find their way out of the maze of reflecting glass, and often kill themselves by flying into windows in their panic. Mortalities at television towers, ceilometers, and the like are the result of birds migrating at night under low ceilings being attracted and baffled by the lights and striking the towers and guy wires. Johnston and Haines (1957) record two particularly disastrous nights in early October 1954 during which over 100,000 migrant birds were killed in only 25 localities sampled from New York to Georgia. Picture windows also exact their toll—although the number of birds killed at any given window is small, the aggregate is undoubtedly enormous. A reasonable estimate of birds killed annually in North America by encounters with buildings, picture windows, and TV towers undoubtedly runs in the millions. Golden Eagles, Mute Swans, Red-tailed Hawks, and other large birds are often killed or fatally injured by flying into or being electrocuted by high-tension power lines.

AUTOMOBILES. In the 1960's it was estimated that about 2.5 million birds were killed annually in collisions with automobiles in *Britain*. The number of birds killed on North America's much more extensive network of highways must be staggering.

BEACH RECREATION. Relatively few species (mainly sand plovers and some terns) breed in what might be called "Frisbee" or "sunbathing" zones of public beaches, and in many instances these areas are recognized and protected from the ravages of feet and tires. Perhaps of greater concern is the need for long-distance shorebird migrants to rest and feed relatively undisturbed at a number of points during their long journeys. Increased development of beach real estate and public demand for recreational access are making such quiet havens scarce along the coast of North America. Clearly there is a compromise to be reached between the legitimate claims of beach users and the equally valid interests of shorebirds. Conceivably banning motorized traffic from most beach areas would find wide support among most beachgoers as well as environmentalists.

INTRODUCED BIRDS. Alien bird species brought to North America for reasons ranging from the wildly frivolous to the well-intentioned and pseudo-scientific have at times threatened populations of native birds. For accounts of such detrimental effects caused by House Sparrows, Common Starlings, and other resident aliens, see INTRODUCED BIRDS.

THREATENING THE WHOLE. As noted earlier, the most alarming of today's man-made threats to birdlife are more subtle but also more far-reaching than the simple destructiveness of men shooting birds. One reason so many people have recently become interested in the welfare of the world's wildlife is that our own fate is inextricably involved with that of our fellow organisms (see Ehrlich and Ehrlich, 1981–EXTINCT BIRDS). We may survive "frail" species such as the Bachman's Warbler or the blue whale, but there are other creatures such as the cockroach which have already demonstrated greater staying powers than our own.

Listed above are a few of the many threats to the environment which *we* have posed quite recently. They are ones which relate particularly to birdlife and in ways which have been clearly documented. Many others, such as air pollution, acid rain, disposal of chemical and nuclear wastes— both alone and in combination—gnaw inexorably away at the abundance and diversity of earthly life. This self-inflicted corrosion afflicts not only our physical well-being but also what we alone have the ability to appreciate—the overall quality of life.

It has long been traditional among coal miners to take a caged canary down into the shaft with them. When the canary falls off its perch—killed by lethal fumes—it's time to get out. If we wake up one morning to find birds falling off their perches, it will be too late to correct earlier miscalculations. And, of course, there is nowhere else to go.

See also CONSERVATION; MORTALITY.

MANOMET. See OBSERVATORY.

MANTLE. The feathers of the back, scapulars, and upper wing coverts; a topographical region sometimes distinctly colored or patterned. The differences in mantle color among large gulls are the object of much intense scrutiny by some field ornithologists.

MARKET GUNNING. Throughout the latter half of the nineteenth century and the early decades of this century, game was shot in great quantities, often by professional gunners, and shipped to city markets. Shorebirds and songbirds were taken as readily as the ducks and upland gallinaceous species we now think of as "game birds." The number of birds taken of all species was so enormous as to bring some species, especially of shorebirds, close to extinction. It was the principal factor in the extinction of the Passenger Pigeon—a bird whose population probably numbered in the billions at the time of Columbus—and has probably sealed the fate of the Eskimo Curlew (see EXTINCT BIRDS; ENDANGERED BIRDS).

MARKING (of live birds). Though it is often possible to differentiate birds on sight into age and sex groups by noting plumage and obvious size characters, individual birds within these large categories remain virtually anonymous—at least to the human eye. Therefore, in studying behavior or movements of particular birds, it is often essential to add distinguishing features artificially. For example, investigators trying to determine which of a number of nearby Herring Gull colonies contributed the most birds to a potentially hazardous roosting area at a coastal airport sprayed the breasts of the birds in question with a harmless dye, a different color for each colony. By observing the proportion of colors which appeared on the runways, it was possible to pinpoint where control measures would be most effective. Ornithologists trying to learn the precise feeding and resting schedules of certain shorebird species which migrate from Canada to South America have color-marked large numbers of birds and solicited the reports of birdwatchers along the migration route.

A number of marking methods have been developed and used with varying degrees of success. The dyeing of breasts or other parts is highly satisfactory so long as the paint or dye used does not mat or otherwise injure the plumage. The marking substance may be applied directly to captured birds; or the dye can be placed in such a way, e.g., near a nest site, that the bird in effect marks itself; or birds can be marked at a distance by squirt gun. Lightweight, colored plastic markers attached to wing or bill or circling the neck or leg serve the same purpose. By using several different colors and spraying different body parts or using different combinations of colored leg bands, a fairly high degree of individual recognition can be achieved. Adult female Least Sandpipers from Churchill, for example, might be marked with a single red band on their left leg, adult males with the same color on their right leg, juvenile females with a green band on their left leg, juvenile females from Cambridge Bay with a green band on the left leg and a yellow band on the right, etc.

All marking schemes are recorded at the Bird Banding Laboratory in Laurel, Maryland, so that no two investigators will use systems simultaneously that might be confused. Marking birds for any reason requires a federal permit. See LAWS and BANDING for further detail.

MARSH. An open, treeless wetland usually supporting a more or less continuous stand of emergent herbaceous vegetation, especially cattails (*Typha*), rushes (Juncaceae), sedges (Cyperaceae), and/or grasses (Gramineae). The ground is typically flooded at least during the wetter seasons or at high tide (see SALT MARSH), and there may be intermittent shallow ponds, islands of higher ground with trees or shrubs, and interwinding streams. Sometimes used as a synonym for the more broadly defined SWAMP.

A number of North American bird species breed in marshland habitats, exclusively in some cases, and many others feed there regularly without nesting. Among the familiar "marsh birds" are the Everglade Kite (mainly rush beds), Northern Harrier, American and Least Bitterns, all native rails, Common and Purple Gallinules, American Coot, Common Snipe, Franklin's Gull, Forster's Tern, Black Tern, Short-eared Owl, Long-billed Marsh Wren (the so-called Short-billed Marsh Wren usually prefers drier grasses or sedges and is more aptly called Sedge Wren), Redwinged, Tricolored, and Yellow-headed Blackbirds, and Sharp-tailed, Seaside, and Swamp Sparrows.

MARTIN. Standard English name for about 23 species of swallows (family Hirundinidae; order Passeriformes). The name has little taxonomic integrity (the species we call Bank Swallow is known as Sand Martin in Britain); however, all the species in the New World genus *Progne* are known as "martins." One of these, the Purple Martin (*P. subis*), breeds continentwide in North America. Four other "martins" have been recorded as extralimital stragglers (see Appendix II).

The Purple Martin has been widely touted as an effective natural mosquito-control agent, but such claims are at best exaggerated. While the species is undeniably a voracious insectivore, it feeds mainly on dragonflies, beetles, butterflies, grasshoppers, small flies and wasps, and other insects which are abroad mainly in the heat of the day. Most martins have gone to roost by the time the bulk of the mosquito population has begun to fly in the cool of the evening and nighttime.

Because of the presumed effectiveness of Purple Martins as "skeeter eaters" as well as their inherent attractiveness, many people erect apartment-type martin houses to attract them (see BIRDHOUSE and Fig. 3).

These are frequently well occupied in spite of the fact, revealed in recent studies, that martins are not by nature truly colonial birds (see Bitterbaum and Brown, *Natural History* [1981], 90:64–69).

Choate (1973–BIOGRAPHY) explains the origin of the Christian name Martin as a diminutive, viz., "little Mars," and speculates at length upon how the term came to be used for swifts as well as swallows. The name has a much broader current application in the Old World, where it is essentially a synonym for swallow, than it does in North America.

For family characteristics, see SWALLOW.

MATING. Either the formation of a pair bond (see COURTSHIP; PAIR FORMATION) or the act of copulation (see REPRODUCTIVE SYSTEM).

MATURITY. The age at which an organism is capable of reproduction. In birds, this varies from as little as 5 weeks (*Coturnix* quail) to 9 (or possibly 12) years in some albatross species. Most small songbirds breed for the first time when just under a year old, and many other species attain sexual maturity near the end of their second year. There is also some variation within species, some individuals maturing a year earlier than others.

Plumage is often taken as an indication of maturity; birds in "adult" (definitive) plumage are said to be "mature"; those not fully in adult plumage are called "immature." In general this is valid, but it should be borne in mind that some birds are capable of reproduction while still in subadult plumage, while others look like adults before they are sexually mature.

See also AGE.

MAURI, Ernesto, 1791–1836 (*Calidris mauri:* Western Sandpiper). An eminent Italian botanist (director of the Rome Botanical Gardens) and a friend of Charles Lucien BONAPARTE, who named this shorebird in a work that compared the birds of Rome with those of Philadelphia.

MAXILLA (mak-SILL-uh) (pl.: maxillae). The upper jaw. In the narrowest technical sense, the bill of a bird can be said to consist of a maxilla (upper mandible) and mandible (lower mandible), though normally both parts of the bill are called mandibles. See Fig. 25.

McCOWN, John C., c. 1817–79 (McCown's Longspur: *Calcarius* [*Rhynchophanes*] *mccownii*). An army naturalist who collected in the West (mainly Texas) for the Philadelphia Academy of Natural Sciences. He collected his longspur on its wintering grounds in Texas, and it was named for him by George N. LAWRENCE. McCown was from Tennessee and graduated from West Point; Gruson (1972–BIOGRAPHY) notes that when the Civil War broke out, he resigned his U.S. commission (captain) to fight for the South. He survived the war and died in Little Rock.

McKAY, Charles L., ?–1883 (McKay's Bunting: *Plectrophenax hyperboreus*). A young soldier (U.S. Army Signal Service) sent to Alaska to collect specimens for the National Museum in addition to performing his official duties—in this case as the keeper of a weather station. He drowned on duty but was commemorated by RIDGWAY in the name of the species first called McKay's Snowflake, now considered a race of Snow Bunting (*P. nivalis*) by some authorities.

M'DOUGALL, Dr. Patrick, c. 1770–c. 1817 (*Sterna dougallii*: Roseate Tern). Dr. M'Dougall is a shade of immortality. He is credited by the author of the species (George Montagu) with shooting the type specimen of the exquisite Roseate Tern. He *may* have been the Dr. M'Dougall who was involved in a fracas at the University of Glasgow Medical School in 1809. And this is all history remembers of him.

MEADOWLARK. Standard English name for 4 or 5 (depending on taxonomy) members of the New World blackbird family (Icteridae; order Passeriformes). Two of these (the only members of the genus *Sturnella*) breed in North America.

The only superficial hint that the meadowlarks are closely related to the blackbirds and orioles is their long, sharply pointed bill. Otherwise they are almost quail-like in proportions, with a stout build, broad wings, a short tail, sturdy, fairly long legs, and large feet adapted to walking on the ground. Both species average 9 to 10 inches in length. They are cryptically patterned in brown and black above and brilliant yellow below. Though nearly identical in appearance, our two meadowlarks (Eastern and Western) have proven to be well-differentiated species that normally do not interbreed where their ranges overlap (see Lanyon, *Auk* [1962], 79:183–207).

As their name correctly implies, the meadowlarks are birds of open, grassy habitats. Three quarters of their diet consists of insect and other invertebrate food, which they pick from vegetation or probe for in the earth. They also eat grass seeds, including grain. One grackle-like trait is the occasional eating of road-kill carrion (Terres, *Auk* [1956], 73:289–90).

The song of the Western Meadowlark is a rich, bubbly fluting; that of the Eastern is less melodious—more "twangy." Song is the best character for separating the two species in the field.

The nest is a rather large structure made of coarse grasses and weed stems. Over the ground cup, the birds construct a canopy that is woven into the surrounding grass stems. The lining is of finer grasses and occasionally hair. As the birds come and go, a tunnel is often formed leading from the nest entrance into the dense surrounding grasses.

The 2–7 (usually 3–5) eggs are white, finely speckled or rather coarsely splotched with brownish, reddish, or purplish.

Like all other icterids, the meadowlarks are restricted to the New

World. The Western Meadowlark reaches the edge of the boreal forest on the northern prairies of central Canada and the Eastern species breeds as far south as northern South America. Between the two, their ranges broadly span North America from coast to coast with a considerable zone of overlap in the Midwest and Southwest.

Meadowlarks are not larks but were so named because of their lark-like preference for open country and their habit of singing exuberantly on the wing.

For characteristics of other icterids, see BLACKBIRD; COWBIRD; ORIOLE; GRACKLE; BOBOLINK. See also Fig. 10.

MEASUREMENTS (of birds). The comparison of external dimensions of a bird's body is often crucial in making taxonomic distinctions, and more general notions of size are key factors in field identification. It is important that measurements be taken according to a consistent method, and some basic bird measurements and the accepted ways of making them follow. Precise measurements are usually made with the aid of dividers or, in the case of eggs, calipers.

Overall Length. Best taken from a fresh (unskinned) specimen. It is laid on its back on a level surface with the bill pointing directly ahead and the tail directly behind. The specimen should be in a "relaxed" or "normal" state, i.e., the neck should be neither stretched nor compressed. Then a straight-line measurement is taken from the tip of the bill to the tip of the longest tail feather. Once a specimen is prepared for preservation in a collection (see BIRD SKIN), it shrinks, or it may be deformed in the skinning and stuffing process. Therefore measurements of skins are in general less reliable than those taken from a fresh specimen.

In many species, lengths yielded by the above method will be greater than is apparent when a bird is standing or perched in its normal posture in life. In order to give a truer impression of the length of the living bird, some field guides give an average "natural" length, which may be considerably shorter than the "standard" length described above.

Wingspan. Wings spread to their fullest *natural* expanse, a straight-line measurement is taken between the tips of the longest primaries with the bird lying on its back. It is not possible, of course, to take this dimension on a prepared skin.

Wing Length. The outer edge of the folded wing from the bend (carpal joint) to the tip of the longest primary. Since birds' wings have a slight natural camber, two measuring methods have been developed, one which calls for flattening the wing on a rule and the other measuring the unflattened wing, i.e., the chord. The latter is the method preferred by North American bird banders for measuring the wings of live birds.

Tail Length. One point of the dividers is placed between the two central rectrices where they emerge from the skin and the other point at the tip of the longest rectrix.

Bill Length. The upper mandible is measured with dividers from the tip to the base, i.e., the point at which it meets the skull. The bill base is feathered in many species and sometimes the measurement is made to the roots of the outermost frontal feathers. In birds which have a cere, the length from its outer (distal) edge to the bill tip is measured. Bills with long nostril openings are sometimes measured from the distal end of the opening to the tip. The type of bill measurement taken should be noted along with recorded dimensions. Note that bill dimensions are not the length of the culmen (except in perfectly straight-billed species), but rather the *chord* of the culmen.

Tarsal (Tarsometatarsus) Length. One point of the dividers is placed at the outside of (i.e., below or behind) the "heel/ankle" joint and the other at the distal end of the last tarsal scale before the toes on the upper surface of the tarsus—the measurement runs diagonally across the side of the tarsus.

Eggs. Length of the long axis is taken with calipers between the poles of the "pointed" ends. Width is measured at the point of greatest diameter.

See Figs. 1 and 25 for anatomical parts mentioned above. See Palmer (1962) for illustrations of how to take these measurements.

MELANISM (MELL-uh-nizm). Dark coloration due to unusually large deposition of the pigment melanin (see COLOR AND PATTERN). Regularly occurring "dark phases" of various species, e.g., Rough-legged Hawk (see Plate 4), are sometimes referred to as "melanistic." However, some authorities restrict the term to cases of *abnormal* excesses of melanin, whether of genetic origin or related to diet or disease. Melanism is recorded from a wide variety of species (see the American Robin in Plate 5).

MERGANSER (mer-GAN-zer, sometimes MER-gan-zer). Standard English name for 7 species (one extinct) of ducks, all in the genus *Mergus* (family Anatidae; order Anseriformes). Three species of mergansers breed and winter in North America and a fourth occurs as a migrant in the Aleutians (Alaska). These distinctive ducks are placed in their own subfamily (Merginae) by some authorities and lumped with the sea ducks by others.

The mergansers are all handsome diving ducks with crested heads and long, cylindrical, serrate bills, adapted for catching and holding small, slippery fish. The Hooded Merganser is a North American endemic; the other two resident species are widespread in the Holarctic region. All of them are migratory.

"Merganser" is a Latin compound meaning "diving goose." This relates to Goosander, the preferred British name for the Common Merganser, which averages an inch longer than a Brant.

For family characteristics, see DUCK.

MERLIN. Standard English name for a single species, *Falco columbarius* (family Falconidae; order Falconiformes), which breeds throughout the Holarctic region. The name has been used by some authors for a few other falcon species, e.g., the Red-headed "Merlin" (Falcon) of Africa and India. In North America the Merlin breeds continentwide in the boreal forest and winters in the southern and southwestern states (as well as to South America). It is a splendidly agile hunter of small land birds and shorebirds.

The ornithological etymologists give little satisfaction on the derivation of "merlin." Not surprisingly, its present form evolved from falconry, but connections with the Arthurian magician are nowhere to be found. The Merlin was once widely known in North America as the Pigeon Hawk, which is not implausible in terms of the species' feeding habits and corresponds to its Latin species name, *columbarius*.

For family characteristics, see FALCON.

METABOLISM. In the broadest sense, *all* of the physiological processes in any living organism, including digestion, reproduction, muscular activity, etc. (see DIGESTIVE SYSTEM; MUSCLES; etc.). Usually, however, metabolism has the more specific meaning of conversion of raw materials (nutriment in food) into the energy which keeps an organism alive and all its systems functioning normally.

The metabolic process in the body of a mammal or bird is extremely complex, involving interaction with a variety of enzymes and all of the body's living tissue. Two basic types of metabolic reaction are recognized: one which *uses* energy to break down raw materials into substances which can in turn be converted into energy (anabolic) and another which actually *releases* the energy (catabolic); clearly the functions of these two processes are intimately interdependent.

One of the major metabolic functions is the breakdown of fats and carbohydrates into heat energy for the maintenance of normal body temperature (see TEMPERATURE, BODY). Another fundamental metabolic sequence is conversion of carbohydrates into stored animal starch (glycogen) which in turn is converted as needed into a sugar (dextrose) which supplies energy for muscular and other activities.

Basal metabolism is the minimum of energy required to keep the body's basic (involuntary) functions operating, and is used in diagnosing the general health of an organism and as a bench mark for measuring metabolism under varying conditions. It is measured in calories per square meter of body surface or per gram of body weight or by amount of oxygen used per gram of body weight.

Metabolism is one of the limitations on the size of animals. Very small birds such as hummingbirds must metabolize food at a fantastic rate in order to supply their energy needs from such a limited "power and storage plant." They must also reduce metabolism to a minimum when food is not available, to keep from exhausting the limited resources of their tiny bodies (see TORPIDITY); they walk a metabolic tightrope, so to speak, and a bird smaller than the smallest hummingbird is probably not physiologically practical. Conversely, a bird the size of a brontosaurus, in spite of great capacity for energy production and storage, would probably be unable to manage its bulk effectively.

See also ENERGY; FAT; SIZE; TEMPERATURE, BODY.

MEW (Gull). "Sea mew" is an archaic British term for "sea gull," making "Mew Gull" redundant in one interpretation. However, "mew" undoubtedly echoes a generalized gull cry (particularly gulls heard at a distance or through a fog) and is thus analogous to "Screech Owl." The unusual, high-pitched call of the Mew Gull (*Larus canus*) is something like *kee-ah*.

MIGRATION (migrant, migratory). See Fig. 13. In the most general sense, any extended movement by an organism from one place to another. The phenomenon is strongly associated with birds, probably because bird migration is relatively conspicuous (more bird species migrate than do species of any other class of animals); many bird migrations are easily and frequently observed; and these migrations take place over virtually the entire surface of the earth.

The term is restricted here to regular, seasonal movements, thus excluding various forms of dispersal and activities such as traveling between feeding and roosting areas, which are sometimes referred to as migrations. See also DISPERSAL; FLIGHT; IRRUPTION; NAVIGATION; NOMADISM.

Migration is arguably the most spectacular and intriguing aspect of bird behavior. In North America, it involves about 80 percent of the approximately 645 species of breeding birds; may be observed anywhere from the High Arctic to the tropics, from the Pacific Ocean to the Atlantic; and is accomplished in as many variations of timing, routes, and techniques as there are migratory species to practice them.

Almost everything we know about bird migration has been learned in this century, prior to which sophisticated men of science could theorize that swallows spent part of the year hibernating in the mud or on the moon without fear of contradiction. Modern techniques (see BANDING; RADAR; MOON WATCHING), the accumulation of basic data on arrivals and departures, and the mobility of modern man, which allows us to observe birds on their summer and winter quarters and en route, are responsible for what we now know. Some of the newfound facts—high altitude, nocturnal migration, for example—are scarcely more credible than the myths they supplant. Still, our knowledge of bird migration is far from comprehensive, and new insights are gained constantly by birdwatchers as well as professional ornithologists.

WHY BIRDS MIGRATE. The reasons for migration will always be sub-ject to speculation and controversy. It seems obvious that the advantages gained through the evolution of migration have been great; otherwise the many dangers and enormous expenditures of energy involved would not have proven worthwhile for so many species of birds. It is also clear on a more observable level that the vast majority of migrant birds worldwide are retreating, on one leg of their journey, from harsh climatic conditions which reduce or eliminate their available food supply. The mystery is why insect- or nectar-eating species don't simply remain where they can obtain food year-round instead of flying hundreds or thousands of miles twice a year at great risk. Most authorities favor one of two general explanations. In considering both, it should be borne in mind that despite the broad scope of present-day migration, each species evolved its migratory pattern in its own way, not as part of a mass phenomenon. (1) One theory argues that about a half million years ago during the last (Pleistocene) ice age, when a third of North America was covered by glaciers, birds dependent on a warm climate for food were forced into what are now tropical regions but retained an innate instinct to return to their original ranges and did so as the ice retreated. Since the predominant pattern of bird migration is north-south and largely involves flight from a cold climate to a warmer, this scheme is logical and is supported by a widespread pattern of well-documented behavior. However, critics point out that many types of birds which migrate today, including those apparently physically adapted for long flights, existed before the ice advanced; they also note that there are other migration patterns, e.g., east-west or within the ever-warm tropics, which cannot be explained by glaciation. (2) Another popular scenario is that present-day migrants which breed in North America originated in the tropics and expanded into northern habitats, where there was less compe-tition for food and territory. From this perspective, the cold, temperate zone weather and consequent lack of appropriate food compel the annual return to (rather than retreat from) a species' place of origin. It is easy to see our relatively few northern species of hummingbirds, flycatchers, ori-oles, and tanagers, all of them migrants, as pioneers escaping pressures created by the diversification of their large tropical families. But this the-ory also fails to account for all cases, nor can we expect any simple explana-tion to do so.

WHEN BIRDS MIGRATE

Season. We justifiably associate bird migration with spring and fall, since peak numbers of many species pass through North America in April-May and September-October. However, significant migration takes place almost throughout the year, with perhaps least activity in January and June. Diversity in migration schedules is predicted by diversity in life styles. Many shorebirds and other tundra breeders time arrivals and departures to and from the Arctic to coincide with the brief period of midsummer insect activity; thus they may arrive as late as early June and depart by mid-July when their young are independent. Arctic seabirds, on the other hand, which can find food as long as there is open water, arrive at breeding colonies as early as April, remain in the area until fall, and may not complete their relatively short migration to wintering grounds off the coasts of northern states until November or December.

The hordes of migrants arriving in the spring from tropical America begin to hit the Gulf coast and other southern borders beginning in late March and peaking in April; peaks in the northern states and Canada follow a month later. These dates can be seen to coincide roughly with the increasing availability of insect food as the season advances. In general, the passage back to winter quarters takes place on a more leisurely and protracted schedule, with some leaving in midsummer and others not heading south until November.

Dates of arrival and departure vary among different populations of the same species: as a rule, northern populations arrive later both on breeding and on wintering grounds. It is not unusual for migrating Blue Jays, for instance, to commingle with jays that are already raising young—contrary to logic, which suggests that southern populations could leave their breeding grounds later as well as arrive earlier.

Adult and immature birds of the same species may migrate on different schedules. In some instances, notably that of arctic shorebirds, adults depart as soon as the young are self-sufficient, with the latter following a month or so after. In most songbird species, adult and young usually migrate at about the same time, although some young birds precede the adults.

In contrast to the great variation in migration schedules among different populations of the same species, individual birds as a rule arrive and depart very punctually, though departures are less conspicuous. The literature abounds in instances of individual birds arriving at specific migration spots, nesting territories, or wintering grounds on the same date year after year.

The Time of Day at which specific birds choose to migrate differs as does the time of year. Birds of prey and other soaring birds which take advantage of warm air currents rising from the earth (see FLIGHT) tend to move in greatest numbers from midmorning until late afternoon. Swallows and swifts which feed on the wing also travel by day. The majority of small songbirds migrate at night, which explains why their sudden annual disappearances have until recently seemed so mysterious. Many species of waterfowl move at any hour, apparently indifferent to the degree of light. And obviously, nocturnal migrants such as warblers or shorebirds which meet the dawn over the deserts or water must keep going regardless of the time of day.

How Birds Migrate

Locomotion. The great majority of bird migrants fly to their destinations, but some species of seabirds supplement flights by swimming significant distances. Turkeys are reputed to have undertaken extensive journeys on foot in times when their habitat was not severely broken up as it is today; modern populations of this species are essentially non-migratory.

Direction. The usual course of bird migration over North America is roughly from north to south after the breeding season and the reverse on the return from the wintering area. There are a number of exceptions however. (1) South-north: Several of "our" species of shearwaters and petrels breed on oceanic islands in the Southern Hemisphere during the northern winter and migrate to the North Atlantic or North Pacific during non-breeding periods. Juvenile birds of many species tend to wander extensively once self-sufficient, and a certain percentage of normally southward-migrating birds will initially move northward (as well as to all other points of the compass) in this haphazard manner. More significantly, the young of some southern species, e.g., egrets and Bald Eagles, *habitually* move north shortly after quitting the nest, frequently as far as Canada. (2) East-west: Many of the White-winged Scoters which breed in central and northwestern Canada migrate *both* due east and due west to the coasts for the winter; some midwestern breeding populations of Evening Grosbeaks (sometimes) move east to winter in New England; and a few pelagic species make east-west oceanic crossings, e.g., Cory's Shearwater (breeds eastern Atlantic and Mediterranean and migrates to northwestern Atlantic), Black-footed Albatross (breeds north-central and western Pacific islands and disperses to northeastern Pacific), and Sooty Tern (breeds Dry Tortugas and disperses to west coast of Africa). (3) Northeast-southwest: essentially Palearctic species (e.g., Rufous-necked Sandpiper, Yellow Wagtail) which breed as far east as extreme northwestern Alaska follow the migration route of their Siberian populations to winter in southern Asia and/or Australasia. (4) Northwest-southeast: Blackpolls and other wood warblers whose breeding ranges extend well into western North America follow an eastern migration route rather than head directly south from their nesting grounds. It is supposed that these species evolved in the East, spreading to the West only fairly recently, and continue to follow their ancestral migration pattern.

Of course, migrants frequently deviate from their intended directions because of environmental influences (see *Effects of Weather,* below).

Routes. Birds migrate over the entire face of the continent but, particularly in the case of daytime migrants, tend to follow topographical features such as mountain chains, river valleys, and coastlines. This tendency has given rise to the speculation that there are four major "flyways"—the Pacific, Central, Mississippi, and Atlantic—along which migration is concentrated. This concept has been a boon to those (e.g., officers of the U.S. Fish and Wildlife Service) whose job it is to keep tabs on numbers of migratory waterfowl and other game species: abundance is much easier to assess if nearly all birds follow only a few unvarying routes. Unfortunately for the census takers, much recent evidence refutes the notion of flyways as a principal pattern of migration.

There are, however, four main flight plans by which birds reach Latin American wintering grounds once across the southern U.S. border: (1) directly into the peninsular extension of Mexico and Central America, (2) across the Gulf of Mexico from the Gulf states to southern Mexico, principally the Yucatán Peninsula, (3) island hopping from Florida across the Caribbean to South America, and (4) direct transatlantic flight from extreme northeastern Canada and U.S. to South America. A great diversity of specific itineraries is included within these broad basic patterns.

Some migrants travel south by one route and north by another; others follow the same route in both directions. Routes tend to be precisely followed and unvarying among individual birds and populations; however, different populations of widespread species may reach similar destinations by two or more different routes. Some pelagic birds with no fixed wintering area use less direct, less clearly defined routes, but wander in broad loops, in some cases taking more than a year to return to their breeding grounds but always doing so on schedule, sometimes even to the day.

Techniques by which routes are followed are discussed under NAVI-GATION.

Manner of Flight. All nocturnal and most diurnal migrants propel themselves by the continual strenuous exertion of beating their wings. Tail winds (see *Effects of Weather*, below) and flying in V formations (see *Flocking*, below) allow modest savings of energy, but most migrants must break their journeys regularly for food and rest. A few groups of birds have evolved methods of travel which are highly energy-efficient. Albatrosses and shearwaters are adapted for "sailing" long distances with little effort using wind currents (see FLIGHT), and species of pelicans, raptors, herons, storks, and cranes move largely by soaring high on updrafts of warm air currents called "thermals" (see *Soaring* under FLIGHT) and then drifting gradually and effortlessly in the direction of their destination. Some of the longest migratory journeys are accomplished using this method, the efficacy of which may be confirmed by a few observations indicating that soaring migrants seldom feed en route. Because thermals are not generated at night or over water, soaring birds migrate only by day and skirt large bodies of water (see *Concentrations*, below).

WHERE MIGRANTS GO. The winter destination of birds varies widely among species and often among different populations of the same species. Overall, North American birds winter throughout the Western Hemisphere from the edge of northern pack ice to the Antarctic. A few species which breed in extreme northwestern Alaska winter in southern Asia and Australasia, and a few oceanic species also reach the Eastern Hemisphere in both oceans. A majority of migrant species winter between the southern half of the U.S. and northern South America. Only about 25 percent of total species winters *exclusively* south of the U.S. border; i.e., the winter range of about 75 percent of migrant species is at least partially within North America. The winter range of about 20 percent of all North American migrants extends as far south as South America, though only about 5 percent winters exclusively on that continent.

Winter ranges tend to be comparable to or greater than breeding ranges in extent, so that the northernmost wintering population of a given species may be hundreds, even thousands of miles away from the southernmost. Despite their extent, the wintering grounds of a particular species are usually well defined: virtually all Hudsonian Godwits winter in the southern third of South America; all Magnolia Warblers from southern Mexico through Panama. A few non-breeding individuals often remain on the wintering grounds through the breeding season, just as stragglers occasionally remain north of the normal wintering range.

Banding has proven that individual birds of many species return to the same relatively restricted breeding *and* wintering areas year after year once adult patterns have been set; stops en route may also be precisely "programmed."

HOW FAR? The world's longest migration route is that of the western arctic populations of the Arctic Tern, some members of which travel as far as 11,000 miles *each way* between breeding grounds and winter range near the Antarctic Circle (see Fig. 13). The Lesser Golden Plover, which flies 2,000–2,400 miles nonstop over the ocean from Alaska to mid-Pacific islands or from northeastern Canada to the West Indies, probably makes the longest *uninterrupted* flight. Wilson's Storm-Petrel, which breeds on subantarctic islands and approaches the Arctic Circle on its "wintering" grounds during the northern summer, holds the distance record for Southern Hemisphere breeders and for its order (the Procellariiformes); the Sooty Shearwater, which follows a similar itinerary, is a close second in both categories.

Few land-bird migrations approach these distances. However, Swainson's Hawk breeds as far north as central Alaska and winters almost exclusively on the Argentine pampas; both Barn and Cliff Swallows nest as far north as the Subarctic and winter regularly south to central Argentina (the former reaching Tierra del Fuego with some frequency); and some Bobolinks commute between southern Canada and northern Argentina. (For distance in relation to time, see *How Fast?* below.)

Why the longest migration routes should have evolved is by no means clear. The notion occasionally advanced that Buff-breasted Sandpipers, for example, can find no suitable feeding habitat between their arctic breeding grounds and the Argentine grasslands where they winter, is belied by their

FIG. 13. *Migration routes.*

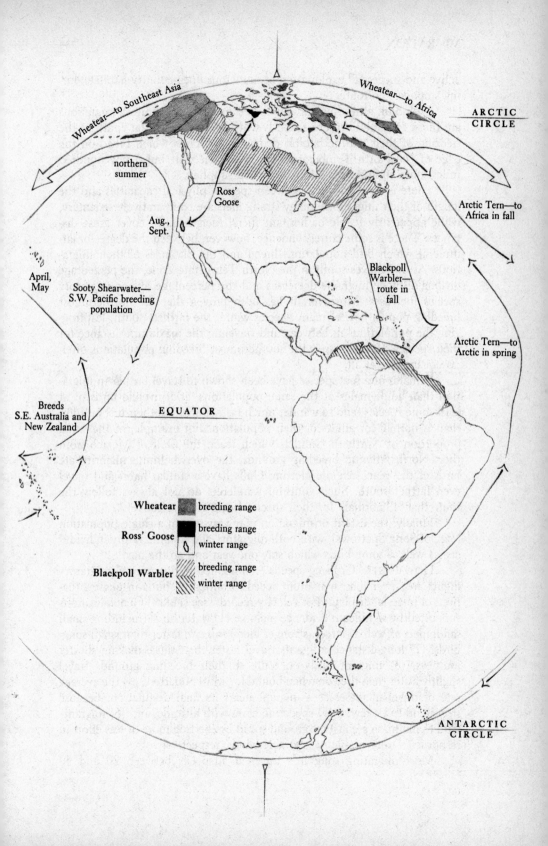

Wheatear—to Southeast Asia

Wheatear—to Africa

ARCTIC
CIRCLE

northern
summer

Ross'
Goose

Aug.,
Sept.

Arctic Tern—to
Africa in fall

Blackpoll
Warbler—
route in
fall

April,
May

Sooty Shearwater—
S.W. Pacific breeding
population

Arctic Tern—to
Arctic in spring

Breeds
S.E. Australia and
New Zealand

EQUATOR

Wheatear | breeding range

Ross' Goose | breeding range
winter range

Blackpoll Warbler | breeding range
winter range

ANTARCTIC
CIRCLE

active and successful exploitation of numerous open-country habitats during stopovers en route.

Excluding altitudinal migrants (see below), the shortest migrations are those of some northern seabirds which move only as far south as the freezing of their marine habitat demands and birds which breed on the edge of the North Temperate Zone and must shift but a few hundred miles south to find adequate winter food supplies.

There is no correlation between species' physical capacities and the length of their migrations: many strong fliers are comparatively sedentary, while apparently feeble or hesitant fliers, such as rails, cover great distances. There is some correspondence, however, between the degree of latitude at which bird populations breed and the distances of their migrations. As one moves south in the North Temperate Zone, the percentage of long-distance migrants decreases and the percentage of non-migratory species increases. Moreover, it has been proven that the northernmost breeding populations of many species winter the farthest south, leapfrogging the populations in between and traveling the maximum distance for their species. In such cases, the southernmost breeding populations often do not migrate at all.

Females of a few species have been shown to travel farther in migration than adult males of the same populations, and juvenile birds of at least some species tend to wander much farther afield in their first autumn than is normal for adults of their population. For example, of the small proportion of Northern Gannets which reach the Gulf of Mexico from their North Atlantic breeding grounds, the overwhelming majority are birds of the year. Juvenile Herring Gulls have a similar habit and travel even farther south. Such youthful wanderers do not always follow the route that is "normal" for their species (see *Direction*, above).

Finally, the extent of migration may vary within a single population (e.g., of Song Sparrows), with both migratory and non-migratory individuals, as well as some birds which stay one year and go the next.

How Fast? "Cruising speeds" maintained during normal migratory flights are lower than maximum speeds attained by birds in chase situations or in aerial display. (For velocity records, see SPEED.) Generalizations supported by significant evidence include: (1) water birds (including small sandpipers as well as larger, stronger fliers) migrate faster than small songbirds; (2) long-distance migrants travel faster than those making shorter journeys; (3) migrant birds en route to their breeding grounds travel slightly faster than they do when bound for winter quarters; (4) the average rate of travel increases as a migrant nears its final destination, because stops tend to be fewer; (5) speed increases with altitude; and (6) migrants tend to maintain a constant ground speed by exerting more or less effort in response to unfavorable or favorable winds, respectively.

Most migrating songbirds travel at airspeeds between 20 and 40

m.p.h., larger species averaging faster than smaller. Species of ducks, pelagic birds, shorebirds, and falcons seem to average between 40 and 60
m.p.h. airspeed, but small shorebirds flying at high altitudes have been
clocked at airspeeds exceeding 100 m.p.h.

Duration of uninterrupted flight is a crucial factor in calculating overall rate of travel. Warblers and other small songbirds may average 30 miles
per day during the first stages of their migration and increase to 200 or
more as they approach their destinations. Likewise, migrants forced to stay
aloft over long water crossings make better time overall than those able to
land regularly.

Homing experiments have produced rates of 250–300+ miles per day
(for albatrosses, shearwaters, and petrels, which can, of course, rest periodically on the water); the Peregrine Falcon is known to be capable of at least
1,350 miles within 24 hours.

HOW HIGH? In general: (1) Nocturnal migrants fly higher than diurnal migrants; in at least some cases the former gradually ascend and then
descend during the course of a night's travel, reaching maximum altitude
around the middle of the night. (2) Migrants tend to fly higher over land
than over large expanses of water. (3) Perhaps obviously, migrants crossing
high mountain ranges tend to fly at greater than average heights. The altitude record for a migrant bird is held by the Bar-headed Goose, flocks of
which regularly cross the Himalayas flying at about 28,000 feet.

Nocturnal songbird migrants normally travel between 3,000 and
5,000 feet, but altitudes of between 8,000 and 10,000 feet are not unusual.
Radar scans have picked up flocks (plausibly of long-distance, transoceanic
migrants) as high as 21,000 feet. Clouds and other atmospheric conditions
obviously affect the altitude at which birds can or prefer to migrate (see
Effects of Weather, below).

At the opposite extreme, many daytime migrants fly well below 100
feet over land and especially over the sea; small, low-flying land birds
sometimes barely clear the waves, and shearwaters regularly touch the surface with their wing tips.

PREPARING TO MIGRATE. Defining a bird's urge to migrate is akin to
explaining various complex urges of our own, such as hunger. We recognize the feeling of hunger, we know it coincides with the body's need for
food, and we realize, at least in some cases, that it is stimulated by some
external source such as the smell of a freshly baked pie. But these observations explain nothing about how the process works. The beginning of a
bird's migratory urge is probably "external," e.g., a change in day length or
temperature. This in turn triggers a physiological reaction, e.g., an "awak-
ening" of the sexual glands in birds returning north in the spring. One
well-documented symptom of the metabolic changes that occur in birds
about to migrate is called "pre-migratory restlessness." As a species' characteristic departure time approaches, it becomes hyperactive and increas-

ingly unable to rest during the night. The increased energy and the greater time in which to expend it are largely directed into a single activity—eating. The result is a prodigious accumulation of fat—the fuel supply for the great flight ahead.

It has been demonstrated, for example (Nisbet et al., 1963–FAT), that Blackpoll Warblers reach New England in September from their breeding grounds to the north and west and, after locating good feeding areas, gorge for several weeks until their weight reaches more than twice what it was on arrival (to 27 grams, up from 11–12 grams). On attaining this "signal" weight they take off as soon as weather conditions permit—typically following a cold front from the northwest—with enough "fuel" on them to fly up to 120 hours without stopping, more than enough to take them from New England to their wintering grounds in northern South America.

FLOCKING. Most migrant birds travel in groups, though individual songbird migrants are known to maintain considerable "flying room" around them and solitary migrants are not unusual. Migrant flocks may be composed of a single species, age, or sex, or a mixture of any or all of the three. Birds of different species which migrate together usually have similar migratory habits: manner of flight, speed, altitude, season, time of day, etc. Flocks of nocturnal migrants keep together by constant calling.

Advantages of flocking in migration include: protection against predators, improved directional bearings due to consensus among experienced birds (particularly advantageous to juvenile birds), and, in the case of birds flying in V formation, energy conservation (see FLIGHT, V Formation).

Except for some waterfowl, little is known about the degree to which flocks remain together during the course of migration, on the wintering grounds, or through successive years.

At least some species of anatids and cranes remain together in family groups from breeding grounds to wintering grounds and back to breeding grounds. Though the young birds usually form their immediate families during their first breeding season, they may still travel with the larger "extended family" group (see FLOCK).

EFFECTS OF WEATHER. Weather in the sense of climatic conditions is an essential element in the major theories on the origins of migration (see Why Birds Migrate, above).

Day-to-day weather conditions affect migrant birds much as they do traveling humans. Clouds, fog, and precipitation often result in poor visibility, greater expenditure of energy, and occasionally physical danger (see Hazards, below). A clear atmosphere frees migrants from these negative factors, produces certain benefits such as thermals for soaring birds (see How Birds Migrate, above, and Soaring under FLIGHT), and is often accompanied by favorable winds.

Wind is the most important single climatic element affecting bird migration. Recent analyses have shown that principal migration directions and routes coincide worldwide with prevailing directions of upper-level winds. It is reasonable to speculate that high-altitude migrants might evolve migration patterns which would coincide with consistent tail winds. And this theory seems to be supported, for example, by the generally northwest-to-southeast direction of fall migration in North America and an absence of migrant concentrations in regions where winds blow consistently contrary to the course of migration. Further evidence of the influence of wind on migration appears in instances of reverse migration in which birds migrating with the prevailing wind will change their course when the wind does, even when this takes them in the opposite direction from their intended destination and exposes them to danger.

The northwest winds which accompany cold fronts in the fall are thought to act as a "green light" for birds which are "ready" to migrate.

See also WEATHER.

HAZARDS. When migrating, birds are more vulnerable due to lack of cover, the stresses and complexities of the long journey, and the vagaries of the weather. Traveling in the open, they are more susceptible than usual to predators. Merlins and Sharp-shinned Hawks, for example, maintain *their* migratory energy by eating smaller birds.

It is well known that juvenile birds on their first migration are beset with problems. Some are led astray by confusing winds, others simply migrate in the wrong direction, while others find themselves far out to sea— where they perish. Both oceans become the final resting place for untold thousands of young migrants. While juveniles may be more vulnerable than adults, all are subject to climatic vagaries that can cause the death of millions of birds (see MORTALITY) or drive them thousands of miles off course. It is by such accidents that Black-and-White Warblers end up in the California desert and Fork-tailed Flycatchers on the coast of Maine, causing excitement among the birding community. "It is an ill wind . . ."

Of increasing concern to conservationists is harassment of coastal migrants, such as terns and shorebirds, which must rest and feed along certain beaches, mud flats, and marshes. The greatly increased recreational use of such places competes with the birds' need to make restorative stops. Other man-made hazards to migrant birds include lighthouses, skyscrapers, and communications towers, the lights of which attract nocturnal migrants, particularly in bad weather. Hundreds of birds frequently become disoriented by the light and injure or kill themselves against the structures as they fly about aimlessly (see MAN-MADE THREATS TO BIRDLIFE).

CONCENTRATIONS. Nocturnal migrants tend to travel in fronts or "waves" which coincide with favorable/unfavorable weather patterns. This phenomenon often results in the arrival of a large number of birds of many species at favorable or opportune stopping points. Spectacular concentrations of migrants often occur as a result of bad weather, as when a "norte" meets a wave of migrants arriving on the U.S. Gulf coast from Mexico. When this happens, millions of exhausted birds concentrate on the first available landfall rather than dispersing northward as they normally would (see NORTHER).

Concentrations also occur at the tips of certain peninsulas which lie in the path of a migration. Migrants following a coastline to the shortest crossing point between two shores "pile up" in the topographical cul-de-sac before they head out across the water (see POINT PELEE). A similar "funnel effect" can be expected where soaring migrants which must avoid long water crossings find a "bridge" or narrows between two large bodies of water (see CAPE MAY).

Soaring birds, particularly raptors, also concentrate along mountain ridges which parallel the migration route, where updrafts help keep the birds aloft (see HAWK MOUNTAIN).

VERTICAL MIGRATION. Many bird species which summer at high elevations move on a regular seasonal basis down to foothills or plains for the winter. Though they travel only a few thousand feet at most, these altitudinal migrants are responding to the same stimulus as the long-distance latitudinal migrants—namely, the need to retreat from a climate which cannot support them.

THE LITERATURE. The complexity and fascination of the migration phenomenon are reflected in the vast literature on the subject, much of it produced within the last twenty years. A brief treatment such as the above can only summarize richly detailed revelations, and the reader is urged to refer to the Bibliography, where some of the classic, most interesting and/or most readable works on migration are listed.

MIMICRY. In a biological context, imitation in form, color, pattern, and/or behavior of one species by another to the advantage of the imitator. So-called Batesian mimicry, in which a relatively uncommon species closely resembles a common but unpalatable or otherwise protected one and thereby gains security by disguise, is fairly common among insects but unknown in birds.

It has been suggested that the Zone-tailed Hawk has evolved to mimic the Turkey Vulture and thereby gains advantage over prey, which ignore vultures as harmless. (A similar claim has been made for the Common Black Hawk and its look-alike, the Black Vulture.) There can be no question that the hawk strongly resembles the vulture in color, pattern, form, and distinctive manner of flight. But it has also been suggested that the similarity is attributable simply to parallel evolution of an aerodynamically sound "design" for a raptor that forages over an extensive area. For a discussion of the question, see Willis (*Condor*, 65:313); Willis (*Condor*, 68:104); Mueller (*Condor*, 74:221); and Zimmermann (*Condor*, 78:420).

For "mimicry" of habitat, see COLOR AND PATTERN, *Concealment*, and Plate 3; for vocal mimicry, see SONG, *Vocal Mimicry*.

MIMIC THRUSH. A standard collective name for all 31 members of the family Mimidae (order Passeriformes), also known as the mockingbird or mockingthrush family. The family includes the catbirds, mockingbirds, thrashers, and tremblers. Ten species of mimic thrushes breed in North America and one other species (Bahama Mockingbird) has been recorded as an accidental straggler (see Appendix II).

The mimic thrushes are medium-sized (8 to 12 inches), mostly elongate songbirds, most of which have fairly long, narrow, decurved bills, pale (yellow, white, red) irises, relatively short, rounded wings, fairly long legs, and a long tail. A number of species are nearly uniform gray, brown, or black, while others are heavily streaked or spotted below.

The mimids are birds of brushy tangles, whether in the shrubby forest understory or sparse desert scrub. Many species inhabit open arid habitats. They forage largely on the ground in leaf litter, stony, dry riverbeds, and the like, feeding on small insects and other invertebrates as well as fruits and seeds. Some of the longer-billed thrashers probe into the soil for subterranean morsels. The butterfly-like flight of most mimids does not seem very efficient, and they are seldom seen to fly long distances, though several species are migratory.

The Northern Mockingbird is an extraordinarily talented vocal mimic, incorporating in its repertoire not only the songs of other birds but mechanical sounds as well, and in captivity readily imitates the human voice and other household noises (see SONG, *Vocal Mimicry*). Other members of the family also practice mimicry but none with the skill and enthusiasm of the Northern Mocker. Some mimids *never* imitate sounds, but all have repetitive, elaborate "bubbly" songs sometimes punctuated with harsher chatterings and abrupt snaps and clucks.

The nests of this family are usually set fairly low in shrubs or small trees and hidden by dense vegetation; some species will nest on the ground. The nests may be basket-like, i.e., loosely woven of sticks or made of finer materials and with a more compact shape, similar to the nests of many finches. The lining is of fine plant fibers, shredded bark, etc. Most species average 4–5 eggs (range: 2–7) but some average only 2–3. The eggs are pale to medium blue, immaculate or with fine or coarse reddish/brownish markings.

The mimic thrushes are a strictly New World family, ranging from southern Canada to the Patagonian desert (Argentina). Several of the North American species range continentwide, but there is an unusual variety of dry-country thrashers with local southwestern distributions.

See also MOCKINGBIRD; CATBIRD; THRASHER.

MIRROR (in wing). Occasionally used to refer (somewhat mysteriously) to the white spots in the black primary tips of many gull species. More rarely (but more plausibly) it is used as a synonym for speculum, the shiny area of feathers in the secondaries of many duck species. Compare WINDOW.

MIST NET. Now the most popular method of catching live birds for banding or marking, mist nets are made of very fine strands of black silk or nylon. They average between 30 and 40 feet in length and are available in various widths (3 to 7 feet) and mesh sizes. When hung between poles against a background of vegetation they are practically invisible, so that birds blunder into them and become harmlessly entangled.

In North America mist nets are available through biological suppliers, but only to licensed bird banders. For further details, see BANDING.

MITE. See FEATHER MITES; ECTOPARASITE.

MOBBING. See Fig. 14. The harassing of a predatory species, usually by mixed flocks of smaller passerines. Perched owls and hawks are frequently victims of noisy groups of tits, nuthatches, warblers, wrens, and other species, which call at, fly at, and, rarely, even strike at the presumed threat. Grackles, jays, and other nest robbers are "mobbed" in flight by tyrant flycatchers and other medium-sized species, and flocks of crows harry owls and hawks in a similar manner. It seems clear that the activity is a collective response to a common danger (participants are known to cross territorial boundaries in joining such mobs), but whether the intention is to drive the enemy away or simply to alert the avian community to the threat is unclear. The degree of feverish displacement activities (feeding, preening) often evident among members of a mob suggests that their response is an ambivalent mixture of fear and aggression. See especially Curio (1978).

MOCKINGBIRD. Standard English name for 16 members of the family Mimidae (order Passeriformes), most of them in the genus *Mimus.* The name is sometimes used as a collective to refer to the family as a whole (the mockingbirds). *The* (Northern) Mockingbird (*Mimus polyglottos*) is a common and widespread resident of the southern half of North America and northern Mexico. It is one of our best-known songbirds and among the

FIG. 14. "*Mobbing*" of owls in their daytime roosts is a strong, innate defensive urge in many forest birds. The beleaguered Screech Owl pictured here is harassed by (clockwise from top left): a Solitary Vireo, a Blue Jay, a Black-capped Chickadee, a Common Yellowthroat, another chickadee, a Hermit Thrush, and a Red-breasted Nuthatch. Notice that one of the chickadees is engaged in feeding actions and the thrush is preening its breast, both "irrelevant" expressions of the birds' ambivalence about whether to flee from the predator or act aggressively toward it (see REDIRECTION).

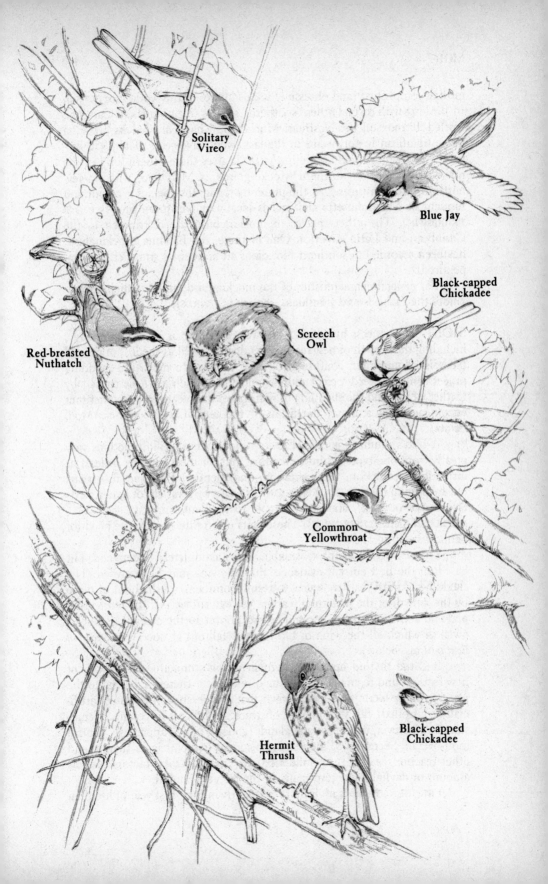

Solitary
Vireo

Blue Jay

Black-capped
Chickadee

Red-breasted
Nuthatch

Screech
Owl

Common
Yellowthroat

Hermit
Thrush

Black-capped
Chickadee

most accomplished (and obsessive) vocal mimics in the world (see SONG).

Along with several other "southern" species (e.g., Northern Cardinal, Tufted Titmouse), the Northern Mockingbird has extended its breeding range significantly northward in the last twenty-five years. The 1956 edition of Peterson's *Field Guide to the Birds* gives the northern limit of the main population of Northern Mockingbirds as Maryland, with "a few north to Massachusetts." At the present writing, the species is a common resident of Massachusetts and breeds locally in Newfoundland (see DISTRIBUTION). The other species of mockingbirds are distributed in the Caribbean and Latin America. One of these, the Bahama Mockingbird, has been recorded in southern Florida as an accidental straggler (see Appendix II).

For general characteristics of the mockingbird family (which also includes the catbirds and thrashers), see MIMIC THRUSH.

MOLT. The process by which a bird renews a part or all of its plumage, including the growth of new feathers (endysis) as well as the loss of the old (ecdysis). Sometimes, confusingly, "molt" is used to mean the shedding process only. Other types of plumage changes—such as those caused by feather wear—and the shedding of parts other than feathers are sometimes encompassed in a looser definition of the term (see *Non-feather Molt,* below).

A bird's plumage is crucial to its survival. Its specific functions vary greatly from one type of bird to another, but for most it serves at least as insulation, protection, transportation, and identity. Plumage also wears out by normal friction (see ABRASION), is eaten by a variety of live-in pests (see ECTOPARASITE), and is vulnerable to accidental damage (see MAN-MADE THREATS TO BIRDLIFE). These facts of birdlife explain the need for periodic molting.

PHYSIOLOGY. Complex, variable, and incompletely understood, but based on the best current evidence, the following may be ventured. The shedding of most feathers seems to result from being pushed out of place by the growth of the incoming feather (see FEATHER), i.e., the old feather plays no active role in the molt. The exceptions are the cases (e.g., ducks, owls) in which all the wing or tail feathers fall out at once (see *Order of Feather Loss,* below).

It is the thyroid hormone thyroxin which stimulates the growth of new feathers and regulates the timing of molt. It is therefore crucial to the process, and experiments have shown that its presence or absence (artificially controlled) can stimulate or obstruct the process in certain circumstances. However, it is the sexual glands (gonads) which apparently control molt overall. Secretion of the sexual hormones (which trigger thyroid and other reactions) is, in turn, influenced by environmental factors such as amount of daylight and (especially in the tropics) rainfall.

FREQUENCY. Birds molt more frequently in their first year of life than in any subsequent year, due to the down and/or juvenal plumages, which are, of course, unique to young birds. In addition to these two relatively brief stages, a first-year bird will also undergo the usual adult molts into a winter plumage and (often) into a "breeding" plumage the following spring (see *Molt/Plumage Sequence*, below). Thus, yearling birds, in many cases, molt three times to an adult's twice. A few birds (kingfishers, woodpeckers, the odd passerine) are completely naked until the juvenal plumage grows in and so *skip* a molt in the first year; other species (e.g., petrels and owls) have *two* down coats and so *add* one.

All adult birds molt at least once annually, though some eagles and cranes molt wing feathers over a span of two years. Many species molt *only* once a year, following the breeding season, at which time they renew their entire plumage. But a significant number—especially those species that migrate long distances or are otherwise subject to heavy feather wear—undergo at least a partial molt *before* the breeding season as well.

Drake Oldsquaws, departing from the normal pattern of male ducks in the Northern Hemisphere (see *Eclipse Plumage*, below), have a distinctive winter plumage (October to April), a "spring" plumage through the end of June, followed by the "eclipse" stage. A complete renewal of all feathers is achieved only after a full year's cycle, but most feathers are changed twice, and the longest scapular feathers are replaced three times in this species.

Ruffs (males) undergo three annual molts—a "supplemental" plumage intervenes in late winter between the basic (winter) and alternate (breeding) plumages—and other species of sandpipers are suspected of doing likewise.

Ptarmigan typically molt before the breeding season into their brown "summer" plumage, then begin a partial molt that leaves blotches of white amid the brown, and finally (in response to low temperature) change into their snow-white plumage. As many as four individual molts are perceived in this sequence by some authorities.

DATE AND DURATION. Timing of molt generally correlates with rhythms of the breeding cycle and therefore varies widely among species. Adults of some arctic-breeding shorebirds begin to molt into basic (winter) plumage as early as June before starting south in July, whereas double-brooded passerines in warmer climates may not begin this pre-basic (postnuptial) molt until August or September. A similar range applies to the pre-alternate (pre-nuptial) molt, which can take place in February for early nesters or not be complete until May for arctic species.

The calendar for birds that breed in the Southern Hemisphere is, of course, reversed, and for some seabirds that skip a breeding season, molt may extend throughout the year. Given the protracted nature of the process, it is clear that something is molting somewhere year-round.

The dropping of any given feather is of course more or less instantaneous—even the simultaneous shedding of the flight feathers of the wing as in ducks usually takes only a matter of hours. It is the growth of the new feathers that takes time—how much time varying greatly among different species according to genetic characteristics, age, climate, and, of course, whether the molt is partial or complete. Individual primaries and tail feathers of House Sparrows can attain full growth in 19–23 days (Zeidler, 1966), whereas those of the Eurasian Kestrel take 45 and 50 days (Welty, 1975–ORNITHOLOGY). Flight feathers of ducks (dropped simultaneously) may not be functional for 3 weeks to a month, and swans can remain flightless for up to 7 weeks. Birds that lose feathers traumatically tend to replace them faster than they would in the course of a normal molt.

With certain exceptions (see *Order of Feather Loss*, below), birds lose feathers gradually rather than all at once, the span of a full molt running from the loss of the first "old" feather(s) until the last "new" one(s) is (are) fully grown. A complete molt in passerines as a rule is encompassed between the dropping of the first flight feather and the full growth of the last one. This period tends to be shorter in long-distance migrants than in sedentary birds. The pre-basic (post-nuptial) molt may take as little as a month for some migrant songbirds, though the 49–56 days recorded for the Northern Wheatear (Williamson, 1957) is probably closer to the average. By comparison, the non-migratory House Sparrow averages 82 days to complete the same molt (Zeidler, 1966). And as noted above, some raptors (and other birds) shed and regenerate some feathers continually and do not complete a cycle for about two years.

Natal down feathers are pushed out on the tips of the incoming juvenal feathers and fall off almost immediately. The scant down of songbird nestlings is lost within a few days of hatching. The precocial chicks of many water birds lose their heavy down coat more slowly and gradually and may retain vestiges of this first plumage for 6 weeks or more. The body feathers of the juvenal plumage are relatively transitory, in some cases yielding to the first basic (winter) plumage before the juvenal wing and tail feathers are fully grown. Often these flight feathers remain until the second complete molt.

Another molt variable is the time required to reach "adult" plumage. There is a measure of ambiguity here since some species achieve adult *plumage* before they are sexually mature, while others are ready to breed though still superficially subadult. However, many small perching birds acquire a "definitive" plumage within three months of hatching. Others (e.g., Rose-breasted Grosbeak) spend a year in a recognizable "immature" plumage. Adult plumages remain "imperfect" (i.e., subadult) for several years in many species, and not a few (e.g., gulls, gannets) pass through distinctive stages over 3, 4, or 5 years. It has been reported that some eagles do not attain a fully "definitive" plumage for 8 to 10 years, though 5 or 6 seems to be the norm.

Most migratory species complete their post-nuptial molt before departing for winter quarters, but swallows and some hawks, falcons, and fly-catchers delay the process until they reach their destination.

EXTENT. The molt of natal down (if any) is, of course, complete. The subsequent juvenal plumage may be shed completely in favor of the first basic (winter) plumage, but in many species the wing and tail feathers of this first coat of contour feathers are retained through the first year. If there is a spring molt, it too is usually partial, omitting the flight feathers. A number of so-called breeding plumages result from feather wear and some heightening of pigment rather than feather renewal. Sharp-tailed Sparrows and Bobolinks, in contrast, are known to undergo a complete pre-nuptial molt.

The molt that follows the breeding period in adults is complete in almost all birds, though it may be delayed (see under *Duration*, above). Long-term, continuous molting of flight feathers in certain eagles and the "eclipse" molt of ducks (see *Sequence*, below) are, of course, not consistent with a single, complete post-nuptial molt.

The extent of molt has been tied, in the Phainopepla (Miller, 1933), to the length of the breeding period. In a late-breeding, migratory population in California, young birds underwent an incomplete post-juvenal molt as compared to the complete molt in juvenals of an early-breeding, resident population of the same subspecies.

There is some evidence that molt is sexually dimorphic in some species. Nolan (1978), for example, notes an apparently more complete pre-alternate (pre-nuptial) molt in male Prairie Warblers than in females.

MOLT/PLUMAGE SEQUENCE AND ITS TERMINOLOGY. Despite many variations in frequency, duration, and extent of molt, all birds change their feathers according to a regular sequence, which is highly predictable for any one species and is surprisingly consistent for all birdlife. To compare the differences, it is obviously necessary to have a standard terminology for referring to each distinctive plumage and the intervening molts. The terminology which has become traditional was proposed by Dwight (1900) on the basis of his studies in New York State. In 1959, Humphrey and Parkes proposed a new terminology intended to be more broadly applicable and to refine certain concepts. The basic differences in the two systems are these: (1) Dwight's terminology has a North Temperate Zone bias. What he calls "winter" plumage can with equal accuracy be called a "summer" plumage in the case of pelagic species which breed in the Southern Hemisphere during their summer and migrate to the Northern for *our* summer (their winter). Furthermore, molts of tropical species are usually correlated with wet and dry seasons which are not completely analogous to our summer and winter. Humphrey and Parkes replace "winter" with "basic" to refer to that plumage which is acquired annually in almost all birds by a complete molt regardless of season. The partial molt undergone annually by many species then produces an "alternate" plumage in the Humphrey-Parkes terminology. (2) Dwight ties his sequence to the breeding season, e.g., "first pre-nuptial molt," "first nuptial plumage." This makes it difficult to compare sequences of tropical species which breed more than once a year and pelagics and others which breed only every other year. Furthermore, many species are not yet ready to engage in nuptial activities in their first "nuptial" plumage. The term "alternate" is proposed to accommodate these anomalies.

Humphrey and Parkes also suggest the following refinements: (1) All molts should be named according to the incoming plumage, e.g., "post-juvenal" becomes "first pre-basic. (2) A "plumage" is defined as only those feathers acquired in the preceding molt. Dwight's nuptial plumage includes all of a bird's feathers worn after the pre-nuptial molt; in the Humphrey-Parkes terminology this "plumage" would not include the flight feathers retained from the basic (winter) plumage. The broad use of "plumage" to mean all the feathers currently worn is replaced in Humphrey-Parkes by "feather-coat." (3) Once the appearance of a bird's plumage has ceased to change with age it is called "definitive." This obviates the necessity of counting plumages after this point: a bird can be said to be in definitive basic plumage rather than its eighth (or eighteenth) winter plumage—unless, of course, its eighth basic (winter) plumage does show a change from the preceding.

The Humphrey-Parkes proposals have not been accepted universally (see Stresemann, 1963), but they are followed in many recent ornithological publications, as is the "traditional" terminology. In the summary of plumage sequences immediately below, the Humphrey-Parkes names are given first, followed by the Dwight names in parentheses; other terms frequently used for the molts and plumages are also noted. In the present work the Humphrey-Parkes terminology is preferred, but the Dwight equivalents are usually noted in parentheses.

NATAL DOWN (NATAL DOWN). Present to some degree in most birds; lacking in woodpeckers, kingfishers, some passerines; scant in cuckoos, trogons, hummingbirds, and most passerines; thick and virtually complete in hawks, owls, gallinaceous birds, and most water birds; some swifts are naked when hatched and acquire a heavy down covering; petrels and many owls have two successive down coats; hawks and eagles have two overlapping down coats of different textures.

PRE-JUVENAL MOLT (POST-NATAL MOLT). Always complete; down feathers attached to tips of juvenal feathers drop off soon after appearance of new feather.

JUVENAL PLUMAGE (JUVENAL PLUMAGE). First true contour feathers, but plumage appears "looser," softer, fluffier than following, and tail feathers often distinctively shaped. Usually a brief stage, with body feathers sometimes molting before flight feathers fully grown.

FIRST PRE-BASIC MOLT (POST-JUVENAL MOLT). May be complete but often flight feathers of juvenal plumage are retained.

FIRST BASIC PLUMAGE (FIRST WINTER PLUMAGE). May closely resemble adult winter plumage or be distinct in color and pattern; this and following plumages which are not "definitive" (see above) are often called "immature" plumages; worn at least through the first winter.

FIRST PRE-ALTERNATE MOLT (FIRST PRE-NUPTIAL MOLT). Does not occur in all species; is usually partial (flight feathers retained) when does occur, but is complete at least in a few species.

FIRST ALTERNATE PLUMAGE (FIRST NUPTIAL PLUMAGE). Also called "breeding," "spring," or "summer" plumage. Usually brighter than basic (winter) plumage, sometimes due to feather wear and/or fading rather than feather renewal (e.g., Common Starling, Snow Bunting); some species acquire special features, e.g., plumes, "extra" patches of color; retained only through the breeding period; yearling birds of some species indistinguishable from adults in this plumage.

SECOND PRE-BASIC MOLT (FIRST POST-NUPTIAL MOLT). Almost invariably complete (some raptors and cranes prolong change of flight feathers over two years); migratory species usually complete before departure; some delay until wintering grounds.

SECOND BASIC PLUMAGE (SECOND WINTER PLUMAGE). Most species show no signs of "immature" plumage by this stage and their plumage can then be called "definitive basic" or "adult winter."

Subsequent molts and plumages follow the same timing and duration pattern as this second cycle, though the plumage patterns of a number of species (e.g., gulls) continue to change for 4 or 5 years and continue to be numbered accordingly.

ECLIPSE PLUMAGE. In most male ducks of the Northern Hemisphere the pre-alternate (pre-nuptial) molt begins in the fall and is completed in the winter rather than occurring near the beginning of the breeding season as in most birds which undergo such a molt.

The basic ("winter") plumage in ducks, which is assumed during summer (after the eggs are laid), is, as in most birds, dull in comparison to the nuptial plumage, resembling, in fact, the relatively unchanging female plumage. Because of this dullness and the "premature" beginning of the pre-alternate (pre-nuptial) molt, the basic plumage seems more like a brief effacing of the drakes' bright breeding plumage than the more usual long-term basic (winter) plumage. However, except for the timing and the fact that ducks drop all their wing and tail feathers simultaneously in the pre-basic (post-nuptial) molt, the term "eclipse" could be applied with equal accuracy to the basic (winter) plumage of the Scarlet Tanager. The latter simply lasts longer.

Exceptions are male Ruddy Ducks, which have a "normal" pre-alternate (pre-nuptial) molt in spring, and Oldsquaws, which have summer, winter, *and* eclipse plumages (see above).

ORDER OF FEATHER LOSS. Except for a slightly unkempt appearance or gaps in the wings of large birds in flight, the molting process seldom comes to our attention. This is because in the vast majority of species it occurs over a period of weeks or months in an overlapping and symmetrical order without sudden changes or conspicuous bare patches.

The order in which feathers are lost is part of a bird's genetic heritage and is so consistent for a given species or group that it has been used as a taxonomic character. However, a few generalities may be ventured regarding molt sequence.

A complete molt (usually the pre-basic/post-nuptial) normally begins with the innermost (first) primaries of each wing (see Fig. 25); when these two feathers have dropped and the new first primaries are partially grown, the two second primaries are shed, and so on. In some cases, the first *and* seventh primaries are shed simultaneously and the molt proceeds outward from two (actually four) starting points. When about half the primaries are molted, the tertials begin to drop from the outermost (first) inward. The first (outermost) secondary falls after the loss of the third (last) tertial and is also succeeded inward. Clearly the gradual, sequential, and symmetrical pattern of this molt is crucial in maintaining the ability to fly—which in turn is a small bird's greatest asset in avoiding predators.

The molt of the tail feathers follows a similar pattern. In most species, it begins with the central pair of rectrices and proceeds outward in opposite directions; in a few, the sequence is exactly the reverse; and in fewer still, an intermediate pair is the first to fall and the sequence proceeds *both* inward and outward. Woodpeckers and Brown Creepers, in which the tail molt proceeds outward, retain the two central feathers for support in perching until the other rectrices are well grown.

The molting of the body feathers begins during the wing molt and has been shown to follow a highly predictable progression in at least some species. Baird (1958) chronicles this progression in male Brown-headed Cowbirds undergoing their (incomplete) first pre-basic (post-juvenal) molt. He finds that the first area of body feathers to complete the molt sequence is the breast, followed by the nape, and that the underwing areas are completed last. Following the nape, the other head feathers of juvenal cowbirds are molted in the order: throat, lores, crown, forehead, chin, malar area, auriculars, and orbital area. Except for the breast, the other regions of the body (back, belly, sides, flanks, rump) progress more or less simultaneously (though gradually). Baird further observed that within each body region feathers are lost and regained in a consistent direction, e.g., the nape feathers from the inside out (centrifugally); the lores from the outside in (centripetally); the back feathers from front to back and from the center toward the edges; and the belly feathers from front to back and from the edges toward the center. In general, the feathers at the periphery of the feather tracts are molted last, and in immature cowbirds the molt process often comes to an end before these last juvenal feathers are shed.

The sudden loss of many feathers at once in healthy birds is characteristic of only a few groups of birds. Loons, grebes, anhingas, flamingos,
ducks, geese, and swans, most rails, many alcids, and dippers lose their
wing feathers simultaneously and so are rendered flightless for a period
ranging from a few days (dippers) to 7 weeks (swans). Ducks, geese, and
swans also lose all their tail feathers at once during this molt, and smaller
owls lose just their tail feathers in this precipitous manner.

The relative helplessness of ducks while flightless is a plausible factor
in the evolution of the dull eclipse plumage which "conceals" their normally conspicuous plumage from potential predators.

A few members of the crow family (e.g., Black-billed Magpie) shed all
head and neck feathers in a very short period.

IRREGULAR AND ABNORMAL MOLTS. It should be clear from the preceding section that most birds seen lacking a tail or other feathers have lost
them accidentally. Such losses regenerate within a few weeks rather than
wait for the next normal molting period. However, it has been demonstrated in some species that the replacement feathers are "subtracted," so
to speak, from the upcoming molt and will not be shed again at that time.
Thus if one were to pluck a Scarlet Tanager in basic (winter) plumage, the
red feathers of the upcoming alternate (breeding) plumage will come in,
producing a splotchy effect. Birds have been made to delay or skip molts in
laboratory experiments, but wild individuals whose plumage is "out of
sync" with that of its fellows can be presumed to be suffering from a disease or other abnormality. For other irregularities of this kind, see PLUM-
AGE, *Abnormal Variation.*

NON-FEATHER MOLT. As noted in the definition (above), "molt" is
sometimes used broadly as a synonym for "shed." Thus puffins and auklets
in the genera *Cerorhinca* and *Aethia* and American White Pelicans, which
acquire bill sheaths or ornaments prior to the breeding season, are said to
"molt" them afterward. This usage is also applied to the egg tooth and
heel pads found in nestling birds.

MONOMOY National Wildlife Refuge (Massachusetts). A 10-mile-long
sandspit extending southward from the "elbow" of Cape Cod into Nantucket Sound. At times Monomoy has been accessible by foot (albeit wet
foot) from the mainland, but its fragile form is subject to the whims of
winter storms, and at present it must be reached by boat. Because it is out
of reach for the casual beachgoer, Monomoy has remained a true coastal
wilderness, combining unspoiled ocean beach, dunes, tidal flats, migrant-
trapping copses of bayberry and beach plum, freshwater "kettle" ponds,
and—because of its seaward-jutting length—excellent vantage points for
watching pelagic birds without risking seasickness. Virtually every species
of bird ever recorded in Massachusetts has been seen on Monomoy, and it
seems to harbor at least one avian rarity—arctic, western, tropical, or

Eurasian—continually. The 2,700-acre refuge includes part of Morris Island (connected by bridge to the mainland at Chatham), where the management office is located. Unless you have boat-owning friends in the area, the best access to Monomoy is by private charter from Chatham.

MONOPHAGOUS (mo-NAH-fa-gus). Tolerant of only a single type of food. The Everglade Kite, for example, apparently feeds on nothing but the large snails in the genus *Pomacea.* Needless to say, the fate of monophagous birds is closely linked with that of their preferred food. If "apple" snails disappear due to disease or draining of wetlands, Everglade Kites may also be doomed. Compare EURYPHAGOUS; STENOPHAGOUS.

MONOTYPIC. Referring to a taxonomic category which contains only a single representative of the category immediately below it. The loon family, Gaviidae, is monotypic since it contains only a single genus, *Gavia.* However, the genus *Gavia* is *polytypic,* since it contains four species. An example of a monotypic genus is *Dolichonyx,* which contains only the Bobolink (*D. oryzivorus*), and the American Avocet, which has not been divided into subspecies, is a monotypic species. It is not possible to have a single subspecies; there must be either none or more than one.

MONTANE. Of the mountains; montane birds are those which are characteristic of elevations at least 1,000 feet (usually higher) above sea level. A montane region is generally determined by the presence of plant or animal life which is distinct from that of the lowlands. This transition takes place gradually, of course, with increase in elevation and consequent change in climate, and it varies from one highland region to another, so that some montane zones begin lower than others. The alpine zone above tree line is sometimes treated as distinct from the montane zone, immediately below.

MONTEREY (California). This region of coastal California, including the Monterey Peninsula, Pacific Grove, Point Lobos, and Big Sur immediately to the south, offers some of the best Pacific water-birding at any season as well as excellent land-birding in adjacent pine-oak and redwood groves. The municipal pier in Monterey has been the starting point for many a fine pelagic trip; boats can be chartered at will, but local bird clubs run a number of trips a year at appreciably less cost to the individual (see Appendix III for species timing). A few of the specialties of the greater Monterey region are (birds marked with an asterisk are best seen at sea): Black-footed Albatross,* a variety of shearwaters* and storm-petrels,* Brandt's and Pelagic Cormorants, numbers of sea ducks, Black Oystercatcher, Black Turnstone, Wandering Tattler, Rock Sandpiper, Western, Glaucous-winged, and Thayer's Gulls, a variety of alcids,* Steller's and Scrub Jays, Chestnut-backed Chickadee, Pygmy Nuthatch, Varied Thrush (winter), Hutton's Vireo, Townsend's and Hermit Warblers, and Cassin's Finch (winter). Sea otters are now common in coastal kelp beds, and the wintering hordes of monarch butterflies at Pacific Grove are another non-avian winter diversion.

MONTEZUMA, c. 1480–1520 (Montezuma, or Harlequin, Quail: *Cyrtonyx montezumae*). Chief of the Aztecs, who were the indigenous rulers of much of Mexico until their empire fell to Cortez and his conquistadors. Most of this quail's range lies in Mexico; it reaches the U.S. only in southernmost Arizona, New Mexico, and western Texas. See Plate 1.

MOON WATCHING. A technique for studying certain aspects of nocturnal bird migration, made popular by Lowery and Newman (Newman, 1952). The procedure for collecting the raw data is quite simple. In a typical instance an observer trains an ordinary 20x spotting telescope on the face of the moon, usually from two days before to two days after the full moon, when the maximum lunar surface is illuminated. Birds seen flying across the moon are recorded in terms of their numbers, the size of their image, the time of their passing, and their direction in relation to the moon face, e.g., "9 o'clock to 3 o'clock." If to this information the observer adds the elevation of the moon—obtained by fastening a protractor to the side of the scope—he can then calculate the *real* direction and number of birds passing on a mile front using a formula and table devised by Nisbet (1959).

Antedating the study of nocturnal migration by RADAR, moon watching yielded much new information on numbers of migrants, the importance of "flyways" (relatively slight), spatial density (individual migrating songbirds tend to maintain wide spacing rather than travel in compact flocks), and the influence of wind (relatively great), among other data.

See MIGRATION.

MORPHOLOGY (morphological, morph). In the strictest sense, morphology is form or the study thereof. However, in zoology, it is now widely applied to any structural aspect of an organism whether external or internal. For example, both the pattern of intestinal loops and the position of the toes in birds are known as "morphological taxonomic characters." A "morph" is a variation (form or "phase") that may occur within a population of a given species (as distinct from racial variations), e.g., the "dark morph" of the Pomarine Jaeger or the "ringed phase" of the Common Murre. Plate 4 shows dark and light morphs of the Rough-legged Hawk.

MORTALITY. Sheltered as most of us now are from the majority of nature's deadliest ravages by recent discoveries in medicine and other technologies, we are inclined to be appalled at the comparatively huge mortality rates sustained by birds and other forms of animal life. It has been estimated, for example, that during the nestling stage, when vulnerability is generally greatest, the *average* mortality rate among passerine birds is about 50 percent (Nice, 1957). Within this average there is enormous variation based on species biology, food supply, weather conditions in a given season, and many other unpredictable factors obtaining only locally. But the average shows that for every circumstance in which 90 percent of passerine nestlings survive, there exists another in which 90 percent perish. Nor does maturity bring any great security. The toll that weather, predation, and the "success" of our own species take on bird populations makes a bird species' normal life span totally inconsistent with its expected longevity in captivity (see AGE).

The many instances of awesomely vast "natural" mortalities of birdlife now documented seem at first to encourage the notion that bird populations must be invulnerable to any threats posed by human agency. But natural mortalities are redressed by long-term counterbalances that have been built into the rhythm of the ecosystem over eons. Species that are subject to heavy predation or that suffer great annual losses due to the many hazards of long-distance migration, for example, tend to compensate for the drain on their overall population with such biological characteristics as large clutch size and number of broods, density within breeding niches, broad total range, colonial nesting, etc. Thus when 148,000 waterfowl succumb to hailstorms in Alberta over a 2½-month period (Smith and Webster, 1955–WEATHER) or untold thousands of songbird migrants are drowned in Lake Huron due to adverse weather conditions during their crossing (Saunders, 1907) or like numbers of Dovekies are stranded ashore by fall gales and die of starvation or predation by gulls (Snyder, 1960)— the populations of the species involved recover fully and, as it were, automatically. We may notice temporary population declines locally, as in the well-documented decimation of the northeastern bluebird population during early-spring ice storms in 1940, but we can confidently predict a rapid recovery from such natural cataclysms, unless, like the California Condor, the species as a whole is reaching the end of its tenure on the planet.

So integrated into the maintenance of population stability are such normal mortality factors as weather and predation that, viewed objectively, they can be seen as beneficial influences that keep us from being buried in warblers or Dovekies (see also POPULATION; PREDATION).

In sharp contrast to the ecological give-and-take that ultimately permits the harmonious coexistence of an unimaginable variety of organisms are the occasional great upsets that devastate a wide range of organisms on many fronts and thereby ultimately alter the whole system profoundly. One good example of this sort of upset is a major ice age. Another is humanity's recent domination of the earth. The resiliency of bird populations is amply demonstrated in their ability to sustain multiple losses such as those cited above, but within the last 300 years or so they have ceased to be a match for our ubiquity and our still increasing efficiency in altering the planet's surface and atmosphere. With one invention alone—firearms—coupled with the insatiable appetite of our burgeoning population, we accomplished in a few decades what no weather condition or non-human predator has ever achieved—the extinction of an entire species. In fact, we did it many times over (see EXTINCT BIRDS). Yet guns are now the least of our life-threatening inventions, and the ability of birds or anything else to "bounce back" from the cumulative effect of deforestation, oil spills, pesticides, radio towers, automobiles, acid rain, picture windows, domestic animals, hydrogen bombs, etc., must be deeply doubted. (See MAN-MADE THREATS TO BIRDLIFE for statistics on some of these hazards.)

Having overwhelmed the natural balance, we rely on our alleged ability to balance the world ecosystem ourselves. Regarding the likelihood of this, the optimist points to our retreat from the wanton slaughter of egrets for hat decorations (see CONSERVATION), the cynic to our retreat from environmental protection policy in the face of minor reductions in the gluttonous living standard to which we in the West have recently become accustomed.

MOULT. See MOLT.

MOUNT LEMMON. See SOUTHEASTERN ARIZONA.

MOUNT PINOS Condor Observation Site (California). Perhaps the best (certainly the best-known) place to glimpse the increasingly rare California Condor (see ENDANGERED BIRDS). Located about 65 miles north of Los Angeles and reached from the town of Gorman, the site is best visited July–September.

MURPHY, Robert Cushman, 1887–1973. One of the most prominent American ornithologists of the twentieth century. Murphy's reputation is inextricably bound to the seabird fauna of South America. Born in Brooklyn, he developed strong passions for both natural history and the nautical life while growing up on Long Island, interests that together formed the basis of his long career. His professional ornithological life began immediately following his graduation from high school when he helped Frank Chapman edit his forthcoming *Warblers of North America* at the American Museum of Natural History in New York City. After receiving his undergraduate degree at Brown University, Murphy at once set sail on the brig *Daisy* to circumnavigate South America on what was perhaps the last commercial whaling voyage ever under sail. From this experience came his classic journal *Logbook for Grace* (1947), kept for the new bride he had left at home, and the inspiration for his lifelong study of pelagic birds. His magnum opus on the subject is *Oceanic Birds of South America* (1936), a two-volume work noted for its meticulous detail, finely written anecdotal text, and evocative illustrations by F. Lee Jaques. Though he never took a Ph.D., he eventually assumed the chairmanship of the department of ornithology at the American Museum, held his share of prestigious offices (e.g., president of the A.O.U., 1948–50), and garnered the awards due our most distinguished ornithologists. He was an ardent conservationist. Writing *in memoriam*, Dean Amadon implies that Robert Cushman Murphy inspired affection as well as respect by achieving an admirable balance of character traits: he was meticulous without being fussy, ambitious but patient, well-to-do yet liberal.

MURRE (rhymes with "fur," not "cure"). Standard English name in North America for the 2 species of auks in the genus *Uria* (family Alcidae; order Charadriiformes), both of which breed and winter in North America.

Like all but a few species of alcids, the murres are birds of arctic and subarctic seas. They nest on narrow ledges on precipitous cliffs or rocky islets and spend the rest of their lives at sea. The Thick-billed Murre is restricted to the North Atlantic, while the Common Murre inhabits the North Pacific as well.

The origin of the name is uncertain; it may come from a Celtic word referring to these and similar birds. In British usage, the murres are called guillemots.

For family characteristics, see AUK.

MURRELET (MERR-lit). Standard English name for 5 or 6 (depending on taxonomy) species of auks (family Alcidae; order Charadriiformes) in 2 or 3 genera, all but one of which breed along the Pacific coasts of North America. Except perhaps for the two members of the genus *Synthliboramphus* (including the Ancient Murrelet), which have a mildly ornate alternate (breeding) plumage, the murrelets do indeed resemble small (under 10 inches) murres (genus *Uria*).

It is in their breeding habits that the murrelets distinguish themselves from the other auks. Xantus' and Craveri's Murrelets (believed by some taxonomists to be conspecific) breed farther south than any other species of alcid—the latter species (or race) nesting on islands in the Gulf of California and ranging *north* for the winter. Kittlitz's Murrelet breeds above the tree line on mountaintops, some distance from the sea, laying its single egg on bare rock. Most remarkable of all is the Marbled Murrelet, which sometimes nests in trees. One nest site 148 feet from the ground on a branch (near the trunk) of a Douglas fir was discovered by accident in 1974 south of San Francisco; another nest was found a mere 20 feet up in a larch tree in taiga near the Soviet coastal city of Okhotsk.

For family characteristics, see AUK.

MUSCLES. In birds as in humans, muscles are the principal mechanisms by which the needs and desires of the body are transformed into action. There are three basic types of muscles: the *visceral* muscles, which control involuntary movement such as those of the internal organs; the *skeletal* muscles, which act in conjunction with the skeleton at the will of the brain; and the specialized *cardiac* muscles, which make up the greatest part of the heart. The skeletal muscles are the most familiar to us. They are the meat or flesh of a bird's body and on average make up about 50 percent of body weight.

Anyone who has eaten a chicken knows that these skeletal muscles come in two colors, one dark and one light. These are composed of different types of muscle fiber which are fueled in different ways and function in different manners. The dark red fiber burns accumulated fat, using oxygen carried by the blood. The muscles thus fueled are capable of strenuous sustained activity, e.g., the wing muscles of strong fliers or the leg muscles of species which walk, run, or paddle. The paler fibers (white meat) are fueled by a carbohydrate (glycogen) which is stored in the liver of most animals; these provide quick bursts of power, which, however, cannot be sustained for long. There is a third type of muscle fiber intermediate between these two in both color and function.

There are 175 skeletal muscles, most of them paired symmetrically, one on each side of the body. They function in virtually all parts of the body, sometimes working in intricate combinations or performing subtle operations, but always on a fundamentally simple principle. Basically, they work by pulling and releasing or, more precisely, contracting and relaxing. The brain transmits an impulse through nerve fibers which are connected to muscle fibers. Given the appropriate signal, the center of the muscle contracts, pulling its extremities inward. The extremities end in strong, fibrous, inelastic *tendons*, which attach the muscles to a bone. These often pass over another bone or through a loop of tissue, so that when the tendons are pulled on by the contracting muscles, they haul on the bone to which they are attached in a manner strongly reminiscent of a rope and pulley. An excellent example of this is the way the wings are raised and lowered by the pectoral muscles (see below and Fig. 10).

To define all of the muscles of a bird, their functions and variations among different groups, and to sort out the nomenclature and confusions which have plagued avian myology from its inception to the present, would require a book larger than this one. However, a few muscular phenomena which are specialized in birds deserve mention.

Not surprisingly, the areas of complex or highly developed musculature in birds are the ones which play the most significant roles in their habits, e.g., the muscles of jaw, neck, wings, and legs. Abdominal muscles and those of the lower back are relatively little used by birds and therefore tend to be less prominent than in mammals.

Control of Body Feathers is achieved by muscles of the skin. These serve to streamline body contours for efficient aerodynamics (see FLIGHT); to "fluff" or raise feathers for preening and drying; to squeeze air from the body feathers to reduce buoyancy, as for the kind of "sinking" dive practiced by some grebes; and to erect and lower crests or other features used in display. Of course, some "motions" used in display, such as the erecting of fleshy wattles or inflating of air sacs, are achieved by engorging the tissue with blood or by respiratory action, rather than by muscle contraction.

Neck Muscles are unusually numerous and complex in birds with long, mobile necks, e.g., herons and anhingas. Birds which plunge from the air into the sea, e.g., gannets and pelicans, have unusually powerful neck muscles capable of absorbing shocks.

In this context of neck motions—many of which are forward or thrusting—it is interesting to reflect that *all* muscular actions are accomplished by "pulling" as described above and *none* by "pushing."

Jaw Muscles. *Adductors* are muscles which move things together, and those controlling the closing of a bird's bill are highly developed in finches, which must crush hard seeds. In some seed-eating species the equivalent of more than 100 pounds per square inch of pressure is applied to the crushing of hard fruit pits (see BILL).

The Breast (Pectoral) Muscles are the muscles which power flight. They are usually the most prominent of a bird's muscles and may account for up to a third of body weight (hummingbirds). They are securely anchored to the broad surface of the breastbone (sternum), pass through scapular and coracoidal bones, and pull the upper wing bone (humerus) up and down in a classic example of the rope-and-pulley action described above (see FLIGHT and Fig. 10).

The Hatching Muscle, attached to the back of the skull, begins to appear early in the development of the embryo and attains full growth in time to aid the young bird in pipping and emerging from the egg (see HATCHING). This specialized muscle disappears gradually after its function has been fulfilled.

Perching Ability. It was long supposed that as a bird flexed its "ankle" (tarsal) joints in perching, the tendons that pass down the leg and over this joint to the tips of the toes were "automatically" pulled, closing the toes like a clenched fist around the perch. This also provided a convenient explanation for how birds are able to cling to a perch while asleep. However, recent research and observation do not support this logical description and reveal in fact that the front toes do not need to be clenched tightly around the perch and the hind toe (hallux) need not necessarily even be in contact with the perch, much less lock around it (see Bock, 1965). On the other hand, a locking mechanism does exist in the tendons of a bird's front toes to hold the toes in whatever position they assume when the bird perches. Hundreds of tiny projections from the undersurface of the toe tendons catch firmly in corresponding ridges on the inner surface of the tendon sheaths when the weight of the bird presses down on the toe bones under which the tendons lie.

Formula Muscles. Late in the nineteenth century the anatomist A. H. Garrod discovered that certain muscles of the pelvis and legs varied extremely and consistently among categories of birds, one species having *more* than another, for example, or the same number in a different combination. This system has been refined by various workers (e.g., George and Berger, 1966) as a method of classification and now uses up to thirteen different muscles, lettered A, B, C, D, E, F, G, M, N, V, X, Y, and Am. The formula represented in the muscles of most passerines, for example, is ACEFMNXY, while that of the Chimney Swift, with scant musculature in the pelvic region, is simply AEN.

MUSEUMS. For the public at large, the relationship between museums and birdlife is discovered in those high-ceilinged halls—known to every schoolchild from at least one "field trip"—in which mounted bird specimens are displayed in glass cases. Such exhibits range in quality from dismal regiments of misshapen avian corpses, made anonymous by a combination of inept taxidermy and years of accumulated dust, to wonderfully vivid re-creations of habitat with birds mounted skillfully in lifelike postures and placed against evocative painted backgrounds, e.g., the famous dioramas at the American Museum of Natural History in New York City. At their best, museum displays are undoubtedly effective in educating visitors about the wonders of the world avifauna or their own local one and in fanning the enthusiasm of young naturalists. But the museum's greater purpose in the study of birdlife is housed beyond those signs which say "Employees Only," in the rooms filled with enormous cases, reeking of fumigants and a variety of other pungent odors, where the collections of scientific specimens are stored. In the largest and best-curated collections, tens of thousands of carefully prepared and meticulously labeled bird skins lie side by side in drawer after drawer, showing (ideally) a complete range of size and age, geographical, plumage, and other variations for each species and arranged in their proper taxonomic order. The uninitiated can be forgiven if he finds the idea of these vast ornithological mortuaries unappealing on first encounter, but eventually he should understand that scientific collections are crucial to the study of phylogeny, evolution, plumage and molt, migration, anatomy, and other subjects that contribute to our understanding of living birds. Even the field guides, without which the increasingly popular sport of birdwatching would not exist, could not have been written or illustrated without the use of specimens. For a more specific discussion of the uses and "ethics" of museum collections, see BIRD SKIN; COLLECTING; and the Bibliography for this entry.

Now that the collecting of specimens is being severely restricted even in the remotest parts of the world, the great bird collections assembled over decades are an increasingly valuable, non-renewable scientific resource.

As of 1973, nine North American museums owned over 100,000 bird skins. Ranked in order of their specimen wealth, they are:

American Museum of Natural History, New York City (900,000 skins)

National Museum, Smithsonian Institution, Washington, D.C. (400,000 skins)

Field Museum of Natural History, Chicago (300,000 skins)

Museum of Comparative Zoology, Harvard University, Cambridge, Mass. (300,000 skins)

University of Michigan Museum of Zoology, Ann Arbor (200,000 skins)

Academy of Natural Sciences, Philadelphia

Carnegie Museum, Pittsburgh

Museum of Vertebrate Zoology, University of California, Berkeley

Royal Ontario Museum, Ottawa

Of course, natural history museums also frequently contain collections of skeletons, specimens preserved in fluid, eggs, etc., in addition to bird skins, all of which fill the needs of particular branches of ornithological research.

For a systematic listing by state of museum collections in North America with statistics on specimens (of all kinds) and the regional or taxonomic "bias" (if any) of each, see Banks et al. (1973).

MUSIC (birds in). See HUMAN CULTURE.

MUSKEG. A term that has been applied to a wide range of boreal/low arctic habitats from open boglands to "forested tundra." Some authorities resolve the ambiguity by describing as many as five different kinds of muskeg. A common element in most definitions is a degree of wetness, which in turn implies the presence of plants such as *Sphagnum* moss and cotton grass and other sedges, but spruces, scrub willows, and alders at borders or on islands of higher ground may also be considered characteristic of muskeg. In its open wetland incarnation, muskeg is typically frequented by a variety of duck and sandpiper species. Hawk Owl, Palm Warbler, and Rusty Blackbird are among the characteristic species of more wooded muskeg. See also TAIGA; TUNDRA; BOREAL; ARCTIC; SUBARCTIC.

MUSTACHIAL STRIPE. A mark running through the malar region, i.e., from the base of the bill back along the side of the throat, as that on the Black-whiskered Vireo (see Fig. 1).

MUTATION. A sudden change in a gene or chromosome which may produce a visible new genetic character; also an individual showing a change in a genetic character possessed by both of its parents. See EVOLUTION; SPECIATION.

MYIARCHUS (my-AR-kuss). A New World genus of about 15 species of tyrant flycatchers (family Tyrannidae; order Passeriformes), 4 of which breed in North America. Two other species have been recorded as accidental stragglers (see Appendix II).

Most *Myiarchus* are fairly large (8 to 9 inches), long-tailed, somewhat crested flycatchers. Most have olive backs and heads, some rufous in wings and tail, some yellow on the belly, and some gray on the throat. North American species are normally sorted out easily on the basis of range and habitat as well as comparatively obvious superficial differences. In the Neotropics, where the ranges of two or more very similar species frequently overlap, they are often best distinguished by voice. This problem also arises when vagrant *Myiarchus* appear in North America out of their normal range.

The *Myiarchus* are cavity nesters, an unusual preference among the tyrant flycatchers.

For family characteristics, see TYRANT FLYCATCHER.

MYNAH (myna). Standard English name for about 22 species of Asian birds in the starling family (Sturnidae). One of these is a popular cage bird, the Hill or Talking Mynah, *Gracula religiosa* (see AVICULTURE; SONG, *Vocal Mimicry*), and another species, the Crested Mynah, *Acridotheres cristatellus*, was introduced to the Vancouver region of British Columbia around the end of the nineteenth century. In its native distribution in Southeast Asia the latter is an open-country bird which has adapted well to cultivated habitats. In northwestern North America it visits farmland and dumps. Like most members of its family, it is a skillful mimic. Its North American distribution is not expanding (see INTRODUCED BIRDS).

The name is generalized from the Hindi word for the common and widespread Indian species of mynahs.

For family characteristics, see STARLING.

MYTHICAL BIRDS. See IMAGINATION.

N

NAIL (of bill). The ducks, geese, and swans (family Anatidae) have a hard hooked tip on the upper mandible. This functions in the cropping of aquatic vegetation—or grass in the case of grazing geese—and is called the "nail" or, more technically, the unguis. Birds also have toenails, though they are usually called claws.

NAMES, COLLOQUIAL. People the world over give names to conspicuous birds or those that have some significant impact on their daily lives. Cultures—even primitive ones—which use birds extensively for food or adornment tend to have a high degree of recognition at least of the "useful" bird species and invent names to differentiate them. These colloquial or local names almost always refer to some distinctive plumage, voice, or behavioral characteristic. In this regard, in fact, they are often more relevant and almost invariably more imaginative and pleasing than standardized vernacular (common) names (see NAMES, VERNACULAR).

Of course, the great majority of "official" or standard English names for North American species derive from colloquial stock, sometimes of ancient lineage. Words like "finch" can only be traced back so far before becoming lost in a tangle of linguistic roots. The American Robin would doubtless have been called Red-breasted Thrush or the like had it not reminded British colonists of the Robin Redbreast of their homeland. "Nuthatch" is only very slightly removed from the original colloquial name "nuthack," based on observed behavior. "Anhinga" and "caracara" come to us virtually unchanged from Tupi, a common language of the natives of the Amazon Basin.

Despite the fact that we have constructed a reasonably standardized English nomenclature for our native (and other) avifauna(s), it should be remembered (probably with considerable gratitude) that the great majority of people have paid not the slightest attention. A few of us insist that this bird here *is* a "Common Nighthawk," but those who know it (in some ways at least) far better than most ornithologists do, know full well that it is a "bullbat," which after all is shorter and hardly less accurate than the "official" name.

The main objection raised against colloquial names, of course, is that they are confusing. One man's Black-bellied Plover is another's "gump" or "chucklehead" and still another's "too-lee-huk." But it is on Latin names that we depend for nomenclatural consistency (see NOMENCLATURE), and the terrible ambiguity exemplified above can usually be relieved with a little conversation. The smorgasbord of regional flavors and the local humor contained in North American bird slang easily outweigh any fancied need to have an ornithological Esperanto.

It is gladdening to think that someone out there still knows the Ruddy Duck as a biddy, blatherskite, butterball, blackjack, bobbler, broadbill, bluebill, daub duck, dipper, dapper, dopper, bullneck, bumblebee buzzer, butter bowl, chunk duck, deaf duck, dinky, dip-tail diver, goddamn, goose teal, greaser, broadbill dipper, creek coot, pond coot, dumb bird, goose wigeon, stiff-tailed wigeon, wigeon coot, hardhead, toughhead, steelhead, sleepyhead, hardheaded broadbill, booby, murre, pintail, hickoryhead, leatherback, leather breeches, lightwood knot, little soldier, muskrat chick, noddy paddy, paddywhack, quill-tail coot, rook, spoonbill, gray teal, bumblebee coot, saltwater teal, shanty duck, shot pouch, spike-tail, spatter, spoon-billed butterball, stiffy, stub-and-twist, water partridge, wiretail, and who knows what else. This is a mere 60-odd names; Terres (1980–BIRD) notes that there are at least 132 "common" names for the Yellow-shafted (Common) Flicker.

Needless to say, it is impossible to give more than a sample of such names here. The names below were selected by the author for their general usage, their historical, anthropological, ornithological, or etymological interest, or because they made him laugh.

Bee-martin: Eastern Kingbird; though it is known to eat honeybees occasionally, this species eats many more insects (such as robber flies) which are injurious to bees.

Beetlehead: Hunter's name for the Black-bellied Plover.

Bluebill: Hunter's name for both species of scaup and, less frequently, for the Ruddy Duck. For other nicknames of the Ruddy Duck, see above.

Bogsucker: American Woodcock; refers to its characteristic probing for earthworms and other invertebrates, though this activity is seldom pursued in bogs and probably involves little or no sucking.

Bos'n (boatswain) bird: Seamen's name referring to the elongated central rectrices of the jaegers and tropicbirds, which are reminiscent of the notched ribbon of old-fashioned boatswain's caps and/or the bos'n's splicing tool, the marlinespike (see below). The name may also refer to the shrill calls of tropicbirds, not unlike the sound of the bos'n's whistle (Palmer, 1962–TROPICBIRD).

Bullbat: Refers to the nighthawks, connoting a large bat and the crepuscular habits of these birds.

Burgomaster: Seamen's name for the Glaucous Gull, which tends to have a well-filled figure and a proprietary bearing.

Butcher bird: Northern and Loggerhead Shrikes, both of which kill large insects, small mammals, and birds and then hang the "meat" in the crotch of a branch or on a thorn.

Butterball: Hunter's name for the Bufflehead, referring to its chubby form and perhaps the presence of large quantities of fat in the fall.

Butterbill: "Coot" shooter's name for the Black Scoter, referring to the bright orange-yellow bill knob of the drake.

Buzzard: Popular name for the Black and Turkey Vultures; a corruption of the traditional British use of this name to refer to medium-sized, broad-winged raptors, mostly in the genus Buteo. For a comprehensive discussion of the corruption in American usage of the names of day-flying raptors, see HAWK.

Calico plover: Hunter's name for the Ruddy Turnstone, referring to its multicolored breeding plumage.

Callithumpian duck: Oldsquaw; a callithumpian band is an amateur musical group which characteristically produces an odd assortment of notes at random; the same may be said of the Oldsquaw.

Carey chicks: Storm-petrels; see Mother Carey's chickens, below.

Chaparral cock: Local name for the (Greater) Roadrunner. Though they belong to the cuckoo family, roadrunners do look and act rather like some gallinaceous birds—whence "cock." For a description of one of the southwestern habitats they frequent, see CHAPARRAL.

Chebec (chi-BEK): Least Flycatcher; a close literal rendering of this species' "song."

Chewink (chuh-WINK): Rufous-sided Towhee. "Chewink" and "towhee" are both intended to resemble one of the calls of the species they refer to.

Chucklehead: Hunter's name for the Black-bellied Plover.

Creaker or creaker pert: Hunter's name for the Pectoral Sandpiper, referring to call(s) often given when flushed.

Dabchick: Pied-billed Grebe.

Devil-downhead: Applied to all of the nuthatches, which frequently forage over tree trunks head downward; the "devil" is a little mysterious, as it is hard to imagine species which present a more benign temperament; perhaps "daredevil" is implied.

Diablotin (dee-AH-blow-TAHN): Applied, in the Caribbean, to the Black-capped Petrel. See also CAHOW and GADFLY.

Doughbird or doebird: Though Thomas Nuttall and many shorebird shooters came to regard this name as generic for many of the larger, longer-billed sandpipers, it originally referred specifically to the Eskimo Curlew, and as A. C. Bent (1929–SHOREBIRD) explains, the name was spelled "doughbird," not "doebird," "for it was so fat when it reached us in the fall that its breast would often burst open when it fell to the ground, and the thick layer of fat was so soft that it felt like a ball of dough."

Dunk-a-doo: American Bittern; echoes its call.

Erne: An old Anglo-Saxon name for the White-tailed Sea Eagle, perpetuated in modern usage in the Scandinavian words for eagle (ørn or örn); well known to all workers of crossword puzzles.

Fish hawk; less frequently, fish eagle: Widespread name for the Osprey, referring, of course, to its preferred prey.

Fool hen: Applied to several members of the grouse family, but especially to the Spruce and Blue Grouse, connoting fearlessness of man, *ergo* stupidity. From a behavioral, if not a taxonomic, point of view, a fool hen is a booby is a dodo.

Garefowl (GAIR-fowl): A colloquial name once in wide usage for the Great Auk (*Pinguinus impennis*). According to Newton (1893–96–ORNI-

THOLOGY), it is either a corruption of a Gaelic name meaning "strong, stout bird with a spot" (referring to a large, white facial spot) or of a general Norse name for all of the alcids.

Goonybird. Seamen's name for the albatrosses, referring to their comical courtship antics.

Grasshopper hawk: Applied locally to the shrikes, which often prey on large insects.

Greenhead: A common hunter's name for the Mallard.

Greenlet: Widespread English name for the vireos before the turn of the century—the Philadelphia Vireo was then known as the Brotherly-love Greenlet. Now restricted to members of the Neotropical genus *Hylophilus,* none of which reaches North America.

Groundbird: Generalized name for sparrows and other ground-feeding, "nondescript" passerines.

Ground warbler: Common Yellowthroat, which habitually feeds and nests on or near the ground.

Grunter: Hunter's name for Wilson's Phalarope, referring to the call sometimes given when flushed.

Gump: Hunter's name for the Black-bellied Plover.

Hagdon, hagdown: Seamen's name for shearwaters, especially the Greater Shearwater; the name is modified when used for other species, e.g., "black hagdon" for Sooty Shearwater.

Harrywicket: One of numerous names applied to the Common Flicker, echoing its distinctive call.

Hell-diver: The smaller grebes, particularly the Pied-billed; grebes often seem to disappear when they dive and this name offers a superstitious opinion as to where they go.

Honker: Canada Goose.

Humility: Fanciful name for the Willet; like the current name, this echoes the species' call.

Ice bird: Seamen's name for both the Dovekie and the Razorbill, possibly referring to their habit (common to many birds of northern seas) of feeding at the edge of the pack ice or in the wake of icebergs, where upwellings of invertebrate food tend to occur.

Jiddy hawk: Seamen's name for the species of jaegers; this is a laundered version of a name which refers to jaegers' alleged habit of eating excrement expelled by terns and other birds that they harass. The Latin family name, Stercorariidae, also means "eaters of excrement."

Linnet: Standard English name for a Eurasian finch (*Acanthis cannabina*), the males of which have a rosy breast and front; this explains the colloquial usage in North America referring to the House Finch and less frequently the Purple Finch.

Logcock: Pileated Woodpecker.

Lord and lady: Describes a *pair* of Harlequin Ducks.

Mackerel goose: Fishermen's name for the two species of seagoing phalaropes, Red and Northern; they are not geese, of course, and are now usually placed in the sandpiper family (Scolopacidae).

Mackerel gull: Widespread seamen's name for species of *Sterna* terns, especially Common, Arctic, and Roseate. These birds and Atlantic mackerel share a taste for small saltwater schooling fishes, such as lances and silversides, and therefore often occur in the same place at the same time.

Man-o'-war bird: A variant of "frigatebird," likewise referring to these birds' majestic "sailing" manner of flight.

Marlin: Hunter's name for the godwits, apparently referring to the resemblance between the upturned bills of these birds and a type of old-fashioned marlinespike which was similarly curved.

Marlinespike: Seamen's name for the Parasitic and Long-tailed Jaegers and the tropicbirds, referring to the resemblance between the elongated central rectrices of these species and the pointed metal rope-splicing tools.

Mollymauk or mollymoke (many other spellings): A widespread seamen's name that may have originally referred to the Northern Fulmar. Used loosely since for many tubenose species (order Procellariiformes), but in its strictest current usage refers specifically to the smaller species of albatrosses in the genus *Diomedea.*

Moorhen: Standard English name in Britain for *Gallinula chloropus,* and occasionally used here colloquially. The standard name in North America is Common Gallinule.

Mosquito hawk: Local name for the nighthawks, from their habit of catching small insects on the wing.

Mother Carey's chickens: Seamen's name for the storm-petrels, particularly Wilson's and Leach's. The name apparently derived from *mater cara,* or "dear mother," i.e., the Virgin Mary. This is somewhat at odds with the usual superstitions about "Carey chicks," which describe them as tormented souls of lost sailors or cruel ship's officers or even avian demons keeping watch over the drowned.

Mud hen: Common Gallinule and several species of rails; refers, of course, to their preferred marshy habitat.

Mutton bird: Name for several medium-sized seabirds, especially the Slender-billed and Sooty Shearwaters, which breed in vast colonies in southeastern Australia (Slender-billed) and New Zealand (Sooty), where the chicks are "harvested" and sold commercially for food. The name comes from their flavor.

Nonpareil: Painted Bunting; literally (French), "without equal"; "uniquely splendid." As in many other instances, the less colorful female was ignored by the coiner of the standard English name of this species.

Ouzel (OO-zul) (water ouzel): An old Anglo-Saxon word for thrush. A popular British name for the Eurasian Dipper is water ouzel and this name is also used colloquially for the American Dipper.

Oxeye: Hunter's name for some of the "peeps," particularly the Semipalmated Sandpiper.

Peabody bird: White-throated Sparrow, one song of which is often verbalized by residents of the U.S. as "Old Sam Peabody-Peabody-Peabody"; Canadian ears hear "Oh, sweet Canada, Canada, Canada."

Peep: See entry in main text.

Prairie pigeon: Franklin's Gull, which breeds on the northern prairies of North America.

Preacher: Colloquial name for the Red-eyed Vireo, which is noted for its monotonous, endlessly repeated song.

Quailhead: Lark Sparrow, referring to the adults' boldly striped head.

Quandy: Hunter's name for a *female* goldeneye.

Quank: White-breasted Nuthatch, in imitation of its nasal calls; the Red-breasted Nuthatch is sometimes called "little quank."

Quawk: Popular nickname for the Black-crowned Night Heron; an excellent literal rendering of this species' characteristic call.

Rain crow: Applied to the Black-billed and Yellow-billed Cuckoos, in the belief that the frequent calling of cuckoos is a reliable prediction of rain.

Redbird: Popular name, particularly in the southern states, for the male Northern Cardinal; the discerning distinguish the Summer Tanager as the *summer* redbird.

Ricebird: Popular name for the Bobolink around the turn of the century, when migratory hordes of this species stopped to feed on southern rice and other grain crops en route to their South American wintering grounds in the fall. Many of the birds killed as crop pests were sold to restaurateurs, so that "Ricebirds" was once a common menu item (see EDIBILITY).

Robin snipe: Hunter's name for the Red Knot and the two species of dowitcher, referring to the red underparts of the alternate (breeding) plumage of these species.

Sawbill: Colloquial name for the mergansers, referring to their prominent bill serrations, useful in grasping slippery fish.

Scissorbill: Black Skimmer; see SKIMMER for a description of the unique bill adaptation of this family; also Fig. 2.

Sea hen: Seamen's name for the Great Skua.

Sea parrot: Seamen's name for the Common Puffin.

Sea pigeon: Seamen's name for the Black Guillemot; also applied to a wide variety of vaguely "dove-like" warm-water seabirds, e.g., tropicbirds, petrels, small gulls.

Sea swallow: Seamen's name for the species of *Sterna* terns with long, forked tails, e.g., Common, Arctic, and Roseate.

Shag: See entry in main text.

Shitepote or shitepoke: Laundered version of a name applied to several species of herons, especially the Green Heron and the Black-crowned Night Heron, referring to their habit of defecating conspicuously when alarmed.

Skunkhead: Hunter's name for the drake Surf Scoter.

Smutty-nosed coot: Hunters of North Atlantic waterfowl call all of the scoters "coots." This variation refers to the fatty orange knob at the base of the bill of the male Black (Common) Scoter.

Snakebird. Describes the sinuosity of the Anhinga, which often swims with only its long, serpentine head and neck above the surface.

Snowflake: A once popular name for the Snow Bunting.

Solan goose: Colloquial and, of course, taxonomically misleading name for the Northern Gannet. "Solan" probably comes from the old Scandinavian name for gannet, *sula,* now the generic Latin name for the boobies.

Specklebelly: Widely used colloquial name for the White-fronted Goose.

Sprig: Hunter's name for the Pintail.

Stib: Hunter's name for several of the larger "peeps," particularly the Dunlin and Sanderling.

Swamp angel: Wood and Hermit Thrushes and perhaps the Veery, referring to the "heavenly" songs of these species.

Teacher bird: Ovenbird (Parulidae), the loud and distinctive song of which sounds like a repetition of the word "teacher" strongly accented on the first syllable; song analysis shows that the phrases, in fact, begin with the unemphasized syllable, so that the species really says "erteach-erteach-erteach."

Teeter-bob: Spotted Sandpiper; refers to its characteristic, nearly continual tail bobbing. Many variations, e.g., teeter-tail, teeter-peep, teeter-arse snipe, tip-up, tip-tail.

Thistlebird: An apt name for the American Goldfinch, deriving from its close association with thistle. Not only do adult goldfinches eat thistle seed; they feed their young on it and line their nest with thistle down. In some regions late-season nesting of this species follows the thistle bloom.

Throat-cut: Rose-breasted Grosbeak (male).

Thunderpump: American Bittern; refers to this species' distinctive call.

Tickle-arse: Seamen's name for the Black-legged Kittiwake; the name is a contraction of "tickle-yer-arse-wit'-a-feather" and is inspired by the giggle-like calls of this northern gull.

Timberdoodle: American Woodcock.

Tinker: Seamen's name for the Razorbill.

Titlark: Name of British origin for the pipits.

Turr: Seamen's name for the species of murres.

Wamp: Hunter's name for species of eider, especially the Common Eider; the King Eider is sometimes called "wamp's cousin."

Water hen: American Coot.

Water witch: Pied-billed Grebe; probably refers to its habit of slowly submerging and apparently not resurfacing.

Wavy: Hunter's name for the Blue/Snow Goose.

Whalebird: Seamen's name for the two species of seagoing phalaropes, Red and Northern. These phalaropes, along with other pelagic birds, often feed in the oily slicks which surround whales feeding or traveling at the surface.

Whiptail: Seamen's name for the Long-tailed Jaeger in breeding plumage.

Whiskey Jack: Popular colloquial name for the Gray Jay; a corruption of an American Indian name ("wiskedjak," or the like) for a trickster god personified by this species.

Whistler: Hunter's name for the goldeneyes. The characteristic "whistling," produced by the birds' wings in flight, is probably discernible at least as far away as the color of the eye. See also WHISTLING DUCK.

Whooper: Nickname for the Whooping Crane or, in Europe, for the Whooper Swan.

Wide-awake: Applied in the Caribbean to the Sooty Tern, in approximation of that species' call.

Wobble: Seamen's name for the Great Auk—describing its penguin-like gait? Not to be confused with "wobbla," the collective name in New England for the members of the family Parulidae, e.g., "a wobbla wave at Mount Awbun Cemetery."

Yellowhammer: Colloquial name for the yellow-shafted race of the Common Flicker; also the standard English name for a species of Eurasian bunting which occurs virtually throughout the Palearctic region and has been successfully introduced in New Zealand but has never occurred in North America.

NAMES, SCIENTIFIC (LATIN). See LATIN NAMES.

NAMES, VERNACULAR or COMMON. Standardized names by which bird species are known in the language of the country or countries where they occur; distinguished here both from technical (scientific) names in Latin and from colloquial names. The "purpose" of vernacular names falls somewhere between that of colloquial and technical names. On the one hand, many common names derive from colloquial usage (e.g., Bobolink); on the other, they are (at least in English) standardized by ornithologists, as are Latin names. They are not meant to reflect the continual process of taxonomic revision as are scientific names, but they are meant to be far more stable—thus much more useful—than the anything-goes usage of local names can ever be. (The function of technical naming is discussed under NOMENCLATURE, and the problems inherent in inconsis-

tency in naming life forms are discussed there and under NAMES, COLLO-
QUIAL.)

Despite the efforts of ornithologists to standardize vernacular names,
inconsistencies tend to remain when a single bird species occurs in two (or
more) countries, each with its own cultural traditions and ornithological
establishment. For example, members of the family Gaviidae have long
been called "divers" in the standard vernacular nomenclature of the British Isles, while the preferred standard English name in North America has
always been "loon." Since all the diver/loon species have a Holarctic distribution, some slight confusion is possible when an American talks to an
Englishman about these birds. The converse problem also occurs in which
two different regions inadvertently come up with the same name for two
distinct species: the Black Duck of Australasia (*Anas superciliosa*) is not
the same as the Black Duck of North America (*A. rubripes*). In the case of
cosmopolitan species, the ambiguity may be bewilderingly compounded.
Egretta alba is variously known as Great Egret (in North America, where it
was formerly called Common Egret and, before that, American Egret),
Great White Egret (in Britain, where it was formerly known as Great
White Heron and Large Egret), and White Egret (in Australia).

Such discrepancies in common names are clearly a bother, though
perhaps not a major stumbling block to the progress of ornithology or
birdwatching. Systematists and birders alike always have recourse to the
Latin nomenclature for resolving ambiguities. Furthermore, the great majority of birdwatchers pursue only the members of their own avifauna, and
most of those who do bird abroad might prefer to say Black-throated Diver
when in Scotland rather than be told by a committee on common bird
names that they *must* learn to say it at home as well in preference to Arctic
Loon. Nevertheless, there doubtless should be a work entitled *Standard
Vernacular Names in English of the Birds of the World* which would
publish the compromises of an international panel of interested ornithologists and give all the accepted synonyms of the common names decided
on. It is a lacuna in the literature which should be filled regardless of
whether an American birder can ever be persuaded to call a Dovekie a Little Auk.

The vernacular-name ambiguities that most often befuddle North
American birdwatchers may be assigned to three categories, as follows:

1. *Different names for the same species in British and American
usage.* All species listed are of regular occurrence in both the United Kingdom and North America.

American	British
Common Loon	Great Northern Diver
Arctic Loon	Black-throated Diver
Red-throated Loon	Red-throated Diver
Horned Grebe	Slavonian Grebe

American	British
Eared Grebe	Black-necked Grebe
Greater Shearwater	Great Shearwater
Great Cormorant	Cormorant
Brant	Brent Goose
Green-winged Teal	Teal
Greater Scaup	Scaup
Common Goldeneye	Goldeneye
Common Eider	Eider
Oldsquaw	Long-tailed Duck
Black Scoter	Common Scoter
White-winged Scoter	Velvet Scoter
Common Merganser	Goosander
Northern Harrier (formerly Marsh Hawk)	Hen Harrier
Hawk (for buteos)	Buzzard (for buteos)
Willow Ptarmigan	Willow Grouse (and Red Grouse)
Rock Ptarmigan	Ptarmigan
Great Egret (formerly Common Egret)	Great White Egret
Black-crowned Night Heron	Night Heron
Common Gallinule	Moorhen
Black-necked Stilt	Black-winged Stilt (sometimes considered a distinct species)
Black-bellied Plover	Grey Plover
Snowy Plover	Kentish Plover
Ruddy Turnstone	Turnstone
Red Phalarope	Grey Phalarope
Northern Phalarope	Red-necked Phalarope
Common Snipe	Snipe
Parasitic Jaeger	Arctic Skua
Pomarine Jaeger	Pomarine Skua
Long-tailed Jaeger	Long-tailed Skua
Skua	Great Skua
Mew Gull	Common Gull
Black-legged Kittiwake	Kittiwake
Least Tern	Little Tern
Common (or Thin-billed) Murre	Guillemot
Thick-billed Murre	Brünnich's Guillemot
Dovekie	Little Auk
Common Puffin	Puffin
Boreal Owl	Tengmalm's Owl
(Northern) Three-toed Woodpecker	Three-toed Woodpecker
Horned Lark	Shore Lark

American	British
Barn Swallow	Swallow
Bank Swallow	Sand Martin
Black-billed Magpie	Magpie
Common Raven	Raven
Chickadee (for most *Parus* species)	Tit (for most *Parus* species)
Brown Creeper	Treecreeper
Winter Wren	Wren
Kinglets	Goldcrest, Firecrest
Bohemian Waxwing	Waxwing
Northern Shrike	Great Grey Shrike
Common Redpoll	Redpoll
Hoary Redpoll	Arctic Redpoll
Red Crossbill	Crossbill
White-winged Crossbill	Two-barred Crossbill
Lapland Longspur	Lapland Bunting

2. *The same (or nearly the same) name for different species in British and American usage.* Included are names which are unmodified in Britain and are often used unmodified for *different* species in America—because a given species is the only one of its kind occurring in a particular region or the continent as a whole. For example, the standard name for the Eurasian Goldfinch in Britain is simply Goldfinch, and because the American Goldfinch is the only goldfinch species which occurs east of the Mississippi, it is usually called simply Goldfinch there.

	American	British
White Pelican	*Pelecanus erythro-rhynchos*	*P. onocrotalus*
Spoonbill	*Ajaia ajaja*: Roseate Spoonbill	*Platalea leucorodia*
Wigeon	*Anas americana*: American Wigeon	*A. penelope*
Coot	*Fulica americana*: American Coot	*F. atra*
Vultures	Family Cathartidae (New World vultures)	Family Accipitridae (incl. Old World vultures)
Sparrow Hawk	Former name for American Kestrel: *Falco sparverius*	*Accipiter nisus*
Kestrel	*Falco sparverius*: American Kestrel	*F. tinnunculus*

Golden Plover	*Pluvialis dominica:* Lesser Golden Plover	*P. apricaria:* Greater Golden Plover
Woodcock	*Scolopax minor:* American Wood-cock	*S. rusticola*
Flycatchers	Family Tyrannidae (tyrant flycatchers)	Family Muscicapidae (Old World fly-catchers)
Dipper	*Cinclus mexicanus*	*C. cinclus*
Robin	Species of *Turdus* thrushes, esp. *T. migratorius:* American Robin	*Erithacus rubecula*
Warblers	Family Parulidae (wood warblers)	Family Sylviidae (Old World warblers)
Redstart	*Setophaga* and *Myioborus* species (family Parulidae: wood warblers)	*Phoenicurus* species (family Turdidae: thrushes)
Chat	*Icteria virens:* Yellow-breasted Chat (family Parulidae: wood warblers)	*Saxicola* and other genera (family Turdidae: thrushes)
Blackbird	Family Icteridae in part (New World blackbirds/orioles)	*Turdus merula*
Redwing	*Agelaius phoeniceus:* Red-winged Black-bird (family Icteridae)	*Turdus iliacus* (thrush family)
Oriole	Family Icteridae in part (New World orioles/blackbirds)	Family Oriolidae (Old World orioles)
Goldfinch	*Spinus* species, esp. *S. tristis:* American Goldfinch	*Carduelis carduelis*
Sparrow	Used for emberizid/fringillid finches as well as ploceid (weaver) finches	Used only for ploceid (weaver) finches
Whitethroat	*Zonotrichia albicollis:* White-throated Sparrow	*Sylvia communis* (family Sylviidae: Old World warblers)

3. *Different names for the same Mexican bird species.* A name coined in a North American context for a species whose range is largely Neotropical and a name coined by Neotropical specialists in the context of the species' native (Neotropical) avifauna.

American	Neotropical
Black Hawk	Common Black Hawk
Chachalaca	Plain Chachalaca
Harlequin Quail	Montezuma Quail
Jacana	Northern Jacana
White-fronted Dove	White-tipped Dove
Roadrunner	Greater Roadrunner
Pygmy Owl	Northern Pygmy Owl
Ferruginous Owl	Ferruginous Pygmy Owl
Ridgway's Whip-poor-will	Buff-collared Nightjar
Rivoli's Hummingbird	Magnificent Hummingbird
Buff-bellied Hummingbird	Fawn-breasted Hummingbird
Coppery-tailed Trogon	Elegant Trogon
Kiskadee Flycatcher	Great Kiskadee
Wied's Crested Flycatcher	Brown Crested Flycatcher
Olivaceous Flycatcher	Dusky-capped Flycatcher
Beardless Flycatcher	Northern Beardless Tyrannulet
Coues' Flycatcher	Greater Pewee
Mexican Jay	Gray-breasted Jay
Mexican Chickadee	Gray-sided Chickadee
Bahama Honeycreeper	Bananaquit
Olive-backed Warbler	Tropical Parula
Lichtenstein's Oriole	Altamira Oriole

NARIS (NAY-riss or NAIR-iss) (pl.: nares [NAY-reez or NAIR-eez]). Technical term for NOSTRIL.

NATIONAL WILDLIFE REFUGE. A parcel of habitat—often including extensive wetlands—owned, protected, and managed by the U.S. Fish and Wildlife Service for the benefit of birds and other life forms. The first federal refuge was Pelican Island, a rookery on the Indian River near the east coast of Florida, acquired in 1903 by executive order of Teddy Roosevelt. As of September 30, 1981, there were 410 refuges, comprising 86,-719,942 acres (including Alaska and Hawaii), contained within the system. Traditionally, the major objectives of our National Wildlife Refuges have been to protect endangered species and to promote the conservation of migratory waterfowl. Accordingly, each refuge is usually strongly identified either with a particular species—the Aransas refuge encompasses most of the wintering range of the Whooping Crane—or as a regular stopping place for large concentrations of migrating water birds, as at the Bear River refuge at Great Salt Lake. Most refuges are actively managed to maintain or improve the habitat favored by the species under protection. For example, dikes may be constructed to increase the area of wetland available for resting ducks and to control water levels. Often blinds, boardwalks, and trails are maintained to encourage the public to enjoy the nation's wild heritage, subject of course to access restrictions imposed for the welfare of protected species. On some refuges, duck shooting is permitted during a limited season.

The Canadian Wildlife Service operates 39 National Wildlife *Areas*, encompassing 76,601 acres.

A free list of National Wildlife Refuges, with their addresses and managers, is available from the main office of the U.S. Fish and Wildlife Service in Washington, D.C., or from the regional office nearest you. For more descriptive material on individual refuges, see Riley and Riley's *Guide to the National Wildlife Refuges* (New York, 1979).

NATURAL SELECTION. The process, articulated by Charles Darwin in 1859, by which evolution proceeds. The theory of natural selection involves many complexities, but, in essence, it holds that inheritable traits which allow an individual organism to cope more successfully with its environment will increase the individual's "survivability," allowing it to produce more offspring with the same advantageous trait(s), thus ultimately perpetuating successful genetic changes. The selection process works in reverse for disadvantageous traits, which appear with the same frequency as advantageous ones but are eliminated because they work against survival and are not perpetuated in a significant percentage of a population. This is "survival of the fittest," although this phrase is often misapplied to predators which kill and eat life forms of which humans are fond. In fact, chickadees are also predators and every bit as "fit" as the Sharp-shinned Hawks that sometimes prey on them. See SPECIATION; PREDATION.

NAVIGATION. Once science confirmed the astonishing fact that most of the birds of the North Temperate Zone travel hundreds or thousands of miles each year to more southerly wintering grounds (see MIGRATION), it was faced with the need to explain how that is possible. How does a bird with its meager intelligence find its way to and from remote and restricted breeding and wintering areas? How does it know in which direction to go? How does it maintain its course, particularly in the dark, when many migrants travel? How can it tell when it has arrived at the right place in the Central American rain forests or Caribbean highlands? Does it really know where "home" is, or does it just follow an innate "flight plan" blindly? Does it know where to go "instinctively" or must it learn by experience?

The sensory processes which encompass these difficult "hows" have so far been only partially explained. What *has* been learned—almost entirely since 1940—is summarized below.

EXPERIMENTS IN BIRD NAVIGATION. The experiments which have been undertaken to determine the extent and nature of birds' navigational capabilities have generated some of the most interesting reading in the ornithological literature. Some of the best-known of these are noted here, and other classic and/or interesting references are listed selectively in the Bibliography.

To begin to assess the accuracy, effectiveness, and extent of a bird's ability to return to where it "wants to be," a number of species have been banded and then transported not only away from breeding or wintering sites but far out of their normal migration route. Manx Shearwaters, known to be long-distance pelagic migrants, have been taken from British breeding colonies and released on the east coast of North America (Mazzeo, 1953) and at various points in southern and western Europe (Matthews, 1953) and were found to return to their nest burrows with remarkable efficiency (12½ days for the Atlantic crossing) and little or no apparent hesitation. Medwalt (1964) made similar tests on White-crowned and Golden-crowned Sparrows which breed in northwestern North America (including Alaska) and winter in southern California. He trapped hundreds of birds on their wintering grounds and released them on the Gulf coast of Louisiana and the east coast of Maryland. A number of these birds were recaptured the following winter in California, presumably having returned to their breeding grounds in the interim.

Displaced juvenile (i.e., inexperienced) birds of migratory species (e.g., Perdeck, 1958) were found to know the direction in which they were "supposed" to travel but apparently did not have any innate notion of their normal destination.

Homing experiments with Common Pigeons (e.g., Matthews, 1963), a non-migratory species, and with other "short-distance" migrants resulted in a higher percentage of disoriented birds and the conclusion that local landmarks are of great importance to the navigating skills of such birds.

Kramer's experiments with starlings in Germany (1952) resulted in the first well-substantiated information on *how* birds migrate. During the period in spring when starlings normally migrate, he placed a bird reared in captivity in a structure from which only the sky was visible through the windows. He found (1) that when the sun was out, the bird would flutter restlessly in the direction of its species' migratory destination at that time of year; (2) that if he changed the position of the sun with the use of mirrors, the starling would alter course accordingly and fly in the "wrong" directions; (3) that the bird remained on course through the sun's normal daily arc, i.e., that its orientation system compensated for this movement; and (4) that on overcast days when the sun's position was obscured, the bird was apparently disoriented.

The first experiments with nocturnal migrants (see Sauer, 1957, and Sauer and Sauer, 1960), using species of Old World warblers (Sylviidae) reared in the lab and a planetarium where the stars in the night sky could be altered, yielded similar findings: (1) Exposed to a clear night sky during a migratory period, the warblers would orient correctly for the season. (2) When, for example, they were shown a fall sky in the spring under the planetarium ceiling, they would "follow the stars" in the "wrong" direction. (3) When the stars were invisible or when the sky of a non-migratory season was displayed, the birds became disoriented.

Emlen (1967) found that the hormonal states which constitute "readiness" in birds about to migrate are not the same in the spring as they are in the fall. When he induced both spring and fall "readiness" in wild-captive Indigo Buntings and exposed them to a spring sky in a planetarium, he found that the hormones won out over the stars, i.e., that the buntings which were "ready" physiologically to go south did so regardless of the celestial configuration.

The myriad experiments which have followed from these classic pioneering ones, as well as uncovering important "new" factors, have tended on the whole to (1) increase respect for the complexity of avian navigation; (2) confirm the importance of celestial guidance; and (3) reinforce a growing awareness that birds' extraordinary homing capability is achieved not by one area of the brain processing one type of information but by combining several kinds of information using several physiological faculties.

GENERAL SUMMARY OF PRESENT KNOWLEDGE. There is experimental evidence to support the following facts and speculations:

1. Some species of birds have been shown incontestably to perform spectacular "homing" feats involving great distances and radical dislocations.

2. Navigational ability varies widely among different species of birds. At least some species which are typically permanent residents (e.g., pigeons) and spend their whole lives within a limited area have comparatively simple "homing" abilities, which would seem to correspond to their limited needs; species which undertake long migrations have evolved more sophisticated techniques, and nocturnal and pelagic migrants which normally must find their way without the aid of landmarks probably have the most highly developed orientation abilities of all.

3. The use of landmarks plays a significant role in homing for many birds. Species of limited range memorize key features of their neighborhood and can be taught to learn landmarks of a wider area. Birds deliberately disoriented (e.g., Griffin and Hock, 1949) often wander at random, apparently searching for familiar places or "clues" such as a coastline which may bring them back into their familiar home range if followed. Birds which depend on the celestial clues described below may follow coasts or mountain ranges (leading lines) when the sky is overcast.

4. The sun is known to be a means of orientation in some birds. Day-flying migrants unable to see the sun's position (as under a heavy overcast) become disoriented.

5. Birds have some form of "internal clock" which allows them to compensate for the sun's normal daily movement and keep a steady course.

6. Birds' use of the sun apparently involves a form of bi-coordinate navigation, perhaps making use of the discrepancy in the sun's azimuth between where they are and where they want to be. (Azimuth is an arc on the horizon measured clockwise from the north or south compass point to the point on the horizon intersected by a vertical circle passing through the center of a celestial body, e.g., the sun.)

7. Nocturnal migrants seem to depend to some extent on the stars for orientation (some experimental birds apparently lose their bearings on overcast nights), but the nature of this star navigation is unclear. There is as yet no evidence that displaced birds can reorient themselves at night as they clearly can during the day. Emlen's planetarium experiments showed somewhat perplexingly that the removal of key celestial features such as the North Star or the Milky Way did not apparently impair Indigo Buntings' confidence that they knew where they were going and that southbound migrants were not even perturbed by the erasure of all the southern constellations but did become disoriented when the whole northern sky was obliterated. Furthermore, some studies indicate that nocturnal migrants *can* navigate under overcast skies.

8. The direction of migration (north or south) is clearly influenced at least in some species by hormonal predisposition.

9. Some navigational ability is acquired from experience at least in some species. Displaced adult birds of some species have been shown to find their "correct" wintering grounds successfully while inexperienced juvenile birds from the same population seemed to know the direction they should follow but could not find their "traditional" route or end point.

10. Several studies (e.g., Bellrose, 1958) have demonstrated that some displaced birds have a tendency to orient decisively in the *wrong* direction (i.e., away from any conceivable "home"). Matthews (1961) terms this "nonsense orientation."

11. It has been convincingly demonstrated that at least some birds can sense and orient according to the earth's magnetic field. This has been shown in controlled experiments both by attaching magnets to birds, thereby disrupting the sensation produced by the earth's magnetism (Keeton, 1972), and by observing birds' reactions to an artificially created field similar in force to the earth's (Lancaster and Johnson, 1976). Walcott et al. (1979) located a small structure between the brain and the skull in pigeons which contains magnetite and which may be used to sense the earth's magnetic field for the purpose of orientation.

12. Many factors in addition to the ones noted above may play a role in bird navigation. Theories linking avian orientation to perception of infrared light rays or the Coriolis force have been hotly debated. The possible influences of wind and the earth's magnetic field continue to be investigated and most workers in the field concede the possibility of influences, or even avian faculties, as yet unimagined.

13. The most sophisticated navigation systems in birds undoubtedly use a combination of orientation aids. Birds that use celestial navigation may, for example, rely on wind direction, sounds from below (i.e., surf sounds indicating a shoreline), or some other perception of which we are still unaware, to maintain their course until they can reorient under a clear sky. Moreover, celestial navigation is only useful for broad orientation, whereas an individual bird's breeding and wintering ranges have been shown to be very restricted in most cases. Once its destination is approached, therefore, birds very probably switch over to the use of landmarks or, in the case of pelagic species that must find tiny isolated breeding islands (see Fig. 13), more "finely tuned" internal mechanisms.

14. Since the navigational techniques of different species each evolved separately along with other characteristics, it is not surprising to find great variation among birds in the importance and priority of any particular method. Wind, for example, may prove to be crucial to some species and merely a backup system for others.

15. Finally, it should be noted that young (inexperienced) birds are the individuals that most often go astray, apparently because of their misreading of physical stimuli, their inability to cope with strong winds or overcast, or simply a genetic aberration.

NEARCTIC REGION (nee-ARK-tik). One of the six major zoogeographic regions of the world. It includes all of North America south to an irregular line across Mexico that marks the northern limits of tropical rain forest. At the edges of the Nearctic, there are zones of overlap with adjacent regions in which the neighboring avifaunas are strongly represented. Western Alaska, for example, shares many species with the contiguous Palearctic region, and the southern borders of the Nearctic are crossed by many species of largely Neotropical distribution.

"Nearctic birds" include those that breed exclusively within the Nearctic region but winter in the Neotropics (e.g., most wood warblers) as well as those that range wholly in North America (e.g., Henslow's Sparrow). Compare NEOTROPICAL; PALEARCTIC; HOLARCTIC; see also ZOOGEOGRAPHY; DISTRIBUTION; and Fig. 24.

NECTIVOROUS (nek-TIH-vor-us). Literally, nectar-eating. Nectivorous birds are those which feed largely on nectar from flowers or the juices of fruits. The most highly specialized of nectivores are, of course, the hummingbirds, with powerful hovering flight and long bills adapted for probing the calyxes of blossoms as a principal feeding technique. The bills of orioles are also adapted for nectar feeding. Both of these families also must seek a protein supplement of insects, which in many cases are easily found around the same flowers from which the birds are feeding on nectar. Many other birds, including warblers, tanagers, and finches, occasionally feed on nectar.

NEOCATHARTES (NEE-oh-cuh-THAR-teez). A fossil genus of long-legged terrestrial vultures (Cathartidae) with apparently limited capacity for flight (short wings). A single species (*N. grallator*) has been described from skeletal remains found in Eocene deposits in Wyoming. See EVOLUTION OF BIRDLIFE.

NEOSPECIES. A modern species, i.e., one that has lived within the recent geological period, whose status as a species can be defined according to the usual biological criteria (see SPECIES; SPECIATION). Compare PALAEOSPECIES.

NEOTROPICAL REGION (Neotropics). One of the six major zoogeographic regions of the world, each of which is distinguishable by broad floral and faunal characteristics. The northern boundary of the Neotropics is an irregular line across Mexico that marks the northern limits of tropical rain forest. The region encompasses everything south of this line in the New World, excepting American Antarctica, but including the islands of the West Indies, the islands of coastal Latin America, and the entire mainland of South America south of the Tropic of Capricorn. The political boundaries of North America largely coincide with the boundaries of the Nearctic region; however, many bird species which breed mainly in the Neotropics reach the southernmost regions of the U.S., e.g.: the Masked Duck, Short-tailed Hawk, Harlequin Quail, Northern Jacana, White-tipped Dove, Mangrove Cuckoo, several hummingbird species, Elegant Trogon, Tropical Kingbird, Mexican Chickadee, Green Jay, Painted Redstart, and Black-headed Oriole, to name but a few. See also NEARCTIC; ZOOGEOGRAPHY; DISTRIBUTION; and Fig. 24.

NERVOUS SYSTEM. The function of any animal nervous system may be compared to an electrical network attached to a control center. In effect it "turns on" all the bodily functions—senses, muscles, internal organs—and regulates and coordinates their activities, enabling most humans, for example, to think, breathe, hear, smell, walk, and chew gum all at the same time. The nerves, like wires, pick up sensations through the sensory organs and either induce an automatic reaction or transmit the signal to the brain or spinal cord, which processes the data and determines an appropriate response. This response is also transmitted by nerves and stimulates muscular action.

A bird's nervous system has the same major parts arranged in the same general pattern as that of other vertebrate animals, but with numerous specific modifications. These relate both to a bird's unique manner of living and to its place on the evolutionary scale.

Nervous systems are usually explained in terms of three "subsystems"—the *central nervous system* (brain and spinal cord), the *peripheral nervous system* (the main voluntary nerves controlling senses, movement, etc.), and the *autonomic nervous system* (the self-controlling or involuntary nerves which operate the heart, glands, blood flow, and other internal functions).

But these are all part of one unified system and are inextricably interconnected with the other systems. It may be easier, therefore, to understand its workings in terms of the major parts and their functions.

THE BRAIN. Despite the derogatory implications of "bird brain," birds have the largest brains in proportion to body weight of all animals except mammals. As in humans, a bird's brain is divided into front, middle, and rear sections (the fore-, mid-, and hindbrain). The arrangement of these parts in a bird's skull is somewhat different from that in the skulls of other animals, and the presence and/or size of specific parts are indications of the physical and intellectual strengths and weaknesses of birds. Brains of different groups of birds vary in adaptation to specialized habits and in general development.

The Front of the Brain is largely taken up by two symmetrical lobes, the cerebral hemispheres or cerebrum, which is composed mainly of a mass of nerve cells called basal ganglia. A distinctive layer of this mass called the hyperstriatum is unique to birds, but the details of its function are imperfectly understood (see INTELLIGENCE, *The Bird Brain*). As a whole, this part of the brain controls instinctive actions such as the impulse to migrate or build nests.

Covering the human cerebral hemispheres is that gray, convoluted and furrowed structure which most of us associate strongly with the physical appearance of the brain. This is the cerebral cortex or pallium and is responsible for man's unique learning capacity and resulting intelligence. Some specialists claim to have found a bit of cortex atop the smooth cerebral lobes of birds, but others can find no trace of one, and this is consistent with what is known of the avian I.Q.; however, see INTELLIGENCE.

Attached to the front of the cerebrum is the olfactory bulb or lobe—the smell center—another feature poorly developed except in a few species (see SMELL).

The rear part of the forebrain (diencephalon) consists in part of the hypothalamus, which is important in the function of the endocrine as well as the nervous system. It regulates body temperature, involuntary sensations such as sleepiness, hunger, and thirst, and certain physical reactions to emotional stimulation.

The Midbrain of a bird consists essentially of the optic lobes, which are located on the sides of and below the cerebrum, rather than on top of it, as in most animals.

Given the importance of sight to most birds, it is not surprising to find that they have large and prominent optic lobes; in species in which vision is less important, the lobes are smaller.

The Rear of the Brain includes the cerebellum and the medulla oblongata. The cerebellum, located behind and below the cerebrum, is relatively large in birds—understandably, as it coordinates muscular activity, controls balance, and determines the quality of each movement, and is thus of prime importance in flight. However, birds lack the two cerebellar lobes controlling execution of skilled movements which only mammals are capable of performing.

The medulla oblongata may be thought of as an enlargement on the top of the spinal column. It functions in voice production, hearing, breathing, and circulation, among other things.

The Cranial Nerves attach in twelve pairs to all three regions of the brain. They are named and numbered (I–XII) exactly as in the human system and activate both senses and muscles in the head and neck: smell, eye functions (five of the cranial muscles are involved with vision and eye movement), hearing, taste, salivation, bill, tongue, neck, larynx, and syrinx.

Spinal Cord and Nerves. The spinal cord runs from the base of the brain to the last vertebra in a narrow canal down the center of the backbone. Pairs of spinal nerves, spaced along the length of the spinal cord, lead to and control the external muscles. The spinal cord is enlarged where the two great pairs of nerve networks (wing plexus and leg plexus) arise to control functions of those limbs. These two major spinal nerve centers vary in size and complexity, depending on the degree to which a species habitually uses its wings or legs. (For reaction of muscles to nerve impulses, see MUSCLES.)

Balance is controlled from the cerebellum through the spinal cord, but the spinal cord itself controls most of the motor activities of the body. This spinal independence from the brain is clearly inferred from the ability of a chicken to run around the barnyard for a short period after it has been decapitated.

In the spinal cord, at the lower lumbosacral enlargement, is found another feature which, like the hyperstriatum of the brain, is unique to birds but poorly understood. This is the rhomboid sinus, a hollow space filled with nerve fibers, a gelatinous substance, and glycogen.

Involuntary Nerves (Autonomic Nervous System). These

nerves stimulate internal functions, such as circulation, digestion, and the secretion of hormones, over which animals have little voluntary control. There are two types of involuntary nerves, which work, as it were, *against* each other. The first type (sympathetic) stimulates those processes appropriate for activity or excitement, e.g., increasing pulse rate and adrenaline secretion but shutting off digestion; the opposing (parasympathetic) does just the reverse. Both types are ultimately connected to the cranial or spinal nervous systems, which integrate their actions with the working of the entire system. They are regulated in part by the hypothalamus (see above).

NEST (nesting). A broad term even when restricted to a zoological context, but most often refers to a place where eggs are laid and develop. Some bird's nests are no more than "a place," but many more are distinctive structures of intricate architecture.

FUNCTION. Since some species construct no enclosure whatever for their eggs, it can be argued that nests are not, strictly speaking, necessary. However, it is clear from their elaborate evolution and general prevalence that nests have aided survival by protecting eggs and young from weather and predation and perhaps by increasing the efficiency of the rearing process.

A single small family of birds, the Australian megapodes, bury their eggs in warm earth or decaying vegetation, thereby relieving themselves of the ennui of INCUBATION. Grebes and a few other species of North American birds cover their eggs with dead plant material when they leave their nests temporarily, and it has been suggested that this, too, is a form of carefree incubation.

Cactus Wrens and Verdins, which build enclosed nests, and many hole nesters use their nests "off season" or in bad weather for night roosting and shelter. Nests may also provide hospitality for an astonishing variety of non-avian creatures. Small rodents frequently take over abandoned bird's nests and legions of invertebrates may be resident, especially while a nest is in use (see NEST FAUNA).

Aside from aesthetic pleasure, humans have found little use for bird's nests; however, see BIRD'S NEST SOUP.

PHYSIOLOGY. Like most other functions of avian life, the nesting urge is tied to a bird's hormonal cycles. The earliest manifestation of this urge—prospecting for a suitable site—coincides with the mating and copulation period and, at least in some species, nest building parallels the development of the fertilized ovum (Riddle, 1911–EGG).

Hormonal triggers (mostly estrogens and androgens) are in turn set off by external phenomena such as temperature and precipitation, so that site selection, for example, may be prolonged due to bad weather.

NESTING BEHAVIOR
Site Selection. Once a pair of birds has mated, choosing a place to lay

the eggs becomes a high priority. Either or both partners may undertake this responsibility, according to the habits of their species, but the female dominates the process in the majority of cases. Birds which return to old nest sites in successive years are, of course, relieved of this responsibility. For some species, e.g., many colonial seabirds, choosing a site is mostly ritual with the final selection apparently quite arbitrary. Most species, however, "shop around" for a while, a process which may include "fitting" the body into prospective tree forks or patches of ground. This prospecting period varies in length from species which seem to take the first site they see and immediately start construction, to tits and others which inspect sites year-round. Specialized, relatively scarce sites, e.g., tree cavities, require more rigorous testing and prolonged searching than more commonplace ones, but for the majority of species site selection probably consumes a few days under optimal conditions.

Nest Building seems on superficial observation to be clear proof of the sophistication of the avian brain. Any human who tries to make a good facsimile of a Northern Oriole's closely woven sack or a Cliff Swallow's gracefully sculptured pottery cell cannot but be impressed by these species' "cleverness." We now know for certain, however, that a bird's intellect is a very limited instrument (see INTELLIGENCE)—so how to explain its routine performance of such a skilled and complicated task? The question has yet to be answered with the thoroughness and documentation required for scientific proof, but a sound hypothesis is as follows.

Birds (especially females) are born with the inclination and ability to perform the complex of activities required to complete a nest. Hormonal changes at the beginning of the breeding cycle induce what might be called the nesting "mood"; the specific actions required for successful completion of the process are then triggered in succession by specific stimuli. The stimulus may be an overt act, such as copulation, which triggers (or at least enhances) the site selection "urge" or it may be simply an innate apprehension that a particular task is complete. In a sense, a bird has a picture in its tiny mind of what its nest should look like at a given stage; when the reality matches the picture, the bird gets reinforcement (what we might think of as a sense of satisfaction) and is "released" to go on to the next innate step in the breeding process. Once the exterior of the familiar cup-type nest reaches a certain stage of completion, for example, the "exterior" urge wanes and the "lining" urge is triggered—all, as it were, "automatically," i.e., without real thought.

The fact that abnormal nests are not uncommon and that young birds are often seen to be less skilled engineers than their elders indicates that some learning of the "practice makes perfect" kind does occur at least in some cases. Clearly, for example, a bird is not born knowing where a particular lining substance can be found. But basic know-how will produce at least an adequate nest, given the normal pattern of stimuli.

The many individual tasks required in nest construction vary greatly among species because of different nesting habits (see below). Birds which live in the ground or in banks must expend time and energy in excavation, unless they colonize another species' hole. Many icterids are unusually skilled in weaving. Some swallows and swifts are expert masons. And except for brood parasites, all passerines (as well as many non-passerines) are natural masters of a variety of building and shaping skills. Ornithologists have defined a number of nest-building gestures, such as "tacking," "drawing," "looping," and "squatting," which are characteristic of many species.

The effort that goes into nest construction also varies among species. Many species forgo the process altogether and simply lay their eggs on a bare surface or take over an abandoned nest without making alterations. Eagles and other members of their family which return each year to old nest sites apparently never lose the urge to build. In some species additions are perfunctory, but Bald Eagles add many new sticks each year, creating an enormous edifice over decades. Male wrens build a series of DUMMY NESTS, and species, such as rails, which nest low near water must continue or resume nest building if the water level rises. Furthermore, in many species these various labors are repeated once or more in a single season (see *Nesting Pattern*, below).

In some species, a young bird from a first brood will help in the construction of its parents' second nest of the season, a practice with apparent benefits to all concerned.

Nesting Pattern and Timing. Most birds build a new nest for each brood they rear, even when double- or triple-brooded, but less time and energy are expended each time in nest construction. The California Condor and a few species of long-distance pelagic migrants which breed in the Southern Hemisphere (e.g., Greater Shearwater) breed only every other year. But the former builds no nest of any kind and the latter usually reoccupy old burrows and make no improvements, so that there is little or no nesting effort by either one in any case.

Whether a species is single- or multiple-brooded depends on both the inherent nature of the species and the climate in which it lives. Some species or families (e.g., wood warblers) tend to be single-brooded even in southern North America, where climate would permit a second or third brood. Most North American birds are single-brooded, but a significant percentage of passerines rear a second brood and a few (e.g., Mourning and other doves, some wrens, mimids, bluebirds, House Finch, and Song and Field Sparrows) are typically treble-brooded in the southern parts of their range. More than three broods is very exceptional, but the Common Ground Dove, with a prolonged breeding season (February–November), is suspected of rearing up to four broods and the Inca Dove, on a similar schedule, is known to have reared five. None of these numbers include re-nesting due to parasitization or loss of eggs or young—not uncommon events in avian life.

The time required to build the nest is also highly variable. None is required, of course, for nestless species. Most passerines do the job in 3–9 days, though the period may be prolonged by cold or otherwise bad weather. As might be expected, nest construction, like the rest of the breeding cycle, is accelerated in the brief arctic summer, and the process tends to be prolonged in the warmer climate of southern areas. The complexity of the nest structure is also a factor: the long, pendulous sack of the Altamira (Lichtenstein's) Oriole may take 3 weeks or more; but in general birds are surprisingly efficient. A Bank Swallow, for example, can excavate a 2-foot tunnel nest in 5 to 6 days, though apparently ill-equipped for digging.

Sexual Roles. Site selection and nest building (as well as other nest activities; see INCUBATION and PARENTAL CARE) tend on the whole to be dominated by the female. On the other hand, males are rarely exempted *entirely* from these duties.

The Red Phalarope may be the only North American species in which the *male alone* is responsible for nest construction, although unmated male cormorants are known to build a nest, which is then rearranged by the female if and when she consents to mate. Among all hummingbirds; most tits, icterids, tanagers, and finches; and some flycatchers, swallows, vireos, and wood warblers, the *female alone* builds the nest. In most species nest building is shared in a variety of ways. Pairs of woodpeckers, waxwings, and some swallows divide responsibility equally; in Mourning and other dove species, the female builds while the male brings materials; among frigatebirds the reverse applies; in some cases the male will build certain parts of the nest and the female the rest; male Phainopeplas begin their nests and their mates finish them; male wrens of some species build a series of nest "shells" and the female selects one and lines it for occupation.

MATERIALS. In general, birds of a given species will use similar materials in making their nest; however, there is considerable variation, depending upon the availability of materials and individual "taste." Great Cormorant nests on offshore islands have a large component of seaweed, for example, while inland arboreal nests of the same species are made mainly of sticks with little or no seaweed. When horses were ubiquitous many species built with horsehair, a scarce material today, which has been replaced by plant fibers. Though the vast majority of nests are made with a small number of "basic" components—mostly plant material—in some cases held together with a binding substance (see below), a few species characteristically incorporate an "odd" item. Great Crested Flycatcher nests, for example, usually contain snakeskin—though not for protective purposes, as is sometimes supposed. Some species seem to like to "decorate" their nests with flowers or man-made materials, such as paper (Blue Jay), rags (Northern Mockingbird, American Robin), or yarn (Northern Oriole). Individual birds learn where certain materials can be found within their home range or territory and will return to the source consistently.

Materials commonly used for basic external nest structure include: sticks, grass, reeds (including cattail, *Phragmites*), sedges (*Scirpus*, etc.), rushes (*Juncus*), seaweed, wet decaying aquatic plants, Spanish moss (*Tillandsia*), bark, foliose lichens, paper, string/yarn, "debris," and mud.

All passerines and many other species line their nests; some ground nesters (e.g., phalaropes, Savannah Sparrow) make no external nest but simply line a scrape or hollow in the earth. Lining is the last stage in the construction of complex nests and the materials used are much finer than those used in the "walls." Typical lining materials are: leaves (dead or fresh), fine grasses, *Usnea* lichens, moss, plant down (thistle, milkweed, etc.), bark fibers, pine needles, contour feathers, down feathers (Anseriformes only), and animal hair/fur.

Some nests are loose and dry—the flimsy platform of sticks typical of most doves and pigeons are the ultimate in this mode. Other nests (e.g., orioles, vireos) are given shape and coherence by careful "sewing" or "weaving" techniques.

A great many species solidify their nests with some form of binding material. This process varies widely in both extent and materials used. Some nests are pure "adobe" (e.g., Cliff Swallow; see below); the phoebes build largely of mud but with a larger proportion of plant material; American Robins "plaster" their interior walls with mud and then add a further lining of fine grasses; crows sometimes use small amounts of mud or animal dung; the excrement of nestlings adds to the solidity of the nest structure in some species; swifts (most species) are unique in cementing their nests with their own gluey saliva (see below); and hummingbirds and other small species use spider and caterpillar silk to bind the fine materials used in their diminutive nests.

Red-breasted Nuthatches daub pine sap around the entrance holes of their nest cavities, and Red-cockaded Woodpeckers create a copious flow of resin around their nest holes by drilling tap holes in the surrounding bark. It is thought that these practices may afford protection from insects, snakes, and/or other nest pests.

NESTING LOCATIONS. Bird's nests are found in virtually every conceivable situation except in midair, on the surface of the sea (the legends of the halcyon to the contrary notwithstanding), and underwater. Placement ranges from 3 or more feet below the earth's surface (Burrowing Owl, some auks) to over 100 feet in trees (kinglets, Lewis' Woodpecker, Marbled Murrelet: 148 feet). The tops of our tallest trees, e.g., the sequoias, which often approach and occasionally exceed 300 feet, seem to be avoided by birds; at least there are no data for these heights. Particular species tend to nest within a characteristic range of heights, which, however, may be quite broad and span two or more niches. Ground nesters never nest in treetops and treetop species do not nest on the ground, but some ground nesters will also build in low shrubs or the lower branches of trees and treetop species may descend to within a few feet of the ground. This variation may be seasonal and geographical as well as individual. Rufous-sided Towhees and Song and Field Sparrows frequently build their first nest of the season on the ground and move up into the shrubbery for successive broods. Species, such as the Osprey, which are typically arboreal where trees exist will nonetheless nest on the ground in barren country.

Requirements as to the kind of situation in which the nest is built are also very generalized in many cases. Long-eared Owls will nest well up in trees (in abandoned raptor or squirrel nests), on the forest floor at the base of a tree, in scrubby growth, or even in open marshland or sand dunes. Some cavity nesters, e.g., the House Wren, will appropriate virtually any hole of the right size regardless of the substance in which it occurs (see Audubon's plate—Havell LXXXIII); the American Robin may prefer a tree branch but will not disdain a rock ledge, the eaves of a house, or even the ground under some circumstances. Many species have come to regard man-made structures as acceptable nest sites (see below) and a few—the Barn Swallow, phoebes, House Sparrow, Chimney Swift—have come to prefer them to what nature offers.

Some birds enhance nesting security—whether by design or chance —by nesting close to other, more aggressive bird species. For example, several species of songbirds have occasionally nested among the twiggy interstices of a raptor's nest, and birds nesting within tern or gull colonies doubtless derive some benefit from the latter's no-nonsense approach to nest defense. A number of Neotropical bird species routinely nest near wasp or ant colonies, thereby deriving protection from predators without apparently incurring any risk to themselves; no North American species is known to take advantage of this technique.

TYPES OF NESTS. Given the great diversity in bird forms, habitats, and habitat preferences, a comparable variety in nesting styles is hardly

FIG. 15. *Nesting habits* are wonderfully varied among different groups of birds. The examples illustrated are (clockwise from top left): stick platforms in an arboreal heronry; tree cavity excavated by woodpeckers; pendulous sack woven by some oriole species; the "standard" cup nest of most songbirds, set on a wide branch, in a crotch, or on a level surface on a building; the cup suspended from a small fork typical of the vireos; the clustered flask-shaped "adobe" homes of Cliff Swallows; the tunnel-and-chamber excavated by kingfishers (shown "cut away"); the floating platform of soggy aquatic plants favored by grebes; the ground burrow of a storm-petrel; the unlined scrape of the Least Tern; a swan's mound of plant material and debris; the spherical basket woven into rushes or cattails by the male Long-billed Marsh Wren; and the massive heap of sticks (with central cup) piled up year after year by Golden Eagles and other diurnal birds of prey.

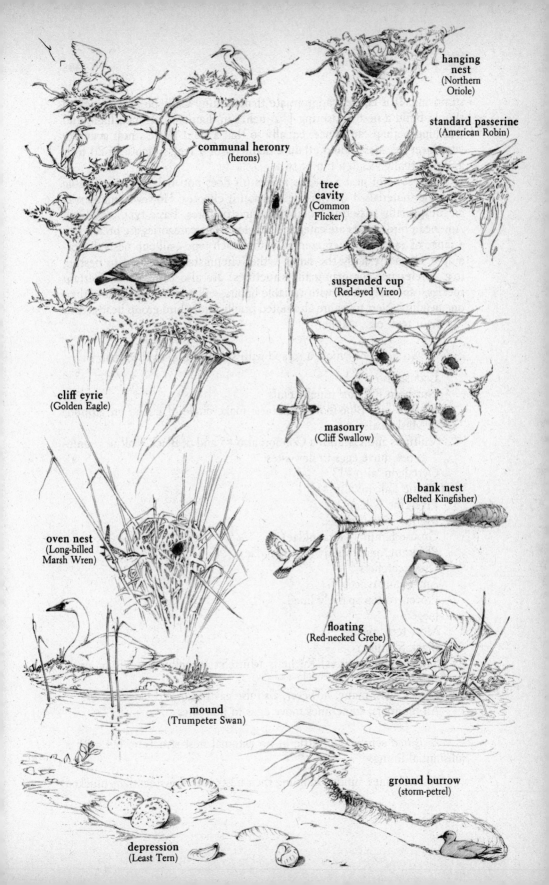

communal heronry
(herons)

hanging nest
(Northern Oriole)

standard passerine
(American Robin)

tree cavity
(Common Flicker)

suspended cup
(Red-eyed Vireo)

masonry
(Cliff Swallow)

cliff eyrie
(Golden Eagle)

bank nest
(Belted Kingfisher)

oven nest
(Long-billed Marsh Wren)

floating
(Red-necked Grebe)

mound
(Trumpeter Swan)

ground burrow
(storm-petrel)

depression
(Least Tern)

surprising. It is entirely appropriate that the tiny Calliope Hummingbird should build a nest measuring 1½ inches in diameter, ⅞ inch high, and weighing perhaps an ounce; equally so that a Bald Eagle's nest accumulated over decades should attain a diameter of 9 feet, a depth of 20 feet, and eventually weigh a ton or two.

The *type* of nest a species makes (or does not make) is less variable than the materials it uses or the location it chooses. However, many species (especially passerines) build similar structures. Basic types of North American bird's nests are categorized below. The categories are broad, i.e., a range of variation is represented within each type—all cup nests, for example, are not exactly the same. Other circumstances related to nesting (e.g., preference for man-made structures) are also categorized. Certain species, especially those with variable habits, will appear under more than one heading. Nest types are also noted briefly under bird group headings in the main text, e.g., GREBE.

1. *No nest* or at most a scrape with scant lining, in the open:

Loons: also #3
Northern Fulmar: usually cliffs
Masked and Blue-footed Boobies: make circle of guano on ground;
    Masked also #7
Vultures and California Condor: also #5 and 6; Black Vultures some-
    times move eggs to new sites
Gyrfalcon: also #13
Prairie Falcon: also #13
Peregrine Falcon
Merlin: very variable
Grouse family (Tetraonidae)
Pheasant/quail family (Phasianidae)
Oystercatchers
American Avocet
Plovers: often sparsely lined
Jaegers
Most tern species
Black Skimmer
Some alcids: murres, Kittlitz's Murrelet (usually on cliffs or open
    ground)
Larger owls: many, however, also use cavities or old hawk nests
All nightjars: sometimes move eggs to new sites

2. *Lined scrape*, i.e., little or no external nest structure, but with a substantial lining:

Anseriformes: unique in lining their nests with down feathers plucked from the breast of the female, except for the whistling (tree) ducks and the stifftails; geese line with plant material as well as down; ducks line with down only (see also #6)

Sandpipers (Scolopacidae): lined with grasses and other dry plant material; depth of scrape variable but Sanderling exceptional in making true cup (see #9); Solitary Sandpiper also exceptional (see #13)

Some gulls: Sabine's, Ring-billed, Mew, and Ivory

Some sparrows: e.g., Savannah and Grasshopper make little more than a cup-shaped lining in a depression in the ground, i.e., midway between this category and #9

3. *Mounds* on open ground or in shallow water:

Loons: also #1

Grebes: also #4

Northern Gannet: largely seaweed

Pelicans: earth and debris

Cormorants: largely seaweed; Great and Neotropic also #7

Herons: in treeless country; most species usually #7; bitterns usually low in dense marsh vegetation

Roseate Spoonbill: rarely (see #7)

All ibises: mainly #7; but also on ground in dense marsh vegetation

Swans: large mounds of plant material, hollowed at top; down-lined; sometimes use muskrat houses

Whistling (tree) ducks: do not line with down; Black-bellied usually #6

Canvasback: also #4

Ruddy Duck: also #4; usually lacks down lining; known to use muskrat house

American Flamingo: low mud cylinders with hollow in top for egg

Bald Eagle: in treeless country; normally #7

Everglade Kite: occasionally; sticks with finer lining; primarily #7

Osprey: in treeless country; normally #7

Northern Harrier: sticks and reeds

Cranes: marsh-plant materials

Limpkin: in marshes; also #7

Gallinules and American Coot: in marsh vegetation

Some gulls: large species, Herring, etc., as well as Laughing and Kittiwake

Forster's Tern: sometimes #4 or on muskrat house

Black Tern: usually #4

Brown Noddy: occasionally; primarily #7

4. *Floating nests*, normally made of dead aquatic vegetation and anchored to living plants:

Grebes: sometimes #3; unlined
Whistling Swan: occasionally; also #3; down-lined
Canvasback: occasionally; also #3; down-lined
Ruddy Duck: also #3; no down
Northern Jacana: loose, wet plant matter lying atop floating vegetation
Franklin's Gull
Forster's Tern: also #3
Black Tern: also #3, 13

5. *Ground holes*, including burrows, bank holes, and crevices in rocks. Some species, e.g., tubenoses, alcids, Burrowing Owl, kingfishers, and swallows, can dig their own holes, though many will also occupy sites that were dug by other members of their species or by different species.

Shearwaters and petrels: burrows or rock crevices of varying depths; scantily lined with debris
Tropicbirds: often in rock holes or crevices, unlined
Some ducks: tree-hole nesters (see #6) will occasionally use a hole in a bank or an old rabbit hole; down lined
Some alcids: most auklets, Dovekie, Xantus' Murrelet, Razorbill, and guillemots usually prefer rock crevices with little or no lining; Rhinoceros Auklet, puffins, and Ancient Murrelet use burrows of varying depths, usually with linings
Burrowing Owl: usually in prairie dog or other mammal burrows; debris-lined
White-throated Swift: rock crevices, old Rough-winged Swallow holes (rarely); varied nest material glued with bird's saliva
Elegant (Coppery-tailed) Trogon: rarely; usually #6
Kingfishers: earth banks; unlined but rank with excrement and food remains
Bank and Rough-winged Swallows
Plain Titmouse: rarely in earthen bank; usually #6
Many wrens (e.g., House, Winter, Carolina, Bewick's): occupy almost any opening of the right proportions, including crevices in banks or rocks; generously lined; also #6, 8, 11, and 16
Canyon and Rock Wrens: often in rock cavity; cup-like construction
Mountain Bluebird: sometimes in rock crevices or earthen banks; lined, cup-like construction; also #6
Wheatear: rocky crevices; loose, cup-like construction
Townsend's Solitaire: sometimes in rocky crevice; cup-like construction (#8) with lining; also #6, 10
White Wagtail: sometimes in rock cavities or holes in earthen banks; very variable; lined, cup-like construction (#8)

Water Pipit: sometimes in shallow bank or rock cavity; lined, cup-like construction (#9); also #10

Common Starling: occasionally in rock crevice; very variable (see #6, 16, etc.); loose, messy cup

Lucy's Warbler: rarely in earthen bank; usually #6

Waterthrushes: sometimes in banks very near water

Rosy finches: occasionally in hole or rock crevice; cup-like construction

6. *Tree holes*, whether natural cavities in rotted trees, stumps, and fallen logs or (frequently) abandoned woodpecker holes. In addition to the woodpeckers, only the tits, nuthatches, and trogons often do their own excavation. While it is possible to define species generally as "tree-hole nesters" or "ground-hole nesters," it should be noted that it is the hole—the fact that it is a cavity, its size and location—rather than the material in which it occurs, or has been dug, that is of prime importance to the prospective occupants. Thus, most of the species below feel equally at home in a woodpecker hole, natural tree crevice, or nest box and a number occasionally fit in category #5.

Vultures, the tree ducks, the owls, and the trogons leave their cavities unlined; the ducks add only down and most of the passerines construct some form of lined cup.

Tree holes are scarce in nature compared with other nest sites, with fewer sites than prospective occupants, at least in some areas. Therefore, the fact that woodpeckers construct new holes each year crucially affects populations of forest and other cavity-nesting species. It is also clear that "cleaning" forests of dead and rotting timber—entrenched dogma among modern tree farmers—has a major detrimental impact on the diversity of these ecosystems.

In view of the normal scarcity and recently accelerated decline of tree holes, the setting of nest boxes (see BIRDHOUSE) is all the more worthwhile and likely to be successful.

Ducks: Black-bellied Whistling, Wood, Bufflehead, goldeneyes, Hooded and Common Mergansers

Merlin: occasionally; very variable; see also #1, 13

Most owls: frequently; see also #13

Elegant Trogon

Woodpeckers

Flycatchers: Sulphur-bellied, Great Crested, and Western (sometimes)

Tree and Violet-green (rarely Rough-winged) Swallows, Purple Martin

All tits

All nuthatches

Brown Creeper: lined cup in crevice under loose bark of tree trunk

Some wrens: House, Bewick's, Carolina, and Winter; but all widely variable; see also #5, 8, 10, 16

All bluebirds: see also #5, 16

Common Starling and Crested Mynah: also #5 (starling) and 16

Prothonotary Warbler

Lucy's Warbler: also #5

Brewer's Blackbird: rarely; usually #8

7. *Stick platforms* in trees or lower vegetation. Non-passerine nests are lined sparsely if at all.

Red-footed (and sometimes Masked) Booby

Great and Neotropic Cormorants: both also build on the ground (#3) in coastal areas, the former more frequently

Anhinga: lined with fresh leaves and moss

Most herons: also under #3

Wood Stork

Roseate Spoonbill

All ibises: also on ground (#3)

Most eagles, hawks, and Osprey: a few nest on ground in open country (#3), Northern Harrier habitually; some (e.g., falcons) use other species' abandoned nests (#13); American Kestrel and Merlin often in tree cavities (#6); mostly lined (except falcons)

Plain Chachalaca: sparsely lined with leaves

Limpkin: sometimes in low trees; mainly #3; loose plant materials rather than sticks

Brown Noddy: sparsely lined with debris

Pigeons and doves: usually loosely constructed and very frail

Yellow-billed Cuckoo: other cuckoos under #8

Large owls: sometimes take over old stick platform built by hawks

Note: The nests of the larger corvids (especially Northern Raven) often seem to be simply large platforms of sticks (and are sometimes taken over by hawks and owls) but are essentially large cup nests (#8).

8. *Cup nests*, the "classic" bird's nest, typically with a coarser outer wall and finer lining, sometimes cemented with mud or dung, and, unless otherwise noted, in trees or shrubs. Species which build ground cups, domed nests, suspended nests, or mud cups—all essentially variations of the cup—are excluded here and listed under #9, 10, 11, and 12.

Bonaparte's Gull: in northern spruce forests; sticks, lined with grasses, lichen, etc.

Cuckoos (except Yellow-billed; #7), anis, Roadrunner: loosely made
Hummingbirds: smallest nests; variable fine materials (e.g., lichen
    flakes) bound with spider silk, caterpillar silk, and/or plant fibers
Most flycatchers: see also #6, 10, 11
Crows and jays: see also #7 (Note) and 12
Brown Creeper: behind tree bark, equivalent to #6?
Wrentit
Red-whiskered Bulbul
All mimic thrushes: occasionally on ground (#9)
Most thrushes
Gnatcatchers
Waxwings
Phainopepla
Shrikes
Many warblers: including most *Dendroicas*, Bachman's, Olive, Mac-
    Gillivray's (near ground), Yellowthroat (low), Yellow-breasted
    Chat, Hooded Warbler, and American Redstart
Some blackbirds: Red-winged and Tricolored (see Note below);
    Rusty, Brewer's (usually, but variable), grackles (often low)
White-collared Seedeater
Fringillid finches (i.e., excluding emberizine finches); tundra breeders
    (e.g., Hoary Redpoll) also on ground (#9)
Tanagers
Cardinal-Grosbeaks (including *Passerina* buntings)
Brown and Abert's Towhees
Many sparrows: some (e.g., Field and Song) nest on ground for first
    brood
Note: Red-winged and Tricolored Blackbirds and Sharp-tailed, Sea-
    side, and Swamp Sparrows, all of which habitually nest in marsh-
    land, usually "weave" cup nests onto standing cattail or sedges,
    well above water level. Chimney and Vaux's Swifts build *half-cups*
    of twigs cemented together with their saliva and fixed to the inside
    of a hollow tree, chimney, or other vertical interior surface.

9. *Ground cups*, similar to #8 but on the earth, in marshland, or on
rock ledges:

Rails: in marshland; with grass canopy, so listed also under #10; also
    affinities with mound-type nests (#3) but cup well made and lined
    with finer material
Sanderling (most sandpipers under #2)
Black Swift: mosses, mud (no saliva), on wet ledges, usually near
    seeping water

Yellow-bellied Flycatcher: in moss clumps or tree roots; often somewhat elevated

Larks

Canyon Wren: on open ledges or shelves; also #5

Some thrushes: Hermit, Veery (sometimes), Townsend's Solitaire (also #5), and Bluethroat

White Wagtail (sometimes)

Yellow Wagtail

Pipits (Water Pipit also #5)

Many warblers: all *Vermivoras* (except Bachman's and Lucy's), plus Black-and-White, Worm-eating, Blackpoll (rarely), Kirtland's, Palm (usually), Kentucky, Mourning, Connecticut, Red-faced, Wilson's, Canada, Painted Redstart, and waterthrushes (also #5)

Bobolink and Brewer's Blackbird (rarely)

Dickcissel

Green-tailed and Rufous-sided Towhees (also #8)

Sparrows: most sparrows nest on the ground, but many will also place their cups in low shrubbery at least occasionally; in some species (e.g., Field and Song) the higher nests are characteristic of later broods; some grassland sparrows (e.g., Savannah) have rather rudimentary nests amounting to little more than a lined scrape (#2)

Longspurs

10. *Domed or enclosed nests*, usually with a well-lined internal cup and either arboreal or on the ground:

Great Kiskadee

Northern Beardless Tyrannulet (Beardless Flycatcher)

Magpies: canopy of twigs

Verdin: spherical; thorny twigs

American Dipper: made of moss; on ledge or bank near river

Winter Wren: in some form of cavity (#5 and 6)

Carolina Wren: dome may be lacking in hole nests (#5 and 6)

Cactus Wren: often in cactus or other thorny plant

Long-billed Marsh Wren: supported among marsh vegetation (cattail, sedges, rushes); relatively high above shallow water

Short-billed Marsh (Sedge) Wren: supported among marsh sedges or rush; generally lower, over drier ground than preceding

Arctic Warbler: ground

Ovenbird: ground; named for its nest

Common Yellowthroat: on or very near ground; sometimes partially canopied

Meadowlarks

House and Eurasian Tree Sparrows: lack dome in cavities (#5, 16)

Olive Sparrow

Seaside Sparrow: in salt-marsh grass clumps; sometimes partially domed

Note: Among the rails, Common Gallinule, some sandpipers (e.g., Upland) and phalaropes, living grasses or other plants near the nest may be pulled over it to form a rough concealing canopy.

11. *Suspended nests,* i.e., attached to and hanging from a branch or other support; form varies from the long, pendulous bags made by some orioles to the cups which the vireos hang between forked branches.

Rose-throated Becard: globular mass; entrance near bottom
Acadian Flycatcher: partially suspended
Bushtit (a penduline tit): a long bag; entrance at top
Kinglets: usually a deep, suspended cup
All vireos: cup suspended in fork
All orioles: Northern, Spot-breasted, and Altamira (Lichtenstein's) weave long, hanging bags attached to branch ends (entrance at top); the other species' nests are more cup-like and are hung from a variety of sites—Hooded Oriole, for example, sometimes "sews" the top of the nest to the underside of a palm frond.
Note: Tropical and Northern Parulas and Yellow-throated Warbler often suspend their cup-like nests in hanging festoons of *Usnea* lichen or Spanish moss in regions where these epiphytic plants are common.

12. *Mud nests,* not including earthen mounds, e.g., Pelicans (#3). Barn and Cave Swallows and Eastern and Black Phoebes make cups (or half-cups) by the accretion of mud pellets mixed with binding substances such as grass, hair, or feathers. Except that the structures are built "wet" rather than of dried bricks, the similarity to human "adobe" construction is striking. By far the most skillful of the North American "potter" birds is the Cliff Swallow, which assembles "pueblos" of graceful beehive-shaped nests beneath overhanging rock faces or eaves. The Cave Swallow also attaches its nest to a vertical surface (in caves and sinkholes) but makes only a half-cup.

The Black Swift, Blue and Steller's Jays, the magpies and crows, Clark's Nutcracker, American Robin, and Varied and Gray-cheeked Thrushes typically use some mud and/or dung in their nests.

13. *Secondhand nesters.* Almost all tree-cavity nesters (#6) use old woodpecker nests. Indeed, most depend on them for maintaining their population, though other kinds of cavities may also be used and some species are capable of hewing out their own. *These species are omitted from the following list* unless they *also* appropriate other nest types. (In the list below, birds whose nests are taken over by a given species appear in parentheses.) A few species not only use another species' nest but also avail

themselves of free incubation service (see BROOD PARASITE); these species are marked "P."

> Anhinga (egret)
> Many ducks, esp. Hooded Merganser, Ruddy Duck, bay ducks: often lay eggs in other species' nests, especially before their own nests are complete; in some cases such birds may not lay a clutch of their own and thus rate a full "P" (see also DUMP NEST)
> Falcons (ravens, Rough-legged and other hawks)
> Solitary Sandpiper (American Robin, Bohemian Waxwing, Rusty Blackbird, Eastern Kingbird, and other songbirds)
> Forster's Tern (grebes; also muskrats) (see also #4)
> Black Tern (grebes, coots) (usually #3 or 4)
> Mourning Dove (in rare cases builds on top of old songbird nests)
> Large owls (ravens, hawks)
> Yellow-billed and Black-billed Cuckoos (P: occasionally—with other cuckoos, Gray Catbird, Wood Thrush, Yellow Warbler, Chipping Sparrow) (usually # 7 or 8)
> Ash-throated Flycatcher (Cactus Wren)
> Violet-green Swallow (Cliff and Bank Swallows)
> Rough-winged Swallow (kingfishers)
> Bluebirds (Cliff and other swallows)
> White Wagtail (other songbirds, Osprey—crevices among sticks)
> Lucy's Warbler (Verdin)
> Great-tailed Grackle (heron rookeries)
> Brown-headed Cowbird (P: wide range of small to medium-sized species, esp. flycatchers, vireos, warblers, and finches)
> Bronzed Cowbird (P: wide range of small to medium-sized species, esp. orioles but also ground doves, flycatchers, thrashers, wrens, warblers, and finches)
> House Finch (many songbirds, including Cliff Swallow)

14. *Communal nesters,* i.e., species which use a single nest for the eggs of several (or many) pairs. Some ducks will deposit "extra" eggs in the nest of another duck of the same or different species (see DUMP NEST). Only the Groove-billed and Smooth-billed Anis and the Acorn Wood-pecker are known to make a habit of communal nesting in North America. In all these species, both sexes and most or all individuals in a communal group incubate. Record numbers of eggs in a single nest of the Smooth-billed Ani is 29; Groove-billed Ani, 15; Acorn Woodpecker, 10.

15. *Colonial nesters,* see COLONY.

16. *Nests in/on man-made structures,* excluding the rarest inci-dences and the use of nest boxes (see #6 for latter). Species which seem

now to *prefer* man-made structures to "natural" ones are marked with an asterisk.

Leach's Storm-Petrel: walls, buildings
Osprey: telephone poles
American Kestrel
Common Pigeon*
Barn Owl
Chimney* and Vaux's Swifts
Phoebes*
Some swallows—Barn,* Cliff, Rough-winged (pipes), and Purple Martin
Some wrens—House, Bewick's, Carolina, Canyon
American Robin
White Wagtail: walls, pipes, buildings
Common Starling and Crested Mynah
Common Grackle
House* and Eurasian Tree Sparrows
House Finch

FINDING AND IDENTIFYING NESTS. Not very long ago one could still mount an expedition to search for a North American bird's nest that no one had ever seen. The last vestige of this frontier passed into history on August 7, 1974, when the nest of the Marbled Murrelet was found—a small cup, made mainly of guano, laid improbably 148 feet up in a Douglas fir in Big Basin State Park, Santa Cruz County, California. Another wet blanket on the ardor of the would-be nest seeker is the fact that the laws which prohibit the collection of most native birds (see LAWS) also protect their nests and eggs.

These realities of the modern era do not, however, prevent the dedicated birdwatcher from both adding to our knowledge of birdlife and having fun with nests. Countless details of nest construction, site preferences, frequency of re-nesting, and the degree of variation shown by any given species remain to be recorded. Properly identified off-season nests can be used in confirming the presence of a particular species in breeding-bird atlas work—a concept which is just beginning to enlist the enthusiasm of North American field ornithologists (see ATLAS).

Looking for nests in winter, when the absence of most leaves makes the beginner's efforts reasonably rewarding, can add a lot to a stroll through your neighborhood or a nearby wilderness. There are now a number of good field guides to help with identification, and most people over twelve will probably not be very disappointed at not being able to bring these treasures home.

Watching nesting activities "live" is also rewarding—once you've watched a Northern Oriole stitching its distinctive bag together, you may find yourself addicted to this benign form of voyeurism.

Caution must always be mentioned in this context, but common sense will guide most people who are taking the trouble to read this. Most birds will abandon their nest without a pang given what they regard as due cause, and some species are much more skittish than others. Birds are particularly liable to disturbance during the early phases of the cycle. Whole colonies of terns, for example, may abandon a site they've used for years for reasons which seem (to us at least) whimsical at best. On the other hand, most birds are quite tolerant of observation and once your presence has been found innocuous you can often count on being ignored.

If a bird flushes off eggs or stops feeding young at your approach, back off; you're too close, at least for the present. If you are the kind of person who wants to fondle, sniff, and eyeball each of life's new wonders, restrain yourself—at least where active nests are involved.

For nesting habits (including descriptions of nest and eggs) of particular families, see ALBATROSS; BOOBY; CORMORANT; etc.

See also EGG; INCUBATION; PARENTAL CARE; YOUNG, DEVELOPMENT OF; BIRDHOUSE; NEST FAUNA.

NEST BOX. See BIRDHOUSE.

NEST FAUNA. As Harold Oldroyd, the British fly specialist, has pointed out succinctly (1964–NEST): "The nests of birds are attractive to a variety of insects because they provide at the same time shelter, concealment, a supply of highly nutritious bird guano and the opportunity to attack the birds themselves." It should be added that invertebrate inhabitants of bird's nests are by no means restricted to insects. Ticks and mites are particularly well represented in terms of both species and numbers, and the boarders may even include an occasional moth larva.

Many of these creatures are harmful to the birds with which they cohabit (see ECTOPARASITE); other species, however, may actually be beneficial to their hosts by helping to clean the nest of feces and other organic debris and by eating or parasitizing the bird parasites. Some species have broadly defined habitats and regard a bird's nest as one of any number of similar cozy niches where food is abundant, but a great many others are restricted exclusively to nests for at least part of their life cycle. In the case of flies, beetles, and moths, it is often the immature stages which are most active in and dependent upon the nest, but adults may also be present. At least one species of louse fly (Hippoboscidae) overwinters in the nest as a pupa and hatches when the occupants return to re-nest.

As might be predicted, large, heavily constructed nests and those in crevices, holes, and nest boxes tend to have a richer, more numerous fauna than open-work nests of flimsy construction.

Adjectives such as "teeming" and "aswarm" barely do justice to the condition of some bird's nests. Hundreds of individual arthropods may be present in a given nest—especially with some species (e.g., Eastern Phoebe); the invertebrate species count can quickly run into the hundreds if a series of nests of different bird species are censused.

NESTLING. A young bird which is helpless at birth and therefore confined to the nest. Not, in the strictest sense, synonymous with CHICK. See also ALTRICIAL; PSILOPAEDIC; NIDICOLOUS; YOUNG, DEVELOPMENT OF.

NETS. See MIST NET; BANDING; CANNON NET; CAPTURE.

NEWBURYPORT/PLUM ISLAND (Massachusetts). An area on the north shore of Massachusetts that encompasses a harbor with vast mud flats (at the mouth of the Merrimack River), extensive salt marshes, freshwater marshes, diked empoundments, dunes with kettle-hole copses, and 9 miles of barrier beach. Most of Plum Island is preserved as the Parker River National Wildlife Refuge. A profitable birding area at any time of year but particularly so during migration, when over a hundred species can be found with relative ease in a day. That the area's diverse habitats are visited constantly by legions of faithful Massachusetts birders ensures that rarities such as Ross' Gull are regularly encountered and widely publicized.

NEWPORT BAY (California). Highly productive water-birding locality on the coast of southern California about 40 miles south of Los Angeles. The mud flats, marshes, and inshore waters attract large numbers and a great variety of loons, grebes, herons, ducks, rails, shorebirds, gulls, and terns.

NEW WORLD. In a strict geographical sense, the landmasses of the Western Hemisphere of the earth. These consist principally of North and South America, but also include a corner of Siberia, New Zealand, part of Antarctica, and most of the smaller Pacific island groups. In the zoogeographic sense, "New World" is generally taken to mean only the Nearctic and Neotropical regions combined (see DISTRIBUTION). Thus references to New World families of plants or animals (e.g., New World vultures, Cathartidae; New World flycatchers, Tyrannidae) are equivalent to "American" families. The fauna and flora of Siberia, New Zealand, and much of Oceania are "Old World" in nature. See ZOOGEOGRAPHY. Compare OLD WORLD.

NICHE (nitch or neesh). In the ecological sense, the *role* an organism plays within the ecosystem; its interrelationship with all of the factors of its environment. Sometimes applied (less usefully) in the sense of place or habitat. See DISTRIBUTION.

NICTITATING (NIK-tuh-TAY-ting) **MEMBRANE.** A kind of "third eyelid" which lies under the "main" eyelids on the inner, i.e., bill, side and is drawn obliquely or horizontally across the cornea to keep it moist and clean. Most birds blink with their nictitating membrane and close their main eyelids infrequently except when asleep. In birds active by day the membrane is transparent, whereas in owls and other nocturnal species it is translucent. In at least some water birds (e.g., loons, alcids) the nictitating membrane is modified with a transparent "window" to aid underwater vision. Reptiles, amphibians, and some mammals also have nictitating membranes. See VISION.

NIDICOLOUS (nye-DIK-uh-lus). The technical term for young birds which remain in the nest completely dependent on the parent birds for a period after hatching. Compare NIDIFUGOUS. See YOUNG, DEVELOPMENT OF.

NIDIFICATION (NID-if-ih-KAY-shun). Technical term for nest building or, in a more general sense, the entire nesting process, including site, construction, clutch size, timing, etc. See NEST.

NIDIFUGOUS (nye-DIFF-yuh-gus). The technical term for young birds which leave the nest soon after hatching. See also PRECOCIAL; PTILOPAEDIC; YOUNG, DEVELOPMENT OF.

NIGHTHAWK. Standard English name for the 3 species of nightjars in the genus *Chordeiles* (family Caprimulgidae; order Caprimulgiformes). The Antillean Nighthawk, once considered a race of the Common Nighthawk, has recently been found to breed in the Florida Keys. The nighthawks are restricted to the New World and differ from other caprimulgids in several details of form and behavior: they have sharply pointed, rather than rounded wing tips; they lack rictal bristles; their calls consist of a nasal *peent* (Common Nighthawk) and a low trill (Lesser) rather than the resonant "articulate-sounding" songs common to other nightjars; they nest and roost in the open or on tree limbs (Lesser) rather than in forest leaf litter; and they habitually fly in broad daylight (as well as at dawn, at dusk, and after dark).

Nighthawks do, of course, "hawk" for insects, but the name probably originated in the same way as "bullbat," another nickname for these birds. They are familiar birds, somewhat falcon-like in form, and hunt in the evening, so that "nighthawk" is an apt enough example of popular taxonomy.

For family characteristics, see NIGHTJAR.

NIGHT HERON. Standard English name for all 8 members of the subfamily Nycticoracinae (family Ardeidae; order Ciconiiformes), 2 of which, the Black-crowned and Yellow-crowned Night Herons, breed in North America.

The night herons are stocky birds with comparatively shorter necks and legs and stouter bills than the other members of their family. They roost communally in trees during the day, fly out to wetland habitats at dusk, and feed during the night—though the Yellow-crowned is less nocturnal in habit than the Black-crowned and both are often seen during the daytime, especially in cloudy weather. The Yellow-crowned Night Heron is generally less common here than the Black-crowned, has a more tropical distribution in the New World (to which it is restricted), is less gregarious, and in the tropics shows a decided preference for mangroves. The Black-crowned Night Heron is nearly cosmopolitan (absent from arctic and subarctic areas and Australasia).

For general physical characters and food preferences, see HERON.

NIGHTINGALE. A small drab thrush, *Luscinia* (*Erithacus*) *megarhynchos*, of the southwestern Palearctic, famous for its plaintive song. Newton (1893–96–ORNITHOLOGY) points out that in romantic literature the species is always referred to as female and its notes interpreted as expressions of anguish, as if "leaning its breast upon a thorn." To North Americans who have never heard it, the charm of the song might be likened to that of the Hermit Thrush, though Nightingales are also capable of a loud, rather raucous bubbling and chattering version which puts one more in mind of a mimic thrush. To the north and east *L. megarhynchos* is replaced by the very similar *L. luscinia,* the Thrush Nightingale or (in German) *Sprosser,* whose song is thought by some to rival "her sister's." Both sing during the day as well as at night. Nightingales reach North America only in reputation.

NIGHTJAR. Standard English collective name for the approximately 70 members of the family Caprimulgidae (order Caprimulgiformes), 7 of which breed in North America. An eighth species (Buff-collared Nightjar) may breed very locally and/or sporadically in the extreme southwestern U.S.

The nightjars range in size from about 7 inches (Poor-will) to slightly over a foot (Chuck-will's-widow). In general form they are strongly tapered from a large head and prominent breast to a long tail. The bill is tiny, but the gape is enormous (see Fig. 9), an adaptation to their habit of feeding on flying insects. This behavior may also explain the presence of long rictal bristles in most species (see TOUCH). The wings are long and rounded or sharply pointed (nighthawks). The legs and feet are very small and weak, but the middle toe is longer than the others and bears a pectinate (comb-like) claw.

The nightjars are among the best examples of cryptic coloration in birds (see Plate 3), their plumage pattern consisting of marvelously intricate vermiculations and irregular splotches in browns and grays which blend beyond perception into leaf litter, branch, or pebbly ground. Most species have white "banner marks" on wings and/or tail.

They have large eyes, as befits their crepuscular/nocturnal habits, and in some species (genus *Caprimulgus*) these give off a brilliant red, orange, or pink "eyeshine" when caught in the beam of headlights or a flashlight.

The nightjars are almost totally insectivorous, taking large moths, beetles, flies, and wasps on the wing while coursing through the air with their huge mouths agape, or darting out from a sedentary position like a flycatcher. These birds probably consume more mosquitoes in a single night's feeding than the average Purple Martin does in a lifetime. Chuck-will's-widows have been known to swallow a small bird on occasion.

The nightjars roost on the ground or in trees (Lesser Nighthawk) during the day and apparently are most active in the dim light before dawn and after dusk, except for the nighthawks, which habitually hunt in early morning and late afternoon as well as after dark. A western nightjar, the Poor-will, is the only bird species in which hibernation has been demonstrated (see TORPIDITY).

Caprimulgids make no nest, laying their eggs directly on the ground; and it has been reported that they occasionally transport their eggs and young from their original nest sites. Their (almost invariably) 2 eggs are white, pink, or buffy. Those of the Poor-will are usually unmarked; those of *Caprimulgus* spp. sparsely to densely marked with rather pale blotches; those of the nighthawks densely marked with dark and light brown and gray speckles.

Nightjars have highly distinctive voices, and the vernacular names of many species echo their "songs." As is true of the owls, the peculiar form, nocturnal habits, and weird cries of the nightjars have given rise to superstitious beliefs, the most tenacious and widespread of which is the fantastic notion that these birds suck milk from the teats of goats and cows, eventually causing the animals' death. (*Caprimulgus* is Latin for "goatsucker," another collective term for the family.)

The nightjars are distributed virtually worldwide (absent from arctic tundra and Patagonia) and throughout North America. All of our species are migratory.

The songs of most caprimulgids indubitably "jar" the stillness of the night; however, it is likely that the derivation of the name is more prosaic and echoes (very imperfectly) the "churring" ("jarring") sound made by the common Eurasian Nightjar (*Caprimulgus europaeus*).

NOCTURNAL. Active at night. Among birds, nocturnal habits vary greatly: there are species which are normally active *only* at night, e.g., many species of owls; those which are normally active both during the day and at night, e.g., many species of petrels and shearwaters; those which may be more active near dawn and dusk than during the dead of night (see CREPUSCULAR), e.g., species of nightjars; and those which, normally active by day (diurnal), undertake nocturnal migrations. Advantages of nocturnal habits include protective concealment and availability of prey which is not active by day.

NODDY. Standard English name for the 2 (or 3, depending on taxonomy) species of terns in the genus *Anous* and the single species in the genus *Procelsterna* (family Laridae; order Charadriiformes). The Brown or Common Noddy breeds in the Dry Tortugas and the Black, White-capped, or Lesser Noddy (sometimes divided into two species) occurs there as a summer visitor.

The noddies are almost perfect negative images of the usual tern pattern, being dark with white caps (rather than light with black caps) and with wedge-shaped rather than forked tails. They are pantropical pelagic terns which typically nest on sandy islands.

"Noddy" is an archaic English word for a simpleton and is thus analogous to "booby," i.e., a bird too dumb to flee from club-wielding sailors.

For family characteristics, see TERN.

NOMADISM. Migrant birds normally move according to orthodox traveling schedules, flying between two highly specific localities, following a standard route, and arriving at and departing from stopping points and ultimate destinations on or near the same dates, year after year (see MIGRATION). Even individuals which stray from the usual migration plan of their species tend to show up in the same places at the same dates for as long as they survive. Certain species are forced to make more or less irregular migrations from their usual ranges due to a combination of high populations and low food supply (see IRRUPTION), but even in these cases, the timing and the direction of travel are predictable to some degree.

In contrast, a few species seem to live according to no fixed schedule, breeding at different times and places and following no established routes. Such birds may be termed "nomadic." Their behavior is not totally haphazard, of course: they conform to given range limitations and biological strictures—a population of temperate zone nesters will never arrive and attempt to breed on the arctic tundra. And nomadic behavior may be confined to a certain part of a species' annual cycle—many pelagic species apparently wander wide expanses of ocean according to where food is available when not breeding but return to specific nesting grounds on a regular schedule. Nomadic movements can usually be related to climatic factors and/or food supplies, their uniqueness lying in the fact that the birds which undertake them seem to react spontaneously rather than according to an inflexible behavior pattern. Further research may well show that nomadic birds are much more strictly "programmed" than they appear to be.

In addition to pelagic species (e.g., Northern Fulmar, Great Skua), Cedar Waxwings, Dickcissels, and Lawrence's Goldfinches are among the few North American avian nomads.

NOMENCLATURE, ZOOLOGICAL. The orderly naming of animal species and subspecies and of the higher taxonomic groupings in which they are placed.

The need for a consistent, universal, centrally governed system of naming life forms as they are differentiated and described should be clear from several standpoints. (1) *Identity.* A unique animal without a unique name is like the philosopher's tree falling unnoticed in the forest—its very existence is in question. Naming something does not, of course, give it its identity, but if it has no name, it is difficult to consider it an entity. (2) *Communication and consistency.* What North Americans call a Parasitic Jaeger, the British call an Arctic Skua; the same bird in Germany is a *Schmarotzerraubmöwe*; in Japan it is called *Kuro-tózoku-kamome* and this name is written in characters that neither the average American nor the average German could read. However, in all of these countries ornithologists and well-informed birdwatchers would understand what species of bird was meant by *Stercorarius parasiticus,* a Latin species name which remains understandable the world over. Even if everyone in the world spoke English (or Italian or Russian), it would still be awkward to discuss different animal species intelligently using vernacular language. When Forbush wrote the *Birds of Massachusetts* (1925–29), he cited the following alternative names for the species then "officially" known as the Florida Gallinule: Gray Pond Hen, Meadow Hen, King Rail (!), and Red-billed Mud Hen. Doubtless this is but a small sample of the names by which this widespread species is called in North America alone. The standard English name here is now Common Gallinule. The same species has another list of colloquial labels in Britain, where it is also common and is "officially" called Moorhen. Many of these names are both colorful and apt, but each identifies the species only to a limited number of people. The scientific name *Gallinula chloropus* was not the first Latin name given to this species and it may change again, but it will change according to the rules of a universal system and will therefore change for *everyone simultaneously.* (3) *Order.* Most American birdwatchers may be indifferent to the fact that there are some 8,000 species and over 25,000 subspecies of living birds which never visit this continent, but an ornithologist studying a particular family of birds needs to be aware of its members worldwide—there are no exclusively North American bird families (the Wrentit, once considered the sole member of the family Chamaeidae, is now widely thought to be a babbler, family Timaliidae). Just defining his subject matter would be a life's work were it not for a system for cataloguing scientifically described species and recording taxonomic changes as they occur. This is no trivial task. The 15 volumes of the *Checklist of the Birds of the World*, the first volume of which appeared in 1931, is a project which has outlived its original author, James Peters; it has been continued by a number of the world's foremost ornithologists and is just now nearing "completion." The quotation marks signify that no such listing is ever truly complete—the early volumes of the *Checklist* were already being revised before the latest were published.

The basis for our present system of zoological nomenclature is the 10th edition of the *Systema Naturae Regnum Animale*, published in 1758. Its author, Carl von Linné (whose name, appropriately, is most familiar in its Latinized version, Carolus Linnaeus), was a Swedish botanist who gave us not only a nomenclature system but a structure for classifying all life forms. Linnaeus' original taxonomic hierarchy and its current, more sophisticated incarnation are given under TAXONOMY. The essence of his method of naming species remains unchanged and in the manner of most great ideas is ingeniously simple. All species are given two names: the second name identifies a species considered to be unique in nature; the first name assigns it—and perhaps other, similar species—to a genus. The process is therefore called the binomial ("double name") system; it was expanded beginning in 1844 into a trinomial system in order to allow for the naming of races or subspecies—forms which, though recognizable, are not specifically distinct (see SPECIATION). The creation of the trinomial does not alter the rules of the basic system. The placement of species in genera and in the higher categories is at the discretion of the "author" (i.e., the describer) of the species or of taxonomists who may later revise the classification on the basis of research into relationships among species, genera, families, etc.

The procedures which govern the use of world zoological nomenclature have expanded in proportion to our knowledge of the planet's life forms. The ultimate authority in these matters is the International Code of Zoological Nomenclature (latest edition, 1964), published by a nomenclatural commission of the International Congress of Zoology. The code is the rule book and standard for current usage of Linnaean principles; it is supplemented by the periodical *Bulletin of Zoological Nomenclature*, which reports recent rulings of the commission.

Precision being crucial to a useful nomenclatural system, the code sets guidelines on every facet of the subject, from the use of diphthongs (eschewed) to fine points of Latin grammar. Such details and the elaboration of technical phenomena such as "secondary homonyms" and "*nomina dubia*" seem impenetrable thickets of nomenclatural jargon to the layman, but their result is clarity, and they are crucial to the orderly and efficient study of animal life.

Though taxonomy would be impossible without nomenclature and nomenclature useless without taxonomy, it should be emphasized that the code governs only the *naming* of life forms, not their classification; also that nomenclature, though it has become complex, is not a discipline unto itself but rather a tool of science.

Some basic nomenclatural considerations are given below; for further details see the Bibliography. Many nomenclature terms are defined under separate entries.

Priority. The first name properly published is the valid name for any taxon (taxonomic category, e.g., family, genus, species; pl.: taxa). The starting point is January 1, 1758, the year the 10th edition of Linnaeus' *Systema Naturae* was published.

It is not uncommon for a zoologist to describe and name what he considers a "new" species which turns out eventually to be a race of a species previously named. In this case, the original name stands, though the second species name may be retained as the *subspecific* name if the race in question has not previously been described.

If two species originally assigned to two different genera are "lumped" together under one of them, the first-coined generic name is used. It takes little imagination to appreciate the potential complexities which arise in maintaining the rule of priority through a constant flood of taxonomic revision. The need for strict rules and periodical nomenclature publications becomes clear.

Uniqueness. All species and subspecies names must be unique within their genera; names of subgenera and higher taxa must be unique in the Animal Kingdom.

Authorship. The author of a species is the person who first publishes a scientific description of it. His or her name may appear after the species binomial, e.g., *Anas penelope* Linnaeus. If the species ends up in a different genus the author's name is put in parentheses, e.g., *Archilochus colubris* (Linnaeus) was originally *Trochilus colubris* Linnaeus. A proper name appearing after a *trinomial* is the author of the *subspecies*, and an author's name may also appear after a generic name standing alone, referring to the person who coined the *genus* name.

Application of the Code. The International Code of Zoological Nomenclature does not include taxa above superfamily, essentially because these higher categories have been defined and used in such a variety of ways that it is impossible to formulate a set of rules which would apply to all cases.

Language. All names must be Latin or "Latinized." Many names are simply Latin nouns which apply to the form being named: *Hirundo*, the generic name for the Barn and other swallows, is the Latin word for swallow. Others are descriptive compounds: the genus of the Vermilion Flycatcher, *Pyrocephalus*, is Latinized Greek, meaning fire (*pyro*)—i.e., red—head (*cephalus*). Still others commemorate a person: *Nuttallornis* (Nuttallbird), *Dendroica graciae* (Grace's tree dweller); a few are words from other languages which happen to have Latin-sounding endings, e.g., *Anhinga*, the Tupi Indian name for the Anhinga (*Anhinga anhinga*), or are simply made up at the whim of the author.

Appropriateness. That a scientific name be appropriate to the animal it labels is preferable but not necessary to the functioning of the system. The specific name of the Red-cockaded Woodpecker is *borealis*, implying that it is a northern species. The fact that it is endemic to *southeastern* North America and many species of woodpeckers range much farther north is of no nomenclatural significance. The usefulness of the name is its published association with the description of a unique species.

Conventions of Form. There are rules governing capitalization, typeface, standardized taxon endings, formation of subgroup names, parts of speech, and agreement of Latin endings for all taxa. Some of these are noted under the separate entries for each category: SPECIES; FAMILY; GENUS; etc.

Types. A mainstay of the present nomenclature system is that each name is associated with a "type." The concept enhances stability and consistency and is best explained by example. The "type" of a species or subspecies is a "type specimen," an actual preserved bird skin from which the species or race was described. Such specimens are so labeled and (barring loss) can be re-examined in museum collections. The "type" of a genus (or subgenus) is a "type species," the characteristic form from which the genus was described. Families are described from "type genera," etc. For more explicit definitions of the terms of the type concept, see GENOTYPE; HOLOTYPE; LECTOTYPE; MONOTYPIC; NOMINATE; PARALECTOTYPE; PARATYPE; POLYTYPIC; TOPOTYPE; TYPE GENUS; TYPE LOCALITY; TYPE SERIES; TYPE SPECIES; TYPE SPECIMEN; SYNTYPE.

NOMINATE (NOM-ih-nit). When a taxon (e.g., family, genus, species) is subdivided into lower taxa, the subdivision which contains the type (see NOMENCLATURE) repeats the name of the higher taxon and is known as the "nominate" subdivision (e.g., subfamily or subspecies). The concept is more easily explained by example than by definition. When the Common Nighthawk, *Chordeiles minor*, was divided into races or subspecies, the subspecies in which the original type *specimen* belongs had to be designated as the "nominate subspecies," and named *Chordeiles minor minor*. Likewise, when a family is subdivided into subfamilies, one subfamily (the one which contains the type of the family) must take its root from the family name and is called the nominate subfamily. For example, the so-called dabbling ducks are the nominate subfamily, Anatinae, of the family Anatidae, which also contains other subfamilies, such as the geese (Anserinae), bay and sea ducks (Aythyinae), etc.

Note that the "nominate" concept has nothing to do with phylogeny or any characteristic of the form in question, but is purely a nomenclatural convention.

NORTHER (in Spanish: norte). For the average Texan or Mexican a norther simply means bad weather—cold, windy, and rainy. But for bird-watchers seeking spring migrants along the upper Texas coast (see ROCK-PORT; GALVESTON ISLAND; HIGH ISLAND), a well-placed norther can mean a bonanza. Land-bird migrants arriving in North America from their Neo-tropical wintering grounds across the Gulf of Mexico tend to continue their flight into the interior when they arrive over the U.S. with the pre-vailing southerly tail winds. But when a cold front hits the coast from the north at the same time the migrants are arriving from the south, millions of birds may be forced to seek shelter from strong contrary winds and heavy rain at their first landfall, e.g., the live oak copses at High Island and Rockport. See also MIGRATION.

NORTH TEMPERATE ZONE. That part of the earth north of the Tropic of Cancer and south of the Arctic Circle. It includes most of North America and Europe, much of Asia, and part of Greenland and Africa. Many bird species reside solely in the North Temperate Zone; many others migrate from the N.T.Z. to the tropics for the winter; but only a few spe-cies—e.g., Swainson's Hawk, Arctic Tern, a number of shorebird species, Barn Swallow, and Bobolink—migrate between the N.T.Z. and the SOUTH TEMPERATE ZONE.

NOSTRILS. As in humans, a bird's nostrils (technically called nares; sing.: naris) are paired, external openings to the RESPIRATORY SYSTEM. They open into passages in the skull which lead ultimately to the windpipe (trachea).

Except for the kiwis of New Zealand, whose nostrils are located near the tip of their long bills, birds' nostril openings are located near the base of the upper mandible. In most cases they are relatively inconspicuous slits or holes, but in some birds they are uniquely modified or accompanied by special appurtenances.

The most elaborate external nostril structure is that of the so-called tubenoses, the pelagic birds of the order Procellariiformes. In shearwaters (family Procellariidae) and storm-petrels (family Hydrobatidae) the base of the culmen consists of two tubes joined along their length like the barrels of a tiny shotgun; in the albatrosses (family Diomedeidae) the tubes are raised separately from the sides of the upper mandible. One explanation for these unusual bill/nostril modifications is that they direct the flow of air over a structure within the nasal passages the purpose of which is to sense slight changes in air currents produced over the sea surface, allowing tubenoses to navigate with great precision over waves and swells even in the most turbulent weather. For another function of these distinctive structures, see SALT GLAND.

Softer, less conspicuous nostril tubes are present in some nightjars.

At the other extreme are members of the order Pelecaniformes (pelicans, cormorants, boobies, anhingas), in most of which the nostril slits are completely closed and obsolete in adulthood, though in some species they are open at hatching. This adaptation presumably evolved in conjunction with these birds' underwater habits, a theory bolstered by the fact that boobies and cormorants have "secondary nostrils" at the corners of their mouths which are closed "automatically" by a special flap when the birds submerge.

In hawks and eagles, falcons, owls, and parrots the nostrils open through a fleshy "saddle" at the base of the bill called a CERE. This structure may be feathered (parrots) or naked and brightly colored (falcons), but its function if any is unclear. Pigeons, gallinaceous birds, and a few passerines (none in North America) have a fleshy flap or "operculum" which partly occludes the nasal passages; its purpose too is debatable.

Corvids (crows, jays, etc.) and grouse have their nostril openings covered by a layer of feather-like bristles, and many flycatchers and other insectivorous birds have nasal bristles (see FEATHER) "screening" the nares.

The nostril openings in the *bone* (as opposed to the rhamphotheca or bill sheath) of the upper mandible have been divided by taxonomists into four major categories based on shape and internal structure and used to posit relationships among birds. See also SMELL.

NOUNS OF ASSEMBLAGE (or collective nouns). "Flock" is the collective noun which is most generally applied to birds and which is appropriate to any species or mixture thereof as long as there are more than two individuals; it is also the usual collective for sheep. Of course, many other general group nouns, e.g., "group," "bunch," "pack," "host," may also be used for birds, and a few terms relating specifically to birds are also in wide use, e.g., "flight" (of any birds in the air); "raft" (of ducks, usually sea or bay ducks); "kettle" or "screw" (of soaring birds, e.g., hawks or storks, referring to the vortex shape flocks assume when riding thermals; see FLIGHT, *Soaring*, and Fig. 20); and "skein" (in flight) or "gaggle" (on land or water) of geese. A few other words, especially "brace" (two dead game birds) and "covey" (a family group of small game birds), are common hunter's terms.

Then there is a long (perhaps endless) list of fanciful, poetical, and/or comical nouns of assemblage which are collected and sometimes coined by aficionados of avian togetherness. A sampling follows. Many of these were also originally sportsman's terms.

Bouquet or nye of pheasants
Building of rooks
Cast of hawks
Charm of finches
Clamor of rooks
Cluster of knots
Commotion or covert of coot
Congregation of plover
Dissimulation of birds
Dule of doves
Exaltation of larks
Fall of woodcock
Gulp of cormorants
Murder of crows
Murmuration of starlings
Mustering of storks

Ostentation of peacocks
Pack of grouse
Paddling of ducks
Parliament of owls
Peep of chickens
Pitying of doves
Rafter of turkeys
Richness of martins
Siege of herons
Spring of teal
Stand of flamingos
Strand of silky flycatchers
Tiding of magpies
Unkindness of ravens
Walk or wisp of snipe
Watch of nightingales

Another flock of collectives applies to bird colonies:

Rookery: originally rooks, now applied to any species of tree-nesting colonial birds

Heronry: herons, egrets, perhaps mixed with ibis, spoonbills, or other species

Shaggery: shags or cormorants

Cormorantry: cormorants or shags

Gullery: gulls

Loomery: alcids, especially murres

NUCHAL (NYEW-kl or NOO-kl). Referring to the back of the neck or nape. "Nucha" is a technical synonym for this region (see Fig. 25). The Band-tailed Pigeon has a narrow white nuchal collar.

NUMBERS. See ABUNDANCE; CENSUS; COUNTING; EVOLUTION OF BIRD-LIFE; POPULATION; SPECIES.

NUPTIAL (NUPP-shul). Referring to some aspect of the breeding cycle, e.g., nuptial plumage. See DISPLAY; MOLT.

NUTCRACKER. Standard English name for the 2 members of the genus *Nucifraga* (family Corvidae; order Passeriformes), 1 of which, Clark's Nutcracker, breeds in North America.

In general form and behavior, both nutcrackers resemble the other members of their family, the crows and jays. However, both have unusual plumage patterns, are essentially birds of coniferous alpine habitat, and show a strong feeding preference for pine seeds, which they pry out from between cone scales with their long, pointed bills. In the absence of their favorite food, they become typical corvine omnivores. They are obsessive food storers (see FOOD).

Clark's Nutcracker nests near the tree line in late winter when the temperature regularly drops below zero and heavy snowfalls are routine. Both nutcrackers are given to irregular winter IRRUPTIONS to the south and east of their normal range.

For family characteristics, see CROW; JAY.

NUTHATCH. Standard English name for all but one (Wallcreeper) of the 22–25 members of the family Sittidae and for the family as a whole; 4 species of nuthatches breed in North America.

The nuthatches are small birds (3 to 7 inches) with a highly distinctive shape—compact and tapered at both ends. The bill is narrow and sharp, somewhat elongated, and though straight, it gives the impression of jutting upward slightly from the horizontal. The wings are fairly long and pointed. The tail is short but broad. The legs are short and the toes are rather long with long, sharp, strongly decurved claws. Most nuthatches are blue-gray above with darker crowns and white to reddish buff below.

The manner in which nuthatches feed is even more distinctive than their form: they scale the trunks of trees in short hops, moving with head pointed downward as readily as in the "normal" vertical ascent of woodpeckers or creepers. Some Old World nuthatches prefer rocks, but all our species are arboreal. They probe in bark crevices for insects and other invertebrate life forms, but also like conifer and other seeds and readily take suet and peanut butter at feeders. Though capable of long-distance movements, nuthatches are usually seen flying only in short, woodpecker-like undulations between tree trunks. They produce no elaborate songs, but may twitter softly and/or give abrupt, regular piping or nasal notes.

Nuthatches construct cups of hair and delicate plant fibers in a tree cavity, the entrance to which is often thickly smeared with resin. The 4–12 eggs are white with fairly fine, dense to sparse reddish-brown speckles (see Fig. 7).

Nuthatches are mainly of Holarctic distribution, though they reach the Neotropics in the highlands (Mexico) and northern Malaysia. At least one species of nuthatch occurs everywhere in North America where there are trees, except the northernmost boreal forest, tropical palm areas, and deserts. Only the northernmost populations of Red-breasted Nuthatch are regular migrants, though other populations are subject to seasonal irruptions. "Nuthatch" is a pleasing corruption of "nuthack," which refers to a characteristic practice of securing a nut in a niche and hammering it open with the bill.

NUTTALL, Thomas, 1786–1859 (*Phalaenoptilus nuttallii:* Poor-will; *Nuttallornis borealis:* Olive-sided Flycatcher). Born in Yorkshire, England, where he worked as a printer's apprentice until his emigration in 1808 to Philadelphia, then the "Athens" of American natural history, Nuttall was chiefly a botanist. He made extensive collecting expeditions alone and on foot across much of North America, especially in the South and West. He worked initially for Dr. Benjamin Barton of the University of Pennsylvania; took an ill-paid curatorial chair at Harvard for eleven years—a period in his life which he described as "vegetating with vegetation"; and accompanied the Philadelphia Academy of Natural Science Columbia River Expedition headed by John K. TOWNSEND. In 1842 he inherited an uncle's estate in England and returned there to live for the rest of his life. Nuttall's greatest works were botanical; however, he also produced an account of some of his travels, called *Journal of a Journey into the Arkansas Territory* (1821), and two small volumes which might qualify as the first field guide to North American birds (see FIELD GUIDE). Despite his botanical bent, his name is memorialized in that of the Nuttall Ornithological Club, the oldest of its kind in North America and the progenitor of the American Ornithologists' Union. His nightjar and flycatcher were named for him by Townsend.

NUTTALL ORNITHOLOGICAL CLUB. Perhaps the most venerable of North American bird clubs. Founded in 1873, it gave rise, through the energies of its distinguished ornithological membership, to the AMERICAN ORNITHOLOGISTS' UNION in 1888. The "Nutt. Club" meets monthly during school term at the Agassiz Museum, Harvard University, and features speakers on avian subject matter. Dues finance a series of ornithological papers, published irregularly. All members are elected. No field trips.

O

OBERHOLSER, Harry C., 1870–1963 (*Empidonax oberholseri:* Dusky Flycatcher). Noted American ornithologist and, as a protégé of RIDGWAY, one of the last-surviving direct links to what Coues called the "Bairdian epoch" in American ornithology. It was a period of furious data collection and obsessive classification, and it therefore seems fitting that Dr. Oberholser was known as a walking ornithological data bank and one of the greatest "splitters" of all time. During his long life, much of which was spent in the U.S. Fish and Wildlife Service, he filled in many gaps in our knowledge of the native avifauna. He was an authority on the birds of Texas (see the Bibliography under STATE BOOKS–Texas).

OBSERVATORY. A bird observatory is a place set aside for the purpose of studying birdlife—especially migration. Typically, observatories are located on coastal points where both land- and water-bird migration can be monitored; they run large-scale banding operations; are staffed by one or a few scientists and a host of enthusiastic, mostly young, volunteers; and periodically publish the results of their studies.

The progenitor of the modern bird observatory was Heinrich Gätke's bird-censusing program undertaken on the North Sea island of Heligoland (Germany) in the mid-nineteenth century. In 1909, Gätke's pioneering project was institutionalized as a major banding station, which trapped migrants by means of a wire contraption bearing the name of its place of origin (see HELIGOLAND TRAP). The first British bird observatory was founded by R. M. Lockley in 1933 on the island of Skokolm, and today there are fourteen observatories in the British Isles and a number of others in northwestern Europe. The two major North American bird observatories are the Point Reyes Bird Observatory, founded in 1965, on a headland just north of San Francisco, and Manomet Bird Observatory, founded in 1969, on a promontory south of Plymouth, Massachusetts.

See BANDING; MIGRATION.

OCEANIC BIRDS. See PELAGIC; ALBATROSS; SHEARWATER; PETREL; STORM-PETREL; TROPICBIRD; BOOBY; JAEGER; PHALAROPE; ALCID; CHUMMING; DISTRIBUTION.

ODOR. *Aviculturist:* I plugged my parrot's nares with cotton yesterday.
    Ornithologist: Really? How does he smell?
    Aviculturist: Terrible!

Not surprisingly, the body odors of birds have so far proven of little general (or even specialized) interest, and literature on the subject is scant. Nevertheless, a few broad comments may be ventured if for no other reason than to encourage pioneers into this ornithological frontier.

It should be obvious that bird colonies or nest sites, where excrement and putrefying food matter are allowed to accumulate, may have a very insistent odor, offensive to humans in many cases. However, birds themselves may also have characteristic odors, ranging from stenches to fragrances. Black and Turkey Vultures at least part of the time carry the unpleasant smell of their preferred food, carrion. Tubenoses have a very distinctive oily or musky odor, a mild version of the strong-smelling stomach oil which they are liable to vomit onto molesters. Alcids have a similar (but distinct) musky air. Most land birds are reputed to have little or no natural odor; however, to the writer's nose many shorebirds and passerines have a pleasant, almost floral (though not sweet) smell.

Banders sometimes notice various smells of our polluted environment (e.g., sulphur dioxide) in the plumage of nocturnal migrants, which have presumably arrived in their nets through city skies.

As a final proof that much work remains to be done in this field, I cite Professor Robert Storer (in Thomson, 1964–ORNITHOLOGY), who states that the bill plates of the Crested Auklet "give out an odor like that of tangerine oranges" (!).

OIL, STOMACH. See STOMACH OIL.

OIL GLAND (oiling of feathers). A small, usually bilobed organ located beneath the rump at the base of the tail in most birds. It contains an oily substance which is secreted via a duct through an external opening at the surface of the skin. Though covered by the feathers of the upper tail coverts, the oil gland can usually be easily located by its nipple-like form and tends to be more prominent among aquatic birds. It is sometimes called the "uropygial (rump) gland" or the "preen gland."

Along with the tiny wax-secreting glands of the outer ear and the little-understood glands surrounding the anus, the oil gland is one of only three localized skin glands in birds—in marked contrast to the vast subcutaneous glandular system in humans.

Though a few birds (e.g., most ratites, some pigeons and woodpeckers) lack preen glands and others have negligible, seemingly useless ones, most birds repeatedly touch the uropygium during PREENING. The bill apparently presses oil from the opening and then spreads it over the contour feathers with the normal preening gestures. Oiling usually follows bathing, and some species typically dip their bills in water before touching the oil gland. It therefore is generally supposed that water facilitates spreading the oil quickly and evenly before it "sets."

The "oil" itself is composed of fat, fatty acid, and wax. In some birds—notably the tubenoses—it has a strong musky odor (or worse) and it may be tinted at certain seasons in some gull, tern, and other species and applied to the breast to produce a nuptial "bloom."

The function of preen oil is still much debated. Logic strongly urges the theory that, applied to the feathers as a surface coating, preen oil aids insulation and waterproofing, a notion supported by the prominence of the gland on many water birds. But while some scientific corroboration of this has been obtained, other experiments indicate that the oil is at best inessential for this purpose in some species. The oil apparently lubricates the horny covering of the bill (rhamphotheca), minimizing flaking deterioration, and it doubtless also prevents the feathers from becoming brittle. The smell and color of the oil present in some birds seem to point to some recognition function. One investigator has shown that, when activated by the sun on the feathers, the oil produces vitamin D, which is absorbed through the skin. This may prevent rickets from developing in some birds—though not, it has been demonstrated, in all.

The evidence increasingly tends to support the theory that the oil gland is an organ with more than one function, variable in its use among different kinds of birds.

OIL POLLUTION. See MAN-MADE THREATS TO BIRDLIFE.

OLDSQUAW. Standard English name in North America for a single species of sea duck, *Clangula hyemalis,* with a nearly Holarctic distribution. The standard English name for the same species in Britain is Longtailed Duck. The Oldsquaw does not undergo the normal "eclipse" plumage (see MOLT). It is one of the fastest-flying ducks, with a recorded speed of up to 72 m.p.h., and one of the deepest-diving birds (to 200 feet). The white-headed winter plumage especially of the drakes suggests a full head of white hair, hence "old"; perhaps the characteristic yodeling gabble of this gregarious species suggests (chauvinistically) "squaw." For family characteristics, see DUCK.

OLD WORLD. The Eastern Hemisphere, including Europe, Africa, Asia, and Australia. In a number of cases used to distinguish groups of birds which have the same English names, e.g., Old World flycatchers (family Muscicapidae) vs. New World flycatchers (family Tyrannidae). The birdlife of the Old World is homogeneous in many respects and may be distinguished as a whole from the birdlife of the New World. See DISTRIBUTION; ZOOGEOGRAPHY. Compare NEW WORLD.

OLD WORLD FLYCATCHER. Standard English name for the Muscicapidae, a very large (approximately 375 species) and diverse family of Old World birds; or, according to some taxonomists, a subfamily (Muscicapinae) under an even larger family, including the thrushes, Old World warblers, babblers, and several other groups and containing 1,250 or more species.

Some Old World flycatchers superficially resemble some New World (tyrant) flycatchers in plumage pattern and coloration and behavior. But many species are brilliantly colored and boldly patterned, which is not the case with the majority of tyrannids, and some muscicapids would probably suggest bluebirds or warblers more than "flycatchers" to a North American birdwatcher unfamiliar with the group.

No species of Old World flycatcher occurs regularly in North America; however, 3 species have occurred as accidental stragglers to Alaska (see Appendix II).

OLD WORLD WARBLER. Standard English collective term for all (approximately 395) members of the large family Sylviidae (order Passeriformes). Some taxonomists classify this group as a subfamily (Sylviinae) in a stupendous passerine family, the Muscicapidae, in which they also "lump" the thrushes, Old World flycatchers, babblers, and other smaller groups. The gnatcatchers have been traditionally considered a subgrouping in the Old World warblers, but some taxonomists place them in a family of their own, the Polioptilidae.

As might be expected from such a vast aggregate of species, the Old World warblers exhibit great diversity in size (3½ to 11½ inches); in coloration (mainly rather dull, but some strikingly plumaged); in external form; in habitat preference (desert, tundra, second-growth and all major types of forest); and in feeding and breeding habits.

The distribution of the family is nearly cosmopolitan, though it is very poorly represented in North America and (if the gnatcatchers and gnatwrens are excluded) absent in South America as well as the remotest oceanic islands.

The one Old World warbler known as a "warbler" that reaches North America is the Arctic Warbler, a typical member of the large genus *Phylloscopus*. Like most of its congeners—known collectively as leaf warblers—*P. borealis* is exceedingly drab and anonymous, with only a faint wing bar and thin eye line emerging from the general greenish-brownish murk of its plumage. Except that there are far more species of them, the *Phylloscopus* might be thought of by field ornithologists as the Palearctic's answer to EMPIDONAX flycatchers; where two or more species overlap in distribution, they are usually distinguished by song or by local experts.

The Arctic Warbler nests in arctic and subarctic conifers as well as in dwarf tundra birches and willows. It is mainly (if not exclusively) insectivorous. Its song, like that of many another leaf warbler, is a "buzzy trill," distinctive if you know all the similar songs. It builds a dome nest of mosses, grasses, and dead vines, lined with fine grass and with an entrance hole at one side. The 3–7 (usually 5–6) eggs are white and finely marked with reddish or brownish speckles.

The Arctic Warbler ranges across all of the northern Palearctic south of the barren lands and reaches the eastern extremity of its range in Alaska. The Alaskan population, like its Siberian counterpart, winters in Southeast Asia.

For details of other members of the small but rather heterogeneous assortment of Old World warblers in the New World, see GNATCATCHER; KINGLET.

OLFACTORY (awl-FAK-ter-ee) **SENSE.** See SMELL.

OLIVACEOUS (ah-lih-VAY-shuss) (Cormorant, Flycatcher). The color of a green olive, i.e., a range of shades between brownish green and greenish brown. Like many species of tyrant flycatchers, including all of those in the genus *Myiarchus,* the Olivaceous (or Dusky-capped) Flycatcher is olive-colored over most of the head and back. However, as so often proves to be the case in birds named for their color, the greenish brown discernible on close examination of some plumages of the Olivaceous Cormorant cannot be said to characterize the species well; Neotropic Cormorant, preferred by many authors, seems a better choice for the standard English name of this species.

OMENS, BIRDS AS. See ORNITHOMANCY; IMAGINATION.

OMNIVOROUS (om-NIH-vuh-rus). Eating anything or at least any kind of normally edible substance. In a zoological context the term usually refers to animals that habitually take both animal and plant food. Many birds, e.g., ducks, eat both but nevertheless have relatively restrictive food preferences. True avian omnivores, such as many gulls and corvids, seem to observe no dietary prohibitions, taking nearly all classes of animal and all forms of plant food with almost equal relish. Specific food sources are described under family entries.

  See FOOD. Compare CARNIVOROUS; EURYPHAGOUS; FRUGIVOROUS; GRAMINIVOROUS; GRANIVOROUS; HERBIVOROUS; INSECTIVOROUS; NECTI-VOROUS; PISCIVOROUS; STENOPHAGOUS.

ONTOGENY (on-TODGE-uh-nee). The development of an individual organism from its conception to its maturity; as compared, for example, with a species' development over time, or the history of animal evolution as a whole (phylogeny).

OOLOGY (oh-AHL-uh-jee). The study of bird's eggs, especially their superficial aspects: color, shape, size, number/clutch, etc., and variations thereof among different species and individuals. Once a very active branch of ornithology, recently much less so, as knowledge of the subject in the North Temperate Zone has approached the exhaustive and interest in external physical aspects of birdlife has diminished. See EGG; EGG COLLECTING.

OPERCULUM (oh-PERK-yuh-lum) (pl.: opercula). A lid, flap, plate, or membrane, often movable, the function of which is to close off an opening in the body of an animal. The fleshy knob that partially covers the nostril openings of the Common Pigeon and other columbids is sometimes referred to as an operculum, though it is not movable and is usually discussed in the context of a CERE. Another kind of flap is found at the upper edge of the nostrils of many gallinaceous birds and at least a few hummingbirds (e.g., Rivoli's). Some owl species have a movable operculum at the ear openings which may be protective and/or aid in the detection of sounds in the same way that cupping our hands behind our ears does (see HEARING).

OPORORNIS (OPP-er-OR-niss) (Warbler). A genus of wood warblers (family Parulidae) containing 4 species: Kentucky, Mourning, MacGillivray's, and Connecticut Warblers. The last three are very similar, particularly in juvenal plumage, and the genus name is frequently used among birdwatchers in speaking of these collectively or of an individual bird that cannot be identified to species: Q.: "Did you get a look at it?" A.: "Briefly; it was an *Oporornis* of some kind."

For family characteristics, see WOOD WARBLER.

OPTICAL EQUIPMENT. The current popularity of birdwatching would simply not exist were it not for the high quality of modern binoculars and telescopes. Less than a hundred years ago the amateur pursued his hobby with the aid of a shotgun and would have been mightily amused at anyone claiming to identify a Cape May Warbler on sight—that is, without examining it "in the hand." Good "glasses" have completely reversed our perspective. Today anyone attempting to point a shotgun barrel into the leafy domains of our feathered friends is likely to be throttled by birders with thousands of dollars' worth of Japanese or German optics hanging about their necks.

Compared to even the best "field glasses" of fifty years ago modern binoculars are marvels of scientific achievement. At their best they provide high magnification and bright, clear, broad images without distortion, all delivered in a compact, lightweight form. Though the jewels of the binocular market command prodigious prices (see *Buying*, below), glasses which can fairly claim to embody the above qualities are affordable by almost everyone living in those countries where birdwatching is most popular (see BIRDWATCHING). Indeed, so many brands and models of binoculars are now on the market that the neophyte is likely to feel intimidated when he arrives at the optics counter. To him and to those who wish to know a little more about the precision instruments they carry so casually into the field, the following may be helpful.

TERMINOLOGY. A few basic optical terms, some of them bandied widely in birdwatching circles, are useful in any discussion of binoculars.

Power is the amount of magnification your binoculars provide. This is expressed in the first part of a numerical formula engraved somewhere on the body of your glasses, e.g., 7x35 or 10x40. 10x means the binoculars magnify the image your eye sees ten times. Through them, a bird 500 feet away will appear to be only 50 feet away. Birders often ask, "What power are your glasses?" Answer: "ten power" or "ten x" or simply "tens."

Ocular Lens. The lens you put your eye to, i.e., the "small end" of your binoculars or telescope is the ocular lens.

Objective Lens. The opposite lens, the "big end," is the objective lens. The second number in the formula described above is the diameter in millimeters of the objective lens. 10x40 binoculars have an objective lens measuring 40 mm. across.

Brightness is the amount of light admitted by your binoculars. This is governed both by power and by the diameter of the objective lens. The lower the power and the wider the objective lens, the greater the amount of light admitted. The pupil of the human eye closes to a diameter of about 2–3 mm. in bright sunlight and opens to 6–7 mm. in low light. Binoculars too have a pupil, which can be seen by holding your glasses about a foot away from your eyes and looking through the ocular lenses. The bright spot you see is called the "exit pupil" and is measured by dividing the objective lens diameter by the power. For 10x40's the diameter of the exit pupil is 4. Binoculars cannot, of course, supply any more light than your pupil can take in, but they may (often do) take in *less* light than your pupil can. At dusk or on a very dark day or when focused on a bird in deep shadow, your 10x40's will let in only "4 mm. worth" of light, when your own pupils would be capable of admitting 6–7 mm. worth. 7x50's, on the other hand, would admit as much light as your eyes, and therefore enable you to see what you were looking at better.

Field (of View) is, in effect, how much you can see when you look through your glasses. This is measured in the breadth of view at a standard distance, e.g., 122 meters at 1,000 meters or the degree of any circle on the earth's plane taken in by your binoculars from the center, e.g., your glasses might take in 8° of the horizon's total of 360°.

Field decreases as magnification increases. The greater the field, the easier it is to pick up small, moving objects such as feeding warblers or distant, fast-moving shorebirds.

Coated Optics. Modern prism binoculars contain at least ten lens and prism surfaces through which light is transmitted to your eye. En route, a significant amount of light is reflected from these surfaces within the binoculars and fails to reach your eye. This reflection is reduced by coating the surfaces (*all* of them in the best glasses) with a transparent chemical (usually magnesium fluoride) to cut glare. This accounts for the bluish or yellowish tint your lenses show at some angles.

Alignment. In order for the images you see through each side of your binoculars to combine precisely into a single stereoscopic image, the optical axes must be parallel, i.e., vertical and horizontal lines should appear at exactly the same angle on both sides. Severe misalignment, caused, for example, by dropping your glasses, would be easy to recognize. But very often slight misalignments occur with long use and may not be noticed unless they are looked for (see below). This can cause an undefinable discomfort due to the slight compensation your eyes must constantly make.

Field Glasses. Strictly speaking, field glasses are non-prismatic binoculars. Their magnification is achieved solely by the opposition of the ocular and objective lenses and is therefore relatively low—often about 5x in portable-sized glasses. They also have a very narrow field by nature. To increase magnification and field, the lenses and the body of such binoculars must be enlarged and lengthened to a size that is too unwieldy for birdwatching. Beginning birdwatchers sometimes try to "make do" with some old field glasses they find in the attic or with "opera glasses," which are constructed the same way. Like other occupations, birdwatching requires adequate tools.

THE RIGHT BINOCULARS FOR YOU. Leaving quality aside for the moment, it is important to choose binoculars that meet your personal needs and that you feel comfortable with. These factors vary with different birding styles and physical capabilities. Here are some points to consider in choosing binoculars that you will be happy with.

• Birders seldom use glasses with a magnification less than 7x or greater than 10x. Any less and the images of distant birds are not enlarged sufficiently; any greater and the field tends to become unduly restricted and the effect of vibration—which increases with power—may outweigh the benefit of the higher magnification. Experience and physical condition should be considered in choosing the proper power for you. Young, experienced field ornithologists often opt for the extra power of 10's, knowing they will have no trouble holding them steady or in adapting their eyes to the limitations of light and field which tend to accompany greater power. Novice and older birders tend to prefer 7's and 8's.

• Is field identification or aesthetic enjoyment your main objective in watching birds? If you will be using your binoculars primarily to pick up field marks, high power may add to your capability. If you like to study birds for long periods at close range, magnification is not as crucial, but you want to be sure that your glasses transmit maximum light (see *Brightness*, above) and that you can focus on near objects. Close-focusing capacity varies greatly among different makes of binoculars and tends to be limited as the power increases, though factory adjustments to allow closer focusing can often be made on the more expensive products.

• There is a little knack to picking up small and/or moving birds in binoculars (see *Using*, below), but in any case it is easier to do using glasses with a wide field. Furthermore, many people feel uncomfortably restricted when looking through glasses with the narrowest of fields. On the other hand, the "wide angle" binoculars now available offer no particular advantage to birdwatchers and may in fact show the novice a bewildering panorama of leafage that makes it difficult to zero in on individual birds.

• Unless you have a well-considered reason for buying binoculars which have individual focus adjustments on each eyepiece, select glasses with a central focusing device.

• If you wear eyeglasses, be sure the binoculars you buy have appropriate eyepieces or ones that can be modified to meet your needs. Wearers of glasses need shallow rims on the ocular lens of their binoculars to be as close to their glasses as possible in order to have an adequate field of view.

• One of the major advantages of modern binoculars is their lightness, but there is still considerable variation in the weights of different styles and makes. How heavy your binoculars are affects how long and steadily you can hold them up to your eyes, and, though it may seem minimal at any given moment, there is a cumulative strain felt by many people from wearing binoculars hung around their necks all day.

USING YOUR BINOCULARS. Looking through binoculars is a pretty straightforward business, but even veteran birders sometimes unwittingly reduce their pleasure and field competence by ignoring a few simple procedures and techniques.

• Because the spacing between our eyes varies from person to person, binoculars are designed to be bent along their long axis to fit your particular "interpupillary distance." Bend your binoculars up or down as you look through them until the separate images in each ocular become one, and the margin of the image is circular, as if you were looking through a telescope. A calibrated scale, located between the eyepieces on most glasses, gives you a setting for your correct interpupillary distance, which will work for any pair of binoculars.

• Even center-focus binoculars have a separate adjustment for the right eye in order to accommodate any difference between your two eyes. To set your binoculars for focusing, close your right eye and look through the left eyepiece only. Aim at a target in the middle distance, such as a printed sign, and turn the central focus wheel (or other device) until the image is perfectly sharp. Then close the *left* eye and adjust the individual focus for your right eye. The focusing mechanism for the right eye is usually on the right eyepiece, but in some glasses it is located at the end of the bridge shaft opposite the central focus wheel. In either case the wheel is calibrated so that you can reset the right ocular without refocusing it every time. Once you have set your glasses for the difference between your eyes, the adjustment is maintained when you focus with the central focus wheel alone. With separate-focus binoculars, it is necessary to change the setting of both eyepieces every time you refocus. For birdwatchers, who refocus constantly, this system is not a practical one.

• It takes a little practice to find birds quickly in your binoculars. The trick is to fix the bird with your eyes and then bring your binoculars up— the same principle as keeping your eye on a baseball when you are trying to hit it. This sequence becomes second nature in no time.

• It is essential that you be able to hold your binoculars steady, and this is made more difficult, of course, if your binoculars are unduly heavy or of high power or if you are moving (e.g., standing on the deck of a ship) or you personally are shaking for whatever reason. The first rule of steadiness is: always hold your binoculars with both hands; one hand simply doesn't provide enough support, and besides, it looks silly—the one-handed grip is the mark of a rank amateur. The eyepieces should be braced gently but firmly against your eye sockets (or glasses). If you can't hold steady with your elbows raised, bring them down and brace them against your sides. Leaning on a fixed surface such as your car roof is also helpful. Many European birdwatchers carry their binocular cases into the field with them and use them for stabilizing their glasses while scanning. The binoculars are placed on top of the case, which is held at the bottom. This allows the elbows to brace more comfortably at your sides and the case can be held and moved more steadily (for some reason) than the binoculars themselves.

• A surprising number of birdwatchers let their lenses become encrusted with a layer of grime and then complain that they can't see anything. At the opposite extreme, some birders carry expensive airbrushes or Windex into the field with them and spend more time polishing than watching birds. Keeping your glasses clean need not be a complex chore—a little warm breath and a clean hanky or Kleenex will do the job. The important thing to remember is that even the finest dust particles can scratch glass, so try to blow off surface dust before wiping. Try to shield your binoculars from excessive dirt and, after birding in sandy or dusty places, it is a good idea to give your glasses a thorough cleaning to prevent grit from clogging the main hinge and focusing wheels and dust from infiltrating the lens housings. While you're at it, check the leather strap periodically to be sure that it is not wearing thin at its points of attachment; more than one birder has pawed the air vainly as he watched his glasses hit the water or pavement after falling from around his neck.

• Most people soon forget that binoculars are precision optical instruments and treat them rather casually. Good (i.e., expensive) binoculars are built to withstand a lot of abuse, but if they are used regularly in the field they are bound to show the strain sooner or later. A common symptom of heavy use is misalignment, which you may sense or can check for (see below). Unfortunately there is little you can do about this or more serious problems except take them to an expert. Even trying to oil your own glasses is courting disaster if your total optical expertise consists of "common sense." Ask birding friends about reliable and (relatively) inexpensive cleaning/repairing services in your area. Often the best solution with high-quality binoculars is to return them to the manufacturer for service. If you drop your binoculars in water, have them examined professionally *at once*. Rust and corrosion can cause irreparable harm.

BUYING BINOCULARS. There is no dearth of variety at the binocular counter these days. The problem is sorting out different styles, qualities, and prices and going home with glasses that suit your needs. Here are some general guidelines and specific caveats.

Price may be the first criterion to check when buying binoculars. 10x40 Leitz Trinovids currently retail for over a thousand dollars. They are ideal for birdwatching and their quality is unexceptionable. Conversely, you can buy a pair of binoculars for thirty dollars which will almost certainly fail you after slight use. It is best to face the fact that there is really no such thing as "good, cheap" binoculars; they represent the kind of merchandise it is best to invest heavily in and keep for a long time. If your intent is the least bit serious, you should probably spend no less than $150 at the current (1982) inflation rate. If you have a serious young naturalist in the house, do everyone a favor and buy him or her good glasses unless he or she is utterly careless with possessions; the cost and headaches of repairing and discarding cheap binoculars should be visited on no one.

Brand names are also useful in selecting binoculars. Leitz, Bushnell, Swift, and Zeiss are purveyors of optical equipment widely favored by North American naturalists. This does not mean that there are not many other companies making fine binoculars—only that their reputation is less well established.

Once you have found a pair of binoculars that seem to suit you, insist on taking them outside and using them in the sunlight. Check off the following criteria in your head:

• Do they come with a warranty?

• Can they be serviced locally? Most glasses are foreign-made, and if the manufacturer is a small one, the nearest parts and repair center may be in Tokyo.

• Do the glasses feel comfortable in your hands?

• Are they too heavy? Hold them to your eyes for several minutes.

• Do they seem to be sturdily constructed? Look for dents and other imperfections in the metal body.

• Shake them gently to see if anything is loose inside.

• Look through the objective lenses (big end) for dirt inside and scratches or other imperfections on the lens and prism surfaces you can see.

• Make sure the ocular and objective lenses are coated (see above) and ask if the other optical surfaces are. In the best glasses *all* are, and this badge of superiority is usually flaunted in the accompanying literature.

• Check how close you can focus and if distant forms are clear when you focus on infinity.

There are also more sophisticated tests you can make, which are especially useful for evaluating binoculars of obscure make and unknown quality. Most of them require a steady surface on which to place the binoculars while you look through them and a straight, dark object, e.g., a telephone pole, on which to focus.

• Alignment: With the glasses on a steady surface focus on a vertical form in the middle distance. Now look through each lens separately and compare them by these criteria: When the vertical object is placed in the center of both lenses, it should stand at the same angle in both, i.e., be parallel; when the vertical is placed off to the side of the field or at the bottom, it should appear in the same place in both oculars.

• Distortion: Start with the vertical object at the center of the field and move the steady surface slowly until the vertical is at the edge of the field. Near the edge, the vertical may appear slightly curved. In general, the greater the curve and the farther from the edge it is apparent, the poorer the optical quality of the binoculars.

• Chromatism: Focus on the dark vertical, and look for edges of any spectral color. There should be no chromatic edge when the vertical is at the center of the field in good glasses and perhaps a slight one at the edge of the field; in poor glasses the color will be visible at the center and broaden markedly toward the edge of the field.

• Coma: With the binoculars resting steadily, focus on a starry sky, then compare the stars in the center of the field with those at the edge. The stars at the edge may appear less sharp than those in the center and perhaps misshapen, i.e., not perfectly round. The greater the "fuzziness" of the edge stars, the poorer the optical quality.

If you can make some or all of these tests on several pairs of binoculars in the store, you will probably have a fairly good idea of which are the best or at least which you *like* best, and you will also have a good basis for comparison with brands carried elsewhere. Once you know the brand and model you want, you can compare prices, which often differ significantly at different retail outlets. Good values can sometimes be had by buying used binoculars of known quality, but you should be aware that some elements, such as lens coating, deteriorate with age and cannot be economically restored.

TELESCOPES. These instruments are crucial to effective and enjoyable water-birding, as when thousands of tiny distant forms must be scanned in search of the unusual species or for separating species of very similar shorebirds on a vast mud flat. They also allow you to become practically intimate with less distant birds.

Many of the basic rules cited above for choosing and using binoculars apply equally to telescopes. What you want is a modern, lightweight prism telescope, not an ancient, bronze spyglass that your seafaring great-uncle left you in his will. A few specific recommendations:

• Telescopes are adapted for interchanging lenses. Some young hotshots prefer a 30x lens, but unequivocally the best choice for all-purpose use is 20x. Power is too slight under 20, and over 30 the narrower field and the distortion of distant images are a bit of a trial (especially if *you're* over thirty).

• Zoom telescopes were big for a while, but their optics were generally poor and the zoom more a gimmick than a genuine advantage. The fad has largely passed. Beware of used zoom scopes at any price.

• A good, new telescope can be purchased (1982 prices) for under $200.

• A good tripod is nearly as important as the scope attached to it. It should combine lightness with stability. You want it to be easy to lug over your favorite dike or beach but not so light that it won't hold the scope in place in a stiff breeze (scopes are often at their most useful in *very* stiff coastal breezes). The legs and neck should be very easy to extend and retract and should not slip or stick unduly. The Fliplock tripod has a wide following among birders.

Parts of this entry were adapted from a Massachusetts Audubon Society public service leaflet entitled "Binoculars for Birders." For more detailed information on many of the topics summarized, see the references noted in the Bibliography, most of which were also used by the author.

ORBITAL (OR-bih-tull) (region, ring). Referring to the region around the eye; an "orbital ring" is identical to an eye ring.

ORD, George, 1781–1866. A Philadelphia aristocrat and a bastion of that city's thriving community of early American naturalists, Ord is best remembered as Alexander WILSON's editor, biographer, and champion in the famous conflict with Audubon about who painted what where and when. He was also the author of a few North American bird species, e.g., Bonaparte's Gull. By most accounts, George Ord was a cold and difficult personality and a pretentious and high-handed editor with little respect for accuracy or the integrity of his author.

ORDER. The major taxonomic category between class and family: classes may be divided into subclasses and orders; orders into suborders and families (see TAXONOMY and Appendix I). An order may also be defined as a grouping of phylogenetically related families. There are two widely recognized ordinal breakdowns of the class Aves (birds): that of Stresemann (1959–TAXONOMY), which proposes 51 orders of modern birds worldwide, and that of Wetmore (1960–TAXONOMY), which proposes only 27. As is customary in North American ornithology, the latter is followed in the present work. In the Wetmore system, all ordinal names end in *-iformes.*

All 21 orders of birds that occur in North America are listed below in alphabetical order. For a "definition" of these—which and how many families and species they contain and their phylogenetic position—note the page number given after each order, which refers to Appendix I.

ORIENTATION. See NAVIGATION.

ORIGINS OF NORTH AMERICAN BIRDLIFE. See DISTRIBUTION, *Origins of Birdlife.*

ORIOLE (OR-ee-ole or OR-ee-yull). Standard English name for 24 members of the New World family Icteridae (order Passeriformes), all in the genus *Icterus*; and also for a similar number of species in the Old World family Oriolidae (order Passeriformes), all in the genus *Oriolus*. (See below for more on the nomenclatural ambiguity.) Of the *Icterus* orioles, 6 species are native to North America, a seventh (Spot-breasted) has been introduced, and 2 more species have been recorded as accidental stragglers (see Appendix II).

The New World orioles range in size from the 6-inch Orchard Oriole to the nearly 10-inch Altamira (Lichtenstein's). They are generally slender birds with a sharply pointed bill of medium length, relatively long tail, and strong, perching legs. The adult male plumage of most species is a bold pastiche of brilliant orange or yellow, black, and white.

Most of our orioles feed primarily on insects, though they are also fond of fruit and adapted for sipping nectar from the corollas of flowers. Despite their bright colors, they are often inconspicuous, spending most of their time hidden beneath the leafy canopies of trees, especially during the breeding season. Their songs consist of loud, clear, rich whistles and warbles in phrases of varying length.

The American orioles are noted for their skillfully woven pendulous nests suspended from the forked end of a branch. Such nests are typical of Northern, Altamira, and Spot-breasted Orioles, but the nests of our other species are more cup-like than bag-like and may be "sewn" to the underside of yucca, palmetto, or other large leaves or surfaces (Hooded and Scott's). The weave is of long grasses, plant fibers, aerial roots, and sometimes string or yarn, and the lining typically consists of plant down, moss, fine plant fibers and grasses, hair, and/or feathers.

The 2–7 (usually 3–5) eggs are very pale blue (to almost white) with rather distinct purplish, reddish, or grayish spots or long scrawls.

The *Icterus* orioles are restricted to the New World and achieve greatest diversity in Middle America. In North America, orioles are essentially birds of deciduous forest and arid scrublands (acacia or pinyon-juniper). Only the Northern Oriole—with its distinct eastern (Baltimore) and western (Bullock's) races—breeds from coast to coast. Most species winter in Latin America.

"Oriole" comes from a Latin root meaning "golden" and the Latin word *oriolus*, which referred specifically to the European oriolid oriole now called Golden Oriole (*Oriolus oriolus*). This redundancy of gold is entirely justified in the case of many of the Old World orioles, but no less so among the brilliant New World birds, which were, of course, named for their superficial similarity in color.

For other icterids, see BLACKBIRD; COWBIRD; GRACKLE; BOBOLINK; MEADOWLARK.

ORNITHICHNITE (OR-nih-THIK-nite). The fossilized footprint of a bird.

ORNITHOLITE (or-NITH-uh-lyte). A bird fossil. See EVOLUTION OF BIRDLIFE.

ORNITHOLOGY (ornithologist). The scientific study of birdlife. The modern academic ornithologist is likely to be a specialist in a particular branch of the field, such as classification (see TAXONOMY and NOMENCLATURE), physiology (see DIGESTIVE, REPRODUCTIVE, and other systems; EMBRYO), DISTRIBUTION (including ecology), or behavior (ETHOLOGY). Ornithologists employed outside the academic sphere, e.g., in wildlife management agencies of the government, though once mainly concerned with control of "nuisance birds" (see PESTS) and management of game species, are increasingly involved in the conservation and management of non-game species. It should also be noted that there is now a class of birdwatchers whose knowledge is so comprehensive as to compare favorably with the ornithologists of fifty years ago, though they may lack advanced degrees and make their living in other professions. Such individuals may with justification be called "field ornithologists" (see also BIRDWATCHING).

Like all scientific disciplines, the study of birdlife has altered its focus and become more complex as succeeding generations of ornithologists have added to the accumulation of knowledge about the class. Scholars of ancient Greece puzzled over the mysteries of flight and migration and made early attempts at scientific description and classification. From the

eighteenth century to the early twentieth, and particularly after the publication of Linnaeus' seminal nomenclatural work, *Systema Naturae* (10th
ed., 1758; see NOMENCLATURE; LINNÉ), most ornithological effort was
concentrated in defining and ordering the world avifauna, a process which
continues today. It has been said that birds are the best-known group of
animals taxonomically, and therefore are frequently cited as examples in
phylogenetic and evolutionary works. The extreme evolutionary divergence displayed by the *Geospiza* finches of the Galápagos Islands off the
coast of Ecuador, for example, figures prominently in Darwin's classic
Origin of Species. Other broad fields of scientific inquiry in which birds
have played significant roles include animal movements (MIGRATION),
communication (SONG), and the relatively new science of animal behavior
(ETHOLOGY).

If we compare an issue of an ornithological journal such as *The Auk*
from 1890 with one from 1981, we find that, while much of the basic subject matter is the same, the emphasis on various aspects of birdlife has
shifted drastically and our methods of studying them have taken enormous
leaps in sophistication, allowing a much more detailed scrutiny. Whereas
ornithologists of the nineteenth century still had their hands full describing species, subspecies, nests, eggs, distributions, and the like, the modern
ornithologist has enough data and technique at his disposal to begin asking
some of the more difficult questions of "how?" and "why?" True, new
species of birds are still being discovered and described, but they tend to
be found in the remotest regions and most difficult habitats of the planet,
such as the mountaintop cloud forests of Peru. Taxonomic theory is beginning to depend heavily on factors such as chemical analysis of egg-white
protein by means of complex techniques such as electrophoresis, rather
than on more superficial characteristics (e.g., bill shape or even skull structure) which are subject to adaptive modification.

Rather than describing simply where a bird builds its nest, and of
what materials, modern bird students attempt to define a species' total
role—how it affects other organisms and how they affect it—within its environment. Now that science has learned what route Blackpoll Warblers
take to their wintering grounds (see Fig. 13) it has proceeded to discover at
least in part how they store energy for such stupendous journeys and what
physiological modifications have evolved to aid the effort.

Given the size of the world avifauna, the number and complexity of
the questions still unanswered, and the rate at which man is altering the
natural laboratory, it is clear ornithologists will not lack new challenges for
the foreseeable future.

The history of science is itself now a branch of knowledge, and the
history of ornithology a well-grown twig. For summaries of the progress of
both world and North American bird study, see Stresemann (1975) and
Coues (1903).

ORNITHOMANCY (OR-nih-tho-MAN-see). Magical prediction of the future by observing the behavior of birds. See IMAGINATION.

ORNITHOPHILOUS (OR-nih-THAH-fih-luss). A botanical term for plants which are distributed, germinated, or fertilized by birds. See POLLINATION; SEED DISPERSAL.

ORNITHOSIS (OR-nih-THO-siss). Once considered a viral disease of birds occasionally transmitted to man, especially those who keep birds for a living or as a hobby. Now redefined as bacterial in origin and renamed CHLAMYDIOSIS. See DISEASE.

OSCINES (OSS-eens; also OSS-synes, OSS-ins; when referring to the Latin subordinal name, OSS-ih-neez is preferred). The so-called songbirds; the largest suborder of the largest order of birds, namely the Passeriformes, or "perching birds." The only non-oscine (see SUBOSCINE) perching birds in North America are the flycatchers (Tyrannidae) and one (perhaps) species of cotinga (Cotingidae). The latter, the Rose-throated Becard (*Platypsaris aglaiae*), is thought by some authorities to be a tyrannid.

OSPREY (OSS-pray). Standard English name for a single, nearly cosmopolitan bird of prey (*Pandion haliaetus*) which is sometimes relegated to a subfamily (Pandioninae) of the Accipitridae, but often given a family of its own, Pandionidae. Taxonomists have found that the Osprey has a number of anatomical features that indicate a sizable evolutionary gap between it and the hawks and eagles—which it otherwise superficially resembles.

In addition to the powerful, broad wings and heavy, hooked bill, traits it shares with other diurnal raptors, the Osprey is equipped with unusually long talons, a reversible fourth (outer) toe, and spines on the soles of its feet, all adaptations for grasping slippery, struggling fish. Ospreys feed almost exclusively on fish and are therefore typically found (except during migration) near water—especially large lakes, rivers, and bays.

Because of their food preference, Ospreys suffered a severe decline during the 1960's from indiscriminate use of pesticides (especially DDT; see MAN-MADE THREATS TO BIRDLIFE), which washed from agricultural lands and sprayed trees into rivers and lakes and concentrated in the tissues of fish. With the banning of DDT in North America (1972), this exquisite raptor is making a good recovery.

The nesting habits of the Osprey are similar to those of its near relatives, the hawks and eagles. The nest is a large, bulky stick platform lined with finer plant material and set in the top of a tree (or utility pole), on a rock ledge, or on the ground where trees or poles are lacking; the site is never far from water. The 2–4 (usually 3) eggs are notably round (short sub-elliptical) and yellowish white, fairly to very heavily spotted and splotched with tan, reddish and/or dark brown.

The most frequently heard Osprey call is a series of clear (shrill at close range) piping notes.

The Osprey is migratory throughout most of its range and nearly cosmopolitan in total distribution; it occurs throughout North America, except for the barrens of the High Arctic.

"Osprey" is a unique ornithological word which disappointingly derives from a series of not very interesting errors and corruptions. Its root is *ossifraga*, or "bone breaker," a term most aptly applied to an Old World marrow-eating vulture, the Lammergeier, which resembles the Osprey not at all.

OSSIFICATION (of birds' skulls). The formation of bone. Like the skull of a human infant, that of a young bird is not fully hardened (ossified) at birth/hatching and becomes thicker with age. Bird banders unable to "age" a bird by plumage or other characters, can detect birds of the year by examining the skull. By wetting and parting the feathers on the top of the head behind the eyes, it is possible to see the skull through the transparent skin. If the top of the skull appears pink and transparent, only one layer of bone has formed, indicating that the bird is immature. If, on the other hand, it is whitish and spotted ("granulate"), the individual is an adult or an immature that is at least 4–6 months old. The rate of skull ossification varies among different groups of birds, and this aging technique is used for the most part on passerine species.

The same test can be made—much more easily, in fact—while making a BIRD SKIN, when the cleaned skull can be held up to a light for a close inspection.

For another aging technique, see BURSA OF FABRICIUS.

OVENBIRD. Standard English name for a single species of wood warbler (Parulidae), *Seiurus aurocapillus.* Its nest is a domed construction of dead leaves and other plant materials. It has a side entrance and overall may be compared to the shape of a Dutch oven. The name "ovenbird" also applies to a large, exclusively Neotropical family of birds, the Furnariidae; many members of this family also build oven-like nests and are somberly colored, forest-haunting species like the North American Ovenbird, but they are not closely related. See WARBLER.

OVIPAROUS (oh-VIP-er-us). Characterizing animals which hatch from eggs outside the body of the female. All birds are oviparous, as are most reptiles, amphibians, fishes, and insects. Mammals, by contrast, are almost exclusively *viviparous*, i.e., bear live young, with the exception of six species in the order Monotremata, e.g., the duck-billed platypus, all endemic to Australia, Tasmania, and New Guinea.

OVIPOSITION (OH-vih-puh-ZISH-un). The act of laying an egg. See EGG.

OVULATION (OH-vyoo-LAY-shun or AHV-yoo-LAY-shun). Production of eggs (ova) in the ovary and/or discharge therefrom into the oviduct. See REPRODUCTIVE SYSTEM.

OWL. Standard English name for all of the approximately 125 members of the family Strigidae (order Strigiformes), 18 of which breed in North America.

Owls are small (5¼ inches) to moderately large (over 2 feet) birds of prey. They mostly appear to be of stocky build, an impression aided by their large heads and extraordinarily soft plumage. Their eyes are large, often with yellow irises, and are placed in the front of their heads rather than on the sides as in most birds. The effect of a human expression is enhanced by facial plumage forming a more or less round visage-like disk. Their bills are short with a strongly decurved upper mandible that normally completely covers the lower one and bears a basal cere largely concealed by feathers. Owls are typically long- and broad-winged and short-tailed (some exceptions); their legs and toes are densely feathered and end in long, sharp claws. The outer, i.e., fourth, toe is reversible, so that they can perch in either a zygodactyl or anisodactyl manner (see LEG/FOOT). Many species have "horns" or "ears," tufts of feathers at the front corners of the head that have no auditory function. In general, owls are somberly colored but heavily patterned with streaks, bars, and spots. "Red" (rufous) and gray (and sometimes intermediate) color phases occur in a number of species.

Most owls hunt exclusively at night or during the twilight hours at dawn and dusk and are peculiarly adapted in several ways to suit this mode of living. Their eyes, in addition to being large, have high concentrations of light-gathering cells (rods) in the retina (see VISION). The ear openings of many species of owls are larger than is usual among birds and are located asymmetrically on the sides of the head, both adaptations to locating prey by sound in the dark (see HEARING). The forward webs (leading edge) of the flight feathers are serrated (i.e., the barbs are separated at the tips), which reduces noise from air passing over the feathers in flight, allowing a stealthy approach to prey.

Owls feed on a wide assortment of animal prey from insects and other invertebrates to birds, reptiles, amphibians, and even fish. Many species depend largely on small mammals, but the largest, most powerful species (e.g., Great Horned Owl) have no hesitation about attacking a skunk or a large domestic cat. They swallow smaller prey and large chunks of larger prey whole and later regurgitate undigestible bones, fur, and feathers in a compact PELLET. A few species of owls gather in winter roosts or at a source of abundant food, but they are mostly solitary.

Owls nest in tree (or cactus) cavities (or nest boxes), abandoned hawk, eagle, or corvid nests, and (less usually) in buildings, on the ground, or in burrows. They lay 2–13 eggs (average 3–6 in most species) that are white or off white, glossy, and in many species almost round (short sub-elliptical; see Fig. 7).

The "songs" of the large owls are usually sonorous hoots or seemingly well-articulated phrases, e.g., the "Who cooks for you-all" of the Barred Owl. Smaller species tend to wail or toot.

Their human expression, nocturnal habits, and variety of "unearthly" calls have made owls the most prominent of birds in myth, folklore, and superstition (see IMAGINATION). They are often thought to portend death.

Owls occur in all major biomes (except marine), though the majority are forest birds. They are present in some diversity on all the major land-masses of the world (except Antarctica) and tolerate the coldest and warm-est, driest and wettest climates. This broad adaptability is evident in the overlapping distributions of North American owls, some of which are very widespread and others very local. Some species are migratory, while others are essentially sedentary, and several arctic species are given to moving south in large numbers during "flight years" when food is scarce within their normal range (see IRRUPTION).

"Owl" is onomatopoeic and descends from the same Latin root as "ululate."

OYSTERCATCHER. Standard English name for all 6–8 members of the family Haematopodidae (order Charadriiformes), 2 of which breed in North America.

Oystercatchers are medium-sized (15 to 20 inches), blackish or blackish-and-white shorebirds with long, laterally compressed, red bills, red fleshy eye rings, and bright golden irises. Their legs are pink and mod-erately long and their feet are narrowly webbed at the bases of the three front toes; the hind toe (hallux) is lacking.

The unusual oystercatcher bill is specially adapted for penetrating the shells of bivalves and snipping their adductor muscle(s) (see BILL; FOOD; and Fig. 2), but these shorebirds also eat crustaceans, limpets, sea urchins, and sea worms.

Oystercatchers make a shallow scrape on beaches, dunes, rocks, or in salt marshes, lining it sparsely if at all with bits of shell, pebbles, weeds, and other debris. In this they lay 2–4 (usually 3) yellowish-buff eggs which may be finely and densely speckled or rather heavily but less densely spotted with dark brown and lighter shades.

The commonest oystercatcher calls are sharp *kleep*'s or *wheep*'s, but lower, more melodious trills are also produced on occasion. The calls of our two species (American and American Black) are rather similar.

Oystercatchers are found along coastlines throughout most of the world (except high arctic regions), and some species also feed routinely in pastures well inland. The American Oystercatcher prefers sandy shores and mud flats, while the American Black Oystercatcher of the Pacific coast favors wave-washed rocks.

P

PAIR. In reference to birds, the word usually means two mated individuals, which normally, of course, are adults of the same species and different sexes.

PAIR FORMATION. An early stage in the breeding cycle, during which male and female birds of the same species establish an intimate bond which facilitates reproduction. The duration and nature of the bond vary greatly among different groups of birds. Species such as the prairie chickens and other grouse in which the males hold no territory and display in communal LEKS form pairs with members of the opposite sex (typically several of them) only for as long as it takes to copulate. Other species, e.g., swans, pair for life and remain together throughout the year, though "widows" and "widowers" may "remarry." Most species, and especially territorial songbirds, form limited, seasonal pair bonds which typically last until the young are independent. The majority of birds are monogamous, but there is a nice variety of exceptions; see, for example, POLYGAMY; POLYANDRY; POLYGYNY.

Pair formation begins in some species before wintering flocks break up in the spring. For many, however, the bonding begins on the breeding ground after a female has been attracted to a male's territory by his singing. At first the male behaves aggressively toward his prospective mate, as he would toward other intruders of his species into his domain (see TERRITORY). The female responds initially by fleeing, but she returns shortly and then hangs around, making non-threatening responses to the aggressive displays of the male. These attacks gradually give way to courtship displays, and soon it is the male that is hanging around (see COURTSHIP). The courtship rituals are highly characteristic for each species and therefore are safeguards against hybridization in addition to cementing the pair bond. Once the bond is established the paired birds usually maintain a close physical proximity and eschew the company of other members of the species.

Copulation may occur soon after pair formation or there may be a chaste "engagement" lasting two weeks or more. See also COURTSHIP; DISPLAY; TERRITORY; and Lack, *Condor* (1940), 42:269–86.

PALAEOSPECIES (PAY-lee-oh-SPEE-sheez). A species known only from fossil remains. Since the present definition of a species depends on the interrelationships of living animals, a palaeospecies has no biological basis. *Archaeopteryx lithographica* is perhaps the best-known avian palaeospecies. See EVOLUTION OF BIRDLIFE.

PALATABILITY. See EDIBILITY.

PALEARCTIC REGION (PAIL-ee-ARC-tik or PAL-ee-ARC-tik). The largest of the six major zoogeographic regions of the world. It includes all of Europe, Asia north of the Himalayas, and Africa north of the Sahara. Iceland, Greenland, and western Alaska are transitional between the Palearctic and Nearctic regions. "Palearctic birds" include those that breed exclusively within the Palearctic region but winter in tropical Africa (e.g., most Old World warblers) as well as those relatively few species that range wholly in Europe, North Africa, or northern Asia (e.g., Crested Tit). Some of the western Alaskan species that are primarily Palearctic in distribution are: Steller's Eider, Bar-tailed Godwit, White and Yellow Wagtails, Arctic Warbler, Bluethroat, and Gray-headed Chickadee (Siberian Tit). Compare NEARCTIC; HOLARCTIC; see also ZOOGEOGRAPHY; DISTRIBUTION; and Fig. 24.

PALLIUM (PAL-ee-yum). A little-used technical term equivalent to MANTLE.

PALMATE. Describes a bird's foot which is webbed between the three forward toes, characteristic of the majority of swimming birds. Compare TOTIPALMATE.

PANTING. Rapid breathing is a frequent method of dissipating excess body heat among birds. See TEMPERATURE, BODY, *Cooling Off.*

PARAKEET. Standard English name for 40–80 (depending on nomenclature) members of the family Psittacidae (order Psittaciformes), one of which, the Carolina Parakeet, was endemic to North America until its extirpation, completed in the early 1920's. "Parakeet" is a diminutive of "parrot" and this is vaguely reflected in size and form among psittacid species, but the name has no taxonomic integrity. For family characteristics, see PARROT.

PARALECTOTYPE. When a particular specimen of a bird (or other animal) has been designated from a type series as a LECTOTYPE (as opposed to

HOLOTYPE), the other specimens in the series are the paralectotypes. See NOMENCLATURE, *Types*.

PARASEMATIC (PAAR-uh-seh-MAT-ik). Refers to appearance or behavior which distracts the attention of a potential predator from a more vulnerable body part or individual (e.g., young bird) to a less vulnerable. Many insects have evolved cryptic forms or patterns which "trick" predators (often birds) into striking at a wing tip or leg under the impression that they are aiming for the head, thorax, or abdomen; the predator may end up with a piece of wing or even a leg, but the insect remains essentially unharmed and has time to escape. This kind of distraction is not so highly developed among birds; however, white rump patches and especially white outer tail feathers may be considered in this context (though not exclusively), and injury feigning, which distracts predators from eggs or young, may be considered parasematic behavior. See COLOR AND PATTERN; DISPLAY.

PARASITISM. In the broadest sense, a parasite is an organism that lives with and obtains food from another organism called a "host"; the host may or may not be harmed by the association. In the narrower construction, the parasite is always harmful to the host. (For other types of relationships, see COMMENSALISM and SYMBIOSIS.) An "obligate" parasite is one that *must* live off another organism, as distinct from a "nonobligate" parasite, which can live parasitically or not. The best North American examples of obligate parasites are our two species of COWBIRDS, which make no nests of their own but invariably lay their eggs in the nests of other species which rear the young blackbirds at the expense of their own brood. Some duck species are nonobligate parasites, occasionally laying one or more eggs in another bird's nest but also rearing broods in their own nests.

Nest parasitism, in which one species of bird takes over the nest of another for its own use, is rare in North America but is known to be practiced occasionally by Black-billed Magpies.

For non-avian organisms that parasitize birds, see ECTOPARASITE; ENDOPARASITE; NEST FAUNA.

For parasitism practiced by birds on other birds, see PIRACY (kleptoparasitism); BROOD PARASITISM.

PARATREPSIS (PAAR-uh-TREP-siss). A technical term encompassing all forms of distraction display. See DISPLAY.

PARATYPE. When a particular specimen of a bird (or other animal) has been designated from a type series as a HOLOTYPE of a species or subspecies, the other specimens in the series are the paratypes. See also PARALECTOTYPE; NOMENCLATURE, *Types*.

PARENTAL CARE. The behavior of parent birds toward their young from hatching to independence. The usual criteria for independence in young birds are (1) the ability to fly and (2) the ability to find food for themselves. For care of eggs, see INCUBATION; for early stages of nest life apart from parental roles, see YOUNG, DEVELOPMENT OF.

DIVISION OF LABOR. Brooding of the young normally follows the same pattern of responsibility as incubation, whether shared or relegated to one parent only. Very often males are active in the feeding of young (see below), whether or not they share brooding. Sometimes they begin bringing food to the nest before the eggs are hatched. As the young grow, and they need less brooding and more feeding, the parental roles usually change accordingly. In the case of two consecutive broods the male may be left to "finish" the first family while the female lays the groundwork for the second.

Virtually all variations of shared responsibility (or lack of it) have been recorded, from all-male or all-female to "equal rights." In some species (e.g., Snow Bunting, Hudsonian Godwit) each parent takes responsibility for part of the brood. Roles have also been seen to vary among different pairs of the same species.

Young of the Common Eider, Sandwich Tern, and a few other species of colonial water birds are combined into a kind of avian nursery school or CRÈCHE. Nestling anis are born and reared communally in a single nest by a number of pairs; all members of the commune, including both sexes, share incubation, brooding, and feeding of young, and the young of early broods often remain to help feed successive ones. In species other than anis a pair is occasionally assisted in various nesting tasks by a young or adult bird of their own or even a different species.

HATCHING. Parent birds are aware when their eggs become "pipped," i.e., cracked from within by the mature embryo. At this point, the usual procedure of turning the eggs ceases, leaving the pipped side up. Parents may occasionally remove a piece of the cracked eggshell or dump the hatchling out of part of the shell once it is completely open, but for the most part, parent birds are passive during hatching.

RECOGNITION OF YOUNG. Colonial seabirds can discriminate their own young with remarkable acuity from among hundreds of apparently identical chicks, and strenuously reject importunate offspring of other pairs. In the communal confusion of a crowded colony, feeding the "right" chick has survival value. Songbirds and other species which tend their young in relative isolation do not "need" to do more than feed whatever asks to be fed in their nest. It is this lack of discrimination which permits the brood parasitism practiced by cowbirds and others, and substitution experiments by humans have shown similar results. (For recognition of parents by young, see YOUNG, DEVELOPMENT OF.)

DISPOSING OF EGGSHELLS. Once they have served their purpose, eggshells become useless clutter in the nest and even a potential hazard to the delicate skin of naked nestlings. If they are simply jettisoned over the side, they advertise the presence of the nest. So most birds eat or carry used eggshells away from the nest. Ducks, geese, and swans and gallinaceous birds, whose young abandon the nest within hours of hatching, simply leave the shells behind, but other "precocial" species, e.g., shorebirds, remove the shells in spite of an early departure. A few species (e.g., Northern Goshawk, cuckoos) simply leave the eggshells as part of the furniture of their nests.

In at least some species there seems to be a generalized "tidying" instinct which urges the disposal not only of eggshells but also of displaced nest material, fallen leaves, or any foreign object. The most obsessive housekeepers will, on occasion, even discard their own young in order to get rid of an unsightly band which has been attached to one of the nestling's legs.

DISPOSING OF NESTLING EXCREMENT. Nests occupied by young birds over a period of weeks have an obvious sanitation problem. Birds use three basic approaches in meeting it. (1) A few species, e.g., kingfishers, some woodpeckers (among other hole nesters), are content to wallow in their own wastes; despite the unwholesomeness we naturally attach to this "solution," it does not seem to affect the success of the species which practice it. (2) Most non-passerine nestlings early develop the habit of defecating over the edge of the nest or from the entrance of the nest hole. (3) Adult passerines and some non-passerines eat their young's excreta or carry it away for disposal. The latter is facilitated by the enclosure of the waste products in a gelatinous mass known as the fecal sac. Parental collection of feces usually occurs following the feeding of the nestlings. In some instances the young raise their tails and "present" the fecal sac to the parent bird, or the young birds may deposit feces conveniently at the edge of the nest.

There is a general tendency, as the nestlings mature, for parents to carry wastes away rather than consume them and also for the zeal for nest sanitation to wane. By the end of the nestling period, therefore, the nests of many species are coated with "lime" around their rims, though others are kept clean for the entire period.

BROODING. Keeping nestlings next to the brood patch and under the insulating feathers of the parent birds serves the same basic function as incubating the eggs, namely, the maintenance of adequate temperature for the developing organism. In addition to transferring their own body heat, adult birds also shield their young from precipitation and the direct rays of the sun. It is often imagined that brooding must be constant and that any disturbance causing a parent bird to leave nestlings uncovered will inevitably result in their premature demise. In fact, nestlings can withstand temperatures considerably lower than their "optimal" body temperature and, on balance, are probably in greater danger from overheating in the sun than from exposure to summer chills.

The brooding rhythm changes as nestlings acquire their juvenal plumage and become less helpless. For the first few days after hatching, the brooding parent leaves the nest only infrequently and adopts behavior consistent with concealing the nest contents. But as the young gain more control over their body temperature, learn to react to signals of danger, and manifest their growing appetites, the parents spend more and more time finding and delivering food—and do less and less brooding.

Environmental conditions affect the brooding rhythm. Birds in enclosed nests are less vulnerable to exposure than those in open ones and need not be covered by the parents as much. The brooding period may be lengthened by unseasonably cold or wet weather. And nestlings tend to be covered more continuously during the night than the day.

FEEDING

Degree of Dependence. So-called nidifugous young—those which leave the nest almost immediately after hatching—are soon able to find their own food with little or no preliminary "coaching" from their parents. The most independent of these, such as ducks and most shorebird chicks, follow their parents away from the nest but almost immediately begin testing the palatability of substances they encounter, apparently with no influence whatever from the parent(s). Parents of gallinaceous species typically pick up edible items and drop them, perhaps several times, while giving a feeding call; the chick at first picks up the items chosen by the parent but very soon begins foraging on its own. Loons, grebes, cranes, and members of the rail family at first procure food—usually in the presence of the young—and give it to them directly or lay it near them. Young diving birds may practice submerging within a few days but may not be able to catch their own food for up to 6 weeks (Common Loon).

Forming a link between these nidifugous young and the nidicolous, or nest-bound, types are species such as the gulls, terns, and other colonial nesters whose chicks become fairly mobile soon after hatching and may wander about their colony, yet remain incapable of procuring their own food and must be fed entirely by the parents until fledged.

Normally one or both parents of nidicolous species start feeding nestlings within a few hours of hatching—as noted, male birds may even begin bringing food before the eggs have hatched. Bad weather or other conditions unfavorable for finding food occasionally delay meals throughout the nesting period. Young passerines can usually withstand a day or so of starvation, while the young of some tubenoses have fat reserves on which they can survive for weeks.

Period. The total period of parental feeding in nidicolous species ranges from about a month for most passerines to 8 months or more in the case of some albatross species. Half—or much more—of this period takes place after the young have quit the nest. As the young birds become more competent physically, a gradual weaning process develops in which parents bring food less frequently. This promotes aggressiveness which fuels the drive to find food rather than beg and wait for it. The point at which a young bird supplies all its own food is probably the best demarcation of independence from parental care, though parent-young encounters often evoke a begging response after this point.

Food supplied to young may correspond to the usual adult diet or differ markedly. Many species which are largely fruit or seed eaters give their nestlings a protein-rich menu of insects and other invertebrates.

Mechanics. That parents should feed their young seems "only human," so perhaps it should not surprise us that the transfer of food from adult birds to nestlings is a rather mechanical ritual which depends not on emotion or ethics but on the exchange of special "releaser" signals. Adult gulls, for example, will not feed their young unless they are stimulated by them to disgorge food. A Herring Gull may be "ready" to feed its chicks but unless it is pecked on the bill near its red spot, the food will remain in its gullet. Adult passerines are moved to feed by the sight of open gapes accentuated by prominent mouth corners (flanges) and (often) brightly colored and patterned mouth interiors, usually accompanied by a characteristic begging call. However, as noted above, this response is very generalized, and at least some species will give food to almost anything that gapes and cheeps. If *nothing* gapes and cheeps at a parent bird holding food, the latter eventually departs with its catch or swallows it on the spot.

The actual transfer of food is accomplished in different ways by different kinds of birds. Most birds of prey deliver an entire carcass to the nest and tear off manageable bits of meat for the nestlings. As the latter mature, they learn to butcher the prey for themselves. Most passerines carry food in their bills and place it in the yawning gapes of their young. Non-passerines and some passerines generally swallow the intended baby food and regurgitate it at the nest in one of three basic ways: (1) gulls, some herons, and others regurgitate into the nest or onto the ground beside the chick and allow it to pick up the food by itself; (2) some passerines disgorge into the nestlings' open mouths, and hummingbirds thrust their bills well down in the young birds' throats in order to "pump" in regurgitated food; (3) herons typically (though not exclusively) practice a kind of beak-to-beak regurgitation in which the young clasps the parent's bill in its own; in pigeons the adult clasps the young bird's bill in a variation on the same principle.

The young of many seabirds (e.g., fulmars, gannets, pelicans, cormorants) and some wading birds (e.g., Roseate Spoonbill) reach into the open mouth or throat of the parent bird and pull or scoop out regurgitated or unregurgitated food.

With all of these methods, the consistency of the food offered becomes coarser as the nestlings mature, the youngest birds sometimes getting a nearly liquid (perhaps predigested) "formula."

Distribution. Generally, parents give food to the nestling which is most aggressive in begging for it. This bird is fed until its gullet is full and it can no longer make the swallowing contraction which stimulates the parent to continue to feed. Once a nestling is "full" its begging ceases and its siblings are then fed in turn. When responses are more or less equal, parent birds may test the degree of hunger by placing the food and judging the swallowing reaction. When hatching is staggered, the oldest bird, if normal, will always get the first meal and the youngest remain unfed until its older siblings are sated; when food is scarce, the younger nestlings are thus "automatically" sacrificed to ensure the survival of the older.

Frequency. Up to a point, feeding increases with growth, i.e., in proportion to the needs of a growing bird, and then it drops off as the weaning process progresses. At the peak of their nutritive need, nidicolous nestlings may be fed as often as every 20 to 30 minutes during the day, with parent birds devoting almost all of their time and energy to foraging and delivery. By contrast, some young seabirds are accustomed to a single daily feeding or one meal every few days; at the end of the nesting period many species of tubenoses are abandoned altogether by their parents and left for weeks to survive on their accumulated fat until they can go to sea and find food for themselves.

Water and Grit. The bringing of pure water—i.e., other than what is contained in food—to nestlings has been recorded in only a very few instances (Eurasian White Storks, large birds which occupy open nests, and sandgrouse, which nest in very arid habitats).

Grit, necessary for digestion in some species, may also be supplied by parent birds.

DEFENSIVE BEHAVIOR. Parent birds defend their nests against predators by methods ranging from total passivity—simply covering the nest and remaining silent and motionless (characteristic of many passerines)—to savage aggression, e.g., brooding Northern Goshawks. Between these extremes, parents protect their young by giving alarm calls, which signal them to scatter, take cover, and/or remain still; by "shepherding" (precocial) young to safety; by distracting the attention of potential predators away from the young and onto themselves or frightening them by raising the feathers and screaming or hissing (see DISPLAY); and by "dive-bombing" or making threatening gestures without actual contact.

In colonies or forest communities, birds of the same or different species sometimes act in concert to sound an alarm and drive predators from the otherwise easy predation on nearly immobile nestlings (see FLOCK; MOBBING).

TRANSPORTATION. Species of loons, grebes, coots, swans, and ducks carry young nestlings on their backs or under their wings while swimming and in some cases even dive with them in this position. Picking up young birds in the bill is much less frequently seen (Virginia and Clapper Rails, ptarmigan) and seems to be a last-ditch rescue measure only. Reports and legends of many other species (e.g., nightjars) walking or even flying around with young tucked in various body crannies are not well substantiated.

TEACHING/URGING. Numerous parent/young interactions are sometimes interpreted from the human point of view as forms of rational communication—the parents "urging" the young to fly, for example, or "teaching" them to dive or preen. While parents of some precocial species (e.g., gallinaceous birds) certainly introduce their chicks to edible substances, the experimental evidence indicates that basic abilities to fly, feed, sing, etc., are innate. These may be refined by practice or trial and error but they are not transferred "intellectually" from one individual to another (see INTELLIGENCE).

PARIS BROTHERS (*Icterus parisorum*: Scott's Oriole). Obscure early-nineteenth-century French businessmen, based in Mexico, who sent numerous zoological specimens back to Paris. One of the latter, now known as Scott's Oriole, was named for the brothers (note the genitive plural) by Charles Lucien BONAPARTE.

PARROT. Standard English name for 100–130 members (depending on taxonomy and nomenclature) of the family Psittacidae (order Psittaciformes); also a collective term for the whole family, including macaws, cockatoos, lories, lorikeets, amazons, conures, rosellas, lovebirds, parakeets, parrotlets, etc., all of which may be considered types of "parrots." In the New World, parrots are generally larger species with shorter, blunt-tipped tails, and parakeets smaller with relatively long, graduated tails. The distinction has no taxonomic integrity, however, many small parrots being smaller than large parakeets. Except for escaped cage birds (see EXOTIC SPECIES), only two species of parrots can be considered North American birds: the Carolina Parakeet, a North American endemic, which bred widely throughout the southeastern region of the continent and was extirpated by the 1920's at the latest (see EXTINCT BIRDS), and the Thick-billed Parrot, which visited the highland pine forests of southeastern Arizona and New Mexico sporadically until 1936 (may once have bred) and is now decreasing alarmingly due to lumbering and other disturbances of its habitat in Mexico.

Parrots vary in size from 3¼ inches to over 3 feet in length. They come in a wide assortment of shapes and colors, with many brilliant green species, but also many with spectacular, multicolored plumage. They typically have short bills with strongly decurved upper mandibles closed over a much shorter lower one. These are used not only in cracking hard nuts but as an extra appendage in climbing from branch to branch. They have short legs and feet with toes I and IV pointing to rearward and the others forward (zygodactyl). Most species feed primarily on fruits, nuts, and seeds and nest in unlined cavities, but there are many exceptions within this large family. The Carolina Parakeet and Thick-billed Parrot are (were) both tree-cavity nesters, the latter at least occasionally occupying abandoned holes of the nearly extinct Imperial Ivory-billed Woodpecker. All parrot eggs are white.

The calls of parrots are typically harsh, shrill, rasping or grating screeches, often given in chorus by flocks in flight. A few species are noted for their ability to mimic human speech (see SONG) and this, together with their brilliant plumage, makes them attractive as pets (see AVICULTURE).

Though there are several species of parrots which endure severe climates in the Southern Hemisphere, parrots achieve their greatest diversity in the tropics, and they occur in this zone throughout the world.

The supposed provenance of "parrot" is too vague and irrelevant to warrant repeating. To "parrot" someone is now, of course, to imitate or repeat him.

PARTIAL MIGRANT. A species in which some members of a population leave the breeding area after nesting while others remain behind. Particularly prevalent in colder climates and as an age phenomenon. Young Herring Gulls and Blue Jays, for example, regularly wander much farther from their nesting area than adults of the same population. For other examples, see MIGRATION.

PARTRIDGE. Standard English name for about 40 members (including wood partridges) of the family Phasianidae (order Galliformes), which also includes the quail, pheasants, francolins, jungle fowl, and peacocks. The name is applied to numerous genera in the family (even to *Francolinus*, most of which are known as francolins) and therefore implies no taxonomic affinities; in fact, it is widely used to refer to the Ruffed Grouse, which is in a different family (Tetraonidae). Except for the grouse, the two "partridges" which occur in North America—the Gray (or Hungarian) Partridge and the Chukar—were introduced as game birds. The former has established itself continentwide in southern Canada and the northern U.S. on well-watered cultivated lands. For the latter, see CHUKAR.

Gruson (1972–BIOGRAPHY) traces the name back through the Latin *perdix* (*Perdix perdix* is the Latin name of the Gray Partridge) and the Greek *perdika*, which is derived from the verb meaning "to fart"—referring (thinks Gruson) to the flatulent sound made by the bird's wings when it flushes.

PARULA (PAA-ruh-luh or puh-ROO-luh). Standard English and Latin name for 2 rather similar species of wood warblers (family Parulidae; order Passeriformes). The Northern Parula (*Parula americana*) ranges throughout most of eastern North America; the Tropical Parula or Olive-backed Warbler (*P. pitiayumi*) is a widespread Neotropical species that reaches the northernmost extent of its range in the lower Rio Grande Valley of Texas. Both parulas are notably small and colorful warblers and prefer to build their nests in pendulous masses of *Usnea* lichen (old-man's-beard) or Spanish moss (*Tillandsia usneoides*).

"Parula" is a diminutive form of *parus*, the Latin word for titmouse. Since "titmouse" itself means a "small, small bird," "parula" might be translated as "tiny bird," which is fair enough.

For family characteristics, see WOOD WARBLER.

PASSAGE. Widely used in Britain and parts of the former empire as a synonym for bird migration, e.g., the "fall passage." In this context a "passage migrant" is a species which migrates through a region but neither breeds nor winters there, i.e., a "transient." The Buff-breasted Sandpiper, for example, is a passage migrant in the United States.

PASSERES (PASS-uh-reez). One of Linnaeus' original ordinal names and an old synonym for the order now called the Passeriformes (perching birds); now widely used as the name for the passerine suborder that encompasses the songbirds, also called the Oscines.

PASSERINE (PASS-er-in or PASS-er-een). A perching bird; in its strictest sense referring to species which belong in the order Passeriformes. It is also defined more loosely as "land bird," but this is somewhat imprecise: all passerines are land birds, but many land birds (e.g., raptors, gallinaceous birds, pigeons, cuckoos, owls, nightjars, swifts, hummingbirds, trogons, and woodpeckers) do not belong to the Passeriformes. Another near synonym is "songbird," but this term is more accurately used for the Oscines (or Passeres), the largest suborder of the Passeriformes. In Europe, there are no passerines which are not oscines and one may call any passerine a songbird without fear of contradiction. In North America, however, two families of birds, the tyrant flycatchers (Tyrannidae) and the cotingas (Cotingidae—one North American species "lumped" by many in the Tyrannidae), are perching birds (passerines) but not songbirds (oscines). These are sometimes referred to as "suboscine passerines." See Appendix I.

PATAGONIA (Arizona). See SOUTHEASTERN ARIZONA.

PATHOLOGY. See DISEASE.

PATRISTIC. Referring to resemblances among species or other taxa which can be attributed to a common origin rather than convergent evolution. The resemblance between gulls and jaegers is patristic; that between Dovekies and diving petrels is not. Compare CONVERGENCE; GENOTYPE.

PAURAQUE (puh-RAH-kee). Standard English name for a single species of nightjar, *Nyctidromus albicollis*, which breeds from southern Texas to northern Argentina. The name apparently is a Spanish rendition of a native Mexican word; it may have been intended originally to echo the species' call, but in its present form, it is not very close except for having three syllables. Another widespread Mexican name, *culejo* or *cuejo*, is a better "translation." For family characteristics, see NIGHTJAR.

PAWNEE GRASSLANDS (Colorado). Approximately 775,000 acres of shortgrass prairie habitat in northeastern Colorado (between Greeley and Sterling), partly owned and administered by the National Forest Service. Bird specialties include Golden Eagle (mainly winter), Ferruginous and Swainson's Hawks, Prairie Falcon, Mountain Plover, Long-billed Curlew, Burrowing Owl, McCown's (short grass) and Chestnut-collared (longer grass) Longspurs, Western Meadowlark, Say's Phoebe, and Brewer's Sparrow. Intermittent wet areas hold Franklin's Gulls and Forster's Terns and attract migrant waterfowl and shorebirds. Pronghorn antelopes, coyotes, jackrabbits (two species), and black-tailed prairie dogs also occur, and the wildflower show is spectacular from April to June, which is also the best period for seeing resident birds. December–January is the peak period for raptors. The Denver Audubon Society has established a grassland nature center in Grover.

PEACOCK. The peacock, which is familiar worldwide as a domesticated ornamental bird, is descended virtually unchanged from the wild Common Peafowl of India, *Pavo cristatus* (family Phasianidae), and has been displaying its remarkable tail fan and metallic-blue body in gardens since before the birth of Christ. Though essentially a lowland forest species in its original range, it frequently forages in the open. It is still a common sight in fields and even along the roadsides in India, where even such highly edible life forms are revered by the Hindu majority and go unmolested.

There are two other species known as "peacocks," the very similar Green Peafowl (*Pavo muticus*), which replaces *cristatus* in Asia, and the very rare, secretive African Peacock (*Afropavo congensis*) of the central Congo.

"Peacock" may be used very strictly to refer to the male peafowl, as opposed to the female or peahen, but the word is also widely used to refer to both sexes, as is "peafowl."

Anyone attracted to the notion that a peacock or two would add a charming touch to his garden should be made aware that their characteristic call is worthy of a banshee in distress and may be likened to the mating yowl of an alley cat amplified a hundred times.

PECK(ING) ORDER. A term deriving from the dominance hierarchy among flocks of domestic chickens, now broadly applied to such hierarchies among other social birds and even to human institutions, as the "pecking order" among the executives of a corporation. In the classic instance the "head chicken" at the top of the peck order has established the right to peck where she chooses and to peck any other member of the flock unchallenged. The hen which is second in line dominates all but the head chicken, and so forth, down to the most subordinate bird, which must submit to the will of the entire flock. See DOMINANCE.

PECTORAL (PEK-turr-ull) (Sandpiper). Pertaining to the breast, e.g., pectoral muscles (see MUSCLES). In the case of the sandpiper, referring to the heavy vertical barring which stops abruptly along the lower margin of the breast. Often shortened by the ornithologically hip to "pec": "Just had a flock of pecs."

PEEP. Originally a hunter's term for all of the small sandpipers, deriving from the high-pitched calls characteristic of several species. Now widely used by birdwatchers for the smallest, most "confusable" species of sandpipers in the genus *Calidris*—in North America: Semipalmated, Western, Least, White-rumped, Baird's, and Rufous-necked. Essentially synonymous with "stint," the standard term for these birds in British usage, which, however, does not include Baird's and White-rumped.

PELAGIC (puh-LADGE-ik) (Cormorant, trip). Oceanic; of the open sea. Pelagic birds are those which prefer a marine habitat beyond the coastal zone and normally visit land only to breed. The most truly pelagic birds are the tubenoses (Procellariiformes)—the albatrosses, shearwaters, petrels, and storm-petrels—many of which spend their entire lives, except for breeding periods, hundreds of miles from any shore. Other birds which may correctly be called pelagic are the tropicbirds, gannets and boobies, phalaropes, jaegers and skuas, certain gulls (kittiwakes), terns (Sooty, Bridled, and the noddies), and many of the alcids. The Pelagic Cormorant, like the other marine members of its family, prefers the coastal zone and its standard English name is therefore something of a misnomer.

A "pelagic trip" is an outing by boat (often to offshore fishing banks) organized by a group of birdwatchers for the purpose of seeing "pelagics," i.e., oceanic birds.

A broader but seldom used definition of "pelagic" includes any wide body of water, salt or fresh, more than 20 meters deep.

PELICAN. Standard English name for all members of the family Pelecanidae (order Pelecaniformes). There are 6 species of pelicans worldwide, 2 of which breed in North America.

Pelicans are very large (see below), peculiarly shaped water birds with heavy, bulky bodies, short, stout legs, long necks, and unusually adapted heads. The bill is very long and hooked at the tip with no external nostril openings (as in most Pelecaniformes). From near the end of the lower mandible to the base of the throat is suspended a great extensible sac of skin capable of holding at least 3 gallons of water—several times more than "its belly can." This unique adaptation acts as a scoop which takes in fish and water together when the bird's head is underwater; when the pelican lifts its head from the surface, the water escapes from the corners of the gape, leaving the catch behind to be swallowed or stored temporarily in the esophagus. Pelicans waddle in an ungainly manner on land but are among the most graceful of birds in the air: riding air currents over coastal wave lines; soaring high over the ocean; migrating effortlessly on extended wings; and (in seagoing species) executing precision aerial dives into shoals of surface-feeding fish.

Most of the world's pelicans are white or whitish, often with black or dark wing tips and yellow-orange bills. One North American species, the American White Pelican, fits this pattern, whereas the other, the Brown Pelican, is handsomely patterned in deep chestnut, black, gray, white, and tawny.

Pelicans are among the world's largest birds, some species attaining a length of 6 feet (North American species, 3½ to 4 feet), a wingspan of 6 to 9 feet, and a weight of 10 to 17 pounds. The Brown Pelican, once common along the Pacific, Gulf, and southeastern Atlantic coasts of the U.S., has declined drastically as the result of indiscriminate use of pesticides (see MAN-MADE THREATS TO BIRDLIFE).

American pelicans are colonial. Their nests are shallow depressions or mounds of mud or debris on flat ground (White and Brown) or stick platforms in trees or bushes (Brown only). They lay 1–4 eggs, averaging 2 (White) and 3 (Brown); these are white with a chalky white outer coating that soon becomes stained in the nest.

Nestling pelicans are notably noisy, the adults much less so; the repertoire of both runs to grunts, groans, barks, and screams.

The pelicans are widespread as a family, absent only from the Arctic and Antarctic, most of South America, and waterless regions. One of the North American species (White) breeds on interior (often saline) lakes and winters in coastal shallows (California and Gulf coast); the other (Brown) breeds along the coasts and ranges into offshore waters.

"Pelican" is very close to the Greek word from which it comes and which refers appropriately to bill characters. Originally, however (cf. *The Birds* by Aristophanes), it described an ax-like tool and, by association, a woodpecker!

PELLET. A mass of indigestible matter—e.g., bones, fur, feathers, shell, stones, hard insect parts (legs, elytra), seed husks, rubber bands—formed in the stomachs of many (perhaps most) birds and eventually regurgitated.

The gray or brown, ovoid owl pellet, consisting of rodent bones embedded in clotted fur, is the most familiar of these "castings," but pellets are also produced by species of grebes, cormorants, vultures, hawks and eagles, herons, rails, shorebirds, gulls and terns, swifts, flycatchers, swallows, crows and jays, dippers, thrushes, catbirds, kinglets, wagtails, shrikes, and wood warblers. The larger pellets and those which accumulate at a roost or nest site are, of course, much better known than the tiny boluses ejected by songbirds and immediately lost in vegetation. Therefore, the list of species known to make pellets can be expected to increase with continued observation.

The details of pellet formation have been studied only recently. In owls, the indigestible materials are apparently separated from the softer food substances in the gizzard (see DIGESTIVE SYSTEM and Fig. 19) and the hard, sharp, and/or linear objects such as bones enclosed in a relatively smooth, rounded mass of fur or feathers. The finished pellet then travels up into the proventriculus, where it is held for a number of hours before being regurgitated. The entire process from ingestion to ejection of pellet takes from 9 to 16 hours in the few species studied, but the actual formation of the pellet may take only half as long. Though a pellet very often contains parts of several food items, it is likely that once it reaches the proventriculus, it must be disgorged before another meal can be swallowed. Thus the stimulus for pellet regurgitation may be hunger, the sight of prey, or other feeding-related phenomena.

From the observer's point of view, the regurgitation process looks like some acute form of respiratory or digestive distress until the pellet emerges from the mouth and the bird settles itself in evident satisfaction.

On cursory inspection, the "pellet system" would seem to be simply a means of eliminating certain kinds of solid wastes by birds which swallow their food whole. However, experience in feeding sick or injured raptors has shown that the "roughage" of bone, fur, and feather is essential to the good health of these species. Pellet regurgitation may, for example, serve to clean the upper digestive tract.

Since pellets neatly collect bones, insect parts, and the like, often intact or in fragments large enough to be identified, they can yield valuable data on feeding habits when carefully dissected and analyzed.

From the birdwatcher's perspective, pellets are useful in locating roosting owls, especially when there is a snow cover.

PEN. A little-used term for the female of any species of swan.

PENDULINE TITS. Standard English collective name for the 9 species of birds in the family Remizidae (order Passeriformes), often considered a subfamily (Remizinae) of the "true" tits (family Paridae). For the single North American representative, see VERDIN.

PENNA (pl.: pennae). Any feather in which the barbs unite (connected by the barbules) to form a continuous surface, i.e., the vane or web; as distinct from a "pluma," in which each barb branches separately from the rachis. See also SEMIPLUME; FEATHER; and Fig. 9.

PERCHING BIRDS. The species of the vast order Passeriformes. The observant reader will remark that all birds perch in one fashion or another. It should therefore be explained that the names (both Latin and English) refer to the characteristic foot structure of passerines, with three forward toes and one behind, which, like the human thumb and finger arrangement, is ideal for grasping (e.g., a perch). See PASSERINE.

PEREGRINE (PAIR-uh-grin) (Falcon). Standard English name for the cosmopolitan bird of prey *Falco peregrinus* (family Falconidae). Its speed, agility, and handsome plumage justify its reputation as one of the most majestic of all birds, which in turn explains its preferred status among falconers and the wide popular support for restoring the eastern North American populations decimated by DDT poisoning (see MAN-MADE THREATS TO BIRDLIFE). The name means "traveler" or "wanderer," referring to its long-distance migrations. See FALCON; FALCONRY; ENDANGERED BIRDS; SPEED.

PERIODICALS, ORNITHOLOGICAL AND BIRDWATCHING. One measure of the current interest in birds in North America is the wide range of available periodical literature dealing specifically with birdlife and related matters. Among them these publications cover every aspect of the subject, from abstruse analyses of avian physiology to the minutiae of listing ethics. The North American periodicals with a continental or international purview are: *The Auk, The Wilson Bulletin, The Condor* (see entries for these three), *The Living Bird, The Journal of Field Ornithology* (formerly *Bird-Banding*), *American Birds* (see entry), *Birding* (see entry), and *The Birdwatcher's Digest.*

In addition to these there are many excellent state and provincial publications devoted to birds, as well as natural history, ecology, and animal behavior periodicals that often contain articles on avian subjects. A selection of periodicals, including all those noted above, is given in the Bibliography along with addresses of subscription offices as of 1982.

PERMANENT RESIDENT. An individual bird or species which both breeds and winters in the same region; a non-migratory form. This concept is a little more complex than might be assumed. Since there are Blue Jays year-round in New England, it is logical to assume that the Blue Jay as a species is a permanent resident there. In fact, however, only *some* Blue Jays reside permanently in the region, while others move south in the fall and return in the spring. Furthermore, the breeding success of Blue Jays during a given year and the abundance of acorns and other food sources affect how many individuals stay or depart. Residency patterns also vary greatly among different species and regions. Many woodpeckers and gallinaceous birds, for example, can essentially be called permanent residents as *species*, so limited are their movements under any normal circumstances. Winter finches, e.g., crossbills, will reside year-round in an area as long as cone crops support the population—often over a number of years—but will move south en masse when a food shortage develops (see IRRUPTION). In general, as one moves south in North America the percentage of species which occur as permanent residents increases because of year-long availability of food. Thus Eastern Bluebirds in the southeastern states tend to be non-migratory and are joined in winter by migratory bluebirds from the northern states and Canada.

Individual birds which overwinter in their breeding area in defiance of the normal habit of their species, e.g., at a feeding station, are not properly called permanent residents.

PERSPIRATION. Birds do not perspire by means of sweat glands in the skin as do humans, but give off excess heat in the form of water vapor, mainly by panting. See TEMPERATURE, BODY, *Cooling Off.*

PESTS, BIRDS AS. This entry attempts to summarize the main instances in which birdlife causes problems for human life, whether as serious threats, e.g., to health or agriculture, or as minor annoyances. Solutions to the problems are noted briefly when known.

It should be emphasized at the outset that on balance birds are far more beneficial to human endeavor than they are detrimental. Birds' greatest crime against humanity, the eating of grain and fruit crops, for example, is easily outweighed by the service birds perform in controlling numbers of insects and other non-avian pests which menace agriculture. Furthermore, studies of the feeding habits of birds reveal that it is not possible to distinguish "good" birds from "bad" birds on the basis of their relationship with people, since birds tend to combine traits which serve our interests with those that are competitive with our purposes. Generally beloved American Robins, for example, often plague blueberry and other fruit crops, while the largely noxious Common Starling eats a great many Japanese beetle grubs. Most "bird problems" in North America are local and temporary in nature, though they may recur in succeeding years. Therefore stopgap solutions usually suffice.

Finally, those silly enough to take bird nuisances personally who contemplate vindictive rather than simple corrective action should be warned that with the exception of a few introduced species all North American bird species are protected to some degree by both state and federal law. All control measures involving possible harm to birds are subject to government regulations that emphasize the desirability of finding humane solutions to problems involving birds (see LAWS).

AGRICULTURAL PESTS. Eighty percent of North American crop damage by birds is attributable to songbirds, especially blackbirds, starlings, and crows. By comparison, damage done by seed-eating ducks, geese, doves, and cranes is of little significance (unless, of course, it is *your* crop which has been attacked). Those who have never seen the hordes of Redwinged Blackbirds, grackles, cowbirds, and starlings that winter in the southeastern states (200 million in the Gulf states alone) should not underestimate the impact of these birds on rice crops and feedlot grains. In other regions, vineyard and orchard owners can suffer serious economic consequences as a result of migrating or dispersing robins, starlings, and other fruit-eaters. *Solution:* There are *no* universal solutions. The ages-old answer to avian crop pests has been to scare them away—with scarecrows, strips of tinfoil that move, gleam, and rustle in the wind, and automatic "guns" that go off at irregular intervals. The fact that large farms and vineyards sometimes employ airplanes to chase off bird flocks is a measure of the cost of the potential damage. The problem with any "unmanned" scarecrow device is that birds learn with surprising rapidity that they are not in any danger no matter how loud, bright, menacing, or irregular the effect. Recordings of the problem species' own alarm or distress calls have been shown to have a longer "scare life," but even these are eventually perceived as innocuous. Periodic chasing to maintain a continuing sense of danger in the birds is still essential in dealing with this problem. Practically speaking, all such cases require their own unique solutions, in many instances involving a combination of techniques. An intelligent citizen confronted with a potential problem should begin by considering the possibility of "exclusion" of pest birds (obviating the necessity for further action), move on, if necessary, to harassment (as described above), and resort to attempts at "radical removal" only in desperation.

LARGE ROOSTS. Congregations of birds near residential areas also usually involve starlings and species of blackbirds. Aside from the relatively trivial nuisances of noise and unsightly droppings, the fear of disease is sometimes aroused. Histoplasmosis, a fungus that thrives in piles of bird droppings and can affect (and in rare instances kill) humans who inhale the spores (see DISEASE), is the only significant potential health hazard connected with roosts and can be contracted only through close contact with the droppings. There have also been instances of large roosts posing threats to aircraft landing and taking off nearby. *Solution:* Harassment of the birds, especially when they first select the roost site, is often effective in forcing them to choose another location where the conflict with human activity is minimal. Unfortunately, starlings have become particularly fond of city structures as night roosts and are therefore likely to move from one urban site to another. A more drastic solution involves altering the roosting habitat of the birds so that it no longer suits their purpose. A grove of trees, for example, might be thinned, thus eliminating the togetherness potential that roosting birds require.

In the late winter of 1975, the U.S. Army undertook the control of a large blackbird roost near Fort Campbell, Kentucky, by spraying the roosting birds with a detergent-like chemical from the air. The "avian stressing agent" used (Tergitol) dissolves the oil in birds' plumage (see OIL GLAND; PREENING) that normally prevents them from becoming "soaked to the skin" and that is essential for maintaining proper insulation in cold and wet weather. When the temperature drops near freezing, sprayed birds die of exposure. In Kentucky, 500,000 blackbirds succumbed to this technique. This action was opposed (unsuccessfully) by conservation and humane organizations—not because they oppose radical control of pest species in all circumstances, but because (1) the Kentucky roost was about to disband naturally, since the birds were within days of departing on their northward migration; (2) the ambient temperature was not low enough on the proposed spraying date to kill the birds quickly, making the humaneness of the operation questionable; and (3) the method inevitably leaves a significant number of birds disabled but not dead, another humanitarian concern.

PIGEON NESTS/ROOSTS. Though pigeons don't usually roost communally in groups containing millions of birds as do starlings and blackbirds, they are very fond of colonizing niches of buildings, where they foul the architecture and present some (slight) risk of disease (chlamydiosis, see DISEASE). They are literally "trash birds," their abundance in cities and towns being commensurate with the tidiness of its streets—as well as the density and enthusiasm of the local pigeon feeders, pigeon breeders, and/or pigeon racers. Pigeons are not native to North America and, aside from providing sustenance for a few urban-dwelling Peregrines, have few redeeming attributes. *Solutions:* Pigeons are not protected by law and may be controlled at the discretion of the citizen. Regrettably, they are indifferent to owl replicas and are highly shoo-resistant, and stronger measures are usually called for. Shooting and poisoning are neither practical, recommended, nor legal in cities or around homes. Metal strips with spikes affixed (Nixalite) or wire "pigeon fences" can be installed where the birds are known to roost or nest, but may be expensive or as unsightly as the pigeons. Some of the fences inadvertently create ideal conditions for the untidy nests of that other urban alien, the House Sparrow. A caustic substance which irritates pigeons' feet is available commercially under several brand names (e.g., Roost-No-Mor, Flyaway, and 4-the-Birds)—it is spread or sprayed where pigeons walk. Pigeons are easily trapped and if you wish to make your solution someone else's problem, you can transport yours out "into the country." But remember that pigeons are famous for their homing abilities and may get back to your house before you do if released too close to home. Reminder: spreading poisoned bait is both dangerous and illegal.

HAZARDS TO AIRCRAFT. Flocks of small birds or single large birds have caused a number of fatal airplane crashes either by clogging jet engines or damaging the hull as a result of impact at high speed. A bird the size of a large gull, goose, or vulture hitting an aircraft traveling at 400–600 m.p.h. can penetrate windshields, wings, tail, or fuselage, causing the pilot to lose control of the aircraft. The worst such accident in history was the crash of an Eastern Airlines Electra jet in Boston on October 4, 1960. A flock of starlings en route to their airport roost were sucked into the jet engines, causing immediate failure in one and loss of power in another two, resulting in a loss of control. Sixty-two of the 72 people on board were killed. Bird-aircraft collisions are very infrequent (Drury, 1966, says 1–3 instances in 10,000 takeoffs and landings) and usually innocuous. However, the costs of a single mishap can, of course, be very high. *Solutions:* At least some jet engines are now so designed as to inhibit the ingestion of birds. Design and construction have also been tested for "bird resistance" and some modifications made accordingly. Airports now actively discourage the presence of birds by employing loudspeaker trucks or other harassing techniques to clear runways periodically of roosting gulls and the like. Concerted efforts to alter the airport habitat to make it less attractive to potential troublemakers and/or to discourage breeding colonies in the immediate vicinity are now standard operating procedures at all major airports.

PREDATION ON LIVESTOCK AND GAME BIRDS. Golden Eagles are known to take sheep or other small stock animals (usually young and/or weak individuals) as well as deer or antelope *on rare occasions.* Ducks, grouse, pheasant, and quail are among the many game birds that Northern Goshawks and other large hawks and owls take. Chicken yards are raided with some regularity by Cooper's Hawks and Great Horned Owls, very rarely by other diurnal or nocturnal raptors. It can now be stated on the basis of much accumulated data and without a hint of sentimental bias that (1) the amount of damage done to livestock and/or game by bird predators is insignificant and amply compensated by these birds' roles in controlling potential pests such as rodents and rabbits; and (2) the vengeful "control" methods practiced by farmers, ranchers, and others based on ignorant prejudice have been vastly out of proportion to the actual threat and a great disservice to the wildlife fauna of North America. Terres (1980–BIRD) notes that *at least* 20,000 eagles were shot (mostly from small airplanes) in the southwestern U.S. between 1940 and 1962, when full protection was accorded. The fact that most of these birds were killed for "sport" masquerading as predator control makes it all the more contemptible.

Fish hatchery managers complain with justification that fish-eating ducks (especially the Common Merganser) and herons sometimes eat significant numbers of fingerlings. The prejudice of commercial marine fishermen against cormorants, on the other hand, has been shown to be unjustified, as these birds eat mostly small "trash fish." *Solutions:* Covered fish tanks and ponds. Harassment or removal of predators caught in the act. Jail sentences and stiff fines for killing raptors.

RAPTORS AT FEEDERS. Northern Shrikes, Sharp-shinned and Cooper's Hawks, and even Northern Goshawks occasionally exploit bird feeders as reliable feeding grounds, reacting to the localized abundance of food in much the same way as the small birds that are attracted to your feeder. There is no danger that your chickadee or junco populations will be decimated, and the larger hawks may also provide squirrel and rat control if you have those problems. Predators are far rarer in nature than the species they feed on and are fully protected by law. They kill to live, without emotion, quickly and with admirable agility. *Solutions:* Tolerance, harassment, or, these failing, stop feeding.

BIRDS AND WINDOWS. During the breeding season, male birds defending their territories often catch sight of themselves in reflective surfaces such as windows, car hubcaps, etc., and thinking their own image to be a rival, attack the reflective surface. *Solutions:* The phenomenon will cease as the breeding season wanes, but if it is seriously bothersome the reflection can be temporarily removed with glass wax, tape, or other means.

Particularly in migration, birds often crash into large windows. They are notably susceptible to situations in which they can look through a room to habitat on the other side or when the window mirrors the vegetation in *front* of it. Large picture windows, especially ones near feeders, are also more than usually hazardous. Normally, of course, this situation does more harm to the birds involved than to the windows, though large birds (hawks, grouse) may crack or shatter panes. Depending on their flight speed, the birds may only stun themselves momentarily or—not infrequently—they may be killed by the impact. *Solutions:* Many stores which sell natural history books or feeder supplies now stock cutout silhouettes of hawks or falcons that can be stuck on the offending windows. These inhibit birds from flying in that direction. Some stores also stock a thin, wide netting that does not substantially mar the view and can be hung in such a way as to prevent birds from reaching the window. Otherwise, any technique which corrects the impression that glass is air or reduces its reflective characteristics, e.g., curtains, tape, wax, will also solve the problem.

BIRDS IN CHIMNEYS. Starlings (rarely other birds) sometimes enter chimneys while prospecting for roosting or nesting sites. Once inside they may find themselves with no place to perch and too little maneuvering space to execute the necessary vertical exit flight. Such birds often arrive in a panic in the living room. As anyone who has had this happen can attest, a frantic starling can knock over a surprising number of objects in a very short time. *Solution:* Keep birds (as well as other uninvited visitors, e.g., raccoons) out of the chimney in the first place by covering it with ¾-inch to 1-inch galvanized wire mesh. If a bird beats you to the chimney, keep in mind that the bird doesn't want to be in your house any more than you want it to be there. Therefore, your goal should be to show your guest the easiest escape route. Accordingly, open the nearest door or large window that leads to the outside and at the same time close or curtain off other windows and doors leading to other parts of the house. *Do not* be afraid of the bird; it has little capacity and no desire whatever to do you any harm. *Do not* chase the bird around with a broom or a butterfly net; this will only cause the bird to panic and to fly into your most precious knickknacks and confuse its perception of the best exit.

HOUSE-EATING WOODPECKERS. Homeowners are justifiably annoyed when they find woodpeckers chipping away at their dearly purchased (or deeply mortgaged) real estate. This is not an uncommon complaint, especially in the fall (mid-September through November in Massachusetts), and usually involves Downy Woodpeckers, which (for unknown reasons) seem to prefer shingles (especially cedar ones) to clapboards and to be particularly destructive of the facing below gutters and at the corners of buildings. Exactly what the woodpeckers think they are doing is still open to conjecture. Of the latter, however, there is an abundance. It has been variously supposed that: (1) Since woodpeckers find their food by listening for the rustlings of insects which live in wood, they may hear noises coming from household appliances and mistake them for the sound of a meal. (2) Inexperienced young birds occasionally choose houses in which to drill roost holes for the winter. (3) The woodpeckers do actually hear insects in the wood of the house—if not termites, carpenter ants, or other house-destroying pests, then harmless hibernating insects such as wasps. *Solutions:* Check to make sure you don't have termites, then harass the offending bird—scare it off, spray it with a hose. If repeated often enough, this will eventually discourage it in many cases. Temporarily placing a sheet of plywood or heavy plastic over the favored area has also proven effective. The above solutions also work (sometimes) in discouraging courting woodpeckers hammering out nuptial messages at dawn on a hollow drainpipe or other metal amplifiers near your bedroom window. Techniques which have *not* worked include: plastic owls, rubber snakes, painting or spraying the affected area with an anti-woodpecker substance—which exists only as a gleam in a con man's eye.

ATTACKS BY BIRDS. Some species of birds defend their nests with unusual ferocity. Terns nesting on your favorite beach will "dive-bomb" you in an intimidating but usually harmless manner if you come too near. Northern Mockingbirds (and rarely other songbirds) will menace people (more frequently dogs and cats) which they perceive as threatening to their eggs or young. Defensive behavior is characteristic of a short segment of the breeding cycle and the best solution is to steer clear of the birds' territory if possible or tolerate the mild nuisance for a few weeks.

One notable exception to the above generalizations is the Northern Goshawk, which defends a circle of several hundred feet around its treetop nest with such ferocity that an unsuspecting human wandering too close at the wrong time could be seriously injured. Because goshawks generally prefer to nest in remote areas far from human habitation, the problem seldom arises, but campers or owners of country cottages arriving in the midst of the breeding season (late spring to early summer is the danger period in most cases) occasionally find their site already occupied and fiercely defended. *Solutions:* Goshawks are among our most magnificent birds of prey and, while they seem to be increasing locally in recent years, they are by no means common. In normal circumstances, seeing a goshawk is a rare treat. Therefore, annoying though it is to be attacked, especially on your home turf, it should be remembered that these birds are not vermin or household pests to be disposed of at will. Goshawks are protected by law, and a special dispensation is required before they can be "controlled." Furthermore, amateur attempts to deal with the goshawk problem often end in a hospital visit for the would-be "controller." In view of these considerations, the best way to deal with usurping goshawks is to (1) stay away during the two or three weeks of the current breeding season, (2) remove the nest when the danger period is past (large raptors tend to re-use old nests), and (3) establish your presence the following year before the birds have taken possession of the site for the new season. If you feel that a more immediate solution is essential, the aid of a local falconer or other expert in handling raptors should be enlisted if possible. He or she could arrange for the removal of the nest in a manner which would serve the best interests of all concerned, once the proper permits have been issued.

Those tempted by the "no bird's going to push me around—where's my shotgun?" approach should remember that the hasty disposal of a goshawk may well create a far greater hassle than dealing with the situation rationally and humanely.

MAYBE YOU'RE THE PROBLEM. Natural history and animal welfare organizations which offer free advice to the public receive a significant number of calls from people who in effect are complaining about the intrusion of nature into our increasingly controlled, human-oriented environment. That Northern Mockingbirds often sing during warm, moonlit nights, for example, seems to be a nuisance rather than a delight to a lot of people; they want to know how to get rid of the noisy pest—which interrupts the soporific hum of passing traffic. Likewise, grazing Canada Geese are strongly resented by some golfers; the birds' droppings foul the fairways and are a detriment to straight putting. A songbird that attacks a house cat in defense of its nest (see above) may be regarded as a species of vermin: "Can't you kill it or trap it or something?" It is difficult to be sympathetic to this point of view in an era when a more legitimate complaint is that machine-made noise shuts out birdsong in many places and that animal life is generally less evident as a result of the human fondness for pavement and the multifarious pollutants that we have released, sprayed, poured, and buried during the recent past.

It is possible to argue that people living in North America today have a better opportunity to enjoy the exquisite complexities of the natural world than anyone ever has or will. We no longer have to fear the wilderness and its inhabitants as threatening to our well-being. Most of us have the leisure to explore and study the natural aspects of our extraordinary planet, aided by a wealth of illustrated books which describe species of plants, birds, mammals, insects, etc. And we have not yet committed ourselves to the necessity of living in "controlled atmospheres" underground or in space. It is pitiful, then, that so many people regard the other animals with which they share space as a menace rather than a rare luxury.

If you have a "bird problem" which is not discussed above, take a minute to consider (1) whether it is really a problem and (2) whether the solution might be found in a slight reassessment of your values rather than a massive disruption in the life of a fellow earthling.

PETREL (PET-truhl). Standard English name for about 35 members of the family Procellariidae (order Procellariiformes). The only tubenoses called simply "petrels" which visit North American waters with any regularity are 2 (possibly 4) species in the genus *Pterodroma* (see GADFLY PETREL). For family characteristics, see SHEARWATER; see also STORM-PETREL; see the latter for the origin of the name.

PEWEE (PEE-wee). Standard English name for all but one of the 10–12 (depending on taxonomy) species of tyrant flycatchers in the genus *Contopus* (family Tyrannidae; order Passeriformes); 3 *Contopus* flycatchers breed in North America. Some authorities suggest that one of these, Coues' Flycatcher (*C. pertinax*), should be "lumped" with a South American form (*C. fumigatus*) under the name Greater Pewee. It has also been suggested that the Olive-sided Flycatcher (*Nuttallornis borealis*) properly belongs in *Contopus*.

Pewees are exceedingly drab, rather small (6 to 7½ inches) flycatchers of the forest and forest edge. Our Eastern and Western Wood Pewees are virtually indistinguishable except by call and replace each other in eastern and western North America. They would seem to represent a classic case of recent species divergence, instigated by the separation of eastern and western populations in the last (Pleistocene) ice age. Where these two forms now overlap in breeding range, they are not known to interbreed.

"Pewee" is a fair imitation of the most frequently heard call of the Eastern Wood Pewee.

For family characteristics, see TYRANT FLYCATCHER.

PHAINOPEPLA (FAY-noh-PEP-la). Standard English name for the sole member of the family Ptilogonatidae (order Passeriformes) that occurs in North America.

The Phainopepla is a small (7½ inches), slender songbird with "silky" plumage similar to that of the waxwings, to which it may be closely related. It has a prominent crest, a short, but moderately broad bill, broad, rounded wings, and a long tail. The sexes are dimorphic: the male glossy blue-black, the female dull olive-brown; both have large pale areas in the primary webs and red irises.

The Phainopepla is a bird of arid mesquite scrub, including cultivated lands. Like many other dry-country songbirds, it is likely to be found along streams, where it feeds mainly on berries (e.g., mistletoe and the fruits of the Peruvian pepper or mastic, *Schinus molle*); it also eats insects, frequently catching them on the wing. Phainopeplas tend to travel in small flocks except when nesting and their broad wings give them a distinctive "butterfly" flight.

The song is somewhat weak and irresolute, often containing squeaks as well as pleasant liquid notes.

A typical nest site is the fork of a low tree (e.g., mesquite). The nest is a shallow cup of comparatively delicate construction—small twigs, stems, and leaves bound with spider silk and lined with down or hair. The 2–3 (rarely 4) eggs are very pale gray to slightly pinkish with moderately dense black and paler subsurface spotting.

The Phainopepla occurs from central California, southern Utah, and western Texas and south with its habitat to the limits of the central plateau of Mexico. Northernmost populations move south after breeding and, like the waxwings, Phainopeplas are somewhat nomadic, probably moving according to food availability; a few stray birds have been recorded in eastern Canada and the New England coast.

Phainopepla (also the Latin name of the monotypic genus) is a classical Greek compound which translates prettily as "shining robe" (Choate, 1973–BIOGRAPHY).

PHALAROPE (FAL-uh-rope). Standard English name for 3 distinctive members of the sandpiper family (Scolopacidae; order Charadriiformes), once thought to constitute a family of their own (Phalaropodidae); all 3 breed in North America.

Phalaropes are small (average 8½ inches) sandpipers with lobed and partially webbed toes evolved for swimming. Two of the three species (Red and Red-necked or Northern Phalaropes) are highly pelagic in habit and spend most of the year resting and feeding in flocks on the ocean. Another notable trait of the phalaropes is their reversal of sexual attributes: females are larger and wear a more brilliant alternate (breeding) plumage, while the male incubates the eggs. The phalaropes also share a unique feeding method. Whether at sea or in tidal pools, the birds spin rapidly in a tight circle, stirring up bottom sediment for surface organisms, which they deftly pick up in quick stabbing motions as they turn. The seagoing species are often seen in the company of marine mammals—presumably benefiting from the small animal life churned up in their wake—and are widely known as "whalebirds" among seamen.

The nests of phalaropes are shallow hollows on the ground lined with grasses and often built into a clump of grass with surrounding vegetation pulled over the top to form a canopy. The 4 (rarely 3) eggs are off white to brownish yellow or olive, covered rather densely (particularly at the large end) with well-defined dark brown speckles and splotches.

The phalaropes are not as songful on the breeding grounds as the sandpipers, but make occasional nasal wheezings, grunts, and quacks. The piping call note of the pelagic phalaropes is loud and sharp enough to be audible over the noise of wind, water, and ships' engines.

Red and Red-necked (Northern) Phalaropes breed on arctic tundra (circumpolar) and winter at sea over most of the globe except antarctic waters. Wilson's Phalarope is the landlubber of the family, nesting largely in northern prairie sloughs and wintering in Central and South America. It breeds exclusively in North America and has expanded its range dramatically eastward (as far as the Atlantic coast) in recent years.

"Phalarope" derives from a Greek compound meaning "cootfooted," referring to the lobed feet of phalaropes—miniature versions of those of the coots.

See references in the Bibliography under SHOREBIRD.

PHANERIC (fuh-NAIR-ik). Referring to conspicuous colors or patterns, e.g., in the plumage of birds, which serve to attract attention to, rather than conceal, their owners. The bright gorgets of male hummingbirds are examples of phaneric plumage. See COLOR AND PATTERN; DISPLAY.

PHASE. A variation—among birds most conspicuous in plumage coloration—which occurs with some frequency *within a population of a species*, and thus not an indication of racial distinction. An example is the dark, light, and many intermediate color phases of the Northern Fulmar. Other North American birds subject to the phenomenon are: Blue/Snow Goose, several species of buteos and falcons, several species of herons, the jaegers, Common Murre ("ringed" or "bridled" and "plain" phases), and Screech Owl. This kind of variation should not be confused with geographical or other variations with taxonomic implications, such as the black *race* of the Brant (*Branta bernicla nigricans*), or with color aberrations, such as melanism.

"Phase" is synonymous with "morph." See COLOR AND PATTERN; SPECIATION; POLYMORPHISM; and Plate 4.

PHEASANT. Standard English name for about 37 members of the family Phasianidae (order Galliformes), which also includes the quail, francolins, partridges, jungle fowl, and peacocks. One species, the Common Pheasant (*Phasianus colchicus*), has been widely introduced in North America as a game bird. Most of these birds are bred in captivity for the express purpose of being shot and are restocked each year in areas where they cannot sustain their populations. The "Ring-necked" Pheasant is the most familiar race. Like most of its kind, the Common Pheasant is native to Asia.

Pheasants have short, rounded wings capable of propelling them almost vertically when flushed but not able to power sustained flight (see MUSCLES). Like most gallinaceous birds, pheasants feed largely on grains, seeds, and some fruit. They forage on the ground and roost in trees during the night.

Like the quail and other members of their family, pheasants make a shallow hollow on the ground in which to lay their large clutches of eggs. This nest is often concealed in ground vegetation and is sometimes sparsely lined with handy plant material. The 7–15 (usually 10–12) eggs are blue-gray to light or dark olive and unmarked. Hens not infrequently lay eggs in nests of other pheasants or other ground-nesting birds, such as ducks or woodcocks.

The pheasant "song" sung by males on territory and at other times is a harsh, abrupt, two-syllable crowing, similar in quality to the first part of a rooster's *cock-a-doodle-doo*. It is generally accompanied by a loud beating of the wings.

The pheasant family is largely restricted to the Palearctic and Oriental regions and reaches its greatest diversity in the Asian highlands.

The Common Pheasant is established locally continentwide in North America.

"Pheasant" comes from a Greek word meaning "bird of the river Phaisos," which flows from the Caucasus, where one race of the Common Pheasant is native.

See references in the Bibliography under GALLINACEOUS BIRDS.

PHENETIC (feh-NET-ik) **CLASSIFICATION.** Arrangement of species in relation to one another based on what they look like, rather than on structural characteristics (often hidden) or chemical analysis. Phenetic characters may or may not be indicative of close phylogenetic relationship among species. See PHYLOGENY; TAXONOMY.

PHENOLOGY (feh-NAHL-uh-jee). The study of visible changes which occur in plants and animals on a regular seasonal basis and in response to climate. Phenological information includes, for example, the arrival and departure dates of bird migrants in a given season; the duration of territorial singing in a given bird species; the flowering dates of species of plants; or the date of first calling of green frogs.

PHENOTYPE (FEE-no-type). The sum of an organism's external characteristics—i.e., its appearance, as opposed to its genetic characterization or GENOTYPE. Mayr (1963–SPECIATION) notes that an individual's phenotype results from "the interaction between genotype and environment." The Great Auk and the Least Auklet share the same genotype, both being members of the auk family (Alcidae), but have very different phenotypes, owing to adaptive modifications each has undergone. On the other hand, the Great Auk had the same general phenotype as the penguins, though the genotypes of the alcids and the penguins are very different.

PHOEBE (FEE-bee). Standard English name for the 3 species of tyrant flycatchers in the genus *Sayornis* (family Tyrannidae; order Passeriformes), all of which breed in North America.

Phoebes are medium-sized (about 7 inches) flycatchers with relatively long tails, which they flick in a characteristic *downward* motion. The phoebes also differ from most other members of their family in their nesting practices. They prefer to build on a flat solid surface (usually with an overhang), such as a rock shelf, the eaves of a house, or a beam beneath a bridge. Eastern and Black Phoebes construct "adobe" cups of mud mixed with plant fibers. Phoebes often (but by no means exclusively) feed and nest near running water (see Plate 1).

The name "phoebe" imitates the call of the Eastern Phoebe.

For family characteristics, see TYRANT FLYCATCHER.

PHOENIX (FEE-nix). Perhaps the best-known of legendary birds, famed for its splendid plumage, its beautiful song, and its association with fire and the sun. Its life history was set down by the Greek historian Herodotus (fifth century B.C.) and the Roman naturalist Pliny the Elder (first century A.D.) among others, and it was believed to be seen occasionally by travelers to the Middle East at least until the Middle Ages. Authorities differ on the details of Phoenix biology, but there is general agreement on its most spectacular characteristics: Only one Phoenix, always a male, inhabits the earth at any given time, living for 500 or perhaps as long as 12,954 years. It ranges in Arabia and/or Egypt or perhaps in a paradise beyond the eastern horizon. At the end of its life, it builds a nest of aromatic vegetation, sings its surpassingly lovely song, enacts some kind of self-fertilization (details obscure), and sets its nest and itself on fire. (One legend says the fire is set by sparks thrown from the hooves of the horses of the sun god, who stops his chariot to listen to the Phoenix sing.) In the ashes of the nest is a white grub which is ultimately transformed into the new Phoenix.

For other fabulous birds and some Phoenix taxonomy, see IMAGINATION.

PHOTOGRAPHY. Increasingly sophisticated photographic technology has had an impact on ornithology and birdwatching as it has on nearly every other facet of life. No attempt will be made here to discuss basic photographic techniques, but only to mention some of the special considerations of photographing birds.

The problems involved in photographing birds might be boiled down to a single irrefutable truth: birds move a lot. In most cases they have an instinctual fear of man and thus move away from the cameraman. They often move rapidly and unpredictably, creating difficulties of finding, focusing, and stopping action. And they are likely to move into inconvenient positions or poor lighting conditions. In the early days of bird photography, the practitioner had little to offset these disadvantages except patience and luck. Since World War II, however, the versatility of camera equipment, the amount of literature on the subject, and the number of photographers out developing new techniques have all increased to such a degree that the bird is more likely to be inconvenienced than the photographer.

USEFUL ACCESSORIES AND SUGGESTIONS in bird photography are those which help the photographer remedy the problems noted above. The neophyte will find that the only constraint on his freedom of choice in selecting accessories is his bank account. In most cases what follows is equally relevant to still photography and movies.

Telephoto Lenses are, of course, most useful in compensating for birds' natural shyness. Unless a blind is used or very patient stalking contemplated, 300 mm. is probably the smallest lens size practical for getting reasonably large images of small birds. Much larger lenses are available, but it should be borne in mind that weight and bulkiness tend to increase with the degree of magnification. This is not a problem if the camera is to remain stationary, as on a tripod, but if the photographer plans to handhold his camera, he must be able to both move easily and remain stable with it.

Zoom lenses which permit quick changes in magnification without changing lenses are increasingly popular with nature photographers, now that some of their inherent optical "bugs" have been eliminated.

Lens Aperture. The more light that can enter through the lens, the greater the photographer's advantage in shooting moving subjects or those in low light. Lenses with low f-stops, e.g., $f1.9$ or $f2.7$, are preferable and lenses with a low stop greater than 5.6 are not recommended for bird photography.

Extension Rings, Tubes, and Bellows are inserted between lens and camera body and are useful for getting closer to your subject than the normal focal length of your lens allows. They permit extreme close-ups and close stalking with a long telephoto lens.

Camera Supports such as tripods and gunstock mounts enhance stability and allow the photographer to use heavier, bulkier equipment than he could hand-hold. In selecting tripods the bird photographer should weigh the convenience of light weight against the stability of a heavier tripod—for example, in high winds. He should also make sure that the tripod is designed to be used outdoors in such conditions as salty air and wet ground. Ease of adjustment may also be crucial in certain kinds of work. Gunstock mounts, which may be nothing more than the name implies, give increased stability, especially in shooting birds on the wing. This technique is made even more efficient by more elaborate gunstock mounts equipped with fingertip focusing systems and cable-release triggers.

Flash, either electric or bulb, enables the bird photographer to shoot in the worst of lighting conditions and to stop motion in his subjects, ensuring clarity of focus. An aesthetic drawback to flash pictures is that they tend to have an artificial look with a brightly lit foreground and a background that is swallowed in darkness. The nature of the artifice is altered, but its presence no less obvious, when an artificial "sky" or other reflecting background is used.

Motor-drive attachments advance your film automatically, which allows rapid-fire shooting of moving subjects and is especially useful for birds in flight. A drawback is the temptation to "lean on the trigger," thus using more frames than necessary and making an expensive hobby even more so.

Blinds are essential for photographing nesting birds, both to ensure unselfconscious subjects and to prevent disrupting the nesting cycle. They are also valuable in getting close to moving subjects, such as shorebirds which "spook" easily. Lightweight collapsible blinds are available commercially or they can easily be made with simple materials (designs can be found in most wildlife photography books; see the Bibliography).

It is usually necessary to accustom birds to the presence of a blind over a period of a few days. For nesting birds the blind should be set up at some distance (Pettingill, 1970–ORNITHOLOGY, recommends 10 feet for small birds) and left for a day, then moved up to shooting distance (no closer than 5 feet) and left again. If no disturbance is evident, the photographer can use the blind. If birds see someone enter a blind, they will often feel threatened by the human presence even if they cannot see into the blind. They can sometimes be deceived if two people enter the blind and one leaves.

USES OF BIRD PHOTOGRAPHY. In addition to the challenge, fun, and aesthetic enjoyment to be had from photographing birds, the modern camera is useful for scientific and educational purposes. Stop action allows analysis of flight and other movements normally too fast for the human eye to see; aerial photos of flocks, roosts, and colonies are an invaluable tool in census work; good photos can in many cases obviate the need of taking specimens of birds as occurrence records—even diagnostic details such as wing formulas can be photographed in birds taken from mist nets; photographs used as text illustrations can be less expensive and (in some cases) more accurate than paintings or drawings; display rituals and other avian activities can now be recorded with complete fidelity on color movie film; and, of course, due in large part to nature films and other popular media using photography, birds are more widely appreciated than ever before.

AESTHETICS. Frame-filling subjects, in pleasing compositions, perfect focus, and (eventually) brilliant color, were once the goal to which bird photographers aspired. This aesthetic was enforced to a certain extent by clumsy, unsophisticated equipment which demanded a relatively stationary subject. Such bird portraits—often recording a nest tableau—are still taken, of course, and, with justification, widely appreciated. But the definition of a good photograph has been expanded. Action pictures, for example, especially "wing shots," now draw praise even if not completely in sharp focus. Photographs showing a species in a characteristic habitat or exhibiting a typical behavioral trait (even if not "full frame") are deemed more interesting than the standard nest shot. And a quality of wildness in a photograph—as of a shy species painstakingly stalked—is more appealing than the tame indifference recorded in "setups." In some camera clubs nature photographs are disqualified if any evidence of human presence appears in the picture, no matter how obscurely.

PHOTOPERIODISM. The effect of light—especially length of day—on animal physiology and behavior. Stimulation of birds' reproductive systems in response to increased hours of daylight has been demonstrated repeatedly in the laboratory and on chicken farms. The phenomenon also plays a role (of debated importance) in the urge to migrate. See MIGRATION; NAVIGATION; and the Bibliography.

PHYLETIC (fye-LET-ik). Referring to evolutionary descent and relationship; phylogenetic. See PHYLOGENY; TAXONOMY.

PHYLOGENY (fye-LODGE-uh-nee) (less frequently, phylogenesis [fye-luh-JEN-ih-sis]). Evolutionary history as a whole or that of any given taxon (species, family, etc.) and therefore the relationships among these units and groupings. The framework of modern taxonomy consists of the attempt to place organisms in phylogenetic order—the order of their descent from common ancestors. Shearwaters are phylogenetically closer to the pelicans than to the gulls though they more resemble the latter. Placing the Yellow-breasted Chat in its proper family involves discovering its phylogenetic (or phyletic) relationships with other birds. Compare ONTOGENY. See also TAXONOMY and Appendix I.

PHYLUM (FYE-lum) (pl.: phyla). The major taxonomic category between kingdom and class. The animal and plant kingdoms are divided into phyla; the phyla into subphyla and classes. Depending on taxonomic interpretation, there are between 10 and 33 phyla in the animal kingdom. Birds (class Aves) belong in the phylum Chordata, which contains all vertebrates and other animals with nerve cords. See TAXONOMY.

PHYSIOLOGY. The study of the *functions* of living organisms as a whole and of their components. Bird physiology is treated here under the various systems (DIGESTIVE, REPRODUCTIVE, etc.), senses (VISION, SMELL, etc.), and specific organs (OIL GLAND, etc.).

PIGEON. Standard English name for about 150 members of the family Columbidae, the only family in the order Columbiformes represented in the New World. Counting the DOVES, the family contains a total of about 295 species worldwide. Nine species of pigeons and doves, including the extinct Passenger Pigeon, are native to North America; three others, including the ubiquitous Common Pigeon, have been "successfully" introduced (see INTRODUCED BIRDS); and five species have occurred as accidental stragglers (see Appendix II). Pigeons are generally larger than doves, with short, blunt rather than long, pointed tails, but the terms have no taxonomic integrity; our feral city columbid, for example, is widely known both as Rock Dove and as Common Pigeon.

Columbids vary in size from 6 to 30 inches (6 to 14 inches in North America). They are plump, small-headed, short-legged birds, usually somberly colored (though often with patches of iridescent feathers). Their bills are slender and short with a cere or operculum above the nostrils at the base.

Pigeons and doves feed largely on fruits and seeds, either in trees or on the ground. They are often gregarious while feeding, and a few species (notably the extinct Passenger Pigeon) nest in colonies. They are capable of drinking without raising their heads as most birds must, and they are unique in producing a secretion from the crop on which they "nurse" nestlings (see PIGEON'S MILK). Their vegetarian eating habits and plump form make them popular "table birds," and there is a season here on several species.

The Common Pigeon (Rock Dove) nests on cliffs when thoroughly wild, but in its more familiar feral state prefers man-made structures: building ledges, eaves, etc. Native pigeons tend to nest fairly low in trees or shrubs (ground doves infrequently on the ground). The typical nest is a flimsy stick platform, several species occasionally using abandoned songbird nests. The usual columbid clutch consists of 2 glossy, white to buff eggs (see Fig. 7).

Pigeon/dove calls are invariably moans, coos, or hoots, some haunting, others mechanical and monotonous.

As a family, the pigeons and doves occur throughout the world except in arctic and antarctic areas, and the native Mourning Dove occurs throughout North America south of the subarctic region. Most of our pigeons and doves are permanent residents, and even in the migratory species some populations are sedentary.

"Pigeon" is descended from the Latin *pipire*, "to peep," through the French *pijon*, a nestling bird.

PIGEON'S MILK. A "cheesy" secretion from the lining of the crop in members of the pigeon family (Columbidae), regurgitated to feed nestlings during their early development. Like the milk of mammals, it is composed mainly of fat and protein, is rich in A and B vitamins, and its production is stimulated by the pituitary hormone prolactin.

Pigeons and doves have very well-developed crops, which, as in other birds, are used for storing food (see DIGESTIVE SYSTEM and Fig. 19). In the last week to 10 days of the incubation period, the interior lining (epithelium) of this sac becomes greatly thickened in both sexes. The "milk" is contained in the cells of this layer, which are progressively shed into the crop cavity ready for regurgitation. For the first 4 or 5 days after hatching, nestlings are fed exclusively on this crop milk, but gradually thereafter it is mixed with increasing amounts of seeds (pigeons do not feed their young any animal food). Milk production continues for up to 18 days, its cessation coinciding roughly with the young's departure from the nest.

PIGMENT. See COLOR AND PATTERN.

PILEATED (PYE-lee-ay-ted or PILL-ee-ay-ted) (Woodpecker). Crowned, capped, or crested, i.e., having feathers in a distinctive shape or color covering the pileum.

PILEUM (PYE-lee-yum or PILL-ee-yum). Technical term for crown; the top of the head between the forehead and the nape. See Fig. 25.

PINFEATHER. An early stage of feather growth in which only the feather sheath is apparent. See FEATHER.

PINION (pinioning). Sometimes used in a literary context to mean simply a bird's wing or a flight feather, but more specifically, it refers to the wrist and hand (carpals and phalanges) of a bird's wing, including the primary feathers. Pinioning involves severing this portion of *one* wing to permanently keep captive birds from flying. Not the same as CLIPPING.

PINTAIL. Standard English name for at least 3 species and a corresponding number of well-marked subspecies of ducks in the genus *Anas*. The pintails all have elongated tails to *some* degree. However, only drakes of the so-called blue-billed pintails and especially *the* Pintail (*Anas acuta*) have the two greatly elongated central rectrices which strongly evoke the English generic name. The latter is also the only pintail that occurs regularly (widespread) in North America. Drake OLDSQUAWS also have "pin tails" but are not pintails. For family characteristics, see DUCK.

PINYON (or Piñon) (Jay). Spanish for "pine nut," the seed of the pinyon pines (*Pinus edulis* and *P. monophylla*), which, along with juniper and yucca, characterize the arid slopes of the mountains of western North America (pinyon-juniper biome) between desert and forest zones. This is the breeding habitat of the Pinyon Jay, which, like the human inhabitants of the region, is fond of eating *piñones*.

PIPIT. Standard English name for 35 members of the family Motacillidae (order Passeriformes), which also includes the WAGTAILS and longclaws (all African), for a family total of 54 species. Except for the unique Golden Pipit of Africa, all pipits belong to the genus *Anthus*. Three species of pipits breed in North America, 1 occurs as a migrant in the Aleutians, and 2 others have been recorded as accidental stragglers in Alaska (see Appendix II).

The pipits are a rather homogeneous group of small (5½ to 7½ inches), drab, ground-feeding birds with slender, pointed bills of medium length, fairly long legs, and toes with an elongated hind claw in most cases. Pipits are typically tan, brown, or olive above with some degree of streaking on the breast and/or sides. Their tails are usually moderately long with white outer margins—the extent varying among species. Though a few species nest in trees, pipits are the quintessential open-country birds, thriving best in arctic barrens, deserts, and especially fields and paddies. They walk—rather than hop, as do most songbirds when on the ground—"pumping" their tails and stopping periodically to pick up worms, insects, snails, and other small invertebrates as well as weed seeds.

On their breeding grounds, pipits perform aerial song flights. The sound, which issues from as high as 500 feet in the air, may be quite melodious or not—e.g., the strange dry rattle or hiss of our Sprague's Pipit. On migration their presence is often evident from their distinctive flight calls.

Most pipits nest on the ground (sometimes in rock crevices), building cup nests of grasses, fiber, hair, and/or mosses. The 3–7 (usually 4–5) eggs are rather glossy and variable in color and markings, the ground color ranging from pale gray to pinkish, finely—but often very densely—speckled or lined. Many pipit species are highly migratory and the family is therefore distributed worldwide, except for some remote oceanic islands. Our native pipits occur in open country (including arctic and alpine barrens) throughout the continent.

The name "pipit" roughly imitates the flight call of the Water Pipit.

PIRACY. Refers to the stealing of food from one bird by another, more technically known as kleptoparasitism. The practice has been recorded in many species, including a variety of songbirds. Some raptors and seabirds obtain a significant proportion of their diet by harassing other birds for food they have caught, but all avian pirates are fully capable of catching or finding their own food. Where Bald Eagles and Ospreys occur together the former will often pursue the latter until it drops the fish it has caught. Frigatebirds specialize in chasing boobies and other seabirds over tropical seas and will even strike a bird reluctant to give up its catch. The food item does not have to be visible; pelagic pirates are aware that a pursued bird will disgorge swallowed food to "lighten its load" and make a faster escape. The most skillful maritime thieves habitually catch regurgitated tidbits before they hit the water. Being among the most resourceful feeders, gulls have also mastered piratic techniques. In addition to chasing other birds, they have learned to accompany fishing Brown Pelicans (Laughing Gulls) or flocks of sea ducks (Herring Gulls), hoping to snatch a free meal when these divers resurface. Perhaps the most dedicated and certainly the most agile of the kleptoparasites are the members of the jaeger family (Stercorariidae). The slightly built Long-tailed Jaeger is the least inclined to thievery. But the Great Skua has been seen to grab gannets by the wing and pull them into the sea and to try to push birds beneath the surface with its feet in order to force regurgitation. Parasitic and Pomarine Jaegers must be the chief bane of seagoing terns and gulls, but the sight of these consummate "aerobats" in pursuit of an uncooperative victim is one of the classic thrills of birdwatching.

For other details of avian piracy, including an account of a "four-way snatch," see Meinertzhagen (1959 and in Thomson, 1964).

PISCIVOROUS (piss-SIV-er-us). Describes organisms which feed largely or exclusively on fish. The Great Cormorant, Red-breasted Merganser, Osprey, and Belted Kingfisher are all piscivorous birds. See FOOD/FEEDING; SWIMMING/DIVING.

PISHING (or spishing). Onomatopoeia for an oral sound made by birdwatchers in the field in the hope of attracting birds or encouraging them to forsake the cover of vegetation. For an analysis of its effectiveness, see BIRD CALLS.

PLANTING FOR BIRDS. See BIRD FEEDING.

PLASTIC (plasticity). A plastic species is one that is highly variable over its range, i.e., one in which many well-defined subspecies can be distinguished. The Ruffed Grouse, with 10 subspecies recognized over its Canadian-Transition Zone distribution, is a notably plastic species, whereas the more widely ranging Pied-billed Grebe is thought to contain at most 2 North American races. Other native exemplars of avian plasticity are: Canada Goose (11 North American subspecies), Rock Ptarmigan (11), Hairy Woodpecker (12), Horned Lark (20), Long-billed Marsh Wren (10), Bewick's Wren (13), Winter Wren (12), Fox Sparrow (18), Song Sparrow (30), Dark-eyed Junco (12), Savannah Sparrow (12), Rufous-sided Towhee (13), Brown Towhee (10), Common Yellowthroat (11), Red-winged Blackbird (14), and Scrub Jay (11). Of course, opinion varies among taxonomists about the validity of some races.

Appendix I gives the number of North American subspecies for all North American species. See also SPECIATION.

PLAY. Many young vertebrate animals are observed to be "playful," a behavior pattern usually associated with "practicing" or preparing for such adult activities as catching and killing of prey and dominance contests. Animal play in young or adults which does not have any clear behavioral context, i.e., play with no apparent "purpose," is sometimes explained as exercise or an innate honing of physical dexterity, both of which can be seen as serving an individual's survival potential without implying that "lower" animals are capable of anything as intellectually sophisticated as frivolity.

Human beings, of course, have raised playing for fun to an art form, but it is impossible to detect with any certainty whether birds and other animals derive anything like the pleasure we get from recreation for its own sake. Certainly they appear to. Nestling birds are clearly not aware that they are "practicing" for adulthood when they spar energetically with nest mates or jump up and flap their wings as fledgling raptors often do. It is therefore not unreasonable to suppose that such activities yield some kind of gratification. Brown and Amadon (1968–HAWK) point out that hawks and eagles often soar with full crops and without enacting any particular courtship ritual, implying that fun rather than hunting or sexual activity is the motive for such flights. Fulmars accompanying ships habitually engage in aerobatics, using the air currents set up by the moving vessel; a favorite trick is to career along the rails or waterline and then dart across the bow as closely as possible. Dolphins do this as well (not to mention young humans racing trains to a crossing), and it is difficult to relate this game, which fulmars play over and over again for hours, to any "practical" purpose other than staying with the ship (see FOLLOWING SHIPS). And this they could do with far less effort. Penguins, sea ducks, and alcids have also been observed engaging in this kind of repetitive, "aimless" sport—riding rapids or ice floes—and it may not be entirely fanciful to speculate that these and other birds spend their few "off-duty" moments simply enjoying themselves, whether or not the activity is "emotionally analogous" to human joy.

Another phenomenon related to the little-studied subject of avian emotions is ecstasy flights and singing performed by certain species at certain times (see SONG).

PLOVER (rhymes with "lover," not "clover"). Standard English name for about 40 members of the family Charadriidae (order Charadriiformes), and the name of the family as a whole. The plover family contains a total of 62 species, some of which are known as lapwings and dotterels. Some taxonomies include the turnstones in the Charadriidae. Ten species of plovers (including the Eurasian Dotterel and Killdeer) breed in North America; another (the Mongolian Plover) may breed very locally in Alaska; and 3 other species have been recorded as accidental stragglers (see Appendix II).

Plovers are small to rather large (6 to 16 inches), plump, compact shorebirds, with short, stubby bills, legs of moderate length, and somberly colored, but usually strikingly patterned, plumage. Many species have prominent breast bands, eye stripes, and wing stripes conspicuous in flight. The bill is typically swollen at the tip, the toes are generally unwebbed (partially webbed in some cases), and the hind toe (hallux) is minute or lacking.

Plovers move over mud flats, beaches, and cultivated fields in a characteristic run-and-stop motion, picking up small invertebrates and plant matter.

Their nest is a shallow scrape in sand, mud, or dry tundra, sometimes sparsely lined with plant debris. The 2–5 (usually 4) eggs are brownish yellow with distinct dark brown spots of variable density (see Fig. 7).

Most plover species have plaintive whistling cries, among the great wild sounds of the world.

Like the SANDPIPERS, the plovers were heavily shot until well into the present century and shipped to market by the wagonload (see CONSERVATION). The populations of many species were severely reduced thereby, but with full protection, they have recovered well.

The plovers are distributed throughout the world from the High Arctic through the tropics to the Antarctic, and occur in all open-country habitats in North America. Some of the longest migration routes are undertaken by plover species, the western race of the Lesser (American) Golden Plover, for example, traversing thousands of miles of open ocean from its arctic Alaskan breeding grounds to its nearest winter quarters on islands of Oceania.

"Plover" comes from a Latin root, *pluv-*, which refers to rain, and various legends figure plovers as "rain birds" in some sense. Some of these are purely superstitious but others may contain some substance. Shorebird shooters along the east coast, for example, knew to expect flocks of Golden Plovers to put down in coastal fields in the fall when there were onshore storms.

PLOWSHARE BONE. The pygostyle, a "tailbone" consisting of the fused vertebrae at the end of the backbone. It is named for its shape. See SKELETON and Fig. 19.

PLUMA (pl.: plumae). Any feather in which the barbs branch separately from the rachis and are not united to form a vane as in a pennaceous feather (penna). See FEATHER and Fig. 9.

PLUMAGE. The collective term for all of the feathers which cover a bird's body; a technical synonym is "ptilosis." All birds eventually wear such a "feather coat," a characteristic which distinguishes them absolutely from all other classes of animal life.

PLUMAGE COMPOSITION. The individual feathers, which together constitute the plumage, vary greatly in both shape and structure. Only major structural variations are described below; many of the italicized specific terms are treated in somewhat greater detail elsewhere under headings of their own, and structural details are discussed at length under FEATHER.

Almost all of the feathers normally visible on a bird, including the relatively large, stiff wing and tail feathers and the smaller, softer feathers which give a bird its smooth outline, are called the *contour feathers*. All of these have a *rachis* and in the great majority the *barbs* are closely "zippered" together to form a unified surface or *vane* on either side of the rachis. However, "plumaceous" contour feathers—with barbs unconnected—are also present in many species.

Beneath the contour feathers there is usually a layer of short, soft, vaneless feathers present in varying degrees and in different locations among different species. These are either *down* feathers or *semiplumes* (see Fig. 9). Down feathers may be no more than rachis-less tufts of barbs, but they intergrade in structure with the slightly more rigid semiplumes, which (though vaneless) in turn intergrade with the softer, more plumaceous type of contour feathers. Down feathers are absent altogether in some species.

In addition to the contour feathers and the undercoat of down and semiplumes, there are *filoplumes*, long, narrow feathers, usually with a few barbs at the tip. These always grow with a contour feather and may be distributed over most of a bird's body, but rarely show at the surface. In some freshly molted passerines, they are visible above the feathers of the nape.

Hardly recognizable as feathers are the *vibrissae*, stiff, hairlike feathers which appear as "eyelashes" in a few species of birds (e.g., Northern Harrier) but more often as *rictal (or nasal) bristles* around the top of the gape and over the nostrils, as in most flycatchers and nightjars (see Fig. 9).

Finally, there are the strongly modified feathers known as *powder down*. These are evenly distributed under the contour feathers of most birds but in a few species occur in concentrated patches; they give off a fine dust made up of minute scale-like particles of keratin, the purpose of which is imperfectly understood.

Contour feathers + down + semiplumes + filoplumes + vibrissae + powder down = plumage. (*Natal down*, as differentiated from the adult down referred to above, is described under DOWN.)

ARRANGEMENT OF FEATHERS. On casual inspection, a bird's body feathers seem to be evenly distributed, much in the way hair covers the human head. The reality, however, more resembles the head of the balding man who combs hair rooted in one place over a bare patch, for the body feathers (and attendant filoplumes) of all but a few species of birds (e.g., Ostrich, penguins; none North American) are rooted in discrete regions of the skin called *feather tracts* or *pterylae,* between which are open patches called *apteria.* The pattern made by the tracts, which varies consistently among different groups of birds and governs how the feathers are distributed, is called *pterylosis.* Typically, major tracts cover most of the head, throat, and neck; run down the center of the back in varying widths from neck to tail; surround the breast and belly; cover the leading margins of the wings above and below and parts of the upper leg. The location and extent of the tracts obviously determine the location, extent, and number of the apteria. As noted, the overall pattern is highly variable among different types of birds; more information on comparative pterylosis, along with a more formal description of the feather tracts and apteria, will be found under FEATHER TRACTS.

Down feathers may occur within both the feather tracts *and* the apteria, i.e., more or less evenly over the body; *or* be restricted to the apteria; *or* be absent altogether. Semiplumes may also be present in the apteria and/or along the edges of the feather tracts. Put another way, the apteria may be bare or covered thinly or thickly with down and semiplumes.

Normally, of course, the contour feathers cover the apteria, so that, unlike most bald human pates, a bird's bare patches are effectively concealed. For the arrangement of the contour feathers of WING and TAIL, see under those entries.

NUMBER OF CONTOUR FEATHERS. There is relatively little data on feather numbers (due in part no doubt to the tedious nature of the research), but a few basic tendencies have been established. As one would expect, small birds have fewer feathers than very large birds. The fewest contour feathers yet recorded is 940 for the Ruby-throated Hummingbird (Wetmore, 1936); the highest, 25,216 for the Whistling Swan (Ammann, 1937). The numbers for passerines studied to date range between about 1,000 and almost 5,000, but, excluding a few extremes, the normal range seems to be between 1,500 and 3,000.

Feathers are not distributed in equal numbers over a bird's body. The abundantly feathered Whistling Swan cited above had 80 percent of its feathers concentrated on its head and very long neck. Small birds tend to have more feathers per square inch (or other measure) and in proportion to their body weight than large birds (Hutt and Ball, 1938). This is consistent with the fact that smaller birds lose heat more rapidly and require more insulation. At least some species which must endure cold winters have up to 11½ percent more feathers during that season (Staebler, 1941).

PLUMAGE VARIATIONS. Most of a bird's color and pattern and much of its form and "personality" are realized in its plumage, but plumage characteristics are not static. They vary enormously from species to species in accordance with specialized life styles; moreover, the plumage of individual birds can vary by sex, age, season, feeding habits, and a wide range of abnormalities. The pattern of normal change is "programmed" genetically in a given species, but the change itself is often triggered by hormonal activity (see MOLT).

Functional Variation. Many details of a bird's plumage reflect its manner of living: most water birds have comparatively dense feathering with thick undercoats of down for added insulation; the flight feathers of migratory populations are often longer than those of sedentary populations of the same species; ptarmigan, which spend much of their life foraging in snow, have heavily feathered legs and feet (see Fig. 12); the cryptic plumage of nightjars which nest and roost on the ground has evolved to camouflage them from potential predators (see Plate 3); the stiff, spiny-tipped tails of woodpeckers and swifts have adapted to support the bodies of their owners as they cling to a vertical surface (see Fig. 21); the tails of many flycatching species are usually long and seem to aid aerial agility (see Fig. 21). Many other plumage characteristics aid recognition and sexual display (see Plate 2). These may be patches of bright color (e.g., the iridescent plumage of many hummingbirds) or accouterments such as the distinctive central rectrices of adult jaegers or the peculiar facial plumes of many alcids. Plumage "flashes" or "banner marks," such as the flicker's white rump or the wing patches of a White-winged Dove, may serve to distract potential predators momentarily and divert their "aim" to less vulnerable parts of the body. Wing or tail feathers (e.g., of the American Woodcock and Common Snipe) may be so shaped as to produce a sound used in courtship or territorial display.

Sexual Differences. Male and female birds of the same species may have strikingly different plumages. The difference may be permanent in adults (e.g., Northern Cardinal) or become accentuated during the breeding season (e.g., American Goldfinch). The plumages of many shorebirds, raptors, swifts, and other birds do not differ sexually; however, in those species which do show a difference, it is almost invariably the female which exhibits the duller plumage, perhaps to make her less conspicuous while nesting. In North America, the only exceptions to this "rule" are the phalaropes, in which the males are the less vividly colored and patterned and also incubate the eggs and perform other tasks usually relegated to female birds, and the Belted Kingfisher, in which the female has a rusty chest band that the male lacks. See also DIMORPHISM.

Seasonal Differences. The acquisition of an alternate (breeding or nuptial) plumage (see MOLT) is most striking in males (again except for the phalaropes) but may also occur in females. It may be only a minor change, e.g., the "cleaner" look of American Robins due to feather wear (see ABRA-SION), or a spectacular total transformation, e.g., the Common Loon or Scarlet Tanager. In sexually dimorphic species, the male often assumes a duller plumage resembling the female's in the pre-basic (post-nuptial) molt, e.g., Indigo Bunting. Seasonal plumages may also be adaptations to habitat, e.g., the white plumages of the ptarmigan and Snow Bunting, which become browner during the period when their habitat is less likely to be snow-covered. In the ptarmigan this period is the months of mid-summer, but the Snow Bunting becomes browner for its stay on more southerly wintering grounds.

Age Differences. All birds go through some degree of plumage change as they mature (see MOLT). In species which hatch with a full, often strikingly patterned covering of natal down, the first plumage change is a total metamorphosis into a full coat of contour feathers. This juvenal plumage may resemble that of one or both of the parents (e.g., Blue Jay); or resemble that of neither parent—whether the adults are sexually dimor-phic (e.g., frigatebirds) or not (Purple Gallinule, Plate 4). With the first pre-basic (post-juvenal) molt some species attain a "definitive" plumage, i.e., one indistinguishable from that of an adult of their species. But in many species the first basic (first winter) plumage is distinct from both the juvenal and the definitive adult plumages. In some sexually dimorphic species (e.g., Rose-breasted Grosbeak), the tendency to revert to a duller plumage after breeding diminishes with age, i.e., the older a male becomes, the less of his bright coloration he loses in the post-nuptial molt.

Streaking and spotting, typical of many juvenal plumages, tends to disappear or diminish with age, regardless of sex (e.g., Cedar Waxwing, Fig. 23). In a very few instances, juvenile birds have *brighter* plumage than adults of either sex. This occurs, for example, in young Downy and Hairy Woodpeckers, which have more extensive red areas on the crown than either parent until their first pre-basic (post-juvenal) molt.

Racial Differences and Phases. Geographical races of species tend to differ consistently in certain adaptive plumage characteristics. Western races of the Fox Sparrow, for example, are dark brown and generally un-streaked above, in striking contrast to their bright rufous and boldly streaked eastern counterparts (see SPECIATION; GLOGER'S RULE; ALLEN'S RULE; KELSO'S RULE). Permanent plumage differences may also occur among individuals of the same population of a single race, e.g., the dark, light, and intermediate "morphs" or phases in the jaegers and some rap-tors, the gray/red variations of the Screech Owl, and the "ringed" and "plain" types of the Common Murre. See POLYMORPHISM.

Externally Caused Differences. Diet is responsible for some plumage coloration, e.g., the bright salmon pink of the American Flamingo and the warm "peachy" color of the underparts of the Common Merganser. When the plants or animals containing these pigments are not consumed regularly, the color fades. Such color loss occurs infrequently in the wild but is fairly common among captive birds.

"Blooms" such as the pink suffusions which appear on the breasts of Roseate Terns and Franklin's Gulls in the breeding season may be produced by a special secretion of the oil gland and applied, like makeup, to the breast. The substance fades in the sun and air and the source presumably "dries up" during the non-breeding season.

An example of a frequent plumage variation which is purely adventitious is the "rusting" of the white head and neck of Snow Geese acquired by feeding in water or mud stained with iron ore. See also COLOR AND PATTERN.

Abnormal Variation. The plumage of hybrids often combines the characteristics of both parents or even produces "original," perhaps atavistic, colors and patterns (see HYBRIDIZATION and Fig. 11).

A disruption in the endocrine system caused by injury or disease can produce "cock-plumaged" females (see SEX, CHANGE OF) and, more rarely, "hen-plumaged" males. Another kind of sexual ambiguity, gynandromorphism, produces individuals with typical male plumage on one side of the body and typical female plumage on the other.

Genetic aberrations can produce: hairy-looking plumage due to an absence of barbicels in the contour feathers (accompanies some cases of albinism); weak wing and tail feathers which break off at the base when the affected bird tries to fly; and wing and tail feathers in which the rachis extends beyond the vane tip, giving an effect similar to the tail of a Chimney Swift.

For other *color* abnormalities, see ALBINISM; MELANISM; LEUCISM; SCHIZOCHROISM; ERYTHRISM; XANTHOCHROISM; and Plate 5.

CARE OF PLUMAGE. A bird's feathers become dirty, are eaten by feather mites and other pests (see ECTOPARASITE), and lose oils essential for insulation and waterproofing. In order to stay healthy, therefore, birds must constantly maintain their plumage by a combination of preventative and corrective measures, such as PREENING; ANTING; BATHING; DUSTING; SMOKE BATHING; OILING; SUNNING; SCRATCHING.

USE. If we ask what benefits a bird derives from its feathers, the first answer likely to occur to us is: the ability to fly. Aerodynamically, plumage is the ideal body covering: it is light; it can be streamlined by compressing the body feathers to minimize drag; the wing and tail feathers are flexible enough to allow high maneuverability yet stiff enough to use wind power for lift and motion (see FLIGHT).

Control of body temperature, especially heat, may be an even more important function of plumage. The semiplume and down "underwear" provides insulation next to the skin, and the overlapping contour feathers can be "fluffed" to trap a maximum of warm air and "closed" to insulate swimming birds from cold water (see TEMPERATURE, BODY). Embryonic temperature and that of naked nestlings are also maintained by the natural insulation of parental plumage in addition to the "direct heat" applied through the brood patch. "Slippery" semiplumes and down may also serve as an "anti-friction" mechanism around the bases of wings and legs.

Plumage colors and patterns play essential roles in recognition, display, and protection against predators (see COLOR AND PATTERN, *Concealment*; DISPLAY; and Plates 2 and 3).

Female ducks, geese, and swans line their nests with down feathers plucked from their breasts, and some songbirds use "found" feathers both for lining and for decoration.

Feathers also serve as a binding material in the pellets regurgitated by bird-eating raptors, and grebes eat their own feathers to serve a similar "digestive" function.

PLUME HUNTERS. Men who shot birds, especially certain species of herons, in order to sell their nuptial plumes to milliners and other purveyors of feather fashions. A thriving occupation well into the twentieth century before it was outlawed. See CONSERVATION for a more detailed account.

PLUM ISLAND National Wildlife Refuge (Massachusetts). See NEWBURYPORT.

PLUMULE (or plumula; pl.: plumulae). An individual down feather. See FEATHER; DOWN; and Fig. 9.

PNEUMATIZATION (NOO-muh-tih-ZAY-shun) **OF BONE.** The remarkable process by which the bones of birds are hollowed and filled with air sacs connected to the respiratory system. See SKELETON.

POCHARD (POACH-erd or POTCH-erd; even POKE-erd or POCK-erd). A name, little used in North America, which here is synonymous with the genus *Aythya*, the bay ducks. The Redhead, which resembles the Eurasian species known simply as Pochard or Common Pochard, has been referred to colloquially as American Pochard. The word has no clear or interesting provenance.

PODOTHECA (POD-uh-THEE-kuh). The leathery or horny "hide" which covers unfeathered parts of a bird's leg and foot; on close inspection it is seen to be textured in arrangements of plates or scales, which vary among different groups of birds. See LEG/FOOT.

POIKILOTHERMAL (POY-kill-oh-THUR-mul) (or poikilothermic or poikilothermous). Cold-blooded; i.e., with body temperature fluctuating with that of the environment. All animals except mammals and birds are "poikilotherms," and the young of bird species which are born naked are in fact "cold-blooded" until at least partially fledged. Opposite of HOMOIOTHERMAL. See TEMPERATURE, BODY.

POINT PELEE National Park (Ontario). A tiny (6 square miles) peninsula jutting south into Lake Erie, 35 miles east of Windsor, Ontario/Detroit, Michigan; famed for the spectacular concentrations of migrant birds during both the spring and the fall passage. The park also encompasses substantial samples of deciduous woodland, marsh, and of course shore and open water, so that on a good day during a migratory wave, seeing over a hundred species of birds at Point Pelee is practically routine. Migration peaks are mid-May and mid-September (see Appendix III for extended period). See also Stewart's guide *Point Pelee* (Detroit, 1977).

POINT REYES. See OBSERVATORY.

POISON. For lead poisoning, pesticides, etc., see MAN-MADE THREATS TO BIRDLIFE; for "food poisoning," e.g., salmonellosis and botulism, see DISEASE.

POLE TRAP. A steel spring-jaw trap fixed to the top of a pole and set where birds of prey are likely to perch. This was once a very popular method of killing "chicken hawks" and other species deemed (usually mistakenly) to be a threat to poultry or livestock. The indiscriminate destruction of any North American predator is now prohibited by federal law and punishable by fines and jail sentences and the use of pole traps *expressly* forbidden (see LAWS).

POLITICS, BIRDS IN. At least one famous North American instance. During the investigation by the House Committee on Un-American Activities of former State Department official Alger Hiss in 1948 as an alleged Communist subversive, it was crucial to establish the veracity of the testimony of Whittaker Chambers, himself a former Communist of questionable character. Chambers claimed intimate association with Hiss and, among many other corroborating details, noted that Hiss was an enthusiastic birdwatcher and had once been excited at having seen a Prothonotary Warbler along the Potomac River. By feigning casual good-fellowship in subsequent interrogation, Richard Nixon and U.S. Representative John McDowell (R.–Pa.), also a birdwatcher, elicited from Hiss a confirmation of his encounter with the species and excitement over it. "Beautiful yellow head," Alger Hiss exclaimed, "a gorgeous bird." He was ultimately convicted on two counts of perjury and sentenced to ten years in jail.

POLLEX. The first digit, or "thumb," of a bird's hand. See SKELETON, *Bones of the Wing,* and Fig. 19.

POLLINATION. Pollination by birds is most prevalent in tropical regions, where a relatively wide range of bird species sip nectar and take insects from the many flowers with deep corollas. In North America, hummingbirds are by far the most effective avian pollinators, though other insectivorous/nectivorous species, e.g., warblers and orioles, doubtless make some contribution to plant reproduction here. However, it should be emphasized that the combined effect of all bird pollinators is insignificant compared to the role played by insects and the wind.

In the southwestern U.S., where hummingbirds are nearly ubiquitous, it is not unusual to see hummers with yellow faces. Visiting bird-watchers unable to find a yellow-headed species in their field guides may be told by locals that they have been seeing "pollinated hummingbirds."

POLYANDRY (PAHL-ee-AN-dree). In general, a female mating with more than one male. With respect to birds, it may refer to the normal breeding behavior of those species wherein the female copulates with two or more males and lays several clutches of eggs which are then incubated exclusively by the males, e.g., as in the case of the Northern Phalarope; or to atypical multiple matings by females in populations which have an excess of males. It is not a common phenomenon among birds in either case.

POLYGAMY (puh-LIG-uh-mee). In general, a member of one sex mating with two or more members of the opposite sex. With respect to birds, the term may be used in a narrow sense to refer to species which normally form pair bonds with more than one mate or more broadly to include any multiple copulation by either sex. It encompasses POLYANDRY and POLYGYNY, but is sometimes used as a synonym for the latter. The occurrence of polygamy (in the broader sense) can be influenced by population densities (an excess of males or females) and seems to be more prevalent in open-country habitats. See also HOMOSEXUALITY.

POLYGYNY (puh-LIDGE-uh-nee). In general, the mating of a male with more than one female. Among birds, wrens are conspicuously polygynous, but it is common behavior in many bird families. Compare POLYGAMY and POLYANDRY.

POLYMORPHISM. The occurrence of two or more stable forms—often called "morphs" or "phases"—existing within a single population of a species. The most familiar form of polymorphism in birds appears in plumage variation, e.g.: the light, dark, and intermediate phases of the Northern Fulmar; the white and "blue" phases of the "Lesser" Snow

Goose; the light and dark phases of the Rough-legged, Ferruginous, Red-tailed, Swainson's, and Short-tailed Hawks; the red and gray phases of the Ruffed Grouse and Screech and Flammulated Owls; the "great white" and gray phases of the Great Blue Heron; the white and red phases of the Red-dish Egret; the light and dark ("Cory's") phases of the Least Bittern; the almost infinite variations in the alternate (nuptial) plumage of the male Ruff; the light, dark, and intermediate phases among the jaeger species (especially Parasitic and Pomarine); and the "ringed" or "bridled" and "plain" phases of the Common Murre. However, the term may also be used to describe the same kind of regularly occurring differences in size, egg coloration or pattern, or even functions such as clutch size. When only two distinct morphs occur—as with the bridled and plain Common Murres—it is not incorrect to refer to the species in question as "dimorphic." However, that term is widely used to describe sexual, racial, seasonal, and age differences which do *not* exemplify true polymorphism. Even cases in which "many morphs" occur within the same species are not always polymorphic in the strict genetic sense, e.g.: the zone of secondary hybridization where "red-shafted" and "yellow-shafted" races of the Common Flicker meet and produce an assortment of hybrids; or the large number of distinct racial variations of the Song Sparrow continentwide; or aberrant populations of a particular species which perpetuate some form of mutation such as albinism in many variations. None of these are genetically permanent variations within a single population.

The fact that variation is constant in a polymorphic species does not mean that the different morphs always occur in equal numbers or equal proportions within the geographical range of the species; rather, the opposite tends to be the case. The "purpose" of polymorphism seems to be to allow a species to "choose" by natural selection the morph which carries the advantage in a particular habitat or climate. Thus gray phases of the Ruffed Grouse apparently have greater survivability in coniferous forest, because that coloration is more cryptic in that habitat, whereas the red morphs survive better in deciduous forest for the same reason (Gullion and Marshall, 1968). Obviously then, the "safer" phase, whether red or gray, will predominate in any given locality. In other species, e.g., the White-throated Sparrow, survivability seems to have little to do with the perpetuation of polymorphism.

POLYTYPIC (PAHL-ee-TIPP-ik). A taxonomic category which contains two or more representatives of the category immediately below it. A polytypic family contains two or more genera; a polytypic genus contains more than one species; etc. Compare MONOTYPIC.

POMARINE (POH-muh-reen) (formerly Pomatorhine) (Jaeger). Literally, "flap-nosed," referring to the cere-like "saddle" unique to the bills of all

skuas and jaegers and not peculiar to the one species. The flap overlaps the
ridge of the upper mandible from the base to just beyond the end of the
nostrils, which it overlaps. See NOSTRILS.

POOR-WILL. Standard English name for a species of nightjar, *Phalaenoptilus nuttallii*, which breeds from southwestern Canada to central
Mexico. The name is a literal approximation of its call. Two other nightjar
species (genus *Otophanes*) of Mexico and northern Central America have
"poor-will" in their names, but "poor-will" is not a good "translation" of
the call of either. See NIGHTJAR.

Phalaenoptilus is the only bird in the world known to "hibernate."
See, however, TORPIDITY.

POPULATION. The total number of individuals in a given area. The
term can be used to describe all of the individuals which occupy a particular plot of habitat at a particular time, e.g., the breeding-bird population of
a specific pine-oak woodland; or to refer to all the living members of a species, e.g., the world population of Brown Creepers. The study of *population dynamics* asks how, why, and to what degree populations change, and
what factors are involved in limiting such changes and maintaining a balance among populations of different organisms.

Answering these questions requires first of all that we accurately
count and recount the number of birds in a population over an extended
period of time—a tedious chore which has yet to be facilitated by any sophisticated labor-saving device. Once the statistics are gathered, the student of populations must evaluate the myriad variables—food availability,
predation, disease, weather, habitat destruction, etc.—which may affect
the stability of the community of birds in question.

Because of these difficulties, irrefutable conclusions about specific
problems in population dynamics are still rare in the literature. However, a
few facts have been established; theories abound; and many intriguing examples of population changes have been recorded.

• A stable population implies a birth rate in balance with the death
rate.

• Birds tend to have as many young as prevailing conditions, such as
the length of season, will allow and do not significantly control their population by manipulating their own birth rates.

• Birds sustain an enormous death rate, particularly as juveniles. The
yearly death rate of *adult* passerines is between 40 and 60 percent or more,
but the percentage of *eggs* which reach full adulthood averages only about
12 percent, on the basis of available information (see also AGE).

• Food availability seems to exercise great influence on population
stability. Birds are known to: (1) time breeding to coincide with maximum
food availability; (2) stagger egg laying (many raptors and large water

birds), so that the younger birds are "automatically sacrificed" when food is scarce; (3) suffer greater mortalities in years or seasons of food shortage due to droughts or other environmental factors; (4) leave areas where food is scarce in proportion to populations (e.g., northern raptors, finches, waxwings); and (5) become more aggressive when feeding in flocks in times of food scarcity.

• Though predation and disease may also be important influences on populations, solid documentation of their effects is difficult to collect and is therefore very thin so far.

• Most population changes seem to be unpredictable, but a few (e.g., Ruffed Grouse) have been thoroughly studied and proven to occur in regular cycles.

• Introduced species are good material for population studies. After the Common Starling became successfully established in North America, it went through a period of alarming increase, but its numbers then tapered off, and its population now seems relatively stable. This pattern is common among introduced animals and seems to indicate that initially alien organisms can "run wild" in an ecosystem in which they are not "naturally" controlled but that such controls rapidly evolve. Introduced species can also be expected to influence populations of native species with which they compete for food and nesting sites (see INTRODUCED BIRDS).

To form a notion of the difficulties inherent in studying bird populations, try to determine exactly how many individuals of a given species visit your feeder regularly. Many people suppose that they are host to a single flock of a dozen chickadees when in fact they are helping to support several times that many, visiting in alternating shifts. This is virtually impossible to notice unless the birds are artificially marked or individual plumage characters can be discerned. See also DISTRIBUTION; TERRITORY; COLONY; ABUNDANCE; AGE; CENSUS.

Many interesting studies have been done in this field; see the Bibliography.

PORTLANDICA. In the broadest sense refers to a distinctive subadult plumage of any tern in the genus *Sterna*. The term's usual context, however, is the problem of recognizing Common and Arctic Terns encountered in this plumage and distinguishing between the two.

Portlandica terns are immature birds (1–3 years old), most of which remain in the Southern Hemisphere wintering area of their species until they are old enough to breed. Exceptional individuals occasionally return prematurely to their natal areas with adult birds, where they often confuse Northern Hemisphere birdwatchers unfamiliar with the plumage.

In typical portlandica, the mantle color is essentially uniform gray as in the adult plumage, but the black carpal ("wrist") bar (above) is retained from the juvenal plumage; the black cap is present to a variable extent, but there is always some degree (usually extensive) of white frontal area (forehead); the underparts lack any trace of gray shading; the bill and legs are black; and the primaries and elongated rectrices are often (not always) less than fully grown. Short-winged, short-tailed birds look distinctly smaller than and fly in a manner different from breeding adults of their own species; they rather suggest some species of marsh (*Chlidonias*) tern in winter plumage. Common and Arctic portlandicas are distinguished chiefly by a difference in rump color—gray in the Common, white in the Arctic—and from below by the pattern of black in the primary tips cited in many guides as a means of separating adults of these species.

Historically, portlandica-plumaged birds have occurred rarely in the Northern Hemisphere, the name deriving from *Sterna portlandica*, the binomial coined by British ornithologists who mistook an individual of this kind for a new species. But within the last decade, there has been a great, inexplicable increase in portlandica records, with over 800 recorded at Monomoy (Cape Cod), Massachusetts, July 6, 1979.

Numerous notes on portlandica have been published in *British Birds* since 1969; see also R. A. Forster, *Bird Observer* (1980) 8:91–93.

POULT (pollt). A young domestic fowl, especially a turkey.

POULTRY. Domestic fowl, especially chickens, turkeys, guinea fowl, pheasants, and, in the very broadest usage, ducks and geese.

POWDER DOWN. A modified type of body feather which disintegrates at the tip into a fine dust made up of scale-like particles. These feathers occur in most birds and may be dispersed evenly among the body feathers, but in a few groups (e.g., herons) they occur in well-developed patches. The powder gives a bloom to the plumage and may play a role in cleaning and/or waterproofing the feathers.

PRAIRIE. A broadly inclusive term used in North America to describe treeless, often "rolling," grassy plains such as once covered much of the continent from the Mississippi Valley to the Rocky Mountains and from the boreal forests of Canada to the deserts of Texas. In addition to grasses, prairies nurture many other characteristic plant species, often including many legumes. More restricted botanical communities are recognized under such names as "tallgrass" prairie. Sadly, these unique plant and animal communities have today largely been replaced by farmland and suburban sprawl and exist in a pristine condition only in a few preserved patches (see *National Geographic*, Vol. 157, No. 1, January 1980, for a map of remnant spots of tallgrass prairie and a glimpse of its former glory).

In central Eurasia, land with the above characteristics is usually called "steppe."

Typical North American "prairie birds" (excluding many water birds typical of prairie marshes) are Swainson's Hawk, Greater and Lesser Prairie Chickens, Sandhill Crane, Mountain Plover, Marbled Godwit, Franklin's Gull, Burrowing Owl, Sprague's Pipit, meadowlarks, Lark Bunting, and McCown's and Chestnut-collared Longspurs.

Prairie Warblers are birds of second-growth and other shrublands and therefore are found in true prairies even less frequently than Connecticut Warblers are found in Connecticut.

PRAIRIE CHICKEN. Standard English name for 2 species of grouse in the genus *Tympanuchus* (family Tetraonidae; order Galliformes), both of which are endemic to North America. The prairie chickens (Greater and Lesser) are famed for the elaborate courtship "dances" performed by males in spring (see DISPLAY; LEK; and Plate 2). The dance is accompanied by an indescribably haunting sound and the inflation of colorful air sacs in the neck.

The prairie chickens have declined as a result of the development of their habitat—which is correctly identified in their name. The eastern race of the Greater Prairie Chicken, known as the Heath Hen, became extinct in 1932 and another race is currently listed as endangered (see ENDANGERED BIRDS).

For general family characteristics, see GROUSE.

PRECOCIAL (pree-KO-shul). Describes young birds which are relatively well-developed at hatching. Typically precocial young have a thick coat of natal down (ptilopaedic), leave the nest soon after hatching (nidifugous), and feed themselves at an early stage. Contrast with ALTRICIAL. See YOUNG, DEVELOPMENT OF.

PREDATION (predator, predacious). The killing and eating of one animal by another (excluding parasites). The word "predator" is often used in a much narrower sense to refer to hawks, eagles, and falcons, owls, and shrikes, i.e., birds which habitually take warm-blooded prey; but it is no less accurate to refer to herons as predacious on fish or flycatchers as predatory on insects.

Though it is one of the most pervasive, ineluctable facts of life on this planet, predation has strong negative connotations for many—perhaps most—people. It suggests a common perception of the world ecosystem as a realm of chaotic cruelty—"nature red in tooth and claw"—where certain "vicious" animals (e.g., wolves, bears, big cats, raptorial birds) prey "mercilessly" on a majority of "gentle creatures" (e.g., mice, antelopes, chickadees). This view is a largely self-serving trick of the human mind rooted in a widespread ignorance of basic biology. For one thing, our anthropomorphism is ludicrously selective. The little songbirds whose "murder" by hawks we find deplorable are themselves highly predatory, the difference being that we have a hard time "feeling sorry" for the invertebrate prey of tits and warblers. The falcon that attacks the "gentle" heron is a brute beast, but the heron is welcome to stab all the "cold," slimy (i.e., inhuman!) fish and frogs it likes without being damned as a "predator." The final irony is that we sensitive humans are the ultimate predators, the only species that deliberately rears other animals for the express purpose of killing and eating them and the only one to kill for fun. Neither these practices nor the kills of wild predators need be condemned; they should simply be viewed in their proper context—as a crucial balance in a biological system that generates an unimaginable mass of matter through continual growth—matter which must be consumed as fast as it is produced if the ecosystem is to remain in equilibrium and a healthy diversity of organisms is to survive.

While the need for predation as a natural "equalizer" can hardly be overstated, specific effects of predation—both good and bad—are often exaggerated. For example, Golden Eagles have been persecuted on the ground that they are a serious threat to livestock, especially sheep, whereas in fact these eagles feed mainly on rabbits. Equally erroneous is the notion that predation by Purple Martins can be an effective means of mosquito control.

The relatively scant data that exist seem to indicate that the impact of insectivorous birds feeding on outbreaks of pest insects or of hawks and owls on "explosions" of rodents is normally quite small, though greater, of course, in proportion to the concentration of predators. In years when northern raptors, e.g., Snowy and Short-eared Owls and Rough-legged Hawks, are particularly abundant on their wintering grounds, rodent populations there presumably suffer a greater mortality rate from predation. However, it is arguable that, since predators characteristically prey on weaker or less competent individuals of a species, the long-term effect of predation may be beneficial to the prey species (see NATURAL SELECTION). For types of prey, see FOOD/FEEDING; for "predatory" in the sense of one species stealing food from another, see PIRACY.

PREEN GLAND. See OIL GLAND; PREENING.

PREENING. The cleaning, manipulation, and arrangement of individual feathers of a bird's plumage using the bill; in the broadest sense, it includes the application of oil from the "preen gland" (see OIL GLAND).

In the course of normal activities, a bird's plumage becomes dirty, wet, matted with old preen oil, infested with parasites (see ECTOPARASITE), and the barbs of individual feathers become separated. All are potentially hazardous to the health and well-being of a bird (see PLUMAGE,

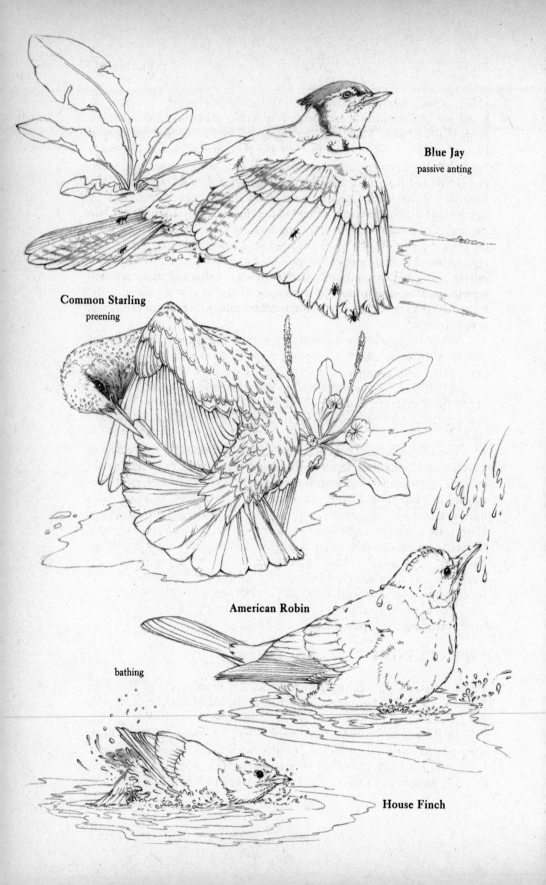

Blue Jay
passive anting

Common Starling
preening

American Robin

bathing

House Finch

Uses), and preening is the innate activity—performed regularly and frequently—by which these conditions are rectified.

The basic preening action involves grasping an individual feather at its base and "nibbling" along its length to the tip or simply drawing the bill along the feather in a single, less meticulous action. This reattaches separated barbs, removes water and dirt, and in some instances applies oil. During preening, birds often come upon ectoparasites, which they usually seize and eat. The process involves all parts of the plumage and requires birds to assume an amusing variety of contorted postures (see, for example, the Common Starling in Fig. 16 and the Hermit Thrush in Fig. 14). Swimming birds which preen while sitting on the surface execute what is known as a "rolling preen," in which they turn over on their side while floating with one leg in the air and preen their belly with their bill, apparently in perfect comfort.

The one area of the body which birds cannot reach with their own bill is the head. This is "preened" by SCRATCHING, by rubbing with the wing, or with the assistance of another bird (see ALLOPREENING).

Birds often engage in prolonged preening sessions during which—barring disturbance—the whole plumage is tended to, virtually feather by feather. A complete preening operation of this kind often follows other plumage-maintenance activities, such as BATHING, DUSTING, or ANTING, and the body feathers are typically "fluffed" for easy access. Birds also may be seen to make preening gestures at any time while in the midst of some other activity, e.g., feeding or simply out of "nervousness" (see REDIRECTION).

PRIBILOF ISLANDS (Alaska). Four islands in the Bering Sea about 250 miles north of the Aleutian chain and 285 miles off the west coast of Alaska. The two largest islands, St. Paul and St. George, have spectacular seabird colonies during the summer months, and in May and September rarities from Siberia are regular. St. Paul has modest tourist facilities (one hotel), some rudimentary roads, and airline connections to and from Anchorage several times a week, weather permitting. The latter is predictably unpredictable and characteristically poor (fog, snow, cold, and wind even during the summer). Seabird specialties include Tufted and Horned Puffins, Parakeet, Crested, and Least Auklets, Red-legged Kittiwake, and Red-faced Cormorant. Palearctic migrants and strays which have been recorded include Whooper Swan, Smew, Steller's Sea Eagle, Mongolian Plover, Greenshank, Spotted Redshank, Sharp-tailed, Common, and Wood Sandpipers, three species of stint, Common and Fork-tailed Swifts, Skylark, Eye-browed Thrush, Siberian Rubythroat, Grey Wagtail, and

FIG. 16. *Plumage maintenance.* It is essential for a bird's well-being that it keep its feathers clean and free of parasites.

Brambling. For more detail, see Kenyon and Phillips, *Auk* (1965), 82:624–35.

PRIMARIES. The flight feathers (remiges) which are attached to the bones of the "hand" (manus). All flying birds have between 9 and 12 primaries and the number tends to be the same within groupings of closely related birds. The primaries are numbered from the innermost to the outermost. Perching (passerine) birds have 10 primaries but in some songbird (oscine) families the 10th (outermost) is greatly reduced, in which case it is known as the remicle. These families, including swallows, pipits, wood warblers, icterids, tanagers, and fringillid finches, and parts of other families are sometimes called 9-primaried songbirds. See WING and Figs. 1, 19, and 25.

PROCRYPTIC. Blending with the natural background; disguised so as to be ignored by potential predators (compare ANTICRYPTIC). The nightjars, bitterns, and rails are notable for their procryptic plumage among North American birds. See also COLOR AND PATTERN, *Concealment,* and Plate 3.

PROLACTIN (pro-LAK-tin). A hormone secreted by the pituitary gland (see ENDOCRINE SYSTEM) which controls the onset of "broodiness," the development of a brood patch, and affects various forms of sexual behavior; also stimulates production of PIGEON'S MILK.

PRONUNCIATION. For treatment of pronunciation of English terms in this book, see p. 10. See also LATIN NAMES.

PROTECTION OF BIRDS. See LAWS; CONSERVATION.

PROTHONOTARY (pruh-THON-uh-tair-ee or PROH-thuh-NOH-tuh-ree) (Warbler). The chief clerk or notary of the English court system and in some U.S. state courts. Also one of seven members of the College of Prothonotaries Apostolic of the Catholic Church, who concern themselves with recording canonizations, signing papal bulls, and other clerical responsibilities. The robe of an English prothonotary includes a saffron-yellow cowl and therefore is an apt metaphor for the brilliant golden head and breast plumage of *Protonotaria citrea.*

PROVENTRICULUS (PRO-ven-TRIK-yuh-luss). The first (uppermost) of two enlargements in a bird's digestive tract which together function like the human stomach. See DIGESTIVE SYSTEM and Fig. 19.

PROXIMAL (PROCKS-ih-mul). Nearest to the main body. The term is little used in ornithology, and then is generally synonymous with BASAL.

For example, the proximal (or basal) portion of a drake King Eider's wing is largely white. Opposite of DISTAL.

PSILOPAEDIC (SYE-low-PEE-dik). Naked when hatched; completely lacking in natal down or with only a few tufts on the head and back. See PTILOPAEDIC; ALTRICIAL; YOUNG, DEVELOPMENT OF.

PSITTACOSIS (SIT-uh-COH-siss). Parrot fever. Once thought to be a viral disease of birds of the parrot family which in rare instances was transmitted to man; a parrot-restricted form of ornithosis. This group of diseases is now thought to be bacterial in nature and has been redefined under the name CHLAMYDIOSIS. See also DISEASE.

PTARMIGAN (TAR-muh-gun). Standard English name for 3 or 4 species (depending on taxonomy) of grouse in the genus *Lagopus* (family Tetraonidae; order Galliformes), one of which (White-tailed Ptarmigan) is endemic to North America.

Ptarmigan are birds of the arctic and subarctic regions, including the arctic-alpine zones of high mountains. They are noted for a sequence of cryptic plumages that are molted to match their habitat; as the tundra turns from variegated brown to snow white, so do the ptarmigan. The Rock Ptarmigan is among the few birds to remain in the High Arctic during the winter, when it survives by feeding on seeds in places which the wind has swept clear of snow or by digging through the snow crust with its sharp claws. These birds are a staple and favorite food of the Innuit.

Choate (1973–BIOGRAPHY) guesses that "ptarmigan" springs from a Gaelic word, *tarmachan*, which he says means "mountaineer" or "white game" (?); he notes that the superfluous "p" was an error in classical scholarship (many Greek words with "t" sounds begin "pt") committed in 1684.

For general family characteristics, see GROUSE.

PTERODACTYL (TAIR-uh-DAK-tull). Any member of an ancient order (Pterosauria) of prehistoric (Jurassic and Cretaceous) flying *reptiles*. Pteranodon, familiar to most young dinosaur enthusiasts, was one of these.

PTERYLA (TERR-ih-luh) (pl.: pterylae). Technical term for FEATHER TRACT(S).

PTERYLOSIS (tair-ih-LOH-siss). Plumage; the distribution and arrangement of feathers over the body. Except in the Ostrich, penguins, and two other small groups of birds (none of which occur in North America), the body feathers all arise from a pattern of tracts, technically known as pterylae. See FEATHER TRACTS; PLUMAGE.

PTILOPAEDIC (TYE-low-PEE-dik). Covered with down when hatched. See PSILOPAEDIC; PRECOCIAL; YOUNG, DEVELOPMENT OF.

PTILOPODY (tih-LOP-uh-dee). A technical term meaning feathered toes and legs, as is characteristic, for example, of the ptarmigan; see Fig. 12 and LEG/FOOT.

PTILOSIS (tuh-LOW-sis). Technical term for plumage; all the feathers of a bird's body. See PLUMAGE.

PUBLICATIONS, ORNITHOLOGICAL AND BIRDWATCHING. See PERIODICALS and the bibliography for that entry.

PUFFIN. Standard English name for 3 species of auks with white, "clown-like" faces and large, laterally compressed bills which acquire highly colored "sheaths" in alternate (breeding) plumage (see BILL). Two of these birds (Horned and Common Puffin) belong to the genus *Fratercula*; the Tufted Puffin is the sole member of the genus *Lunda* (family Alcidae; order Charadriiformes). All breed and winter in North America.

The puffins all nest in burrows which they excavate in the usually shallow soil of sea islands or remote coasts; they winter at sea. The Common Puffin inhabits the North Atlantic and is replaced by the Horned and Tufted Puffins in the North Pacific.

"Puffin" is thought to derive either from the bloated, i.e., "puffed up," appearance of the adult birds or from the powder-puff appearance of the chicks in down.

For family characteristics, see AUK.

PULLET. A young domestic hen; in the strictest sense, one under a year old.

PULLUS (POOL-us). A young bird from the time of hatching until it is more or less independent of its parents.

PYGMY OWL. Standard English collective name for the 13 species of small (about 7 inches), mainly diurnal and crepuscular owls in the genus *Glaucidium* (family Strigidae; order Strigiformes), 2 of which, the Ferruginous (Pygmy) Owl and the (Northern) Pygmy Owl, are resident in western North America.

To most birdwatchers, these little owls are irresistible, though they are widely shunned as omens of death in Latin America. They can often be readily attracted by imitating their staccato tooting, which in turn often attracts a "mob" of small songbird species (see Fig. 14).

For family characteristics, see OWL.

COLOR PLATES 4–6

Plate 4. *Plumage variations.* All species of birds exhibit some form of variation in the color and/or pattern of their plumage, but the variations are related to a number of different phenomena and occur with varying degrees of frequency. Almost all birds have a distinctive juvenal plumage, and many have a first basic (winter) plumage which bears little resemblance to the adult plumage. The latter is exemplified by the Purple Gallinule [1], in which the immature birds are drably colored whereas adult birds *of both sexes* are arrayed in identical splendor. Many species exhibit a pronounced *sexual* "dimorphism," in which the male (in the great majority of cases) wears the more spectacular plumage—as with the pair of Vermilion Flycatchers [2]. In these instances, the first basic (winter) plumage of immature birds usually resembles that of the females. Another common form of plumage variation is *seasonal* dimorphism, in which a striking change of appearance is effected with the pre-alternate (pre-nuptial) and pre-basic (post-nuptial) molts. All ages and both sexes of Black Guillemots [3] are largely white in basic (winter) plumage, and all acquire a mainly black alternate (breeding) plumage. Wide-ranging species often evolve distinctive plumage (and other) *"racial"* differences in the extremities of their range (see SPECIATION). The males of the eastern and western races of the Northern Oriole [4] are so differently marked that until recently they were considered to be separate species, called Baltimore (lower) and Bullock's Orioles. The females of these two subspecies are also readily identified, but birds in first basic (winter) plumage are nearly identical. The two races of Savannah Sparrow [5] also exemplify subspecific or racial variation, but their differences also demonstrate *adaptive coloration.* The "Ipswich" race (lower) is notably pale, matching the pallid earth tones of its preferred coastal beach and dune habitat; the "Labrador" Savannah Sparrow lives in more richly colored open country of the interior. There is a general tendency for races of a given species which breed in warmer, more humid habitats to be darker than those breeding in cool, dry ones (Gloger's Rule). Finally, populations of certain species exhibit color variations unrelated to sex, age, season, or geography—a phenomenon called *polymorphism.* Polymorphic species such as Rough-legged Hawks [6] contain markedly contrasting individuals in light and dark (or red and gray as in Screech Owls) "phases" or "morphs." In many cases a full range of "intermediate" plumages also occurs. See PLUMAGE; POLYMORPHISM.

Plate 5: *Aberrant plumages.* In rare instances, we encounter birds which, due to some physiological malfunction or dietary deficiency, wear a plumage bearing little or no resemblance to their normal one. The commonest of these color disorders is ALBINISM, as exemplified by two of the Purple Martins [1] shown next to a normal bird. Partial albinism is much more frequent than total. Abnormal paleness such as that of the Dovekie [2] is termed SCHIZOCHROISM or LEUCISM; it results from an absence of pigment and in some cases is closely akin to albinism, but its causes apparently vary. The barely recognizable American Robin [3] is afflicted with MELANISM, the deposition of an excess of dark pigment in the feathers. The golden Evening Grosbeak [4] pictured next to a normal male is known as a "lutino" among aviculturists, but XANTHOCHROISM is the more technical term for its condition; its body has failed to produce the darker pigments which normally combine with yellow in some parts of its plumage. ERYTHRISM is the term for high concentrations of red pigment in plumage. The commonest examples are normal birds, such as the red race of Ruffed Grouse [5] shown next to one of the gray extremes. The red "phases" or "morphs" of Screech Owls, Least Bitterns, and other species also occur normally, but there are references in the literature to (mostly galliform) birds which are abnormally "erythristic." This is not to be confused with the red stain sometimes acquired by birds (e.g., Snow Geese) feeding in water or earth with a high iron content.

1

2

3

4

5

Plate 6. *Endangered birds of North America* are those considered to be "in danger of extinction throughout all or a significant portion of [their] range." There are currently eight such species: California Condor [1], Bald Eagle [2], Kirtland's Warbler [3], Bachman's Warbler [4], Whooping Crane [5], Ivory-billed Woodpecker [6], Red-cockaded Woodpecker [7], and Eskimo Curlew [8]. In addition, we have illustrated three endangered subspecies: American Peregrine Falcon [9], Dusky Seaside Sparrow [10], and Florida Everglade (Snail) Kite [11]. For accounts of the present status of these birds, see ENDANGERED BIRDS.

PYGOSTYLE (PYE-guh-style). A "tailbone" consisting of the fused vertebrae at the end of a bird's backbone; the plowshare bone. See SKELETON and Fig. 19.

PYRRHULOXIA (peer-uh-LOCKS-ee-uh). Standard English name for a single species of large, crested finch, *Cardinalis* (*Pyrrhuloxia*) *sinuata* (family Fringillidae or Emberizidae; order Passeriformes). It breeds from southern Arizona and Texas south to central Mexico; it prefers arid scrublands. The name is a somewhat muddy classical compound which refers to the red in the plumage and the curved, somewhat parrot-like mandibles; something like "crooked-billed cardinal" may have been intended. See FINCH.

Q

QUAIL. Standard English name for about 23 members of the family Phasianidae (order Galliformes), which also includes the wood quail, partridges, francolins, jungle fowl (wild chickens), pheasants, and peacocks. Six species of quail (including the Bobwhite) breed in North America, several of which are North American endemics.

The relatively few species of American quail have been placed in a subfamily of their own, the Odontophorinae. These are small (7 to 9 inches), squat, ground-hunting, largely herbivorous birds (seeds, fruit, some insects) that prefer open woodland or scrub habitats. They are somberly colored on the whole but strikingly patterned, and all have distinctive, loud whistled calls. Most are decorated with improbable head plumes.

Quail make a shallow scrape on the ground, often concealed under a bush or other cover. This nest may be unlined or contain fragments picked from nearby plants. The eggs are characteristically numerous (to 28 in a single clutch; 8–15 average) and very variable in color and pattern among different species: white to dark buff; immaculate, finely speckled or heavily splotched with buff, reddish, or dark brown.

Quail vocalizations comprise a great variety of distinctive, penetrating whistles and "well-articulated" phrases (e.g., *bob white*) as well as low "conversational" cluckings and sharp, abrupt alarm calls. Males of some species have characteristic breeding "songs," and a few species are known to engage in DUETTING.

The quail are distributed nearly worldwide (absent from southern South America—except for game-bird introductions—and the most northerly parts of the Holarctic region). The American quail achieve their greatest diversity in the West and Southwest, with only one species, the

Bobwhite, occupying most of the continent east of the Mississippi and south of the coniferous forest zone.

"Quail" originated with a distinctive call of the Eurasian *Coturnix* quail, but catches the effect of the sounds made by the American species.

See references in the Bibliography under GALLINACEOUS BIRDS.

QUILL. In the vernacular, an entire long feather such as a primary or tail feather, the former used in colonial times and earlier as a pen. In respect to the technical anatomy of a feather, it may refer to the stiff, but light, central "spine" (calamus and rachis together), i.e., the "shaft," or to the calamus alone. See FEATHER and Fig. 9.

R

RACE. An "unofficial" alternative term for subspecies. The subspecies *Seiurus noveboracensis notabilis* is known in English as the Grinnell's "race" of the Northern Waterthrush. See NOMENCLATURE.

RACHIS (RAY-kiss). The stiff central spine of a feather from the point where the vane begins to the tip (distal end), i.e., excluding the calamus. See FEATHER and Fig. 9.

RADAR. The development of increasingly powerful and sophisticated radar technology beginning during the Second World War (1940) has greatly advanced our knowledge of specific details of nocturnal migration which were once undetectable.

Essentially, radar (radio detecting and ranging) involves sending into the air very high-frequency radio waves which reflect off the surface of any object they encounter. The returning images are collected by a large dish-like receiver and projected onto a viewing screen.

Radar was developed, of course, to detect enemy aircraft at long range and at night, but even in the earliest days, an unexpected type of "echo" was picked up. These "angels," as radar technicians named them, were eventually proven to be migrating birds.

Using this system to detect high-flying nocturnal migrants (see MIGRATION), ornithologists have been able to "see" for the first time the number of birds involved in migratory movements (far greater than previously suspected); to detect specific directions and routes taken (often more varied than imagined); and to obtain accurate data on timing, speed, elevation, and correlation with weather patterns. When combined with ground observation of migrants in the daytime, radar information allows a close monitoring of migratory activity.

The short history of migration study by radar (see the Bibliography) is an exciting one to read because of the scope of the phenomenon and the continual succession of unexpected revelations. And anyone who has an opportunity to watch a radar screen fill up with the illuminated "shadows" of small birds on a night of heavy migration can experience one of the few benign miracles of modern technology.

Some of the best-known migration studies conducted with the use of radar are listed in the Bibliography.

RADIATION. In the context of bird distribution, used to describe the movement over time of species, families, etc., out from the regions in which they originally evolved; or the shorter-term range expansions such as the recent conspicuous movement of certain southern species, e.g., the Northern Cardinal, north of breeding limits defined previously.

Adaptive radiation is a concept of evolution describing how a grouping of closely related but highly diverse organisms (the family Icteridae, which includes oropendolas, orioles, cowbirds, meadowlarks, Bobolink, a number of blackbird types, and perhaps Dickcissel, is a good example) diverges markedly from a common ancestor by adapting to particular modes of life. This kind of radiation is the "opposite" of CONVERGENCE.

See DISTRIBUTION; IRRUPTION; INVASION.

RAIL. Standard English name for 50 or more members of the family Rallidae (order Gruiformes), which also includes the crakes, coots, and gallinules. Six species of rails breed in North America, including the Sora, and 5 other members of the family have been recorded as accidental stragglers (see Appendix II).

Rails range in size from 5½ to 20 inches (6 to 16 inches in North America). Their legs are moderately long—adapted to wading in shallow water—but not *very* long, as in the herons and cranes. Their toes are unwebbed, but are peculiarly lobed in the coots. They may have relatively long, slender bills or shorter, stubby ones, and their bodies are typically compressed laterally, apparently an adaptation to walking amid dense marshland vegetation (see illustration, Terres, 1980–BIRD, p. 757).

Though there are a few upland and forest species, rails are essentially secretive marshland birds. They are usually somberly colored (see Plate 3); frequently of crepuscular habits; and tend to walk while foraging along muddy marshland edges. They are also adept swimmers, and though loath to fly any great distance when flushed, many species undertake long-distance migrations. Like their near relatives the cranes, rails eat almost anything of the right size—animal or vegetable—which comes along.

The nests of rails, coots, and gallinules are piles of marsh vegetation, in some species shaped into a rather neat, deep cup. They are placed on clumps of emergent marsh plants or in shallow water and may be built up as rising water levels demand. Typically, surrounding vegetation is pulled over the top of the nest to form a dome or canopy. Common Gallinules lay from 2 to 21 eggs, but 8–10 is more usual in this family. They are off white, buffy, pinkish, or olive and generally rather sparsely spotted and speckled with reddish or dark brown and paler subsurface markings.

Rails call mainly between dusk and dawn, making a wide variety of whinnies, clicks, cackles, and pumping sounds more suggestive of frogs or insects than birds. Because rails are so secretive by nature, their presence is often revealed first by their vocalizations.

Like many other bird names, "rail" is supposed to derive from the birds' cries, specifically from *raelare*, a Latin verb meaning "to scrape," a good description of one call of several North American rails.

See also CRAKE; COOT; GALLINULE.

RAMSEY CANYON (Arizona). See SOUTHEASTERN ARIZONA.

RAMUS (RAY-muss) (pl.: rami). One of the two lateral halves of the lower mandible; or the barb of a feather. See BILL; FEATHER.

RANGE. The geographical area normally occupied by a given organism or group of organisms beyond which they are entirely absent. In migratory species well-defined breeding and wintering ranges are discernible as well as a total or "gross" range including the area over which a particular species migrates. Ranges are normally described or mapped in terms of geographical extremities; however, it should be recognized that most species are restricted to habitats within their broader range, so that no range is uniformly occupied. No two species occupy exactly the same range. For specifics such as disjunct ranges, cosmopolitan ranges, etc., see DISTRIBUTION.

RAPTOR. Generally refers to the hawks, eagles, falcons, and their relatives (except for the vultures) and the owls. However, see discussion under BIRD OF PREY, which is essentially synonymous.

RARA AVIS (RARE-uh AY-vis or [Latin] RAH-ruh AH-wiss). Latin for "rare bird." Often used metaphorically to describe any bizarre creature, and therefore as applicable in some cases to birdwatchers as to birds.

RARE BIRD ALERT. Also known as Dial-A-Bird. A recorded telephone message, available at any hour of the day or night, providing an up-to-date account of what birds—especially rarities—have recently been reported in a particular area. In the case of "super rarities," explicit directions to the bird's last known perching place may be given. Initiated by the Massachusetts Audubon Society in November 1954 as the VOICE OF AUDUBON, the

FIG. 17. *Ranges* of several "North American" species.

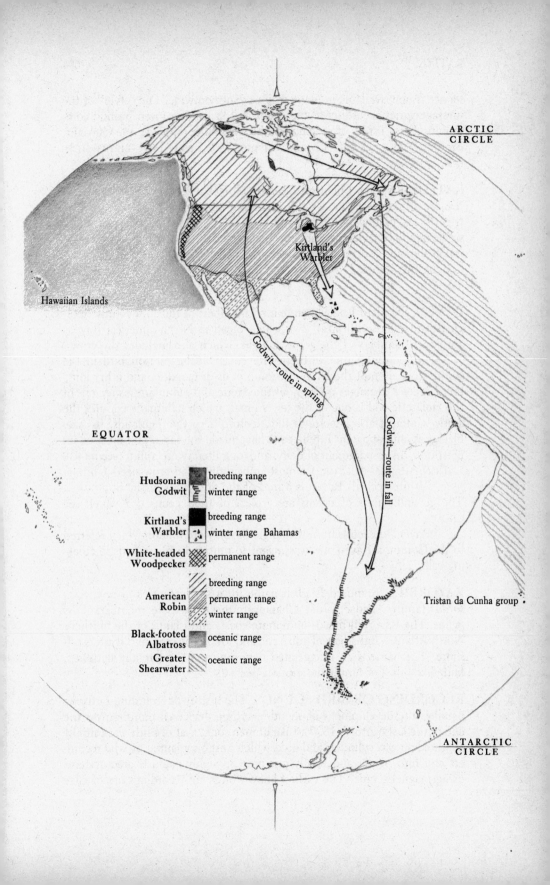

ARCTIC
CIRCLE

Hawaiian Islands

Kirtland's
Warbler

Godwit—route in spring

Godwit—route in fall

EQUATOR

Hudsonian
Godwit — breeding range
— winter range

Kirtland's
Warbler — breeding range
— winter range Bahamas

White-headed
Woodpecker — permanent range

American
Robin — breeding range
— permanent range
— winter range

Black-footed
Albatross — oceanic range

Greater
Shearwater — oceanic range

Tristan da Cunha group

ANTARCTIC
CIRCLE

service is now available in many regions continentwide. The "style" of the message varies according to the needs and tastes of a given birding community. For a listing of specific numbers to call nationwide, see Cutright, *Birding* (1980), 12:110–12, and Chapter 7 of Kress, 1981–BIRDWATCHING.

RATITE (RAT-ite). Flightless birds which lack a keel down the center of the breastbone (see SKELETON), including among living species the Ostrich, rheas, cassowaries, Emu, and kiwis. These were once lumped into a single family (Ratidae) but are now placed in different *orders*. There are no ratites living in North America except in zoos. See de Beer's "The Evolution of the Ratites," *Bull. Brit. Mus. (Nat. Hist.)*, Zool. Ser. (1956), 4:57–76.

RAVEN. Standard English name for 7 members of the crow family (Corvidae; order Passeriformes), 2 of which breed in North America. Ravens are larger members of the genus *Corvus*, which also includes the crows.

The Common (or Northern) Raven is the largest songbird in the world, if we exempt the lyrebirds, some birds of paradise, and other long-tailed species. It ranges throughout the Arctic and mountainous regions of the Holarctic and is one of the few animals which habitually endures the arctic winter; it also penetrates the Neotropics in the highlands. Its size, blackness, and apparent intelligence have made the raven an object of superstition, an embodiment of deity, and/or a literary metaphor (see IMAGINATION; HUMAN CULTURE) almost universally. The crow-sized Chihuahuan (White-necked) Raven is a bird of the arid lands of the Southwest. The general habits of ravens are typical of their genus, for which see CROW.

"Raven" descends from the Anglo-Saxon word *hraetn*, which referred to the Common Raven and was meant to imitate its characteristic croaking call.

RAZORBILL. Standard English name for a single species of auk, *Alca torda* (family Alcidae; order Charadriiformes), the sole member of its genus. The Razorbill breeds on remote coasts and islands of the northern North Atlantic and adjacent subarctic and low arctic seas, and winters offshore. The name is an exaggerated description of the laterally flattened, knife-like bill. For family description, see AUK.

RECORDING OF BIRD SOUNDS. The history of recording birdsong parallels the development of sound-recording devices beginning near the end of the last century (1877). Like human song, that of birds was initially captured on wax cylinders and disks which were supplanted by wire recorders and film media and finally our present highly sophisticated systems using magnetic tape. The earliest-known birdsong recordings are of cage birds in Europe (late 1880's) and soon afterward (1898) a record of a captive Brown Thrasher was being played before a congress of the American Ornithologists' Union.

The recording of wild birdsong in North America owes much to the efforts of the fascinating Albert Rich Brand, a successful businessman who began recording songs with fanatical zeal in his forties and by the time of his death in 1940 had collected the songs of over 300 North American species. This collection provided the beginning of the song library at Cornell's LABORATORY OF ORNITHOLOGY, which remains the most comprehensive in the world.

The modern scientific birdsong technician goes into the field with high-fidelity tape recorders capable of picking up the full range of avian sounds, including those inaudible to the human ear (see HEARING). His microphone is fixed at the center of a parabolic reflector—a gently and uniformly curving metal disk a yard or more in diameter. This allows him to "concentrate" a bird's song from as far away as several hundred feet under ideal conditions and to exclude many extraneous noises; elongated "shotgun" mikes are also used to "zero in" on a particular singer.

Since we cannot hear certain bird sounds, either because they are uttered too rapidly or at a frequency beyond our perception, recordings are often made into "sonograms," which look like cardiograms and represent in effect a written record of a given sound. With these, variations within and between species can be compared and can provide clues to phylogeny and the nature of song development.

The sounds of all North American bird species are now on tape and most of them are available to the public on records or tape cassettes. Many song variations and calls remain to be captured and many species in remote parts of the world have not been taped at all.

Birdwatchers have discovered that professionally produced tapes or even songs recorded "on location" can be very effective in arousing secretive birds. Nothing outrages a singing male bird more than playing his own voice back to him within his own territory, and in many cases he will appear immediately to challenge the presumed intruder. It is particularly useful for seeing such species as owls, rails, and reclusive forest or brush birds, whose secretive habits are thought by some competitive birders to give such species an unfair advantage. Owl calls (especially Screech and Pygmy) are also played to evoke a "mobbing" response and bring in a variety of songbirds for close inspection. Used with sensitivity and in moderation these techniques are effective and probably harmless. However, a callous fringe of the bird-listing community has occasionally disrupted nesting activities, particularly in cases of rarer, more sought-after species. The local populations of Elegant (Coppery-tailed) Trogons in southeastern Arizona have been victimized, for example, and tapes are now banned in some refuges.

See the Bibliography for more on technique and a selected listing of available records and tapes of North American birds.

RECTRICES (REK-truh-seez or rek-TRY-zeez) (sing.: rectrix). The main feathers of the tail not including the coverts (see Fig. 25); usually more or less long and stiff (the grebes are notable exceptions) and serving the functions of steering, balance, and maneuvering in flight. They are paired and overlap fan-wise, with the central rectrices topmost. Most species have 12 rectrices, but a few typically have 20 or more. See TAIL.

REDHEAD. Standard English name for a single species of bay duck, *Aythya americana*, which breeds exclusively in North America. The name, of course, refers to the rufous head of the drake. See DUCK; POCHARD.

REDIRECTION. A term frequently encountered in behavioral literature, referring to an action substituted for a more appropriate one in a situation calling for a definite response but involving some ambiguity. For example, a sexually motivated bird may "redirect" its amorous attention to a male of its species or even an inanimate object; chickadees and other species mobbing an owl (see Fig. 14) often glean and peck at branches or preen, redirecting the hostility meant for the predator, which they dare not attack directly, into substitute modes of behavior.

REDPOLL. Standard English name for 2 species of cardueline finches (family Fringillidae; order Passeriformes), both of which have a circumpolar arctic breeding distribution. In North America, redpolls remain largely in the Arctic and Boreal zones, even in winter, but like other "winter finches" are subject to periodic "irruptions" during which they appear in large numbers and range as far south as southern South Carolina (Common Redpoll).

The "poll" is the crown of the head (to take a poll is to count heads); both male and female redpolls have red polls.

For general family characteristics, see FINCH.

REDSTART. Standard English name for the members of the wood warbler genera *Setophaga* and *Myioborus* (family Parulidae; order Passeriformes), 2 of which breed in North America. It is also the standard English name for 12 species of small Old World thrushes (family Turdidae; order Passeriformes), all but two in the genus *Phoenicurus*.

"Start" is cognate with the Anglo-Saxon word *steort*, meaning tail, and the Old World redstarts, including *the* Redstart of Europe, do indeed have red (bright rufous) tails which they bob and "shiver" conspicuously and habitually. The American Redstart was named by association after the Old World species because of the characteristic fanning of its red (orange) marked tail, despite the fact that it is a wood warbler and not closely related to the thrush redstarts. The other tail-fanning wood warblers—e.g., the Painted Redstart—were in turn named for their congener despite the fact that none have any red in the tail. Alden and Gooders (1981–BIRD FINDING) suggest the name "whitestart" for the majority of the *Myioborus* and *Setophaga* warblers.

For family characteristics, see WOOD WARBLER.

REELFOOT LAKE (Tennessee). Once a 12-by-4-mile lake formed when an area of forest was drowned in a spate of earthquakes in 1811–12. Now several basins of shallow (maximum depth: 20 feet) water surrounded by lush cypress swamp. It is Tennessee's most extensive water-birding area and one of the most spectacular wilderness habitats of its kind in North America. Avian highlights of Reelfoot include: breeding "southern" species, e.g., Purple Gallinule, Mississippi Kite, and Kentucky, Swainson's, and Prothonotary Warblers; grebes, rails, herons, and other water birds, nesting or visiting from nearby "rookeries"; large concentrations of migrant and wintering waterfowl; vast winter blackbird roosts containing millions of birds; and wintering Bald Eagles (often 50 or more). A total of 23,000 acres of this wilderness is protected by the state, which leases 9,586 acres to the federal government as the Reelfoot National Wildlife Refuge. Access mainly from State Highway 22 via Samburg and Tiptonville; visitor center, nature trails, and boat trips from several points.

REEVE. The female RUFF; a usage similar to the familiar gander and goose, though referring to one species only. Choate (1973–BIOGRAPHY) thinks "reeve" preceded "ruff" as the species name, pointing out that it is an old English term for an overseer or bailiff. This fits with the male's breeding-plumage "ruff," which might be seen as a "coat of office," and with the apparently aggressive male courtship displays (see LEK), which also inspired the Latin generic and specific names, *Philomachus pugnax*, or "combative war-lover."

REFUGE. In the broadest sense, similar to "sanctuary" or "reserve," i.e., a parcel of land set aside for the protection of birds and other wildlife. However, the word is strongly associated with the NATIONAL WILDLIFE REFUGE system administered by the Fish and Wildlife Service of the U.S. Department of the Interior and consequently carries a connotation of extensive wetland habitat preserved and managed for the benefit of migratory waterfowl and the conservation of endangered species. See also SANCTUARY.

RELEASER. The behaviorists' term for a sound, gesture, or plumage character which signals another bird that a particular action—fighting, courting, feeding, etc.—is appropriate. The red spot on a Herring Gull's bill "releases" nestling gulls' urge to peck at it, which in turn "releases" the adult's urge to regurgitate food. Such sequences of stimulus and response are innate and immutable and therefore essential to the basic routines of a bird's life. See also FIXED ACTION PATTERN; INTELLIGENCE.

RELICT (RELL-ikt or ruh-LIKT). Refers to a population of birds or other organisms contained within a limited range and isolated from other populations of that species or from any similar form. The word also implies that such a population is "left behind" from a once wider distribution.

The Caspian Tern ranges nearly worldwide, but today breeds largely in local "relict" populations which presumably were more continuous in prehistory. In North America, for example, it nests in widely scattered colonies on Great Slave Lake, N.W.T.; in Labrador; on the Great Lakes; at the mouth of the St. Lawrence; and along southeastern coasts. See DISTRIBUTION.

REMEX (REM-eks or REE-mecks) (pl.: remiges). One of the flight feathers of a bird's wing: primary or secondary. See WING and Fig. 25.

REMICLE (REM-uh-cl). A small feather attached to the second phalanx of the second digit of the wing (see SKELETON, *Bones of the Wing,* and Figs. 1 and 19). It occurs in a wide spectrum of families (passerine and non-passerine) and is generally believed to be a vestigial outermost (10th, 11th, or 12th) primary. So inconspicuous is it in small songbirds that the many species of songbirds in which it makes a 10th primary are known as 9-primaried oscines.

An alternative explanation of the remicle's origin is that it was a covert for the wing claw of ancestral forms.

REMIGES (REM-ih-jeez or REM-ih-jiz). Plural of REMEX.

REPRODUCTIVE ISOLATION. The condition of being unable to interbreed with another organism because of some physical or behavioral incompatibility. As a hypothetical example, a bird species which normally forms pairs in March would probably be reproductively isolated from one which did so in May, whatever their similarities; incompatible genital structure which makes copulation physically impossible would also enforce reproductive isolation. This is not to be confused with the situation in which species are prevented from interbreeding by *spatial* isolation, e.g., total discontinuity of range. See SPECIATION.

REPRODUCTIVE SYSTEM. See Fig. 18. In animals which reproduce sexually, the essence of the process is the uniting of a cell (spermatozoon) from the male parent and a cell (ovum) from the female parent to form a single third cell (zygote). The resulting fertilized ovum contains the genetic material of both parents and will, if all goes well, develop into a unique individual. In humans and most other mammals, the embryo develops within the body of the female; all birds and most reptiles, however, lay a hard-shelled egg almost immediately following fertilization, so that embryonic development takes place outside the female's body.

Perhaps the most notable structural differences between the avian and mammalian reproductive systems are (1) the virtual lack of external sexual organs in birds and (2) the prodigious enlargement which birds' internal reproductive organs undergo during the breeding season. (The sexual organs of birds may truly be called private parts; the ones on the inside are difficult to find during most of the year, and there is nothing significant to conceal on the outside.)

MALE REPRODUCTIVE ORGANS. The testes are a pair of glands (in birds they are attached to the abdominal wall and lie near the top of the kidneys) in which the sperm cells are produced. A bird's testes are usually roughly egg-shaped and, unlike the main *female* reproductive organs, are *both* functional, though one may be larger than the other. The sperm cells develop within the mass of tiny tubules which make up the interior of each testis. When mature, they travel along a tube (one from each testis) called the deferent duct (vas deferens) to the cloaca, from which ejaculation (as well as urination and defecation) takes place. The ejaculatory duct, which is simply the cloacal end of the deferent duct, is made of erectile tissue, but only a few orders of birds (the ducks and geese and perhaps the Wood Stork in North America) have an organ resembling a penis, and this remains within the cloaca until copulation (see below).

During the breeding season the testes of birds increase in size by hundreds or even thousands of times and the deferent ducts may quadruple in length, becoming heavily coiled and with a much greater diameter. In most land birds this enlargement of the ducts makes an external bulge in the lower abdomen, the cloacal protuberance; this is the birds' only claim to an external genital character, and it is sometimes used by banders and others to determine the sex of species in which this is impossible on the basis of plumage. Because the bulge fills with semen, which may cool somewhat in its partially external sac, the structure has been compared to the semen storage sacs (seminal vesicles) and scrotums of mammals, but this does not seem otherwise justified by either structure or function.

FEMALE REPRODUCTIVE ORGANS. Like the testes, a bird's ovaries are reproductive glands attached to the abdominal wall and situated near the top of the kidneys. Except in certain hawks, only the left ovary functions in birds; the right ovary ceases to develop in an early stage and degenerates. In about half of female accipiters, harriers, and falcons, both ovaries develop but are apparently only rarely capable of ovulation. If ova do mature on the right, they continue development in the left oviduct (see also SEX, CHANGE OF). The ovary produces thousands of ova (female germ cells) of which only a few reach maturity. From the ovary, an ovum falls into the enlarged mouth (infundibulum) of the oviduct, a tube which ends, like the male's deferent duct, at the cloaca. There are four major sections of the oviduct, the first three of which contribute significantly to the production of a finished bird's egg. The ovum, essentially the egg yolk, is fertilized by the sperm cells in the uppermost part of the oviduct, called the magnum. Following fertilization the ovum travels through the magnum, which makes up about half the entire length of the oviduct. Mucous glands lining the magnum secrete several layers of egg white (albumen) around the yolk, which then passes into the narrower isthmus. In the isthmus two shell membranes are secreted: an inner one to enclose the nearly liquid yolk and albumen and an outer one to adhere to the shell-to-be. Beyond the isthmus is the wider shell gland, which occupies the same position in the female bird's oviduct as the uterus does in the human female's genital tract, and is often so named. But a bird's shell gland does not function as a womb any more than the mammalian womb secretes a shell, so the comparison is not exact. After the shell, including its distinctive coloration, is added, the egg is ready to be laid. However, below the shell gland is a final short segment of the oviduct, a "vagina," constricted above and below by a ring-like closing (sphincter) muscle. In domestic hens at least, the walls of the uterus invert through this last section of oviduct into the cloaca, so that the egg is laid, as it were, from the "uterus." The whole process from the time the ovum enters the oviduct to laying takes only about twenty-four hours. See also EGG, *Formation and Structure.*

COPULATION AND FERTILIZATION. The striking development of the reproductive organs which characterizes the onset of breeding condition in birds is triggered by hormonal secretion of the pituitary gland. Once the ova have been released from the ovary into the oviduct of the female and the male's sperm cells are mature, the stage is set for copulation. From the

FIG. 18. *Reproduction.* The herons demonstrate the rather awkward (at least by human standards) position most birds assume in copulation. The female must raise her tail and twist her lower abdomen acutely to one side in order to present her cloacal opening to the male above. The "cloacal kiss" which passes for intercourse among most birds is essentially performed "sideways" and "at right angles." In many smaller species, the male actually stands on the back of the female during copulation, a procedure known as "treading." The "dissected" urogenital systems show: the male system "off season," with the testes only partially enlarged (upper left); the contrasting system in breeding condition (upper right), with greatly enlarged testes and deferent duct; and a female system in an early stage of ovulation. The inactive female system would show no egg mass whatever at the ovary, and the right oviduct little larger than the normally useless left one shown. In full breeding condition, however, some of the eggs and the oviduct itself become 3–4 times the size illustrated. The figure also shows the main elements of the urinary system (see EXCRETORY SYSTEM).

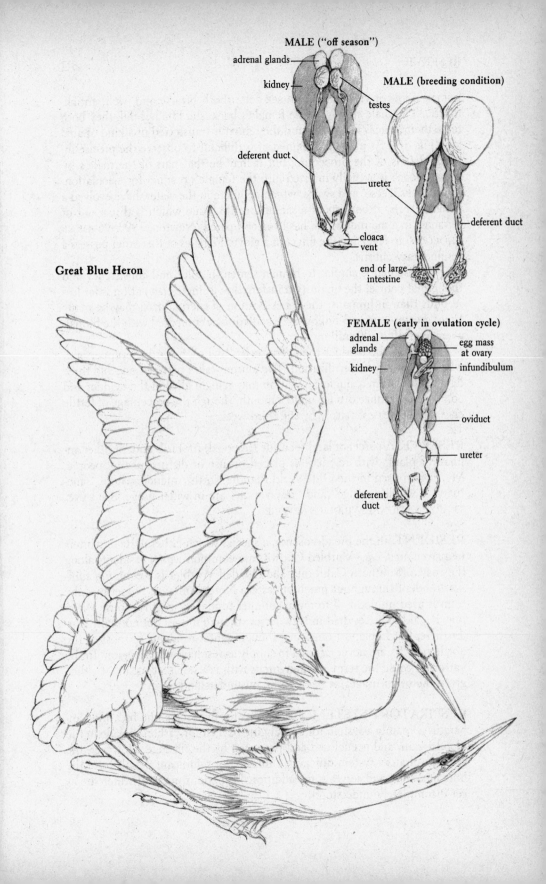

MALE ("off season")
adrenal glands
kidney
testes

MALE (breeding condition)

deferent duct
ureter
deferent duct

cloaca
vent

end of large
intestine

Great Blue Heron

FEMALE (early in ovulation cycle)
adrenal glands
egg mass at ovary
kidney
infundibulum

oviduct

ureter

deferent duct

human point of view, the avian sex act is both bizarre and, well, anticlimactic. The male stands on the female's back; she lifts her tail; they both force their cloacas inside out and the semen is transferred in a kind of anal kiss (Fig. 18). As may be imagined, it is difficult to observe the precise internal details of the procedure, but it may be that part of the male's inverted cloaca is actually inserted into the female's oviduct for ejaculation. Male ducks, geese, and swans, which copulate in the water, have evolved a penis of sorts. It consists of a sac of erectile tissue which is thrust out or retracted in a manner which has been compared (Newton, 1893–96–ORNITHOLOGY) to reversing the finger of a glove. Females of this order possess a rudimentary clitoris.

Bird semen is similar to human semen in color and consistency and though, of course, the quantity transferred in a single ejaculation is far less in birds than in humans, the concentration of spermatozoa may be many times greater—up to 3 billion per ejaculation as compared with the human average of 300–500 million.

Once in the oviduct the sperm cells "swim" toward the upper end, where the ova await fertilization. The journey takes between one and three days. Sperm from a single copulation may remain alive in the oviduct and continue to fertilize ova for up to a month, though the percentage of fertile eggs laid decreases sharply by the third week.

RESERVE. A parcel of land set aside (reserved) for birds and/or other animals or plants with restrictions placed on use or disturbance by people. More often used in the Old World than in North America, where "sanctuary," "wildlife refuge" and "reservation" are in wider usage. See SANCTUARY; NATIONAL WILDLIFE REFUGE.

RESIDENT. In the broadest sense, a species which either nests or winters in a given area, e.g., Marbled Godwits are common *winter* residents along the coast of southern California; the Hooded Warbler is a common *summer* resident throughout much of eastern North America. Sometimes the term is used unmodified to mean summer resident, e.g., the House Wren may be said to be resident in New Jersey, though it does not normally winter there; but Lapland Longspurs, though winter residents of most of the northern U.S., are never referred to simply as resident in that region. In the narrowest sense the term is synonymous with PERMANENT RESIDENT; this, given the other usages, is likely to be misunderstood.

RESPIRATORY SYSTEM. For birds as for mammals, the breathing apparatus is mainly a system for exchanging oxygen for carbon dioxide in the bloodstream, and is enclosed and protected by the rib cage. However, the avian respiratory system differs in a number of significant details from the human system and serves some additional functions, most of which are as yet incompletely understood.

AIR ROUTES. Except for gannets, boobies, and cormorants, which have closed external nostrils and must take air into the mouth through the sides of the bill, birds inhale and exhale through openings at the base of the bill, the nares or nostrils. In a few groups these nasal openings are peculiarly modified (see NOSTRILS; CERE; OPERCULUM). Then the air passes through the mouth cavity into the pharynx. As in humans, this is the throat passage connecting the mouth with both the gullet (esophagus) and the windpipe (trachea). The entrance to the windpipe is a slit called the glottis; birds lack an epiglottis, the one-way flap of cartilage which normally prevents food from going down the human windpipe. At the top of the windpipe is a structure called the larynx, which holds the vocal cords in mammals but is not the voice-producing organ in birds. This function is performed by the SYRINX, a mechanism unique to birds. It too is a modification of the windpipe and is located at its lower end, where it divides into two main bronchi. The main bronchial tubes enter the lungs, where they divide and redivide into a fine network which intermeshes with the capillary network carrying blood laden with carbon dioxide (see CIRCULATORY SYSTEM). The bronchi exchange oxygen for carbon dioxide and carry the latter back to the nostrils to be exhaled into the atmosphere. In the human system, the finest of the bronchial tubes (bronchioles) end up in tiny air sacs called alveoli. But birds' bronchi are interconnected and the passage of air is apparently continuous in one direction.

The lungs of birds are comparatively small, usually taking up less than half the proportion of space in the body that human lungs occupy. But this is more than compensated for by another feature unique to birds—a system of balloon-like extensions of the lungs, called simply air sacs.

AIR SACS. These fill most of the extra space left between organs and muscles in a bird's body cavity, amounting to about 20 percent of the total space. In the majority of bird species the main air sacs are located symmetrically: (1) along the upper spinal column (cervical), (2) between the shoulder blades (interclavicular), (3) in the upper chest cavity (anterior thoracic), (4) in the lower chest cavity (posterior thoracic), and (5) in the belly (abdominal). The abdominal, thoracic, and in a few cases the cervical sacs occur in pairs; the single interclavicular sac spans the space between the shoulder blades; and the cervical sac, though usually unpaired, branches in some species into a pair of sacs (median clavicular) partway along its length. Left and right members of the paired sacs may be of different shapes and are sometimes numbered separately, so that birds may be said to have 4–5 main air sacs on the average or 8–9; as many as 14 have been recorded. These main sacs extend into the remotest crannies of the body, reaching under the skin in a few cases and, most remarkably, entering into the bones of many species (see PNEUMATIZATION OF BONE).

The functions of the air sacs are much debated. There can be little doubt that the evolution of partially hollowed bones is an advantage in flight. Authorities also seem to agree that birds can give off excess heat by water vaporization from the air-sac surfaces (see TEMPERATURE, BODY) and get rid of fluid wastes by the same method. The neck pouches which are inflated for display in male frigatebirds and various grouse species, for example, are also connected to this system.

Additionally, it should be noted that birds which are constantly airborne seem to have more or bigger sacs than more earthbound species and that birds which must make deep and long dives tend to have fewer and smaller sacs. It has been demonstrated that the capacity of the sacs is not great enough to allow a hot-air balloon effect, but other arguments relating air sacs and buoyancy remain unresolved. It is also debated whether birds can use the sacs as "spare air tanks" when diving.

BREATHING RATE AND RHYTHM. Birds normally breathe much faster than human beings, but the rates of both vary similarly for reasons of physical and emotional stress. In general, smaller birds breathe faster than larger ones, and torpid birds breathe much more slowly than normal (see TORPIDITY). The average human respiration rate is 11–12 breaths per minute; small birds average over 100 per minute but with a wider range (50–200) among different species. Very large birds and torpid ones may take fewer than 10 breaths per minute.

Some birds have been shown to breathe and flap their wings in a synchronized rhythm, leading to speculation that the two functions are interconnected in all species. Though certain muscles are shared between lungs and wings, it is now known that the number of beats per breath is odd, rather than even, so that it is at least certain that the two actions are not perfectly simultaneous.

RETROMIGRATION. A relatively new term coined to describe the migratory movement of birds which are misled into taking a course which is divergent from—even opposite to—their normal direction as the result of following a coastline or other topographical feature or "leading line." Not to be confused with "reverse migration" (see MIGRATION; LEADING LINE).

RHAMPHOTHECA (RAM-fo-THEE-ka). The horny sheaths covering the bones of the bill, i.e., the part of the bill we normally see and refer to when we note the color or texture. The upper and lower sheaths may be referred to separately as the rhinotheca and the gnathotheca, respectively. See BILL.

RHOMBOID SINUS. A cavity in the lower spinal cord containing a gelatinous substance, nerve fibers, and glycogen. It is unique to birds, but its function is poorly understood (see NERVOUS SYSTEM).

RICHMOND, Charles W., 1868–1932 (*Richmondena* [*Cardinalis*] *cardinalis:* Northern Cardinal). A protégé of William BREWSTER and Robert RIDGWAY, Richmond was a scholar-bibliographer, not a field man. He helped Ridgway with his great work, *The Birds of North and Middle America*, and was a loyal slave to the bureaucracy of natural science at the National Museum, but his most significant achievement was the completion of a meticulous and thorough card catalogue of the vast bird collection of that institution. Gruson (1972–BIOGRAPHY) describes Richmond as "generous and gentle." His commemorative genus, *Richmondena*, has recently given way to a taxonomic revision making the Northern Cardinal the type species of the genus *Cardinalis*.

RICTAL (bristles). The "rictus" is the mouth opening, the gape. Rictal bristles in birds are hair-like feathers which project over the gape from above. They are present in many insectivorous species and are perhaps most conspicuous in some nightjars. See FEATHER and Fig. 9.

RIDGWAY, Robert, 1850–1929 (*Caprimulgus ridgwayi*: Ridgway's Whip-poor-will or Buff-collared Nightjar). One of the young men whom Spencer BAIRD sent West to collect birds in the latter half of the nineteenth century, Ridgway began as a shy, ill-educated boy artist-naturalist from Illinois and ended as a shy ornithologist at the top of his profession: Curator of Ornithology at the U.S. National Museum in Washington, president of the A.O.U., and author of a large scientific oeuvre. The bulk of his achievement was accomplished at his desk, but he accompanied the survey expedition to Utah, Nevada, and Wyoming in the late 1860's, the Harriman Expedition to Alaska in 1899, and made early exploratory forays to Central America (Costa Rica) in 1904 and 1908. He described a number of "new" North American bird species and many others from Mexico. His multi-volume opus *Birds of North and Middle America*, 1901–50 (completed by Herbert Friedmann), a "descriptive catalogue" containing keys and detailed descriptions of all taxa (including subspecies) of the birds of North America, Mexico, Central America, the West Indies, and the Galápagos, remains authoritative. Ridgway was also the author of the single-volume *Manual of North American Birds* (Philadelphia, 1887), consisting mainly of keys and technical drawings "for determining the character of any given specimen" of North American bird species or subspecies.

RINGING. The preferred British term for BANDING.

RING SPECIES. A species which varies over a more or less circular range to such a degree that at the point where the divergent forms rejoin (through subsequent range expansion) they are no longer inclined to interbreed. Visualize an imaginary species (with a circular range) which is gray at due north, becomes progressively darker in geographical races to the west and south, and progressively paler as it ranges to the east and south;

when the races overlap in the south they have become so different (one black, one white) as in effect to be two separate species though originating as one. This is an oversimplification, but it illustrates the general concept.

The distribution of Herring Gulls today forms a continuous ring around the Holarctic and consists of a number of intergrading racial variations. It is thought that many of the variations on the Herring Gull "theme" that now exist—e.g., Iceland Gull, Western Gull, etc.—evolved when parts of a similar ring were isolated during the Pleistocene glacial advance. See Mayr (1963–SPECIATION) for a fuller account and illustration of this phenomenon.

RIO GRANDE VALLEY (Texas). Literally, of course, the valley cut by the Rio Grande from its source in the San Juan Mountains of Colorado to its mouth at the Gulf of Mexico. In Texas, however, *the* Valley is the *lower* Rio Grande Valley, beginning somewhere south of San Antonio. This corresponds fairly well to the birdwatcher's Rio Grande Valley, which connotes an avifauna typical of the arid mesquite scrublands of northern Mexico that extend north of the national boundary. Among the Tex-Mex species which fire the imaginations of birders visiting the Valley for the first time are: Least Grebe, Neotropic Cormorant, Black-bellied Whistling (Tree) Duck, Hook-billed Kite, White-tailed Hawk, Plain Chachalaca, Red-billed Pigeon, White-tipped Dove, Pauraque, Buff-bellied Hummingbird, Ringed and Green Kingfishers, Golden-fronted Woodpecker, Brown Crested Flycatcher, Great Kiskadee, Green and Brown Jays, Mexican Crow, Long-billed Thrasher, Black-headed and Altamira Orioles, White-collared Seedeater, and Olive Sparrow.

Several specific localities in the Valley are de rigueur as birding stops, among them: Santa Ana National Wildlife Refuge (tame Plain Chachalacas, nesting Hook-billed Kites [sometimes at Bentsen], and a wide selection of other Valley birds on 2,000 acres); Brownsville (Mexican Crows at the dump); Bentsen State Park; and Falcon Dam (Ringed and Green Kingfishers and Brown Jays).

For birding highlights of the *upper* Rio Grande Valley in Texas, see BIG BEND.

RITUAL. The characteristic and stylized movements and gestures of birds' courtship displays—for example, the elaborate nuptial "rituals" among species of albatrosses, gulls, grouse, and cranes—are believed to be "ritualizations" evolved from such innate commonplace activities as preening, pecking, or taking flight. See DISPLAY.

RIVOLI (RIV-uh-lee), François Victor Masséna, Duc de, 1799–1863 (Rivoli's Hummingbird: *Eugenes fulgens*). Son of André Masséna, who rose from cabin boy to become the greatest of Napoleon Bonaparte's marshals and was made a duke following his great victory at Rivoli and Prince d'Essling for a later triumph. These titles passed on to his son, who became a patron of natural history (introduced Audubon to French society and bought a subscription to *The Birds of America*) and collector of bird specimens (one of the largest private collections of his time). His wife was also commemorated in the name of a North American hummingbird (see ANNA).

ROADRUNNER. Standard English name for 2 very similar species of large ground cuckoos (family Cuculidae; order Cuculiformes), 1 of which breeds in North America.

Roadrunners are large (about 2 feet), long-tailed, crested, brown-striped terrestrial birds that live in open, arid country (to nearly 9,000 feet in the tropics) and feed on a wide assortment of large invertebrates (e.g., beetles, caterpillars, tarantulas), small vertebrates (e.g., rodents, lizards, rattlesnakes, and nestling birds), as well as some fruits, seeds, and bird's eggs. They fly well, but prefer to flee and chase their prey on foot. They are very agile and have attained running speeds of at least 15 m.p.h.

Roadrunners nest in low trees, shrubs, and cactus clumps; rarely on the ground. They fashion a well-made cup of sticks lined with finer plant material, leaves, feathers, and "decorative" debris, e.g., shed snakeskin. The eggs are white or off white and unmarked and usually number 3–6, though larger clutches have been recorded—possibly resulting from contributions from more than one female.

The roadrunners' vocal repertoire is quite extensive and contains an assortment of whining and crowing noises as well as cuckoo-type staccato hoots and clucks.

Roadrunners are a New World phenomenon. The North American species (properly called Greater Roadrunner) resides in the deserts and dry scrublands of the Southwest; it is non-migratory.

See references in the Bibliography under CUCKOO.

ROBIN. Standard English name used by itself or in combinations such as "scrub robin" or "robin chat" for over 70 species worldwide. Most of these are thrushes (family Turdidae; order Passeriformes), especially those in the Old World genus *Erithacus* and the widespread genus *Turdus*; but the name is also standard for some of the Old World flycatchers (family Muscicapidae), e.g., the "yellow robins" (*Eopsaltria* spp.) of Australasia. Some nomenclators would call all of the *Turdus* thrushes "robins"; others would call all the *Turdus* robins "thrushes."

The American Robin (*Turdus migratorius*) is arguably the most familiar and best-loved songbird of North America. It has entered enthusiastically with humankind into the pursuit of the American dream—pulling worms from suburban lawns, nesting near us in shade trees and eaves, and serving as chief herald of the beginning and end of our summer days. Though we have at times responded ungratefully by spraying deadly insecticides into the American Robin's arboreal habitat in the vain hope of ridding ourselves of insect pests (see MAN-MADE THREATS TO BIRDLIFE), our more sensitive children spend untold hours yearly rescuing nests, eggs, and young of this species from the dangers of life in general and suburbia in particular. When their efforts fail, the ensuing funerary rites are frequently elaborate and affecting. Two Neotropical (*Turdus*) robins have been recorded here as accidental stragglers (see Appendix II).

The original "robin" is Robin Redbreast (*Erithacus rubecula*), a widespread Palearctic species named in England in the tradition of "Jenny Wren," "Jack the Daw," and "Mag the Pie." English colonists, seeing the American red-breasted *Turdus*, which both looked and behaved somewhat like the friend of their birthplace, transferred the name along with their affection.

For general characteristics of the Turdidae, see THRUSH.

ROC (originally Rukh). A gigantic bird of Arabic legend, said to be able to carry off elephants in its talons. In the Western world, it is best known from the second and fifth voyages of Sinbad in *A Thousand and One Nights*. In the phylogeny of myth, the Roc is closely related to other avian giants such as the Anka (Arabia), Simurgh (Persia), and Phoenix (classical legend). It was thought to nest on an island in the Indian Ocean and eventually became identified with the Elephant Bird of Madagascar (*Aepyornis titan*), which, though flightless, was the heaviest bird we know of and laid eggs with a capacity of two gallons (see SIZE). The enormous fronds of the *Raphia* (*Sagus*) palm of Madagascar were passed off (on the Great Khan among others) as feathers of the Roc. Compare PHOENIX and see IMAGINATION.

ROCKPORT (Texas). A small town and famous birding area on the Texas coast north of Corpus Christi; many individual bits of habitat, including ponds, marshes, beaches, and live oak copses, have contributed to Rockport's reputation, originally created by a local bird lady, Connie Hagar. The copses are flooded at times with exhausted northern land-bird migrants returning over the Gulf in spring, and the wetlands contain at one season or another a majority of the water-bird species of North America. In addition, Rockport is handy to Whooping Cranes in winter (boat tours from the Sea-Gun Sports Inn); marks the northern boundary for some Rio Grande Valley species (e.g., Least Grebe, White-tailed Hawk); and is not far from the Welder Wildlife Refuge in Sinton, where Greater Prairie Chickens can be seen. See Appendix III for timing.

ROCKY MOUNTAIN National Park (Colorado). 412 square miles of unspoiled American highland habitat between 7,500 and 14,255 feet (65 peaks over 10,000 feet), including deciduous woodland (aspen, willow), open ponderosa pine woods, dense spruce and fir forest, stunted "wind timber" above 10,000 feet, alpine meadows and tundra (both with unique and spectacular floral displays in season), snowfields, icy tarns, and swift, rocky streams. Avian specialties are boreal and western montane species such as: Northern Goshawk, Golden Eagle, Prairie Falcon, Blue Grouse, White-tailed Ptarmigan, Black Swift, Broad-tailed and Rufous Hummingbirds, Williamson's Sapsucker, Northern Three-toed Woodpecker, Hammond's, Dusky, Western, and Olive-sided Flycatchers, Violet-green Swallow, Gray and Steller's Jays, Clark's Nutcracker, Mountain Chickadee, American Dipper, Rock Wren, Mountain Bluebird, Townsend's Solitaire, MacGillivray's Warbler, Western Tanager, Cassin's Finch, Pine Grosbeak, rosy finches, and Lincoln's Sparrow.

Mammals of note include mule deer, elk, bighorn sheep, and pika.

The peak of birdsong in the mountains is around mid-June and the road to the tundra area is usually not open until the beginning of that month. Wildflower spectacles continue from late June to September; tourists peak in high summer.

Access on U.S. Highway 34 is via Loveland and Estes Park from the east and from Granby from the southwest.

For other western mountain birding, see YELLOWSTONE; YOSEMITE.

ROOKERY. Originally referring to the communal nesting colonies of the European crow called the Rook. Expanded in North American usage to other tree-nesting colonial species, e.g., a heron or water-bird rookery, and occasionally even to colonies of ground nesters, e.g., pelicans.

ROOST (roosting). A place where birds congregate to rest or sleep, by day or (usually) night, in trees, on water, or on the ground. Some roosts are stupendously large—Common Starlings and blackbird species regularly gather by the millions in dense roosts in the southeastern states (see PESTS)—but it is also correct to speak of a single bird "roosting for the night." Roost sites often become part of a population's habitual behavior pattern, some sites being known to have existed for over 100 years, and to attract birds from feeding areas as far as 30 miles away (Common Starlings).

Some birds, e.g., herons, may roost in the same place where they nest, following the breeding season; however, a clear distinction exists between "roost" and terms such as "colony," "rookery," and "heronry," all of which are used for breeding as opposed to resting.

"Roosting" is frequently used to mean "sleeping," but, as noted, the two words are not synonymous; sleeping behavior is discussed under SLEEP.

ROSEFINCH. Standard English name for 18 of the 21 species of cardueline finches (family Fringillidae; order Passeriformes) in the genus *Carpo-*

dacus. The exceptional species are the three American ones: Purple Finch, Cassin's Finch, and House Finch.

Carpodacus is a fairly homogeneous genus, with males ranging in color from pink to scarlet to slightly purplish, the streaky females and juveniles usually lacking any trace of "rose."

They range throughout the Palearctic region south of the Arctic in coniferous and deciduous woodland, desert, and montane barrens; two of the North American species reach the Neotropics (Mexico) in the highlands.

For general family characteristics, see FINCH.

ROSS, Bernard Rogan, 1827–74 (Ross' Goose: *Anser* [*Chen*] *rossii*). Born in England, and a lifelong naturalist, Ross became head trader for the Hudson's Bay Company. This gave him the opportunity to collect the type specimen of his goose (named for him by John CASSIN) near Great Slave Lake, N.W.T., in 1861. For the Ross of gull fame, see the following entry.

ROSS, Sir James Clark, 1800–62 (Ross' Gull: *Rhodostethia rosea*). Great British naval explorer of the Arctic and Antarctic who sailed with Booth and Parry as a young man and commanded the *Endeavor* expedition to look for John Franklin. No more fitting avian memorial to an explorer of polar seas can be imagined than the high arctic gull which bears Ross' name. For the Ross of goose fame, see the preceding entry.

ROSTRUM. Technical term for the bill; it is also the Latin word for "bill" and is combined in the scientific names of many species with distinctive bills, e.g., *Rostrhamus*, literally "hooked bill," is the genus of the Everglade Kite.

ROSY FINCH. Standard English name for 2 to 5 species of finches (family Fringillidae; order Passeriformes) all in the genus *Leucosticte*. The taxonomy of this genus is much disputed. Several distinctive populations of rosy finches are isolated on alpine peaks where they have no breeding contact with other forms, so that their degree of biological differentiation is never tested (see SPECIATION). Many authorities now believe, however, that all of the North American rosy finches constitute a single variable species (see Appendix I).

Whatever their taxonomic status, the rosy finches are fascinating birds, among the few songbirds adapted to the harsh conditions of the alpine barrens above tree line on our highest mountains. They generally arrive on still-snowy peaks by early April. Their bulky nest of grasses, sphagnum moss, and stems, lined with finer plant fibers, fur, hair, and feathers, is tucked under rocks on talus slopes or into crevices or on ledges of cliff walls. They feed (themselves and nestlings) almost exclusively on seeds, for which they forage in alpine meadows, at the edge of the snowfields and along the shores of frigid tarns. In winter, some populations descend to the plains, but others remain above 6,000 feet, where large roosts have been recorded, individual birds huddling in rock crevices or abandoned Cliff Swallow nests to conserve heat. The rosy finches also breed on rocky arctic barrens at sea level (Alaska).

Rosy finches are found in alpine and arctic regions only in the eastern Palearctic and western Nearctic regions; their migrations are almost exclusively altitudinal. In North America they are confined to the highest western mountains (and adjacent plains) and the Arctic.

Male birds in breeding plumage are subtly handsome with distinct patterns of rose on wings, belly, and rump, but this color is less evident or absent in females, during other seasons, and at different ages. The name Mountain Finch—in current use for the Eurasian species of *Leucosticte*—is perhaps more apt and avoids confusion with the ROSEFINCHES (*Carpodacus* spp.).

For general family characteristics, see FINCH.

ROUNDUP. A birdwatching event in which a given area is covered as thoroughly as possible by teams of birders. For most participants, a roundup is a dawn-to-dusk affair, though some of the "hard core" can usually be counted on to start earlier and go out after dinner for night birds. There is no limitation on number of participants or area covered. Traditionally, there is an evening gathering to compare notes and combine the team lists into a total count.

RUFF. Standard English name for the male of a single species of medium-sized sandpiper, *Philomachus pugnax*. The name is also used for the species as a whole; however, females are often distinguished as "reeves." In spring migration, this species now occurs regularly in small numbers almost wherever concentrations of shorebirds occur in North America—inland as well as along both coasts—and recently has been found nesting in Alaska (Gibson, *American Birds* [1977], 25 [4]). There are also records from South America and Australia/New Zealand, and yet the single breeding site noted above is the only one known beyond the Palearctic region.

The provenance of this name is a kind of etymological chicken-egg quandary. A natural assumption is that this species was named for the spectacular varicolored "ruff" of colorful feathers which adorns the male's head and neck in breeding plumage, but Newton (1893–96–ORNITHOLOGY) opines that the various types of frilly collars called "ruffs" may have been named for the bird! See also REEVE.

For family characteristics, see SANDPIPER.

RUFOUS (ROO-fuss) (Hummingbird, -sided Towhee, -crowned Sparrow, -winged Sparrow). Ideally, the bright orangy-brown exhibited by adult male Rufous Hummingbirds, but often generalized as any shade of reddish brown. The crown of a Rufous-crowned Sparrow, for example, is different from either the hummingbird's shade or the sides of a Rufous-sided Towhee.

RUMP. The area between the end of the lower back and the base of the tail. A "rump patch" of contrasting color is cited as a good field mark, especially in flight, for various bird species, e.g., Common Flicker (white), Yellow-rumped Warbler. A "rump patch" may include the upper tail coverts but extends beyond them onto the back. See TOPOGRAPHY.

RUNNING. See WALKING.

S

SABINE, Sir Edward, 1788–1883 (Sabine's Gull: *Larus* [*Xema*] *sabini*). English general, physicist, and astronomer, veteran of the War of 1812, and member of the Ross and Parry expeditions to the Arctic (1818 and 1819). An early authority on the earth's magnetic field and its use in navigation. His gull was named for him by Joseph Sabine, Sir Edward's younger brother naturalist.

Birders frequently say SAY-byne's Gull and other variations are also heard. Sir Edward, however, pronounced his name SABB-un.

SAGE (Grouse, Thrasher, Sparrow) (i.e., sagebrush). A dominant shrub (*Artemesia tridentata;* family Compositae) of a distinctive type of "cool" desert which occurs at higher elevations than the low "hot" scrub deserts in the western mountain states of North America. It is the preferred breeding habitat of three bird species which are named for it: Sage Grouse (*Centrocercus urophasianus*), Sage Thrasher (*Oreoscoptes montanus*), and Sage Sparrow (*Amphispiza belli*). The breeding ranges of the grouse and the thrasher, like the occurrence of sagebrush, are restricted to North America; the sparrow also breeds in lower desert scrub as far south as northern Baja California.

The leaves, buds, and shoots of sagebrush are an enormously nutritious food source on which the Sage Grouse depends almost entirely during the winter months.

See BIOME; DISTRIBUTION; and Fig. 5.

SALMONELLOSIS. A common bacterial "food poison" which infects a wide variety of animals, including birds as well as men. See DISEASE.

SALT GLAND. Humans must void excess salt in urine via the kidneys. Flushing the salt from our system requires fresh water, which explains why drinking sea water is counterproductive to the castaway dying of thirst.

It has been demonstrated that the capacity of birds' kidneys to deal with excess salt is even poorer than our own, and yet seabirds frequently drink quantities of their preferred habitat with no ill effects.

The solution to this apparent paradox was revealed fairly recently (Schmidt-Nielsen et al., 1958) in experiments performed on the so-called nasal gland—since renamed the salt gland. This paired, linear structure lies in grooves in the skull over and/or in front of the eyeholes (orbits) and is connected to the nasal openings by a duct. The salt is transferred from the bloodstream to the glands and is then secreted in a highly concentrated solution via the ducts and nostrils. The tubenoses (order Procellariiformes) "fire" the salt solution through their double-barreled nostrils, but in most seabirds the colorless liquid dribbles along the bill and drops off the tip. This accounts for the frequent head shaking seen in oceanic birds and perhaps the perpetual drop adorning the bill tips of fulmars at sea. Not surprisingly, seabirds have been shown to possess the most well-developed salt glands, but ducks and other water birds that inhabit interior salt lakes also have them (Cooch, 1964).

SALT MARSH. A coastal wetland habitat, regularly flooded at high tide, dominated by species of *Spartina* grass and containing other salt-loving plants, such as glassworts (*Salicornia* spp.), sea lavender (*Limonium nashii*), and marsh elder (*Iva frutescens*). It is the preferred breeding habitat of the Seaside Sparrow (*Ammospiza maritima*) and coastal populations of the Sharp-tailed Sparrow (*Ammospiza caudacuta*). See *Dusky Seaside Sparrow* under ENDANGERED BIRDS.

SALTON SEA (California). A large lake in the southern California desert (southeast of Palm Springs) formed early in this century by a combination of hydrological experimentation and natural flooding. This oasis is home to tens of thousands of wintering waterfowl and shorebirds as well as interesting land birds attracted to the (relatively) lush vegetation. In fall "Mexican" vagrants such as the Blue-footed Booby often stray northward from the Gulf of California, and rarities of all kinds are sought—and frequently found—by local birders during spring and fall migration. A profitable birding area at any season—*very* hot in summer.

SANCTUARY. A parcel of land of any size where human use is restricted for the benefit of birds and other organisms. The term is very general, as are related terms—reserve, refuge, conservation land—and does not carry any implications of management policy. Some sanctuaries are little more than public parks with restricted vehicle access, while others may be visited only by obtaining a written permit. Some contain rare organisms; others are simply green spaces or resting areas for migrant birds. See the

Bibliography for listings of specific sanctuaries and other conservation lands. See also NATIONAL WILDLIFE REFUGE.

SANDERLING. Standard English name for a single species of sandpiper, *Calidris* (*Crocethia*) *alba* (family Scolopacidae; order Charadriiformes). The breeding distribution of the Sanderling is circumpolar arctic, and since they regularly winter as far south as the southern antipodes, they are among the most cosmopolitan of birds. They are among the few birds to breed exclusively in the stony barrens of the High Arctic, and while the migration of many individuals is among the longest of any bird species, others winter farther north (e.g., coast of New England) than almost any other shorebird. Though in many ways the quintessential sandpiper familiar to beachgoers the world over, the Sanderling is something of an anomaly. It is unique in the sandpiper family in lacking a hind toe (hallux), and its nesting habits are also atypical (see NEST; INCUBATION). The name is a corruption of an Icelandic name translatable as "sand wagtail"; it also evokes a preferred feeding habitat—the wave edge of sandy beaches. For family characteristics, see SANDPIPER.

SANDHILL (Crane). Sandhill Cranes normally nest and forage in marshland, prairie, or tundra habitats; however, in migration across interior North America they rest and feed in many of the extensive areas of dunes commonly called "sandhill country" by Midwesterners.

SANDPIPER. Standard English name for about 23 members of the family Scolopacidae (order Charadriiformes) as well as the name for the family as a whole. The sandpiper family contains a total of 85 species, which include the CURLEWS, GODWITS, YELLOWLEGS, WILLET, TATTLERS, DOWITCHERS, TURNSTONES, SURFBIRD, SNIPES, WOODCOCKS, KNOTS, SANDERLING, STINTS, and PHALAROPES, in addition to the species which are named "sandpipers."

Members of the sandpiper family come in a wide assortment of shapes and sizes (5 inches to 2 feet) with great variation in leg length and bill length and shape. They are mostly somberly colored in earth tones, usually marked in cryptic patterns of lines, spots, and "scales." Legs are sometimes brightly colored and the toes are unwebbed or partially webbed; all except the Sanderling retain the hind toe (hallux).

Sandpipers feed on a wide variety of plant and animal food from berries of arctic plants (e.g., *Empetrum nigrum*, an abundant arctic ground cover widely known as "curlewberry") to large sea worms pulled from mud flats by the long probing bills of the godwits. Many smaller, shorter-billed species dab on surf-washed beaches, picking up tidbits too small to identify even with binoculars.

The nests of sandpipers are usually shallow scrapes in the open or concealed in ground vegetation and typically lined fairly heavily with moss, lichens, leaves, and the like. The Solitary Sandpiper nests in a tree in an abandoned songbird's nest. The Sanderling makes an unusually deep, tidy cup. The 3–6 (usually 4) eggs are very variable in color and markings among different species: pale yellow-buff, yellow-olive, brownish yellow, or greenish; sparsely or densely marked with dark brown, reddish, or purple—usually rather distinct—speckles and/or splotches.

On the breeding grounds many sandpiper species utter extended trills and warbles, comparable to those of wood warblers, finches, or larks. Snatches of these songs are sometimes heard on migration, but most birdwatchers who have not visited the Arctic are familiar only with the shorter calls, which range in quality from abrupt, staccato chirps or pipings (peeps) to strident yelps (yellowlegs) and pleasing, mellifluous yodels (curlews).

These shorebirds are distributed worldwide (several cosmopolitan species) and a significant proportion breed in the Arctic and undertake long migrations to tropical wintering grounds or pass through the tropics en route to antipodean winter quarters (see, for example, the Hudsonian Godwit route, Fig. 17). They occur in virtually all water-edge situations as well as upland habitats such as shortgrass prairies and cultivated fields.

Sandpiper and other shorebird populations in North America had been decimated by market gunners by late in the last century (see CONSERVATION; EXTINCT BIRDS; EDIBILITY). Most species have made good recoveries with full protection, but the Eskimo Curlew (see ENDANGERED BIRDS) may have been shot beyond its ability to recover.

Only a few sandpipers prefer sandy habitats, but most utter characteristic piping notes.

SANDWICH (Tern). *Sterna* (*Thalasseus*) *sandvicensis* was named for the English town in Kent where the type specimen was collected in the eighteenth century and not for the famous earl, known to us for his islands and lunchtime staple.

SANIBEL ISLAND (Florida). A once pristine, now extensively developed island-cum-causeway off the Gulf coast of Florida near Fort Myers. The beaches and wetlands still contain numbers of shorebirds and wading birds, and the mangrove swamp of the Ding Darling National Wildlife Refuge holds the Mangrove Cuckoo, Gray Kingbird, and Black-whiskered Vireo during the breeding season and an impressive number of herons and egrets which come (spectacularly) home to roost in the evening. Shell collecting is another attraction of Sanibel.

SANITATION (of nest). See NEST.

SANTA ANA National Wildlife Refuge (Texas). See RIO GRANDE VALLEY.

SAPSUCKER. Standard English name for the 3 species of woodpeckers in the genus *Sphyrapicus* (family Picidae; order Piciformes), all of which breed and winter (in part) in North America.

The sapsuckers differ from other woodpeckers in their highly specialized method of feeding. They drill lines (horizontal or vertical) of round or square holes in a wide variety of woody plants (conifers as well as broadleaf species) and lick the sap that accumulates, using the brush-like modification on the tip of their extensible tongue. They also eat the green inner bark called the cambium and a wide variety of insects. Many species of songbirds as well as other woodpeckers have learned to visit fresh sapsucker holes, both for the accumulated sap and the insects that it attracts (see Foster and Tate, 1966–FOOD/FEEDING).

For family characteristics, see WOODPECKER.

SAPSUCKER WOODS (New York). A patch of deciduous woodland not far from the campus of Cornell University in Ithaca. Famed not so much for its birdlife, which is typical of upstate New York—Ruffed Grouse, American Woodcock, Pileated Woodpecker, Great Horned Owl, Brown Creeper, Black-throated Green Warbler, etc. (in addition to the Yellow-bellied Sapsucker)—as for the Cornell ornithologists—Arthur A. Allen, Frank Chapman, Albert Brand, and the consummate bird portraitist Louis Agassiz Fuertes—with whom it is closely associated.

SAUROPSIDA (saw-ROPP-sid-uh). An informal taxonomic grouping containing birds and reptiles, including most of their ancestors and emphasizing the close relationship between these now distinct classes of vertebrates.

SAVANNA(H) (Sparrow). This term originated in the tropics and has been used in various specific contexts (especially South America and Africa) to describe relatively flat or "rolling" areas with rank grasses and scattered shrubs or low trees with or without marked seasonal rainfall and sometimes bridging forest and pure grassland. The origins and life spans of savannas are disputed by plant ecologists, but they are at least a stable subclimax plant association maintained by poor soil. In a much looser sense, the word is sometimes applied to any grassland.

Like the definition of savanna, the habitat preferences of the Savannah Sparrow are highly flexible. It prefers open, usually grassy country and scattered scrubs under which to nest, usually near water (salt or fresh). Its name, however, has nothing to do with habitat, but refers to Savannah, Georgia, where Alexander Wilson first noted this species. Its range is continentwide.

See BIOME; DISTRIBUTION; and Fig. 5.

SAY, Thomas, 1787–1834 (*Sayornis phoebe:* Eastern Phoebe; *S. nigricans:* Black Phoebe; and *S. saya:* Say's Phoebe). Perhaps the most brilliant and most broadly knowledgeable of the early Philadelphia naturalists. Say's main interests and contributions were in entomology and conchology (mollusk shells). However, his general expertise was exercised as professor of natural history at the University of Pennsylvania; as expedition zoologist in the West; and as editor of Charles Lucien BONAPARTE'S *American Ornithology.* Collecting excursions took him all over the U.S. and into parts of Mexico; on one of these to the Rockies, the Black Phoebe was first collected and became the type for the genus which was eventually named for Say by Bonaparte. Say's Phoebe had already been described by Bonaparte as *Muscicapa saya,* and when the taxonomy of the flycatchers was revised, Say became the only man to be binomially commemorated in the name of a species of North American bird.

SCANSORIAL (skan-SOR-ee-yul). Specially adapted for climbing. Woodpeckers, Brown Creeper, nuthatches, and Black-and-White Warbler are examples of scansorial North American birds. See CLIMBING.

SCAPULARS (SKAP-yuh-lerz). Prominent feathers along the margins of the back (i.e., above the shoulders) which also overlap the lesser coverts and tertials. They provide a smooth transition of plumage from the feathers of the upper wing surface to those of the back. See Fig. 25.

SCAPUS (SKAY-pus). A little-used term for the stiff tapering shaft of a contour feather, i.e., the CALAMUS and RACHIS combined. See also FEATHER.

SCAUP (skawp). Standard English name for 2 species of the so-called BAY DUCKS in the genus *Aythya.* The Greater and Lesser Scaups are impossible to distinguish in the field except under the most favorable circumstances, most of the standard field marks proving unreliable by themselves. However, the habits of the two species are more distinctive than their respective plumages. The Greater breeds largely in marshy tundra above tree line and winters along the seacoasts of the continent. The Lesser prefers muskeg ponds and lakes below the tree line and ranges as well into prairie marshes; it tends to winter farther south than its congener and is then more characteristic of inland bodies and sheltered coastal waters.

"Scaup" comes from "scalp," an old British term for the beds of mud and grasses on which mussels grow. Mussels and other shellfish are preferred foods of these ducks on coastal wintering grounds. Both species are aptly called "bluebills" by hunters.

For family characteristics, see DUCK.

SCHIZOCHROISM (SKIZ-oh-CROH-izm). An abnormal lack of one of a bird's normal plumage pigments (see COLOR AND PATTERN), resulting in an oddly colored individual (normally green birds turn blue in the absence of yellow) or an unusually pale individual (recorded in alcids and other species). See Plate 5; also LEUCISM; ALBINISM.

SCLATER (SKLAY-ter), Philip L., 1829–1913 (*Parus sclateri*: Mexican or Gray-sided Chickadee). Eminent British ornithologist (a founder of the British Ornithologists' Union and secretary of the Zoological Society of London) who traveled in North America but whose main contribution to our ornithology was as the describer and author of many species and subspecies. See also under ZOOGEOGRAPHY.

SCLEROTIC (skleh-ROT-ik) **or SCLERAL** (SKLAIR-ul) **RING.** A circle of overlapping bony plates in the eyes of birds, reptiles, and certain fishes; it helps to stabilize the eye during focusing. See VISION.

SCOTER. Standard English name for 3 species of sea ducks, all in the genus *Melanitta* (family Anatidae; order Anseriformes). All of these—the Black (Common), Surf, and White-winged Scoters (*M. nigra, M. perspicillata,* and *M. fusca* [*deglandi*])—occur in North America.

The scoters are large black diving ducks which breed on arctic tundra and subarctic muskeg and winter along both coasts—to Baja California in the West.

On their wintering grounds the scoters eat prodigious numbers of shellfish—especially blue mussels—which are pulverized by the powerful muscles of their gizzards. Shellfishermen accuse these birds of competition for more valuable species such as oysters and scallops, but these have proven not to be very significant items of the scoter diet. "Coots," as hunters of sea ducks call scoters, migrate to their wintering grounds in long lines and are shot for sport—especially on the east coast of North America—during this fall passage. Their flesh is not generally esteemed; however, see recipe under EDIBILITY. On shoals such as those off Cape Cod, Massachusetts, scoters winter in great rafts consisting of hundreds of thousands of birds; such concentrations are particularly vulnerable to oil spills (see MAN-MADE THREATS TO BIRDLIFE).

The Surf Scoter is a North American endemic; the Black and White-winged (including the "Velvet") range throughout most of the Holarctic region.

The best speculation on the origin of "scoter" is that it is derived from "coot" owing to the superficial resemblance between these common members of the rail family and the black sea ducks.

SCOTT, General Winfield, 1786–1866 (Scott's Oriole: *Icterus parisorum*). Hero of the War of 1812 and Mexican War, a brave and intelligent soldier, famed for his talents as a peacemaker. Sometimes called the greatest American general between Washington and Lee, Scott was also known as "Old Fuss and Feathers" because of his personal vanity and an obsessive punctilio. He was a national political figure during his entire career, but failed (rather badly) as the Whig candidate for President in 1852, running against Franklin Pierce.

SCRAPE. The most rudimentary nest form, a mere depression in sand or earth scraped out by the feet of the parent birds, unlined or lined with a few bits of shell or pebbles, or scraps of plant material. The Least Tern, Black Skimmer, and several of the *Charadrius* plovers make this kind of nest along the coast; most grouse species make scrapes in their appropriate habitats. See NEST and Fig. 15.

SCRATCHING (of head with foot). One of birds' basic, innate behavior patterns, often practiced or attempted within hours of hatching. It is often, as in humans, a straightforward response to an itch. But since birds cannot reach the head with their main preening tool, the bill, scratching also serves to control lice and other ECTOPARASITES, to clean and straighten the feathers, and to spread preen oil in this region (see PREENING).

There are two stereotyped head-scratching methods: direct and indirect. *Direct* scratchers raise their foot directly to the head below the wing, i.e., without requiring any adjustment in the position of the wing. *Indirect* scratchers extend the wing downward and extend the leg *over the wing base* to reach the head. Most (though not all) passerines scratch indirectly. Most birds overall—including what are considered more primitive forms—are direct scratchers. There is much controversy over which scratching method is "better" (i.e., easier to perform, more efficient) and how much variation exists in scratching technique among different orders, families, genera, and even individual birds. It is widely held that one method or the other is fairly consistent among the larger taxonomic groupings and that the character is therefore of some use in confirming phylogenetic relationships.

See Nice and Schantz, *Auk* (1959), 76:339–42.

SCREECH OWL. See Fig. 14. Standard English name for many of the approximately 40 species of small, nocturnal owls in the genus *Otus* (family Strigidae; order Strigiformes), 4 of which breed in North America. The term is also used as a collective name for this group, especially in the New World; in the Old World most *Otus* owls are called "scops" owls.

On the whole, *Otus* owls do more wailing, hooting, and whistling than screeching.

SCUTELLATE (SKYOO-teh-late). Scaly; referring, for example, to the overlapping horny plates covering the legs and feet of many species of birds; see LEG/FOOT.

SEABIRD. In the broadest sense, any bird species which habitually frequents the ocean. However, often used in a more restrictive sense to refer to pelagic birds, i.e., those characteristic of offshore waters, e.g., the tubenoses, gannets and boobies, jaegers, two phalaropes, and some gulls, terns, and alcids. This narrower definition excludes such essentially coastal "seabirds" as SEA DUCKS and cormorants.

SEA DUCK. Collective name for ducks belonging to the subfamily Aythyinae or the tribe Mergini, including the eiders, scoters, goldeneyes, Bufflehead, Oldsquaw, Harlequin Duck, and mergansers (not included in the Aythyinae). All of these ducks live primarily at sea—largely coastally or over shoals—when not on their breeding grounds.

For further description, see DUCK; EIDER; SCOTER; etc.

SEA GULL. A vernacular name for any species of gull, including those which breed inland. Many people think it is the specific name for the commonest gull of their region.

SECONDARIES. The flight feathers (remiges) that are attached to the "forearm" (ulna), less frequently referred to as the "cubitals." The number of secondaries is much more widely variable than that of the primaries and is apparently proportional to attachment space, i.e., the length of the ulna: hummingbirds have as few as 6, while some albatross species have more than 30; most passerines have 9. The secondaries are numbered from the outermost (i.e., that nearest the innermost primary) to the innermost (that nearest the body). For distinction of the innermost secondaries, see TERTIALS; WING. See also Figs. 19 and 25.

SEDENTARY. May be used in the same sense as "permanent resident," i.e., referring to a bird species which does not migrate.

SEED DISPERSAL. The majority of birds at least occasionally play some role in plant dispersal by carrying seeds from one place and depositing them in another. Obviously, birds which feed most heavily on fruits and seeds are the most effective dispersers, and long-distance migrants may distribute seeds over hundreds or even thousands of miles. The briefest consideration of some of the ways in which birds transport seeds shows the resourcefulness of plant adaptation and the "interconnectedness" of organisms.

• Some plants, e.g., jewelweeds (*Impatiens* spp.), have "explosive" seed pods which scatter their contents when touched by foraging birds and other animals.

• Seed-eating birds scatter seeds from dry pods in a local area simply by landing on a plant and shaking it while feeding.

• Many frugivorous birds remove and swallow only the fleshy outer part of a fruit, letting the seed fall to the ground.

• A number of plants have sticky, fuzzy, or barbed seeds which cling to plumage (and fur) and may thereby be transported considerable distances.

• Seeds or other reproducing parts of plants which grow in or near water readily adhere to the plumage and/or legs and feet of ducks, shorebirds, and other aquatic species and then float or brush off in another pond or marsh.

• Jays, nutcrackers, etc., bury acorns and other nuts, sometimes far from their place of origin.

• Some hard seeds are regurgitated hours after being eaten, following the digestion of the soft part of the fruit (see PELLET).

• Many seeds pass through a bird's digestive tract unharmed and land in suitable habitat many miles from the parent plant. Some seeds may *require* the action of strong digestive acids in order to germinate properly.

• Raptors which kill seed/fruit-eating animals determine the ultimate destination of the contents of their prey's digestive tract.

• Some plant features such as brightly colored fruits and sticky seeds may have evolved specifically to "encourage" dispersal by birds and other animals, either externally or internally.

SEEDEATER. In the broadest sense, a descriptive term for members of the family Fringillidae (and Emberizidae)—i.e., "birds which eat seeds." Also the standard English name for about 12 species of African cardueline finches (Fringillidae) in the genus *Serinus*; for the approximately 30 members of the New World emberizine finch genus *Sporophila* (family Emberizidae; order Passeriformes); and for the 2 members of another New World emberizine genus, *Amaurospiza*.

One member of the essentially Neotropical *Sporophila* seedeaters, the White-collared Seedeater, breeds sporadically in the lower Rio Grande Valley of Texas.

All *Sporophila* species are noted for their distinctive short, deep, conical bills. White-collared Seedeaters feed on grass and weed seeds up to about 5,000 feet in the tropics.

For more on the nomenclature and general characteristics of the finches, see FINCH.

SEMATIC (seh-MAT-ik). Signal-like; acting as a warning or attracting device, such as the colors, patterns, or devices in the plumage of some birds. See APOSEMATIC; EPISEMATIC; PARASEMATIC.

SEMIPALMATED (Plover, Sandpiper). Having partial webbing between the front toes. The Willet (*Catoptrophorus semipalmatus*) bears this characteristic along with the Semipalmated Plover, the Semipalmated Sand-piper, and other species.

SEMIPLUME (also semipluma; pl.: semiplumae). A type of feather intermediate between adult down feathers and contour feathers, i.e., they have a well-developed rachis (longer than the longest barb) but no or little cohesive vane owing to the lack of barbules (see Fig. 9). Semiplumes typically occur at the margins of feather tracts/apteria and—like down—apparently function mainly as insulation. See PLUMAGE for other plausible functions. See also FEATHER for comparison with other feather types.

SEMISPECIES. A term coined by Mayr (1942–TAXONOMY) to refer to forms which are obviously closely related but totally isolated geographically. Since the two (or more) populations never meet under natural circumstances, it is impossible to judge by the usual criterion of interbreeding whether they consist of fully distinct species or subspecies. See also SUPER-SPECIES; SPECIATION.

SENSES. See HEARING; NAVIGATION; SMELL; TASTE; CIRCADIAN RHYTHM; TOUCH; VISION.

SET (of eggs). Same as CLUTCH.

SETOSE (SEE-tohs). Having bristles, which in birds are modified feathers. See FEATHER; RICTAL.

SEX. See REPRODUCTIVE SYSTEM; COPULATION; DIMORPHISM; HOMOSEX-UALITY.

SEX, CHANGE OF. The sexual glands (gonads) of bird embryos in early stages have the potential to develop into either testes (male organs) or ovaries (female organs). Vestiges of potential testes are retained in mature females and in rare instances, when the left ovary (the only one which normally develops in most birds) is damaged or diseased, a healthy testis may develop on the right. The bird may then become a fully functional male with the plumage and behavioral characteristics of that gender. This is a rare phenomenon and would, of course, go unnoticed in most cases in wild birds; the known instances are recorded in domestic hens and pigeons. See REPRODUCTIVE SYSTEM.

SEXUAL DIMORPHISM. See DIMORPHISM and Plate 4.

SHAFT. The stiff central spine of a contour feather, i.e., the calamus and rachis together. A little-used synonym is "scapus." See FEATHER and Fig. 9.

SHAG. The preferred name for cormorants in much of the English-speaking world and in British ornithological literature. This arbitrary usage doubtless owes its origin to the two resident British species in the genus *Phalacrocorax*, one known simply as Shag (*P. aristotelis*) and the other with equal majesty as Cormorant (*P. carbo*). In North America the standard English name for all birds in this family is cormorant; however, Atlantic fishermen often refer to all species indiscriminately as shags. See also CORMORANT.

SHEARWATER. Standard English name for 17 species (mostly in the genus *Puffinus*) of the family Procellariidae (which also includes the PETRELS and FULMARS) and used here to designate that family as a whole. Fifteen species (including 11 shearwaters) occur as regular visitors in North American waters and another 7 as stragglers (see Appendixes I and II).

The shearwaters and petrels comprise a varied segment of the order Procellariiformes, i.e., the tubenoses. They vary considerably in size (10 inches to 3 feet worldwide), though species which visit North America are in the middle range (12 to 20 inches). They are patterned in shades of black, white, gray, and brown, sometimes relieved by a touch of yellow or pink on bill and/or feet. They have relatively short (stubby or slender), hooked bills, with nostril tubes situated on the top of the bill at its base (see SALT GLAND; NOSTRILS). The front three toes are webbed and the hind toe (hallux) is vestigial. All species are awkward on land, where they must waddle on their tarsi rather than walk erect. The shearwaters and fulmars are graceful fliers adapted, like the albatrosses, to soar on ocean wind currents (see FLIGHT, *Dynamic Soaring*, and Fig. 22). GADFLY and other smaller petrels, however, may fly in a more erratic, jerky manner. Many species profit from the refuse of offshore fishing operations. When molested, shearwaters will often vomit forth whatever is in their gullet, along with a musky STOMACH OIL, which effectively repulses most would-be captors.

The skill with which shearwaters can sail at the very edge of the waves even in the roughest weather is one of the wonders of birdlife and one of the joys of birdwatching. On a calm day, when the sea is glassy, it is often possible to see that shearwaters do indeed "shear" the surface with their wing tips from time to time. It is thought that their ability to maneuver so accurately is assisted in great measure by their elaborate nostril modifications (see NOSTRILS).

Like the storm-petrels, these tubenoses are colonial nesters that dig their own burrows, take over abandoned ones, or simply occupy crevices on rocky slopes. The chamber may be thinly or heavily lined with plant material and normally contains a single immaculate white egg.

On a calm day at sea, where shearwaters are gathered in flocks they are often heard to utter various squawks, grunts, cackles, and even "buzzes." Bizarre nocturnal wailing and moaning are characteristic sounds at breeding colonies.

The shearwaters and petrels range over all the oceans of the world, but are most diverse and abundant in colder waters, where marine life is especially prolific—particularly around the Antarctic.

The majority of our shearwaters and petrels are non-breeding summer visitors to North American waters and nest in the Southern Hemisphere during the northern winter. The Northern Fulmar, which breeds in the Arctic in both the Atlantic and the Pacific, Audubon's Shearwater, which breeds in the Bahamas, and the Manx Shearwater, which breeds off Baja California and in the northeastern Atlantic (one nesting record for eastern North America), are the exceptions.

For the derivation of "shearwater," see above.

SHIELD, FRONTAL. See FRONTAL SHIELD.

SHOREBIRD. On the whole, synonymous with the suborder Charadrii with the exception perhaps of the jacanas. It therefore includes the oyster-catchers, stilts and avocets, plovers, turnstones, and sandpipers (including godwits, curlews, woodcock, snipe, yellowlegs, etc.), and phalaropes. The perspicacious reader will not fail to notice that many undisputable "birds of the shore," e.g., gulls, terns, ducks, are not "shorebirds," while many "shorebirds," e.g., Upland Sandpiper, woodcock, and snipe, are not, for the most part, "birds of the shore."

SHOVELER. Standard English name for 4 species of dabbling ducks worldwide, all of which have distinctive long, wide bills. One species, the Northern Shoveler, *Anas* (*Spatula*) *clypeata*, occurs throughout most of North America (as well as the Old World). The name, of course, refers to the shape of the bill, which, however, is used not as a shovel but rather as a strainer (see FOOD/FEEDING). For family characteristics, see DUCK.

SHRIKE. Standard English name for most of the approximately 70 members of the family Laniidae (order Passeriformes), as well as the collective term for the family as a whole.

Shrikes are small to moderately large birds (6¼ to 14½ inches) with a short, heavy, strongly hooked bill; rather large head; strong, rounded wings; long tail; and powerful legs, feet, and claws. Their overall shape is somewhat accipiter-like. Shrikes are usually boldly patterned with dark facial markings, wings, and tail, contrasting with pale underparts and white "flashes" on wings and tail. Some tropical African groups are brilliantly colored; the two resident North American species (Northern and Loggerhead Shrikes) are black, gray, and white, with brown tones in the juvenal plumage. An Asian species, Brown Shrike, has been recorded as an accidental straggler to Alaska.

The subfamily Laniinae, to which the North American shrikes belong, comprises the only species of songbirds that prey habitually on vertebrate animals (birds, mammals, reptiles, amphibians, fish). They are birds of open country and forest edge and tend to seek prominent perches where they can scan for their prey, which also includes large insects and crustaceans. Both of our species of "butcher birds" practice the famous shrike habit of hanging "meat" on thorns or in narrow crotches, sometimes returning to the mummified remains as long as months afterward. Loggerhead and Northern Shrikes are usually silent, except for a few harsh calls, but both have true songs which are often likened to those of the mockingbirds, with sweet, melodic phrases interspersed with harsh chatters and squeaks as well as mimicry of other birds.

The cup nest has a bulky exterior of sticks and stems lined with fine plant fibers, plant down, hair, and feathers. It may be placed in the crotch of a low, dense, thorny shrub or high (over 50 feet) in a tree. The 5–9 (usually 4–7) eggs are white or off white, densely marked with comparatively pale, brownish and grayish blotches and speckles.

Shrikes occur throughout North America, Europe, and Asia, achieve greatest diversity in Africa, are absent in Australia and New Zealand (present in New Guinea), and reach only the edge of the Neotropics at the southern end of the high central plateau of Mexico. Together, the distributions of our two shrikes cover all of North America except the most barren, treeless parts of the Arctic, the breeding range of the more southerly Loggerhead picking up roughly where that of the Northern leaves off. The Northern Shrike also occurs widely in the Palearctic, where its English name is Great Grey Shrike. Both of our shrikes are migratory from the northernmost parts of their range.

The notion that shrikes were so named because they "shriek" is not very satisfactory, but there is some evidence of early confusion with the Eurasian Jay, which is similarly proportioned, quite predatory, and shrieks *a lot.*

SIBLING SPECIES. Species which are very closely related but which do not normally interbreed where their ranges overlap. Eastern and Western Meadowlarks exemplify the phenomenon in North America. See SUPERSPECIES; REPRODUCTIVE ISOLATION.

SIGHT. See VISION.

SIGHT RECORD. The occurrence of a bird species in a given locality corroborated only by one or more eyewitnesses and perhaps their notes and sketches made at the scene; sightings not confirmed by a specimen, photograph, or tape recording. See VERIFICATION OF RECORDS.

SIGN STIMULUS. A phenomenon, usually visual (e.g., an action, shape, or color), to which birds (or other animals) can be expected to respond predictably. Such stimuli may be so broad as to elicit a mistaken response—flocks of ducks or other birds sometimes "spook" at the passing shadow of a Great Blue Heron, which they mistake for the threatening presence of an eagle. Or, as in many forms of recognition among members of the same species, they may be too subtle to be perceived by human senses.

SILKY FLYCATCHER. Standard English collective name for the 4 species of birds in the family Ptilogonatidae (order Passeriformes); 3 of these species reside exclusively in the highlands of Central America. For the single species which breeds in North America, see PHAINOPEPLA.

SINGING. See SONG.

SISKIN. Standard English name for about 20 species of small cardueline finches (family Fringillidae; order Passeriformes), 4 in the Old World genus *Carduelis* and 16 in the New World genus *Spinus.* (Some taxonomies include all in *Carduelis.*) One species of *Spinus* siskin, the Pine Siskin, breeds throughout most of the boreal and montane coniferous forest of North America; it also winters mainly in the Nearctic region, though wandering as far south as Guatemala in "irruption" years.

The Pine Siskin feeds mainly on small, soft seeds and insects, as befits its comparatively narrow bill. It often nests in loose colonies and in flight years may remain south of its normal summer range to breed.

"Siskin" was first applied to the Eurasian (*Carduelis*) Siskin, one of whose calls may be rendered as *tsyzing*. It is possible that this sound is related to the Scandinavian words—e.g., *sidsken* and *zieske*—from which the English form followed.

For general family characteristics, see FINCH.

600 CLUB. An elite organization open only to those members of the bird-listing fraternity who have seen 600 or more species in North America in accordance with the geographical and ethical guidelines articulated by the American Birding Association. Since only about 650 species of birds breed in North America, eligibility for the 600 Club is achieved only by thorough and fortunate coverage of all of the continent's major biomes and at least most of the specialized avian habitats (see BIRD FINDING). The club's headquarters travel from year to year. See S. Keith, *Audubon* (1963), 65:376–77.

SIZE (including length, weight, and wingspan). Birds as a class exhibit an enormous variation in the several size criteria (see below), the more so if we consider the gigantic extinct birds, known from fossil skeletons. Before noting some of the extremes, a few generalizations about size in birds:

• Many more very large bird forms existed in earlier geological epochs than have occurred in recent times. Like many of the largest mammals, some bird giants perished during the Pleistocene ice age, but the extinction of huge modern birds, such as the Elephant Bird of Madagascar and the moas of New Zealand, seems to be more related to the ascendancy of humanity than to unfavorable climatic changes. See *Extremes of Size*, below; also DIATRYMA; TERATORNIS; EVOLUTION OF BIRDLIFE.

• Bird species (and other "warm-blooded" animals) tend to be larger in overall body size in the northern parts of their range than in the southern (Allen's Rule). This is probably related to the fact that the ratio of surface area to weight decreases as size increases, so that proportionally less heat is lost from larger bodies.

• Sexual differences in size tend to be slight among the great majority of bird species. When sexual dimorphism in size does occur, however, it is the male which is slightly larger in the majority of cases (noticeable in many gallinaceous birds). However, female hawks, eagles, etc., and falcons (order Falconiformes) are conspicuously larger than their mates in many species.

• There is some evolutionary correlation between size of predator and size of prey: Northern Goshawks hunt grouse; Sharp-shinned Hawks prey on small land birds.

• There is some correlation between size (body weight) and flying ability. The heaviest birds are flightless, and the largest of flying birds (albatrosses, condors) have extreme wing adaptations (see FLIGHT).

• There are also limitations to smallness. Hummingbirds can store very little energy in their tiny, but comparatively heavy, vertebrate bodies and must therefore feed almost constantly (or become torpid) in order to maintain basic metabolism. A hummingbird any smaller than the smallest species (see below) could probably not eat enough to meet the energy needed to feed.

EXTREMES OF SIZE. It should be noted here that disparities in records and opinions of various sources lend a still broad margin of ambiguity to many of these "records."

Largest Bird Known to Have Lived. The Giant Moa (*Diornis maximus*) of New Zealand, a wingless ratite which stood as high as 13 feet with neck extended and weighed over 500 pounds, is the tallest known bird, while the Elephant Bird of Madagascar (*Aepyornis titan*), which stood a mere 9–10 feet tall but probably weighed over 950 pounds, is the heaviest known.

Largest Living Bird. The African Ostrich (*Struthio camelus*), some of which stand 8–9 feet tall and weigh at least 345 pounds. Other living ratites, e.g., cassowaries, Emu, rheas, are also far from petite.

Largest Flying Bird Known to Have Lived. A recently discovered species of prehistoric condor in the genus TERATORNIS had a wingspan of 25 feet and is thought to have weighed about 175 pounds.

Largest Living Flying Birds. Species of bustards, pelicans, swans, and condors. The Kori Bustard of Africa weighs up to at least 40 pounds, and Mute and Trumpeter Swans equal or exceed this weight (the ability of an alleged 49.5-pound Mute Swan to become airborne has been officially doubted, however; McWhirter, 1980). In North America, the Trumpeter Swan may be the largest native bird overall, males attaining weights of up to 38 pounds, a length of 6 feet, and a wingspan exceeding 8 feet.

Birds with Greatest Wingspan. See above for the largest flying bird known to science. Among living species, the Marabou Stork of Africa may have the greatest wingspan—to 12 feet (Fisher and Peterson, 1964–BIRD), though 9 feet is more usual for this species. Wandering and Royal Albatrosses, on the other hand, *average* wingspans of over 10 feet and some individuals may achieve a 13-foot span (11 feet 4 inches *confirmed* for Wandering). The native California Condor has a wingspan of up to 9 feet 7 inches (Koford, 1953–ENDANGERED BIRDS), which exceeds that of even our regularly occurring Black-footed Albatross (7–7½ feet), and with a weight of up to 31 pounds, the condor has a reasonable claim to be the largest flying bird in the world.

Smallest Living Birds. The Bee Hummingbird (*Mellisuga helenae*), endemic to Cuba and the Isle of Pines, is generally acknowledged to be the smallest living bird, males measuring 2¼ inches from bill tip to tail end. The Calliope Hummingbird is the smallest North American bird at 2¾ inches. Both of these species weigh about ⅒ of an ounce (3 grams).

For other mensural figures, see BILL; EGG; for standards of calculation, see MEASUREMENTS.

See also SEXUAL DIMORPHISM.

SKELETON. See Fig. 19. In the broadest sense, the skeleton of a bird serves the same basic functions as it does in all the other animals which possess one: it is a more or less rigid frame to which the muscles are attached and in which the softer, more delicate organs of the body are supported and protected. In its overall design and the structure of many of its parts, however, the bird skeleton is unique, and most of its singular features are related to the ability to fly. Not surprisingly, lightness and a flexible but unified framework have been the principal skeletal adaptations to flight. Many bones present in earthbound animals are absent altogether in birds or have become fused into less cumbersome units. In addition, the larger bones of most strong-flying species are essentially hollow (see *Pneu-*

FIG. 19. *Digestive system and skeleton.*

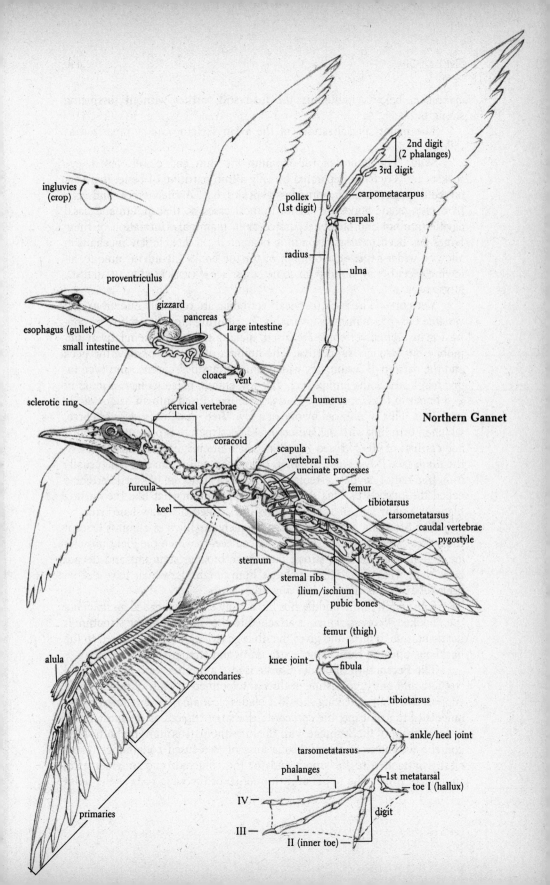

ingluvies
(crop)

2nd digit
(2 phalanges)

3rd digit

pollex
(1st digit)

carpometacarpus

carpals

radius

ulna

proventriculus

gizzard

pancreas

esophagus (gullet)

small intestine

large intestine

cloaca

vent

humerus

Northern Gannet

sclerotic ring

cervical vertebrae

coracoid

scapula

vertebral ribs

uncinate processes

femur

tibiotarsus

tarsometatarsus

caudal vertebrae

pygostyle

furcula

keel

sternum

sternal ribs

ilium/ischium

pubic bones

alula

secondaries

femur (thigh)

knee joint

fibula

tibiotarsus

ankle/heel joint

tarsometatarsus

phalanges

IV

III

II (inner toe)

1st metatarsal

toe I (hallux)

digit

primaries

matization, below), lightening the load still further without sacrificing strength.

The major specializations of the avian skeleton are summarized as follows:

Skull. The bones of the cranium are thin and closely fused; eye sockets are very large, separated by only a thin partition of bone; there are no teeth (present only in some fossil species, e.g., *Archaeopteryx* and *Hesperornis*); palate bones are narrow in most cases, so that mouth and nasal cavities are not completely separated as in mammals (formation of these bones has been used as taxonomic characters); a flexible jaw mechanism allows a wider gape; development of tongue bones (hyoids) is unique, allowing exceptional mobility in some cases (see WOODPECKER; HUMMING-BIRD; TONGUE).

Vertebrae. The neck (cervical) vertebrae are relatively numerous and variable (13–25; mammals invariably 7), allowing great flexibility; by contrast many *spinal* vertebrae are fused, making the backbone relatively immobile but strongly supportive. The number of vertebrae below the neck and the pattern of fusion vary widely among families, species, and even individual birds. Some groups (e.g., falcons, cranes, pigeons) have a series of 2–5 bones in the upper back (dorsal vertebrae) fused into an *os dorsale* or *notarium*. This is followed by one or a few "free" (i.e., unfused) vertebrae, which in turn link with the *synsacrum*. This structure is present in all birds and consists of 10–23 fused vertebrae which in most cases are also fused to the *ilium* (see *Pelvic Girdle*, below). Below the synsacrum are 4–9 (usually 6–7) free tail or caudal vertebrae and finally a structure of fused vertebrae called the *pygostyle*. This structure is shaped somewhat like the cutting blade of a plow and therefore is sometimes called the plowshare bone.

The Sternum, or breastbone, is uniquely modified in all birds (except the ratites) with a more or less pronounced *keel* to which the flight muscles are attached. In general, strong fliers have broader sternums and deeper keels than weak fliers. This includes hummingbirds, which have deeper keels relative to body size than any other birds.

Ribs. Each of the middle ribs has a bony extension called an *uncinate* (i.e., hooked) *process*, which is attached to the rib behind; the structure is nearly unique to birds and gives the rib cage (which is also anchored to the backbone and the breastbone) extra unity and strength.

The Pectoral or Shoulder Girdle is also a modification for structural strength and unity, consisting of three interconnected pairs of bones which support the wings: the long shoulder blades (*scapulae*) are anchored by ligaments to the rib cage; the *coracoids*, the largest bones of the girdle, connect the front of the scapulae with the breastbone (sternum) on both sides; and the *wishbone* or *furcula*, consisting of two fused collarbones (clavicles), is attached to the upper ends of the coracoids and provides extra support in front. The upper arm (humerus) of the wing rests at the point of maximum support where these three paired structures join. At this same juncture is located the triosseum canal, the "pulley" through which the "rope"—the tendon of the supracoracoideus muscle—passes and attaches to the base of the humerus, allowing the wing to be "hoisted" in flight (see MUSCLES; FLIGHT; and Fig. 10).

The Pelvic or Hip Girdle consists of a plate not unlike the sternum in general shape but made up of three fused bones (*ilium, ischium,* and *pubis*). This plate is anchored firmly along the major fused part of the backbone (synsacrum); it bears the socket of the upper leg bone (femur) and, like the sternum, provides a broad surface for the attachment of important muscles, in this case those of the legs. In addition to support, it is a kind of shock absorber for the "landing gear." The conjunction of the femur and the pelvic girdle is specially modified to enable some birds to stand comfortably on one leg.

The Bones of the Wing conform very closely to the bones of the human arm, at least down as far as the wrist. The bone of the upper arm (*humerus*) is the strongest bone of the arm/wing and, together with the appropriate muscles, bears the main burden of moving it. Its heavy appearance is belied by its essentially hollow interior in most species (see *Pneumatization,* below). In some long-winged birds (e.g., the Northern Gannet in Fig. 19) a series of long feathers (sometimes called tertials or tertiaries) are attached to the humerus. Beyond the humerus come the bones of the forearm (*radius* and *ulna*), also rather similar to the corresponding human structure. The ulna bears the secondary feathers. Starting at the bend of the wing the modifications of bird wing and human arm diverge strikingly. Where man has 27 bones in his wrist and hand, birds make do with 7–9. The human wrist is an agglomeration of 8 bones (*carpals*) and is followed by 5 hand bones (*metacarpals*); these in turn are attached to five digits, each consisting of 3 finger bones (*phalanges*), except for the thumb, which has only 2. A bird has only 2 distinct wrist bones. The other wrist bones and all of the hand bones are fused into a "double" bone called the *carpometacarpus*. At the base of the carpometacarpus is attached the avian "thumb" (first or "alular" digit or *pollex*), which usually consists of 1 phalanx, rarely 2 (loons, some geese). At the end of the carpometacarpus, two more digits are attached: the larger consists of either 2 or 3 phalanges; the smaller invariably has only 1. The bird's hand bones (except the two tiny carpals) hold the primary feathers and the "thumb" holds the alula (see Fig. 19).

The Bones of the Leg. At first glance the leg of a bird seems more like a human leg than a wing seems like an arm. Particularly on a long-legged bird such as a heron, we can see clearly what appears to be a thigh ending in a prominent knee followed by a very plausible shin, ankle, and foot with toes. Except for the toes, this is a misreading of the anatomy of a bird's leg. The real thigh bone (*femur*) is short and stout and rests close to the body under the feathers and skin, where it is hidden from view unless you are making a bird skin or carving a roast. The femur ends at the knee joint, which is also normally buried under the feathers of the belly. The first exposed part of a bird's leg corresponds to our shin or lower leg and, like it, is made up largely of two bones (*tibia* and *fibula*) which are partly fused. Thus the conspicuous knob which we at first take for a bird's knee is really its ankle (or heel) joint and bends in the opposite direction from the knee. A bird's ankle bones (*tarsals*), like those of the wrist, are reduced in number and strongly modified. Some of them are fused with the lower end of the tibia, so that this bone is properly called the *tibiotarsus*. Other ankle bones are fused with bones of the foot (*metatarsals*) to make what looks to be a shin but in reality is more like the human instep and is properly called the *tarsometatarsus*. To ensure confusion, this precise term is often shortened to *metatarsus* or, in birding jargon, simply *tarsus* (see Fig. 25).

The tibiotarsus (the leg bone above the ankle) is feathered in most birds though bare in many long-legged species such as herons and shorebirds. The rest of the leg is naked in most species, but a few hawks have feathered "tarsi," and owls and some grouse have feathered "tarsi" and toes (see Fig. 12).

Most birds, then, stand and walk on the balls of their feet and their toes, of which, with a few exceptions, there are four. The "little toe" (fifth digit) is missing and the "big toe" (first digit or *hallux*) usually points rearward, leaving three toes in front, (for other arrangements, see LEG/FOOT). In many species the hallux is thumb-like in that it is crucial for grasping perches or prey; in others, it is much reduced in size and functionless; and in a very few cases (e.g., the plovers) it has disappeared altogether. All of the toes bear claws, which, like the toes themselves, may be greatly modified in accordance with the habits of different species (see LEG/FOOT).

Pneumatization. As noted above, one striking skeletal adaptation to flight is the evolution of "hollow" bones—particularly well developed in large, strong fliers, in which the weight-saving advantages are obvious. The process by which the phenomenon occurs is called pneumatization (i.e., filling with air). It is a function of the respiratory system and indisputably one of the most astonishing "miracles" of animal physiology.

Late in the incubation period, air sacs connected to the ear and nasal cavities and the lungs (see RESPIRATORY SYSTEM) invade the bones of the embryo by way of natural openings such as those through which veins pass. At this point, possibly due to the release of certain hormones, part of the bone core "dissolves," allowing the air sac to penetrate the entire core and leaving only a tracery of thin, interlocking bony struts to retain internal strength. The process may continue up to two years after hatching and occurs in varying degrees among different species of birds. It is usually best developed in the bones of the upper arm (humerus), thigh (femur), ribs, and vertebrae, but in some birds the process extends to the skull and "fingers." For reasons which seem obvious in some cases but remain obscure in others, pneumatization is less prevalent in many deep-diving birds (e.g., loons), in fast-flying birds (e.g., shorebirds), and in parts of the body which must withstand unusual stresses (e.g., the heads of woodpeckers).

SKIMMER. Standard English name for all 3 members of the family Rynchopidae (order Charadriiformes), all of which belong to a single genus, *Rynchops*. One species, the Black Skimmer, breeds in North America.

Skimmers are peculiar-looking water birds whose closest relatives are the gulls and terns (Laridae). They have long powerful wings attached to a comparatively short body; their legs are short (tern-like) with partial webbing between the front three toes. The Black Skimmer is about 20 inches long. All species are dark above, white below, with yellow or red legs and mandible bases. The most distinctive skimmer characteristic is the bill, which is deep but compressed laterally to knife-like thinness with the lower mandible extending a quarter of its length beyond the upper. See FOOD/FEEDING and Fig. 2 for a description and illustration of the use of this apparatus.

Like most terns, skimmers are colonial and lay their eggs in an unlined, shallow scrape. The 2–5 eggs are white to buff and boldly splotched with blackish-brown and paler (grayish) subsurface markings and some smaller speckles.

Skimmers make a very distinctive, low *kaup* and *aur*, reminiscent of a dog's bark and frequently heard in the still air of dawn and dusk, when they prefer to feed.

Skimmers are essentially tropical birds (New World, Africa, Asia) and frequent quiet bays, estuaries, and river mouths where they can feed most effectively. The single North American species breeds only along the Atlantic and Gulf coasts, reaching as far north as Massachusetts; some populations winter along the Gulf.

SKIN. The bodies of birds, like those of other vertebrates, are encased in skin. Except at the dinner table, this feature of a bird's anatomy is inconspicuous because of the thick layers of feathers which are rooted in it and which cover it almost completely. Even those features which are usually unfeathered—bill, legs, and feet—have a horny or leathery covering over the true skin, so that we normally see bird skin only in those species which have bare face patches or adornments such as wattles, combs, pouches, and fleshy eye rings.

The skin of both birds and humans consists of upper and lower layers (epidermis and dermis), but bird skin is a less complex organ than human skin. It lacks self-lubricating glands; it cannot perspire and therefore plays only a minor part in controlling body temperature. It is also probably less sensitive to touch than human skin.

However, it is capable of "blushing," at least in some species. As in humans, this phenomenon is associated with emotional excitement and results from blood rushing to vessels at the skin's surface. It accounts, in part, for the transitory brightening of legs, bills, and colored areas on the faces of many heron species during the breeding season. See also BIRD SKIN; TOUCH; COLOR AND PATTERN; TEMPERATURE, BODY.

SKUA (SKEW-uh). Standard English name in North America for the 2 members of the genus *Catharacta* (family Stercorariidae; order Charadriiformes), and frequently used as a collective name for the skua/jaeger family. Both species occur in offshore waters of North America, though neither breeds here.

The skuas are large, plump, brown, aggressive pelagic predators which in general habits greatly resemble the other members of their family, the JAEGERS. The Brown or Great Skua (*C. skua*) breeds on islands and remote coasts of both the Arctic/Subarctic and the Antarctic/Subantarctic and occurs regularly off both coasts of North America. The South Polar Skua (*C. maccormicki*) breeds only on the Antarctic continent and the South Shetlands but has recently been recorded off both coasts of North America; its status here is uncertain.

"Skua" was apparently coined in the Faroe Islands (where the Brown Skua breeds) and may have been meant to echo the species' gull-like cry. In British usage, the jaegers (genus *Stercorarius*) are also called skuas.

For general family characteristics, see JAEGER.

SKULL. See SKELETON.

SKYLARK. Standard English name for 2 of the 3 members of the lark genus *Alauda* (family Alaudidae; order Passeriformes). *The* Skylark is native to Eurasia. It is one of the Western world's best-known songbirds, and inspired one of the best poems on an avian theme in English literature, Shelley's "To a Skylark" (see HUMAN CULTURE). The species has been widely introduced wherever Englishmen have settled, which accounts for its presence on Vancouver Island, British Columbia, where it was introduced in the first decade of this century. It has since spread to the adjacent San Juan Islands, Washington.

Its name derives from its song flight, a characteristic of most members of its family.

For further family characteristics, see LARK.

SLEEP. As with most other animals, including humans, birds pause at intervals during their daily routines and become inactive. Such resting periods do not always involve the relatively deep dormancy of sleep—birds are often seen to sit motionless at midday with their eyes open. And birds are also known to "nap," i.e., close their eyes and sleep for a matter of minutes in the midst of feeding or other activities. However, it is with the more or less prolonged, regular periods of true sleep that this entry is concerned.

There is much variation in sleeping behavior, not only among different species but among individuals of the same species. Many of the sleeping styles which have been recorded are adaptations to two fundamental survival requirements: the need to keep warm and the need to remain secure from predators—to which animals are particularly vulnerable when not fully alert.

POSTURE. One of the most widespread misconceptions about birds is that they sleep with their heads under their wings. In fact, the commonest sleeping posture, especially among songbirds, is with the head turned and resting on the back and the bill tucked under the feathers of the shoulder (scapulars). Not all birds sleep in this position, however, and even species which normally do, sometimes don't. Members of some groups, e.g., grebes, storks, doves, *never* sleep this way, but adopt the second most frequent posture—with the back of the head retracted and apparently resting on the shoulders and the bill pointing forward. Swifts, woodpeckers, and Brown Creepers sleep as they perch, clinging to a vertical surface.

Whether on the ground or grasping a branch, land birds normally squat down over their legs and feet while sleeping. Many water birds will do this as well, but will also stand erect with their bills tucked in. A great many species, including songbirds, habitually sleep standing or perching with one foot while the other is tucked up into the plumage, and it has been shown (Berger, 1968) that at least some species shift, flex, and alternate the perching/standing foot frequently. Fluffing the feathers to retain maximum body heat is also characteristic of sleeping birds.

It has long been believed and widely repeated that perching birds are held fast to their sleeping perches by the "automatic" action of the flexor tendons of the legs and feet. The theory was that the more a bird relaxed, closing its heel joint as it squatted, the stronger the pull on the tendon, which passes across this joint and runs to the toes. This was supposed to pull the toes together in an immovable grasp on the branch. It has recently been demonstrated, however, that in at least some songbirds the rear toe is not flexed and in fact does not even touch the perch (Van Tyne and Berger, 1976–ORNITHOLOGY).

Nestling birds simply close their eyes and sleep as they are, perhaps resting their heads on nest mates; there is evidence that they are not capable of assuming an adult sleeping posture for two weeks or more after hatching.

WHERE BIRDS SLEEP. Birds tend to sleep in the same habitat they prefer when awake and in a way which enhances their security. Many water birds sleep sitting on or standing in their native element or on predator-free islands. Horned Larks and many quail, partridge, and sparrow species sleep on the ground. Cavity nesters tend to sleep in their trees, chimneys, nest boxes, etc. The Common Swift of Eurasia vindicates its reputation as the most aerial of birds by sleeping on the wing (also in cavities). It is no accident that the majority of bird species—including pheasants, herons, and other non-arboreal species—prefer to sleep in trees or dense shrubbery, where they are out of reach of those predators which cannot climb and are warned by vibration long before more agile carnivores can reach them. Species such as some swallows and blackbirds which roost in emergent aquatic vegetation, such as cattails, are doubly protected.

Some birds require more structured sleeping accommodations. These may use their nests of the year to sleep in during the off season, or use cup nests or cavities abandoned by other species, or in a few cases (Cactus Wren, some woodpeckers) build separate "dormitory" nests near the ones in which they rear their young.

In many cases sleeping habits change with the seasons. Territorial birds usually sleep on their territories (including in their nests) during the breeding season. Thereafter, some species remain solitary in their sleeping habits, but roost in many different sites (especially on migration), while others sleep communally (see below) and return to the same sites year after year. Woodpeckers sometimes excavate new sleeping cavities in the fall instead of roosting in their breeding-season holes. Ruffed Grouse, which usually prefer the cover of dense conifers, sometimes burrow into the snow to sleep, and begin their excavation by diving into a snowbank from the air, a tactic also used to escape hungry Northern Goshawks.

COMMUNAL SLEEPING ROOSTS. Birds which are gregarious in their nesting habits (e.g., herons, ibises, gulls and terns, swifts) or feeding habits (e.g., shorebirds, starlings, blackbirds) or both (crows) often sleep together in large (sometimes gigantic) aggregations. Such roosts may contain a single species only but more frequently are mixed, and single winter roosts in the southeastern states consisting of four blackbird species and starlings may contain a million or more birds. The chief benefit of sleeping in this manner would appear to be defensive, since the slightest disturbance in any quarter of the roost inevitably sends the entire assembly into a noisy panic.

Other (mainly passerine) birds huddle together in crevices or cavities to sleep on winter nights. Swifts, tits, nuthatches, (tree) creepers, and other birds known to congregate in this manner are not typically gregarious (or only mildly so); this and the fact that all are also known to sleep individually suggest that the principal motivation for this kind of roost is heat conservation. Coveys of some quail and partridge species huddle in a similar way, but on the ground and in the open, and they compensate for their apparent vulnerability by clustering in a circle with all heads pointed outward, so that the birds can make an instantaneous escape, each in a different direction (see Audubon's plate: Havell LXXVI).

The occasional communal sleeping arrangements of eagles, vultures, Rough-legged Hawks, Northern Harriers (on the ground), Long- and Short-eared Owls, Wood Ducks, and nighthawks (sometimes large, all-male roosts) are not as easily explained as the above examples. None of these species is typically gregarious, none huddles for warmth, and all are less vulnerable to predation than many non-communal sleepers. In at least some cases, local abundance, combined with a favorable roosting site and the proximity of a reliable food supply, may suffice to explain propinquity.

WHEN AND HOW LONG BIRDS SLEEP. In general, the sleeping rhythms of birds correlate with their feeding habits. Species which are active throughout the hours of daylight (most birds) tend to sleep relatively soundly and uninterruptedly through the night.

Nocturnal species such as owls and nightjars follow the opposite rhythm. Shorebirds and other water birds whose feeding habits are often governed by the tides sleep accordingly. One frequently sees large flocks of sandpipers sleeping on the upper beach at midday when high water covers the flats, and since most feed by "feeling" for prey with their bills, they easily adapt to being active at night when the tide is favorable. Food preferences and requirements and feeding methods also affect sleeping schedules. At least a few insectivorous species may "sleep in" until the air temperature is warm enough to activate their preferred prey. Arctic species which are normally diurnal must feed in darkness or near darkness in the northern fall and winter in order to get enough food to sustain them. And birds which soar in search of food (vultures, hawks and eagles, etc.) need thermals generated by the sun's rays in order to hunt effectively (see FLIGHT) and therefore tend to leave their roosts later and return earlier than most other birds.

The sleeping/feeding rhythms of birds are not static schedules but change according to environmental factors. The same arctic species which must feed in darkness in the winter could be active constantly in the northern summer with twenty-four hours of daylight. Yet they do have regular sleeping periods—though these tend to be shorter or more sporadic than their winter sleeps. As noted, many water birds feed and roost with the tides.

These examples raise the question of how birds know when they are supposed to do what. There is some good evidence that specific light intensities trigger the urge to wake or roost in many species. Many songbirds do not become active at the same hour each morning but alter their schedule according to the sun's. On cloudy days, songbird activity is conspicuously diminished, and heavy overcast often brings normally crepuscular/nocturnal night herons out to feed. As we have seen, however, this model would not work for arctic species, nor does it explain sensitivity to tidal changes.

Experiments have shown that at least some birds have an "internal clock" which guides their behavior (at least temporarily) in the absence of all normal environmental stimuli (see CIRCADIAN RHYTHM; NAVIGATION). The question warrants much more study.

SMELL. Although most birds are equipped with an adequate or even well-developed sensory apparatus for perceiving odors, both in the nasal passages and in the brain, they clearly depend on their sense of smell far less than mammals do.

Experiments calculated to make birds respond to strong odors have either failed or resulted in conflicting evidence from different smells, species, and/or investigators.

Birds rarely exhibit behavioral traits which might imply reliance on smell, but there are a few noteworthy exceptions. Albatrosses, shearwaters, and storm-petrels seem to be attracted to fishy odors from considerable distances; rancid cod livers spread on the sea at a favorable place and season can rapidly attract flocks of such birds from beyond the horizon (see CHUMMING). In the early 1800's, John James Audubon, in an interesting, but unscientific experiment, proved to his satisfaction that Turkey Vultures found his painting of an eviscerated sheep more attractive than a genuine "ripe" (but invisible) carcass. However, more recent experiments have proven that this species is capable of finding at least certain types of decaying flesh by odor alone, so that it probably uses a combination of sight and smell in its normal foraging activities. The olfactory acuity of the Black Vulture, on the other hand, is apparently poorly developed.

For how birds smell *to humans,* see ODOR.

SMITH, Gideon B., 1793–1867 (Smith's Longspur: *Calcarius pictus*). According to Gruson (1972–BIOGRAPHY), Smith was an early authority on the propagation of silkworms in the U.S., a friend of Audubon's, and one of the many doctors prominent in the annals of American ornithology (see BAIRD; BIOGRAPHY). His medical career was marred by expulsion from the Baltimore Medical Society for "unprofessional conduct," but Gruson was unable to discover the reason for his disgrace.

SMOKE/FIRE (birds' reaction to). It is well documented that forest fires drive a great variety of organisms from their burning habitat, thereby exposing them to predation. It is also known that certain insects (e.g., some species of long-horned beetles, family Cerambycidae) are *attracted* to smoke, especially that generated by pine-woods blazes. Both the flight and the attraction phenomena are at times exploited for food by kites and other insectivorous birds, which catch and eat their prey on the wing.

Birds are also known to use smoke and even burning twigs or live flames in a way that resembles anting, i.e., to derive some sort of heat stimulation and possibly to help control ectoparasites. This playing with fire has led to more than one case of accidental arson. See ANTING.

It is not inconceivable that one of the above phenomena helped inspire the legend of the PHOENIX.

SNIPE. Standard English name for about 17 members of the subfamily Scolopacinae (family Scolopacidae; order Charadriiformes), which also includes the woodcocks and (in some taxonomies) the dowitchers. One species, the Common Snipe, breeds in North America and another has occurred as an accidental straggler (see Appendix II).

Snipe are long-billed "shorebirds" of marshes, bogs (where they often breed), swamps, and muddy banks and fields. They are cryptically colored—often overlooked until flushed—and sometimes gather in groups traditionally known as "wisps." They probe for earthworms but also pick small insects and other invertebrates as well as plant matter from the surface of the ground. At dawn, at dusk, on moonlit nights and overcast days during the breeding season, male snipe perform a courtship flight consisting of a relatively direct ascent to as high as 300 feet and a zigzagging return to earth. On the descent the wings are folded, but the tail is spread wide and the outermost pair of rectrices moved beyond the penultimate pair, leaving a space at the outer ends (base) of the fan. Air rushing across these two last feathers makes them vibrate, which, in interaction with the flow of air over the wings, produces an eerie tremulous whistle called "winnowing" or "bleating."

There is still a hunting season on Common Snipe, which test marksmen by their erratic zigzag flight when flushed.

The Common Snipe is nearly cosmopolitan in distribution (absent from Australasia) and in North America breeds from the Arctic to the northern U.S. and winters in most of the remainder of the continent as well as farther south.

"Snipe" derives from old European words and is cognate with "snip" and "snap," referring to the action of their elongate bill in picking up food. In the days of the shorebird gunners many sandpiper species were known as "snipe" (e.g., "robin snipe" for dowitchers) and the root is retained in the many Swedish sandpiper names which end in *-snäppa.*

For family characteristics, see SANDPIPER; references in the Bibliography under SHOREBIRD.

SOARING. Sustained flight without wing flapping and therefore aided by some form of air movement such as thermals or updrafts. Pelicans, anhingas, cranes, vultures, hawks, eagles, falcons, and gulls are among the bird groups which soar habitually in search of food or as a method of long-distance migration. See FLIGHT; WING; MIGRATION; and Figs. 20 and 22.

SOCIAL PHENOMENA. See FLOCK; COLONY; ROOST; COMMENSALISM; DISPLAY; FOOD/FEEDING; MOBBING; MIGRATION; NEST.

SOCIETIES, ORNITHOLOGICAL. See AMERICAN ORNITHOLOGISTS'
UNION; WILSON ORNITHOLOGICAL SOCIETY; COOPER ORNITHOLOGICAL
SOCIETY; BIRD CLUB.

SOFT PARTS. Exposed, unfeathered parts of a bird's body, including the
bill, legs and feet, fleshy eye rings, facial skin, combs, wattles, and iris. In
some species, soft-part colors can change rapidly—becoming more intense
during courtship or the breeding season, fading to a subtler hue during the
rest of the year. At any season, soft-part colors fade after death and therefore must be noted on the labels of museum specimens. As Thomson
points out (1964–ORNITHOLOGY), the name is not very apt, since, excepting the skeleton, many of the "soft" parts are in fact among the hardest
parts of the bird's body. Soft-part colors are sometimes useful field marks
for identifying bird species.

SOLITAIRE. Standard English name for the 7 members of the genus
Myadestes and 2 others in *Entomodestes* (family Turdidae [thrushes] or
perhaps—based on egg-white proteins—Ptilogonatidae [silky flycatchers];
order Passeriformes). One species, the Townsend's Solitaire, breeds and
winters largely in North America.

　　Solitaires are notably short-billed, long-tailed, somberly colored, arboreal thrushes. They feed mainly on insects—sometimes "flycatching" on
the wing—and berries, but often sit with uncanny stillness in the shadows—all but invisible, though in plain view.

　　The solitaires are noted songsters, some of them uttering ethereal,
ventriloquial, harmonic pipings which seem to ascend and descend the
musical scale simultaneously. The song of the Townsend's Solitaire is neither preeminent nor untypical and is sometimes delivered in a song flight.

　　The native solitaire nests in the coniferous forests (or sometimes
above the tree line) of the western mountains, especially where there are
rocky slopes. It descends to cedar canyons in the winter. The nest is a
loose, rather messy cup made of coarse grasses, twigs, stems, and pine needles, lined with moss and finer plant fibers. It is placed in a tree stump,
among roots, in an earthen niche, on a bank, or in a rock crevice—often
highly inaccessible to human investigators.

　　The 3–5 (usually 4) eggs are white or pale blue, green, yellowish, or
pinkish and densely speckled, splotched, and/or scrawled with brownish,
purplish, reddish, and/or grayish.

　　The solitaires are confined to the New World, and Townsend's is the

FIG. 20. *Thermal soaring.* Many hawks, such as these soaring "buteos," and other broad-
winged birds (cranes, pelicans, etc.) gain almost effortless "lift" by seeking out ascending
"bubbles" of hot air which rise in a widening cone from the sun-warmed earth. Once they
have soared to the desired height in a swirling "kettle" or "screw" formation, the birds leave
the air mass and fall gradually in the direction they wish to follow. For a more detailed description of this technique, see FLIGHT, *Thermal Soaring.*

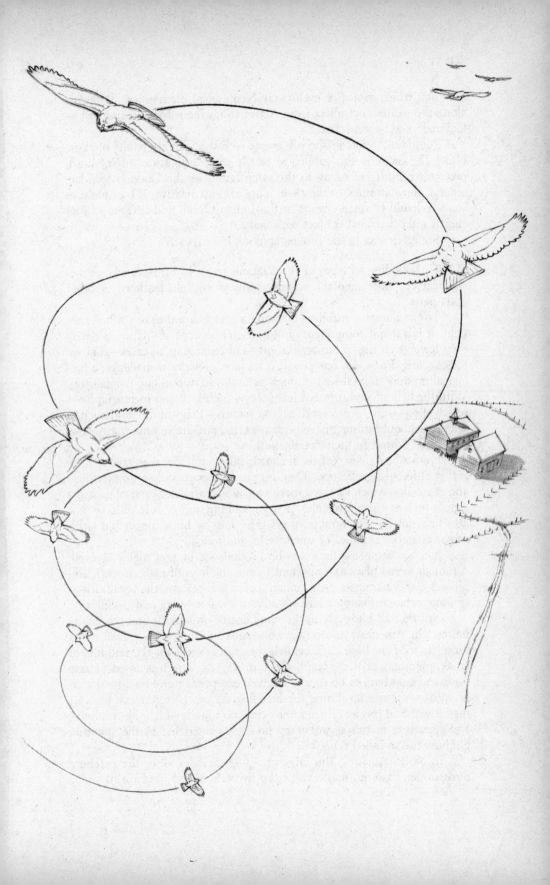

only one which is not of exclusively Neotropical distribution. It occurs along the western cordillera from Alaska to northern Mexico and east to Colorado and western Texas.

"Solitaire" refers to the somewhat reclusive, solitary habits of these birds. The name is also applied to two species of flightless, turkey-sized, pigeon-like birds belonging to the same family as the Dodo (Raphidae; order Columbiformes). Like their more famous relative, these solitaires were endemic to small islands in the Indian Ocean and became extinct shortly after their first contact with man.

See references in the Bibliography under THRUSH.

SONG. Including all types of vocalizations made by birds, as well as mechanical or "instrumental" sounds produced by bill, feathers, or other body parts.

To the human sensibility, birdsong is mainly a source of aesthetic delight. It is a major component of our general concept of "nature"; it may even have given rise to our realization—not reliable in all cases—that we too can sing. For a very few people it has also provided a challenge, a biological mystery to be solved through patient observation and comparison. With the help of sophisticated technology, such as sound spectography— which allows us to "see" as well as hear sounds—many of the fundamental questions about birdsong have been answered and are summarized below. Many more await further investigation.

From a bird's perspective, of course, the sounds it makes have an altogether different significance. They are practical means of communication and expression which for most species are as necessary for survival as *visual* signals such as distinctive color, pattern, and physical gesture. Bird sounds also help fill the "communications gap" left by birds' negligible (with minor exceptions) senses of smell, taste, and touch.

It is not surprising then that bird sounds are by now highly evolved. Although sound plays an important role in the lives of many insects, amphibians, and mammals, only human speech and perhaps the vocalizations of some cetaceans surpass bird sounds for vocal subtlety and complexity.

Not that all birds rely to the same degree on making and perceiving noises. The American vultures have no syrinx and storks lack crucial syrinx muscles (see *How Birds Sing*, below); therefore, except for the rare hiss or croak, members of these families live in silence. The tubenosed pelagic birds and auks tend to be vocally reserved except for weird nocturnal arias given by some species during the breeding season. Nevertheless, the vast majority of bird species rely to some extent on sounds which they produce, and versatility in this regard is by no means restricted to the suborder Oscines, the so-called songbirds.

In North America, this large grouping includes all of the perching birds (order Passeriformes) except the flycatchers and (perhaps) a single species of COTINGA. The Oscines are technically distinguished by their relatively numerous and intricately arranged syrinx muscles. This anatomical complexity, however, is not always reflected in the sounds produced. True, some of our finest songsters, e.g., the Hermit Thrush, belong to the Oscines, but so do the crows and jays. Conversely, virtuosi among the shorebirds, owls, and nightjars are not even in the same order as the "official" songbirds.

HOW BIRDS SING. Regardless of how the singers are labeled, virtually all vocal bird sounds are produced in an organ called the *syrinx*, which is unique to birds. The human voice is produced in the larynx, a modification of the upper part of the windpipe (trachea) which holds the vocal cords. In birds, the upper part of the trachea is called the larynx but it contains no vocal cords and does not produce sound. In a few species the syrinx is located at the lower end of the trachea just above where the bronchi divide (an arrangement found only in suboscine species of the American tropics—none of which occurs in North America); or it is a paired structure, in effect two syringes, one modifying the top of each of the two bronchi (cuckoos, nightjars, and some owls); or, as is the case in the majority of birds, it involves both the trachea and the bronchi at their juncture. The syrinx can therefore be thought of structurally as a second larynx, lacking in humans, or functionally as the uniquely avian organ analogous to the human voice box (larynx).

Attached to the syrinx are pairs of muscles which control the quality of sound production. The songbirds (Oscines) have a maximum complement of syringeal muscles, up to 8 or 9 pairs (depending upon which authority is counting), whereas most other birds make do with 1 or 2 pairs. Within the syrinx are elastic membranes which can be stretched and relaxed both by air pressure and by the workings of the syringeal muscles. The membranes can also be manipulated within the air passages of the bronchi to regulate the amount of air passing through. When air is forced through the syrinx from the lungs, the membranes are made to vibrate, producing a sound in the way that a blade of grass held between the thumbs will "scream" if air is blown across it. The sound can be modified (1) by stretching or loosening the membranes (for higher and lower pitch); (2) by making them vibrate slowly or rapidly (for tonal qualities); (3) by altering the direction of the air passage (for loudness or softness); and (4) by stopping and starting air flow (for rhythm).

It will be noticed that birdsong, unlike human speech, is not inflected much (if at all) by resonating in nasal, mouth, or throat cavities. This is dramatized by the ability of many species to sing full, rich songs with their mouths full or their bills closed.

Perhaps the most remarkable feature of a bird's voice is the ability to sing through both bronchi simultaneously or separately. This twin voice is responsible for the harmonic sounds present in most songs and can also produce two distinct themes at the same time, giving songs like the Veery's their unearthly quality.

As with a wind instrument, the versatility of the syrinx depends on the diversity of means and combinations by which the state of the membrane and air passage can be modified. Therefore, there is a general correlation between the complexity of the syringeal muscles—which in effect "play" the syrinx with greater or lesser virtuosity—and the complexity of a bird's "music." In many cases vocal ability is more real than apparent— the negligible *stlick* of a Henslow's Sparrow does scant justice to the evolution of its syrinx. On the other hand, splendid sounds such as the Common Loon's wail or the trumpeting of cranes can be produced on comparatively simple instruments. It must be admitted, however, that the truly fabulous songsters—the thrushes, wrens, and some larks, icterids and wood warblers—owe their renown to the Stradivarian subtlety of their vocal anatomy.

Cranes and swans have greatly elongated tracheas, which loop down into specially adapted hollows in the breastbone (sternum). Traditionally these have been supposed to function in voice production and have been likened to the tubes of instruments such as the trombone, but recent evidence (Greenewalt, 1968) makes such theories dubious—without, however, supplying an alternative hypothesis.

For production of non-vocal sounds, see below.

HOW BIRDS ACQUIRE THEIR SONGS. The answer to whether birds *inherit* their characteristic repertoire of sounds or *learn* them through imitation and practice appears to be: *both.* Early experiments involving birds hatched and reared in total isolation from any contact with their species have shown that with the passage of time these birds not only know as many songs and calls as their normal counterparts and know when to sing them but also—at least to the ears of the experimenters—give them the same intonations heard in wild birds (Sauer, 1954). Subsequent experiments on different species, however, indicate that young birds hatch knowing a sort of generalized song but must listen to adult birds singing it "correctly," and then imitate them, before they perfect their vocal technique. Such birds deprived of this learning experience may stick with the simple "baby song" or they may invent the missing elements and end up with a full complex song which, however, does not conform closely to the characteristic song of their species. If they are exposed when young to the song of a different species they may "adopt" its song or use elements of it to devise an original composition. How to make particular call notes (see definitions of song vs. call below) may be more firmly fixed genetically at hatching, yet untutored individuals may not understand in what circumstances they should be used and must learn this from experience, i.e., by hearing other birds use them in the appropriate situation.

The development of the vocal faculties has as yet been studied in only a relatively few species. Given the different results obtained (even allowing for the foibles of the experimenters) and the great diversity birds exhibit in other forms of behavior, it is not unrealistic to speculate that the proportional influence of nature and nurture in song development varies significantly from species to species.

Passerines typically make "begging" sounds within the first couple of days after hatching, and the first generalized singing may begin as early as the 13th day in some species, but not for 8 weeks in others (see Nice, 1943–PARENTAL CARE, and Thorpe, 1961). Young male Song Sparrows appear to advance gradually—during a period when they are exposed to the adult song of their species—from a nondescript warble to shorter phrases to a recognizable adult song. Males singing on territory their first spring may begin with a rather crude rendition, but improve noticeably as they listen to and conform with the songs of neighboring males. At least in some species, the entire vocal repertoire is completely acquired and "fixed" within the first year. Once this happens birds seem to have an infallible vocal memory and can, for example, reproduce their territorial songs precisely after a winter of silence or even if deafened.

WHY BIRDS SING. As a class, birds are perhaps the most vocal of animals. The majority of species have an elaborate vocabulary equaled by only a few gregarious mammals and conspicuously surpassed only by ourselves. Not long ago it would have seemed pointless to ask *why* birds sing. But since Darwin the inquisitive have been schooled to realize that the presence of such a conspicuous trait in many successful species must imply significant survival value. That there must be advantages in making loud noises is further urged by very apparent disadvantages. What better way, after all, to attract the attention of predators than to sing a lengthy song over and over from a prominent perch? As we shall see, some birdsongs seem to be purely expressive, serving no obvious function other than the expenditure of "emotional" energy, but overall the sounds made by birds confer the same broad advantage as human speech—the ability to efficiently communicate a wide range of essential information, all of which contributes to the "survivability" of an individual bird and its species.

Bird sounds, like other languages, take a variety of distinctive forms which in many cases imply a particular usage. The major forms of vocalizations and their functions are as follows:

Song. Anyone who has paid any attention to the sounds birds make is aware of two broad categories of vocalization. The one we call "song" typically contains a series of different notes uttered in a cohesive sequence so that they form a characteristic phrase with a recognizable rhythm and "tune" like a line of music. Some songs, such as the abrupt *chebec* of the Least Flycatcher, don't fit this description very well but are still defined as songs because of their function.

Most of the birdsongs we hear are those of male birds advertising their presence on their territories to prospective mates and to potential rivals of their own sex and species (see PAIR FORMATION; TERRITORY). Neighboring males may engage in singing contests to establish their invisible boundary lines. They may "escalate" their song battles by adding aggressive motifs, but they almost always come to terms vocally without resorting to physical violence. Wandering males are also warned efficiently when they trespass on occupied territory. This territorial song usually continues through the breeding cycle and seems to cement the pair bond after mating. When a similar (or identical) song is sung by a male to communicate with its mate and serves no aggressive or advertising functions, it is sometimes distinguished as a "signal song."

Another type of song, usually very distinct in phrasing from the territorial/signal song, seems to be unrelated to the breeding cycle, but rather to be pure release of energy of the kind that Shelley attributed to his Skylark. "Emotional-release songs" of this kind have been recorded for many passerine species. They usually happen at random; they may be accompanied by an "ecstasy flight" (not to be confused with territorial song flights characteristic of many open-country species); in some species (e.g., several tyrannid flycatchers), they are likely to be performed at twilight; but they may also be given at night during migration or on the wintering ground. They often contain many improvised elements. The function of this category of song is unclear. But even sober scientists, who eschew anthropomorphism by profession, acknowledge its expressive quality and have even suggested that it contains a germ of artistic invention (!).

In certain circumstances, birds also sing extraordinarily softly. This form of song may be simply a *sotto voce* rendition of the territorial song ("whisper song") or be completely distinct. The different variations are often lumped together as "subsongs" or "secondary songs" and are often lower in pitch and more extended as well as lower in volume than ordinary songs. Adult birds sometimes sing a whisper song in bad weather or during the heat of the day. The early warblings and hesitant imitations of adult songs sung by young birds (see above) and weak territorial songs sung by males which have yet to attain full gonadal development in spring are also categorized as subsongs.

Calls are typically brief, as befits their function of conveying immediate information within the routine activities of a bird's daily life. They consist of single "call notes," such as the familiar *snap* of the Common Yellowthroat, or a short phrase—rarely more than 5 notes—such as the Willet's *bill-will-willet*.

There is a great variation among species in richness of call vocabulary. All birds are capable of producing some kind of call, if only a hiss or grunt elicited under the direst stress. Many species (e.g., grebes, cormorants, herons) have no true song as defined above, but produce a fair diversity of calls, especially on the breeding grounds. The precise import of each of these sounds has not been defined for many species, but some of them clearly serve a function not unlike that of signal songs. Songbirds are the most articulate, with more than 20 distinct vocalizations recorded for several species.

The distinction between a long call (the bugling call of a Herring Gull) and a short song (Kiskadee) is best defined by function. Among the commonest functions of calls are: defense, warning, distress, begging (by nestlings), flock cohesion (e.g., on migration), identification of a food source (e.g., in foraging birds), gathering (e.g., by parents of precocial broods), and comfort. Within these broad categories there may be two or more distinct calls appropriate to slightly different situations. For example, a number of bird species give a soft, hard-to-place "seeping" call that alerts nearby birds to a passing hawk without drawing attention to the caller's location. The same species, however, may utter a loud scold to warn of a perched owl or cat and rally birds in the vicinity to "mob" it (see Fig. 14).

Certain calls may be used exclusively by birds of a certain age or sex, or in highly specific situations (e.g., for maintaining contact within a migratory flock), or, like the hawk or mobbing call, they may be used and recognized among many different species.

Though experience may be required to learn the precise "etiquette" of using some specific calls, the ability and inclination to make and respond to most calls is innate. This helps to explain the instantaneous response to an alarm call given among a flock of birds feeding in the open. Blackbirds and starlings, for example, are frequently seen to rise as if linked to a single nervous system, close into tight formation, and dodge erratically in unison even when no apparent threat exists, as if to be safe rather than sorry (see FLOCK).

WHEN AND HOW OFTEN BIRDS SING

Season. Whereas calls tend to be uttered "as needed," song is under the influence of the hormonal rhythms of the breeding cycle and therefore has a pronounced seasonality. In most species, full male territorial song begins shortly (rarely immediately) after arrival on the breeding ground, wanes briefly during the mating period, picks up again after copulation, drops off after the young hatch, and stops altogether as a bird's reproductive system enters its dormant phase in late summer/early fall. Of course, there are departures in many cases from this basic pattern. Snow Buntings and Brown Thrashers, for example, apparently stop singing altogether after mating is established, whereas a number of species show undiminished enthusiasm throughout the breeding cycle.

A few species—e.g., Northern Mockingbird, Carolina Wren, Northern Cardinal—sing regularly throughout the year, especially in the southern parts of their ranges. This is true of many species which stay on their breeding territories year-round. Partial, muted, and/or infrequent songs are given by some males: (1) after the pre-basic (post-nuptial) molt; (2) on migration; (3) on the breeding grounds before the territorial drive has reached full throttle.

Time of Day. The "dawn chorus" of birdsong is familiar to anyone who is awake that early or who reads romantic poetry. The hour around sunrise on a clear morning during the breeding season is likely to contain the voices of all the resident species of a given locality. In some cases dawn songs are given more rapidly and/or frequently than normal, which adds a sense of extra enthusiasm to the performance.

There is a close correlation between when birds start and stop singing and the light level. This varies from species to species and according to weather conditions (see below).

There is also a "dusk chorus" during which birds are generally more songful than at midday, though less spectacularly so than at sunrise. A number of species have a distinctive "evening song." Many thrushes sing such variations beginning after sunset and continuing into darkness; and, as already noted, some species of tyrant flycatchers add an exuberant song flight to their evensong which is not normally performed at other times of day.

Night singing is characteristic of most owls and nightjars, and again there is often a notable intensification of effort near dawn and dusk. The American Woodcock is a crepuscular songster—the males beginning their nuptial ritual well after sunset but continuing till midnight only when the moon provides enough light to trigger their urge to perform. A few day singers regularly sing at night as well—the famous Nightingale is supreme in this category. Its North American counterpart is the Northern Mockingbird, though in the modern suburb its efforts are probably more likely to be associated with insomnia than with romance. Occasionally during the breeding season, other species will give out with a nighttime "emotional song" (see above) which bears little or no resemblance to their day songs. Thoreau's mysterious "nightsinger" turned out to be an Ovenbird demonstrating this phenomenon.

Weather. Because they reduce light levels, clouds obscuring the sun tend to retard and diminish the dawn chorus and hasten the end of evening songs. However, they also ameliorate the heat of midday, when many birds seek shade and stop singing or murmur a whisper song. A cloudy day, then, tends to have a more even level of song throughout.

Wind and precipitation can shut off birdsong completely if heavy enough, but there is considerable tolerance for low levels of both. There are a few recorded instances of very specific responses to particular weather conditions. Tinbergen (1939) recorded that male Snow Buntings stop singing as soon as snow begins to fall, and he interpreted this behavior as a response to the possibility that the birds' food source would soon be covered, a signal that they should therefore stop singing and start feeding. By contrast, spring snowstorms often *stimulate* song in recently arrived migrants, which apparently sing as a redirected activity (see RE-DIRECTION).

Number of Songs. The Red-eyed Vireo, with its short phrase uttered seemingly without pause through the day, appears to hold the North American record for most songs sung per unit of time: 22,197 in 10 hours (de Kiriline, 1954). Other such patiently gathered statistics indicate that the norm for passerine species may be closer to 1,000–2,500 songs per day. Birds involved in disputes over territorial boundaries sing more frequently than more "secure" members of the same species. Therefore, there is individual variation in number of songs sung per day as well as the obvious variations caused by weather and the breeding rhythms.

WHERE BIRDS SING. Territorial songs must, of course, be heard over a sizable range in order to attract a mate and warn off trespassers, and audibility is affected not only by the volume and carrying quality of the song but also by the location of the singer. In most species, males choose several conspicuous singing perches within their territories from which they habitually broadcast their message. These may be the tops of high trees, shrubs, rocks, or telephone poles, depending upon the habitat of the species. Some species which nest in tundra or other types of flat, open country (e.g., many sandpipers, most longspurs, Horned Lark) compensate for the lack of good song posts by singing from the air; these territorial song flights are performed as regularly as their earthbound counterparts and are not to be confused with "ecstasy songs" described above.

Not all birds sing from a conspicuous open perch. Some arboreal species (e.g., vireos, tanagers), birds of the forest floor (e.g., Ovenbird), and those which favor dense cover (e.g., wrens, Mourning Warbler) remain within their preferred habitat while singing, but their songs tend to be notably loud and/or carrying. Thrushes which may sing either from an open perch or from deep within the forest have a wide volume range and may adjust it to suit their location.

Regardless of whence territorial song issues, there appears to be a rough correlation between its range and the average territory size of the species singing—i.e., a song emanating from the center of a territory tends to be audible roughly to the boundaries of the territory and no farther. It follows that birds with smaller/larger territories should have quieter/louder songs (or vice versa), and while there is some evidence that this tends to be so, the great variations in territory size and song volume among different individuals and situations often obscure the validity of this generalization.

Another tendency which appeals to human logic is that males usually sing at some distance from their nest. However, males of a few species (e.g., Warbling Vireo, Black-headed Grosbeak) have been observed giving a full song while sitting on the nest—a practice which is hard to rationalize in terms of survival value.

VARIATION IN SONG. Even excluding the few bird sounds which the human ear cannot discern (see HEARING), the variety of utterances of which birds as a class are capable is sufficiently impressive. Consider for a moment the range in pitch, volume, meter, tune, harmonics, and length represented by: the Common Loon's wail, the various honkings of geese and quackings of ducks, the scream of an eagle, the cluckings of gallinaceous birds, the "pumping" of the American Bittern, the trumpeting of cranes, the clattering of rails, the pipings of shorebirds, the hootings of owls and doves, the explosive name-calling of nightjars, the twitterings of swifts and hummingbirds, the staccato exclamations of woodpeckers, and the apparently infinite assortment of lisps, buzzes, chirps, tweets, and warbles by which passerines express themselves. Like other characteristics, these vocal variations have evolved according to adaptation and selection pressure over eons (see NATURAL SELECTION), but it should not be assumed that the course of vocal evolution is always in the direction of greater complexity. It is true that the relatively "recent" songbirds have the most highly developed vocal organs (see How Birds Sing, above), but there are many non-songbirds with relatively simple vocal instruments which nevertheless make elaborate sounds, just as there are songbirds which are practically songless in spite of their highly evolved "voice box."

Extent of vocal repertoire is another obvious variation among different species. We have already seen that some species are normally mute, while a vocabulary of more than 20 distinct songs and calls is probably not unusual among songbirds. Many of the sounds made by the more articulate species are very similar or used relatively infrequently in situations that humans seldom observe. Therefore only the student of a species' life history or of birdsong is likely to become aware of the full scope of a species' vocal capabilities. Even skilled and experienced birdwatchers are familiar with (or distinguish) only a single call for many species or, in the case of songbirds, one territorial song and one frequently used call. Many wood warblers have two or more distinct territorial songs which are sung—apparently interchangeably—by all males of the species.

Within genera and families, there tends to be much divergence in song pattern, which no doubt aids recognition and reproductive isolation in closely related forms. There are also cases of convergence of songs between two unrelated species. Thus the Warbling Vireo sounds more like a Purple Finch than like any other North American member of its own family.

Different geographical races often sing distinctive variations of the basic song of their species—one often hears birdwatchers from out of state say, "That doesn't sound like our Song Sparrow"—and it is not unusual to detect different "dialects" even among different populations of a single race. The difference between "song races" can be so great that members of one race do not recognize and respond to some calls made by the other.

The degree to which a different race alters or expands its vocal repertoire sometimes depends upon other species with which it coexists. If it does not have to distinguish itself by song from other closely related species, it may evolve a range of musical variations, some of which may resemble by chance the song of a related species; but if a near relative with a similar song occupies the same range, it may be obliged to give a very typical, "conservative" rendition of its species' song as a reinforcement of reproductive isolation.

In contrast to males of different races or populations, males within a single population tend to sing very much like their neighbors and indeed imitate each other in defending their territories; young birds establishing new territories generally fall in with the local dialect.

Despite this tendency toward similarity of song among the members of a population, sensitive recording devices and spectrographic analysis have revealed that relatively subtle *individual variations* of the "basic" song seem to be more the rule than the exception. A single male bird may sing more than 50 versions of his territorial song (Borror, 1961); he may share *some* of these variations with other males of the same population; he will tend to sing some versions more frequently than others; and his offspring will not inherit his variations.

On the whole, individual variations are seldom obvious enough to attract the attention of the casual listener. However, those who listen habitually to the songs of common species in their yard may notice a change in phrasing or the absence of one or more striking "motifs" as generations of singers succeed each other.

The fact that individual birds routinely invent new versions of the basic song patterns they inherit raises some provocative questions about learning, creativity, and language, the more so in the case of "talented" vocal mimics (see below).

FEMALE SONG. Among female birds as a whole, the singing of a full (i.e., territorial-type) song is unusual and it has even been demonstrated that there is some causal relationship between sex hormones and the development of the syrinx. Females which *do* sing tend to do so much less frequently than the males and only in specific situations.

It is now clear, however, that female song is by no means rare. It is practiced in some form by species of thrushes, mimic thrushes, dippers, wrens, orioles, tanagers, finches, and the Wrentit, and in a few species (e.g., Northern Cardinal, Rose-breasted Grosbeak, several thrushes) the female's song is equal to her mate's in complexity and intensity.

As might be expected, female Northern Phalaropes (and perhaps the other two species) give a display "song" on the breeding grounds, while the male's vocal repertoire is restricted to terse calls.

MULTIPLE VOCALIZATIONS. A few bird species habitually sing duets, either giving the same phrases simultaneously or alternating *different* phrases in such close synchronization that the effect is of a single "antiphonal song." Duetting seems to be commonest among species living in dense habitats (e.g., many tropical wrens) and may be a means of reinforcing pair bonds in birds which often lose sight of each other in thick vegetation.

Only a few North American bird species are known to sing duets, among them the Bobwhite, California and Gambel's Quail, and Brown-headed Cowbird (see Brackbill, 1961, and Stokes and Williams, 1968).

Family groups of Plain Chachalacas engage in cackling choruses, especially at dawn and dusk. Voice quality varies in this species according to age and sex (Delacour and Amadon, 1973–GALLINACEOUS BIRDS), and when mature males and females and young birds "sing" together, a distinct (though unpredictable) antiphonal rhythm emerges. The well-known American naturalist and "bird finder" Jim Lane translates this cracid din as: Male chacha: "Gonna catchya, gonna catchya, gonna catchya." Female chacha (antiphonally): "Betcha can't, betcha can't, betcha can't." Anyone who has heard this performance can vouch for the phonetic (if not the biological) accuracy of this analysis.

Some species of swifts that nest in colonies engage in communal flights accompanied by intermittent bursts of simultaneous twittering.

Roosts of starlings, blackbirds, and other communal species often produce a high level of noise, especially when individuals are flying in and settling down for the night, but whether we are hearing an intentional "concert" or simply the accumulation of many individual calls is hard to judge. On the other hand, it seems clear that the chorus of calls produced by migrating flocks results from individuals contributing to flock cohesion.

The territorial song of a single male sometimes "sets off" neighboring males; in colonial species, e.g., gulls, this may result in a choral effect.

VOCAL MIMICRY. As we have seen, many birds "perfect" their species' song by imitating their parents or other adult birds of their own kind and are also capable of improvising individual song variations. This kind of learning and ability reaches its greatest avian development in the so-called vocal mimics—birds which can (and habitually do) reproduce the sounds made by other birds and animals, including human speech, and even the "inanimate" sounds of the modern world. The phenomenon in its several variations has long been a rich source of fanciful speculation; its biological "hows" and "whys" come much less readily, however, and are still far from completely understood.

Forms of Vocal Mimicry. Two types of vocal mimicry can be distinguished fairly sharply on a circumstantial basis. The first type consists of "natural" mimics such as the Northern Mockingbird, some other mimic thrushes (family Mimidae), and the Common Starling. Such species use imitated sounds along with motifs characteristic of their species to create a unique individual song, the functions of which are analogous (with some differences; see *Why*, below) to normal territorial songs. This type of mimic may incorporate train whistles or other non-bird sounds and can, if kept in captivity, imitate human speech, but normally has significant non-imitative components in its song as well. (The composition of these songs varies widely among individuals and it has been suggested [Borror, 1964] that the degree of mimicry in a song may vary geographically in some species.)

The other type of avian mimics are the "talking birds." Certain members of the parrot family and the Hill (or Talking) Mynah (*Gracula religiosa*) are in such wide demand as pets because of their imitative talent that their populations are subject to significant pressure. Unlike the first type of mimic, talking birds *never* (as far as is known) use their mimetic faculty in the wild.

Blue Jays are known to imitate the calls of hawks and crows in the wild, though these are not incorporated into any kind of song; and other corvids, e.g., ravens, crows, and magpies, readily learn to talk in captivity.

The ability and/or inclination to mimic varies widely among species. Northern Mockingbirds, for example, are much more versatile and enthusiastic imitators than the other North American representatives of their family. One mocker may appropriate 30 or more different sounds from other birds as well as ones from other sources; and it has been suggested (Borror, 1964) that northern mockers use more mimicry in their songs than southern.

Among talking birds, the Gray Parrot (*Psittacus erithacus*) of Africa, the Yellow-headed Amazon (*Amazona ochrocephalus*) of Middle America, and the little Budgerigar (*Melopsittacus undulatus*) of Australia are widely known as superior mimics, while many other psittacids show little or no such ability. The Hill Mynah, which can not only repeat human words but also give a very accurate rendering of a person's particular inflections and tone of voice, is probably supreme in this category. Many other mynahs and starlings and at least some crows exhibit some degree of imitative proficiency in captivity, though only a few (e.g., the Common Starling) use this ability in the wild. It should be noted here that the cruel practice of "splitting the tongues" of captive birds in order to enhance their speaking ability does nothing to achieve this end (see *How Birds Sing*, above) and in fact will cause the pet's death.

How. A great many, if not all, songbirds show some skill in vocal mimicry in their ability to learn the nuances of their species' song (see *How Birds Acquire Their Songs*, above). Moreover, a number of species which we do not normally think of as mimics have been heard to sing notes or phrases of other birds in subsongs, which, however, are dropped when they sing their full territorial songs. In rare instances (Thomas, 1943, and Short, 1966) wild birds not known as vocal mimics have learned to sing the songs of a different species (in the same family) in place of their own song. Taken as a whole, these records begin to suggest that the ability and inclination to imitate sounds is widely developed in birds, albeit in varying degrees. If we add the well-documented fact that many birds routinely "compose" individual song variations based on motifs in their species' basic song, it is only a short jump to mockingbirds, which use imitation of other sounds *and* innovative composition together to make up their characteristic song type.

The best of the "natural" mimics have the greatest possible number of syringeal muscles (8–9 pairs), so that their physical ability to reproduce a wide variety of bird sounds does not seem very surprising.

The imitation of human speech, however, is a different matter. Our ability to produce a wide range of vowel sounds is attributable to the ample resonating chambers of our throat, mouth, and nose; and our tongue, teeth, and other mouth structures give us considerable versatility in producing consonants. Birds, by contrast, seem to have few of these speech-producing modifications, and even animals, such as the great apes, which seem far better equipped in this department never utter anything that resembles a word.

Some talking birds resolve this problem in part by "faking it," i.e., using changes in pitch to simulate the variations of vowel and consonant sounds. In addition, human vocal coaches can often hear their bird say the things they have taught them with much greater clarity than an impartial auditor. These two factors in combination explain why "Budgie" says "Good morning, gorgeous," as clear as a bell to Aunt Lulu while all you can hear is a jumble of psittacine squawks and gargles. Nevertheless, Hill Mynahs and other species can reproduce human speech with extraordinary fidelity, emitting vowels and consonants which are unmistakable even under audiospectrographic analysis. Exactly how they do this with their limited equipment is still poorly understood.

Why. Since many of the favorite talking birds never mimic any sounds in the wild and begin imitating speech only when confined in close contact with humans and away from their own species, it would seem that "talking" may be a form of social adjustment. Parrots are known to "pine" and die if deprived of association with their fellows, and talking may be a way of creating a necessary attachment to their captors. Once this is accepted, it is easy to explain apparently intelligent uses of language—speaking to people they "like," saying, "Come back here!" when you leave the room, and making other apt or amusing comments. It is simple conditioning: when they perform well, they are rewarded with attention.

The explanation for "natural" mimicry is not so apparent. If anything, the inherent random quality seems to diminish some of the functions of territorial song. It has been suggested (Marshall, 1950) that many mimics live in dense habitats and, in effect, need more sound for attraction and defense to compensate for less visibility; but does a bird need to mimic other species in order to sing loud and/or long? Perhaps a more plausible theory (Thorpe, 1961) is that mimicry gives an edge in developing highly individual sounds which would help in *individual* recognition and thus reinforcement of pair bonds in dense habitats. What then of the open-country mimics?

Much remains unresolved. For the present, perhaps the most attractive theory—which has been advanced quite seriously—is that birds imitate sounds for positive self-reinforcement—that is, in essence, for fun.

NON-VOCAL SOUNDS. The syrinx is not the only sound-producing mechanism available to birds. Even species such as the vultures and storks, which essentially lack a syringeal sound system, nevertheless can produce a few rudimentary sounds from the throat; the American Bittern makes its unique pumping sound by forcing air in and out of its esophagus; several gallinaceous birds and a few other species make noise with their air-sac system, specifically modified in most cases; bills become percussion instruments when snapped or hit against each other; and the sounds made by air passing through feathers in different ways are wonderfully diverse. Of course, some sounds made by birds are purely incidental. The whoosh made by the flapping of the wings of large birds and the audible snapping shut of a flycatcher's bill when it is feeding are simply by-products of routine behavior. But some wing and bill noises, as well as many other specialized sounds, have evolved—either in part or totally—as functional sounds, most often in association with courtship rituals.

North American species which produce significant non-vocal sounds are listed on pp. 666–69 along with the sounds they produce and their function.

LEARNING BIRDSONGS. All field guides make a heroic effort to teach the novice birdwatcher what various species sound like. Three methods are widely favored: (1) The rendering into words (or at least syllables) of a song or call. Except for the "talking birds" (see *Vocal Mimicry*, above), birds are generally inept at forming vowels and consonants and this "verbalization" technique is therefore doomed to more or less fanciful approximation. Once you know what a Chestnut-sided Warbler sounds like, you may or may not be willing to concede that it "says" "I wish to see Miss Beecher." But it is extremely difficult to apply "Skip-teer Rea-cheer-for You, Cheet-weigh get-yuWhip . . . ReeChee-raVeer-chWoo" or the like (Spot-breasted Wren; Davis, 1972) to a bird with whose song you are unfamiliar. (2) Only slightly more helpful are attempts to *explain* what a bird sounds like: a thin, nasal, but "airy" trill or rattle ending in four melodious but eerie notes. This may be compared to the song of another species with which the novice is, of course, also unfamiliar. (3) Finally there is the "sonogram," which shows us indubitably what a birdsong *looks* like—even parts of it which are inaudible to the human ear. Except for bird-minded audiospectrographers, however, no one has yet been able to apply these fascinating, meticulously graphed runes to learning what birds *sound* like.

In fairness, all of these methods become more useful as the novice bird listener gains some experience—even a sonogram will help you confirm that the insect-type trill you have just heard is more likely to originate in a Prairie Warbler than a Barred Owl.

NON-VOCAL SOUNDS

SPECIES	SOUND	FUNCTION
Black-footed Albatross	Bill snapping by individuals and "bill-ing" by pairs	Courtship
Red-throated Loon	"Rushing train" noise made by wings when gliding down	Courtship flight
Grebes, several species	Bill "fencing"	Courtship
Great (and other) Cormorants	"Gurgles" and other sounds made by vibration of throat pouch	Courtship
Magnificent Frigatebird	Bill clacking, perhaps using inflated throat pouch as a resonator	Male on nest; part of courtship (?)
Herons: most N. Amer. species	Bill snapping and/or mutual "billing"; Great Blue makes (non-vocal?) gurgling	Courtship
American Bittern	"Swallows air" and releases, making 2–3-note "pumping" or "stake-driv-ing" sound	Territorial "song" (?)
Wood Stork	Hissing ("fizzing"); bill nibbling and clacking; loud wing "whoosh" in flight, esp. on down-swoop	Nest ritual; courtship; incidental
White Ibis	Bill snapping	Courtship

Species	Sound	Function
Waterfowl: many species, esp. swans, whistling ducks, and goldeneyes ("whistlers")	Whistling noise from air through wings in flight; variable in pitch and volume; also foot splashing	Courtship
Ruddy Duck	"Bubbling" and other water sounds and perhaps clucking notes produced with aid of tracheal air sac	Courtship
American vultures	Hisses, grunts, cooing, etc., from throat and mouth	Alarm, threat, etc.
Spruce Grouse	Wing "whirring"	Courtship
Ruffed Grouse	"Drumming" sound made by wings beating rapidly over (but not touching) breast	Courtship, but heard year-round
Prairie chickens, and Sage, Sharp-tailed, and Spruce Grouse	Weird cooing, plopping, and booming sounds made with the aid of esophagus and air-sac system	Courtship: male lek display
Many gallinaceous species, e.g., pheasant	Notable, explosive whir or whistle on takeoff.	Surprise predators (?); incidental
Some rails	Esophageal (?) "pumping" sounds similar to American Bitterns' (see above)	Territorial "song" (?)
Pectoral (and other?) sandpiper species	"Booming," not unlike prairie chickens' made by pumping air in and out of esophagus	Courtship

NON-VOCAL SOUNDS (Cont.)

SPECIES	SOUND	FUNCTION
American Woodcock	Soft twittering made by passage of air through modified outer 3 primaries	Made during ascent in males' territorial/courtship flight
Common Snipe	Stiffened outer pair of tail feathers held at right angle to body in steep descent; air passing over wings causes these feathers to vibrate, producing an intermittent, tremulous "winnowing" or "bleating" sound	Territorial/courtship flight
Auks, some species	Bill "fencing"	Nest ritual
Pigeons and doves, most species	Generally noisy flight	Incidental
Columba pigeons, incl. Common Pigeon	Wing clapping: explosive sound made by carpal area of wings meeting over back; bill sounds also recorded	Takeoff (predator surprise?); also part of courtship ritual
Greater Roadrunner	"Rattles" mandibles	Courtship (?)
Most owls	Bill snapping	Defense/threat
Long- and Short-eared Owls	Clap carpal joint of wings *below* body	Courtship flight and nest defense
Nightjars (known in Chuck-will's-widow and Poor-will)	Wing clapping	Courtship/territorial display

Common Nighthawk	"Booming," like blowing over mouth of empty bottle, caused by air rushing through wings on sharp upswing	Courtship (?)
Hummingbirds (in general)	Clearly audible hum or whirring noise made by rapidly beating wings in normal flight	Incidental
Broad-tailed Hummingbird	Two outer primary tips of male modified to produce trill/rattle in flight	Courtship/territorial display
Rufous and Allen's Hummingbirds	Wing buzz or whine; Allen's modifies with tail bobbing and makes ripping noise at climax of courtship flight	Courtship
Most woodpeckers	Drumming noises with bill	Incidental while feeding but also using hollow logs, metal surfaces, or other "sounding boards," in courtship
Some species of waxwings, thrushes, crows, and finches	Various bill noises	Mostly associated with nest rituals
Many (most?) insectivorous birds	Bill snapping	Incidental while feeding

Excellent records and tapes including all North American birdsongs (with variations in some cases) are now available (see the Bibliography under RECORDING OF BIRD SOUNDS for a list of titles) and are invaluable aids to learning songs. However, by far the best method of acquiring this arcane expertise is to search out the singer of every song you don't recognize. The effort will help fix the sound in your memory, and you will have eliminated at least one machine from your effort to make contact with nature.

The wealth of literature on birdsong befits the intricacy and fascination of the subject. Some of the classic, most interesting, and/or most readable books and papers are listed in the Bibliography.

SONGBIRD. Widely used English name for the Oscines (or Passeres), the largest suborder of the Passeriformes, or "perching birds." All North American perching birds except for the tyrant flycatchers and one species of cotinga (considered a flycatcher by many authorities) are "songbirds."

SONOGRAM (or audiospectrogram). Written reproduction of birdsong (or other sounds) made by a stylus which transfers the complex patterns of pitch and frequency from a recording to a moving belt of graph paper. The result is an interrupted series of smudges which purport to show what birdsong sounds like; in reality they show what birdsong *looks* like and are of limited value for field use except for audiospectrographers and a few birdwatcher-musicians. See, however, J. C. Beaver, "Sonograms as Aids in Bird Identification," *American Birds* (1976), 30:899.

SORA. Standard English name for a single species of short-billed rail, *Porzana carolina*, which breeds exclusively in North America. Short-billed rails in this and other genera are for the most part called "crakes." The name is a mystery; possibly of native American origin. See RAIL; CRAKE.

SOUTHEASTERN ARIZONA. In birders' terms, the highlands from Tucson south, including the Santa Catalina, Santa Rita, Huachuca, and Chiricahua Mountains and the intervening arid lowlands. An impressive variety of "Mexican" bird species reach the northernmost extent of their range in this region (including adjacent New Mexico) and occur nowhere else in North America, except in southwestern Texas (see BIG BEND), where, however, they are generally much less common and less easily found. Among these specialties are: Zone-tailed, Gray, and Common Black Hawks, Montezuma (Harlequin) Quail, Flammulated and Whiskered Owls, Magnificent (Rivoli's), Blue-throated, Violet-crowned, White-eared, and Broad-billed Hummingbirds, Elegant (Coppery-tailed) Trogon, Arizona (Brown-backed) Woodpecker, Rose-throated Becard, Sulphur-bellied Flycatcher, Thick-billed Kingbird, Dusky-capped (Olivaceous) Flycatcher, Northern Beardless Tyrannulet (Beardless Flycatcher),

Coues' Flycatcher, Mexican (Gray-breasted) Jay, Mexican (Gray-sided) Chickadee, Bridled Titmouse, Brown-throated Wren, Olive and Red-faced Warblers, Painted Redstart, Yellow-eyed (Mexican) Junco, and Rufous-winged and Five-striped Sparrows. In addition to these "highlights," southeastern Arizona has a fine variety of other "western" birds, an abundant and cooperative avifauna generally, a vastly interesting flora and fauna apart from birds, and enjoys a superb climate and some of the most pleasing landscapes in North America (see Plate 1).

A number of place names come readily to the lips of birders who visit the region, among them *Mount Lemmon*: 9,185-foot peak of the Catalinas with a paved road traversing four life zones to the top; *Madera Canyon* in the Santa Ritas: trogon, hummers, and other pine-oak birds plus a lodge in which to stay; *Patagonia*: a small town about 15 miles north of the Mexican border and the region of excellent roadside birding surrounding it; Patagonia is also the "address" of the Nature Conservancy's *Sonoita Creek Sanctuary*: a fine patch of arid scrub and gallery woodland which contains most of the lowland bird specialties of the region along with a great many others; *Ramsey Canyon* in the Huachucas: best known for the Nature Conservancy's Mile Hi Ranch, where dozens of hummingbird feeders are maintained for the benefit of hundreds of hummingbirds and visitors; *Cave Creek Canyon* in the Chiricahuas: home of the American Museum's Southwest Research Station and a locality from which virtually all of the southeastern Arizona specialties (desert and montane) can be seen within a 5-mile radius.

See Lane's guide to the region (1979–BIRD FINDING).

SOUTH TEMPERATE ZONE. That part of the earth south of the Tropic of Capricorn and north of the Antarctic Circle. It includes the southern half of South America, the southern tip of Africa, the southern half of Australia, and all of New Zealand. A small percentage of the bird species which breed in the S.T.Z. migrate north to the tropics for the southern winter; of these only a few pelagic species, e.g., the Greater Shearwater, Wilson's Storm-Petrel, regularly reach the NORTH TEMPERATE ZONE.

SPARROW. Standard English name for a broad assortment of finches in at least two families. In British usage the name is restricted to the WEAVERS in the family Ploceidae (some of which are placed by many in the family Passeridae), e.g., House Sparrow. In North America it is applied to most of the drabber (brown and gray) emberizine finches in 8–13 genera (depending on taxonomy) comprising 32 species which breed on the continent.

Other New World emberizines, such as the juncos, are sometimes referred to as types of "sparrows."

The New World sparrows are analogous in many ways to the Old

World "buntings" and their general characteristics are considered under the heading *Sparrow-Buntings* (FINCH).

The New World sparrows are mostly birds of open habitats—tundra, deserts, grasslands, and shrubby savanna—but a number of species are forest birds and several prefer fresh or salt marshes.

They achieve their greatest diversity in North America and a number of species are endemic to the Nearctic region. Several species range continentwide, most are migratory, but the majority also winter at least partially in North America.

"Sparrow" comes initially from the Indo-European word *sper*, meaning "flutter," thence to the Anglo-Saxon *spearwa*, meaning any small (fluttering) bird.

SPECIATION (spee-she-AY-shun). The process by which new life forms evolve from those already in existence.

All plants and animals—including birds and humans—have always been, and continue to be, ever-changing.

The "opportunity" to change is offered by the regular occurrence of random gene MUTATION which is controlled, according to its survival value (or lack of it), by NATURAL SELECTION. In a small unified population of a species any advantageous mutation which arises in an individual tends to be acquired in time through interbreeding by the whole population. In this case, the species in question changes in character but it remains a single entity made up of like individuals. However, if two or more populations of a species become separated from one another, the characteristics of each begin to change in their own unique ways, and because the isolated populations can no longer interbreed, the new mutations cannot be shared. Differences between separate populations first begin to appear as barely discernible tendencies, e.g., a greater number of slightly paler, longer-billed individuals in one population than in another. If the tendencies continue in opposite directions, the populations become readily recognizable races or subspecies—one long-billed and pale, the other short-billed and dark—but would still interbreed freely and successfully if the populations were reunited. As the populations continue to "grow apart," however, their willingness and ability to interbreed continue to decline, and when the sharing of genetic traits becomes impossible (or at least highly unlikely), the populations have evolved into distinct species. Though this process is called speciation, it begins, as we see, with individual variation and does not stop with the evolution of a new species. Each new species has the potential for continued divergence, and since there are few limitations on the degree of change possible, the process can continue up the phylogenetic ladder. The same "system" which produced that slightly paler, longer-billed individual was also responsible, as it were, for making birds from reptiles.

Needless to say, speciation takes time. *Archaeopteryx* did not go to bed a reptile and wake up a bird. The traditional view of biological change (evolution) is that it takes place very gradually over eons, but many modern theorists now believe that it may occur in (relatively) quick adaptive bursts, interspersed with long periods during which the organism in question remains genetically static. Of course, fundamental and complex changes, e.g., skeletal modifications or the transformation of scales into feathers, are still long-term processes. But relatively superficial, yet conspicuous changes in color and size can be noticed within a few decades. House Sparrows, for example, which were first introduced into North America around 1850, have already evolved distinctive forms in response to ecological influences so universal in their effect on bird morphology that zoologists have names for them (see, for example, the several biological "rules" noted under *The Ways of Changing*, below).

HOW POPULATIONS BECOME ISOLATED. The separation of animal populations can result from sudden cataclysms, gradual, relatively confined processes, or anything in between. A few major and frequent phenomena should be mentioned:

Continental Drift separated populations of hundreds of thousands of organisms, giving rise to what are now the highly distinctive faunas of South America, Africa, Australia, etc.

Glacial Advances moving southward across the landmasses of the Northern Hemisphere split continents and habitats into eastern and western regions. It is theorized, for example, that a great coniferous forest once transcontinental in North America was divided during one of the Pleistocene advances, allowing bird and other faunas to plot separate genetic courses. This explains in part why it is now practical to have eastern and western field guides.

Mountaintop Islands of habitat into which populations retreat and begin to change can result from glacial invasion or geological events such as uplift and vulcanism. The races (or species?) of rosy finches isolated in different parts of the Rockies exemplify this kind of genetic isolation in North America. Some high mountains in the tropics have evolved their own unique avifaunas by this process.

Oceanic Islands can also be hotbeds of speciation—witness the many species which are unique to one or a small group of islands in the West Indies or Polynesia. Most of these island "endemics" are probably descendants of storm-driven vagrants from mainland populations. Some (e.g., Darwin's famous finches of the Galápagos Islands and many forms on Madagascar) have evolved with such abandon for so long that they no longer have any close off-island relatives. The Bermuda race of the White-eyed Vireo, on the other hand, has just begun its evolutionary divergence from the other members of its species. In the relatively recent past, a population of White-eyes established a resident population on Bermuda. The so-called Chick-of-the-Village never leaves the islands, and mainland White-eyes passing through in the fall never remain to breed. At present the Bermuda birds are distinguished from other races only by such inconspicuous differences as shorter wings, but over time its physiology and/or behavior will likely become so changed as to render it unable or unwilling to mate with any form of White-eyed Vireo. It will have evolved from *Vireo griseus bermudianus* (the Bermuda White-eyed Vireo) to *Vireo bermudianus* (the Bermuda Vireo).

Distance. Species with very broad ranges may evolve in different directions toward the extremities of their range, even though they remain genetically linked. Changes in color or size, for example, tend to be graduated geographically between poles in such cases, so that it is often impossible to draw sharp boundaries between the end of one race's range and the beginning of another's (see CLINE). In rare instances the diverging range of such a species is circular, with the extremities meeting, and the races being sexually incompatible (see RING SPECIES). This makes a quandary for the taxonomist, who must decide whether he is dealing with one species or two, and if the latter, how to define their breeding ranges. The Song Sparrow may be the champion North American "diverger," with about 30 recognized races within its unified range; interestingly, other species almost equally widespread change little over their range.

RESPECTING BARRIERS. The factors which separate populations, thus encouraging speciation, need not be vast oceans or thousands of miles of glacial ice. Particularly in tropical regions, the barriers between populations of different races of birds may be no more formidable than a river or narrow strait. Ecological barriers such as an intervening "wall" of forest between two deserts (or vice versa) often remain unbroached even though the width of the barrier is negligible. However, such barriers are not equally respected by all forms. Some yield to the isolating forces and become distinct, while others interact with the wider "gene pool" beyond and retain their species' homogeneity.

THE WAYS OF CHANGING. Given the different scenarios which can produce genetic isolation and the adaptive "cunning" of mutation/selection, it is not surprising that speciation progresses in a number of different ways.

To begin with, there seem to be some biological formulas which govern animal form and coloration according to differences in climate (see ALLEN'S, BERGMANN'S, GLOGER'S, and KELSO'S RULES). For example, populations of bird species tend to be smaller and paler in hot, dry regions than their counterparts in cool, humid regions. The validity of these generalizations is much more apparent in a tray of museum specimens from different climates than in the field, and there are numerous exceptions, but there is no doubt that they play a role in speciation.

A more "inventive" force for change is called adaptive *radiation*, the tendency of animals to diversify in accordance with the available ecological niches. If we placed a population of robins on a birdless island with a variety of habitats, and returned after a few million years, we might find no sign of the bird that pulls worms from our lawn. We might, however, find a species of robin with a long tail which caught flying insects from a tree-top perch, another which lived deep in the forest and fed only on fruit, a third with longer bill and legs which waded in shallow water and caught fish, etc. These fanciful robins are not so different, in fact, from the Drepanididae, a family (honeycreepers) which apparently evolved in isolation in the Hawaiian Islands in just this way.

As species evolve in different ways away from their common ancestors, the adaptations they acquire to suit a particular life style may make them look strikingly different from other species to which they are really closely related. This is called adaptive *divergence* and is well illustrated among the members of the American blackbird family (Icteridae): the Bobolink has developed the appearance and habitat and food preferences common to many finches; orioles, on the other hand, are more like tanagers or warblers in these respects; the meadowlarks, also icterids, resemble neither the Bobolink nor the orioles, but look and act a great deal like some African species in the pipit family called longclaws. This chance development of similar characteristics in families of birds only distantly related is called adaptive CONVERGENCE (which see for other examples.)

Testing the Theories. It is all very well to spin hypotheses about speciation and reproductive isolation, but how can we know for sure whether long-separated populations would or would not interbreed—whether, that is, they are races of the same species or genetically distinct forms? Do divergent populations ever reunite? What happens when they do? The simple answer to the first question is: We can't. The taxonomic status of forms such as the Brown-capped Rosy Finch, whose breeding range nowhere overlaps with its closest relatives, cannot be asserted beyond doubt.

The close similarity in many instances between fully distinct species (e.g., Willow and Alder Flycatchers; Greater and Lesser Scaup) and the marked dissimilarity among many subspecies (races of the same species) (e.g., eastern and western Fox Sparrows) clearly rule out appearance as a decisive criterion. But we must form some judgment in these cases, for nomenclatural reasons if for no other, and ornithologists can make highly educated guesses based on such criteria as song pattern, nesting and feeding habits, social structure, as well as "conservative" morphological characters (see TAXONOMY). In addition, biologists are developing increasingly sophisticated techniques to compare the structure of body proteins for the determination of genetic relationships (see ELECTROPHORESIS).

Of course, long-separated bird populations are sometimes reunited "naturally": glaciers melt, rivers alter their courses, habitat changes, etc., resulting in the elimination or bridging of former barriers between breeding ranges. What happens in the areas where populations of closely related species overlap varies depending upon how far they have evolved away from each other. They may, for example, have developed different songs, plumage, courtship rituals, and/or feeding habits—*isolating mechanisms* which work against the possibility of genetic reunion. At one extreme, differentiation is complete and reunited forms do not recognize even the possibility of interbreeding, though they share a close common ancestry. Or initial attempts at hybridization may result in infertile eggs or sterile offspring due to genetic incompatibility, and separation is automatically enforced. The small, dull flycatchers in the genus *Empidonax* are obviously very closely related, yet each species has evolved an effective repertoire of isolating mechanisms, so that hybrids among them are (virtually) unknown, though the breeding ranges of two or three species overlap almost everywhere in North America.

At the opposite extreme, forms reunited after a relatively brief separation and little opportunity for change could interbreed with complete abandon, so that both populations would merge into one, consisting entirely of hybrids.

Many cases fall between the two extremes. If hybrids produced by the union of related forms turn out to be less satisfactory than the "pure" forms on either side of the family, new isolating mechanisms will evolve relatively quickly to keep the populations from merging completely. Sometimes there is a relatively stable zone of overlap in which nearly all individual birds are hybrids. The classic North American example of this model is that of the "yellow-shafted" (eastern) and "red-shafted" (western) races of the Common Flicker, which were probably forced to go their own ways by Pleistocene glaciers, a barrier enforced after the withdrawal of the ice by the treeless central prairies. Trees planted in midwestern farmlands and suburbs have bridged the gap, and a wide zone of "orange-shafted" and parti-colored flickers has developed in the northern plains states. It may be too soon to predict, but unless the hybrid zone expands, distinctive eastern and western forms of flickers will continue to be much more numerous than mixed individuals. Baltimore and Bullock's Orioles, now classified as races of a single species (called Northern Oriole), may be responding to their recent reunion with less relish than the flickers. They seem to be hybridizing less freely than they did when they first met, which could indicate the development of isolating mechanisms and perhaps a reinforced separation. See also HYBRIDIZATION.

PITY THE TAXONOMIST. The transitional nature of speciation poses occasional problems for the professional classifier, part of whose job is to assign a fixed status to evolving organisms. How, for example, is one to define ranges of bird races which intergrade into one another along a cline as described above? Or to decide at what point a population is distinct enough to rate subspecific status? Or whether Baltimore and Bullock's Orioles are one species or two?

In part, ornithologists and other specialists are guided by scientific convention. There is an arbitrary rule, for example, which holds that characters meriting subspecific distinction must be present in 75 percent of a population before it can be described as a geographical race.

It is more important, however, to realize that the whole structure of systematics (see TAXONOMY) is a man-made convention which allows us to deal with organisms as concrete entities even as they change. It is a "given" of any such system that it is continually subject to revision, and a glance at taxonomic literature is all that is needed to demonstrate that this is so. In 1975, a committee of distinguished ornithologists *decided*, based on the present scientific evidence, that Baltimore and Bullock's Orioles should be considered races of a single species. None of these men would be embarrassed if they had to reverse themselves on the basis of new or better data.

See the Bibliography for full accounts of several of the speciation examples given above; also under HYBRIDIZATION.

See also DISTRIBUTION.

SPECIES (sing. and pl.) (SPEE-shees). The fundamental unit of taxonomy, defined biologically by free interbreeding among the organisms it contains and reproductive isolation from other such groups of organisms. All other taxonomic categories are artificial groupings defined (and continually redefined) by human beings to classify related groupings of species. A GENUS, for example, is an aggregation of what taxonomists believe to be phylogenetically closely related species. In the vernacular, "species" is often used to mean simply a "kind" of animal, but this loose usage sometimes creates confusion about the true biological meaning of the term. It is impossible to deny that the Bullock's and Baltimore races (subspecies) of the Northern Oriole (see Plate 4) are different "kinds" of birds—typical individuals are easily distinguished by a number of characters. But ornithologists have recently decided that these two forms are in fact striking variations of the same "kind," i.e., species (see SPECIATION).

A world total of between 8,600 and 8,700 species of birds is now recognized by most authorities, the precise number being subject to taxonomic interpretation. Perhaps another 50–100 remain to be discovered, mostly in isolated mountain habitats in tropical South America. About 650 bird species breed in North America (north of the Mexican border), about 50 more occur here regularly but do not breed, and about 140 species have been reliably recorded as accidental stragglers from other avifaunas. All species of regular occurrence in North America are listed in phylogenetic order in Appendix I. Accidental species are listed in Appendix II.

In modern biological nomenclature, a species is designated by two Latin (or "Latinized") names, a generic name followed by a specific name, e.g., *Somateria spectabilis*, the species name for the King Eider (see NOMENCLATURE).

The abbreviations "sp." (sing.) and "spp." (plural) are sometimes used for "species" when species identity is unknown or when one wishes to refer collectively to some or all species in a higher category. For example, "Peep sp." or "*Calidris* sp." refers to one or more unidentified shorebirds of a single species; "*Calidris* spp." indicates that more than one species is involved. The total number of a raft of scoters containing all three species might be expressed as "Scoters, spp.—500."

SPECIFIC. In a biological context, refers (specifically) to a species. For example: "It was decided that the form should be elevated from subspecific to specific level."

SPECIMEN (of a bird). Usually, the preserved skin of a bird, stored in a museum collection and vital to the pursuit of numerous ornithological objectives, including, for example, comparison of forms for taxonomic purposes and the making of accurate illustrations for field guides. In matters of critical determination, whether in the field or the lab, birders and ornithologists alike are heard to discuss the desirability of collecting or examining "specimens." See BIRD SKIN.

Occasionally whole birds (not just their skins) are preserved in fluid, when continued reference to internal structures is wanted. These too, of course, are "specimens."

In recent years some successful experiments have shown that it is possible to preserve satisfactory specimens of some (especially small) birds by freeze-drying, thus eliminating the considerable time and effort consumed in making bird skins.

SPECULUM (SPEK-yuh-lum). A patch of contrasting color on the wing, especially that on the upper surface of the secondary feathers of dabbling ducks. See WING.

SPEED. In normal, traveling flight most birds proceed at between 20 and 50 miles per hour, but are generally capable of much higher speeds at least for short distances, as when they are being chased by a predator. Racing pigeons and the Red-breasted Merganser have been reliably clocked at air speeds of 80 m.p.h., and doubtless many other species have a similar capacity.

The characteristics shared by the fastest-flying birds are: powerful flight (pectoral) muscles (see Fig. 10); streamlined bodies; flat wings (i.e., little camber); a high aspect ratio and no slots (see FLIGHT). The ultimate "high-speed" wings are those of the swifts, but falcons, many shorebirds, hummingbirds, and swallows share most if not all of these characteristics.

There is evidence that the fastest birds may at times attain speeds reaching or exceeding 200 m.p.h.; however, such speeds have never been recorded in a controlled scientific procedure. Many velocity records come from pilots who check their speedometers as their planes are passed by birds; while many of the highest speeds thus recorded have yet to be scientifically confirmed, there is little reason to doubt their validity in most cases. Some alleged and confirmed speed records are as follows:

Fastest Bird Worldwide (flapping flight). This record so far belongs to the White-throated Needle-tailed Swift (*Hirundapus caudacutus*), an Asian species, whose speed has been reliably clocked at 106.25 m.p.h.; the same species is also said to reach 219.5 m.p.h. (ground speed), but the method of recording this statistic has been called into question.

Fastest North American Bird. The speed record for flapping flight here may well belong to the White-throated Swift, which has been *estimated* to attain 200 m.p.h. Dunlins have been clocked from a plane (McCabe, 1942) at "not less than 110 m.p.h." The Peregrine Falcon in a stoop has long been credited with a speed of at least 175 m.p.h. and possibly over 200 m.p.h. by several pilots. However, experimenters who recently attached small air speedometers to this species were unable to confirm a diving speed over 82 m.p.h.

Fastest Running Birds. The Ostrich holds the world record, which is at least 44 m.p.h. and may well reach 50 or 60 m.p.h. In North America the Wild Turkey may attain 30 m.p.h. for short periods and frequently travels on foot at 15 m.p.h. Cottam et al. (1942) give speeds of 15 m.p.h. for the Greater Roadrunner and up to 21 m.p.h. for the Common Pheasant.

Fastest Swimming Bird. The Gentoo Penguin has been timed underwater at 22.3 m.p.h. (McWhirter, 1980).

SPISHING. See PISHING; BIRD CALLS.

SPLITTING (splitter). In an ornithological context, the practice of separating bird forms (especially species) into smaller taxonomic units (especially subspecies). The taxonomist who performs this kind of dissection is known as a "splitter." The splitter is the bird listers' champion, because, in effect, he adds species to the avifauna. Compare LUMPING.

SPOONBILL. Standard English name for all 5 members of the subfamily Plataleinae (family Threskiornithidae [ibises]; order Ciconiiformes), 1 of which, the Roseate Spoonbill, breeds in North America.

The most notable of spoonbill characteristics is, of course, their peculiar spatulate bill, which is really more a sensory device than a spoon.

The inside of the broad, flattened tip is lined with sensitized tissue that feels small food items as the birds swing their partially opened bills through shallow, murky water. When small prey such as insect larvae, shrimps, or shellfish are encountered the "spoon" snaps shut on them.

All spoonbills except the New World species are largely white. The unique roseate plumage of our species put its owners' existence in peril during the days of the plume trade (see CONSERVATION).

Like their near relatives the ibises, spoonbills are colonial nesters and make a platform of sticks in low trees (e.g., mangroves) or shrubs or (less usually) rush beds or on the ground. They often occupy mixed "rookeries" with herons, ibises, etc. The 2–4 eggs are whitish with both fine speckles and larger splotches of light reddish brown, the latter concentrated near the large end.

Spoonbills are generally silent but make low grunts and clucks when alarmed or at the nest site.

The small, local North American spoonbill populations in Florida and Texas are now fairly stable or on the increase; the species also occurs throughout the New World tropics.

SPORT (bird-related). See BIRDWATCHING; COCKFIGHTING; FALCONRY; HUNTING; LISTING.

SPRAGUE (sprayg), Isaac, 1811–95 (Spague's Pipit: *Anthus spragueii*). Prominent nineteenth-century illustrator from Massachusetts. His chief fame (aside from the pipit) lies in his fine drawings for Asa Gray's *Botanical Textbook*. He was a friend of Audubon, who was the author of Sprague's Pipit.

SPRAYING (chemical). See MAN-MADE THREATS TO BIRDLIFE.

SPURS (on wings and legs). See WING; LEG/FOOT.

SQUAB. In the broadest sense, any nestling bird without down or feathers; more specifically, a nestling pigeon, sometimes cooked and eaten as a delicacy.

STARLING. Standard English name for about 78 of the approximately 110 members of the family Sturnidae (order Passeriformes), which also includes the mynahs, oxpeckers, and (perhaps) bald crows (rock fowl); also the standard name for the family as a whole. There is no taxonomic or precise vernacular distinction between a starling and a mynah. Two species of starlings, the Common Starling and the Crested Mynah, have been "successfully" introduced into North America (see INTRODUCED BIRDS).

Worldwide, the starlings range in length between 7 and 17 inches;

the Common Starling measures about 8 inches and the Crested Mynah about 10 inches. Our two alien starlings are typical of many of their kind, being compact with a fairly long, straight, sharp bill; short tail; and strong legs and feet. Both have dark, glossy, iridescent plumage as adults. In North America, starlings are widely and justly characterized as overabundant nuisance birds. Were they less common, they might be deemed as decorative as some of the African starling species that are among the most brilliantly plumaged and elegantly proportioned birds in the world.

Starlings roost and feed in flocks, sometimes very large ones (see PESTS). They often feed in fruiting trees, but are equally at ease walking (not hopping) on the ground, probing for beetle grubs and picking up other invertebrates and seeds. Both the Common Starling and the Crested Mynah are well known for their fondness for garbage dumps, stockyards, and cultivated fields. And both are attracted to man-made urban structures (bridges, office buildings) as roosts. Starling song tends to be raucous and rather chaotic, though with some musical notes or phrases, and many species, including our two, add motifs mimicked from other birds. Mynahs, of course, are famed as "talking birds" (see SONG; MYNAH), and captive Common Starlings readily pick up human sounds.

Starlings are mostly cavity nesters and will occupy rock crevices, holes in earthen banks, and niches in houses as well as tree cavities. One of the reasons our introduced starlings are considered banes rather than blessings is that they are too successful in competing with "nicer" native species such as bluebirds for nest sites. By contrast, in parts of rural Europe, where the Common Starling is indigenous and not inordinately prolific, bird-houses are erected specifically to attract them. The nest cavity typically contains an untidy lining of coarse plant materials as well as paper and other debris. Mynahs lay 6–7 (usually 4–5) eggs, starlings 4–9 (usually 5–7). In both cases the eggs are pale to darker greenish blue.

The starling family is native to Eurasia, Africa, New Guinea, northern Australia, and much of Oceania. The Common Starling now ranges coast to coast in North America south of the boreal forest and southward to central Mexico. The Crested Mynah has remained a localized resident of Vancouver City and Vancouver Island, B.C.

Recognizable forms of the name "starling" are found at least as far back as Old English, referring specifically to the Common Starling. Choate (1973–BIOGRAPHY) notes the theory that it may mean "little star" because of the somewhat star-shaped silhouette of a starling in flight. Another suggestion put forward is that the name comes from the buff-colored spots in the basic (winter) plumage, which some observers have likened to "little stars."

STATE/PROVINCIAL BIRDS. The "official" bird species of a given political unit, proclaimed or voted into law in most cases. The North American roster of honored species is as follows:

United States (National Bird: Bald Eagle)
Alabama: Common Flicker
Alaska: Willow Ptarmigan
Arizona: Cactus Wren
Arkansas: Northern Mockingbird
California: California Quail
Colorado: Lark Bunting
Connecticut: American Robin
Delaware: Blue Hen (chicken)
District of Columbia: Wood Thrush
Florida: Northern Mockingbird
Georgia: Brown Thrasher
Hawaii: Nene (Hawaiian Goose)
Idaho: Mountain Bluebird
Illinois: Northern Cardinal
Indiana: Northern Cardinal
Iowa: American Goldfinch
Kansas: Western Meadowlark
Kentucky: Northern Cardinal
Louisiana: Brown Pelican
Maine: Black-capped Chickadee
Maryland: Northern (Baltimore) Oriole
Massachusetts: Black-capped Chickadee
Michigan: American Robin
Minnesota: Common Loon
Mississippi: Northern Mockingbird
Missouri: Eastern Bluebird

Montana: Western Meadowlark
Nebraska: Western Meadowlark
Nevada: Mountain Bluebird
New Hampshire: Purple Finch
New Jersey: American Goldfinch
New Mexico: Greater Roadrunner
New York: Eastern Bluebird
North Carolina: Northern Cardinal
North Dakota: Western Meadowlark
Ohio: Northern Cardinal
Oklahoma: Scissor-tailed Flycatcher
Oregon: Western Meadowlark
Pennsylvania: Ruffed Grouse
Rhode Island: Rhode Island Red (chicken)
South Carolina: Carolina Wren
South Dakota: Common Pheasant
Tennessee: Northern Mockingbird
Texas: Northern Mockingbird
Utah: California Gull
Vermont: Hermit Thrush
Virginia: Northern Cardinal
Washington: American Goldfinch
West Virginia: Northern Cardinal
Wisconsin: American Robin
Wyoming: Western Meadowlark

Score: Northern Cardinal, 7; Western Meadowlark, 6; Northern Mockingbird, 5.

In 1982 the U.S. Postal Service issued a block of 50 stamps commemorating the state birds and state flowers.

Few (if any) Canadian provinces have official birds, though all have official flowers; the Federation of Ontario Naturalists has proposed the Black-capped Chickadee as the avian emblem of Ontario.

STATE/PROVINCIAL BOOKS. See the Bibliography under this heading for major works on the avifauna of North American states and provinces, with illustrators noted where exceptional.

STELLER, Georg Wilhelm, 1709–46 (Steller's Eider: *Polysticta stelleri;* Steller's Jay: *Cyanocitta stelleri*). A doctor-naturalist (see BIOGRAPHY), Steller was born in Germany and spent much of his short life chronicling the natural history of Siberia/Alaska. He was a member of the Bering expedition of 1740–42 and his extensive field work and writings on the flora and fauna of the northeastern Palearctic easily merit his present nomenclatural prominence. He died appropriately (though apparently despondently) in Siberia. For a fuller biography, see Sutton and Sutton, *Natural History* (1956), 65:485–91.

STENOECIOUS (sten-EE-shus). Able to exist only in one or a few habitats. The Golden-cheeked Warbler is stenoecious on its breeding grounds, nesting only in a cedar and scrub oak formation typical of the limestone hills of the Edwards Plateau of central Texas.

STENOPHAGOUS (steh-NAH-fa-gus). Tolerant of only certain forms of food. Woodcocks feed almost exclusively on earthworms, and their bills are strongly adapted to find and capture this prey; however, 25 percent of their diet consists of other foods, such as insects, snails, and the occasional small vertebrate. The Brant population of the Atlantic coast almost perished during the early 1930's due to a catastrophic blight of eelgrass, their preferred food. Both the woodcock and the Brant are stenophagous—but not MONOPHAGOUS—species. As the Brant example shows, there are clear disadvantages to stenophagous habits. See EURYPHAGOUS.

STERNUM. The breastbone. See SKELETON and Fig. 19.

STIFFTAIL DUCK. Collective name for all members of the subfamily Oxyurinae or the tribe Oxyurini (family Anatidae; order Anseriformes). There are 9 species of "stifftails" worldwide, 2 of which, the Ruddy Duck and Masked Duck, breed in North America. The former is a lake and pond species widespread in the New World south of the Arctic, and the latter is a secretive marsh species largely confined to the American tropics but just reaching the southern U.S. in southern Florida and Texas.

The name refers to the long tail, characteristic of most members of the group; it is often held erect and plays a part in certain courtship rituals (see DISPLAY).

STILT. Standard English name for 2–4 (depending on taxonomy) members of the family Recurvirostridae (order Charadriiformes), which also includes 4 species of avocets and is sometimes called the avocet family. One species, the Black-necked Stilt, breeds in North America. Some authorities believe that three of the four stilt forms, including the Black-necked Stilt, are variations of a single species.

The stilts are tall (average 14 inches), gracefully elongated black-and-white shorebirds with bright pink legs and a long, thin, slightly upturned bill. They wade (and sometimes swim) in shallow water, feeding on small vertebrates (fish, frogs) and large invertebrates (shrimp, insects) as well as some plant matter. They usually feed in flocks.

They nest colonially, making a shallow depression in mud or sand, in a shortgrass marsh or in the open, sparsely or fairly heavily lined with plant debris. The nest is typically placed near or even in shallow water and in the latter case additional "walls" are added. The 3–5 (usually 4) eggs are brownish yellow, rather heavily marked with prominent dark brown spots.

The frequently uttered stilt call consists of sharp, loud, piping notes: *pep* or *ip*.

The stilts are most prevalent throughout the warmer regions of the world but range well into the Temperate Zone—e.g., to southern Oregon and Delaware in North America. Northern populations are migratory.

"Stilt," of course, refers to these birds' extraordinary legs.

STINT. Standard English name in Britain and its former empire for the smaller sandpipers in the genus *Calidris* (incl. *Erolia*). As a collective term, essentially synonymous with PEEP (slightly more restrictive).

STOMACH. See DIGESTIVE SYSTEM.

STOMACH OIL. A fatty, usually pinkish liquid produced in the stomachs (proventriculi) of the tubenosed birds (order Procellariiformes). The substance is apparently similar to the oils found in the heads and stomachs of some whales and dolphins and, when cooled, hardens to a waxy consistency like that of ambergris or spermaceti. It has a strong, distinctive (some say "foul") musky odor, and is used in self-defense by nestlings and adults, which expel it violently from mouth and nostrils onto would-be molesters. The plumage of albatrosses, shearwaters, petrels, and their allies usually smells strongly of musk, and while the oil secreted from the uropygial gland (see OIL GLAND) is also strong-smelling, it has been suggested that stomach oil too may be applied to the feathers (see PREENING). It may also aid in the metabolic production of fresh water in the bodies of the strictly oceanic tubenoses.

STOOP. The characteristic dive of some species of falcons onto their prey from above. It was once widely stated with authority that Peregrine Falcons attained speeds of up to 180 m.p.h. (passing an airplane diving at 175 m.p.h.) and even to 275 m.p.h.! (Brown and Amadon, 1968–HAWK). But recent attempts to confirm such velocities, using air speedometers attached to stooping birds, have been unable to prove speeds in excess of 82 m.p.h.

Because large birds (e.g., Great Blue Heron, Red-tailed Hawk) have been seen killed instantaneously on impact by a stooping Peregrine, it has long been surmised that death is effected by a blow from the falcon's large, powerful feet. Recent evidence indicates that a raking action by the long claw of the hind toe may also play a role.

STORAGE OF FOOD. See FOOD/FEEDING.

STORK. Standard English name for all 17 members of the family Ciconiidae (order Ciconiiformes), of which 1 species, the Wood Stork, breeds in North America; 1 other, Neotropical species (the Jabiru) has occurred as a vagrant (see Appendix II).

Storks are among the largest water birds (30 to 60 inches), with a long neck, legs, and bill and a short tail, characters which sometimes lead to confusion with the HERONS and CRANES. The three front toes are webbed at the bases and their bills are particularly massive: the Wood Stork has the largest bill of any North American bird, to 9 inches in length.

Many of the world's storks are at home in relatively dry uplands, including tilled fields, where they feed on a wide range of small vertebrates and large insects. The Wood Stork is equally undiscriminating in its diet (it will gladly swallow a young alligator), but is by preference a water bird and often wades up to its belly, "feeling" with its bill below the surface for any living edible. The sight of broad-winged, black-and-white Wood Storks soaring over a broad wetland is one of the great sights of the warmer parts of the New World, though fast becoming a rare one in North America.

Our native stork typically builds its stick platform in trees rooted in water, e.g., cypresses and mangroves. It lines the nest with finer twigs and leaves and lays 3–4 (rarely 5) off-white, unmarked eggs.

Storks are usually silent and in fact are ill-equipped vocally, capable only of hissing when alarmed or disturbed. According to Palmer (1962), the young also make "goose-like" calls. Adults not infrequently snap their great bills loudly and make an impressive "whooshing" sound as they flap overhead.

The Wood Stork once bred across the southern border of the U.S. from California to the east coast and north to Tennessee. It now breeds only in Florida, where its population is currently dwindling.

"Stork" as a name for these distinctive birds—especially the White Stork of Europe—has an ancient lineage. Etymologists speculate that origins may have related to "stark," i.e., "strong" or "starch," as in the rigid posture and form of storks.

Only the Eurasian White Stork is known to deliver babies.

STORM-PETREL. Standard English name for all 22 members of the family Hydrobatidae (order Procellariiformes), of which 3 breed in North

America. Three more occur as regular visitors to our offshore waters in either the Atlantic or the Pacific and yet another 4 have occurred as accidental stragglers (see Appendix II).

The storm-petrels are small (5 to 10 inches), usually sooty-black, pelagic birds with a rather short, slender, hooked bill, tubular nostrils located above at the bill base, and rather long, slender legs, which they characteristically dangle in the water while hovering. The front three toes are webbed (the webbing yellow in one of our species) and the hind toe (hallux) is vestigial. On land, they hobble awkwardly on their tarsi, rather than walk erect.

Storm-petrels are seldom seen from land but are often common on offshore fishing banks, where they flit over the waves like swallows, butterflies, or bats. In rough weather, they seem to survive by giving themselves up to the will of the winds. Seamen traditionally regard these Mother Carey's chickens (Carey chicks) as the souls of the drowned and as omens of ill fortune or bad weather. Like other tubenoses, storm-petrels have a musky odor and are able to confer it on molesters by vomiting forth a strong-smelling STOMACH OIL or wax similar to the "head oil" of sperm whales. Some species habitually follow ships, others never do.

The storm-petrels nest colonially in rock crevices (including walls) or in ground burrows abandoned by other animals or dug by themselves (see Fig. 15). The site is lined in some cases with bits of plant material; the single egg is white and sometimes has a "wreath" of fine blackish or reddish speckles at the larger end.

The voices of the Carey chicks are seldom heard at sea except on calm nights near breeding colonies. However, most species have a great repertoire of twitters, chirps, wails, gasps, whistles, etc., and sometimes give extended weird "songs"—all of which enhances their reputation as demons.

The family ranges over all the oceans of the world, but shows greatest diversity and abundance in colder waters where marine food sources are most prolific. This is particularly true of the Antarctic Ocean.

"Petrel" is usually supposed to be associated with St. Peter and his walk on the lake of Gennesaret (Matthew 14), owing to the birds' foot-dangling habit noted above.

STRUTTING GROUNDS. The open sagebrush plains used for courtship display by the Sage Grouse. Like the prairie chickens, male Sage Grouse gather in spring, sometimes in hundreds, to perform a dawn prenuptial ritual involving a characteristic "dance" with accompanying sounds. See also BOOMING; LEK; DISPLAY.

STUDY SKIN. A specimen of an animal, especially a bird or mammal, prepared in such a manner as to be easily stored in a museum collection.

Bird skins which are mounted in lifelike poses by taxidermists are *not* study skins. See BIRD SKIN.

SUBADULT. Not fully mature. Commonly used to describe an intermediate plumage that immediately precedes that of a fully adult bird. For example, the immature male American Redstart in the fall and winter closely resembles a female (of any age), but by spring—following a pre-alternate (pre-nuptial) molt—it has acquired a blotchy black-and-olive-brown plumage that readily identifies it as a male. It will not assume the fully adult black-and-orange plumage until its next molt at the end of the summer. Species such as the Herring Gull and Northern Gannet pass through a similar sequence of plumage changes, but the process takes three or more years to complete, and the result is a bewildering array of motley variations made even more confusing by feather wear (see ABRASION). In referring to such "long sequence" species, birdwatchers frequently call birds in the earlier plumages (i.e., those which more resemble juveniles than adults) "immatures" and the later ones "subadults." See also MATURITY; MOLT.

SUBARCTIC. The region south of the arctic isotherm in which the mean temperature does not exceed 10° C. for more than *four* months in summer and does not rise above 0° C. during the coldest month. In this definition, the Subarctic roughly coincides with the combined Hudsonian and Canadian life zones and with the coniferous forest biome. It is the region of the boreal forest and is sometimes called the taiga. For birds typical of the North American Subarctic, see BOREAL; compare ARCTIC; see also TAIGA; MUSKEG.

SUBCLASS. Secondary taxonomic category between CLASS and ORDER. Formerly, birds have been divided into three subclasses: the Sauriurae—toothed, reptile-like birds represented by a single species, *Archaeopteryx lithographica*; the Odontoholcae—diving birds with teeth set in grooves in the jaws (see HESPERORNIS); and Ornithurae—all "modern" (untoothed) birds, fossil and recent. This and most other current works follow Wetmore (1960–TAXONOMY) in placing all known birds (fossil and recent) in a single subclass, Neornithes (usually referred to as the "true birds"), with the single exception of ARCHAEOPTERYX, which alone occupies a second subclass, Archaeornithes. See TAXONOMY.

SUBGENUS. Secondary taxonomic category sometimes interposed between GENUS and SPECIES. For example, *Cerchneis* is sometimes recognized as a subgrouping encompassing the kestrels under the genus *Falco*. See TAXONOMY.

SUBFAMILY. Secondary taxonomic category between FAMILY and GENUS or between family and TRIBE when the latter category is used. In zoological nomenclature subfamily names invariably end in *-inae*. For example, the Polyborinae is the subfamily in which the caracaras are distinguished within the family Falconidae, containing the falcons and caracaras (see TAXONOMY). For "definitions" of all North American subfamilies, see Appendix I.

SUBORDER. Secondary taxonomic category between ORDER and FAMILY or between order and SUPERFAMILY when this last category is used. In zoological nomenclature, subordinal names take the appropriate Latin plural ending rather than bearing a fixed ending in all cases. See TAXONOMY. The 22 suborders of North American birds (following Wetmore, 1960–TAXONOMY) are listed alphabetically below along with the numbers of the pages on which they are "defined" in Appendix I.

Accipitres, p. 799	Charadrii, p. 804	Oscines, p. 813
Alcae, p. 807	Ciconiae, p. 798	Pelecani, p. 797
Alcedines, p. 811	Columbae, p. 808	Phaethontes, p. 797
Anseres, p. 800	Cuculi, p. 809	Pici, p. 811
Apodi, p. 810	Falcones, p. 800	Trochili, p. 810
Ardeae, p. 798	Galli, p. 802	Tyranni, p. 812
Caprimulgi, p. 810	Grues, p. 803	
Cathartae, p. 799	Lari, p. 806	

SUBOSCINE. Perching birds (Passeriformes) which are not songbirds (i.e., not members of the suborder Oscines), and which are theoretically "below" them on the phylogenetic tree, are called suboscine passerines or simply suboscines. In North America there is only one suboscine family, the Tyrannidae (tyrant flycatchers), including one species, the Rose-throated Becard, often placed in the Cotingidae, another suboscine family. For pronunciation, see OSCINES.

SUBSONG. A song which differs from the main characteristic song of a species; typically softer, of generally lower frequency, often longer, and with a different pattern. See SONG and compare especially the "whisper song" described in that entry.

SUBSPECIES (sing. and pl.). A population of a species in which individuals show the same structurally definable variation from other populations of the same species. The breeding areas of subspecies or "races" of the same species are normally separated geographically and represent early stages in the process of speciation. No matter how distinctive in appearance, races of the same species are presumed to be able to interbreed freely if given the opportunity. Failure to do so would indicate that effective isolating mechanisms had evolved, thereby defining the forms in question as distinct species (however, see RING SPECIES). Often, species vary gradually over a wide geographical range (see CLINE); in such cases racial boundaries cannot be sharply defined and subspecies must be described on the basis of *averages* in size, coloration, song dialect, etc., or combinations of these characters. It should be clear from this example that the subspecies is an invention of taxonomists and not a natural biological entity. The term allows for description and discussion of variation within species.

By biological convention, characters meriting subspecific distinction must be present in 75 percent of a given population before it can be described as racially distinct.

In modern biological nomenclature, a subspecies is designated by a "trinomial," a name consisting of the species designation (genus plus specific name) modified by a third name which identifies the race. For example, *Catoptrophorus semipalmatus* designates the species known in English as the Willet; *Catoptrophorus semipalmatus semipalmatus* is the subspecies known as the Eastern Willet, which breeds along most of the Atlantic and Gulf coasts from Nova Scotia to southern Texas; and *C. s. inornatus* describes the paler, longer-legged Western Willet, which occupies a geographically isolated breeding range in the western interior of the continent. Some species are subject to much racial variation—11 North American subspecies of the Rock Ptarmigan are currently recognized—while other species, e.g., the Ring-billed Gull, do not vary enough to warrant the description of any subspecies, despite a wide distribution consisting of several discrete populations.

The number of North American subspecies currently recognized for each North American species is given in parentheses after the species names in Appendix I. For the names and distributions of these races, see the A.O.U. *Check-list of North American Birds*, 5th ed. (1957).

See also SPECIES; SPECIATION.

SUMMER RESIDENT. A species which breeds in a given area but spends the winter elsewhere. Obviously the use of the term in reference to a given species varies geographically, i.e., the Palm Warbler is a summer resident throughout much of Canada but not in the central U.S., where it occurs only as a migrant, or in the southeastern U.S., where it winters. All North American breeding birds are summer residents *somewhere* on the continent. Compare SUMMER VISITOR.

SUMMER VISITOR (or visitant). A species which regularly spends the warmer months of the year in a given area but breeds elsewhere. Wilson's Storm-Petrel, which breeds during the Southern Hemisphere summer (our winter) in subantarctic waters, is a summer visitor to the North Atlantic during the southern winter. Compare SUMMER RESIDENT.

SUNNING. Many species of birds, both passerine and non-passerine, are known to assume "peculiar" postures, spreading and fluffing their feathers in order to expose their plumage to the light and/or heat of the sun. Though the behavior is sometimes observed on cool days, a number of witnesses record that the assumption of a sunning posture seems to be triggered when a bird suddenly experiences a rise in heat (and light?) intensity.

Sunning behavior varies among species and apparently also according to the sun's intensity. Among songbirds, a typical posture involves squatting on the ground at a right angle or facing away from the sun with wings drooped or outspread, tail fanned, and body feathers (especially those of the head and tail) erected, i.e., fluffed (not unlike the anting jay in Fig. 16). In this position the bird's head, neck, mantle, rump, and the upper surfaces of wings and tail receive the full impact of the sun's rays. Another posture, assumed by some swallows, pigeons, and others, is to roll over on one side, raise the wing, and expose the undersurface to the sun. Many water birds simply stand with their backs to the sun, perhaps with their wings drooped or necks stretched. Especially when the heat is most intense, sunning birds frequently open their bills and pant. As in water bathing and dusting, birds often have favorite sunning spots to which they return regularly.

While sunning, birds often seem to go into a kind of trance, allowing people to approach much more closely than normal. The bizarre posture and behavior strongly suggest to the human observer that sunning birds are injured—or perhaps suffering from sunstroke!

The main theories which have been advanced to date to explain sunbathing in birds are: (1) that exposure to heat and light activates ECTOPARASITES such as bird lice and perhaps drives them from areas of the body which the bird has most trouble reaching and/or to areas where they can be captured most easily in the bill; (2) that the sun's ultraviolet rays release vitamin D from the preen oil, which in turn is ingested by the bird in the preening which typically follows a sunbath; (3) that the sun dries and fluffs the feathers by evaporating moisture and oils from the plumage (as may be true of DUSTING), thus maintaining good insulation; (4) that birds may be able to increase energy reserves by absorbing solar radiation directly through the skin (Storer et al., 1975); and (5) that it feels good, especially when molting causes skin irritations.

For related behavior, see BATHING; PREENING; DUSTING; ANTING; OIL GLAND.

SUPERCILIARY (line or stripe; supercilium). A linear, usually pale mark running immediately above the eye; referred to in the vernacular as the eye stripe or eye line. See Figs. 1 and 25.

SUPERFAMILY. A secondary taxonomic category between SUBORDER and FAMILY. In zoological nomenclature names of superfamilies end in

-oidea. For example, the superfamily Falconoidea falls under the suborder Falcones and encompasses the families Accipitridae and Falconidae. See TAXONOMY.

SUPERORDER. Secondary taxonomic category between SUBCLASS and ORDER. Wetmore (1960–TAXONOMY), followed here, recognizes four superorders of birds: the Odontognathae, which contains only the extinct order Hesperornithiformes (see HESPERORNIS); the Ichthyornithes, containing only the Ichthyonithiformes (see ICHTHYORNIS), also extinct; the Impennes, containing only the penguins (order Sphenisciformes); and the Neognathae, containing all other birds, recent and fossil. A previous arrangement recognized another superorder, the Paleognathae, which contained the primitive, keel-less RATITES and the tinamous, but these are now included in Neognathes. See TAXONOMY.

SUPERSPECIES. A taxonomic concept referring to groups of distinct species that are presumed to have evolved relatively recently from a common ancestor and that occupy distinct (often separate) ranges and/or ecological niches. For example, the so-called Black-throated Green Warbler Group—including the Black-throated Green, Townsend's, Golden-cheeked, Hermit, and Black-throated Gray Warblers—conforms to the definition of a superspecies. The term is not an "official" nomenclatural category as is the species or subspecies, but as a grouping of species, it applies below subgenus. See TAXONOMY.

SUPRASPECIFIC. Referring to any taxonomic category (taxon) higher than a species, e.g., genus, family, order, etc.

SURFBIRD. Standard English name for a single species of shorebird, *Aphriza virgata* (order Charadriiformes). The Surfbird is sometimes placed taxonomically with the smaller sandpipers in the subfamily Calidrinae (family Scolopacidae) or in the turnstone subfamily Arenariinae—which in turn may be placed with the sandpipers or the plovers (family Charadriidae).

Surfbirds are short-legged, gray shorebirds (speckled in summer, rather uniform in winter) with plover-like bills. They are almost exclusively birds of the rocks, both on their breeding grounds, where they nest in alpine fell-fields, and in winter, when they seldom stray from wave-washed coastal rocks. They are known to eat many insects on the breeding grounds and seemingly prefer mussels on the coast.

Palmer (1967–SHOREBIRD) notes their defensive habit of "sitting tight" on their nest until almost stepped on and then flying in the face of the intruder—a behavioral trait he supposes may have evolved due to frequent disturbance by mountain (white) sheep (*Ovis dalli*).

Surfbirds are known to breed only in Alaska but probably also do so in the adjacent mountains of the Yukon; they winter along the Pacific coast as far south as the Straits of Magellan.

SWAINSON, William, 1789–1855 (Swainson's Hawk: *Buteo swainsoni*; Swainson's Thrush: *Catharus ustulatus*; Swainson's Warbler: *Limnothlypis swainsonii*). A brilliant and prolific English writer-artist-naturalist who was dogged by misfortune for much of his life. His collecting trip to Brazil in 1816–17 was stymied by a revolution; he was seldom able to make ends meet despite his great effort and achievements; and he swam all his life against the increasingly prevailing current of Linnaean classification, preferring a long-forgotten alternative called the Quinary System (Gruson, 1972–BIOGRAPHY). Hoping to make a new start, he emigrated to New Zealand, only to lose his precious collections en route. Audubon named his warbler, Bonaparte his hawk.

SWALLOW. Standard English name for most of the 70–75 members of the family Hirundinidae (order Passeriformes), some of which are called MARTINS. Eight species of swallows and martins breed in North America, and 5 others have occurred as accidental stragglers (see Appendix II).

Swallows are small (3¾ inches) to medium-sized (to 9 inches) songbirds with short, flattened bills, wide gapes, long wings, and short legs. The three forward-pointing toes are partially fused at the base. Many species are brightly colored, often with glossy metallic green or blue backs.

Swallows are adapted for catching insects on the wing and are therefore among the most graceful and agile birds in the world. Unlike the swifts, with which they share their food preference, swallows are capable of perching horizontally in the normal songbird manner.

Many swallows (Cliff, Cave, Bank, and the martins in North America) nest colonially. Some (e.g., Barn, Cliff, and Cave) make "adobe" cups or vase-like structures from pellets of mud mixed with plant fibers (see NEST and Fig. 15) and affix them to cliff faces, cave walls, or buildings, while others are cavity nesters that use old woodpecker holes, dry pipes, bird boxes, or excavate burrows in earthen banks (Bank Swallow). Inside the "adobe" or cavity, there is a loose cup of plant material, lined with feathers, fine grasses, hair, and the like. The eggs number 3–8 (average 4–5) in most species. They are white and unmarked in all but the "adobe" species; the latter's eggs are sparsely to densely speckled and spotted with varying shades of brown and gray.

Most swallow species make pleasant, liquid chirping sounds or twitters. Rough-winged and Bank Swallows are at the drier, buzzier end of this range.

The swallows are among the most thoroughly cosmopolitan of bird families. They range from the Arctic throughout the tropics to the subantarctic islands and are absent only from the most barren tundra and desolate ocean islands. Several species undertake long transoceanic migrations, and the Alaskan populations of the Barn Swallow undertake perhaps the greatest such journey of any native passerine—7,000 miles one way to Argentine wintering grounds. Certain swallow species are among the first migrants to return to the Temperate Zone in the spring and therefore have long been considered heralds of that season. All but two North American swallow species breed continentwide; all are migratory and only the southernmost populations of a few species winter here.

The origin of "swallow" is lost in the tangle of Old World etymological roots. See also MARTIN.

SWAMP. A general term referring to any of a variety of habitats in which the ground is inundated; though swamps may have stretches of open water during the wetter seasons, it is never deep (though the mud below may be very deep) and emergent vegetation predominates. Wooded swamps (e.g., red maple, cypress, mangrove), marshes (e.g., cattail), and bogs may all be thought of as types of swampland. These variations provide habitat for many species of birds. Wooded swamps are particularly congenial to the Wood Duck, several species of herons, the Veery, and Prothonotary, Bachman's, and Swainson's Warblers, among other species. The Swamp Sparrow prefers marshes. See also MARSH.

SWAN. Standard English name for 5–8 members of the family Anatidae (order Anseriformes), including 2 which are native to North America (Whistling [Tundra] and Trumpeter), 1 which occurs as a migrant from Eurasia (Whooper), and 1 which has been successfully introduced from Europe (Mute). They are sometimes included with the geese in the subfamily Anserinae or the tribe Anserini or distinguished in a subfamily of their own (Cygninae).

Swans are among the largest living birds (see SIZE). All of our species are wholly white except for "soft parts" and are distinguished by bill characteristics and posture. Like most other members of their family, swans have a broad, flat bill with a terminal "nail" and sieve-like lamellae along the internal edges; the front three toes are webbed. The characteristic long neck of swans is an adaptation for feeding on bottom vegetation in the shallows of lakes, ponds, and estuaries. Swans are among the world's most graceful and splendid wild creatures and have always captured people's imaginations, e.g., the Leda myth (see IMAGINATION), Tchaikovsky's ballet *Swan Lake*, and Yeats's "The Wild Swans at Coole."

They have also long been popular game birds (see SWAN SONG), and the Trumpeter Swan was shot to the brink of extinction in the nineteenth century for its feathers (see CONSERVATION) and flesh. There is still a hunting season on the Whistling Swan.

For their nests swans construct large piles of vegetation on the bank or in the shallows of a lake, pond, or river (see Fig. 15). They occasionally use the ready-made piles of muskrat lodges, and Whistling Swans sometimes make floating nests. Females line their nests sparsely with down from their breasts and lay 2–12 (usually 5–7) white to yellowish, unmarked eggs (Mute Swan, pale gray, blue, or green).

Mute Swans generally live up to their name, though they can hiss impressively when disturbed. Whistling Swans make a melodious bugling, often heard in chorus from a flock in the air. Trumpeter Swans give a distinctive, deep, bisyllabic honking call. See also SWAN SONG.

The swans are birds of the Temperate Zone and are mostly distributed in the Holarctic region, though there is a single Australian species (the Black Swan, popular as an ornamental here) and two in southern South America.

The word "swan" comes to us unchanged from Old English.

SWAN SONG. Debate about the nature—or very existence—of a unique "song" uttered by some swan species with their last breath has raged at least since classical times. Plato did not doubt that swans sang in their last hour but argued that this was simply a final affirmation of their cheerful, musical disposition—a description that few present-day swan watchers would recognize. Other commentators have contended that the swan song is as mythical as the lustful anserine that ravished Leda.

There can be no doubt that swans are capable of a variety of vocalizations—most notably "bugling" or "trumpeting" notes, possibly facilitated by their unusually long, coiled tracheas, but also muted "conversational" sounds and (especially in the Whistling and the Eurasian Bewick's Swans) pleasing, musical tones; pairs of Whistling Swans are known to engage in prolonged "duets" with the two sexes taking different parts. Delacour (1954–WATERFOWL) opines that the swan song is simply (unpoetically) the expulsion of air from the trachea of a shot swan as it plummets to earth, but there are several authoritative accounts of an extended, melodious, but rarely heard call made by Whistling Swans, sometimes (but not always) during their death agony. The waterfowl expert A. H. Hochbaum (1955–BIRDWATCHING) records what he calls a "departure song"—a soft, beautiful series of notes uttered before takeoff—and this description agrees well with the account of the nineteenth-century naturalist Dr. D. G. Elliot, who recorded a similar "song" from a Whistling Swan he brought down out of the North Carolina sky.

In vernacular usage, the swan song is a metaphor for a last earthly act, usually a creative one, e.g., a poet's last sonnet or an actor's last role. Even a politician's last speech may be so described by the broad-minded.

SWIFT. Standard English name for most of the approximately 70 members of the family Apodidae (order Apodiformes), 4 of which breed in

North America. Five other species have been recorded as vagrants (see Appendix II).

Some swifts measure as little as 3½ inches in length, but North Americans may be surprised to learn that others reach 9½ inches (larger than a robin). Swifts have very small bills and wide gapes, like the nightjars, which have similar feeding habits (see below). Their wings are very long and pointed, most of the length extending from the "wrist" (bend of the wing), giving the swifts a characteristic fluttering flight. The spine-tailed swifts (subfamily Chaeturinae), to which our two commonest species belong, have very short tails, the rachises of which extend beyond the vanes at the tips. This series of rigid spines that forms the end of the tail acts as a prop when the birds perch on vertical surfaces (see Fig. 21). Even the longer-tailed species have a generally fusiform body shape and suggest "flying cigars."

The feet of swifts are very small (one of the few obvious characters they share with their order mates, the hummingbirds) and strongly modified for clinging—the only kind of perching that swifts do. All four toes are directed forward (pamprodactyl) and bear long, strong, hooked claws. Most swifts (all in North America) are somberly plumaged in white, black, grays, and browns.

Swifts are the most aerial of birds, capable of fast (see below), agile, and high-altitude flight. They feed exclusively on airborne invertebrates (mainly insects and "ballooning" spiders), which are carried in surprising numbers thousands of feet into the air. Many of the routine activities of everyday life that most birds perform on the ground—e.g., bathing, drinking, gathering nesting material, even sleeping and copulation—swifts can accomplish in flight.

Swifts often feed in flocks and nest colonially, placing cup or half-cup nests on cliff faces, inside hollow trees, or in chimneys. Many species glue their nest materials together with their sticky saliva (see BIRD'S NEST SOUP) and affix the structure to vertical surfaces by the same method.

Black Swifts lay but a single egg, other North American species 3–7 (usually 4–5). All are white to pale yellowish and unmarked.

Because of their dependence on live, airborne prey, swifts are vulnerable to cold or wet spells during which insects, etc., are not flying. Both adults and nestlings of at least some species respond to such emergencies by assuming a temporary state of dormancy (see TORPIDITY) in which bodily functions are "shut down" almost completely, thus requiring little sustenance.

The songs and calls of swifts are typically high-pitched, often metallic or bell-like twitters, chatters, or shrill screeches with occasional single sharp chips. Many swifts engage in communal flight displays in which the flock breaks into a choral tintinnabulation that can be quite earsplitting at close range or when reverberating from the walls of a narrow gorge.

Swifts are distributed worldwide (absent from the coldest northern and southern extremes and some oceanic islands). In North America, swifts are absent from tundra, boreal forest, and central plains (except in migration). Except for the White-throated Swift, which is a permanent resident in parts of the Southwest, all of our species are long-distance migrants.

The name "swift" is apt. The greatest natural flight speed on record anywhere is that of the White-throated Needle-tailed Swift (*Hirundapus caudacutus*) (see Appendix II), which *may* reach 219.5 m.p.h. (however, see SPEED) in straight flapping flight. The North American White-throated Swift may attain comparable speeds.

SWIMMING/DIVING. Over 20 percent (about 150 species) of the regular North American avifauna habitually swim and/or dive. However, not all swimming birds dive, nor do all divers swim. And of course there are numerous water-bird species (e.g., plovers, herons) which seldom do either (see below, however).

Evolution has wrought an impressive number of avian variations and combinations with these two forms of behavior. The loons, grebes, some tubenoses, cormorants, anhingas, coots, alcids, and about 60 percent of native duck species are highly adept at both swimming and diving from the surface. The albatrosses, shearwaters, storm-petrels, White Pelican, gulls, swans, geese, dabbling (surface-feeding) ducks, and phalaropes swim as a way of life, but in most cases dive only infrequently and near the surface, if at all. Most tubenoses and gulls will force themselves a few feet beneath the surface to attack a school of fish, and the non-diving anatids "tip up" in a kind of halfhearted dive to pluck bottom vegetation, but otherwise dive only in a panic to escape a Peregrine or other predator.

Tropicbirds, Manx Shearwater (occasionally), boobies and gannets, Brown Pelican, most terns, Osprey, and all our native kingfishers plunge from the air into the water after fish. This technique varies from the gannets—which may begin their plunge from over 100 feet in the air and pursue fish to moderate depths once submerged—to the kingfishers—which often hover only a relatively few feet above the water and barely penetrate the surface on their splash-downs. Among this group of divers, Brown Pelicans swim habitually, the Osprey and kingfishers not at all, and the others sit on the water relatively infrequently or for short periods only.

Though adapted most conspicuously for walking and wading, the flamingos, rails, and most shorebirds swim well. Some have partially webbed toes, and a few species (e.g., yellowlegs, Stilt Sandpiper) swim routinely while feeding. Avocets and stilts not only swim well but also dive expertly. Even herons will "swim" on occasion: Great Blue Herons have been seen to alight on the open sea (briefly), presumably to rest.

The only truly aquatic songbirds are the dippers, which, however, behave uniquely in the water. Their feet are not webbed and they more "drift" or "ride" than "paddle" when traveling on a surface current. Though they swim or "fly" using their wings underwater, their actual feeding behavior largely involves *walking* on the bottom (see DIPPER).

The swimming ability of other passerine birds is decidedly limited. They have a certain natural buoyancy due to the air trapped in their plumage and body cavity (see RESPIRATORY SYSTEM) and are usually capable of flapping a short distance to shore if accidentally dunked. But their feathers rapidly become waterlogged and drag them down, and many thousands of exhausted migrants perish by drowning in the ocean in spring and especially in fall (see MIGRATION, *Hazards*).

PHYSICAL ADAPTATIONS

• A bird's source of locomotion when swimming at the surface is its legs and feet and these are strongly modified in all true swimming/diving birds. The most frequent swimming modification is, of course, webbing between the toes, but phalaropes and coots have scalloped lobes along the margins of each toe, and in the grebes, each toe is a flat, mobile paddle which can be "feathered" like oars when in use (see LEG/FOOT and Fig. 12).

The feet of water birds which *don't* swim are often clues to behavior. Though frigatebirds belong to the same order as the pelicans and boobies (Pelecaniformes), which have webbing between all four toes, the former have relatively tiny, only partially webbed feet, reflecting the fact that they are essentially aerial birds which don't swim and which perch awkwardly.

• When progressing normally at the surface, swimming birds paddle with alternating strokes, one foot pushing the water behind as the other returns forward. However, birds which use foot power while diving (see below) push with both feet at once. Most swimming birds also have laterally flattened legs to allow minimum drag when paddling. The "engines" which permit this kind of paddling locomotion are appropriately enlarged thigh muscles.

• Wings modified for diving are not common among birds, since most adaptations of these limbs are related to flight. The most striking exception to this rule is the penguins, whose forelimbs have become flippers—useless for flying in air, but perfectly adapted for "flying" underwater. Of all birds, penguins are by far the most at home in the water. They are as agile as any marine mammal (or more so) and can swim underwater faster than some birds can fly (more than 22 m.p.h.—Gentoo Penguins). Among North American birds only the alcids have wings which seem strongly adapted for use underwater. Though fully feathered and capable of flight, these appendages are notably narrow and flipper-like when extended.

• Birds which both swim and dive habitually should ideally be both buoyant and have a high specific gravity. This seemingly contradictory condition is achieved in most swimmers/divers by a combination of ana-

tomical specialization and behavior. Birds' body cavities are lined with a
system of air sacs which fill the spaces between the other organs and can be
inflated and deflated, as the lungs are, by inhaling and exhaling (see RESPI-
RATORY SYSTEM). These air sacs even penetrate many bones (see SKELE-
TON, *Pneumatization*), so that even a bird's skeleton is partially air-filled.
The buoyancy thus achieved is, of course, an advantage in flight and, when
combined with the air-trapping capacity of the plumage, also makes birds
natural floaters. In addition, most swimming/diving birds have particularly large oil glands, from which they continually coat their feathers,
making them waterproof—sealing in the trapped air and preventing them
from becoming waterlogged while active in their preferred habitat. We
take it for granted that water "naturally" rolls off a duck's back and the
same can be said of loons, grebes, gulls, and most other water-inhabiting
species. Two peculiar exceptions—one of nature's apparent oversights—
are the cormorants and anhingas, neither of which have adequate waterproofing in spite of the fact that they feed mostly or wholly submerged.
This explains the characteristic "spread-eagle" posture of members of
these two families, which rely largely on the sun to keep their feathers dry.

When it comes to diving, buoyancy becomes a liability, working
against a bird's efforts to penetrate water, which becomes ever denser with
increasing depth. Species which plunge into the water from the air depend
partly on gravity to counteract their natural "floatability," and those which
dive from the surface and pursue prey once submerged push themselves
under, using their legs and feet. More subtle is the ability of many water
birds to compress their plumage, squeezing the trapped air out and raising
their specific gravity. It is this trick which permits the grebes to sink like a
submarine, apparently without exerting any effort. In preparing for a dive,
birds also expel air from their air sacs, further reducing buoyancy. Loons
and other birds which dive often and deep also tend to have heavier—i.e.,
less pneumatized—bones.

• Anyone who has watched a gannet plummet headfirst into the sea
from high in the air is likely to wonder how the impact can be sustained
time after time without resulting in a broken neck or at least a bad head-
ache. In its practical way, evolution has given gannets unusually powerful
neck muscles, a thickened and strongly supported skull, and air sacs lying
under the skin of the head which act as a kind of padded crash helmet.

• If diving birds expel air from their respiratory systems before submerging, where is their oxygen supply contained? Answer: In the red pigment of red blood corpuscles (oxyhemoglobin), which are more numerous
in divers than in other types of birds. In a dive, the flow of oxygenated
blood can be regulated—so that the brain and the rest of the nervous system continue to receive oxygen from the blood, which is being supplied
temporarily at a much slower rate to muscular tissue.

• The eyes of diving birds are modified to see prey accurately underwater (see VISION).

• The nostril openings of pelicans, cormorants, and gannets and boobies are either closed at birth or become so by adulthood and breathing is done through openings at the corners of the gape (see NOSTRILS); this is probably an adaptation to underwater habits.

DIVING "STYLES." The beginning of a standard "surface dive"—i.e., one that starts from a sitting position on the water—is a strong push forward—sometimes almost a leap upward—followed by a downward bowing of the neck and back, so that the bird breaks the surface in an arc, striking it almost vertically. Loons, grebes, and anhingas sometimes perform a sinking dive by "squeezing" the air from their body feathers and emptying their air sacs (see above). The "plungers" use gravity instead of muscle power to penetrate the water surface, but hit the water and "recover" in a variety of ways. The terns and kingfishers, which take fish from near the surface, make shallow splash-downs and return to the air with a shake (and perhaps a fish) almost at once. Tropicbirds as well as the terns and kingfishers often hover before plunging, and kingfishers frequently dive from fixed perches. Ospreys hit first with their feet, extended at the last moment by their long legs to grasp the unsuspecting fish. Their weight and the momentum of the dive may submerge them completely, but only momentarily, after which they too regain the air. Brown Pelicans and the gannets and boobies enter the water bill-first with neck extended and often from considerable heights (gannets from more than 100 feet at times).

The pelicans fold their wings and push them far back just before entry; their great mass prevents them from submerging very deeply and they almost immediately bounce back to the surface with a "pouch" full of fish (see BILL). The gannets and boobies fold their wings tightly as they begin their dives and then open them slightly just before impact. Palmer (1962–BOOBY) notes that Northern Gannets rotate slightly during their descent and also that the greater their starting altitude, the steeper is their angle of entry. Members of this family (Sulidae) also sometimes dive from the surface. Though they hit the water with great force, pursue fish underwater, and may stay submerged for up to 40 seconds, most of their dives (whether from the surface or from "on high") are short and relatively shallow (to 6 feet or less).

A variety of techniques are also used by birds in underwater swimming. Loons and grebes have legs set at the extreme tail end of their bodies and propel themselves with maximum efficiency torpedo-like through the water, wings tightly folded and neck extended. By contrast, the alcids use their feet little, if at all, when submerged but rather use their wings as penguins do to "fly" at relatively high speed underwater.

The gannets and boobies, cormorants and anhingas, and diving ducks use *mainly* their feet for propulsion underwater but also use their wings to varying degrees and in various ways (there is little information on the sulids). The ducks may use their wings to steer with to some extent. The

White-winged Scoter is known to dive with wing tips crossed over its tail, its "wrist" joints protruding, and its long alulas extended.

DEPTH AND DURATION OF DIVES. The farther down a bird dives, the harder and slower the going, and therefore there is some correlation between the depth of a dive and its duration. However, long dives are not necessarily deep dives: one Western Grebe submerged for 63 seconds in 5½ feet of water (Palmer, 1962–GREBE).

The majority of diving birds are not deep or long divers; most species rarely exceed 10 feet or stay under more than 10–20 seconds. Even the champion deep divers, such as the loons, grebes, sea ducks, and alcids, rarely approach their full diving potential. The record-holding Common Loon (see below) *usually* dives to a depth not exceeding 35 feet and takes less than a minute (sometimes much less) to resurface. Also, birds under duress (e.g., chased or shot) will typically stay submerged much longer than normal.

World's Record Dive. It has been well documented that the Emperor Penguin can reach at least 265 meters (869 feet) below the surface and stay under for at least 18 minutes (Kooyman et al., 1971).

North American Record Dives. The Common Loon and Oldsquaw (duck) are tied for the deepest-diver record, both having been trapped in fishing nets at depths of 180–200 feet and perhaps slightly deeper. Though their average dives are much shorter (see above), these birds are apparently little taxed by dives lasting 3 minutes and the loon has survived forcible submersion for 15 minutes. Except for the penguin record noted above, these are also world records.

SYMBIOSIS (sim-bih-YO-sis). In the broadest sense, any association between two different organisms, including parasitism, commensalism, etc. In the narrower usage, a symbiotic relationship is one in which both partners derive benefit. Anis picking ticks from the backs of cows is an avian example of the latter. For examples of the broader usage relating to birds, see COMMENSALISM; BROOD PARASITISM; ECTOPARASITE; PIRACY.

SYMBOLIC BIRDS. See IMAGINATION.

SYMPATRIC (sim-PAT-rik). Referring to closely related species or subspecies whose geographical ranges overlap. Sympatry is often cited in questions of speciation. In Texas and Louisiana where the Great-tailed and Boat-tailed Grackles are sympatric, they do not normally interbreed (see Selander, *Condor* [1961], 63:29–86). Converse of ALLOPATRIC. See SPECIATION.

SYNANTHROPIC (SIN-an-THRO-pik). Showing a preference for habitat altered by man, e.g., yards or farmland. The Killdeer, Mourning Dove, and

American Robin, among many other species, exemplify synanthropic behavior in North America. Compare EUSYANTHROPIC; EXANTHROPIC.

SYNONYMS. In a taxonomic context, two or more names for the same species or other taxon. Synonyms are created, for example, when a species is mistakenly redescribed by an author under the impression that he is dealing with a new species; in such cases, the law of priority holds that the first name is the valid one and the new synonym is discarded. Synonyms are also created by taxonomic revision. The original Latin name given to the White-rumped Sandpiper was *Tringa fuscicollis*, thus placing it in a genus with nearly all of the other sandpipers, including, for example, the yellowlegs. More recently the smaller sandpipers were "split" into several different genera, e.g., *Erolia*, *Ereuntes*, and *Calidris*, at which time the White-rumped became *Erolia fuscicollis*. In 1976, the A.O.U. Committee on Taxonomy and Nomenclature ruled that most of the small sandpipers (including the three genera noted above) should be "lumped" into a single one. As the earliest name used among these birds, *Calidris* was the generic name of choice and the White-rumped Sandpiper became, and remains today, *Calidris fuscicollis*. All of these Latin name variations are "synonyms."

SYNTYPE (SIN-type). When the author of a species designates a type series as the criterion for his original description but does not designate a particular type specimen, all of the specimens in the series are called "syntypes." See NOMENCLATURE, *Types*.

SYRINX (SEER-inks) (pl.: syringes [suh-RIN-jeez]). The organ of voice production unique to birds; a bird's "voice box." It is located either (1) near the lower end of the windpipe (trachea); (2) over the junction of the trachea and the fork of the bronchi (most birds); or (3) as a paired organ, one syrinx on each of the two bronchi. In general, species with the most highly evolved syringes produce the most complex sounds. Birds also have a larynx, the voice box of humans (and other mammals). It is located above the syrinx but is little developed and is not involved (or only marginally so) in voice production. The syrinx is sometimes referred to as the lower of a bird's two larynges. For more detail on the structure and function of the syrinx, see SONG.

SYSTEMATICS. The study, description, and orderly arrangement of life forms. Frequently used interchangeably with "taxonomy," though in the strictest sense the latter refers only to classification. See TAXONOMY.

T

TAIGA (tye-GAH or TYE-guh). Subarctic coniferous forest such as is typical of most of Siberia and most of Canada south of the tundra. In North America it consists largely of black and white spruce (*Picea mariana* and *P. glauca*), balsam fir (*Abies balsamea*), tamarack (*Larix laricina*), and jack pine (*Pinus banksiana*) and is typically interspersed with lakes, bogs (muskeg), and bare outcroppings of rock. It is essentially synonymous with "boreal forest" and spans the Canadian and Hudsonian life zones. For characteristic birds, see BOREAL.

TAIL. Like many of man's primate ancestors, the earliest birds, such as *Archaeopteryx*, had long, bony tails. This reptilian appendage has long since ceased to be part of avian anatomy, however, and when we speak of the tail of a modern bird, we usually mean a more or less elongated group of feathers extending rearward from the end of its body. Birds which lack these feathers by accident or have very short ones by nature are likely to be labeled "tailless." This is not quite accurate, however, for the tail feathers are embedded in skin covering muscles which govern tail movements. The muscles in turn are anchored to the plowshare bone (pygostyle) at the end of the backbone and the series (usually 6) of unfused vertebrae which precede it. Speaking precisely then, a bird's tail is all of these—bones, muscle, skin, and feathers—beginning at an imaginary circle drawn from the end of the rump down through the vent and back up to the rump on the other side and ending at the tips of the longest tail feathers.

 Arrangement of Tail Feathers. The main "flight" feathers of the tail are known collectively as the *rectrices*. In most birds these take the form of a fan made up of pairs of closely overlapping feathers: the outer pair is overlapped by the pair immediately inside and so on until the innermost pairs meet at the center of the tail, usually overlapping each other completely, giving the illusion of a single central feather. The number of rectrices varies among different species from 8 (e.g., anis) up to 32 (a species of snipe) but most birds have a total of 12. The number is not necessarily consistent within families or even within genera.

 Overlapping the bases of the rectrices from above are the greater upper tail coverts (the number varies: one covert per rectrix, or less, or

FIG. 21. *Specialized tails* are adapted to suit particular forms of bird behavior. The greatly elongated rectrices of the Scissor-tailed Flycatcher aid the quick stops and turns crucial to the life style of an insectivorous "aerobat." The broad fan of the Red-tailed Hawk is likewise essential as a "rudder" but also provides an extra "lifting" surface for this soaring species (see FLIGHT). By contrast, the tail of the Chimney Swift is of scant use in flight but serves as an indispensable prop or brace in the swifts' characteristic vertical clinging posture—the only form of perching these birds do.

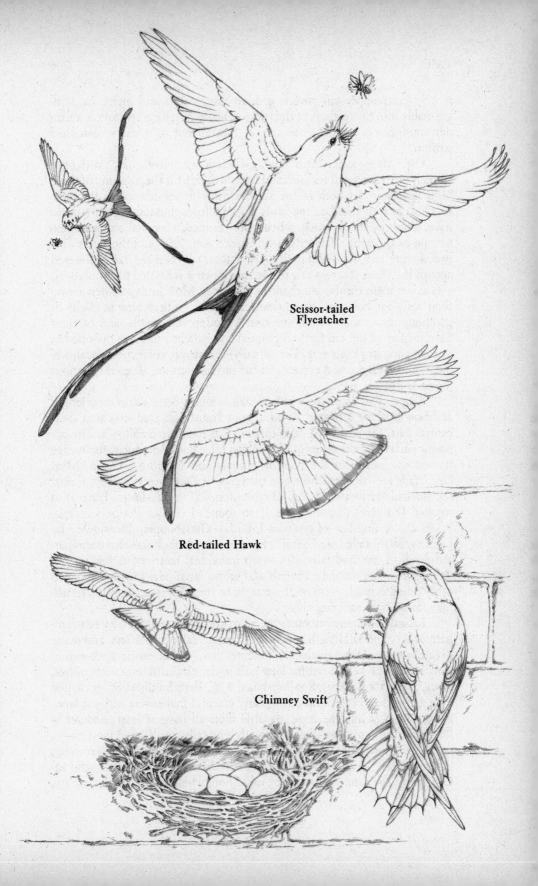

Scissor-tailed
Flycatcher

Red-tailed Hawk

Chimney Swift

more); lesser upper tail coverts overlap the greaters and merge indistinguishably into the feathers of the rump. The undertail coverts follow a similar arrangement on the underside of the tail but in a less well-defined pattern.

Use. Many water birds (e.g., grebes, loons, most auks, rails) have scarcely any visible tail feathers and have little use for them. Many of these birds use their feet both in the air and while diving to replace the tail's function as a rudder. Soaring birds (e.g., vultures, buteos, eagles) tend to have very broad tails which, when fully "fanned," become almost an extension of the wing. This extra surface increases "lift" and the "slots" between wing and tail aid stability (see FLIGHT). When the tail is lowered against the wind, it serves as a brake. And when it is twisted horizontally, it acts as the main turning mechanism or rudder. Most birds also depend on their tails for balance—the awkwardness of a tailless bird in flight or perching on a phone wire is obvious. Woodpeckers, swifts, and creepers have the tips of the tail feathers pointed and stiffened to brace their bodies as they cling or climb vertically. Finally, the shape, color, pattern, movement, and even musical capacity of the tail feathers are all used in various forms of display.

Shape. The shape the rectrices take as a unit depends on their length and how they are arranged. If a long outermost pair graduates to a short central pair, the result is a deep fork such as the Barn Swallow's. The opposite pattern (short outer graduating to long inner) produces the wedge (cuneiform) shape of the tails of gannets and Mourning Doves. Most birds' tails are between these two extremes of shape, varying from forked (Scissor-tailed Flycatcher, Fig. 21) to notched (Purple Martin, Plate 5) to squared (Elegant Trogon, Plate 1) to rounded (Lesser Prairie Chicken, Plate 2). A number of grassland birds—Grasshopper, Henslow's, Le Conte's, Sharp-tailed, and Seaside Sparrows and Bobolinks—have comparatively short, pointed tails with sharp individual rectrices. A few species (tropicbirds, jaegers, male Pintails and Oldsquaws) have greatly elongated or modified central rectrices; these seem to function in recognition or display rather than as flying aids.

Length. In many instances there is a strong correlation between aerobatic agility and tail length. Accipiters, jaegers, falcons, harriers, and many flycatchers would be unable to execute their characteristic split-second stops and turns were it not for long tails under powerful muscular control. Long, *forked* tails (terns, Swallow-tailed Kite, Barn Swallow, Scissor-tailed Flycatcher) seem to permit particularly graceful maneuvers without sacrificing speed. While the most versatile fliers all have at least moderately long tails, the converse—that birds with long tails are all aerial masters—is not true. Chachalacas, cuckoos, and thrashers, all of which have long, "loose-jointed" tails, are birds of trees and dense shrubbery and spend little time on the wing except during migration, when endurance, not agility, is required. Magpies, wagtails, and grackles feed mostly on the ground and make little use of their long tails in flight maneuvers.

The evolution of the Anhinga's long tail is interesting to contemplate, since swimming, diving, and soaring birds tend to have comparatively (or *very*) short tails. The species does cock and spread the tail during courtship rituals; in addition, perhaps it counterbalances the species' extraordinarily long neck.

Position and Gesture. Most birds at rest hold their tails in roughly the same plane as their backs—which may be parallel or perpendicular to the ground depending on the bird's posture. However, some ducks, Razorbill, rails, dippers, and wrens "cock" their tails more vertically even in repose. The tails of woodpeckers and treecreepers, because of their function as props, are normally cocked downward (i.e., inward against the tree trunk), and the Bushtit, tits, and Verdin flex their tails toward the belly for equilibrium when they hang from branches.

Almost constant tail movements are common among many passerines, e.g., flycatchers, thrushes, thrashers, and warblers, and the exact nature of the gesture (whether flicked up or down and in what sequence) is a clue to field identification of some of the difficult *Empidonax* flycatchers. Most tail wagging is vertical, but anis, mimic thrushes, and a few other species have extremely mobile tails, which they habitually move through nearly all points of the compass.

The Spotted Sandpiper, wagtails and pipits, Kirtland's and Palm Warblers, Ovenbird, and the waterthrushes "pump" their tails and, to varying degrees, the whole of their hindquarters, almost without interruption. This motion is distinct from the more abrupt bobbing or "teetering" of dippers and many shorebirds (especially *Tringa* spp.), but no clear-cut explanation of its function has yet emerged. It has often been noted that many bobbing or wagging species frequent watery habitats.

Tail cocking is a common gesture of the courtship displays of many species and its effect is heightened in some cases by special tail features (e.g., the elongated central rectrices of male Oldsquaws and Pintails) or by beautifully patterned and colored tails, which are fanned to show them off (e.g., Wild Turkey, Ruffed and Sage Grouse, Killdeer). Tail fanning is not a common habit among North American songbirds, the conspicuous exceptions being the American and Painted Redstarts, both of which keep their boldly patterned tails (and wings) spread while catching insects in the air, scolding potential predators, courting, or simply foraging.

TALKING BIRDS. See SONG, *Vocal Mimicry*.

TALON. In the broadest sense, the claw of any animal. Usually, however, talons refer to the relatively long, sharp claws of birds of prey. See LEG/FOOT and Fig. 12.

TAMENESS. Like other "wild" animals, birds are generally wary of close contact with human beings, yet the degree to which some species or individual birds will tolerate our company is by no means uniform, and cases of extraordinary tameness are common in the literature. In many cases it is clear that birds sometimes relinquish much of their wariness not from any desire for intimate contact with people themselves, but rather because human society makes food and shelter available either inadvertently (cleaning fish) or by design (birdhouses). Yet there are numerous other instances of both fear and tameness in birds which cannot be explained as learned behavior and which therefore seem to have some genetic basis. So many phenomena have been cited under the heading of "tameness," and so little effort made so far to relate one to another, that it seems best simply to list some of the more conspicuous facts in the matter.

• Birds which are wary of humans *per se* often overcome their seemingly innate fear when compensation in the form of food or nesting sites is available. There are innumerable examples: gulls coming on board fishing boats; gulls, crows, and other birds following on the heels of a plowman; Barn Swallows, phoebes, robins, wrens, and others nesting over a much-used doorway or inside someone's porch; Gray Jays raiding campers' rations; and of course the enthusiastic response of many species to being fed store-bought seeds and other "bird food."

• This self-interested tameness can be heightened to the point of intimacy by training birds to take food from the hand, mouth, etc. (see Martin, 1963–BIRD FEEDING, for techniques).

• Certain families and species of birds seem to be "naturally" tamer than others and need no training by or experience with humans in the matter. Many seabirds, grouse, owls, shorebirds, corvids, tits, kinglets, waxwings, and "winter finches" seem not to recognize a human being as a threat and are thought variously to be "friendly," "bold," or "stupid" by the objects of their trust.

• Many of the species and individuals in the preceding groups breed in remote areas of the world where their contact with humans can be presumed to be limited. The birds (and other animals) of the Galápagos and other remote oceanic islands are notably fearless. The species of grouse, owls, waxwings, and finches which have the greatest reputation for tameness breed largely in remote boreal forests, many shorebirds in a vast wilderness of uninhabited tundra.

• There are numerous cases of apparently inexplicable geographical variation in tameness within a single species or among like ones. American birdwatchers are always struck by the reclusiveness of many woodland birds (e.g., woodpeckers) in the British Isles as compared with the U.S.— where persecution of songbirds has if anything been far greater than Britain's in recent time—or with other parts of Europe, where ancient traditions of trapping songbirds for food are still intact.

• There is much variation in wariness among individuals of a species:

not all Pine Grosbeaks may be closely approached; American Robins breeding in forested areas are likely to be shyer than their suburban counterparts.

• It has been demonstrated that organisms tend to have an innate negative response to sizes, shapes, and movements which correspond to those of their natural predators. Some species may be genetically "programmed" to respond in this way to humans, whereas others may have to learn this fear. In this connection it is interesting to note that birds which are very wary of a man on foot are often not nearly so wary when approached in a car or on horseback.

• To the extent that this can be fairly judged, some individual birds seem to "enjoy" human company over and above the practical benefits (food) they derive therefrom. There are numerous records of birds in captivity being petted and ultimately seeking out their captor and "begging" to be stroked. This may be referable to some birds' urge to preen other birds and be preened (see ALLOPREENING).

• The "tameness" of birds which stay on their nests and allow themselves to be touched or which attack a human being who trespasses on breeding territory is probably best interpreted as defensive behavior, which represents a distinctly different response to the human presence than the other reactions discussed here.

• The "tameness" of birds which become imprinted by a human at hatching (see INTELLIGENCE) should probably also be considered as a separate phenomenon, due to its abnormality.

TAMIAMI TRAIL (Florida). The highway (U.S. 41) which crosses southern Florida from the Gulf at Naples to Miami. En route, it traverses vast marshlands crisscrossed by drainage canals in which thousands of herons, egrets, storks, and ibises can be seen with great ease along with other Florida specialties, such as Anhinga, Limpkin, Swallow-tailed and Everglade Kites (especially in winter), and Short-tailed Hawk (uncommon, winter).

TANAGER (TAN-uh-jur). Standard English name for most of the approximately 230 members of the family Thraupidae (order Passeriformes); about 30 smaller tropical tanager species are called chlorophonias or euphonias. Many authorities now consider the tanagers a subfamily (Thraupinae) of the family Emberizidae, placing them among certain of the finches (see FINCH). Four species of tanagers are native to North America, one other has been introduced, and a third has been recorded with some frequency as a vagrant.

Though a few tanagers are as small as 3 inches and others as long as a foot, most species, including all North American species, measure 6 to 8 inches. They are well-proportioned songbirds with long, conical bills, usually with a slight hook and a "tooth" (i.e., a single serration) along the cutting edge of the upper mandible. Their legs are relatively short. Some drab tanagers exist, and in many species (including native North American ones) females and juvenal and basic (winter) plumage males are less than spectacular. But overall this mainly tropical family can be said to contain a better than average share of the surpassing splendor of birddom. Our native tanagers display only the red/yellow end of the spectrum; still, for sheer "dazzle" few birds can compete with a male Scarlet Tanager in nuptial plumage.

Tanagers are mainly arboreal birds which feed on a wide variety of insects, other invertebrates (spiders, snails), and fruit, especially berries. Only a few tropical tanagers forage in flocks of mixed species.

Some tanagers have extended, warbling songs, others raspy, squeaky ones; our native species all have songs popularly described as "robin-like," but with more of a "burr," i.e., hoarser.

The nests of North American tanagers are typically fairly shallow cups of twigs, stems, coarser grasses, sometimes moss, lined with finer grasses, plant fibers, and/or hair. The 3–5 (usually 4) eggs are pale blue to greenish and finely to fairly coarsely marked with brown and/or reddish and/or lavender.

The tanager family is restricted to the New World and achieves exuberant diversity in the Neotropics, especially in South America. In North America, the native tanager species are largely segregated in northeastern (to midwestern) deciduous forest (Scarlet); southern deciduous and mixed forest, continentwide (Summer); western conifers and aspen (Western); and southwestern montane pine-oak (Hepatic). All but the Hepatic winter exclusively in the Neotropics, except for laggard Western Tanagers which try to survive at temperate zone feeders.

Like many tropical bird names, "tanager" comes to us via Portuguese (or Spanish) from Tupi, a common language of the natives of the Amazon Basin. It may well have referred originally to any small, brightly colored bird.

TARGET SPECIES. An avian specialty of a given locality at which bird listers take particularly careful aim. It is both natural and intelligent, of course, to study and hope to see birds endemic to a limited region to be visited. However, the term has an unfortunate acquisitive ring, as when some birders speak of "getting" some rarity; it seems to imply that the target species exists chiefly to fill a space on a list.

TARSOMETATARSUS (pl.: tarsometatarsi). The bone of a bird's leg between the ankle and the toes; a fusion of tarsal and metatarsal bones. See SKELETON and Fig. 19.

TARSUS (pl.: tarsi). The part of a bird's leg between the ankle and the toes. See LEG/FOOT; SKELETON; and Fig. 25.

TASTE. From a human perspective, taste is a sophisticated sensation blending the four basic "flavors"—salty, sour, bitter, sweet—in various strengths combined with a much broader range of perceptions received through our sense of smell. The main organs of taste in all vertebrate animals are collections of cells—the taste buds—that send and receive signals to and from the brain via aggregations of nerve fibers. Human taste buds are located mainly on the tongue—where they are readily visible to the naked eye—and in the wall of the pharynx (upper throat).

The taste sense in birds is much simpler structurally, with an average of only 30–70 inconspicuous taste buds (humans have about 9,000) located mainly in the throat and the softer areas of the palate, and usually only a few in the relatively soft back of the TONGUE; taste buds have also been detected in the bill edges of some species. Among the exceptional aspects of the large fleshy tongues of parrots is the presence of some 400 taste buds.

The physiology of taste is not completely understood in humans and little studied in birds. It is known that individual human nerve fibers transmitting taste sensations respond differently to salt, bitter, sour, and sweet—each sensing only one or two (and none responding directly to sweet stimuli)—and it has also been shown that there is a range of taste acuity and values among people. This information doubtless plays a role in taste tests on birds in which some are found to have little or no response to bitter or sweet, while sour seems to be readily detected in small amounts, and food or water to which salt has been added may be preferred to the unaltered substance. Since most birds seem to have a poorly developed sense of SMELL and since the avian mouth and upper throat hold food only briefly during normal feeding in most birds (in marked contrast to humans; see DIGESTIVE SYSTEM), it is reasonable to assume that taste holds little or none of the subtle gratifications for birds that it does for us. However, it may play a significant role in discriminating appropriate from inappropriate foods. It has been suggested that birds feeding at winter roosts of monarch butterflies in the central Mexican highlands may learn to detect the presence or absence of toxic cardiac glycocides by making quick "taste tests" on the insects' wings. This kind of discrimination is apparently rather limited, however, and no one has yet found a harmless substance that, for example, will make grain taste bad to flocks of blackbirds.

For "how birds taste" in another sense, see EDIBILITY. See also SMELL; TONGUE; FOOD/FEEDING.

TATTLER. Standard English name for the 2 species of sandpipers in the genus *Heteroscelus* (family Scolopacidae; order Charadriiformes), 1 of which, the Wandering Tattler, breeds in Alaska and winters along the coast of southern California (as well as widely over the Pacific). The other species, the Grey-tailed or Polynesian Tattler, occurs as a migrant in the Aleutians (Alaska).

Tattlers have gray upperparts with heavily barred underparts in alternate (breeding) plumage. They frequent swift rocky streams on their breeding grounds and wave-washed rocks in their coastal winter quarters. Like other stream-haunting birds, tattlers habitually and constantly "pump" their tails.

The name refers to their clear, loud call notes.

For family characteristics, see SANDPIPER.

TAUTONYM (TAW-tuh-nim). A Latin binomial in which the generic and specific names are the same. *Nycticorax nycticorax* (Black-crowned Night Heron) is an example of tautonymy.

TAVERNER (TAV-er-ner), Percy A., 1875–1947. Perhaps Canada's best-known ornithological figure, Taverner was for most of his life ornithologist-zoologist-curator of the National Museum of Canada. His chief interests and achievements were not in taxonomy. Rather, he excelled as a "popularizer" of nature (especially birds), as a "museum builder," and as an instigator of scientific and conservation efforts. He published a number of comprehensive works on the avifauna of Canada— e.g., *Birds of Canada* (Toronto, 1947)—which were unique in North America for their time in being profusely illustrated in color.

Taverner was noted for his sense of humor and was an enthusiastic contributor to the facetious edition of *The Auk*, known as *The Auklet*.

TAXIDERMY. The craft or skill of skinning and then mounting birds and other animals in lifelike poses. Stuffed exhibits of virtually any species of bird were once popular either as parlor decorations or sport trophies. Mail-order courses in taxidermy, showing how to mount clocks in the bellies of owls as well as more practical techniques, were once highly popular with adolescent boys. It is now illegal to make or own stuffed specimens of protected birds without a federal permit (see LAWS), and avian application of the taxidermist's art is now largely confined to game birds and museum exhibitions. See also BIRD SKIN.

TAXONOMY (tax-ON-uh-mee). The classification and arrangement of plants and animals based on their similarities and differences. Modern systems of taxonomy are based on phylogeny; i.e., life forms are theoretically grouped in the order of descent from common ancestors, oldest forms coming first, most recently evolved, last. Any classification structure is inextricably dependent on a formal system of names by which individual organisms or groups thereof can be labeled once they have been distinguished (see NOMENCLATURE). In the strictest sense, taxonomy refers solely to classification, whereas SYSTEMATICS includes identification and naming as well as classification, but these two terms are now often used interchangeably.

Together, taxonomy and nomenclature define biological subject matter, allowing scientists to communicate as precisely as possible about the objects of their studies. They can, therefore, be seen as a basis for all other aspects of biology, but also as tools for extracting knowledge rather than categories of knowledge unto themselves.

HISTORY OF TAXONOMY. Men have undoubtedly been classifying birds (and other organisms) from earliest times. The oldest categories likely lumped species which were good to eat, had usable parts, or were dangerous. Aristotle (384–322 B.C.) devised a system which categorized birds largely by behavioral traits—swimming birds, singing birds, birds of the fields—and of course we still place birds of disparate origins in such categories when we speak of "seabirds" or "marsh birds" or "birds of prey." This system was used with modifications until the late seventeenth century, when physical features such as the shape of bill or type of foot began to be compared. With the publication of Darwin's *Origin of Species* (1859), it became logical to try to arrange living things according to the sequence of their evolution. It also became evident that closely related birds might have very different types of bills (e.g., Darwin's finches—subfamily Geospizinae—or the sandpiper family) or conversely that relatively unrelated birds might have evolved a similar type of foot (e.g., albatrosses and gulls). By the end of the nineteenth century taxonomists were looking for structural characters in plants and animals which reliably indicated evolution rather than mere adaptation—not always an easy distinction to make (see discussion of convergence below).

In 1735, a Swedish botanist, Karl von Linné (Linnaeus), proposed a hierarchical system of grouping and naming life forms. All names were to be in Latin, the language of science, and his original categories were:

Classis
  Ordo
    Genus
      Species
        Varietas

Each species was referred to by a binomial name consisting of the genus and species.

The combination of classification by evolved anatomical structures and the Linnaean system of nomenclature forms the basis of modern taxonomy. This is not to say that methods have remained unimproved. Other characters are now considered as valid as or more so than structural ones (see *Taxonomic Characters*, below), and the nomenclature of Linnaeus has been greatly expanded and modified to adequately denote the relationships among different kinds of organisms. Not all of the taxonomic categories that have been erected have been applied to birds. Those that have are given in descending sequence below, using a single bird species as a model. Primary taxonomic categories appear in boldface.

Kingdom. Animales (all animals, as opposed to plants or minerals)
  Phylum: Chordata (animals with a hollow dorsal nerve cord)
    Subphylum: Vertebrata (animals with a well-developed brain encased in a bony skull and, in all living vertebrates, a segmented vertebral column)
      Class: Aves (birds)
        Subclass: Neornithes (true birds, including all fossil species except *Archaeopteryx lithographica*)
          Superorder: Neognathae (recent birds, including all living species, except the penguins, as well as some fossil forms)
            Order: Falconiformes (American vultures, Old World vultures, hawks and eagles, Secretary Bird, and falcons and caracaras)
              Suborder: Falcones (all of the above except the American vultures)
                Superfamily: Falconoidea (all of the remainder except the Secretary Bird)
                  Family: Falconidae (falcons and caracaras)
                    Subfamily: Falconinae (falcons)
                      (Tribe: not applicable here but sometimes interposed between subfamily and genus)
                      Genus: *Falco* (true falcons)
                        Subgenus: *Cerchneis* (a grouping of species within the true falcons)
                          (Superspecies: not applicable here but sometimes used to distinguish a group of closely related species within a given genus)
                          Species: *F. sparverius* (American Kestrel)
                            Subspecies: *F. s. paulus* ("Florida" Kestrel)

For further information, see entries for taxonomic categories: SUPERORDER; FAMILY; etc.

For further discussion of the use of the categories and the naming process, see NOMENCLATURE.

THE CLASSIFICATION PROCESS. Applying the system described above to living organisms may be compared to doing the kind of crossword puzzle in which you must figure out where the words fit as well as discover their definitions. The taxonomist must first differentiate true species and then group them in larger and larger categories—genus, family, order, etc.—in the desired phylogenetic order. Of all the categories, only the species is a scientifically definable—"real" or "natural"—entity. All the other categories both above and below are completely subjective and defined solely by the taxonomist's theories about which species are closely related to each other. These theories are based on documentable evidence (see *Taxonomic Characters*, below), but interpreting such evidence to prove relationships between organisms is an exercise of human intellect which does not mirror any objectively discernible natural design. Nature proceeds energetically by random invention and the results cannot always be forced into the tidy systems of which man is so fond.

DIFFERENTIATING SPECIES. Since the species is the objective foundation of the whole system, it is not surprising that a great deal of ornithological taxonomic effort to date (perhaps most of it) has gone into "simply" differentiating the world's bird species. We are apt to underestimate this task. As we glance through a field guide of North American birds, things seem to be sorted out much as we would have done it had we been asked—drab, fat-billed birds over with the sparrows; a brightly colored, fast-moving, slender-billed bird must be a warbler; the Wrentit doesn't look like anything in particular—give it a family of its own. Nothing to this taxonomy business.

One way to dispel the illusion that differentiating species is not challenging work is to imagine yourself Catesby or Audubon newly arrived in North America with only your eye and your intuition to help you decide what is a species and what is not. Would you have recognized all the plumages of a Yellow Warbler (age, sex, and season) as variations within a single species or would you have called them three different species as Audubon did (Havell Plates XXV, LXV, and XCV)? How about the light, dark, and intermediate phases of the Rough-legged Hawk? Would you have guessed that the large, pale Ipswich Sparrow, which breeds only on Sable Island, Nova Scotia, was a race of the same species as the small, dark Labrador Savannah Sparrow? Having learned this lesson, would you have been sure that the Western Bluebird was *not* a geographical color variation of the Eastern Bluebird? How many *Empidonax* flycatcher species would you allow if museum specimens of all the North American species were laid before you? Three? Six? There are ten. And Brewster's Warbler—a highly distinctive species in the same genus as the Golden-winged and Blue-winged Warblers? Wrong again—a hybrid between the two! These and other problems of species differentiation (see DIMORPHISM; POLYMORPHISM; GEOGRAPHICAL VARIATION; SIBLING SPECIES; HYBRIDIZATION) remain to be resolved in many cases and continue to be a vital part of taxonomic work. But the attention of the sophisticated modern taxonomist focuses more on taxa above and below the species. The creation and ordering of genera, families, orders, and their subgroupings require a thorough knowledge of the broad patterns and intricate details of evolutionary and zoogeographic theory as well as facility in applying the now numerous criteria by which relationships between organisms can be assessed (see *Taxonomic Characters*, below). A central question in judging similarities between different life forms is whether such likenesses really imply a close phylogenetic relationship or are the result of adaptations to similar environments taking place "coincidentally" in widely separated places and/or times. It would be reasonable to assume, for example, that the Great Auk and the other alcids of the northern oceans are closely related to the penguins of the southern. Taxonomists now generally agree, however, that today's penguins descend from an ancient line of birds and among living relatives are closer to the loons, whereas the alcids have evolved much more recently and so are placed near the gulls on the phylogenetic tree. Their obvious similarities are explained by the need to evolve physical attributes well adapted to the seagoing, fish-eating way of life common to both (for other examples, see CONVERGENCE). Many subtle structural characters as well as obvious superficial ones have evolved in this confusing manner, and taxonomists have always sought features which verify lines of evolution and cannot be explained by convergence. Biochemical analysis has recently produced significant progress in solving this problem.

Studying how species evolve is another way of learning about evolutionary relationships, and therefore populations of subspecies or races—i.e., forms apparently in the process of becoming distinct species—are of particular interest to taxonomists. In this regard it is important to realize that some species are "better" than others, i.e., further separated by evolution from their closest relatives and therefore less likely to interbreed with any but their own kind. In populations which are connected across a large area and many habitats, it is often possible to see a progress of intermediate forms, for example, between the darkest or largest race of a species and the palest or smallest (see CLINE). But when populations are geographically isolated or nearly so, the closeness of relationships is more difficult to test.

Study of such cases sometimes changes a widely accepted view of the taxonomy of the species involved. The recent "lumping" of Baltimore and Bullock's Orioles due to the high incidence of hybridization in the narrow zone where their ranges overlap involves two diverging forms which have not quite become fully distinct species. This change in the taxonomy of the two birds, the males of which appear totally different throughout most of their respective eastern and western ranges, was confusing and frustrating to many birdwatchers, but a good lesson in taxonomy and speciation for those who took the trouble to understand the circumstances.

TAXONOMIC CHARACTERS. It should be clear by now that differentiating species and placing them in their proper phylogenetic sequence no longer involve a casual comparison of bill shape or general habits. The criteria now used have all been the subject of serious research, testing, and debate and are used in combination as well as separately in the attempt to determine affinities. Four major types of taxonomic characters may be distinguished:

Structural (Morphological) Characters have, of course, been used since the earliest attempts at classification and they still account for the bulk of taxonomic distinctions. When specific and subspecific questions are being considered, the taxonomist often compares vast series of museum specimens for differences in color, size, and more subtle details such as relative length of primary feathers (see WING FORMULA). Relationships among the higher taxa are investigated with the aid of numerous details of a bird's body which have been shown to evolve in a consistent pattern. Morphologists tend to concentrate on the "conservative" aspects of an animal's anatomy, i.e., those that are not as subject to adaptive changes as external features, such as bills, which are notably "responsive" to selective pressures. Some of the parts of a bird's anatomy that are most frequently analyzed are: the shape of the breastbone, and whether it has a keel or not; number of neck vertebrae; shape of the nostril opening in the bill and whether open or closed; form of the bony palate; structure of the columella, the single bone in the bird's middle ear; form and number of jaw, wing, and thigh muscles (see MUSCLES, Formula Muscles); form of the syrinx; number, symmetry, and pattern of the carotid arteries; the pattern in which the small intestine is coiled; the form of scaling on the legs; the number and position of toes; the pattern in which the feathers grow from the skin (see FEATHER TRACTS); the color patterns of downy chicks; and the presence or absence of a tuft of feathers on the oil gland.

Behavioral (Ethological) Characters—such as type of nest built; the nature of the pair bond; type of courtship display; song; care of young (e.g., whether both parents brood and/or feed)—also provide clues to avian lineages.

Habitat and Distribution may reveal distinctions not exhibited by dead specimens or internal structure. Much of the evidence supporting the "split" of the Thayer's from the Herring Gull rested on nest-site preferences and change of iris and eye-ring color in zones of range overlap.

Biochemical Analysis of various bodily substances, notably egg-white proteins, by subjecting them to an electrical current and comparing genetically reliable patterns which are produced (see ELECTROPHORESIS). These methods require a high degree of technology, but since they analyze basic genetic structures, they are free from confusion related to convergence.

These methods have confirmed taxonomic relationships determined by morphological and other characters but have also suggested some surprises in relationships between various groups.

WHITHER TAXONOMY? It may seem that the modern taxonomist, armed with the battery of techniques outlined above, must have answered all the major questions or will do so within the year. This is far from the case.

The German taxonomist Dr. Erwin Stresemann divided the world's birdlife into 51 orders as of 1959, whereas his equally respected American colleague Dr. Alexander Wetmore proposed a mere 27 in his 1960 analysis.

The work of unraveling the relationships among the members of the huge order containing all the world's perching birds (Passeriformes) has barely begun. Are the finches really the last-evolved among living birds as recent tradition has held, or does the crow family deserve this distinction? And what is a finch anyway? Some taxonomists put the longspurs, sparrows, and some grosbeaks in a family which includes the tanagers (Emberizidae) and place it phylogenetically before the wood warblers, leaving the rest of the "finches" to follow the American blackbirds but precede the crows. This may puzzle an American birdwatcher familiar with his 700-odd species. He would never confuse a sparrow with a tanager. But the taxonomist familiar with the world avifauna—as well as all the forms known to us only through fossils—knows that there are birds which might aptly be called sparrow-tanagers, so evenly do they combine characteristics of both.

There are also many species whose family affiliations are only guessed at. The Yellow-breasted Chat, for example, is customarily placed among the wood warblers, yet its large size, heavy bill, mockingbird-like song, and un-warbler-like habits argue otherwise, even to a non-specialist. Some think it may be a tanager; perhaps it belongs in a family of its own; or maybe it should be dumped into the Cotingidae, a family containing more than its share of taxonomic misfits. At present, its exact origins—its place in the avian family tree—remain mysterious, and such problems will provide work for taxonomists for generations to come.

For other points of controversy about taxonomic relationships among North American birds, see Appendix I.

TEAL. Standard English name for about 16 species of small dabbling ducks in the genus *Anas*, of which 3 commonly breed in North America. Three others (including the Garganey, usually thought of as a teal) have occurred as migrants or vagrants in Alaska and elsewhere. The word has no taxonomic significance, but only a general implication of small size, and in some species it is interchangeable with "duck"—e.g., the Falcated Teal is sometimes called the Falcated Duck. "Teal" is of venerable provenance in several languages, but its original "meaning," if any, is uncertain. For family characteristics, see DUCK.

TECTRIX (pl.: tectrices). An individual feather of wing or tail coverts; in the plural, equivalent to "coverts."

TEETH. No modern birds have any ("scarce as hens' teeth"), and with the notable exceptions of some early fossil forms, toothless jaws are among the major departures in the evolution of birdlife away from reptilian ancestry. The earliest-known bird, ARCHAEOPTERYX, had individual teeth set in sockets in the jawbones, and a later fossil species, HESPERORNIS, had teeth set in grooves. The latter was once held to be one of an entire superorder of toothed birds (Odontognathae) which lived during the Cretaceous Period (see EVOLUTION OF BIRDLIFE), but the presence of teeth in other Cretaceous birds (e.g., ICHTHYORNIS) has not been proven.

A number of modern birds have tooth-*like* bill modifications, e.g., the serrations of mergansers' bills which help them grasp and manipulate slippery fish and the "tomial tooth" of the falcons' bills (see Fig. 1). Though these "bill teeth" may serve some of the same purposes as true "jaw teeth," the two structures are not homologous.

See also EGG TOOTH.

TEMPERATURE, BODY. Birds, like man and other mammals, are warm-blooded, i.e., capable of maintaining a relatively constant body temperature by means of their own heating and cooling systems, rather than depending on external heat sources as, for example, do reptiles. Three major differences between the avian heating system and our own stand out: (1) all birds have higher normal body temperatures than we do; (2) the body temperatures of birds normally fluctuate during the day to a greater degree than do ours; and (3) birds lack our principal cooling mechanism, the ability to sweat.

RANGE AND RHYTHM. The normal body temperature of all species of birds falls between 100° and 112° F., with small perching birds generally at the higher end of the range. The temperature of an individual bird may fluctuate a few degrees in either direction in response to various stimuli in its normal daily routine, such as physical activity, emotional stress, eating, a rise in air temperature, and the reverse of all these. It has also been demonstrated that there is a usual daily rhythm to these variations in body temperature. The lowest temperatures in most species have been recorded while they were roosting or sitting on the nest during the cool of midnight; their temperature rises and peaks coincident with a peak of avian activity and atmospheric heat around midday and then declines again. As one might guess, the rhythm is more or less reversed in nocturnal birds.

Body temperature does not fluctuate in relation to climate; birds of the Arctic and the tropics have similar normal temperatures, though their respective adaptations to temperature *control* may vary.

MAKING HEAT. Like mammals, birds produce heat by transforming nutrients and stored fats into energy; therefore, keeping warm is directly dependent upon taking in sufficient food.

In extreme cold, birds must eat constantly to produce at least as much heat as they lose, and those which perish in subzero temperatures may thus be said, with equal truth, to die of the cold or of starvation. Larger birds have an advantage in this respect, since the ratio of their body surface to total volume is less than that of smaller species. They therefore have less area from which heat can escape and do not have to eat as much in proportion to their weight as do smaller birds (see BERGMANN'S RULE).

KEEPING WARM. As anyone who lives north of the 40th parallel knows, good insulation is the key to staying warm.

Seabirds in particular rely to some extent on a layer of fat below the skin to retain body warmth, but by far the most important insulator for all birds is their feathers. The several types of body feathers (see FEATHER) are layered and overlapped in such a way as to trap and stabilize a layer of air next to the body and greatly slow the outward radiation of body heat. These feathers are under muscular control and can be raised to increase the air space and amount of insulation—this explains the familiar cold-weather sight of birds "fluffing out" their feathers.

The oil with which birds coat their feathers when preening helps create a surface shield which protects the inner layer of insulation against wind and water. Birds inhabiting cold regions often have notably deep and thick coverings of feathers and may exhibit behavioral traits such as huddling together in communal roosts, sleeping in caves or tree cavities, or burrowing into the snow (ptarmigan) to stay warm.

Inasmuch as temperature is controlled to a great extent by the feathers, young birds which are born naked cannot maintain a steady body temperature. Such "psilopaedic" species are essentially "cold-blooded" at birth, and therefore dependent on the parent birds to keep them warm enough or shaded from the sun. Passerine nestlings gain significant control of their own heating plant within their first week but are not in full command until fledged. Species born with a covering of down are less dependent on parental warmth and rapidly become thermally self-sufficient.

Heat loss from unfeathered parts of the body such as legs and feet can be reduced by slowing circulation selectively to these extremities—in some instances to just above freezing. Conversely, a temperature increase may be achieved by "shivering," which produces heat from muscular activity.

Perhaps the ultimate in metabolic control is practiced by a few species which "shut down" almost completely during cool periods and lapse into a state similar to hibernation (see TORPIDITY).

COOLING OFF. Lacking sweat glands in the skin, birds must avoid overheating by other means. To some degree their air-conditioning system is simply the reverse of their heating system. Instead of "fluffing" feathers to increase insulation, for example, they compress their plumage to retain as little body heat as possible. Or they can increase circulation to unfeathered parts to give off more heat rather than reduce circulation to retain it.

Many temperate zone species molt into a thinner plumage for the summer or achieve one gradually by normal feather loss and/or wear. Birds also adapt their *behavior* to the air temperature, often seeking rest and shade during the hottest part of the day.

Though they cannot perspire, birds do vaporize water in the lungs and internal air sacs (see RESPIRATORY SYSTEM) and release it by panting. Another cooling device is known in ornithological jargon as "gular flutter." The skin of the throat is quivered rapidly while the blood flow to the region is increased, thus letting off internal heat. This practice is especially prominent in birds with fleshy throat pouches, e.g., cormorants, frigatebirds, pelicans, and boobies. A good place to witness either or both of these phenomena is at a seabird colony at midday when parent birds must sit on their nests and endure the full force of the sun while protecting their eggs or young from it.

By human standards, practicality has always characterized the species of American vultures far better than fastidiousness. Their method of cooling off is consistent with their reputation—they defecate on their feet. Wood Storks also practice this untidy method of evaporative cooling.

See also ENERGY; METABOLISM; DESERT.

TERATORNIS (TAIR-uh-TOR-nis). A fossil genus of enormous vultures that lived during the Pleistocene Epoch and are known from skeletal remains recovered from the famous natural asphalt pools at Rancho La Brea, California, and elsewhere. A recently discovered species had a wingspan of 25 feet and probably weighed about 175 pounds; it is therefore the largest known flying bird. See EVOLUTION OF BIRDLIFE.

TERN. Standard English name for almost all (approximately 40) members of the subfamily Sterninae (family Laridae [gulls and terns]; order Charadriiformes). Four species are called by the name NODDY. Fourteen species of terns breed in North America, an additional species (Black Noddy) occurs as a regular visitor (may breed) at Dry Tortugas, Florida, and 2 or 3 others have occurred as accidental stragglers (see Appendix II).

Terns are slender, graceful water birds with long wings; short neck and legs; slender, pointed bill; and the front three toes fully webbed. They range in length from 8 inches (Least) to nearly 2 feet (Caspian). Many species have crested heads and most have notched or strongly forked tails. The plumage of the majority of tern species is gray above and white below with a black cap in alternate (nuptial) plumage. But there are a number of exceptions, some of which—the noddies—are almost perfect "negatives" of the usual tern coloration, being *dark* below with a *white* cap and a *wedge-shaped* rather than forked tail. Many species of terns have bright red or yellow bills and/or legs.

In general, terns feed by diving on fish and other surface-swimming organisms from the air. Unlike their near relatives the gulls, they are picky eaters, often preferring particular types of fish and never taking plant food or refuse. Most species are primarily inhabitants of the coastal zone; however, there are several highly pelagic tropical species (Sooty, noddies) and others (Black, Forster's) that also breed on freshwater marshes of the interior.

The Gull-billed Tern feeds by coursing over marshes, where it catches insects on the wing and picks up small invertebrates and even small frogs or lizards from the ground—a notable exception to the aerial-diving habit of most terns.

Terns usually nest in densely populated colonies near water, most species laying their eggs in a shallow scrape, either unlined or sparsely lined with some pebbles, shells, or other handy debris. Black and Forster's Terns nest on floating mats of accumulated marsh vegetation anchored to emergent plants, on marshy ground among reeds or rushes, or on abandoned muskrat lodges or the abandoned nests of other water birds (e.g., grebes). The Brown Noddy builds a stick or seaweed platform on low trees, shrubs, cacti, rocks, or on the ground, often with coral, shells, and other debris as lining. Royal, Sooty, and Noddy Terns typically lay only a single egg; 2 or 3 are usual for most species, but as many as 5 have been recorded for a few. The color and markings are very variable, even within a species: white, pale pink, buff, or olive with sparse or dense speckles and/or splotches in reddish, purplish, or dark brown.

Most terns are very vocal, typical sounds being drawn-out nasal cries and sharp, staccato pipings.

The terns are distributed worldwide from the Arctic to the Antarctic and over most landmasses where there are wetlands as well as over the oceans. Several species of terns (Gull-billed, Caspian, Sandwich) are cosmopolitan in distribution, and one population of Arctic Terns makes one of the longest migrations of any bird species—22,000 miles or more round trip from its breeding grounds in high arctic Canada to the Antarctic via the coasts of Africa and South America (see Fig. 13). The majority of tern species breed colonially on sandy beaches.

"Tern" comes from very similar words in Old Norse and Swedish referring specifically to these birds (especially, perhaps, to the larger species).

TERRITORY (territoriality). In the broadest sense, simply a defended area, but usually implies distribution of available habitat among members of the *same species*. Though its importance as a zoological phenomenon was pointed out only fairly recently (Howard, 1920), territoriality is common in the animal kingdom, with many examples among mammals, fish, insects, etc., as well as birds. The behavior patterns associated with territory (see below) are conspicuous among many species of birds, but the territorial urge is apparently lacking in some species (e.g., the Sharp-tailed Sparrow) and not very evident in others. The form that territoriality takes, the purposes that it serves, and the strength or weakness with which it is enforced are extremely variable among different species and individuals.

DIFFERENT KINDS OF TERRITORIES. As a result of studies on territoriality (e.g., Nice, 1941, and Hinde, 1956), four basic types of *breeding* territories are now widely recognized:

1. A relatively large area (see *Size of Territory*, below) in which a pair of birds court, mate, feed, and rear their young. This is the commonest form of territoriality and is practiced by a wide variety of passerine species, e.g., the wood warblers.

2. Another type of territory is much like the preceding except that the adult birds leave the territory to do most of their feeding and food finding for their young. Many shorebirds and at least a few passerines (e.g., the Red-winged Blackbird) follow this pattern. There is much intergradation between this kind of territory and the first-described, and some authorities believe that few if any species restrict themselves entirely to their own territory while searching for food during the breeding season.

3. A very restricted area which barely extends beyond the actual nest site. Most easily observed among colonial seabirds (e.g., gannets, murres) and herons, but also characteristic of a few solitary nesters (e.g., the Mourning Dove). In this case it is hard to distinguish defense of territory from defense of "person," mate, eggs, or young.

4. A relatively small area used only for the courtship ritual and mating, but not for nesting or (except casually) for feeding. This is exemplified by male grouse and hummingbirds which perform "dances" in arenas called LEKS (see also DISPLAY) or flights from conspicuous perches. The courtship area is not defended and the nest site of the female may not be considered a breeding territory.

Non-breeding territories include: defended feeding areas outside the breeding territory; night roosts, which are defended in some cases; and winter territories, which may or may not correspond closely to the breeding territory (see below).

SIZE OF TERRITORY. The amount of defended breeding territory varies widely not only among different species but among members of the same species.

In the densest seabird colonies the distance from one nest to another is equivalent to the reach of the nestlings and the total territory of a pair can therefore be measured in square inches. Many birds of prey, by contrast, vigilantly defend a square mile or more, and have more or less exclusive hunting rights for their own species over much more of the landscape (see HOME RANGE). The territories of most passerines are measured in acres, but again the variation is great: some American Robins are content with (or must settle for) as little as a tenth of an acre, while some Black-capped Chickadees patrol more than 17 acres.

Perhaps the most fundamental variation among species is dictated by innate behavior patterns: cliff-nesting kittiwakes never claim more than their foothold of ledge, while Song Sparrows, given their preference, will energetically defend an acre or more.

Birds which maintain the first type of territory described above must, of course, have enough habitat to supply an adequate amount of the right kind of food for themselves and their young. In general though, such species are apt to defend more than the minimum space needed to survive. It has been observed that species breeding on islands, where space is limited, tend to have much smaller territories than the same species breeding on the mainland. Accidents of topography on the mainland (e.g., water, geological formations) can also leave "islands" of habitat which may be sufficient as territories even though they measure smaller than the average for the species in question. The "personality" of individual birds is another influence on size of territory. More aggressive proprietors tend to claim larger areas than meeker members of their own species and may annex part of a neighbor's territory by winning boundary disputes.

It is sometimes stated that size of territory is roughly proportional to species size: the bigger the bird, the bigger the territory. Many examples can be found to support this notion, e.g., House Wren vs. Peregrine Falcon, but these discrepancies in territorial size have more to do with food preferences and species characteristics than size, and exceptions to the proposed rule are numerous. Many large birds, for example, are colonial nesters with far smaller breeding territories than the average wood warbler, though of course their feeding ranges are much wider (see HOME RANGE). Even among passerines, however, size correlation does not hold: the territory of the Red-eyed Vireo averages five times as large as the American Robin's.

The difficulty of measuring territorial space adds to the difficulty of making such comparisons, because territories have volume as well as linear dimensions. The ground-nesting Ovenbird has no occasion to repel rivals in the forest canopy above it, where a Scarlet Tanager's territory starts and ends.

TERRITORIAL BEHAVIOR. The duties of establishing and maintaining a territory largely fall to the male of the species. (As in other matters involving avian sexual roles, the phalaropes are exceptional.) Females may participate to a limited degree in territorial rituals, but on the whole they play a backup position and consent to the males' initiatives. (Feminists will appreciate the female Eurasian Blackbird in England which refused to be courted within the boundaries set by her mate, forcing him to alter his invisible fences.) When females do participate in territorial defense, they concentrate on members of their own gender.

Males of some species arrive back on their breeding grounds several days ahead of the females; in other species both sexes arrive at the same time. In some cases, males remain silent for a brief time after arrival and wander around the general area without "acting territorial." Males in flocks will stay together during this period until the territorial urge turns their flocking companions into rivals and they begin singing and defending their own parcels of habitat.

A male attempting to establish a territory for the first time begins with an innate recognition of the proper habitat for its species. This ensures, for example, that pipits don't end up colonizing cliff faces and that puffins eschew cattail marshes. In addition to its general aspect, a prospective territory may have to include certain specific features, such as a conspicuous song perch or, in the case of colonial species, the presence of other birds. A newcomer prospecting for a territory in an area where its species is already common will be driven from most of the likely sites by males whose land titles are established from previous seasons' occupations. If the young male finds an unoccupied territory at all in this situation, it is likely to be less favorable than those of its older neighbors. But there is strong evidence that many young males simply do without. When 81 percent of territorial male birds on a 40-acre plot of Maine forest were systematically "removed" in two successive years (Stewart and Aldrich, 1951; Hensley and Cope, 1951), replacement males filled the vacancies with revealing alacrity in both years.

Most "land" birds (including owls) announce their dominion over their territory by uttering their characteristic (often surprisingly loud) song from a conspicuous perch. Open-country species, such as the Horned Lark, which lack permanent perches broadcast their claim while hovering high in the air. It has been shown in at least a few instances that the range of a species song corresponds roughly to its normal territory size.

Display of bright plumage or other distinctive characteristics is also essential for holding territory in some species. For example, some male Red-winged Blackbirds, deprived of their red "epaulets" experimentally, quickly lost their credibility as landowners. Display *postures* are also part of the territorial apparatus of some species.

A few species (e.g., among the corvids and hawks) maintain their territories simply by being in residence, without any elaborate song or display activities.

Once a male has declared his sovereignty over a territory, he must defend its borders against potential usurpers *of his own species*. Different species using different "niches" in the same habitat are usually ignored, but similar species may evoke at least some defensive reaction from territorial males. (And, of course, predators recognized as threats to eggs or young are also harassed, though the urge here is not territorial—see MOBBING; FLOCK). Territorial boundaries may be marked by particular trees or other features prominent to the human eye, but often there is simply an intangible line perceivable only to the defenders of adjacent lots. If an ambitious neighbor or wandering landless male trespasses, he is likely to be met by the owner with feathers erected in indignation (see DISPLAY, *Threat*) and issuing a characteristic vocal threat. If "words" do not suffice, the defender may chase the intruder off his territory and may even attack physically (see AGGRESSION), though this is usually unnecessary. Birds have an innate sense of territorial rights and it has often been shown that when a defending male chases an interloper onto the latter's side of the fence, the roles automatically reverse: the former interloper becomes the righteous chaser, and the former defender, the submissive chasee. Ornithologists disagree on whether the aggressive defending urge or the instinct to avoid conflict is more important in maintaining territories.

Not that the outcome of territorial disputes is always inevitable. The strength of the aggressive urge varies among different individuals of the same species, and, as noted, weaker males are known to yield acreage to stronger neighbors. There is also a kind of seniority system, enforced by an increase of aggressiveness in males as they age, so that, as in our own society, it is often the successful old birds who hold the best and biggest sites.

The passion for territorial defense is at its height between the males' arrival and the hatching of the eggs. After this point, aggressive urges usually cool somewhat; border incidents become less frequent, less prolonged, and less apoplectic. The male's protective instincts often shift focus from the territory to mate and young; in some species, family and not territory is apparently the object of male defenses from the beginning of the breeding cycle.

PURPOSES OF TERRITORIALITY. Territorial instincts are so elaborate, well developed, and widespread that we must assume they confer significant advantages on the practitioners. A number of *possible* functions suggest themselves very readily and many subtler ones have been offered by behaviorists. However, the phenomenon includes so many variables and intangibles that it is difficult to collect meaningful data, much less come to definitive conclusions. Some of the most widely articulated speculations about why territoriality evolved follow. It is reasonable to suppose that territoriality has a combination of advantages and that the combination differs from species to species.

Distribution of Birdlife. Experiments (noted above) strongly suggest that, at least in some habitats, there are many more prospecting males than available territories. In this context, territoriality seems to provide a kind of natural "spacing" which prevents overcrowding and the food and other shortages which it might cause. It also forces younger males to accept less desirable habitat, so that the ecosystem runs, so to speak, at peak capacity.

Familiarity. Returning to the same territory year after year, birds inevitably learn the best alternatives for feeding, gathering nesting material, and escaping from predators. These small efficiencies doubtless add up to significant survival value.

Self-sufficiency. It was once widely assumed that a territory was analogous to a family farm and provided all the necessities of life for a family of birds. But observations now suggest that few if any species rely *completely* on the resources (food, nesting material, cover, etc.) of their territories.

Reservation of Specialized Nest Sites. Isolated cliffside eyries favored by certain raptors and holes in banks or trees are in shorter supply than other sites. "Single family" occupancy is obviously essential in these cases and there is probably an advantage to the species in having such scarce housing "reserved" by older, successful individuals.

Mating Efficiency. The territorial songs of males also serve to attract females of the species. The courtship and mating rituals can proceed inside the territory without interference from other individuals of the species. The relationship between males and females (pair bond) is reinforced year after year, so that time which might be spent searching for new mates in new locations can be applied to the breeding cycle. Young males prospecting for unoccupied territory are, in effect, ushered to any available territory by the rapid aggressive responses of defending males.

Protection. Widely spaced nests and individuals are harder for predators to find. Even cryptically colored ground nesters, such as Whip-poorwills, would be much more vulnerable to trial-and-error hunting by predators if they were more densely distributed. Colonial nesters mount a collective defense of their territories which helps offset their conspicuousness.

It is also logical to suppose that incidence of disease might be lowered by wide spacing, but as yet there is no evidence that this is a factor in territoriality.

Social Interaction. Notably gregarious species (e.g., parrots) have been known to despair and die if deprived of the company of their fellows. It has been suggested that the interaction among holders of neighboring territories may provide essential social stimulation.

WINTER TERRITORIES. Certain species that winter in the same area where they nest continue to defend their territory throughout the year, though much less vigorously than in the breeding season; male and female Northern Mockingbirds each defend their own separate winter territories. It has also been established (see, for example, Schwartz, 1964) that many long-distance migrant species defend territories on their tropical wintering grounds.

*   *   *

During the breeding season you can readily test the territorial defenses of birds in your neighborhood with a few simple props. A mirror or other reflective surface placed where a territorial male is likely to notice his own image will provoke paroxysms of rage in mockingbirds, robins, and many other species. In fact, shiny windowpanes and hubcaps provoke many such performances each spring, usually to the perplexity of the home or car owner (see PESTS for what to do). A similar response can be obtained with a paper "dummy" of a breeding-plumage male—it need not be a particularly good likeness as long as the right colors and patterns are prominent (see INTELLIGENCE; RELEASER). A tape recording of a breeding song is also effective, particularly if you can arrange to play back the male's own song. If you present your mirror, model, or tape in different locations and observe the response (active or passive) of a particular male, you can establish the border lines of his territory. Such experiments should, of course, be performed with the welfare of the bird in mind. Too much disturbance can disrupt a pair's essential breeding activities.

See also SONG; DISPLAY; COURTSHIP; PAIR FORMATION; AGGRESSION.

TERTIALS (TURR-shuls) (also tertiaries [TURR-shee-air-eez]). Alternative name for the three innermost secondary feathers of the wing (see Fig. 25); in certain groups (e.g., ducks) these feathers are often shaped, colored, and molted differently from the other secondaries but they are attached to the same bone (ulna) and in some groups are indistinguishable. In another usage, the long, covert-like feathers which are attached to the humerus and fill the space between the secondaries and the body of some long-winged birds; see, for example, the Northern Gannet in Fig. 19.

THAYER, John Eliot, 1862–1933 (Thayer's Gull: *Larus thayeri*). According to his eulogizer, G. M. Mathews, John Thayer was "amply supplied by inheritance with this world's goods" and after graduating from Harvard largely gave himself over to the occupation of "gentleman farmer." He was generously supportive of his alma mater and (due to a strong interest in natural history) especially of its Museum of Comparative Zoology. He financed expeditions to Latin America, China, Siberia, and Alaska and was an active collector of bird skins and eggs. He built a museum near his home in Lancaster, Massachusetts, to house these and other treasures, but later donated them—28,000 skins, 15,000 eggs, including many rarities—to the M.C.Z.

Thayer has been cruelly buffeted by the changeable winds of taxonomic theory. His gull was first described as a new species in 1915, then reclassified as a race of the Herring Gull. Smith's work (1966–SPECIATION) convinced the A.O.U. Committee on Taxonomy and Nomenclature to restore full species rank, but more recent studies now in preparation may argue that it is properly regarded as a race of the Iceland Gull!

THERMALS. "Bubbles" of warm air rising from the heated surface of the earth. For relation to birdlife, see FLIGHT, *Thermal Soaring.*

THERMOREGULATION. See TEMPERATURE, BODY.

THRASHER. Standard English name for 14 species of mimic thrushes (family Mimidae; order Passeriformes), all but four of them in the genus *Toxostoma.* Seven species of thrashers breed in western (mainly southwestern) North America and one additional species (Brown Thrasher) is widespread east of the Mississippi.

As a group, the thrashers have shown particular resourcefulness in exploiting the ecological niches of arid habitats—witness the assortment of pale (desert-colored) forms of the American Southwest. For other characteristics of the family (including the catbirds and mockingbirds), see MIMIC THRUSH.

Disappointingly, "thrasher" is simply a variant of "thrush"; thrashers do not "thrash"—despite long, mobile tails—nor do they "thresh"—despite the scythe-like bills of some species.

THREAT. See DISPLAY.

THRUSH. Standard English name for about a third of the approximately 305 members of the large family Turdidae (order Passeriformes), and also used to refer to the family as a whole. The group is also widely considered a subfamily (Turdinae) under a gigantic family (Muscicapidae) which also holds the babblers, Old World warblers, Old World flycatchers, and other smaller groups. Thirteen species of thrushes breed in North America, and another 8 species have been recorded as accidental stragglers (see Appendix II).

Thrush species go by a wide variety of names besides the familial one—e.g.: robins, bluebirds, solitaires, wheatears, akalats, nightingales, chats, alethes, shamas, redstarts, forktails, even warbler (!), as well as by a variety of one-species names such as Veery. Some of these standard English names refer reliably to specific genera or subfamilies, but others are used ambiguously. The thrushes are such a heterogeneous group that it is difficult to make family-wide generalizations about either their form or their behavior, even among the comparatively few North American species. They range in size between 4½ and 13 inches (5½ to 11 inches in North America). Their bills are usually short to medium-length and may be narrow or fairly heavy. Their wings, tails, and legs may be short to fairly long. Many species are somberly colored in browns and grays and/or finely spotted and streaked, but many others are brilliantly colored and boldly patterned. Despite the variations, however, there is a generalized "thrush shape" which closely corresponds to the generalized "songbird shape," i.e., the image many people would make if asked to draw a bird. And members of other families are frequently described as "thrush-like."

Thrushes occupy all land habitats from barren, stony tundra (Northern Wheatear) to rain forest (Varied Thrush), though there are no true desert thrushes in North America and the family shows a bias here for woodland and woodland edge (including farmland and suburbs). All our thrushes prefer insects, worms, and other invertebrates when the climate makes them available, but are also fond of fruits and readily shift to them when convenient or necessary.

Virtually all thrushes have pleasing, melodious songs, and some (the NIGHTINGALE comes inevitably to mind) are among the world's preeminent avian virtuosi. The cheerful warbling of the American Robin may be the most familiar birdsong in America, and the caroling of several of our forest thrushes (especially the Wood and Hermit Thrushes and the Veery) ranks with the finest in the world.

Most thrush nests epitomize the common notion of a bird's nest, i.e., a rather neat cup of woven sticks and grasses, lined with finer plant fibers. Many species use mud as a kind of interior wall between the stick shell and the inner lining. Most species place their nests in a crotch or on a branch near the trunk of a tree, but others nest on the ground, in rock crevices, or in tree cavities (see NEST). Bluebirds readily occupy birdhouses, and American Robins will build on a properly placed nest "shelf" (see BIRD-HOUSE). Elsewhere in the world, thrushes lay white eggs, but in North America, all are blue (pale to moderately dark); those of some species are immaculate, others are finely to heavily speckled or splotched (see Fig. 7). The distribution of the thrush family approaches the truly cosmopolitan; they are absent only from New Zealand (where, however, two Eurasian thrush species have been introduced) and some islands of Oceania. The North American species occupy virtually the whole of the continent at one season or another, and several species breed from coast to coast. All of these are migratory in at least part of their range and several are long-distance migrants—see especially the Northern Wheatear routes mapped in Fig. 13.

"Thrush" is of ancient and fairly clear—but, alas, not very interesting—provenance, and its oldest known antecedents may have referred to birds in general (Greek) or to a particular thrush (Latin) or perhaps to "twittering."

See also BLUEBIRD; BLUETHROAT; ROBIN; SOLITAIRE; VEERY; WHEAT-EAR.

THUNDERBIRD. A bird deity recognized widely among native North American tribes; the guardian of fire, war spirit, and protector of mankind. Thunderbird figures appear in many Amerind rituals, and the power of the image even inspired the American auto industry to name a car after this bird spirit. For a further description in context, see IMAGINATION.

TIBIOTARSUS (pl.: tibiotarsi). With the fibula, the leg bones of a bird between the knee and ankle; a fusion of the tibia with some of the tarsal bones. See LEG/FOOT; SKELETON; and Fig. 19.

TICK. A check mark. Used by British birders in referring to birds added to their life lists. Particularly rare or spectacular birds are sometimes said to be "good ticks." Also in a (somewhat derogatory) personal context: "ticker" (or "tick hunter"), and a joyous exclamation upon seeing a "new" species: "Tick!" "Twitch" is an equivalent word. All of these are little used in North America. See LISTING; BIRDWATCHING; "CHECK!"

Also, of course, a noisome arachnid pest which locks its jaws into the flesh of birdwatchers (and others) whose business takes them into rank grasses and shrubbery during the summer months.

TIME SENSE. See CIRCADIAN RHYTHM; NAVIGATION.

TIT (titmouse). Standard English name for most of the 46–47 members of the family Paridae (order Passeriformes) and a collective term for the family as a whole. Many taxonomies include the long-tailed tits (family Aegithalidae) and the penduline tits (Remizidae) as subfamilies under the "true" tits; the single North American representative of each of these groups is considered separately here under BUSHTIT and VERDIN. In North America, tits with crests are called "titmice" and those with dark caps and "bibs" which lack crests are called "chickadees." Ten species of chickadees and titmice breed in North America, if Black-crested Titmouse is considered a race of Tufted.

Except for the Sultan Tit of Asia, which is 8 inches long, tits are all small birds (average 5 inches) with short, sharp bills (a fairly deep base in some species), short, but strong legs, and (in North American species) moderately long tails. Tits are highly active birds of forests and their edges and often forage with flocks of their own or mixed species. They feed mainly on small insects and other invertebrates, but also eat fruits and seeds, particularly in winter. They tend to be among the first birds to discover a newly erected feeding station.

The tits' preferred nest site is a tree cavity, which chickadees usually excavate for themselves in rotten wood. Old woodpecker holes, dry pipes, and bird boxes are also acceptable. Within the cavity, most tits lay down a thick base of moss, on top of which they place a cup of fine plant fibers, down, fur, hair, and/or feathers. The 4–13 (average 6–8) eggs are white to slightly yellowish and either unmarked (Mountain Chickadee, Bridled

Titmouse) or finely speckled with reddish or dark brown over the whole surface or in a "wreath" at the large end.

Many tits have two distinct call types, one that includes a variety of buzzy and tinkling sounds and another consisting of a series of clear, whistled notes. In several species one of the first type sounds something like *chick-a-dee-dee.*

Tits are essentially birds of temperate zone forests (including tropical highlands). They are widely distributed in the Holarctic region, absent from most of the Neotropics, Madagascar, Australia, and Polynesia. In North America they are absent only from treeless regions, e.g., arctic tundra and desert (however, see VERDIN).

"Tit" connotes anything small, and the "mouse" of "titmouse" is from an Anglo-Saxon word, *mase,* which referred to any small bird. Choate (1973–BIOGRAPHY) points out that "titmouses" rather than "titmice" should be the correct plural of "titmouse"—yet another good reason to dispense with the "mouse" and hang on to the "tit."

TITMOUSE. See TIT.

TOLMIE, William, 1812–86 (*Oporornis tolmiei:* MacGillivray's Warbler). A Scottish physician who emigrated to Canada when he was twenty, eventually becoming the head of the Hudson's Bay Company. He was the first man to conquer Mount Rainier. He owes his ornithological immortality to a meeting with John TOWNSEND in British Columbia in 1836.

TOMIUM (TOH-mee-yum) (pl.: tomia). The cutting edge of both mandibles of the bill.

TONGUE. In birds as in humans, the tongue is a muscular organ attached to the floor of the mouth. The human tongue is a fleshy member supported by a single hyoid (U-shaped) bone. It is crucial to our manipulation of food, our highly developed sense of taste, and the articulation of our speech. By contrast, the avian tongue is usually tough (cartilaginous) in texture, especially toward the tip, and the hyoid apparatus has evolved into a series of small narrow bones, most of them paired, which in some species is prodigiously elongated (see below). Birds' tongues come in a great variety of sizes and shapes. In pelecaniform species (pelicans, boobies, cormorants, etc.), ibises, and storks, it is reduced to a vestige, while ducks, flamingos, parrots, and many finches have comparatively large and even fleshy tongues. In general the shape of birds' tongues conforms with the shape of the bills which enclose them and accordingly are subject to great variation: long and thin, short and wide, spoon-shaped or globular, rounded to nearly rectangular.

The tongue modifications which appear most frequently (but by no means universally) among different forms of birdlife are: (1) surface spines or barbs which are directed back toward the throat and probably aid the movement of food in that direction and (2) barbed edges (e.g., woodpeckers) and/or split tips (e.g., tits, hummingbirds, nuthatches, crows) which facilitate the picking up or prizing out of food items.

With a few possible exceptions (parrots?) birds apparently have little sense of TASTE nor do their tongues play a role in voice production (again possibly excepting parrots). Thus it is in dealing with food that human and avian tongues have most in common, and in this we are vastly outdone by many bird species in complexity of structure and versatility.

It has been demonstrated that many birds have great concentrations of tactile sensors on the tips of their tongues (see TOUCH), perhaps a heritage from their reptilian ancestors which, like modern reptiles, used their tongues routinely as "feelers." Birds do not "wag" their tongues like snakes and lizards, but some doubtless find food and judge its suitability by touch, and the Australian Mallee Fowl may gauge the temperature of its peculiar "nest" with its tongue (see INCUBATION).

A few "famous" bird tongues deserve special emphasis:

Woodpecker tongues tend to be unusually long and extensible. Their hyoid apparatus is elaborated into long, flexible pairs of branchial bones or "horns" which extend from near the base of the tongue around the back of the skull and find their ultimate attachment (in some species) inside the nostril openings of the bill. Extensibility is apparently achieved by the ability of the hyoid mechanism to "fold up" accordion style. Along with sensitive tissue, the tongue tops of woodpeckers are fixed with backward-projecting barbs and a sticky saliva. Thus equipped, woodpeckers can probe deep into holes, locate insect prey, and extract it with great efficiency.

The longest tongues of the bird world (in proportion to body size) are probably those of the woodpecker-like wrynecks (family Jyngidae) of the Old World, whose apparatus measures more than half its owner's total body length. The Common Flicker, a ground-loving, ant-eating woodpecker, may have the longest tongue (proportionate to body size) of any North American bird, measuring over 5 inches from the tip to the end of the hyoid horns anchored at the back of the skull. The tongues of the sapsuckers are not particularly long, but are covered with fine bristles which soak up sap by capillary action.

Hummingbird tongues are also long and extensible by means of a hyoid system like that of the woodpeckers. In addition, the tongues of most hummers are deeply split at the tip, bilaterally grooved, and capable of being furled into a tube. This last feature led observers to believe that hummingbirds sucked nectar from flowers as if drinking through a straw, but it has since been demonstrated (Weymouth et al., 1964) that this is not the case; the liquid is drawn onto the tongue (probably by capillary action), then the tongue is returned to the mouth and the nectar is swallowed in the usual manner. Some hummers also have fringes on the tongue tip(s) which aid in gleaning insects from vegetation or picking them from the corollas of flowers.

Flamingo tongues are fat and fleshy with serrated edges and bear numerous small, soft protuberances (papillae). This unusual organ is used in conjunction with the lamellae of the bill to sieve minute food items from mud (see BILL; FLAMINGO). The tongues of surface-feeding ducks (especially the shovelers), which also have lamellate bills, are also large and papillate. The serrations on the tongue edges of grazing geese are used in conjunction with the bill to hold and break off vegetation.

Many seed-eating finches have large (fat) tongues with which they manipulate seeds or fruits so that they may be "husked" inside the bill (see BILL for description). Crossbill tongues are thick and bear a cutting "tool" at the tip with which they detach conifer seeds once the cone scales have been separated (see FOOD and Fig. 2).

The notably large, thick, mobile tongues of parrots may play a part in the ability of some species to produce "articulate" sounds (see SONG).

TOOL USE. See INTELLIGENCE.

TOOTH. See TEETH; EGG TOOTH.

TOPOGRAPHY. In zoology, the delineation and identification of the external features and areas of the body surface of a bird or other animal. See topographic diagrams, Figs. 1 and 25.

TOPOTYPE. A specimen collected at the same place where the original type specimen or type series was taken. See NOMENCLATURE, *Types.*

TORPIDITY. A slowing down or reduction in bodily function usually as a reaction to cold or stress or as a technique for conserving energy.

Torpidity in birds has been reported in three closely related families: the hummingbirds, the swifts, and the nightjars (and, in one instance, a species of swallow). In all cases, body temperature is greatly reduced, breathing and heartbeat become negligible, and the birds can be handled without arousing them.

Because of their small size and extremely high metabolism when active, most hummingbird species can barely sustain themselves overnight without feeding. To reduce energy requirements, some species of hummingbirds become dormant each night and return to normal at daylight, when they can resume feeding.

Flocks of White-throated Swifts of the western mountains are known to roost in rock crevices in a torpid state during periods of cold weather when insect food is unavailable. This survival technique is also practiced by swift nestlings, which become torpid during the night in times of food scarcity.

The longest known period of torpidity—amounting to hibernation—is endured by the Poorwill, which is known to "sleep" for nearly three months in rock crevices in the American Southwest. As with the swifts, the Poorwill's torpidity coincides with cold weather and the consequent lack of insect food. Its temperature drops to 40° F. below normal and it survives on stored fat. Though this is the only species of bird found hibernating in the wild so far, torpidity has been observed in other species of nightjars in captivity. See also TEMPERATURE, BODY.

TOTIPALMATE (TOH-tuh-PAHL-mate). Describes a bird's foot which is webbed between all four toes, thus bringing the fourth (usually hind) toe forward. Characteristic of the Pelecaniformes (pelicans, boobies, gannets, tropicbirds, frigatebirds, cormorants, and anhingas)—the "totipalmate swimmers."

TOUCH. Much remains to be learned about the extent to which birds feel pressure, pain, vibration, and variations in temperature. Present assumptions about tactile sensations are based on physiological evidence such as concentrations of nerve endings in the skin, bill, feet, and elsewhere and observations of behavior which implies a sense of touch.

Nerve endings in the bill tips of shorebirds which probe deep in the mud for invertebrates, which they cannot see, are reasonably supposed to help locate food by touch, as are those in the tongues of woodpeckers and at the base of rictal bristles. Concentrations of presumed tactile receptors in the bills of ducks may serve to sort food by texture.

Apparently unique to birds are two bodies of encapsulated nerve endings, called Herbst's and Grandry's corpuscles, which are located in the lower skin layer (dermis) at various points in the body. Since they do not lie at the surface, they may be responsible for birds' observed sensitivity to vibrations and changes in atmospheric pressure. The ability of barnyard fowl or cage birds to "predict" earthquakes, presumably by feeling vibrations not perceptible to human beings, has often been observed; and it is suspected that birds may be able to "feel" weather changes approaching in their migration path.

We infer from watching gulls and ducks standing on the ice that their feet are either insensitive to cold or that the tactile receivers in these extremities can be "turned off" when necessary. We are probably justified in concluding, when we see a bird scratch an area beneath feathers which it cannot see, e.g., on its face, that it is reacting to the attacks of an ectoparasite or other felt stimulus.

TOWHEE (TOE-ee; however, see below). Standard English name for about 6 species of large New World emberizine finches (family Emberizidae or

Fringillidae; order Passeriformes), all (or all but one) in the genus *Pipilo*. Four of the towhees breed in North America.

In addition to being relatively large, towhees are distinguished from most other North American finches by their long tails and preference for forest or scrubland underbrush and leaf litter. Two of our species are colorful, boldly patterned birds.

The towhees eat a great many insects (even some small vertebrates, e.g., lizards) as well as seeds and fruit.

The name derives from the nasal, whistled call of the Rufous-sided Towhee, and if intended to echo the bird, should properly be pronounced "too-WHEE."

For family characteristics, see FINCH.

TOWNSEND, John Kirk, 1809–51 (Townsend's Solitaire: *Myadestes townsendi*; Townsend's Warbler: *Dendroica townsendi*). Well-to-do and well-educated son of a Quaker family and a member of the flourishing natural history establishment in Philadelphia in the early 1800's. He is chiefly remembered for his expedition to the Pacific Northwest, on which he was accompanied by Thomas NUTTALL. The trip resulted in the discovery and collection of several "new" North American bird species. Townsend was fated to be a contemporary of Audubon, whose *Birds of America* overshadowed a similar comprehensive work attempted by Townsend but never completed. He abandoned natural history for dentistry in 1845 but apparently failed at this and a number of other things before his early demise. Not to be confused with Dr. Charles W. Townsend, a rather prolific (amateur) ornithologist, author of *Birds of Essex County, Massachusetts*, and a number of the "biographies" in BENT'S *Life Histories of North American Birds* series. For a fuller biography of J. K. Townsend, see Stone, *Cassinia* (1903), 7:1–5.

TOXIC CHEMICALS. For effects on birds, see MAN-MADE THREATS TO BIRDLIFE.

TRAILL, Thomas S., 1781–1862 (*Empidonax traillii*: Willow Flycatcher). A doctor-zoologist (see BIOGRAPHY), Traill was a professor of medical jurisprudence and a light of the cultural and intellectual life of Liverpool, England, and Edinburgh, Scotland, where he was born and died. The obscure flycatcher that once bore Traill's name in both English and Latin was named by AUDUBON, whose cause Traill championed in Britain. Recently, the species was "split" into two obscure flycatchers, now called Willow and Alder in standard English usage.

TRANSIENT. A species (or population) which migrates through a given area but neither breeds nor winters there. Obviously, the use of the term in reference to a particular species varies geographically; i.e., the Palm Warbler is a transient in most of the east-central U.S. but not in the eastern boreal zone of Canada, where it breeds, or in Florida, where it winters.

TRANSITION ZONE. One of Merriam's life zones; called the Alleghenian Zone east of the 100th meridian. See LIFE ZONES and Fig. 6.

TRAPPING (of birds). See HELIGOLAND TRAP; CANNON NET; BANDING; LIME; and POLE TRAP for specific trapping methods. A brief discussion of bird catching in general is given under CAPTURE.

TRASH BIRD. In some (very hard-core) birding circles, applied to any abundant species regardless of its beauty, grace, or charm, sometimes with the express purpose of infuriating the sentimental element of the bird-watching community. Typical usage as follows:

Novice birder (first trip to Texas): "Oh, I just think that little Vermilion Flycatcher is the most BEE-OO-TEE-FUL bird I've ever seen."

Veteran birder (trying to "get" 300 species in 24 hours): "Forget the trash birds and listen for the Botteri's Sparrow that's supposed to be here."

TREAD. "Treading" refers to the male bird's action in copulation, based on the fact that in many cases he stands on the back of the female. See REPRODUCTIVE SYSTEM; COPULATION.

TREECREEPER. Standard English collective name for the 6 members of the family Certhiidae (order Passeriformes), 1 of which, the Brown Creeper, breeds in North America. The term "creeper" is used alone or in combination to refer to many species in a wide range of families, e.g., wallcreeper (Sittidae), woodcreeper (Dendrocolaptidae), Australian tree-creeper (Climacteridae), etc., while "treecreeper" is used as the standard English generic name for all species in the genus *Certhia*, except in North America, where the species *Certhia americana* is called Brown Creeper. Vernacular nomenclature might be well served by combining these two names into Brown Treecreeper.

Treecreepers are small (average 6 inches), delicately built birds, colored and patterned cryptically to resemble the surface of a rough-textured tree trunk above and white or off white below. The bill is typically fairly long, narrow, and decurved; the legs are (usually) slender with long toes and sharp, strongly decurved claws; and the longish tail has stiff, pointed woodpecker-like rectrices which act as a prop as the bird climbs.

Unlike the nuthatches, treecreepers are exclusively *vertical* climbers, typically following a spiral course upward from the base of a tree and then flying down to the base of a nearby tree. They are essentially forest birds but will also glean walls and buildings. Their food preferences run to small insects, spiders, and other animal matter—e.g., insect eggs prized from crevices—but they also eat seeds occasionally and take suet at feeders.

Most treecreepers, including the North American one, have a surprisingly clear, sweet, high-pitched melodious song, and frequently thin lisping or piping calls.

The Brown Creeper stuffs its loose cup nest behind a section of loose bark on a tree trunk (rarely among rocks). The construction is of moss, small sticks, and grass and the lining is typically of feathers and soft plant down. The 3–9 (usually 6) eggs are white with fine reddish-brownish speckling at the "blunt" end.

The distribution of treecreepers is mainly Holarctic, though they reach the Neotropics (Central America), India, and Africa, mainly in the highlands. The Brown Creeper breeds from southwestern Alaska to Nicaragua and occurs at some season throughout most wooded areas of North America south of the boreal forest.

TREE DUCK. Once the standard English generic name for members of the genus *Dendrocygna*, only a few of which nest and/or roost regularly in trees. WHISTLING DUCK is now officially preferred. See also DUCK.

TRIBE. Taxonomic category between SUBFAMILY and GENUS. In zoological nomenclature, tribal names invariably end in *-ini*. The tribe is a tertiary category below subfamily. The ducks, for example, are sometimes classified with all species placed in a large subfamily (Anatinae), which is then subdivided into a number of tribes (e.g., Mergini: sea ducks) as an alternative to dividing the ducks into smaller subfamilies, viz., Anatinae (typical ducks), Merginae (sea ducks), etc. See TAXONOMY.

TRINOMIAL. A three-word scientific name, the third word of which designates the subspecies of a plant or animal. The binomial *Dendroica petechia* designates the *species* of the Yellow Warbler as a whole. The several races or *subspecies* of the Yellow Warbler each bear a trinomial, e.g., *Dendroica petechia rubignosa*, the Alaskan Yellow Warbler.

TRITURATION. Crushing or grinding into fine particles. Used to describe the muscular action of a bird's gizzard which pulverizes hard seeds, mollusk shells, etc. See DIGESTIVE SYSTEM.

TROGON (TROH-gun). Standard English name for most of the 35 members of the family Trogonidae, the sole family in the order Trogoniformes

(5 species of large Neotropical trogons are called quetzals). One species of trogon, the Elegant (or Coppery-tailed), breeds in North America, and one other has occurred as a vagrant (see Appendix II and Plate 1).

Though in many respects they exemplify quintessential "tropical birds," trogons are unique in appearance. They are medium-sized (9 to 12 inches), very colorful, usually with iridescent metallic (often green) upperparts, a brilliant red or yellow belly, a conspicuously barred or spotted undertail pattern, and a brightly colored fleshy eye ring. The bill is short but rather broad and deep, the nostrils heavily bristled, the feet extraordinarily small, and the tail long and (in most cases) abruptly squared at the end. They are the only birds to have toes I and II turned backward, III and IV frontward (heterodactyl).

The trogons are fruit-eating forest birds capable of sitting with uncanny stillness while croaking in a ventriloquial manner and screwing up their courage to launch an attack on an unsuspecting berry. They vary their diet occasionally with insects or even small reptiles or amphibians.

Many trogons excavate their own nest cavities in rotten tree trunks or wasp nests, but the Elegant (Coppery-tailed) prefers to occupy natural tree cavities (exceptionally holes in earthen banks) or abandoned woodpecker holes, which it lines sparsely (if at all) with a little plant down, grass, and/or other debris. The 3–4 (rarely 2) eggs are white or pale blue.

Trogon calls consist of short or long series of hoots, croaks, or clucks; our native species typically gives 4–6 notes in the second category.

Trogons are pantropical (except for Australia and Oceania), though they range well into the Temperate Zone on tropical mountains. The single North American representative reaches the northernmost limit of its extensive Mexican and Central American range (to northwestern Costa Rica) in the pine-oak zone of the highlands of southeastern Arizona and New Mexico (see Plate 1), from which most individuals depart in the winter. In the tropics trogons are non-migratory.

"Trogon" is Greek for "the gnawer," an odd characterization probably meant to refer to the way they hollow out their nest cavities.

TROPICBIRD. Standard English name for all members of the family Phaethontidae (order Pelecaniformes). There are 3 species of tropicbirds worldwide, 2 of which occur with some degree of regularity in North American offshore waters. The third species has been recorded off California and Baja California. None is resident here, though the White-tailed Tropicbird (*Phaethon lepturus*) breeds in Bermuda.

Tropicbirds are graceful, largely white seabirds with yellow or orange bills and greatly elongated central tail feathers (rectrices), a feature that contributes to their ethereal bearing. They are about 18 inches long excluding the elongated tail feathers, which contribute an additional foot and a half or more. Like the other Pelecaniformes, tropicbirds have webs between all four toes. Their legs are very short and on land they hobble along on their tarsi rather than walk upright as do the pelicans and boobies. Tropicbirds sail high over tropical seas looking for shoals of fish or squid, which they hover over and then dive into. They are partially migratory.

All three species are loosely colonial and lay their eggs in an unlined natural cavity or crevice in rock, an abandoned (or pirated) petrel burrow, or a hollow on the ground amidst vegetation. They lay only a single egg which is very variable in color and markings: white to reddish brown with darker spots and blotches of yellowish to dark red-brown or purple.

Unlike most members of their order, tropicbirds are rather noisy, making a variety of loud, shrill screams, rattles, and clicks. A rasping call given at sea, *clik-et-clik-et*, gave rise to the nickname "bos'n bird" according to Palmer (1962).

The name is an apt reflection of their pantropical distribution.

TROUPIAL (TROO-pee-yul). The first-named (*Icterus icterus*) and largest of the New World orioles. It has been suggested that the icterid orioles of the New World be called troupials to avoid confusion with the oriolid orioles of the Old World; or that the term be used collectively to refer to *all* members of the family Icteridae, i.e., blackbirds, cowbirds, meadowlarks, etc. The name is of French derivation and refers to flocking, which, though typical of many American blackbirds as well as most of the caciques and oropendolas of Latin America, is *not* characteristic of most icterid orioles including *the* Troupial.

TUBENOSES. Standard English name for the order Procellariiformes, which includes the albatrosses, shearwaters, petrels, and storm-petrels. For further reference to this bill structure and other characteristics of this order, see SALT GLAND; NOSTRILS.

TUBERCULOSIS. See DISEASE.

TUBINARES (TOO-buh-NAH-reez). Formerly a suborder comprising the albatrosses, shearwaters, petrels, and storm-petrels under the old order Longipennes (long-winged swimmers), which also included the gulls, terns, jaegers, and skimmers. The "tubenoses" have now been elevated to ordinal rank and their collective name changed from Tubinares to Procellariiformes; thus Tubinares is now obsolete, but its English version is a handy vernacular term for the group described.

TUNDRA. Treeless barrens characteristic of arctic regions between the permanent glacier zone and the tree line. When poorly drained, as it is in vast areas underlain by permafrost, it is swampy, but in upland areas it is dry and "turfy." Botanically it is characteristically made up of a great abundance and variety of mosses and lichens, as well as grasses and sedges (particularly in wetter areas), many species of uniquely arctic flowers, decumbent matted shrubs of the heath family (Ericaceae), and small sprawling "trees," mostly willows and birches, which in sheltered localities may reach the proportions of small bushes. In North America, virtually all land between the Arctic Circle and the north polar sea ice is tundra and it accounts for perhaps half of the landscape north of the 60th parallel. Below 60° N., it occurs in western Alaska, northern Quebec, and a narrow strip along the western shore of Hudson Bay to below 55° N. A similar condition prevails on the highest peaks of the Rockies and other high mountains and is often called "alpine tundra." In general, tundra regions are frozen solid with a relatively thin snow cover for at least nine months of the year; they spring into riotous life during the height of summer.

Tundra birdlife is characterized by many water-bird species, especially loons, ducks, the majority of North American shorebird species, jaegers, a few gulls, and the Arctic Tern; other typical species include the ptarmigans, Snowy Owl, Common Raven, Smith's and Lapland Longspurs, and Snow Bunting. Where cliffside nest sites are available, the Peregrine Falcon, Gyrfalcon, Rough-legged Hawk, and Golden Eagle often occur, and where the vegetation reaches shrub proportions, a few other hardy passerines such as Harris' Sparrow can be expected.

See also ARCTIC and the Bibliography under same.

TURKEY. Standard English name for the only 2 members of the New World family Meleagrididae (order Galliformes). Both turkeys are large birds, standing to 4 feet tall with neck stretched normally. They have a bare, colored, carunculated head, neck wattles, spurs on the tarsi, and gorgeous iridescent plumage including a magnificent tail fan.

Turkeys fly well, but, like other gallinaceous birds, do so only in short bursts, usually when alarmed. They are birds of the forest and forest edge, foraging in flocks at a stately pace, scratching in leaf litter for grain, nuts, and other seeds, picking fresh fruits and buds, and nabbing the occasional invertebrate. Turkeys roost for the night in trees.

The nest is a shallow depression on the ground, scantily lined with handy plant material. The 8–12 eggs (up to 20 recorded) are white to pale buff or yellowish and densely but rather finely speckled and spotted with reddish or darker brown.

The voice of the Wild Turkey cock has changed little with domestication; "gobble-gobble" does not begin to do it justice.

The Wild (or Northern) Turkey (*Meleagris gallopavo*), once resident throughout most of North America south of the coniferous forest zone, was reduced to remnant populations due largely to its appeal as a game and table bird. Ironically, the turkey's popularity with sportsmen has also been its salvation, for it has been artificially reestablished in many states by fish and game agencies at the urging of turkey shooters. The Wild Turkey is a magnificent American species which has made its mark in the history of the Republic: the Pilgrim fathers gave thanks to it (and *with* it); Ben Franklin nominated it as the national bird; and it has become a staple of the American poultry industry.

Opinions vary about the relationship (if any) between turkey, the bird, and Turkey, the country. Gruson (1972–BIOGRAPHY) says that it is a Tartar word (meaning "brave") used in the sixteenth century to refer both to part of Asia Minor and, very generally, to any form of exotica. Other sources (including at least one Turk) insist that the connection has to do with Turkish prowess in breeding turkeys. Perhaps the most plausible explanation is the one which holds that guinea fowl were the original avian "turkeys," so named because they were imported from Africa to Europe via Turkey. When another exotic fowl arrived from America, it fell under the same misnomer.

For Thanksgiving-type turkeys see DOMESTICATED BIRDS. See also references in the Bibliography under GALLINACEOUS BIRDS.

TURNSTONE. Standard English name for the 2 shorebirds belonging to the genus *Arenaria* (order Charadriiformes), both of which breed in North America. The subfamily Arenariinae is sometimes reserved for the turnstones exclusively or may include the SURFBIRD. Some taxonomies include the turnstones in the plover family (Charadriidae) and others with the sandpipers (Scolopacidae).

Turnstones are small (7 inches), strikingly patterned shorebirds with somewhat wedge-like, slightly upturned bills, which they use to turn over small rocks and debris in search of anything edible; sometimes these birds will join forces to flip a stone too heavy or too securely embedded for one. They are by no means restricted to this manner of feeding, however, and in fact appear to be among the most resourceful of shorebirds: digging with bill and feet in sand for buried eggs of marine invertebrates, taking maggots from putrefying seal carcasses, rooting vigorously in piles of rotting seaweed and other beach detritus; they are even known to take bread crumbs from people's hands (Palmer, 1967–SHOREBIRD). Their strong, stout bills are used for breaking into mollusk shells and eggshells of nesting birds as well as for turning. Like other shorebirds, they readily eat fruit on their breeding grounds. Their manner of walking is similar to the step-and-stop movement characteristic of plovers.

The Black Turnstone is almost exclusively a bird of wave-washed rocks (except when nesting), and though the Ruddy Turnstone is also inclined to prefer this habitat, it is much more tolerant of sandy beaches, mud flats, and even marsh pools.

Black Turnstones breed only in coastal Alaska and the northwestern

Yukon and winter at least as far south as the coast of Sinaloa, Mexico. The Ruddy Turnstone is one of the few shorebirds (along with the Red Knot and Sanderling) to nest on the stony barrens of northernmost Greenland. Its breeding distribution is circumpolar arctic and it migrates or winters over most of the rest of the world, to as far south as Tierra del Fuego and New Zealand.

For family characteristics, see PLOVER; SANDPIPER.

TURTLE DOVE. Standard English name for some of the doves in the Old World genus *Streptopelia*, including *the* Turtle Dove, *S. turtur*. *Turtur* is the Latin word for "turtle" and echoes the gentle, purring call of this species. Two species of *Streptopelia* doves have been introduced more or less successfully in North America: the Barbary or Ringed Turtle Dove, *S. "risoria,"* an aviary-bred form of the African Collared Dove, *S. roseogrisea* (southern California and Florida), and the Spotted Dove, *S. chinensis*, a widespread Asian species (Los Angeles and Orange counties, California).

TWITCH. In British, a check mark; a "twitcher" is one whose chief interest in birds is checking them off on lists, i.e., a lister. See TICK; LISTING.

TYPE GENUS. A genus of birds or other animals designated by the author as the basis for his description of a new family, superfamily, subfamily, or tribe. If a type genus is not published by an author, one is subsequently designated. See NOMENCLATURE, *Types*.

TYPE LOCALITY. Ideally, the exact place where the type specimen of a bird or other animal species was collected. If a type locality is not designated by an author when he publishes the description of a species (as was the case in many early species descriptions), one is chosen and published by a later authority. See NOMENCLATURE, *Types*.

TYPE SERIES. Two or more specimens of a bird or other animal from which a type specimen is selected as the basis for the description of a new species or subspecies. See NOMENCLATURE, *Types*.

TYPE SPECIES. A species designated by an author as the basis for his description of a new genus (or subgenus). If a type species is not published by an author, one is subsequently designated. See TYPE SPECIMEN; NOMENCLATURE, *Types*.

TYPE SPECIMEN. An actual specimen of a bird (or other animal), usually in the form of a museum "study skin," to which the scientific description of a species or subspecies (both in the case of a nominate subspecies) refers in the "type" system. See NOMENCLATURE, *Types*; also HOLOTYPE; LECTOTYPE; SYNTYPE; PARATYPE; TYPE SERIES.

TYRANNULET (tuh-RAN-yuh-let). Standard English generic name for many species of tiny flycatchers of several genera in the family Tyrannidae. All but one of these are residents of the American tropics. The exception is the Northern Beardless Tyrannulet (*Camptostoma imberbe*), which breeds from southernmost Texas and Arizona to northwestern Costa Rica; it is called the Beardless Flycatcher in North America.

TYRANT FLYCATCHER. Standard English collective name for the approximately 390 species of suboscine passerine birds in the family Tyrannidae (order Passeriformes), 34 of which (counting one BECARD) breed in North America. Five other species have occurred as accidental stragglers (see Appendix II).

The tyrant flycatchers are such a varied group that few characters apply to all the species. They range in size from 3 to 16 inches (4 to 9½ inches in North America). Most have relatively large heads and tails of medium length (some moderately long to very long). Larger species tend to have broad, heavy, hooked bills (all species show some degree of hook at the tip). The great majority have well-developed rictal bristles (absent in the Northern Beardless Tyrannulet). The legs and feet of all North American species are relatively small and weak. The coloration of most species is drab—combinations of grays, browns, and olives. But some species have brilliant yellow breasts; the kingbirds have brilliant orange or red crown patches (usually concealed) and some *Myiarchus* and the Great Kiskadee have areas of bright rufous in wings and tail. The male of one North American species is vivid vermilion. Many species have conspicuous wing bars and eye rings.

As their name implies, tyrant flycatchers tend to be active, often aggressive birds, many of which habitually sit in conspicuous perches and sally into midair after flying insects or to chase potential nest robbers, such as crows and jays. They are usually solitary. They feed mainly on insects, but all species take some fruit and a few are primarily frugivorous.

Tyrannids typically build cup nests, usually in a tree in the open, but in some species in cavities (*Myiarchus*) or on buildings or rock ledges (phoebes); a few (e.g., Kiskadee) build enclosed nests. The eggs are white to buff-yellow, immaculate, finely speckled/streaked, boldly streaked, or spotted with dark brown, reddish, and/or grayish.

The calls of tyrant flycatchers are distinctive but unmusical, usually short, often harsh and abrupt.

The tyrant flycatchers are an exclusively New World family which achieves its greatest diversity in the Neotropical region, where it undoubtedly evolved. In North America, they inhabit all major biomes except arctic tundra; a few species range continentwide.

See also EMPIDONAX; KINGBIRD; MYIARCHUS; OLD WORLD FLYCATCHER; PEWEE; PHOEBE; TYRANNULET.

U

UNCINATE (UN-sin-et) **PROCESS.** A bony projection from a rib, linking by means of a tendon to the rib behind; present only in birds and a few reptiles. See SKELETON and Fig. 19.

UNDERPARTS. Strictly interpreted, synonymous with "ventrum," i.e., everything below a lateral midline including, for example, the underside of the tail. However, normally used to describe general pattern or coloration of the throat, breast, belly, and undertail coverts—or the greater part thereof. The Yellow-breasted Chat may be said to have bright yellow underparts even though the lower belly and vent are white.

UNGUIS (UNG-gwis). Technical term for the bill NAIL present in the ducks, geese, and swans.

UPPER AUSTRAL ZONE. One of Merriam's life zones; called Upper Sonoran Zone west of the 100th meridian. See LIFE ZONES and Fig. 6.

UPPERPARTS. Strictly interpreted, synonymous with "dorsum," i.e., everything above a lateral midline including, for example, the forehead. However, normally used to describe general pattern or coloration of the head, back, wings, rump, and tail—or the greater part thereof. The Red-eyed Vireo may be described as having olive-green upperparts even though it has a gray crown.

URINARY SYSTEM. See EXCRETORY SYSTEM.

UROPYGIUM (YOOR-uh-PIDGE-ee-yum). Technical term for a bird's rump, where the uropygial, i.e., oil or preen, gland is located. See OIL GLAND.

V

VAGRANT. In an ornithological context, a bird which has wandered or been blown (see WEATHER) or otherwise transported to a locality beyond its normal range. As a term of abundance (or lack thereof) it is essentially synonymous with "accidental." The term varies, of course, according to context: a Lark Bunting would be a vagrant in Alaska or Florida, but not in Nebraska or in North America as a whole. For a list of verified vagrants which have occurred in North America (excluding BAJA CALIFORNIA, GREENLAND, and BERMUDA), see Appendix II.

A less frequent use of the term refers to species, such as Bohemian Waxwings, which appear beyond (usually south of) their normal ranges in IRRUPTIONS at irregular intervals.

VANE. The flat, relatively soft area of a feather extending outward on both sides from the central shaft (rachis). The vane is also called the web (inner and outer) or the vexillum and is made up of a series of interlocking barbs. See FEATHER and Fig. 9.

VARIETY. In botany, a taxonomic category below subspecies, but in zoology refers to individuals within a population which differ from the norm; also used more loosely for any variation within a species.

VAUX (vawks), William S., 1811–82 (Vaux's Swift: *Chaetura vauxi*). A pillar of the hyperactive natural history community of Philadelphia in the nineteenth century. His specialties were archaeology and mineralogy, not birds; his commemorator was William TOWNSEND.

VASCULAR SYSTEM. See CIRCULATORY SYSTEM.

VEERY. Standard English name for a single species of thrush, *Catharus* (*Hylocichla*) *fuscescens* (family Turdidae or Muscicapidae), that breeds exclusively in North America, occupying wet deciduous woodlands of the Transition Zone continentwide. The name gives a feeble suggestion of the species' inimitable, ethereal song. For family characteristics, see THRUSH.

VENT. A single anal opening (cloacal aperture) through which pass solid and liquid wastes as well as the products of the reproductive system. Characteristic of birds, as well as reptiles, amphibians, most fishes, and a few untypical Australasian mammals in the subclass Prototheria (e.g., the duck-billed platypus).

VENTRAL. Lower or under, as: the "ventral surface" of an animal's body; in birds, "ventral surface" is synonymous with "underparts." Opposite of DORSAL.

VENTRICULUS (ven-TRIK-yuh-luss). The second of two enlargements in a bird's digestive tract which together function like the human stomach; it could also be described as the lower of a bird's two stomachs. Also called the GIZZARD. See DIGESTIVE SYSTEM and Fig. 19.

VERDIN. Standard English name for a single species, *Auriparus flaviceps*, traditionally classified in a subfamily (Remizinae) among the tits (family Paridae; order Passeriformes). Some authorities have raised this group, known collectively as the penduline tits, to full family rank (Remizidae); the Verdin is its only New World member.

The Verdin is a small bird (4 inches) with a short, pointed (tit-like) bill. In its generally grayish plumage and active, often gregarious feeding behavior, it resembles the "true" tits, but the yellow head and chestnut "shoulder" patch of the adults distinguish it from any other North American bird species.

Verdins are birds of arid *Acacia* scrub, through which they forage, probing bark and twigs and gleaning leaves for insects, as well as taking berries when available. The species apparently never bathes or drinks and gets all necessary moisture from its food.

Its song is a series of loud, clear, whistled notes which carry well through the still desert atmosphere, and it also gives a number of buzzy calls which recall its kinship with the chickadees.

The Verdin nest is placed from 2 to 20 feet (usually about 5 feet) up in a cactus or thorny desert shrub and consists of a ball of thorny twigs with a side entrance, lined with spider silk, grasses, leaves, feathers, and plant down. In addition to its usual function, the nest is used as a night and winter roost.

The 3–6 (usually 4) eggs are pale blue or greenish blue, finely marked around the larger end with reddish speckles.

The Verdin is resident in desert or semi-desert habitats from southern California to western Texas south through Baja California and to central Mexico. It is endemic to this range and non-migratory. The other penduline tits occur in Eurasia and Africa.

The provenance of "verdin" is obscure, but it is a colloquial French name for the Eurasian bunting called the Yellowhammer (*Emberiza citrinella*) and doubtless refers to the yellow head of *Auriparus*.

See Bent (1946–TIT).

VERIFICATION OF RECORDS. Not very long ago, the only satisfactory means of verifying the occurrence of a particular bird in a particular place was to shoot the bird, prepare it as a specimen (see BIRD SKIN), label it, and preserve it in a museum drawer for future reference. Good (i.e., clearly recognizable) photographs are now widely accepted as proof of the occurrence of rare species, but it should be noted that in many cases subspecific determination is impossible from a photograph and still requires a bird "in the hand." Of course, anyone wishing to falsify such a record could easily do so using a bogus photograph or specimen. Hoaxes of this kind have been perpetrated (see, for example, the fascinating cases of the "Hastings Rarities," *British Birds* [1962]), but the crime is such an absurd one that it evokes more amusement than indignation.

Since the advent of good optical equipment and the resulting improvement in our ability to identify birds by sight, it has been recognized that there should be a system for evaluating "sight records," i.e., those for which no corroborating specimen or photograph could be obtained. Such a standard became all the more necessary with the exponential increase in the number of competent (and incompetent) field observers and with the increasing prohibitions, both legal and moral, against shooting birds in most places.

The main criteria which have evolved over the years for the consideration of sight records are: (1) That the record be within some parameter of possibility. A novice may be heard to explain his report of a non-migratory Andean endemic in his backyard in Texas by saying: "Well, birds fly, don't they?" The fact is that, without in any way belittling birds' well-documented capacity for long-distance travel, a James' Flamingo in El Paso is either an escape or a mistake. (2) The competence and reputation of the observer. Field identification is an acquired skill; the more accomplished the observer, the more credible his records, especially if he is known to be "reliable." It may surpass the imagination of the uninitiated to contemplate an adult human being getting any satisfaction out of "fudging" the identification of a bird, but unfortunately the phenomenon is by no means rare even among birders of known competence. (3) Corroboration from other witnesses. The more competence and reliability present, the better, especially since two people with impeccable credentials in field identification have been known to stand side by side, look at the same bird, and call it a different species. (4) Previous experience with the species in question as well as the species it might be confused with. If you have studied birds in both Australia and North America, your record of a Sharp-tailed Sandpiper in New Jersey is more credible. (5) Field notes and sketches. In this, British birders have far outstripped their American counterparts. Even the most distinguished British field ornithologist would not expect to have his record of a rare bird considered for acceptance without submitting detailed notes—preferably with a sketch indicating the basis for his identification and *made on the spot without reference to guides.* Details such as weather conditions and power of optical equipment are also relevant. In the U.S. it is often considered insulting to question a sight record, especially one made by someone who has more than 600 species on his life list, and the field notebook is practically unknown here. As a result, a great many erroneous records slip into our literature. (6) An evaluation committee to pass judgment on all of the above.

See BIRDWATCHING.

VERMILION (Flycatcher). A vivid red hue on the yellow rather than the blue side of the spectrum. Not very different from scarlet and, like most color descriptions, used rather loosely (though not incorrectly) in English bird names. Only the *adult male* Vermilion Flycatcher is largely brilliant red. See Plate 4.

VERREAUX (vair-OH), Jules Pierre, 1807–73 (*Leptotila verreauxi*: White-tipped [-fronted] Dove). A widely traveled French naturalist who, along with his brother, established in Paris the Maison Verreaux, "one of the greatest, if not the greatest emporium of natural history the world has ever seen" (quoted by Gruson, 1972–BIOGRAPHY). As a youth Verreaux studied with Baron Cuvier, collected an impressive number of specimens during his peregrinations, and applied himself seriously to taxonomic work in Paris. He seems never to have traveled in the Americas. The largely Neotropical dove was named by a fellow French naturalist, Charles Lucien BONAPARTE.

VEXILLUM (VEK-sill-um). Synonymous with "web" or "vane" of a feather. See FEATHER and Fig. 9.

V FORMATION. A distinctive flock configuration in flight, characteristic of certain large water birds, e.g., cormorants, pelicans, cranes, ducks, geese, and swans and sometimes gulls. Conventional wisdom has it that birds flying in V formation (except for the leader) gain additional lift (and perhaps reduced drag) by flying in the "slipstream" of the bird in front. See FLIGHT.

VIBRISSA (vih-BRISS-uh) (pl.: vibrissae). A bristle; in birds such bristles are modified feathers which occur around the gape, nostrils, and eyes. See FEATHER; RICTAL; and Fig. 9.

VIEILLOT (VYEH-yoh), Louis Jean Pierre, 1748–1831. Master taxonomist of France, whose influence on the study of North American birdlife is abundantly recorded throughout its technical nomenclature. He named 26 genera and 32 species of North American birds, a remarkable number of which have not been altered by taxonomic revision, attesting to the acuity of Vieillot's perception. In an obituary, Lesson called him the "dean of ornithologists," but the details of his life are little known. His ornithological career began in the then French colony of Santo Domingo (Hispaniola) but he fled to the U.S. from a revolution on the island. He spent a number of years studying the U.S. avifauna and produced (in French) an early (1807) work on the birds of North America. He also published an illustrated volume on beautiful tropical birds (*Oiseaux Dorés*), an ornithology of France, and a book on mammals. His life was apparently a constant struggle to survive, and Lesson notes that he died "on the brink of poverty."

VIREO (VEER-ee-oh). Standard English name for about 25 of the approximately 40 members of the family Vireonidae (order Passeriformes) and the collective term for the family as a whole. The smaller members of the vireo family are known as greenlets. Depending on taxonomy, 11 or 12 species of vireos breed in North America and 1 other has been recorded as an accidental straggler (see Appendix II). Recent chemical analysis (Sibley and Ahlquist, 1982) has confirmed that the vireos are not closely related to the wood warblers or other New World 9-primaried oscines, but should be placed near the drongos and cuckoo-shrikes.

The vireos are all small (4 to 6½ inches) songbirds, typically with a rather heavy, hooked bill, large head, and moderately short tail. They are generally dull-plumaged (olives, grays, browns), but some have patches of bright yellow and a few have white, yellow, or red irises. They are arboreal birds of woodland and scrub, where they actively (though more deliberately than wood warblers) glean foliage for insects and other small invertebrate food. They are also known to take small vertebrates (e.g., small lizards) and regularly eat berries.

Most vireo songs are abrupt, distinctive, whistled phrases, but some are more extended and "warbling."

The nests of all vireos are cups suspended from forks of narrow branches. They tend to be tidy structures, woven of grasses, fibers, and hair and bound with spider silk. The site may be as low as 2 feet in dense shrubbery or 60 feet up in a tall tree. Eggs normally number 3–5 (rarely 2) and are either immaculate white or sparsely marked with dark brown or black spots. The vireo family is restricted to the New World and reaches its greatest diversity in the Neotropics. In North America, vireos are distributed from the subarctic to the subtropics. All but one species (Hutton's) are migratory at least from the northern parts of their breeding range, and most winter in the tropics.

Aristotle apparently used the Latin word *vireo*, from the verb *virere*, "to be green," to refer to the Eurasian Greenfinch. The name was next used by VIEILLOT as the Latin genus for the birds presently called vireos. This is fair enough, as most vireos are as green as greenfinches, i.e., not very.

VIRGINIA Anderson (Virginia's Warbler: *Vermivora virginiae*). Spencer BAIRD named this warbler for the wife of the army surgeon who sent him the specimen of this dry-country species. Dr. William Wallace Anderson collected his wife's warbler near Fort Burgwyn, New Mexico, c. 1858. For other army doctors who played a significant role in American ornithology—a small army of their own—see BIOGRAPHY and Hume (1942–BIOGRAPHY).

VISION. The vertebrate eye is a very complex organ about which much remains to be learned. This entry is restricted to some conspicuous peculiarities of the avian eye and its function in comparison with the human eye. However, a rudimentary description of how vision works for both men and birds will be useful in understanding some of the details described.

The eye of higher animals is a modified sphere, most of which is concealed from view within the eye sockets (orbits) of the skull. Covering the surface of the part of the eye through which we see is a layered transparent membrane called the *cornea*. Beneath the cornea is a (usually) round, col-

ored membrane, the *iris*, with a hole in the middle, the *pupil*. The iris is
made up of muscle fibers which control the size of the pupil and thus the
amount of light allowed into the eye. Beneath the iris is an ovoid *lens*, behind which is a clear gelatinous mass, the *vitreous* (glass-like) *body* or
humor, which takes up the greatest part of the eye's interior. Lining
the back wall of the eye is a layered membrane of nerve fibers (formed
by the expansion of the optic nerve) called the *retina*. The eye is connected
to the brain by the optic nerve and its movements are controlled by a
complex of external muscles.

Light rays entering the eye are refracted (bent) by the cornea and
again by the lens, which also focuses the incoming image. The image
passes through the vitreous body (with little or no further refraction) and is
projected upside down on the sensitive retina. One layer of the retina is
made up of perceptor cells, called rods and cones because of their shape.
The rods are effective in perceiving low levels of light, as in night vision;
the cones permit perception of detail and color in high levels of light.
Cones are distributed relatively sparsely over the retina except in depressions (usually one to each eye, but see below) called *foveae*, where fine
cones are closely concentrated to perceive the sharpest details of an image.

THE AVIAN EYE IN GENERAL. Before offering generalities, it should
first be noted that there is an enormous variation among eyes of different
kinds of birds, so that the eye of a Dickcissel is as different from the eye of
a goshawk as either is from the eye of an owl or a human. Nevertheless, it
is broadly accurate to say that birds have proportionately very large eyes
and acute vision and depend on this sense more than any other.

Though we normally see only a small portion of them, a bird's eyes
take up far more room than any other part of its head; certain large predators have eyes as large as or larger than man's; and it has been stated that
the Ostrich's eyes (diameter 2 inches) may be the largest of all terrestrial
vertebrates. Another oft-quoted measure of avian eye size is that the eyes
frequently outweigh the brain—but in view of the limited capacity of a
bird's brain, this is perhaps less impressive.

There is much disagreement about various types of visual competence (resolution, light sensitivity, focusing, etc.) in birds as compared
with humans. There is no doubt, however, that *some* birds "see better"
than we do—how much better is disputed—and that some have specialized powers—highly developed night vision, good accommodation underwater—which we lack. It may also be true that many passerine species in a
general sense see less well than we do. Some details are discussed below.

Birds require sight to find food, to orient themselves when traveling,
and to perform basic functions, such as landing and flying between trees
rather than into them. Other senses may assist these actions but cannot
compensate for blindness. A bird which has lost both eyes is doomed,
though there are cases of apparently healthy birds surviving with just one.

ABILITY TO DISTINGUISH DETAIL, technically called "visual acuity" or "resolving power," is best developed in birds (e.g., flycatchers and hawks) which must be able to see very small (or distant) moving objects. Birds with high acuity tend to have relatively large eyes with flat lenses at a greater distance from the retina—a combination which allows the projection of a larger image—and a very high concentration of cones in the foveae. It is widely published and repeated that the most keen-eyed day-flying raptors have resolving power *eight* times greater than that of a human, but this is probably an exaggeration. By comparing the number of cones in the foveae of raptors (about 1 million per sq. mm.) with the human concentration (a mere 200,000 per sq. mm.), some authorities deduce that the disparity may be only ×5; and others contend (for different reasons) that ×2 or ×3 is more like it. If you try to imagine seeing twice or three times "as well"—i.e., acutely—as you now do, the visual competence of hawks and their relatives remains sufficiently impressive even by the most conservative standards. In fact, it is probably the most highly developed eyesight that exists.

The range of visual acuity in other types of birds ranges from significantly (perhaps ×2 to ×3) poorer than ours to measurably—but not dramatically—better.

LIGHT-GATHERING ABILITY, or "visual sensitivity," makes it possible to see well when very little light is present. It is most highly evolved in owls but is present to a significant degree (i.e., greater than in humans) in a great many birds. The eyes of owls are large and elongated (tubular) with comparatively wide corneal and lens surfaces, allowing a maximum amount of light to reach the retina. As would be expected, the concentration of light-sensitive rods is very high; cones are proportionately few, which means that owls have low visual acuity compared to day-flying raptors. (Rods and cones tend to be present in inverse proportions.)

Contrary to what is sometimes supposed, owls cannot see prey in total darkness and at least some species depend heavily on sound as well as sight. It is also a mistake to believe that nocturnal owls are "blind," or nearly so, during the day simply because they are inactive; the visual acuity, at least of some species, is better than ours, night or day.

Night vision in birds, though in general superior to humans', usually takes longer to "turn on"—perhaps an hour or more as compared to about 10 minutes for us.

Birds which make deep dives (e.g., loons) have increased rods for finding prey in nearly sunless depths.

FOCUSING, or "accommodation," is the ability to retain a sharp image at varying distances or under changing refractory conditions. It is mainly achieved by muscular action on the lens, stretching it flatter for seeing into the distance, making it more convex for examining the foreground. The cornea may also be moved in this way for focusing in a few birds, notably raptors.

A wide range of accommodation and the ability to focus rapidly are of special importance to fast-flying birds and particularly to those which make fast dives from the air to catch prey. Species such as cormorants, which make long dives underwater, must be able to focus through water was well as air. Birds with such special needs may have a focal range five times that of humans, but the capacity of more sedentary land birds may be less than or about equal to ours.

The chief factors which allow exceptional powers of accommodation in birds are (1) high development in the muscle apparatus (ciliary body) which controls the shape of the lens; (2) a very soft lens; and (3) a ring of small overlapping bones, the scleral ossicles (sclerotic ring), which stabilizes the eyeball while the lens is being pushed and squeezed.

Terns, which dive on fish from the air, cannot focus underwater and must rely on a "preset" aim. Penguins, by contrast, see well *only* in the water, where their eyes have evolved to follow fast-swimming fish.

SIZE OF FIELD AND DEPTH AND DISTANCE PERCEPTION. How much of the surrounding visible sphere one sees at a given time, the sense of three-dimensionality, and judgment of relative distances depend on where the eyes are placed in the head, the extent to which they can be moved, and the ability (or lack of it) to turn the neck.

Human eyes are located close together in the front of the head. We therefore command a relatively narrow total field without moving the eyes or turning the neck. This field is significantly enlarged if we turn the neck without moving the rest of the body, but it is still by no means total. Because we receive a slightly different image in each eye, and the two images are combined by the brain (binocular vision), we readily perceive the depth as well as the length and width of objects (stereoscopic vision) and can tell how far away things are and the degree to which they get closer as we approach them. The field of binocular vision is, of course, always narrower than the total field, but the ratio of one to the other varies among different animals according to eye placement and other factors.

The eyes of owls are placed like humans' and have similar field (110° total; 70° binocular) and depth and distance perception. The fact that their eyes are rigidly fixed in their sockets is compensated for by an extraordinarily mobile neck. (This is true to a lesser extent of most birds.) The eyes of day-flying raptors are set somewhat more to the sides, so that their total field is wider (about 250°), but their binocular field is reduced to 35° to 50°. The eyes of most birds, however, are placed almost opposite each other on either side of the head. This gives them an enormous total field (up to 340°) but a very narrow binocular field (as low as 6° with an average of about 20° to 25°). Most birds, then, see most things with only one eye and have little depth perception. This may explain why ground-feeding birds will often cock their heads sideways—to see if that is really a seed or just a yellow spot on the ground—and why shorebirds (and others) turn one eye to the sky to appraise the threat posed by a form passing over, rather than cock their necks backward as we would do. It may also explain why some birds bob their heads when a potential threat approaches—to get a quick double-angle fix on an object in order to gauge its form and distance.

No discussion of visual field is complete without mentioning the woodcocks and the bitterns. The large eyes of the former are so set in the skull that except for small "blind spots" directly in front and behind, their visual field is nearly total, even including the area directly above them; this may be an adaptation for perceiving danger from above. The eyes of bitterns, on the other hand, are angled downward when the head is horizontal—so that they can see food on the ground without cocking or nodding the head—and forward when the head is upraised in their characteristic cryptic "freeze" posture. If you think this is easy, try looking someone in the face while your nose is pointed to the ceiling.

SEEING COLOR. Day-flying birds generally see a color spectrum similar to the one we see. Some, however, have colored oil droplets ranging from yellow to red on the retina which act as filters, shutting out some (not all) of the blue/violet values and increasing sensitivity to yellow/red; it is interesting in this context to note the high percentage of avian display features which are yellow/red. The droplets also help to cut glare.

Because color is perceived by the cones, nocturnal birds which have relatively few are believed to be color-blind.

The speculation that owls can perceive infrared light and thus "see" the heat generated by their prey in the "dark" is unproven.

IRIS COLOR AND "EYESHINE." Birds, of course, have no eye "whites" as do humans, and eye color (exclusive of external eye rings) is that of the iris. In most birds the iris is dark brown or black, but a significant number of species have colored eyes. In some cases this color is sexually dimorphic—males having the brighter color—and bright eye color is usually characteristic of adult birds and may heighten during the breeding season.

The function of iris color is undetermined but it may play a part in display.

"Eyeshine" is a brilliant red or yellow (more rarely white or pale green) reflection emanating from the eyes of some birds (especially members of the nightjar family) when a light hits them. The familiar shine from the eyes of cats and other mammals is produced by a thin iridescent surface behind the retina called a tapetum. This feature is absent in birds, however, and both the origin and the function of avian eyeshine remain mysterious.

OTHER FEATURES unique to or conspicuous in the avian eye deserve brief mention.

The Nictitating Membrane lies under the main eyelids of all birds and moves across the cornea at an angle from the lower inside of the eyeball (near the bill) to the upper outside. It is transparent in most birds (exceptions among nocturnal species) and used for regularly moistening the eye and perhaps for protection in the same way that we use our outer eyelids. (Birds rarely close their eyelids except to sleep.) The nictitating membrane of some diving birds is modified to aid accommodation underwater. It has been suggested that the transparent membrane may act as a "windshield" for birds in flight.

Frogs, all reptiles, and some mammals also have nictitating membranes.

The Pecten is a small membranous organ filled with blood vessels which is attached to the optic nerve and extends out into the vitreous body. It is unique to birds. A great many theories have been advanced as to its function—the most plausible having to do with supplying sustenance to the retina—but none is conclusive.

Pupil Dilation in most animals is an involuntary function performed by the nervous system in conjunction with the iris muscles in response to the amount of light available. The pupils of birds open and close in a rapid and complex manner, but not particularly in response to light changes, and it has been suspected, but not proved, that the pupils of birds may be under voluntary control.

VISITOR (visitant). See SUMMER VISITOR; WINTER VISITOR.

VOCALIZATION. See SONG.

VOICE OF AUDUBON. The first automated telephone answering service to give details of recent bird occurrences. It was begun by the Massachusetts Audubon Society in November 1954. The original "voice" was that of Ruth Emery, a pillar of the venerable Massachusetts birding establishment. It has always been traditional for the Voice of Audubon to relay reports of common as well as rare birds, thereby conveying, however sketchily, the avian "state of the state" to callers. Some RARE BIRD ALERTS ignore the "trash birds" and concentrate on giving specific directions for finding rarities and up-to-the-minute accounts of their whereabouts. Such recordings are thus more of a service to "hard-core listers" than to the bird-loving community at large.

VOLANT (VOH-lunt). Capable of flight. A bird, like a bat or bee, is a volant organism; also, rarely, rather poetically, "in flight," "on the wing."

VULTURE. Standard English name for 5 of the 7 members of the family Cathartidae (order Falconiformes); the two largest members of this family are called CONDORS. The cathartids are the New World vultures, confined in distribution to the Americas, and are not to be confused with the Old World vultures, which belong to the family Accipitridae (order Falconiformes) along with the hawks and eagles, and are restricted to the Old World. Two species of vultures (Black and Turkey) breed in North America in addition to the California Condor. There is a detailed old record of the Neotropical King Vulture by the distinguished botanist William BARTRAM from southern Florida in 1774–75, but it is difficult to interpret the former status of the species here (if any) based on a single report. There is also a 1968 sight record of this species from Arizona.

The New World vultures are large birds (2 to nearly 4 feet in length), the California Condor having the greatest wingspan (to 9½ feet) of any North American land bird (see SIZE). They have broad as well as long wings adapted for slow soaring over wide areas in search of their preferred food, carrion. Their heads are unfeathered, a trait which doubtless evolved from their habit of probing with their heads into the greasy, decomposing entrails of carcasses. Except for the Black Vulture, members of this family have fairly heavy bills for tearing flesh, but all have weak feet unsuitable for grasping prey. In addition to carrion, garbage, and offal, vultures will occasionally take weak (i.e., young or injured) live animals, some fruit, and in rare cases will kill a healthy small animal. It has finally been proven that Turkey Vultures do find at least some of their food by scent (see SMELL), though other cathartids are less talented in this regard. Though many people regard "buzzards" as unsavory, these scavengers do yeomanly service as unpaid garbage men. Brown and Amadon (1968–HAWK) opine that the Black Vulture probably has the largest total population of any bird of prey in the Western Hemisphere.

Vultures sometimes nest in small, loose groupings. They make no nest but lay their egg(s) in a cave, rock crevice, hollow tree trunk, stump, or on the ground under the cover of vegetation. The eggs may be moved within the general nesting area. Black and Turkey Vultures lay 2 (rarely 1 or 3), off-white, yellowish, buff, gray, or greenish eggs, sparsely to rather densely marked with reddish or dark brown speckles and splotches. The California Condor lays a single white to pale green/blue egg—the largest of any North American bird (see EGG).

Vocal apparatus is almost totally lacking in the vultures, and it is therefore unsurprising that they are normally silent and only rarely utter faint hisses, grunts, and barks—usually when alarmed.

As a family the vultures range nearly throughout the Nearctic and Neotropical regions (excepting the highest latitudes) and over almost all biomes. The northern distribution of the Turkey Vulture stops roughly at the southern edge of the Canadian Zone coniferous forests; the Black Vulture's center of abundance here is more to the south and east.

The name was taken from the distantly related Old World vultures, which our species resemble in general form and habits. The word derives from the Latin infinitive *vellere*, "to tear," and the noun *vultur*, which referred to the accipitrid vultures of Europe.

W

WADERS. In North America, a little-used word referring collectively to long-legged wading birds such as herons, ibises, storks, etc. In Britain and throughout the rest of the English-speaking world, the standard term for "shorebirds."

WAGTAIL. Standard English name for 12 members of the family Motacillidae (order Passeriformes), all but one in the genus *Motacilla*. The family also includes the pipits and the African longclaws. The wagtails are essentially an Old World group, but 2 species breed in western Alaska, another occurs as a migrant there, and a fourth has been recorded there as a vagrant (see Appendixes I and II).

The wagtails are implausibly slender, graceful, ground-haunting birds, their elongate form accentuated by their characteristic energetic tail wagging. Our species range between 6½ and 7 inches in length. As with other terrestrial birds, their legs are relatively long and sturdy. Adult males of most species are strikingly colored and/or patterned.

The wagtails forage methodically on the ground, typically in open country and mainly for insect food, but also for other small invertebrates (e.g., snails) and fruit.

Wagtail songs, often given on the wing up to several hundred feet above the ground, are generally buzzy or twittery; more often heard are their sharp call notes.

The White Wagtail is comfortable in a wide range of breeding habitats and nest sites. It will build in grass clumps in dunes, in cultivated fields, in rock crevices, walls, niches in buildings, dry pipes, abandoned nests of other bird species, even crevices in an inhabited Osprey nest. The Yellow Wagtail is more particular, preferring a ground site on tundra or grassland, sometimes nestled in shrub roots or under a bank. Both species usually nest near water.

The 3–7 (usually 5–6) eggs are off white (buff, bluish, or grayish), densely and finely speckled with gray or brown (White Wagtail) or buff-brown (Yellow Wagtail).

The North American wagtail populations winter in Southeast Asia. For other facts of distribution, see above. See also PIPIT.

WALKING/RUNNING. The usual manner of locomotion for non-passerine birds on the ground.

Many water birds which are superbly adapted for moving efficiently in the water are extremely awkward when called upon to move on land, as they are during the nesting season. Loons and grebes, with their short legs placed far to the rear, cannot walk on their toes as most birds do (see SKELETON) but must push themselves along on their bellies, giving the impression of having had some injury to their legs.

The shearwaters and large petrels (Procellariidae) and the storm-petrels (Hydrobatidae) must also, as it were, crawl along on their "ankles" when going to and from their nesting burrows, and the upright waddle of the alcids is only slightly more graceful and effective. Primarily aerial birds are also poorly equipped for terrestrial movement. Most hawks, eagles, and falcons manage little more than a slow waddle, though vultures, the Crested Caracara, and a few others have long legs and walk habitually and easily. The legs and feet of swifts and hummingbirds are practically non-existent (hence the name of their order, Apodiformes, which denotes foot-lessness) and they are capable only of clinging and grasping, respectively.

Other non-passerine families with strikingly deficient ambulatory capacity are the tropicbirds, frigatebirds, anhingas, cuckoos (except the road-runners), owls (except the Burrowing and Barn), nightjars, trogons, and kingfishers. The remaining species walk adequately (some, e.g., pelicans, boobies, and swans, barely so) to skillfully.

The gallinaceous birds (chachalacas, turkeys, grouse, quail, and pheasants), the rails, and the roadrunners should perhaps be singled out as species which often prefer to walk (or run) from danger rather than fly. These and the long-legged waders (storks, herons, ibises, and cranes), the shorebirds, and most of the doves also walk a great deal while feeding.

Most passerines hop rather than walk (see HOPPING); however, there are the following noteworthy exceptions: most corvids (jays do both), the Horned Lark, pipits and wagtails, starlings, the ground-haunting icterids (meadowlarks, grackles, etc.), and the Savannah Sparrow.

Though many birds run, either from danger or in the course of feeding (e.g., the Snowy Egret, yellowlegs), only one species can be referred to with any conviction as a "running bird." The Greater Roadrunner has been clocked at speeds of up to 15 m.p.h. and uses this talent rather than flight to catch fast-moving prey such as small rodents and reptiles.

The physiology of avian walking is quite different from that of humans. In order to maintain our balance when one foot is off the ground, we use muscle contractions from the hip to shift our center of gravity over one leg or the other. Birds keep their balance by rotating their lower leg inward at the knee to place their foot under their center line. This motion is easily seen in the "pigeon-toed" waddle of an oncoming goose.

Many birds that walk habitually—especially the gallinaceous birds and doves—accompany their strides with a pronounced, synchronous back-and-forth head-bobbing motion that allows the head to remain effectively motionless for most of the time that the bird is moving and thus allows it to see food and predators more effectively while walking. The plovers may achieve the same end with their characteristic run-and-stop locomotion.

See also LEG/FOOT; HOPPING.

WARBLER. See OLD WORLD WARBLER (family Sylviidae); WOOD WARBLER (family Parulidae).

WATER BIRD. A term of convenience, without taxonomic or other scientific significance, for birds that habitually frequent fresh or salt water, including many species, e.g., certain shorebirds, that feed at the water's edge but never (or rarely) wade, swim, or dive. It excludes certain water-haunting species: the Osprey, kingfishers, dippers, and waterthrushes are not generally called "water birds," though they are more closely associated with aquatic habitats than some species that are so called. The water-bird families represented in North America are: the loons, grebes, albatrosses, shearwaters, storm-petrels, tropicbirds, pelicans, frigatebirds, gannets and boobies, cormorants, anhingas, ducks, geese, and swans, herons, storks (many largely terrestrial), ibises and spoonbills, flamingos, cranes, Limpkin, rails, oystercatchers, stilts and avocets, plovers (several largely terrestrial), sandpipers, phalaropes, jaegers, gulls and terns, skimmers, and auks.

See also SEABIRD; PELAGIC; SWIMMING/DIVING; LAND BIRD.

WATERFOWL. In North America, the ducks, geese, and swans collectively; the members of the family Anatidae. Used both more and less specifically elsewhere in the English-speaking world. Compare WILDFOWL; WATER BIRD.

WATERTHRUSH. Standard English name for 2 of the 3 members of the wood warbler genus *Seiurus* (family Parulidae; order Passeriformes). Despite their, phylogeny, the waterthrushes are named aptly enough. They frequent watery habitats, particularly forest streams and rivers, and their coloration and preference for shady situations suggest the true thrushes (family Turdidae).

Like other birds which frequent running-water habitats, the waterthrushes bob their tails continuously. The "reason" behind this characteristic is imperfectly understood, but it may enhance the cryptic effect of the waterthrushes against the changing pattern of moving water (see Plate 3).

For family characteristics, see WOOD WARBLER.

WATTLE. Any of a variety of fleshy or leathery, unfeathered, usually wrinkled or warty processes on the head of a bird (or reptile). These are often brightly colored, particularly during courtship rituals (see DISPLAY).

Though the red patch on the face of the cock Common Pheasant may be referred to as a wattle, the word often implies a pendulous quality, e.g., the dangling folds of skin which hang from the throat and neck of the Wild Turkey. Few North American birds have wattles, but the phenomenon is characteristic of certain groups in other avifaunas.

WAVE. A birdwatching term which refers to an abundance of migrant land birds of many species putting down in a particular locality. Since bird migration tends to coincide with the passage of weather fronts, the metaphor is not inappropriate. At favorable localities and under the right weather conditions, a "warbler wave" can be a truly spectacular event, particularly in spring, with thousands of birds in brilliant plumage and stunning variety all vying for tree space or even "littering the ground."

WAXWING. See Fig. 23. Standard English name for all 3 members of the family Bombycillidae (order Passeriformes) as well as for the family as a whole. The unique Hypocolius of arid Middle Eastern scrublands is sometimes included. Two species of waxwings breed in North America.

The waxwings are all rather similar in appearance, with a smooth, elegant form; short, fairly thick bill; crested head; and short legs with two of the forward-pointing toes (III and IV) joined at the base. The wings are fairly long and pointed, the tail of medium length with a squared end. The basic plumage coloration is soft browns and grays highlighted with areas of red, yellow, and/or white.

Waxwings typically feed and travel in flocks when not nesting.. They are mainly (and voraciously) frugivorous (berries, crab apples) but are highly competent "flycatchers" during the warmer seasons and feed their young exclusively on insects. The most commonly heard sound waxwings make is a high, thin, almost whispering monotone.

Waxwing nests are cups made from twigs, grasses, fruticose lichens, etc., and lined with pine needles, fine fibers, and/or plant down. The site is usually 5 feet or more up in a tree. The 3–5 (rarely 6) eggs are pale bluish gray with sparse to moderately heavy "ink spots" as well as paler subsurface spots.

As a family, the waxwings breed throughout the northern Holarctic region. The Bohemian Waxwing is an almost cosmopolitan resident of boreal forest/taiga; the Cedar Waxwing replaces it to the south (in North America only) and winters as far as northern South America. Waxwings are somewhat nomadic; one can expect Cedar Waxwings to appear unexpectedly at any season, and Bohemian Waxwings are given to irregular "irruptions" south of the Subarctic. These movements are at least partially related to food availability (see IRRUPTION; NOMADISM).

"Waxwing" refers to the brightly colored (red or yellow) waxy secretions produced at the tips of the secondary feathers and to a lesser extent on the tail tip. What function these peculiar decorations serve, if any, is unknown.

WEATHER. In the broadest sense of climatic conditions, weather has been one of the formative influences of the planet, profoundly affecting EVOLUTION, DISTRIBUTION, ABUNDANCE, and species diversity, not only of birdlife but of the entire world biota. However, this entry concentrates on the immediate effects of present-day weather conditions on various aspects of birdlife.

OUTRIGHT DESTRUCTION. Severe weather conditions not infrequently kill birds directly. Hailstorms have been responsible for the deaths of vast numbers of birds, for example: more than 1,000 Sandhill Cranes in 30 minutes (Merrill, 1961), 148,000 waterfowl in Alberta over a 2½-month period (Smith and Webster, 1955), and 2 California Condors (Rett, 1938). Lightning is known to have dispatched flying birds (Zimmer, 1951). Freezing rain or mist occasionally traps prairie chickens under the snow, where they habitually roost on winter nights (Linsay, 1967). Tornadoes can destroy up to 96 percent of breeding-bird populations locally (McClure, 1945). And of course sudden or unseasonable shifts in temperature, wind, or precipitation often fatally complicate bird migration or breeding success (see below).

EFFECT ON FOOD SUPPLY. Many kinds of insects, especially flying forms (e.g., odonata, diptera, hymenoptera) that make up a significant part of the diet of flycatchers, warblers, and other insectivores, cannot survive below certain temperatures and are inactive below others. Their availability as food is also greatly reduced by strong winds or heavy precipitation. Unseasonable cold or drought can also adversely affect supplies of plant foods such as nectar, fruits, and seeds. Heavy snow cover may make it difficult or impossible for ground-feeding birds (e.g., gallinaceous species, doves, sparrows) to reach their food supply. And the freezing of water cuts off usual food sources for such birds as herons, rails, and many species of waterfowl. Many of these effects in turn influence bird movements (see below).

EFFECT ON BREEDING SUCCESS. Nesting is often timed to coincide with the availability of a food source necessary for nourishing young (see NEST). In unusually cold seasons, reduced food supplies may result in a smaller percentage of young birds surviving. This is especially true in the short summers of the Arctic, when breeding shorebirds and other species depend on a few weeks of warm weather during which insect food is abundant. Less usually, cold and wet weather can be the proximate cause of bird deaths (see, for example, Stewart, 1972).

EFFECT ON BIRD MOVEMENTS. In many instances, bird migrants

take advantage of beneficial weather conditions. Major migration routes tend to coincide closely with patterns of favorable upper-level winds that both guide migrants and help them conserve energy. Conversely, contrary winds or severe storms may drive birds far from their normal range or migratory course and sometimes cause "wrecks" involving the deaths of many thousands of birds (see MORTALITY). Migrants dependent on favorable winds for guidance are known to follow winds blowing in the "wrong" direction to their doom (see MIGRATION). Clouds obscuring the sky can also cause disorientation in migrants dependent on celestial NAVIGATION, and fog or low ceiling is usually implicated in the deaths of small migrants that are attracted to or blunder into radio towers or illuminated office buildings. Bagg (1967) has plausibly demonstrated how exceptionally cold weather in western Europe coinciding with broad transatlantic depressions apparently carries Northern Lapwings to the Newfoundland/St. Lawrence region, but seldom farther south. Arrival times of migrants in northern areas coincide with the onset of mean temperatures at which insect food becomes available in life-sustaining quantity.

The effect of weather on fluctuations in crops such as conifer seeds indirectly influences the irregular movements of certain birds, e.g., winter finches (see IRRUPTION).

EFFECT ON FLIGHT. Because of specialized physical adaptations, large seabirds such as albatrosses are dependent to a great extent on wind to travel over their marine habitat (see FLIGHT, *Dynamic Soaring*). Hawks, vultures, storks, and other birds that depend on soaring to find food and migrate require thermals, which are best generated on sunny days (see FLIGHT, *Thermal Soaring*); such birds are at a severe disadvantage in dark, cold, rainy weather. As implied above, small birds and weak fliers (e.g., Dovekies) occasionally find themselves at the mercy of severe windstorms.

EFFECT ON BIRDWATCHING. It is well known that some of the best birdwatching takes place in the worst of weather conditions. Onshore gales along the coast routinely drive large numbers of pelagic species within easy "scoping" distance. Along the Gulf coast of Texas, birders are alert to storms (see NORTHER) that force exhausted land-bird migrants to seek the first available refuge after making the long flight across the Gulf of Mexico in the spring. At times, incredible numbers of migrants crowd a few stands of live oaks or even "crash" on coastal roads and dunes, unable to proceed inconspicuously inland as they would do under favorable conditions.

Days on which the sun's rays penetrate a thin, low overcast may be the ideal hawk-watching conditions, providing enough ground-warming heat to create thermals (see above) but not enough to permit the birds to disappear into the firmament; a uniform cloud cover also makes it easier to locate groups of migrating raptors.

Because of the above-mentioned effect on insect life, rain can put a damper on watching warblers and other insectivorous species. But far worse is wind, which above a certain velocity can reduce song and activity almost to zero.

Feeder attendance becomes frantic before storms and is usually much improved when a snowfall covers other food sources.

For further details of the relationship between weather and birdlife, see MIGRATION; MORTALITY.

WEAVERBIRD, WEAVER FINCH. Standard English names for about 70 members of the family Ploceidae (order Passeriformes), which in some taxonomies incorporates the waxbills, grass finches, mannikins, and whydahs, otherwise classified separately in the family Estrildidae (waxbill or weaver finch family) or elsewhere. "Weaverbird" usually signifies the Ploceidae with weavers and waxbills combined.

The only relevance of these taxonomic and nomenclatural tangles to North America is that (1) waxbill finches are among the most popular birds to be kept as pets here (see AVICULTURE) and (2) two species of weavers, the Eurasian Tree Sparrow and the House (or English) Sparrow, have been "successfully" introduced. The latter are sometimes placed in a smaller family, the Passeridae (Old World sparrows).

In view of the mundaneness of our two alien-resident weavers, it is worth noting that many members of their family (no matter how defined) are highly attractive birds, boldly colored and patterned. Many weavers breed in colonies and construct large, elaborate (and handsome!) nests.

The House Sparrow (see INTRODUCED BIRDS for its North American history) is a small (average 6 inches), rather stocky songbird with a moderately large head, conical seed-eating bill, short legs, and tail of medium length. On the whole, it is an unimposing little creature, though the optimists among us are often at pains to point out how handsome we we would find the males if only the species weren't so damnably abundant.

The House Sparrow is arguably *the* wild bird of the urban habitat— wilder than pigeons and far more integrated with town life than starlings. They thrive on potato-chip crumbs, spilled popcorn, and other detritus of the city streets and in suburbia find crabgrass and other grass seeds and of course bird feeders very much to their taste. To their credit, they also consume significant numbers of cutworms, aphids, Japanese beetles, and other insect pests.

The species rarely sings extended songs but cheeps ("cheerfully" to some ears) almost continually.

House Sparrows occasionally nest in tree cavities, but, as their name implies, what they have come to prefer are niches in human habitations and birdhouses. Notably undiscriminating in their choice of nesting material, they will use grass, cloth, paper, cotton, feathers, etc., in which to lay their 3–5 (exceptionally 8) white or pale green, sparsely to densely marked eggs. Occasionally they will build a globular nest with a side entrance in conifers, tangled vegetation (e.g., ivy vines), or even an Osprey nest. After breeding, House Sparrows roost and feed in flocks—sometimes large ones.

From its native range in northern Eurasia the House Sparrow has been transported by man nearly worldwide. It is now present wherever enough dwellings are gathered to deserve the name "town," including communities on remote islands such as the Falklands in the South Atlantic Ocean.

The Eurasian Tree Sparrow belongs to the same genus (*Passer*) as the House Sparrow and resembles it in most aspects of appearance and behavior. However, it is not nearly so fond of humanity. It breeds in tree cavities and rocky crevices and (in Europe at least) prefers abandoned country houses to inhabited city ones. It is also native to Eurasia. It was introduced in St. Louis, Missouri, in the 1870's, and has remained a local resident in eastern Missouri and neighboring Illinois.

For derivation of "sparrow," see SPARROW.

WEB. An alternative name for the vane or vexillum of a feather, as, for example, "the inner or outer webs of the primaries." Also the flexible skin connecting the toes in various groups of water birds. See FEATHER; LEG/FOOT; and Figs. 9, 11, and 25.

WEIGHT. See SIZE.

WETMORE, Alexander, 1886–1978. Arguably the most versatile and prolific of all American ornithologists, Alexander Wetmore began modestly enough as a boy naturalist from North Freedom, Wisconsin. But he soon showed the promise of a distinguished future by publishing his first ornithological paper (on Red-headed Woodpecker behavior) at the age of thirteen. After earning a B.A. at the University of Kansas, he went to Washington, D.C., where he naturally fell in with Robert RIDGWAY and his circle of eminent zoologists at the National Museum. Wetmore took his Ph.D. at Georgetown University and four years after (1924) was appointed Assistant Secretary of the Smithsonian Institution, head of the National Museum. Like other ornithologists of his stature, Wetmore presided over a number of professional organizations (president of the American Ornithologists' Union, 1926–29) and received his share of awards. But the real measure of his career is his bibliography, which includes authoritative papers on avian physiology, pathology, behavior, distribution, migration, taxonomy, and paleontology (155 titles on the last subject alone). He also wrote the text for several popular bird books published by the National Geographic Society (see the Bibliography under BIRD), but his magnum opus in book form is his four-volume *Birds of the Republic of Panama* (Smithsonian Misc. Coll. No. 150), for which he displayed his considerable skill as a field man and on which he was working at the time of his sudden death at the age of ninety-two; the last volume is currently being edited for publication by Wetmore's colleagues at the Smithsonian. See also the Bibliography under EVOLUTION OF BIRDLIFE and TAXONOMY.

WHEATEAR. Standard English name for about 21 species of small thrushes in the genus *Oenanthe* (family Turdidae or Muscicapidae). Only one of these, *the* Wheatear or Northern Wheatear, *Oenanthe oenanthe*, occurs in North America. It seems to have reached the eastern Canadian Arctic (at least as far west as the Boothia Peninsula) from the east via Greenland—and Alaska from the Palearctic. The eastern population follows the European population south to Africa in the winter; the Alaskan population winters in southern Asia.

One explanation of the name makes a case for the species' fondness for wheat, but wheatears are largely insectivorous, and while they occasionally eat fruits and seeds, it seems unlikely that their fondness for wheat grains would stand out as characteristic. A much more plausible theory relates to the strikingly white rump of the Northern Wheatear and all its relatives. This holds that "wheatear" is a corruption of "white arse." For family characteristics, see THRUSH.

WHIMBREL (WIM-brul). Standard English name for a single species of CURLEW, *Numenius phaeopus* (family Scolopacidae; order Charadriiformes), which has a Holarctic breeding range and winters in most of the other regions of the world. For general characteristics of the family, see SANDPIPER.

The name supposedly derives from a call which sounds like "whim," but this is not the species' usual call, a lonely plaintive fluting which more resembles "curlew."

WHIP-POOR-WILL. Standard English name for a single species of nightjar, *Caprimulgus vociferus*, which breeds from central and eastern Canada south to the highlands of Honduras. The name is an approximation of its call.

Another species of nightjar, *Caprimulgus ridgwayi*, just reaches North America in southwestern Arizona and New Mexico. It is sometimes called Ridgway's Whip-poor-will, but in view of the fact that its call does not sound at all like "whip-poor-will" and that two other English names are available and widely used throughout the greater part of its range, one of these latter may be preferable. They are: Buff-collared Nightjar and Cookacheea. Irby Davis' consistency in naming nightjars for their distinctive calls seems well considered (see his *Field Guide to the Birds of Mexico and Central America*, Austin, 1979).

For family characteristics, see NIGHTJAR.

WHISTLING DUCK. Standard English name for 8 members of the family Anatidae (order Anseriformes), all belonging to the genus *Dendrocygna* and placed in a subfamily (Dendrocygninae) or tribe (Dendrocygnini) of their own. Two species of whistling ducks breed in North America and a third (West Indian Whistling Duck) has been recorded as a straggler in Bermuda.

Until recently, the New World members of the group have traditionally been called "tree ducks," and while this is a misnomer in the majority of cases, one of our species, the Black-bellied Tree Duck, does nest in tree cavities up to 30 feet from the ground and in the American tropics can be seen perching atop giant ceibas of 100 or more feet. Unlike almost all other anatids, the whistling ducks do not line their nests with down—or with anything else.

Whistling ducks are long-necked and long-legged, which gives them a somewhat goose-like appearance, and they also share some behavioral traits with the geese. They are essentially (but not exclusively) a tropical group and are migratory (sometimes erratic) in the northern extremities of their range. They are named for their high-pitched, piping calls.

WHITE-WINGED GULL. A birdwatching term for large gulls which have no black in the tips of the primaries as adults. The term—strictly one of convenience—embraces the Glaucous and Iceland Gulls and, on the west coast, the Glaucous-winged Gull, but not the smaller Ivory Gull, the whitest-winged of all.

WHITNEY, Josiah Dwight, 1819–96 (*Micrathene whitneyi*: Elf Owl). A prominent geologist (founder of the Harvard School of Mines) and early worker on the U.S. Geological Surveys.

WIED (veedt, in German; weed, in North American), Maximilian, Prince of Wied-Neuwied, 1782–1867 (Wied's [Brown] Crested Flycatcher: *Myiarchus tyrannulus*). A German aristocrat, officer (Napoleonic Wars), and naturalist-explorer who pursued his interests in Brazil and North America, collecting thousands of bird and mammal specimens and later writing (brilliantly) of his adventures.

WIGEON (WIDGE-n) (formerly spelled widgeon). Standard English name for 3 species of dabbling ducks in the genus *Anas* (formerly *Mareca*; family Anatidae; order Anseriformes). One of these, the American Wigeon (*A. americana*), breeds exclusively in North America and ranges nearly throughout the continent; it is also widely known as the Baldpate. Another species, the Eurasian Wigeon (*A. penelope*), ranges essentially throughout the Palearctic region, but has occurred annually in small numbers in North America for over half a century at least; despite the strong circumstantial evidence, breeding has never been verified here.

According to Gruson (1972–BIOGRAPHY) "wigeon" may be traceable to a Latin bird name meaning "little crane" (Pliny) and to a later Italian form referring to a "whistling duck." In corroboration of the latter, wigeons do make a characteristic pleasant, high-pitched, piping sound.

For family characteristics, see DUCK.

WILDFOWL. The preferred British term for the ducks, geese, and swans collectively; little used in North America, where WATERFOWL is the preferred synonym.

WILLET. Standard English name for a single species of long-legged sandpiper, *Catoptrophorus semipalmatus*, which breeds exclusively in North America along inland lakes and in east coast salt marshes; it winters along all of our southern coasts and south to Peru and Brazil. A nondescript shorebird at rest, the Willet gains a measure of glamour in flight when it spreads its boldly patterned black-and-white wings. The species' characteristic cry is often rendered as "bill-will-*willet*." For family characteristics, see SANDPIPER.

WILLIAMSON, Robert Stockton, 1824–82 (Williamson's Sapsucker: *Sphyrapicus thyroideus*). West Point graduate, "military engineer," distinguished Civil War veteran, and participant in surveying the railway route to the Pacific (see BAIRD). The woodpecker which bears his name was so designated by one of his junior officers, one Dr. Newbury, yet another of the legion of ornithological "surgeons" of nineteenth-century North America (see BIOGRAPHY).

WILSON, Alexander, 1766–1813 (Wilson's Storm-Petrel: *Oceanites oceanicus*; Wilson's Plover: *Charadrius wilsonia*; Wilson's Phalarope: *Steganopus tricolor*; Wilson's Warbler: *Wilsonia pusilla*). Perhaps even more than CATESBY or AUDUBON, deserving of the title "father of American ornithology." Wilson produced the first comprehensive, systematic, illustrated account of North American birdlife, and the greatest natural history publication to its time in America. His *American Ornithology* in nine volumes was produced between 1808 and 1814, the last two volumes being published posthumously and the final one written by Wilson's friend, patron, and editor, George ORD. The work includes drawings of 320 individual birds in 76 plates, which amount, according to current taxonomy, to about 279 species. Wilson's accomplishment is all the more impressive given his humble beginnings as the son of a weaver in Paisley, Scotland; the interruption of his education at the age of thirteen; his struggles to survive as a surveyor and teacher in Pennsylvania; and his complete ignorance of science and drawing prior to undertaking the writing and illustration of his *Ornithology*. As with Audubon, some clue to his success may be found in his personality. He was a romantic poet in the tradition of Robert Burns and, as he said of himself in a letter to his future engraver, Alexander Lawson of Philadelphia, "long accustomed to the building of Airy Castles and brain Windmills." He was also possessed of strong convictions, which got him jailed in Scotland for writing political poetry in support of mill workers—probably largely responsible for his emigration to America. His personal stubbornness and intolerance of criticism made him a touchy friend but were probably crucial to the completion of his life's work. He was also fortunate in attracting the support of William BARTRAM, prominent botanist and sometime ornithologist of the day; of the famous painter and curator Charles Willson Peale; of Samuel E. Bradford, his employer as editor of *Ree's New Cyclopedia*, who eventually published *American Ornithology*; and of George ORD, the wealthy and influential naturalist of Philadelphia, who championed Wilson's work, acted as his editor, wrote the final volume after Wilson's death, and defended his reputation against Audubon's inferences of ornithological plagiarism.

The famous rivalry between the two artist-naturalists arose (mainly after Wilson's death) from Audubon's assertion that Wilson's "Small-headed Flycatcher" was copied from his own drawing of 1808. Ironically, the controversy centered on an anonymous immature-warbler-like form which no one has seen (or recognized) since Audubon and/or Wilson encountered it. In defending his protégé's scruples, Ord pointed out with undeniable accuracy that a number of Audubon's portraits bear a striking likeness to ones of Wilson. Why Audubon, an infinitely superior draftsman, should have been tempted to copy Wilson is mysterious, but the resemblance between his Bald Eagle (Havell XXXI), his Mississippi Kite (Havell CXVII), and his Red-winged Blackbirds (Havell LXVII) and the indisputably prior drawings by Wilson of these species is beyond coincidence. Wilson died of dysentery and/or tuberculosis.

WILSON BULLETIN, THE. See next entry.

WILSON ORNITHOLOGICAL SOCIETY. A nonprofit organization which promotes the scientific study of birdlife. It was founded in 1902 under its present name, which commemorates Alexander WILSON, one of the several "fathers of American ornithology." Originally a midwestern group, the W.O.S. now has a national, if not international membership. The society publishes a quarterly journal, *The Wilson Bulletin*, containing scientific papers, bird notes of more general interest, book reviews, etc. Membership is open to the public by subscription. See the Bibliography under PERIODICALS for current address.

WINDOW (in wing). A pale, translucent area at the base of the primaries. Such a "window" is, for example, a good field mark for immature Red-shouldered Hawks.

For the relationship between birds and real windows, see PESTS; MAN-MADE THREATS TO BIRDLIFE.

WING. In birds, the front legs or arms modified for flight. By comparison, insect wings evolved from the upper sides of the thorax and have no direct relationship with the limbs., Bat wings, like those of birds, are modified forelimbs but are characterized by great elongation of the bones of the hand and an elastic membrane of skin which stretches not only between the fingers and arm but along the sides of the body and hind legs. The structure of bird wings is restricted to the front limbs, and the bones of the hand, rather than being extended and elaborated, are drastically reduced and/or fused.

BASIC STRUCTURE. See Fig. 19. The wing skeleton consists of an upper arm bone (humerus), two parallel bones (ulna and radius) which make up the forearm, and a wrist/hand arrangement which, as noted, is greatly modified. (For a more detailed analysis of these bones, see SKELE-TON, *Bones of the Wing*.) The wing muscles attached to the bones are analogous to human arm muscles (see MUSCLES) but, of course, strongly modified for flight. Over bone and muscle lies a covering of skin (*ala membrana*) out of which grow the wing feathers.

PLUMAGE. See Figs. 1 and 25. The plumage of the wing consists of distinguishable series of feathers which overlap closely and neatly from front to back and inside to outside.

The Flight Feathers, or remiges, consist of the *primaries* and *secondaries*. The primaries are all attached to the bones of the "hand" and vary consistently in number among different groups of birds between 9 and 12, including the sometimes tiny last primary, or remicle. They are usually numbered from the inside outward toward the wing tip, though another system reverses this (!). The secondaries (or cubitals) are more numerous and variable in number depending on the length of the "forearm": hummingbirds have as few as 6, most passerines have only 9, whereas albatrosses may have over 30. They are usually numbered from the bend of the wing inward toward the body. All of the secondaries are attached to the ulna. The innermost secondaries, which in certain groups (notably ducks) are differently shaped and colored and may molt in a different sequence, are often called the *tertials* or *tertiaries*. (See TERTIALS for another use of the term.)

All flight feathers overlap in continuous sequence, the innermost secondary covering part of its immediate neighbor (on the upper surface) and so on to the last primary.

The Alula is a group of relatively short feathers attached to the "thumb" bone (pollex). These vary in number from 2 to 7 (usually 3–4) and serve as a stabilizing mechanism in flight and underwater for some diving birds.

The Coverts are small contour feathers which overlap the bases of the flight feathers and then each other, covering the entire surface of the forewing both above (*upper wing coverts*) and below (*lower wing coverts* or *wing lining*). The rows of coverts are subdivided and named. Thus the largest coverts which cover the bases of the primaries are called the *greater primary coverts*, those that overlap the g.p.c.'s are called the *median primary coverts*, which in turn may be overlapped by the *lesser primary co-*

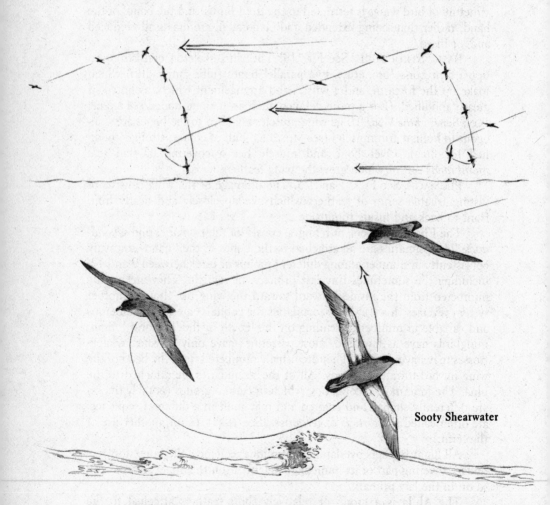

Sooty Shearwater

FIG. 22. *Dynamic soaring*. Many of the larger seabirds with high "aspect ratios" travel almost effortlessly over their oceanic habitat by letting the wind hurl them into the air and then gliding gradually back to sea level, aided by decreasing wind speed over the water as they descend. For a detailed description of this and similar techniques, see FLIGHT, *Dynamic Soaring*.

verts. The coverts of the secondaries have a similar sequence and names (*greater secondary coverts,* etc.). The rows of coverts on the undersurface of the wing are less distinctly differentiable but follow the same pattern. Covering the lesser coverts (both primary and secondary) are the *marginal coverts,* which cover the entire forward inner corner of the wing, from shoulder to beyond the bend and merging indistinguishably with the lesser coverts above and below.

Each quill of the alula has a covert feather at its base.

The Scapulars are "shoulder feathers" which overlap the base of the wing and the tertials.

The Axillaries, or axillars, are the usually elongated feathers covering the armpit, i.e., the area between the base of the underwing and the body.

USE. See Fig. 10. Wings have evolved primarily as adaptations for flight (for details of function, see FLIGHT), though in a few cases the ability to fly has been lost in the evolution of completely terrestrial habits (e.g., Ostrich) or aquatic ones (penguins). However, birds also put their wings to a number of secondary uses. Wing surfaces are often brightly colored and patterned (e.g., Willet) or their shape modified (e.g., the elongated, curled secondaries of cranes) for use in courtship displays; and a number of sounds (the explosive wing clapping of pigeons, the "drumming" of Ruffed Grouse) are also produced by the wings as part of a display ritual (see SONG, *Non-vocal Sounds*).

The wings are also used for fighting, and some species (only the Northern Jacana in North America) have sharp spurs at the bend of the wing, turning this seemingly innocent member into a deadly weapon. Some diving birds, notably the auks and some sea ducks, propel or steer themselves underwater with their wings rather than folding them and relying only on the paddle power of their feet as do other divers, such as the loons (see SWIMMING/DIVING).

VARIATION. One has only to think of the wings of hummingbirds, albatrosses, condors, falcons, and owls to realize that the evolutionary variations which have been wrought on the "alar theme" are numerous and highly specialized.

The function of different wing shapes is discussed under FLIGHT.

WING BAR(S) (wing patch). One or (often) two contrasting (almost always paler) lines running across a bird's folded wing (see Fig. 1). This effect, cited with great frequency as a mark of identification, results from pale tips of the greater and middle (median) covert feathers. Generally used quite specifically and *not* synonymous with "wing patch," in which most or all of the greater coverts are pale or white (e.g., adult male Magnolia Warbler), or WING STRIPE.

WING FORMULA. A method of recognizing certain hard-to-identify bird species by noting the comparative length of the primary feathers and the presence or absence of emargination. Needless to say, use of this technique requires either a live bird taken from a mist net or a museum specimen. In North America, wing formulas are consistently useful in determining species of *Empidonax* flycatchers as well as some immature warbler species (e.g., MacGillivray's, Mourning, and Connecticut). See, for example, the warbler section of Peterson et al. (1954–FIELD GUIDE) for a figure of comparative wing formulas. Wing formula is reliable as long as the feathers measured are full-grown and unworn.

WINGSPAN. The distance between the tips of a bird's extended wings. See SIZE; MEASUREMENTS.

WING STRIPE. Normally refers to a pale (usually white) margin running along the base of the primaries and secondaries of the wing and sometimes including the edges of the greater coverts. Often very inconspicuous on a bird at rest but striking when the wing is unfolded in flight. The presence or absence of a wing stripe is cited frequently as a field mark, especially among the sandpipers and plovers. Compare WING BAR.

WINTER FINCHES. Usually applied to certain seed-eaters which breed in the boreal forest and move south in large numbers during winters when their populations are high, the cone crop is poor, or both. "Classic" winter finches are the Evening Grosbeak, Purple Finch, Pine Grosbeak, the redpolls, Pine Siskin, and the crossbills. Juncos, longspurs, and other finches which arrive on their wintering grounds on a somewhat more regular schedule are not usually included under the term. All winter finches visit feeding stations, some much more regularly than others.

WINTERING GROUNDS (or winter quarters). The place where a given species or individual spends the winter. In North America, a majority of bird species move south from their breeding grounds during the colder months of the year, though the tendency becomes less pronounced as one moves south into zones of milder winters. In general, ranges of species and territories of individuals are as well defined in their winter quarters as during the breeding season (see MIGRATION; DISTRIBUTION; TERRITORY). Birds which live at high elevations (e.g., rosy finches) may descend to foothills or lowlands for the winter instead of migrating south; some, while moving south out of their breeding range, remain in the North Temperate Zone (e.g., Tree Sparrow); some populations remain in the same locality the year round even in regions of extreme cold and heavy snow (e.g., Black-capped Chickadee); and some have fluctuating winter ranges as food availability dictates (e.g., Pine Siskin and other "winter finches").

WINTER PLUMAGE. The plumage acquired in the first pre-basic (post-juvenal) molt and thereafter in successive pre-basic (post-nuptial) molts; on the whole, synonymous with "basic" plumage. The winter plumage is less colorful in many species than the "breeding" or "nuptial" or "alternate" plumage. See MOLT.

WINTER RESIDENT. A species that regularly spends the winter in a given area but breeds elsewhere. Usage varies, of course, geographically: Harris' Sparrow is a winter resident in parts of Texas, a SUMMER RESIDENT in parts of arctic Canada, and a TRANSIENT or VAGRANT elsewhere. The term might also be used in the same sense as "summer resident" to describe those few species (e.g., Red Crossbill, Mourning Dove) that sometimes nest during the winter months. Compare WINTER VISITOR.

WINTER VISITOR (or visitant). A species that is present on an irregular basis in a given area only during the winter. Usage varies, of course, geographically: Common Redpolls are winter visitors throughout much of the northern U.S. but SUMMER RESIDENTS in parts of arctic and subarctic Canada and Alaska and TRANSIENTS or VAGRANTS elsewhere in North America. Because it implies irregularity, "winter visitor" is usually applied to irruptive species and those at the edge of their wintering ranges, i.e., as a term complementary to WINTER RESIDENT.

It is possible for a species to be both a summer resident and a winter visitor in a given area. For example, Northern Goshawks breed in New England, but more northerly populations may also be present in winter during flight years (see IRRUPTION).

WIREBIRDS. Species that characteristically perch on telephone, fence, and other roadside wires: American Kestrel, Belted Kingfisher, swallows, many flycatchers, magpies, shrikes, Northern Mockingbird, bluebirds, Common Starling, meadowlarks, blackbirds, and many open-country finches are typical wirebirds. Watching wires for such species is a helpful diversion for a birdwatcher driving cross-country. Endpapers of the Peterson field guides (birds) show silhouettes of wirebirds.

WISHBONE. The fused clavicles or collarbones characteristic of birds; the furcula; the merrythought (British). See SKELETON and Fig. 19.

WOLLWEBER (Christian names and dates unknown) (Bridled Titmouse: *Parus wollweberi*). A little-known collector who sent specimens—including the one which immortalizes him—from Mexico back to his native Germany. Nothing of his biography has survived (Gruson calls him "a traveler"). His tit was named by Charles Lucien BONAPARTE.

WOOD BUFFALO NATIONAL PARK (Northwest Territories and Alberta). A 17,300-square-mile park in the muskeg of north-central Canada; it contains the breeding area of the world's only wild population of

Whooping Cranes. The nesting site was discovered in 1954 after a ten-year search. The western border of the park lies less than 50 miles south of Great Slave Lake and can be visited from the town of Fort Smith (connected by air and road to Edmonton). Visitors should not expect to see whoopers, but an interesting variety of subarctic land and water birds are present along with the park's namesake, the woodland race of the American bison.

WOODCOCK. Standard English name for 5 members of the subfamily Scolopacinae (family Scolopacidae; order Charadriiformes), which also includes the snipes and (in some taxonomies) the dowitchers. One species, the American Woodcock (*Scolopax* [*Philohela*] *minor*), breeds in North America and another has occurred here as an accidental straggler (see Appendix II).

Woodcocks are chubby "shorebirds" with long bills, short legs and tail, and rounded wings. They inhabit the edges of wet wooded areas (e.g., alder and red maple), though seldom mature forest. They are nocturnal and are usually encountered near dawn and dusk, when they emerge to court and feed, and remain inactive and concealed by their cryptically patterned plumage by day. They feed almost exclusively on earthworms, for which they "feel" in soft earth and mud with their long, sensitive, probing bill. The large, protruding eyes of woodcocks are set rather high in the skull and are centered on either side, so that except for small "blind spots" directly in front and behind, their visual field is nearly total, even including the area directly above them.

A requirement of a woodcock's breeding site is the proximity of an open field, where the males come to perform their courtship flight during a couple of months in spring. Emerging from cover just before dark, the male first sits in the open and utters a distinctive buzzy *peent* at regular intervals. Periodically he takes to the air, making a staccato whistling sound which results from air passing through "slots" of the peculiarly narrowed outer primary feathers. He flies in widening spirals, rising 100–200 feet from the earth, and then circles at the highest point, uttering an almost songbird-like chirping-twittering sound. This he continues for the first part of his descent, made in a series of precipitous zigzags. Back at his ground station, he resumes his *peent*-ing. This performance continues until after dark (more prolonged on moonlit nights) and is repeated before dawn.

The American Woodcock was once far more abundant than it is at present, especially in fall migration, when 1,000 birds might be shot in a day's hunting. Overshooting reduced their numbers drastically by the early twentieth century, but with hunting restrictions (seasons, bag limits) they are once more fairly common throughout their range—though they are vulnerable to pesticides such as DDT (see MAN-MADE THREATS TO BIRDLIFE) which accumulate in the tissue of their preferred food.

The American Woodcock is endemic to North America and largely restricted to the eastern half of the country. It breeds into southeastern Canada and winters to the tip of the Florida peninsula.

For family characteristics, see SANDPIPER; see also references in the Bibliography under SHOREBIRD.

WOODPECKER. Standard English name for most of the approximately 210 members of the family Picidae (order Piciformes), of which 21 (including the sapsuckers and the nearly extinct Ivory-billed Woodpecker) breed in North America.

Worldwide, woodpeckers range in size from 3½ inches to nearly 2 feet (5¾ to 18 inches in North America). Most species have a dominant plumage pattern of black (or brown) and white, usually highlighted by bright splashes of red or yellow; a few species are largely metallic green. Not a few species are crested. The typical woodpecker form and behavior are highly distinctive and familiar to everyone. And most of the specific characteristics of the family are adaptations to the birds' mode of living, consisting in most cases of climbing trees and "drilling" and probing for insects or sap. The bill is hard, straight, and chisel-shaped. The skull is specially reinforced to withstand continual shocks and vibrations. The unusually long, mobile tongues of most species can be extended to an extraordinary degree into drilled holes to extract wood-boring insects; this ability is effected by a unique elongation of a set of special small bones and muscles in the skull known as the hyoid apparatus (see TONGUE). The tongues of woodpeckers also have barbed tips with sticky secretions, facilitating the extraction of their prey or, in the case of sapsuckers, brush tips for soaking up tree juices. The neck muscles are unusually strong. The legs are short and the feet are "yoke-toed" (zygodactyl), with toes I and IV pointing to rearward and II and III forward (some species with only one rear toe). The claws are notably long, decurved, and pointed to maintain a firm grip on vertical surfaces. The tail is usually wedge-shaped and the tail feathers are very stiff and pointed, acting as a prop and stabilizer in climbing.

Woodpeckers are primarily arboreal and insectivorous, though several species (e.g., the flickers) are primarily ground feeders (ants) and the sapsuckers show the preference that their name implies. Insectivorous species usually also eat a significant amount of fruit, nuts, bark, and/or other plant matter. Most species are solitary in behavior, but the Acorn Woodpecker nests, roosts, and often feeds in groups.

All woodpeckers nest in unlined tree cavities (less usually in earthen banks or termite nests) that they excavate. Typically, they construct a new site each year, and abandoned woodpecker holes are the chief source of sites for other cavity-nesting birds (see NEST). Woodpecker eggs are white, glossy in most species, and the average clutch is 3–5 (extremes: 1–14).

Woodpecker calls are loud, often staccato, metallic or "laughing," and are supplemented in the breeding season by courtship "drumming" with the bill on hollow trees or otherwise resounding surfaces.

Woodpeckers are distributed throughout the world with the notable exceptions of Madagascar, Australia, New Zealand, and Oceania. In North America, several species occur wherever there are trees or tree cacti (i.e., absent from arctic tundra) and some species are very widespread; most are essentially non-migratory; the three-toed woodpeckers are given to periodic IRRUPTIONS.

WOOD WARBLER. Standard English collective name for all 107–123 members of the family Parulidae (order Passeriformes) and for the family as a whole. Individual species of wood warblers are called simply warblers (e.g., Yellow Warbler) and thus may be confused with the superficially similar OLD WORLD WARBLERS (e.g., Arctic Warbler), which belong to the family Sylviidae. A total of 53 species of wood warblers breed in North America, including 2 species whose taxonomic place is uncertain.

Excluding the 7½-inch Yellow-breasted Chat (which is included in this family only provisionally; see CHAT), the wood warblers are all small (4¼ to 5¾ inches), well-proportioned songbirds, typically with a moderately short, slender, pointed bill and tail of medium length. Many species are brilliantly colored (yellow predominates, but blue, orange, and red also occur) and/or boldly patterned with black and white. A few species forage largely on the ground, but most are arboreal and actively glean leaves, limbs, and trunks for insects and other invertebrate prey. Parulids are also fond of nectar, sap (including pine pitch), and berries, and those which occasionally winter in temperate climates (e.g., Pine and Yellow-rumped Warblers) will eat seeds and suet at feeding stations. Wood warbler songs are highly distinctive and immensely variable, ranging from rich melodies to nearly inaudible lisps and trills reminiscent of cricket or cicada sounds. Many parulid "chips" are also distinctive.

Nests of wood warblers are small cups (sometimes domed: Ovenbird, Common Yellowthroat), which in most species are neat and compact, made with fine grasses, plant down, and spider silk—but may also be more bulky and loose, made with twigs, stems, bark, and dead leaves. The lining is usually of fine grasses, plant fibers, hair, moss, and plant down. Most wood warblers build in shrubs or trees, but some are habitual ground nesters. Two North American species (Prothonotary and Lucy's) are cavity nesters, and the parulas build in pendant festoons of *Usnea* lichen or Spanish moss (*Tillandsia*). Eggs number 3–8, but clutches of most species average 4–5. Eggs may have a white, gray, blue, or green (pale) ground color and be immaculate to heavily speckled or blotched in reddish or brownish.

The wood warbler family is confined to the New World, with about an equal number of species breeding in the Nearctic and Neotropical regions. They occur in all major biomes, occupying a great variety of specific breeding niches, and range from the Arctic to the South Temperate Zone of Argentina. All North American wood warblers are migratory (at least in part of their range) and the great majority winter exclusively in the tropics.

One of the great, uniquely American, birdwatching experiences is a spring "warbler wave" when hundreds—occasionally thousands—of wood warblers of many species, all clad in gorgeous nuptial plumage, descend from their nocturnal migration to rest and feed in favorable areas (see WAVE; HIGH ISLAND; NORTHER; MIGRATION).

Relatively few warblers warble, a practice much more typical of the FINCH family.

For the warblers of the family Sylviidae, see OLD WORLD WARBLER.

WORMS, PARASITIC. See ENDOPARASITE.

WRECK. When migration coincides with strong onshore winds, the result may be "wrecks" of pelagic birds. The term is of British origin, implies large numbers of birds incapacitated on land, and is therefore most usually applied to alcids, which require a watery "runway" to become airborne. Dovekies are particularly susceptible to these conditions and are often blown far inland, sometimes by the thousands. Many such casualties fall prey to cars, cats, penguin-loving humans, and starvation. For a vivid account of a Dovekie wreck, see Snyder (1960–MORTALITY).

WREN. Standard English name for all 59 members of the family Troglodytidae (order Passeriformes) and for the family as a whole. Depending on taxonomy, 9 or 10 species of wrens breed in North America.

The "basic" wren form is a familiar one to North Americans: generally small (4 to 5 inches; Cactus Wren to 8¾ inches); brown above, paler below; compact shape; wings short and rounded; tail long or short but characteristically "cocked up." The wrens' preference for dense shrubbery, their active feeding habits, and their "bubbly," often rather long and chaotic songs are also widely known. They feed mainly on insects and other invertebrates, but larger species are known to take small lizards and the like and they readily take to fruit in cold seasons.

Wrens frequently build rather large, loose, domed nests in trees, shrubs, cacti, or cattails, but they also often nest in cavities (including birdhouses), where they may omit the superfluous dome. The lining may be of feathers, hair, plant fiber or down, and other soft materials. Male wrens of some species build a series of DUMMY NESTS, one of which the female selects and lines. House Wrens are famous for nesting in unusual man-made localities, such as hats, cans, teapots, and shoes, and they will also use abandoned nests of swallows and other bird species. Wren eggs are variable: white to brown; immaculate to heavily marbled with reddish-brown speckles.

The wrens are generally supposed to have evolved in North America and spread southward into the Neotropics, where they currently attain their greatest diversity. Only one species, the Winter Wren, ever reached the Old World, where, however, it is widespread; it is presumed to have spread via the now submerged land bridge across the Bering Strait, and it is currently the only North American wren species to reach as far north as Alaska. Several other North American wrens range widely on the continent but only a few reach southern Canada.

The name "wren" comes to us essentially unchanged from the Anglo-Saxon and similar words in old Scandinavian languages. In addition to referring to the one Old World wren (Winter), it has traditionally carried a connotation of lasciviousness (Gruson, 1972–BIOGRAPHY), which perhaps originated in observation of the polygamy of the males.

WRENTIT. Standard English name for the single North American member of the babbler family (Timaliidae; order Passeriformes). The Wrentit was long identified with the tits (Paridae), though in many structural and behavioral characteristics it seemed to fit neither there nor anywhere else in the native avifauna. Recently, it has usually been assigned to a family of its own (Chamaeidae), but analysis of its egg-white proteins by ELECTRO-PHORESIS indicates that it should be grouped with the enormously diverse Old World family the babblers.

Like a number of babblers, the Wrentit has what North Americans and Europeans think of as wren-like characteristics: a thin, sharp bill; short, rounded wings; a long, "cocked-up" tail; generally brown coloration; a loud, clear, trilled song; and a fondness for dense, brushy habitat. As with wrens, tits, and many other small passerines, Wrentits feed largely on insects and other invertebrates when they are available but switch readily to fruit and other plant matter in cold weather.

Wrentits nest in dense shrubbery, building a shallow, compact cup of twigs, bark, dead leaves, grasses, etc., bound with spider silk, lined with fine fibers (including hair), and decorated with bits of lichen. The 3–5 (usually 4) eggs are unmarked and greenish blue.

The species is strongly associated with the coastal chaparral scrub west of the Sierra Nevada in California and in northern Baja California, but it also occupies other types of brush north to western Oregon. It is non-migratory. The name, of course, reflects the taxonomic confusion that long surrounded the Wrentit.

WRIGHT, Charles, 1811–85 (*Empidonax wrightii:* Gray Flycatcher). Wellborn, self-taught botanist and consummate plant collector, whose work in Texas was published by Asa Gray as *Plantae Wrightianae*. He also collected in the Pacific Northwest, Japan, China, and Africa. He was briefly curator of the herbarium at Harvard. While in the West, Wright also collected a few birds and sent them to Spencer BAIRD, who named one for him.

X

XANTHOCHROISM (ZAN-thoh-CROH-izm). An abnormal dominance of yellow coloration in the absence of normal amounts of darker pigments. The condition is seen only rarely in wild birds but occurs regularly among cage birds, especially parrots. Both red and green portions of some plumages are apt to turn yellow as a result of a deficiency in diet. Birds in this condition are called "lutinos" in avicultural jargon. A few presumed xanthochroistic birds have been recorded in the wild, however; for example, see Plate 5.

XANTUS (ZAN-toose), John, 1825–94 (Xantus' Murrelet: *Endomychura hypoleuca*). A Hungarian lawyer, soldier, impostor, and, after emigration to the U.S., a jack-of-all-trades, including naturalist-collector. Considering his lack of credentials, his résumé bespeaks no small intelligence and/or a persuasive personality, for he managed to win the confidence of Spencer BAIRD; became (briefly) a U.S. consul in Mexico; posed as a captain in the Navy; and ended respectably as the director of the Zoological Garden of Budapest (see Gruson, 1972–BIOGRAPHY, for further details). On a trip to Baja California, Xantus collected the southernmost-ranging alcid, described it, and, given his style, was probably at least influential in choosing its name.

XEROPHILOUS (zer-OFF-uh-luss). Literally, loving dryness. In reference to birds and other organisms, it describes a preference for arid habitats, especially deserts. Le Conte's Thrasher is a North American example of a xerophilous species.

Y

YELLOWLEGS. Standard English name for 2 of the 11 species of long-legged sandpipers in the genus *Tringa* (formerly *Totanus*). Greater and Lesser Yellowlegs breed only in North America and generally nest in low arctic and subarctic muskeg habitat. They are common migrants on both coasts, and some populations winter on marshes, flats, and interior wetlands along the southern shores of the continent. Other populations reach the southern tip of South America. Their loud, piping calls are among the most distinctive of American shorebird notes.

For family characteristics, see SANDPIPER.

YELLOWSTONE National Park (Wyoming). Famous worldwide for its spectacular scenery, large mammals, and hordes of summer tourists, Yellowstone is both the oldest and the largest (3,472 square miles) of U.S. national parks (excepting the great Alaskan ones). It is also an excellent place to see a wide range of the breeding-bird specialties of the western highlands as well as northern forest species, e.g.: Trumpeter Swan, Golden Eagle, Blue Grouse, Sandhill Crane, Williamson's Sapsucker, Hammond's and Western Flycatchers, Violet-green Swallow, Gray and Steller's Jays, Black-billed Magpie, Clark's Nutcracker, Mountain Chickadee, American Dipper, Mountain Bluebird, Townsend's Solitaire, Bohemian Waxwing (winter), Townsend's and MacGillivray's Warblers, Western Tanager, Cassin's Finch, rosy finches, and Green-tailed Towhee. Accommodations are available year-round; be sure to write for reservations (including camping) during the peak season, Memorial Day to Labor Day.

YELLOWTHROAT. Standard English name for about 11 species of wood warblers (family Parulidae), all but one in the genus *Geothlypis*. One of these, *G. trichas*, the Common or Northern Yellowthroat, is one of the most familiar of North American songbirds and breeds across the entire continent and south to southern Mexico. Another species, *Geothlypis (Chamaethlypis) poliocephala*, the Gray-crowned Yellowthroat, or Ground Chat, is mainly Neotropical in distribution but has bred in the past in the lower Rio Grande Valley of Texas. All yellowthroats in all plumages have yellow throats.

For family characteristics, see WOOD WARBLER.

YOLK. In birds, a yellow or orange mass of protein and fat granules produced by the ovary, enclosed in a thin, transparent membrane. After passage through a bird's oviduct, it is surrounded by a clear gelatinous substance (the albumen) and a hard eggshell. The yolk is the "food" which sustains the embryo until hatching. See EGG; EMBRYO; REPRODUCTIVE SYSTEM.

YOLK SAC. A membranous pouch containing the egg yolk and connected by a tube (the yolk stalk) to the underside of the embryos of fishes, reptiles, and birds. The yolk is largely consumed by the embryo during the incubation period. Just before hatching, the yolk sac is forced by muscular contraction inside the abdomen of the embryo. Thus all birds are born with an internal yolk sac, which, however, disappears within the first week after hatching. Humans and other mammals have a similar structure, but it contains no yolk.

See EMBRYO and Fig. 8.

YOSEMITE National Park (California). One of the venerable jewels in the crown of the U.S. national park system and the best possible refutation of the widely repeated ornithological maxim that the best birding is always to be found in garbage dumps and sewer beds. The park contains almost 700,000 of the Sierra Nevada's most spectacular acres, beginning at an elevation of about 4,000 feet on the floor of the Yosemite Valley and climaxing in an array of alpine peaks, eight of them exceeding 10,000 feet, the two highest over 13,000. To the public at large, Yosemite is probably best known for its spectacular rock formations such as Half Dome and Cathedral Spires; waterfalls such as the 1,430-foot Upper Yosemite; Mirror Lake; multicolored alpine meadows; and groves of giant sequoias. To the birdwatcher interested in highland bird species of the American West, however, it offers a wide range of habitats from the dipper-infested rapids of the Merced River to the rocky edges of the snowfields preferred by (Gray-crowned) Rosy Finches. In between there are both coniferous and deciduous woodlands holding specialties such as: Blue Grouse, Band-tailed Pigeon, Great Gray Owl, Northern Pygmy Owl, Black Swift, White-headed Woodpecker, Williamson's Sapsucker, Western Flycatcher, Steller's Jay, Clark's Nutcracker, Canyon Wren, Mountain Bluebird, Townsend's Solitaire, Western Tanager, and Black-headed Grosbeak. Overhead look for Golden Eagle, White-throated Swift, and Violet-green Swallow.

The park is easily reached by following State Highway 140 about 70 miles east from Merced. Early summer offers the appealing combination of breeding-bird activity and less than peak tourist activity.

For other western mountain birding, see ROCKY MOUNTAIN; YELLOWSTONE.

YOUNG, DEVELOPMENT OF. Details of a bird's maturation from the time it is hatched until it becomes functionally independent of its parents, i.e., can fly and/or find its own food.

It is natural and convenient to consider the development of young birds beginning with the moment they leave the egg. When we do this we find that birds at hatching divide into two main types: (I) those which are essentially helpless and totally dependent on their parents (altricial) and (II) those which are relatively well developed and able to fend for themselves to some degree (precocial). In addition, there are two fairly distinct "subtypes," types III and IV, which are a little less helpless than type I and a little less independent than type II, respectively. In one sense, these differences at hatching are more apparent than real, for in general those birds which emerge helpless from the egg have a markedly shorter incubation period than those which emerge more or less ready to face the world. In other words, some birds hatch sooner and develop longer in the nest, whereas others hatch later and spend little or no time in the nest, having developed longer in the egg. There are many factors which influence incubation and post-hatching development time, but among comparable species development follows a generally similar schedule and the time from *laying* to independence is likely to match fairly well even though the time from *hatching* to independence is very different.

Before proceeding to a schematic comparison of the main development patterns just described, here are a few more generalities about the development of young birds.

• Birds grow rapidly in early stages, at the end of which they cease to grow. Most birds attain adult proportions and size well before independence and are only slightly short of adult weight when ready to fend for themselves. Many people used to the mammalian (especially the human) growth pattern will say, when faced for the first time with an adult kinglet or other diminutive species: "How sweet, is it a baby?" Answer: No.

• Larger species generally have longer development periods than smaller.

• Birds with "safe" nesting habits, e.g., hole nesters, develop at a slower rate than more vulnerable forms such as ground nesters.

• In defiance of the above "rule" by which altricial species have shorter "egg lives" and precocial species shorter "nest lives," some groups (see especially type III below) have both long incubation periods and long stretches of post-hatching dependency. The Black-footed Albatross, for example, remains in the egg for more than 2 months, yet does not become independent for 5 months or more *after hatching*.

The following is a schematic comparison of the major aspects of the basic development patterns of young birds. For convenience, the North American avifauna is divided into four "types" of development, though, as noted above, types III and IV are probably more accurately regarded as "subtypes" of I and II, respectively. The data included have been gleaned from a variety of sources which are listed in the Bibliography. For thor-

FIG. 23. *Growth and plumage development.* The young of songbirds, such as the Cedar Waxwing, are altricial (helpless for a period after hatching); nidicolous (confined to the nest during the helpless period); and psilopaedic (naked or with scant down at hatching). The young of some other bird families (e.g., ducks, rails, sandpipers) are precocial (able to walk and look for their own food almost immediately); nidifugous (leave the nest soon after hatching); and ptilopaedic (covered in a thick coat of natal down). The Laughing Gull chick is semi-precocial, because, although it is downy and is able to move almost immediately, it stays near its nest and depends on its parents for food for a period of weeks after hatching.

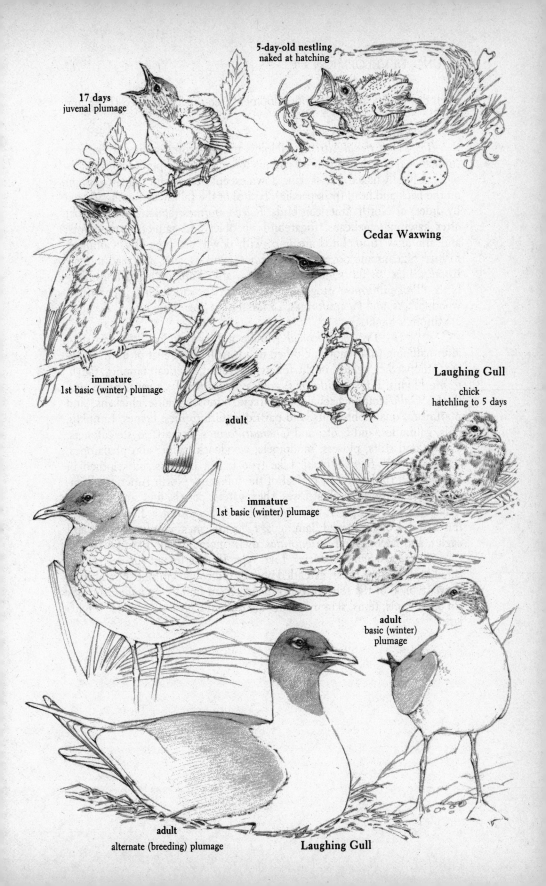

5-day-old nestling
naked at hatching

17 days
juvenal plumage

Cedar Waxwing

immature
1st basic (winter) plumage

adult

Laughing Gull

chick
hatchling to 5 days

immature
1st basic (winter) plumage

adult
basic (winter)
plumage

adult
alternate (breeding) plumage

Laughing Gull

ough day-by-day accounts of development, see especially Nice (1943 and 1962).

DESCRIPTION OF TYPES

Type I—Typical Altricial: Helpless and therefore confined to the nest (nidicolous) and dependent on parents for an extended period after hatching; essentially naked, i.e., lacking down except perhaps for a small amount on the back and head (psilopaedic); typical of the following families (listed by order) of North American birds: *Pelecaniformes* (acquire a down coat after hatching): pelicans, frigatebirds, boobies and gannets, cormorants, and anhingas (tropicbirds are *born* with down, see type III); *Columbiformes:* pigeons and doves; *Cuculiformes:* cuckoos, anis, and roadrunners; *Apodiformes:* swifts (some acquire down after hatching) and hummingbirds; *Trogoniformes:* trogons; *Coraciiformes:* kingfishers; *Piciformes:* woodpeckers; and *Passeriformes:* 25 families of "perching birds," flycatchers through finches.

Type II—Typical Precocial: Mobile and ready to leave the nest soon after hatching (nidifugous); clothed in a usually thick coat of down feathers (ptilopaedic); typical of the following North American families: *Gaviiformes:* loons; *Podicipediformes:* grebes; *Anseriformes:* swans, geese, and ducks; *Galliformes:* chachalacas, turkeys, grouse, prairie chickens, and ptarmigan, quail, pheasants, and partridge; *Gruiformes:* cranes, Limpkin, rails, gallinules, and coots; and *Charadriiformes* (in part): oystercatchers, avocets and stilts, plovers, sandpipers, woodcock, snipe, and phalaropes.

Type III—Semi-altricial: Like type I, i.e., helpless, but clothed in heavy down (ptilopaedic); typical of the following North American families: *Procellariiformes:* albatrosses, shearwaters, petrels, and storm-petrels; *Pelecaniformes* (in part): tropicbirds *only; Ciconiiformes:* herons, storks, ibises and spoonbills, and flamingos; *Falconiformes:* vultures, hawks and eagles, and falcons; and *Strigiformes:* owls (including the Barn Owl).

Type IV—Semi-precocial: Like type II, but remain in nest to be cared for by parent for an extended period (nidicolous) in spite of ability to move; typical of the following North American families: *Charadriiformes* (in part): gulls, terns, skimmers, and alcids; and *Caprimulgiformes:* nightjars.

	TYPE I	TYPE II	TYPE III	TYPE IV
1. Incubation Period	25–55 days (Pelecaniformes); 11–19 all others; most passerines 11–16.	17–37 days; most 3–4 weeks.	Variable: 41–65 days (tubenoses); 17–32 (herons); 38–42 (vultures and condors); 21–34 (owls).	20–39 days (gulls, terns, skimmers, and alcids); 19–20 (nightjars).
2. Condition at Hatching	Naked or minimal down dorsally; eyes closed (open within 3–5 days); helplessly confined to nest; large head and belly, small wings and legs; skin usually pinkish; prominent whitish or yellowish mouth corners (rictal flanges); bill, legs, and mouth lining often brightly colored/patterned; raises head and "gapes" almost immediately.	Down-covered; eyes open; mobile immediately or nearly so; proportions more like adult except for small wings; no rictal flanges; bill, leg, and mouth color usually dark; unable to lift head at first.	Superficially like II, but confined to nest and dependent on parents for extended period; petrels and owls have eyes closed at hatching, unlike most of type III.	Like II, but stays in or near the nest and is tended by parents in spite of early mobility.
3. Plumage Growth	First adult feathers "sprout" within first 4 days (passerines), especially on wings and back; full growth of feathers more or less coincides with leaving the nest.	First adult feathers "sprout" within first 5–6 days, especially on wings and tail; in swimming birds, feathers on ventral surfaces appear first (1–3 weeks); head and pelvic regions often last to lose down; timing/sequence variable among groups—e.g., ducks, geese, etc., retain down longer than most.	Most if not all tubenoses have 2 coats of nestling down; in some cases the second is paler and curlier than the first. Fulmars begin to show juvenal plumage at 4–5 weeks, but albatrosses take much longer and this plumage is not fully developed until 5 or 6 months (Palmer, 1962). Most owls and at least some diurnal raptors also have 2 down coats, but the juvenal plumage develops rapidly in the nest within 3 weeks (small hawks and owls) to 2–3 *months* (large owls, con-	Gulls and terns lose most down for juvenal plumage before fully grown, but species which take longer to mature can still appear largely downy after 3 weeks or more and not be fully fledged for 7.

	TYPE I	TYPE II	TYPE III	TYPE IV
		dors), depending on the species. Heron down is generally thinner than typical precocials' and molts into juvenal plumage within first third of nest life, or about 2 weeks.		
4. Body Temperature Control	Lacking at hatching but developed rapidly and acquired essentially by midpoint of nest life, i.e., well before adult feather coat is complete.	Partially developed at hatching because of down, but continued development slower than in type I and not complete for about a month after hatching.	Generally as in type II.	Generally as in type II.
5. Motor Activities	Very limited at first; within few days grips floor of nest tightly; by middle of nest life begins to yawn, stretch, preen, etc.	Well developed from start and practiced within hours of hatching.	Similar to type I.	Similar to type II, but nevertheless remains in or near the nest for long period dependent on parental feeding.
6. Vocalization	May not call immediately but begins "begging" sounds within first 2–3 days; capable of "distress calls" by midpoint of nest life but may not utter first "adult" calls until near independence.	Often begins to call *before* hatching; "brood call" continues throughout "family period." Other distinctive calls rapidly developed include alarm, begging (if fed by parents), distress (when molested), threat (mostly in sibling rivalry), and "contentment" (while being brooded).	Generally as in type I.	Generally as in type I.

7. Leaves the Nest			
As early as 7–8 days for vulnerable ground nesters (e.g., Ovenbird, Mourning Warbler); later for more secure cavity nesters, such as woodpeckers (20–30 days), kingfishers (30–38 days). In more secure nesters, the leaving of the nest is often simultaneous with first flight, but ground nesters may vacate before able to fly. The majority of passerine species leave the nest in 10 days to 2 weeks, but there are many exceptions, e.g., most corvids don't leave for 3 or more weeks, likewise the two large grackles and some wrens.	As soon as down dries (a few hours) or within the first day (24 hours).	In tubenose species which have open nest sites (e.g., Black-footed Albatross), young birds begin to wander from the nest area at about 2–3 months, but are coaxed back into the nest territory for feeding by parents. However, this wandering precedes independence by several months (see #8 and #10). Burrow-nesting tubenoses (e.g., Greater Shearwater, Leach's Storm-Petrel) emerge in the evening or at night for a few days before first flight but reenter the burrow during the day. After first flight, they may return to the nest site but not reenter the burrow. In herons, departure generally coincides with first flight, but young birds may climb around on the nest tree (usually returning to the nest) for as much as a week before first flight. In the Wood Stork and many hawks, eagles, etc., leaving coincides with first flight, but in some species, young return to the nest	Gull and tern chicks usually wander from the nest site within a few days of hatching, but remain within the parental territory. The young of Royal and Sandwich Terns form groups (crèches) within 2–3 days (Royal) or in 2nd week (Sandwich) where they continue to be fed by their own parents; first flight does not occur until much later (see #8). The young of many alcid species go to sea several weeks *before* first flight, either alone or with parents, which continue to feed them. Young nightjars may be moved by the parents from the nest site in response to danger; they also may wander on their own almost immediately; but remain close enough to be located by parents for feeding.

	TYPE I	TYPE II	TYPE III	TYPE IV
8. First Flight	Very variable among "types," families, and even species; ranges from 8 days (wood warblers) to 190 (frigatebirds); the Pelecaniformes all take between 1 and 3 months to fly; kingfishers and crows may take more than a month; most passerines fly between the 2nd and 3rd weeks after hatching.	Fairly consistent at family level; range great, from gallinaceous birds—some can fly as early as 7 days after hatching and all are normally airborne in less than 3 weeks—to swans, which may not fly until their 108th day; loons fly at 70–80 days; Anseriformes (except swans) anywhere between 35 and 77; cranes 60–70. Arctic-breeding sandpipers may fly within 2 weeks, while plovers of more southern distribution can take as long as 40 days.	for a period of up to 3 weeks to roost for the night and be fed. Most nestling owls may climb out of nests and onto adjacent branches well before they are able to fly (1 to several weeks). Black-browed Albatross at 5–6 months; Leach's Storm-Petrel 2–2½ months. Herons 3 (Green) to 5 (larger species) weeks; Wood Stork 7–8 weeks; American Flamingo 10–11 weeks. Small falcons 2–3 weeks; eagles about 2 months; Black and Turkey Vultures 10–11 weeks; California Condor about 5 months. Owls 3 weeks to 2 months, generally with larger species taking longer.	Gulls 5 to 7 weeks; terns about a month; alcids 5–6 weeks; nightjars 3–4 weeks.
9. Finds Own Food	Begins tentatively soon after leaving the nest (see #7) and continues as parent begins "weaning," until young is self-sufficient: about	As soon as departure from nest (see #7) or with some parental guidance within a few days of hatching for most precocial species, but	Tubenoses begin to find own food only after having flown to sea; this follows a period of starvation and weight loss (in many	Gulls and terns begin fishing (or scavenging) for themselves soon after their first flights; alcids begin diving for food soon after

they leave the nest site, i.e., *before* they can fly in many cases. Nightjars' self-sufficiency in catching insects follows shortly after first flight.

species) after abandonment by parents. Most heron young fly to feeding grounds with adults as soon as able. Hawks and eagles learn to tear up prey by end of nestling period and learn gradually to kill for a period of weeks after, while still being fed by parents. Owls also depend on parental feeding while learning to hunt for themselves.

Independence in gulls and terns closely follows ability to fly and find food; alcids may be fed briefly on the ocean during their early flightless period but soon learn feeding techniques and become functionally self-sufficient. Nightjars also gain independence more or less simultaneously with ability to fly and find food.

loons and grebes may continue to be fed by their parents for 6 weeks or more, though they are active and follow their parents from the beginning.

Many tubenoses are abandoned by their parents weeks before they are fledged or can find food for themselves; they live on large fat reserves, complete fledging, and are ultimately forced to fly to sea to avoid starvation. In herons, hawks, and owls, feeding by parents continues after first flight and departure from the nest; full independence may exist within a few weeks (some herons and hawks), but many are dependent for 6 weeks or more and California Condor young are fed by their parents for more than a year after hatching.

a month for passerines, but possibly more than a year for frigatebirds.

Variable. There is a tendency in several groups of precocial birds for the young to remain with the parents after they are functionally independent (i.e., can fly and feed themselves). Geese and crane families are known to remain together in migration and winter quarters and not split up until the return to the breeding grounds the following spring. Young Red-throated Loons may be abandoned on nest ponds by parents before they can fly and then rejoin them on salt water when able (Palmer, 1962). At least some arctic-breeding

10. Full Independence from Parents

In about a month for most passerines; much longer for Pelecaniformes: gannets and cormorants become independent in 3-4 months, and frigatebirds may be partially fed by parents for more than a year after hatching (Palmer, 1962).

	TYPE I	TYPE II	TYPE III	TYPE IV
11. Weight Pattern	In majority of passerines, weight is 6–8% that of adult female at hatching; rises very rapidly to 50–80% of adult female's weight at departure from the nest; then rises more gradually until near adult weight at independence. Weight may decline slightly during "weaning," (Nice, 1943).	Less at hatching than type I:1–6% of adult female weight as compared to 6–8%. Precocials drop in weight slightly just after hatching when learning to feed themselves, as altricials do just after they leave the nest. But precocials are still 30–40% short of adult weight when able to fly. shorebirds abandon young before they can fly and migrate south, leaving the young to follow with their peers a month or more later.	Tubenoses are exceptional in reaching a weight which *exceeds* that of the parents well before fully fledged; these large fat stores help see the chicks through the period of parental abandonment, which usually occurs weeks before independence, and may also serve as a hedge against bad weather when parents are unable to obtain food or return to the nest. Most other type III species generally similar to type II.	Generally similar to type II.

Z

ZÉNAIDE (zeh-NED). Princess Zénaide Charlotte Julie Bonaparte (White-winged Dove: *Zenaida asiatica*; Mourning Dove: *Zenaidura macroura*). Charles Lucien Bonaparte named two genera of doves after his wife, who was also his cousin.

ZOOGEOGRAPHY (ZOH-uh-gee-OG-ruh-fee). The study of the distribution of animal species over the surface of the earth. Put simply, the zoogeographer asks how a given species has come to occur where it presently does and what factors keep it there. Such judgments involve broad, long-term phenomena such as continental drift, the uplifting of mountains, changes in the level of the seas, and animal evolution.

The concept of zoogeographic regions or realms was articulated by the eminent British ornithologist Philip L. SCLATER in 1851. The notion was elaborated and refined by Alfred Wallace in 1857 into the system of the six major areas we recognize today: Nearctic, Neotropical, Palearctic, Ethiopian, Oriental, and Australasian. (See NEARCTIC, NEOTROPICAL, and

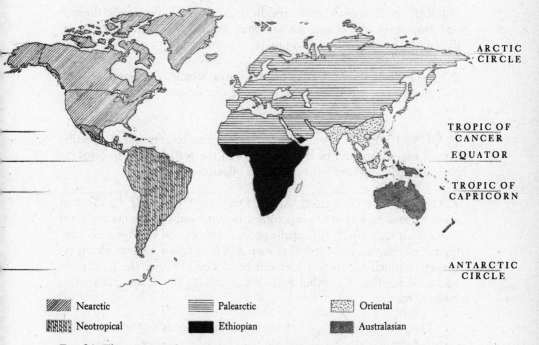

FIG. 24. *The zoogeographic regions of the world*. The Nearctic and Palearctic together make up the Holarctic region. Madagascar, Oceania, Antarctica, and the marine environment are usually considered apart from the six major regions. See DISTRIBUTION.

PALEARCTIC for descriptions; see Fig. 24 for boundaries.) Subregions have been proposed for a number of isolated landmasses and island groups such as Madagascar and New Zealand.

There are, of course, broad transition zones between regions, and the regions are not meant to indicate strict range limitations. Virtually all migrating species range across two zoogeographic regions, and many wide-ranging species occur normally in three or more. The numerous discrepancies and exceptions which are inevitable in such a broad concept have led to criticism of the theory as a whole, but it clearly embodies enough general truth to be at least useful for basic reference.

North America lies entirely within the Nearctic region but has many species in common with the Palearctic and Neotropical regions and particularly strong influences from these regions in western Alaska and along the Mexican border, respectively. See DISTRIBUTION.

ZOOLOGY (zoh-AHL-uh-jee). The study of animal life or the science which derives therefrom; a subdivision of biology (plant and animal life); divided into specialized branches, such as ornithology, the study of bird-life.

ZOOME (ZOH-ome). A major worldwide community of animals; the animal component of a biome; animals characteristic of rain forests make up the rain forest zoome. See also BIOME; DISTRIBUTION.

ZOONOSIS (ZOH-uh-NOH-siss). Any disease which is transmitted from animals to man, e.g., rabies. Certain bird diseases are zoonotic. See DISEASE.

ZUGUNRUHE (TSOO-gun-ROO-uh). A German term meaning, literally, "travel urge." Applied by ornithologists to the restlessness exhibited by birds immediately before they begin to migrate.

ZYGODACTYL (ZYE-goh-DAK-tull). Describes the form of a bird's foot when the first and fourth toes point to rearward and the second and third forward. Among North American species, cuckoos and woodpeckers have typical zygodactyl feet; the feet of owls and the Osprey are considered zygodactyl though their outer toes can be moved to either the forward or backward position. For other foot types, see LEG/FOOT; also SKELETON, *Bones of the Leg*.

FIG. 25. *Topography of a bird*. Mostly technical terms; for field terms, see Fig. 1.

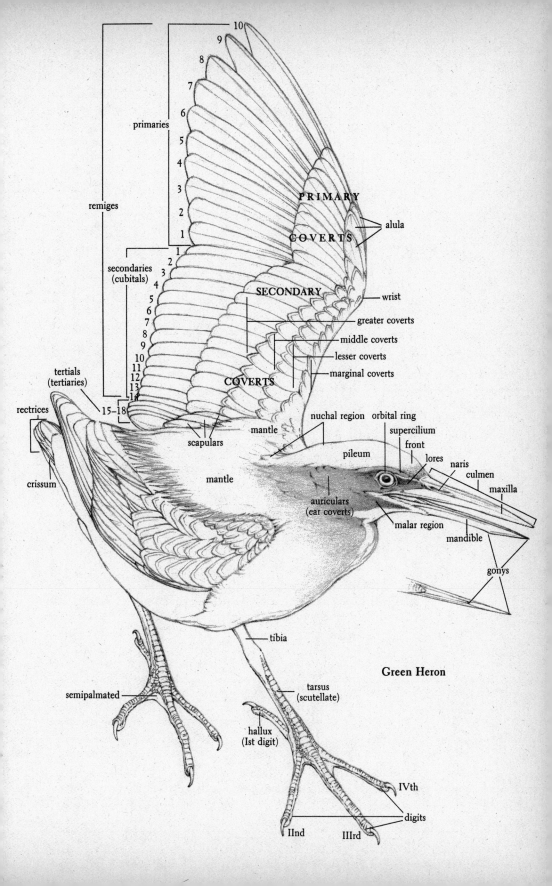

primaries

remiges

secondaries
(cubitals)

tertials
(tertiaries)

rectrices

crissum

PRIMARY

COVERTS

alula

SECONDARY

wrist

greater coverts

middle coverts

lesser coverts

marginal coverts

COVERTS

scapulars

mantle

mantle

nuchal region

pileum

auriculars
(ear coverts)

malar region

orbital ring

supercilium

front

lores

naris

culmen

maxilla

mandible

gonys

tibia

Green Heron

semipalmated

tarsus
(scutellate)

hallux
(Ist digit)

IVth

digits

IInd

IIIrd

Appendix I

The list that follows contains several "layers" of information:

1. It includes all species of birds known to occur regularly in North America, as the continent is defined on p. 3. These fall into two broad categories: species that breed here and those that occur regularly during part of the year but breed elsewhere. The latter species are marked "(visitor)"; those not so marked can be assumed to breed here. In a few cases in which breeding is sporadic, very recently established or discovered, uncertain, or merits comment otherwise, a longer note appears.

The meaning of the term "regular" applied to the occurrence of bird species is not always clear. The goal here has been to include all species that can reasonably be counted as integral parts of the North American avifauna and to exclude those that occur here only unpredictably, even though the latter may have been recorded dozens of times. Therefore, I have not used the principle followed elsewhere that any species which has occurred more than 10 times is a rare visitor rather than an accidental straggler. Following this rule, the Fork-tailed Flycatcher (a straggler from the Neotropics that has occurred with surprising frequency) is accorded a status comparable to that of Wilson's Storm-Petrel (an abundant summer visitor) rather than to that of, say, the Variegated Flycatcher (an accidental straggler from the Neotropics that has occurred but once). Rather I have used the criterion of regularity of occurrence (no matter how sparse) rather than frequency (no matter how often) in including species in Appendix I. With the recent increase in competent observers combing the avifaunal peripheries of the continent—especially western Alaska and the Mexican border—many species formerly thought to occur only irregularly as vagrants are now being encountered on an annual basis or nearly so. In addition to "transforming" some species from vagrants into regular visitors, this demonstrates that a few species, e.g., the White-tailed Tropicbird or the Terek Sandpiper, may *occur* annually—probably a fair criterion for inclusion in the avifauna—but not be *seen* so often. In categorizing such cases, I have been guided by the record and knowledge of the species in question, but will not claim that a few of the judgments made are anything but subjective. Species that occur regularly only as spring and/or fall migrants in the Aleutians (often in the westernmost Aleutians only) are marked "(migrant Aleutians)." Also included in Appendix I are well-established introduced species (e.g., European or Common Starling), extinct

species (e.g., Passenger Pigeon), and species that were once of regular occurrence in North America but are now rarely seen (e.g., Short-tailed Albatross); and the status of all such species is noted. Species deemed vagrants (accidental) by the above criteria are listed in Appendix II.

2. The list can also be used to learn the "definition" of particular
taxa (orders, suborders, families, subfamilies, genera, and species), i.e.,
their relationship to other taxonomic groupings and their size both worldwide and in North America. The numbers following the major taxa signify
as follows:

Orders: The number of families an order contains worldwide/in
North America follows the ordinal names. The first order listed, Procel-
lariiformes, contains 4 families worldwide, 3 of which occur regularly in
North America.

Suborders: No numerical breakdown given.

Families: The number both of genera and of species a family contains
worldwide/in North America follows the familial names. The first family
listed, Diomedeidae, contains 2 genera worldwide, 1 of which occurs regularly in North America. It also contains 13 species worldwide, 3 of which
occur regularly in North America.

Subfamilies: No numerical breakdown given.

Genera: The number of species a genus contains worldwide/in North
America follows the generic names. The first genus listed, *Diomedea,* contains 11 species worldwide, 3 of which occur (or have occurred) regularly
in North America.

Species: The number of *North American* subspecies into which a
species has been divided follows the specific name. The fourth species
listed, *Fulmarus glacialis,* is represented by 3 subspecies (races) in North
America. When only a single race of a polytypic species occurs regularly in
North America the species name is followed by "(1 N.A.)." Species followed by "(1)" are monotypic (worldwide).

Any taxon (order, family, genus, or species) followed by "(1)" is
monotypic, i.e., it contains only one immediately subordinate taxonomic
unit, except for monotypic species, which contain *no* subordinate units
(subspecies). The second order listed, Gaviiformes (1), contains only a single family, the Gaviidae (1), which in turn contains only a single genus,
Gavia. The genus of the California Condor, *Gymnogyps* (1), contains only
a single species, *G. californianus* (1), which is also monotypic.

Definitions of taxonomic categories—CLASS, SUBCLASS, ORDER,
etc.—including their significance in avian taxonomy, appear as entries in
the main text. Definitions of bird groups also have entries of their own
under their English names: TUBENOSE, ALBATROSS, FULMAR, etc. Definitions of specific Latin taxa, Procellariiformes, Diomedeidae, *Diomedea,*
etc., are defined only here in Appendix I. For the convenience of
readers wishing to look up a particular Latin order, suborder, or family,
these are listed alphabetically under ORDER, SUBORDER, and FAMILY

along with the numbers of the pages on which they appear in Appendix I.

3. To a limited extent, the list mirrors recent debate on avian taxonomy. A great many changes—in relationships among various bird taxa, the phylogenetic order in which they are listed, and the names accorded them—have been authoritatively proposed since the publication in 1957 of the 5th edition of the A.O.U. *Check-list of North American Birds*, which, however, is still the major source of taxonomy and nomenclature for most of the popular bird books now on the market. The present list incorporates many of the most widely accepted revisions and notes others proposed, but also records "traditional" names and concepts, so that the reader familiar with the taxonomy and nomenclature of his field guide will not be baffled. The list is not intended to express any taxonomic opinion, but rather to lay some of the prevailing ones before the reader. Major sources used in compiling Appendix I are listed in the Bibliography under CHECKLIST and TAXONOMY.

As this book went into the final stages of publication a list of the taxonomic and nomenclatural changes that will appear in the forthcoming 6th edition of the A.O.U. *Check-list* became available. Regrettably it has not been possible to revise Appendix I in complete accordance with the new standard and there remain many discrepancies between the two lists, particularly in matters of phylogenetic sequence, preferred names in both Latin and English, and changes in the higher taxa, such as the replacement of most of the subfamilies of the Anseriformes and Charadriiformes with a concept using tribes. Many alterations proposed in the literature and adopted here were *not* ratified in the new A.O.U. list, so that in a sense Appendix I sometimes reflects more "radical" taxonomic theory than that adopted by the A.O.U. Of course, revision and divergent opinion are mainstays of systematics, and there will never exist a list of the birds of anywhere on the details of which all authorities agree. Regardless of the many technical differences, however, the *species* in Appendix I have been made to agree with those proposed in the new A.O.U. list, and in virtually all cases in which two or more recent names/concepts have been in contention, I have included the principal alternatives in Appendix I.

Readers unfamiliar with the premises on which phylogenetic lists are based may want to see TAXONOMY and NOMENCLATURE and also perhaps to review terms such as MONOTYPIC.

Appendix I lists 21 orders, 75 families, 300+ genera, and 702 species of birds that occur regularly (as defined above) in North America (as defined on p. 3). Appendix II lists an additional 6 families and 140 species that have occurred here as vagrants. Any disparity between these totals and others that have been published are readily explained by the differences in taxonomic opinion discussed above and by legitimate differences of opinion about the status of some species in North America. The reader would do well to append the adverb "about" to all such broad numerical summaries.

Class **AVES**: All birds, living and extinct
Living orders: 25–28/21
Living families: ±170/65–75
Living species: ±8,650/±700 (regular)

ORDER
    SUBORDER
        FAMILY
            SUBFAMILY
                Genus
                    Species

PROCELLARIIFORMES: Tubenoses—Albatrosses, Shearwaters & Petrels, Storm-Petrels, and Diving Petrels. Families: 4/3
    DIOMEDEIDAE: Albatrosses. Genera: 2/1; species: 13/3
        Diomedea: Albatrosses (11/3)
            D. *albatrus,* Short-tailed Albatross (1) (formerly regular visitor)
            D. *nigripes,* Black-footed Albatross (1) (visitor)
            D. *immutabilis,* Laysan Albatross (1) (visitor)
    PROCELLARIIDAE: Fulmars and Shearwaters & Petrels. Genera: 12/4; species: 53–60/15
        Fulmarus: Fulmars (2/1)
            F. *glacialis,* Northern Fulmar (3)
        Pterodroma: Gadfly Petrels (26/3)
            P. *hasitata,* Black-capped Petrel (1 N.A.) (visitor)
            P. *cahow,* Cahow (Bermuda Petrel) (1) (pelagic range unknown; perhaps regular in N.A. waters)
            P. *inexpectata,* Scaled (Mottled) Petrel (1) (visitor)
        Calonectris: Shearwaters (2/1)
            C. (*Puffinus*) *diomedea,* Cory's Shearwater (1 N.A.) (visitor)
        Puffinus: Shearwaters (13/10)
            P. *bulleri,* New Zealand (Buller's, Gray-backed) Shearwater (1) (visitor)
            P. *carneipes,* Pale-footed (Flesh-footed) Shearwater (1) (visitor) (sometimes regarded as conspecific with *creatopus*)
            P. *creatopus,* Pink-footed Shearwater (1) (visitor) (sometimes considered conspecific with *carneipes*)
            P. *gravis,* Greater Shearwater (1) (visitor)
            P. *griseus,* Sooty Shearwater (1) (visitor)
            P. *tenuirostris,* Slender-billed (Short-tailed) Shearwater (1) (visitor)
            P. *puffinus,* Manx Shearwater (1 N.A.) (mainly visitor; has bred *very* locally off N.E. coast)
            P. *opisthomelas,* Black-vented Shearwater (1) (visitor; formerly lumped with *puffinus*)
            P. *auricularis,* Townsend's Shearwater (1) (visitor; formerly lumped with *puffinus*)
            P. *lherminieri,* Audubon's (Dusky) Shearwater (1 N.A.) (visitor; breeds in Bermudas)

HYDROBATIDAE: Storm-Petrels. Genera: 8/3; species: 22/6
  Oceanites (2/1)
   O. oceanicus, Wilson's Storm-Petrel (1 N.A.) (visitor)
  Halocyptena (1)
   H. microsoma, Least Storm-Petrel (1) (visitor)
  Oceanodroma (12/4)
   O. leucorhoa, Leach's Storm-Petrel (2)
   O. (Loomelania) melania, Black Storm-Petrel (1)
   (visitor; breeds off Baja Calif.)
   O. homochroa, Ashy Storm-Petrel (1)
   O. furcata, Fork-tailed Storm-Petrel (2)
GAVIIFORMES: Loons (1)
  GAVIIDAE: Loons (1). Species: 4/4
   Gavia (4/4)
    G. stellata, Red-throated Loon (1)
    G. arctica, Arctic Loon (2)
    G. immer, Common Loon (1)
    G. adamsii, Yellow-billed Loon (1)
PODICIPEDIFORMES: Grebes (1)
  PODICIPEDIDAE: Grebes. Genera: 6/4; species: 20/6
   Tachybaptus (5/1)
    T. (Podiceps) dominicus, Least Grebe (1 N.A.)
   Podilymbus (2/1)
    P. podiceps, Pied-billed Grebe (1 N.A.)
   Podiceps (8/3)
    P. auritus, Horned Grebe (1 N.A.)
    P. grisegena, Red-necked Grebe (1 N.A.)
    P. nigricollis, Eared Grebe (1 N.A.)
   Aechmophorus (1)
    A. occidentalis, Western Grebe (1 or 2 N.A.)
PELECANIFORMES: Tropicbirds, Frigatebirds, Cormorants, Darters, Boobies
& Gannets, and Pelicans. Families: 6/6
 PHAETHONTES: Tropicbirds
  PHAETHONTIDAE: Tropicbirds (1). Species: 3/2
   Phaethon (3/2)
    P. aethereus, Red-billed Tropicbird (1) (visitor S. Calif.)
    P. lepturus, White-tailed Tropicbird (1 N.A.) (rare but
    regular visitor offshore, esp. Gulf Stream)
 PELECANI: Frigatebirds, Cormorants, Darters, Boobies & Gannets, and
 Pelicans
  FREGATIDAE: Frigatebirds (1). Species: 5/1
   Fregata (5/1)
    F. magnificens, Magnificent Frigatebird (1)
  PHALACROCORACIDAE: Cormorants. Genera: 1–2/1; species: 29/6
   Phalacrocorax (29/6)
    P. carbo, Great Cormorant (1 N.A.)
    P. auritus, Double-crested Cormorant (4)
    P. olivaceus, Neotropic (Olivaceous) Cormorant (1
    N.A.)
    P. penicillatus, Brandt's Cormorant (1)
    P. urile, Red-faced Cormorant (1)
    P. pelagicus, Pelagic Cormorant (2)

ANHINGIDAE: Darters (1). Species: 1–4/1
  Anhinga (1–4/1)
   A. *anhinga,* Anhinga (1 N.A.)
SULIDAE: Gannets and Boobies (1). Species: 7–9/2
  Sula (9/2)
   S. (*Morus*) *bassana*(*-us*), Northern Gannet (1) (some-
    times regarded as conspecific with the two Southern
    Hemisphere gannets)
   S. *leucogaster,* Brown Booby (1 N.A.) (rare but regular
    visitor to Fla. Keys)
PELECANIDAE: Pelicans (1). Species: 6/2
  Pelecanus (6/2)
   P. *erythrorhynchos,* American White Pelican (1)
   P. *occidentalis,* Brown Pelican (2)
CICONIIFORMES: Herons, Hammerheads, Storks, Whale-billed Storks, and
Ibises & Spoonbills. Families: 5/3
 ARDEAE: Herons
  ARDEIDAE: Day Herons, Night Herons, Tiger Herons, and Bitterns.
  Genera: 15–32/7; species: 62–63/12
   ARDEINAE: Day Herons
    Ardea (11/2)
     A. *herodias,* Great Blue Heron (3, incl. Great White
      Heron)
     A. (*Casmerodius*) *alba,* Great (Common) Egret (1 N.A.)
    Egretta (15/5)
     E. (*Dichromanassa*) *rufescens,* Reddish Egret (2)
     E. (*Hydranassa*) *tricolor,* Louisiana (Tricolored) Heron
      (1 N.A.)
     E. (*Bubulcus*) *ibis,* Cattle Egret (1 N.A.)
     E. (*Florida*) *caerulea,* Little Blue Heron (1)
     E. (*Leucophoyx*) *thula,* Snowy Egret (2)
    Ardeola (7/1)
     A. *striata* (*Butorides striatus*), Green (Green-backed)
      Heron (2)
   NYCTICORACINAE: Night Herons
    Nyctanassa (1)
     N. *violacea,* Yellow-crowned Night Heron (1 N.A.)
    Nycticorax (6/1)
     N. *nycticorax,* Black-crowned Night Heron (1 N.A.)
   BOTAURINAE: Bitterns
    Ixobrychus (8/1)
     I. *exilis,* Least Bittern (2)
    Botaurus (4/1)
     B. *lentiginosus,* American Bittern (1)
 CICONIAE: Storks, Shoebills, and Ibises & Spoonbills
  CICONIIDAE: Storks. Genera: 3–11/1; species: 17/1
   Mycteria (4/1)
    M. *americana,* Wood Stork (Ibis) (1)
  THRESKIORNITHIDAE: Ibises and Spoonbills. Genera: 13/3;
  species: 28–30/4
   THRESKIORNITHINAE: Ibises
    Eudocimus (2/1)
     E. *albus,* White Ibis (1)

Plegadis (3/1)
   P. *falcinellus,* Glossy Ibis (1 N.A.)
   P. *chihi,* White-faced Ibis (1)
PLATALEINAE: Spoonbills
   Platalea (5/1)
   P. *(Ajaia) ajaja,* Roseate Spoonbill (1)
PHOENICOPTERIFORMES: Flamingos (sometimes regarded as part of Ci-coniiformes) (1)
   PHOENICOPTERIDAE: Flamingos. Genera: 3/1; species: 4–5/1
   Phoenicopterus (2/1)
      P. *ruber,* Greater (American) Flamingo (1 N.A.) (for-merly a regular visitor to S. Fla.)
FALCONIFORMES: American Vultures, Hawks & Eagles, Secretary Bird, and Falcons & Caracaras. Families: 4/3
   CATHARTAE: American Vultures
   CATHARTIDAE: American Vultures. Genera: 5/3; species: 7/3
      Coragyps (1)
         C. *atratus,* Black Vulture (1)
      Cathartes (3/1)
         C. *aura,* Turkey Vulture (3)
      Gymnogyps (1)
         G. *californianus,* California Condor (1)
   ACCIPITRES: Osprey and Hawks & Eagles
   ACCIPITRIDAE: Osprey and Hawks & Eagles. Genera: 59–64/13; species: 205–218/25–26
      PANDIONINAE: Osprey (sometimes regarded as a separate family)
      Pandion (1)
         P. *haliaetus,* Osprey (1 N.A.)
      ACCIPITRINAE: Hawks (incl. Buteos, True Hawks, Kites, and Harriers) and Eagles
      Chondohierax (1–2/1)
         C. *uncinatus,* Hook-billed Kite (1 N.A.) (recently resident S. Tex.)
      Elanoides (1)
         E. *forficatus,* American Swallow-tailed Kite (1 N.A.)
      Elanus (4/1)
         E. *leucurus,* Black-shouldered (White-tailed) Kite (1 N.A.)
      Rostrhamus (2/1)
         R. *sociabilis,* Everglade (Snail) Kite (1 N.A.)
      Ictinia (2/1)
         I. *mississippiensis,* Mississippi Kite (1)
      Haliaeetus (8/2)
         H. *leucocephalus,* Bald Eagle (2)
         H. *albicilla,* White-tailed (Sea) Eagle (1) (breeds very locally, Aleutians)
      Circus: Harriers (13/1)
         C. *cyaneus,* Northern Harrier (Marsh Hawk) (1 N.A.)
      Accipiter (48/3)
         A. *striatus,* Sharp-shinned Hawk (3)
         A. *cooperii,* Cooper's Hawk (1)
         A. *gentilis,* Northern Goshawk (2)
      Buteogallus (5/1)
         B. *anthracinus,* Common Black Hawk (1 N.A.)

Parabuteo (1)
 P. unicinctus, Harris' (Bay-winged) Hawk (2)
Buteo (25/10)
 B. nitidus, Gray Hawk (1 N.A.)
 B. lineatus, Red-shouldered Hawk (5)
 B. platypterus, Broad-winged Hawk (1 N.A.)
 B. brachyurus, Short-tailed Hawk (1 N.A.)
 B. swainsoni, Swainson's Hawk (1)
 B. albicaudatus, White-tailed Hawk (1 N.A.)
 B. jamaicensis, Red-tailed Hawk (incl. Harlan's Hawk)
  (7)
 B. regalis, Ferruginous Hawk (1)
 B. lagopus, Rough-legged Hawk (1 or 2 N.A.)
 B. albonotatus, Zone-tailed Hawk (1)
Aquila (9/1)
 A. chrysaetos, Golden Eagle (1 N.A.)
FALCONES: Caracaras and Falcons
 FALCONIDAE: Caracaras and Falcons. Genera: 10/2; species: 58/7
  POLYBORINAE: Caracaras
  Polyborus (1)
   P. plancus (*Caracara cheriway*), Crested Caracara (1)
  FALCONINAE: Falcons
  Falco (38/6)
   F. sparverius, American Kestrel (2)
   F. femoralis, Aplomado Falcon (1 N.A.) (formerly resi-
    dent in S.W.; now very rare; status uncertain)
   F. columbarius, Merlin (3)
   F. mexicanus, Prairie Falcon (1)
   F. rusticolus, Gyrfalcon (2)
   F. peregrinus, Peregrine Falcon (3)
ANSERIFORMES: Swans, Geese & Ducks and Screamers. Families: 2/1
 ANSERES: Swans, Geese, and Ducks
  ANATIDAE: Pied Geese, Whistling Ducks, Swans & Geese, Shel-
  ducks, Typical Ducks, Sea Ducks, and Stifftail Ducks. Genera:
  ±44/16; species: ±150/52 (incl. 1 introduced and 1 extinct)
  DENDROCYGNINAE: Whistling (Tree) Ducks
  Dendrocygna (8/2)
   D. bicolor, Fulvous Whistling (Tree) Duck (1 N.A.)
   D. autumnalis, Black-bellied Whistling (Tree) Duck (1
    N.A.)
  ANSERINAE: Swans and Geese
  Cygnus (6/4)
   C. olor, Mute Swan (1) (introduced)
   C. (Olor) buccinator, Trumpeter Swan (1)
   C. (Olor) columbianus, Tundra (incl. Bewick's and
    Whistling) Swan (1 N.A.)
   C. (Olor) cygnus, Whooper Swan (1) (migrant Aleu-
    tians)
   Some authorities consider Bewick's (see Appendix II),
    Whistling, Trumpeter, and Whooper Swans to be
    races of a single species, *C. cygnus*.
  Anser (9/5)
   A. albifrons, White-fronted Goose (3)
   A. fabalis, Bean Goose (1 or 2) (migrant Aleutians)

A. (Chen) caerulescens (incl. *A. hyperborea*), Snow/
Blue Goose (2)
A. (Chen) rossii, Ross' Goose (1)
A. (Philacte or Chen) canagicus, Emperor Goose (1)
Branta (5/2)
B. canadensis, Canada Goose (11)
B. bernicla, Brant (2, incl. *nigricans*, Black Brant)
ANATINAE (incl. Athyinae): Typical Ducks
Aix (2/1)
A. sponsa, Wood Duck (1)
Anas: Dabbling Ducks (37/12)
A. crecca, Green-winged Teal (2)
A. (Mareca) penelope, Eurasian Wigeon (1) (numerous
records annually, but breeding not proven)
A. (Mareca) americana, American Wigeon (1)
A. strepera, Gadwall (1 + another extinct race)
A. platyrhynchos (incl. *diazi*), Mallard (incl. Mexican
Duck—sometimes regarded as separate species) (2)
A. fulvigula, Mottled Duck (2)
A. rubripes, Black Duck (1)
A. acuta, Pintail (1 N.A.)
A. discors, Blue-winged Teal (1)
A. querquedula, Garganey (1) (migrant Aleutians)
A. cyanoptera, Cinnamon Teal (1 N.A.)
A. (Spatula) clypeata, Northern Shoveler (1)
Aythya: Bay Ducks (12/7)
A. valisineria, Canvasback (1)
A. americana, Redhead (1)
A. ferina, Common Pochard (1) (migrant Aleutians)
A. collaris, Ring-necked Duck (1)
A. marila, Greater Scaup (1 N.A.)
A. affinis, Lesser Scaup (1)
A. fuligula, Tufted Duck (1) (migrant Aleutians)
MERGINAE: Sea Ducks
Somateria: Eiders (3/3)
S. mollissima, Common Eider (4)
S. spectabilis, King Eider (1)
S. (Lampronetta) fischeri, Spectacled Eider (1)
Polysticta (1)
P. stelleri, Steller's Eider (1)
Camptorhynchus (1)
C. labradorius, Labrador Duck (1) (extinct)
Histrionicus (1)
H. histrionicus, Harlequin Duck (1)
Clangula (1)
C. hyemalis, Oldsquaw (1)
Melanitta: Scoters (3/3)
M. (Oidemia) nigra, Black (Common) Scoter (1 N.A.)
M. perspicillata, Surf Scoter (1)
M. fusca (*deglandi*), White-winged Scoter (1 N.A.)
Bucephala: Goldeneyes (3/3)
B. clangula, Common Goldeneye (1 N.A.)
B. islandica, Barrow's Goldeneye (1)
B. albeola, Bufflehead (1)

Mergus: Mergansers (6/4)

   M. albellus, Smew (1) (migrant Aleutians)

   M. (Lophodytes) cucullatus, Hooded Merganser (1)

   M. serrator, Red-breasted Merganser (1 N.A.)

   M. merganser, Common Merganser (Goosander) (1 N.A.)

OXYURINAE: Stifftail Ducks

Oxyura (6/2)

   O. dominica, Masked Duck (1)

   O. jamaicensis, Ruddy Duck (1 N.A.)

GALLIFORMES: Gallinaceous Birds and Hoatzins. Families: 7/4

  GALLI: Gallinaceous Birds—Megapodes, Guans & allies, Grouse & allies, Pheasants & Quail, Guinea Fowl, and Turkeys

CRACIDAE: Currassows, Guans, and Chachalacas. Genera: 11/1; species: 44–45/1

Ortalis (9/1)

   O. vetula, Plain Chachalaca (1 N.A.)

TETRAONIDAE: Grouse, Ptarmigan, and Prairie Chickens (now widely considered a subfamily, Tetraoninae, of the Phasianidae). Genera: 11/7; species: 18/10

Dendragapus (1)

   D. obscurus, Blue Grouse (8)

Lagopus: Ptarmigan (3/3)

   L. lagopus, Willow Ptarmigan (7)

   L. mutus, Rock Ptarmigan (11; 7 in Aleutians)

   L. leucurus, White-tailed Ptarmigan (5)

Canachites (1)

   C. (Dendragapus) canadensis, Spruce Grouse (5)

Bonasa (1)

   B. umbellus, Ruffed Grouse (10)

Pedioecetes (1)

   P. (Tympanuchus) phasianellus, Sharp-tailed Grouse (6)

Tympanuchus: Prairie Chickens (1–2/1–2)

   T. cupido, Greater Prairie Chicken (2 + 1 extinct)

   T. pallidicinctus, Lesser Prairie Chicken (1) (regarded by some authorities as conspecific with *cupido*)

Centrocercus (1)

   C. urophasianus, Sage Grouse (2)

PHASIANIDAE: Pheasants, Quail, and Partridges. Genera: 57/9 (incl. 4 introduced); species: 175/10 (incl. 4 introduced)

ODONTOPHORINAE: American Quail

Oreortyx (1)

   O. pictus, Mountain Quail (5)

Callipepla (1)

   C. squamata, Scaled Quail (2)

Lophortyx (3/2)

   L. (Callipepla) californicus, California Quail (7)

   L. (Callipepla) gambelii, Gambel's Quail (3)

Colinus (3/1)

   C. virginianus, Northern Bobwhite (4 + 1 extinct, Ariz.)

Cyrtonyx (1–3/1)

   C. montezumae, Montezuma (Harlequin) Quail (1 N.A.)

PHASIANINAE: Partridges, Quail, and Pheasants
    Alectoris (7/1)
        A. chukar, Chukar Partridge (many races; now interbred)
        (introduced)
    Francolinus (40/1)
        F. francolinus, Black Francolin (1 N.A.) (introduced)
    Perdix (3/1)
        P. perdix, Gray (Hungarian) Partridge (1 N.A.)
        (introduced)
    Phasianus (2/1)
        P. colchicus, Common Pheasant (hybrids of several
        races) (widely introduced)
MELEAGRIDIDAE: Turkeys (now widely considered a subfamily,
Meleagridinae, of the Phasianidae). Genera: 2/1; species: 2/1
    Meleagris (1)
        M. gallopavo, Wild Turkey (4)
GRUIFORMES: Mesites & Monias, Bustard Quail & Hemipodes, Collared
Hemipodes, Cranes, Limpkin, Trumpeters, Rails (incl. Gallinules and Coots),
Sun Grebes, Kagu, Sun Bittern, Seriemas, and Bustards. Families: 12/3
  GRUES: Cranes, Limpkin, Trumpeters, and Rails (incl. Gallinules and
  Coots)
    GRUIDAE: Cranes and Crowned Cranes. Genera: 4/1; species: 14/2
    GRUINAE: Cranes
    Grus (10/2)
        G. canadensis, Sandhill Crane (3)
        G. americanus, Whooping Crane (1)
    ARAMIDAE: Limpkin (1). Species: 1/1
    Aramus (1)
        A. scolopaceus (*guarauna*), Limpkin (1 N.A.)
    RALLIDAE: Rails & Gallinules and Coots. Genera: 52/7; species:
    ±130 (many recently or soon to be extinct)/9
    RALLINAE: Rails
    Rallus (8/3)
        R. longirostris, Clapper Rail (8)
        R. elegans, King Rail (1 N.A.)
        R. limicola, Virginia Rail (1 N.A.)
    Porzana (12/1)
        P. carolina, Sora (Rail) (1)
    Laterallus (10/1)
        L. jamaicensis, Black Rail (2)
    Coturnicops (3/1)
        C. noveboracensis, Yellow Rail (1 N.A.)
    Gallinula (6–7/1)
        G. chloropus, Common Gallinule (1 N.A.)
    Porphyrio (5/1)
        P. (*Porphyrula*) *martinica*, Purple Gallinule (1)
    FULICINAE: Coots
    Fulica (9/1)
        F. americana, American Coot (1 N.A.)
CHARADRIIFORMES: Jacanas, Painted Snipes, Oystercatchers, Sandpipers &
Phalaropes, Avocets & Stilts, Plovers, Crab Plover, Thick-knees, Coursers &
Pratincoles, Seedsnipes, Sheathbills, Skuas & Jaegers, Gulls & Terns, Skim-
mers, and Auks. Families: 16/9

CHARADRII: Jacanas, Painted Snipes, Oystercatchers, Plovers, Sandpipers & Phalaropes, Avocets & Stilts, Crab Plover, Thick-knees, Coursers & Pratincoles, Seedsnipes, and Sheathbills

JACANIDAE: Jacanas. Genera: 7/1; species: 7–8/1

Jacana (1–2/1)

J. spinosa, Northern Jacana (1 N.A.) (breeds irregularly S. Tex.)

HAEMATOPODIDAE: Oystercatchers (1). Species: 6–8/2

Haematopus (6–8/2)

H. bachmani, American Black Oystercatcher (1)

H. palliatus, American Oystercatcher (1 N.A.)

CHARADRIIDAE: Plovers and Lapwings. Genera: 8–20/3; species: ±62/11

CHARADRIINAE: Plovers

Pluvialis (4/2)

P. (Squatarola) squatarola, Black-bellied Plover (1)

P. dominica, Lesser (American) Golden Plover (2)

Charadrius (21/8)

C. hiaticula, Common Ringed Plover (1 N.A.)

C. semipalmatus, Semipalmated Plover (1) (sometimes considered conspecific with *hiaticula*)

C. melodus, Piping Plover (2)

C. alexandrinus, Snowy Plover (2)

C. mongolus, Mongolian Plover (1 N.A.) (rare breeder Alaska; migrant Aleutians)

C. vociferus, Killdeer (1 N.A.)

C. wilsonia, Wilson's Plover (1 N.A.)

C. montanus, Mountain Plover (1)

Eudromias (2/1)

E. (Charadrius) morinellus, Eurasian Dotterel (1)

SCOLOPACIDAE: Sandpipers, Turnstones, Surfbird, and Phalaropes. Genera: 27/17; species: 85/48

TRINGINAE

Bartramia (1)

B. longicauda, Upland Sandpiper (Plover) (1)

Numenius: Curlews (8/4)

N. borealis, Eskimo Curlew (1) (close to extinction)

N. phaeopus, Whimbrel (1 N.A.)

N. tahitiensis, Bristle-thighed Curlew (1)

N. americanus, Long-billed Curlew (2)

Limosa: Godwits (4/3)

L. haemastica, Hudsonian Godwit (1)

L. lapponica, Bar-tailed Godwit (1 N.A.)

L. fedoa, Marbled Godwit (1)

Tringa (11/6)

T. erythropus, Spotted Redshank (1) (migrant Aleutians)

T. flavipes, Lesser Yellowlegs (1)

T. melanoleuca, Greater Yellowlegs (1)

T. nebularia, Common Greenshank (1) (migrant Aleutians)

        T. solitaria, Solitary Sandpiper (2)

        T. glareola, Wood Sandpiper (1) (breeding record for
          Pribilofs, Alaska)

  Actitis (2/2)

        A. hypoleucos, Common Sandpiper (1) (migrant Aleu-
          tians)

        A. macularia, Spotted Sandpiper (1)

  Catoptrophorus (1)

        C. semipalmatus, Willet (2)

  Heteroscelus: Tattlers (2/2)

        H. brevipes, Grey-tailed (Polynesian) Tattler (1) (migrant
          Aleutians)

        H. incanus, Wandering Tattler (1)

SCOLOPACINAE

  Limnodromus: Dowitchers (3/2)

        L. griseus, Short-billed Dowitcher (3)

        L. scolopaceus, Long-billed Dowitcher (1)

  Gallinago (15/1)

        G. (Capella) gallinago, Common Snipe (1 N.A.)

  Scolopax (6/1)

        S. (Philohela) minor, American Woodcock (1)

CALIDRINAE

  Calidris: Stints (18/16)

        C. canutus, Red Knot (2)

        C. (Crocethia) alba, Sanderling (1)

        C. (Ereuntes) pusilla, Semipalmated Sandpiper (1)

        C. (Ereuntes) mauri, Western Sandpiper (1)

        C. (Erolia) ruficollis, Rufous-necked Sandpiper (Stint)
          (1)

        C. (Erolia) temminckii, Temminck's Stint (1) (migrant
          Aleutians)

        C. (Erolia) subminuta, Long-toed Stint (1) (migrant
          Aleutians)

        C. (Erolia) minutilla, Least Sandpiper (1)

        C. (Erolia) fuscicollis, White-rumped Sandpiper (1)

        C. (Erolia) bairdii, Baird's Sandpiper (1)

        C. (Erolia) melanotos, Pectoral Sandpiper (1)

        C. (Erolia) acuminata, Sharp-tailed Sandpiper (1)
          (visitor, esp. to Alaska)

        C. (Erolia) maritima, Purple Sandpiper (1)

        C. (Erolia) ptilocnemis, Rock Sandpiper (3)

        C. (Erolia) alpina, Dunlin (1 N.A.)

        C. (Erolia) ferruginea, Curlew Sandpiper (1) (breeds very
          locally, Alaska; rare visitor elsewhere)

  Micropalama (Calidris) (1)

        M. himantopus, Stilt Sandpiper (1)

  Tryngites (1)

        T. subruficollis, Buff-breasted Sandpiper (1)

  Philomachus (1)

        P. pugnax, Ruff (1) (breeding recently established,
          Alaska)

ARENARIINAE: Turnstones
    Arenaria (2/2)
        A. interpres, Ruddy Turnstone (2)
        A. melanocephala, Black Turnstone (1)
APHRIZINAE
    Aphriza (1)
        A. virgata, Surfbird (1)
PHALAROPODINAE
    Phalaropus (3/3)
        P. fulicarius, Red Phalarope (1)
        P. (Steganopus) tricolor, Wilson's Phalarope (1)
        P. (Lobipes) lobatus, Red-necked (Northern) Phalarope (1)

RECURVIROSTRIDAE: Stilts, Avocets, and Ibisbills. Genera: 3/2; species: 7/2
    RECURVIROSTRINAE: Stilts and Avocets
        Himantopus (1–3)
            H. mexicanus, Black-necked Stilt (1 N.A.)
        Recurvirostra (4/1)
            R. americana, American Avocet (1)
LARI: Skuas & Jaegers, Gulls & Terns, and Skimmers
STERCORARIIDAE: Skuas and Jaegers (now widely considered a subfamily, Stercorariinae, of the Laridae). Genera: 2/2; species: 4–5/4
    Catharacta: Skuas (2–4/1)
        C. skua, Great or Brown Skua (2–4; poorly understood) (visitor)
    Stercorarius: Jaegers (3/3)
        S. pomarinus, Pomarine Jaeger (1)
        S. parasiticus, Parasitic Jaeger (1)
        S. longicaudus, Long-tailed Jaeger (1)
LARIDAE: Gulls and Terns. Genera: 17/6; species: ±83/38
    LARINAE: Gulls
    Pagophila (1)
        P. eburnea, Ivory Gull (1)
    Larus (44/22)
        L. heermanni, Heermann's Gull (1) (visitor; breeds off Baja Calif.)
        L. delawarensis, Ring-billed Gull (1)
        L. canus, Mew Gull (1 N.A.)
        L. argentatus, Herring Gull (1 N.A.)
        L. thayeri, Thayer's Gull (1) (formerly lumped with *argentatus*)
        L. fuscus, Lesser Black-backed Gull (1) (now regular visitor locally)
        L. livens, Yellow-footed Gull (1) (visitor; formerly lumped with *argentatus*)
        L. californicus, California Gull (1)
        L. occidentalis, Western Gull (3)
        L. schistisagus, Slaty-backed Gull (1) (migrant Aleutians)
        L. marinus, Great Black-backed Gull (1)
        L. glaucescens, Glaucous-winged Gull (1)
        L. hyperboreus, Glaucous Gull (2)
        L. glaucoides, Iceland Gull (2)
        L. atricilla, Laughing Gull (1)
        L. pipixcan, Franklin's Gull (1)

        L. ridibundus, Common Black-headed Gull (1 N.A.)
        L. philadelphia, Bonaparte's Gull (1)
        L. minutus, Little Gull (1) (recently established Eurasian
          species)
        L. (Rissa) tridactyla, Black-legged Kittiwake (2)
        L. (Rissa) brevirostris, Red-legged Kittiwake (1)
        L. (Xema) sabini, Sabine's Gull (2)
    Rhodostethia (1)
        R. rosea, Ross' Gull (1)
STERNINAE: Terns
    Chlidonias (3/1)
        C. niger, Black Tern (1 N.A.)
    Sterna (32/12)
        S. (Gelochelidon) nilotica, Gull-billed Tern (2)
        S. (Hydroprogne) caspia, Caspian Tern (1)
        S. hirundo, Common Tern (1 N.A.)
        S. paradisaea, Arctic Tern (1)
        S. forsteri, Forster's Tern (1)
        S. dougallii, Roseate Tern (1 N.A.)
        S. aleutica, Aleutian Tern (1)
        S. fuscata, Sooty Tern (1 N.A.)
        S. albifrons, Least Tern (3)
        S. (Thalasseus) maximus, Royal Tern (1 N.A.)
        S. (Thalasseus) elegans, Elegant Tern (1)
        S. (Thalasseus) sandvicensis, Sandwich Tern (1 N.A.)
  Anous: Noddies (3/2)
        A. stolidus, Noddy Tern (1 N.A.)
        A. minutus (tenuirostris), Black (Lesser) Noddy (an-
          nually in summer in Dry Tortugas, Fla., but breeding
          not yet proven)
RYNCHOPIDAE: Skimmers (1) (now widely considered a subfamily,
  Rynchopinae, of the Laridae). Species: 3/1
    Rynchops
        R. niger (nigra), Black Skimmer (1 N.A.)
ALCAE
  ALCIDAE: Auks. Genera: 14/14; species: 23/21 (incl. 1 extinct)
    Alle (1)
        A. (Plautus) alle, Dovekie (1)
    Pinguinus (1)
        P. impennis, Great Auk (1) (extinct)
    Alca (1)
        A. torda, Razorbill (1 N.A.)
    Uria: Murres (2/2)
        U. lomvia, Thick-billed Murre (2)
        U. aalge, Common (Thin-billed) Murre (3)
    Cepphus (3–4/2)
        C. grylle, Black Guillemot (3)
        C. columba, Pigeon Guillemot (2)
    Brachyramphus (2/2)
        B. marmoratus, Marbled Murrelet (1 N.A.)
        B. brevirostris, Kittlitz's Murrelet (1)
    Endomychura (Synthliboramphus) (2/2)
        E. hypoleucus, Xantus' Murrelet (1)
        E. craveri, Craveri's Murrelet (1) (rare visitor)
          (sometimes regarded as conspecific with *hypoleucus*)

Synthliboramphus (2/1)
 S. antiquus, Ancient Murrelet (1)
Ptychoramphus (1)
 P. aleuticus, Cassin's Auklet (1 N.A.)
Cyclorrhynchus (1)
 C. psittacula, Parakeet Auklet (1)
Aethia (3/3)
 A. cristatella, Crested Auklet (1)
 A. pusilla, Least Auklet (1)
 A. pygmaea, Whiskered Auklet (1)
Cerorhinca (1)
 C. monocerata, Rhinoceros Auklet (1)
Fratercula (2/2)
 F. arctica, Common Puffin (1 N.A.)
 F. corniculata, Horned Puffin (1)
Lunda (Fratercula) (1)
 L. cirrhata, Tufted Puffin (1)

COLUMBIFORMES: Sandgrouse, Pigeons & Doves, and Dodo & Solitaires (extinct). Families: 3/1
 COLUMBAE: Pigeons & Doves and Dodo & Solitaires (extinct)
  COLUMBIDAE: Pigeons & Doves, incl. Fruit Pigeons, Typical Pigeons & Doves, Crowned Pigeons, and Tooth-billed Pigeons. Genera: ±58/7; species: ±295/12 (incl. 3 introduced and 1 extinct)
   COLUMBINAE: Typical Pigeons and Doves
    Columba (50/4)
     C. livia, Rock Dove or Common Pigeon (1) (introduced and widely domesticated)
     C. leucocephala, White-crowned Pigeon (1)
     C. flavirostris, Red-billed Pigeon (1 N.A.)
     C. fasciata, Band-tailed Pigeon (2)
    Ectopistes (1)
     E. migratorius, Passenger Pigeon (1) (extinct)
    Zenaida (5/2)
     Z. asiatica, White-winged Dove (2)
     Z. (Zenaidura) macroura, Mourning Dove (2)
    Streptopelia (17/2)
     S. chinensis, Spotted Dove (1 N.A.) (introduced)
     S. "risoria," Ringed Turtle Dove (introduced; feral aviary-bred stock derived from *S. roseogrisea* of Africa or *S. decaocto* of Eurasia)
    Scardafella (Columbina) (2/1)
     S. inca, Inca Dove (1)
    Columbina (7/1)
     C. passerina, Common Ground Dove (2)
    Leptotila (10/1)
     L. verreauxi, White-tipped (White-fronted) Dove (1 N.A.)

PSITTACIFORMES: Parrots & allies (1)
  PSITTACIDAE: Owl Parrots, Keas, Lories, Pygmy Parrots, Cockatoos, and Typical Parrots & Macaws. Genera: 80/3; species: ±320/3 (1 extinct, 1 introduced, 1 no longer occurs)

ARINAE
    Rhynchopsitta (2/1)
        R. pachyrhyncha, Thick-billed Parrot (1) (formerly a spo-
        radic visitor to Ariz./N.M.)
    Conuropsis (1)
        C. carolinensis, Carolina Parakeet (2) (extinct)
    Myiopsitta (1)
        M. monachus, Monk Parakeet (1 N.A.) (introduced)
    Other exotic parrots, escaped from captivity, have established
    themselves locally, esp. in S. Fla.; see EXOTIC SPECIES.

CUCULIFORMES: Plantain-eaters (Turacos, etc.) and Cuckoos & allies. Families: 2/1
   CUCULI: Cuckoos & allies
     CUCULIDAE: Cuckoos, Anis, Guiras, Roadrunners, Ground
    Cuckoos, Couas & Coucals. Genera: 38/3; species: ±127/6
     COCCYZINAE: Cuckoos
       Coccyzus (8/3)
          C. erythropthalmus, Black-billed Cuckoo (1)
          C. americanus, Yellow-billed Cuckoo (2)
          C. minor, Mangrove Cuckoo (1 N.A.)
     CROTOPHAGINAE: Anis
       Crotophaga (3/2)
          C. ani, Smooth-billed Ani (1)
          C. sulcirostris, Groove-billed Ani (1 N.A.)
     NEOMORPHINAE: Ground Cuckoos and Roadrunners
       Geococcyx: Roadrunners (2/1)
          G. californianus, Greater Roadrunner (1)

STRIGIFORMES: Owls—Barn Owls and Typical Owls. Families: 2/2
  TYTONIDAE: Barn Owls. Genera: 2/1; species: 10–11/1
    TYTONINAE
      Tyto (8/1)
         T. alba, Common Barn Owl (1 N.A.)
  STRIGIDAE: Typical Owls. Genera: 23/10; species: ±125/18
    BUBONINAE
      Otus: Screech Owls (±40/4)
        O. flammeolus, Flammulated (Screech) Owl (1 N.A.)
        O. asio, Eastern Screech Owl (15)
        O. kennicottii, Western Screech Owl (1) (formerly
        lumped with *asio*)
        O. trichopsis, Whiskered (Screech) Owl (1 N.A.)
      Bubo (12/1)
        B. virginianus, Great Horned Owl (9)
      Nyctea (1)
        N. scandiaca, Snowy Owl (1)
      Surnia (1)
        S. ulula, Northern Hawk Owl
      Glaucidium: Pygmy Owls (15/2)
        G. gnoma, (Northern) Pygmy Owl (4)
        G. brasilianum, Ferruginous (Pygmy) Owl (1 N.A.)
      Micrathene (1)
        M. whitneyi, Elf Owl (2)
      Speotyto (1)
        S. cunicularia, Burrowing Owl (2)
    STRIGINAE
      Strix (11–12/3)
        S. occidentalis, Spotted Owl (3)

S. varia, Barred Owl (3)

S. nebulosa, Great Gray Owl (1 N.A.)

Asio (5–6/2)

A. otus, Long-eared Owl (2)

A. flammeus, Short-eared Owl (1 N.A.)

Aegolius (4/2)

A. funereus, Boreal Owl (1 N.A.)

A. acadicus, Northern Saw-whet Owl (2)

CAPRIMULGIFORMES: Oilbird, Frogmouths, Potoos, Owlet-Nightjars, and Nightjars (Goatsuckers). Families: 5/1

CAPRIMULGI: Frogmouths, Potoos, Owlet-Nightjars, and Nightjars (Goatsuckers)

CAPRIMULGIDAE: Nightjars. Genera: 19/4; species: ±70/8

CHORDEILINAE: Nighthawks

Chordeiles (5/2)

C. acutipennis, Lesser Nighthawk (1 N.A.)

C. minor, Common Nighthawk (8)

C. gundlachii, Antillean Nighthawk (1) (recent breeding records from S. Fla.; formerly lumped with *minor*)

CAPRIMULGINAE

Nyctidromus (1)

N. albicollis, Pauraque (1 N.A.)

Phalaenoptilus (1)

P. nuttallii, Poor-will (4)

Caprimulgus (±46/3)

C. carolinensis, Chuck-will's-widow (1)

C. vociferus, Whip-poor-will (2)

C. ridgwayi, Buff-collared Nightjar (Ridgway's Whip-poor-will) (1 N.A.) (rare resident [?] S.W.)

APODIFORMES: Swifts, Crested Swifts, and Hummingbirds. Families: 3/2

APODI: Swifts and Crested Swifts

APODIDAE: Swifts—Spine-tailed Swifts and Typical Swifts. Genera: 8–13/3; species: ±70/4

CHAETURINAE: Spine-tailed Swifts

Chaetura (±21/2)

C. pelagica, Chimney Swift (1)

C. vauxi, Vaux's Swift (2)

Cypseloides (±8/1)

C. niger, Black Swift (1 N.A.)

APODINAE: Typical Swifts

Aeronautes (2/1)

A. saxatalis, White-throated Swift (2)

TROCHILI: Hummingbirds

TROCHILIDAE: Hummingbirds. Genera: 123/10; species: ±320/15

Cynanthus (2/1)

C. latirostris, Broad-billed Hummingbird (1 N.A.)

Hylocharis (8/1)

H. leucotis, White-eared Hummingbird (1 N.A.) (visitor to S.W.)

Amazilia (±32/2)

A. yucatanensis, Buff-bellied hummingbird (1 N.A.)

A. violiceps (verticalis), Violet-crowned Hummingbird (1 N.A.)

    Lampornis (7/1)
        L. clemenciae, Blue-throated Hummingbird (2)
    Eugenes (1)
        E. fulgens, Magnificent (Rivoli's) Hummingbird (1 N.A.)
    Calothorax (2/1)
        C. lucifer, Lucifer Hummingbird (1)
    Archilochus (2/2)
        A. colubris, Ruby-throated Hummingbird (1)
        A. alexandri, Black-chinned Hummingbird (1)
    Calypte (2/2)
        C. anna, Anna's Hummingbird (1)
        C. costae, Costa's Hummingbird (1)
    Stellula (1)
        S. calliope, Calliope Hummingbird (1)
    Selasphorus (8/3)
        S. platycercus, Broad-tailed Hummingbird (1 N.A.)
        S. rufus, Rufous Hummingbird (1)
        S. sasin, Allen's Hummingbird (2)
TROGONIFORMES: Trogons (1)
    TROGONIDAE: Trogons. Genera: 8/1; species: 35/1
        Trogon (16/1)
            T. elegans, Elegant (Coppery-tailed) Trogon (1 N.A.)
CORACIIFORMES: Kingfishers, Todies, Motmots, Bee-eaters, Hoopoes, Rollers, Cuckoo-Rollers, Hoopoes, Woodhoopoes, and Hornbills. Families: 9/1
    ALCEDINES: Kingfishers, Todies, and Motmots.
        ALCEDINIDAE: Kingfishers. Genera: 14/2; species: 86/3
        CERYLINAE
        Ceryle (5/2)
            C. (Megaceryle) torquata, Ringed Kingfisher (1 N.A.)
            C. (Megaceryle) alcyon, Belted Kingfisher (2)
        Chloroceryle (4/1)
            C. americana, Green Kingfisher (2)
PICIFORMES: Jacamars, Puffbirds, Barbets, Honeyguides & Toucans, and Woodpeckers & allies. Families: 6/1
    PICI: Woodpeckers and allies
        PICIDAE: Woodpeckers, Wrynecks, and Piculets. Genera: 38/9; species: ±210/21 (incl. 1 near extinction)
        PICINAE: Woodpeckers
        Colaptes: Flickers (5/1)
            C. auratus (incl. *cafer* and *chrysoides*), Common (Northern) Flicker (incl. Yellow-shafted, Red-shafted, and Gilded) (7)
        Dryocopus (6/1)
            D. pileatus, Pileated Woodpecker (4)
        Asyndesmus (Melanerpes) (1)
            A. lewis, Lewis' Woodpecker (1)
        Melanerpes (4–18 depending on taxonomy/2)
            M. erythrocephalus, Red-headed Woodpecker (2)
            M. formicivorus, Acorn Woodpecker (2)
        Centurus (or *Melanerpes*) (14/3)
            C. carolinus, Red-bellied Woodpecker (4)
            C. aurifrons, Golden-fronted Woodpecker (2)
            C. uropygialis, Gila Woodpecker (2)

Sphyrapicus: Sapsuckers (3/3)
    S. varius, Yellow-bellied Sapsucker (5)
    S. thyroideus, Williamson's Sapsucker (2)
    S. ruber, Red-breasted Sapsucker (1) (formerly lumped
      with *varius*)
Picoides (12/9) (all but last 2 species formerly *Dendrocopus*)
    P. albolarvatus, White-headed Woodpecker (2)
    P. villosus, Hairy Woodpecker (12)
    P. pubescens, Downy Woodpecker (7)
    P. borealis, Red-cockaded Woodpecker (2)
    P. nuttallii, Nuttall's Woodpecker (1)
    P. scalaris, Ladder-backed Woodpecker (2)
    P. stricklandi (incl. *arizonae*), Strickland's Woodpecker
      (incl. Arizona) (1 N.A.)
    P. tridactylus, (Northern) Three-toed Woodpecker (2)
    P. arcticus, Black-backed (Three-toed) Woodpecker (1)
Campephilus (3/1)
    C. principalis, Ivory-billed Woodpecker (1 N.A.) (near
      extinction)

PASSERIFORMES: Perching Birds. Suborders in Latin are followed by English family names: suborders or families that do not occur in North America (except as vagrants in a few cases) are in parentheses: (suborder Eurylaimi: Broadbills); (suborder Furnarii: Woodcreepers, Ovenbirds, Antbirds, and Tapaculos); suborder Tyranni: Tyrant Flycatchers, (Cotingas), (Manakins), (Sharpbills), and (Plantcutters); (suborder uncertain: Pittas, New Zealand Wrens, and Asities); (suborder Menurae: Lyrebirds and Scrubbirds); suborder Passeres [or Oscines], Songbirds: Larks, Swallows, (Cuckoo-Shrikes), Crows & Jays, (Bellmagpies), (Bowerbirds), (Birds of Paradise), (Mudnest-builders),Tits, Penduline Tits, Long-tailed Tits, Nuthatches, (Australian Nuthatches), Treecreepers, (Philippine Creepers), (Australian Treecreepers), (Drongos), (Old World Orioles), Bulbuls, (Leafbirds), Wrens, Dippers, Muscicapids [including former families of Old World Warblers, Old World Flycatchers, Thrushes, Babblers, and other smaller groups sometimes accorded full family rank], Mimic Thrushes, (Accentors), Wagtails & Pipits, Waxwings, Silky Flycatchers, (Palmchat), (Wood Swallows), (Coral-billed Nuthatch), (Vangas), Shrikes, (Wood Shrikes), Starlings & Mynahs, (Wattlebirds), (Honey-eaters), (Sunbirds), (Flowerpeckers), (White-eyes), Vireos, (Wrenthrush), Emberizids [now including former families of Wood Warblers, Honeycreepers, Tanagers, Fringillid Finches in part, and New World Orioles & Blackbirds according to the A.O.U. *Check-list,* 6th ed.], Fringillids [now including former family of Hawaiian Honeycreepers, but excluding many species now in Emberizidae; see above], Old World Sparrows [Passeridae], (Weavers [Ploceidae]), and Waxbills [Estrildidae]. Families: ±62/23–28
  TYRANNI: Tyrant Flycatchers, Cotingas, Manakins, Sharpbills, and Plant-
  cutters
    TYRANNIDAE: Tyrant Flycatchers. Genera: 89–100+/10; species:
  ±390/34 (incl. Cotingas)
      ELAENIINAE
        Camptostoma (2/1)
          C. imberbe, Northern Beardless Tyrannulet (Beardless
          Flycatcher) (2)
      FLUVICOLINAE
        Contopus (10–12/4)
          C. (*Nuttallornis*) *borealis,* Olive-sided Flycatcher (1)
          C. fumigatus (*pertinax*), Coues' Flycatcher (Greater
          Pewee) (1 N.A.)

       C. sordidulus, Western Wood Pewee (2)
       C. virens, Eastern Wood Pewee (1)
    Empidonax (16/10)
       E. flaviventris, Yellow-bellied Flycatcher (1)
       E. virescens, Acadian Flycatcher (1)
       E. alnorum, Alder Flycatcher (1) (formerly lumped in Traill's Flycatcher with *traillii*)
       E. traillii, Willow Flycatcher (1) (formerly lumped in Traill's Flycatcher with *alnorum*)
       E. minimus, Least Flycatcher (1)
       E. hammondii, Hammond's Flycatcher (1)
       E. wrightii, Gray Flycatcher (1)
       E. oberholseri, Dusky Flycatcher (1)
       E. difficilis, Western Flycatcher (2)
       E. fulvifrons, Buff-breasted Flycatcher (1 N.A.)
   Sayornis: Phoebes (3/3)
       S. phoebe, Eastern Phoebe (1)
       S. saya, Say's Phoebe (3)
       S. nigricans, Black Phoebe (1 N.A.)
   Pyrocephalus (1)
       P. rubinus, Vermilion Flycatcher (2)
TYRANNINAE
   Myiarchus (15/4)
       M. tuberculifer, Dusky-capped (Olivaceous) Flycatcher (1 N.A.)
       M. cinerascens, Ash-throated Flycatcher (1 N.A.)
       M. crinitus, Great Crested Flycatcher (2)
       M. tyrannulus, Brown (Wied's) Crested Flycatcher (2)
   Pitangus (2/1)
       P. sulphuratus, Great Kiskadee (Kiskadee Flycatcher) (1 N.A.)
   Myiodynastes (5/1)
       M. luteiventris, Sulphur-bellied Flycatcher (1 N.A.)
   Tyrannus (13/8)
       T. melancholicus, Tropical Kingbird (1 N.A.)
       T. couchii, Couch's Kingbird (1) (formerly lumped with Tropical Kingbird)
       T. vociferans, Cassin's Kingbird (1 N.A.)
       T. crassirostris, Thick-billed Kingbird (1 N.A.)
       T. verticalis, Western Kingbird (1)
       T. forficatus, Scissor-tailed Flycatcher (1)
       T. tyrannus, Eastern Kingbird (1)
       T. dominicensis, Gray Kingbird (1 N.A.)
  TITYRINAE (formerly part of Cotingidae)
   Pachyramphus (16/1)
       P. (Platypsaris) aglaiae, Rose-throated Becard (2)
OSCINES (or *PASSERES*): Songbirds
  ALAUDIDAE: Larks. Genera: 15/2 (incl. 1 introduced); species: 66–75/2 (incl. 1 introduced)
   Alauda (2/1)
       A. arvensis, Eurasian Skylark (1 N.A.) (introduced resident Vancouver Is., B.C., and vicinity; migrant Aleutians)
   Eremophila (2/1)
       E. alpestris, Horned Lark (20)

HIRUNDINIDAE: Swallows. Genera: 20/6; species: 70–75/8
>HIRUNDININAE
>>*Tachycineta* (6/2)
>>>T. *(Iridoprocne) bicolor*, Tree Swallow (1)
>>>T. *thalassina*, Violet-green Swallow (1 N.A.)
>>*Progne:* Martins (5/1)
>>>P. *subis*, Purple Martin (2)
>>*Stelgidopteryx* (1)
>>>S. *serripennis*, Northern Rough-winged Swallow (2)
>>*Riparia* (4/1)
>>>R. *riparia*, Bank Swallow (1 N.A.)
>>*Hirundo* (13/1)
>>>H. *rustica*, Barn Swallow (1 N.A.)
>>*Petrochelidon (Hirundo)* (10/2)
>>>P. *pyrrhonota*, Cliff Swallow (4)
>>>P. *fulva*, Cave Swallow (1 N.A.)

MOTACILLIDAE: Wagtails and Pipits. Genera: 5/2; species: 54/7
>*Motacilla:* Wagtails (10/3)
>>M. *flava*, Yellow Wagtail (1 N.A.)
>>M. *alba*, White Wagtail (1 N.A.)
>>M. *lugens*, Black-backed Wagtail (1) (migrant Aleutians; formerly lumped with *alba*)
>*Anthus:* Pipits (34/4)
>>A. *hodgsoni*, Olive (Indian) Tree Pipit (1) (migrant Aleutians)
>>A. *cervinus*, Red-throated Pipit (1) (breeds locally Alaska)
>>A. *spinoletta*, Water Pipit (3)
>>A. *spragueii*, Sprague's Pipit (1)

PYCNONOTIDAE: Bulbuls. Genera: 15/1 (introduced); species: 119–120/1 (introduced)
>*Pycnonotus* (47/1)
>>P. *jocosus*, Red-whiskered Bulbul (introduced)

LANIIDAE: Shrikes and Helmet Shrikes. Genera: 12/1; species: 65–74/2
>LANIINAE: Shrikes
>>*Lanius* (22/2)
>>>L. *ludovicianus*, Loggerhead Shrike (7)
>>>L. *excubitor*, Northern Shrike (2)

BOMBYCILLIDAE: Waxwings. Genera: 1/1; species: 3/2
>BOMBYCILLINAE: Waxwings
>>*Bombycilla* (3/2)
>>>B. *garrulus*, Bohemian Waxwing (1 N.A.)
>>>B. *cedrorum*, Cedar Waxwing (1)

PTILOGONATIDAE: Silky Flycatchers (sometimes considered part of the Bombycillidae). Genera: 3/1; species: 4/1
>*Phainopepla* (1)
>>P. *nitens*, Phainopepla (2)

CINCLIDAE: Dippers (1). Species: 4–5/1
>*Cinclus* (4/1)
>>C. *mexicanus*, American Dipper (1 N.A.)

TROGLODYTIDAE: Wrens. Genera: 14/6; species: 59/9
>*Campylorhynchus* (11/1)
>>C. *brunneicapillus*, Cactus Wren (1 N.A.)

Salpinctes (2/2)
  S. obsoletus, Rock Wren (1 N.A.)
  S. (Catherpes) mexicanus, Canyon Wren (2)
Cistothorus (4/2)
  C. platensis, Sedge (Short-billed Marsh) Wren (1 N.A.)
  C. (Telmatodytes) palustris, (Long-billed) Marsh Wren
    (10)
Thryomanes (2/1)
  T. bewickii, Bewick's Wren (13)
Thryothorus (21/1)
  T. ludovicianus, Carolina Wren (3)
Troglodytes (5/2)
  T. troglodytes, Winter Wren (12)
  T. aedon (incl. *brunneicollis*), House Wren (incl.
    Brown-throated Wren) (4)
MIMIDAE: Mimic Thrushes. Genera: 13/4; species: 31/10
Dumetella (1)
  D. carolinensis, Gray Catbird (1)
Mimus: Mockingbirds (9/1)
  M. polyglottos, Northern Mockingbird (2)
Oreoscoptes (1)
  O. montanus, Sage Thrasher (1)
Toxostoma: Thrashers (10/7)
  T. rufum, Brown Thrasher (2)
  T. longirostre, Long-billed Thrasher (1 N.A.)
  T. bendirei, Bendire's Thrasher (1)
  T. curvirostre, Curve-billed Thrasher (3)
  T. lecontei, Le Conte's Thrasher (1 N.A.)
  T. redivivum, California Thrasher (2)
  T. dorsale, Crissal Thrasher (2)
MUSCICAPIDAE: Traditionally this family has contained about 375
species called Old World Flycatchers, including a number of uncer-
tain forms of Australasia and elsewhere. More recently it has been
suggested that the Thrushes (family Turdidae), Babblers (Timaliidae), Parrotbills (Panuridae or Paradoxornithidae), Bald Crows (Pi-
cathartidae), Old World Warblers (Sylviidae), and Gnatcatchers (Polioptilidae) be added as subfamilies to make a single gigantic family,
containing some 1,250 species, and this model has been adopted in
the 6th edition of the A.O.U. *Check-list of North American Birds.*
Because the traditional family concepts are so familiar, they are re-
tained here (with appropriate annotation) and their genera and spe-
cies breakdowns included.
TURDIDAE: Thrushes (now regarded by many as a subfamily, Tur-
dinae, of the family Muscicapidae). Genera: 49/8; species: ±305/13
Luscinia (Erithacus) (25/1)
  L. svecicus, Bluethroat (1 N.A.)
Sialia: Bluebirds (3/3)
  S. sialis, Eastern Bluebird (4)
  S. mexicana, Western Bluebird (2)
  S. currucoides, Mountain Bluebird (1)
Myadestes: Solitaires (7/1)
  M. townsendi, Townsend's Solitaire (1 N.A.) (may be-
    long with silky flycatchers in family Ptilogonatidae)

Oenanthe: Wheatears (18/1)
> *O. oenanthe,* Northern Wheatear (2)

Zoothera (29/1)
> *Z. (Ixoreus) naevia,* Varied Thrush (2)

Catharus (10/4)
> *C. (Hylocichla) fuscescens,* Veery (3)
> *C. (Hylocichla) minimus,* Gray-cheeked Thrush (2)
> *C. (Hylocichla) ustulatus,* Swainson's Thrush (4)
> *C. (Hylocichla) guttatus,* Hermit Thrush (8)

Hylocichla (1)
> *H. mustelina,* Wood Thrush (1)

Turdus (62/1)
> *T. migratorius,* American Robin (5)

TIMALIIDAE: Babblers. Genera: 44/1; species: 244–282/1
> *Chamaea* (1)
> > *C. fasciata,* Wrentit (5) (formerly thought to belong to a monotypic family, Chamaeidae)

POLIOPTILIDAE: Gnatcatchers and allies (sometimes regarded as a subfamily, Polioptilinae, of the family Sylviidae or Old World Warblers, or as a tribe, Polioptilini, of the subfamily Sylviinae, in the family Muscicapidae). Genera: 3/1; species: 11–12/2–3
> *Polioptila* (9/3)
> > *P. caerulea,* Blue-gray Gnatcatcher (2)
> > *P. melanura,* Black-tailed Gnatcatcher (3–4)
> > *P. nigriceps,* Black-capped Gnatcatcher (1) (sometimes merged with *melanura*) (breeds irregularly S. Ariz.)

SYLVIIDAE: Old World Warblers (excluding Australasian families, Maluridae, Acanthizidae, etc.) (now regarded by many as a subfamily, Sylviinae, of the Old World Flycatcher family, Muscicapidae). Genera: ±127/2; species: ±395/3
> *Regulus:* Kinglets (5–6/2) (sometimes placed in a separate family, Regulidae)
> > *R. satrapa,* Golden-crowned Kinglet (4)
> > *R. calendula,* Ruby-crowned Kinglet (4)

> *Phylloscopus* (±40/1)
> > *P. borealis,* Arctic Warbler (1 N.A.)

See Appendix II for other sylviid species that have occurred in North America.

AEGITHALIDAE: Long-tailed Tits (sometimes regarded as a subfamily, Psaltriparinae, of the Tit family, Paridae). Genera: 3/1; species: 8/1
> *Psaltriparus* (1)
> > *P. minimus* (incl. *melanotis*), Bushtit (6, incl. Black-eared Bushtit, once considered a separate species)

REMIZIDAE: Penduline Tits (sometimes regarded as a subfamily, Remizinae, of the Tit family, Paridae). Genera: 4/1; species: 9/1
> *Auriparus* (1)
> > *A. flaviceps,* Verdin (2)

PARIDAE: Tits (Titmice). Genera: 4/1; species: 46–47/10
> *Parus* (44/10)
> > *P. atricapillus,* Black-capped Chickadee (9)
> > *P. carolinensis,* Carolina Chickadee (5)
> > *P. sclateri,* Mexican (Gray-sided) Chickadee (1 N.A.)
> > *P. gambeli,* Mountain Chickadee (5)

P. *cinctus*, Gray-headed Chickadee (Siberian Tit) (1 N.A.)

P. *hudsonicus*, Boreal Chickadee (5)

P. *rufescens*, Chestnut-backed Chickadee (3)

P. *wollweberi*, Bridled Titmouse (1 N.A.)

P. *inornatus*, Plain Titmouse (8)

P. *bicolor* (incl. *atricristatus*), Tufted Titmouse (5, incl. Black-crested Titmouse)

SITTIDAE: Nuthatches and allies. Genera: 4/1; species: 22–25/4

Sitta (21/4)

S. *pygmaea*, Pygmy Nuthatch (4)

S. *pusilla*, Brown-headed Nuthatch (2)

S. *canadensis*, Red-breasted Nuthatch (1)

S. *carolinensis*, White-breasted Nuthatch (6)

CERTHIIDAE: Treecreepers. Genera: 2/1; species: 6/1

CERTHIINAE: Treecreepers

Certhia (5/1)

C. *americana*, Brown Creeper (7)

EMBERIZIDAE: Once restricted to a group of Old World "finches," the "buntings," this family is now understood by most authorities to encompass many American "finches" (family Fringillidae in part) and the Tanagers (Thraupidae). It has also been suggested that the Wood Warblers (Parulidae), Honeycreepers (Coerebidae), and New World Blackbirds (Icteridae) belong here as well, and this model has been adopted in the 6th edition of the A.O.U. *Check-list of North American Birds.* Because the traditional family concepts of the tanagers, wood warblers, and icterids are so familiar, they are retained here (with appropriate annotation) and their genera and species breakdowns included. Therefore the Emberizidae is here shown to contain only two subfamilies: the Emberizinae (genera: ±65/15; species: ±315/48) and the Cardinalinae (genera: 9/4; species: ±37/10).

EMBERIZINAE: Longspurs, Snow Bunting(s), Lark Bunting, Old World Buntings, New World Sparrows, Juncos, Seedeaters, and Towhees

Emberiza (34/1)

E. *rustica*, Rustic Bunting (1 N.A.) (migrant Aleutians)

Calcarius: Longspurs (4/4)

C. (*Rhynchophanes*) *mccownii*, McCown's Longspur (1)

C. *lapponicus*, Lapland Longspur (2)

C. *pictus*, Smith's Longspur (1)

C. *ornatus*, Chestnut-collared Longspur (1)

Plectrophenax (1–2/1–2)

P. *nivalis*, Snow Bunting (2)

P. *hyperboreus*, McKay's Bunting (1) (sometimes regarded as a race of Snow Bunting)

Calamospiza (1)

C. *melanocorys*, Lark Bunting (1)

Zonotrichia (9/8)

Z. (*Passerella*) *iliaca*, Fox Sparrow (18)

Z. (*Melospiza*) *melodia*, Song Sparrow (30)

Z. (*Melospiza*) *lincolnii*, Lincoln's Sparrow (3)

Z. (*Melospiza*) *georgiana*, Swamp Sparrow (3)

Z. *querula,* Harris' Sparrow (1)
Z. *leucophrys,* White-crowned Sparrow (5)
Z. *albicollis,* White-throated Sparrow (1)
Z. *atricapilla,* Golden-crowned Sparrow (1)
Junco: Juncos (3/2)
J. *hyemalis* (incl. *aikeni, caniceps,* and *oreganus*), Dark-eyed Junco (12, incl. Slate-colored, White-winged, Gray-headed, and Oregon Juncos)
J. *phaeonotus,* Yellow-eyed (Mexican) Junco (1 N.A.)
Ammodramus (10/7)
A. (*Passerculus*) *sandwichensis* (incl. *princeps*), Savannah Sparrow (12, incl. Ipswich Sparrow)
A. (*Ammospiza*) *maritimus* (incl. *nigrescens* and *mirabilis*), Seaside Sparrow (9, incl. Dusky and Cape Sable Seaside Sparrows)
A. (*Ammospiza*) *caudacutus,* Sharp-tailed Sparrow (5)
A. *lecontei* (*Passerherbulus caudacutus*), Le Conte's Sparrow (1)
A. *bairdii,* Baird's Sparrow (1)
A. (*Passerherbulus*) *henslowii,* Henslow's Sparrow (2)
A. *savannarum,* Grasshopper Sparrow (5)
Spizella (6/6)
S. *arborea,* American Tree Sparrow (2)
S. *passerina,* Chipping Sparrow (3)
S. *pusilla,* Field Sparrow (3, incl. Worthen's Sparrow, which formerly bred in New Mexico)
S. *atrogularis,* Black-chinned Sparrow (3)
S. *pallida,* Clay-colored Sparrow (1)
S. *breweri,* Brewer's Sparrow (2)
Pooecetes (1)
P. *gramineus,* Vesper Sparrow (3)
Chondestes (1)
C. *grammacus,* Lark Sparrow (2)
Amphispiza (2/2)
A. *bilineata,* Black-throated Sparrow (3)
A. *belli,* Sage Sparrow (4)
Aimophila (14/6)
A. *aestivalis,* Bachman's Sparrow (3)
A. *botterii,* Botteri's Sparrow (2)
A. *cassinii,* Cassin's Sparrow (1)
A. (*Amphispiza*) *quinquestriata,* Five-striped Sparrow (1 N.A.)
A. *carpalis,* Rufous-winged Sparrow (1 N.A.)
A. *ruficeps,* Rufous-crowned Sparrow (6)
Sporophila: Seedeaters (31/1)
S. *torqueola,* White-collared Seedeater (1 N.A.) (local and irregular resident S. Tex.)
Pipilo: Towhees (7/4)
P. (*Chlorura*) *chlorurus,* Green-tailed Towhee (1)
P. *erythrophthalmus,* Rufous-sided Towhee (13)
P. *fuscus,* Brown Towhee (10)
P. *aberti,* Abert's Towhee (2)

Arremonops (4/1)
>   *A. rufivirgatus,* Olive Sparrow (1 N.A.)

CARDINALINAE: Dickcissel, Cardinal-Grosbeaks, and *Passerina* Buntings
>   *Spiza* (1)
>>   *S. americana,* Dickcissel (1) (possibly belongs in the New World Blackbird family, Icteridae)
>   *Pheucticus* (4/2)
>>   *P. ludovicianus,* Rose-breasted Grosbeak (1)
>>   *P. melanocephalus,* Black-headed Grosbeak (2)
>   *Cardinalis* (3/2)
>>   *C. (Richmondena) cardinalis,* Northern Cardinal (5)
>>   *C. (Pyrrhuloxia) sinuatus,* Pyrrhuloxia (2)
>   *Passerina* (12/5)
>>   *P. (Guiraca) caerulea,* Blue Grosbeak (3)
>>   *P. cyanea,* Indigo Bunting (1)
>>   *P. amoena,* Lazuli Bunting (1)
>>   *P. versicolor,* Varied Bunting (2)
>>   *P. ciris,* Painted Bunting (2)

THRAUPIDAE: Tanagers (widely thought to be a subfamily, Thraupinae, of the Emberizidae, above). Genera: 51/2 (incl. 1 introduced); species: ±230/5 (incl. 1 introduced)
>   *Piranga* (9/4)
>>   *P. flava,* Hepatic Tanager (2)
>>   *P. rubra,* Summer Tanager (2)
>>   *P. olivacea,* Scarlet Tanager (1)
>>   *P. ludoviciana,* Western Tanager (1)
>   *Thraupis* (8/1)
>>   *T. episcopus (virens),* Blue-gray Tanager (1) (introduced S. Fla.)

PARULIDAE: Wood Warblers (regarded by many as a subfamily, Parulinae, of the Emberizidae, above). Genera: 27/15; species: 107–123/53
>   *Mniotilta* (1)
>>   *M. varia,* Black-and-White Warbler (1)
>   *Vermivora* (11/9)
>>   *V. bachmanii,* Bachman's Warbler (1) (near extinction)
>>   *V. chrysoptera,* Golden-winged Warbler (1)
>>   *V. pinus,* Blue-winged Warbler (1)
>>   *V. peregrina,* Tennessee Warbler (1)
>>   *V. celata,* Orange-crowned Warbler (4)
>>   *V. ruficapilla,* Nashville Warbler (2)
>>   *V. virginiae,* Virginia's Warbler (1)
>>   *V. crissalis,* Colima Warbler (1)
>>   *V. luciae,* Lucy's Warbler (1)
>   *Parula* (2/2)
>>   *P. americana,* Northern Parula (1)
>>   *P. pitiayumi,* Tropical Parula (Olive-backed Warbler) (1 N.A.) (resident very locally S. Tex.)
>   *Dendroica* (26/21)
>>   *D. petechia,* Yellow Warbler (6)
>>   *D. pensylvanica,* Chestnut-sided Warbler (1)
>>   *D. cerulea,* Cerulean Warbler (1)
>>   *D. caerulescens,* Black-throated Blue Warbler (2)

D. *pinus*, Pine Warbler (2)
D. *graciae*, Grace's Warbler (1 N.A.)
D. *dominica*, Yellow-throated Warbler (3)
D. *nigrescens*, Black-throated Gray Warbler (1)
D. *townsendi*, Townsend's Warbler (1)
D. *occidentalis*, Hermit Warbler (1)
D. *chrysoparia*, Golden-cheeked Warbler (1)
D. *virens*, Black-throated Green Warbler (2)
D. *discolor*, Prairie Warbler (2)
D. *tigrina*, Cape May Warbler (1)
D. *fusca*, Blackburnian Warbler (1)
D. *magnolia*, Magnolia Warbler (1)
D. *coronata* (incl. *auduboni*), Yellow-rumped Warbler
(4, incl. Myrtle and Audubon's Warblers)
D. *palmarum*, Palm Warbler (2)
D. *kirtlandii*, Kirtland's Warbler (1)
D. *striata*, Blackpoll Warbler (1)
D. *castanea*, Bay-breasted Warbler (1)
Setophaga (1)
S. *ruticilla*, American Redstart (2)
Seiurus (3/3)
S. *aurocapillus*, Ovenbird (3)
S. *noveboracensis*, Northern Waterthrush (3)
S. *motacilla*, Louisiana Waterthrush (1)
Limnothlypis (1)
L. *swainsonii*, Swainson's Warbler (1)
Helmitheros (1)
H. *vermivorus*, Worm-eating Warbler (1)
Protonotaria (1)
P. *citrea*, Prothonotary Warbler
Geothlypis: Yellowthroats (14/6)
G. *trichas*, Common Yellowthroat (11)
G. (*Chamaethlypis*) *poliocephala*, Gray-crowned Yel-
lowthroat (Ground Chat) (1) (formerly resident S.
Tex.; now very rare; status uncertain)
G. (*Oporornis*) *formosa*, Kentucky Warbler (1)
G. (*Oporornis*) *agilis*, Connecticut Warbler (1)
G. (*Oporornis*) *philadelphia*, Mourning Warbler (1)
G. (*Oporornis*) *tolmiei*, MacGillivray's Warbler (2)
Wilsonia (3/3)
W. *citrina*, Hooded Warbler (1)
W. *pusilla*, Wilson's Warbler (3)
W. *canadensis*, Canada Warbler (1)
Cardellina (1)
C. *rubrifrons*, Red-faced Warbler (1)
Myioborus (11/1)
M. (*Setophaga*) *pictus*, Painted Redstart (1 N.A.)
Icteria (1)
I. *virens*, Yellow-breasted Chat (2) (probably *not* a paru-
lid)
Peucedramus (1)
P. *taeniatus*, Olive Warbler (1) (regarded by some as a
sylviid)

VIREONIDAE: Vireos, Peppershrikes, and Shrike Vireos (the two latter groups sometimes regarded as separate families). Genera: 4/1; species: ±40/11 (Vireos only, species: 37/11)

    VIREONINAE: Vireos

        Vireo (25/11)

            V. huttoni, Hutton's Vireo (4)

            V. atricapillus, Black-capped Vireo (1)

            V. griseus, White-eyed Vireo (4)

            V. bellii, Bell's Vireo (4)

            V. vicinior, Gray Vireo (1)

            V. solitarius, Solitary Vireo (4)

            V. flavifrons, Yellow-throated Vireo (1)

            V. philadelphicus, Philadelphia Vireo (1)

            V. olivaceus (incl. *flavoviridis*), Red-eyed Vireo (incl. Yellow-green Vireo) (2)

            V. altiloquus, Black-whiskered Vireo (1 N.A.)

            V. gilvus, Warbling Vireo (3)

ICTERIDAE: American Orioles, Blackbirds & Meadlowlarks and Bobolink (regarded by many as a subfamily, Icterinae, of the Emberizidae, above). Genera: 25/8; species: 90–92/20

    ICTERINAE: American Orioles, Blackbirds, and Meadowlarks

        Icterus: American Orioles (24/7)

            I. pectoralis, Spot(ted)-breasted Oriole (1 N.A.) (introduced S. Fla.)

            I. gularis, Altamira (Lichtenstein's) Oriole (1)

            I. cucullatus, Hooded Oriole (4)

            I. galbula (incl. *bullocki*), Northern Oriole (3, incl. Baltimore and Bullock's Orioles)

            I. spurius, Orchard Oriole (1)

            I. graduacauda, Audubon's (Black-headed) Oriole (1 N.A.)

            I. parisorum, Scott's Oriole (1)

        Xanthocephalus (1)

            X. xanthocephalus, Yellow-headed Blackbird (1)

        Agelaius (8/2)

            A. phoeniceus, Red-winged Blackbird (14)

            A. tricolor, Tricolored Blackbird (1)

        Sturnella: Meadowlarks (2/2)

            S. magna, Eastern Meadowlark (4)

            S. neglecta, Western Meadowlark (2)

        Quiscalus: Grackles (7/3)

            Q. (*Cassidix*) *mexicanus*, Great-tailed Grackle (3) (formerly merged with *major*)

            Q. major, Boat-tailed Grackle (2) (formerly merged with *mexicanus*)

            Q. quiscula, Common Grackle (3)

        Euphagus (2/2)

            E. carolinus, Rusty Blackbird (2)

            E. cyanocephalus, Brewer's Blackbird (1)

        Molothrus: Cowbirds (5/2)

            M. (*Tangavius*) *aeneus*, Bronzed Cowbird (2)

            M. ater, Brown-headed Cowbird (3)

DOLICHONYCHINAE: Bobolink
   Dolichonyx (1)
      D. oryzivorus, Bobolink (1)
FRINGILLIDAE: Traditionally defined in North America as encompassing the New World Sparrows, Cardinal-Grosbeaks, and other forms now included by most authorities in the family Emberizidae (see above); this model comprises some 436 species. The family is here defined as including only two subfamilies, the Fringillinae (genus [1]; species: 3/1) and the Carduelinae (genera: 18/7; species: 129/15 [incl. 1 introduced]). Both of these subfamilies are sometimes considered to be distinct families.
   FRINGILLINAE: Chaffinches and Brambling
      Fringilla (3/1)
         F. montifringilla, Brambling (1 N.A.) (migrant Aleutians)
   CARDUELINAE: Siskins, Goldfinches, Redpolls, Rosefinches, Rosy Finches, Grosbeaks, and Crossbills
      Carduelis: Siskins and Goldfinches (24/5)
         C. carduelis, Eurasian Goldfinch (1 N.A.) (widely introduced but poorly established except in Bermuda)
         C. (Spinus) pinus, Pine Siskin (1 N.A.)
         C. (Spinus) tristis, American Goldfinch (4)
         C. (Spinus) psaltria, Lesser Goldfinch (2)
         C. (Spinus) lawrencei, Lawrence's Goldfinch (1)
      Acanthis (6/2)
         A. (Carduelis) flammea, Common Redpoll (3)
         A. (Carduelis) hornemanni, Hoary Redpoll (2)
      Leucosticte: Rosy Finches (3/1)
         L. arctoa (incl. *tephrocotis, atrata,* and *australis*), Common Rosy Finch (8, incl. Gray-crowned, Black, and Brown-capped Rosy Finches)
      Carpodacus: Rosefinches (21/3)
         C. purpureus, Purple Finch (3)
         C. cassinii, Cassin's Finch (1)
         C. mexicanus, House Finch (3)
      Pinicola (2/1)
         P. enucleator, Pine Grosbeak
      Loxia: Crossbills (3/2)
         L. curvirostra, Red Crossbill (7)
         L. leucoptera, White-winged Crossbill (1 N.A.)
      Coccothraustes (9/1)
         C. (Hesperiphona) vespertinus, Evening Grosbeak (3)
PLOCEIDAE: Weaverbirds. Genera: 18–19/1 (introduced); species: ±155 (excluding Estrildidae)/2 (introduced)
   PASSERINAE: Old World Sparrows (now widely considered a family, Passeridae)
      Passer: Old World Sparrows (15/2)
         P. domesticus, House Sparrow (1 N.A.) (introduced)
         P. montanus, Eurasian Tree Sparrow (1 N.A.) (introduced)
STURNIDAE: Starlings and Mynahs. Genera: 26/2 (introduced); species: ±110/2 (introduced)
   STURNINAE

Sturnus (16/1)
    S. vulgaris, Common (European) Starling (1 N.A.) (introduced)
Acridotheres (6/1)
    A. cristatellus, Crested Mynah (1 N.A.) (introduced)
CORVIDAE: Crows, Ravens, Magpies, and Jays (family often placed earlier in the phylogenetic sequence, between the Swallows and the Tits). Genera: 26/9; species: 103–104/17
    Gymnorhinus (1)
        G. cyanocephalus, Pinyon Jay (1)
    Cyanocitta (2/2)
        C. cristata, Blue Jay (4)
        C. stelleri, Steller's Jay (6)
    Psilorhinus (*Cyanocorax*) (1)
        P. morio, Brown Jay (1 N.A.) (recently established S. Tex.)
    Aphelocoma (3/2)
        A. coerulescens, Scrub Jay (11)
        A. ultramarina, Mexican (Gray-breasted) Jay (2)
    Cyanocorax (11/1)
        C. yncas, Green Jay (1 N.A.)
    Perisoreus (3/1)
        P. canadensis, Gray Jay
    Pica: Magpies (2/2)
        P. pica, Black-billed Magpie (1 N.A.)
        P. nuttalli, Yellow-billed Magpie (1)
    Nucifraga: Nutcrackers (2/1)
        N. columbiana, Clark's Nutcracker (1)
    Corvus: Crows and Ravens (36/6)
        C. brachyrhynchos, American (Common) Crow (4)
        C. caurinus, Northwestern Crow (1)
        C. imparatus, Mexican Crow (1 N.A.) (visitor)
        C. ossifragus, Fish Crow (1)
        C. cryptoleucus, Chihuahuan (White-necked) Raven (1)
        C. corax, Common Raven (2)

Appendix II

The following list contains 140 species of birds whose normal ranges do not include North America. Some have been recorded irregularly with surprising frequency (more than ten times in a number of cases), and a few may turn out to be of regular occurrence in remote extremities of the continent, especially western Alaska; however, all at present are found here only rarely and irregularly.

The majority of species are included on the basis of specimen confirmation or definitive photographs, but a few well-documented sight records are also listed at the author's discretion. Judgments on occurrence status and validity of records are based on the sources given in the Bibliography under CHECKLIST as well as basic references cited under family headings.

Brief details are given in column form on the native distribution of the species (Native); the state(s) or province(s) in which the vagrant species have been recorded (Locality); and Remarks about species or records in a few cases. Where no Remarks appear, it can be assumed that a specimen exists for the species in question.

SPECIES	NATIVE	LOCALITY	REMARKS
White-capped (Shy) Albatross *Diomedea cauta*	S. Hemis. oceans	Calif., Ore., Wash.	
Yellow-nosed Albatross *Diomedea chlororhynchus*	S. Hemis. oceans	Que., N.B., N.S., Me., N.Y., Md. La., Tex., Fla.	
Black-browed Albatross *Diomedea melanophris*	S. Hemis. oceans	Mass., N.C., Nfld.	Sight
Wandering Albatross *Diomedea exulans*	S. Hemis. oceans	Calif.	Photo
Cape Petrel *Daption capense*	S.Hemis. oceans	Calif.	Sight
Streaked Shearwater *Calonectris leucomelas*	N. Asian oceans	Calif.	
Little Shearwater *Puffinus assimilis*	Widespread oceanic	N.S., S.C.	
Murphy's Petrel *Pterodroma ultima*	Trop. Pacif.	Ore.	
Herald Petrel *Pterodroma arminjoniana*	Local, S. oceans	N.Y., N.C.	

SPECIES	NATIVE	LOCALITY	REMARKS
Cook's Petrel *Pterodroma cookii*	S. Pacif.	Calif., Alas.	Many sight recs., photos; may be regular off W. coast
Stejneger's Petrel *Pterodroma longirostris*	S. Hemis. oceans	Calif.	Sight
White-faced Storm-Petrel *Pelagodroma marina*	Widespread oceanic	Mass., N.Y., N.C., Del., Conn., N.J., Va.	Possibly regular, W. Atlan., fall
British Storm-Petrel *Hydrobates pelagicus*	N.E. Atlan.	N.S.	
Wedge-rumped (Galápagos) Storm-Petrel *Oceanodroma tethys*	Ocean, vic. Galápagos Is.	Calif.	
Harcourt's (Band-rumped) Storm-Petrel *Oceanodroma castro*	Widespread Atlan. & Pacif.	Pa., Ind., Ont., D.C., Fla., S.C., N.C., Del., Tex., Calif.	
Red-tailed Tropicbird *Phaethon rubricauda*	Tropical Pacif. & Indian oceans	Calif.	Sight
Lesser Frigatebird *Fregata ariel*	Tropical oceans	Me.	Photo
Blue-footed Booby *Sula nebouxii*	Tropical E. Pacif.	Calif., Wash.	
Masked (Blue-faced) Booby *Sula dactylatra*	Tropical oceans	Gulf & Atlan. coasts	
Red-footed Booby *Sula sula*	Tropical oceans	Fla., La., Tex., Calif.	
Little Egret *Egretta garzetta*	Eurasia	Nfld., Que.	
Chinese Egret *Egretta eulophotes*	E. Asia	Alas.	
Jabiru (Stork) *Jabiru mycteria*	Neotrop.	Tex., Okla.	Photo
Scarlet Ibis *Eudocimus ruber*	Trop. S. Amer.	Fla., Tex.	
King Vulture *Sarcoramphus papa*	Neotrop.	Fla.	Old sight rec.

SPECIES	NATIVE	LOCALITY	REMARKS
Roadside Hawk *Buteo magnirostris*	Neotrop.	Tex.	
Steller's Sea Eagle *Haliaeetus pelagicus*	N.E. Asia	Alas.	
Eurasian Kestrel *Falco tinnunculus*	Eurasia	Mass., N.J., Alas.	
Bewick's Swan *Cygnus bewickii*	Eurasia	Ore., Calif., Alas.	Now lumped with Whistling Swan (*C. co- lumbianus*) as Tundra Swan
Pink-footed Goose *Anser brachyrhynchus*	Europe	Nfld.	Photo; for- merly consid- ered a race of Bean Goose (*A. fabalis*)
Barnacle Goose *Branta leucopsis*	Greenland, N. Europe	Many recs. E. coast	
White-cheeked (Bahama) Pintail *Anas bahamensis*	Caribbean	Del., Va., Fla., Ala., Tex., Wisc.	
Spot-billed Duck *Anas poecilorhyncha*	E. Asia	Alas.	
Baikal Teal *Anas formosa*	N.E. Asia	Alas., B.C., Wash., Ore., Calif.	
Falcated Teal *Anas falcata*	E. Asia	Alas.	May occur annually, W. Aleutians
Eurasian (Common) Crane *Grus grus*	Eurasia	Alta., Nebr., Alas., N.M.	Photos
Corn Crake *Crex crex*	Eurasia	Many recs. Lab. to Md.	
Spotted Rail *Rallus maculatus*	Neotrop.	Pa.	
Paint-billed Crake *Neocrex erythrops*	S. Amer.	Tex.	
Eurasian Coot *Fulica atra*	Eurasia	Lab., Nfld., Alas.	

SPECIES	NATIVE	LOCALITY	REMARKS
Caribbean Coot *Fulica caribaea*	Caribbean	Fla.	
Double-striped Thick-knee *Burhinus bistriatus*	Neotrop.	Tex.	
Northern Lapwing *Vanellus vanellus*	Eurasia	Many recs. N.E. coast to S.C.	
Greater Golden Plover *Pluvialis apricaria*	N. Europe	Nfld.	
Little Ringed Plover *Charadrius dubius*	Eurasia	Alas.	
Slender-billed Curlew *Numenius tenuirostris*	C. Asia	Ont.	
Eurasian Curlew *Numenius arquata*	N. Eurasia	N.Y., Mass., N.S.	
Far Eastern Curlew *Numenius madagascariensis*	N.E. Asia	Alas.	May occur annually W. Aleutians
Black-tailed Godwit *Limosa limosa*	Eurasia	Nfld., Mass., N.J., Alas., Pa., N.C., Fla.	Probably regular in W. Aleutians
Marsh Sandpiper *Tringa stagnatilis*	Eurasia	Alas.	
Green Sandpiper *Tringa ochropus*	Eurasia	Alas.	Sight
Terek Sandpiper *Tringa (Xenus) cinereus*	Mainly N. Asia	Alas.	May occur annually W. Aleutians
Jacksnipe *Lymnocryptes minimus*	Eurasia	Lab., Calif., Alas.	
Eurasian Woodcock *Scolopax rusticola*	Eurasia	Nfld., Que., N.J., Va., Pa., Ohio, Ala.	
Great Knot *Calidris tenuirostris*	N. E. Asia	Alas.	
Little Stint *Calidris minuta*	N. Eurasia	Ont., Alas., N.B., Mass., Del.	
Spoon-bill(ed) Sandpiper *Eurynorhynchus pygmeus*	N.E. Siberia	Alas.	
Broad-billed Sandpiper *Limicola falcinellus*	N. Eurasia	Alas.	

SPECIES	NATIVE	LOCALITY	REMARKS
South Polar Skua *Catharacta maccormicki*	Antarctic	Offshore, Atlan. & Pacif.	May occur regularly
Band-tailed Gull *Larus belcheri*	S. Amer.	Fla.	Photo
Black-tailed Gull *Larus crassirostris*	E. Asia	Alas.	Sight
White-winged (Black) Tern *Chlidonias leucopterus*	Eurasia	N.B., Ga., Mass., Wisc., Alas., Ind., Va., Del.	
Large-billed Tern *Phaetusa simplex*	S. Amer.	Ill., Ohio	Photo
Trudeau's Tern *Sterna trudeaui*	S. Amer.	N.J.	Old Audubon rec.
Scaly-naped Pigeon *Columba squamosa*	Caribbean	Fla.	
Zenaida Dove *Zenaida aurita*	Caribbean	Fla.	
Ruddy Ground Dove *Columbigallina talpacoti*	Neotrop.	Tex.	Photo
Ruddy Quail Dove *Geotrygon montana*	Neotrop. & Caribbean	Fla.	
Key West Quail Dove *Geotrygon chrysia*	N. Caribbean	Fla.	
Red-crowned Parrot *Amazona viridigenalis*	N.E. Mex	Tex.	Sight; escapes?
Eurasian (Common) Cuckoo *Cuculus canorus*	Eurasia	Alas., Mass.	
Oriental Cuckoo *Cuculus saturatus*	N. Asia	Alas.	
Oriental Scops Owl *Otus sunia*	Asia	Alas.	
Grey (Jungle) Nightjar *Caprimulgus indicus*	E. Asia	Alas.	
White-collared Swift *Streptoprocne zonaris*	Neotrop.	Fla., Tex.	
White-throated Needle-tailed Swift *Hirundapus caudacutus*	Widespread Asia	Alas.	
Eurasian (Common) Swift *Apus apus*	Eurasia	Alas.	

SPECIES	NATIVE	LOCALITY	REMARKS
Fork-tailed Swift *Apus pacificus*	E. Asia	Alas.	
Antillean Palm Swift *Tachornis phoenicobia*	N. Caribbean	Fla.	Photo
Green Violetear *Colibri thalassinus*	Neotrop.	Tex.	Photo
Cuban Emerald *Chlorostilbon ricordii*	Bahamas, Cuba	Fla.	Sight
Rufous-tailed Hummingbird *Amazilia tzacatl*	Neotrop.	Tex.	Old recs.; 2 specimens
Berylline Hummingbird *Amazilia beryllina*	Mexico & C. Amer.	Ariz.	Photo; bred once
Plain-capped Starthroat *Heliomaster constantii*	Mexico & C. Amer.	Ariz.	Photos
Bahaman Woodstar *Calliphlox evelynae*	Bahamas	Fla.	
Bumblebee Hummingbird *Atthis heloisa*	Mexico	Ariz.	
Eared Trogon *Euptilotus neoxenus*	Mexico	Ariz.	Photo
Eurasian Hoopoe *Upupa epops*	S. Eurasia	Alas.	
Eurasian Wryneck *Jynx torquilla*	Eurasia	Alas.	
Fork-tailed Flycatcher *Tyrannus savana* (*Muscivora tyrannus*)	S. Amer.	±20 recs., incl. N.E. states	
Loggerhead Kingbird *Tyrannus caudifasciatus*	Caribbean	Fla.	Photos
Variegated Flycatcher *Empidonomus varius*	S. Amer.	Me.	Photo
Pale-throated (Nutting's) Flycatcher *Myiarchus nuttingi*	Mexico & C. Amer.	Ariz.	
La Sagra's Flycatcher *Myiarchus sagrae*	Caribbean	Ala.	
Bahaman Swallow *Callichelidon cyaneoviridis*	Bahamas, Cuba	Fla.	May breed
Cuban Martin *Progne cryptoleuca*	Cuba	Fla.	
Gray-breasted Martin *Progne chalybea*	Neotrop.	Tex.	

SPECIES	NATIVE	LOCALITY	REMARKS
Southern Martin *Progne elegans*	S. Amer.	Fla.	
Common House Martin *Delichon urbica*	Eurasia	Alas.	
Grey Wagtail *Motacilla cinerea*	Eurasia	Alas.	
Brown Tree Pipit *Anthus trivialis*	Eurasia	Alas.	
Pechora Pipit *Anthus gustavi*	N.E. Asia	Alas.	
Brown Shrike *Lanius cristatus*	Asia	Alas.	Sight
Bahaman Mockingbird *Mimus gundlachii*	Bahamas, Cuba, Jamaica	Fla.	Photo
Mountain (Siberian) Accentor *Prunella montanella*	N.E. Asia	Alas.	
Grey-spotted Flycatcher *Muscicapa griseisticta*	N.E. Asia	Alas.	May occur annually, W. Aleutians
Siberian Flycatcher *Muscicapa sibirica*	N. Asia	Alas., also Bermuda	
Red-breasted Flycatcher *Ficedula parva*	Eurasia	Alas.	
Siberian Rubythroat *Erithacus (Luscinia)* *calliope*	N. Asia	Alas.	May occur annually, W. Aleutians
Aztec Thrush *Ridgwayia pinicola*	Mexico	Ariz., Tex.	Photos
(Eurasian) Redwing *Turdus iliacus*	Eurasia	Nfld., N.Y., Alas.	Photo; N.Y. bird possibly an escape
Eye-browed Thrush *Turdus obscurus*	N. Asia	Alas.	May occur annually, W. Aleutians
Fieldfare *Turdus pilaris*	Eurasia	Lab., N.W.T., Nfld., N.S., Ont., Que., N.Y., Conn., Del., Alas.	

SPECIES	NATIVE	LOCALITY	REMARKS
Dusky Thrush *Turdus naumanni* *(eunomus)*	Asia	Alas.	May occur annually, W. Aleutians
Clay-colored Robin *Turdus grayi*	Neotrop.	Tex.	
Rufous-backed Robin *Turdus rufopalliatus*	Mexico	Ariz., Calif.	
Dusky Warbler *Phylloscopus fuscatus*	N. Asia	Alas., Calif.	Sight
Wood Warbler *Phylloscopus sibilatrix*	Europe	Alas.	
Middendorff's Grasshopper Warbler *Locustella ochotensis*	N.E. Asia	Alas.	
Black-faced Grassquit *Tiaris bicolor*	Caribbean, S. Amer.	Fla.	
Blue Bunting *Cyanocompsa parellina*	Mid. Amer.	La., Tex.	
Yellow Grosbeak *Pheucticus chrysopeplus*	Neotrop.	Ariz.	Photos
Little Bunting *Emberiza pusilla*	N. Eurasia	Alas.	
Grey Bunting *Emberiza variabilis*	N.E. Asia	Alas.	
Eurasian Reed Bunting *Emberiza schoeniclus*	Eurasia	Alas.	
Pallas' Reed Bunting *Emberiza pallasi*	Asia	Alas.	
Stripe-headed Tanager *Spindalis zena*	N. Caribbean	Fla.	Photo; perhaps regular; may have bred
Bananaquit (Bahama Honeycreeper) *Coereba bahamensis*	Neotrop. & Caribbean	Fla.	
Slate-throated Redstart *Myioborus miniatus*	Neotrop.	N.M., Ariz.	
Fan-tailed Warbler *Euthlypis lachrymosa*	Mexico & C. Amer.	Ariz.	
Rufous-capped Warbler *Basileuterus rufifrons*	Mexico & C. Amer.	Tex., Ariz.	

SPECIES	NATIVE	LOCALITY	REMARKS
Golden-crowned Warbler *Basileuterus culicivorus*	Neotrop.	Tex.	
Thick-billed Vireo *Vireo crassirostris*	Caribbean	Fla.	Sight
Streak-backed (Scarlet-headed) Oriole *Icterus sclateri*	Mexico & C. Amer.	Ariz., Calif.	
Black-vented Oriole *Icterus wagleri*	Mexico & C. Amer.	Tex.	Photo
Tawny-shouldered Blackbird *Agelaius humeralis*	Cuba, Haiti	Fla.	
(Eurasian) Hawfinch *Coccothraustes coccothraustes*	Eurasia	Alas.	
Eurasian Bullfinch *Pyrrhula pyrrhula*	Eurasia	Alas.	
Common Rosefinch (Scarlet Grosbeak) *Carpodacus erythrinus*	Eurasia	Alas.	May occur annually W. Aleutians
Grey-capped (Oriental) Greenfinch *Carduelis sinica*	N.E. Asia	Alas.	

Appendix III

Timing is very important in planning excursions to see particular bird species or avian events. The westerner wishing to experience an eastern warbler wave will be disappointed if he plans a visit to New England in April. California Condors may be resident in southern California, but they are not stationary and favor different feeding areas at different seasons. These and other temporal aspects of bird finding are addressed in the schedule below. It lists birding dates in three ways: by event (mainly migrations)—e.g., when best to see shorebird migrants on the Great Plains; by locality—e.g., when the greatest variety of species is to be found in Churchill; and by species—e.g., the period during which Kirtland's Warbler is singing on territory and thus is most easily located. The three categories overlap, of course, in numerous instances.

Fortunately birding adventures cannot be planned with absolute precision. No one can predict on which days the best "waves" will hit the Texas coast in spring; you may arrive at the very peak of the puffin season at Machias Seal Island only to find that the birds are invisible behind a dense fog bank. "Fortunately" because without a strong element of chance the sport of birding would, like viewing historical monuments or visiting the zoo, lack the special piquancy of *la chasse*.

For locality information, see BIRD FINDING.

PASSERINE MIGRATION (spring and fall). In general, the autumn passage of land birds tends to be more protracted than the spring. It involves greater numbers of individuals due to the addition of the young birds of the year, and it tends to contain a greater variety of species with a higher proportion of extralimital rarities in many localities (for the reason, see MIGRATION). Waves of warblers and other songbirds result from parallel patterns of weather fronts and migration which prevail only over eastern North America, and consequently waves do not occur regularly west of the foothills of the Rockies. *N.B.*: The dates given for migration periods are intended to encompass the time of greatest activity, not the much longer span between the arrival of the earliest migratory species and the departure of the latest.

Maritimes/New England. Late April to early June, with biggest waves usually between May 10 and June 1; most warblers, thrushes, etc., mid-August to mid-October; sparrows and other late migrants through early November, peaking in October.

Cape May (New Jersey). See under *Localities,* below.

Central South (North Carolina/Tennessee). Late March through early May; second week in September to early November.

Southern Florida. Late March to early May (peaks April); mid-September to early November.

Point Pelee (Ontario). See under *Localities,* below.

Gulf Coast (Texas/Louisiana). Spring migration much more spectacular than fall, especially when cold fronts from the north put down migrant flocks arriving from across Gulf of Mexico; first wave usually occurs late March; southern specialties (e.g., Swainson's Warbler) peak before April 15; greatest movement and best chance of waves between mid-April and first week in May; fall passage September to October.

Great Plains (Kansas/Nebraska). Spring passage more concentrated, spectacular; fall more diffuse. Scattered copses in prairie regions often harbor large concentrations of migrants. Second week in April to third week in May; late August to early November (main peaks September to October).

Central Rockies (Colorado). Spring peaks usually late April to early May; waves regular only in eastern foothills, but late snowstorms sometimes force down large numbers of migrants locally in mountains; eastern rarities and concentrations sometimes to late May; fall passage early September to early November.

Southern Arizona. Diffuse and unspectacular, without waves. Main movements April to May and August to September; note that many resident "Mexican" specialties do not arrive until mid-May or later.

Washington State. Generally unspectacular compared to East, without waves. Peaks mid-April to early June and mid-August to early October.

California. North-south migration generally diffuse and protracted, without waves. Bulk of passerines pass early April to mid-May and late August to early November. Much altitudinal movement of both highland species retreating from winter weather or returning to breeding areas and migrant wanderers. Concentrations may be encountered in foothills. For more detailed description and breakdown by species, see California in Pettingill (1980–BIRD FINDING).

SHOREBIRD MIGRATION. Spring peaks generally parallel those of land-bird migration, but fall passage even more protracted than that of passerines, with first adult shorebirds returning from arctic breeding grounds only weeks after the last of the spring stragglers have moved north. Many species winter in part along southern coasts. Migratory concentrations of shorebirds occur continentwide.

New England/Maritimes. Late April through May and early July to early November, with greatest species variety in September and early October.

Gulf Coast. Late March to early May (best numbers and variety in late March and April); August through October (best numbers and variety in September); many species overwinter.

Great Plains (Kansas/Nebraska). Late April to June 1 and early August to early October.

Central Rockies (Colorado). April to late May (peak late April to early May); late July to early October (peak August to September).

Washington State. Late April to June 1; fall passage peaks between late July and mid-September.

California Coast. Many species resident from mid-August to early May along southern coast; transients peak April to early May and late July through October.

WATERFOWL MIGRATION. The majority of North American swans, geese, and ducks breed in the northern half of the continent (many reaching the Arctic) and winter in the southern half. Some species migrate only far enough south to find open water (fresh or salt); others continue until they reach southern extremities of the U.S. or beyond. Peaks of waterfowl movements occur in early spring and late fall.

New England. Late March to late April and late September to mid-November. Most North American sea duck species winter along the coast.

Great Plains (Kansas/Nebraska). Early March to mid-April and mid-October to early December (or earlier, depending on date of freeze-up).

Washington State. Late March to late April and mid-September to mid-November. Most North American sea and bay duck species winter along the coast.

Southern Half of U.S. Most North American freshwater species are winter residents, many continentwide, some restricted to east, west, or Gulf coast.

HAWK MIGRATION. Peak numbers of hawks tend to pass earlier in the spring than the peaks of passerine and shorebird migrations. Thermal soarers (including cranes and pelicans as well as diurnal raptors) concentrate along mountain ridges, coastlines, land bridges, and other places offering favorable air conditions (see MIGRATION; FLIGHT). These conditions are not always present in a given locality in both spring and fall, and some hawk-watching points are therefore good only at one season or the other. The most spectacular movements often occur on only a few days during a season, and these events can never be precisely predicted. As with passerine migration, raptor passage seems to be more dispersed (therefore less spectacular) in the West, but good new localities continue to be discovered and the spectacle may "improve" with better coverage.

For a listing of North American hawk-watching areas, see Heintzel-man (1979–BIRD FINDING).

New England/Great Lakes. Late March to mid-May (peaks in late April); September through mid-November (peak numbers mid to late September).

Derby Hill (New York). Perhaps the most spectacular *spring* (peak in April) flight in the Northeast.

Hawk Mountain (Pennsylvania). See under *Localities*, below.

Cape May (New Jersey). See under *Localities*, below.

Florida Keys. Good to excellent flights recorded for Key West in October.

Rio Grande Valley. Peak numbers of Broad-winged and Swainson's Hawks late March to early April and September to October (much less spectacular). Because of the valley's generally flat terrain, movements are seen at many points over a wide front, but coastal concentrations are reported from the Aransas area to the north, especially in the fall.

Utah (especially Wellsville Mountain near Logan). September to late October.

Pacific Northwest (British Columbia/Washington/Oregon). September to mid-October.

California (especially Mount Diablo and Mount Tamalpais [*Point* Diablo] near San Francisco). Mid-September to late October; spring flights are less impressive.

COASTAL WATER-BIRD MIGRATION. This is essentially a phenomenon of coastal regions in the fall when large concentrations of loons, grebes, gannets, cormorants, sea ducks, pelagic gulls, and alcids stream southward to offshore or inshore wintering grounds. Since the winter ranges of most of these species are largely northerly, the number of birds involved diminishes to the south. The northward return of these birds in the spring tends to be more protracted and diffuse and thus far less spectacular in most places; however, see below. The phenomenon tends to be most rewarding when onshore gales push migrating birds toward the coast. Under these conditions, tubenoses, jaegers, and other pelagic species are often seen.

Fall sea watches are a very popular activity among birders of northern European coastal countries—much less so in North America, either because there are fewer known coastal watch points or because the best sea watching often requires exposing oneself to the worst weather conditions. Localities where this type of migration has *traditionally* been observed include southeastern Nova Scotia; several offshore islands in the Gulf of Maine; a few points along the Massachusetts coast (Rockport, Manomet, various localities on Cape Cod); Montauk Point, New York; Cape May, New Jersey; Cape Hatteras, North Carolina; Cape Flattery, Washington;

and Point Reyes, California. In all of these places peaks for most species occur in October and November. An exception to the generality about the superiority of the *fall* coastal migration, St. Lawrence Island, Alaska, witnesses an excellent northward movement of the area's unique waterfowl and alcid species in May and early June—conveniently coinciding with the best period for finding Palearctic migrants and vagrants there.

It is worth reemphasizing that many fine North American sea-watch localities are never graced by the presence of birders with telescopes. Birders unaware of the joys of trying to distinguish species of loons or alcids while staring into the teeth of an ocean gale (see HARD CORE) are missing one of the great thrills of their sport.

PELAGIC BIRDS. Most tubenoses in North American waters are summer visitors from the Southern Hemisphere. Many of these species arrive in early spring, but only far offshore (e.g., the spectacular concentrations of Greater Shearwaters present on the Grand Banks by May); however, they become more prevalent on the inner shoals in late summer and fall, when they are joined by arctic-breeding jaegers and phalaropes. Occurrence fluctuates radically with changes in the abundance and location of marine food sources.

North Atlantic. Outer banks (e.g., Grand and Georges) have good to great numbers of northbound pelagics (residents and visitors) late April to early June; inner shoals better in late summer (July on) and fall (through October; best variety in September). Alcids mid-November through early April.

Gulf Stream. Warm-water pelagic birding from the east coast has become popular only recently, perhaps because marine life thrives best in cold water and tropical seabirding is therefore often excruciatingly dull. Big concentrations do occur, however, and it is in or near the Gulf Stream that North American birders have the best chance of seeing tropical visitors such as tropicbirds, boobies, Black-capped Petrels, Audubon's Shearwaters, and Bridled Terns. Seasonal bird distribution in these areas is still poorly understood, but pelagic trips off Florida and Cape Hatteras seem to have the best overall luck from midsummer to fall. Black-capped Petrels may be regular off Florida in April and May and off Hatteras in mid-August through October. If you can take the swell you may have better than average variety in the Gulf Stream after southerly gales.

Washington State. Offshore birding can be very good at all seasons, but winter weather seldom allows access. Boats generally available late April through early October (hundreds of thousands of Sooty Shearwaters late August through September), and this coincides with the best birding, but heavy swells often prevail even in summer.

Southern California. Best numbers and variety mid-August through

October; winter for alcids and Northern Fulmar. As in other areas, highly unpredictable.

VAGRANTS. Young birds tend to wander beyond their "normal" ranges after fledging, and many birds of the year lose their way while undertaking long-distance migrations. Migrants and seabirds are particularly vulnerable to strong winds and other unfavorable weather conditions. All of these phenomena have a recognizable seasonality and are most regular in certain localities.

Western North American Vagrants in the East. Late September through winter. Western vagrants of several species are routine in small numbers where migrants "pile up" on the east coast; some of these show up at feeding stations as the season progresses.

Eastern North American Vagrants in the West. Localities such as the Tijuana River valley, Death Valley (California), and other areas characterized by general barrenness relieved occasionally by isolated copses of vegetation where lost eastern forest species are forced to congregate are most productive during migration in April and May; coastal areas (Farallon Islands, Monterey) are better in fall. Number and variety of vagrants fluctuate greatly from year to year.

Palearctic Vagrants in Alaska. Spring best overall, especially mid-May to mid-June. Fall more protracted, August to November, with shorebirds, warblers, and thrushes better earlier, finches and gulls later. The western Aleutians are more within Siberian–Asian migration patterns than North American–Neotropical ones, and many species once thought of as Palearctic vagrants are now known to be regular during the above periods. See Appendixes I and II.

West Indian Vagrants in Florida. Most prevalent August through November.

Neotropical Vagrants Along Mexican Border. Many occur in midsummer, though the intense heat of this season may discourage tenderfoot northern birders; summer rains cool things off in southern Arizona beginning in July; also fall and winter. Mexicans are very fond of keeping the more colorful or songful of their native species as cage birds; these can escape at any season.

LOCALITIES. Like the birding hot spots or regions described in the main text (see p. 9), those listed alphabetically below are not necessarily the best in North America (though all are excellent); rather they are the best known.

1. *Alaska.* See under *Aleutian/Pribilof Bird Colonies* and *High Arctic*, below, and under *Vagrants, Palearctic*, above.

2. *Aleutian/Pribilof Bird Colonies.* Activity best mid-May through August; many species resident in Alaskan waters year-round.

3. *Arizona.* Good year-round, but many resident specialties of the

southern mountains do not arrive until mid-May and Mexican visitors tend to appear in July and August; April and early May are good for migrants, winter lingerers, and ideal weather. June is the hottest month, with summer rains beginning in July.

4. *Cape May* (New Jersey). Early August (Tree Swallows) to early December; passerines peak late September to early October; hawks early September to mid-November (peak numbers and variety around mid-October). Spring (late April to May) is not as varied or spectacular, but can be very exciting nonetheless.

5. *Churchill* (Manitoba). Earliest migrants (e.g., Snow Buntings) arrive late April; waterfowl begin to appear in numbers with first melts in late May; prime birding time is first two weeks in June, when bulk of high arctic migrants pass through, all resident species are in, and mosquitoes have not yet emerged in full force; unpredictable weather before June 15 sometimes makes for spectacular concentrations of "grounded" migrants. Adult shorebirds take off as early as mid-July and all ages are mostly gone by mid-August; passerine and waterfowl migration mid-August through September. Wildflowers best late June and July. Polar bears begin to gather in mid-September and depart in November when Hudson Bay freezes over.

6. *Dry Tortugas* (Florida). A few Sooty and Noddy Terns arrive in March, most not until mid-April, and Black Noddies and boobies (up to three species) best after mid-May; good through early September.

7. *Everglades* (Florida). Most water birds and Everglade Kite are present during the main tourist season, December 15 to April 15, and many (including the kite) are permanent residents. For seasonal specialties, see under *Florida Keys*, below; for migrants, see under *Passerine Migration*, above.

8. *Florida Keys*. Most summer resident specialties present late March to September; see other Florida listings under *Dry Tortugas* and *Everglades* and under *Passerine Migration*, above.

9. *Hawk Mountain* (Pennsylvania). First movement (Bald Eagle, Osprey) by late August; peak numbers mid to late September (usually around the 20th); best variety mid-October to mid-November.

10. *High Arctic*. Local conditions very variable, but in general mid-June to August 1 is peak time for resident specialties (many of which begin to head south around July 15) and the often spectacular arctic wildflower display. In wet tundra areas mosquitoes often become a serious hindrance after mid to late June. For Alaska, see also under *Vagrants* and *Aleutian/Pribilof Bird Colonies*, above.

11. *Northeastern Seabird Colonies* (Bonaventure Island, Machias Seal Island, etc.). Birds arriving in most cases by late April, but mid-May to mid-August best for seeing birds onshore as well as offshore; other pelagic birding in adjacent waters improves in July.

12. *Point Pelee* (Ontario). Late April to early June (big waves usually mid-May); fall peaks in mid-September.

13. *Rio Grande Valley* (Texas). Good year-round, but some resident specialties do not arrive in Big Bend until May and Neotropical vagrants best in summer and fall. Midsummer temperatures often in excess of 100° F. April to May perhaps best all around for first visit; see also under *Passerine Migration (Gulf Coast)*, above, and under *Species*, below.

14. *Rocky Mountains*. June through early August for resident highland specialties (song best to early July); wildflowers best in June and July. See also under *Passerine Migration* and *Shorebird Migration*, above.

15. *Southern California*. Good birding and weather year-round. April to early May best for migrants and winter lingerers (April) and therefore perhaps best all around for first visit, since most specialties are permanent residents; August to November for fall vagrants; midsummer is the dullest season and many forested areas closed due to fire hazard.

16. *Southern Florida*. Mid-May best for seeing as many Florida specialties as possible; however, see other Florida localities in this section, above, and under *Passerine Migration*, above.

SPECIES. Virtually all bird species—even permanent residents—are more readily found at certain times of the year than at others. Those listed below are very local "target species" whose behavior or movements do not, however, fit within the schedules of migration or localities given above. Someone visiting Texas to see the spectacular coastal migration and the summer resident specialties, for example, will probably want to plan an itinerary that takes in the Whooping Cranes at Aransas National Wildlife Refuge before they depart in early April.

White-tailed Tropicbird (Bermuda). Resident mid-March through October; birds disperse to sea in winter; may be absent for days at a time during cold spells in March and April; best seen inshore 8 a.m. to noon.

California Condor. July through September (especially August) at Mount Pinos and points north, e.g., Valle Vista; winter months best for (generally less productive) Sespe Creek Refuge.

Sage Grouse. Displaying mainly March through early May.

Greater Prairie Chicken. Displaying March to May (April best) in Colorado; December to May (early spring best) in Texas.

Lesser Prairie Chicken. Displaying March to May (April best).

Whooping Crane. On breeding grounds in Wood Buffalo National Park (Northwest Territories) from late April–early May until October; winter on Aransas National Wildlife Refuge near Rockport, Texas, from late October until early April.

Eskimo Curlew. Best chance currently is probably the shortgrass fields of West Galveston Island, Texas, from late March to mid-April.

Ross' Gull. Irregular (sometimes impressive) passage of this species at

Point Barrow, Alaska, in late September and October; Ivory Gulls have also occurred in this region at the same time. Ross' Gull has bred at Churchill, Manitoba, in recent years; present continuously late June to early August.

Boreal Owl. Found with notable regularity in recent years in Toronto region in March and is now known to nest in Minnesota and Colorado.

Elegant (Coppery-tailed) Trogon. Most readily seen May through August; most vocal in May; a few (silent) birds remain through winter. For localities, see SOUTHEASTERN ARIZONA.

Bachman's Warbler. Arrives in North America in March and may stop singing as early as mid-May. For localities, see ENDANGERED BIRDS.

Colima Warbler. Singing late April to early June on Boot Springs Trail. See BIG BEND.

Golden-cheeked Warbler/Black-capped Vireo. Warbler present early March to late July; males sing mid-March to late June. Vireo arrives slightly later and does not depart until August (stragglers to September). See EDWARDS PLATEAU.

Kirtland's Warbler. Singing mid-May to mid-July. For localities, see ENDANGERED BIRDS.

Bibliography

ABNORMALITY

Hicks, L. E. 1934. Individual and sexual variation in the European Starling. *Bird-Banding*, 5:103–18.

Michener, H. 1936. Abnormalities in birds. *Condor*, 38:102–9.

Nickell, W. P. 1965. Adaptive behavior under handicaps of several species of Michigan birds. *Wilson Bull.*, 77:396–400.

Pomeroy, D. E. 1962. Birds with abnormal bills. *Brit. Birds*, 55:49–72.

ABUNDANCE

Aldrich, J. W., and Robbins, C. S. 1970. Changing abundance of migratory birds in North America. In *The Avifauna of Northern Latin America*, ed. H. K. and J. H. Buechner. Washington, D.C.

Meanley, B., and Webb, J. S. 1965. Nationwide population estimates of blackbirds and starlings. *Atlantic Naturalist*, 20:189–91.

Merikallio, E. 1958. *Finnish Birds, Their Distribution and Numbers.* Fauna Fennica no. 5. Helsinki.

ACCENTOR

Bent, A. C. 1950. *Life Histories of North American Wagtails, Shrikes, Vireos, and Their Allies.* U.S. Natl. Mus. Bull. no. 197. Washington, D.C. Reprinted New York, 1965.

AGE

Bergstrom, E. A. 1956. Extreme old age in birds. *Bird-Banding*, 27:128–29.

Fisher, H. I. 1975. Longevity of the Laysan albatross, *Diomedea immutabilis*. *Bird-Banding*, 46:1–6.

Kennard, J. H. 1975. Longevity records of North American birds. *Bird-Banding*, 46:55–73.

Moreau, R. E. 1966. On estimates of the past numbers and of the average longevity of avian species. *Auk*, 83:403–15.

Rydzewski, W. 1962. Longevity of ringed birds. *Ring*, 3:147–52.

Schumacher, D. M. 1964. Ages of some captive wild birds. *Condor*, 66:309.

Tickell, W. L. N. 1968. *The Biology of the Great Albatrosses,* Diomedea exulans *and* D. epomophora. Amer. Geophys. Union Antarc. Res. Ser., 12:1–55.

AGGRESSION

Andrew, R. J. 1957. Influence of hunger on aggressive behavior in certain buntings of the genus *Emberiza. Physiol. Zool.,* 30:177–85.

Cottrille, B. D. 1950. Death of a Horned Lark in territorial combat. *Wilson Bull.,* 62:134–35.

Dilger, W. C. 1956. Hostile behavior and reproductive isolating mechanisms in the thrush genera *Catharus* and *Hylocichla. Auk,* 73:313–53.

———. 1960. Agonistic and social behavior of captive redpolls. *Wilson Bull.,* 72:115–32.

Hamilton, III, W. J. 1959. Aggressive behavior in migrant Pectoral Sandpipers. *Condor,* 61:161–79.

Johnson, R. R. 1961. Turkey attacks hawk. *Auk,* 78:646.

Kilham, L. 1961. Aggressiveness of migrant Myrtle Warbler toward woodpeckers and other birds. *Auk,* 78:261.

ALBATROSS

Bent, A. C. 1922. *Life Histories of North American Petrels and Pelicans and Their Allies.* U.S. Natl. Mus. Bull. no. 21. Washington, D.C. Reprinted New York, 1964.

Palmer, R. S., ed. 1962. *Handbook of North American Birds.* New Haven. Vol. 1, pp. 116–36.

See also references under SEABIRD.

ALBINISM

Deane, R. 1876, 1878, 1879. Albinism and melanism among North American birds. *Bull. Nuttall Ornith. Club.* Vols. 2, 3, and 5.

Edson, J. M. 1928. An epidemic of albinism. *Auk,* 45:377–78.

Frazier, F. P. 1952. Depigmentation of a robin. *Bird-Banding,* 23:114.

Gross, A. O. 1965. The incidence of albinism in North American birds. *Bird-Banding,* 36:67–71.

Nero, R. W. 1954. Plumage aberrations of the Red-wing (*Agelaius phoeniceus*). *Auk,* 71:137–55.

Sage, B. L. 1962. Albinism and melanism in birds. *Brit. Birds,* 55:201–22.

ALLOPREENING

Harrison, C. J. O. 1965. Allopreening as agonistic behavior. *Behavior,* 24:161–209.

———. 1969. Further records of allopreening. *Avicultural Magazine,* 75:97–99.

ALTITUDE

Laybourne, R. C. 1974. Collision between a vulture and an aircraft at an altitude of 37,000 feet. *Wilson Bull.,* 86:461–62.

McWhirter, N., et al., eds. 1980. *Guinness Book of World Records.* New York.

Swan, L. W. 1970. Goose of the Himalayas. *Natural Hist.*, 70:68–75.

Tucker, V. A. 1968. Respiratory physiology of House Sparrows in relation to high altitude flight. *Jour. Exper. Biol.*, 48:55–66.

ANHINGA

Bent, A. C. 1922. *Life Histories of North American Petrels and Pelicans and Their Allies.* U.S. Natl. Mus. Bull. no. 21. Washington, D.C. Reprinted New York, 1964.

Palmer, R. S., ed. 1962. *Handbook of North American Birds.* New Haven. Vol. 1, pp. 357–65.

ANTING

Goodman, J. M. 1960. *Aves incendaria. Wilson Bull.*, 72:400–1.

Hauser, D. C. 1973. Comparison of anting records from two localities in North Carolina. *Chat*, 37:91–102.

Mayfield, H. 1966. Fire in birds' nests. *Wilson Bull.*, 78:234–35.

Potter, E. F. 1970. Anting in wild birds, its frequency and probable purpose. *Auk*, 87:692–713.

———— and Hauser, D. C. 1974. Relationship of anting and sunbathing to molting in wild birds. *Auk*, 91:537–63.

Simmons, K. E. L. 1966. Anting and the problem of self-stimulation. *Jour. Zool.*, 149:145–62.

Terres, J. K. 1962. Anting behavior of a Wood Thrush with a snail. *Wilson Bull.*, 74:187.

Whitaker, L. M. 1957. A résumé of anting, with particular reference to a captive Orchard Oriole. *Wilson Bull.*, 69:195–262.

ARCTIC

Karplus, M. 1952. Bird activity in the continuous daylight of arctic summer. *Ecology*, 33:129–34.

Parmelee, D. F.; Stephens, H. A.; and Schmidt, R. H. 1967. *Birds of Southeastern Victoria Island and Adjacent Small Islands.* Natl. Mus. Can. Bull. no 222, Biol. Ser. 78. Ottawa.

Salomonsen, F. 1972. Zoogeographical and ecological problems in arctic birds. *Proc. (XVth) Internatl. Ornith. Congr., Leiden.*

Snyder, L. L. 1957. *Arctic Birds of Canada.* Toronto.

Stonehouse, B. 1971. *Animals of the Arctic, the Ecology of the Far North.* London.

Sutton, G. M. 1971. *High Arctic.* New York.

AUDUBON

Arthur, S. C. 1937. *Audubon: An Intimate Life of the American Woodsman.* New Orleans.

Audubon, J. J. 1831–39 (several subsequent editions). *Ornithological Biography: or an Account of the Habits of the Birds of the United States of America; Accom-*

panied by Descriptions of the Objects Represented in the Work Entitled the Birds of America, and Interspersed with Delineations of American Scenery and Manners. 5 vols. Edinburgh.

————. 1966. *The Original Water-color Paintings by John James Audubon for The Birds of America.* Intro. by M. B. Davidson. 2 vols. New York. (Best available reproductions of Audubon's work; many editions of prints are available in a wide range of qualities and prices.)

————. 1979. *The Art of Audubon.* New York. (Complete birds and mammals, with an introduction by Roger Tory Peterson.)

Audubon, M., ed. 1897. *Audubon and His Journals* (with notes by Elliott Coues). Reprinted New York, 1960.

Fries, W. H. 1973. *The Double Elephant Folio: The Story of Audubon's Birds of America.* Chicago.

Herrick, F. H. 1938. *Audubon the Naturalist: A History of His Life and Time.* 2nd ed. New York.

Peattie, D. C. 1940. *Audubon's America.* Boston.

AUK

Bent, A. C. 1919. *Life Histories of North American Diving Birds.* U.S. Natl. Mus. Bull. no. 107. Washington, D.C. Reprinted New York, 1946 and 1963.

Lockley, R. M. 1953. *Puffins.* New York.

Storer, R. W. 1952. A comparison of variation, behavior and evolution in the sea-bird genera *Uria* and *Cepphus. Univ. Calif. Publ. Zool.,* 52:121–222.

Tuck, L. M. 1961. *The Murres: Their Distribution, Populations, and Biology.* Canadian Wildlife Serv. Ser. no. 1. Ottawa.

See also references under SEABIRD.

AVICULTURE

The A.F.A. Watchbird (bimonthly publication of the American Federation of Aviculture). 2208 "A" Artesia Blvd., Redondo Beach, CA 90278.

American Cage-bird Magazine. 3448–51N Western Ave., Chicago, IL 60618.

Banks, R. C. 1970. *Birds Imported into the United States in 1968.* U.S. Fish and Wildlife Serv., Spec. Sci. Rept.—Wildlife, no. 136. Washington, D.C.

Crandall, L. S. 1917. *Pets: Their History and Care.* New York.

Nilsson, G. 1980. *The Bird Business: A Study of the Importation of Birds into the United States.* Washington, D.C.

Ripley, S. D. 1957. *A Paddling of Ducks.* New York. (Memoirs of a waterfowl collector.)

Rutgers, A., and Norris, K. A. 1970. *Encyclopedia of Aviculture.* London. (All birds known to be kept by humans, treated by family.)

BAIRD

Baird, S. F.; Cassin J.; and Lawrence, G. N. 1859. *The Birds of North America.* Philadelphia.

———; Brewer, T. M.; and Ridgway, R. 1874 and 1884. *A History of North American Birds.* (Land Birds and Water Birds, 5 vols.) Boston.

Dall, W. H. 1915. *Spencer Fullerton Baird.* Philadelphia.

BANDING

Anonymous. 1960. *Bird-Banding: The Hows and Whys.* U.S. Fish and Wildlife Serv. *Conservation Notes.* Cir. 79. Washington, D.C.

Lincoln, F. C. 1933. Bird banding. In A.O.U., *Fifty Years Progress of American Ornithology.* Lancaster, Pa.

BARTRAM

Cruickshank, H. G., ed. 1957. *John and William Bartram's America.* New York.

Harper, F., ed. 1958. *The Travels of William Bartram.* New Haven.

BATHING

Harrison, C. J. O. 1961. Rain-bathing. *Avicultural Magazine,* 67:90–92.

Slessers, M. 1970. Bathing behavior of land birds. *Auk,* 87:91–99.

BECARD

Bent, A. C. 1942. *Life Histories of North American Flycatchers, Larks, Swallows, and Their Allies.* U.S. Natl. Mus. Bull. no. 179. Washington, D.C. Reprinted New York, 1963.

BENT

Taber, W. 1955. In memoriam: Arthur Cleveland Bent. *Auk,* 72:332–39.

BERGMANN'S RULE

Kendeigh, S. C. 1969. Tolerance of cold and Bergmann's rule. *Auk,* 86:13–25.

BERMUDA

Wingate, D. B. 1973. *A Checklist and Guide to the Birds of Bermuda.* Privately publ. in Bermuda.

BIOGRAPHY

Barnhart, C. L., and Halsey, W. D., eds. 1954. *New Century Cyclopedia of Names.* 3 vols. New York.

Choate, E. A. 1973. *The Dictionary of Bird Names.* Boston.

Eifert, V. 1962. *Men, Birds and Adventure.* New York.

Geiser, S. W. 1948. *Naturalists of the Frontier.* Dallas.

Gruson, E. S. 1972. *Words for Birds.* New York.

Hanley, W. 1977. *Natural History in America from Mark Catesby to Rachel Carson.* New York.

Heintzelman, D. S. 1980. *The Illustrated Bird Watcher's Dictionary.* Tulsa, Okla. (Thumbnail sketches and photos of many contemporary American ornithologists.)

Hume, E. E. 1942. *Ornithologists of the United States Army Medical Corps.* Baltimore.

Milne, L. J., and Milne, M. 1952. *Famous Naturalists.* New York.

Palmer, T. S. 1928. Notes on persons whose names appear in the nomenclature of California birds. *Condor*, 30:261–307.

———— et al. 1954. *Biographies of Members of the American Ornithologists' Union.* Washington, D.C.

Terres, J. K., ed. 1961. *Discovery: Great Moments in the Lives of Outstanding Naturalists.* New York.

Welker, R. H. 1955. *Birds and Men.* Cambridge, Mass.

Wynne, O. E. 1969. *Names of Birds of the World: Biographical Key to Authors and Those Commemorated.* Fordingbridge, Hants., England (published by the author).

BIRD

Amadon, D. 1966. *Birds Around the World: A Geographical Look at Evolution and Birds.* New York.

Austin, Jr., O. L., and Singer, A. 1961. *Birds of the World.* New York.

———— and ————. 1971. *Families of Birds.* New York.

Campbell, B. 1974. *The Dictionary of Birds in Color.* New York.

Cruickshank, A. D., and Cruickshank, H. G. 1958. *1001 Questions about Birds.* New York.

Fisher, J. 1954. *A History of Birds.* Boston.

———— and Peterson, R. T. 1964. *The World of Birds.* New York.

Fitter, R., ed. 1969. *Reader's Digest Book of British Birds.* London.

Forbush, E. H., and May, J. B. 1925 (and current reprint). *A Natural History of American Birds.* New York. (Plates by Louis Agassiz Fuertes and Allan Brooks from *Birds of Massachusetts*; see STATE BOOKS).

Gilliard, E. T. 1958. *Living Birds of the World.* New York.

Gooders, J. 1969–71. *Birds of the World* (serialized magazine). London.

————. 1975. *The Great Book of Birds.* New York.

Grzimek, B., ed. 1972–73. *Grzimek's Animal Life Encyclopedia.* Vols. 7–9 (Birds). New York.

Pasquier, R. F. 1977. *Watching Birds: An Introduction to Ornithology.* Boston.

Peterson, R. T. 1977. *The Birds.* Morristown, N.J.

Stefferud, A., and Nelson, A. L., eds. 1966. *Birds in Our Lives.* U.S. Fish and Wildlife Serv., Washington, D.C.

Terres, J. K. 1980. *The Audubon Society Encyclopedia of North American Birds.* New York.

Wetmore, A., et al. 1937. *The Book of Birds.* Washington, D.C. (Illustr. by Allan Brooks.)

————. 1964. *Song and Garden Birds of North America.* Washington, D.C.

————. 1965. *Water, Prey and Game Birds of North America.* Washington, D.C.

See also references under ORNITHOLOGY and BIRDWATCHING.

BIRD CALLS

Tucker, J. 1978. Swishing and squeaking. *Birding*, 10:83–87.

BIRD CLUB

Fink, L. C. 1958. Want to start a bird club? *Audubon*, 60:20–23.

Rickert, J. E. 1978. *A Guide to North American Bird Clubs*. Elizabethtown, Ky.

BIRD FEEDING

Arbib, R., and Soper, T. 1971. *The Hungry Bird Book*. New York.

DeGraaf, R. M., and Thomas, J. 1974. *Wildlife in an Urbanizing Environment*. Natural Resource Center Planning and Resource Development Series 28. Amherst, Mass.

Dennis, J. V. 1975. *A Complete Guide to Bird Feeding*. New York.

Geis, A. D. 1980. *Relative Attractiveness of Different Foods at Wild Bird Feeders*. U.S. Fish and Wildlife Serv. Spec. Sci. Rept.—Wildlife, no. 233. Washington, D.C.

Grant, K. A., and Grant, V. 1968. *Hummingbirds and Their Flowers*. New York.

Harrison, G. H. 1979. *The Backyard Bird Watcher*. New York.

Martin, A. G. 1963. *Hand-taming Wild Birds at the Feeder*. Portland, Me.

Terres, J. K. 1977. *Songbirds in Your Garden*. 3rd ed. New York.

BIRD FINDING

Alden, P. C., and Gooders, J. 1981. *Finding Birds Around the World*. Boston. (14 North American localities.)

Drennan, S. R. 1981. *Where to Find Birds in New York State*. Syracuse. (The top 500 sites.)

Gart, J. 1975. Supplement: Bird-finding guides. *Amer. Birds*, 29:1050–54.

Heintzelman, D. S. 1972. *A Guide to Northeastern Hawk Watching*. Lambertsville, N.J.

————. 1979. *A Guide to Hawk Watching in North America*. University Park, Pa.

Kitching, J. 1976. *Birdwatcher's Guide to Wildlife Sanctuaries* (North American). New York.

Lane, J. A. 1979. *A Birder's Guide to the Rio Grande Valley of Texas*. Denver.

————. 1979. *A Birder's Guide to Southeastern Arizona*. Denver.

————. 1979. *A Birder's Guide to Southern California*. Denver.

————. 1980. *A Birder's Guide to Florida*. Denver.

———— and Holt, H. R. 1979. *A Birder's Guide to Eastern Colorado*. Denver.

———— and Tveten, J. 1980. *A Birder's Guide to the Texas Coast*. Denver.

McElroy, Jr., T. P. 1974. *The Habitat Guide to Birding*. New York.

Pettingill, Jr., O. S. 1977. *A Guide to Bird Finding East of the Mississippi*. 2nd ed. Boston.

————. 1980. *A Guide to Bird Finding West of the Mississippi*. 2nd ed. Boston.

Stirling, D., and Woodford, J. 1975. *Where to Go Bird Watching in Canada*. Saanichton, B.C.

BIRDHOUSE

Jackson, J. A., and Tate, Jr., J. 1974. An analysis of nest box use by Purple Martins, House Sparrows and Starlings in eastern North America. *Wilson Bull.*, 86:435–45.

Kale, II, H. W. 1968. The relationship of Purple Martins to mosquito control. *Auk*, 85:654–61.

MacNeil, D. 1979. *The Birdhouse Book.* Seattle.

Pushel, B. 1981. The bluebird house that Bauldry built. *Birding*, 13:14–15.

BIRD SKIN

Anderson, R. M. 1965. *Methods of Collecting and Preserving Animals.* Natl. Mus. Can. Bull. no 69. Biol. Ser. no. 18.

Coues, E. 1890. Field ornithology. Part I of *Key to North American Birds.* Rev. ed., p. 28.

BIRDWATCHING

Allen, R. P. 1957. *On the Trail of Vanishing Birds.* New York.

Brandt, H. 1940. *Texas Bird Adventures.* Cleveland.

Burroughs, J. 1871. *Wake-robin.* Boston. (A good example of nineteenth-century "nature writing.")

Chapman, F. M. 1933. *Autobiography of a Birdlover.* New York.

Delacour, J. 1966. *The Living Air: The Memoirs of an Ornithologist.* London.

Fisher, J. 1951. *Watching Birds.* Rev. ed. Harmondsworth, England.

Heintzelman, D. S. 1979. *A Manual for Bird Watching in the Americas.* New York. ("How to.")

Hickey, J. J. 1943. *A Guide to Birdwatching.* New York. (The unsurpassed classic on "how to.")

Hochbaum, H. A. 1955. *Travels and Traditions of Waterfowl.* Minneapolis.

Homes, R. C. 1964. Bird-watching. In *A New Dictionary of Birds*, ed. A. L. Thomson. New York.

Hudson, W. H. 1918. *Far Away and Long Ago.* New York.

———. 1920. *Adventures Among Birds.* New York.

Huxley, J. S. 1934. *Bird-watching and Bird Behavior.* London.

Kieran, J. 1952. *Footnotes on Nature.* New York.

Kress, S. W. 1981. *The Audubon Society Handbook for Birders.* New York.

Krutch, J. W., and Eriksson, P., eds. 1962. *A Treasury of Bird Lore.* New York.

Lack, D. 1965. *Enjoying Ornithology.* London.

Laycock, G. 1976. *The Bird Watcher's Bible.* New York

Matthiessen, P. 1959. *Wildlife in America.* New York.

———. 1973. *The Wind Birds.* New York.

McElroy, Jr., T. P. 1974. *The Habitat Guide to Birding.* New York.

Murphy, R. C. 1947. *Logbook for Grace.* New York.

Nero, R. W. 1961. The gentle art of bird watching. *Canadian Audubon*, 23:168–73.

Nice, M. M. 1939. *The Watcher at the Nest.* New York.

Ogburn, C. 1975. *The Adventure of Birds.* New York.

Peterson, R. T. 1948. *Birds Over America.* New York.

———, ed. 1957. *The Bird Watcher's Anthology.* New York.

——— and Fisher, J. 1955. *Wild America.* Boston.

Pettingill, O. S. 1974. *The Bird Watcher's America.* New York.

Richards, A. J. 1980. *The Birdwatcher's A–Z.* London.

Scofield, M. 1978. *The Complete Outfitting and Source Book for Bird Watching.* New York.

Scott, P., and Fisher, J. 1954. *A Thousand Geese.* Boston.

Stokes, D. N. 1979. *A Guide to the Behavior of Common Birds.* Boston.

Sutton, G. M. 1936. *Birds in the Wilderness: Adventures of an Ornithologist.* New York. (Dr. Sutton has many other titles to his credit and illustrated most of his writings; see under ILLUSTRATION.)

———. 1951. *Mexican Birds: First Impressions.* Norman, Okla.

Teale, E. W. 1951. *North with the Spring.* New York.

BLACKBIRD

Bent, A. C. 1958. *Life Histories of North American Blackbirds, Orioles, Tanagers, and Their Allies.* U.S. Natl. Mus. Bull. no. 211. Washington, D.C. Reprinted New York, 1965.

Lanyon, W. E. 1957. *The Comparative Biology of the Meadowlarks* (Sturnella) *in Wisconsin.* Nuttall Ornith. Club Publ. no. 1. Cambridge, Mass.

Orians, G. H. 1961. The ecology of blackbird (*Agelaius*) social systems. *Ecol. Monogr.,* 31:285–312.

BOOBY

Bent, A. C. 1922. *Life Histories of North American Petrels and Pelicans and Their Allies.* U.S. Natl. Mus. Bull. no. 21. Washington, D.C. Reprinted New York, 1964.

Fisher, J., and Vevers, H. G. 1943. The breeding distribution, history, and population of the North Atlantic gannet (*Sula bassana*). Part I: A history of gannet colonies and the census in 1939. *Jour. Anim. Ecol.,* 12:173–213. Part II: The changes in the world numbers of the gannet in a century. *Ibid.,* 13:49–62.

Kepler, C. B. 1969. *Breeding Biology of the Blue-footed Booby.* Nuttall Ornith. Club Publ. no. 8.

Nelson, J. B. 1970. The relationship between behavior and ecology in the Sulidae with reference to other seabirds. *Oceanogr. Marine Biol.,* 8:501–74.

———. 1978. *The Gannet.* Vermillion, S.D.

Palmer, R. S., ed. 1962. *Handbook of North American Birds.* Vol. 1. New Haven.

See also references under SEABIRD.

BREEDING SEASON

Kuroda, N. 1960. Notes on the breeding season in the Tubinares (Aves). *Jap. Jour. Zool.,* 12:449–64.

Orians, G. H. 1960. Autumnal breeding in the Tricolored Blackbird. *Auk*, 77:379–98.

Snow, D. W. 1955. The abnormal breeding of birds in the winter 1953–54. *Brit. Birds*, 48:121–26.

BREWSTER

Brewster, W. 1906. *Birds of the Cambridge Region.* Memoirs of the Nuttall Ornith. Club no. 4. Cambridge, Mass.

———. 1936. *October Farm.* Cambridge, Mass.

BROOD PARASITISM

Friedmann, H. 1930. Social parasitism in birds. *Smithsonian Rep.*, 1929, pp. 385–95.

———. 1964. The history of our knowledge of avian brood parasitism. *Centaurus*, 10:282–304.

Many other titles on brood parasitism by the same author, especially 1948, 1955, 1960, and under COWBIRD.

Hamilton, III, W. J., and Orians, G. H. 1965. Evolution of brood parasitism in altricial birds. *Condor*, 67:361–82.

Keith, L. B. 1961. Parasitic egg laying by ducks. *Auk*, 78:93.

Smith, N. G. 1968. The advantage of being parasitized. *Nature*, 219:690–94.

Weller, M. W. 1959. Parasitic egg laying in the Redhead (*Aythya americana*) and other North American Anatidae. *Ecol. Monogr.*, 29:333–65.

———. 1968. The breeding biology of the parasitic Black-headed Duck. *Living Bird*, 7th annual, pp. 169–207.

BULBUL

Carleton, A. R., and Owre, O. T. 1975. The Red-whiskered Bulbul in Florida: 1960–71. *Auk*, 92:40–57.

BURSA OF FABRICIUS

Gower, C. 1939. The use of the bursa of Fabricius as an indication of age in game birds. *Trans. (4th) N. Amer. Wildlife Conf.*, pp. 426–30.

Hochbaum, H. A. 1942. Sex and age determination of waterfowl by cloacal examination. *Trans. (7th) N. Amer. Wildlife Conf.*, pp. 299–307.

CANNIBALISM

Ingram, C. 1959. The importance of juvenile cannibalism in the breeding biology of certain birds of prey. *Auk*, 76:218–26.

Parsons, J. 1971. Cannibalism in Herring Gulls. *Brit. Birds*, 64:528–37.

CANNON NET

Dill, H. H., and Thornsberry, W. H. 1950. A cannon-projected net trap for capturing waterfowl. *Jour. Wildlife Management*, 14:132–37.

Thompson, M. C., and DeLong, R. L. 1967. The use of cannon and rocket-projected nets for trapping shorebirds. *Bird-Banding*, 38:214–18.

CAPE MAY

Allen, R. P., and Peterson, R. T. 1936. The hawk migrations at Cape May Point, New Jersey. *Auk*, 53:393–404.

Stone, W. 1937. *Bird Studies at Old Cape May.* 2 vols. Proc. Delaware Valley Ornith. Club. Philadelphia.

CAPTURE

MacPherson, H. A. 1897. *History of Fowling: An Account of Devices for Capturing Wild Birds.* Edinburgh.

CARACARA

Bent, A. C. 1938. *Life Histories of North American Birds of Prey.* U.S. Natl. Mus. Bull. no. 170, pt. 2. Washington, D.C. Reprinted New York, 1961.

Brown, L., and Amadon, D. 1968. *Eagles, Hawks and Falcons of the World.* New York. Vol. 2, pp. 727–39.

CARE OF DISTRESSED BIRDS

Hamerstrom, F. H. 1970. Care and feeding of young raptors. *Raptor Res. News*, 4:75.

Laughlin, P. A. 1978. Care and treatment of injured birds. *Birding*, 10:300–4. (Shows splinting technique.)

Mutchler, T. 1972. Surgical treatment, by pinning, of longbone fractures in raptors. *Hawk Mt. Sanctuary Assoc., News Letter to Members*, no. 44.

Terres, J. K. 1980. Care and feeding of abandoned or injured wild birds. In *The Audubon Society Encyclopedia of North American Birds.* New York. Pp. 83–84 (and species accounts).

CASSIN

Cassin, J. 1856. *Illustrations of the Birds of California, Texas, Oregon, British and Russian America.* Philadelphia.

Stone, W. 1901. John Cassin. *Cassinia*, 5:1–7.

See also references under BAIRD.

CATESBY

Catesby, M. 1731–43 (Appendix 1748). *The Natural History of Carolina, Florida, and the Bahama Islands, Containing the Figures of Birds, Beasts, Fishes, Serpents, Insects, and Plants.* 2 vols. London.

See also in Hanley (1977–BIOGRAPHY).

CENSUS

Dobinson, H. M. 1976. *Bird Count: A Practical Guide to Bird Surveys.* New York.

Mikol, S. A. 1980. *Guidelines for Using Transects to Sample Non-Game Bird Populations.* Rept. of Office of Biological Services, U.S. Fish and Wildlife Service. Washington, D.C.

See also Pettingill (1970–ORNITHOLOGY) for a good bibliography of census techniques (pp. 410–12).

CHACHALACA

Delacour, J., and Amadon, D. 1973. *Curassows and Related Birds.* New York.

CHAPMAN

Chapman, F. M. 1930. *Handbook of Birds of Eastern North America.* New York.
————. 1933. *Autobiography of a Birdlover.* New York.

CHECKLIST

American Birding Association. 1982. *A.B.A. Checklist: Birds of Continental United States and Canada.* 2nd ed. Austin, Tex.

American Ornithologists' Union. 1957. A.O.U. *Check-list of North American Birds.* 5th ed. Baltimore. Supplements: 32nd (1973), *Auk,* 90:411–19; 33rd (1976), *Auk,* 93:875–79. Also skeleton list (1982) from 6th ed.

Clements, J. F. 1974. *Birds of the World: A Checklist.* New York.

Edwards, E. P. 1974. *A Coded List of Birds of the World.* Sweet Briar, Va.

Gruson, E. S., and Forster, R. A. 1976. *A Checklist of the World's Birds.* New York.

Kessel, B., and Gibson, D. D. 1978. Studies and distribution of Alaskan birds. *Studies in Avian Biology,* no. 1. Cooper Ornith. Soc. Berkeley.

Peters, J. L., et al. 1931–   (ongoing). *Checklist of Birds of the World.* Vols. 1–10 and 12–15; vol. 1 revised 1979. Cambridge, Mass. Editors: D. Amadon; E. R. Blake, G. W. Cottrell, H. G. Deignan, J. C. Greenway, T. R. Howell, G. H. Lowery, Jr., E. Mayr, B. L. Monroe, Jr., R. E. Moreau, R. A. Paynter, A. L. Rand, S. D. Ripley, F. Salomonsen, D. W. Snow, R. Storer, M. A. Traylor, C. Vaurie, and J. T. Zimmer.

Roberson, D. 1980. *Rare Birds of the West Coast.* Pacific Grove, Calif.

Walters, M. 1980. *The Complete Birds of the World.* London.

CHRISTMAS COUNT

Peterson, R. T. 1955. The Christmas count. *Audubon,* 57:52–53, 64–65.

Robbins, C. S. 1966. The Christmas count. In *Birds in Our Lives,* ed. A. Stefferud and A. L. Nelson. Washington, D.C.

CIRCADIAN RHYTHM

Gwinner, E. 1975. Circadian and circannual rhythms in birds. In *Avian Biology,* ed. D. S. Farner et al. Vol. 4. New York.

Harker, J. E. 1958. Diurnal rhythms in the animal kingdom. *Biol. Rev.,* 33:1–52.

CIRCULATORY SYSTEM

Calder, W. A. 1968. Respiratory and heart rates of birds at rest. *Condor,* 70:358–65.

Clark, A. J. 1927. *Comparative Physiology of the Heart.* New York.

Jones, D. R., and Johansen, K. 1972. The blood vascular system of birds. In *Avian Biology,* ed. D. S. Farner et al. Vol. 2. New York.

Norris, R. A., and Williamson, F. S. L. 1955. Variation in relative heart size of certain passerines with increase in altitude. *Wilson Bull.,* 67:78–83.

Odum, E. P. 1941. Variations in the heart rate of birds: A study in physiological ecology. *Ecol. Monogr.,* 3:299–326.

Simons, J. R. 1960. The blood-vascular system. In *Biology and Comparative Physiology of Birds,* ed. A. J. Marshall. Vol. 1. New York.

Stresemann, E. 1927–34. Aves. In *Handbuch der Zoologie,* ed. Kukenthal and Krumbach. Vol. 7, Part II. Berlin.

CLIMBING

Spring, L. W. 1965. Climbing and pecking adaptations in some North American woodpeckers. *Condor,* 67:457–88.

COLOR AND PATTERN

Armstrong, E. A. 1951. The nature and function of animal mimesis. *Bull. Anim. Behav.,* 9:46–58.

Averill, C. K. 1923. Black wing tips. *Condor,* 25:57–59.

Cott, H. B. 1941. *Adaptive Coloration in Animals.* London.

Ficken, R. W.; Matthiae, P. E.; and Herwich, R. 1971. Eyemarks in vertebrates: Aids to vision. *Science,* 173:936–39.

Fox, D. L. 1953. *Animal Biochromes and Structural Colors.* Cambridge.

Fox, H. M., and Vevers, G. 1960. *The Nature of Animal Colours.* London.

Gower, C. 1936. The cause of blue color as found in the bluebird (*Sialia sialis*) and the Blue Jay (*Cyanositta cristata*). *Auk,* 53:178–85.

Meinertzhagen, R. 1951. Desert coloration. *Proc. (Xth) Internatl. Ornith. Congr., Uppsala, 1950,* pp. 155–62.

Sumner, F. B. 1934. Does "protective coloration" protect? Results of some experiments with fishes and birds. *Proc. Natl. Acad. Sci.,* 20:559–64.

Thayer, G. H. 1909. *Concealing-coloration in the Animal Kingdom.* New York.

CONSERVATION

American Ornithologists' Union. 1975. Report of the American Ornithologists' Union Committee on Conservation, 1974–75. *Auk* (Supplement), 92:1B–16B.

Buchheister, C. W., and Graham, Jr., F. 1973. From the swamps and back: A concise and candid history of the Audubon movement. *Audubon,* 75:4–43.

Doughty, R. W. 1975. *Feather Fashions and Bird Preservation: A Study in Nature Protection.* Berkeley.

Elliott, H. F. I. 1970. Outlook for bird conservation. *Bird Study,* 17:81–94.

Leedy, D. L. 1961. Some federal contributions to bird conservation during the period 1885–1960. *Auk,* 78:167–75.

Pearson, T. G. 1933. Fifty years of bird protection in the United States. In A.O.U., *Fifty Years Progress of American Ornithology: 1883–1933.* Lancaster, Pa.

Samuels, E. A. 1868. *Among the Birds.* Boston.

Teague, R. 1971. *Manual of Wildlife Conservation.* Washington, D.C.

CORMORANT

Bent, A. C. 1922. *Life Histories of North American Petrels and Pelicans and Their Allies.* U.S. Natl. Mus. Bull. no. 21. Washington, D.C. Reprinted New York, 1964.

Palmer, R. S., ed. 1962. *Handbook of North American Birds.* Vol. 1. New Haven. See also references under SEABIRD.

COUES

Coues, E. 1874. *Birds of the Northwest: A Handbook of Ornithology.* Washington, D.C.

————. 1884 and 1903. *Key to North American Birds.* Boston.

Cutright, P. R., and Brodhead, M. J. 1980. *Elliott Coues: Naturalist and Frontier Historian.* New York.

COURTSHIP

Burton, M. 1954. *Animal Courtship.* New York.

Hinde, R. A. 1955. A comparative study of the courtship of certain finches. *Ibis,* 97:706.

Lack, D. 1940. Courtship feeding in birds. *Auk,* 57:169–78.

Royama, T. 1966. A re-interpretation of courtship feeding. *Bird Study,* 13:116–29.

COWBIRD

Byers, G. W. 1950. Black-and-White Warbler's nest with eight cowbird eggs. *Wilson Bull.,* 62:136–68.

Friedmann, H. 1929. *The Cowbirds.* Springfield, Ill.

————. 1963. *Host Relations of the Parasitic Cowbirds.* U.S. Natl. Mus. Bull. no. 233. Washington, D.C.

————. 1971. Further information on the host relations of the parasitic cowbirds. *Auk,* 88:239–55.

Hann, H. W. 1941. The cowbird at the nest. *Wilson Bull.,* 53:209–21.

Nice, M. M. 1949. The laying rhythm of cowbirds. *Wilson Bull.,* 61:231–34.

Payne, R. G. 1965. Clutch size and numbers of eggs laid by Brown-headed Cowbirds. *Condor,* 67:44–60.

Walkinshaw, L. H. 1949. Twenty-five eggs apparently laid by a cowbird. *Wilson Bull.,* 61:82–85.

CRANE

Bent, A. C. 1926. *Life Histories of North American Marsh Birds.* U.S. Natl. Mus. Bull. no. 135. Washington, D.C. Reprinted New York, 1963.

Walkinshaw, L. 1973. *Cranes of the World.* New York.

CROW

Amadon, D. 1944. The genera of the Corvidae and their relationships. *Amer. Mus. Novit.* no. 1215:1–21.

Angell, T. 1978. *Ravens, Crows, Magpies and Jays.* Seattle.

Bent, A. C. 1946. *Life Histories of North American Jays, Crows, and Titmice.* U.S. Natl. Mus. Bull. no. 191. Washington, D.C. Reprinted New York, 1964.

Goodwin, G. G. 1976. *Crows of the World.* Ithaca, N.Y.

CUCKOO

Bent, A. C. 1940. *Life Histories of North American Cuckoos, Goatsuckers, Hummingbirds, and Their Allies.* U.S. Natl. Mus. Bull. no. 176. Washington, D.C. Reprinted New York, 1964.

Sheldon, H. 1922. Top speed of the Roadrunner. *Condor,* 24:180.

DIGESTIVE SYSTEM

Bock, W. J. 1961. Salivary glands in the Gray Jays (*Perisoreus*). *Auk,* 78:355–65.

McBee, R. H., and West, G. C. 1969. Caecal fermentation in the Willow Ptarmigan. *Condor,* 71:54–58.

Stevenson, J. 1933. Experiments on the digestion of food by birds. *Wilson Bull.,* 45:155–67.

Worden, A. N. 1964. Alimentary system. In *A New Dictionary of Birds,* ed. A. L. Thomson. New York.

Ziswiler, V., and Farner, D. S. 1972. Digestion and the digestive system. In *Avian Biology,* ed. D. S. Farner et al. Vol. 2. New York.

DIMORPHISM

Amadon, D. 1959. The significance of sexual differences in size among birds. *Proc. Amer. Phil. Soc.,* 103:531–36.

Reynolds, R. T. 1972. Sexual dimorphism in accipiter hawks: A new hypothesis. *Condor,* 74:191–97.

Sibley, C. G. 1957. The evolutionary and taxonomic significance of sexual dimorphism and hybridization in birds. *Condor,* 59:166–91.

Snyder, N. F. R., and Wiley, J. W. 1976. Sexual size dimorphism in hawks and owls of North America. *Ornith. Monogr.* no. 20.

Storer, R. W. 1966. Sexual dimorphism and food habits in three North American accipiters. *Auk,* 83:423–36.

DIPPER

Backus, G. J. 1959. Observations in the life history of the dipper in Montana. *Auk,* 76:90–207.

Bent, A. C. 1948. *Life Histories of North American Nuthatches, Wrens, Thrashers, and Their Allies.* U.S. Natl. Mus. Bull. no. 195. Washington, D.C. Reprinted New York, 1964.

Goodge, W. R. 1959. Locomotion and other behavior of the dipper. *Condor,* 61:4–17.

————. 1960. Adaptations for amphibious vision in the dipper (*Cinclus mexicanus*). *Jour. Morphol.,* 107:79–92.

DISEASE

Arnall, L., and Keymer, I. F. 1975. *Bird Diseases*. Neptune City, N.J. (Abundantly illustrated.)

Burkhart, R. L., and Page, L. A. 1971. Chlamydiosis (ornithosis-psittacosis). In Davis et al. (below).

Davis, J. W.; Anderson, R. C.; Karstad, L; and Trainer, D. O., eds. 1971. *Infectious and Parasitic Diseases of Wild Birds*. Ames, Ia.

Herman, C. M. 1966. Birds and our health. In *Birds in Our Lives*, ed. A. Stefferud and A. L. Nelson. Washington, D.C.

Jennings, A. R. 1964. In *A New Dictionary of Birds*, ed. A. L. Thomson. New York.

Leibovitz, L. 1971. Duck plague. In Davis et al. (above).

Meyer, K. E. 1959. Ornithosis. In *Diseases of Poultry*, ed. A. E. Biester and L. H. Schwarte. Ames, Ia.

Terres, J. K. 1980. Diseases (and assoc. entries). *The Audubon Encyclopedia of North American Birds*. New York.

Worth, C. B.; Hamparian, J.; and Rake, G. 1957. A serological survey of ornithosis in bird banders. *Bird-Banding*, 28:92–97.

DISPLAY

Armstrong, E. A. 1942. *Bird Display and Behavior*. New York.

Duffy, E.; Creassey, O. N.; and Williamson, K. 1950. Distraction display of certain waders. *Ibis*, 92:27–33.

Morris, D. 1956. The feather postures of birds and the problem of the origin of social signals. *Behavior*, 9:75–113.

Moynihan, M. 1955. Remarks on the original sources of displays. *Auk*, 72:240–46.

Smith, D. J. 1972. Role of the epaulets in the Red-winged Blackbird, *Agelaius phoeniceus*, social system. *Behavior*, 41:251–68.

DISTRIBUTION

Balda, R. P. 1969. Foliage use by birds of the oak-juniper woodland and ponderosa pine forest in southeastern Arizona. *Condor*, 71:399–412.

Berger, A. J. 1954. Association and seasonal succession in the use of nest sites. *Condor*, 56:164–65.

Bowen, V. T., and Nicholls, G. D. 1968. An egret observed on St. Paul's rocks, equatorial Atlantic. *Auk*, 85:130–31.

Cracraft, J. 1973. Continental drift, paleoclimatology, and the evolution and biogeography of birds. *Jour. Zool. London*, 169:455–545.

Crosby, G. T. 1972. Spread of the Cattle Egret in the Western Hemisphere. *Bird-Banding*, 43:205–12.

Darlington, Jr., P. J. 1957. *Zoogeography: The Geographic Distribution of Animals*. New York.

Dice, L. R. 1943. *The Biotic Provinces of North America*. Ann Arbor, Mich.

Hesse, R.; Allee, W. C.; and Schmidt, K. P. 1951. *Ecological Animal Geography*. 2nd ed. New York.

Humboldt, A. von. 1845–62. *Kosmos.* Stuttgart.

Johnstone, D. W. 1971. Niche relationships among some deciduous forest fly-catchers. *Auk,* 88:796–804.

Klopfer, P. H., and MacArthur, R. H. 1960. Niche size and faunal diversity. *Amer. Nat.,* 94:293–300.

Lack, D. 1937. The psychological factor in bird distribution. *Brit. Birds,* 31:130–36.

———. 1971. *Ecological Isolation in Birds.* Cambridge, Mass.

MacArthur, R. H. 1959. On the breeding distribution of North American migrant birds. *Auk,* 76:318–25.

———. 1964. Environmental factors affecting bird species diversity. *Amer. Nat.,* 98:387–97.

———. 1971. Patterns of terrestrial bird communities. In *Avian Biology,* ed. D. S. Farner et al. Vol. 1. New York.

——— and Wilson, E. O. 1967. *The Theory of Island Biogeography.* Princeton, N.J.

Marshall, Jr., J. T. 1957. *Birds of Pine-Oak Woodland in Southern Arizona and Adjacent Mexico.* Pacific Coast Avifauna no. 32. Cooper Ornith. Soc. Berkeley.

Mayr, E. 1946. History of North American bird fauna. *Wilson Bull.,* 58:3–41.

Milstead, W. W. 1972. Toward a quantification of the ecological niche. *Amer. Midland-Nat.,* 87:346–54.

Odum, E. P. 1971. *Fundamentals of Ecology.* 3rd. ed. Philadelphia.

Pitelka, F. A. 1941. Distribution of birds in relation to major biotic communities. *Amer. Midland-Nat.,* 25:113–37.

Ricklefs, R. E. 1966. The temporal component of diversity among species of birds. *Evolution,* 20:235–42.

Sclater, P. S. 1858. On the general geographical distribution of the members of the class Aves. *Jour. Proc. Linn. Soc. London Zool.,* 2:130–45.

Udvardy, M. D. F. 1958. Ecological and distributional analysis of North American birds. *Condor,* 60:50–66.

Wallace, A. R. 1876. *The Geographical Distribution of Animals.* 2 vols. London.

Wiens, J. A. 1969. An approach to the study of ecological relationships among grassland birds. *Ornith. Monogr.* no. 8.

See also some references under SPECIATION.

DOMESTICATED BIRDS

Jull, M. A. 1927. Races of domestic fowl. *Natl. Geographic Magazine,* 51:379–452.

Schorger, A. W. 1966. *The Wild Turkey: Its History and Domestication.* Norman, Okla.

Zeuner, F. E. 1963. *History of Domesticated Animals.* London.

DOMINANCE

Crook, J. H. 1964. Dominance (2). In *A New Dictionary of Birds,* ed. A. L. Thomson. New York.

Noble, G. K. 1931. The role of dominance in the social life of birds. *Auk,* 53:269–82.

Smith, S. M. 1976. Ecological aspects of dominance hierarchies in Black-capped Chickadees. *Auk,* 93:95–107.

DUMP NEST

Weller, M. W. 1959. Parasitic egg laying in the Redhead (*Aythya americana*) and other North American Anatidae. *Ecol. Monogr.,* 29:333–65.

Wiens, J. A. 1971. "Egg-dumping" by the Grasshopper Sparrow in a Savannah Sparrow nest. *Auk,* 88:185–86.

DUSTING

Healy, W. M., and Thomas, J. W. 1973. Effects of dusting in plumage of Japanese Quail. *Wilson Bull.,* 85:442–48.

Simmons, K. E. L. 1964. Feather maintenance. In *A New Dictionary of Birds,* ed. A. L. Thomson. New York.

ECTOPARASITE

Beer, R. E. 1970. Ectoparasites of birds: A brief review. In *Ornithology in Laboratory and Field,* by O. S. Pettingill, Jr. Minneapolis.

Boyd, E. M. 1951. The external parasites of birds: A review. *Wilson Bull.,* 63:363–69.

Malcolmson, R. O. 1960. Mallophaga from birds of North America. *Wilson Bull.,* 72:182–97.

EDIBILITY

Cott, H. B. 1946. The edibility of birds. *Proc. Zool. Soc. London,* 116:371–524.

———. 1951 and 1954. The palatability of the eggs of birds. *Proc. Zool. Soc. London,* 121:1–41 and 124:335–463.

Garland, J. E. 1978. *Boston's North Shore.* Boston.

EGG

Cody, M. L. 1966. A general theory of clutch size. *Evolution,* 20:174–84.

Crowell, K. L., and Rothstein, S. I. 1981. Clutch sizes and breeding strategies among Bermudan and North American passerines. *Ibis,* 123:42.

Lack, D. 1947–48. The significance of clutch size. *Ibis,* 89:302–52 and 90:25–45.

———. 1958. The significance of the colour in turdine eggs. *Ibis,* 100:145–66.

Phillips, C. L. 1887. Egg-laying extraordinary in *Colaptes auratus. Auk,* 4:346.

Preston, F. W. 1969. Shapes of birds' eggs: extant North American families. *Auk,* 86:246–64.

Ricklefs, R. E. 1980. Variation in clutch size among passerine birds: Ashmole's hypothesis. *Auk*. 97:38–49.

Riddle, O. 1911. On the formation, significance and chemistry of the white and yellow yolk of ova. *Jour. Morphol.*, 22:455–90.

Romanoff, A. L., and Romanoff, A. J. 1949. *The Avian Egg.* New York.

Rothstein, S. I. 1974. Mechanism of avian egg recognition: Possible learned and innate factors. *Auk*, 91:796–807.

Skutch, A. F. 1949. Do tropical birds rear as many young as they can nourish? *Ibis*, 91:430–55.

Taylor, T. G. 1970. How an eggshell is made. *Scientific American*, 222:88–95.

For field guides, see NEST.

EMBRYO

Portmann, A., and Stingelin, W. S. 1964. Development, embryonic. In *A New Dictionary of Birds*, ed. A. L. Thomson. New York.

Romanoff, A. L. 1960. *The Avian Embryo.* New York.

ENDANGERED BIRDS

Agey, H. N., and Heinzmann, G. M. 1971. The Ivory-billed Woodpecker found in central Florida. *Florida Nat.*, 44:46–47, 64.

Arbib, R. 1971–78. The Blue List: An "early warning system" for birds. *Amer. Birds*, Vols. 25–32.

Bass, K. H. 1979. I'on Swamp revisited: A 1979 update. *Birding*, 11:275.

Cade, T. J., ed. 1931. *Eastern Peregrine Falcon Reintroduction Program—Summary Report.* Cornell University Lab. of Ornith.

Hagar, J. A., and Anderson, K. S. 1977. Sight record of Eskimo Curlew (*Numenius borealis*) on west coast of James Bay, Canada. *Amer. Birds*, 31:135–36.

Halliday, J. 1978. *Vanishing Birds.* New York.

Harwood, M. 1981. Kirtland's Warbler—a born loser? *Audubon*, 83:99–111.

Hickey, J. J., ed. 1969. *Peregrine Falcon Populations: Their Biology and Decline.* Madison, Wisc.

King, W. B., comp. 1981. *Endangered Birds of the World: The ICBP Red Data Book.* Washington, D.C.

Koford, C. B. 1953. *The California Condor.* Natl. Audubon Soc. Rept. no. 4. New York.

Ligon, J. D. 1970. Behavior and breeding biology of the Red-cockaded Woodpecker. *Auk*, 87:255–78.

Mayfield, H. 1960. The Kirtland's Warbler. *Cranbrook Inst. Sci. Bull.*, no. 40. Bloomfield Hills, Mich.

McMillan, I. 1968. *Man and the California Condor: The Embattled History and Uncertain Future of North America's Largest Free-Living Bird.* New York.

McNulty, F. 1966. *The Whooping Crane: The Bird That Defies Extinction.* New York.

Ripley, S. D., and Moreno, A. 1980. A recent sighting of Bachman's Warbler in Cuba. *Birding*, 12:211–12.

Shuler, J. 1977. Bachman's phantom warbler *and* Bachman's Warbler habitat. *Birding*, 9:245–54.

Snyder, N. F. R. 1980. The California Condor conservation program: An overview. In *Transcript of California Condor Information Session*, Aug. 1980.

Stevenson, H. M. 1972. A recent history of Bachman's Warbler. *Wilson Bull.*, 84:344–47.

Stieglitz, W. O., and Thompson, R. L. 1967. *Status and Life History of the Everglade Kite in the United States.* Bureau of Sport Fisheries and Wildlife, Spec. Sci. Rept.—Wildlife, no. 109. Washington, D.C.

Sykes, Jr., P. W. 1976. The Everglade Kite. In *Inventory of Rare and Endangered Biota of Florida*, ed. J. N. Layne. Gainesville, Fla.

Tanner, J. T. 1942. *The Ivory-billed Woodpecker.* Natl. Audubon Soc. Res. Rept. no. 1. New York.

Temple, S. A., ed. 1977. *Endangered Birds: Management Techniques for Preserving Threatened Species.* Madison, Wisc.

Thompson, R. L., ed. 1971. *The Ecology and Management of the Red-cockaded Woodpecker: Proceedings of a Symposium at Okefenokee National Wildlife Refuge, Folkston, Ga., May 26–27.* Tallahassee, Fla.

ENDOCRINE SYSTEM

Boss, W. R. 1943. Hormonal determination of adult characters and sex behavior in Herring Gulls. *Jour. Exp. Zool.*, 94:181–203.

Hartman, F. A., and Albertin, R. H. 1951. A preliminary study of the avian adrenal. *Auk*, 68:202–9.

Höhn, E. O. 1961. Endocrine glands, thymus, and pineal body. In *Biology and Comparative Physiology of Birds*, ed. A. J. Marshall. Vol. 2. New York.

Marshall, A. J. 1964. Endocrine system. In *A New Dictionary of Birds*, ed. A. L. Thomson. New York.

Wolfson, A. 1945. The role of the pituitary . . . in bird migration. *Condor*, 47:95–127.

ENERGY

Kendeigh, S. C. 1970. Energy requirements for existence in relation to size of bird. *Condor*, 72:60–65.

Lasiewski, R. C. 1962. The energetics of migrating hummingbirds. *Condor*, 64:324.

Odum, E. P.; Connell, C. E.; and Stoddard, Sr., A. L. 1961. Flight energy and estimated flight ranges of some migrating birds. *Auk*, 78:515–27.

Paynter, R. A., ed. 1974. *Avian Energetics.* Nuttall Ornith. Club Pub. no. 15. Cambridge, Mass.

Tucker, V. A. 1969. The energetics of birds' flight. *Scientific American*, 220:70–78.

West, G. D. 1960. Seasonal variation in the energy balance of the Tree Sparrow in relation to migration. *Auk*, 77:306–29.

ERYTHRISM

Cole, L. J.; Stoddard, H. L.; and Komarek, E. V. 1949. Red Bobwhite: A report and a correction. *Auk,* 66:28–35.

Greenlaw, J. S. 1973. An erythristic specimen of the Rufous-sided Towhee. *Auk,* 90:428–29.

ESCAPES

Bolen, E. G. 1971. Some views on exotic waterfowl. *Wilson Bull.,* 83:430–34.

Ryan, R. 1972. A guide to North American waterfowl escapes. *Birding,* 4:159–60.

———. 1974. European escapes in northeastern U.S. *Birding,* 6:3–4.

———. 1976. Escapes, exotics and accidentals. *Birding,* 8:223–28.

ETHOLOGY

Dilger, W. C. 1962. Methods and objectives of ethology. *Living Bird,* 1st annual, pp. 83–92.

Ficken, R. W., and Ficken, M. S. 1966. A review of some aspects of avian field ethology. *Auk,* 83:637–61.

Lorenz, K. 1962. *King Solomon's Ring.* New York.

Thorpe, W. H. 1951. The definition of some terms used in animal behavior studies. *Bull. Anim. Behav.,* 9:34–40.

Tinbergen, N. 1953. *The Herring Gull's World: A Study of the Social Behavior of Birds.* New York.

———. 1969. Ethology. In *Scientific Thought 1900–1960,* ed. R. Harre. Oxford. (Reprinted in *The Animal in Its World,* Vol. 2, 1973. Cambridge, Mass.)

ETIQUETTE

Balch, L. G. 1981. Birding ethics. *Birding,* 13:171–73.

Glinski, R. L. 1976. Bird-watching etiquette: The need for a developing philosophy. *Amer. Birds,* 30:655–57.

Naveen, R. 1980. Birding ethics. *Birding,* 12:60–61.

Tucker, J. A. 1981. Slob birders (editorial). *Birding,* 13:112.

Wauer, R. 1974. Moral obligations of birders. *Birding,* 6:227–29.

EVOLUTION OF BIRDLIFE

Brodkorb, P. 1960. How many species of birds have existed? *Bull. Florida State Mus.,* 5:41–53.

———. 1960–71. Catalogue of fossil birds. *Bull. Florida State Mus.* Gainesville.

———. 1971. Origin and evolution of birds. In *Avian Biology,* eds. D. S. Farner et al. Vol. 1. New York.

de Beer, G. 1954. *Archaeopteryx lithographica.* London.

Howard, H. 1962. *Fossil Birds.* Los Angeles County Mus., Science Ser. no. 17, Paleontology no. 10.

Marsh, O. C. 1880. *Odontornithes: A Monograph of the Extinct Toothed Birds of North America.* Washington, D.C.

Nopsca, F. 1923. On the origin of flight in birds. *Proc. Zool. Soc. London,* pp. 223–36.

Osborn, H. F. 1900. Reconsideration of the evidence for a common dinosaur-avian stem in the Permian. *Amer. Nat.,* 34:777–99.

Ostrum, J. H. 1974. *Archaeopteryx* and the origin of bird flight. *Quart. Rev. Biol.,* 49:27–47.

Parkes, K. C. 1966. Speculations on the origins of feathers. *Living Bird,* 5th annual, pp. 77–87.

Selander, R. K. 1965. Avian speciation in the Quaternary. In *The Quaternary of the United States,* ed. H. E. Wright, Jr., and D. G. Frey. Princeton, N.J. Pp. 527–42.

Stock, C. 1961. *Rancho La Brea: A Record of Pleistocene Life in California.* Los Angeles County Mus., Sci. Ser. no. 20.

Swinton, W. E. 1960–61. The origin of birds. In *Biology and Comparative Physiology of Birds,* ed. A. J. Marshall. Vol. 1. New York.

Wetmore, A. 1956. *A Checklist of the Fossil and Prehistoric Birds of North America and the West Indies.* Smithsonian Misc. Coll. 131, no. 5. Washington, D.C.

————. 1959. *Birds of the Pleistocene of North America.* Smithsonian Misc. Coll. 138:1–24. Washington, D.C.

EXCRETORY SYSTEM

Shoemaker, V. H. 1972. Osmoregulation and excretion in birds. In *Avian Biology,* ed. D. S. Farner et al. Vol. 2. New York.

Sperber, I. 1960. Excretion. In *Biology and Comparative Physiology of Birds,* ed. A. J. Marshall. Vol. 1. New York.

EXOTIC SPECIES

Banks, R. C. 1970. *Birds Imported into the United States in 1968.* U.S. Fish and Wildlife Serv. Spec. Sci. Rept.—Wildlife, no. 136. Washington, D.C.

Hardy, J. W. 1973. Several exotic birds in southern California. *Wilson Bull.,* 84:506–12.

Owre, O. T. 1973. A consideration of the exotic avifauna of southeastern Florida. *Wilson Bull.,* 85:491–500.

Ryan, R. 1979. Established exotics in the ABA area. *Birding,* 11:116–21, 164–66, 244–45.

Trimm, W. 1972. The Monk Parakeet. *Conservationist,* 26:4–5.

See also references under ESCAPES and INTRODUCED BIRDS.

EXTINCT BIRDS

Ehrlich, P., and Ehrlich, A. 1981. *Extinction.* New York.

Greenway, Jr., J. C. 1958. *Extinct and Vanishing Birds of the World.* Amer. Committee for Internatl. Wildlife Protection, Spec. Publ. no. 13. New York. (Rev. ed.; New York: Dover, 1967.)

Gross, A. O. 1928. The Heath Hen. *Memo. Boston Soc. Nat. Hist.*, 6:491–588.

Nicholson, D. J. 1948. Escaped paroquets found breeding in Florida. *Auk*, 65:139.

Schorger, A. W. 1973. *The Passenger Pigeon*. Norman, Okla.

FALCON

Bent, A. C. 1938. *Life Histories of North American Birds of Prey*. U.S. Natl. Mus. Bull. no. 170, pt. 2. Washington, D.C. Reprinted New York, 1961.

Brown, L., and Amadon, D. 1968. *Eagles, Hawks, and Falcons of the World*. New York. Vol. 2, pp. 727–856.

Cade, T. J. 1960. Ecology of the Peregrine and Gyrfalcon populations in Alaska. *Univ. Calif. Publ. Zool.*, 63:151–290.

See also Hickey (1969–ENDANGERED BIRDS)

FALCONRY

Ap Evans, H. 1960. *Falconry for You*. Newton Centre, Mass.

Beebe, F. L. 1976. *Hawks, Falcons and Falconry*. Passaic, N.J.

—— and Webster, H. M., ed. 1976. *North American Falconry and Hunting Hawks*. 4th ed. Denver.

Fuertes, L. A. 1920. Falconry, the sport of kings. *Natl. Geographic Magazine*, 38:429–60.

Peeters, H. J., and Jameson, Jr., E. W. 1970. *American Hawking: A General Account of Falconry in the New World*. Davis, Calif. (published privately).

White, T. H. 1951. *The Goshawk*. New York.

Wood, C. A., and Fyfe, F. M. 1943. *The Art of Falconry*. Stanford, Calif.

FAT

Helms, C. W., and Drury, Jr., W. H. 1960. Winter and migratory weight and fat: Field studies of some North American buntings. *Bird-Banding*, 31:1–40.

King, J. R. 1972. Adaptive periodic fat storage by birds. *Proc. (XVth) Internatl. Ornith. Congr., Leiden*, pp. 200–17.

Nisbet, I. C. T.; Drury, Jr., W. H.; and Baird, J. 1963. Weight-loss during migration: Parts I and II (Blackpoll Warbler, *Dendroica striata*). *Bird-Banding*, 34:107–59.

FEATHER

'Espinasse, P. G. 1964. Feather. In *A New Dictionary of Birds*, ed. A. L. Thomson. New York.

Lederer, R. J. 1972. The role of avian rictal bristles. *Wilson Bull.*, 84:193–97.

Lillie, F. R. 1940. Physiology of development of the feather. *Physiol. Zool.*, 13:143–75.

Stettenheim, P. 1973. The bristles of birds. *Living Bird*, 12th annual, pp. 201–34.

For origins of feathers, see references under EVOLUTION OF BIRDLIFE.

FIELD GUIDE

Bond, J. 1971. *Birds of the West Indies.* 2nd ed. Boston.

Bruun, B., and Singer, A. 1970. *Birds of Europe.* New York.

Bull, J., and Farrand, Jr., J. 1977. *The Audubon Society Field Guide to North American Birds: Eastern Region.* New York. (Photos.)

Fitter, R.; Heinzel, H.; and Parslow, J. 1972. *Birds of Britain and Europe.* Philadelphia.

Godfrey, W. E. 1966. *The Birds of Canada.* Natl. Mus. Can. Bull. no. 203. Ottawa. (Large format but includes a wealth of field identification material and comprehensive illustrations.)

Nuttall, T. 1832–34. *A Manual of Ornithology of the United States and Canada.* Vols. 1 and 2. Boston.

Peterson, R. T. 1947. *A Field Guide to the Birds* (Eastern North America). Boston. ("Classic" edition.)

————. 1960. *A Field Guide to the Birds of Texas and Adjacent States.* Boston.

————. 1961. *A Field Guide to Western Birds.* Boston.

————. 1980. *A Field Guide to the Birds East of the Rockies.* Boston.

————; Mountfort, G.; and Hollom, P. A. D. 1954. *A Field Guide to the Birds of Britain and Europe.* Boston.

———— and Chalif, E. 1973. *A Field Guide to Mexican Birds.* Boston.

Pough, R. H. 1949. *Audubon Land Bird Guide.* New York.

————. 1951. *Audubon Water Bird Guide.* New York.

————. 1957. *Audubon Western Bird Guide.* New York.

Prater, A. J.; Marchant, J. H.; and Vuorinen, J. 1976. *Guide to the Identification and Ageing of Holarctic Waders.* London.

Robbins, C. S.; Bruun, B.; and Zim, H. 1966. *Birds of North America: A Guide to Field Identification.* New York.

Scott, P. 1957. *A Colored Key to the Waterfowl of the World.* Slimbridge, England.

Tuck, G., and Heinzel, H. 1978. *A Field Guide to the Seabirds of Britain and the World.* London.

Udvardy, M. D. F. 1977. *The Audubon Society Field Guide to North American Birds: Western Region.* New York. (Photos.)

FINCH

Bent, A. C., et al., comps. 1968. *Life Histories of North American Cardinals, Grosbeaks, Buntings, Towhees, Finches, Sparrows, and Their Allies,* ed. O. L. Austin, Jr. U.S. Natl. Mus. Bull. no. 237, pts. 1–3. Washington, D.C. Reprinted New York, 1968.

Newton, I. 1973. *Finches.* New York.

FLAMINGO

Allen, R. P. 1956. *The Flamingoes: Their Life History and Survival.* Natl. Audubon Soc. Res. Rept. no. 5. New York.

Bent, A. C. 1926. *Life Histories of North American Marsh Birds*. U.S. Natl. Mus. Bull. no. 135. Washington, D.C. Reprinted New York, 1963.

Palmer, R. S., ed. 1962. *Handbook of North American Birds*. New Haven. Vol. 1, pp. 542–50.

FLIGHT

Cone, Jr., C. D. 1962. Thermal soaring of birds. *Amer. Scientist,* 50:180–209.

Heppner, F. H. 1974. Avian flight formations. *Bird-Banding,* 45:160–69.

Pennycuick, C. J. 1975. Mechanics of flight. In *Avian Biology,* ed. D. S. Farner et al. Vol. 5. New York.

Poole, E. L. 1938. Weights and wing areas in North American birds. *Auk,* 55:511–17.

Raspet, A. 1960. Biophysics of bird flight. *Annual Rept. Smithsonian Inst.,* pp. 191–200.

Stillson, B. 1954. *Wings: Insects, Birds, Men.* Indianapolis.

Storer, J. H. 1948. The flight of birds analysed through slow-motion photography. *Cranbrook Inst. Sci. Bull.* no. 28.

―――. 1952. Bird aerodynamics. *Scientific American,* 186:25–29.

Tucker, V. A., and Schmidt-Koenig, K. 1977. Flight speeds of birds in relation to energetics and wind directions. *Auk,* 88:97–108.

Woodcock, A. H. 1942. Soaring over the open sea. *Scientific Monthly,* 55:226–32.

FLOCK

Allee, W. C. 1931. *Animal Aggregations.* Chicago.

―――. 1936. Analytical studies of group behavior in birds. *Wilson Bull.,* 48:145–51.

Emlen, Jr., J. T. 1952. Flocking behavior in birds. *Auk,* 69:160–70.

Goldman, P. 1980. Flocking as a possible predator defense in Dark-eyed Juncos. *Wilson Bull.,* 92:88–95.

Meyerriecks, A. J. 1957. "Bunching" reactions of Cedar Waxwings to attacks of a Cooper's Hawk. *Wilson Bull.,* 69:184.

Nichols, J. T. 1931. Notes on the flocking of shorebirds. *Auk,* 48:181–85.

Sabine, W. S. 1959. The winter society of the Oregon Junco: The flock. *Condor,* 61:110–35.

Wynne-Edwards, V. C. 1962. *Animal Dispersion in Relation to Social Behavior.* London.

FOOD/FEEDING

Baldwin, W. P. 1946. Clam catches oystercatcher. *Auk,* 63:589.

Beecher, W. J. 1951. Adaptations for food-getting in the American blackbirds. *Auk,* 68:411–40.

Betts, M. M. 1955. The food of titmice in oak woodland. *Jour. Anim. Ecol.,* 24:282–323.

Broun, M. 1941. Gulls eating fruit of cabbage palmetto. *Auk,* 58:579.

Chettleburgh, M. R. 1952. Observations on the collection and burial of acorns by jays in Hainault Forest. *Brit. Birds*, 45:359–64.

Cottam, C. 1939. *Food Habits of North American Diving Ducks.* U.S. Dept. Agric. Tech. Bull. no. 643. Washington, D.C.

———— and Uhler, F. M. 1937. *Birds in Relation to Fishes.* U.S. Dept. Agric. Wildlife Res. and Management Leaflet no. BS-83. Washington, D.C.

————; Williams, C. S.; and Sooter, C. A. 1942. Cooperative feeding of White Pelicans. *Auk*, 59:444–45.

Dickson, J. G., et al., eds. 1979. *The Role of Insectivorous Birds in Forest Ecosystems.* New York.

Dusi, R. L. 1968. "Ploughing" for fish by the Greater Yellowlegs. *Wilson Bull.*, 80:491–92.

Evenden, Jr., F. G. 1943. Food-washing habit of the Dipper. *Condor*, 45:120.

Fitzpatrick, I. W. 1980. Foraging behavior of Neotropical tyrant flycatchers. *Condor*, 82:43–57.

Foster, W. L., and Tate, Jr., J. 1966. The activities and co-actions of animals at sapsucker trees. *Living Bird*, 5th annual, pp. 87–113.

Gibb, J. A. 1960. Populations of tits and Goldcrests and their food supply in pine plantations. *Ibis*, 102:163–208.

Heppleston, P. B. 1971. Feeding techniques of the oystercatcher. *Bird Study*, 18:15–20.

Heppner, F. H. 1965. Sensory mechanisms and environmental clues used by the American Robin in locating earthworms. *Condor*, 67:247–56.

Lang, H. 1924. *Ampullarius* and *Rostrhamus* at Georgetown, British Guiana. *Nautilus*, 37:73–77.

MacRoberts, M. H. 1970. Notes on the food habits and food defence of the Acorn Woodpecker, *Condor*, 72:196–204.

————. 1975. Food storage and winter territory in Red-headed Woodpeckers in northwestern Louisiana. *Auk*, 92:382–85.

Meng, H. 1959. Food habits of nesting Cooper's Hawks and Goshawks in New York and Pennsylvania. *Wilson Bull.*, 71:169–74.

Meyerriecks, A. J. 1959. Foot-stirring feeding behavior in herons. *Wilson Bull.*, 71:153–58.

————. 1966. Additional observations on "foot-stirring" feeding behavior in herons. *Auk*, 83:471–72.

Moffit, J., and Cottam, C. 1941. *The Eel-grass Blight and Its Effect on Brant.* U.S. Fish and Wildlife Service Leaflet, 204:1–26.

Nice, M. M., and Nice, C. 1950. The appetite of a Black-and-White Warbler. *Wilson Bull.*, 62:94–95.

Richardson, F. 1942. Adaptive modifications for tree-trunk foraging in birds. *Univ. Calif. Publ. Zool.*, 46:317–68.

Smith, S. M. 1971. The relationship of grazing cattle to foraging rates in anis. *Auk*, 88:876–80.

Snyder, N. F. R., and Snyder, J. A. 1969. A comparative study of mollusk predation by Limpkins, Everglade Kites, and Boat-tailed Grackles. *Living Bird*, 8th annual, pp. 177–223.

Sperry, C. C. 1940. *Food Habits of a Group of Shorebirds: Woodcock, Snipe, Knot and Dowitcher.* U.S. Dept. Agric., Bur. Biol. Surv. Wildlife Res. Bull. no. 1. Washington, D.C.

Tinbergen, N. 1962. Foot-paddling in gulls. *Brit. Birds,* 55:117–20.

Tomback, D. F. 1978. Foraging strategies of Clark's Nutcracker. *Living Bird,* 16th annual, pp. 123–62.

———. 1980. How nutcrackers find their seed stores. *Condor,* 82:10–19.

Turner, R. R. A. 1964. Social feeding in birds. *Behavior,* 24:1–46.

Wetmore, A. 1920. A peculiar feeding habit of grebes. *Condor,* 22:18–20.

FRIGATEBIRD

Bent, A. C. 1922. *Life Histories of North American Petrels and Pelicans and Their Allies.* U.S. Natl. Mus. Bull. no. 121. Washington, D.C. Reprinted New York, 1964.

Palmer, R. S., ed. 1962. *Handbook of North American Birds.* Vol. 1. New Haven.

See also references under SEABIRD.

GALLINACEOUS BIRDS

Beebe, N. 1918–22. *A Monograph of the Pheasants.* 4 vols. London.

Bent, A. C. 1932. *Life Histories of North American Gallinaceous Birds.* U.S. Natl. Mus. Bull. no. 162. Washington, D.C. Reprinted New York, 1963.

Delacour, J. 1951. *The Pheasants of the World.* New York. (2nd ed., 1977, Hindhead, England.)

——— and Amadon, D. 1973. Chachalacas. In *Curassows and Related Birds.* New York.

Edminster, F. C., et al. 1947. *The Ruffed Grouse: Its Life Story, Ecology and Management.* New York.

Johnsgard, P. A. 1973. *Grouse and Quails of North America.* Lincoln, Neb.

Schorger, A. W. 1966. *The Wild Turkey: Its History and Domestication.* Norman, Okla.

GENETICS

Dobzhansky, T. 1957. *Genetics and the Origin of Species.* New York.

Goldstein, P. 1947. *Genetics Is Easy.* New York.

Sinnott, E. W.; Dunn, L. C.; and Dobzhansky, T. 1958. *Principles of Genetics.* New York.

GREBE

Bent, A. C. 1919. *Life Histories of North American Diving Birds.* U.S. Natl. Mus. Bull. no. 107. Washington, D.C. Reprinted New York, 1946 and 1963.

Palmer, R. S., ed. 1962. *Handbook of North American Birds.* New Haven. Vol. 1, pp. 62–113.

Storer, R. W. 1963. Courtship and mating behavior and the phylogeny of the grebes. *Proc. (XIIIth) Internatl. Ornith. Congr., Ithaca, N.Y., 1962,* pp. 562–69.

See also Wetmore (1920–FOOD/FEEDING).

GREENLAND

Salomonsen, F. 1950. *Grønlands Fugle* (Birds of Greenland). With Eng. text. Copenhagen.

GRISCOM

Griscom, L. 1932. The distribution of birdlife in Guatemala. *Bull. Amer. Mus. Nat. Hist.*, 64:1–439.

———. 1945. *Modern Bird Study.* Cambridge, Mass.

———. 1949. *The Birds of Concord.* Cambridge, Mass.

———; Friedmann, H.; Miller, A. H.; and Moore, R. T. 1950 (Part I) and 1957 (Part II). *Distributional Checklist of the Birds of Mexico.* Pacific Coast Avifauna no. 29. Cooper Ornith. Soc. Berkeley.

——— and Snyder, D. E. 1955. *The Birds of Massachusetts.* Salem, Mass.

——— and Sprunt, Jr., A., eds. 1957. *The Warblers of North America.* New York. Reprinted 1979.

GRIT

Jenkinson, M. A., and Mengel, R. M. 1970. Ingestion of stones by goatsuckers (Caprimulgidae). *Condor,* 72:236–37.

McCann, L. J. 1961. Grit as an ecological factor. *Amer. Midland-Nat.,* 65:187–92.

GULL

Bent, A. C. 1921. *Life Histories of North American Gulls and Terns.* U.S. Natl. Mus. Bull. no. 113. Washington, D.C. Reprinted New York, 1963.

Dwight, Jr., J. 1925. The gulls (Laridae) of the world: Their plumages, moults, variations, relationships, distribution. *Bull. Amer. Mus. Nat. Hist.,* 3, art. III, 63–401.

Tinbergen, N. 1960. Comparative studies of the behavior of gulls (Laridae). *Behavior,* 15:1–70.

Vickery, P. D. 1977. Northeast maritime region. *Amer. Birds,* 31:1112.

See also references under SEABIRD.

GYNANDROMORPHISM

Brodkorb, P. 1935. A Sparrow Hawk gynandromorph. *Auk,* 52:183–84.

Laybourne, R. C. 1967. Bilateral gynandrism in an Evening Grosbeak. *Auk,* 84:267–72.

HATCHING

Armstrong, E. A. 1964. Parental care. In *A New Dictionary of Birds,* ed. A. L. Thomson. New York.

Fisher, H. I. 1958. The "hatching muscle" in the chick. *Auk,* 75:391–99.

Skutch, A. F. 1952. On the hour of laying and hatching of birds' eggs. *Ibis,* 94:49–61.

Hawk

Bent, A. C. 1937. *Life Histories of North American Birds of Prey.* U.S. Natl. Mus. Bull. no. 167, pt. 1. Washington, D.C. Reprinted New York, 1961.

Brown, L. 1976. *Birds of Prey.* New York.

—— and Amadon, D. 1968. *Eagles, Hawks, and Falcons of the World.* 2 vols. New York.

Newton, I. 1979. *Population Ecology of Raptors.* Vermillion, S.D.

Hawk Mountain

Broun, M. 1949. *Hawks Aloft: The Story of Hawk Mountain.* New York.

Harwood, M. 1973. *A View from Hawk Mountain.* New York.

Hearing

Kreithen, M. L., and Quine, D. B. 1979. Infrasound detection by the homing pigeon. *Jour. Comp. Physiol.,* A 129:1–4.

Payne, R. S. 1962. How the Barn Owl locates prey by hearing. *Living Bird,* 1st annual, pp. 150–59.

Pumphrey, R. J. 1964. Hearing and balance. In *A New Dictionary of Birds,* ed. A. L. Thomson. New York.

Ramp, W. K. 1965. The auditory range of a Hairy Woodpecker. *Condor,* 67:183–85.

Schwartzkopff, J. 1955. On the hearing of birds. *Auk,* 72:340–47.

Thorpe, W. H. 1963. Antiphonal singing in birds as evidence for avian auditory reaction time. *Nature,* 197:774–76.

Heron

Bent, A. C. 1926. *Life Histories of North American Marsh Birds.* U.S. Natl. Mus. Bull. no. 135. Washington, D.C. Reprinted New York, 1963.

Hancock, J., and Elliott, H. 1978. *The Herons of the World.* New York.

Meyerriecks, A. J. 1960. *Comparative Breeding Behavior of Four Species of North American Herons.* Nuttall Ornith. Club Publ. no. 2. Cambridge, Mass.

Palmer, R. S., ed. 1962. *Handbook of North American Birds.* New Haven. Vol. 1, pp. 381–508.

Homosexuality

Brackbill, H. 1941. Possible homosexual mating of the Rock Dove. *Auk,* 58:581.

Conover, M. R.; Miller, D. E.; and Hunt, Jr., G. L. 1979. Female-female pairs and other unusual reproductive associations in Ring-billed and California Gulls. *Auk,* 96:6–9.

Hunt, Jr., G. L.; Wingfield, J. C.; Newman, A.; and Farner, D. S. 1980. Sex ratios of Western Gulls on Santa Barbara Island, California. *Auk.* 97:473–79.

Starkey, E. E. 1972. A case of interspecific homosexuality in geese. *Auk,* 89:456–57.

HUMAN CULTURE

Clark, Sir K. 1977. *Animals and Men: Their Relationship as Reflected in Western Art.* New York.

Friedmann, H. 1946. *The Symbolic Goldfinch: Its History and Significance in European Devotional Art.* Washington, D.C.

Gelkie, A. 1916. *The Birds of Shakespeare.* Glasgow.

Howes, F. S. 1964. Music, birds in. In *A New Dictionary of Birds,* ed. A. L. Thomson. New York

Massingham, H. J., ed. c. 1922. *Poems about Birds from the Middle Ages to the Present Day.* New York.

Welker, R. H. 1955. *Birds and Men.* Cambridge, Mass.

See also many references in the text of this entry.

HUMMINGBIRD

Bent, A. C. 1940. *Life Histories of North American Cuckoos, Goatsuckers, Hummingbirds, and Their Allies.* U.S. Natl. Mus. Bull. no. 176. Washington, D.C. Reprinted New York, 1964.

Greenewalt, C. H. 1960. *Hummingbirds.* New York.

Scheithauer, W. 1967. *Hummingbirds.* New York.

Skutch, A. F. 1973. *The Life of the Hummingbird.* New York.

HYBRIDIZATION

Banks, R. C., and Johnson, N. K. 1961. A review of North American hybrid hummingbirds. *Condor,* 63:3–27.

Cockrum, E. L. 1952. A checklist and bibliography of hybrid birds of North America north of Mexico. *Wilson Bull.,* 64:140–59.

Davis, I., and Webster, F. S. 1970. An intergeneric hybrid flycatcher (*Tyrannus X Muscivora*). *Condor,* 72:37–42.

Dickerman, R. W. 1961. Hybrids among the fringillid genera *Junco, Zonotrichia,* and *Melospiza. Auk,* 78:627–32.

Gill, F. B. 1980. Historical aspects of hybridization between Blue-winged and Golden-winged Warblers. *Auk.* 97:1–18.

Gray, A. P. 1958. *Bird Hybrids.* Tech. Communication no. 13. Commonwealth Agricultural Bureaux. London.

Harris, M. P. 1970. Abnormal migration and hybridization of *Larus argentatus* and *L. fuscus* after interspecies fostering experiments. *Ibis,* 112:488–98.

Martin, R. F. 1980. Analysis of hybridization between the hirundid genera *Hirundo* and *Petrochelidon* in Texas. *Auk,* 97:148–59.

Short, Jr., L. L. 1963. Hybridization of the wood warblers *Vermivora pinus* and *Vermivora chrysoptera. Proc. (XIIIth) Internatl. Ornith. Congr., Ithaca,* N.Y., pp. 147–60.

———. 1965. Hybridization of the flickers (*Colaptes*) of North America. *Bull. Amer. Mus. Nat. Hist.,* 129:307–428.

——— and Robbins, C. S. 1967. An intergeneric hybrid wood warbler (*Seiurus X Dendroica*). *Auk,* 84:534.

Sibley, C. G. 1957. The evolutionary and taxonomic significance of sexual dimorphism and hybridization in birds. *Condor*, 59:166–91.

———. 1958. Hybrids of and with North American Anatidae. *Proc. (Xth) Internatl. Ornith. Congr., Rouen, France*, pp. 327–55.

——— and Short, Jr., L. L. 1959. Hybridization in the buntings (*Passerina*) in the Great Plains. *Auk*, 76:443–63.

IBIS

Bent, A. C. 1926. *Life Histories of North American Marsh Birds*. U.S. Natl. Mus. Bull. no. 135. Washington, D.C. Reprinted New York, 1963.

Palmer, R. S., ed. 1962. *Handbook of North American Birds*. New Haven. Vol. 1, pp. 515–41.

ILLUSTRATION

Alexander, W. B. 1953. Ornithological illustration. *Endeavor*, 12:144–53.

Anker, J. 1938. *Bird Books and Bird Art*. Copenhagen.

Audubon, J. J. 1966. *The Original Water-color Paintings by John James Audubon for The Birds of America*. Intro. by M. B. Davidson. 2 vols. New York. (Best available reproductions of Audubon's work; many editions of prints are available in a wide range of qualities and prices.)

Buerschaper, P., comp. *Animals in Art: An International Exhibition of Wildlife Art*. Royal Ontario Museum. Toronto, Canada. Oct. 7–Dec. 14, 1975.

Catesby, M. 1731–43 (Appendix 1748). *The Natural History of Carolina, Florida, and the Bahama Islands, Containing the Figures of Birds, Beasts, Fishes, Serpents, Insects, and Plants*, 2 vols. London. (Illustr. by the author.)

Delacour, J., and Amadon, D. 1973. *Curassows and Related Birds*. New York. (Illustr. by A. E. Gilbert and George M. Sutton.)

Eckelberry, D. R. 1963. Birds in art and illustration. *Living Bird*, 2nd annual, pp. 69–82.

Forshaw, J. M. 1973. *Parrots of the World*. New York. (Illustr. by William T. Cooper.)

Fuertes, L. A. 1930. *Album of Abyssinian Birds and Mammals*. Field Museum of Natural History, Chicago. (32 plates.)

Harris, H. 1926. Examples of recent American bird art. *Condor*, 28:191–206.

Hill, M. 1978. Liljefors of Sweden: The peerless eye. *Audubon*, 80:70–104. (Many examples of the master's work in color.)

Jaques, F. P. 1973. *Francis Lee Jaques: Artist of the Wilderness World*. New York.

Lansdowne, J. F., and Livingston, J. A. 1966. *Birds of the Northern Forest*. Boston.

——— and ———. 1968. *Birds of the Eastern Forest: I*. Boston. Also three other titles in this series: *Eastern Forest II, Northern Forest*, and *Pacific Coast*.

Leslie, C. W. 1980. Birds. Ch. 7 in *Nature Drawing: A Tool for Learning*. Englewood Cliffs, N.J. (Examples of many artists' work in black and white; bibliography; also "how to.")

The Living Bird. All issues of annual format (1962–81) include many examples of the work of modern bird illustrators.

Marsham, F. G., ed. 1971. *Louis Agassiz Fuertes and the Singular Beauty of Birds.* New York.

Mengel, R. M. 1980. Beauty and the beast: Natural history and art. *Living Bird.* 18th annual, pp. 27–70.

Murphy, R. C. 1936. *Oceanic Birds of South America.* New York. (Illustr. by F. Lee Jaques.)

National Geographic Magazine. Many issues included fine examples of bird illustration before the advent of color photography; see especially the series on North American birds (July 1932–August 1937) with illustrations by Allan Brooks.

Norelli, M. R. 1975. *American Wildlife Painting.* New York.

Peterson, R. T. 1942. Bird painting in America. *Audubon,* 44:166–76.

Sitwell, S.; Buchanan, H.; and Fisher, J. 1953. *Fine Bird Books, 1700–1900.* London.

Stout, G. D., ed. 1967. *The Shorebirds of North America.* New York. (Illustr. by Robert Verity Clem.)

Sutton, G. M. 1951. *Mexican Birds: First Impressions.* Norman, Okla. (Illustr. by the author.)

——. 1962. Is bird-art art? *Living Bird,* 1st annual, pp. 73–78.

——. 1971. *High Arctic.* New York. (Illustr. by the author.)

Many other examples of Sutton's fine watercolor and scratchboard illustrations are scattered profusely throughout popular and technical bird literature of the twentieth century, including many titles under the artist's name.

Tunnicliffe, C. F. 1979. *A Sketchbook of Birds.* New York.

For other examples of bird illustration, see references under STATE BOOKS, BIRD, and FIELD GUIDE. See also all issues of *The Living Bird* (PERIODICALS).

IMAGINATION

Armstrong, E. A. 1958. *The Folklore of Birds.* London.

Carrington, R. 1957. *Mermaids and Mastodons.* London.

Coffin, T., and Cohen, H. 1966. *Folklore in America.* New York.

Fraser, J. G. 1922. *The Golden Bough.* New York.

Ingersoll, E. 1923. *Birds in Legend, Fable and Folklore.* New York.

Leach, M., ed. 1949. *Dictionary of Folklore, Mythology and Legend.* New York.

—— and Fried, J., eds. 1949. *Funk and Wagnall's Standard Dictionary of Folklore, Mythology and Legend.* 2 vols. New York.

Lum, P. 1951. *Fabulous Beasts.* New York.

Wakefield, J. 1964. *The Strange World of Birds.* Philadelphia.

White, T. H., trans. 1954. *The Book of Beasts: A Latin Bestiary of the 12th Century.*

INCUBATION

Bailey, R. E. 1952. The incubation patch of passerine birds. *Condor,* 54:121–36.

Drent, R. 1975. Incubation. In *Avian Biology,* ed. D. S. Farner et al. Vol. 5. New York.

Frith, H. J. 1956. Breeding habits in the family Megapodiidae. *Ibis,* 98:620–40.

Irving, L., and Krog, J. 1956. Temperature during the development of birds in arctic nests. *Physiol. Zool.,* 29:195–205.

Kendeigh, S. C. 1963. New ways of measuring the incubation period of birds. *Auk,* 80:453–61.

Nice, M. M. 1954. Problems of incubation periods in North American birds. *Condor,* 56:173–97.

Parmelee, D. F. 1970. Breeding behavior of the Sanderling in the Canadian High Arctic. *Living Bird,* 9th annual, pp. 97–146.

Skutch, A. F. 1957. The incubation patterns of birds. *Ibis,* 99:69–93.

———. 1962. The constancy of incubation. *Wilson Bull.,* 74:115–52.

Taft, J. E. 1970. Possible seven-day incubation period in the Robin, *Turdus migratorius. Audubon Field Notes,* 24:652.

Tucker, B. W. 1943. Brood-patches and the physiology of incubation. *Brit. Birds,* 37:22–28.

INTELLIGENCE

Alcock, J. 1970. The origins of tool-using by Egyptian Vultures, *Neophron percnopterus. Ibis,* 112:542.

Green, C. 1972. Use of tool by Orange-winged Sitella. *Emu,* 72:185–86.

Hess, E. H. 1964. Imprinting in birds. *Science,* 146:1128–39.

Jones, T. B., and Kamil, A. C. 1973. Tool-making and tool-using in the Northern Blue Jay. *Science,* 180:1076–77.

Kohler, O. 1950. The ability of birds to "count." *Bull. Anim. Behav.,* 9:41–45.

Morse, D. H. 1968. The use of tools by Brown-headed Nuthatches. *Wilson Bull.,* 80:220–24.

Pastore, N. 1954. Discrimination learning in the Canary. *Jour. Comp. Physiol. Psychol.,* 47:288–89, 389–90.

Thorpe, W. H. 1956. *Learning and Instinct in Animals.* London.

Tinbergen, N. 1951. *The Study of Instinct.* Oxford.

———. 1953. *The Herring Gull's World: A Study of the Social Behavior of Birds.* New York.

van Lawick-Goodall, J. 1969. Tool-using bird, the Egyptian Vulture. *Natl. Geographic Magazine,* 133:630–41.

INTRODUCED BIRDS

Chapman, F. M. 1925. The European Starling as an American citizen. *Natural Hist.* (reprinted April 1980 number, 89:60–65).

Elliott, J. J., and Arbib, Jr., R. S. 1953. Origin and status of the House Finch in the eastern United States. *Auk,* 70:31–37.

Kinkead, E. 1978. In numbers too great to count. *The New Yorker*, May 22, "Profiles," pp. 40–88. (House Sparrow.)

Phillips, J. C. 1928. *Wild Birds Introduced or Transplanted in North America.* U.S. Dept. Agric. Tech. Bull. no. 61. Washington, D.C.

Robbins, C. S. 1973. Introduction, spread, and present abundance of the House Sparrows in North America. In *A Symposium of the House Sparrow* (Passer domesticus) *and European Tree Sparrow* (P. montanus) *in North America.* Amer. Ornith. Union. Monogr. no. 14.

Stott, Jr., K. 1959. The Starling arrives in San Diego, California. *Condor*, 61:373.

Weisbrod, A. R., and Stevens, W. F. 1974. The Skylark in Washington. *Auk*, 91:832–35.

IRRUPTION

Baird, J. 1964. The irruptive phenomenon. *Audubon Field Notes*, 17:6–8.

Cornwallis, R. C. 1964. Irruption. In *A New Dictionary of Birds*, ed. A. L. Thomson. New York.

Davis, D. E. 1974. Emigration of Northern Shrikes, 1959–1970. *Auk*, 91:821–25.

Davis, J., and William, L. 1964. The 1961 irruption of the Clark's Nutcracker in California. *Wilson Bull.*, 76:10–18.

Mueller, H. B.; Berger, D. D.; and Allez, G. 1977. The periodic invasions of Goshawks. *Auk*, 94:652–63.

Reinikainen, A. 1937. The irregular migrations of the Crossbill (*Loxia curvirostra*) and their relation to the cone crop of the conifers. *Ornis Fennica*, 14:55–64.

Shelford, V. E. 1945. The relation of Snowy Owl migration to the abundance of the collared lemming. *Auk*, 62:592–96.

JAEGER

Bent, A. C. 1921. *Life Histories of North American Gulls and Terns.* U.S. Natl. Mus. Bull. no. 113. Washington, D.C. Reprinted New York, 1963.

Maher, W. J. 1974. *Ecology of Pomarine, Parasitic and Long-tailed Jaegers in Northern Alaska.* Pacific Coast Avifauna no. 37. Cooper Ornith. Soc. Los Angeles.

See also references under SEABIRD.

JAY

Amadon, D. 1944. The genera of the Corvidae and their relationships. *Amer. Mus. Novit.*, no. 1215:1–21.

Angell, T. 1978. *Ravens, Crows, Magpies and Jays.* Seattle.

Bent, A. C. 1946. *Life Histories of North American Jays, Crows, and Titmice.* U.S. Natl. Mus. Bull. no. 191, pt. 1 (Pinyon Jay in pt. 2). Washington, D.C. Reprinted New York, 1964.

Goodwin, G. G. 1976. *Crows of the World.* Ithaca, N.Y.

KINGFISHER

Bent, A. C. 1940. *Life Histories of North American Cuckoos, Goatsuckers, Hummingbirds, and Their Allies.* U.S. Natl. Mus. Bull. no. 176. Washington, D.C. Reprinted New York, 1964.

Fry, C. H. 1980. The evolutionary biology of kingfishers (Alcedinidae). *Living Bird*, 18th annual, pp. 113–60.

LARK

Bent, A. C. 1942. *Life Histories of North American Flycatchers, Larks, Swallows, and Their Allies.* U.S. Natl. Mus. Bull. no. 179. Washington, D.C. Reprinted New York, 1963.

Meinertzhagen, R. 1951. Review of the Alaudidae. *Proc. Zool. Soc. Lond.*, 121, 81:132.

LATIN (SCIENTIFIC) NAMES

Borror, D. J. 1960. *Dictionary of Word Roots and Combining Forms.* Palo Alto, Calif.

Buhrman, C. B. 1977. Endangered pronunciations. *Birding*, 9:164–65.

Jaeger, E. C. 1955. *A Source Book of Biological Names and Terms.* 3rd ed. Springfield, Ill.

———. 1960. *The Biologists' Handbook of Pronunciations.* Springfield, Ill.

Staloff, C., and Willoughby, H. 1981. Call them as you see them—but pronounce their names correctly. *Birding*, 13:96–98.

LAYING

Skutch, A. F. 1952. On the hour of laying and hatching of birds' eggs. *Ibis*, 94:49–61.

Weidmann, U. 1964. Laying. In *A New Dictionary of Birds*, ed. A. L. Thomson. New York.

LEG/FOOT

Bock, W. J., and Miller, W. D. 1959. The scansorial foot of the woodpeckers, with comments on the evolution of perching and climbing feet in birds. *Amer. Mus. Novit.*, no. 1931:1–45.

Delacour, J. 1951. The significance of the number of toes in some woodpeckers and kingfishers. *Auk*, 68:49–51.

Harrison, J. G. 1964. Leg. In *A New Dictionary of Birds*, ed. A. L. Thomson. New York.

LEK

Crawford, J. A., and Bolen, E. G. 1975. Spring lek activity of the Lesser Prairie Chicken in West Texas. *Auk*, 92:808–10.

Shepard, J. M. 1975. Factors influencing female choice in the lek mating system of the Ruff. *Living Bird*, 14th annual, pp. 87–111.

LIFE ZONES

Daubenmire, R. F. 1938. Merriam's life zones of North America. *Quart. Rev. Biol.*, 13:327–32.

Merriam, C. H. 1894. Laws of temperature control of the geographical distribution of terrestrial animals and plants. *Natl. Geographic Magazine*, 6:229–38.

————. 1898. *Life Zones and Crop Zones of the United States*. U.S. Dept. Agric., Bur. Biol. Surv. Bull. no. 10. Washington, D.C.

LIMPKIN

Bent, A. C. 1926. *Life Histories of North American Marsh Birds*. U.S. Natl. Mus. Bull. no. 135. Washington, D.C. Reprinted New York, 1963.

LINNÉ

Blunt, W. 1971. *The Compleat Naturalist. A Life of Linnaeus*. New York.

LISTING

Emerson, G. 1940. The lure of the list. *Bird-Lore*, 42:37–39. Reprinted in Peterson (1957–BIRDWATCHING).

Piatt, J. 1973. *Adventures in Birding: Confessions of a Lister*. New York.

Short, Jr., L. L. 1970. Bird-listing and the field observer. *Calif. Birds*, 1:143–55.

Vardeman, J. 1980. *Call Collect, Ask for Birdman*. New York.

LOON

Bent, A. C. 1919. *Life Histories of North American Diving Birds*. U.S. Natl. Mus. Bull. no. 107. Reprinted New York, 1949 and 1963.

Palmer, R. S., ed. 1962. *Handbook of North American Birds*. New Haven. Vol. 1, pp. 21–61.

MAGPIE

Bent, A. C. *Life Histories of North American Jays, Crows, and Titmice*. U.S. Natl. Mus. Bull. no. 191. Washington, D.C. Reprinted New York, 1964.

Linsdale, J. M. 1937. *The Natural History of the Magpies*. Pacific Coast Avifauna no. 25. Cooper Ornith. Soc. Berkeley.

See also references under CROW.

MAN-MADE THREATS TO BIRDLIFE

Ames, P. L., and Mersereau, G. S. 1964. Some factors in the decline of the Osprey. *Auk*, 81:174–85.

Banks, R. C., 1979. *Human-related Mortality of Birds in the United States*. U.S. Fish and Wildlife Serv., Spec. Sci. Rept.—Wildlife, no. 215. Washington, D.C.

Bellrose, F. C. 1964. Spent shot and lead poisoning. In *Waterfowl Tomorrow*, ed. J. P. Linduska and A. L. Nelson. Washington, D.C.

Bourne, W. R. P. 1970. Special review, after the *Torrey Canyon* (oil spill) disaster. *Ibis*, 112:120–25.

Cade, T. J.; Lincer, J. L.; White, C. M.; Roseneau, D. G.; and Schwartz, L. E. 1971. DDE residues and eggshell changes in Alaskan falcons and hawks. *Science*, 172:955–57.

Carson, R. 1962. *Silent Spring*. Boston.

Cochran, W. W., and Graber, R. R. 1958. Attraction of nocturnal migrants by lights on a television tower. *Wilson Bull.*, 70:378–80.

Cornwall, G., and Hochbaum, H. A. 1971. Collisions with wires—a source of anatid mortality. *Wilson Bull.*, 83:305–6.

Cott, H. B. 1953–54. The exploitation of wild birds for their eggs. *Ibis*, 95:409–49, 643–75; 96:129–49.

Hickey, J. J. 1966. Birds and pesticides. In *Birds in Our Lives*, ed. A. Stefferud and A. L. Nelson. Washington, D.C.

——— and Anderson, D. W. 1968. Chlorinated hydrocarbons and eggshell changes in raptorial and fish-eating birds. *Science*, 162:271–73.

Hodson, N. L., and Snow, D. W. 1965. The road deaths inquiry, 1960–61. *Bird Study*, 12:90–99.

Johnston, D. W., and Haines, T. P. 1957. Analysis of mass bird mortality in October 1954. *Auk*, 74:447–58.

Knopf, F. L., and Street, J. C. 1974. Insecticide residues in White Pelican eggs from Utah. *Wilson Bull.*, 86:428–34.

Porter, R. D., and Wiemeyer, S. N. 1969. Dieldrin and DDT: Effects on Sparrow Hawk eggshells and reproduction. *Science*, 165:199–200.

Stewart, P. A. 1973. Electrocution of birds by an electric fence. *Wilson Bull.*, 85:476–77.

Stoddard, H. L., and Norris, R. A. 1967. *Bird Casualties at a Leon County, Florida, TV Tower: An Eleven-Year Study*. Tall Timbers Res. Sta. Bull. no. 8. Tallahassee, Fla.

Temple, S. A. 1972. Chlorinated hydrocarbon residues and reproductive success in eastern North American Merlins. *Condor*, 74:105–6.

Tull, C. E., et al. 1972. Mortality of Thick-billed Murres in the West Greenland salmon fishery. *Nature*, 237:42–44.

Wetmore, A. 1919. *Lead Poisoning in Waterfowl*. U.S. Dept. Agric. Bull. no. 793. Washington, D.C.

MARKING

Marion, W. R., and Shamis, J. D. 1977. An annotated bibliography of bird marking techniques. *Bird-Banding*, 48:42–61.

See also bibliography in Pettingill (1970–ORNITHOLOGY), pp. 437–38.

MEASUREMENTS

Palmer, R. S., ed. 1962. *Handbook of North American Birds*. Vol. 1. New York.

MELANISM

Gross, A. O. 1965. Melanism in North American birds. *Bird-Banding*, 36:240–42.

Sage, B. L. 1962. Albinism and melanism in birds. *Brit. Birds*, 55:201–22.

Sealy, S. G. 1969. Color aberrations in some alcids on St. Lawrence Island, Alaska. *Wilson Bull.*, 81:213–14.

MIGRATION

Able, K. P. 1970. A radar study of the altitude of nocturnal passerine migration. *Bird-Banding*, 41:282–90.

Austin, Jr., O. L. 1928. Migration routes of the Arctic Tern (*Sterna paradisaea*). *Bull. Northeastern Bird-Banding Assoc.*, 4:121–25.

Baird, J., and Nisbet, I. C. T. 1959. Observations of diurnal migration in the Narragansett Bay area of Rhode Island in fall 1958. *Bird-Banding*, 30:171–81.

Bellrose, Jr., F. C. 1971. The distribution of nocturnal migrants in the air space. *Auk*, 88:397–424.

Dixon, K. L., and Gilbert, J. D. 1964. Altitudinal migration in the Mountain Chickadee. *Condor*, 66:61–64.

Dorst, J. 1962. *The Migrations of Birds*. Boston.

Dunn, E. H., and Nol, E. 1980. Age-related migratory behavior of warblers. *Jour. Field Ornith.*, 51:254–69.

Farner, D. S. 1955. The annual stimulus of migration: Experimental and physiologic aspects. In *Recent Studies in Avian Biology*, ed. A. Wolfson. Urbana, Ill.

Griffin, D. R. 1974. *Bird Migration*. New York.

Hamilton, III, W. J. 1962. Bobolink migratory pathways and their experimental analysis under night skies. *Auk*, 79:208–33.

Harris, M. P 1970. Abnormal migration and hybridization of *Larus argentatus* and *L. fuscus* after interspecies fostering experiments. *Ibis*, 112:488–98.

Keast, A., and Morton, E., eds. 1980. *Migrant Birds in the Neotropics: Ecology, Behavior, Distribution and Conservation*. Washington, D.C.

Lack, D. 1943. Partial migration. *Brit. Birds*, 36:22.

————. 1960. The height of bird migration. *Brit. Birds*, 53:5–10.

————. 1960. The influence of weather on passerine migration: A review. *Auk*, 77:171–209.

Lackley, R. M. 1973. *Ocean Wanderers: The Migratory Sea Birds of the World*. Harrisburg, Pa.

Lincoln, F. C. 1928. The migration of young North American Herring Gulls. *Auk*, 45:49–59.

————. 1945. *The Waterfowl Flyways of North America*. U.S. Dept. Agric. Circ. no. 342. Washington, D.C.

————. 1979. *Migration of Birds*. Rev. ed. U.S. Fish and Wildlife Circ. no. 16. Washington, D.C.

Lowery, Jr., G. H. 1945. Trans-Gulf spring migration of birds and the coastal hiatus. *Wilson Bull.*, 57:92–121.

————. 1951. A quantitative study of the nocturnal migration of birds. *Univ. Kansas Publ. Mus. Nat. Hist.*, 3:361–472.

———— and Newman, R. J. 1966. A continent-wide view of bird migration on four nights in October. *Auk*, 83:547–86.

Nickell, W. P. 1968. Return of northern migrants to tropical winter quarters and banded birds recovered in the United States. *Bird-Banding*, 39:107–16.

Robertson, W. B. 1969. Transatlantic migration of juvenile Sooty Terns. *Nature*, 222:632–34.

Snow, D. W., and Snow, B. K. 1960. Northern Waterthrush returning to same winter quarters in successive winters. *Auk*, 77:351–52.

Williams, T. C., and Williams, J. M. 1978. An oceanic mass migration of land birds. *Scientific American*, 239:166–76.

Wolfson, A. 1959. The role of light and darkness in regulation of the spring migration and reproductive cycles of birds. In *Photoperiodism and Related Phenomena in Plants and Animals.* Amer. Assoc. Adv. Sci. Publ., no. 55: 679–716. Washington, D.C.
See also references under NAVIGATION.

MIMIC THRUSH

Bent, A. C. 1948. *Life Histories of North American Nuthatches, Wrens, Thrashers, and Their Allies.* U.S. Natl. Mus. Bull. no. 195. Washington, D.C. Reprinted New York, 1964.

Engels, W. L. 1940. Structural adaptations in thrashers (Mimidae: genus *Toxostoma*) with comments on interspecific relationships. *Univ. Calif. Publ. Zool.,* 42:341–400.

MOBBING

Altmann, S. A. 1956. Avian mobbing behavior and predator recognition. *Condor,* 58:241–53.

Curio, E. 1978. The adaptive significance of avian mobbing. *Z. f. Tierpsychol.,* 48:175–202.

MOLT

Amadon, D. 1966. Avian plumages and molts. *Condor,* 68:263–78.

Baird, J. 1958. Post-juvenal molt of male Brown-headed Cowbirds. *Bird-Banding,* 29:224–28.

Dwight, Jr., J. 1900. The sequence of plumages and moults of the passerine birds of New York. *Ann. N.Y. Acad. Sci.,* 13:73:360.

Harrison, J. M. 1964. Molt. In *A New Dictionary of Birds,* ed. A. L. Thomson. New York.

Höst, P. 1942. Effect of light on the molts and sequences of plumage in the Willow Ptarmigan. *Auk,* 59:388.

Humphrey, P. S., and Parkes, K. C. 1959. An approach to the study of molts and molting. *Auk,* 76:1–31.

Lewis, J. C. 1967. Molt of the remiges of *Grus canadensis.* In *Proceedings of the 1978 Crane Workshop,* pp. 255–59. Fort Collins, Colo.

Mayr, E., and Mayr, M. 1954. The tail molt of small owls. *Auk,* 71:172–78.

Miller, A. H. 1933. Postjuvenal molt and the appearance of sexual characters of plumage in *Phainopepla nitens. Univ. Calif. Publ. Zool.,* 38:425–46.

Nolan, V. 1978. *The Ecology and Behavior of the Prairie Warbler* Dendroica discolor. Lawrence, Kans.

Palmer, R. S. 1972. Patterns of molting. In *Avian Biology,* ed. D. S. Farner et al. Vol. 2. New York.

Payne, R. B. 1972. Mechanisms and control of molt. In *Avian Biology,* ed. D. S. Farner et al. Vol. 2. New York.

Potter, E. F., and Howser, D. C. 1974. Relationship of anting and sunbathing to molting in wild birds. *Auk,* 91:537–63.

Stresemann, E. 1963. Taxonomic significance of wing molt. *Proc. (XIIIth) Internatl. Ornith. Congr., Ithaca, N.Y., 1962,* pp. 171–75.

Watson, G. E. 1963. The mechanism of feather replacement during natural molt. *Auk,* 80:486–95.

Williamson, K. 1957. The annual post-nuptial moult in the Wheatear, *Oenanthe oenanthe. Bird-Banding,* 28:129–35.

Zeidler, K. 1966. Untersuchungen über Flügelbefiederung und Mauser des Haussperlings, *Passer domesticus. Jour. Ornith.,* 107:113–53.

MOON WATCHING

Newman, R. J. 1952. *Studying Nocturnal Bird Migration by Means of the Moon.* Special Publ. Mus. Zool. Louisiana State Univ., Baton Rouge.

Nisbet, I. C. T. 1959. Calculation of flight directions of birds observed crossing the face of the moon. *Wilson Bull.,* 71:237–43.

MORTALITY

Fay, L. D.; Kaufmann, O. W.; and Ryel, L. A. 1965. *Mass Mortality of Waterbirds in Lake Michigan, 1963–64.* Univ. Mich. Mus. Zool. Misc. Publ. no. 13. Ann Arbor.

Lincoln, F. S. 1931. Some causes of mortality among birds. *Auk,* 48:538–46.

Nice, M. M. 1957. Nesting success in altricial birds. *Auk,* 74:305–21.

Saunders, W. E. 1907. A migration disaster in western Ontario. *Auk,* 24:108–10.

Snyder, D. E. 1960. Dovekie flights and wrecks. *Bull. Mass. Aud. Soc.,* 44:3.

MUSCLES

Berger, A. J. 1960. The musculature. In *Biology and Comparative Physiology of Birds,* ed. A. J. Marshall. Vol. 1. New York.

Bock, W. J. 1965. Analysis of the avian perching mechanism. *Amer. Zool.,* 5:251.

George, J. C., and Berger, A. J. 1966. *Avian Myology.* New York.

Hudson, G. E. 1957. Studies on the muscles of the pelvic appendage in birds. *Amer. Midland-Nat.,* 18:1–108.

Owre, O. T. 1967. *Adaptations for Locomotion and Feeding in the Anhinga and the Double-crested Cormorant.* Amer. Ornith. Union Monogr. no. 6.

MUSEUMS

Banks, R. C.; Clench, M. H.; and Barlow, J. C. 1973. Bird collections in the United States and Canada. *Auk,* 90:136–70. Addenda and corrigenda: *Auk,* 93:126–29.

Parkes, K. C. 1963. The contribution of museum collections to knowledge of the living bird. *Living Bird,* 2nd annual, pp. 121–30.

Van Tyne, J. 1952. Principles and practices in collecting and taxonomic work. *Auk,* 60:27–33.

NAMES, COLLOQUIAL

Choate, E. A. 1973. *The Dictionary of Bird Names.* Boston.

Forbush, E. H. 1925–29. *Birds of Massachusetts and Other New England States.* 3 vols. Boston.

Kortright, F. H. 1943. *The Ducks, Geese and Swans of North America.* Washington, D.C.

McAfee, W. L. 1955. Folk names of Georgia birds. *Oriole,* 20:1–14.

———. 1955–56. Folk names of Florida birds. *Florida Nat.,* 28:35–37, 64, 83–87, 91; 29:25–28.

———. 1955–56. Folk names of New England birds. *Bull. Mass. Audubon Soc.,* 39:307–16, 375–79, 441–46; 40:17–22, 79–84, 127–30, 253–56.

Newton, A. 1893–96. *A Dictionary of Birds.* London.

Trumbull, G. 1888. *Names and Portraits of Birds which Interest Gunners with Description in Language Understanded of the People.* New York.

NAMES, VERNACULAR

Choate, E. A. 1973. *The Dictionary of Bird Names.* Boston.

Eisenmann, E. 1955. *The Species of Middle American Birds.* Trans. Linn. Soc. New York, no. 7.

——— and Poor, H. H. 1946. Suggested principles of vernacular nomenclature. *Wilson Bull.,* 58:100–15.

Gruson, E. S. 1972. *Words for Birds.* New York.

Skutch, A. F. 1950. On the naming of birds. *Wilson Bull.,* 62:95–99.

NAVIGATION

Able, K. P., and Dillon, P. M. 1977. Sun compass orientation in a nocturnal migrant, the White-throated Sparrow. *Condor,* 79:393–95.

Bellrose, Jr., F. C. 1958. Celestial navigation by wild Mallards. *Bird-Banding,* 29:75–90.

———. 1972. Possible steps in the evolutionary development of bird navigation. In *Animal Orientation and Bird Navigation.* National Aeronautics and Space Administration. NASA SP-261, pp. 223–57.

Emlen, S. T. 1967. Migratory orientation in the Indigo Bunting, *Passerina cyanea.* Part I: Evidence for use of celestial cues. Part II: Mechanism of celestial orientation. *Auk,* 84:309–42, 463–89.

———. 1970. Celestial rotation: Its importance in the development of migratory orientation. *Science,* 170:1198–1201.

———. 1975. The stellar-orientation system of a migratory bird. *Scientific American.* 233:102–11.

Griffin, D. R. 1969. The physiology and geophysics of bird navigation. *Quart. Rev. Biol.,* 44:255–76.

———. 1973. Oriented bird migration in or between opaque cloud layers. *Proc. Amer. Philos. Soc.,* 117:117–41.

——— and Hock, R. J. 1949. Airplane observations of homing birds. *Ecology,* 30:176–98.

Keeton, W. T. 1972. *Effects of Magnets on Pigeon Homing.* National Aeronautics and Space Administration. NASA SP-262, pp. 579–94.

Kramer, G. 1952. Experiments on bird orientation, *Ibis,* 94:265–85.

————. 1961. Long-distance orientation, In *Biology and Comparative Physiology of Birds*, ed. A. J. Marshall. Vol. 2. New York.

Lancaster, D. A., and Johnson, J. R., 1976. Birds navigate by magnetic field. *Cornell Laboratory of Ornith. Newsletter* no. 82:5.

Matthews, G. V. T. 1953. Navigation in the Manx Shearwater. *Jour. Exper. Biol.,* 30:370–96.

————. 1961. "Nonsense" navigation in the Mallard (*Anas platyrhynchos*) and its relation to experiments in bird navigation. *Ibis,* 103a;211–20.

————. 1963. The orientation of pigeons as affected by learning of landmarks and by the distance of displacement. *Animal Behavior,* 11:310–17.

————. 1968. *Bird Navigation.* 2nd ed. Cambridge, England.

Mazzeo, R. 1953. Homing of the Manx Shearwater. *Auk,* 70:200–1.

Mewaldt, L. R. 1964. California sparrows return from displacement to Maryland. *Science,* 146:941–42.

Perdeck, A. C. 1958. Two types of orientation in migrating Starlings, *Sturnus vulgaris,* and Chaffinches, *Fringilla coelebs,* as revealed by displacement experiments. *Ardea,* 46:1–37.

Ralph, C. J., and Mewaldt, L. R. 1976. Homing success in wintering sparrows. *Auk,* 93:1–14.

Sauer, E. G. F. 1957. Die Sterneorientierung nächtlich ziehender Grasmücken (*Sylvia atricapilla, borin, curruca*). *Z. f. Tierpsych.,* 14:29–70.

Sauer, F., and Sauer, E. 1960. Orientation of nocturnal bird migrants by the stars. *Proc. (XIIth) Internatl. Ornith. Congr., Helsinki, 1958,* pp. 645–48.

Schmidt-Koenig, K. 1960. The sun-azimuth compass: One factor in the orientation of homing pigeons. *Science,* 131:826–27.

————. 1979. *Avian Orientation and Navigation.* London.

Southern, W. E. 1972. Influence of disturbances in the earth's magnetic field on Ring-billed Gull orientation. *Condor,* 74:102–5.

Tatum, J. B. 1980. The effect of the Coriolis force on the flight of a bird. *Auk,* 97:99–117.

Walcott, C.; Gould, J. L.; and Kirschvink, J. L. 1979. Pigeons have magnets. *Science,* 205:1027.

Walcott, C., and Green, R. P. 1974. Orientation of homing pigeons altered by a change in the direction of an applied magnetic field. *Science,* 184:180–82.

NERVOUS SYSTEM

Bennett, T. 1974. The peripheral and autonomic nervous systems. In *Avian Biology,* ed. D. S. Farner et al. Vol. 4. New York.

Cobb, S. 1960. Observations on the comparative anatomy of the avian brain. *Perspect. Biol. Med.,* 3:383–408.

Goldby, F. 1964. Nervous system. In *A New Dictionary of Birds,* ed. A. L. Thomson. New York.

Pearson, R. 1972. *The Avian Brain.* New York.

Portmann, A., and Stingelin, W. H. 1961. The central nervous system. In *Biology and Comparative Physiology of Birds*, ed. A. J. Marshall. Vol 2. New York.

Stettner, L. J., and Matyniak, K. A. 1968. The brain of birds. *Scientific American*, 218:64–76.

Nest

Beer, J. R.; Frenzel, L. D.; and Hansen, N. 1956. Minimum space requirements of some nesting passerine birds. *Wilson Bull.*, 68:200–9.

Berger, A. J. 1968. Clutch size, incubation period, and nesting period of the American Goldfinch. *Auk*, 85:494–98.

Collias, N. E. 1964. The evolution of nests and nest building in birds. *Amer. Zool.*, 4:175–90.

Cruickshank, A. D. 1956. Nesting heights of some woodland warblers in Maine. *Wilson Bull.*, 68:157.

Davis, D. E. 1940. Social nesting habits of the Smooth-billed Ani. *Auk*, 57:179–218.

Grubb, Jr., T. C. 1970. Burrow digging techniques of Leach's Petrel. *Auk*, 87:587–88.

Harrison, C. 1978. *A Field Guide to the Nests, Eggs and Nestlings of North American Birds.* London.

———. 1979. *A Field Guide to Western Birds' Nests.* Boston.

Harrison, H. H. 1975. *A Field Guide to Birds' Nests.* Boston.

Holcomb, L. C., and Twist, G. 1968. Ecological factors affecting nest building in Red-winged Blackbirds. *Bird-Banding*, 39:14–22.

Kendeigh, S. C. 1945. Nesting behavior of wood warblers. *Wilson Bull.*, 57:499–513.

Nickell, W. P. 1944. Studies of habitats, locations, and structural materials of nests of the Robin. *Jack Pine Warbler*, 22:48–64.

———. 1958. Variations in engineering features of the nests of several species of birds in relation to nest sites and nesting materials. *Butler Univ. Bot. Stud.*, 13:121–40.

Oldroyd, H. 1964. *The Natural History of Flies.* New York.

Parmelee, D. F., and Payne, R. B. 1973. On multiple broods and the breeding strategy of arctic Sanderlings. *Ibis*, 115:218–26.

Slack, R. D. 1976. Nest-guarding behavior of male Gray Catbirds. *Auk*, 93:135–41.

Swennen, C. 1968. Nest protection of eider ducks and shovellers by means of faeces. *Ardea*, 56:248–58.

Nightjar

Bent, A. C. 1940. *Life Histories of North American Cuckoos, Goatsuckers, Hummingbirds, and Their Allies.* U.S. Natl. Mus. Bull. no. 176. Washington, D.C. Reprinted New York, 1964.

Ganier, A. F. 1964. The alleged transportation of its eggs and young by the Chuck-will's-widow. *Wilson Bull.*, 76:19–27.

Kilham, L. 1957. Egg-carrying by the Whip-poor-will. *Wilson Bull.*, 69:113.

NOMENCLATURE

Coble, M. F. 1954. *Introduction to Ornithological Nomenclature.* Los Angeles.

Jaeger, E. C. 1955. *A Source Book of Biological Names and Terms.* 3rd. ed. Springfield, Ill.

Skutch, A. F. 1950. On the naming of birds. *Wilson Bull.*, 62:95–99.

See also references under LATIN NAMES.

NOSTRILS

Macdonald, J. D. 1960. Secondary external nares of the Gannet. *Proc. Zool. Soc. London,* 135:357–63.

Thomson, A. L. 1964. Naris. In *A New Dictionary of Birds,* ed. A. L. Thomson. New York.

NUTHATCH

Bent, A. C. 1948. *Life Histories of North American Nuthatches, Wrens, Thrashers, and Their Allies.* U.S. Natl. Mus. Bull. no. 195. Washington, D.C. Reprinted New York, 1964.

Norris, R. A. 1958. Comparative biosystematics and life history of the nuthatches *Sitta pygmaea* and *Sitta pusilla. Univ. Calif. Pub. Zool.,* 56:119–300.

OIL GLAND

Elder, W. H. 1954. The oil gland of birds. *Wilson Bull.*, 66:6–31.

Hou, H. C. 1929. Relation of the preen gland (glandula uropygialis) of birds to rickets. *Chinese Jour. Physiol.,* 3:171–82.

OLD WORLD WARBLER

Bent, A. C. 1949. *Life Histories of North American Thrushes, Kinglets, and Their Allies.* U.S. Natl. Mus. Bull. no. 196. Washington, D.C. Reprinted New York, 1964.

OPTICAL EQUIPMENT

Anonymous. 1980. Binoculars. *Consumer Reports,* March, pp. 196–203.

Entwhistle, B. 1973. The secret language of binoculars. *Birding,* 5:5–8.

Howard, D. V. 1973. *Binoculars for Birders.* A Massachusetts Audubon Society Public Service Leaflet. Lincoln, Mass.

Koehler, H. 1973. Everything you've always wanted to know about binocular care . . . *Birding,* 5:85–92.

Reichert, R. J., and Reichert, E. 1951. Know your binoculars. *Audubon,* 53:45–50, 105–9.

ORNITHOLOGY

Allen, J. A. 1925. *Birds and Their Attributes.* Francistown, N.H.

Coues, E. 1903. Historical preface and general ornithology. In *Key to North American Birds.* 5th ed. Boston.

Dorst, J. 1974. *The Life of Birds.* 2 vols. New York.

Farner, D. S.; King, J. R.; and Parkes, K. C., eds. 1971–75. *Avian Biology.* 5 vols. New York.

Griscom, L. 1945. *Modern Bird Study.* Cambridge, Mass.

James, F. C.; Cooch, F. G.; Ficken, M. S.; Knoder, C. E.; Lanyon, W. E.; and Springer, P. F. 1974. Career opportunities in ornithology. *Amer. Birds,* 28:741–46.

Lanyon, W. E. 1964. *Biology of Birds.* New York.

Marshall, A. J., ed. 1960–61. *Biology and Comparative Physiology of Birds.* 2 vols. New York.

Newton, A. 1893–96. *A Dictionary of Birds.* London.

Pasquier, R. F. 1977. *Watching Birds: An Introduction to Ornithology.* Boston.

Pettingill, Jr., O. S. 1970. *Ornithology in Laboratory and Field.* 4th ed. Minneapolis.

Rand, A. L. 1967. *Ornithology: An Introduction.* New York.

Ridgway, R., and Friedmann, H. 1901–50. *Birds of North and Middle America.* U.S. Natl. Mus. Bulls. Washington, D.C.

Stresemann, E. 1975. *Ornithology: From Aristotle to the Present.* Cambridge, Mass.

Sturkie, P. D., ed. 1976. *Avian Physiology.* 3rd. ed. New York.

Terres, J. K. 1980. *The Audubon Society Encyclopedia of North American Birds.* New York.

Thomson, A. L. ed. 1964. *A New Dictionary of Birds.* New York.

Van Tyne, J., and Berger, A. J. 1976. *Fundamentals of Ornithology.* 2nd ed. New York.

Wallace, G. J., and Mahan, H. D. 1975. *An Introduction to Ornithology.* 3rd ed. New York.

Welty, J. C. 1975. *The Life of Birds.* 2nd ed. Philadelphia.

Wilson, B. W., ed. 1980. *Birds: Readings from Scientific American.* San Francisco. (Contains many of the *Scientific American* articles cited elsewhere in the Bibliography.)

Wolfson, A., ed. 1955. *Recent Studies in Avian Biology.* Urbana, Ill.

See also references under BIRD.

OSPREY

Ames, P. L., and Mersereau, G. S. 1964. Some factors in the decline of the Osprey. *Auk,* 81:174–85.

Bent, A. C. 1937. *Life Histories of North American Birds of Prey.* U.S. Natl. Mus. Bull. no. 167, pt. 1. Washington, D.C. Reprinted New York, 1961.

Brown, L., and Amadon, D. 1968. *Eagles, Hawks and Falcons of the World.* New York. Vol. 1, pp. 195–200.

Henny, C. J., and Ogden, J. C. 1970. Estimated status of Osprey populations in the United States. *Jour. Wildlife Management,* 34:214–17.

OWL

Bent, A. C. 1938. *Life Histories of North American Birds of Prey.* U.S. Natl. Mus. Bull. no. 170, pt. 2. Washington, D.C. Reprinted New York, 1961. ·

Burton, J. A., ed. 1973. *Owls of the World.* New York.

Clark, R. J.; Smith, D. G; and Kelso, L. H. 1978. *Working Bibliography of Owls of the World with Summaries of Current Taxonomy and Distributional Status.* Natl. Wildlife Fed. Tech. Ser. no. 1. Washington, D.C.

Eckert, A. E., and Karalus, K. E. 1974. *The Owls of North America.* New York.

Graham, R. R. 1934. The silent flight of owls. *Jour. Roy. Aeronaut. Soc.,* 38:837–43.

Hocking, B., and Mitchell, B. L. 1961. Owl vision. *Ibis,* 103a:284–88.

Jonishi, M. 1973. How the owl tracks its prey. *Amer. Scientist,* 61:414–24.

PALEARCTIC

Cramp, S., chief ed. 1977. *Handbook of the Birds of Europe, the Middle East and North Africa.* Vol. 1. London.

Vaurie, C. 1959. *The Birds of the Palearctic Fauna: A Systematic Reference.* London.

PARENTAL CARE

Eisner, E. 1960. The relationship of hormones to the reproductive behavior of birds, referring especially to parental behavior: A review. *Jour. Anim. Behav.,* 8:155–79.

Johnsgard, P. A., and Kear, J. 1968. A review of parental caring of young by waterfowl. *Living Bird,* 7th annual, pp. 89–102.

Kendeigh, S. C. 1952. *Parental Care and Its Evolution in Birds.* Urbana, Ill.

Nice, M. M. 1937 and 1943. *Studies in the Life History of the Song Sparrow.* Parts 1 and 2. Trans. Linn. Soc. New York, nos. 4 and 6.

Silver, R., ed. 1977. *Parental Behavior in Birds.* Stroudsburg, Pa.

Skutch, A. F. 1935. Helpers at the nest. *Auk,* 52:157–69.

———. 1954–55. Parental stratagems of birds. *Ibis,* 96:544–64; 97:118–42.

———. 1976. *Parent Birds and Their Young.* Austin, Tex.

PARROT

Bent, A. C. 1940. *Life Histories of North American Cuckoos, Goatsuckers, Hummingbirds, and Their Allies.* U.S. Natl. Mus. Bull. no. 176. Washington, D.C. Reprinted New York, 1964.

Forshaw, J. M. 1973. *Parrots of the World.* New York. (Brilliantly illustr. by W. T. Cooper.)

PELICAN

Bent, A. C. 1922. *Life Histories of North American Petrels and Pelicans and Their Allies.* U.S. Natl. Mus. Bull. no. 121. Washington, D.C. Reprinted New York, 1964.

Palmer, R. S., ed. 1962. *Handbook of North American Birds.* New Haven. Vol. 1, pp. 264–80.

See also references under SEABIRD.

PELLET

Chitty, D. 1938. A laboratory study of pellet formation in Short-eared Owls, *Asio flammeus. Proc. Zool. Soc. London.,* 108 (series A):267–87.

Grimm, R. J., and Whitehouse, W. M. 1963. Pellet formation of a Great Horned Owl: A roentgenographic study. *Auk,* 80:301–6.

Marti, C. D. 1973. Food consumption and pellet formation rates in four owl species. *Wilson Bull.,* 85:178–81.

Storer, R. W. 1961. Observations of pellet casting by Horned and Pied-billed Grebes. *Auk,* 78:90.

Tucker, B. W. 1944. The ejection of pellets by passerine and other birds. *Brit. Birds,* 38:50–52.

PERIODICALS

The following ornithological journals or birdwatching magazines contain articles of continentwide or international interest. They are listed alphabetically by title.

American Birds (incl. *Audubon Field Notes*; 6/yr.). National Audubon Society, 950 Third Ave., New York, NY 10022.

The Auk (quarterly). American Ornithologists' Union, c/o K. P. Able, Irish Hill Rd., P.O. Box 44, Berne, NY 12023.

Bird-Banding. See *The Journal of Field Ornithology.*

Birding (bimonthly). American Birding Association, P.O. Box 4335, Austin, TX 78765.

Birding News Survey (quarterly). Avian Publications, Inc., P.O. Box 310, Elizabethtown, KY 42701.

Bird Study (quarterly). British Trust for Ornithology, Beech Grove, Tring, Hertfordshire, HP23 5NR, England.

Bird-Watch. Bird Populations Institute, Division of Biological Sciences, Kansas State University, Manhattan, KS 66506.

The Birdwatcher's Digest. P.O. Box 110, Marietta, OH 45750.

British Birds (monthly). Macmillan Journals Ltd., 4 Little Essex St., London, WC2R 3LF, England.

The Condor (quarterly). Ornithological Societies of North America (O.S.N.A.), P.O. Box 21160, Columbus OH 43221.

Continental Birdlife (bimonthly). P.O. Box 43294, Tucson, AZ 85733. (Discontinued publication after completing second [1981] volume.)

The Ibis (quarterly). British Ornithologists' Union, 141 S. Second St., Decatur IN 46733.

The Journal of Field Ornithology (formerly *Bird-Banding;* quarterly). P.O. Box 797, Manomet, MA 02345.

The Living Bird (annual; became a quarterly in 1982). Laboratory of Ornithology, 159 Sapsucker Woods Rd., Ithaca, NY 14850.

Newsletter of the Hawk Migration Association of North America. c/o Mrs. N. Clayton, 95 Martha's Point Rd., Concord, MA 01742.

North American Bird Bander (quarterly; merger of major continental banding publications, including *Western Bird Bander, E.B.B.A. News, Inland Bird Banding News,* and *Ontario Bird Banding*). Edison Publishing Co., Carefree, AZ 85331.

Raptor Report (formerly *California Condor;* 3/yr.). Society for the Preservation of Birds of Prey, Pacific Palisades, CA 90272.

The Wilson Bulletin (quarterly). c/o J. C. Barlow, Department of Ornithology, Royal Ontario Museum, 100 Queen's Park, Toronto, Ont., Canada M5S 2C6.

The following state, provincial, or regional publications concentrate mainly on local avifaunas and birding activities. They are listed alphabetically by state, province, or region. The position of corresponding secretary for many bird clubs shifts frequently, so that the addresses given below may already be out of date; however, they will usually lead to a source of up-to-date information regarding the publication in question. For a more complete listing of local newsletters, see Rickert (1978–BIRD CLUB) and Ch. 7 of Kress (1981–BIRDWATCHING).

ALABAMA: *Alabama Birdlife.* Alabama Ornithological Society, c/o Mr. J. R. Bailey, 18 Peachtree St., Birmingham, AL 35213.

ALBERTA: *The Alberta Naturalist.* Federation of Alberta Naturalists, P.O. Box 1472, Edmonton, Alta., Canada 75J 2N5.

ARIZONA: *The Roadrunner.* Maricopa Audubon Society, c/o Dr. R. Witzeman, 4619 East Arcadia Lane, Phoenix, AZ 85108.

————: *The Vermilion Flycatcher.* Tucson Audubon Society, P.O. Box 3981, Tucson, AZ 85717.

BRITISH COLUMBIA: *The Federation of British Columbia Naturalists Newsletter.* P.O. Box 33797, Station D, Vancouver, B.C., Canada V6J 4L6.

CALIFORNIA: *Western Birds* (formerly *California Birds*). Western Field Ornithologists, c/o E. Copper, P.O. Box 595, Coronado, CA 92118.

————: *The Western Tanager.* Los Angeles Audubon Society, 7737 Santa Monica Blvd., Los Angeles, CA 90046.

COLORADO: *The Colorado Field Ornithologists' Quarterly.* P.O. Box 109, Berthoud, CO 80513.

————: *The Lark Bunting.* Denver Field Ornithologists, Denver Museum of Natural History, Denver, CO 80522.

DELMARVA (Delaware/Maryland/Virginia): *Delmarva Ornithologist.* Delmarva Ornithological Society, P.O. Box 4247, Greenville, DE 19807.

FLORIDA: *The Florida Naturalist* and *The Florida Field Naturalist.* Florida Ornithological Society, P.O. Drawer 7, Maitland, FL 32751.

GEORGIA: *The Oriole.* Georgia Ornithological Society, P.O. Box 38214, Atlanta, GA 30334.

IDAHO: *The Prairie Owl.* Palouse Audubon Society, P.O. Box 3156, University Station, Moscow, ID 83843.

ILLINOIS: *Illinois Audubon Bulletin.* Illinois Audubon Society, P.O. Box 608, Wayne, IL 60184.

INDIANA: *The Indiana Audubon Quarterly.* Indiana Audubon Society, Mary Gray Bird Sanctuary, R.R. #6, Connersville, IN 47331.

IOWA: *Iowa Bird Life.* Iowa Ornithologists' Union, 235 McClellan Blvd., Davenport, IA 52803.

KANSAS: *Kansas Ornithological Society Bulletin.* c/o J. L. Zimmermann, Division of Biological Sciences, Kansas State University, Manhattan, KS 66056.

KENTUCKY: *The Kentucky Warbler.* Kentucky Ornithological Society, Department of Biology, University of Louisville, Louisville, KY 40208.

MAINE: *The Guillemot.* Sorrento Scientific Society, c/o W. Townsend, P.O. Box 373, Sorrento, ME 04677.

———: *Maine Audubon Quarterly.* Maine Audubon Society, 118 U.S. Route 1, Falmouth, ME 04105.

———: *Maine Bird Life.* c/o M. K. Lucey, P.O. Box 280, R.F.D. #3, Bangor, ME 04401.

MANITOBA: *The Manitoba Naturalist.* Manitoba Naturalists Society, 190 Rupert Ave., Winnipeg, Man., Canada R3B 0N2.

MARYLAND: *Maryland Birdlife.* Maryland Ornithological Society, 4915 Greenspring Ave., Baltimore, MD 21209.

See also under *Delmarva.*

MASSACHUSETTS: *The Bird Observer of Eastern Massachusetts.* 462 Trapelo Rd., Belmont, MA 02178.

———: *Sanctuary.* Massachusetts Audubon Society, South Great Rd., Lincoln, MA 01773.

MICHIGAN: *The Jack Pine Warbler* and *Michigan Audubon.* Michigan Audubon Society, 7000 N. Westnedge, Kalamazoo, MI 49001.

MINNESOTA: *The Loon* (formerly *The Flicker*). Minnesota Ornithologists' Union, James Ford Bell Museum of Natural History, University of Minnesota, Minneapolis, MN 55455.

MISSISSIPPI: *The M.O.S. Newsletter.* Mississippi Ornithological Society, Museum of Natural Science, 111 N. Jefferson St., Jackson, MS 39202.

MISSOURI: *The Bluebird.* Audubon Society of Missouri, c/o Mrs. K. Wade, 2202 Missouri Blvd., Jefferson City, MO 65101.

MONTANA: *Yellowstone Valley Flyer.* Yellowstone Valley Audubon Society, P.O., Box 1075, Billings, MT 59103.

NEBRASKA: *Nebraska Bird Review.* Nebraska Ornithologists' Union, University of Nebraska State Museum, Lincoln, NE 68588.

NEVADA: *The Pelican.* Lahontan Audubon Society, P.O. Box 2304, Reno, NV 89505.

NEW BRUNSWICK: *The New Brunswick Naturalist.* New Brunswick Museum, 277 Douglas Ave., St. John, N.B., Canada E2K 1E5.

NEWFOUNDLAND: *N.N.H.S. Newsletter.* Newfoundland Natural History Society, P.O. Box 1013, St. John's, Nfld., Canada, A1L 5M3.

NEW HAMPSHIRE: *Newsletter* and *Journal* (annual) *of the Audubon Society of New Hampshire.* 3 Silk Farm Rd., Concord, NH 03301.

NEW JERSEY: *Records of N.J. Birds* and *Journal of the New Jersey Audubon Society.* 790 Ewing Ave., Franklin Lakes, NJ 07417.

NEW MEXICO: *N.M.O.S. Field Notes.* New Mexico Ornithological Society, c/o D. A. McCallum, Rte. 2, P.O. Box 3, Thoreau, NM 87323.

NEW YORK: *The Kingbird.* Federation of New York State Bird Clubs, 20 Drumlins Terrace, Syracuse, NY 13224.

———: *Linnaean Newsletter.* Linnaean Society, 15 W. 77th St., New York, NY 10024.

NOVA SCOTIA: *Nova Scotia Birds.* Nova Scotia Bird Society, Nova Scotia Museum, 1747 Summer St., Halifax, N.S., Canada B3H 3A6.

OHIO: *The Bulletin of the C.A.S.* Cleveland Audubon Society, 2063 E. Fourth St., Cleveland, OH 44115.

OKLAHOMA: *The Scissortail, O.O.S. Newsletter* and *Bulletin of the O.O.S.* Oklahoma Ornithological Society, Department of Biology, Cameron University, Lawton, OK 73505.

ONTARIO: *The Bluebill.* Kingston Field Naturalists, P.O. Box 831, Kingston, Ont., Canada K7L 4X6.

———: *The Ontario Naturalist.* Federation of Ontario Naturalists, Moatfield Park, 355 Lesmill Rd., Don Mills, Ont., Canada M3B 2W8.

OREGON: *Oregon Birds.* South Willamette Ornithological Club, P.O. Box 3082, Eugene, OR 97403.
See also next entry.

PACIFIC NORTHWEST: *The Murrelet.* Pacific Northwest Bird and Mammal Society, Department of Zoology, Washington State University, Pullman, WA 99194.
See also under *British Columbia, Oregon,* and *Washington.*

PENNSYLVANIA: *Bulletin of the A.S.W.P.* Audubon Society of Western Pennsylvania, Beechwood Farms Nature Reserve, 614 Doseyville Rd., Pittsburgh, PA 15238.

———: *Cassinia.* Delaware Valley Ornithological Club, Academy of Natural Sciences, 19th and the Parkway, Philadelphia, PA 19103.

QUEBEC: *Bulletin Ornithologique.* Club des Ornithologues du Québec, 8191 de Zoo, Orsainville, Que., Canada G1G 4G4.

———: *Tchebec* (annual) and *Newsletter.* Province of Quebec Society for the Protection of Birds, P.O. Box 43, Station B, Montreal, Que., Canada H3B 3J5.

RHODE ISLAND: *Field Notes of Rhode Island Birds.* Rhode Island Ornithological Club, c/o S. Dana, 106 E. Manning, Providence, RI 02907.

SASKATCHEWAN: *The Blue Jay.* Saskatchewan Natural History Society, P.O. Box 1784, Saskatoon, Sask., Canada S7K 3S1.

SOUTH CAROLINA: *C.A.S. Newsletter.* Columbia Audubon Society, P.O. Box 5923, Columbia, SC 29250.

SOUTH DAKOTA: *South Dakota Bird Notes.* South Dakota Ornithologists' Union, P.O. Box 236, Highmore, SD 57345.

TENNESSEE: *Audubon Flyer.* Chattanooga Audubon Society, P.O. Box 245, Chattanooga, TN 37401.

————: *The Migrant.* Cumberland Museum and Science Center, 800 Ridley Ave., Nashville, TN 37203.

TEXAS: *T.O.S. Bulletin* and *Newsletter.* Texas Ornithological Society, P.O. Box 19581, Houston, TX 77024.

UTAH: *The Stilt.* Bridgerland Audubon Society, 1722 Saddle Hill Dr., Logan, UT 84321.

VERMONT: *Record of Vermont Birds* and *Newsletter.* Vermont Institute of Natural Science, Woodstock, VT 05091.

VIRGINIA: *The Raven.* c/o J. Dalmas, 520 Rainbow Forest Dr., Lynchburg, VA 24502.
See also under *Delmarva.*

WASHINGTON: *S.A.S. Notes.* Seattle Audubon Society, 714 Joshua Green Bldg., Seattle, WA 98040.

WEST COAST: *Bulletin.* Pacific Seabird Group, c/o Point Reyes Bird Observatory, 4990 Shoreline Highway, Stinson Beach, CA 94970.
See also under *California, Oregon, Washington,* and *British Columbia.*

WEST VIRGINIA: *The Redstart* and *Newsletter.* Brooks Bird Club, 707 Warwood Ave., Wheeling, WV 26003.

WISCONSIN: *The Passenger Pigeon.* Wisconsin Society for Ornithology, W.330 N.8275 West Shore Drive, Hartland, WI 53029.

WYOMING: *Plains and Peaks.* Newsletter of the Murie Audubon Society, P.O. Box 2112, Casper, WY 82602.

YUKON: *Y.C.S. Newsletter.* Yukon Conservation Society, P.O. Box 4163, Whitehorse, Yukon Territory, Canada.

The following widely circulated journals and magazines often contain interesting articles on birdlife pertinent to North America. Current subscription information is available from any recent periodical guide. Listed alphabetically by title.

The American Midland-Naturalist (University of Notre Dame)

American Zoologist (American Society of Zoologists)

Animal Behavior (Association for the Study of Animal Behavior, London, England)

Animal Kingdom (New York Zoological Society)

Audubon (National Audubon Society)

Behavior (publ. in Holland)

Bulletin of the Ecological Society of America

The Canadian Field Naturalist (Ottawa Field Naturalists' Club)

Canadian Journal of Zoology (National Research Council of Canada)

Defenders (Defenders of Wildlife)

Ecology and *Ecological Monographs* (Ecological Society of America)

Evolution (U.S.)

The Great Basin Naturalist (Brigham Young University)

The Journal of Animal Ecology (British Ecological Society)

The Journal of Wildlife Management (Wildlife Society)

National Geographic Magazine

National Wildlife (National Wildlife Federation)

Natural History (American Museum of Natural History)

Nature (England)

The Ontario Naturalist (Federation of Ontario Naturalists)

Sanctuary (Massachusetts Audubon Society)

Science (American Association for the Advancement of Science)

Scientific American

The Southwestern Naturalist (Southwestern Association of Naturalists)

Smithsonian (U.S.)

Wildlife Monographs (Wildlife Society)

PESTS, BIRDS AS

Anderson, T. E. 1969. Identifying, evaluating, and controlling wildlife damage. In *Wildlife Management Techniques,* ed. R. H. Giles, Jr. Washington, D.C.

Beale, F. E. L. 1897. *Some Common Birds in Their Relation to Agriculture.* U.S. Dept. Agric. Farmer's Bull. no. 9. Washington, D.C.

Besser, J. F., et al. 1968. Costs of wintering Starlings and Red-winged Blackbirds at feedlots. *Jour. Wildlife Management.,* 32:179–80.

Buchheister, C. W. 1960. What about problem birds? *Audubon,* 62:116–18.

Dennis, J. B. 1963. Preventing bird damage. *Proc. Southeastern Wood Pole Conf., Univ. of Florida, Gainesville,* pp. 89–93.

Drury, Jr., W. H. 1966. Birds at airports. In *Birds in Our Lives,* ed. A. Stefferud and A. L. Nelson. Washington, D.C.

Dykstra, W. W. 1960. Nuisance bird control. *Audubon,* 62:118–19.

Graham, Jr., F. 1976. Blackbirds: A problem that won't go away. *Audubon,* 78:118–25.

Jackson, J. A. 1976. Blackbirds, scare tactics and irresponsible legislation. *Wilson Bull.,* 88:159–60.

Kalmbach, E. R. 1920. *The Crow in Its Relation to Agriculture.* U.S. Dept. Agric. Farmer's Bull. no. 1102. Washington, D.C.

———. 1937. *Suggestions for Combating Starling Roosts.* U.S. Dept Agric. Wildlife Res. and Management Leaflet no. BS-81. Washington, D.C.

———. 1940. *Economic Status of the English Sparrow in the United States.* U.S. Dept. Agric. Tech. Bull. no. 711. Washington, D.C.

McAfee, W. L., and Piper, S. E. 1936. *Excluding Birds from Reservoirs and Fish Ponds.* U.S. Dept Agric. Bot. Biol. Surv. Leaflet no. 120. Washington, D.C.

Meanley, B., and Webb, J. S. 1965. Nationwide population estimates of blackbirds and Starlings. *Atlantic Naturalist,* 20:189–91.

Mott, D. F. 1980. Dispersing blackbirds and Starlings from objectionable roost sites. *Proc. Ninth Vertebr. Pest Conf., Fresno, Calif.*, ed. J. P. Clark, pp. 38–42.

Murton, R. K., and Wright, E. N., eds. 1968. *The Problems of Birds as Pests.* New York.

Williams, C. S., and Neff, J. A. 1966. Scaring makes a difference. In *Birds in Our Lives*, ed. A. Stefferud and A. L. Nelson. Washington, D.C.

PHAINOPEPLA

Bent, A. C. 1950. *Life Histories of North American Wagtails, Shrikes, Vireos, and Their Allies.* U.S. Natl. Mus. Bull. no. 197. Washington, D.C. Reprinted New York, 1965.

Crouch, J. E. 1943. Distribution and habitat relationship of Phainopepla. *Auk,* 60:319–33.

Sibley, C. G. 1973. The relationships of the silky-flycatchers. *Auk,* 90:394–410.

PHOTOGRAPHY

Allen, A. A. 1961. *Stalking Birds with a Color Camera.* Washington, D.C.

Blaker, A. A. 1976. *Field Photography.* San Francisco.

Campbell, B. 1974. *The Dictionary of Birds in Color.* New York.

Cruickshank, A. D. 1977. *Cruickshank's Photographs of Birds of America.* New York.

Hosking, E., and Newberry, C. 1961. *Bird Photography as a Hobby.* London.

Kinne, R. 1962. *The Complete Book of Nature Photography.* New York.

Line, L., and Russell, F. 1976. *The Audubon Society Book of Wild Birds.* New York.

Linton, D. 1964. *Photographing Nature.* New York.

Maye, P. 1974. *Fieldbook of Nature Photography.* San Francisco.

Osolinski, S. 1981. *Nature Photography.* Englewood Cliffs, N.J.

Terres, J. K. 1980. *The Audubon Society Encyclopedia of North American Birds.* New York.

PHOTOPERIODISM

Bartholomew, Jr., G. A. 1949. The effect of light intensity and day length on reproduction in the English Sparrow. *Bull. Mus. Comp. Zool.,* 101:433–77.

Bissonnette, T. H. 1937. Photoperiodicity in birds. *Wilson Bull.,* 64:197–220.

Karplus, M. 1952. Bird activity in the continuous daylight of arctic summer. *Ecology,* 33:129–34.

Wolfson, A. 1959. The role of light and darkness in regulation of the spring migration and reproductive cycles of birds. In *Photoperiodism and Related Phenomena in Plants and Animals.* Amer. Assoc. Adv. Sci. Publ. no. 55: 679–716. Washington, D.C.

PIGEON

Bent, A. C. 1932. *Life Histories of North American Gallinaceous Birds.* U.S. Natl. Mus. Bull. no. 162. Washington, D.C. Reprinted New York, 1963.

Goodwin, D. 1970. *Pigeons and Doves of the World.* New York.

Levi, W. M. 1977. *The Pigeon*. Sumter, S.C. (An exhaustive work on the domesticated Common Pigeon, *Columba livia*, in all its forms, abundantly illustrated.)

PIPIT

Bent, A. C. 1950. *Life Histories of North American Wagtails, Shrikes, Vireos, and Their Allies*. U.S. Natl. Mus. Bull. no. 197. Washington, D.C. Reprinted New York, 1965.

PIRACY

Meinertzhagen, R. 1959. *Pirates and Predators: The Piratical and Predatory Habits of Birds*. London. See also Meinertzhagen's "Piracy" entry in *A New Dictionary of Birds*, ed. A. L. Thomson. New York, 1964.

Van Tyne, J. 1946. Starling and Brown Thrasher stealing food from Robins. *Wilson Bull.*, 58:185.

PLAY

Kilham, L. 1974. Play in Hairy, Downy, and other Woodpeckers. *Wilson Bull.*, 86:35–42.

PLUMAGE

Ammann, G. A. 1937. Number of contour feathers of *Cygnus* and *Xanthocephalus*. *Auk*, 54:201–2.

Brodkorb, P. 1949. The number of feathers in some birds. *Quart. Jour. Fla. Acad. Sci.*, 12:241–45.

Buckley, P. A. 1973. Plumage aberrancies. *Amer. Birds*, 27:585.

Fabricius, E. 1959. What makes plumage waterproof? *Report of the Wildfowl Trust*, 10:105–13.

Hutt, F. B., and Ball, L. 1938. Number of feathers and body size in passerine birds. *Auk*, 55:651–57.

Markus, M. B. 1965. The number of feathers on birds. *Ibis*, 107:394.

Staebler, A. E. 1941. The number of feathers in the English Sparrow. *Wilson Bull.*, 53:126–27.

Wetherbee, D. K. 1957. Natal plumages and downy pteryloses of passerine birds of North America. *Bull. Amer. Mus. Nat. Hist.*, 113:339–436.

Wetmore, A. 1936. The number of contour feathers in passeriform and related birds. *Auk*, 53:159–69.

For other references, see under MOLT; ALBINISM; COLOR AND PATTERN.

POLLINATION

Meeuse, J. D. 1961. *The Story of Pollination*. New York.

Melville, R. 1964. Pollinators and distributors. In *A New Dictionary of Birds*, ed. A. L. Thomson. New York.

Pickens, A. L. 1929. Bird pollination problems in California. *Condor*, 31:229–32.

POLYANDRY

Hann, H. W. 1940. Polyandry in the Ovenbird. *Wilson Bull.*, 53:69–72.

Jenni, D. A. 1974. Evolution of polyandry in birds. *Amer. Zool.*, 14:129–44.

Oring, L. W., and Knudson, M. L. 1972. Monogamy and polyandry in the Spotted Sandpiper. *Living Bird,* 11th annual, pp. 59–73.

POLYGAMY

Haartman, L. von. 1951. Successive polygamy. *Behavior,* 3:256–74.

Verner, J. 1964. Evolution of polygamy in the Long-billed Marsh Wren. *Evolution,* 18:252–61.

———— and Willson, M. F. 1966. The influence of habitats in mating systems of North American passerine birds. *Ecology,* 47:143–47.

Zimmermann, J. L. 1966. Polygamy in the Dickcissel. *Auk,* 83:534–46.

POLYMORPHISM

Ford, E. B. 1945. Polymorphism. *Biol. Rev.*, 20:73–88.

Gullion, G. W., and Marshall, W. H. 1968. Survival of Ruffed Grouse in a northern forest. *Living Bird,* 7th annual, pp. 117–67.

Huxley, J. S. 1955. Morphism in birds. *Proc. (XIth) Internatl. Ornith. Congr., Basel and Stuttgart,* pp. 309–27.

Mosher, J. A., and Henny, C. J. 1976. Thermal adaptiveness of plumage color in Screech Owls. *Auk,* 93:614–19.

POPULATION

Baker, J. A., and Brooks, R. J. 1981. Distribution patterns of raptors in relation to density of meadow voles. *Condor,* 83:42–47.

Dunning, Jr., J. B., and Brown, J. H. 1982. Summer rainfall and winter sparrow densities: A test of the food limitation hypothesis. *Auk,* 99:123–29.

Haartman, L. von. 1971. Population dynamics. In *Avian Biology,* ed. D. S. Farner et al. Vol 1. New York.

Lack, D. 1954. *The Natural Regulation of Animal Numbers.* Oxford.

————. 1966. *Population Studies of Birds.* London.

MacArthur, R. H. 1958. Population ecology of some warblers of northeastern coniferous forests. *Ecology,* 39:599–619.

Skutch, A. F. 1967. Adaptive limitation of the reproductive rate of birds. *Ibis,* 109:579–99.

Watson, A., ed. 1970. *Animal Populations in Relation to Their Food Resources.* Oxford.

Wynne-Edwards, V. C. 1959. The control of population density through social behavior. *Ibis,* 101:436–41.

See also some references under TERRITORY.

PREDATION

Errington, Jr., P. L. 1967. *Of Predation and Life.* Ames, Iowa.

Hamerstrom, Jr., F. N. 1939. What eats what? *Bird-Lore,* 41:31–33.

Nicholson, A. J. 1933. The balance of animal populations. *Jour. Anim. Ecol.,* 2:131–78.

PRIMARY

Ashmole, N. P.; Dorward, D. F.; and Stonehouse, B. 1961. Numbering of primaries. *Ibis,* 103a:297–98.

Stresemann, E. 1963. Variations in the number of primaries. *Condor,* 65:444–59.

RADAR

Eastwood, E. 1967. *Radar Ornithology.* London.

Gauthreaux, Jr., S. A. 1971. A radar and direct visual study of passerine spring migration in southern Louisiana. *Auk,,* 88:343–65.

———. 1972. Behavioral responses of migrating birds to daylight and darkness: A radar and direct visual study. *Wilson Bull.,* 84:136–48.

Nisbet, I. C. T. 1963. Measurements with radar of the height of nocturnal migration over Cape Cod, Massachusetts. *Bird-Banding,* 34:57–67.

Schnell, G. H. 1965. Recording the flight speed of birds by Doppler radar. *Living Bird,* 4th annual, pp. 79–87.

RADIATION

Bedard, J. 1969. Adaptive radiation in the alcids. *Ibis,* 3:189–98.

Storer, R. W. 1971. Adaptive radiation in birds. In *Avian Biology,* ed. D. S. Farner et al. Vol. 1. New York.

RAIL

Bent, A. C. 1926. *Life Histories of North American Marsh Birds.* U.S. Natl. Mus. Bull. no. 135. Washington, D.C. Reprinted New York, 1963.

Ripley, S. D. 1977. *Rails of the World: A Monograph of the Family Rallidae.* Boston.

RECORDING OF BIRD SOUNDS

Borror, D. J. 1967. *Common Bird Songs.* Dover Records. New York.

———. 1970. *Songs of Eastern Birds.* Dover Records. New York.

———. 1971. *Songs of Western Birds.* Dover Records. New York.

———. 1972. *Bird Song and Bird Behavior.* Dover Records. New York.

The above four records come with explanatory manuals.

——— and Gunn, W. W. H. *Songs of Warblers of Eastern North America.* Federation of Ontario Naturalists' Sounds of Nature Series. Vol. 4. Don Mills, Ont. (Definitive.)

——— and ———. *Songs of Thrushes, Wrens and Mockingbirds.* F.O.N. Sounds of Nature Series. Vol. 5. Don Mills, Ont.

——— and ———. *Songs of Finches.* F.O.N. Sounds of Nature Series. Vol. 6. Don Mills, Ont.

Boswall, J. 1961 and 1963. A world catalogue of gramophone records of bird voice. *Bio-Acoustics Bull.,* 1:1–2, 25–29.

Davis, L. I. 1971. Birding with sound. *Birding*, 3:123–50.

Davis, T. 1974 and 1978. Cassette tape recorders. *Birding*, 6:166–68; 10:185–92.

————. 1979. Microphones and headphones for bird-recording. *Birding*, 11:240–43.

Gulledge, J. L. 1976. Recording bird sounds. *Living Bird*, 15th annual, pp. 183–203.

Gunn, W. W. H. *A Day in Algonquin Park*. F.O.N. Sounds of Nature Series. Vol. 2. Don Mills, Ont. (Songs of many birds of the northern forests.)

Kellogg, P. P. 1962. Bird-sound studies at Cornell. *Living Bird*, 1st annual, pp. 37–48.

Kellogg, P. P., and Allen, A. A. 1959. *A Field Guide to Bird Songs* (Eastern and Central North America). Kellogg, P. P. *A Field Guide to Western Bird Songs.* Boston. (Sets of records that follow the format of the Peterson field guides.)

King, B. 1980. The magic wand ("shotgun" microphone). *Birding*, 12:106–8.

Margoschis, R. 1977. *Recording Natural History Sounds.* Barnett, England.

National Audubon Society. 1977. *Audible Audubon.* New York. (A compact, 3″ x 5″ set of microphonograph cards and player with appropriate illustrations and brief text on cards to be used in the field for "instant recognition," not for attracting birds.)

Sinderson, Jr., S. W. 1975. Making your own parabolic reflector for sound recording, *Birding*, 7:1–3.

REPRODUCTIVE SYSTEM

Burger, J. W. 1949. A review of experimental investigations on seasonal reproduction in birds. *Wilson Bull.*, 61:211–30.

Fitzpatrick, F. L. 1930. Bilateral ovaries in Cooper's Hawk. *Anat. Rec.*, 46:381–83.

Lofts, B., and Murton, R. K. 1973. Reproduction in birds. In *Avian Biology*, ed. D. S. Farner et al. Vol. 3. New York.

Witschi, E. 1935. Origin of asymmetry in the reproductive system of birds. *Amer. Jour. Anat.*, 56:119–41.

————. 1935. Seasonal sex characters in birds and their hormonal control. *Wilson Bull.*, 47:177–88.

Wolfson, A. 1954. Notes on the cloacal protuberance, seminal vesicles and a possible copulatory organ in male passerine birds. *Bull. Chicago Acad. Sci.*, 10:1–23.

————. 1960. The ejaculate and the nature of coition in some passerine birds. *Ibis*, 102:124–25.

RESPIRATORY SYSTEM

Berger, M.; Hart, J. S.; and Roy, O. Z. 1970. Respiration, oxygen consumption, and heart rate in some birds during rest and flight. *Zeit. Vergleich Physiol.*, 66:201–14.

Berger, M.; Roy, O. X.; and Hart, J. S. 1970. The co-ordination between respiration and wing beats in birds. *Zeit. Vergleich Physiol.*, 66:190–200.

Casler, C. L. 1973. The air sac systems of the Anhinga and Double-crested Cormorant. *Auk*, 90:324–40.

Duncker, H. R. 1971. The lung air sac system of birds: A contribution to the functional anatomy of the respiratory apparatus. *Ergeh. Anat. Entwickl. Gesch.*, 45:171.

Gier, H. T. 1952. The air sacs of the loon. *Auk*, 69:40–49.

Lasiewski, R. C. 1972. Respiratory function in birds. In *Avian Biology*, ed. D. S. Farner et al. Vol. 2. New York.

Salt, G. W., and Zeuthen, E. 1960. The respiratory system. In *Biology and Comparative Physiology of Birds*, ed. A. J. Marshall, Vol. 1. New York.

Schmidt-Nielson, K. 1971. How birds breathe. *Scientific American*, 225:72–79.

Tomlinson, J. T. 1963. Breathing of birds in flight. *Condor*, 65:514–16.

RIDGWAY

Ridgway, R. 1895. *Manual of North American Birds.* 2nd ed. Washington, D.C.

—— and Friedmann, H. 1901–50. *Birds of North and Middle America.* U.S. Natl. Mus. Bulls. Washington, D.C.

See also under BAIRD.

ROOST

Smith, S. M. 1972. The roosting aggregations of Bushtits in response to cold temperatures. *Condor*, 74:478–79.

Swinebroad, J. 1964. Nocturnal roosts of migrating shorebirds. *Wilson Bull.*, 76:155–59.

SALT GLAND

Cooch, F. G. 1964. A preliminary study of the survival value of a functional salt gland in prairie Anatidae. *Auk*, 81:380–93.

Schmidt-Nielson, K. 1959. Salt glands. *Scientific American.* 200:109–16.

——; Jorgensen, C. B.; and Osaki, H. 1958. Extrarenal salt excretion in birds. *Amer. Jour. Physiol.*, 193:101–7.

SANCTUARY

Kendeigh, S. C., et al. 1950–51. Nature sanctuaries in the United States and Canada. *Living Wilderness*, 15:1–46.

Kitching, J. 1975. *Birdwatcher's Guide to Wildlife Sanctuaries.* New York.

Perry, J., and Perry, J. G. 1980. *The Random House Guide to Natural Areas of the United States.* New York.

SEABIRD

Alexander, W. B. 1928. *Birds of the Ocean.* New York.

Ashmole, N. P. 1971. Seabird ecology and the marine environment. In *Avian Biology*, ed. D. S. Farner et al. Vol. 1. New York.

Bourne, W. R. P. 1963. A review of oceanic studies of the biology of seabirds. *Proc. (XIIIth) Internatl. Ornith. Congr., Ithaca, N.Y., 1962*, pp. 831–54.

Fisher, J., and Lockley, R. M. 1954. *Sea-birds.* Boston.

Murphy, R. C. 1936. *Oceanic Birds of South America.* New York.

Tuck, G., and Heinzel, H. 1978. *A Field Guide to the Seabirds of Britain and the World.* San Diego.

See also references under seabird families: ALBATROSS, SHEARWATER, STORM-PETREL, etc.

SEED DISPERSAL

Melville, R. 1964. Pollinators and distributors. In *A New Dictionary of Birds,* ed. A. L. Thomson. New York.

Owen, H., and Owen, P. 1956. Tufted Titmice plant sunflower seeds. *Kentucky Warbler,* 32:62.

See also food storage by various species in FOOD/FEEDING and its bibliography.

SHEARWATER

Bent, A. C. 1922. *Life Histories of North American Petrels and Pelicans and Their Allies.* U.S. Natl. Mus. Bull. no. 121. Washington, D.C. Reprinted New York, 1964.

Fisher, J. 1952. *The Fulmar.* London.

Lockley, R. M. 1942. *Shearwaters.* London.

Palmer, R. S., ed. 1962. *Handbook of North American Birds.* New Haven. Vol. 1, pp. 136–217.

See also references under SEABIRD.

SHOREBIRD

Bent, A. C. 1927 and 1929. *Life Histories of North American Shorebirds.* U.S. Natl. Mus. Bull. nos. 142 and 146, pts. 1 and 2. Washington, D.C. Reprinted New York, 1962.

Bock, W. J. 1958. A generic review of the plover (Charadriinae, Aves). *Bull. Mus. Comp. Zool.,* 118:27–97.

Drury, W. H. 1961. The breeding biology of shorebirds on Bylot Island, Northwest Territories, Canada. *Auk,* 78:176–219.

Gibson, D. 1977. First North American nest and eggs of the Ruff. *Western Birds,* 18:25–26.

Hamilton, R. B. 1975. Comparative behavior of the American Avocet and the Black-necked Stilt (Recurvirostridae). *Ornith. Monogr.,* no. 17.

Höhn, E. O. 1969. The phalarope. *Scientific American,* 220:104–9, 111.

Johnsgard, P. A. 1981. *The Plovers, Sandpipers and Snipes of the World.* Lincoln, Nebr.

Palmer, R. S. 1967. Species accounts. In *The Shorebirds of North America.* New York.

Tuck, L. M. 1972. *The Snipes: A Study of the Genus* Capella. Canadian Wildlife Serv. Monogr. Ser. no. 5. Ottawa.

SHRIKE

Bent, A. C. 1950. *Life Histories of North American Wagtails, Shrikes, Vireos, and Their Allies.* U.S. Natl. Mus. Bull. no. 197. Washington, D.C. Reprinted New York, 1965.

Miller, A. H. 1931. Systematic revision and natural history of the American shrikes (*Lanius*). *Univ. Calif. Publ. Zool.*, 38:11–242.

SIZE

Kendeigh, S. C. 1970. Energy requirements for existence in relation to size of bird. *Condor*, 72:60–65.

————. 1972. Energy control of size limits in birds. *Amer. Nat.*, 106:79–88.

McWhirter, N., et al., eds. 1980. *Guinness Book of World Records*. New York.

SKELETON

Bellairs, A. d'A. 1964. Skeleton. In *A New Dictionary of Birds*, ed. A. L. Thomson. New York.

Harrison, J. G. 1960 and 1961. A comparative study of the method of skull pneumatisation in certain birds. *Bull. Brit. Ornith. Club.*, 80:167–72; 81:12–17.

See also Owre (1967–MUSCLES).

SKIMMER

Bent, A. C. 1921. *Life Histories of North American Gulls and Terns*. U.S. Natl. Mus. Bull. no. 113. Washington, D.C. Reprinted New York, 1963.

Zusi, R. L. 1962. Structural adaptations of the head and neck in the Black Skimmer. *Linnaeus Publ. Nuttall Ornith. Club* no. 3. Cambridge, Mass.

See also references under SEABIRD.

SKIN

Rawles, M. E. 1960. The integumentary system. In *Biology and Comparative Physiology of Birds*, ed. A. J. Marshall. Vol. 1. New York.

Stettenheim, P. 1972. The integument of birds. In *Avian Biology*, ed. D. S. Farner et al. Vol. 2. New York.

SLEEP

Berger, A. J. 1968. Behavior of hand-raised Kirtland's Warblers. *Living Bird*, 7th annual, pp. 103–16.

Goodman, I. J. 1979. The study of sleep in birds. In *Birds: Brain and Behavior*, ed. I. J. Goodman and M. W. Schein. New York.

SMELL

Audubon, J. J. 1826. Account of the habits of the Turkey Buzzard, *Vultor aura*, particularly with the view of exploding the opinion generally entertained of its extraordinary power of smelling. *Edinb. New Phil. Jour.*, 2:172–84.

Bang, B. G. 1971. Functional anatomy of the olfactory system in 23 orders of birds. *Acta Anat.*, Suppl., 58:1–76.

———— and Cobb, S. 1968. The size of the olfactory bulb in 108 species of birds. *Auk*, 85:55–61.

Grubb, Jr., T. C. 1972. Smell and foraging in shearwaters and petrels. *Nature*, 237:404–5.

Henton, W. W.; Smith, J. C.; and Tucker, D. 1966. Odor discrimination in pigeons. *Science*, 153:1138–39.

Stager, K. E. 1964. The role of olfaction in food location by the Turkey Vulture (*Cathartes aura*). *Contr. in Science*, no. 81, Los Angeles County Museum.

————. 1967. Avian olfaction. *Amer. Zool.*, 7:415–19.

SONG

Ames, P. L. 1971. *The Morphology of the Syrinx in Passerine Birds*. Peabody Mus. Nat. Hist. Bull. no. 37.

Armstrong, E. A. 1963. *A Study of Bird Song*. London.

Borror, D. J. 1961. Intraspecific variation in passerine bird songs. *Wilson Bull.*, 73:57–78.

————. 1964. Songs of the thrushes (Turdidae), wrens (Troglodytidae) and mockingbirds (Mimidae) of eastern North America. *Ohio Jour. Sci.*, 64:195–207.

———— and Reese, C. R. 1956. Vocal gymnastics in Wood Thrush songs. *Ohio Jour. Sci.*, 56:177–82.

Brackbill, H. 1961. Duetting in Brown-headed Cowbirds. *Auk*, 78:97.

Chapin, J. P. 1922. The function of the esophagus in the bittern's booming sound. *Auk*, 39:196–202.

Davis, L. I. 1972. *A Field Guide to the Birds of Mexico and Central America*. Austin, Tex.

de Kiriline, L. 1954. The voluble singer of the treetops. *Audubon*, 56:109–11.

Emlen, Jr., J. T. 1960. Introduction to *Animal Sounds and Communication*, ed. W. E. Lanyon and W. N. Tavolga. Amer. Inst. Biol. Sci. Publ. no. 7. Washington, D.C.

Falls, J. B. 1963. Properties of bird song eliciting responses from territorial males. *Proc. (XIIIth) Internatl. Ornith. Congr., Ithaca, N.Y.*, 1:259–27.

Frings, H., and Frings, M. 1959. The language of crows. *Scientific American*, 201:119–31.

Greenewalt, C. H. 1968. *Bird Song: Acoustics and Physiology*. Washington, D.C.

Hartshorne, C. 1958. *Born to Sing: An Interpretation and World Survey of Bird Song*. Bloomington, Ind.

Jellis, R. 1977. *Bird Sounds and Their Meaning*. London.

Johnsgard, P. A. 1971. Observations on sound production in the Anatidae. *Wildfowl*, 22:46–59.

Kellogg, P. P., and Hutchinson, C. M. 1964. The solar eclipse and birdsong. *Living Bird*, 3rd annual, pp. 185–92.

Kroodsma, D. E. 1980. Winter Wren singing behavior: A pinnacle of song complexity. *Condor*, 82:357–65.

————. 1981. Geographical variation and functions of song types in warblers (Parulidae). *Auk*, 98:743–51.

Lanyon, W. E., and Tavolga, W. N., eds. 1960. *Animal Sounds and Communication*. Amer. Inst. Biol. Sci. Publ. no. 7. Washington, D.C.

Leopold, A., and Eynon, A. E. 1961. Avian daybreak and evening song in relation to time and light intensity. *Condor*, 63:209–93.

Marler, P. 1957. Specific distinctness in the communication signals of birds. *Behavior*, 11:13–39.

———. 1967. Comparative study of song development in sparrows. *Proc. (XIVth) Internatl. Ornith. Congr., Oxford, 1966*, pp. 231–44.

Marshall, A. J. 1950. The function of vocal mimicry in birds. *Emu*, 50:5–16.

Mathews, F. S. 1904. *Field Book of Wild Birds and Their Music.* New York. (Transpositions of birdsongs into traditional musical notation.)

Mowrer, O. H. 1950. The psychology of talking birds: A contribution to language and personality theory. In *Learning Theory and Personality Dynamics*, ed. O. H. Mowrer. New York.

Nice, M. M. 1937 and 1943. *Studies in the Life History of the Sparrow.* Parts 1 and 2. Trans. Linn. Soc. New York, nos. 4 and 6.

Nottebohm, F. 1972. The origins of vocal learning. *Amer. Nat.*, 106:116–40.

Perrone, Jr., M. 1980. Factors affecting the incidence of distress calls in passerines. *Wilson Bull.*, 92:404–8.

Sauer, F. 1954. Die Entwicklung der Läutausserungen vom Ei ab schalldicht gehaltener Dorngrasmücken (*Sylvia c. communis*) im Vergleich mit später Isolierten und mit wildebenden Artgenossen. *Z. f. Tierpsychol.*, 11:10–93.

Saunders, A. A. 1947. The seasons of birdsong: The beginning of song in spring. *Auk*, 64:97–107.

———. 1948. The seasons of birdsong: The cessation of song after the nesting season. *Auk*, 65:19–30.

———. 1951. *A Guide to Bird Songs.* New York.

Short, L. L. 1966. Field Sparrow sings Chipping Sparrow song. *Auk*, 83:665.

Stokes, A. W., and Williams, H. W. 1968. Antiphonal calling in quail. *Auk*, 85:83–89.

Thielcke, G. 1969. Geographic variations in bird vocalizations. In *Bird Vocalizations: Their Relation to Current Problems in Biology and Psychology*, ed. R. A. Hinde. Cambridge, England.

———. 1976. *Bird Sounds.* Ann Arbor, Mich.

Thomas, E. S. 1943. A wren singing the songs of both Bewick's and House Wren. *Wilson Bull.*, 55:192–93.

Thomson, W. L. 1970. Song variation in a population of Indigo Buntings. *Auk*, 87:58–71.

Thorpe, W. H. 1959. Talking birds and the mode of action of the vocal apparatus of birds. *Proc. Zool. Soc. London*, 132:441–55.

———. 1961. *Bird Song: The Biology of Vocal Communication and Expression in Birds.* Cambridge, England.

———. 1972. Duetting and antiphonal song in birds: Its extent and significance. *Behavior*, Suppl. 18 (187 pp.). See also *Auk*, 90:451–53 (1973).

——— and Pilcher, P. M. 1958. The nature and characteristics of sub-song. *Brit. Birds*, 51:509–13.

Tinbergen, N. 1939. *The Behavior of the Snow Bunting in the Spring.* Trans. Linn. Soc. New York, no. 5.

For a listing of birdsong records and tapes, see under RECORDING OF BIRD SOUNDS.

SPECIATION

Dilger, W. C. 1956. Hostile behavior and reproductive isolating mechanisms in the thrush genera *Catharus* and *Hylocichla. Auk,* 73:313–53.

Hubbard, J. P. 1969. The relationship and evolution of the *Dendroica coronata* complex. *Auk,* 86:393–432.

————. 1973. Avian evolution in the aridlands of North America. *Living Bird,* 12th annual, pp. 155–96.

MacArthur, R. H., and MacArthur, J. W. 1961. On bird species diversity. *Ecology,* 42:594–98.

Mayr, E. 1942. *Systematics and the Origin of Species.* New York.

————. 1963. *Animal Species and Evolution.* Cambridge, Mass.

Mengel, R. M. 1964. The probable history of species formation in some northern wood warblers (Parulidae). *Living Bird,* 3rd annual, p. 943.

————. 1970. The North American central plains as an isolating agent in bird speciation. In *Pleistocene and Recent Environments of the Central Great Plains,* ed. W. Dort, Jr., and J. K. Jones, Jr. Lawrence, Kans.

Smith, N. G. 1966. *Evolution of Some Arctic Gulls* (Larus): *An Experimental Study of Isolating Mechanisms.* Amer. Ornith. Union Monogr. no. 4. Washington, D.C.

Selander, R. K. 1971. Systematics and speciation in birds. In *Avian Biology,* ed. D. S. Farner et al. Vol. 1. New York.

See also some references under DISTRIBUTION.

SPEED

Broun, M., and Goodwin, B. V. 1943. Flight speeds of hawks and crows. *Auk,* 60:486–92.

Cooke, M. T. 1937. *Flight Speed of Birds.* U.S. Dept. Agric. Circ. no. 428. Washington, D.C.

Cottam, C.; Williams, C. S.; and Sooter, C. A. 1942. Flight and running speeds of birds. *Wilson Bull.,* 54:121–31.

Davis, R. A. 1971. Flight speed of Arctic and Red-throated Loons. *Auk,* 88:169.

Hayes, Jr., S. P. 1929. Speed of flying hummingbirds. *Auk,* 46:116.

Howell, A. B. 1944. *Speed in Animals.* Chicago.

McCabe, T. T. 1942. Types of shorebird flight. *Auk,* 59:110–11.

McWhirter, N., et al., eds. 1980. *Guinness Book of World Records.* New York.

Meinertzhagen, R. 1955. The speed and altitude of bird flight. *Ibis,* 97:81–117.

Pearson, O. P. 1961. Flight speed of some small birds. *Condor,* 63:506–7.

Thompson, M. C. 1961. The flight speed of a Red-breasted Merganser. *Condor,* 63:265.

Youngsworth, W. 1936. The cruising speed of the Golden Plover. *Wilson Bull.,* 48:53.

See also Schnell (1965–RADAR).

STARLING

Bent, A. C. 1950. *Life Histories of North American Wagtails, Shrikes, Vireos, and Their Allies.* U.S. Natl. Mus. Bull. no. 197. Washington, D.C. Reprinted New York, 1965.

See also references under PESTS, BIRDS AS.

STATE/PROVINCIAL BOOKS

(in alphabetical order by state or province)

For regional and local works and checklists, see Ch. 8 of Kress (1981–BIRD-WATCHING).

ALABAMA: Imhof, T. A. 1962. *Alabama Birds.* Birmingham. (Illustr. by Richard A. Parks and David C. Hulse.)

ALASKA: Armstrong, R. H. 1980. *A Guide to the Birds of Alaska.* Anchorage.

————: Brandt, H. 1943. *Alaska Bird Trails.* Cleveland. (Illustr. by Allan Brooks and E. R. Kalmbach.)

————: Gabrielson, I. N., and Lincoln, F. C. 1959. *The Birds of Alaska.* Harrisburg, Pa.

ALBERTA: Salt, W. R., and Wilk, A. L. 1966. *The Birds of Alberta.* 2nd rev. ed. Gov't of Alberta. Edmonton.

ARIZONA: Brandt, H. 1951. *Arizona and Its Birdlife.* Cleveland. (Illustr. by Allan Brooks, Roger Tory Peterson, Terrence Shortt, and George M. Sutton.)

————: Phillips, A.; Marshall, J.; and Monson, G. 1964. *The Birds of Arizona.* Tucson. (Illustr. by George M. Sutton and photos by Eliot Porter.)

CALIFORNIA: Grinnell, J., and Miller, A. H. 1944. *The Distribution of the Birds of California.* Pacific Coast Avifauna no. 27. Cooper Ornith. Club. Berkeley.

————: Small, A. 1974. *The Birds of California.* New York.

COLORADO: Bailey, A. M., and Niedrach, R. J. 1965. *Birds of Colorado.* 2 vols. Denver. (Illustr. by 23 artists including D. Eckelberry, Roger Tory Peterson, and Peter Scott, plus many full-page photos.)

FLORIDA: Sprunt, Jr., A. 1954. *Florida Bird Life.* New York. (Illustr. by F. Lee Jaques and John Henry Dick.)

GEORGIA: Burleigh, T. D. 1958. *Georgia Birds.* Norman, Okla. (Illustr. by George M. Sutton.)

KENTUCKY: Mengel, R. M. 1965. *The Birds of Kentucky.* Amer. Ornith. Union. Ornith. Monogr. no. 3. (Illustr. by the author.)

LOUISIANA: Lowery, Jr., G. H. 1974. *Louisiana Birds.* Baton Rouge. (Illustr. by Robert E. Tucker.)

MAINE: Palmer, R. S. 1949. *Maine Birds.* Bull. Mus. Comp. Zool., 102:1–656.

MARYLAND AND THE DISTRICT OF COLUMBIA: Stewart, R. E., and Robbins, C. S. 1958. *Birds of Maryland and the District of Columbia.* N. Amer. Fauna no. 62:1–401. U.S. Fish and Wildlife Service. Washington, D.C.

MASSACHUSETTS: Forbush, E. H. 1925–29. *Birds of Massachusetts and Other New England States.* 3 vols. Boston. (Illustr. by Louis Agassiz Fuertes and Allan Brooks.)

MICHIGAN: Wood, N. A. 1951. *The Birds of Michigan.* Univ. Mich. Mus. Zool. Misc. Publ. no. 75.

MINNESOTA: Roberts, T. A. 1932. *The Birds of Minnesota.* Minneapolis. (Illustr. by George M. Sutton, Walter Weber, F. Lee Jaques, and Louis Agassiz Fuertes; plates also published separately as *Bird Portraits in Color,* Minneapolis, 1960.)

NEVADA: Linsdale, J. M. 1936. *The Birds of Nevada.* Pacific Coast Avifauna no. 23. Cooper Ornith. Club. Berkeley. (Also: Supplement 1951, *Condor,* 53:228–49.)

NEW BRUNSWICK: Squires, W. A. 1952. *The Birds of New Brunswick.* N.B. Mus. Monogr. Ser. no. 4.

NEWFOUNDLAND-LABRADOR: Peters, H. S., and Burleigh, T. D. 1951. *Birds of Newfoundland.* Boston. (Illustr. by Roger Tory Peterson.)

————: Todd, W. E. C. 1963. *Birds of the Labrador Peninsula and Adjacent Areas.* Toronto. (Illustr. by George M. Sutton.)

NEW MEXICO: Bailey, F. M. 1928. *Birds of New Mexico.* Albuquerque. (Illustr. by Allan Brooks and Louis Agassiz Fuertes.)

NEW YORK (STATE): Bull, J. 1974. *Birds of New York State.* Garden City, N.Y. (Illustr. by Don Eckelberry, A. E. Gilbert, Roger Tory Peterson, Arthur Singer, Guy Tudor, and others.)

————: Eaton, E. H. 1909 and 1914. *Birds of New York.* New York State Mus. Memoir no. 12. 2 vols. (Illustr. by Louis Agassiz Fuertes.)

NEW YORK CITY: Bull, J. 1964. *Birds of the New York Area.* New York.

NORTH CAROLINA: Pearson, T. J.; Brimley, C. S.; and Brimley, H. H. 1942. *Birds of North Carolina* (and revision by D. L. Wray and H. T. Davis, 1959). N.C. Dept. Agric. Raleigh. (1959 edition illustr. by Roger Tory Peterson—field guide plates—and by Bruce Horsfall.)

NOVA SCOTIA: Tufts, R. W. 1961. *The Birds of Nova Scotia.* Halifax. (Illustr. by John Crosby, John Henry Dick, and Roger Tory Peterson.)

OKLAHOMA: Sutton, G. M. 1967. *Oklahoma Birds.* Norman, Okla. (Illustr. by the author.)

OREGON: Gabrielson, I. N., and Jewett, S. G. 1940. *Birds of Oregon.* Corvallis, Ore.

PENNSYLVANIA: Todd, W. E. C. 1940. *Birds of Western Pennsylvania.* Pittsburgh. (Illustr. by George M. Sutton.)

SOUTH CAROLINA: Sprunt, Jr., A., and Chamberlain, E. B. 1949. *South Carolina Bird Life.* Columbia, S.C. (Illustr. by F. Lee Jaques, Roger Tory Peterson, and John Henry Dick.)

SOUTH DAKOTA: Over, W. H., and Thomas, C. S. 1946. *Birds of South Dakota.* Rev. ed. Univ. S.D. Mus. Nat. Hist. Study no. 1.

TEXAS: Oberholser, H. C., and Kinkead, Jr., E. B., eds. 1974. *The Bird Life of Texas.* 2 vols. Austin. (Illustr. by Louis Agassiz Fuertes.)

WASHINGTON: Aldrich, J. W.; Jewett, S. G.; Shaw, W. T.; and Taylor, W. D. 1953. *Birds of Washington State.* Seattle.

WISCONSIN: Gromme, O. J. (artist). 1963 and 1974. *Birds of Wisconsin.* (Plates only.) Madison.

CONTINENTAL AVIFAUNAS

CANADA: Godfrey, W. E. 1966. *The Birds of Canada.* Natl. Mus. Canada Bull. no. 203. Ottawa. (Illustr. by J. A. Crosby.)

NORTH AMERICA: Pearson. T. G., ed. in chief. 1937. *Birds of America.* Garden City, N.Y. (Illustr. by Louis Agassiz Fuertes.)

————: Reilly, Jr., E. M., and Pettingill, Jr., O. S., eds. 1968. *The Audubon Illustrated Handbook of American Birds.* New York.

PACIFIC NORTHWEST: Rogers, J. E. 1974. *Shorebirds and Predators—Birds of the Pacific Northwest.* (B.C., Wash., and northern Ore.) Vol. 1. Vancouver. (Despite the title, covers loons through owls.)

STOMACH OIL

Dennis, R. 1970. The oiling of large raptors by Fulmars. *Scot. Birds,* 6:198–99.

Sweenen, C. 1974. Observations on the effects of the ejection of stomach oil by the Fulmar, *Fulmarus glacialis,* on other birds. *Ardea,* 62:111–17.

STORK

Bent, A. C. 1926. *Life Histories of North American Marsh Birds.* U.S. Natl. Mus. Bull. no. 135. Washington, D.C. Reprinted New York, 1963.

Kahl, M. P. 1971. Social behavior and taxonomic relationships of the storks. *Living Bird,* 10th annual, pp. 151–70.

Palmer, R. S., ed. 1962. *Handbook of North American Birds.* New Haven. Vol. 1, pp. 508–15.

STORM-PETREL

Bent, A. C. 1922. *Life Histories of North American Petrels and Pelicans and Their Allies.* U.S. Natl. Mus. Bull. no. 121. Washington, D.C. Reprinted New York, 1964.

Palmer, R. S., ed. 1962. *Handbook of North American Birds.* New Haven. Vol. 1, pp. 217–54.

See also references under SEABIRD.

SUNNING

Barlow, J. D.; Klass, E. E.; and Lenz, J. L. 1963. Sunning of Bank Swallows and Cliff Swallows. *Condor,* 65:438–40.

Cade, T. J. 1973. Sunbathing as a thermoregulatory aid in birds. *Condor,* 75:106–8.

Hauser, D. C. 1957. Some observations on sun-bathing in birds. *Wilson Bull.,* 69:78–90.

Kennedy, R. J. 1969. Sun-bathing behavior of birds. *Brit. Birds,* 62:249–58.

Lanyon, W. E. 1958. The motivation of sun-bathing in birds. *Wilson Bull.*, 70:280.

Potter, E. F., and Hauser, D. C. 1974. Relationship of anting and sunbathing to molting in wild birds. *Auk*, 91:537–63.

Storer, R. W.; Siegfried, W. R.; and Kinahan, J. 1975. Sunbathing in grebes. *Living Bird*, 14th annual, pp. 45–56.

SURFBIRD

Dixon, J. S. 1927. The Surfbird's secret. *Condor*, 29:3–16.

Jehl, Jr., J. R. 1968. The systematic position of the Surfbird, *Aphriza virgata. Condor*, 70:206–10.

SWALLOW

Bent, A. C. 1942. *Life Histories of North American Flycatchers, Larks, Swallows, and Their Allies*. U.S. Natl. Mus. Bull. no. 179. Washington, D.C. Reprinted New York, 1963.

SWIFT

Bent, A. C. 1940. *Life Histories of North American Cuckoos, Goatsuckers, Hummingbirds, and Their Allies*. U.S. Natl. Mus. Bull. no. 176. Washington, D.C. Reprinted New York, 1964.

Lack, D. 1956. *Swifts in a Tower*. London. (Eurasian Swift, *Apus apus*.)

SWIMMING/DIVING

Brooks, A. 1945. The underwater actions of diving ducks. *Auk*, 62:517–23.

Chase, R. M. 1926. Crow alighting in the water. *Auk*, 43:237.

Dow, D. D. 1964. Diving times of wintering waterbirds. *Auk*, 81:556–58.

Heard, W. R. 1960. A record of swimming in Bobwhites. *Wilson Bull.*, 72:201.

Heintzelman, D. S., and Newberry, C. J. 1963. Some waterfowl diving times. *Wilson Bull.*, 76:291.

Kelso, J. E. H. 1926. Diving and swimming activities displayed by Limnicolae. *Auk*, 43:92–93.

Kooyman, G. L.; Drabek, C. M.; Elsner, R.; and Campbell, N. B. 1971. Diving behavior of the Emperor Penguin, *Aptenodytes forsteri. Auk*, 88:775–95.

McWhirter, N., et al., eds. 1980. *Guinness Book of World Records*. New York.

Merrell, Jr., T. R. 1970. A swimming Bald Eagle. *Wilson Bull.*, 82:220.

Prange, H. D., and Schmidt-Nielsen, K. 1970. The metabolic cost of swimming in ducks. *Jour. Exper. Biol.*, 53:763–77.

Schorger, A. W. 1947. The deep diving of the loon and Oldsquaw and its mechanism. *Wilson Bull.*, 59:151–59.

Speich, S., and Speich, M. A. 1972. Floating and swimming in passerines. *Calif. Birds*, 3:65–68.

Storer, R. W. 1960. Evolution in the diving birds. *Proc. (XIIth) Internatl. Ornith. Congr., Helsinki, 1958*, pp. 694–707.

Townsend, C. W. 1909. The use of the wings and feet of diving birds. *Auk*, 24:234–48.

TAMENESS

Huxley, J. S. 1947. Notes on the problem of geographical differences in the tameness of birds. *Ibis*, 89:539–52. (Subsequent *Ibis* volumes carry responsive notes:
90:312–15; 91:108–10; 356–58, 528.)

Ivor, H. R. 1944. Birds' fear of man. *Auk*, 61:203–11.

Martin, A. G. 1963. *Hand-taming Wild Birds at the Feeder.* Portland, Me. (See
also in Terres, 1977–BIRD FEEDING.)

TANAGER

Bent, A. C. 1958. *Life Histories of North American Blackbirds, Orioles, Tanagers,
and Their Allies.* U.S. Natl. Mus. Bull. no. 211. Washington, D.C. Reprinted
New York, 1965.

Storer, R. W. 1969. What is a tanager? *Living Bird,* 8th annual, pp. 127–36.

TASTE

Duncan, C. J. 1960. Preference tests and the sense of taste in the feral pigeon
(*Columba livia*). *Animal Behavior,* 8:54–60.

––––––. 1964. Taste. In *A New Dictionary of Birds,* ed. A. L. Thomson. New
York.

TAXONOMY

Berger, A. J. 1959. Leg-muscle formulae and systematics. *Wilson Bull.,* 71:93–94.

Blackwelder, R. E. 1967. *Taxonomy: A Text and Reference Book.* New York.

Mayr, E. 1942. *Systematics and the Origin of Species.* New York.

––––––, ed. 1957. *The Species Problem: A Symposium.* Amer. Assoc. Adv. Sci.
Publ. no. 50. Washington, D.C.

––––––; Linsley, E. G.; and Usinger, R. L. 1953. *Methods and Principles of Systematic Zoology.* New York.

–––––– and Short, L. L. 1970. *Species Taxa of North American Birds.* Nuttall
Ornith. Club Publ. no. 9. Cambridge, Mass.

Parkes, K. C. 1975. Notes on taxonomy. In *Avian Biology,* ed. D. S. Farner et al.
Vol. 5. New York.

Selander, R. K. 1971. Systematics and speciation in birds. In *Avian Biology,* ed.
D. S. Farner et al. Vol. 1. New York.

Sibley, C. G. 1960. The electrophoretic patterns of avian egg-white proteins as taxonomic characters. *Ibis,* 102:215–85.

––––––. 1970. *A Comparative Study of the Egg-white Proteins of Passerine Birds.*
Peabody Mus. Nat. Hist. Bull. no. 32. New Haven.

Simpson, G. C. 1961. *Principles of Animal Taxonomy.* New York.

Storer, R. W. 1969. What is a tanager? *Living Bird,* 8th annual, pp. 127–36.

––––––. 1971. Classification of birds. In *Avian Biology,* ed. D. S. Farner et al. Vol.
1. New York.

Stresemann, E. 1950. The development of theories which have affected the taxonomy of birds. *Ibis,* 92:123–31.

————. 1959. The status of avian systematics and its unsolved problems. *Auk*, 76:269–80.

————. 1963. Taxonomic significance of wing molt. *Proc. (XIIIth) Internatl. Ornith. Congr., Ithaca, N.Y., 1962*, pp. 171–75.

Wetmore, A. 1960. A classification for the birds of the world. *Smithsonian Misc. Coll.*, 139:1–37.

TEMPERATURE, BODY

Bartholomew, G. A., and Dawson, W. R. 1954. Temperature regulation in young pelicans, herons and gulls. *Ecology*, 35:466.

————; Lasiewski, R. C.; and Crawford, Jr., E. C. 1968. Patterns of panting and gular flutter in cormorants, pelicans, owls, and doves. *Condor*, 70:31–34.

Brenner, F. S. 1965. Metabolism and survival time of grouped Starlings at various temperatures. *Wilson Bull.*, 77:388–95.

Calder, W. A., and King, J. R. 1974. Thermal and caloric relations in birds. In *Avian Biology*, ed. D. S. Farner et al. Vol. 4. New York.

Dawson, W. R., and Evans, F. C. 1957. Relation of growth and development to temperature regulation in nestling Field and Chipping Sparrows. *Physiol. Zool.*, 30:315–27.

Dawson, W. R., and Hudson, J. W. 1970. *Comparative Physiology of Thermoregulation*. Vol. 1 (Birds). New York.

Dawson, W. R., and Tordoff, H. B. 1964. Relation of oxygen consumption to temperature in Red and White-winged Crossbills. *Auk*, 81:26–35.

Hatch, D. E. 1970. Energy conserving and heat dissipating mechanisms of the Turkey Vulture. *Auk*, 87:111–24.

Kahl, Jr., M. P. 1963. Thermoregulation in the Wood Stork with special reference to the role of the legs. *Physiol. Zool.*, 36:141–51.

McNab, B. K. 1966. An analysis of the body temperatures of birds. *Condor*, 68:47–55.

Nickell, W. P. 1964. The effects of probable frostbite on the feet of Mourning Doves wintering in southern Michigan. *Auk*, 81:56.

Norris-Elye, L. S. T. 1945. Heat insulation in the tarsi and toes of birds. *Auk*, 62:455.

Odum, E. P. 1942. Muscle tremors and the development of temperature regulation in birds. *Amer. Jour. Physiol.*, 136:618–22.

Ricklefs, R. E., and Hainsworth, F. R. 1969. Temperature regulation in nestling Cactus Wrens: The nest environment. *Condor*, 71:32–37.

Udvardy, M. D. F. 1951. Heat resistance in birds. *Proc. (Xth) Internatl. Ornith. Congr. Uppsala, Sweden, 1950*, pp. 595–99.

TERN

Bent, A. C. 1921. *Life Histories of North American Gulls and Terns*. U.S. Natl. Mus. Bull. no. 113. Washington, D.C. Reprinted New York, 1963.

See also references under SEABIRD.

TERRITORY

Brown, J. L. 1969. Territorial behavior and population regulation in birds: A review and re-evaluation. *Wilson Bull.*, 81:293–329.

Condee, R. W. 1970. The winter territories of Tufted Titmice. *Wilson Bull.*, 82:177–83.

Emlen, Jr., J. T. 1973. Territorial aggression in wintering warblers at Bahama agave blossoms. *Wilson Bull.*, 85:71–74.

Hensley, M. M., and Cope, J. B. 1951. Further data on removal and repopulation of the breeding birds in a spruce-fir community. *Auk*, 68:483–93.

Hinde, R. A. 1956. The biological significance of the territories of birds. *Ibis*, 98:340–69.

Howard, H. E. 1920. *Territory in Bird Life*. Reprinted London, 1948.

Ibis, 98: no. 3. (Collection of 18 papers on territory.)

MacQueen, P. M. 1950. Territory and song in the Least Flycatcher. *Wilson Bull.*, 62:194–205.

Nice, M. M. 1941. The role of territory in bird life. *Amer. Midland-Nat.*, 26:441–87.

Schoener, T. W. 1968. Sizes of feeding territories among birds. *Ecology*, 49:123–41.

Schwartz, P. 1964. The Northern Waterthrush in Venezuela. *Living Bird*, 3rd annual, pp. 169–84.

Stewart, R. E., and Aldrich, J. W. 1951. Removal and repopulation of breeding birds in a spruce-fir forest community. *Auk*, 68:471–82.

Tinbergen, N. 1957. The functions of territory. *Bird Study*, 4:14–27.

Woolfenden, G. E., and Fitzpatrick, J. W. 1978. The inheritance of territory in group-breeding of birds. *Bio-Science*, 28:104–8.

THRUSH

Bent, A. C. 1949. *Life Histories of North American Thrushes, Kinglets, and Their Allies*. U.S. Natl. Mus. Bull. no. 196. Washington, D.C. Reprinted New York, 1964.

TIT

Bent, A. C. 1946. *Life Histories of North American Jays, Crows, and Titmice*. U.S. Natl. Mus. Bull. no. 191, pt. 2. Reprinted New York, 1964.

Dixon, K. L. 1961. Habitat distribution and niche relationship in North American species of *Parus*. In *Vertebrate Speciation*. Austin, Tex.

Hartley, P. H. T. 1953. An ecological study of the feeding habits of the English titmice. *Jour. Anim. Ecol.*, 22:261–88.

TONGUE

Gardner, L. L. 1927. On the tongues of birds. *Ibis*, ser. 12: 185–96.

Harrison, J. G. 1964. Tongue. In *A New Dictionary of Birds*, ed. A. L. Thomson. New York.

Weymouth, R. D.; Lasiewski, R. C.; and Berger, A. J. 1964. The tongue apparatus in hummingbirds. *Acta Anat.*, 58:252–70.

TORPIDITY

Bartholomew, G. A.; Howell, T. R.; and Cade, T. J. 1957. Torpidity in the White-throated Swift, Anna's Hummingbird, and the Poor-will. *Condor*, 59:145–55; 61:180–85.

Bartholomew, G. A.; Hudson, J. W.; and Howell, T. R. 1962. Body temperature, oxygen consumption, evaporative water loss, and heart rate in the Poor-will. *Condor*, 64:117–25.

Huxley, J. S.; Webb, C. S.; and Best, A. F. 1939. Temporary poikilothermy in birds. *Nature*, 143:683–84.

Lasiewski, R. C., and Thomson, A. J. 1966. Field observation of torpidity in the Violet-green Swallow. *Condor*, 68:102–3.

Matthews, G. V. T. 1964. Torpidity. In *A New Dictionary of Birds*, ed. A. L. Thomson. New York.

Pearson, O. P. 1960. Torpidity in birds. *Bull. Mus. Comp. Zool.*, 124:93–103.

TOUCH

Duncan, C. J. 1964. Touch. In *A New Dictionary of Birds*, ed. A. L. Thomson. New York.

Schaeffer, F. S. 1973. Tactile bristles of Saw-whet Owl are sensitive to touch. *Bird-Banding*, 44:125.

TREECREEPER

Bent, A. C. 1948. *Life Histories of North American Nuthatches, Wrens, Thrashers, and Their Allies.* U.S. Natl. Mus. Bull. no. 195. Washington, D.C. Reprinted New York, 1964.

TROGON

Bent, A. C. 1940. *Life Histories of North American Cuckoos, Goatsuckers, Hummingbirds, and Their Allies.* U.S. Natl. Mus. Bull. no. 176. Washington, D.C. Reprinted New York, 1964

TROPICBIRD

Bent, A. C. 1922. *Life Histories of North American Petrels and Pelicans and Their Allies.* U.S. Natl. Mus. Bull. no. 121. Washington, D.C. Reprinted New York, 1964.

Palmer, R. S., ed. 1962. *Handbook of North American Birds.* New Haven. Vol. 1, pp. 255–64.

See also references under SEABIRD.

TYRANT FLYCATCHER

Bent, A. C. 1942. *Life Histories of North American Flycatchers, Larks, Swallows, and Their Allies.* U.S. Natl. Mus. Bull. no. 179. Washington, D.C. Reprinted New York, 1963.

Smith, W. J. 1966. *Communications and Relationships in the genus* Tyrannus. Nuttall Ornith. Club Publ. no. 6. Cambridge, Mass.

VIREO

Bent, A. C. 1950. *Life Histories of North American Wagtails, Shrikes, Vireos, and Their Allies.* U.S. Natl. Mus. Bull. no. 197. Washington, D.C. Reprinted New York, 1965.

Sibley, C. G., and Ahlquist, J. E. 1982. The relationship of the vireos (Vireoninae) as indicated by DNA-DNA hybridization. *Wilson Bull.,* 94:114–28.

VISION

Curtis, E. L., and Miller, R. C. 1938. The sclerotic ring in North American birds. *Auk,* 55:225–43.

Donner, K. O. 1951. The visual acuity of some passerine birds. *Acta. Zool. Fennica,* 66:1–40.

Goodge, W. R. 1960. Adaptations for amphibious vision in the Dipper (*Cinclus mexicanus*). *Jour. Morphol.,* 107:79–92.

Hocking, B., and Mitchell, B. L. 1961. Owl vision. *Ibis,* 103a:284–88.

Miller, R. S., and Miller, R. E. 1971. Feeding activity and color preference of Ruby-throated Hummingbird. *Condor,* 73:309–13.

Shaler, R. 1972. An eagle's eye: Quality of the retinal image. *Science,* 176:920–22.

Sillman, A. J. 1973. Avian vision. In *Avian Biology,* ed. D. S. Farner et al. Vol. 3. New York.

Tansley, K. 1964. Vision. In *A New Dictionary of Birds,* ed. A. L. Thomson. New York.

Van Rossem, A. J. 1927. Eye shine in birds, with notes on the feeding habits of some goatsuckers. *Condor,* 29:25–28.

Walls, G. L. 1942. *The Vertebrate Eye and Its Adaptive Radiation.* Cranbrook Inst. Sci. Bull. no. 19. Bloomfield Hills, Mich.

VULTURE

Bent, A. C. 1937. *Life Histories of North American Birds of Prey.* U.S. Natl. Mus. Bull. no. 167, pt. 1. Washington, D.C. Reprinted New York, 1961.

Brown, L., and Amadon, D. 1968. *Eagles, Hawks and Falcons of the World.* Vol. 1. New York.

WATERFOWL

Bellrose, F. C. 1976. *The Ducks, Geese and Swans of North America.* Harrisburg, Pa. (Update of Kortwright, 1943—DUCK.)

Bent, A. C. 1923 and 1925. *Life Histories of North American Waterfowl.* U.S. Natl. Mus. Bull. nos. 126 and 130, pts. 1 and 2. Washington, D.C. Reprinted New York, 1962.

Delacour, J. 1954–64. *Waterfowl of the World.* 4 vols. London. (Illustr. by Peter Scott.)

———— and Mayr, E. 1945–46. The family Anatidae. *Wilson Bull.,* 57:3–55; 58:104–10.

Johnsgard, P. A. 1968. *Waterfowl: Their Biology and Natural History.* Lincoln, Nebr.

———. 1975. *Waterfowl of North America.* Bloomington, Ind.

———. 1978. *Ducks, Geese and Swans of the World.* Lincoln, Nebr.

Kortright, F. H. 1943. *The Ducks, Geese, and Swans of North America.* Washington, D.C.

Palmer, R. S., ed. 1976. *Handbook of North American Birds.* Vols. 2 and 3 (Waterfowl: pts. 1 and 2). New Haven.

Scott, P. 1957. *A Colored Key to the Waterfowl of the World.* Slimbridge, England.

Wilmore, S. B. 1974. *Swans of the World.* New York.

WAXWING

Bent, A. C. 1950. *Life Histories of North American Wagtails, Shrikes, Vireos, and Their Allies.* U.S. Natl. Mus. Bull. no. 197. Washington, D.C. Reprinted New York, 1965.

Putnam, L. S. 1949. The life history of the Cedar Waxwing. *Wilson Bull.,* 61:141–82.

WEATHER

Bagg, A. M. 1967. Factors affecting the occurrence of the Eurasian Lapwing in eastern North America. *Living Bird,* 6th annual, pp. 87–121.

Lack, D. 1960. The influence of weather on passerine migration: A review. *Auk,* 77:171–209.

Linsay, G. 1967. Prairie Chickens died under crusted snow. *Passenger Pigeon,* 29:25–28.

McClure, H. E. 1945. Effects of a tornado on birdlife. *Auk,* 62:414–18.

Merrill, G. W. 1961. Loss of 1,000 Lesser Sandhill Cranes. *Auk,* 78:641–42. (Nov. 10, 1960.)

Rett, E. Z. 1938. Hailstorm fatal to California Condors. *Condor,* 40:255.

Smith, A. G., and Webster, H. R. 1955. Effects of hail storms on waterfowl population in Alberta, Canada—1953. *Jour. Wildlife Management,* 19:368–74.

Stewart, P. A. 1972. Mortality of Purple Martins from adverse weather. *Condor,* 74:480.

Zimmer, J. T. 1951. Birds and lightning. *Natural Hist.,* 60:143.

WEAVER FINCH

Bent, A. C. 1958. *Life Histories of North American Blackbirds, Orioles, Tanagers, and Their Allies.* U.S. Natl. Mus. Bull. no. 211. Washington, D.C. Reprinted New York, 1965.

See also references under PESTS, BIRDS AS and INTRODUCED BIRDS.

WILSON

Burns, F. L. 1908–10. Alexander Wilson. *Wilson Bull.,* 20:1–18, 63–79, 130–45, 165–85; 21:16–35, 132–51, 165–86; and 22:79–96.

Plate, R. 1966. *Alexander Wilson: Wanderer in the Wilderness.* New York.

Wilson, A. 1808–14. *American Ornithology, or the Natural History of the Birds of the United States.* 9 vols. Philadelphia. (A number of more recent editions in fewer volumes.)

WING

Harrison, J. G. 1964. Wing. In *A New Dictionary of Birds*, ed. A. L. Thomson. New York.

Rand, A. L. 1954. On the spurs on birds' wings. *Wilson Bull.*, 66:127–34.

WOODPECKER

Bent, A. C. 1939. *Life Histories of North American Woodpeckers.* U.S. Natl. Mus. Bull. no. 174. Washington, D.C. Reprinted New York, 1964.

Burt, W. H. 1930. Adaptive modifications in the woodpeckers. *Univ. Calif. Publ. Zool.*, 3:455–524.

Lawrence, L. de K. 1967. *A Comparative Life History Study of Four Species of Woodpeckers.* Amer. Ornith. Union Ornith. Monogr. no. 5.

WOOD WARBLER

Bent, A. C. 1953. *Life Histories of North American Wood Warblers.* U.S. Natl. Mus. Bull. no. 203, pts. 1 and 2. Washington, D.C. Reprinted New York, 1963.

Ficken, M. S., and Ficken, R. F. 1962. The comparative ethology of wood warblers: A review. *Living Bird*, 1st annual, pp. 103–22.

Griscom, L., and Sprunt, Jr., A., eds. 1957. *The Warblers of North America.* New York. Reprinted 1979.

Kendeigh, S. C. 1945. Nesting behavior of wood warblers. *Wilson Bull.*, 57:499–513.

Mengel, R. M. 1964. The probable history of species formation in some northern wood warblers (Parulidae). *Living Bird*, 3rd annual, p. 943.

WREN

Bent, A. C. 1948. *Life Histories of North American Nuthatches, Wrens, Thrashers, and Their Allies.* U.S. Natl. Mus. Bull. no. 195. Washington, D.C. Reprinted New York, 1964.

WRENTIT

Bent, A. C. 1948. *Life Histories of North American Nuthatches, Wrens, Thrashers, and Their Allies.* U.S. Natl. Mus. Bull. no. 195. Washington, D.C. Reprinted New York, 1964.

XANTHOCHROISM

Harrison, C. J. O. 1966. Alleged xanthochroism in bird plumages. *Bird-Banding*, 37:121.

Saunders, A. A. 1958. A yellow mutant of the Evening Grosbeak. *Auk*, 75:101.

YOUNG, DEVELOPMENT OF

Nice, M. M. 1943. *Studies in the Life History of the Song Sparrow*. Parts 1 and 2. Trans. Linn. Soc. New York, nos. 4 and 6.

————. 1962. *Development of Behavior in Precocial Birds*. Trans. Linn. Soc. New York, no. 8.

Palmer, R. S., ed. 1962. *Handbook of North American Birds*. Vol. 1. New Haven.

Rabinowitch, V. E. 1968. The role of experience in the development of food preferences in gull chicks. *Animal Behavior*, 16:425–28.

ZOOGEOGRAPHY

Darlington, Jr., P. J. 1957. *Zoogeography: The Geographic Distribution of Animals*. New York.

Udvardy, M. D. F. 1969. *Dynamic Zoogeography*. New York.

Vuilleumier, F. 1975. Zoogeography. In *Avian Biology*, ed. D. S. Farner et al. Vol. 5. New York.

See also references under DISTRIBUTION.